the world of
Children

Joan Littlefield Cook

University of Wisconsin, Whitewater

Greg Cook

University of Wisconsin, Whitewater

PEARSON

Boston • New York • San Francisco
Mexico City • Montreal • Toronto • London • Madrid • Munich • Paris
Hong Kong • Singapore • Tokyo • Cape Town • Sydney

Senior Series Editor: Stephen Frail
Series Editorial Assistant: Allison Rowland
Director of Development: Sharon Geary
Marketing Manager: Pamela Laskey
Supplements Editor: Elizabeth DiMenno
Production Supervisor: Karen Mason
Editorial Production Service: Stratford Publishing Services
Composition Buyer: Linda Cox
Manufacturing Buyer: Megan Cochran
Electronic Composition: Stratford Publishing Services
Interior Design: Joyce Weston
Photo Researchers: Annie Pickert, Naomi Rudov, and Katherine S. Cebrik
Cover Administrator: Kristina Mose-Libon

For related titles and support materials, visit our online catalog at www.ablongman.com.

Between the time website information is gathered and then published, it is not unusual for some sites to have closed. Also, the transcription of URLs can result in typographical errors. The publisher would appreciate notification where these errors occur so that they may be corrected in subsequent editions.

Library of Congress Cataloging-in-Publication Data

Cook, Joan Littlefield.
  The world of children / Joan Littlefield Cook, Greg Cook.
    p. cm.
  ISBN 0-205-44743-0
  1. Child development. 2. Children. I. Cook, Greg (Greg L.) II. Title.
  HQ767.9.C666 2007
  305.231—dc22

                                                            2006033356

Printed in the United States of America

10 9 8 7 6 5 4 3 2   [RRD-OH]   10 09 08 07

Text and photo credits are on page 621, which constitutes a continuation of the copyright page.

To our children: Lily, Rachel, Will, and Andy.
They bring child development to life for us every day!

Brief Contents

Contents

chapter 5
Cognitive Development in Infants and Toddlers 153

chapter 6
Socioemotional Development in Infants and Toddlers 189

part two
Summary 221

chapter 11
Cognitive Development in Middle Childhood 363

chapter 12
Socioemotional Development in Middle Childhood 401

part four
Summary 437

chapter 15
Socioemotional Development in Adolescence 517

part five
Summary 557

Preface

As researchers and university professors with a combined 40 years' experience, we have witnessed exciting changes in the field of child development. From the new research on brain development to behavior genetics to new theories of the intricacies of social interactions, developments in this area of psychology continue to provide great insights, challenges, and debates. Bringing these issues to the classroom on a daily basis in a manner that is meaningful to students is our greatest professional achievement. It is, after all, the connection with students—and their efforts to realize personal and professional aspirations as future psychologists, health care professionals, educators, social workers, day care workers, and parents—that we try to convey in the pages of this textbook.

Translating psychological research into clear and practical applications is an instructor's (and a textbook author's) biggest challenge. Most of our text focuses on contemporary science and on what is happening in the field today—but in order to understand the present, we must reflect on the past. Included in the text are both the classic studies within their historical context and an overview of how these studies have influenced, and continue to influence, how psychologists think about the field of child development. This review helps explain how particular scientific approaches emerged or were adapted or rejected over time. We want to remind students that just as adults are influenced by childhood experiences, the science of child development has been shaped by its past.

Built upon this strong foundation of psychological research, *The World of Children* adopts five important goals for the text and the user:

- To present child development issues within the context of real people facing real-world challenges in a diverse world;

- To teach students to think critically about the content and about other people's perspectives, backgrounds, and beliefs;

- To help students make connections between science and practice;

- To equip students with a foundation in child development that they can use to change lives professionally and personally;

- To help students become active learners as they prepare and succeed in this course.

We wrote our textbook from the ground up to accomplish these goals. Every feature in our book is thoughtfully designed as part of an integrated system to support active learning, and we hope you will agree that our textbook satisfies these goals.

Goal 1: Present Child Development Issues within the Context of Real People Facing Real-World Challenges in a Diverse World

We want students to see an important purpose in studying child development. We are convinced, and we know you are too, that the science of child development can be very useful in helping real families and real children. This is one of the exciting things about teaching our courses, and we show this potential to the students in every chapter of *The World of Children*. Every chapter begins with an opening story about a family or a child who is in a situation where more knowledge of child development can be beneficial. We encourage students to take what they are learning in each chapter and apply it in creating advice for the characters in these stories. We use margin notes, real-life examples in the text, and other features to consistently remind students that the science of child development can have an important impact in changing real lives.

Goal 2: Teach Students to Think Critically about the Content and about Other People's Perspectives, Backgrounds, and Beliefs

Critical thinking is a hallmark of higher education. We want students to learn new facts and information, but more importantly we want students to understand how these new facts and information are generated in our field. Throughout the textbook, we take opportunities to show students how research methods work in our field, and we remind them of the important limitations in the methods. The ability to think critically about information, its sources, and its limitations is essential if students are to be effective psychologists, educators, nurses, social workers, or parents in our world of fast-paced and ever-changing information. In every chapter, we ask students to think about why certain results were found, what they mean for the student personally or the world in general, and to explain limitations of the research they are reading.

We also encourage students to consider different perspectives as they study the information. We designed each chapter to illustrate how child development principles and concepts are useful from many different perspectives—from the perspectives of different careers, different personal situations, different social policy issues—and how child development directly impacts all of our lives. By exploring different perspectives, students are better able to understand both the "why" and "how" of child development issues and information. Individuals, theorists, even entire professions see things differently—they notice different details, frame issues and problems differently, and propose different solutions. This field contains many different theories, research findings, ideas, and viewpoints. What we have come to appreciate over our years of teaching is that this diversity is a wonderful learning tool. Trying to take others' points of view broadens and deepens students' comprehension of information, helping them develop a richer understanding of the content and issues in child development. Thinking about different perspectives also helps students see the many ways in which child development information is useful, both to others and to their own lives.

By looking at things from different perspectives, students come to understand more completely and more personally—and, ironically, this approach may help students appreciate the many similarities in development across children. In *The World of Children* we introduce students to people involved in child development in all walks of life: from parents, teachers, and social workers to scholars, researchers, and therapists. Weaving together and understanding the many perspectives on how to raise children, how best to work with children, and how to effect change in our society to better accommodate children are invaluable tools.

Goal 3: Help Students Make Connections between Science and Practice

The field of child development has much to offer students and society in terms of practical advice as well as guidance on social policy issues, and this advice is based on a solid foundation of research. Every chapter in our book has explicit prompts to encourage students to make these important connections. We ask students periodically to think about how the content is relevant for their own lives and those of their family and friends. In each chapter, we highlight a specific social policy issue for which child development theory and research has important implications. Many students who take child development courses plan to enter professions in which they will work with children every day. It is important that they see the connection between the research and theory they are learning from textbooks and their daily lives.

Goal 4: Equip Students with a Foundation in Child Development That They Can Use to Change Lives Professionally and Personally

One primary goal of any course in child development is that students leave the course with a solid foundation of knowledge about child development theory and content. Our book presents information in an engaging writing style and encourages students to be active in their thinking about the material they are learning. We also include in every chapter several pedagogical tools (e.g., "Let's Review" questions after each major section and a "Thinking Back to . . ." section at the end of each chapter) that encourage students to thoughtfully review the main concepts as they apply to one specific situation.

Many students want to work with children and teens, but often they are not aware of the career options that are available. Each chapter in our book includes an interview with a real person who uses knowledge of child development in his or her profession. The interviews help students think more broadly about the many different occupational possibilities open to them. There are so many ways in which knowledge of child development can be used to change lives, and these interviews are one way to help students realize the tremendous impact they can have on children and teens.

We are also proud to include the voices of many families, children, and teens as they talk about child development issues and how those issues relate to their real lives. Some of their stories are amusing, some very touching; they all help students appreciate the diverse perspectives that people bring to child development issues. The personal interviews are another way in which we encourage students to make a meaningful connection between the content they are learning and how it impacts the lives of real people.

Goal 5: Help Students Become Active Learners as They Prepare and Succeed in This Course

Another primary goal of ours was to create an *active learning system* to help students better understand, apply, and retain key concepts. We want students to take an active role in understanding the principles of child development—because the more involved they become, the more they will think about what they are learning on different levels. Our book engages students in the critical thinking process from the very first page. We employed the principles of constructivism, active learning, and the importance of context in learning to provide students with several opportunities to apply and reinforce key concepts throughout each chapter.

One thing we have learned from educational research and personal experience is that people tend to learn better when they can see clear relationships between facts and real life. Students can read and memorize facts and theories, but seeing how information relates to everyday life adds a critical dimension to the learning process and, ultimately, a deeper understanding of the material. This active approach to learning is similar in many ways to how a child develops. Just as children are immensely active in their own process of physical development—by jumping, climbing, and running, their muscles grow stronger and more coordinated—learning is more effective when students are actively involved in the process.

Our active learning system features work together to support learning that is contextualized, meaningful, and motivating. Additionally, several features encourage students to connect the chapter material to real-life scenarios and activate their critical thinking skills.

One of the strengths of these features is that the situations we describe are realistic—they are the typical kinds of problems that people face when they work with or raise children and adolescents.

To achieve this goal, every chapter includes the following pedagogical tools:

Chapter Opening Story Each chapter begins with an individual or family facing a challenging or unstable situation, stimulating students to begin thinking about the concepts they're about to study. Beyond this introduction, the text encourages students to go beyond one person's viewpoint and explore the views and experiences others bring to the issues—including their own.

Thinking About . . . Then, throughout the chapter, **Think About . . .** questions in the margins ask students to provide advice or solutions in response to the opening situation, actively applying what they have learned thus far.

Your Perspective Notes One of the most valuable features of our book is **Your Perspective Notes**. Each of these marginal notes asks students to think about how the material they just read applies to their own lives and reinforces the importance of different opinions and ideas. These questions are designed not only to stimulate inner thought and actually involve the student with the material but also to ignite classroom discussion.

Thinking Back to . . . To tie it all together, at the end of each chapter, **Thinking Back to . . .** offers suggestions on how the chapter content could be used to advise the people described in the chapter's opening story. Students begin to realize that there are no hard-and-fast answers as they work to make key connections between research and practice.

Preview Questions Each major section of a chapter begins with several **preview questions** that will orient students' thinking toward the material and provide a framework students can use for learning. The questions help students recognize the important points and see the organization of the section in advance.

Key Terms Key vocabulary terms are highlighted in **bold print** in the text and are repeated, with their definitions, in the margins. An alphabetical list of these terms also appears at the end of each chapter so students can review any terms that are still unfamiliar. These key terms include both the concepts that are most important and the vocabulary most likely to be unfamiliar to anyone studying child development for the first time.

Let's Review Questions Each of the major sections in the chapters ends with a set of **Let's Review** questions, which include multiple-choice and true/false questions concerning the material. These questions are meant to be relatively general and moderately easy—not brain-busters, which students usually learn to avoid. We provide the answers below the questions, printed upside down, so in just a few seconds this feature can give students quick feedback on their understanding of the material.

Chapter Summary A **Chapter Summary** in a question-and-answer format appears at the end of each chapter. It reminds students about the main questions addressed in the chapter and gives a quick summary of the most important concepts. It is by no means a substitute for reading the chapter, but it is an effective review tool.

mydevelopmentlab *Where human development comes to life!*

Strengthened by MyDevelopmentLab, a powerful interactive, online program that provides multimedia tools all in one place, *The World of Children* offers students many opportunities to practice and master what they're learning. MyDevelopmentLab's unique Individualized Study Plan works together with these features as part of the active learning system. This personalized study and review strategy allows students to actively track their progress in a topic and to prepare for the end-of-chapter test.

Exploring Different Perspectives

To further our goal of teaching students to think critically about other people's perspectives, backgrounds and beliefs, we created three boxed features that appear in each chapter and further explore various perspectives on child development. These features, *A Professional Perspective, A Personal Perspective,* and *A Social Policy Perspective,* help students try on the various hats that those who deal with children and development issues must wear in different situations. Beyond this, these features encourage students to approach problems and debates from a more informed position of understanding and empathy for other people's struggles or achievements.

A Professional Perspective

In **A Professional Perspective,** a real professional discusses how he or she uses child development information. Using an interview format, each of these features introduces students to a different career; by the end of the book, students have explored 15 different career paths (among them social work, genetic counseling, clinical and counseling psychology, school psychology, and marketing) that involve work with children, adolescents, and development. Students should get plenty of career ideas from these boxes.

Chapter	Professional Perspective Box
1	Meet a Child Social Worker
2	Meet a Genetic Counselor
3	Meet a Certified Nurse–Midwife
4	Meet a Physical Therapist
5	Meet a Speech–Language Pathologist
6	Meet a Toy Company Executive
7	Meet a Family Nutrition Counselor
8	Meet a Constructivist Teacher
9	Meet the Director of a Child Care Center
10	Meet a Pediatrician
11	Meet a Child and Family Therapist
12	Meet a Marketing Executive
13	Meet an Eating Disorders Counselor
14	Meet a School Psychologist
15	Meet a Juvenile Probation Officer

A Personal Perspective

Also presented as an interview, **A Personal Perspective** allows students to connect with the personal feelings of an actual parent, child, or adolescent who is experiencing an issue discussed in the chapter. For example, in the chapter where we discuss ethnic identity, an African American adult gives an insightful explanation of how her childhood and early experiences influenced the formation of her own ethnic identity. This feature allows students to see how real people of all backgrounds relate to child development issues.

Chapter	Personal Perspective Box
1	Meet First-Time Parents
2	Meet a Mother Who Used Artificial Insemination
3	Meet a Family Who Adopted a Child with Fetal Alcohol Syndrome
4	Meet the Parents of a Very Premature Baby

A Social Policy Perspective

We designed **A Social Policy Perspective** to give students an understanding of how work in the field of child development can inform government officials, community service agencies, and others who have wide-ranging effects on the lives of children. This feature focuses on many of the controversial issues in society, examining the perspectives of both sides of each debate. It highlights the ways in which programs, laws, regulations, and other factors can affect children and asks students to think about the impact of social policies.

Taken together, these different *perspective* features help students see how child development information is useful in a wide variety of professional, personal, and controversial situations. They also help students understand the real-life challenges faced by professionals, parents, volunteers, and policy makers whose work relates to the field of child development.

Our Own Personal Perspective

In addition to our training and research in child development, we call on our practical experience from raising our own four children. As this book is going into press, our oldest son, Andy, is 16 and a junior in high school. He has his driver's license and spends a great deal of his time now out and about with friends. He looks eagerly toward college, and we are proud of his achievements but at the same time we worry about all of his new freedoms. Our second son, Will, is 12. He looks up to his older brother, loves sports, and excels in most school topics. He is making the transition into middle school, enjoying the increased freedom and responsibility. Our twin daughters, Rachel and Lily, are 10. They are fraternal twins and couldn't be more different from each other. Rachel is quiet and shy at first, and she is very coordinated and graceful in athletic activities. Lily is rambunctious and outgoing, and she thinks homework is the best part of school. We have thoroughly enjoyed watching our children's first steps, first words, first days of school, first dates, and all the many joys of living with children and young teens. Like most families, we have also struggled as we try to balance home life with work, and we have dealt with premature infants, speech and physical therapy, school problems, sibling rivalry, and many of the other challenges that can appear in family life.

Through our children we have learned the practical side of child development. We know that even the grandest theories fail to capture the complexities and practicalities of real life with children. We have used these experiences to inform our writing—they helped us focus on the practical applications of what we teach and what we write. We encourage students to bring their personal perspective to the study of child development; and we do the same thing, including our personal perspective at times throughout the book. We hope that our own experiences will offer students another perspective to consider.

How to Use This Book

When reading textbook chapters, students often ask: "Why should I know this material?" or "How is it useful in real life?" Let us show you.

Maria is the mother of two boys, ages 4½ and 6. She and her children recently moved into a new community that has a school-choice program, allowing families to place their children in any school in the district. Maria wants to pick the best school for her sons, so she plans to observe and interview teachers and school officials at several schools. She's heard a lot about the importance of starting children in school early, but her younger son will have just turned 5 when the school year begins. Maria is concerned that he may not really be ready for formal schooling. She is also concerned because her boys are learning both Spanish and English at home. She wants both boys to continue to learn Spanish (Maria's first language) but she doesn't want it to interfere with their work in school and with their mastering of the English language.

What should Maria look for when visiting schools and teachers? What kinds of classroom activities and teaching methods would best foster both of her sons' cognitive development? How should she decide whether her younger son

Every chapter in the book begins with a story of life from another person's perspective—a realistic, often challenging situation that shows you how child development relates to you or to the people around you.

Each of these stories is linked to **Think About . . .** margin questions placed at critical points throughout the chapter. The **Think About . . .** questions ask you how you might advise the characters described in the opening story, based on what you have learned thus far. By the time you finish studying the chapter, you should have a good idea about how to answer all of the questions.

Think About Maria . . .

For Maria's 4½-year-old son, how would language, art, and play activities be important in his cognitive development? Would art and play be important in his preschool and kindergarten classrooms? Explain.

At the end of the chapter, **Thinking Back to . . .** summarizes some of the possibilities for how you could have answered the margin questions—but try answering the questions yourself before checking our summary!

Thinking Back to Maria . . .

Now that you have studied this chapter, you should be able to explain how Maria can use cognitive development concepts to identify schools and teachers that would facilitate her sons' learning and development. You should be able to list at least a dozen specific concepts and explain how each would relate to Maria's situation.

Using Piaget's theory, Maria would want to find classroom environments that promote active learning and look for teachers who use hands-on activities. Her sons are in the

We include several other perspectives as well, to help you think about the content from personal, professional, and social points of view. To support the personal perspective, we offer **Your Perspective Notes** in the margins where you can stop and think about how the chapter material relates to *your own life*.

To help you understand the professional side of this field, every chapter has **A Professional Perspective,** a one-on-one interview with someone whose job is related to child development. These professional interviews will not only allow you to understand how professionals view children, but they will also show you many of the career options that exist. Working with children is extremely rewarding, and we are excited to be able to show you numerous ways in which you can contribute to children's healthy development.

Surviving Child Sexual Abuse: One Survivor's Story

Dawn
A small town in the Midwest

Dawn is a survivor. She endured years of horrific treatment at the hands of people who should have protected her. But her main message is one of hope. She wants those who have been abused to know that help is available to stop the abuse and cope with the physical and emotional scars that remain. It is ongoing and difficult work, but it is possible. Here is her story.

My earliest memories of abuse are of my alcoholic father beating my mother and me. I even remember him beating my infant brother because he was crying—I was about 4 years old. My parents divorced, and my stepfather began immediately grooming our family for many, many years of severe sexual abuse. He would play seemingly innocent games with me, always physical, which happened mostly when my mother was at work. The games quickly led to rape a few times every week. My stepfather was violent and beat us, so I took seriously his threats to hurt us if I told. In third grade I stayed with my aunt in another state for a while. My teenage cousin, who had many behavior problems, babysat every day while my aunt worked. He soon began raping me, causing great pain and kidney infections. I wet the bed almost every night, which my aunt and uncle regularly embarrassed me about. Finally when I was 13, I told my mother about the abuse. She cursed at me and told me to leave, even after my stepfather admitted his guilt. From then on, I stayed with friends or slept outside. I married soon after I turned 18.

Why didn't anyone help? My mother could be quite violent when she was angry, so maybe she saw my stepfather's violence as acceptable. We lived in a very small town where it was just not acceptable to make waves, and the issue of abuse was only beginning to become public. I once told my best friend's mother and she became irate, accusing me of horrific lies—so I never mentioned it again. And my stepfather was respected in the community. He was from the largest family in town, taught Sunday school, and was a Boy Scout leader.

The effects of sexual abuse are pervasive. A person does not just "get over it," as has been suggested to me many times. It seeps into every part of a person's soul, mutating every cell and thought until there is nothing resembling normalcy, but this may not be evident from the outside. As an adult, I've been diagnosed with Major Depressive Disorder, Obsessive/Compulsive Disorder, Post-Traumatic Stress Disorder, and Generalized Anxiety Disorder. These are all linked to the abuse in my past, as are my lifelong eating disorders and weight-related problems. I have many issues when it comes to relationships, especially with trusting others. But the most precious thing that was ripped away from me was my true identity. I don't know the things I liked or disliked as a child, what my favorite colors were, or if I had favorite cartoon characters. I am 37 years old today and still attempting, on a daily basis, to learn who I am. Abuse strips away your identity and leaves only feelings of worthlessness, self-doubt, guilt, and shame.

In order to move on in life, it is important to seek professional help. I have been going to therapy for many, many years. I know I will need therapy on-and-off for life. I also use meditation, as well as reading just about everything I can about abuse. The biggest gift I have given myself, though, is continuing to learn who I am.

Adults need to know that if they were abused as children, there is no need to continue this terrible cycle. There are thousands of great books on parenting available, and classes are offered in almost every community. The cycle of abuse will not stop by itself; it takes conscious effort and much hard work, but it can be done. I feel it is important to speak out loudly about what happened to me as a child with the hope that more victims will do the same, so that people will become more aware of the extent of the effects of the abuse many children suffer. It is through awareness that we can work together to help stop the victimization of more innocent children.

Q *What could teachers, relatives, neighbors, and other adults in Dawn's life have done to prevent her suffering? What signs of abuse could they have looked for?*

In addition, each chapter contains **A Personal Perspective,** an interview feature that introduces you to real-life parents and children.

The Sex Education Debate

In 2001 the surgeon general of the United States, David Satcher, released a report about sex education in U.S. schools. After reviewing hundreds of scientific studies of teenage pregnancy, teen rates of sexually transmitted disease, and adolescent sexual activity, Satcher recommended that sex education programs teach the importance of abstaining from sex but also teach teens who are already sexually active how to prevent STDs and unintended pregnancies (Alan Guttmacher Institute, 2002).

The issue of teaching teens how to use condoms and other methods of pregnancy and disease prevention has been hotly debated since the federal government began playing a role in sex education in the 1980s. In 1981 Congress passed the Adolescent Family Life Act (AFLA), creating a federally funded program to prevent teen pregnancy by teaching abstinence and self-discipline in the schools. Later, a welfare reform law passed in 1996 and a maternal and child health block grant passed in 2000 began providing additional federal funds to promote *abstinence-only* programs in schools. Abstinence-only programs condemn all sex outside of marriage (for people of any age), and they completely prohibit any positive discussion of contraception. Abstinence-only programs may discuss condoms and other contraceptive methods

about birth control and STDs before their first sexual intercourse (Lindberg et al., 2000). Less than half had instruction on how to say no to sex, and fewer than 40 percent were taught how to put on a condom. Only half said they spoke to their parents about these issues. Girls are more likely to get these messages, with about 70 percent reporting formal education about birth control, HIV/AIDS, STDs, and abstinence before their first intercourse. Other surveys indicate that 81 percent of parents want their children's schools to provide comprehensive sex education that includes abstinence as well as condom use, birth control, abortion, and disease prevention. About half of all teens say they want more information about these and other sex-related topics (Kaiser Family Foundation, 2002).

Satcher's report pointed out that there was no available research evidence that abstinence-only programs work in preventing or delaying teen sex. Comprehensive programs that teach abstinence and contraception, however, have been associated with slight delays in the onset of sexual activity, reductions in the numbers of sexual partners, and increased contraceptive use among sexually active teens. The teenage pregnancy rate did decline slightly during the

To demonstrate the importance of child development information for current social issues and policies, we include **A Social Policy Perspective.** This feature highlights many specific controversies and debates surrounding children in our society. After reading these, you will see that different perspectives and opinions are everywhere. What's your take on the issues?

As you study this section, ask yourself these questions:

- How much growth in vocabulary do we see during early childhood?

- How do young children learn grammar and the other complex rules that are part of any language?

- What are the advantages and disadvantages to learning two languages at the same time? Are bilingual children at a disadvantage?

There are many tools in this book to help you check your learning. As you begin each major section of every chapter, you'll find **preview questions** designed to help you recognize the important points as you read.

Then, at the end of each section, you'll find **Let's Review** questions to help you make sure you've mastered the material. The answers to these questions accompany them, printed upside down.

■ Let's Review . . .

1. Which of the following is true about early childhood education programs such as Head Start, High/Scope Perry Preschool, and the Abecedarian Project?
   a. These programs are not cost effective.
   b. These programs regularly produce permanent gains in IQ scores.
   c. These programs produce improved academic progress and graduation rates.
   d. These programs have little effect on social measures such as arrest records or employment.

2. According to a national survey of kindergarten teachers, what percentage of their students were fully ready for kindergarten?
   a. 65 percent   b. 75 percent
   c. 85 percent   d. 95 percent

3. When it comes to gauging a child's readiness for kindergarten, which characteristic is emphasized more by parents than by teachers?
   a. enthusiasm   b. social skills
   c. physical health   d. academic knowledge

4. **True or False:** Research shows that the Early Head Start Program that enrolls infants and toddlers is less effective than the regular Head Start Program.

5. **True or False:** Research suggests that it is best to "redshirt" children who do not seem to be socially and cognitively ready for kindergarten.

Answers: 1. c, 2. a, 3. d, 4. F, 5. F

The **marginal glossary** offers you a quick way to find definitions. Because the glossary terms are set in the margin of the text, you can study the important vocabulary and definitions for each chapter without having to hunt for them.

attention
The ability to focus on a particular stimulus without becoming distracted by other stimuli.

metacognition
The understanding or knowledge that people have about their own thought processes.

■ Chapter Review . . .

Where does conception normally take place? What are two of the general processes that occur during prenatal development?
Conception normally occurs when the ovum and sperm meet in the upper part of the fallopian tube. After fertilization, prenatal development proceeds with *mitosis* (copy division) and *differentiation* (in which cells take on specific structures and functions).

What are the stages of prenatal development and the major events that take place in each?
The three stages are the germinal, the embryonic, and the fetal stages. During the germinal stage (0 to 2 weeks), the first cell divisions take place, and the embryo implants in the uterine lining. During the embryonic stage (3 to 8 weeks), the ectoderm, mesoderm, and endoderm form and later give rise to the major organs and parts of the body. The placenta, umbilical cord, and other structures form to support the developing baby. The body forms in a cephalocaudal (head-to-tail) and proximodistal (midline-to-outer) pattern. Organogenesis is complete by the end of the embryonic stage, so this stage includes most critical periods in organ and tissue formation. During the fetal stage the baby grows in size and the body systems gradually become more functional.

What effects do legal and illegal drugs have on the developing baby?
Several legal and illegal drugs can harm the developing baby. Alcohol is the leading known cause of mental retardation. It can also cause growth retardation, facial deformities, and FAS. Cocaine can cause growth retardation, cognitive deficits, and defects in the brain, intestines, and genital–urinary tract. Cigarette smoking is associated with low birth weight, hyperactivity, poor school performance, and increased risk of miscarriage, stillbirth, and neonatal death.

If a pregnant woman has an infectious disease, will this harm the developing baby?
Several sexually transmitted diseases and other infectious diseases can harm the developing baby. Sometimes the baby is born infected with a disease; in other cases the disease causes birth defects. If the mother has rubella, the baby can become infected with rubella or can be born with cataracts, heart defects, deafness, or lowered intelligence. Cytomegalovirus can cause embryonic death, retarded growth, microcephaly, blindness, mental retardation, and cerebral palsy. If the mother has HIV, the baby can be born infected with HIV and may show growth retardation and head and facial deformities.

Does the age of the mother affect pregnancy?
Infants of teenage mothers are at higher risk for low birth weight, prematurity, and neonatal death, especially when the mother is younger than 15. Risks of prematurity, fetal death, and pregnancy complications increase slightly after age 30.

What are critical periods, and why are they important in prenatal development?
Critical periods are times when developing organs and tissues are most vulnerable to defects. They usually occur when the organs and tissues are first forming, differentiating from surrounding cells. Most critical periods occur during the embryonic stage (weeks 3 to 8) and are therefore complete by the time most women know that they are pregnant. Parents should avoid exposure to teratogens during pregnancy.

Can fathers expose developing babies to teratogens?
In most cases, no—or at least not directly. Elements in the father's bloodstream do not pass to the developing baby, but some toxic substances can reduce the mobility and viability of sperm. Research with rats indicates that fathers' alcohol consumption may increase activity level in offspring and that cocaine can bind to sperm cells and be carried to the fertilized egg. Men can help to support healthy pregnancies in women.

What are the stages of labor, and what happens in each?
In Stage 1 the cervix dilates (widens) and the fetus moves downward to the birth canal. In Stage 2 the baby moves through the birth canal and is delivered. In Stage 3 the placenta and all membranes (the afterbirth) are delivered.

What is a newborn baby like?
The newborn baby has a large head and may be covered with a cheesy coating. Newborns can see, but their vision is fuzzy. They have reflexes that help them learn to feed, and they will grasp your finger if you touch their palms. They turn their heads to the sound of voices and gaze into the faces of their parents. The Apgar test, given 1 and 5 minutes after birth, identifies newborns who are at risk and need special medical attention.

Finally, the **Chapter Review** reminds you of the main questions addressed in the chapter and gives you a quick review of the most important concepts. This summary is not meant to be a replacement for reading the chapter, but it is an effective study tool.

mydevelopmentlab
Where human development comes to life!

If you are using MyDevelopmentLab, you have access to an ebook version of this textbook, along with dozens of valuable resources per chapter—including video and audio clips, simulations and activities, self-assessments, practice tests, and other study materials. Here is a sampling of the resources available for this chapter.

Explore
Physiological, Evolutionary, and Cognitive Theories of Emotion

Simulate
Attachment Classifications in the Strange Situation

Watch
Contact Comfort
Attachment in Infants
Redefining Fatherhood

If you did not receive an access code to MyDevelopmentLab with this text and wish to purchase access online, please visit www.mydevelopmentlab.com.

At the end of each chapter, you will be reminded to go online for additional study and practice within **MyDevelopmentLab.** Videos, animations, simulations, and other tools help you better understand the concepts presented in the chapter, while practice quizzes and a personalized study plan help you prepare for your exams.

All of these features work together as a learning system, designed to be educational, enlightening, thought-provoking, and memorable. Take what you learn here with you in life: It could help you in your next job, could improve your relationships at home, and surely will influence how you interact with every child you meet.

Supplements

Allyn & Bacon is pleased to offer the following supplements to qualified adopters.

Instructor Supplements

Instructor's Classroom Kit, Volumes I and II   Our unparalleled Classroom Kit includes every instructional aid a child development professor needs to manage the classroom. We have made our resources even easier to use by placing all of our print supplements in two convenient volumes. Organized by chapter, each volume contains chapters from the Instructor's Manual, Test Bank, Grade Aid Study Guide, and slides from the Cook/Cook PowerPoint™ Presentation.

Instructor's Classroom Kit CD-ROM   This exciting new supplement for instructors brings together electronic copies of the Instructor's Manual, Test Bank, Grade Aid Study Guide, PowerPoint™ Presentation, and images from the text for easy instructor access. Highly practical, the CD is organized by chapter and searchable by key terms.

Instructor's Manual   Created by Jeanne Malmberg of Saginaw Valley State University and Jackie Adamson of The University of La Verne, this robust teaching resource can be used by first-time or experienced instructors. Included are numerous handouts, detailed chapter outlines, lecture material, suggested reading and video resources, teaching objectives, and classroom activities and demonstrations.

Test Bank   Cheri Kittrell of Manatee Community College, Deborah Harris-O'Brien of Trinity University of Washington, and Jennifer Leszczynski of Eastern Connecticut State University have created a comprehensive test bank featuring more than 100 questions per chapter and fully reviewed by experienced professors. The test bank includes multiple choice, true/false, short answer, and essay questions, each coded with difficulty rating, page references, and answer justifications. The test bank is also available in TestGen 5.5 computerized version, for use in personalizing tests.

MyDevelopmentLab   MyDevelopmentLab is a state-of-the-art interactive and instructive solution for human development. This multimedia resource can be used to supplement a traditional lecture course or to administer a course entirely online. It is an all-inclusive tool, a text-specific e-book plus multimedia tutorials, audio, video, simulations, animations, and controlled assessments to completely engage students and reinforce learning. Fully customizable and easy to use, MyDevelopmentLab meets the individual teaching and learning needs of every instructor and every student. Visit the site at *www.mydevelopmentlab.com.*

PowerPoint™ Presentation   Mary Beth Miller of Fresno City College has created an exciting interactive tool for use in the classroom. The PowerPoint™ Presentation for *The World of Children* pairs key points covered in the chapters with images from the textbook to encourage effective lectures and classroom discussions. The PowerPoint™ is included on the Instructor's Classroom Kit CD-ROM, and can also be downloaded from our Instructor Resource Center at *http://www.ablongman.com/irc/.*

Allyn & Bacon Transparencies for Human Development   Designed to enhance your classroom presentations, these transparencies contain color acetates drawn from the figures in *The World of Children* and other Allyn & Bacon textbooks.

Digital Media Archive for Child Development   This comprehensive source of images includes charts, graphs, tables, and figures to enhance your lecture.

Course Management   Use these preloaded, customizable content and assessment items to teach your online courses. Available in CourseCompass, Blackboard, and WebCT formats.

Insights into Human Development Video   This new video highlights important high-interest topics in human development across the lifespan, including imagination in early childhood, motivation and school success, and aggression in adolescent romantic relationships. A video user's guide with critical-thinking questions and web resources is available to support the use of the video in the classroom.

Student Supplements

Grade Aid Study Guide with Practice Tests   Developed by Carolyn Morgan of the University of Wisconsin, Whitewater, this is a comprehensive and interactive study guide. Each chapter includes: "Before You Read," with a brief chapter summary and chapter learning objectives; "As You Read," a collection of demonstrations, activities, and exercises; "After you Read," containing three short practice quizzes and one comprehensive practice test; "When You Have Finished," with web links for further information, and crossword puzzles using key terms from the text. An appendix includes answers to all practice tests and crossword puzzles.

mydevelopmentlab

MyDevelopmentLab   This online all-in-one study resource offers a dynamic, electronic version of *The World of Children* textbook with over 160 embedded video clips (2 to 4 minutes in length) and over 60 embedded animations and simulations that dynamically illustrate chapter concepts. With over 100 text-specific practice test questions per chapter, MyDevelopmentLab helps students master the concepts and prepare for exams. After a student completes a chapter pre-test, MyDevelopmentLab generates a customized Study Plan for that student to help focus study efforts where they are needed the most. MyDevelopmentLab is available in both course management and website versions, and can be used as an instructor-driven assessment program and/or a student self-study learning program. Visit the site at *www.mydevelopmentlab.com.*

Development Journey through Childhood and Adolescence CD-ROM   This multimedia learning tool includes eight interactive units that cover development from the prenatal period through adolescence and literally brings development to life. Through the use of unscripted, real video footage, students will see everything from live births to a toddler taking its first steps to a teen mom discussing how her life has changed since becoming a mother. The Flash and 3-D video animations teach students visually about the inner workings of the human body, including the reproductive organs, conception, and pregnancy. Written by Dr. Kelly Welch of Kansas State University, the CD-ROM includes several exercises for students, such as "drag-and-drop" activities, multiple-choice quizzes, flash-cards of glossary terms, journal writing, and instant feedback exercises called "Mad Minutes."

Study Card for Child Development   Colorful, and packed with useful information, the Study Card makes studying easier, more efficient, and more enjoyable.

Research Navigator™ www.ablongman.com/researchnavigator   Allyn & Bacon's new Research Navigator™ is the easiest way for students to start a research assignment or research paper. Complete with extensive help on the research process and three exclusive databases of credible and reliable source material including EBSCO's ContentSelect Academic Journal Database, New York Times Search by Subject Archive, and "Best of the Web" Link Library, Research Navigator™ helps students quickly and efficiently make the most of their research time.

Companion Web Site for Child Development   A unique resource for connecting the child development course to the Internet. Each topic in the course table of contents includes learning objectives, Flash Card glossary terms, and online practice tests. Visit the site at *www.abchilddevelopment.com.*

Acknowledgments

We continue to be impressed with the enormous amount of time, attention, and resources that it takes to bring a textbook like this into print. Literally hundreds of people have been involved. We thank our many partners at Allyn & Bacon Publishers for their guidance and support throughout this project. Stephen Frail, our editor, has great talent in organizing our team, keeping the project moving along smoothly, and balancing the many tensions that are involved in creating a quality product within the realities of publishing timelines. Sharon Geary, our supervising development editor, was one of many people at Allyn & Bacon who read every word and worked with us to improve our writing to communicate information to students in the best possible way. Susan Hartman, Karen Mason, Pamela Laskey, Joyce Weston, and many others played critical roles in the design and execution of this textbook. Annie Pickert coordinated our photo research and Sarah Bylund coordinated our copyright permissions. Allison Rowland did an exceptional job organizing the many interviews with professionals, families, children, and teens that give a unique voice to our chapters. We also thank Susan McNally and Stratford Publishing for their work in getting our book into print. The authors of our textbook supplements worked tirelessly to create materials that are useful for students and instructors, and we are proud that these supplements work so well with our textbook in the spirit of active student learning.

We also acknowledge all of the love and support we received from our family and friends. They were there to share our joys and also to support us when things were difficult. We were too busy, too often, but their understanding and compassion allowed us to push on with a project we truly loved. We are especially indebted to our children, Andy, Will, Rachel, and Lily. They have helped us understand child development with our hearts as well as with our minds.

Manuscript Reviewers

Of course, the most important part of the book is the content, and we want to express our deep appreciation for all of the time and effort provided by the faculty and instructors who reviewed our manuscript pages and offered feedback. Many of their suggestions became strengths of our chapters and our supplements. These individuals include:

Kimberley F. Alkins, Queens College
Kathleen Bey, Palm Beach Community College
Jean Burr, Colby College
Jacquline Cottle, Texas Tech University
Marcie Coulter-Kern, Manchester College
Steven A. Dennis, Brigham Young University—Idaho
Ruth Doyle, Casper College
Patricia S. Eason, Monroe Community College
Michelle M. Englund, University of Minnesota
Karen Falcone, San Joaquain Delta College
Dr. Colleen Fawcett, Palm Beach Community College
Judith M. Geary, University of Michigan—Dearborn
Sabine Ferran Gerhardt, University of Akron
Rebecca Griffith, College of the Sequoias
Loreen Huffman, Missouri Southern State University

David P. Hurford, Pittsburg State University
Brandis Brooke Judkins, Indiana University of Pennsylvania
Sara Lawrence, California State University
Jennifer Leszczynski, Eastern Connecticut State University
Ronald Mulson, Hudson Valley Community College
Annette Nolte, Tarrant County College
Amy Obegi, Grossmont College
Cathy Pollock, Asheville Buncombe Technical Community College
Linda S. Raasch, Normandale Community College
Mary Kay Reed, York College of Pennsylvania
Mark P. Rittman, Cuyahoga Community College
Matthew Schlesinger, Southern Illinois University
Lila Snow, Los Angeles Pierce College
Teraesa Vinson, Bronx Community College

Perspective Boxes Interviewees

Our special thanks go to the individuals, professionals, and families who were incredibly generous enough to share their stories, experiences, challenges, and advice in an effort to inform and educate. We believe their insightful contributions will help students further their understanding of the text's concepts as well as help shape their personal and career decisions. These contributors are:

Lea Adams
Nola and Akindele Akala
Stacie Anderson
Robin L. Bennett
Deena Bernstein
Abbi Beuby
Sharon Buenaventura
Douglas Bunnell
Betsy Carroll
Kim Davenport
"Dawn"
Harlan Gephardt
Patrick, David, and Lori Glenn
Mariana Hertel
Deborah Koshansky
Carolyn and Bob Landers
Paul, Jacqueline, and Paul David Lewis
Nancy Magowan
Sophia Martin
"Mary Jane"
Iris and Manual Matos
Kim Miller
Kristin and Marc Petraluzzi
Kim Powell
Sandy Roland
Donna Rowland
Cheri and Allan Scott
Hannah and Asher Shapiro
Larry Sikkink
Jan Craige Singer
Pamela Talbot
Susan Tice
Kathryn Tromblay

Anne Upgrove
Hanna Lee Vestal
Deanna Walsh
Angela Watkins

Design Focus Group Participants

The visual presentation in any textbook works on many levels to create a learning environment that is easy to use, pleasing to look at, and easy to navigate. We would like to thank the following individuals who participated in our design review focus group. Their review, discussion, and helpful suggestions for the text's design resulted in an aesthetically pleasing and pedagogically sound visual learning platform for students. We are grateful to the following individuals:

Sharon De Leon, Fullerton College
Mark Jacobs, Palomar College
April Juarez, Long Beach City College
Lynda Roberts, Cerritos College
Whitney Scott, California State University at Northridge
April Taylor, California State University at Northridge

Survey Participants

We are grateful to the following instructors who responded to our survey and reviewed several pre-publication chapters. Their input helped finalize the manuscript and we are grateful to them. Thanks to the following participants:

Melanie Arpaio, Sussex County Community College
Jane Baker, Tennessee Tech University
Alfred W. Baptista, Massasoit Community College
Dr. Terri Barrett, Lenoir-Rhyne College
Lynne A. Bond, University of Vermont
Dr. Janine P. Buckner, Seton Hall University
Janice Cataldo, Henry Ford Community College
Mary Anne Chalkley, University of St. Thomas
Sarah Changnon, Southeast Community College
Donna Cohn, Pima Community College
Susan Eilason, Anna Maria College
Miriam Folk, Florida Community College at Jacksonville
Sabine Ferran Gerhardt, University of Akron
Bonnie Good, Delta College
Jill A. Harrison, Delta College
Sharon Hirschy, Collin College
Gary E. Krolikowski, State University of New York at Geneseo
Mary Mallory, Chapman University College
Michael Martinsen, Edgewood College
Cathleen McGreal, Michigan State University
Kelly McKown, Saint Paul College
Maryam Mehran, Chapman University College at Concord
Elizabeth Page, Lurleen B. Wallace Community College
Samantha Ramsay, University of Idaho
Elizabeth Kelley Rhoades, West Texas A&M University
Dr. Betsye Robinette, Indiana Wesleyan University
Carole L. Sanetti, Eastern Connecticut State University
Eulis Sawney, Howard University
Maria K. Schmidt, Indiana University

Pamela Schuetze, Buffalo State College
Stephanie Scroggins, Tarrant County College, Northeast
Chris Seifert, Montana State University
Jamie Simpson, Iowa Lakes Community College
Paulo Sudhaus, University of Arizona
Kim Sutton, Ozarks Technical Community College
April Taylor, California State University at Northridge
Margaret Torrie, Iowa State University
Susan Walker, University of Maryland at College Park
Elizabeth Wall, Wilmington College
Kathryn M. Westcott, Juniata College
Glenna Zeak, Penn State

Class Testers

The following instructors deserve special thanks for their willingness to class test the chapters with their students. Their enthusiasm for teaching and by extension our text is contagious and we thank the following individuals for their participation:

Dr. Gregory Boers, West Los Angeles College
Juanita Cordero, De Anza College
Tim Croy, Eastern Illinois University
Bonnie Good, Delta College
Janet Hale, Porterville College
Nancy Hartshorne, Central Michigan University
Barbara J. Myers, Virginia Commonwealth University
Cathy Proctor-Castillo, Long Beach Community College
April Taylor, California State University at Northridge
Bonnie L. Voth, University of Central Oklahoma
Angela Williamson, Tarrant County College, Northwest

About the Authors

Joan Littlefield Cook is an Associate Professor in the Psychology Department at the University of Wisconsin–Whitewater. As an undergraduate she majored in psychology at Tennessee Technological University. She earned a Ph.D. in psychology and human development at Vanderbilt University. Over the past 20 years she has taught courses related to child and adolescent development, educational psychology, and cognitive psychology at the University of Wisconsin–Whitewater, the University of Wisconsin–Madison, and Middle Tennessee State University. Her classes have ranged from large lecture courses (with 300 or more students) to small seminars. Joan's students have always appreciated her knowledge of the field and her ability to present information in a way that is useful, motivating, and friendly. The Student Association at the University of Wisconsin–Madison voted her as one of their most outstanding professors and the psychology students at University of Wisconsin—Madison also gave her their teaching award. Joan's research is on mathematical problem solving and cognitive development. She and her colleagues have published papers in the *Journal of Educational Psychology, Intelligence, Cognition and Instruction, Memory & Cognition,* the *Gifted Child Quarterly, Reading Psychology*, and the *Journal of Experimental Psychology.* She has co authored three other books and numerous instructional materials.

Greg Cook is a Professor of Psychology at the University of Wisconsin–Whitewater. Greg majored in psychology at the University of Dayton and later received his Ph.D. in psychology at Vanderbilt University. For the past 20 years he has taught courses in child development, research methods, statistics, and related topics at Whitewater as well as at Vanderbilt University and at the Madison and Richland Center campuses in the University of Wisconsin system. At Whitewater Greg received a departmental award for teaching excellence. Students consistently comment on his ability to present difficult information in a clear and understandable way. Greg's research on cognitive development has been published in scholarly journals such as *Child Development, Developmental Psychology,* and the *Journal of Experimental Child Psychology.* He has also collaborated with colleagues in the College of Education on studies published in the *Journal of Experimental Education*, the *Journal of Research and Development in Education,* and the *Journal of Reading Education.*

Joan and Greg also co-authored *Child Development: Principles and Perspectives,* a fresh and widely-acclaimed textbook (published by Allyn & Bacon) that explores child development within a topical framework.

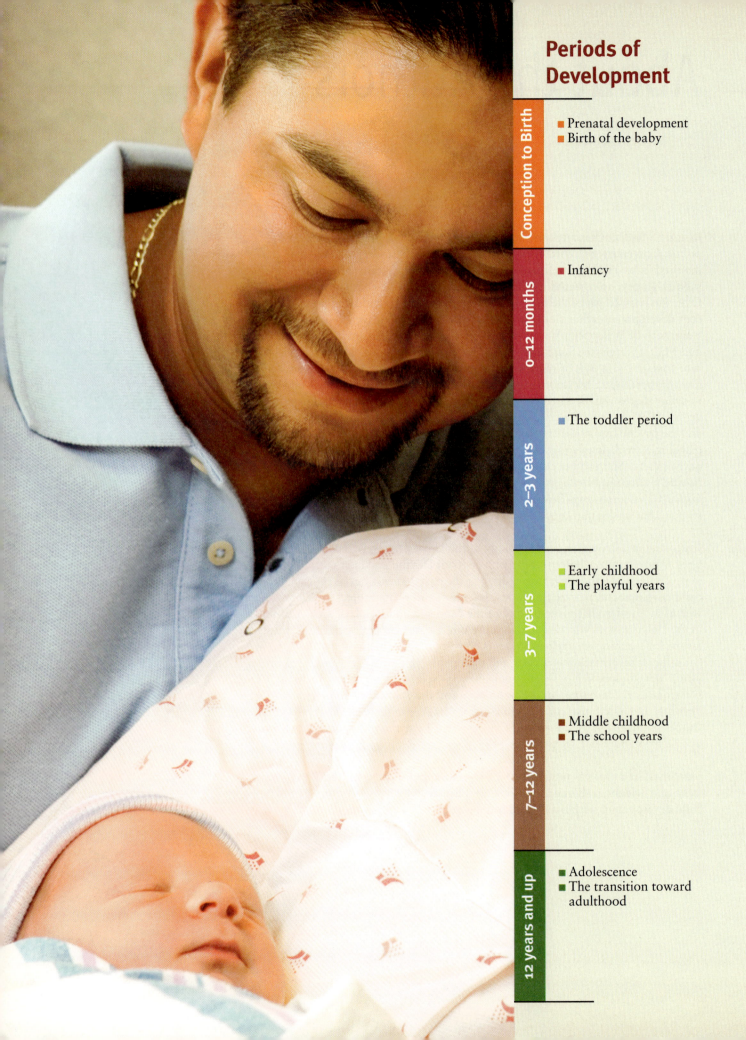

Periods of Development

Conception to Birth

- Prenatal development
- Birth of the baby

0–12 months

- Infancy

2–3 years

- The toddler period

3–7 years

- Early childhood
- The playful years

7–12 years

- Middle childhood
- The school years

12 years and up

- Adolescence
- The transition toward adulthood

part one

Beginnings

The *Beginnings* section of this book launches you on your quest to explore child and adolescent development. **Chapter One** introduces this area of study and summarizes the major theories and theorists who have influenced the field and the methods used to collect scientific information about child and adolescent development. It also shows you how child development research and theory can be useful in your own life. **Chapter Two** covers the interplay between genetics and the environment and how these forces shape the life course of children and adolescents. Understanding how genes and the environment interact is critical to understanding how each of us can intervene in the lives of children to improve their chances of maximizing their developmental potentials. **Chapter Three** covers the period from the time of conception to the birth of the baby. Although still developing in its mother's womb, there are many developmental processes taking place that are setting the stage for the child's future growth and development. Taken together, these first three chapters describe the *Beginnings* of child and adolescent development, and they give you the tools you need to understand the *First Years,* the *Playful Years,* the *School Years,* and the *Transition toward Adulthood* that will all be discussed in later chapters. We hope you enjoy your journey. . . .

chapter 1
Exploring Child Development

Jennifer, who recently gave birth to a baby girl, is also raising her 6-year-old son, Diego. As she watched Diego grow, Jennifer was amazed at his progress. He was crawling at 7 months and walking independently by 1 year. Also around his first birthday, he began speaking his first real words, including "Momma," "Dadda," "cup," and "ball." Diego's progress was typical for children during their first year, but Jennifer was still amazed to see how quickly he was developing. By 3 years Diego was holding fluent conversations and had a vocabulary of more than 1,000 words. By age 5 he was beginning to read and work with numbers, he was riding a bicycle, and he was beginning to make new friends in his kindergarten class. Now Diego is in first grade, and Jennifer continues to be amazed at the progress of his physical, cognitive, and social development.

With the birth of her new daughter, Jennifer has the chance to watch another child grow through similar phases. As she looks ahead, she wonders if her daughter will follow a similar path. What kinds of people will her children become? Will they be graceful and coordinated? Will they do well in school? Will they have lots of friends? How will they be similar to or different from each other? Like most parents, Jennifer wants to help her children as much as possible, and she wonders how she can use her opportunities as a parent to help her children develop to their fullest potentials.

As you read through this introductory chapter, think about the information from Jennifer's perspective. What advice could you give to Jennifer regarding her children? What do researchers know about children's development that could help Jennifer make decisions? In other words, what are the stages of development as children grow and mature, and what are the forces that drive development? After studying this chapter, you should be able to give Jennifer specific answers to these questions.

As you read this chapter, look for the "Think About Jennifer . . ." questions that ask you to consider what you're learning from Jennifer's perspective.

Differences in physical development are obvious when you compare the children in this photo. Size, strength, and coordination all increase with development.

There are few things more amazing to watch than the growth and development of a child. Babies are tiny and helpless at birth, but in just a few short months they are crawling about, feeding themselves, and exploring everything in sight. The changes in children are often undetectable, but many of the milestones are cause for celebration: when they say their first words, take their first steps, wave good-bye on their first days of school, and go out on their first dates.

Have you had the opportunity to closely watch a child grow and mature? If not, you can reflect on your own development. You are certainly different now than you were as a young child. You are obviously larger, stronger, and more coordinated. You also have much more factual knowledge and more effective and efficient problem-solving skills than when you were younger. Your social relations are very different, especially if you have moved away from your family or have started a family of your own. Yet in other ways you have kept many of the qualities you had at the outset. For example, maybe you were shy as a child and continue to be reserved and reflective today, or perhaps you were very active as a child and are still energetic and athletic.

This chapter introduces you to the field of child development. First we'll define the field of child development, examining the basic issues and questions addressed in this field. Then we will give you a thumbnail sketch of some of the most important theories and scientific methods used in the field, and show you how this information applies to the real lives of children.

Defining the Field

child development
Field of study in which researchers from many disciplines work to describe and understand the important changes that take place as children grow through childhood.

In the field of **child development,** professionals from psychology, sociology, anthropology, social work, biology, medicine, economics, and other related fields work together. Their shared purpose is to describe and understand the important changes that take place as children move from infancy through childhood. Children are changing every day—growing, gaining knowledge, and learning new skills. Yet in some ways children remain the same across their development. For example, a child who was happy and outgoing as a toddler may remain happy and outgoing throughout the rest of his childhood.

Understanding child development is important for everyone who wants to work with or help children. Parents naturally have a personal stake in providing the best environment and support they can. Teachers, counselors, social workers, psychologists, nurses, and other professionals who help children also need to understand the fundamental principles of development as well as the various ways that development can be disrupted or affected. Understanding child development can also help you understand your own progression into adulthood: Knowing more about where you came from can help you appreciate your current phase of life and may give you insights about where you are headed next.

your perspective

In what ways are you different now as an adult than you were as a young child? In what ways are you still the same?

As you study this section, ask yourself these questions:

■ What characteristics and processes do researchers study?

■ What are the main forces that drive child development? Do we have influence over these forces? If yes, which ones and how?

■ What is the "nature–nurture debate"? What positions have prominent figures taken in this debate over the years?

■ How has research in behavior genetics contributed to our understanding of nature and nurture?

What Develops?

A child's development is multifaceted. The most obvious component, of course, is **physical development.** Children grow in size, and their muscles become stronger and more coordinated. At birth, newborn babies cannot even hold their heads up, but over the following months, they will make tremendous gains in muscle strength and coordination. Later they will crawl, take their first steps, and eventually learn to ride bicycles and play sports. Many children go through a "lanky" period—a time when a rapid gain in height outpaces the gains in weight and muscle mass. During adolescence sexual maturity is attained, and the adolescent's physical appearance becomes more adult-like. The brain and nervous system grow and mature across childhood too, contributing to many of the changes we see in coordination and skill.

Cognitive development consists of numerous changes in how children perceive the world, think, process information, store and retrieve memories, solve problems, and communicate with language. Infants explore the world all around them, and they begin to speak their first words as they learn names for common objects and events. Later, we see cognitive growth most easily in the progress children and adolescents make in their academic work in school: learning to read and write and learning mathematics, social studies, science, art, and other topics. Underlying and supporting this growth are gains in perception, information processing, memory, and problem solving.

Children also make rapid progress in **socioemotional development.** As infants they depend on their parents and other family members for food, safety, and entertainment. As they grow, they begin to meet and interact with childhood peers, and this helps improve communication and emotional skills. Toddlers play readily with mates of both genders, but by middle childhood true friendships are established and most playmates are same-sex. Later, most adolescents will struggle with the problem of meeting potential partners and dating, exploring their own sexual identities, and forming intimate relationships.

This textbook explores the many changes and similarities we see as we track child development from birth through childhood and the adolescent period. After these first chapters on beginnings, we divide the book into the following parts:

■ *Infants and Toddlers: The First Years,* covers birth through age 2 as infants and toddlers get their starts in life;

■ *Early Childhood: The Playful Years,* covers ages 3 through 6 as children play, make friends, and explore the world around them;

■ *Middle Childhood: The School Years,* covers ages 7 through 11 as children focus on school and learning; and

■ *Adolescence: The Transition toward Adulthood,* covers ages 12 and up as children move into puberty and teenagers emerge into adulthood.

How do cognitive activities change with development? Researchers study how perception, memory, intelligence, problem solving, language, and other thinking skills develop during childhood and adolescence.

physical development
Component of development related to growth in size, strength, and muscle coordination.

cognitive development
Component of development related to changes in how children think, remember, and communicate.

socioemotional development
Component of development related to changes in how children interact with other people (e.g., family members, peers, and playmates) and manage their emotions.

How do social skills change with age? Friendship patterns, play, and cooperation are just a few of the topics that researchers study in the area of socioemotional development.

...cs) that govern
development.

nurture
The environmental conditions
and supports that impact
development.

your perspective

Think back to your own childhood,
and identify several examples of
nature and nurture and how they
influenced your development.

behavior genetics
Field of study that compares the
influence of genetics (nature) to
the influence of learning and the
environment (nurture), and
examines how these forces
interact to influence development.

Each section includes one chapter on physical development, one chapter on cognitive development, and one chapter on socioemotional development. Putting these chapters together should give you a feel for the developmental challenges and advances that take place within each age level.

What Drives Development? Nature *and* Nurture

What are the forces that govern or drive the processes, characteristics, and behaviors that develop across childhood? Basically, these forces are a combination of nature and nurture. The term **nature** refers to the biological forces that govern development. To a certain extent our development is programmed by the genetic codes we inherit. This biological program unfolds throughout childhood. In some respects, child development can be compared to the blossoming of a flower: A seed sprouts, grows into a fragile seedling, and eventually becomes a mature flowering plant. Nature provides the genetic program contained in the seed—and in the child. By now you know that genes influence the color of your eyes, but did you also know they play a role in determining your height and weight, your level of intelligence, and your basic personality?

Nurture refers to the environmental conditions and supports that influence development. A plant needs sunlight, water, and the proper temperature to grow—and it helps if someone pulls the surrounding weeds and adds fertilizer. It is the same for children. Hopefully, the child will receive love and support from parents, siblings, extended family, teachers, peers, and other people important in the child's life. Children can be greatly affected by how these important people nurture them.

Other elements of *nurture* include a child's economic and sociocultural environments. Poverty, malnutrition, and a lack of adequate medical care can obviously alter a child's developmental path. Cultural heritage and diversity can enrich a child's life, and the neighborhood where the child lives can determine the type of schooling and peer group that a child will have.

Through the ages, philosophers and scientists have debated the relative roles of nature and nurture. John Watson, a renowned American psychologist of the early twentieth century, was a strong proponent of the *nurture* school. He wrote:

[G]ive me a dozen healthy infants, well formed, and my own specified world to bring them up and I'll guarantee to take any one at random and train him to become any type of specialist I might select—doctor, lawyer, artist, merchant-chief and, yes, even beggar-man and thief, regardless of his talents, penchants, tendencies, abilities, vocations, and ancestors (1930/1924, p. 104).

Watson argued that experience and learning—nurture—determined what children would become. But other researchers have disagreed, pointing out that characteristics such as personality are determined more by genetics (nature) than by nurture. Today, however, developmental scientists understand that nature and nurture work together and it is impossible to distinguish their separate effects (Lerner, 2006; Rutter, 2002). Rather than arguing about which one is most important, we are interested in learning exactly how the two groups of factors interact with each other. The interacting effects of nature and nurture are evident in the field of *behavior genetics*.

In **behavior genetics** researchers study the relative roles of nature and nurture in development. By studying twins and adopted children, behavior geneticists have been able to estimate that many psychological traits and behaviors, including intelligence, emotionality, and basic personality variables, are approximately 40 percent to 60 percent inherited. For example, researchers have shown that IQ scores of identical twins are much more similar than scores of nonidentical twins (Bouchard & McGue, 1981). Because identical twins come from the same fertilized egg, their genes are exact copies (give or take a few errors in cell division). However, nonidentical twins come from separate fertilized eggs, so they are no more alike genetically than any other sibling pairs. Given the fact that both identical and nonidentical twins tend to share similar family and learning environments, scientists attribute the greater similarity in IQ between identical twins to their greater genetic similarity. Adoption studies also show a strong genetic component in IQ. Studies of children who were adopted as young infants have shown that these children's IQs at age 18 are more similar to the IQs of their biological mothers than to the IQs of the adoptive mothers who nurtured them (Loehlin et al., 1994; Scar et al., 1993).

The impact of nature, or genetic inheritance, is obvious when children are born with genetic disorders such as Down syndrome or cystic fibrosis. Research also has shown genetic links to conditions such as schizophrenia, depression, and severe obesity. The role of *nurture*, however, also emerges in many of these same studies. For example, inheriting genes linked to schizophrenia, depression, or obesity does not guarantee that a person will actually develop the condition. Many people who inherit these genes manage to overcome or avoid them. Also, nurture certainly has an impact on traits such as IQ. IQ scores for identical twins, for example, are more similar when the twins grow up together than when they are raised in separate families (Bouchard & McGue, 1981). Both identical and nonidentical twins show similar patterns of emotional attachment to their parents, indicating that shared family experiences (nurture) play a larger role than genetics (nature) in establishing attachment patterns (O'Connor & Croft, 2001).

Rather than arguing about whether development is controlled completely by nature or completely by nurture, thanks to the results of behavior genetics research, we are now beginning to understand the interactive roles played by both of these forces. We will describe more of this research, and discuss its implications, in Chapter 2.

Think About Jennifer . . .

How could you use behavior genetics research to understand how nature and nurture influenced the development of Jennifer's son?

■ Let's Review . . .

1. Which of the following professions contributes to the field of child development?
   - a. psychology
   - b. sociology
   - c. economics
   - d. all of the above

2. Learning new strategies for solving problems and remembering information is part of:
   - a. cognitive development.
   - b. physical development.
   - c. social development.
   - d. natural development.

3. What was John Watson's position on the nature–nurture debate?
   - a. Nature plays the biggest role in child development.
   - b. Nurture plays the biggest role in child development.
   - c. Nature and nurture play equal roles in child development.
   - d. You can never tell which force (nature or nurture) is playing the biggest role.

4. The main finding from behavior genetics research is that:
   - a. nature governs most of child development.
   - b. nurture governs most of child development.
   - c. nature and nurture both interact to govern child development.
   - d. neither nature nor nurture play strong roles in child development.

5. **True or False:** Genetics is an example of how *nature* can influence a child's development.

6. **True or False:** The fact that IQ scores are more similar between identical twins than between nonidentical twins shows the influence of *nurture* on children's intellectual development.

Answers: 1. d, 2. a, 3. b, 4. c, 5. T, 6. F

Theories of Child Development

Now that we've outlined the main issues studied in child development, let's take a look at the main theories that have been offered to explain how child development occurs. Over the years, researchers have gathered countless observations and facts about all facets of children's development. There are data on everything from average heights and weights to IQ scores to friendship and play patterns to the effects of discipline and divorce. This vast array of facts would be incomprehensible if the data were not organized in some coherent fashion. In this section, we explain why researchers develop theories to organize the facts. We also describe some of the most important theories that have influenced the field of child development.

As you study this section, ask yourself these questions:

- What do researchers mean when they use the word *theory*? How are theories useful in a field such as child development?

- Which theories have been most important in the field, and what are their main ideas?

- How might your view of children change if you adopted each of the theories described in this section?

- How could you use each of these theories to guide you when working with children? What research questions might each theory suggest?

What Is a Theory, and Why Are Theories Useful?

theory
An explanation of how facts fit together, allowing us to understand and predict behavior.

A **theory** is an explanation of how facts fit together. Theories provide frameworks that show how the facts are organized and related, and these frameworks can serve several useful functions (Thomas, 2000).

- Theories *summarize the facts as currently known.* By understanding contemporary theories you can see what researchers currently know about child development. Also, by tracing important theories through history, you can see what experts once thought and how knowledge and ideas have changed over time.

- Theories also *allow prediction of future behavior and events.* Theories tell us how the facts tend to be related in most situations; so if we know some of the facts in a particular case, then we can predict the related facts. For example, an accurate theory of discipline should tell us how children tend to respond to harsh punishment versus nurturing forms of punishment. Then, if we know that a particular child is receiving harsh punishment, we can predict what the child's response may be.

- By allowing prediction, theories *provide guidance* to parents, teachers, counselors, therapists, social workers, and others who work with children.

hypotheses
Specific inferences drawn from theories; researchers test hypotheses by collecting scientific observations.

- Theories also *stimulate new research and discoveries.* By definition theories cannot be directly verified—so researchers test theories by drawing specific inferences, or **hypotheses,** from the general theories and then collecting scientific observations to find out if the hypotheses are valid. In the course of testing hypotheses, researchers collect many new facts, make observations, and may make new discoveries. This process often leads to revisions in the initial theories or perhaps to the development of new theories.

- Finally, theories *act as filters for identifying relevant information, observations, and relationships.* Theories influence how we look at children and their development, and they even influence the kinds of questions researchers ask about development. In this way, theories act to filter out questions and observations that don't seem relevant to the theory; what does seem relevant is allowed to pass on to the next level of consideration. A researcher will see the simple act of a child's helping his or her father, for example, very differently depending on whether the researcher views the behavior through the filtering lens of a psychoanalytic, behavioral, or ecological theory.

Table 1.1 on page 12 provides an overview of some of the major theories of child development. Psychoanalytic theories were among the earliest in the field; they had a major influence in shaping our early notions of child development. The development field has largely discarded these theories, however, as later theories have proved to be more accurate and useful. The behavioral and social learning theories were prominent in the mid-twentieth century. Although newer approaches have emerged since, professionals who work with children still rely on these theories to design programs to modify children's behavior. Cognitive theories rose to prominence in the late 1900s. Neuropsychology and dynamic systems theories are relatively new; their potential is still being explored.

As you read about these various theories, keep in mind that each one offers a summary of what researchers knew and suspected about child development at a given time. Theories change as science progresses. Also, don't expect any one theory to explain everything about child development. Most theories are targeted at certain aspects of child development—such as how children learn, how they think about things in the world, or how they interact with the people around them. No theory by itself is sufficient to explain the myriad of processes and changes that occur as children grow and develop. Today, many psychologists and researchers take an eclectic view that combines the main concepts across several theories at once. With these thoughts in mind, let's explore some developmental theories. We'll begin with the earliest and end with the most recent.

Psychoanalytic Theories

Psychoanalytic theories focus on the structure of personality and on how the conscious and unconscious portions of the self influence behavior and development. The two most prominent psychoanalytic theories were developed by Sigmund Freud and Erik Erikson.

Sigmund Freud (1856–1939) was an Austrian physician, specializing in neurology, who treated patients for a variety of ailments. Some of his patients experienced symptoms (e.g., paralysis) that seemed to be caused by neurological abnormalities—but when Freud carefully examined these patients, he found no evidence of physical problems. After puzzling over these cases, Freud concluded that the symptoms sprang from unconscious psychological conflicts. They were similar to what we might today call psychosomatic illnesses. Over several decades, Freud used hypnosis, free association, dream interpretation, and detailed clinical interviews with his patients to explore their unconscious desires and conflicts. In the process he created his famous (and controversial) theory of psychoanalysis and child development.

According to Freud, the mind contains three basic components: the id, the ego, and the superego.

■ The *id* lies completely below the level of conscious awareness and represents the primitive sexual and aggressive instincts that humans inherited in evolution.

■ The *ego* is the rational branch of personality; it tries to negotiate realistic ways to satisfy the id's impulses.

■ The *superego* represents the moral branch of personality and contains our ethical principles, ideals, and conscience.

psychoanalytic theories
Theories that focus on the structure of personality and how the conscious and unconscious portions of the self influence behavior and development.

Sigmund Freud, the originator of psychoanalysis, proposed five stages of personality development.

TABLE 1.1 An Overview of Major Developmental Theories

PSYCHOANALYTIC THEORIES	BEHAVIORAL AND SOCIAL LEARNING THEORIES	COGNITIVE THEORIES	BIOLOGICAL THEORIES	SYSTEMS THEORIES
Focus on personality development and effects of conscious and unconscious mind on behavior and development	Focus on observable conditions in environment and how they relate to observable behaviors	Focus on how children learn to think	Focus on biological and physical explanations of development	Focus on complex interactions among layers of systems and variables
Psychoanalytic (Sigmund Freud) • Mind contains the id, ego, and superego; all are in constant conflict • Five stages of psychosexual development • Personality is well developed by end of adolescence	**Classical Conditioning (Ivan Pavlov, John Watson)** • Behavior controlled by stimulus-response connections • Unconditioned stimulus reflexively elicits unconditioned response; unconditioned stimulus paired with neutral stimulus; conditioned stimulus comes to elicit conditioned response • Explains the development of many fears	**Cognitive Developmental (Jean Piaget)** • Children actively construct their own understanding • Children develop mental schemas to represent their understanding • Children assimilate and accommodate their schemes • Four major stages of cognitive development	**Ethology (Konrad Lorenz)** • Based on Darwin's theory of evolution and natural selection • Study behaviors that help animals (including humans) compete and survive	**Ecological Systems (Urie Bronfenbrenner)** • Layers of systems affect the development of the child • Layers include interactions among family, friends, schools, neighborhoods, government agencies, parents' workplace, and the values, laws, and customs of the larger society • These interactions change over time
Psychosocial (Erik Erikson) • Focus on development of healthy ego identity • Series of eight psychosocial crises • More positive or more negative crisis resolution dependent on interactions with other people • Personality development is lifelong	**Operant Conditioning (B. F. Skinner)** • Behavior influenced by the consequences of actions • Reinforcement increases probability of a behavior being repeated; punishment decreases the probability of a behavior being repeated • Children adjust behavior to gain reinforcement and avoid punishment	**Sociocultural (Lev Vygotsky)** • Emphasized roles of culture and social interaction in cognitive development • Children adopt the psychological tools created and encouraged by their cultures • Social speech is internalized as private speech; eventually becomes inner speech	**Neuropsychology** • Direct observation of brain and nervous system structures and functions during thought • Uses technological advances to identify specific areas of brain activity during cognitive tasks	**Dynamic Systems** • Theories based on models used by mathematicians and physicists to understand complex systems • Complex interactions of multiple factors can appear chaotic, but stable patterns can emerge as the system self-organizes • Patterns change over time
	Social Learning (Albert Bandura) • Children learn by observing and imitating others' behavior; they do not always need reinforcement or punishment • Reinforcement and punishment give information to help children think about which behaviors to imitate	**Information Processing** • Detailed analysis of processes used in thinking • Emphasis on roles of basic processing efficiency and prior knowledge base		

These three components are in a perpetual state of conflict. When arguing with another person, for example, you might experience an impulse (from the id) to shove the person. At the same time you would recall (thanks to the superego) that it is not polite to assault people. You might arrive at a compromise (negotiated by the ego) to let a few angry words fly and then avoid seeing the person for a while. To have a healthy personality, we need the morality of the superego to balance the primitive instincts of the id. We also need an ego that is strong, realistic, and able to conduct swift and delicate negotiations among the id, the superego, and the demands of the world at large.

How do these components develop during childhood? Freud believed that we are born with the id, inherited from our ancestors. He then proposed five stages of psychosexual development to explain how the ego and superego emerge to tame the id. Figure 1.1 summarizes these stages. During the *oral and anal stages,* feedback from parents helps infants and toddlers curb their instincts for oral and anal gratification. Freud believed that children need an appropriate amount of stimulation in these *erogenous zones* (pleasure-sensitive zones). Receiving too much or too little stimulation can cause a *fixation* where development is blocked and the child's psychological energy becomes stuck at that developmental level. As young children learn to delay gratification—for example, to use the bathroom appropriately and to wait until morning to eat—the ego gradually begins to emerge to help keep the id in check.

Freud's most controversial proposal involved the *phallic stage.* He proposed that children have unconscious sexual desires for their opposite-sex parents. Eventually they realize that they cannot have the parent for themselves, in part because the other parent is too big and powerful to remove. Children then accept a compromise solution: They identify with their same-sex parents. Boys begin to mimic their fathers and girls their mothers. This way, they avoid confrontation (which the child would surely lose) and "join ranks" with the same-sex parent (who is having sex with their opposite-sex parent—the true object of their desires). Through *identification,* the child acquires the superego of the same-sex parent. In other words, to be like these parents, children copy their morals, ideals, and values—these become the conscience of the child. Along with children's new sense of morality come feelings of shame and guilt for the incestuous feelings they have had. So the phallic stage is followed by a period of *latency,* or dormancy. During the *latency stage* children's sexual feelings are repressed, and they prefer to play with same-sex peers and to engage in pursuits that are not sexually threatening. Sexual desires will reawaken in the *genital stage* as children mature into adolescents and begin to explore their sexual identities.

Think About Jennifer . . .

From a Freudian perspective, what would you want to know about the dynamics in Jennifer's family in order to understand her son's development?

Oral: Age 0 to 2
Infant seeks oral gratification by sucking, biting, and babbling.

Anal: Age 2 to 3
Potty training helps toddlers balance their needs for anal gratification with society's demand to be clean and neat.

Phallic: Age 3 to 7
In early childhood an unconscious desire for the opposite-sex parent is controlled by identification with the same-sex parent.

Latency: Age 7 to 11
Sexual urges are repressed, and the child prefers same-sex companions.

Genital: Age 11 to adult
With puberty sexual urges reappear, and the adolescent learns about mature relationships.

Figure 1.1 • Freud's Five Stages of Psychosexual Development

Freud proposed his theory to account for his patients' difficulties—many of which involved anxieties about sexuality or about sexual disturbances from childhood. Critics of Freud have argued that his theory focuses too much on the unconscious mind and sexual impulses, and many experts today do not view his theory as an adequate explanation for normal development in children. Still, Freud was one of the earliest thinkers to propose an elaborate theory of child development. Many of Freud's concepts have become permanent fixtures in our popular culture—the id, the ego, the superego, and the Oedipal complex are just a few examples. There is no question that Freud's theory has had an enormous impact on how we think about child development and psychology.

Erik Erikson (1902–1994) offered a revision of Freud's psychoanalytic theory. Erikson focused more on healthy child development, especially the development of ego identity. Erikson's *psychosocial theory* involves

> conflicts, inner and outer, which the vital personality weathers, re-emerging from each crisis with an increased sense of inner unity, with an increase of good judgment, and an increase in the capacity to "do well" according to his own standards and to the standards of those who are significant to him (Erikson, 1968, p. 92).

Erikson believed that our identity develops as we pass through a series of psychosocial stages. He proposed eight stages, representing eight major crises (Table 1.2). As children interact with significant other people in their social environments, they resolve the stage at hand by adopting an identity oriented more toward one end of the crisis than the other. For example, in stage one infants struggle with trust versus mistrust. If they have positive interactions with nurturing parents or caretakers, infants learn that the world is dependable and that people are basically trustworthy. If their parents are rejecting or neglecting, however, infants learn to mistrust them. These children then tend to mistrust almost everyone they meet. Erikson also believed that resolutions in earlier stages affect later stages. For example, a child who develops a basic sense of trust in stage one is more likely to develop a healthy sense of autonomy in stage two, and so forth. Unlike Freud, Erikson believed that personality development continued long after adolescence, and he proposed stages that covered early, middle, and later adulthood periods.

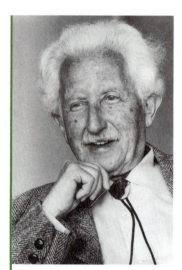

Erik Erikson proposed eight stages of psychosocial development.

your perspective

Which of Erikson's psychosocial stages are you currently in? How have the resolutions of the previous stages gone for you? How might those resolutions influence the remaining stages for you?

behaviorism
An American movement to develop a psychology that was objective and scientific, focusing on the principles of classical conditioning and operant conditioning.

Behavioral and Social Learning Theories

A major criticism of psychoanalytic theories is that these theories' important concepts are difficult, if not impossible, to test scientifically. How do we observe, measure, or verify the existence of the id, for example? **Behaviorism** began as an American movement aimed at developing a more objective and scientific psychology. John Watson (1878–1958) was the "father of American behaviorism." Watson argued that

John Watson demonstrated that children can learn fears through classical conditioning. Here, Watson and his research assistant demonstrate Little Albert's conditioned fears.

TABLE 1.2 Erikson's Eight Stages of Psychosocial Development

STAGE (CRISIS)	AGE	POSITIVE RESOLUTIONS	NEGATIVE RESOLUTIONS
Basic trust versus mistrust	0 to 1 year	With responsive caregiving, infant learns to trust parents or primary caregivers; acquires basic sense that the world and other people are trustworthy; develops self-confidence.	If caregiving is unresponsive or neglectful, infant can develop a basic sense of mistrust in caregivers, other people, and self.
Autonomy versus shame and doubt	2 to 3 years	Child gains independence from caregivers by walking, talking, toilet training; learns pride in independence ("Me do it!").	When independence is stifled or punished, child can develop basic sense of shame in self and doubt about his/her abilities.
Initiative versus guilt	4 to 5 years	Child initiates activities to meet larger goals; learns to take initiative to set own goals, design projects, interact with peers.	When initiative is stifled, child can learn guilt that own desires conflict with those of parents.
Industry versus inferiority	6 to 12 years	School years involve frequent comparisons with peers; confidence and sense of industry emerge when comparisons are favorable.	When comparisons are unfavorable, a sense of inferiority can develop; children feel their work and abilities do not measure up.
Identity versus role confusion	Adolescence	Sense of central identity emerges through sexual, emotional, educational, ethnic/cultural, and vocational exploration.	Sense of self can be confused or diffuse if a core identity does not solidify.
Intimacy versus isolation	Early adulthood	One or more intimate relationships form; may lead to marriage and family.	Without intimate relationships, feeling of isolation can develop; sense of being alone.
Generativity versus stagnation	Middle adulthood	Individual makes a positive contribution to the next generation by raising children, teaching, and volunteering.	Without a positive connection to others, can feel sense of stagnation, fear that life is wasted on selfish pursuits.
Integrity versus despair	Later adulthood	When other stages are resolved positively, an integrated sense of self has emerged; positive view of life and healthy attitude about death.	When other stages are resolved negatively, a negative sense of self emerges; despair that life was wasted, goals unfulfilled; fear of death.

psychology needed to focus on observable conditions in the environment and how they are related to overt, or observable, behaviors.

Watson began by adapting Ivan Pavlov's work on **classical conditioning.** Pavlov, a Russian physiologist, conducted experiments on the digestive system in dogs. He showed that when a dog tastes or smells meat powder, which in this case is the *unconditioned stimulus,* the dog automatically salivates, which is the *unconditioned response.* Further, when a researcher repeatedly pairs a previously neutral stimulus, like the sound of a bell, with the meat powder, the bell can begin to elicit salivation even when the meat powder is no longer present. The bell has become a *conditioned stimulus* and elicits salivation as a *conditioned response.*

Watson studied how children learn stimulus–response connections by classical conditioning. In his most famous demonstration, Watson conditioned an 11-month-old named Albert to fear a white rat (Watson & Rayner, 1920). At first, Albert showed no fear and would readily reach out to touch the rat. When Albert reached

classical conditioning
Process where neutral stimuli are paired with unconditioned stimuli until they come to evoke conditioned responses.

your perspective

Think of examples of classical conditioning from your life. Identify the unconditioned stimulus, unconditioned response, conditioned stimulus, and conditioned response in your examples.

for the rat, however, Watson clanged a steel bar loudly with a hammer behind Albert's head, frightening little Albert. After several interactions like this, Albert would not touch the rat and began to cry whenever he saw it. Albert's fear was a conditioned response. Later, Albert *generalized,* or extended, this fear to a rabbit, a fur coat, a dog, and even a Santa Claus mask! Watson warned that children might learn a great many fears through classical conditioning. He argued that parents and others should harness the powers of conditioning to set children on positive developmental paths. If environments could be controlled properly, children had unlimited potential. Remember Watson's guarantee about "a dozen healthy infants," quoted earlier?

Whereas Watson focused on children's reflexive responses to stimuli, B. F. Skinner (1904–1990) pointed out that children also learn through the consequences of their actions. He called this process **operant conditioning.** As an example, consider a girl who happens to clean her room. Her father, seeing the great deed, gives her a big hug and says, "What a great job—thanks for being so helpful!" After receiving such praise, the child may be more likely to clean her room again in the future. If so, Skinner would say that the child's helpful behavior has been "reinforced" by the hug and praise. In operant conditioning terms, *reinforcement* is any characteristic in the environment that serves to increase the probability that a person will repeat a behavior in the future. *Punishment,* on the other hand, is any characteristic that decreases the probability that a person will repeat a behavior. When a 17-year-old boy comes home late, missing his curfew, his parents may ground him or suspend his driving privileges. If these punishments are effective, the boy will be less likely to come home late in the future. According to Skinner, children "operate" on their environments (hence the term *operant conditioning*), adjusting their behaviors to attract more reinforcements and to avoid punishments.

Adding to the theories of classical and operant conditioning, Albert Bandura (1925–) demonstrated that children also learn by **social learning**—by *observing* and *imitating* the behaviors of other people. For example, when Theresa's father smiles at a visitor, young Theresa smiles too. After watching a television superhero battle with evil villains, Jamie solves his problem at school the next day by picking a fight. After seeing another girl drop a coin into a donation box, Sara asks her mother for a coin that she can donate. Bandura emphasized that children do not always need reinforcements or punishments to shape their behavior; sometimes

B. F. Skinner explored the principles of operant conditioning. He is shown here giving reinforcement for a rat's correct behavior.

operant conditioning
Process where reinforcing or punishing consequences of actions affect behaviors.

social learning
Process where children learn by observing and imitating the behaviors of other people.

Albert Bandura developed a theory of social learning that focuses on how children learn new behaviors by observing and imitating the actions of other people.

they act in imitation of the behaviors that they observe around them. In more recent years, Bandura's social learning theory has evolved into a social cognition theory. The social cognition approach emphasizes how children think about the behaviors and interactions they observe. In this view, reinforcements and punishments provide information that can help the child decide which behaviors to imitate. If children see someone receive reinforcement for a behavior, they are more apt to imitate that behavior in the future. This emphasis on how children think about events is part of a trend away from behavioral theories and toward cognitive theories of development.

Think About Jennifer . . .

Using the behavioral and social learning theories, what advice could you give Jennifer to help her work more effectively with her children?

Cognitive Theories

Jean Piaget (1896–1980), a Swiss psychologist, created a **cognitive developmental theory** to explain how children actively adjust their own understandings as they learn about the world. Piaget proposed that children represent what they understand about the world in cognitive structures that he called *mental schemes*. For example, the infant in Figure 1.2 on page 18 understands how to grasp the ball—he has a grasping scheme. As the baby acquires new experiences, however, his grasping scheme may be challenged. What would happen, for example, if he tried to grasp a larger ball? Most likely, he would first try to grasp the larger ball with one hand, as he had grasped the smaller ball before. But the one-hand-grasp scheme would not work. To hold the larger ball successfully, the infant would need to use trial-and-error practice to learn to use two hands.

cognitive developmental theory A theory that focuses on how children adjust their own understanding as they explore and learn about the world.

In this scenario Piaget would say that the infant tried to assimilate the larger ball into his grasping scheme.

- *Assimilation* is the process of bringing new objects or information into a scheme that already exists in the mind. If the assimilation is not successful (e.g., if the infant drops the ball), then the scheme needs to be accommodated.

- *Accommodation* is the process of adjusting or adapting a scheme so it better fits the new experience. Through accommodation the infant would learn that grasping sometimes requires two hands. Now the infant has a more powerful and flexible grasping scheme. He understands how to grasp smaller objects with one hand and larger ones with two hands.

Jean Piaget (standing between the two children) created a theory of cognitive development that focused on how children adjust their mental schemes as they learn to understand the world. His theory included major stages of development.

As children continue to gain new experiences, they adapt their cognitive structures, or schemes, through a continual cycle of assimilation and accommodation. Piaget also believed that children's cognitive structures develop through four major stages or phases of development: *sensorimotor, preoperational, concrete operational,* and *formal operational* thought. We'll look more closely at these stages, and at the rest of Piaget's cognitive developmental theory, in Chapter 5.

Another cognitive theory that we'll discuss in Chapter 5 is Lev Vygotsky's **sociocultural theory.** Vygotsky (1896–1934) was a Russian psychologist and a contemporary of Piaget. Vygotsky's theory emphasized how children adopt the thought structures represented in the language and culture that surrounds them. Cultures create psychological tools to solve problems and handle information, and these tools become reflected in the language of the culture. As children acquire the language, they also adopt the psychological tools embedded in it. Children in the United States,

sociocultural theory A theory that focuses on how language and culture influence the growth of thought in children.

Figure 1.2 • Assimilation and Accommodation
This infant seems pleased to be able to grasp and hold the ball. How would he adjust his grasping scheme to assimilate a larger ball?

Lev Vygotsky was a prominent Russian psychologist notable for developing a sociocultural theory of child development.

information-processing approach
A theoretical approach focusing on how children perceive, store, and retrieve information, and on the strategies they use to solve problems.

for example, often hear the words *freedom* and *democracy*. As they learn and internalize these words, they may become optimistic that they can shape their own destinies and make contributions to society. Contrast this with an experience one of the authors had in East Germany (formerly a Communist country). It was 1990, just months after the Communist government fell. I frequently heard citizens say, "It's not possible," as in "It's not possible to go there" (because the store was closed) or "It's not possible to do that" (because a sign was posted prohibiting parking or loitering). The phrase sounded odd to me. As a U.S. citizen, I of course knew that it was "possible" to do those things: I could break in, park illegally, or loiter anywhere I wanted! Under Communism, however, citizens had learned that government regulations were not mere requests—they were absolute requirements. Through language, cultures communicate expectations and influence how people think about society and the larger world.

Vygotsky's theory reminds us that language is a powerful tool that we all use when thinking. Children take the social speech spoken by people around them and turn it into their own private speech. At first children speak private speech aloud, as in "Now I cross the laces, then I make a bow." Later this private speech becomes silent inner speech, or what most of us would consider true mental thinking. Our inner thoughts therefore derive from the social speech that we hear in the culture around us. Vygotsky's theory emphasizes the important role that culture and society plays in the cognitive growth of children.

Piaget and Vygotsky had a tremendous impact on our understanding of child development. Piaget, in particular, wrote hundreds of books and articles on children's cognitive development, and his work stimulated countless investigations by other researchers. Since Piaget, researchers have continued investigating cognitive development, often using an **information-processing approach.** This approach focuses on how children perceive information in the world, store and retrieve information from their memory systems, and learn and use strategies to solve complex problems. Information-processing psychologists often emphasize the roles of *basic processing efficiency,* or a child's speed and accuracy in carrying out cognitive processes, and of *changes in the knowledge base,* or changes in the knowledge a child already has. Researchers also have studied how children process academic information such as spelling, science, and mathematics. Although this newer research has not always supported Piaget's theory (see criticisms of Piaget's theory in Chapter 5), the field is indebted to Piaget, the founder of cognitive developmental theory.

Biological Theories

Another group of child development theories focuses on biological explanations. One important biological theory is **ethology,** which examines the adaptive significance or survival value of behaviors. Ethology has its roots in Charles Darwin's (1809–1882) theory of evolution and his concept of natural selection ("survival of the fittest"). Ethologists often study animals in their natural environments, carefully observing behavior patterns and instincts that help the animals compete and survive. Two European zoologists, Konrad Lorenz and Niko Tinbergen, were especially important in formulating the basic tenets of ethology. Lorenz (1903–1989) is most known for his work on *imprinting*. Lorenz showed that baby goslings become attached to the first guardian figure they observe after hatching from their eggs. In his famous demonstration, Lorenz himself served as the guardian, and the goslings imprinted on him and followed him everywhere. Ethologists believe that the purpose of imprinting is to create a bond of attachment between goslings and mother geese so that goslings will be more likely to remain close to their mothers for protection. Extending ethology to humans, researchers have investigated bonding between human infants and their mothers. Some have speculated that the first hours after birth represent a critical period for developing a healthy bond (Klaus & Kennell, 1976). Other researchers believe that attachment bonds develop more gradually in humans, extending across the first year or so of life. We have much more to say about attachment in Chapter 6.

Beyond bonding and attachment, ethologists have wondered if other behavior patterns have adaptive significance for humans. Aggression, dating rituals, and emotional responses are just a few of the areas they have studied. *Sociobiology*, a subarea within ethology, focuses on the evolutionary development of social interactions among humans and among animals. *Behavior genetics* is another area related to ethology. As we discussed earlier in this chapter, behavior genetics asks to what degree particular behaviors are genetic (inherited) as opposed to learned. Each of these areas of study contributes to our knowledge by helping us understand the biological origins and history of important traits and behaviors.

Technological advances in recent decades have allowed more direct observation of the brain and nervous system than was ever possible before. **Neuropsychology,** a growing field in which psychologists, biologists, and other scientists are studying the structure and function of the brain and nervous system, has especially benefited from these advanced technologies. *Computerized tomography (CT)* scans can give computer-enhanced three-dimensional X-ray images of the brain. With *positron emission tomography (PET)*, clinicians inject radioactive markers in a person's

ethology
Area of study focusing on the adaptive significance or survival value of behaviors.

Konrad Lorenz is one of the "fathers of ethology." In this demonstration of imprinting, these baby geese follow him as if he is their father too!

neuropsychology
An area of study that focuses on the brain and nervous system; researchers often observe brain function using technology such as CT scans, PET, and *f*MRI.

This *f*MRI/PET scan shows a composite image of brain activity taken as children think about a problem. Notice how the frontal lobe is especially active in this task. Neuropsychologists use technologies like this to study how the brain functions and changes as children grow and learn new skills.

bloodstream and then trace them through the brain as the person engages in certain cognitive tasks. For example, with PET scans researchers can tell which areas of the brain are most active when a student is reading versus speaking, or doing math versus trying to recall vocabulary words. One problem with PET scans is that they are not precise—they only indicate which gross areas are involved in processing. A newer technology is *functional magnetic resonance imaging (fMRI),* which can detect changes in the rate of metabolism, or energy consumption, in smaller areas of the brain. With fMRI researchers can precisely identify the specific parts of the brain that become more active as people process different types of information. With these and other technologies, researchers are gaining a better understanding of the biological underlying layer of cognitive processing. Knowledge gained in neuropsychology will undoubtedly both inform and challenge the various theories of cognitive development.

Systems Theories

Urie Bronfenbrenner proposed the ecological systems theory of child development.

As children develop, their behaviors become very complex. Clearly, development cannot be explained by a single concept such as genes, instinct, reinforcement, or the id. The newest wave of theories attempt to capture the complexity of child development by focusing on the rich network of systems that operate in and around the child. According to *systems theories,* development emerges from complexity; we cannot understand development by reducing the world into a small set of simple terms. Urie Bronfenbrenner's (1917–2005) *ecological systems theory* is an excellent example of this type of theory. Several other researchers also have used *dynamic systems theories* that take a similar approach.

ecological systems theory
Theory focusing on the complex set of systems and interacting social layers that can affect a child's development.

Ecological Systems Theory. In the 1930s, Lev Vygotsky taught us about the important role that cultural context plays in children's cognitive development. More recently, experts in child development have begun looking at culture and the environment as a complex set of systems and interacting social layers. Bronfenbrenner (1989, 1995, 2005) proposed an **ecological systems theory** to explain how the systems and interrelationships that surround a child affect all aspects of a child's development. Figure 1.3 shows the layers of systems described in Bronfenbrenner's theory:

- The *microsystem,* or inner layer, represents the direct relationships and interactions children have with people in their immediate environment (parents, siblings, friends, teachers, etc.). Parents who are warm and nurturing have a different effect on a child's development than do parents who are cold and distant. Aggressive friends have a different effect than friends who are more peaceful. These relationships go both ways, because a child's own characteristics can influence how others respond to him or her. An easygoing child, for example, may elicit increased warmth and affection from parents. Parents may respond to a child with a difficult temperament by becoming more harsh and punishing.

- The *mesosystem* represents the connections among home, neighborhood, school, day care, and other elements in the larger social environment. Parental involvement in school and increased communication between home and school can have a positive effect on children's school performance. Although children may not take part directly in such communications, the interactions among these larger elements certainly affect their development.

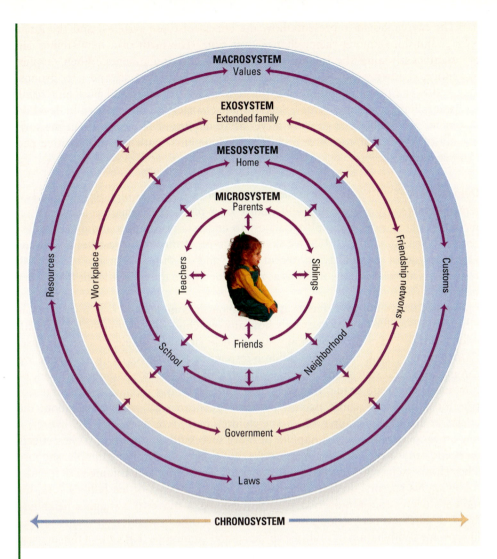

Figure 1.3 • Ecological Systems Theory Urie Bronfenbrenner proposed layers of systems that influence a child's development.

■ The *exosystem* represents even larger social settings and networks. Extended family networks, friendship networks, governmental regulations, social service programs, and even workplace rules regarding family leave and flexible hours are examples of elements in the larger social environment that have bearings on child development.

■ At the widest level, the *macrosystem* represents the values, customs, laws, and resources of the culture at large. Cultures that are more individualistic (e.g., that of the United States) tend to stress early independence in children and competition with peers. In collectivist cultures (e.g., those of China and Japan), however, the emphasis is on community and cooperation. In impoverished countries, malnutrition and inadequate health care can compromise children's development. Affluent nations, where resources abound, can offer more support for optimal development (provided that children have access to the resources).

Think About Jennifer . . .

How could Jennifer use Bronfenbrenner's ecological systems theory to better understand her children's development? What factors within this theory will be the same for both of her children? What factors might differ?

■ The *chronosystem* represents how the effects of these systems, and the inter-relationships among them, change over time. The birth of a new sibling can significantly alter the relationship between child and parents. When families move, children must deal with new schools, neighborhoods, and peer groups. And economies change, moving through cycles of boom and bust and rising and falling employment rates. Any of these changes can influence child development. Bronfenbrenner's theory serves as an important reminder about the variety of forces that can alter a child's developmental path in both positive and negative ways.

dynamic systems theories
Theories that use models from mathematics and physics to understand complex systems of development.

Dynamic Systems Theories. Dynamic systems theories also focus on how layers of systems interact with one another and change over time. These theories are based on models mathematicians and physicists use to understand complex and dynamic systems (Thelen & Smith, 2006). We saved this type of theory for last because it has gained a lot of popularity in recent years and it shows promise for helping researchers integrate many of the ideas they gained from the other theories and other research.

As you know, human behavior is extraordinarily complex and rich in variety. It is virtually impossible to predict exactly how any one child will respond to a given situation, and we can rarely explain any specific behavior by pointing to a single cause. As an example, think about how children respond to the divorce of their parents. We can make general statements about how *most* children become sad or depressed, or how *many* children's grades drop in school, but obviously these statements are not true for all children whose parents divorce. (You can read much more about the effects of divorce in Chapter 12.) Some children may seem unaffected by divorce; a few others may even become happier or more successful after divorce. When effects do occur, can we ever identify their precise cause? Usually not. For example, suppose a boy shows an increase in aggressiveness (fighting at school and arguing with friends) following his parents' divorce. The reason could be the loss of his father figure, his mother's depression, a reduction in family income, a move to a rougher neighborhood, a shift to a new school, or a whole host of other variables. In reality, it was likely some combination of multiple variables and conditions that caused the increase in aggression, not any single variable alone.

According to dynamic systems theory, then, the boy's response to divorce emerges from the complex interaction of elements from multiple layers both in and around the child. Inside the child, we would consider his self-esteem, his ability to cope with intense emotions, and his skills in interacting with peers. Outside the child, factors might include a network of extended family, the aggressiveness of his peers, the quality of his school interactions, and the types of interactions he has with his parents. At the broadest level, the prevailing attitudes about divorce in his culture and society may be important. And at the most elemental levels, we could look at genetic tendencies toward aggression and at how the child's emotions relate to biochemical changes in his brain and nervous system. At first, combining all of these variables may yield a picture that is too chaotic to interpret. But eventually patterns begin to emerge out of the chaos. For example, soon after the divorce, the child may be confused and his behavior may be erratic. Later, as he digests the various pushes and pulls from all of these levels of variables, he may settle into a stable pattern of behavior—such as meeting common frustrations with acts of aggression. Other children, experiencing different combinations of pushes and pulls, may settle into different patterns, such as withdrawal or depression.

In dynamic systems theories, the stable patterns that emerge are called *attractor states*. Attractor states represent the preferred mode of behavior or the dominant psychological attitude or emotion. These states tend to emerge as the whole system *self-organizes* dynamically due to a variety of inputs. It isn't any one variable that causes the aggression to emerge—it isn't the loss of the father alone or the mother's depression alone. Rather, the aggression emerges as a relatively stable and persistent response to the mix of inputs. The system is also dynamic because it *changes with time*. The father may begin to visit the child more frequently, the mother may gradually become less depressed, the child may learn more effective ways of coping with frustration, and even societal attitudes may change (albeit slowly). A change in any variable may affect the system, and in the real world it is common to see complex changes along multiple variables. Strong influences also can disrupt the system, causing a move out of one stable state and into another. An intense instance of racial injustice or an assault by a bully, for example, might push a child's reaction pattern from mild aggression to outright hostility and physical violence. On the other hand, an intimate friendship or the warmth of a caring adult role model could move the pattern in a more positive direction.

Researchers are interested in how systems become stable, when they change, and what makes them change. As Thelen and Smith (2006) put it,

> all components of the developing system are continually linked and mutually interactive in the individual and between the individual and the environment . . . mental and physical activity are assembled in the moment and always as a function of the system's history. Actions done in this moment, in turn, set the stage for behavior in the next second, minute, week, and year. With this formulation, it makes no sense to ask what part of behavior comes from stages, mental structures, symbol systems, knowledge modules, or genes because these constructs do not exist in timeless, disconnected form. There is no time and no level when the system ceases to be dynamic (p. 307).

In recent years dynamic systems theories have helped us understand how infants learn to walk, reach for objects, and perceive forms, as well as how children learn new word meanings, understand emotions, and move across Piaget's stages of cognitive development (Fischer & Bidell, 1998; Gershkoff-Stowe & Thelen, 2004; Thelen & Smith, 2006). Researchers are just beginning to use dynamic systems thinking to model the complexity of child development. Rather than debating nature versus nurture, we now have the opportunity to consider how all of the elements affecting development work in complex interaction. In the coming years it will be interesting to see how well this type of theory performs.

As you can see, theorists have proposed a wide variety of ideas to explain how children and adolescents develop. We hope that these brief sketches have given you a glimpse of the different theories' usefulness in explaining what is (or was) known about children. Each theory offers some degree of prediction and guidance for people working with children. These theories also guide future research efforts by suggesting new factors and variables that need to be explored. As you consider these theories, don't expect any single approach to be the only one that is "right" or "correct." Many theories address narrow or specific aspects of child development. For example, Piaget's cognitive developmental theory focused on how children think, whereas Bronfenbrenner's ecological systems theory focuses more on how children interact with other people. So it wouldn't make sense to pit these two theories against each other and ask which one is better. Each theory offers at least some valuable insight about children and adolescents, yet no single theory captures all of the complexities of human development. As research continues, we will continue to gain information that favors (or discredits) one or another line of thought, and new theories will continue to emerge. In the next section we will describe the most important research techniques used to study child development.

Using the Scientific Method: Research in Child Development

How do researchers identify patterns in child development? How do we know what types of behaviors are typical of children at different ages? How do we gather information to test theories and to generate solutions to the practical problems faced by children and families? In the field of child development, we rely on the *scientific method*. With the **scientific method,** researchers collect data by making systematic observations of children and their behaviors, and they use these data to test their research hypotheses. When their hypotheses are confirmed by the data, then the researchers have reason to believe that their theories are correct. If their hypotheses are not confirmed, then they need to modify or replace their theories. In this section, we introduce you to the research methods that are used most commonly in child development research.

scientific method
Process where researchers test hypotheses by making systematic observations.

As you study this section, ask yourself these questions:

- ■ What are some examples of descriptive research methods, and how are they useful in studying development?

- ■ What is the proper way to interpret a correlation, and what are the advantages and disadvantages of correlational research?

- ■ How do researchers determine cause and effect? How is the experimental method different from correlation? Why don't all research studies employ the experimental method?

- How do cross-sectional, longitudinal, and hybrid research designs differ in how they assess developmental effects?
- What steps do researchers take to protect the rights and privacy of children who participate in their studies?

Descriptive Research Methods

Descriptive methods attempt to describe something about a behavior, such as how often and under what conditions it occurs. One way to describe a behavior is simply to observe it. In *naturalistic observation* researchers watch children in their natural environments (such as at home, in school, or on the playground) and record what they do, when, with whom, and other details. For example, if you want to know how often preschoolers look at books and engage in "prereading" activities, you can go to a day care center and watch the children. But what if the children never show the behavior? Or what if the particular setting or the activities going on while you observe aren't conducive to reading (such as nap time or Play-Doh play)? The biggest advantage of naturalistic observation is that a researcher can gather information about real-life behaviors—but a major disadvantage is that the researcher cannot control the situation to ensure that the behavior of interest will occur. By contrast, in *structured observation,* the researcher creates a suitable situation, arranges for children to be placed in it (often in a laboratory or in a specially prepared space within the home or school), and observes their behavior. For example, to observe reading interest and prereading activities, you could set up a room with a variety of toys, including many interesting books. You could watch children and see if they chose to look at the reading materials, for how long, and in what ways. So in structured observation the researcher has more control than in naturalistic observational settings. However, this method does not answer questions about the real-life occurrences and forms of the behavior. In both types of observation, it's very important that the person collecting the information not know what the expected results are. Otherwise, that person's knowledge could influence his or her observations and the outcome of the research—a situation called *observer bias.*

As an alternative to observing children, researchers can also ask children to give self-reports, or direct answers to questions about a topic or process. For example, you could ask children how much they like to read, how often they look at books, and the like. You could do this in face-to-face interviews or through written questionnaires. The major drawback of self-reports involves participants' abilities to remember accurately and to verbalize their answers. Some children are stronger in these abilities than others are, and these differences can lead to inaccurate conclusions. In addition, children will sometimes give the answers they think the interviewer wants to hear, rather than answers that are more accurate but that they believe are less desirable in some way. Interviewers must also be very careful to not lead children to give certain kinds of responses. This kind of unintentional prompting can occur through the kinds of questions asked, through the phrasing of questions, or through unconscious nonverbal signals such as body movements or facial expressions.

Finally, researchers can do *case studies*—intensive studies of one child or a small number of children. The goal of a case study is to create a detailed description of the individual(s), usually focusing on some particular behaviors. Case studies often focus on children who are exceptional in some way, such as children with some sort of developmental delay or unusually high level of competence or achievement. These studies may employ a variety of different measures. Examples include detailed and repeated observations (both naturalistic and structured); standardized tests and informal assessments; self-reports; and/or physiological measures such as brain activity, heart rate, or respiration patterns during specific activities. For example, you could study a child who is clearly advanced in reading skill so as to understand

descriptive methods
Research methods that describe a behavior of interest, such as how often it occurs and under what conditions.

why and how the skill is developing, or a child who is delayed in reading in order to identify factors that might be contributing to the delay.

Descriptive research methods are valuable in providing information about a behavior, and they are often a useful starting point for understanding some aspect of development. These methods often help researchers develop hypotheses, or specific predictions, about what causes or affects a given behavior. But these methods do not answer questions about relationships among variables; other methods are needed for this.

Correlational Research Methods: Measuring Associations

Suppose we wanted to answer this question: Is reading ability in the early grade school years related to the amount of time parents spend reading to children during the preschool years? What kinds of observations would we need to make? One approach we might take would be to ask parents of preschoolers to keep careful notes (reading logs) on the number of minutes they spent each time they read to their children. After 6 weeks we could collect the logs and calculate the average number of minutes per week that each child was read to by a parent. Later, when the children were in second grade, we could take each child's score on a standardized reading test and match it with his or her average number of minutes of preschool reading. Figure 1.4 presents hypothetical data like those that we might collect if we actually conducted this study. The graph shows that the children who were read to most in preschool tended to have higher reading scores in second grade. The children read to least tended to have lower scores. With the **correlational method,** researchers measure the degree to which two or more variables are related or associated.

A *correlation coefficient* is a number that indicates the direction and strength of an association between two or more variables. In our example, we could compute a correlation coefficient for the association between average minutes of preschool reading and second-grade reading scores. Correlation coefficients (symbolized by the letter r) can range from -1.0 to $+1.0$. *Positive coefficients* ($r = 0.0$ to $+1.0$) indicate that the scores on the two variables tend to run in the same direction. In other words, higher scores on one variable tend to be linked with higher scores on the other variable, and lower with lower. Line A in Figure 1.4 clearly shows a positive correlation, and we calculated the

correlational method
Research method that measures the degree to which two or more variables are related or associated.

Figure 1.4 • Two Positive Correlations Both correlations are hypothetical. The correlation in Line A is stronger ($r = +.81$) than the correlation in Line B ($r = +.32$). The blue data points go with Line A; the yellow points go with Line B.

Notice that greater amounts of preschool reading tend to be associated with higher standardized reading scores. The positive correlation in Line A is stronger than the positive correlation in Line B.

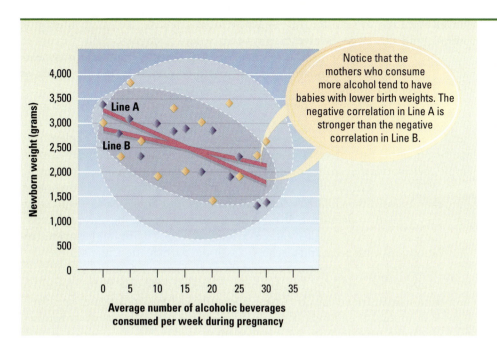

Figure 1.5 • Two Negative Correlations Both correlations are hypothetical. The correlation in Line A is stronger (r = –.84) than the correlation in Line B (r = –.26). The blue data points go with Line A; the yellow points go with Line B.

coefficient to be +.81. The *magnitude* of the coefficient indicates the strength of the correlation. Line A shows a fairly strong positive relationship (+.81)—a fairly strong tendency for greater preschool reading time to be linked with higher second-grade reading scores. Contrast this with the data in Line B of Figure 1.4. Here, the correlation coefficient is +.32. That is, second-grade reading scores still tend to rise along with preschool reading (i.e., the correlation is still a positive one), but the relationship is weaker than in Line A (i.e., the numerical value is smaller).

Now consider an example of a negative correlation. What if we asked mothers of newborn babies to estimate the number of alcoholic beverages they drank per week, on average, during their pregnancies? Would their alcohol consumption be related to the birth weights of their babies? Line A in Figure 1.5 shows hypothetical data with a correlation coefficient of –.84. *Negative coefficients* (r = 0.0 to –1.0) indicate that the two variables have an inverse relationship: Higher scores on one variable tend to be linked with lower scores on the other variable and vice versa. You can see that there is a relatively strong pattern in the data—birth weights tend to decrease as alcohol consumption increases. Line B in Figure 1.5 also shows a negative correlation, but here the relationship is weaker (r = –.26).

From these examples you can see the usefulness of correlational studies. If these were actual studies, we could learn that children tend to score higher in reading in second grade when their parents read more to them as preschoolers, and that alcohol consumption is related to lower birth weights in newborn babies. Both of these results would suggest important advice for parents. But at this point we need to emphasize a key limitation of correlational studies: *Correlation does not prove causation!* On the basis of correlational studies alone, we can determine that two variables are linked but we cannot determine what is the cause and what is the effect. For example, compared to nondrinkers, women who drink larger amounts of alcohol also tend to smoke more cigarettes and tend to have poorer nutrition. Was it the alcohol that caused the reduction in birth weight, or was it the cigarette smoking, or poor nutrition, or some other factor that we did not measure? In the reading study, it seems plausible that reading more to preschoolers would enhance their reading ability—but the real causal direction might be the reverse. For example, children might inherit "reading aptitude," with some children destined to become better readers and some poorer readers. Children with greater "reading aptitude"

Think About Jennifer . . .

How would correlational research help you understand the factors involved in the development of Jennifer's children? Given that this research method cannot determine cause and effect, is this type of research still useful?

might be more fun to read to; they might be more attentive, ask more interesting questions, and otherwise behave in ways that would encourage their parents to spend more time reading to them. If so, then increased "reading aptitude" (as measured in the second-grade standardized tests) would be the cause, not the effect, of increased parental reading time.

Researchers recognize the complex ways that variables can interrelate to influence the behavior and development of children. As we mentioned in our discussion of systems theories, more and more research is trying to describe this complexity by measuring multiple variables. Sometimes researchers compute *path analyses*—sets of multiple correlations that show how several variables relate to each other. Ladd et al., (1999), for example, investigated a large group of kindergarten children. First they assessed the children's cognitive maturity and family background when they entered kindergarten. As the school year progressed, the researchers took measures of prosocial (helpful) behaviors, antisocial (harmful) behaviors, relationships with peers and teachers, classroom participation, and achievement (measured by a kindergarten readiness test). Figure 1.6 shows correlations among these variables. For example, prosocial behavior relates positively with mutual friendships ($r = .35$), and antisocial behavior relates negatively with mutual friendships ($r = -.14$). The strongest relationship is between classroom participation and achievement ($r = .43$). But classroom participation is itself related to several other variables such as cognitive maturity and mutual friendships. As you can see, children's success in kindergarten involves a whole array of interrelated factors.

Even when we measure an array of complicated relationships, we still cannot be sure which are the causes and which are the effects. Do children participate more in kindergarten because they have more friends in class, or do they have more friends because they participate more? Do children achieve more because they participate

your perspective

What other factors can you think of that might have direct or indirect relationships with school achievement in kindergarten? How would a path analysis help you understand the relative contributions of these factors and their interactions?

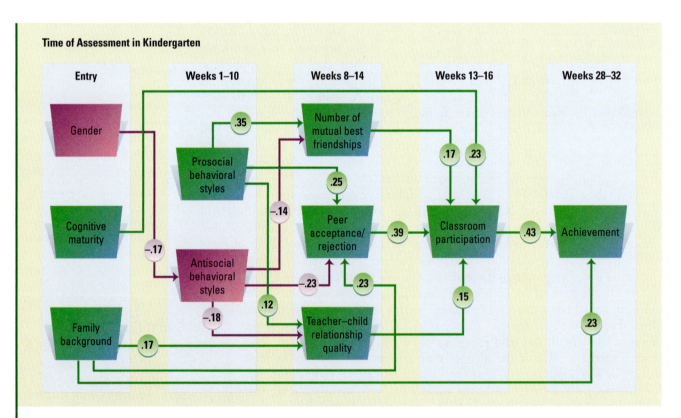

Figure 1.6 • Path Analysis Model This diagram shows correlations among several variables that are related to greater achievement in kindergarten. *Note:* Correlations ≤ .12 are not statistically significant. (Ladd, Birch, & Buhs, 1999.)

more in class, or do they participate more because they are performing well and already feel confident? We can hypothesize several different ways to explain the same correlation. So again, correlation in itself is not sufficient for determining cause and effect. But ultimately, of course, researchers would like to determine cause and effect. To accomplish this they use the experimental method.

Experimental Research Methods: Determining Cause and Effect

How could we demonstrate that increasing alcohol consumption during pregnancy actually *causes* a reduction in birth weight? Consider the hypothetical experiment diagrammed in Figure 1.7. Researchers randomly assign 50 pregnant rats either to an experimental group or to a control group. The 25 rats in the experimental group have water bottles that contain a mixture of water and pure grain alcohol. The 25 rats in the control group have bottles with pure water. Other than this difference, the researchers treat all 50 rats as much alike as possible. They provide identical cages, offer the same food, and follow the same feeding schedules with all the rats. Their aim is to have the two groups differ systematically along only one variable: alcohol versus pure water. This variable is the *independent variable*—the variable that the researchers systematically manipulate in the experiment. The idea is to manipulate this variable independently of other factors (e.g., diet) that might affect pregnancy. In the hypothetical experiment, after the rat pups are born, we can weigh each pup and compare the average birth weights in the experimental and control groups. Birth weight is the *dependent variable*. That is, it represents the outcome that we measure, an outcome that is dependent on the manipulation of the independent variable.

With **experiments,** then, researchers systematically manipulate the independent variable to determine if it causes a difference in the dependent variable. If we conduct this experiment properly, the only systematic difference between the two groups will be exposure to alcohol: The experimental group is exposed to alcohol, and the control group is not. If we observe that the pups in the groups differ reliably in birth weight (e.g., if the birth weights in the experimental group are substantially lower than those in the control group), then we can conclude alcohol exposure caused this difference. What else could be the cause? Rats in both groups got the same diet, were on the same feeding schedules, and had the same experience in every way possible other than alcohol exposure.

Of course, researchers cannot perfectly control every factor in the experiment. Individual rats will differ in their metabolisms and appetites, for example. And each

experiment
Method where researchers systematically manipulate an independent variable to determine if it causes a difference in a dependent variable.

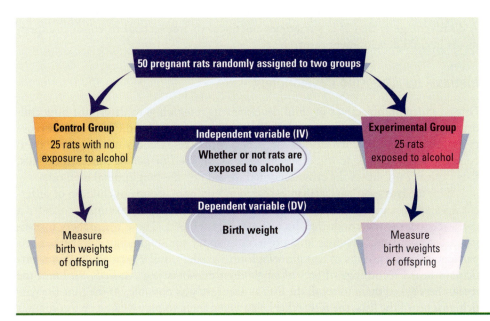

Figure 1.7 • Hypothetical Experiment In a hypothetical experiment to study the effects of alcohol consumption during pregnancy on the birth weight of newborns, the researcher systematically manipulates the independent variable (IV) to determine its effects on the dependent variable (DV). If the only difference between the control and experimental groups is alcohol exposure versus non-exposure, then any reliable difference in birth weights can be attributed to the alcohol exposure. Experiments are the only method that can determine cause–effect relationships. Why would this experiment never be conducted with human participants?

mother rat will weigh a different amount even before pregnancy. Because these factors may affect the birth weights, we use *random assignment* to groups to prevent such factors from differing systematically between the groups. With random assignment, each participant (in this case, each rat) has an equal chance of being assigned to any of the groups in an experiment. It is therefore unlikely that all of the heavier mother rats would be assigned to the control group or that all of the rats with lighter appetites would be assigned to the experimental group.

If experimenters can show a systematic relationship between an independent variable and a dependent variable, then they can demonstrate cause and effect. In our example, we might be able to show that alcohol consumption during pregnancy actually causes reduced birth weight in rat offspring. But of course, we experimented on rats, not humans. It would obviously be unethical for us to require that some women consume alcohol during pregnancy just so we could observe the effect on human newborns.

This highlights the main disadvantage of the experimental method: Researchers always must ask whether it is ethical to manipulate the independent variable that is of interest in the experiment. For example, think back to the discussion of a correlation between preschool reading and second-grade reading scores. The correlation was not sufficient to establish cause and effect. Would it be appropriate or ethical to conduct an experiment in this situation? Could we, for example, require that some parents read more to their preschool children and that some parents read only a little or not at all? Could we, ethically, randomly assign parents and their children to these two experimental conditions? If any of the experimental conditions might conceivably have a negative effect on a child's development, then ethically it is difficult to justify the experiment. Sometimes we turn to animal research to study variables that would be unethical to manipulate with humans. Research on the effect of alcohol consumption on pregnancy, for example, has utilized rats and other animal species. (Animal rights activists have argued that those types of experiments are also unethical, and there are now strict guidelines for conducting research using animals.) In other situations, however, animal research would not be appropriate. For example, it wouldn't make sense to study the effects of preschool reading with monkeys. And it surely wouldn't make sense to study how mutual friendships affect class participation and school achievement in a rat colony! With these types of questions, for which it would be unethical or impractical to conduct human experiments, we have to stick to correlational research methods.

In summary, correlational methods have the advantage of demonstrating and measuring associations among variables, even for variables that we cannot ethically manipulate. The main disadvantage of correlational research is that correlations alone cannot prove causation. A major advantage of the experimental method is that experiments, if conducted properly, can demonstrate cause-and-effect relationships. A disadvantage is that it is sometimes unethical or impractical to conduct experiments in child development research.

Methods for Assessing Development

One of the main objectives in child development research is to determine how children do and do not change as they grow through childhood. Whether they use descriptive methods, correlations, or experiments, researchers need some way to compare observations across different ages of children or across time. To do this, they typically use either the cross-sectional method or the longitudinal method.

cross-sectional method
A type of research design that studies development by comparing groups of children of different ages against one another at the same point in time.

With the **cross-sectional method,** researchers compare groups of children of different ages against one another at the same point in time. As an example, consider a cross-sectional study conducted by Cowan et al. (1999). These researchers investigated developmental changes in short-term memory for single-digit numbers. Their participants were groups of first graders, fourth graders, and young adults. Each participant heard recordings of lists of single-digit numbers (e.g., 3, 7, 5, 9). Later the researchers asked them to recall the lists as accurately as possible. At the time the participants heard the lists, the researchers also asked them to play a game on a computer screen; this activity was intended to distract them from verbally repeating, or rehearsing, the series of digits. The goal was to see how well the participants could remember the digits when they couldn't rehearse them. On average, the first graders recalled approximately 3.6 digits correctly, the fourth graders 4.5 digits, and the adults 5.4. Using this cross-sectional study design, these researchers were able to demonstrate that increasing age coincides with increases in short-term memory.

Another approach is to use the **longitudinal method** by comparing performance or observations across ages by taking repeated measurements from the same people across time. Researchers can then compare the measurements or observations to see how they are changing (or remaining the same) as the participants age. Consider, for example, a longitudinal study conducted by Nancy Eisenberg and her colleagues (1999). These researchers used a variety of measures to assess how frequently children engaged in prosocial, or helping, behaviors. They followed a group of 32 children, taking measurements approximately every 2 years from the time the children were 4 years old until they reached 24 years. The results? Individual differences in prosocial behavior tended to be relatively consistent and stable across development. The children who tended to be the most helpful during preschool (age 4) also tended to show more prosocial behaviors and attitudes during later childhood, in adolescence, and even into early adulthood.

The cross-sectional and longitudinal methods offer different advantages and disadvantages to researchers. The longitudinal method allows a more direct test of development. By following the same children as they age, researchers can observe how behaviors, attitudes, and other dispositions change or remain the same in those children. A disadvantage, however, is that it is difficult to get participants to remain in a study across long periods of time. For example, Eisenberg and her colleagues actually began their study with 37 children. Over the years a few children moved away and could not be contacted; one person participated all the way through adolescence and then refused to complete the study as an adult. You can imagine that participants might drop out of a study for a variety of reasons—from simple boredom and loss of interest to a lack of time due to expanding responsibilities as participants mature to illness or even death.

This factor, called *differential dropout*, poses an especially serious problem with longitudinal studies. If the reason for the dropout is related to the nature of the study itself, then the validity of the results is compromised. If the least prosocial participants were the ones who dropped out of Eisenberg's study, for example, then the results would represent an overestimate of how prosocial most people tend to be. Further, some people might start out being helpful (and agree to participate as children) but then become less helpful (and therefore drop out of the study). If this happened, then the researchers would end up with an overestimate of the stability of prosocial behaviors: The participants who would have demonstrated the most instability would have removed themselves from the study. Clearly, the longer it takes to conduct a longitudinal study, the more likely it is that participants will drop out. Also, the sheer time that it takes to conduct this type of study can make it impractical. Can most researchers really wait 20 years to finish their study? Will they (or the field) even be interested in the same developmental questions 20 years in the future?

The main advantage of the cross-sectional study is that it can be completed in a relatively short period of time. Instead of waiting until participants grow and develop, researchers using the cross-sectional approach take a "cross section" of different ages at one point in time. A disadvantage of this approach, however, is that the participant groups will differ not only in age but also in intelligence, physical strength, and many other qualities that make people unique—and these differences could affect the study results. In the short-term memory study we described, obviously the first graders were not the same children as the fourth graders, and the adults were still another group of people. When we compare the groups on memory performance, how can we be sure that the differences were due to differences in age rather than simply to differences among individuals?

longitudinal method
A type of research design that studies development by measuring or observing the same children across time as they grow and mature.

Think About Jennifer . . .
How might cross-sectional and longitudinal research help Jennifer understand her children's development? What concerns should she have with these methods?

Figure 1.8 • Hybrid Research Design In a hybrid design to assess development, researchers study children of different ages at the same time (the cross-sectional component), then follow and retest the same children as they age (the longitudinal component). These designs are rare in developmental research, in part because they are complicated and time consuming.

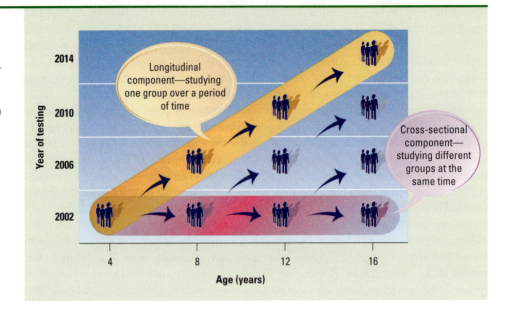

When the age groups differ substantially, as they did in the short-term memory study, there also can be a problem with cohort effects. *Cohort effects* are differences in behavior or other attributes that result from the unique experiences of people who grow up in different periods. Changes in education, technology, medicine, the economy, and the cultural climate are just a few of the factors causing children growing up today to have a different developmental experience than did children several decades ago. For example, we cannot assume that the first graders of today will grow up in the same way as children did during the Great Depression of the 1930s or during the Vietnam War era. Consider the terrorist attacks on the United States on September 11, 2001. Some claim that September 11 was "the day the world changed forever" or the day that freedom and innocence were lost. Would it be fair to compare children raised after the attacks to children raised before? In what ways might their experiences differ?

Some researchers try to balance the advantages and disadvantages of cross-sectional and longitudinal research by using *hybrid designs*. Figure 1.8 shows an example. When the study begins (in the year 2002), groups of 4-, 8-, 12-, and 16-year-olds are all studied at the same time. This part of the study is cross-sectional. Then the researchers track the children's progress by repeating the study with the same children every 4 years. Notice that the children who were 4 years old in 2002 are 8 years old in 2006, and so on. This is the longitudinal component. These types of designs are sometimes called *cross-lag* or *sequential designs*.

Whether researchers use the correlational or experimental method, and whether they use cross-sectional, longitudinal, or hybrid designs, they need to carefully protect the rights of everyone who participates in their studies. Let's turn now to the ethical treatment of children in research.

Ethics in Research with Children

Researchers who work with children must follow the ethical guidelines of the American Psychological Association and the Society for Research in Child Development. The full text of their guidelines can be found at the following Web sites: www.apa.org /ethics and www.srcd.org/about.html. Here is a summary of the most important ethical standards.

- *Risks versus benefits.* Researchers should conduct studies only when the potential benefits outweigh any known risks. Research designs and procedures must be sound enough that the information to be gained has sufficient value to out-weigh any harm, stress, or inconvenience that participants might experience. In some cases participants even receive compensation or other benefits for taking part in the study.

■ *Nonharmful procedures.* Researchers may not use procedures that could harm a child either physically or psychologically. They must use the least stressful research procedures at all times. If there is any question about possible harm to a child, researchers must consult with appropriate authorities or colleagues.

■ *Informed consent.* Researchers must explain the purposes, procedures, and all known risks and benefits of their studies to the potential participants. When working with minors, researchers must obtain informed consent from both the children and their parents or guardians. Children over 6 and their parents must give written consent. Younger children must give verbal consent.

■ *Unforeseen consequences.* If a research procedure results in any negative consequence for a child, the researcher must do whatever is necessary to correct the situation. Also, if during the study the researcher collects information that could have a bearing on a child's well-being, the researcher must discuss this with the child's parents or guardians and with appropriate experts who might be able to assist the child.

■ *Confidentiality.* Researchers must keep all information obtained from participants confidential. They must never reveal participants' names or other identifying information to anyone else, and they may not include this information in any written research reports unless the participants have given prior consent. Most research reports give only group averages or scores accumulated across many participants. Reports that give data from individuals must be anonymous.

■ *Implications of research.* Researchers must be aware of social, political, and human implications—not only of their research but also of how it is presented to colleagues and to the public. Research on sensitive topics is certainly not forbidden, but researchers must take special care when the results may be alarming to groups or individuals.

To ensure compliance with these ethical guidelines, all researchers must get advance approval for their projects from an *institutional review board* (IRB). At most universities, for example, IRBs of trained professionals review research proposals. Before approving any study, the IRB must be satisfied that the potential benefits outweigh any potential risks and that the researchers will follow proper procedures for obtaining informed consent, protecting confidentiality, and adhering to all other ethical standards. Ethical guidelines also exist for research conducted with animals.

your perspective

Regarding the ethics of conducting research with children, do you think these guidelines provide enough protection to child participants? Why or why not?

■ Let's Review . . .

1. Attendance in school tends to decline as drug use increases. This is an example of:
    a. a positive effect.   b. a negative correlation.
    c. lack of a correlation.   d. a cohort correlation.

2. Which of the following is the most important limitation of correlational research?
    a. It is difficult to obtain positive correlations.
    b. Correlation does not prove causation.
    c. Correlational research cannot describe the complex relations among three or more variables.
    d. Correlation coefficients do not tell you anything about the strength of the relationship between variables.

3. Dr. Jorgenson conducted an experiment to test the effectiveness of a new parent training program. She randomly assigned 40 parents to two groups. One group received the new parent training program, and the other group received the old standard program. After the training programs were finished, Dr. Jorgenson asked each parent to rate their interactions with their children. In this scenario, what is the *independent variable*?
   a. The two parent training programs (new versus standard).
   b. The interaction rating given by each parent after the training.
   c. The number of parents assigned to each training program.
   d. The amount of time each parent spent in the training program.

4. Which of the following research methods is capable of demonstrating a cause-and-effect relationship?
   a. correlational methods   b. experimental methods
   c. path analysis methods   d. all of the above

5. **True or False:** Differential dropout is a problem that plagues the cross-sectional method of assessing development.

6. **True or False:** Before working with children, all researchers must have their studies approved by an institutional review board so that the rights and privacy of the children will be protected.

Answers: 1. b, 2. b, 3. a, 4. b, 5. F, 6. T

Applications of Child Development Research and Careers Related to Children

One goal of science is to advance knowledge for its own sake, but another important goal is to provide information that can help people with practical challenges in life. And we can't think of any practical challenge that is more important than raising and educating children! You may already have a clear idea about the work you would like to do, perhaps as a teacher, counselor, psychologist, social worker, or researcher. If you have not yet chosen a career but do have an interest in working with children, then we hope that this section will give you several interesting ideas. What could be more rewarding than a job in which you have the opportunity to help the next generation attain a healthy and satisfying life?

As you study this section, ask yourself these questions:

■ What kinds of child development research could help parents and families with the practical problems involved in raising children?

■ What is *social policy,* and how can child development research influence it?

■ How can psychologists, counselors, educators, and other professionals use child development research to guide their work with children?

■ What career opportunities are available for people who want to work with or for children?

Practical Applications of Child Development Research

Family and Parenting. How do you discipline children while at the same time show that you love and care for them? Should parents have special concerns about raising an only child or about raising a large number of children? How does divorce affect children? And what about children in blended stepfamilies or with single parents?

There are an infinite number of questions and concerns related to family life and parenting. Parenting a child is the most important responsibility that any of us will ever have, and most parents want to improve their knowledge and skills. Almost all of the topics in this book can offer some advice to parents. Researchers continue to collect new data to answer the latest questions (e.g., how to protect children from the dangers of the Internet) and to continue to probe the age-old issues (e.g., whether genes or upbringing influence children more). We will cover many of these issues as we move through this textbook. Also, in each chapter of this book, a boxed feature called *A Personal Perspective* will present interviews with people about their real-life experiences with children. These boxes give examples of how people think about child development or of how people can use topics in child development to improve their understanding of children or their work with children. For your first box, look at the A Personal Perspective box called "Meet First-Time Parents."

a personal perspective

Meet First-Time Parents

Carolyn and Bob Landers
Dallas, Texas
Just gave birth to their first child, Connor

What is the biggest question that you have about your child's future and development?
We wonder what we can do on a daily basis that will enhance our son's development. We want to offer a variety of new experiences without creating a rigid schedule or to-do list for him. It seems like children get overcommitted and spread very thin at an early age—it seems to start shortly after birth. But we also worry we'll miss something that everyone else is doing that gives their child an advantage, and as a result, Connor will be behind in some way. It's all of the short-term things that can have very long-term consequences that concern us.

What are the main hopes and worries you have for your child?
Above everything, we wish good health for our son. That is the foundation that makes everything else possible. We also hope to impart to him at an early age a love of learning and an understanding of the importance of a good education that ultimately results in a fulfilling career. We also hope that he'll find his own path (even if it's different from our vision) so he'll know real happiness and be true to himself. We hope to give him a happy childhood full of wonderful memories and the knowledge that he is very loved and cherished. This will hopefully give him a sense of self-worth and confidence, help him make his own decisions, and develop true friendships. A friend sent a beautiful blessing which sums it up nicely: "May love be the first awareness of Connor's life, and the last. And may all that lies between be filled with discovering its many faces."

Our son's personal safety and health are our main worries. Childhood is a more dangerous time now than it was for both of us. We didn't worry (much) about abduction, molestation, weapons at school, etc. I hope we can give him enough information to be aware and to protect himself without taking away the innocence of his childhood or making him afraid of everyone he meets.

Where will you go for answers to practical questions about raising your child?
We'll go mainly to family and friends who have children. We'll do a lot of reading, too, but there's nothing like those who have gone before for getting the real scoop about what to expect and how to solve problems. I know we'll rely on our gut instincts a lot, too.

Q *If you were expecting your first child, what questions, hopes, and worries would you have? Where would you turn for information about raising children? What would you say to reassure new parents like Carolyn and Bob?*

Social Policy. How does living in poverty affect children's development, and how can we all work together to reduce the negative effects? When parents have new babies, should they receive paid time off from work to stay home? What should the role of the federal government be in testing and monitoring children's progress in school? When children are being abused or neglected, when should government agencies step in and remove the children from their environment? These are just a few of the many questions that relate to the relationship between child development and government policies. In the area of **social policy,** officials at the federal, state, and local levels try to use knowledge provided by child development research to improve the lives of children and families. From President Lyndon B. Johnson's "War on Poverty" in the 1960s to George W. Bush's "No Child Left Behind" legislation, government agencies have tried to intervene to improve the lives of children. Private organizations and individuals can also affect social policy. Charities, service organizations, and private individuals contribute by donating money or offering services to children and families in need.

Research in child development affects social policy in two ways. First, research findings can stimulate changes in social policy. Research showing that children from disadvantaged families fared poorly in school, for example, stimulated the creation of Project Head Start, an enrichment program designed to give disadvantaged preschoolers the skills they will need in the classroom. Second, after public policies and programs have come into being, child development researchers play an important role in evaluating their effectiveness.

Every chapter in this textbook includes *A Social Policy Perspective* box that highlights an important social policy issue relevant for that chapter. For this chapter, take a look at the A Social Policy Perspective box called "Every Day in America." As you will see, more can be done to protect the lives and healthy development of children.

social policy
Attempts to improve the lives of children and families by using child development research to affect laws, regulations, and programs.

your perspective

When you vote in elections, do you consider the impact of social policy on children's lives? What political issues now being debated in your local area might have an impact on children?

a social policy perspective

Every Day in America

- 5 children or adolescents commit suicide
- 8 children are killed by firearms
- 77 babies die before their first birthdays
- 181 children are arrested for violent crimes
- 367 babies are born to mothers who had late or no prenatal care
- 888 low birth weight (weighing less than 5½ pounds) babies are born
- 1,154 babies are born to teen mothers
- 1,701 babies are born without health insurance
- 2,447 babies are born into poverty
- 2,482 children are confirmed as abused or neglected
- 2,756 teens drop out of high school
- 4,356 children are arrested

- more than 9 million children live without health insurance
- 12.4 million children live in poverty

Q *Think about how these statistics are reflected in the city, neighborhood, or area where you live. Which of these problems is most significant in your area? Why do you think these problems exist? Have welfare reforms or any other changes in social policy been effective in reducing these numbers? What government programs, policies, or laws would you enact to address these problems?*

(Data from the Children's Defense Fund, 2006.)

Psychology, Counseling, Education, and Other Uses. Child development research also has many practical uses in therapeutic, educational, and other settings. Child therapists and counselors need to have a thorough understanding of the typical (and atypical) pathways that child development can take. They must be able to tailor their interventions and therapy techniques to the developmental needs of the individual child. Teachers need to understand development so they can help all children maximize their learning potential. It is important that teachers know how children learn new information, how they work independently and in groups, and how they relate with friends and peers. Day care providers, nurses, camp counselors, and anyone else who works professionally with children can benefit by studying what researchers have learned about children and their development.

Careers Related to Children

Another feature you will encounter in each chapter is a box called *A Professional Perspective* in which we present interviews with professionals who work with children. For this chapter, see the Professional Perspective box on page 38 called "Career Focus: Meet a Child Social Worker." A great many career opportunities allow you to work with children or on behalf of children. In therapeutic settings, psychiatrists, clinical psychologists, school psychologists, counselors, and clinical social workers help children who suffer from mental illness or from the abuse or stress they face in life. Social service agencies also employ people to work with children—for example, in domestic violence shelters, at boys and girls clubs, in halfway houses, and in criminal justice or delinquency programs. Teachers work with children on a daily basis, and day care providers help families manage the balance between work and child care. Many corporations also hire people to work with children or to help inform the corporation about children. Marketing, advertising, and the development of children's products are a few examples of business applications. Government agencies hire people trained in child development to direct, manage, or supervise projects designed to help children and families. And of course, to keep the field up to date, scientists and researchers conduct new studies and develop and test new theories of child development. Research scientists provide the database that all of the other professionals can use to decide how best to help children.

In this chapter we introduced the field of child development. We described the basic issues and theories that have shaped the field, and we explained how researchers use the scientific method to study child development. In the remaining chapters you will learn about many of the important trends and research findings in this exciting field. Along the way you will discover many interesting things that can guide your work with children—and perhaps as a bonus, you will gain insight into your own development.

Career Focus: Meet a Child Social Worker

Pamela Talbot
Flat Rock, Michigan
Social worker who evaluates foster homes
for licensing in the state of Michigan

What do you do in your work to help children and families?

I review the financial stability, safety, and suitability of homes for people who want to be foster parents. This involves social history interviews, getting state and local criminal clearances, and medical clearances then making a recommendation as to whether the person should receive a foster care license. I also provide training to potential foster parents to help prepare them for dealing with children, birth parents, the court system, and our agency. I investigate allegations of abuse, neglect, or rule noncompliance and make recommendations about what to do if an allegation is true.

What aspects of child development do you use in your work?

I use information on family structures, discipline, abuse and neglect, separation and attachment, and the effects of drug and alcohol abuse as I train prospective foster parents, with a strong emphasis on discipline. We also address how all of the factors within the family affect the child's stage of development so foster parents can be better prepared to deal with the children's behaviors and needs. Most foster children are not at an average stage of development due to environmental, educational and/or emotional neglect and physical abuse. Many people expect the children to adjust to their homes with no problems and be just like their own kids were. They don't understand the life the kids were exposed to.

From what you see, what is the most important problem faced by children and families?

Drug and alcohol abuse, physical abuse, and neglect. Kids come into care for a lot of different reasons, usually more than one. It's not uncommon for a drug-addicted parent to be physically abusing a child and leaving them home alone. Educational and environmental neglect are also issues; the kids aren't going to school and the house is unsafe (for example, with excessive roaches, no heat or lights, and no furniture). Sexual abuse is also fairly common, but not nearly as common as the other areas.

What advice do you have for students who are considering a career in your field?

First you have to clear up any unresolved personal issues. A lot of people are not able to work effectively with all parties involved because of biases, and some even end up in therapy themselves. Also, you can't personalize the things that are going on, and you can't expect to save the world. But it is very rewarding when you are able to make that difference! To know that you have helped to break the cycle and hopefully made the future better for many generations is wonderful. It's just a long road to get there.

What education and training is needed to work in your area?

You need at least a bachelor's degree in a related area (social work, psychology, child development, etc). State-mandated training (in Michigan, about 24 hours for caseworkers and 16 hours for licensing workers) and ongoing yearly training is required. There is also training at the agency.

Q *If you were working in a career like Pamela's, what information would you need about child development? What do you think are the most important problems faced by children and families today? How can families best be helped?*

■ Let's Review . . .

Students: Now that you have finished the chapter, look back to the questions we posed about Jennifer at the beginning of this chapter. You should be able to use a large amount of the chapter material to answer the questions. Use the "Think About" notes in the margin as a guide to help you. After you have considered your own answers, check them against the suggestions in the "Thinking Back" summary below.

Thinking Back to Jennifer . . .

Now that you have studied this chapter, you should be able to give Jennifer some general guidance on raising her children, answer the questions she had, and explain how researchers study child development. Compare your thoughts to the following comments.

Child development researchers study physical, cognitive, and social development in children and adolescents. They also study how nature and nurture interact to influence development. Because Jennifer's son and daughter share a similar genetic heritage, their paths of development will probably be similar. Their genes do differ, however, and their environmental experiences will also differ, so their developmental paths will not be identical.

Jennifer can use several of the major developmental theories to guide her parenting. For example, behaviorism can help her learn to reinforce appropriate behaviors in her children. Social learning theory can give Jennifer ideas on modeling appropriate behavior for her children to imitate. She can also be mindful of how negative fears and anxieties can be classically conditioned. With an awareness of psychoanalytic theories, Jennifer can encourage positive ego development in her children by establishing trust in infancy and allowing her children to express their autonomy, initiative, and industry. Jennifer can draw on ecological systems theory to understand how her neighborhood, schools, family and friendship networks, ethnic background, and other elements of the larger social systems affect her children's development.

■ Chapter Review . . .

What aspects of development does the field of child development investigate? What are the main forces that drive development?

Child development is a multidisciplinary field that studies physical, cognitive, and social development in children and adolescents. Both nature (including biology and genetics) and nurture (including the environment, parents, and culture) influence development.

What is a theory, and why are theories useful?

A theory is an explanation of how the facts fit together. Theories provide frameworks that summarize the facts as currently known, allow prediction of future behavior and events, provide guidance, stimulate new research and discoveries, and give researchers filters for identifying relevant information and relationships.

Which theories have had the most influence on the field of child development throughout its history?

The psychoanalytic theories of Sigmund Freud and Erik Erikson focused, respectively, on unconscious processes and the development of ego identity. Freud described five stages of personality development that involved the id, ego, and superego. Erikson described eight stages of identity development. Behavioral theories focused on observable behaviors and environmental conditions. Classical conditioning theories (Ivan Pavlov and John Watson) described how organisms learn reflexive responses, and the theory of operant conditioning (B. F. Skinner) described how reinforcement and punishment affect behavior. Albert Bandura's social learning theory emphasized imitation and modeling of behavior. Jean Piaget's cognitive developmental theory proposed that children actively construct and adapt their own structures of thought and logic through four stages of cognitive growth. Lev Vygotsky described how the internalization of language brings the culture's psychological tools to the developing minds of children. Ethologists study the adaptive and survival values of behaviors, and neuropsychologists use modern technology to study the structure and function of the brain and nervous system. Urie Bronfenbrenner's ecological systems theory identifies layers of systems that influence the child, from the child's interaction with immediate family members to the larger context of culture and society. Other dynamic systems theories use math and physics models to understand the complex systems that affect child development.

What are descriptive research methods, and how do they help us understand development?

Descriptive research methods include observation, self-reports, and case studies. The goal of descriptive methods is to provide information and describe some aspect of development. These methods help researchers gather information and develop hypotheses, but they do not answer questions about relationships among variables.

What is the correlational research method, and what are its main strengths and weaknesses?

With the correlational method, researchers measure the degree to which two or more variables are related or associated. Correlation is especially useful in situations in which it would be unethical to manipulate an independent variable experimentally (e.g., to investigate the effects of prenatal alcohol consumption on the development of the fetus). This method also can be used to describe the complex array of interactions among many variables. Its main weakness is that correlation alone does not prove causation.

What is the experimental research method, and what are its main strengths and weaknesses?

With the experimental method, researchers manipulate an independent variable to test its effect on a dependent variable. The main strength of experimentation is that, if conducted properly, experiments can determine cause-and-effect relationships. The main weakness is that it would be unethical to manipulate many of the variables that are of interest in child development. We cannot randomly assign families to live in poverty, children to suffer abusive forms of punishment, or women to use alcohol or drugs during pregnancy, for example. To investigate these types of situations, researchers usually use correlational methods.

What methods do researchers use to assess development, and what are these methods' main strengths and weaknesses?

The cross-sectional method compares groups of children of different ages against one another at the same point in time. With the longitudinal method, researchers follow the same children across time and retest or evaluate them as they age. The longitudinal method provides a more direct test of development, but it can be very time-consuming and is compromised when participants drop out of the study. The cross-sectional method is more efficient, and participants are less likely to drop out, but cohort effects can be a problem when the groups differ substantially in age. Hybrid designs try to use the strengths of both types of methods.

What steps must researchers take to protect the rights and privacy of children who participate in their studies?

All researchers must get approval for their studies from an institutional review board. The IRB evaluates proposals to determine if the potential benefits outweigh the risks. Researchers must use nonharmful procedures, obtain informed consent from participants (and from parents or guardians of minor participants), report unforeseen consequences, protect the privacy of information, and consider the implications of their research.

What are some of the areas of practical application for child development research and theory?

The knowledge provided by child development research can help people deal with family and parenting concerns. It also has important implications for all social policy involving children. It also improves the services offered to children in therapeutic, educational, and medical settings.

What are some careers related to children?

A wide variety of careers involve work with children. Therapy, social service, education, and day care are examples of settings that involve direct work with children and families. Corporations and government agencies hire people to develop products or programs that affect children. Scientists and researchers investigate child development and evaluate the impact that social policies have on children and families.

■ Key Terms

behavior genetics (8)

behaviorism (14)

child development (6)

classical conditioning (15)

cognitive development (7)

cognitive developmental theory (17)

correlational method (26)

cross-sectional method (30)

descriptive methods (25)

dynamic systems theories (22)

ecological systems theory (20)

ethology (19)

experiment (29)

hypotheses (10)

information-processing approach (18)

longitudinal method (31)

nature (8)

neuropsychology (19)

nurture (8)

operant conditioning (16)

physical development (7)

psychoanalytic theories (11)

scientific method (24)

socioemotional development (7)

social learning (16)

social policy (36)

sociocultural theory (17)

theory (10)

mydevelopmentlab
Where human development comes to life!

If you are using MyDevelopmentLab, you have access to an ebook version of this textbook, along with dozens of valuable resources per chapter—including video and audio clips, simulations and activities, self-assessments, practice tests, and other study materials. Here is a sampling of the resources available for this chapter.

Explore

Race and Ethnicity in Psychological Inquiry

Correlations Do Not Show Causation

Simulate

Ethics in Psychological Research

Distinguishing Independent and Dependent Variables

Watch

Human Cloning—The Ethics

Genetic Schizophrenia

If you did not receive an access code to MyDevelopmentLab with this text and wish to purchase access online, please visit www.mydevelopmentlab.com.

chapter 2

Heredity and the Environment

Daniel and Teri have been married for 6 years and have tried desperately to have their own baby. Two years ago Teri found out that she is not able to conceive children, so she and Daniel decided to try to adopt a baby. Last month their adoption came through, and they now have a baby boy! He is perfectly healthy and has a huge smile, and Daniel and Teri are showering him with love and attention. Because the adoption agency keeps adoption information confidential, Daniel and Teri don't have much information about the baby's background. They know only that he came from a teenaged single mother who

gave the baby up so she could go back to school. Someday, Daniel and Teri may be able to meet the baby's biological mother, if both sides agree to meet. Until then, Daniel and Teri wonder if their baby will grow up to be more like them or more like his biological parents.

Already they can see that their baby's physical features will be different from theirs. The baby has blue eyes and light-colored hair, whereas Daniel and Teri both have brown eyes and darker hair. But what about the baby's psychological features? Will his temperament, personality, and level of intelligence resemble Daniel and Teri's? Or will he grow up to be more like his biological parents in these characteristics? What influence will Daniel and Teri have on the development of their baby?

As you read through this chapter, think about the information from Daniel and Teri's perspective. What would you tell Daniel and Teri to help them understand how their new baby will be influenced by the nurturing care that they provide and by the genes inherited from his biological parents? What roles will both nature and nurture play in determining the baby's developing temperament, personality, and intelligence? After studying this chapter, you should be able to give Daniel and Teri a relatively detailed and concrete explanation of how genetics and the environment will influence their baby's physical and psychological traits. You should be able to use at least a dozen specific concepts in your answer.

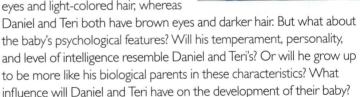

As you read this chapter, look for the "Think About Daniel and Teri . . ." questions that ask you to consider what you're learning from their perspective.

The questions Daniel and Teri face cut to the very core of child development research. How much does a child's personality, intellectual functioning, and other characteristics depend on genes inherited from the child's biological parents? How much are these characteristics learned or modified from experiences with the parents who raise the child or with teachers, peers, and other elements of the environment? In Chapter 1 we introduced this as the nature–nurture question—a question that philosophers have debated for centuries and that is still one of the most fundamental questions scientists research today. We begin this second chapter by focusing on the nature side. We review what we know about genes, chromosomes, human reproduction, and cell division. Then we discuss how these elements of nature interact with the nurture side. How does the environment interact with genetics to influence child development? Will the way Daniel and Teri raise their baby have an influence on the baby's personality, level of intelligence, and other traits? How will the nurturing care they provide interact with the baby's genes to govern the child's development? This chapter will help you appreciate human inheritance and illustrate the important interactions between genes and the environment.

your perspective

To what degree do you believe that your level of intelligence was inherited versus learned? What about the basic components of your personality? In general, do you believe that traits like these are more inherited or more learned? Why do you believe this?

Genes and Human Reproduction

Each one of us began as a single cell—a fertilized egg cell. By the time we reach adulthood, that cell has multiplied into several trillion cells. And the structure and function of every cell in the body is governed by genes. Genes are molecules that dictate how our cells develop and coordinate to form the basic tissues that come together to form a human body. These genes exist in every cell in the body. We inherit some of these genes from our mother and some from our father, but the specific combination of genes that governs our cells is unique to each one of us and distinguishes us from other living things as well as all other human beings. What are genes, and how are they passed down from one generation to the next?

As you study this section, ask yourself these questions:

- What are chromosomes, DNA, and genes? How are these structures different, and how do they function to determine our genetic codes?

- What is the Human Genome Project? What are the potential benefits of the project? Are there potential dangers?

- What is the difference between mitosis and meiosis? How do these processes ensure that every cell in our body has the same genes and that each person inherits genes that are different from everyone else's?

- What is the difference between identical and nonidentical twins?

Genes and the Magical Four-Letter Code

chromosomes
Strands of deoxyribonucleic acid (DNA) molecules that contain the genetic codes.

DNA
Two strands of molecules that twist around each other like a spiral staircase. Connected by a series of nucleotide bases (adenine, thymine, guanine, and cytosine).

Inside the nucleus of most any cell in the human body are 46 chromosomes. **Chromosomes** are structures made of long strands of deoxyribonucleic acid (DNA). Chromosomes operate in pairs, so we have 23 pairs of chromosomes, as you can see in Figure 2.1. Twenty-two of the pairs are the same across males and females—these are called *autosomes*. The remaining pair is the *sex chromosomes*, and they differ between the sexes. Females have two X chromosomes and males have one X and one Y chromosome. Figure 2.1 shows a male.

As Watson and Crick (1953) first discovered, **DNA** consists of two strands of sugar and phosphate molecules that twist around each other like a spiral staircase.

In Figure 2.2, you can see the staircase and the "stairs" that connect the two sides. The stairs are made out of four different varieties of a *nucleotide base molecule*. The four varieties are adenine (A), thymine (T), guanine (G), and cytosine (C). The different nucleotide bases on one side of the staircase pair with specific bases on the other side to form each stair. As you can see in the figure, the DNA strand is simply a series of these connecting stairs or base pairs. Also notice that *adenine always pairs with thymine,* and *guanine always pairs with cytosine.* Thus, if you have a sequence of ACCACT on one side of the staircase, the complementary sequence on the other side will be TGGTGA.

Within the 46 chromosomes in each human cell, there are approximately 3 billion pairs of nucleotide bases (Human Genome Program, 1992, 2001; Venter et al., 2001). It is the specific sequence of these base pairs that makes up our individual *genetic code,* or *genome,* which is a set of instructions that determines which traits and characteristics are inherited. The entire code is divided up into smaller pieces called *genes.* A **gene** is a segment of the DNA strand that provides an instruction for a particular trait, tissue, or other structure. There are approximately 20,000 to 30,000 genes (depending on how they are identified and counted) aligned somewhere along the set of 46 chromosomes in each human cell (Human Genome Project, 2006). It is also important to note that only about 10 percent of the nucleotide base pairs actually provide active instructions. Some of the inactive sequences play a role in cell division, but the function of many of the remaining sequences is not yet known.

Finding specific genes and discovering their functions is a hugely complicated task. For example, Figure 2.3 shows part of the sequence of bases on one side of the DNA strand that makes up just one of the genes related to one form of mental retardation. This form of mental retardation is associated with fragile X syndrome, a genetic disorder we'll discuss later in the chapter. This particular gene contains 39,057 bases. And remember, this is only one side of the DNA strand! To complete the picture, you need to add the complementary strand (the complementary strand is not shown in the figure)

Figure 2.1 • Karotype Showing 46 Paired Chromosomes In this karotype (or picture of chromosomes), there are 22 similar pairs and 1 with different X and Y chromosomes (the boxed pair).

gene
A segment of DNA that provides an instruction for a particular structure, function, or trait.

Cell Nucleus   Chromosome

Side "rails" made of sugar and phosphate molecules.

DNA

Nucleotide base "stairs." A always pairs with T. G always pairs with C.

Figure 2.2 • Chromosomes, DNA, and Genes The nucleus of each cell contains the chromosomes. Chromosomes are made up of highly twisted strands of DNA. The DNA is constructed like a staircase, with each side of the staircase connected by "stairs" made up of pairs of nucleotide bases. Adenine (A) always pairs with thymine (T), and guanine (G) always pairs with cytosine (C). Genes are shorter segments of chromosomal DNA, usually several thousand base pairs in length.

Figure 2.3 • One-Tenth of the Sequence of Nucleotide Bases Needed to Form One of the Genes Related to Fragile X Mental Retardation (FMRI1 on Chromosome X) The total sequence contains 39,057 bases, and this represents only one side of the DNA strand. Each of these bases would be paired with its complementary mate on the second strand, resulting in 39,043 base *pairs* (or 78,086 individual base molecules) for the gene. (National Center for Biotechnology Information, 2003.)

```
GGCGTGCGGCAGCGCGGCGGCGGCGGCGGCGGCGGCGGCGGCGGCGGAGGCGGCGGCGGCGGCGGCGGCGGCG
GCGGCTGGGCCTCGAGCGCCCGCAGCCCACCTCTCGGGGGCGGGCTCCCGGCGCTAGCAGGGCTGAAGAG
AAGATGGAGGAGCTGGTGGTGGAAGTGCGGGGCTCCAATGGCGCTTTCTACAAGGTACTTGGCTCTAGGG
CAGGCCCCATCTTCGCCCTTCCTTCCCTCCCTTTTCTTCTTGGTGTCGGCGGGAGGCAGGCCCGGGGCCC
TCTTCCCGAGCACCGCACCTGGGTGCCAGGGCACGCTCGGCGGGATGTTGTTGGGAGGGAAGGACTGGAC
TGGGGGCCTGTTGGAAGCCCCTCTCCGACTCCGAGAGGCCCTAGCGCCTATCGAAATGAGAGACCAGCGA
GGAGAGGGTTCTCTTTCGGCGCCGAGCCCCGCCGGGGTGAGCTGGGGATGGGCGAAGGACTGGGCAGGT
ACTAGAGCCGGGCGGGAAGGGCCGAAATCGGCGCTAAGTGACGGCGATGGCTTATTCCCCCTTTCCTAAA
CATCATCTCCCAGCGGGATCCGGGCCTGTCGTGTGGGTAGTTGTGGAGGAGCGGGAGGCGGCTCAGCCGG
GCCGCCTCCTGCAGCGCCAAGAGGGCTTCAGGTCTCCTTTGGCTTCTCTTTTCCGGTCTAGCATTGGGAC
TTCGGAGAGCTCCACTGTTCTGGGCGAGGGCTTGAAGAAAGAGTAGTAAGAAGCGGTAGTCGGCACCAA
ATCACAATGGCAACTGATTTTTAGTGGCTTCTCTTTGTGGATTTCGGAGGAGATTTTAGATCCAAAAGTT
TCAGGAAGACCCTAACATGGCCCAGCAGTGCATTGAAGAAGTTGATCATCGTGAATATTCGCGTCCCCCT
TTTTGTTAAACGGGGTAAATTCAGGAATGCACATGCTTCAGCGTCTAAAACCATTAGCAGCGCTGCTACT
TAAAAATTGTGTGCGTGTGTGTTAAGTTTCCAAAGACCTAAATATATGCCATGAAACTTCAGGTAATTAAC
TGAGAGTATATTATTACTAGGGCATTTTTTTTTAACTGAGCGAAAATATTTTTGTGCCCCTAAGAACTT
GACCACATTTCCTTTGAATTTGTGGTGTTGCAGTGGACTGAATTGTTGAGGCTTTATATAGGCATTCATG
GGTTTACTGTGCTTTTTAAAGTTACACCATTGCAGATCAACTAACACCTTTCAGTTTTAAAAGGAAGATT
TACAAATTTGATGTAGCAGTAGTGCGTTTGTTGGTATGTAGGTGCTGTATAAATTCATCTATAAATTCTC
ATTTCCTTTTGAAGTTGCTATAACCTCTTTCAATAAATATCCCACCTTACTACAGTATTTGGCAATAGAAG
GTGCGTGTGGAAGGAAGGCTGGAAAATAGCTATTAGCAGTGTCCAACACAATTCTTAAATGTATTGTAGA
ATGGCTTGAATGTTCAGACAGGACACGTTTGGCTATAGGAAAAATAAACAATTGACTTTATTCTGTGTTT
ACCAATTTATGAAGACATTTGGAGATCAGTATATTTCATAAATGAGTAAAGTATGTAAACTGTTCCATA
CTTTGAGCACAAAGATAAAGCCTTTTGCTGTAAAAGGAGGCAAAAGGTAACCCCGCGTTTATGTTCTTAA
CAGTCTCATGAATATGAAATTGTTTCAGTTGACTCTGCAGTCAAAATTTTAATTTCATTGATTTTATTGA
TCCATAATTCTTCTGGTGAGTTTGCGTAGAATCGTTCACCGTCTAGATTAGTGGTTTTGGTCACTAGA
TTTCTGGCACTAATAACTATAATACATATACATATATATGTGTGAGTAACGGCTAATGGTTAGGCAAGAT
TTTGATTGACCTGTGATAAAACTTAGATTGGAATAGGTTGGTTGCCCCTTAGTCCCTGAGGAGAAATG
TTAATACTTGAACAAGTGTGTGTCAGACAAATTGCTGTTATGTTTATTTAATTAAGTTTGATTTCTAAGA
AAATCTCAAATGGTCTGCACTGATGGAAGAACAGTTTCTGTAACAAAAAGCTTGAAATTTTTATATGAC
TTATAATAACTGCTGTGAGTTTTAAAAGTAAAGCAAAAGTAAACTGAGTTGCTTGTCCAGTGGGATGGACA
GGAAAGATGTGAAATAAAAACCAATGAAAAATGAACTGCTGTGGAAGAAGTGTTACATTTATGGAAAAAGA
AATAGGGAACCTTGTTCATCAAATTGATAGAAAAGCTTTTAAAACTAAACAAATCAAACAACTTGAGTATA
ATGGAATTCAGACTTTGATTTGCCTAACATAACCACCATATTTGCAAGGACAGCTCTCTATCTTCTGGTG
TTTATTCTTAAAAACTTAAAAGTTAGATTTAGCGATCACCAGAGCCACTACTTTTATGCTTAGGTATTTG
TTTGACTTAGAAAAAATTGGTCACGTGTACCACTTTATAGTGCCCTGCAGGTGTTAAGATATGAAGGCAC
TTTGACTTACACCTCATAAAATCTTTACAAAGTATTTTCTAAATGAATAATGATGAAATAAAGTCTTTAT
TCTAGGTGCATCTGCCCCACATAATTTGTTTTCTTTGGACTAGAAGTTTTGATGTGTTGAGAATGGTAAT
GAATTAACTCCATTTTAAATGTAGAATGCGTATCACTCCAATATGAATGCCCTAATGAATCCTAAGATTT
GTAGGTTTTGTGTACTAGTATGAAAATTACTAAAGATGGAAAAATCACATGTTGGAGACATAAGATACAA
ACCTTTTTGTTTTCTGAAAATACAACCTCTGATTTCTGATTCCTTGTTGTAAATGGTGTAATTATACTA
GATTGTAATTTTGTTGTTAGATATACTTTTTAAGTTCAGTGTTTGAGGACAGACTTTCATTTGGTTAG
TAGTATTATGGCAGCTAGCAGCTAAATATGAAAAGTGTACAATCAAAAGGATATTTTTAATGAAGATAT
TAGTGGTCTAACATGTCATTTCAGATACATAGCTGAAATGTAGTAAAATCAGTTTTACTACAAATAAACT
TGCATAAGGTTTATAAATTTATAAGTTTATAAATCAACTTGGGTAAAGTGTAAATAAACTTGCACTCGTG
GTTTCTCTGAAGTCTCCTGAGCTAACTTTGCATAAAGGTGTTATTCTGTACTTCGAGGAAGTGAATTATT
GGGGTCAACCACATTTTTTTCCTTCCTAACAGTCTGATTGCCCTTTTTAGTTTTTAGGGATCTTTGTGGCT
GCATCATTTTTCCCCTTTTGAACTGTGCATTTTCTAACCCCATACTTAAATATTCTCATAACCTCCAAAT
TATTAATTAGATGCAACATTCAGTGGTATATTACTGGAGTTTCTGATTTCTGCCCACATATAGGAATGTGC
TTCCTGAGAAGATTGGGATCGTGATTATAAATAATAGTTAACAGGGGATGAGTACTTTCTAGGTGCCAGGC
ACTGTTCTCTCTGATACTTTATTTGATGTATTGTTGTTATTCCCATTCTTTAAATGATGCACAGAGAGGT
TAGGTAAGTGACTTACTACCAAGTGTCAGGGCCATTAAGGGTCAGGATTCTGAATTCCTGAAATGATGAA
ATTTAGCTTGAAGAAATTGGTTTGATTTCCTGCTTAGTTTTCAATTTCATGGTGGT . . .
```

Human Genome Project
A multinational effort by governments and scientists to map the 3 billion pairs of nucleotide bases and the genes contained in human chromosomes.

Researchers from around the world are working to decipher the human genetic code—one of the most complex tasks scientists have ever attempted.

where each A connects to a T, each G to a C, and so on. So really this gene has 39,057 base *pairs*, or a total of over 78,114 base molecules. Can you imagine how complicated it must be to decode this type of sequence for every human gene?

In April 2003, scientists announced a historic milestone: The sequencing of a human genome was now complete (Human Genome Program, 2005)! Perhaps you have heard about the **Human Genome Project,** a multinational effort among governments and scientists to map the order of every nucleotide base (AGCT) and locate the position of every gene in the human genome. This project began in 1990 and was the most ambitious and technically challenging project ever undertaken by scientists. Though scientists have completed their mapping and positioning of the order of 3 billion pairs of nucleotide bases in the human genome, they still don't know what all of the base sequences mean. Scientists still need to determine which sequences of nucleotide bases define most of our 20,000 to 30,000 genes. Figure 2.4 shows a few examples of the many thousands of genes that have been located so far. Researchers are still working hard to identify and determine the function of many of the remaining genes.

Over the coming decades, the impact of the Human Genome Project will be staggering. Scientists are working toward finding genetic markers for every disease that can be inherited. This information may then help save or prolong millions of lives. For example, if hemophilia (a rare disorder that prevents blood from clotting) runs in your family, you will be able to take a genetic test to find out if you carry the gene associated with this disease. The location of this gene is marked in Figure 2.4. If you do carry the gene, you will know to work with your physician to learn how to prevent injuries that might otherwise lead to fatal bleeding. In addition, physicians might be able to use gene therapy to alter some of your cells' genetic functions. What if they could give you an injection of healthy genes to counteract the destructive effects of disease genes in your body or replace destructive genes entirely? Or what if they could selectively turn off the function of disease genes, preventing you from developing the diseases in the first place?

Already, parents can select the sex of embryos by using certain reproductive technologies. Clinicians first grow embryos in test tubes using the mother's eggs and the father's sperm. The embryos with the preferred set of sex chromosomes (XX for a female or XY for a male) can then be implanted in the mother's uterus. Embryos carrying disease genes can be selected out in a similar manner. Embryos conceived by more "natural" means can also be tested while they are in the

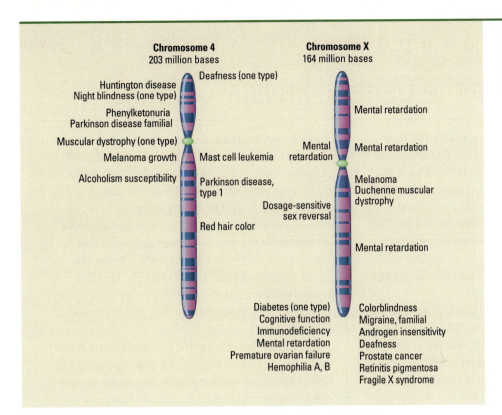

Later in the chapter, we will discuss Huntington disease (on chromosome 4) and sex-linked genes (on X). For a more complete catalog, see McKusick (1998) or the online version that is kept up to date through the Genome Data Base at Johns Hopkins University. (U.S. Department of Energy, 2005.)

mother's womb. Based on the results, couples can make informed decisions regarding their developing embryo. In the future, couples could have their embryos tested for a variety of genetically based diseases before birth. Coming generations could potentially escape the devastating effects of a large number of genetically determined diseases.

But where do we draw the line? As you can see, there are profound moral questions in this area that will test our abilities to make sound ethical decisions. Inheriting a disease gene usually just gives us the tendency to develop the disease at some time in our life. It does not guarantee that we will develop the disease, given that the onset of many diseases can depend on additional changes, diet, exposure to risk factors, and other environmental factors. Should parents selectively discard embryos that have *tendencies* toward certain diseases? Maybe we can agree that future generations should be spared from diseases that lead to early and painful deaths, but what about diseases such as colon cancer or Alzheimer's that tend to emerge late in life? What about embryos carrying other traits that are not desirable? What if an embryo has genes related to low intelligence or a violent personality? Remember, too, that genetic tests are not foolproof. What if an embryo falsely tests positive for a fatal disease? Our growing understanding of genetics raises exciting possibilities but also brings many complicated questions.

Another issue relates to the privacy of individuals after they have had genetic tests. To read more about privacy and ethics in genetic research, read the Social Policy Perspective box on page 48 called "Protecting the Genetic Privacy of Citizens."

As we learn more about the genes related to inherited diseases and medical conditions, physicians will be able to help patients identify their predispositions and may be able to help them avoid the risks. Designer medications may also be produced to more effectively handle multiple health conditions.

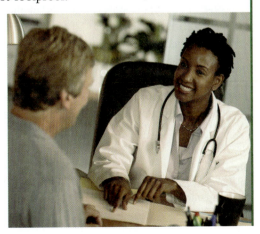

Human Reproduction and Cell Division

In human reproduction, a new embryo is formed when a sperm cell from the father fertilizes an egg cell from the mother. When the sperm and egg cells join, chromosomes from the father and mother combine to

Protecting the Genetic Privacy of Citizens

Wouldn't it be helpful to know if you were carrying genes linked to a serious disease like diabetes, breast or prostate cancer, or heart disease? If you knew at a young age that you inherited the tendency to develop one or more of these diseases, you could alter your lifestyle to avoid the risk factors that might trigger the onset of the disease. With diet, exercise, and the early use of hypertension medication, for example, you might be able to avoid a heart attack that might otherwise have surprised you at age 48.

But what if your genetic predisposition were revealed to your employer or your health insurance company? Could you be fired from your job or lose the next big promotion because your employer was afraid you couldn't take the pressure of the work? Might future employers be reluctant to hire you for fear you would become sick or disabled? Could your health insurance company drop your coverage because it saw you as too great a risk? Would anyone give you health coverage?

These questions are at the center of a national debate about the privacy of genetic information. Even before the first draft of the human genome was complete, the U.S. government issued an order prohibiting federal agencies from using genetic information in any decisions to hire, promote, or dismiss workers. Legislatures in 23 states quickly followed suit by passing laws against "genetic discrimination" in hiring (Uhlmann, 2000). How should genetic information be used, and what limits are necessary?

From one perspective, many employers and insurance companies already use health-risk assessments when considering applicants. How many times have you been asked about "preexisting conditions" or about your smoking and drinking habits? If cigarette smoking causes health problems, isn't it reasonable to ask smokers to pay more for their health insurance? Who pays more for car insurance, a 20-year-old single male or a 40-year-old married female? So we already classify people into groups based on relative risks. Lacking reliable ways to predict the future for any individual, we lump together all of those who share certain risk-related characteristics. Is it really fair to lump every 20-year-old male into a high-risk driving category? Some argue that genetic testing will allow us to assess risks in a way that is more fair, reliable, and objective. An editorial in the *New York Times* suggested that "as the potential for rational discrimination grows, the space for old-fashioned bias may shrink. Men and women will increasingly be judged not by the color of their skin but by the content of their chromosomes" (Sullivan, 2000).

Francis Collins, head of the Human Genome Project in the United States, presented another perspective. Collins predicted that the main legacy of the project will be the use of genetics to tailor and improve health care for individuals (Altman, 2000). But he warned that these benefits will not occur unless we pass effective laws to prevent organizations from denying individuals insurance or jobs based on genetic information. Many people already fear the potential negative effects of genetic testing. One telephone poll found that 63 percent of respondents would not want to take genetic tests if the results would be available to employers and insurers (Uhlmann, 2000). If people avoid genetic tests, they will lose the opportunity for early detection of risks. Millions may suffer or die from diseases that could have been prevented.

Q *Even if every state passes laws preventing genetic discrimination, how effective will the laws be? Will companies have loopholes? Can we really force employers to overlook health risks when choosing among applicants? How will insurance companies remain profitable if they are forced to accept more risky and costly applicants? How do you think we should balance the need for early risk detection against other potential uses and misuses of genetic information?*

allele
An alternative version of a gene; alleles operate in pairs across matched chromosomes.

give the embryo a unique combination of genes. The chromosome from the father has one version of a gene and the chromosome from the mother has another version of the same gene. The versions differ somewhat in the sequence of nucleotide bases (A, T, G, and C). These versions are called the **alleles** of a particular gene. The alleles determine the unique traits of each individual. It isn't always easy for this unique embryo to develop, however. A variety of problems can cause some couples to have difficulty conceiving babies. Low sperm count in the father and damage to the mother's reproductive system are two of the more common problems. In other situations, single individuals or gay or lesbian couples may want to have children. In all these cases, artificial insemination and the other alternative techniques described in Table 2.1 can help people conceive babies. To learn about one mother's experience with alternative techniques, read the Personal Perspective box on page 50 called "Meet a Mother Who Used Artificial Insemination."

So far, research on artificial insemination and in vitro fertilization does not indicate any particular developmental problems when children are conceived by these methods (Golombok et al., 2004a; Golombok et al., 2004b; Golombok et al., 2001; Golombok et al., 2002). Children have been studied all the way into adolescence, and they are well adjusted in their emotions, friendships, school performance, and other behaviors as rated by themselves, their parents, and their teachers. One difference that has been noted is that mothers who use these techniques tend to be more warm and involved with their children, compared to other mothers. This may reflect the difficulties they had conceiving children or their strong desire to overcome barriers in having their own children. Most of the parents who have been studied have not told their children about how they were conceived, and many say they regret not telling them. They worry that their children may hear the truth from another source, or they worry that it will only get more difficult for them to reveal the secret as time goes on. However, attitudes toward openness in telling children how they were conceived may be changing. One recent study found that about half the parents surveyed planned to tell their children the truth, often because they believed the child had a right to know. More than 75 percent

Here human sperm and embryos are being frozen in liquid nitrogen to preserve them to be used later for *in vitro fertilzation*. When parents have fertility problems, this is one of several techniques they can use to conceive a baby.

your perspective

Do you know anyone who used an "alternative" method of conception? If so, why do you believe they chose that particular method? How has it worked for them?

TABLE 2.1 Alternative Techniques for Conception

Artificial insemination	• Sperm are collected from the father and then injected into the mother's reproductive system for fertilization. • If the father cannot produce viable sperm, sperm can be collected from another man or a sperm bank.
In vitro fertilization	• Several eggs are removed from the mother's ovary. • Eggs and sperm are placed in a petri dish for fertilization and initial cell divisions. • Several embryos (each with four to eight cells) are placed in the mother's uterus for further development.
Cryopreservation	• Sperm can be collected and frozen and are still viable even if thawed several years later. • Embryos from in vitro fertilization can be frozen and thawed later to be placed in the mother's uterus.
Assisted in vivo fertilization	• Eggs are collected from the mother's ovary. • Sperm are collected from the father. • Eggs and sperm are injected into the fallopian tube of the mother for fertilization and further development.
Surrogate mothers	• In vitro fertilization is used to combine the sperm and eggs from a mother and father. • The embryo is placed into the uterus of another woman (surrogate) who then grows and delivers the baby for the biological parents.

(Moore & Persaud, 1998.)

Meet a Mother Who Used Artificial Insemination

Lea Adams
Derwood, Maryland
Mother of a 15-year-old conceived through artificial insemination

Why did you decide to use artificial insemination to have your baby?
I was an unmarried professional woman who was 30-something and making more money than most of the men I knew. Only certain agencies would allow single-parent adoption, and many of those would only place at-risk kids with single parents. That didn't make much sense to me, since I couldn't stay home to take care of a child with severe disabilities.

How did the procedure work? Did you want to know who the sperm donor was?
It was very straightforward for me because I got pregnant with the first insemination. I didn't use a sperm bank because the closest one was too far away. I convinced an infertility practice, which had a set of donors, to take me on as a patient. The procedure is like a typical internal exam, only they inject sperm into a little tube that is attached to a cap that fits over the cervix. That tube gets clamped and later you remove it. No big deal. I don't know who the donor was. I had a lawyer work with my doctor to make sure the donor could not track down my child or vice versa. I was fearful some stranger could show up and take away my baby, but I also wanted to protect the donor.

What have you told your child regarding the identity of his father?
I told him I don't know the identity of the donor. I have always been careful to talk about "donor" rather than "father." I have always answered any questions he's asked like, "How did you have a baby if you weren't

married?" I told my son that I wanted him so much that I went to the doctor and the doctor gave me some sperm so I could get pregnant and have a baby. With the diversity of family types in the world today, I don't think he thinks there is anything unique about his situation. He doesn't tell his friends that he was artificially inseminated. He simply says he doesn't have a father.

What was the typical reaction to your decision from friends, family, and others?
I think most people viewed me as "brave." My divorced friends whose ex-husbands aren't cooperating parents have all said I "did it the right way." Sometimes when I was pregnant and morning sick, or exhausted with a sick baby, or frustrated with a petulant 3-year-old, and so on, people would say, "Well, you asked for it!" It's hard to say whether they were commenting on single parenthood or artificial insemination, but I always retorted, "You mean if I were married and became a parent, I wouldn't have asked for it?" The further we move away from the point of conception, the fewer of those kinds of things I hear.

Do you have any advice for others considering artificial insemination?
If you want a baby and will love it and be a wonderful mother, then do whatever it will take. Don't focus on the donor or worry about it. Just enjoy your child!

Q *Would you consider artificial insemination or another alternative to conception? Do you think parents should inform their children about their use of these techniques? Why or why not?*

---

had told at least one other person, and fewer than 25 percent of these parents said they would definitely not disclose information about their child's conception (Golombok et al., 2004a).

To fully appreciate genetic inheritance, you need to understand a few facts about cell division. After the sperm and egg unite, the fertilized cell begins to divide. After the first division occurs, the organism is referred to as a **zygote.** Cells within the zygote will then continue to divide countless times, and with each division, an exact copy of the genetic material is created in each new cell. To explore this process, let's

zygote
Term used to refer to the human organism after the fertilized egg cell begins to divide.

first look at how genes are copied into every cell in your body. **Mitosis** ("copy division") occurs when a cell copies its own chromosomes, then divides to form two cells. During cell division the DNA material on each chromosome "unzips." The weak bonds between the nucleotide bases on opposite sides of the staircase break. Figure 2.5 diagrams how the DNA strand first unzips and then replicates itself. It forms two new strands that then link up with the two old strands and wrap up again to make two new chromosomes. When this process is completed, we have a duplicate set of chromosomes. If all goes well, an exact copy of the DNA goes into each new cell. Mitosis doesn't just occur in a developing embryo, it occurs continually throughout the body as it grows, functions, and heals. Except in mutations—changes in the order of nucleotide bases—and sex cells, every cell in our body contains an exact copy of the 46 chromosomes that originated from our single fertilized egg cell.

One exception to mitosis occurs with our sex cells, or *gametes*. Gametes are the sperm and egg cells, and these specialized cells form through a different process called *meiosis*. **Meiosis** ("reduction division") occurs when sperm and egg cells form. Meiosis reduces the number of chromosomes in these cells from 46 to 23. The entire process of meiosis is shown in Figure 2.6. At the beginning of meiosis, the sex cell duplicates all of its DNA. Each of the original 46 chromosomes unzips its DNA, doubles it to make a duplicate chromosome, and remains connected to the duplicate. Now the cell has 46 doubled chromosomes— each has twice the normal amount of DNA. The 46 doubled chromosomes pair up as usual to form 23 pairs of duplicate chromosomes. Each pair then exchanges genetic

This human cell is finishing the process of mitosis. It has copied itself and all its genetic material to form a second cell.

mitosis
"Copy division," the type of cell division that occurs when chromosomes are copied into each new cell.

meiosis
"Reduction division," the type of cell division that occurs during the formation of gametes (sperm and eggs).

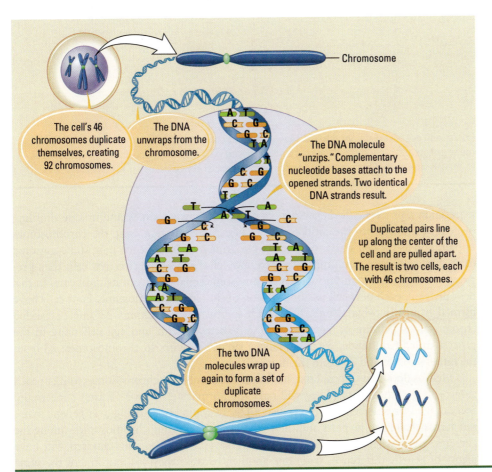

Chromosome

The cell's 46 chromosomes duplicate themselves, creating 92 chromosomes.

The DNA unwraps from the chromosome.

The DNA molecule "unzips." Complementary nucleotide bases attach to the opened strands. Two identical DNA strands result.

Duplicated pairs line up along the center of the cell and are pulled apart. The result is two cells, each with 46 chromosomes.

The two DNA molecules wrap up again to form a set of duplicate chromosomes.

Figure 2.5 • Mitosis
During replication the DNA strand "unzips," and a new complementary strand forms for each original parent strand. This is how each chromosome duplicates itself (with its genetic code) during cell division.

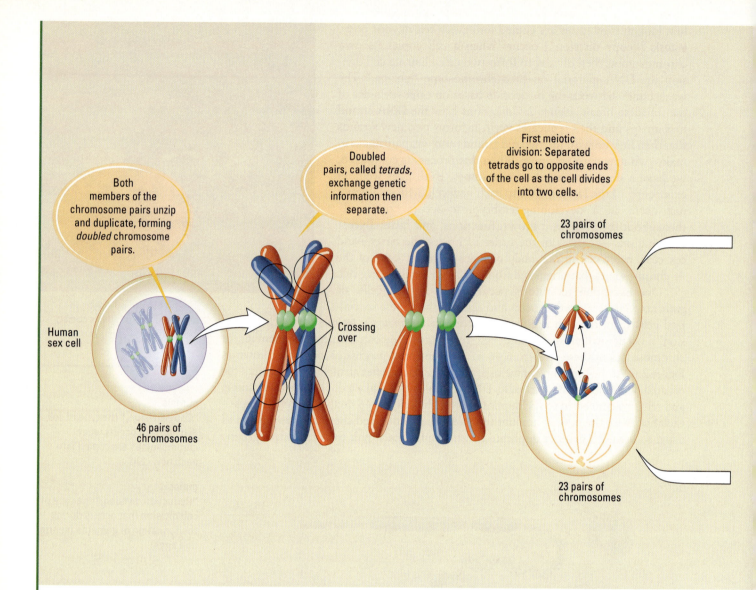

Figure 2.6 • Meiosis The gametes (sperm and egg cells) form via meiosis. Meiosis reduces the number of chromosomes from 46 to 23 in each cell. Crossing over of chromosome segments and random shuffling of chromosomes to cells ensure genetic diversity in the species. After fertilization, cell division occurs with mitosis where all 46 chromosomes are copied into each new cell.

fertilization

The union of the father's sperm cell with the mother's egg, yielding one fertilized cell with a unique combination of genes along 46 chromosomes—23 from the father and 23 from the mother.

material in a process called *crossing over.* This will ensure a new and unique shuffling of genes coming from the mother and father. After crossing over, the chromosomes unpair; and as the cell starts to divide in two, one member of each pair, still connected to its duplicate, goes randomly into each new cell. Each of the two new cells then prepares to divide again, and now each chromosome separates from its duplicate. In this next division, each new cell has one version of the single chromosome. Four cells have formed from the original one. Now each sperm or egg contains 23 single-stranded chromosomes (Moore & Persaud, 1998). When a sperm and egg cell unite in the process called **fertilization,** we again have a single cell with 46 chromosomes: 23 from the father's sperm and 23 from the mother's egg.

Meiosis does two things. First, it reduces the number of chromosomes to 23 in each gamete so that the fertilized egg will have the normal number of 46 after conception. Second, it ensures diversity in the gene pool by swapping or crossing over genetic material across chromosome pairs and then randomly distributing chromosomes among the gametes. Even when the same parents have several children, the children will have plenty of genetic differences from one another, because they will not inherit the same combinations of chromosomes or genes.

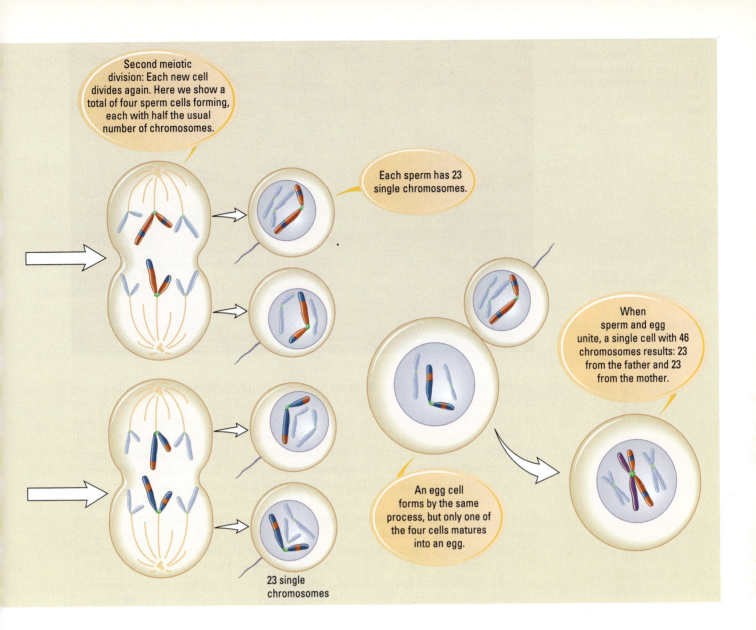

Second meiotic division: Each new cell divides again. Here we show a total of four sperm cells forming, each with half the usual number of chromosomes.

Each sperm has 23 single chromosomes.

When sperm and egg unite, a single cell with 46 chromosomes results: 23 from the father and 23 from the mother.

An egg cell forms by the same process, but only one of the four cells matures into an egg.

23 single chromosomes

Identical twins are the one exception—these children do have the same genetic codes. Identical twins are twins who grow from the same zygote. At some point, as cells in the zygote divide, it separates into two separate zygotes that will develop into two babies. Scientists refer to identical twins as **monozygotic (MZ) twins,** because they come from one zygote. Developing from the same fertilized egg, MZ twins have copies of each other's 46 chromosomes and therefore share the same genetic code. MZ twins are always the same sex and tend to be very similar in appearance. MZ twins occur in about 1 in every 260 births (this rate is virtually the same in all segments of the population), and MZ twins do not seem to run in families (Thompson et al., 1991).

Nonidentical twins, sometimes called *fraternal twins,* grow from two separate conceptions. That is, the mother releases two eggs, and two different sperm from the father fertilize them. Because they come from two separate conceptions and therefore form two separate zygotes, we refer to nonidentical twins as **dizygotic (DZ) twins.** DZ twins are no more alike genetically than are any other brothers or sisters from the same parents. They can be different sexes, and their appearance can also be very different. Theoretically, they could even have different fathers. How? If the mother has intercourse with two different men within a short span of time, it is possible that two eggs she released could be fertilized by different fathers. Although this doesn't happen very often, it demonstrates just how different nonidentical twins can be.

Think About Daniel and Teri . . .

Explain to Daniel and Teri how their son inherited a unique combination of chromosomes from his biological mother and father. What events happened during meiosis to ensure that the genetic material inherited by the baby was unique to him?

monozygotic (MZ) twins
Identical twins. These twins form when one zygote divides to make two zygotes.

dizygotic (DZ) twins
Nonidentical twins. These twins form when two eggs are fertilized by two different sperm cells.

This ultrasound image shows twins. If they are identical twins, they will have the same genetic code as each other. If they are nonidentical, they will share only 50% of their genes, on average.

For reasons that scientists don't yet understand, different ethnic groups have different rates of DZ twinning. DZ twins occur in about 1 in every 500 births for Asians, in 1 in 125 births for Caucasians, and in as many as 1 in 20 births in some African populations (Thompson et al., 1991). Because DZ twinning results from the release of multiple eggs, the mother's genetics and the functioning of her ovaries and reproductive system govern its occurrence. Consequently, higher rates of DZ twinning tend to run on the mother's side of the family. DZ twinning also increases as the mother ages.

Earlier in this chapter we discussed fertility problems that some couples can have. Some women take fertility drugs when they are having difficulty conceiving children. The drugs stimulate the ovaries to release extra eggs. Sometimes several of the eggs become fertilized by multiple sperm from the father, resulting in twins, triplets, quadruplets, and other sets of multiple births. Most of the babies born this way are nonidentical (nonidentical twins, nonidentical triplets, etc.). Sometimes, however, one or more of the nonidentical zygotes divide to form a set of identical twins within the larger set of multiples.

A final note about reproduction and cell division concerns sex determination. As we have already mentioned, among the 23 pairs of chromosomes in a normal cell is a specialized pair, called the **sex chromosomes**. Sex chromosomes are designated as the X and Y chromosomes. Females have two X chromosomes, and males have one X and one Y. When the sex cells form, females can pass only X chromosomes to their eggs. Males, however, pass the X chromosome to half of their sperm and the Y to the other

sex chromosomes
The 23rd pair of chromosomes (in humans), specialized to determine the sex of the child and other characteristics. Males are XY and females are XX.

(a)   **(b)**

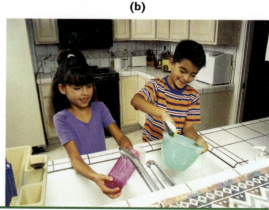

Identical twins (a) are much more alike genetically than are nonidentical twins (b). Later in the chapter, you will see that these differences are used to estimate how much influence genetics has on people's traits and characteristics.

half. The sex of the offspring therefore depends on which type of sperm fertilizes the egg. If the sperm is carrying an X chromosome, the fertilized egg will be XX and will produce a girl. If the sperm is carrying a Y chromosome, the fertilized egg will be XY and will produce a boy. X and Y chromosomes also have implications for genetic defects, as you will see in the next section.

■ Let's Review . . .

1. Each cell in the human body typically has 46:
   a. genes.　　　　　　　　b. gametes.
   c. chromosomes.　　　　　d. nucleotide base pairs.

2. If one strand of base pairs has the sequence of A, T, C, C, G, what will the complementary sequence be on the other strand?
   a. A, T, C, C, G　　　　　b. G, C, T, T, A
   c. C, G, A, A, T　　　　　d. T, A, G, G, C

3. *Mitosis* is the type of cell division that ensures that:
   a. almost every cell in the human body has 23 chromosomes.
   b. almost every cell in the human body has 46 chromosomes.
   c. crossover occurs to exchange genes across chromosomes.
   d. random shuffling of chromosomes occurs to increase genetic diversity.

4. What is the name of the type of cell division that creates sperm and egg cells?
   a. meiosis　　　　　　　　b. mitosis
   c. crossing over　　　　　d. DNA replication

5. **True or False:** Each pair of nucleotide bases forms one gene.

6. **True or False:** The rate of dizygotic (nonidentical) twins varies across ethnic groups and tends to be higher in some family lines.

Answers: 1. c, 2. d, 3. b, 4. a, 5. F, 6. T

How Traits and Genetic Abnormalities Are Inherited

Imagine how complicated the genetic code that forms each unique individual human being must be. More than 3 billion pairs of nucleotide bases must be ordered properly to form thousands of genes stretched across our 46 chromosomes. And all of this code must be copied accurately into each one of our trillions of cells. Errors, or mutations, do occur, and some of these then get passed down to the next generations. In some cases the errors involve only a few base pairs; sometimes, however, whole chromosomes are damaged, lost, or duplicated too many times.

In this section we describe a few examples of diseases that people can inherit when genetic errors occur. Scientists have identified several thousand such diseases, but here we'll present just a few examples to give you a better understanding of how genes can cause human diseases and abnormalites. As the Human Genome Project progresses, we continue to learn more about the specific codes involved. There is hope that someday genetic therapies or other interventions may provide cures or treatments for these terrible and sometimes deadly conditions.

As you study this section, ask yourself these questions:

■ How do dominant and recessive disease traits operate? What is the relative likelihood that children will inherit a disease if their parents have the disease or carry the disease gene?

- How do X-linked or sex-linked traits operate? Why are males more likely to inherit some X-linked traits, but females more likely to inherit others?

- What are some of the most common examples of disorders caused by extra or missing chromosomes?

- What are the most common procedures doctors use to test the health of fetuses, and what are the relative advantages and risks of each procedure?

Dominant–Recessive Traits

We have already mentioned that chromosomes come in pairs. Many human traits are governed by **dominant–recessive relationships** between alleles—the two different versions of a gene—acting across pairs of chromosomes. That is, if a person inherits a dominant allele on one chromosome and a recessive allele on the corresponding chromosome, the dominant allele will rule and determine the trait. For example, the allele for arched feet is dominant, and the allele for flat feet is recessive (Starr & Taggart, 1998). If you inherit two dominant alleles, or a mix of one dominant and one recessive allele, your feet will be arched. To inherit flat feet, you would need to inherit two of the recessive alleles, one on the chromosome that came from your father and one on the chromosome from your mother. Because of this dominant–recessive relationship, traits governed by dominant alleles are much more likely to be expressed than are traits from recessive alleles. Other examples of dominant-allele traits are given in Table 2.2. Which of these traits do you have?

Dominant Gene Diseases. Huntington disease is the most common example of a genetic disorder that is governed by a dominant allele. Although Huntington disease is genetic, the symptoms usually do not appear until age 30 or after. The disease causes progressive damage to the brain and nervous system, leading to deteriorating intelligence, muscle control, balance, and speech. The gene for Huntington disease has been identified on chromosome 4 (refer back to Figure 2.4). The disease occurs in about 4 to 7 out of every 100,000 births, with the highest rate among populations from western Europe (Gulli, 2005; Thompson et al., 1991). At this time there is no cure for Huntington disease.

Figure 2.7 shows the likelihood that offspring will inherit Huntington disease when one or both parents have the disorder. On the left side of the figure, one parent has the dominant allele for Huntington (H) and also has one recessive allele (h) that is healthy. Because the disease gene is dominant, this parent will develop the disease. The other parent carries two recessive healthy alleles (hh), so this parent will not develop Huntington. When these two parents have children, we would expect half of their offspring (on

dominant–recessive relationship Relationship between genes where the dominant allele will govern a particular trait, and the recessive allele will be repressed. To express a recessive trait, the individual needs to inherit two recessive alleles—one on each chromosome.

TABLE 2.2 Common Traits Governed by Dominant–Recessive Gene Relationships

DOMINANT TRAITS	RECESSIVE TRAITS
Detached earlobes	Attached earlobes
Ability to roll tongue	Inability to roll tongue
Dimpled cheeks	Non-dimpled cheeks
Longer eyelashes	Shorter eyelashes
Larger eyeballs	Smaller eyeballs
Arched feet	Flat feet

(Starr & Taggart, 1998.)

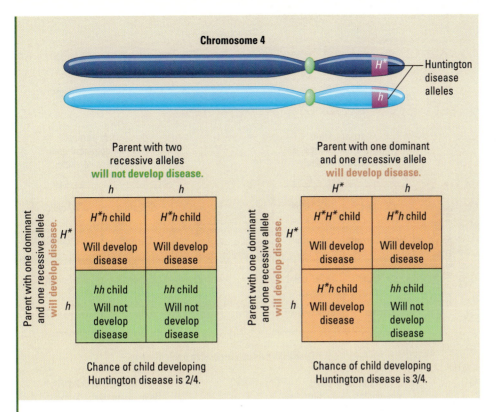

Figure 2.7 • Dominant Disease Alleles With dominant allele traits, individuals only need *one* dominant allele to inherit the trait. Here, the dominant allele causes Huntington disease. Dominant alleles are represented by the uppercase H and recessive alleles by the lowercase h. The asterisk is a reminder of which allele causes the disease (*H**). On the left, one parent with the disease (*H*h*) and one healthy parent (*hh*) have a 50 percent chance of having a child who inherits the disease. On the right, both parents have the disease (both are *H*h*), and they have a 75 percent chance. What would be the odds if one parent carries two dominant disease genes (*H*H**)?

average) to inherit the dominant allele and therefore the disease. On average, we would expect the remaining half to inherit two recessive alleles and be healthy. On the right side of the figure, you can see that having both parents with the dominant allele dramatically increases the likelihood that their children will inherit the disease.

Recessive Gene Diseases. Recessive gene diseases work a bit differently because two recessive alleles need to be inherited before the individual shows the condition. In other words, for a child to inherit a recessive trait, both parents must either have the trait (with two recessive alleles) or at least carry the trait (with one recessive allele). One relatively common recessive disorder is cystic fibrosis. This disease is controlled by genes on chromosome 7. Cystic fibrosis affects tissues in the body that produce mucus secretions. The lungs, gastrointestinal tract, pancreas, and liver are often affected. People with cystic fibrosis usually experience serious respiratory problems and lung infections, and without lung transplants most do not live past the age of 30. Cystic fibrosis is the most common recessive disease among Caucasians, occurring in approximately 1 in every 2,000 Caucasian children (Thompson et al., 1991). Nearly 1 in every 25 Caucasians carries the recessive allele (Rosick, 2005). The disease is virtually unknown in Asian populations and is very rare among people of African descent. Figure 2.8 shows the inheritance patterns for recessive traits such as cystic fibrosis.

Sickle cell disease (SCD) is the most common genetic disorder worldwide (Embury et al., 1994). SCD is actually a group of diseases involving defective hemoglobin, the substance in all red blood cells that carries oxygen from the lungs to the rest of the body. The best-known form of the disease is sickle cell anemia. SCD is

Chromosome 7

Cystic fibrosis alleles

C

c*

Carrier parent has one dominant and one recessive allele.

	C	*c**
Carrier parent has one dominant and one recessive allele. *C*	*CC* child — Not a carrier	*Cc** child — Carrier
c*	*Cc** child — Carrier	*c*c** child — Sick with CF

Carrier parent has one dominant and one recessive allele.

	C	*c**
Parent sick with CF has 2 recessive alleles. *c**	*Cc** child — Carrier	*c*c** child — Sick with CF
c*	*Cc** child — Carrier	*c*c** child — Sick with CF

Cystic fibrosis is a recessive gene disease.

Chance of child developing cystic fibrosis is 1/4; 2 are carriers.

Chance of child developing cystic fibrosis is 2/4; 2 are carriers.

Figure 2.8 • Recessive Disease Alleles With recessive allele traits, individuals must inherit *two* recessive alleles (one from each parent) to show the trait. Here, inheriting two recessive alleles (*c*c**) causes cystic fibrosis. On the left, both parents are carriers (*Cc**), but neither has the disease because they both have the dominant healthy allele. Their children, however, have a 25 percent chance of inheriting two recessive alleles (*c*c**) and developing the disease. On the right, the risk is increased to 50 percent when one parent has the disease. What would the risk be if both parents had the disease? What if one parent carried the disease (*Cc**) but the other parent did not (*CC*)?

most common in people of African and Hispanic descent. About 1 in 400 African American babies and 1 in 1,000 Hispanic babies are affected (Bojanowski, 2005). It also occurs in people with Mediterranean, Middle Eastern, and Native American heritage. In SCD a gene on chromosome 11 causes the production of a defective form of hemoglobin. Unlike normal red blood cells, which are soft and round, red blood cells with the defective form of hemoglobin become stiff and distorted after they deliver oxygen, curving into the shape of a sickle (a tool used to cut wheat). Sickled cells are sticky and can form clots in small blood vessels throughout the body, causing damage to the tissues. In many states, hospitals routinely test for SCD among newborns using a simple blood test, and the condition can even be detected through prenatal genetic testing. As of now there is no cure; but many treatments are available to manage the disease, and genetic researchers hope to develop a cure through gene therapy (Kaslow et al., 2000; "Sickle Cell Anemia," 2002).

Tay–Sachs disease is another recessive allele disorder. Tay–Sachs is controlled by a gene on chromosome 15 that causes damage to the brain and central nervous system. The disease begins in infancy and causes mental retardation, blindness, and loss of muscle control; it is usually fatal by the age of 2 or 3 years (McKusick, 1998; Starr & Taggart, 1998). At present there is no effective cure or treatment. This disease is extremely rare except among certain segments of the Jewish population. Because this disease is

your perspective

As you can imagine, families who carry fatal diseases like Huntington disease, cystic fibrosis, sickle cell disease, or Tay–Sachs can face serious ethical dilemmas. Would you have your fetus tested for potential fatal diseases during pregnancy if you knew you were a carrier? What information would you use to make such a decision?

fatal in childhood, people with Tay–Sachs do not live to reproductive age. Parents who carry the recessive gene, however, can pass it along to their children. If both parents are carriers, there is a 25 percent chance that their children will inherit the disease. If only one is a carrier, their children will not inherit the disease, but they can inherit the recessive allele and therefore become carriers themselves.

X-Linked Traits. **X-linked (sex-linked) traits** are traits that differ in rate of occurrence between males and females because of dominant and recessive alleles on the X and Y chromosomes. Recall that females have two X chromosomes (XX), but males have one X and one Y (XY). The Y chromosome is very small and does not contain much genetic material (look back at Figure 2.1 and find the Y chromosome). Most of the alleles on the X chromosome therefore do not have a corresponding allele on the Y chromosome, and this causes males to be much more likely than females to suffer the *recessive* types of disease traits.

A well-known example is hemophilia (Type A, or classic hemophilia). People with hemophilia lack a clotting agent in their blood, and they can bleed to death from cuts and serious bruises. When males inherit the recessive hemophilia allele on their X chromosome, they do not have an opportunity to mask the disease with the dominant allele for healthy blood clotting on the Y, so they develop the disease. Females are more fortunate. Even if they inherit the recessive hemophilia allele on one X, they almost always have the dominant allele for normal blood clotting on their other X. These females will not get the disease, although they can pass the allele to their children. To have hemophilia, a female would need to inherit the recessive allele on both X chromosomes—a very rare occurrence. One famous case of hemophilia involved the Russian Prince Alexis. His father, Czar Nicholas II, did not carry the disease allele, but his mother, Czarina Alexandra, did. She was a descendant of England's Queen Victoria, who was also a carrier. (It is estimated that 18 members of the British royal family had hemophilia or carried the allele.) Prince Alexis and his family were eventually executed in the Russian Revolution of 1917.

Other examples of X-linked recessive traits include Duchenne muscular dystrophy, color blindness, and some forms of retinitis pigmentosa (a major form of blindness). All of these conditions are more common among males than females. *Dominant* disease alleles on the X chromosome are another matter. Females have two chances to inherit these disease alleles (having two X chromosomes), but males have only one chance (one X chromosome). Because the allele is dominant, having the allele on either X can cause the disease in females. Females are therefore twice as likely as males to show these diseases. Fortunately, dominant X-linked diseases are very rare. Vitamin D–resistant rickets is one example, occurring twice as often among females as among males (Thompson et al., 1991). With this form of rickets, children have kidney problems that block the production of calcium for bone growth. By one year of age, infants begin showing limb deformities and decreased growth (D'Alessandro, 2002). Rett syndrome (causing severe mental retardation) is another example; it occurs only among females, because the few males who do inherit the disease die before birth (Smith, 2001). Girls who have the disease allele on one X chromosome usually have the recessive (nondisease) allele on their other X chromosome. The nondisease allele operates enough to allow survivability for female fetuses. With male zygotes, however, the small Y chromosome does not carry the nondisease allele, so only the disease allele operates. The allele causes such severe damage that these male zygotes are miscarried.

Fragile X syndrome is another special case involving the sex chromosomes. It is linked to a defective part of the X chromosome—the chromosome is weakened at the tip and also contains a defective allele that contributes to the syndrome. This syndrome causes facial deformities; it also damages the brain, causing mental retardation. Fragile X syndrome occurs in about 1 in every 4,000 to 6,000 males and it occurs twice as often in males as females (Quercia, 2005). It is one of the leading inherited causes of mental retardation among males, second only to Down syndrome (described in the next section).

X-linked (sex-linked) traits Traits that differ in rate of occurrence between males and females, caused by dominant and recessive alleles on the X and Y chromosomes.

Chromosome Abnormalities

Abnormalities in the structure or number of whole chromosomes are present in 1 of every 160 live births. They also account for the majority of all miscarriages (Thompson et al., 1991). Normally, each sperm and egg cell has 23 chromosomes. As the gametes form during meiosis, however, errors can occur that cause the sperm or egg cell to have a missing chromosome or an extra chromosome. In most cases, this causes a miscarriage early in pregnancy. Nature seems to have a way of weeding out these serious genetic defects. One exception is with chromosome 21, one of the smallest chromosomes (look back to Figure 2.1).

Down syndrome occurs when babies are born with an extra 21st chromosome. Another name for Down syndrome is *trisomy 21*, as the disorder is due to the presence of three (*tri*) chromosomes (*somy*) at location 21. Individuals with Down syndrome typically have the facial characteristics shown in Figure 2.9. They are short in stature, have short and broad hands, and tend to have heart problems and a shortened life span. Also, people with Down syndrome have mental retardation, with IQs typically between 25 and 50 (compared to the average IQ of 100 in the rest of the population). Down syndrome is the most common genetic cause of mental retardation, accounting for 40 percent of the moderate to severe cases of retardation in the general population (Pennington et al., 2003). In adulthood, the typical person with Down syndrome has the mental ability of an average 7-or 8-year-old child.

In about 95 percent of Down syndrome cases, the extra 21st chromosome exists because the 21st chromosome pair did not separate normally when the egg was formed. The mother's age is a strong risk factor. As Figure 2.10 indicates, the risk increases dramatically by the age of 35. We still do not know the reasons for this increase. Perhaps the eggs have deteriorated in older mothers, leading to problems in chromosome formation. After the mother reaches 35, the risk is high enough that doctors usually recommend genetic testing early in pregnancy to determine if the fetus has the extra chromosome. We'll describe the methods and alternatives for genetic testing later in this chapter. Although most sources emphasize the increased risk for

Figure 2.9 • Down Syndrome Features Down syndrome is caused by an extra chromosome at the 21st pair. Flattened nose, tightened eyelids, low-set ears, and short neck are typical features. Lower IQ is one of the main problems faced by children with Down syndrome.

Down syndrome
Trisomy 21, a genetic disorder that occurs when there is an extra 21st chromosome. Lower IQ, facial defects, heart problems, and shortened life span are characteristic problems.

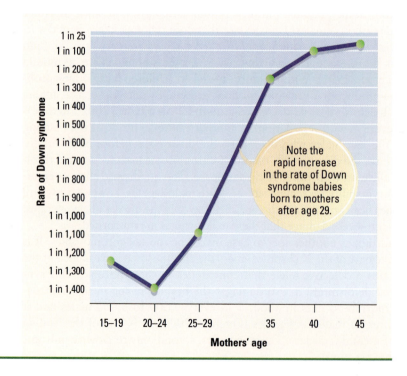

Note the rapid increase in the rate of Down syndrome babies born to mothers after age 29.

Figure 2.10 • Risk of Down Syndrome Due to the Mothers' Age The rate of Down syndrome births increases dramatically as mothers age. (Data from Thompson et al., 1991.)

women of "advancing age," you should keep in mind that the birthrate for younger women is so much higher that more than half of all babies with Down syndrome are born to mothers who are actually *younger* than 35 (Thompson et al., 1991).

Sex Chromosome Abnormalities. With the exception of trisomy 21 (Down syndrome), having an extra chromosome usually leads to pregnancy loss or death of the infant within the first few months of life. Another exception, however, involves the X and Y chromosomes. Babies can survive with extra or missing sex chromosomes—and abnormalities in the number of sex chromosomes are among the most common of all human genetic disorders. They occur in about 1 in every 500 live births (Thompson et al., 1991). Table 2.3 describes several sex chromosome abnormalities. In the next section we describe the most common techniques doctors use to determine if a developing fetus has inherited or developed any of these or other genetic disorders.

Prenatal Screening and Genetic Testing

Many parents are concerned and anxious during pregnancy, especially if a genetic disorder runs in the family or the baby is at risk in some other way. Fortunately, medical experts today can assist expectant parents who have these concerns. Several procedures can detect genetic diseases and abnormalities, and many other potential problems, before the baby is born. *Ultrasonography, amniocentesis,* and *chorionic villus sampling* (CVS) are the procedures most frequently used. An obstetrician may recommend these tests during the mother's prenatal visits, and the obstetrician or another specialist usually performs the procedure.

TABLE 2.3 Summary of Sex Chromosome Abnormalities

DISORDER	SEX CHROMOSOME ARRANGEMENT	FREQUENCY	MAJOR CHARACTERISTICS
Klinefelter syndrome (in males)	XXY, extra X chromosome	1/650 males	Small testicles, infertility; learning problems, shyness, and social immaturity
XYY syndrome (in males)	XYY, extra Y chromosome	1/1,000 males	Tall stature; learning problems; individuals remain fertile
Trisomy X (in females)	XXX, extra X chromosome	1/1,000 females	Tall stature; individuals remain fertile
Turner syndrome (individual develops as female)	X, missing chromosome	1/2,000 females	Short stature, webbed neck, broad shoulders, spatial perception and motor skill deficits; infertility; various other health problems
XX males (reversal)	XX	1/20,000 males	Sex reversal (normally males are XY). A part of the Y chromosome breaks off during meiosis and attaches to one of the X chromosomes. Because this part of the Y chromosome contains the genes that determine male sexual development, the individual develops male sexual characteristics. All XX males are infertile.
XY females (reversal)	XY	1/20,000 females	Sex reversal (normally females are XX). Part of the Y chromosome breaks off and is lost during meiosis. Now the XY individual does not have the genes required for normal male development, and the default is to develop female sexual characteristics. XY females do not develop secondary sex characteristics and are infertile.

(The Gale Encyclopedia of Genetic Disorders, 2005; Thompson et al., 1991.)

Figure 2.11 • Ultrasound Image of a Fetus Using ultrasound, physicians can monitor the growth of the fetus and can detect hundreds of potential defects.

ultrasonography (ultrasound)
Images of the fetus inside the mother's womb produced by sound waves. Ultrasound can be used to help physicians monitor fetal growth and detect physical defects.

amniocentesis
Procedure used to detect chromosomal and genetic abnormalities in the fetus. A needle is inserted through the mother's abdomen and uterus and into the amniotic sac, and fetal cells are withdrawn from the amniotic fluid.

Think About Daniel and Teri . . .

What would Daniel and Teri be able to learn if they had access to the karyotype and other results of genetic tests that may have been performed with their baby? If they knew in advance which diseases or conditions their baby may be susceptible to, what might they be able to do to intervene or help him?

With **ultrasonography (ultrasound)**, a technician uses an instrument that sends sound waves into the mother's abdomen. By reading the return of the sound waves, the instrument produces an image of the fetus and the surrounding structures. Ultrasound measurements help physicians determine if the fetus is growing properly. They also can reveal many structural defects (e.g., heart defects or neural tube or spinal defects). Ultrasound can be performed any time during pregnancy. In the ultrasound picture shown in Figure 2.11, you can clearly see the shape of the fetus.

We will never forget the ultrasound session from our third pregnancy (we already had two boys). As the technician moved the instrument over the abdomen, an image of two tiny side-by-side fetuses appeared on the monitor. At first we thought we were seeing an echo of one baby—echoes are common with ultrasounds. But the technician assured us that it was no echo. Instead, we were seeing the first picture of our twin girls, DZ twins. Two boys, and now two girls! Once we knew that both fetuses looked healthy, our thoughts immediately turned to other things . . . like how to feed and diaper two babies at once and how to fit six people into our small car. (We traded it for a van.)

If the parents are at high risk for passing a genetic defect to the baby, or if the mother's age is 35 or older, then the doctor will usually suggest genetic screening. With **amniocentesis**, a doctor or technician inserts a needle through the mother's abdomen and uterus and into the amniotic sac that surrounds the fetus. The technician also uses ultrasound during this process to show the position of the fetus and to guide the needle to an open pocket of amniotic fluid. The needle draws a small amount of fluid from the amniotic sac. Cells that the fetus has sloughed off into the fluid are then cultured in a laboratory for genetic testing. Technicians remove the chromosomes from these cultured cells and arrange them by size to form a picture called a *karyotype*. The picture of chromosomes in Figure 2.1 at the beginning of this chapter is a karyotype. By examining the karyotype, experts can detect any of several hundred disorders, especially those caused by missing, extra, or broken chromosomes. If a single-gene disease or other genetic disorder runs in the family, specific tests check for DNA markers or other indications of the disease.

Amniocentesis can be conducted after the 14th week of pregnancy, and the results are usually available in 1 to 2 weeks. There is about a 1 in 200 chance that the procedure itself will cause a serious problem. Inserting the needle near the fetus can cause early labor contractions and a miscarriage, and bacteria or injury caused by the needle can lead to serious infection. Because of these risks, doctors usually do not perform amniocentesis unless the fetus is already at a high risk for a serious genetic disorder or other complication.

Chorionic villus sampling (CVS) can be performed earlier than amniocentesis, beginning around the 8th week of pregnancy. With CVS the results can be available in just a few days. In this procedure a technician usually inserts a long catheter (tube) through the vagina and into the uterus. Or a needle may be inserted through the abdomen and uterus (similar to amniocentesis). The technician takes a few cells from the chorionic layer of the placenta that surrounds the fetus. As you will see in the next chapter, this layer of cells originates from the zygote, so the chromosomes and genetic codes in these cells will be the same as those in the fetus. By culturing these cells, specialists can construct a karyotype and perform genetic tests as with amniocentesis. The advantage of CVS is that it can be conducted earlier in pregnancy and parents can have results several weeks sooner than with amniocentesis. If parents must decide whether to terminate the pregnancy because of a serious defect found in the fetus, this earlier diagnosis is helpful. One disadvantage of CVS is that the risk of inducing miscarriage is about twice as high as with amniocentesis. Because CVS is performed earlier, the fetus is smaller and more vulnerable to the invasion than with amniocentesis. The risks associated with both procedures are decreasing, however, as the techniques improve and experts gain experience. Figure 2.12 shows how technicians collect cells using CVS and amniocentesis. To learn more about a career that involves working with genetic tests, read the Professional Perspective box on page 64 called "Career Focus: Meet a Genetic Counselor."

chorionic villus sampling (CVS) Procedure used to detect chromosomal and genetic abnormalities in the fetus. A catheter (tube) is inserted into the uterus, and cells are taken from the chorionic layer of the placenta around the fetus. Chromosomes are removed to conduct genetic tests.

your perspective

Imagine that there was a 1 in 300 chance that you would pass a fatal or very serious genetic disease to your children. Would you want to have amniocentesis performed knowing that there is a 1 in 200 risk that the test itself could lead to serious problems? What if you had a 1 in 100 chance of passing a fatal disease to your child? How would you make difficult decisions like these?

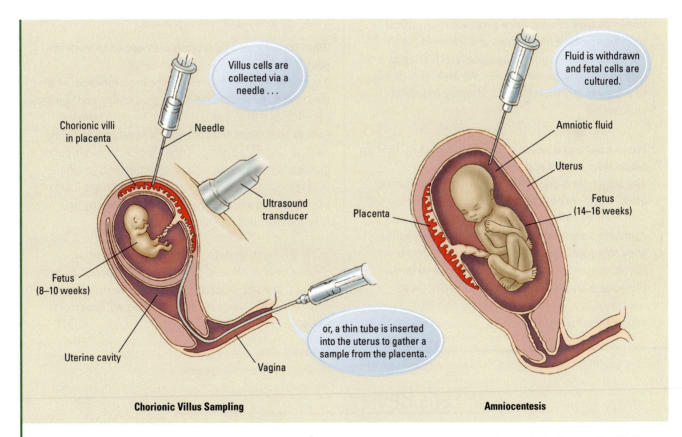

Figure 2.12 • Two Ways Fetal Cells Are Collected for Genetic Testing During Pregnancy With chorionic villus sampling (CVS) (left), either a catheter is inserted through the vagina and into the uterus to take placental villus cells for testing or villus cells are extracted using a needle inserted into the placenta. With amniocentesis (right) a needle is inserted through the mother's abdomen and into the amniotic sac. Amniotic fluid is withdrawn, containing cells from the fetus. (Bee & Boyd, 2000.)

Career Focus: Meet a Genetic Counselor

Robin L. Bennett, MS, CGC
Seattle, Washington
Genetic counselor; president of the National Society of Genetic Counselors (www.nsgc.org); and author of The Practical Guide to the Genetic Family History *(1999), published by John Wiley & Sons*

What are the main roles and job duties of genetic counselors?

We help people at risk for or affected with a genetic disorder. We translate complicated genetic facts into practical information to help clients understand a disorder, the available courses of action, how heredity contributes, and the testing options that are available. During a visit, we create a family *pedigree,* which is a summary of the medical conditions and family relationships over at least three generations. A critical role is discussing the feelings and concerns the clients have about genetic and prenatal testing as well as potential consequences. We also refer clients to community resources and appropriate medical specialties.

When a serious disease or defect is detected, how do counselors inform and assist clients?

The diagnosis is discussed face-to-face, and clients are strongly encouraged to have a support person with them (a partner, relative, or friend). Genetic counselors are trained in grief and crisis counseling. They try to anticipate clients' reactions and refer clients to specialists (such as individual and family therapists) and support groups as needed (see www.geneticalliance.org for information on support groups).

What are the newest techniques and trends in your field?

Presymptomatic or *susceptibility* genetic testing is now available, where people can be tested for the potential of a genetic disorder. Genetic counseling for these individuals is extremely important, because these are healthy individuals at risk of developing the condition, but the tests do not predict when a person will be affected or how their disease will progress. Interpreting these tests is quite complex both medically and emotionally. *Pharmacogenomics,* where people can be tested for a cluster of susceptibilities so that "designer medications" can be prescribed, is also new. Hopefully this will significantly reduce the incidence of adverse reactions to drugs, but it's very expensive. Gene therapy continues to be in the news, but these therapies are still a ways off in terms of clinical practice.

What training and education are needed to work in your field?

A master's degree in genetic counseling is required, which involves course work in medicine, psychology, and human genetics, as well as over a thousand hours in fieldwork. Genetic counselors work in a variety of settings including medical centers, private practice, medical research, public health and policy, pharmaceutical companies, genetic testing laboratories, and in instructional settings. If they work in clinical practice, they must be certified by the American Board of Genetic Counseling.

Q *Do any genetic disorders run in your family? Would you like to be tested to see if you have the predisposition for developing any of the diseases that are linked to genetics? Why or why not?*

■ Let's Review . . .

1. Which combination of alleles below is necessary for a person to inherit a disease such as cystic fibrosis? (*Note:* In this example, "C" refers to the healthy allele and "c" refers to the disease allele.)

   a. cc   b. Cc   c. cC   d. CC

2. Hemophilia, Duchenne muscular dystrophy, and color blindness are examples of:
   a. X-linked dominant diseases.
   b. X-linked recessive diseases.
   c. diseases caused by missing chromosomes.
   d. diseases caused by a broken X chromosome.

3. Which of the following is more common among females than males?
   a. X-linked recessive traits   b. X-linked dominant traits
   c. Fragile X syndrome   d. Klinefelter syndrome

4. Which test below could be used earliest in pregnancy to identify missing or extra chromosomes?
   a. amniocentesis   b. ultrasonography
   c. chorionic villus sampling   d. human genome mapping

5. **True or False:** Children will inherit Huntington disease if they inherit a disease allele from one parent and a healthy allele from the other parent.

6. **True or False:** Down syndrome is caused by a missing chromosome.

Answers: 1. a, 2. b, 3. b, 4. c, 5. T, 6. F

How Genes and Environments Interact

The first part of this chapter introduced you to some of the basic concepts of genetics and inheritance. Any human trait requires more than genetics, however: An environment of some kind is necessary for development to occur. In this context, *environment* refers to the interactions children have with the people, events, and situations in their lives. Children are nurtured by parents, educated by teachers, and influenced in countless ways by their siblings, playmates, and role models. Even the temperature, sunlight, and the presence or absence of toxic chemicals can influence development, and these too are considered part of the child's environment. In this section, we discuss how genetics and the environment interact to produce the complex traits, characteristics, and behaviors that we observe in children.

As you study this section, ask yourself these questions:

■ How do genetics and the environment act together to determine our traits?

■ How do the concepts of *range of reaction, canalization,* and *niche-picking* help explain the interaction of genetics and environment?

■ What is *probabilistic epigenesis*? How does it help explain developmental outcomes?

Developmental psychologists call the interaction of genetics and the environment the **G × E interaction.** Pronounced "G by E interaction," this term refers to the ways in which nature (represented by genetics and heredity) combines with nurture (the influences from a person's environment) to produce a given outcome. As you learned in Chapter 1, philosophers and scientists have long been interested in the relative roles of nature and nurture. For centuries the emphasis has shifted back and forth between nature and nurture, but it is now clear that both are essential for development to take place (de Waal, 1999). There are several ways to think about how genes and the environment interact. We will describe three common ways—range of reaction, canalization, and niche-picking. Then we'll introduce one newer approach, probabilistic epigenesis.

G × E interaction
The interacting effects of genetics and the environment on the development of traits and characteristics.

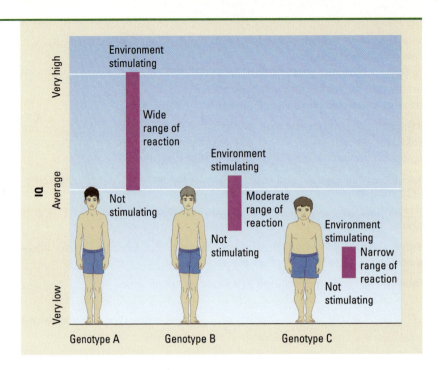

Figure 2.13 • Range of Reaction for Cognitive Skills (IQ) of Three Children (Hypothetical) Child A shows a large range of reaction (RR). When the environment is not stimulating, his IQ is average. But if the environment was more stimulating, this child's IQ could be much higher. Child C, however, has a very limited RR. The genotype for this child has set narrow limits, and his IQ will be low regardless of environment. A child with Down syndrome might have such a genotype, leading to low IQ. The RR for Child B falls in between these two, with more moderate changes as the environment is altered.

genotype
The genetic code a person inherits.

phenotype
The observable trait a person shows, resulting in part from the genotype they inherit.

range of reaction
The range of possible phenotypes that exist for a particular genotype.

canalization
Genetic limits on the effects of the environment. In experiential canalization, in contrast, it is the environment that limits the expression of genes.

Range of Reaction

One way to understand the interaction between genes and the environment is to recognize that an individual's **genotype** (or actual genetic code) establishes boundaries on the possible **phenotype** (or observable traits) that can occur. For any individual, the various possible phenotypic outcomes are the **range of reaction** for that genotype (Gottesman, 1963). The key idea is that genes set the boundaries for the range of reaction, but influences from the environment determine which possible outcomes actually materialize. Figure 2.13 illustrates the hypothetical range of reaction for cognitive skills for three children. Remember that the range of reaction is a theoretical construct. It is useful for helping us think about the ways in which genes and the environment interact. We can never know for certain the range of reaction for a specific individual, because it is impossible to know or manipulate all of the environmental possibilities during the limited time of one person's development.

Canalization

A second way to think about G × E interactions emphasizes how genetics can help protect children from the effects of the environment. **Canalization** refers to the way genes limit developmental outcomes (Waddington, 1942, 1957). In other words, genes provide a strong buffer against environmental variations, limiting the effects that the environment can have. The result is that development can proceed along only a few species-specific paths and can produce only outcomes that are typical for that species. Figure 2.14 diagrams this concept. Genetics provides a small number of pathways, or canals, through the hills and valleys of the developmental landscape. The environment can be thought of as a force (like the wind) that moves the individual around within the developmental landscape. The deeper the canal, the more genes predetermine the developmental pathway. In this model, choice points where one canal splits into two, offering two different developmental directions, represent critical periods in development.

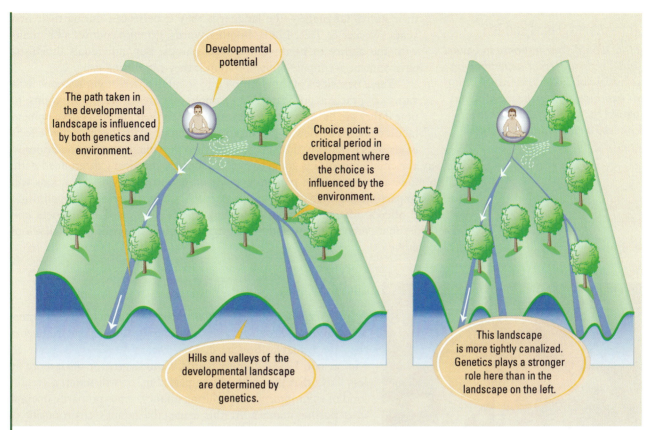

Figure 2.14 • Canalization The hills and valleys in the diagram represent the developmental "landscape" through which an individual progresses. The individual's development is represented by the path of the ball moving through this landscape. Genetics determines the shape of the landscape, while forces in the environment move the ball through the critical choice points. The width of each valley represents the range of phenotypes possible for that genotype (as with range of reaction). Notice that the landscape on the right is more strongly canalized—genetics plays a stronger limiting role in the individual's development. (Adapted from Waddington, 1974.)

The view of canalization presented in Figure 2.14 emphasizes the protective role of genetics (especially the landscape on the right side of the figure). It explains how an individual can physically and psychologically survive despite fairly extreme environmental conditions. Most infants begin walking at about one year of age, for example, and this holds true pretty much regardless of whether the infant receives relatively supportive or nonsupportive parenting and regardless of whether the infant receives poor, mediocre, or excellent nutrition. In this way we say that walking is a relatively canalized activity—it occurs at about one year of age across a wide spectrum of environmental conditions. It would take a severe environmental influence to alter this genetic timetable; walking might be delayed, for example, if the infant was severely abused or malnourished. Notice, however, that this theory places a heavy emphasis on *genetic determinism*—environmental conditions must be strong to change an individual's developmental path.

A more recent interpretation places less emphasis on genetic determination. This newer model gives more weight to the role of the environment, particularly prenatal and early experiences (Gottlieb, 1997). This interpretation is called *experiential canalization*. In this view, genetics provides a fairly wide range of possible developmental outcomes (more like the landscape on the left side of Figure 2.14) and it is the environment that plays the limiting role. For example, think about speech perception. Until about one year of age, infants respond similarly to the basic sounds used in all languages. After that, they can detect subtle differences in language sounds only in

Think About Daniel and Teri . . .

How would your response to Daniel and Teri be different depending on whether you emphasize canalization or experiential canalization? What would the implications of each concept be for Daniel and Teri?

their native languages—the languages they experienced during their first years (Werker & Tees, 1984). In other words, genetics endows all humans with the ability to perceive language sounds, but individuals' linguistic environment eventually limits the sounds they can distinguish.

These two views of canalization lead to quite different implications for a variety of practical problems. For example, all parents wonder from time to time if they are having any important impact on their children's developmental outcomes. The view of canalization that emphasizes the protective effects of genetics would say that unless a parent is providing extreme conditions in some way, the child's outcome is going to proceed along a genetically determined path. Small to moderate variations in parenting style and day-to-day living conditions will have little impact on the child's outcome (Scarr, 1992). The experiential canalization view would offer a different opinion. According to this view, early experiences and opportunities that parents offer would have a significant impact in the child's developmental outcome.

Niche-Picking: I Gotta Be Me . . .

It may surprise you to learn that one way a child's genes interact with the environment is by affecting the kinds of environments that are available (Bouchard, 1997; Scarr, 1992, 1993; Scarr & McCartney, 1983). In other words, a child's genes make it more or less likely that the child will be placed in, or will select, a certain kind of environment. First, during infancy, genes primarily operate in a *passive* manner. At this stage, the infant's environment is almost totally controlled by his or her parents. However, the child and parents share many genes, so the home environment is usually consistent with and supportive of the child's genes. Second, as the child gets older, genes play a more *evocative* role. This means that the child's genetic tendencies evoke certain responses from parents and others. For example, if a child likes to be physically active, parents tend to provide more opportunities for physical activities. They may offer more frequent trips to the playground, or encourage the child to join sports teams. These activities are evoked by and tend to support the child's genetic tendencies.

People who inherit high activity levels tend to select activities and environments to suit this disposition. Can you see here how genetics has an influence on the role played by the environment?

niche-picking
The tendency to pick activities and environments that fit with our genetic predispositions.

Third, as children get older and have more freedom to choose their own activities, genes work in an *active* way. Older children can actively seek out the specific *niches,* or activities and environments, that suit them best. That is, they engage in **niche-picking.** Given a choice, shy children tend to choose more quiet and passive activities, such as going to movies and reading books. Active children gravitate to physical sports and noisy settings. A child's genetic predisposition toward being shy or active leads the child to pick niches that support his or her tendencies. So genes influence behavior not only by predisposing children to develop certain traits or characteristics, but also by affecting the kinds of environments that surround them.

Our twin daughters offer an example of passive, evocative, and active gene influences. When they were infants, we provided an environment that suited our own interests—we read lots of books to them, played music for them, and held and rocked them. Our interests and skills reflected our own genes, and given that we shared a lot of genes with our daughters, the environment we provided was reasonably consistent with their genetic tendencies. But as the girls grow older, they are clearly evoking different kinds of influences from their environments. Rachel is very active and prefers fast-paced physical activities. Lily is much happier playing with computer games or with Barbie dolls, or sitting in someone's lap. We respond to the differences so that Rachel is able to spend more time in physical activities and Lily more time

Think About Daniel and Teri . . .

How will the genetics of Daniel and Teri's baby affect the environment that they provide for him? What about when their son begins picking his own activities and environments?

in quieter kinds of play. The girls are now old enough to begin active niche-picking, and their different preferences will almost certainly lead them to select different kinds of environments as they develop hobbies, choose friends, and decide how to spend their spare time.

Probabilistic Epigenesis: Activating Your Genes

Though researchers have investigated G × E interactions for some time now, they continue to discover increasingly complex ways in which genes and environment interact to influence our traits and characteristics. The concept of *probabilistic epigenesis* provides a good example. The term *epigenesis* refers to the emergence of a trait, characteristic, or behavior over the course of development (as opposed to its presence from the beginning). *Probabilistic* means that there is some probability that a given characteristic or trait will develop depending on certain conditions in the environment (as opposed to a certainty that it will occur regardless of the environment). According to the concept of **probabilistic epigenesis,** the likelihood of a given behavioral outcome depends on the existence of specific genetic potential that must be activated by specific environmental conditions, or "life experiences" (Gottlieb, 1997, 2003). The idea of such an interaction is not new, but awareness of the central role of the environment in activating specific genes is. Researchers agree that only about 10 percent to 15 percent of an individual's total genome is actually expressed, or made active. This means that every individual has many more potential developmental pathways than are ever realized, and *it is the individual's environment that controls which parts of the genome are activated*. Figure 2.15 illustrates the complex interactions that take place. For example, we know that certain environmental conditions (e.g., light, stress, nutrition, and length of the day) affect levels of numerous hormones in the body. Hormones in turn enter the nuclei of cells and affect protein production, which essentially "turns on" or "turns off" certain genes. So not only do our genes affect behavior, as we have long realized (see the upper-left arrow in Figure 2.15), but our environment influences which parts of our vast genetic potential are actually activated and expressed (the lower two arrows in Figure 2.15).

probabilistic epigenesis
The likelihood that specific environmental conditions will activate specific genes that lead to particular traits or behavioral outcomes.

Think About Daniel and Teri . . .
How can the concept of probabilistic epigenesis explain differences in the outcomes of Daniel and Teri's baby in his adopted environment and potential outcomes in other possible environments?

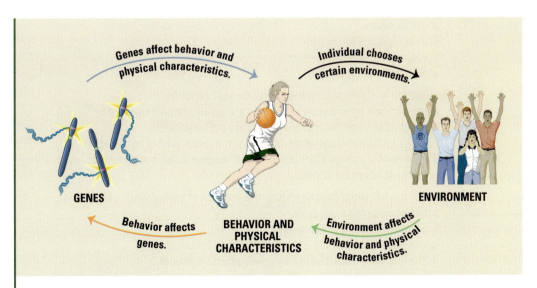

Figure 2.15 • Probabilistic Epigenesis Genes can determine physical and behavioral characteristics (such as high activity level) causing the child to select certain environments (e.g., active and stimulating sports). But the environment also stimulates changes in the body (e.g., hormones) that selectively turn genes on and off. (Based on Gottlieb, 1991.)

An interesting implication of probabilistic epigenesis is that a significant change in the environment will change which genes are expressed. This can create a situation in which characteristics or behaviors not normally seen in a species can develop, even though the actual genetic material has stayed the same. For example, certain changes of the developmental environment of bird embryos can result in the birds' developing teeth, which they normally do not have (Kollar & Fisher, 1980). Because the embryos were already formed, the genetic potential for the abnormal characteristic must already have been present, but the characteristic does not appear in the normal course of development for birds. The environmental changes activated genes that are normally "turned off." In another example, exposure of fruit flies to ether during prenatal development causes them to grow an extra set of wings (Ho, 1984). The altered genetic activation can be passed along to future generations as well—the offspring of fruit flies with extra wings also develop the second set of wings.

What does this mean for human development? Clearly humans have a vast genetic potential, and only a small portion of it is expressed. Which portion is expressed depends on the child's environment. Though researchers continue to make progress, we do not yet have a good understanding of which environmental factors are most important in affecting gene expression. Nor can we pinpoint (yet) precisely how environmental factors shape complex traits like intelligence and personality. But the concept of probabilistic epigenesis makes a strong statement about the relationship between genes and the environment. It emphasizes that this relationship does affect development—that the two factors are truly interdependent.

■ Let's Review . . .

1. In the range of reaction concept, which of the following sets the upper and lower boundaries for the range of possible developmental outcomes?
   - a. genes
   - b. environment
   - c. G × E interactions
   - d. proximal processes

2. A child likes to draw and sketch pictures whenever she can. This is an example of:
   - a. canalization.
   - b. passive G × E interaction.
   - c. evocative G × E interaction.
   - d. active G × E interaction.

3. Canalization is *different* from experiential canalization in that:
   - a. canalization emphasizes that limits are set by the environment.
   - b. canalization emphasizes that limits are set by genetics.
   - c. experiential canalization emphasizes that limits are set by genetics.
   - d. experiential canalization places equal emphasis on both genetics and the environment in setting limits.

4. Which of the following best describes the concept of probabilistic epigenesis?
   - a. Genes determine behavior.
   - b. Genes do not affect behavior.
   - c. Genes activated by the environment affect behavior.
   - d. The environment activated by genes affects behavior.

5. **True or False:** The concept of *niche-picking* is the idea that our genes can influence the kinds of environments that we select for ourselves.

6. **True or False:** We never know what the range of reaction will be for any particular child.

Answers: 1. a, 2. d, 3. b, 4. c, 5. T, 6. T

Behavior Genetics: Measuring the Heritability of Traits

How different are you from your siblings and parents? What accounts for the differences and similarities? Behavior genetics is a field that tries to answer these questions.

As you study this section, ask yourself these questions:

- What is behavior genetics, and how does this field help explain development?

- How do behavior geneticists obtain heritability estimates? What does *heritability* mean, and what does it *not* mean?

- What are shared and nonshared environments, and how does each contribute to development?

- What are the heritabilities of cognitive skills and personality? What do these heritabilities tell us about the causes and developmental courses of these traits?

Behavior Genetics, Heritability, and Shared and Nonshared Environments

In Chapter 1 we introduced you to the field of behavior genetics to show you the relationship between nature and nurture. Behavior geneticists often talk about the *heritability* of certain behavioral outcomes. **Heritability** is a mathematical estimate of the degree of genetic influence for a given trait. Heritability estimates range from 0.00 to 1.00; higher values mean that there is a stronger genetic influence on the trait. For example, the estimated heritability for height is .90, which means that a great deal of the variance in height in a population is due to genetic variance in that population. Contrast this with the estimated heritability of some attitudes, such as religiosity or attitudes toward racial integration. The heritability estimate for religiosity ranges from .04 to .22, depending on how religiosity is assessed; for attitudes on integration it is .06 (Loehlin & Nichols, 1976). These low heritability estimates mean that very little, if any, of the variation in these attitudes is genetic. Instead, the variation is due mostly to learning experiences and other differences in the environment. Though it is theoretically possible for heritability estimates to be as high as 1.0, the complex traits that behavioral geneticists study never show heritabilities this high. In general, heritability estimates over .50 are considered fairly high (Plomin, 1990).

In recent decades, behavior geneticists have become more interested in estimating the influence of the environment on development. As you read earlier in this chapter, an actual developmental outcome reflects both a genetic influence and an environmental influence. But there are two types of environments that we must consider when explaining differences in behavioral outcomes. **Shared environment** consists of experiences and aspects of the environment that are common to all individuals living together (Plomin, 1986). These shared experiences tend to produce similarities in behavioral outcomes. Within a family, shared environments include such things as the existence of lots of reading material at home, the cultural or sporting events the family attends, or the overall socioeconomic level of the household.

The shared environment cannot explain behavioral differences among family members, however. To explain differences we must examine the aspects of the environment that differ from one person to another. The **nonshared environment** consists of experiences and aspects of the environment that are unique to an individual (Hetherington et al., 1994). Nonshared environments differ across people, and they produce differences in behavioral outcomes. For example, perhaps one child in a family spends lots of time listening to music CDs and playing musical instruments, whereas another spends more

These twins are genetically identical and they will share some features of their environments. Not all of their life experiences will be identical, however, so there will be features of their environments that they do not share.

heritability
A mathematical estimate of the degree of genetic influence for a given trait or behavior.

shared environment
Experiences and aspects of the environment that are common across all individuals who are living together.

nonshared environment
Experiences and aspects of the environment that differ across people.

your perspective

In what ways are you and your siblings or other close relatives similar? Different? Identify environmental factors you have shared with these relatives, then ones you have not shared. How do these shared and nonshared environmental factors contribute to the behavioral similarities and differences you identified?

twin studies
Comparisons between measurements of identical and nonidentical twins, used to estimate the genetic contribution to traits and characteristics.

adoption studies
Comparisons between measurements of children and their adoptive and biological parents used to estimate the genetic contribution to traits and characteristics.

time watching and participating in sports activities. Although they are growing up in the same family, these children spend much of their time in different types of environments.

How Is Heritability Estimated?

Two methods that researchers have used to estimate heritability are *twin studies* and *adoption studies*. **Twin studies** estimate the genetic contribution to a given trait by comparing measurements from identical and nonidentical twins. Think about the genetic makeup of these two different kinds of twins and you will see the logic of this method. As you recall from earlier in this chapter, identical twins form when a single zygote splits, resulting in two zygotes. The two individuals that develop from these zygotes are *genetically identical*—they must be, because they came from the same fertilized egg. Nonidentical twins, on the other hand, come from two different eggs fertilized by two different sperm. Therefore, they are no more genetically alike than are any other siblings, having on average 50 percent of their genetic material in common.

In twin studies, researchers estimate heritability by taking measurements (e.g., IQ or personality measures) of both kinds of twins. They compute correlations between the members of each pair of twins; then they compare the correlations for identical twins to the correlations for nonidentical twins. (Recall from Chapter 1 that a correlation is a number representing the amount of association between two scores.) If there is an important genetic influence on the trait measured, then the correlation for the identical twins should be significantly higher than the correlation for the nonidentical twins.

Adoption studies estimate the genetic contribution to a given trait by studying adopted children, their biological parents and siblings, and their adoptive families. Correlations between the children and their biological relatives are compared with correlations between the children and their adoptive families. If there is an important genetic influence on the trait measured, the correlation with the biological relatives should be significantly higher than the correlation with the adoptive relatives.

These two methods provide a way to estimate heritabilities. They are sometimes combined, as in studies that calculate estimates of heritability from measures of identical twins adopted into different families. But remember that both twin studies and adoption studies, no matter how they are used, provide only *estimates* of heritability. Remember, too, that several factors can affect these estimates. For example, adoption studies have the potential problem of *selective placement*, in which agencies place adopted children in homes that are similar in important ways to those of the biological parents. Agencies may well take into consideration factors such as racial and cultural background, overall socioeconomic status, and level of education when they select adoptive homes for children. What effect do you think selective placement would have on heritability estimates? Some adoption studies have reported that selective placement was not an important factor for the traits under consideration. Many, however, provide no information (Plomin, 1990). In twin studies, there is an assumption of *equal environments*. This means that researchers generally assume the similarity of the environment for identical twins to be the same as for nonidentical twins. Do you think this assumption is valid? Or are identical twins likely to share a more similar environment than nonidentical twins? If identical twins share a more similar environment, then heritability estimates may well be inflated (Kendler et al., 1993; Pam et al., 1996).

Finally, remember that in many cases children are exposed to or select certain environments based on their genetic tendencies. This leads to a correlation between genetics and environment that current research methods are not able to unravel. It is difficult to say how heritability estimates are affected, because such correlations are not clearly the effect of either heredity or the environment but result from their interaction. Newer statistical techniques such as path analysis, which you learned about in Chapter 1, can help describe these kinds of relations between genetics and heredity and account for the possible effects of selective placement and unequal environments (e.g., Crosnoe & Elder, 2002). We can now obtain more accurate heritability estimates through these techniques than through simple comparison of correlations.

Heritability of Complex Characteristics

Using the methods just described, researchers have studied a wide variety of different human characteristics to understand the influences of genetics and the environment. Table 2.4 summarizes the estimated heritability for various traits or behaviors. Almost all show small to moderate heritability.

TABLE 2.4 Heritability Estimates for a Variety of Traits and Characteristics

TRAIT OR CHARACTERISTIC	HERITABILITY ESTIMATE	SOURCE
Cognitive Skills		
General intelligence	.52	1
Verbal reasoning	.50	1
Reasoning	.48	2
Spatial visualization	.46	2
Perceptual speed	.46	2
Vocational interests (in adolescence)	.42	1
Spatial reasoning	.40	1
Verbal comprehension	.38	2
Scholastic achievement		1
(in adolescence)	.38	2
English usage	.40	3
Mathematics	.52 to .56	10
Social studies	.34	3
Natural sciences	.38	3
Memory	.32	2
Verbal fluency	.30	2
Processing speed	.22	1
Divergent thinking	.22	2
Personality and Temperament		
Anxiety	.70	4
Sociability	.64	4
Activity-impulsivity	.62	4
Dominance	.60	4
Emotionality	.54	4
Extraversion	.51	1
Task orientation	.50	4
Conservatism	.50	5
Neuroticism	.46	1
Control	.44	4
Agression	.40	4
Masculinity/femininity	.32	4
Sexual orientation	.30 to .70	9
Belief in God	.22	3
Attitude toward racial integration	.06	3
Involvement in religious affairs	.04	3

continued

TABLE 2.4 *continued*

TRAIT OR CHARACTERISTIC	HERITABILITY ESTIMATE	SOURCE
Problem Conditions		
Hyperactivity (adolescent males)	.75	7
Schizophrenia (risk of)	.70	6
Obesity (Body Mass Index)	.50 to .90	8
Alcoholism (risk of)	.50 to .71	9

(1. Plomin et al., 1994; 2. Nichols, 1978; 3. Loehlin & Nichols, 1976; 4. McCartney et al., 1990; 5. Martin et al., 1986; 6. Plomin, 1990; 7. Stevenson, 1992; 8. Maes et al., 1997; 9. Rose, 1995; 10. Walker et al., 2004.)

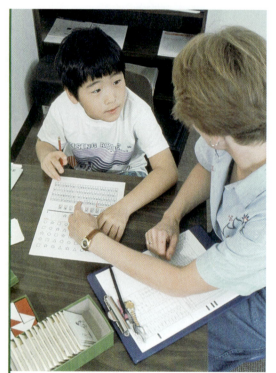

Scores from IQ tests tend to be more similar among identical than among nonidentical twins. Generally speaking, scores are more similar when the genetic relationship is more similar.

Think About Daniel and Teri . . .

According to these data, would we expect Daniel and Teri's child to have an IQ that is more similar to Daniel and Teri's or more similar to his biological parents'?

Heritability of Cognitive Skills. Probably the most extensively studied behavioral trait is intelligence. Researchers often measure intelligence using scores on standardized intelligence tests (e.g., IQ scores). Table 2.5 shows the average IQ correlations taken across 216 different studies. These data indicate that heredity has a significant influence on IQ scores. The correlations for identical twins are substantially higher than those for nonidentical twins, and the correlations for biological relatives are higher than the correlations for adoptive relatives. Based on data like these, behavior geneticists generally estimate that the heritability of IQ is about .50 (Devlin et al., 1997; Plomin & DeFries, 1998; Rose, 1995). As Table 2.4 showed, there have been similar findings for a variety of specific cognitive skills (such as spatial reasoning, verbal reasoning, and perceptual speed) and achievement scores (such as English usage, mathematics, social studies, and natural sciences).

So it seems that a variety of cognitive skills have a significant hereditary component. Does this component change across age? After all, different genetic systems may become more or less important at different ages. Also, environmental influences change as children age. Several studies have shown that heritability estimates for some cognitive skills do change—they *increase* with age, as shown in Figure 2.16 (Alarcón et al., 1998; Bishop et al., 2003; Boomsma, 1993; McGue, Bacon, & Lykken, 1993; Petrill et al., 2004; Plomin & DeFries, 1998; Plomin & Spinath, 2004). In other words, the relative influence of genetics on cognitive skills appears to become stronger the older a person gets! When this result came out, it surprised many researchers. For decades it had been assumed that genes are particularly important in setting an individual's initial developmental path (remember the concept of canalization?), but that the environment exerts more and more influence with age (because we encounter more and more aspects of the environment with age). However, think back to the idea of niche-picking. Niche-picking theory says that individuals' genes affect their environment by guiding the environments they select. This effect then becomes stronger as people become more independent and make more of their own choices of environments. Perhaps the increase in heritability estimates reflects this indirect influence of genetics. It is also possible that the specific genes exerting their effects are different at different points in the life span. In other words, though the overall influence of genetics seems to increase, we do not know which genes are involved. Some may become more influential; others may become less important. Further work is needed to identify the contributions and interactions of specific genes at different points in time. It's also

TABLE 2.5 Correlations Used to Estimate the Heritability of IQ

RELATIONSHIP	AVERAGE CORRELATION IN IQ SCORES
Identical twins, raised together	.85
Nonidentical twins, raised together	.59
Identical twins, adopted apart	.74
Biological parent with child, living together	.41
Biological parent with child, adopted apart	.24
Adoptive parent with adopted child	.20
Biological siblings, living together	.46
Adoptive siblings	.24

(Devlin et al., 1997.)

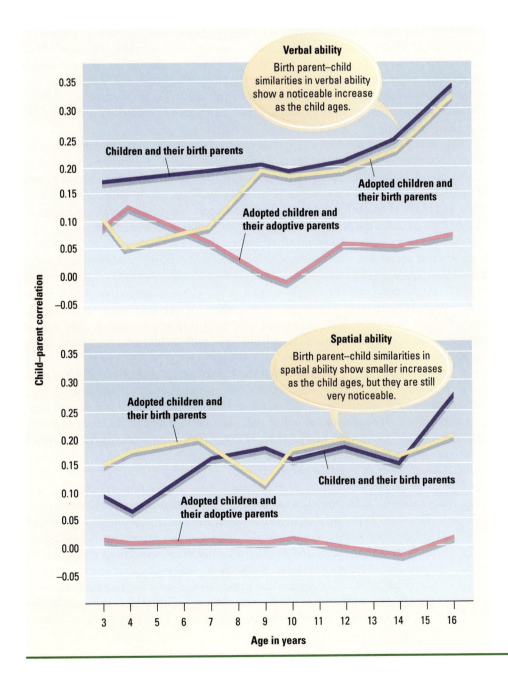

Figure 2.16 • Heritability of Verbal and Spatial Abilities
Heritability estimates for some cognitive skills increase with age, perhaps because niche-picking increases. The specific genes exerting their effects may also differ at various points in the life span. (Plomin & DeFries, 1998.)

important to understand that research on heritability of cognitive skills is often controversial. There are concerns about such issues as bias or inappropriate measures used to assess the skills. We will return to this controversy when we talk about intelligence in Chapter 14.

Heritability of Personality and Temperament. Behavior geneticists also have studied the heritability of many aspects of personality. As with research on cognitive skills, most studies of personality indicate that genetics is an important influence. Heritability estimates from twin and adoption studies go as high as .70, as summarized in Table 2.4. Averaging across the major dimensions of personality, it seems that 40 percent to 50 percent of variation in personality is due to genetic factors (Bouchard, 1994; Carey & DiLalla, 1994; Plomin, 1990).

Estimated heritabilties for personality measures also change across age. For example, for such measures as extraversion, neuroticism, emotionality, activity level, and sociability, heritability estimates appear to decline after late adolescence (McGue et al., 1993; Pedersen, 1993; Plomin et al., 1993; Viken et al., 1994). But note that researchers have calculated the vast majority of personality heritability estimates based on self-report or parent-report questionnaires. Can we trust the accuracy of self-reports, and are they consistent across time? More recent studies that use observational methods yield a wider range of heritability estimates—and lower heritability estimates overall (Emde et al., 1992; Plomin et al., 1993; Robinson et al., 1992). Research into specific genes or gene markers for aspects of personality is only beginning, and this work has identified no specific markers so far.

One dimension of personality that has received much attention from developmental psychologists is *temperament,* or a child's activity level and pattern of response to stimulation. Children clearly differ from an early age in how irritable, sociable, and active they are. Many of these differences have significant effects on a child's interactions, and many persist into adulthood. We will discuss this topic in detail in Chapter 6, but for now consider the evidence for a genetic influence on temperament.

As you saw in Table 2.4, several aspects of temperament show moderate heritability (e.g., anxiety, sociability, activity–impulsivity, and emotionality). Studies with children as young as 3 months of age show persistent genetic influence on traits such as attention, activity, involvement, and shyness (Braungart et al., 1992; Cherny et al., 1994; Emde et al., 1992). Temperament differences are important for a child's interpersonal interactions. Perhaps you know from experience how your interactions with a child who is easygoing, smiling, and responsive differ from those with a child who is irritable, fussy, and difficult to soothe.

Some researchers have suggested that the role of genes in temperament has even broader, cultural-level implications. Jerome Kagan has proposed that societies may differ in the typical underlying temperament of their people. These differences in temperament may then predispose different cultures to adopting certain kinds of philosophical approaches (Kagan et al., 1993, 1994). This hypothesis leads to Kagan's suggestion that a basic aspect of cultural difference, each culture's underlying philosophical orientation, may reflect genetic factors. For example, Buddhist philosophies place more emphasis on serenity and harmony than do Western approaches, and those traits are much more common in people in Asian cultures than in Western ones.

This may seem far-fetched, but consider the fact that Caucasian and Asian babies consistently show cultural differences in aspects of temperament such as activity level and vocalizing—and many aspects of temperament have a clear genetic influence. Kagan is not suggesting that one philosophical orientation is better than the other is. Nor is he arguing that the environment is unimportant for temperament or philosophical orientation. But it is interesting to consider that an aspect of culture that has always been

Think About Daniel and Teri . . .
What can you tell Daniel and Teri about the heritability of personality traits and the role played by the environment?

assumed to be environmental in origin may actually reflect some basic genetically influenced tendencies.

In Table 2.4 you can see that the heritability estimates for hyperactivity, schizophrenia, obesity, and alcoholism are fairly high. Researchers have reported preliminary evidence for specific genetic markers and linkages for a few of these conditions, but they will have to do much more research before we can draw confident conclusions (Cloninger et al., 1996; Holden, 1995; Plomin & McGuffin, 2003; Plomin et al., 2003; Rose, 1995).

In this chapter we discussed the basics of how genes work. We considered the structure of genes, how they are transmitted from one generation to the next, and how they influence complex traits such as intelligence and personality. The current work in behavior genetics is exciting, and the astonishing pace of progress on the Human Genome Project virtually ensures that in a few years we will know much more about genetic influences on behavior. We hope you will keep several important points in mind as you think about the information on genes and environment. First, it is becoming increasingly clear that genes and the environment interact in complex ways. The central question for those interested in the development of children has evolved from "Which factor?" to "Which factor has the biggest effect?" to the current "How do the two factors work together to influence complex traits and characteristics?" Second, we must reiterate that just because a trait is influenced by genetics does not mean that the environment is unimportant; nor does it take away an individual's free will. As Gottlieb notes, "genes do not make behavior happen, even though behavior won't happen without them" (1997, p. xiii). Finally, much of the work currently under way investigates genetic contributions to controversial traits and characteristics such as intelligence, sexual orientation, and aggression. Fully as important as research on the role of genes is the issue of how societies interpret and use the information that researchers discover. Behavior geneticists hope that society will use new discoveries to develop and implement informed and humane policies—but it is the responsibility of thoughtful policy makers and an informed public to make this happen.

Could cultural differences in philosophical approaches reflect genetically influenced differences in temperament?

■ Let's Review . . .

1. Mr. Cho consistently treats all of his students in the same way, and all of the students respond in the same way to his classroom structure. In this case, Mr. Cho's classroom treatment is part of his students':
   a. shared environment.
   b. nonshared environment.
   c. neither shared nor nonshared environment.
   d. nonevocative niche.

2. A twin study measured the political attitudes of identical twins and of nonidentical twins. Which of the following would be the most reasonable conclusion if the correlation between attitudes for identical twins was *not* different from the correlation between nonidentical twins?
   a. Political attitudes are strongly influenced by genetics.
   b. Political attitudes are not at all influenced by genetics.
   c. Political attitudes are influenced equally by genetics and environment.
   d. Political attitudes are more strongly influenced by the environment than by genetics.

3. Suppose researchers estimated the heritability of smoking addiction at 0.95. Based on this heritability estimate, which of the following is true?
   a. There is a "smoking" gene.
   b. Some people have a genetic predisposition to smoking addiction.
   c. If you have the "smoking gene," you will become addicted to nicotine.
   d. The environment has no effect on whether smoking addiction develops.

Thinking Back to Daniel and Teri . . .

Now that you have studied this chapter, you should be able to give Daniel and Teri a detailed explanation of how nature and nurture will operate together to influence the development of their adopted son. First, you could review the process of meiosis to explain how crossing-over and the random shuffling of chromosomes ensure that each new baby receives a unique combination of chromosomes and genetic material. The baby will not be a clone of either of his biological parents, but instead will inherit a portion of the genes from each parent. If the biological parents carry any inherited disease, there is a chance that the baby will develop the disease. If Daniel and Teri have access to the results of any genetic tests (e.g., amniocentesis or CVS) that were performed, they could learn if their baby is susceptible to certain diseases. With some inherited diseases (e.g., hemophilia) early knowledge and intervention may save the child's life. With others (e.g., Tay–Sachs disease), Daniel and Teri may not be able to do much.

Daniel and Teri will likely be especially interested in the effect that the environment they provide will have on their adopted baby. You can explain the complex kinds of G × E interactions that take place, including the ideas of range of reaction, experiential canalization, and probabilistic epigenesis. Each of these concepts suggests how an enriched environment may help their child realize a greater amount of his genetic potential. In fact, environment can even affect which particular genes are expressed. Yet it also important to help Daniel and Teri understand that although the environment they provide is critical, even this environment will be affected in important ways by their baby's genetics. You can describe how evocative G × E interactions and niche-picking work.

Finally, you can help Daniel and Teri understand the idea of heritability. Remember that heritability estimates indicate genetic influence but do not imply that the environment is unimportant for the development of specific traits or behaviors. By helping Daniel and Teri understand heritability in terms of genetic predispositions that might or might not be activated by the environment, you can help them watch for opportunities to foster skills they see in their child. It will be important to communicate that their child's development depends on his genetics and his environment—neither factor can operate alone.

■ Chapter Review . . .

What are chromosomes, DNA, and genes? What is the Human Genome Project, and what can we learn from it?

Most cells in the human body contain 46 chromosomes (23 pairs). DNA molecules are arranged along each chromosome. DNA is a string of nucleotide bases (adenine, thymine, guanine, and cytosine) linked in complementary pairs (A–T and G–C). A gene is a segment of DNA, usually several hundred to several thousands of base pairs long. Each gene provides the code for a trait, tissue, or other structure. The aim of the Human Genome Project has been to identify the full genetic code for human beings. From the project we already know about specific gene codes for a wide variety of diseases and other traits.

What is the difference between mitosis and meiosis? How are identical and nonidentical twins formed?

In mitosis, the 46 chromosomes in the original cell are copied into two cells. With meiosis, however, the number of chromosomes is reduced to 23 in each sex cell (sperm and egg). With crossing-over and the random shuffling of chromosomes to cells, meiosis increases the genetic diversity in offspring. Identical (monozygotic) twins form when one fertilized egg splits later in development to form two zygotes. MZ twins share the same genetic code. Nonidentical (dizygotic) twins come from two separate eggs fertilized by separate sperm. DZ twins are no more alike genetically than are any other sibling pairs.

How do dominant–recessive gene traits work, and what are some of the more common examples?

Chromosomes operate in pairs, and the genes on each member of the pair work to influence our traits. If you inherit one dominant and one recessive allele, the dominant allele will determine the trait. For a recessive allele to be expressed, you need to carry the recessive allele on both chromosomes. Arched feet, dimpled cheeks, and detached earlobes are examples of dominant traits. Flat feet, nondimpled cheeks, and attached earlobes are recessive. Huntington disease is an example of a dominant-gene disease. Cystic fibrosis, sickle cell disease, and Tay–Sachs disease are recessive. Recessive diseases carried on the X chromosome (e.g., hemophilia, Duchenne muscular dystrophy, color blindness, and some forms of retinitis pigmentosa) are more likely to be expressed in males. Dominant X-linked diseases (e.g., vitamin D–resistant rickets, Rett syndrome) occur more in females. Fragile X syndrome is caused by a weakened tip on the X chromosome and is more likely to occur in males.

What are the major chromosome abnormalities?

Chromosome abnormalities involve missing, extra, or damaged chromosomes. Down syndrome occurs when children have an extra chromosome at location 21 (trisomy 21); it causes mental retardation and other problems, and the risk of having a baby with Down syndrome increases dramatically as the mother's age passes 35. Klinefelter syndrome usually occurs when males have an extra X chromosome (XXY); males can also have an extra Y (XYY). In trisomy X (XXX) females are born with an extra X chromosome. Females can also have a missing sex chromosome (only one X), leading to Turner syndrome. Sex reversal sometimes occurs when part of the Y chromosome is lost (leading to XY females) or becomes attached to the X chromosome (leading to XX males).

What are the main procedures doctors use to identify structural defects and genetic abnormalities in developing fetuses?

Ultrasonography (ultrasound) sends sound waves through the mother's abdomen to produce images of the fetus. Through ultrasound the doctor can monitor the growth of the fetus and can detect many structural defects and other problems. In amniocentesis fluid is removed from the amniotic sac and fetal cells are retrieved for genetic testing. In chorionic villus sampling (CVS), cells are removed from the chorionic layer of the placenta. Amniocentesis and CVS allow clinicians to detect chromosome abnormalities and several hundred genetic diseases.

In what ways do genes and environment interact to influence behavior?

Several concepts have been proposed to explain how genes and the environment interact. Some concepts, like range of reaction and canalization, emphasize the limits that genes set on possible developmental paths. Others emphasize the role of the environment in limiting outcomes (experiential canalization) or in activating certain genes (probabilistic epigenesis). The interactions are complex: Sometimes the environment works to "turn on" or "turn off" certain genes, and sometimes genes influence the child's environment. Researchers agree that both genes and the environment are essential and that they interact in very complex ways to produce behavior.

What are shared and nonshared environments? How does each contribute to development?

A shared environment involves experiences that are shared by all those who live together, while a nonshared environment is unique to a particular individual. Behavior geneticists conclude that shared environment contributes to behavioral similarities to only a small degree and that most similarity in behavior is due to shared genetics. The major environmental effect comes from nonshared environment, which contributes to differences between people's behaviors.

How is a heritability estimate obtained? What are the heritabilities of cognitive skills and personality?

Heritability is a numerical estimate of the degree of genetic influence on a particular trait. Twin and adoption studies estimate the heritability of human traits by comparing correlations in various ways. Modern path analyses provide more accurate heritability estimates by statistically accounting for such problems as unequal environments, selective placement, and relations between genes and environments. Many cognitive skills and personality traits show small to moderate heritabilities. Surprising levels of heritability have been found for some very specific behaviors, probably because of genetic influence on more general underlying traits. Even high heritabilities, however, do not mean that the environment does not have an important influence.

■ Key Terms

adoption studies (72)
allele (48)
amniocentesis (62)
canalization (66)
chorionic villus sampling (CVS) (63)
chromosomes (44)
dizygotic (DZ) twins (53)
DNA (44)
dominant–recessive relationship (56)
Down syndrome (60)
fertilization (52)
G × E interaction (65)
gene (45)
genotype (66)
heritability (71)

Human Genome Project (46)
meiosis (51)
mitosis (51)
monozygotic (MZ) twins (53)
niche-picking (68)
nonshared environment (71)
phenotype (66)
probabilistic epigenesis (69)
range of reaction (66)
sex chromosomes (54)
shared environment (71)
twin studies (72)
ultrasonography (ultrasound) (62)
X-linked (sex-linked) traits (59)
zygote (50)

If you are using MyDevelopmentLab, you have access to an ebook version of this textbook, along with dozens of valuable resources per chapter—including video and audio clips, simulations and activities, self-assessments, practice tests, and other study materials. Here is a sampling of the resources available for this chapter.

Explore
Dominant and Recessive Traits
Neuronal Transmission

Simulate
Genetic and Chromosomal Disorders

Watch
How the Human Genome Map Affects You
Down Syndrome

If you did not receive an access code to MyDevelopmentLab with this text and wish to purchase access online, please visit www.mydevelopmentlab.com.

chapter 3
Prenatal Development and Birth

Kendra is 17 years old and has been dating 18-year-old James for 6 months. Kendra recently learned that she is pregnant, and Kendra and James have decided to keep the baby. Kendra's mother is very worried—not only are Kendra and James too young to have a baby, but they also drink alcohol frequently and may use other drugs as well. In addition, there is a family history of premature babies and Kendra's mother is worried that Kendra's young age makes this more likely. Kendra seems serious about doing what is best for her baby, but she knows little about prenatal development. James wants to be supportive and help in any way he can after the baby is born, but he believes there isn't much he can do to help during the pregnancy and birth. What concerns should they have about the health of the baby? What are some of the most significant risk factors that you see in their situation? What are the potential effects of their behavior on the developing baby? What steps can Kendra and James take now that would improve the chances of the baby being born full term and healthy?

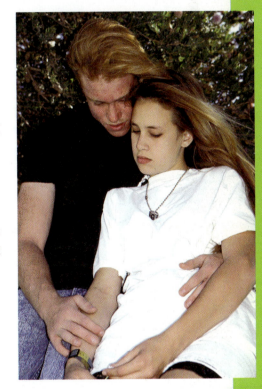

After reading this chapter, you should be able to identify more than a dozen potential risks, and you should also know how to advise Kendra and James so they can minimize some of the risks they might face during pregnancy. What advice would you give to Kendra's mother and the teenage couple?

As you read this chapter, look for the "Think About Kendra and James . . ." questions that ask you to consider what you're learning from their perspective.

As in many unplanned pregnancies, Kendra, James, and their families worry about the health and development of the baby. Although Kendra and James are young and did not plan to start a family, they want to do what they can so their baby will be healthy. But many couples do not have much information about how a baby develops in the womb, or about how their behavior can affect the developing fetus. In this chapter we discuss the basics of conception, prenatal development, and birth. We also detail a variety of factors that can adversely affect the developing fetus. As you read, it may seem that the odds are stacked against a new baby's ever being born healthy! It's true that many things can harm a developing fetus, but we hope you will also notice that many important influences are controllable. That is a very positive thing in our view, because it means that any woman and her partner can greatly increase their odds of having a healthy baby—by making positive, healthy lifestyle choices. And the truth is that the vast majority of pregnancies do produce healthy, full-term babies.

Prenatal Development

prenatal development
Development of the organism that occurs before (*pre*) its birth (*natal*).

Prenatal development is the development of an organism before (*pre*) its birth (*natal*). Prenatal development includes the creation of the organism through fertilization as well as the typical course of development up to birth. In this section we will discuss how conception occurs, then trace the events that take place as the organism develops.

As you study this section, ask yourself these questions:

- What happens during fertilization? What events must precede and follow fertilization for a pregnancy to take place and continue?

- What events mark the beginning and end of each prenatal stage? What kinds of problems can occur in each stage?

- Which stage is most critical for the formation of the baby? Why?

Conception

ovulation
Release of an egg (ovum) from the female ovary.

The female reproductive system, shown in Figure 3.1, contains two ovaries. Each ovary will nourish several hundred egg cells (ova) as they mature and become ready for fertilization. During a woman's reproductive years, an egg cell (ovum) will come to maturity approximately every 28 days. When the ovum has matured, the ovary releases it in a process called **ovulation.** During a typical menstrual cycle, only one ovum matures and is released. But when more than one ovum is released, nonidentical twins or triplets can be conceived. Experts estimate that two ova are emitted 1 in 80 times and that three ova are emitted 1 in 6,500 times (Nathanielsz, 1992).

After ovulation the ovum moves into the fallopian tube adjacent to the ovary. It is in the upper and wider part of the fallopian tube that fertilization normally occurs. As many as 500 million sperm cells can be ejaculated during intercourse, but only a few hundred will survive the journey through the woman's uterus and into the fallopian tube containing the ovum. Recall from Chapter 2 that during *fertilization* the 23 chromosomes from one sperm cell combine with the 23 chromosomes from one ovum to create a single fertilized egg cell. As soon as the first sperm cell penetrates the ovum's outer membrane, a reaction immediately seals the membrane, making it impermeable to other sperm. This is nature's way of ensuring that only 23 chromosomes from the father, carried by one sperm, join with 23 chromosomes from the mother.

At fertilization, 23 chromosomes from the father's sperm cell join 23 chromosomes from the mother's egg to produce a unique combination.

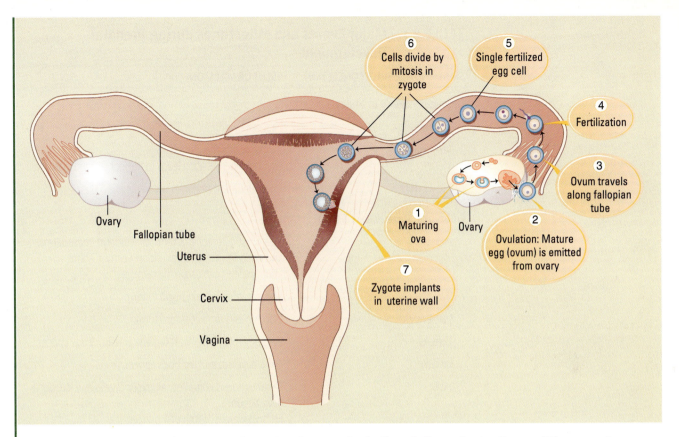

Figure 3.1 • Fertilization and Germinal Stage Development in the Female Reproductive System When an egg is mature, it is emitted from the ovary and moves down the fallopian tube. If fertilized, the egg will form a zygote that will travel to the uterus and become implanted in the inner lining, where it will continue its development.

Following fertilization, prenatal development will proceed according to an intricate schedule of cell division and differentiation. All of the cell divisions throughout prenatal development occur by mitosis. As we described in Chapter 2, *mitosis* is a "copy division" that results in a complete copy of the genetic material in all 46 chromosomes in every new cell. The fertilized cell divides and forms 2 identical cells. Then those 2 cells divide forming 4 identical cells, those 4 divide resulting in 8 identical cells, and so on. During this early phase of cell division researchers refer to the organism as a *zygote*. Notice that mitosis is different from *meiosis* (the "reduction division" process we discussed in Chapter 2.)

How do we get from a jumble of cells to the formation of a human body? **Differentiation** is the important process whereby each new cell, as it divides, forms a particular structure—such as a muscle cell, a heart cell, or a brain cell—that serves a particular function. How each dividing cell "knows" which structure and function to acquire is one of the great mysteries of life. Geneticists are trying to discover how certain segments of DNA selectively "turn off" and other segments "turn on" to program the cell for its specialized purpose.

differentiation
Process that occurs during cell division in which each new cell, as it divides, is committed to becoming a particular structure and serving a particular function.

Here is a zygote only 4 days after fertilization. At this point, it contains only about a dozen cells and may still be traveling through the fallopian tube on the way to the mother's uterus.

Stages of Prenatal Development

Researchers typically organize the major prenatal events into three stages: the *germinal stage*, the *embryonic stage*, and the *fetal stage*. Table 3.1 provides a summary of the major events and milestones that occur as mitosis and differentiation proceed. Let's look at these stages in more detail.

TABLE 3.1 Major Events and Milestones during Prenatal Development

STAGE AND AGE SINCE CONCEPTION	EVENT OR MILESTONE
Germinal Stage (0 to 14 days)	
12 hours	First cell division of fertilized egg (zygote is now two cells).
3 to 4 days	Zygote enters the uterus. First cell differentiation leads to trophoblast and blastocyst.
8 to 12 days	Implantation of zygote in uterine lining.
Embryonic Stage (weeks 3 to 8)	
14 days	Blastocyst differentiates to form ectoderm, mesoderm, and endoderm. Major genetic and chromosomal abnormalities can cause miscarriage.
3 weeks	Spinal cord and brain begin to form.
3 to 4 weeks	Placenta and umbilical cord form.
4 weeks	Eyes begin to form, heart flutters, and arm buds appear.
5 weeks	Arms develop, and leg buds appear.
8 weeks	Organogenesis complete; all major organs and structures have begun. Embryo weighs 1/30th of 1 ounce.
Fetal Stage (weeks 8 to birth)	
9 to 12 weeks	First arm and leg movements (not detected by mother). First reflexes appear. Sex can be determined with ultrasound.
17 to 20 weeks	Mother feels fetal movements. Heartbeat can be heard with stethoscope. Fetus weighs about 1 pound.
24 weeks	Fat begins to form; rapid weight gain begins.
26 to 28 weeks	Lungs mature enough to support breathing. Fetus weighs approximately 2 pounds.
38 to 40 weeks	Normal gestational age for birth. Newborn weighs 7.5 pounds on average.

germinal stage
The first stage of prenatal development, from conception to 2 weeks.

The Germinal Stage: Conception to 2 Weeks. The **germinal stage** spans the first 2 weeks of pregnancy, beginning at conception and ending when the zygote implants itself in the mother's uterine lining. Approximately 12 hours after conception, the fertilized egg cell divides for the first time, resulting in two identical cells. The zygote will take 3 to 4 days to travel through the fallopian tube before reaching the uterus, where the first cell differentiation takes place. The outer layer of cells divides rapidly and elongates to form an outer layer called the *trophoblast*. The inner cells, or *blastocyst*, remain more rounded in appearance. Over the next few weeks, cells in the trophoblast will differentiate further to become the placenta, umbilical cord, amniotic sac, and other structures that support the developing baby. The blastocyst will later develop into the fetus itself. The fact that the placenta and other support structures develop from cells in the zygote has important implications for genetic counseling. Recall from Chapter 2 that in chorionic villus sampling (CVS), specialists sample cells from the placental membrane. Because these cells originated from the zygote, they have the same genes and chromosomes as the baby.

Between 8 and 12 days after conception, **implantation** occurs: The zygote embeds itself in the inner lining of the mother's uterus. To generate energy to support the rapid cell divisions that take place in these early days, the zygote can absorb oxygen and nutrients from direct contact with the mother's blood. The zygote irritates the mother's uterine lining, burrowing into the tissue that lines the inner surface of the uterus. Blood from the mother's tissue covers the zygote, and oxygen and nutrients can then "leak" into the zygote. At this point the zygote does not yet have its own circulatory system (a heart or blood vessels). Even when it does, later in development, the mother's blood never mixes directly with the blood in the fetus; the two blood supplies are kept separate within the placenta. Hormonal changes in the mother allow the uterine lining to be most nourishing at about 9 days after conception, so this is the optimal time for implantation. After 9 days hormonal changes cause the lining to be less nourishing. As a result, the risk of pregnancy loss (*miscarriage*) increases rapidly unless the zygote implants by the 9th day (Wilcox et al., 1999). After the zygote implants into the uterine lining, the organism is referred to as an *embryo*.

Of course, once the embryo makes contact with the uterine lining, it becomes vulnerable to any toxins that might exist in the mother's bloodstream. For healthy development to proceed, the mother's blood needs not only to be rich in healthy nutrients and oxygen but also to be free from harmful substances such as alcohol, cocaine, and nicotine. We will discuss the harmful effects of such substances later in this chapter.

The Embryonic Stage: Weeks 3 to 8. The **embryonic stage** begins after the second week of pregnancy. At this point the blastocyst differentiates to form three cell layers in the embryo: the ectoderm, the mesoderm, and the endoderm. The *ectoderm* is the outer layer of the cell mass, and during the embryonic stage it gives rise to the nervous system (including the brain and spinal cord), sensory receptors, and outer skin layers. The *mesoderm,* or middle layer, becomes the circulatory system, skeleton, muscles, excretory system, reproductive system, the outer layer of the digestive tract, and the inner layer of skin. The *endoderm,* or inner layer, will eventually become the respiratory system and the remainder of the digestive system. This differentiation is critically important. If major genetic abnormalities exist at this point in development, a *miscarriage* is likely to occur. A **miscarriage** is any naturally occuring loss of pregnancy that occurs before a baby is born alive. Miscarriages are also referred to as *spontaneous abortions,* and are different from *induced abortions,* which are terminations that are chosen by the parent(s). Remember, this differentiation occurs early in pregnancy, only 2 weeks or so after conception. A miscarriage at this early stage is unlikely even to be noticed by the mother.

Soon after the initial differentiation of cells in the embryo, the embryo becomes elongated and folds over to form a neural tube. During the 3rd week the brain and spinal cord begin to form from the neural tube. At the time when the first brain cells are differentiating from the neural tube, they are extremely vulnerable to toxins in the uterine environment. If the first brain cells are damaged, irreversible alterations can jeopardize normal brain development.

During weeks 3 to 4 the placenta and umbilical cord form. Their function is to provide a more efficient supply of oxygen and nutrients to the growing embryo. The *placenta* is spongy tissue that grows out of the trophoblast layer and into the uterine lining of the mother. After just a few

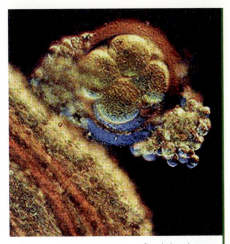

Here is a zygote after it has begun to implant itself into the inner wall of the mother's uterus. Blood supply from the uterus will soon be able to carry more oxygen and nutrients to the growing organism.

implantation
Process where the zygote embeds itself into the inner lining of the mother's uterus.

Think About Kendra and James . . .

What would you want to know about Kendra and her health habits in order to determine if her blood carries the nutrients and oxygen needed for a healthy pregnancy? Will she deliver unhealthy substances to the developing embryo?

embryonic stage
The 2nd stage of prenatal development, weeks 3 through 8. The embryo forms tissue representing every system and major part of the body.

miscarriage
Naturally occurring termination of a pregnancy before the baby is born alive. Also referred to as *spontaneous abortion.*

your perspective

Do you have a close friend or relative who has been pregnant? At what time in her pregnancy did she first become aware that she was pregnant?

Organogenesis is complete by 8 weeks after conception. All of the major structures in the body have already begun to form.

weeks, it surrounds most of the embryo and provides a surface where the mother's blood comes into very close proximity to the blood cells from the baby. The *umbilical cord* connects the placenta to the developing embryo. It contains two arteries and one vein that carry materials back and forth between the mother and the developing baby. Oxygen and nutrients are carried to the embryo, and waste materials produced by the embryo (or later the *fetus*) are carried back to the mother to be excreted.

Now supplied with greater fuel and oxygen, the embryo can undergo even more rapid and complex development. By 4 weeks the eyes begin to form, the torso continues to form, and the heart tissue begins to "flutter" in a primitive heartbeat. Arm buds also appear. By 5 weeks the arms have developed and leg buds begin to form.

If you look across these early weeks of development, you can see two patterns that describe the formation and growth of the embryo. One of these is the **cephalocaudal pattern.** *Cephalo* refers to head and *caudal* to tail, so the cephalocaudal pattern is the tendency of the areas in the head and upper body to form and grow before the areas in the tail or lower body grow. As you've seen, the brain and eyes form before the arms, and the arms before the legs. The second is the **proximodistal pattern.** *Proximo* refers to nearness (to the body's midline) and *distal* to distance away (from the midline). Heart tissue, for example, is near the midline, and it begins to form before the arms, which are away from the midline. These patterns help us estimate the **critical periods** in development—the times when structures are first forming, and when they are most vulnerable to damage if the initial cell divisions are disrupted by environmental events. We will encounter the cephalocaudal and proximodistal patterns again in Chapter 4, because they also describe the pattern that occurs as infants gain control and coordination over their muscles—first in the upper body and along the midline, and later in the lower body and away from the midline.

During the 8th week after conception, organogenesis is complete. **Organogenesis** is the process through which each important body structure differentiates within the embryo. At the conclusion of this process, each structure is represented by its own unique cellular tissue. Brain, heart, lungs, kidneys, fingers, genitals, and even toenails are now identifiable in the embryo. Although most of the important organs are not yet functioning, all of the major structures exist. The embryo is now just over one inch long and weighs only a 30th of an ounce. The completion of organogenesis signals the end of the embryonic stage, and the organism is then called a *fetus.*

The fetal stage of prenatal development lasts from 8 weeks until birth. These photos show the fetus at 3 months (left side) and at 5 months (right side). Notice the growth in size and amount of detail of body structures. You can also see the amniotic sac that surrounds the fetus and the umbilical cord.

The Fetal Stage: Week 9 to Birth (38 to 40 weeks). The **fetal stage** spans a period of about 30 weeks and represents by far the longest period during prenatal development. During this time the fetus grows dramatically in size and weight. Meanwhile, the tissues and organs differentiate further (gaining detail) and gradually become functional. During weeks 9 through 12, the first arm and leg movements begin, although the mother cannot yet feel them. The first reflexes also appear—usually the startle and sucking reflexes—and the sex organs develop enough that an ultrasound examination can reveal the sex of the fetus. During weeks 17 through 20, the mother begins to feel movements as the fetus rolls around within the amniotic sac and moves its arms and legs. The heartbeat can now be heard with a stethoscope.

At 18 weeks the fetus weighs less than 1 pound and is not yet mature enough to survive outside the uterus. By week 24, fat begins to form, and now rapid weight gain begins. Weight gain is critically important for survival, as the newborn baby will live off of accumulated fat during the first few days until the mother's breast-milk supply is well established. By 26 to 28 weeks the lungs are mature enough to allow successful breathing. At approximately 2 pounds, the fetus may now be viable if born early, but development that occurs during the final weeks is still important, increasing the chances of survival and vastly improving the health of the newborn baby. During weeks 28 through 40 the fetus typically gains more than 5 pounds. The major organ systems become more functional and strong, and the brain develops very rapidly. At its peak during the fetal stage, the brain produces more than 250,000 new cells per minute (Kolb, 1999), and it will total over 80 billion cells by birth! At the end of a normal gestational period (38 to 40 weeks), the average newborn weighs 7½ pounds and is approximately 21 inches long.

fetal stage
The 3rd and final stage of prenatal development, lasting from 8 weeks after conception until birth.

Think About Kendra and James . . .

Kendra will gain weight rapidly while her baby is in the fetal stage. Can you explain why it is important for her baby that Kendra gains a healthy amount of weight during this stage?

A fetus at 20 weeks. The sucking reflex is evident and the heartbeat can be heard, but the lungs are not yet mature enough to allow breathing. It will be another 18 to 20 weeks before the fetus reaches full term.

■ Let's Review . . .

1. The process of fertilization normally occurs in the _____.
   a. ovary   b. fallopian tube   c. uterus   d. placenta

2. What is the process whereby each new cell, as it divides and forms, commits to becoming a particular structure and serving a particular function?
   a. organogenesis   b. mitosis   c. implantation   d. differentiation

3. Major genetic abnormalities normally lead to a miscarriage at the beginning of the _____.
   a. germinal stage   b. embryonic stage   c. fetal stage   d. baby's birth

4. All of the major organs and tissues in the body have started to form by the _____ week after conception.
   a. 8th   b. 12th   c. 20th   d. 24th

5. **True or False:** The sex organs of the fetus can be detected by ultrasound beginning around 3 to 4 weeks after conception.

6. **True or False:** At around 26 to 28 weeks after conception, the lungs are mature enough to support breathing if the baby is born early.

Answers: 1. b, 2. d, 3. b, 4. a, 5. F, 6. T

Teratogens: Health Risks for the Baby

Each year hundreds of thousands of babies are born with birth defects that threaten their lives or compromise their future development. Some babies are born with malformations of the head, face, heart, or other body tissues. Others are born seriously low in birth weight, and others may not show any defects until later in life when they begin to have problems with memory, attention, physical coordination, or other health problems related to their birth defects. Most defects occur from unknown causes. About one-third, however, are related to environmental factors that threaten the fetus while it is still developing in the mother's womb (Moore & Persaud, 1998).

your perspective

What aspects of your current lifestyle would you be willing to change to prevent future birth defects in your children?

Because we have some control over mothers' exposure to these factors, we can greatly reduce the incidence of these birth defects. But to do so, we need to know what the factors are and how people can avoid them. This section will explain some of the most important changes that we can make to protect the health of developing babies.

During most of its prenatal development, the fetus (or earlier, the embryo) is surrounded by structures that support and protect it. The fetus floats within the amniotic sac, where the amniotic fluid buffers it against temperature changes, loud noises, and the mother's sudden movements. The placenta and umbilical cord deliver the oxygen and nutrients the fetus needs. Blood from the mother and baby does not actually mix, but the smaller molecules (such as oxygen and nutrients) squeeze into the baby's bloodstream in the placenta. Waste products that build up on the baby's side of the placenta are eliminated in the reverse process—they squeeze into the mother's bloodstream and are processed and eliminated by the mother. At one time people believed that these structures fully protected the fetus from harmful elements in the environment. Today, however, we know that the fetus is not fully protected. We have learned this lesson the hard way—by seeing countless babies born with serious birth defects.

During the 1960s a new area of research emerged: *teratology*, or the study of teratogens. A **teratogen** is any substance or environmental factor that might cause birth defects. For example, when toxins such as alcohol and cocaine get into the mother's bloodstream, they cross the placenta and damage the developing fetus. Pollution in the environment can build up in the mother's tissues, and many of these harmful chemicals can be transmitted to the fetus. Infectious viruses and diseases in the mother also can reach the fetus.

teratogen
Any substance or condition that might disrupt prenatal development and cause birth defects.

As you study this section, ask yourself these questions:

- If a mother drinks alcohol, smokes cigarettes, or uses legal or illegal drugs during pregnancy, how does this affect her fetus? Why do these substances have the effects that they do?

- Are there times during pregnancy when these substances are more or less harmful? Why?

- What is the impact on a fetus of any infectious disease that the mother might carry?

- Do teenage mothers, or mothers who delay childbearing until their late 30s or 40s, face special risks?

- What about the roles and responsibilities of men and fathers? Are teratogens matters of concern for them, too, or only for women?

The most common teratogens and risk factors are summarized in Table 3.2. In the next several sections, we highlight a few of these risk factors and describe why their associated birth defects occur.

As you read further, you will often see the terms *premature, preterm birth,* and *low birth weight,* so let's define these now. **Premature** (or *prematurity*) is a general

premature (or prematurity)
Refers to babies who are born earlier or smaller than average.

TABLE 3.2 Teratogens and Risk Factors

TERATOGEN OR RISK FACTOR	POTENTIAL EFFECTS
Legal and Illegal Drugs	
Alcohol	The leading known cause of mental retardation. Fetal alcohol syndrome (FAS) includes growth deficiency, head and facial deformities, and central nervous system dysfunction. Fetal alcohol effects (FAE) include retarded growth, microcephaly (smaller head circumference), hyperactivity, lowered IQ, and other effects occurring alone or in combination.
Cocaine	Preterm birth, growth retardation, malformations in brain, intestines, and genital–urinary tract. Hemorrhage, lesions, and swelling in the fetal brain. Irritability, muscle tremors, rigidity, decreased spontaneous movement, visual problems, sleep disturbance in newborns.
Cigarette smoking	Low birth weight is the most common problem. Increased risk of spontaneous abortion, stillbirth, neonatal death, hyperactivity, and poor school performance.
Marijuana	Low birth weight, muscle tremors, increased startle response, visual problems. Increased risk of leukemia has been reported.
Heroin	Low birth weight, jaundice, respiratory distress in newborns. Also withdrawal symptoms that include restlessness, agitation, muscle tremors, and sleep disruption that can continue for 4 to 6 months. Increased fetal and neonatal deaths.
Environmental Pollution	
Mercury	When absorbed by pregnant women, can cause the fetus to develop brain damage, blindness, mental retardation, and cerebral palsy. Found in some industrial settings; accumulates in fish from contaminated waters.
Polychlorinated biphenyls (PCBs)	When consumed during pregnancy can cause prematurity, low birth weight, microcephaly, lower scores on infant measures of neurological health, and visual and short-term memory problems. PCBs come from industrial settings and material such as electric insulators; leach into groundwater. Many water sources and fish in the industrial midwest are contaminated with PCBs.
Lead	Lower levels are associated with cognitive impairment in infancy; moderate to higher levels are associated with growth retardation and miscarriage. Lead is found in industrial settings, air pollution, and old paint in many homes.
Electromagnetic radiation	No measurable effects have been found for exposure to the small doses associated with computer monitors, microwave ovens, radio waves, or electric blankets or to medical procedures such as ultrasound, magnetic resonance imaging (MRI), and most medical X-rays. Large doses (e.g., as in repeated pelvic X-rays) should be avoided.
Maternal Diseases	
Herpes simplex virus (HSV)	Preterm birth, microcephaly, eye disorders, and mental retardation.
Cytomegalovirus (CMV)	Embryonic death, growth retardation, microcephaly, blindness, deafness, mental retardation, and cerebral palsy.
Syphilis	Syphilis infection in the infant, deafness, malformations of teeth and bones, facial deformities, excess fluid in the brain, and mental retardation.
Human immunodeficiency virus (HIV)	Effects not clear but include infant HIV infection, growth retardation, microcephaly, and head and facial deformities.
Rubella (German or three-day measles)	Rubella in the infant, cataracts, heart defects, deafness, glaucoma, and lowered IQ.
Chicken pox	Brain damage; mental retardation; muscle atrophy; skin scarring; and malformations of the eyes, limbs, fingers, and toes.
Other Maternal Conditions	
Stress	Studies are mixed. Some show low birth weight, early labor, and increased labor complications. Animal studies show more serious effects, including pregnancy loss.
Age	Teen pregnancy has been associated with low birth weight, early delivery of the baby, and increased rates of neonatal death. Risks of preterm birth, fetal death, and complications during birth increase slightly as women move through their late 30s and into their 40s.
Paternal Considerations	
Alcohol	Studies with rats and mice have shown damage to genetic material in sperm and increased activity levels in offspring.
Cocaine	May bind to sperm cells and be carried to the egg. May disrupt development in the embryo or jeopardize its survival.
Indirect effects	Pregnancies are threatened when fathers or men contribute to the risky behaviors of women. Men must consider the extent to which they encourage or promote women's use of legal or illegal drugs, contribute to environmental pollution, and spread sexually transmitted and other diseases. Healthy pregnancies are the responsibility of men as well as women.

(*Marijuana:* Dalterio & Fried, 1992; and Robinson et al, 1989. *Heroin:* Kaltenaback & Finnegan, 1992; and Wilson, 1992. *Environmental pollutants:* Bentur, 1994; Bentur & Koren, 1994; J. Jacobson & S. Jacobson, 1996; J. Jacobson, S. Jacobson, & Humphrey, 1990; and Moore & Persaud, 1998. *Maternal diseases:* Moore & Persaud, 1998. *Stress:* Anderson, Rhees, & Fleming, 1985; Barlow et al., 1979; Berkowitz & Kasl, 1983; Burstein et al., 1974; Ching & Newton, 1982; DiPietro et al., 2006; Falorni et al., 1979; Istvan, 1986; Newton & Hunt, 1984; and Standley et al., 1979.)

preterm birth
Births that occur before 37 weeks of gestation.

low birth weight
Weight less than 5½ pounds at birth (2 pounds lighter than average).

term that refers to babies who are born earlier or smaller than they should be. **Preterm birth** refers more specifically to a baby who is born before 37 weeks of gestation (remember that the normal gestational period is 38 to 40 weeks). **Low birth weight** refers to babies born weighing less than 5½ pounds (2 pounds lighter than average). Babies who are premature—either preterm or low in birth weight—are at greater risk for a variety of serious health problems and even infant death. Many teratogens disrupt fetal growth and are therefore associated with prematurity, preterm births, and low birth weights.

Alcohol

More than half of all women in the United States consume alcohol, and 10 percent of all pregnant women report that they drink alcohol during their pregnancies (Centers for Disease Control [CDC], 2004). Unfortunately, alcohol use during pregnancy can be catastrophic. Numerous studies with both humans and animals have established that alcohol exposure during pregnancy can cause physical deformities, growth retardation, damage to the central nervous system, and even miscarriage and fetal death (Cornelius et al., 2002; Institute of Medicine, 1996).

Alcohol damages the fetus in several ways. The alcohol in the mother's bloodstream does cross the placenta; once it reaches the fetus it can disrupt cell division and kill fetal cells. Cells in the brain and nervous system are particularly vulnerable to alcohol—and once destroyed, these cells are not replaced. Alcohol in the mother's bloodstream also causes vessels in the placenta to constrict, reducing the flow of blood through the placenta. This reduced blood flow deprives the developing fetus of the oxygen and important nutrients needed for healthy development.

Alcohol-exposed children are at greater risk for being impulsive, easily distracted, and hyperactive (Mattson & Riley, 1998; Mick et al., 2002). Retarded brain growth and lowered IQ are prominent features of alcohol exposure. In fact, *experts believe that prenatal alcohol exposure is the leading known cause of mental retardation in the United States* (Abel & Sokol, 1987; Institute of Medicine, 1996). Once a baby is born with mental retardation, there is no cure. Abstinence from drinking during pregnancy, however, would prevent every single case of alcohol-induced mental retardation as well as every case of the even more serious problem—fetal alcohol syndrome.

Fetal alcohol syndrome (FAS) was first identified in 1968 (Lemoine et al., 1968, as cited in Mattson & Riley, 1998). An FAS newborn shows all of the following conditions: (1) overall growth deficiency, (2) head and facial malformations, and (3) dysfunction of the central nervous system (brain and spinal cord) often resulting in some degree of mental retardation (Institute of Medicine, 1996). Babies exposed to alcohol are typically born with low birth weights indicating a disruption in overall growth during pregnancy. Tight eyelids, flattened midface, short nose, and thin upper lip are typical head and face malformations associated with FAS. Lowered IQ, hyperactivity, and poor motor coordination are examples of deficits that indicate dysfunction of the central nervous system. The combination of these conditions defines the syndrome known as FAS.

In the United States the estimated incidence of FAS is about 1.5 out of every 1,000 live births (CDC, 2005). FAS is part of *fetal alcohol spectrum disorder* (FASD). In FASD, the effects of alcohol exposure can be severe, as in full-blown FAS we described earlier. More frequently, babies are born without the full syndrome but still show one or more of the individual symptoms, such as lowered IQ and hyperactivity, lowered IQ alone, or problems with specific neuropsychological functions such as attention, cognitive flexibility, planning ability, memory, or language.

This child has fetal alcohol syndrome (FAS), a combination of birth defects that includes facial deformities (notice the tight eyelids and flattened nose), growth deficiency, and nervous system dysfunctions that can include lower IQ and hyperactivity. FAS is completely preventable if women avoid alcohol consumption during pregnancy.

fetal alcohol syndrome (FAS)
A syndrome of birth defects caused by prenatal exposure to alcohol. Includes growth deficiencies, head and facial malformations, and central nervous system dysfunction.

your perspective
Did you know that the leading known cause of mental retardation is completely preventable? Do you think drinking behaviors would change if more people were aware of this?

These conditions are commonly referred to as **fetal alcohol effects (FAE)** (Korkman et al., 2003; Jacobson & Jacobson, 2002; Sokol et al., 2003). The physical defects and the cognitive and behavioral deficits associated with FAE may be subtle and may not even become apparent until later in childhood. As a result, it is hard to estimate their incidence. Still, researchers believe that as many as 6 out of every 1,000 live births show FAS or FAE (CDC, 2005); this estimate does not include the number of miscarriages and fetal deaths attributable to alcohol damage. To learn about one family's experience with FAS, read the Personal Perspective box on page 94 called "Meet a Family Who Adopted a Child with FAS."

FAS and the more severe forms of FAE tend to occur when mothers are chronic alcoholics (consuming at least six drinks per day) or engage in regular binge drinking (consumption of four or more drinks per occasion, at least once per week). The effects depend on a variety of factors. These include the timing of the exposure, the genetic health of the fetus and mother, the alcohol metabolism and tolerance of the mother, and the pattern of drinking during pregnancy. You should be aware, however, that noticeable attention deficits and hyperactivity have been reported with babies whose mothers consumed only three drinks, on average, per week (Mattson & Riley, 1998). When it comes to protecting the health and developmental integrity of the baby, there really is no safe level of alcohol consumption.

fetal alcohol effects (FAE)
Individual or multiple birth defects caused by prenatal exposure to alcohol. Lowered IQ, hyperactivity, growth deficiencies, and physical malformations can exist alone or in combinations but not in a way that indicates FAS.

your perspective
Binge drinking and drug use are frequent on college campuses. What dangers are associated with these behaviors?

Cocaine

About 1 out of every 100 women responding to a nationwide survey reported using cocaine during pregnancy (National Institute on Drug Abuse [NIDA], 2001). As you might imagine, however, women tend to underreport use of illegal drugs such as cocaine. When researchers analyzed the fecal material of newborns to detect prenatal cocaine exposure, they found that 6.3 percent of privately insured and 26.9 percent of Medicaid or underinsured babies tested positive for cocaine exposure (Schutzman et al., 1991). It is evident that a large number of babies are being exposed to cocaine, especially those born to lower-income mothers.

Fetal exposure to cocaine retards growth, can cause preterm birth, and can cause malformations in the baby's brain, intestines, and genital–urinary tract (Moore & Persaud, 1998). In adults cocaine causes blood vessels to constrict and can dramatically increase blood pressure. Therefore, sudden heart failure, stroke, and brain hemorrhage are possible in any adult who consumes a large dose of cocaine—and the effects are similar in the developing fetus. Cocaine-exposed newborns can show evidence of hemorrhage, lesions, swelling in the brain, and other brain abnormalities. Cocaine also alters the function of neurotransmitters in the brain (this is how it produces the euphoric effect in adults). This can disrupt how the fetus's brain grows and forms connections during the prenatal period. As a result, cocaine-exposed newborns tend to show increased irritability, muscle tremors, rigidity, and decreased spontaneous movement. They also show impaired sensory function, decreased visual attention, and trouble regulating their own state of arousal (asleep, awake, or attentive). Long-term effects of prenatal cocaine exposure have been harder to determine. Some studies indicate negative effects of cocaine exposure on language, visual skill, or overall cognitive development. However, others have found no relationship with problems during early childhood, or that the effect interacts with other factors such as gender (e.g., boys show behavioral and emotional regulation problems during early childhood while girls do not) or a nonsupportive caregiving environment (Arendt et al., 2004; Delaney-Black et al., 2004; Lewis et al., 2004; Lewis, Singer, & Short, 2004; Messinger et al., 2004; Morrow et al., 2004; Singer et al., 2002).

This tiny baby was born too early to a mother who used cocaine during pregnancy. She will be at a very high risk for a variety of health problems. Only time will tell if she can even survive.

Meet a Family Who Adopted a Child with Fetal Alcohol Syndrome

Cheri and Allan Scott
Anchorage, Alaska
Adopted a child, Justin, with fetal alcohol syndrome

Cheri and Allan Scott adopted Justin when he was an infant. Justin's biological mother was a chronic alcoholic. She was abused as a child, ran away from home, and lived on the streets. Justin was her third child, and she abused alcohol during all three pregnancies. After Justin she had two more pregnancies that ended in miscarriage due to severe alcohol exposure. Justin was still in the neonatal intensive care unit of the hospital at one month of age, and that is when his biological mother visited him for the last time. She returned to live on the streets. She later died from alcohol and drug abuse when she was only 24 years old.

At the time of this interview, Justin had grown up to be 19 years old. Here is some of his story told by his adoptive parents, Cheri and Allan Scott.

We were told that Justin had prenatal alcohol exposure and wasn't expected to live to be a year old. He was medically stable and didn't need to take up a hospital bed—he just needed a safe place to be until he died. His birth records described him as a successfully resuscitated spontaneous miscarriage; he was born at 26 weeks of gestation. His blood alcohol level at birth was 0.236.

We knew that Justin's brain and body had been affected by prenatal alcohol exposure, but having it finally confirmed that he had FAS meant we couldn't pretend the trouble was going to go away with time and love—these differences would impact him for life. The grief was intense. We cried for the little boy that might have been, for his mom who died and would never see her three surviving children grow up, and for ourselves and our fear that we wouldn't know how to help him learn and grow. We worried that people would judge him based on his diagnosis and not give their best effort to help him achieve all he could do and be. We were also relieved, because now we had an answer to one of the many questions about Justin's development and it gave us some direction as we started to pull together the many players who would support Justin and our family over the years.

Justin experiences cerebral palsy, which affects his gross and fine motor skills. He cannot stand or take steps without holding someone's arm, using his crutches, wheelchair, or walker. He can feed himself, but has difficulty using a knife to cut food. He can dress himself, but cannot effectively button, tie, or snap his clothing and shoes. He has vision and hearing problems, brain seizures, and a cleft palate. His preferred communication methods are sign language and his Lightwriter, a handheld electronic voice output device. The hardest thing to deal with is the developmental delay. At 19 years of age, testing shows his cognitive skill level to be between 4 and 7 years. He doesn't have many typically developing friends, and most of the people he spends time with are either family members or paid service providers.

The amazing thing is that in spite of all Justin's developmental differences, he is a very loving, happy, and fun kid to be around. He's very empathetic, funny, and musical, and he appreciates any attention.

Justin's disabilities have impacted everyone in our family, in both positive and negative ways. We have all learned to work through disagreements without raising our voices, as yelling always startles and frightens Justin. My husband Allan has learned to share his feelings more clearly and to be more animated when showing emotion. He's much more patient now and has learned how good it can feel to offer support to other dads raising children with special needs. Our oldest daughter has been Justin's Independent Care Provider for the last 4 years, helping him learn to get around in the community, work on social, self-help, and independent living skills. She realized before any of the rest of us that Justin needed someone close to him who could use sign language, and took it upon herself to sign up for ASL throughout high school.

Through their experiences with Justin, the Scotts began working with *Stone Soup Group*, a nonprofit organization providing support to families of children with special needs and the service providers working with them all over the state of Alaska. The Scotts also created *Parent Navigation*, a service that pairs families of special needs children with experienced parents who can offer support.

Q *What do you think it would take to significantly reduce the number of children and families who are affected by prenatal alcohol exposure? What kinds of programs are needed? Will they work?*

Cigarette Smoking

Approximately 11.5 percent of pregnant women smoke cigarettes. These rates vary widely by age and race, however. For example, among all of the U.S. births registered in 2002 to mothers who were 18 to 19 years old, 30 percent of Caucasian mothers smoked while pregnant (Martin et al., 2003). The rate was only 8 percent among African American mothers and 3 percent for Mexican American mothers.

Cigarette smoke contains more than 450 different harmful chemicals, including nicotine, carbon monoxide, carbon dioxide, and cyanide (Martin, 1992). These chemicals damage the placenta and reduce the blood supply to the placenta and uterus, and this cuts down the supply of oxygen and nutrients available to the fetus. In addition, nicotine is an addictive stimulant that tends to suppress appetite, so women who smoke tend to eat less and gain less weight during pregnancy. But pregnant women need to gain sufficient weight to properly support the nutritional needs of the baby. During healthy pregnancies, women gain at least 20 to 25 pounds. When they gain less weight, their babies are more likely to be premature and are at greater risk for health complications.

Low birth weight is the most common problem associated with newborns of mothers who smoke. In addition, children born to mothers who smoked during pregnancy are more likely to be hyperactive and to have short attention spans, and they tend to score lower in reading, spelling, and math (Fogelman, 1980; Linnet et al., 2003; Naeye & Peters, 1984; Thapar et al., 2003). Finally, cigarette smoke can damage the placenta. As a result, women who smoke during pregnancy are at increased risk for spontaneous abortions, stillbirths, and neonatal deaths. The good news is that more women are learning about the dangers of smoking. Since 1989 there has been a 42 percent decrease in the number of women who smoke during pregnancy (Cnattingius, 2004; Martin et al., 2003).

So far, we have discussed the effects of alcohol, cocaine, and cigarettes. The additional effects from marijuana and heroin are summarized in Table 3.2. All of these are drugs of choice, and if pregnant women chose to avoid these substances, many millions of children could be born without related birth defects. As a society, what can we do to reduce drug use during pregnancy? To see how one state tries to protect developing babies, read the Social Policy Perspective box on page 96 called "The Case of Malissa Ann Crawley."

> **Think About Kendra and James . . .**
> *What concerns would you have if Kendra and James continue to abuse alcohol and drugs? What would the potential risks be for the fetus?*

Maternal Health

If a woman is carrying an infectious disease while pregnant, it can endanger the fetus. The virus or microorganism that causes the disease in the mother will usually cross the placenta to the fetus and can cause birth defects or infectious disease in the baby. In other cases, the disease can be passed to the baby during the birthing process. Let's look at three sexually transmitted diseases: herpes, syphilis, and HIV/AIDS.

Herpes. *Herpes simplex virus* (HSV) is a sexually transmitted disease that, in adults, causes blisters around the mouth and lips ("cold sores") and blisters and sores in the genital areas. HSV is contagious and is passed between partners by oral and genital contact such as kissing, intercourse, and oral sex. The virus spreads most easily when sores are present, but it also can spread before the sores emerge and when there are no noticeable symptoms. About half of the American population is infected with HSV, but two-thirds of those infected are not aware that they have the disease (Herpes.com, 2002). Although HSV is mostly a nuisance disease for adults, it can have serious consequences for developing fetuses and newborn babies. When a woman contracts HSV in early pregnancy, her risk of miscarriage increases threefold (Moore & Persaud, 1998).

The Case of Malissa Ann Crawley

From Anderson, South Carolina: When Malissa Ann Crawley gave birth to her third child, Antwon, his blood tested positive for cocaine. Crawley was arrested for unlawful neglect of a child (Associated Press, 1999). Crawley pleaded guilty to the neglect charge and was sentenced to 5 years in prison. After serving 2 months, she was released to appeal her case.

The South Carolina State Supreme Court upheld Crawley's conviction, stating that a pregnant woman can be charged for harming a viable fetus. The United States Supreme Court refused to hear the appeal, so Crawley went back to prison. After serving approximately 1 year and completing a 6-month addiction treatment program, Crawley was released under the conditions that she must find suitable employment and housing and that she must submit to frequent home visits and drug testing.

South Carolina takes a strong stand in prosecuting pregnant women who use illegal drugs, and most other states have passed similar legislation. For example, in Florida, Indiana, Minnesota, Oklahoma, and Utah, mothers can be charged with abuse if their babies are born with FAS or addicted to drugs (Gostin, 2001; Tomkins & Kepfield, 1992). These get-tough policies are gaining wide attention—and raising thorny questions. In light of what we know about the harmful effects of teratogens, it seems that there is a growing trend to hold pregnant women responsible for their unhealthy behaviors. But are these laws appropriate? That is, will they protect the health of developing fetuses?

Many are concerned that the burden falls completely on the mother. In Nebraska the laws focus on the entire family as a unit, and it is possible to prosecute fathers who drink alcohol with their pregnant wives or girlfriends (Roth, 2000; Tomkins & Kepfield, 1992). Does this seem like an appropriate response? And should men be prosecuted for delivering drugs to "minors" (i.e., fetuses) when they provide pregnant women with illegal substances? Finally, there is also concern about the "slippery slope." After we protect fetuses from the harmful effects of illegal drugs and alcohol, where do we stop? Do we prosecute women for smoking cigarettes, eating contaminated fish, working in stressful environments, eating poorly, or exercising too much or too little?

Q *Do you agree that Malissa Ann Crawley should have served time in prison for delivering cocaine to her unborn baby? If so, how far do you think such legal actions should go? And in the end, will laws be effective in discouraging people from engaging in behaviors that contribute to unhealthy pregnancies?*

Babies born with HSV usually contract the virus during delivery rather than through the exchange of blood elements through the placenta during prenatal development. If they receive antiviral medications, about half of HSV-infected newborns will escape permanent damage. The remaining half are at risk for serious neurological damage, mental retardation, and even death (Herpes.com, 2002). When mothers are not showing symptoms (such as open sores) at the time of birth, the risk of infecting the baby is very small (as low as 4 in 10,000 births). The risks are high, however, if the mother is showing symptoms at birth. In these cases doctors recommend a **cesarean section (C-section)** delivery. Cesarean section is a surgical procedure where the baby is removed through an incision made through the mother's abdomen and into the uterus. This reduces the baby's exposure to the virus (Herpes.com, 2002).

Cytomegalovirus (CMV), another member of the herpes family of viruses, is carried by 50 percent to 75 percent of U.S. adults (Mayo Clinic, 2003). Among adults, CMV spreads the same way as HSV: through kissing and other intimate contact. CMV remains dormant in most adults with healthy immune systems, so infected adults rarely experience any symptoms of the virus. For fetuses, however, the virus is very dangerous (Moore & Persaud, 1998). When CMV infection occurs during the embryonic stage of development (weeks 3 to 8), the embryo usually dies. If CMV infects a fetus later in pregnancy, the baby usually is born alive but is at risk for retarded growth, microcephaly

cesarean section (C-section) births
Surgical procedure in which the baby is removed through an incision made through the mother's abdomen and into the uterus.

(small head circumference, associated with delayed motor, speech, and mental development), blindness, deafness, mental retardation, and cerebral palsy.

Syphilis. *Syphilis* is another sexually transmitted disease. Fortunately, the incidence rate of syphilis infection has declined steadily since 1997 (CDC, 2001a). If the mother contracts syphilis while she is pregnant and does not receive treatment, the baby will almost always be born with birth defects and infected with the disease. It is estimated that 1 in every 10,000 babies born alive in the United States has syphilis. Birth defects include deafness, malformations of teeth and bones, facial deformities, excess fluid in the brain, and mental retardation (Moore & Persaud, 1998). But prompt and adequate treatment of the mother can completely protect the baby from the ill effects of syphilis.

HIV/AIDS. The teratogenic effects of *HIV,* the virus that causes AIDS, are not yet clear, but they may include growth retardation and head and facial deformities. Babies born with HIV usually contract the virus at or near delivery, and the chances of infecting the baby with HIV increase if the mother breast-feeds the baby. During the early 1990s approximately 3,000 infants were infected with HIV each year in the United States. More than 80 percent of those babies' mothers abused drugs or had sexual partners who abused drugs (Kaltenbach & Finnegan, 1992). More recently, antiviral medications such as zidovudine (ZDV) have dramatically reduced the transmission of HIV from infected mothers to infants. Treatment of infected mothers with ZDV cuts the rate of transmission in half (CDC, 2001b).

> **Think About Kendra and James . . .**
> *How can Kendra and James reduce the chances of spreading a sexually transmitted disease to their baby?*

Maternal Age

In the United States, approximately 850,000 teenage girls become pregnant each year, and nearly one-quarter of all first births are to teenage mothers (Ventura et al., 2001; Ventura et al., 2003). At the other end of the spectrum, many women delay childbirth to complete their educations and pursue careers. Are infants at greater risk when they are born to younger or older mothers? Is there a biological advantage if a woman gives birth in her 20s or 30s? For the most part, research has indicated that pregnancies tend to proceed in a healthy manner across all of the reproductive years.

As you can see in Figure 3.2, however, the percentage of babies born low in birth weight is highest for mothers under the age of 15 and over 44. Low-birth-weight

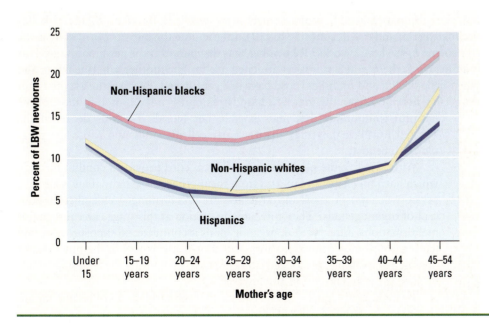

Figure 3.2 • Percentage of Low-Birth-Weight (LBW) Newborns The percentage of babies born low in birth weight (less than 5½ pounds) is greatest for mothers under age 15 and 45 and older. Data are based on all births registered in the United States during the year 2000 for non-Hispanic black, non-Hispanic white, and Hispanic mothers. (Data from Martin et al., 2002.)

Teenage mothers are at higher risk for giving birth to babies who are premature and low in birth weight. Problems are compounded by factors such as low income, inadequate access to prenatal care, and poor nutrition. Many teens are not psychologically or emotionally prepared for the responsibilities of caring for a new baby.

percentages decline steadily through the teen years and begin to rise again in the 30s. You can also see that non-Hispanic blacks have a greater percentage of low-birth-weight babies across the entire range of ages—a racial and ethnic difference that needs to be addressed with better prenatal care and education.

Many adolescents are not socially and cognitively mature, and this may limit their ability to cope with the stress of an early pregnancy. Low income, poor education, social isolation, drug and alcohol use, and lack of early prenatal care are factors that tend to be associated with teenage pregnancy—and with negative birth outcomes. There is also some question as to whether young teenagers, who may only recently have started menstruation, are biologically ready to carry a pregnancy to full term. Fortunately, the pregnancy rate for younger teens (ages 15 to 17) has fallen 40 percent since 1991, and the rate is now at its lowest point since the government started recording the statistic in 1976 (Martin et al., 2003; Ventura et al., 2001). We will have much more to say about the risks and developmental effects associated with teenage pregnancy in Chapter 13.

Women in the later years of their reproductive lives also have concerns. High blood pressure, diabetes, and other health conditions occur more frequently as women age. Whether because of biological health or as a result of other indirect factors (such as increased stress), the risks of prematurity, fetal death, and complications during birth increase slightly as women move through their late 30s and into their 40s (Berkowitz et al., 1990; Cnattingius et al., 1992; Fretts et al., 1995). Among women who give birth in their 40s, mothers who are giving birth for the first time tend to have more problems than those who have already had one or more children. Older mothers have an increased risk of having a baby with Down syndrome (see Chapter 2). (Most of the other known chromosomal abnormalities are not associated with increased maternal age, however.) Yet even with some increased risks, we should emphasize that the vast majority of pregnancies do proceed normally and result in the birth of a happy and healthy newborn, even when the mother is over 40 years of age.

Critical Periods

At what point do you think the developing baby is most vulnerable to toxins such as alcohol, cocaine, and cigarette smoke? Are the defects more severe when the exposure occurs early in prenatal development? Or are they more severe when the baby is exposed closer to birth? You will find answers to these questions in Figure 3.3. Notice that the risk of birth defects is small during the first 2 weeks after conception but rises dramatically and peaks shortly after week 3. By week 8, the risk has declined again, and it will continue to fall until the time the baby is born. Why is the risk so low in the first 2 weeks? Remember that this period is the germinal stage. This is a time when the zygote has not yet attached itself to the mother's uterine lining and when the placenta and umbilical cord have not yet formed. Because the zygote is not yet getting nutrition from the mother's bloodstream, it is not exposed to most of the harmful compounds that may exist in her blood. If toxins do reach the zygote, however, they may disrupt early cell divisions and cause the pregnancy to be lost.

After week 3, the placenta and umbilical cord provide a conduit through which harmful elements can pass from the mother to the baby. This is also the period when most organs and structures are first forming—remember the concept of organogenesis? Therefore, any disruption at this stage can cause major malformations. After week 8, organogenesis is complete, so exposure now will tend to cause more minor malformations or disturbances in the functions of organs. For example, prolonged exposure to toxins during the fetal stage tends to cause growth retardation and lowered IQ.

By looking at Figure 3.3, you can see that the early weeks of pregnancy are crucial to the baby's health. The problem, of course, is that most women are

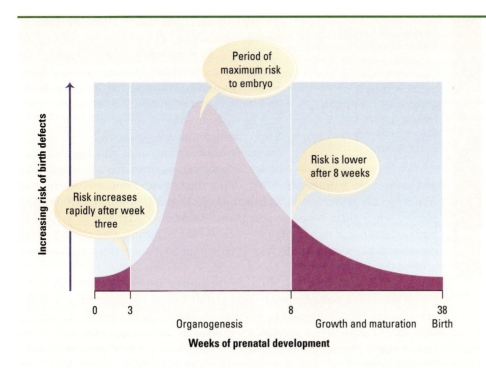

Figure 3.3 • Relative Risk of Birth Defects During Prenatal Development When exposed to teratogens, the developing organism is at greatest risk while the organs and tissues are forming during the embryonic stage (weeks 3 to 8). Abnormalities during the germinal stage (weeks 1 to 2) are not frequent but are often fatal. Risks are lower during the fetal stage (weeks 8 to birth) after the basic organs and tissues have formed. (Moore & Persaud, 1998.)

not even sure that they are pregnant until they are near (or even past) the 8th week of pregnancy. By then the critical periods for the major organ systems have passed. Ideally, women who think they may be pregnant can make healthy changes in their lifestyles even before they are sure to avoid the harmful effects of teratogens. We hope you can see that, to prevent the harmful effects of teratogens, women with risky habits really need to make changes even before they know that they are pregnant.

The Role of Fathers

So far, we have discussed the birth defects that can occur when mothers expose their babies to toxic substances and risky conditions during pregnancy. Can babies also be born with birth defects because the father used or was exposed to teratogens? In most cases, when toxic substances affect sperm cells, the damaged sperm do not survive the long journey to the egg. Nature often seems to select out unhealthy sperm before they have a chance to fertilize an egg. Still, studies with rats and mice have shown that alcohol damages the genetic material in sperm (Abel, 1992). Rat offspring also show increased levels of activity when their fathers consumed alcohol before the conception. Decreased litter size, greater likelihood of low birth weight, and greater susceptibility to infection in the offspring also occurred. Studies with humans show that alcohol use by fathers before or at conception is associated with children's later learning and memory problems, hyperactivity, and difficulties dealing with stress, though the exact causal mechanisms are not clear (Abel, 1993, 2004).

Another study found that cocaine accumulates in the testes and other organs and can bind to human sperm cells (Yazigi et al., 1991). Because cocaine does not destroy the mobility and viability of the sperm cells, this means that cocaine ingested by the father can be carried to the egg cell during fertilization. Although human studies have not yet confirmed the effects, researchers suspect that cocaine can then directly disrupt development in the zygote, probably jeopardizing its survival. The vast majority of birth defects, however, result from the mother's exposure to toxins, because it is elements in the mother's bloodstream that cross the placenta to the developing baby.

Many people consider it to be a romantic overture to offer someone an alcoholic drink. Given what we know about the catastrophic effects of alcohol on the developing fetus, can't we find a better way for people to have fun and get to know each other?

Think About Kendra and James . . .

What can James do to help Kendra have a healthy pregnancy and reduce risks to the developing baby? Are the habits of Kendra's friends and other family members also important?

Putting aside the direct effects of fathers' exposure to toxins, can fathers be responsible for birth defects in other ways? Think about alcohol, for instance. In the United States, 14 percent of men consume two or more drinks on average per day, but only 3 percent to 4 percent of women drink at this level (Abel, 1992). Also consider that 69 percent of women who are alcoholics have husbands who are also alcoholics. When men support the alcohol culture and encourage women to drink, don't they share responsibility for the results? Many fathers do reduce their alcohol consumption, or abstain completely, while their wives are pregnant. Remember that the most serious birth defects occur during organogenesis—that is, during weeks 3 to 8 of the pregnancy. Most women are not even aware that they are pregnant until around the second month.

Men as well as women should realize that many of our exposures to toxins are due to our personal habits, and that these habits develop over the many years before pregnancy occurs. To ensure a healthy pregnancy, a woman of reproductive age can avoid harmful substances even before she knows she is pregnant—or plan her pregnancy so she can take precautions ahead of time. Men should strongly consider how their actions, habits, or attitudes might encourage or contribute to women's use of alcohol, drugs, and tobacco. Men should also consider how they contribute to other prenatal hazards, from environmental pollution to sexually transmitted diseases. Healthy pregnancies are the responsibility of both women and men.

■ Let's Review . . .

1. Drugs, environmental pollutants, and viruses are examples of elements in the environment that can cause birth defects when they come into contact with a developing fetus. These elements are more generally referred to as _____.
   a. teratogens
   b. oncogens
   c. critical periods
   d. differentiation agents

2. The three conditions needed to diagnose a baby as having fetal alcohol syndrome are overall growth deficiency, head and facial malformations, and _____.
   a. preterm birth
   b. detectable blood alcohol levels
   c. central nervous system dysfunction
   d. sign of stroke or hemorrhage in the brain

3. Which drug is known to cause babies to be born with hemorrhages, lesions, and swelling in the brain as well as with intestinal and genital–urinary tract disorders?
   a. alcohol   b. cocaine   c. heroin   d. marijuana

4. What is the most common problem associated with prenatal cigarette exposure?
   a. brain damage in the newborn   b. lung damage in the newborn
   c. low birth weight in the newborn   d. death of the newborn

5. **True or False:** The leading known cause of mental retardation in the United States is completely preventable—it is prenatal alcohol exposure.

6. **True or False:** When it comes to teratogens, the risk of birth defects increases continuously as the fetus gets nearer to birth.

Answers: 1. a, 2. c, 3. b, 4. c, 5. T, 6. F

The Process of Birth

It's been almost 9 months and the time is nearly here. The baby's room is ready, the hospital bag is packed, and everyone is eagerly awaiting the birth of the new baby. Mom has been feeling a vague tightening in her uterus off and on for weeks or even months now, but these *false labor contractions* are only "practice," not as regular as real labor contractions will be. Eventually the contractions become more regular, closer together, and more intense. Within hours the baby will be born.

As you study this section, ask yourself these questions:

■ What are the stages of labor, and what important events take place during each stage?

■ What are some of the potential complications of the birth process, and what can be done to avoid or reduce them?

■ What is the newborn baby like? What are the common treatments and tests given to the newborn?

■ What are some of the psychological adjustments that parents and siblings must make after the birth of a baby?

Stages of Birth

Exactly what triggers the start of the birth process is still a mystery. Researchers believe that when the fetal brain reaches a certain point of maturity, it sends a signal that prompts hormonal changes in the mother (Nathanielsz, 1992). These changes cause the mother's uterine muscles to contract, and the contractions create an ever-increasing feedback loop of hormones that stimulate more frequent and more intense contractions until the baby is born. As shown in Figure 3.4, physicians typically divide the birth process into three stages of labor: dilation, delivery, and afterbirth.

Stage 1 of labor is the longest, lasting on average from 6 to 14 hours. This stage is usually longer for first-time mothers but varies significantly from one woman to another. This stage begins when the uterus starts regular contractions. The contractions are gentle and infrequent at first but eventually occur every 2 minutes or so (with each contraction lasting up to 2 minutes) and become much more intense. The contractions cause **dilation,** the gradual opening of the cervix. The *cervix* is a tough ring of tissue that has remained tightly closed throughout pregnancy to keep the fetus securely inside the uterus and help protect it from infection. During Stage 1 of labor, the cervix must dilate to 10 cm, which is about 100 times its normal diameter, to allow for passage of the baby. Contractions also push the baby downward so the baby's head presses firmly against the cervical opening.

During Stage 2 of labor, the baby actually moves through the birth canal and is delivered. This stage is much shorter than the first, lasting an average of 30 minutes to 2 hours. Contractions push the baby through the birth canal for delivery. During this stage the mother feels an overwhelming urge to bear down strongly to help push the baby out. This stage ends with the delivery of the baby.

In Stage 3 the placenta and other membranes emerge through the birth canal in a process referred to as **afterbirth.** During this stage, which usually lasts less than an hour, the mother continues to experience contractions as her uterus expels the placenta. These contractions are much less intense than those of the first and second stages. Mothers are usually quite preoccupied with their newborn baby, so their attention is not on the contractions.

dilation
The gradual opening of the cervix caused by labor contractions during the first stage of birth.

your perspective

Do you know someone who gave birth recently? How long was her labor? Was this her first delivery? If not, was her labor shorter this time than it was for her first delivery?

afterbirth
The 3rd and last stage of birth, in which the placenta and other membranes are delivered through the birth canal.

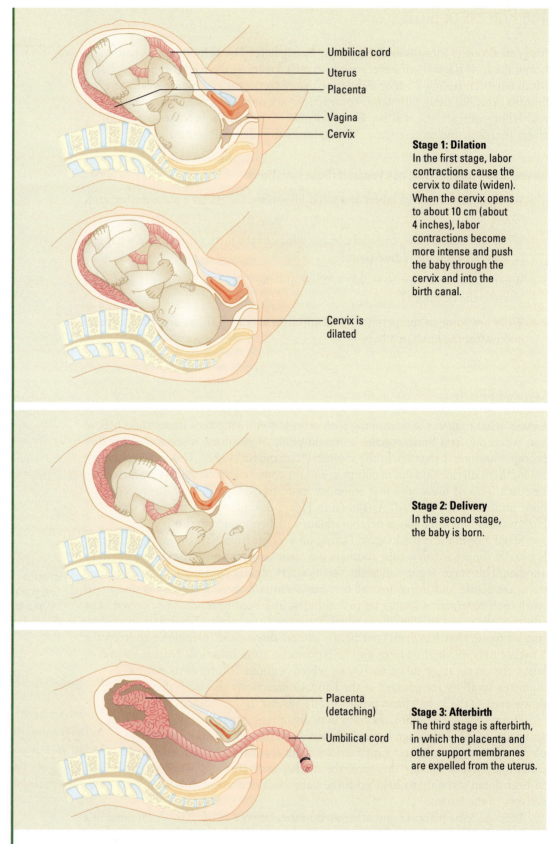

Umbilical cord
Uterus
Placenta
Vagina
Cervix

Stage 1: Dilation
In the first stage, labor contractions cause the cervix to dilate (widen). When the cervix opens to about 10 cm (about 4 inches), labor contractions become more intense and push the baby through the cervix and into the birth canal.

Cervix is dilated

Stage 2: Delivery
In the second stage, the baby is born.

Placenta (detaching)
Umbilical cord

Stage 3: Afterbirth
The third stage is afterbirth, in which the placenta and other support membranes are expelled from the uterus.

Figure 3.4 • The Stages of Birth In Stage 1 labor contractions cause the cervix to dilate (widen). When the cervix opens to about 10 cm, labor contractions become more intense and push the baby through the cervix and into the birth canal. In Stage 2 the baby is born. Stage 3 is afterbirth, in which the placenta and other support membranes are expelled from the uterus. (Adapted from Moore & Persaud, 1998.)

Birthing Complications: Something Isn't Right

The vast majority of pregnancies end happily, producing a healthy infant. Occasionally, however, birthing problems occur—although we have learned a tremendous amount in the last half century about how to deal with these complications.

Malpresentation. One complication during birth involves the position of the fetus. The optimal fetal position is head down. This position allows the head to move through the birth canal first and minimizes risk to both mother and baby. About 4 percent of the time, however, the fetus is positioned differently in the uterus, a situation called **malpresentation** (Fogel, 1997). In a *breech position* the buttocks or the feet are lowest in the uterus. In a *transverse position* the baby lies sideways inside the uterus. Both of these positions pose serious dangers during delivery.

Physicians or midwives can easily detect malpresentations before delivery by ultrasound procedures or by physical examination. Experienced obstetricians will often try to "turn" an ill-positioned fetus, though this is not always successful. In some cases the fetus turns on its own, sometimes just as labor begins, but it is impossible to predict if and when this change will take place. Malpresentation is a complication of birth, but it need not have serious consequences if it is detected and monitored carefully. To prevent potentially serious harm to the baby and mother, many practitioners choose a planned *cesarean section (C-section)* delivery for malpresented babies.

Fetal Distress. **Fetal distress** occurs when the fetus experiences a sudden lack of oxygen, change in heart rate, or change in respiration. Any one of these can indicate that the fetus is at risk. Practitioners can identify these conditions by using electrodes or other devices to monitor the fetus during birth. One type of distress that can have very serious consequences is *anoxia,* or deprivation of oxygen. A fetus can withstand brief oxygen deprivation with no ill effects, but more than a few minutes of decreased oxygen can lead to permanent brain damage (Stechler & Halton, 1982). Anoxia can occur for any of several reasons. These include deterioration or premature separation of the placenta, maternal fatigue or hyperventilation during labor, sudden compression of the umbilical cord during labor, or failure of the baby to begin breathing immediately after birth. The possibility of anoxia is one reason practitioners become concerned during longer labors, and it is a big reason for the increased amount of fetal monitoring done during labor. Early identification and prompt treatment of fetal distress are common reasons for C-section deliveries.

The Newborn Baby

The long-awaited moment has arrived, and the newest member of the family is here! Physicians and nurses immediately examine the newborn to identify any potential problems. They monitor the baby's breathing and temperature regulation, and often treat the newborn's eyes with silver nitrate; this prevents visual problems due to diseases such as gonorrhea that the baby may have contracted from the mother during birth. Hospital or birthing center staffers also monitor the mother to ensure that she does not experience excessive blood loss or develop infections. They often encourage her to nurse the baby very soon after delivery.

The typical newborn baby is not a Gerber-baby look-alike—but is beautiful nonetheless. Infants' heads may seem huge in comparison to their bodies, and their skulls are usually misshapen from being squeezed during birth. Babies are born wet with amniotic fluid, and some may still have remnants of the white, cheesy coating (called *vernix caseosa*) that protected their skin before birth.

Newborns will turn their heads and eyes toward voices and will gaze into their parents' faces. Although their vision is still a little fuzzy, they can see. They also possess

malpresentation
Improper positioning of the fetus in the mother's uterus.

fetal distress
A condition that indicates that the fetus is at risk; usually includes a sudden lack of oxygen (anoxia), a change in fetal heart rate, and/or a change in fetal respiration.

Most newborns are given the Apgar Test at 1 and 5 minutes after birth to identify those who need immediate medical attention. This newborn has a healthy pink color.

Apgar test
A brief assessment of the newborn conducted at 1 and 5 minutes after birth; used to identify newborns who are at risk and need medical attention.

The family system changes dramatically with the introduction of a new family member. Factors to consider in the adjustment include issues between the mother and father, and issues involving siblings who have a new baby (or two!) with whom to share everything. What can this family do to ease their transition?

several adaptive reflexes. If you touch newborns' cheeks, they will turn their heads in the direction of the touch. Touch their lips, and they will suck. Both of these reflexes help a newborn find the nipple and begin feeding. And if you put your finger in the newborns' hand, the infant will reflexively grasp your finger and hold on tight. We will give a more complete description of newborns' reflexes and sensory abilities in the next chapter, along with a description of babies' growth and the development of their brains and nervous systems.

The first formal test administered to almost all newborn babies right after birth is the **Apgar test,** by far the most widely used newborn screening assessment (Apgar, 1953). Practitioners conduct this brief assessment 1 minute after delivery and again 5 minutes after delivery. The reason for giving the assessment twice is to make sure that changes in a newborn's condition will be noticed—because subtle changes can be overlooked in the bustle surrounding a delivery. The Apgar test gives the infant a score of 0, 1, or 2 (2 being the best) on each of five dimensions: heart rate, respiration, muscle tone, color, and reflex irritability. The newborn's total score indicates overall condition. The maximum score is 10. A score from 7 to 10 means that the baby does not need any immediate assistance or close monitoring. A score of 4 to 6 indicates some potential problems: The baby needs close monitoring and possibly some intervention. A score of 0 to 3 indicates a serious risk and calls for immediate action.

Becoming a Family: Psychological Adjustments to Having a Newborn

For most families, having a baby is an exciting and happy event. Even so, the addition of a new person to the family requires a great deal of adjustment. Sleeping and eating patterns, family members' amount of free time, and attention to different individuals' needs and desires are all affected. Jealous siblings may even wish that the parents would "take him back"!

The Transition to Parenthood. A successful transition to this new phase of family life involves a wide range of factors. Parents or partners who are welcoming their first-born child must adjust their self-perceptions: They are now parents, not simply a couple. They must learn to share their time, energy, and emotion with this very needy newcomer. Success in this transition does *not* mean that the new parents experience no stress or problems—such a situation is probably impossible. Instead,

in a successful transition the couple manages to identify and deal in positive ways with stressors and problems so that all the family members' needs are adequately met. Parents who have a supportive, positive relationship and well-developed coping skills can discuss and solve problems rather than avoid or deny them (Belsky et al., 1988; Frosch et al., 1998; Heinicke & Guthrie, 1996). Families that have made a successful transition show more warmth toward one another, greater sensitivity to one another's needs, and more positive interactions with one another than families that have difficulties with the transition. The amount of time needed for this transition varies depending on the family, but it usually takes about 6 months to a year after the baby's birth.

The transition to parenthood also seems to bring to the forefront any issues that a new parent has with his or her own parents. For example, if a new father recalls the relationship with his own parents as cold or rejecting, such feelings can cast a shadow on his attitudes toward his new role as a parent (Belsky & Isabella, 1985). The same is true of identity issues. During the period of adjustment new parents incorporate a parental dimension in their self-concepts—sometimes starting this process even before conception if the pregnancy is planned. The more secure each parent is in who he or she is and in what is important to each person individually and to the family as a whole, the more successful the transition to parenthood seems to be (Diamond et al., 1996). Finally, the transition is easier if the new parents are realistic in their expectations, both of themselves and of their baby. Having a newborn can certainly be an exciting and joyous experience, but it also involves an incredible amount of hard work and sacrifice. To believe otherwise is to set yourself up for frustration and disappointment. And the bigger the gap between the expectation and the reality, the more difficult the transition will be.

In addition, there are *child factors*. The transition to parenthood can be made more or less difficult by several aspects of the newborn himself or herself. After all, infants arrive with temperaments and needs all their own. Some babies have sweet, compliant, happy temperaments. Some do not. Some babies do not sleep for more than 30 minutes at a time, never nap when the parents would like, do not eat well, spit up their food three times a day, and fuss from 5 p.m. to 7 p.m. every night. For the parents of more difficult babies, the transitional period can be easier if the parents (either together or alone) have regular breaks from the infant care. It's also important for them to remember that most families do find a workable routine eventually (McHale et al., 2004).

> **Think About Kendra and James . . .**
> *What can Kendra and James do to help prepare for the transition to parenthood? What role can their families play to ease this transition?*

The Transition to Becoming a Sibling. An older sibling, once the "king of the hill," can have a difficult time coming to grips with the fact that he or she is no longer the center of everyone's concerns after a new baby arrives. Increases in whininess, sleeping difficulties, withdrawal, clinginess, aggressive behaviors, and toileting problems are common in older siblings during the first few months after the birth of a new baby. Most of these changes are short-term, lasting only a few months. Some studies, however, have found correlations between the birth of a sibling and lower levels of verbal development, achievement, and socioemotional adjustment several years later. These findings seem to apply particularly to children in economically disadvantaged families (Baydar & Greek, 1997; Baydar & Hyle, 1997). Such problems are probably due more to changes in the family's overall context and interaction patterns (e.g., poorer parenting strategies, less one-on-one time with the older child, increased financial stress, decreased opportunities for skill development) than to the actual birth of the newborn. And many children adjust quite well to a newborn sibling, showing few negative and even some positive changes. For example, some siblings show greater independence in feeding and toileting habits, improved language abilities, or better peer relations.

Though the transition to being a sibling is not likely to be conflict free, parents can help children adjust. It is important for parents to recognize that becoming a sibling is a major change and can be especially tough for preschool children. It makes sense to prepare the child as much as possible. Talk with the child about changes, acknowledge any negative feelings, and try to provide as much one-on-one time as possible. Help the child develop coping skills by suggesting positive ways to gain attention. Make sure the child has adequate opportunities to play with friends, and encourage more parent–child interaction. Point out the many ways in which the older child is needed and can be helpful. And finally, parents should model positive coping skills and positive attitudes themselves, thereby helping the child see that the transition can lead to a new phase of family life that is as happy and secure as the phase before.

1. What is the purpose of the contractions during Stage 1 of labor?
    a. to open the cervix
    b. to push the baby through the birth canal
    c. to push the placenta and other membranes through the birth canal
    d. to push the baby into a transverse position

2. Which stage of labor is typically the shortest and least intense for the mother?
    a. Stage 1   b. Stage 2   c. Stage 3   d. dilation

3. What is the main event that happens in Stage 2 of labor?
    a. dilation of the cervix
    b. beginning of labor contractions
    c. delivery of the placenta and other membranes
    d. delivery of the baby

4. What condition exists when a fetus is deprived of oxygen during the birth process?
    a. hypoxia   b. anoxia   c. malpresentation   d. breech birth

5. **True or False:** The correct order of events during the birth process is dilation of the cervix, delivery of the baby, and afterbirth.

6. **True or False:** An Apgar score of 5 indicates that the newborn is at serious risk and that immediate attention is needed to save the baby.

Answers: 1. a, 2. c, 3. d, 4. b, 5. T, 6. F

Options in Giving Birth: Choices and Alternatives

When a woman gives birth in the United States today, she has many options available to her that were not possible even 50 years ago. One of the biggest changes in recent decades has been the increasing control that a woman has over the circumstances surrounding the birth. In this section we will discuss many of the options that mothers and their families have for giving birth.

As you study this section, ask yourself these questions:

■ What specific things can mothers and fathers do to prepare for labor and delivery? What birthing options are available, and what are the advantages and disadvantages of each?

■ What are the advantages and disadvantages of the use of drugs during labor and delivery? What effects do these drugs have on mothers and their babies?

■ What can the father do to help during labor and delivery? What are the effects of his presence during labor?

Approaches to Labor and Delivery

In the early 1900s, few babies born in this country were born in a hospital. Women gave birth at home attended by friends, family, and sometimes a midwife. There were few doctors in attendance, no harsh lights, no isolation from those who could offer emotional support. But there were also no drugs for pain relief and no medical assistance in cases of problematic deliveries. By midcentury, hospital births had become the norm. Women labored either alone in a room or in a ward full of other laboring women trying their best to cope with each contraction. Partners and other family members were not allowed to be with the women. Women lay in bed, often flat on their backs. When birth was imminent, hospital staff wheeled a woman to a delivery room and gave her a general anesthetic that rendered her unconscious. Her baby was born in a sterile and brightly lit operating room. Then nurses took the baby to the hospital nursery, where the mother could come and visit. Mother and baby often stayed in the hospital (though not in the same room) for up to a week.

How things have changed! Today, although 99 percent of babies are born in hospitals (Martin et al., 2003), there is much more awareness of the importance of personal support, pain management techniques (both drug- and non–drug-based), and the overall comfort level of the birthing environment. Today's modern *birthing centers* attempt to combine the advantages of a hospital—access to medical expertise and equipment in case of difficulties—with the comforts of a home birth. Rooms have rocking chairs and couches, and partners and family members are encouraged to stay with the laboring woman. Lighting is soft, staffers encourage relaxation techniques and moving around during labor, and even whirlpool baths are available in many places. Unless there are complications, labor and birth take place in the same room. *Rooming-in* lets the baby stay in the same room with the mother so that parents can begin getting to know their newest family member as soon as possible. As a society we have come to realize that having a baby is, in most cases, a normal life event rather than a medical condition. Today's birthing environment often reflects this change in view.

In addition, many births today are attended by *certified nurse–midwives* instead of physicians. To learn more about the midwifery profession, read the Professional Perspective box on page 108 called "Career Focus: Meet a Certified Nurse–Midwife."

Prepared Childbirth. One common approach to labor and delivery is **prepared childbirth.** This approach is largely based on the work of Grantly Dick-Read (Dick-Read, 1972) and of Frederick Lamaze (1958). Dick-Read believed that women become fearful of labor and delivery, partly because they do not know what to expect. This fear increases muscle tension during contractions, and the tension in turn creates pain. It becomes a negative cycle: Increased pain results in more fear and more tension, which increases the pain, and so on. Dick-Read theorized that if women could develop accurate and positive expectations about childbirth, they would experience far less pain.

The *Lamaze method* is one prepared childbirth approach. Lamaze builds both on Dick-Read's theory of pain during childbirth and on the theory of classical conditioning first described by Ivan Pavlov. According to Lamaze, women have been conditioned to believe that labor contractions will be painful. Just the thought of a contraction can cause women to tense up, making the pain of real contractions more intense. To break the conditioning cycle, in Lamaze birthing classes women learn selective relaxation of muscles and controlled breathing. During labor, obviously the uterine muscles contract strongly—they have to in order to push the baby out. But most women instinctively tense other muscles in the body as the contractions begin. Lamaze training in selective relaxation helps women learn *not* to tense other muscles during uterine contractions. The tension and therefore the pain are reduced. Controlled breathing during contractions helps lessen pain by serving as a distraction from the contractions. Together, these two Lamaze techniques can greatly reduce the fatigue and pain experienced during childbirth.

So prepared childbirth involves education about labor and delivery to reduce fear of childbirth, and it also involves practicing selective relaxation and controlled breathing to reduce muscle tension and pain. The final element in prepared childbirth is the presence of a labor coach or companion. This is often the father of the baby.

prepared childbirth
Use of birthing techniques designed to reduce muscle tension, promote relaxation, and reduce pain during labor and delivery.

your perspective
Tighten the muscles in your arm as much as you can. (But don't hurt yourself!) Now hold your muscles tight for a full 2 minutes. Describe how it felt and how you coped with the sensations you experienced. Now think about doing this every 3 minutes for 12 hours! How would you cope?

Career Focus: Meet a Certified Nurse–Midwife

Abbi Beuby
Kailua, Hawaii
Certified nurse–midwife working in a private OB/GYN practice

What does a midwife do? Why did you become one?

Delivering babies makes up about 5 percent of a typical midwifery practice. I work with pregnant patients from their first visits to their last visits, and I do all the follow-up visits and postpartum checks. I am able to spend more time with them and do far more teaching than the physician has time for. I usually spend a half hour with them on the first visit and then 15 to 20 minutes each subsequent visit. I do the initial ultrasounds and the third-trimester ultrasounds to check fluid and size of the baby. The rest of my day is spent doing annual visits, contraceptive counseling, and some primary care.

I was an RN in labor and delivery for 8 years, working with high- and low-risk patients, and I had my master's degree. I mostly thought this was the next step after being a nurse for so long. The most fun part of my job is when I do the first ultrasound that looks like "something" and the parents see their baby for the first time. (On the first ultrasounds the babies are usually too small to see anything.) I used to love doing deliveries, but that's very stressful. Essentially, you have two lives in your hands. It also requires a lot from your family, being on call all the time and up all night sometimes.

Why do some parents choose midwives? How is the birthing approach different?

Most women choose a midwife because we take a more natural approach to childbirth. Physicians see what can go wrong all the time; we see what is going right. We are taught that giving birth is a natural thing; women have been doing it forever. These days, doctors realize that women want a more natural birth and have been striving to achieve that, but this is relatively new. We spend more time with women in labor, coaching and helping them through, and in the total care, including office visits and postpartum care. We spend more time talking to them rather than at them. A midwife strives to remember not only their names but the names of their other kids, parents, spouse, what they do for a living, vacation, and so on.

Are there situations or conditions in which you're not allowed to or would refuse to serve?

I do not take care of women with pregnancy-induced hypertension (preeclampsia/toxemia). I do not take care of those who go into preterm labor, before 36 weeks, and those who are severe diabetics. There are some women who come into the pregnancy with problems, and those are chosen case by case.

What advice would you give to prospective parents who are considering the midwife option?

Look at their credentials, meet them, and discuss their philosophy. Not all midwives believe the same thing or do things the same. Some are very natural and believe no pain medications should be administered. This works for some, but not everyone can handle that. Some do deliveries at home, others in hospitals, and everything in between, so there are lots of options. I also think it is important for the parents to meet with the midwife's backup physician. If things turn ugly, this is the person who they will need to trust to bring their child into the world.

What training and education are usually needed to work in your field?

There are a number of ways to become a midwife. The classic way is to become an RN first then get a master's degree. Certificate-only programs don't give a master's, but both of these routes give the title "certified nurse–midwife." Some programs don't require a nursing degree; those midwives are "certified midwives." Both of these certifications require a national board examination, and the certification must be renewed every 8 years. There is the "lay" midwife, which is the "learn-on-the-job" midwife. They are illegal in most states; however, they have a big following. In the midwest, many of the Amish use them. Here in Hawaii they are considered "a-legal"—not illegal, but also not legal.

Q *What do you see as the advantages to using a nurse–midwife during pregnancy and the delivery of a baby? What cautions should you keep in mind? What approach would you prefer to take?*

The coach attends the childbirth preparation classes with the woman, helps her practice the relaxation and breathing techniques, and is on hand and ready to offer assistance throughout labor and delivery. The coach can help the woman remember how and when to use the relaxation and controlled breathing she has learned, and can help talk her through the more difficult contractions (hence the name "coach").

Achieving a truly pain-free labor and delivery is not common, but women who use prepared childbirth methods experience less pain during childbirth, especially when they are accompanied throughout labor by husbands or partners (Davenport-Slack & Boylan, 1974; Nettlebladt et al., 1976). Some studies also indicate that women who engage in prepared childbirth need less pain medication and enjoy childbirth more (Hodnett & Osborn, 1989; Moir, 1986). However, it is not clear whether these positive effects are due to increased knowledge of what to expect during birth, to relaxation techniques and controlled breathing, to the presence of a support person, or to existing differences between women who choose to participate in prepared childbirth and those who do not.

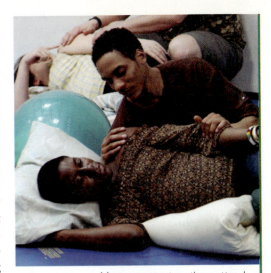

Many expectant mothers attend prepared childbirth classes to learn about techniques they can use to ease the pain and anxiety of childbirth. The birthing partner seen here is learning how to help the mother relax during labor.

The Leboyer Method.

Another interesting approach to childbirth was developed by Frederick Leboyer, who argued that the hospital birth experience is unnecessarily traumatic for the baby (Leboyer, 1975). According to Leboyer, the environment and practices of the surgical-type delivery room (typical prior to Leboyer's time) created a decidedly uncomfortable "first impression" for newborns. There were harsh lights, loud sounds, and cold air; practitioners held the newborn upside down, put drops in his or her eyes, briskly cut the umbilical cord, and promptly removed the baby from the mother. All these events combined to create a highly traumatic experience. The *Leboyer method* carries out any necessary procedures, but in a calmer, quieter, and more respectful way. Typically, the Leboyer delivery room is quiet and softly lit. Helpers place the baby on the mother's abdomen immediately after birth, encourage skin-to-skin contact, and refrain from cutting the umbilical cord until it stops pulsing. They give the baby a bath in warm water (simulating the amniotic fluid that comforted the baby during pregnancy), then return the newborn to the mother and encourage nursing as soon as possible. Leboyer claimed that such practices produce babies who are more relaxed and alert. Research has not supported these advantages for Leboyer-born babies, but these practices do not seem to harm mothers or babies either (Nelson et al., 1980). Leboyer's methods have been extended by those who suggest that *underwater delivery* would be less harmful to both mother and baby. There is no evidence to suggest that this is correct, however (Moir, 1986).

Today couples have a wide variety of options to choose from when deciding how to give birth to their babies. This mother has given birth underwater to relieve strain and ease the transition of the baby through the birth canal.

Home Births and Other Helpful Techniques.

More and more women in this country are returning to what was the norm in the early 1900s: giving birth at home rather than in a hospital or birthing center. A *home birth* offers many advantages to both mothers and babies. These include a comfortable and familiar environment, no concern about making it to the hospital in time, often extensive support from the mother's partner and other family members, and immediate and constant infant–family contact. The obvious disadvantage is that if problems develop for mother or baby, the equipment and personnel to deal with them are not immediately available. Home births can be a satisfying, comfortable, and safe choice if a woman has a trained professional (such as a midwife) on hand, has received thorough screening during pregnancy to identify potential problems, and has quick access to help in case of an emergency (Ackermann-Liebrich et al., 1996; Cohen, 1981; Hazell, 1975).

Upright birthing positions have been used for centuries in certain cultures as seen in this Aztec statue. It was not until the early 1900s that hospital procedures required mothers to lay flat on their backs as a way to ease the process for *physicians.*

Finally, one further positive influence during labor and delivery can start long before the contractions begin: physical fitness. Many cultures encourage women to remain active and to get moderate regular exercise throughout their pregnancies. The traditional reasons for this cultural practice may not be accurate in some cases—for example, some cultures believe that maternal exercise during pregnancy results in a smaller, and therefore easier-to-deliver, baby. Even so, research has provided support for this tradition. The more physically fit a woman is, the fewer complications she is likely to experience, the better she will feel during her pregnancy, and the faster her recovery time is likely to be (Hatch et al., 1993; Khanna, 1998; Stevenson, 1997). The American College of Obstetricians and Gynecologists says that women can benefit from mild to moderate regular exercise during pregnancy, with no apparent ill effects on the fetus, as long as they have no preexisting risk factors or complications (Marble, 1995). Pregnant women should avoid excessive physical exertion, however.

In summary, the alternative approaches to birthing allow families some choice in deciding what their birth experiences will be. Simply having some degree of control over the event may help women and their partners develop a more positive attitude and feel more confident going into labor and delivery. This in turn may enable the mother to relax more; may reduce her tension, anxiety, and perhaps her pain; and may contribute to a more positive birth experience for the entire family.

Drugs During Labor and Delivery

Even with the use of the prepared childbirth techniques we've described, most women experience significant pain and discomfort as labor contractions continue—sometimes for 12 hours or more—and the baby moves through the birth canal. Various studies have documented that anywhere from 68 percent to 95 percent of all hospital-based deliveries in the United States involve some type of medication for the relief of the mother's pain (Gibbs et al., 1986; Rosenblith & Sims-Knight, 1985).

During the middle part of the twentieth century, general anesthetics and major tranquilizers were used for pain relief. However, doctors later realized that many of these drugs crossed the placenta and placed the fetus at significant risk. Today there is a focus on minimizing the use of drugs during labor and delivery. Physicians administer the smallest doses possible and as late in labor as possible, and many women use prepared childbirth techniques to eliminate or decrease their needs for pain medication. A popular approach is to use *epidural anesthesia,* the injection of a mixture of pain-relieving drugs into spaces along the spine of the mother. Usually physicians give epidurals low in the spine so that the drugs block sensations only from the waist down. Over the years, research studies assessing the effects of pain-relieving drugs on the health of the newborn baby have shown mixed results. Based on several reviews of this work, however, we offer the following general conclusions (Brackbill et al., 1985; Coalson & Glosten, 1991; Curran, 1991; Rosenblith & Sims-Knight, 1985):

■ Many of the drugs tested have short-term effects on the newborn's behavior. These include respiratory distress; abnormal variations in heart rate; increased or decreased activity levels; difficulties nursing; and difficulties controlling sleeping, waking, and alert states. Most drugs have not shown measurable long-term consequences, however.

■ Different babies react to medications in different ways. Newborns with preexisting problems (such as premature babies) are at higher risk for detrimental effects of drug exposure.

- When long-term effects of medication have been found, they have generally been relatively small—typically, smaller than the effects of other factors such as low birth weight and lower socioeconomic status.

- The overall amount of medication administered is important; higher amounts are associated with more adverse outcomes.

Epidural administration seems to be a relatively safe and effective way to deliver pain medication during labor. The most commonly used combinations of medications have not shown significant detrimental effects on the newborn. One complication, however, is that a mother who uses epidural medication loses sensation in the pelvic region and therefore cannot feel the normal urge to push. Women can be instructed when to push, of course, but the use of these medications can still prolong labor. Sometimes practitioners have to use forceps to assist the baby through the birth canal.

Think About Kendra and James . . .
Help Kendra decide about the use of pain-relieving drugs during labor. What questions should she ask her doctor about drugs and labor? What can she do to avoid using pain-relieving drugs or to reduce the dosages needed?

The Partner's Role: Helping During Birth

One aspect of the birthing experience that has undergone tremendous change is the family's role, especially the role of the father or partner. Throughout much of the twentieth century, in this country as in many others, the father's traditional role was to wait, pacing anxiously in the hospital halls, and maybe to hand out cigars after the baby's birth was announced. Even back when home births were the norm in this country, the father typically did not assist during labor and delivery—that task was left to midwives and female relatives. Since the advent of prepared childbirth, however, many women's partners have taken more active roles. Today, most partners participate at least to some degree in the birth of their children.

What do partners do during labor and delivery? Typically partners perform four tasks. First, they help the expectant mother remain as comfortable as possible during labor, helping her walk around, change positions, and continue slow but normal breathing through contractions as long as possible. Second, partners coach the laboring woman to use the selective relaxation and controlled breathing techniques she has practiced during the pregnancy. This becomes an ever more important job as the contractions increase in frequency and intensity. Toward the end of Stage 1, the

Partners today can be fully involved in the births of their children. This father coached his wife as she delivered their baby.

Think About Kendra and James . . .

Help Kendra and James think about their options during labor and delivery. What preparation do they need? How can James help during the birth process?

mother is often very tired. Perhaps she is a bit disoriented if the labor has been long, and she may feel anxious and unsure if she will be able to make it through the delivery. The coach/partner's help—in reminding her to take one contraction at a time, switch from one form of breathing to another, and relax—can make a tremendous difference in keeping the mother calm and in control. Third, the partner can offer great emotional support simply by being with the mother. Partners often know better than anyone else what kinds of things the laboring woman finds soothing or irritating, and what kinds of encouragement will be effective. Finally, partners often may assist with the actual birth. They sometimes "catch" the baby when he or she is born, and they can even cut the umbilical cord.

Though some partners may worry that they are not really being helpful, mothers report that their presence during labor is comforting and useful. Studies have found that when partners are present during labor, mothers experience less pain, need less pain medication, and enjoy the birth process more. Partners report benefits as well, expressing more positive feelings about the birth and feeling greater emotional closeness to both the baby and the mother (Bondas-Salonen, 1998; Broome & Koehler, 1986; Cronenwett & Newmark, 1974; Davenport-Slack & Boylan, 1974; Dragonas, 1992; Nettleblad et al., 1976; Szeverenyi et al., 1995).

In this chapter we have gone from the conception through the birth of a baby. We have discussed the normal course of prenatal development, the stages of labor and delivery, and many of the options and choices that a pregnant woman has. We have also covered problems that can occur during the prenatal and birth periods, describing teratogens and other risk factors that can endanger the developing fetus. From these details we hope you clearly see two main points. First, pregnant women and their families can greatly increase their odds of having a healthy baby by making healthy lifestyle choices and avoiding risk factors such as teratogens and teenage pregnancy. *Much is under their control!* Second, although problems can occur, most babies develop normally and are born healthy, robust, and ready to proceed with rapid development of their physical, cognitive, and socioemotional skills. In the next chapters we'll turn to these exciting realms of postnatal development.

■ Let's Review . . .

1. In the early 1900s most babies were born _____.
   a. at home
   b. in hospitals
   c. in birthing centers
   d. in community clinics

2. In prepared childbirth, the purpose of controlled breathing and selective relaxation is:
   a. to speed up the delivery of the baby.
   b. to improve the effectiveness of pain-relieving drugs.
   c. to reduce the mother's experience of pain during contractions.
   d. to slow down the labor contractions.

3. When partners participate in prepared childbirth, their main role is to:
   a. coach the mother through selective relaxation and controlled breathing techniques.
   b. help the physician deliver the baby.
   c. be available to bond with the baby after birth.
   d. wait outside of the birthing room and inform the family of the mother's progress.

Thinking Back to Kendra and James …

Now that you have studied this chapter, you should be able to identify more than a dozen risk factors that Kendra and James might face. You should know the possible effects of these risk factors, and you should be able to give the couple some sound advice on how to reduce their risks.

One factor that you probably noticed is Kendra's age. In her late teens, Kendra's risk of having a low-birth-weight baby is elevated (compared to that of mothers in their 20s and 30s), but it is not as high as it would have been if she were younger than 15. Proper prenatal care and nutrition can reduce the health risks of teenage pregnancy. Also, given that teenagers tend to be less informed about childbirth, babies, and parenting, it would help if Kendra and James would take classes or otherwise prepare themselves for parenthood.

Like all potential parents, Kendra and James should be concerned about their lifestyles and the teratogens to which they may be exposed. Alcohol, cigarette smoke, and cocaine and other illegal drugs all can harm the developing baby. Sexually transmitted and other infectious diseases can cause the baby to be born infected or with birth defects, so Kendra and James should take precautions to avoid these diseases. If Kendra and James continued drinking alcohol, using drugs, and exposing themselves to other potential teratogens until they knew Kendra was pregnant, the baby may already be affected.

Kendra should receive good prenatal care. Both parents should also take childbirth classes. There they can learn about the stages of labor and things they can do to control Kendra's experience of pain. By taking active roles in the birth, both parents can have a more satisfying experience and enhance their attachment to the new baby.

Like Kendra and James, all potential parents should consider the risk factors that they might face and take steps to reduce or avoid them. A great many pregnancy problems and birth defects are prevented when parents take the proper precautions.

■ Chapter Review . . .

Where does conception normally take place? What are two of the general processes that occur during prenatal development?

Conception normally occurs when the ovum and sperm meet in the upper part of the fallopian tube. After fertilization, prenatal development proceeds with *mitosis* (copy division) and *differentiation* (in which cells take on specific structures and functions).

What are the stages of prenatal development and the major events that take place in each?

The three stages are the germinal, the embryonic, and the fetal stages. During the germinal stage (0 to 2 weeks), the first cell divisions take place, and the embryo implants in the uterine lining. During the embryonic stage (3 to 8 weeks), the ectoderm, mesoderm, and endoderm form and later give rise to the major organs and parts of the body. The placenta, umbilical cord, and other structures form to support the developing baby. The body forms in a cephalocaudal (head-to-tail) and proximodistal (midline-to-outer) pattern. Organogenesis is complete by the end of the embryonic stage, so this stage includes most critical periods in organ and tissue formation. During the fetal stage the baby grows in size and the body systems gradually become more functional.

What effects do legal and illegal drugs have on the developing baby?

Several legal and illegal drugs can harm the developing baby. Alcohol is the leading known cause of mental retardation. It can also cause growth retardation, facial deformities, and FAS. Cocaine can cause growth retardation, cognitive deficits, and defects in the brain, intestines, and genital–urinary tract. Cigarette smoking is associated with low birth weight, hyperactivity, poor school performance, and increased risk of miscarriage, stillbirth, and neonatal death.

If a pregnant woman has an infectious disease, will this harm the developing baby?

Several sexually transmitted diseases and other infectious diseases can harm the developing baby. Sometimes the baby is born infected with a disease; in other cases the disease causes birth defects. If the mother has rubella, the baby can become infected with rubella or can be born with cataracts, heart defects, deafness, or lowered intelligence. Cytomegalovirus can cause embryonic death, retarded growth, microcephaly, blindness, mental retardation, and cerebral palsy. If the mother has HIV, the baby can be born infected with HIV and may show growth retardation and head and facial deformities.

Does the age of the mother affect pregnancy?

Infants of teenage mothers are at higher risk for low birth weight, prematurity, and neonatal death, especially when the mother is younger than 15. Risks of prematurity, fetal death, and pregnancy complications increase slightly after age 30.

What are critical periods, and why are they important in prenatal development?

Critical periods are times when developing organs and tissues are most vulnerable to defects. They usually occur when the organs and tissues are first forming, differentiating from surrounding cells. Most critical periods occur during the embryonic stage (weeks 3 to 8) and are therefore complete by the time most women know that they are pregnant. Parents should avoid exposure to teratogens during pregnancy.

Can fathers expose developing babies to teratogens?

In most cases, no—or at least not directly. Elements in the father's bloodstream do not pass to the developing baby, but some toxic substances can reduce the mobility and viability of sperm. Research with rats indicates that fathers' alcohol consumption may increase activity level in offspring and that cocaine can bind to sperm cells and be carried to the fertilized egg. Men can help to support healthy pregnancies in women.

What are the stages of labor, and what happens in each?

In Stage 1 the cervix dilates (widens) and the fetus moves downward to the birth canal. In Stage 2 the baby moves through the birth canal and is delivered. In Stage 3 the placenta and all membranes (the afterbirth) are delivered.

What is a newborn baby like?

The newborn baby has a large head and may be covered with a cheesy coating. Newborns can see, but their vision is fuzzy. They have reflexes that help them learn to feed, and they will grasp your finger if you touch their palms. They turn their heads to the sound of voices and gaze into the faces of their parents. The Apgar test, given 1 and 5 minutes after birth, identifies newborns who are at risk and need special medical attention.

What are some complications that can occur during labor and delivery?

In malpresentation the fetus's position in the womb makes delivery difficult and dangerous. In fetal distress the fetus experiences a serious change in vital signs that put it at risk. Anoxia, a serious birth complication in which the fetus does not receive enough oxygen, can lead to permanent brain damage.

What kind of help is available to a woman in labor?

Women usually choose either an obstetrician or a midwife to provide medical help during labor and delivery. The continuous presence of a labor companion, usually the baby's father, has beneficial effects. In prepared childbirth women learn selective relaxation and controlled breathing techniques to help them relax and to reduce the pain of contractions.

Is it safe to use drugs for pain relief during labor and delivery?

Most of the drugs used today to reduce anxiety or pain may have short-term negative effects on the fetus and newborn but have not been shown to have long-term consequences. Epidural anesthesia, in which medications are injected into spaces along the spine, is increasingly common and appears to have few negative effects on the baby.

What role do fathers or other partners play during labor and delivery?

Fathers or partners help during labor and delivery by helping mothers relax, use selective relaxation techniques and controlled breathing, and remain calm. Both mothers and fathers report that fathers' presence during labor and delivery has beneficial effects.

■ Key Terms

afterbirth (101)
Apgar test (104)
cephalocaudal pattern (88)
cesarean section (C-section) births (96)
critical periods (88)
differentiation (85)
dilation (101)
embryonic stage (87)
fetal alcohol effects (FAE) (93)
fetal alcohol syndrome (FAS) (92)
fetal distress (103)
fetal stage (89)
germinal stage (86)

implantation (87)
low birth weight (92)
malpresentation (103)
miscarriage (87)
organogenesis (88)
ovulation (84)
premature (prematurity) (90)
prenatal development (84)
prepared childbirth (107)
preterm birth (92)
proximodistal pattern (88)
teratogen (90)

mydevelopmentlab

Where human development comes to life!

If you are using MyDevelopmentLab, you have access to an ebook version of this textbook, along with dozens of valuable resources per chapter—including video and audio clips, simulations and activities, self-assessments, practice tests, and other study materials. Here is a sampling of the resources available for this chapter.

 Explore
The Embryonic Period

 Simulate
Teratogens and Their Effects

 Watch
Fetal Development
Labor and Birth
Doulas

If you did not receive an access code to MyDevelopmentLab with this text and wish to purchase access online, please visit www.mydevelopmentlab.com.

Beginnings

Exploring Child Development

Child development is an interdisciplinary field aimed at understanding the important changes that take place as children grow through childhood and into adolescence. At the heart of child development lies the complex interplay between nature (the genes we inherit) and nurture (the environment that supports our growth and development). From Freud to Skinner and from Piaget to Bronfenbrenner, many theorists have shaped the field and advanced our understanding of development. Along the way, researchers have relied on scientific methods to catalog, describe, and explain the developmental processes that shape children's lives. The evidence they gather is very useful for parents and families who are raising children; for government officials and citizens who shape the social policies and laws that affect children and families; and for the many teachers, day care workers, counselors, psychologists, social workers, and others who are involved daily with the important task of helping children learn and grow in healthy ways. The field of child development is varied in its history, in its goals, and in its applications for children's lives, and its study continues to evolve even today.

Heredity and the Environment

Throughout life, growth and development are shaped by the genes children inherit from their parents and by the environments and situations in which children live. Nature provides the biological blueprints, while nurture provides the physical supports and social interactions that children need to reach their developmental potentials. Unfortunately, some children inherit diseases and conditions that present serious challenges to their positive growth and may even challenge their ability to survive. In an ideal world, children inherit healthy genes and have the support and nurturing care they need to grow, learn, and thrive. Genes and the environment interact in complex ways. To some extent, genes influence the situations and contexts children choose in life, but in other ways the situations and activities children engage in influence the actions of their genes. We cannot separate the forces of nature and nurture into two distinct camps—we must instead understand how they interact so we can enhance the positive growth and development of children in our lives.

Prenatal Development and Birth

After conception, the cells in the zygote begin dividing and forming the tissues and structures that will become the fetus and later the baby. Along the way, development can be seriously disrupted if the mother consumes alcohol, uses cocaine or other illegal drugs, smokes cigarettes, or has diseases or is otherwise exposed to unhealthy conditions and environments. The most serious risks tend to occur between the third and eighth weeks after conception, during a time when the basic organs and tissues are forming in the embryo. Hopefully all conditions are relatively healthy, and the baby can grow to a healthy size before being born. When birth arrives, the baby will make the transition from the protection of the mother's womb into the welcoming arms of a new family. The baby is ready to enter the phase of *Infants and Toddlers: The First Years*.

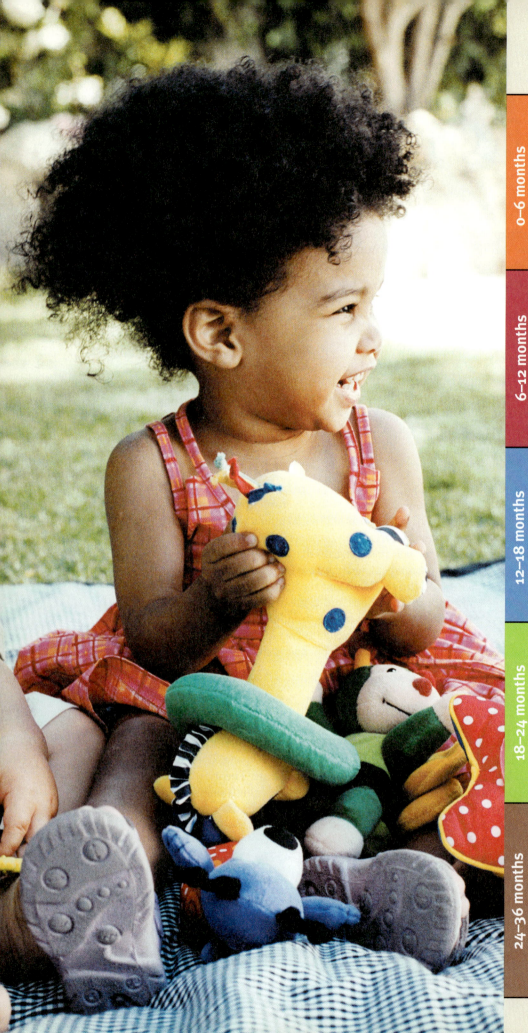

Some Developmental Landmarks

0–6 months
- Strong sucking reflex
- Imitates facial expressions
- Holds head upright
- Recognizes familiar faces and voices
- Will not look for object after it is hidden
- Coos and babbles
- Rolls over

6–12 months
- Sits upright without help
- Begins eating solid foods
- Imitates speech sounds
- Creates own nonsense words
- Crawls
- Afraid of strangers and separation from parents

12–18 months
- Takes first steps
- Speaks first words
- Can find object, if watches where it was hidden
- Attachment with caregivers has formed
- Can pretend play
- Scribbles on paper

18–24 months
- Uses two- and three-word sentences
- Frequent conflicts with other toddlers
- Begins toilet training

24–36 months
- Already reached half of adult height
- Finds object, even if didn't watch where it was hidden
- Imitates other playmates
- Plays turn-taking games
- Makes friends

part two

Infants and Toddlers: The First Years

The First Years, from birth through 2 years, give children their start in the adventurous exploration of life! We refer to the first year as *infancy* (from birth through 12 months). Infants depend completely on their parents and caregivers for survival, and they form special emotional attachments to the people who take care of them most. It's hard to know what's going on inside the minds of young infants, but researchers have used ingenious methods to find out! At home, parents celebrate their baby's first steps and first words, and these milestones signal that the infants are growing into unique and independent little children.

From 12 months through 2 years of age we refer to children as *toddlers*—and that term aptly captures the image of wobbly steps, uncoordinated movements, and the early and sometimes awkward attempts at play and social interaction. Toddlers are still learning to master the complex skills of walking, running, and climbing. They love to explore, and since everything is new to them they have many curiosities to satisfy. Toddlers enjoy playing with others their size, although they sometimes fuss and fight when their playmates don't share toys freely. They have a lot to learn, but they are more skilled to begin with than you might think, and they make rapid progress as you will discover in the next three chapters.

chapter 4

Physical Development in Infants and Toddlers

Beverly is eight months into her first pregnancy, and she is very excited about becoming a mom. She has been avidly reading magazine articles about infant brain development—she wants to help her baby get off to the best start possible. From what Beverly has read, it seems that the baby's brain gets "wired" during the first three years after birth. She wonders how this happens and what she can do to make sure her baby doesn't miss important opportunities during the first years. One of her friends had a baby recently and frequently played classical music around her baby. Her friend says that Mozart's music is supposed to help babies wire their brains for math and science. Can this be true? Can music and other sounds possibly have any effect on a child's development? Also, Beverly has heard that other mothers enroll their infants in yoga classes in which they stretch and exercise their babies' muscles. The sessions sound like a fun way to bond with infants. But will exercising the babies' arms and legs and helping the babies bend their trunk muscles really help the babies to sit up, crawl, and walk? And what about some of the more basic questions, such as nutrition? Is breastfeeding better than using infant formulas? If Beverly chooses to breastfeed her baby, what are the recommendations about when she should wean her baby from the breast?

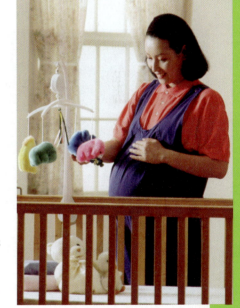

Like most new and prospective parents, Beverly is eager to support her baby's development. What would you suggest? After studying this chapter, you should be able to give Beverly sound advice. Using at least a dozen research findings or concepts, you should be able to help Beverly sort out fact from the fiction and get her baby off to a great start.

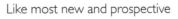

As you read this chapter, look for the "Think About Beverly . . ." questions that ask you to consider what you're learning from Beverly's perspective.

This baby seems healthy, happy, and off to a great start in life. What major developmental milestones can infants be expected to pass through before age 2?

Infancy is an exciting time that contains an impressive run of *firsts*: the first time parents see their baby; the first cuddles, first feeding, and first smiles; and, by the end of the first year, the first steps and the baby's first spoken words. Infants begin life completely helpless and dependent on other people for care. By their second birthday, they are walking, running, climbing, and talking and have developed a sense of autonomy and independence from their parents and caregivers. Most babies end their toddler years with a solid foundation for moving into early childhood. Given the tremendous pace of change during the infant and toddler years, you can understand Beverly's desire to get her baby off to the best start.

In Chapter 3, you learned several things parents can do to avoid teratogens, prevent birth defects, and have healthier pregnancies. In this chapter, we focus on physical development during the first 2 years after birth. We begin by looking at infants who are at risk because they were born too early or too small. We also look at infants who don't survive their first year after birth. What lessons can be learned from these cases? Next we look at the typical patterns of physical growth and at nutrition during infancy and the toddler years. We also look at research on brain development. Neurons in the brain form complex networks of interconnections that allow the brain to process information and govern behavior. How important are the early years in the formation of the brain's structure and neural connections? After discussing brain development, we will explore the sensory capabilities of infants—how well do babies see and hear after they are born, and how do these abilities develop in the early months? We end the chapter by turning to motor development, starting back in infancy with babies' first reflexes. As children grow in size, they also learn to control their muscles, and we review some of the major motor development milestones that we see during these first years. Throughout the chapter, you can see how these developments in physical size, shape, and coordination lay the foundation for the other types of development we cover in the next chapters.

Infants at Risk: Prematurity and Infant Mortality

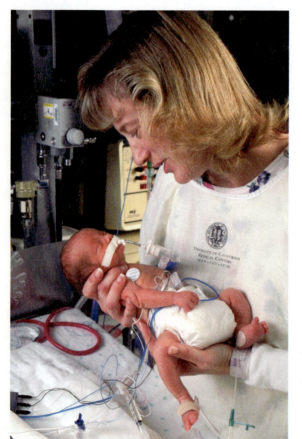

Figure 4.1 • Premature Infant This baby was born at approximately 27 weeks' gestation and weighs only 2 pounds. Usually, babies born at this age and size experience limbs that jerk and twitch, erratic breathing, and shrink from human touch. Their tiny bodies can't properly regulate temperature, and their sucking reflex isn't strong enough for breastfeeding or bottle feeding.

Take a look at the premature baby in Figure 4.1. Prematurity is one of the biggest threats faced by infants in our country. Only 11 percent of babies are born preterm, but these babies account for up to 67 percent of infant deaths in the United States (McCormick, 1985; Nathanielsz, 1992). Although the United States ranks first in the world in health technology, it ranks 17th among industrialized countries in the rate of low-birth-weight births, often associated with preterm birth (Children's Defense Fund, 2001), and the rates of both preterm and low-birth-weight births are increasing. The incidence of preterm birth rose from 9.4 percent in 1981 to 11.6 percent in 2000. The rate of low-birth-weight births now stands at 7.6 percent, the highest level since 1973. The statistics for some groups within the U.S. population are even grimmer. For example, African American women have a low-birth-weight rate of 13 percent and a 17.3 percent prematurity rate; both of these percentages are nearly double those of whites (Matthews, Menacher, & MacDorman, 2002).

Clearly, there is reason for concern. But what do we know about the causes and effects of preterm birth and low birth weight? More important, what have we learned about how to prevent these serious problems?

As you study this section, ask yourself these questions:

■ What are the differences among preterm birth, low birth weight, very low birth weight, and the designation "small for gestational age"?

■ What are the risk factors and possible effects associated with preterm and low-birth-weight babies?

■ What is the relationship between prematurity and infant mortality?

■ How can the rates of prematurity and infant mortality be reduced?

What Is Prematurity?

There is sometimes confusion about the meaning of the term *premature*. A full-term pregnancy is about 38 to 40 weeks long, and the average weight for full-term babies is 7½ pounds. Birth within two weeks of the expected due date (2 weeks early or late) is considered full-term. A **preterm birth** is birth before 37 weeks' gestation, or more than 3 weeks before the expected due date. A baby who is born weighing less than 5½ pounds is considered to have a **low birth weight**. Newborns who weigh less than 3½ pounds are classified as being at **very low birth weight** and are at even greater risk for serious problems. Infants who are **small for gestational age** (SGA) are those who are below the 10th percentile of birth weight for their gestational age (i.e., among the lightest 10 percent of babies born at a particular number of weeks since conception).

Why bother to distinguish among all these classifications? The reason is that their outcomes differ. In other words, different babies face different levels of immediate and long-term risk. Although preterm birth is certainly not good, many babies who are born preterm are at an appropriate level of development and weight, given their length of gestation. As long as birth weight is not too low and is appropriate for the gestational age—and provided that the infant receives appropriate treatment—many preterm babies go on to develop normally. Babies who are SGA, however, are particularly worrisome. Something has kept them from growing as well as they should have, given how long they were in the uterus. It is difficult to know what has gone wrong in these cases, but poor prenatal nutrition of the fetus is a likely factor. Perhaps the maternal diet was poor, there were problems with the placenta, or problems in the fetus prevented it from being able to utilize nutrients. As you read in Chapter 3, teratogens such as alcohol and cocaine also retard fetal growth, causing babies to be born small for their gestational age. SGA babies fare much worse than other preterm infants. They show greater rates of infection, brain damage, and death during their first year and are more likely to show long-term problems in academic achievement (Copper et al., 1993; Korkman, Liikanen, & Fellman, 1996).

In about half of the cases of preterm birth and low birth weight, the causes are not known. Research has identified numerous risk factors, however. Table 4.1 lists some of these along with the most common effects of prematurity.

If you look closely at the list in Table 4.1, one of the most striking things you will notice is that several of the risk factors are controllable. This is good news: It means that it might be possible to reduce the risk of serious birth complications to some extent. That might not be a simple task, however. For example, lack of prenatal care consistently correlates with preterm birth and low birth weight. The reason for this correlation could be that detection of early warning signs or high-risk behaviors cannot be addressed if the pregnant woman is not receiving regular prenatal monitoring. High-quality preventive

This woman is about 36 weeks along in her pregnancy. If her baby were born now, it would be preterm. Babies need their last few weeks in the womb to gain more size and strength before birth.

preterm birth
Birth that occurs before 37 weeks of gestation, or about 3 weeks earlier than the normal due date.

low birth weight
Weight less than 5½ pounds at birth (2 pounds lighter than average); indicates potential for health risks.

very low birth weight
Weight less than 3½ pounds at birth (4 pounds lighter than average); indicates greater potential for health risks.

small for gestational age (SGA)
Born below the tenth percentile of birth weight for gestational age; indicates serious health risks.

your perspective
Do you know anyone who was or who had a preterm or low-birth-weight baby? What were the suspected causes? What have the long-term effects been?

Table 4.1 Risk Factors and Effects of Premature Births

RISK FACTORS WITH PREMATURE BIRTH	EFFECTS OF PREMATURE BIRTHS
Lack of prenatal care	Increased risk of infant mortality
Vaginal infection	Increased risk of difficulties in
Short interval between birth and subsequent pregnancy (less than 3 months)	• respiration (e.g., respiratory distress syndrome, apnea, anoxia)
Malnutrition	• circulation, leading to brain hemorrhage
Cigarette smoking	• feeding, due to poor sucking ability
Drug use (e.g., alcohol, cocaine)	• social interactions (difficult to rouse, difficult to calm, ambiguous interpersonal signals)
Maternal age (especially younger than age 15)	• regulating sleep, awake, alert cycles
Marital status (unmarried)	Increased longer-term risk of
Maternal illness affecting blood vessels (e.g., diabetes, high blood pressure)	• cerebral palsy
Membership in certain ethnic groups	• lowered academic achievement, lowered IQ
Genetic background and family history	• attentional problems
Personal history of spontaneous abortion or preterm labor	• poor language development
Multiple gestations (i.e., twins, triplets, etc.)	• motor and perceptual difficulties
	• specific learning disabilities

Think About Beverly…

Describe three or four things that Beverly could have done during her pregnancy to reduce her risk of having a premature baby.

prenatal care is available, but many women who stand to benefit from this kind of care either do not have access to it or do not use it. To find out what it is like to have a baby who is very premature, read the Personal Perspective box entitled "Meet the Parents of a Very Premature Baby."

Infant Mortality

infant mortality
Deaths that occur between birth and 1 year of age.

The term **infant mortality** refers to deaths that occur before the age of 1 year. In spite of the medical community's best efforts, many infants die each year. As you can see in Figure 4.2, the United States does not rank well when compared to other

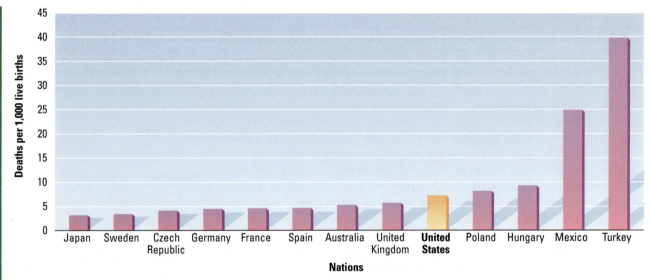

Figure 4.2 • Infant Mortality This graph shows infant mortality rates for selected nations. All data are for the year 2000 except the data for the United States, which are for 1999. (Organisation for Economic Cooperation and Development, 2002.)

Meet the Parents of a Very Premature Baby

Kim Powell and Larry Sikkink
Decorah, Iowa
Parents of Senia, born at 28 weeks'
gestation weighing 1 pound, 15 ounces

When did you learn that your baby would be premature? What were your first thoughts? Do you know what caused the prematurity?

Kim: I experienced a healthy pregnancy up to my sixth month. Then, at a prenatal exam, the doctor found I had high blood pressure as well as protein in my urine. The next day I was admitted to a hospital with a neonatal intensive care unit (NICU). At 28 weeks' gestation, on the way to my first ultrasound, I began feeling light-headed and felt a sudden pain in my upper abdomen. I began throwing up and had a severe headache. The doctor said I had to have an emergency cesarean section if my baby and I were to live. I had HELLP syndrome (hemolysis, elevated liver enzymes, low blood platelets). There is no known cause or predictor for HELLP syndrome, and some mothers and babies die from the complications. I knew my baby would be born prematurely, but I was too sick to realize what that meant. Immediately after her birth, Senia was whisked away to the NICU, intubated, placed on a warming table, and connected to an IV feeding tube and breathing and heart monitors. My husband was still on the 90-minute drive from our home. Senia's left lung collapsed after birth, requiring three days of lung massage therapy. At 2 weeks she was moved to an incubator, where she stayed for 4 weeks.

Larry: Senia had been delivered about 15 minutes before my arrival. The NICU team was attending to her, and I was told I would be allowed to see her in about 30 minutes. I was shocked. How could I be the father of a baby girl already? A NICU doctor assured me that given time, care, and love, our daughter's chances for survival were very good.

Has your baby needed or used any special services? What is your baby like today?

Kim: At 4 pounds and 1 ounce, after seven weeks in the NICU, Senia came home on an apnea and bradycardia monitor. For $2\frac{1}{2}$ months, Senia had episodes in which her breathing would stop and her heart rate would lower. She also had several bouts of pneumonia in her first year. It took 2 years for Senia to perform like others her age, but she is now all caught up. She is tall for her age and is at the fiftieth percentile in weight. Cognitively, she tests above age level. Senia started kindergarten at age 5 and loves writing, books, music, and dancing.

What advice do you have for other parents who may have a premature or low-birth-weight baby?

Kim: Educate yourself and read about other premature babies. Kim Wilson and I wrote *Living Miracles: Stories of Hope from Parents of Premature Babies* (Griffin Trade Paperbacks) so parents could share their situation. Above all else, though having a preemie is very stressful, parents should try to focus on the baby and enjoy every minute of watching the baby develop.

Q *What can parents do to reduce their risk of having a premature baby? Which risk factors can they control in their lives?*

industrialized countries with respect to infant mortality, even with our sophisticated medical technology. The African American infant mortality rate in 2002 was 13.8, almost twice the overall rate of 7.0 deaths per 1,000 live births. The rate for whites and Hispanics was about 5.7 deaths per 1,000 live births (National Center for Health Statistics, 2005). Infant mortality is related to poor or absent prenatal care, teenage pregnancy, poor nutrition, risky health behaviors during pregnancy, and higher rates of prematurity and low-birth-weight births. Experts agree that the steps that would reduce rates of prematurity and low birth weight would also reduce the rates of infant mortality.

Prenatal care is important for all pregnant mothers and their babies. Physicians can monitor the mother's health and the baby's growth and development, and they can help the mother understand how to avoid risks and maintain a healthy pregnancy.

Having a Healthy Baby

Although it is not possible to prevent all of the problems that newborns face, one thing is for certain: Access to and appropriate use of good-quality prenatal care results in healthier babies. In prenatal visits, practitioners can effectively identify and address many risk factors for problems during pregnancy. Again, these include poor nutrition; smoking, alcohol use, and drug use; exposure to environmental toxins; and maternal infections, illnesses, and pregnancy-related conditions that put the fetus at risk. Another important component of prenatal care is education. Education can increase the mother's knowledge of how the baby is developing, what she and her partner can do to improve their odds of having a healthy baby, and what options she has for labor and delivery. Participation in prepared childbirth classes and the supportive involvement of the woman's partner and family can enhance this education. Further, making healthy lifestyle choices even before a woman becomes pregnant can often avert some birth complications. Although the medical community has made astonishing strides in the treatment of many problems suffered by newborns, it is far more effective and desirable to prevent such problems from happening in the first place.

We have some good news to report on this point: More women are now getting prenatal care. Overall, in 2003, 84 percent of pregnant women received prenatal care, and this was up from 76 percent in 1990. The percentage of Hispanic and African American women who received care increased from about 60 in 1990 to nearly 77 percent in 2003 (National Center for Health Statistics, 2005). Although there is a way to go before all women have early prenatal care, rates of care are clearly improving.

Think About Beverly...

How would Beverly benefit by receiving good prenatal care? List several specific risks that might be avoided or reduced if she had good care.

■ Let's Review . . .

1. Preterm births are defined as all births that occur before _____ weeks of gestation.
   - a. 40
   - b. 38
   - c. 37
   - d. 35

2. Very low-birth-weight babies are those who are born weighing less than:
   a. 2 pounds.   b. 3½ pounds.
   c. 5½ pounds.   d. 7½ pounds.

3. Generally, the babies who are at the greatest risk are those who are born:
   a. preterm.
   b. low in birth weight.
   c. small for their gestational age.
   d. before 36 weeks of gestation and under 5 pounds.

4. Which of the following is NOT a risk factor related to infant mortality?
   a. poor prenatal care
   b. poor nutrition
   c. premature and low-birth-weight births
   d. births that occur between 38 and 40 weeks of gestation

5. **True or False:** In the United States, there are no ethnic differences in the rates of prematurity or infant mortality.

6. **True or False:** With good prenatal care, it is possible to control or avoid some of the risk factors associated with infant mortality and preterm and low-birth-weight births.

Answers: 1. c, 2. b, 3. c, 4. d, 5. F, 6. T

Growth of the Body and Brain

Whether they are full-term and healthy or premature and small, most babies grow very rapidly during the first year. In this section, we focus on physical growth. We look first at changes in height and weight, and then we discuss the importance of breastfeeding and other issues related to nutrition. We continue by exploring the intricate processes related to the growth of the brain and nervous system.

As you study this section, ask yourself these questions:

- What changes occur in height and weight during the infant and toddler years?

- Is bottlefeeding just as nutritious as breastfeeding? Why or why not?

- What are the main parts of the brain, and what are their basic functions?

- How does the brain shape the complex neural circuits that are necessary to process information and organize behavior?

Physical Growth

At birth, the average newborn weighs 7½ pounds, males weighing about half a pound more than females. Newborns lose a slight amount of weight in the first days after birth. During these early days, newborns spend almost all of their time sleeping; also, it takes time for newborns to adjust to the process of feeding. If they are breast-fed, their mothers' milk production is low the first few days. The main benefit of the initial breastfeedings is to pass antibodies from the mother's milk to the baby. These antibodies will help the newborn fend off illnesses and infections. After the mother's milk production increases and the newborn adjusts to life outside the womb, weight returns to birth levels—usually by about 2 weeks of age.

Figure 4.3 graphs weight and length gain across the first three years after birth. As you can see, babies double their birth weight by the time they are 5 months old. Changes in length are even more rapid. On average, newborns measure just under

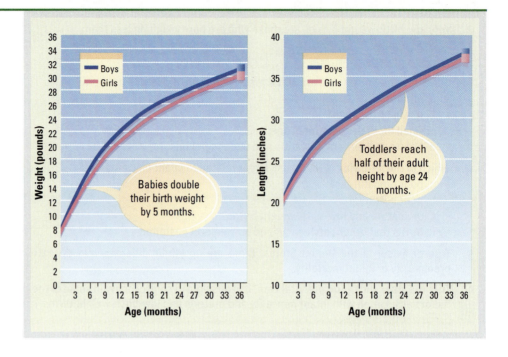

20 inches in length and add another 50 percent in their first year. By 2 years of age, children have already attained about half of their adult height.

Feeding and Nutrition

Nearly all health officials agree that human breast milk provides the best form of nutrition for most infants. Considering the scientific evidence, the American Academy of Pediatrics (2005) noted that human milk is better than any other form of infant formula or supplement for the general growth, health, and development of infants. Breast milk provides all of the nutrients, calories, protein, and fat that young infants need, in a balance that is easy for new babies to digest.

During the first few days of breastfeeding, the mother's milk contains a high concentration of **colostrum,** a thick, yellowish substance that contains important

colostrum
A thick, yellowish substance in breast milk containing important antibodies.

Newborn babies average about 20 inches in length and weigh an average of 7½ pounds. Children reach half of their adult height by the time they are 2 years old.

antibodies that are passed to the newborn baby. These antibodies offer infants protection against a variety of infections, viruses, and illnesses. After about three days, mothers produce a higher volume of milk, and the milk becomes thinner and lighter in color. Although the milk is now not as concentrated with colostrum, important antibodies continue to be passed from the mother to the baby for the duration of breastfeeding.

Babies who are breastfed are at lower risk for a variety of infant diseases and illnesses, including diarrhea, respiratory infections, ear infections, diabetes, lymphoma, and sudden infant death syndrome (American Academy of Pediatrics, 2005). There are also important health benefits for the mother, which may include faster recovery of the uterus, less blood loss after delivery, earlier return to prepregnancy weight, reduced risks of ovarian and breast cancers, and a delay in the next ovulation (which can help to increase the spacing to the next pregnancy). The academy noted that by improving the health of both infants and mothers, breastfeeding can reduce health care costs and the number of days parents miss from work to care for themselves or sick infants.

The academy also concluded that

Breast milk has many benefits for young infants.

- breastfeeding should begin as soon as possible after birth, preferably within the first hour;

- during the first six months after birth, breast milk is usually all that is needed to provide nutrition for optimal growth and development for the infant (water, juice, and other supplements are not necessary these first six months for most infants who are breastfed);

- from 6 to 12 months of age, iron-rich solid foods should be introduced gradually;

- breastfeeding should continue at least until the infant is 12 months of age and as long thereafter as the infant and mother desire.

Infants weaned before 12 months of age should receive iron-enriched infant formula (not cow's milk). Breastfeeding might not be convenient when mothers are working or are away from their babies for long periods during the day. In many of these situations, mothers can still pump their breast milk and store it so it can be given to infants by bottle.

How many babies are breastfed? Results from a recent U.S. survey are presented in Figure 4.4. As you can see, fewer than half are being breastfed at 3 months, and well less than one quarter at 12 months. Younger mothers and mothers who are African American are less likely to breastfeed their babies. Although this is not shown in the figure, the survey also found that mothers are more likely to breastfeed when they are married, have more education, or have higher family incomes. They are also more likely to breastfeed when their choice is supported by their husbands or partners. In one recent study, mothers' choices to breastfeed were related more strongly to what their partners thought they should do than to the mothers' own attitudes or intentions about breastfeeding (Rempel & Rempel, 2004). Although the choice is ultimately the mothers', it is clear that partners play an important role in supporting women's choices to breastfeed or bottle-feed.

Worldwide, there is a push to increase the rates of breastfeeding, especially in poor countries, where many infants are malnourished. In the poorer areas of central Africa, for example, only about 5 percent of infants under 4 months of age are exclusively breastfed, while in the more affluent countries of Egypt and Saudi Arabia, the rate is just over 60 percent (World Health Organization, 2003). A challenge in poorer countries is to provide proper nutrition to women who are pregnant and nursing so that they can produce sufficient breast milk. When babies are bottle-fed, a challenge is to

your **perspective**
Think about any families you know that have young babies. Are they feeding breast milk to their babies, or are they using infant formulas? What are the main factors that you think led to their choice?

Figure 4.4 •
Breastfeeding Rates by
Age and by Ethnicity
Percent of U.S. infants being breastfed at 3, 6, and 12 months of age. At 3 months, "exclusive breastfeeding" means that the infant receives breast milk alone (no supplements). At 6 and 12 months, percentages are for infants receiving breast milk as part of their nutrition. (National Center for Chronic Disease Prevention and Health Promotion, 2004.)

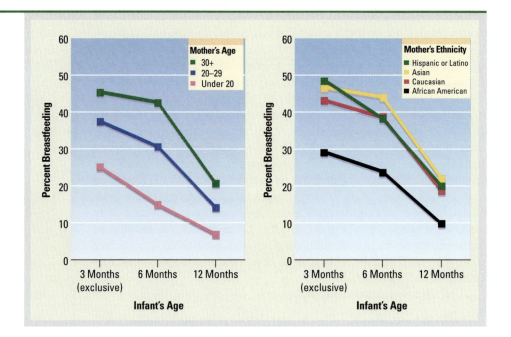

educate mothers to mix formulas properly so that they use clean water and do not try to stretch their supply by watering down the infant formula. Watered-down formulas do not provide infants the calories, nutrients, and other nutritional elements they need for healthy growth.

Although breast milk is the healthy choice for most infants, there are a few situations in which mothers are advised to use infant formulas instead of breastfeeding. Some infectious diseases can be spread through breast milk. Mothers with HIV, for example, should not breastfeed their babies. Mothers with conditions such as tuberculosis, hepatitis B, and chickenpox should consult their doctors before breastfeeding. Mothers who are receiving medications for high blood pressure, cancer, anxiety, depression, and even migraine headaches should also consult their physicians because harmful products from some of these medications can be passed to the infant through

Breastfeeding rates are low in many of the poorer nations of the world. When mothers use infant formulas, a challenge is to find sanitary water to mix with the formula. Mothers sometimes dilute the formula to try to stretch their supply, but this deprives infants of the calories, nutrients, and other nutritional elements they need.

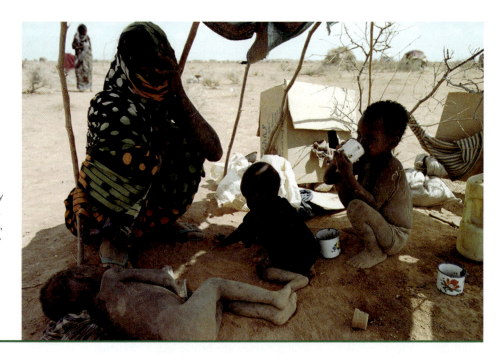

breast milk. In other cases, infants who inherit certain metabolic disorders (e.g., phenylketonuria or galactosemia) might require special formulas designed to help them avoid problems with their disorders. Finally, in Chapter 3, we mentioned that polychlorinated biphenyls (PCBs) are toxic industrial chemicals that can leach into groundwater and enter the food chain. These chemicals are absorbed by fish and eventually consumed by some pregnant and nursing mothers. The chemicals then pass to infants through breast milk. Exposure to PCBs has been linked to a variety of neurological and cognitive impairments in infants. This is just one of many reasons why a clean and healthy environment is important.

Except for conditions such as those that we just described, infants should receive only breast milk for the first four to six months. After that, baby cereals, mild-flavored vegetables, and fruits are good choices for first solid foods that can be added to the diet. Avoid foods that are high in sugar, fat, or salt. Also foods should be soft or diced small enough to avoid choking. Toward the end of the first year, infants enjoy finger foods such as cheese, plain crackers, cooked vegetables, and sliced fruits. By 2 years of age, most toddlers are having meals at the table, eating most of the same foods as the rest of the family. Although the toddlers might still be breastfeeding, breast milk is no longer their main source of calories and nutrition.

Think About Beverly...

What would you recommend to Beverly about breastfeeding her baby? What would you need to know about her situation to make a good recommendation?

Structure of the Brain and Nervous System

The brain and nervous system are the structures that give rise to all of our thoughts, emotions, and behaviors. The most complicated organ in the body, the brain is one of the first structures to form when tissue differentiation begins in the embryo, and at birth, the brain and head are already more than half their adult sizes. In Figure 4.5, you can see that the head represents one fourth of the newborn's total length but only one eighth of the adult's height. The cephalocaudal (head-to-tail) pattern is evident here. At birth, the brain and head region are much further along in growth and development than the trunk and legs are.

The study of how the brain grows and forms the intricate web of connections necessary to code our thoughts, memories, and motor actions is one of the most fascinating areas of science today. How does the brain grow and form internal connections? If the proper experiences are not available for infants, will their brains develop normally? In this section, we outline the major structures in the brain and describe how the brain forms in early development.

The major structures in the human brain are shown in Figure 4.6. The brain and the spinal cord together form the central nervous system. The *spinal cord* is the body's "information superhighway"—it allows vast amounts of information to be exchanged between the body and the brain. At the top of the spinal cord, the *brain stem* controls automatic functions (such as breathing and heart rate) and regulates the general level of alertness throughout the higher levels of the brain. The *cerebellum*, on the back of the brain, controls posture, body orientation, and complex muscle movements. The *cerebral cortex* is the "gray matter" that forms the top portion of the brain; it is divided into four major lobes (frontal, temporal, parietal,

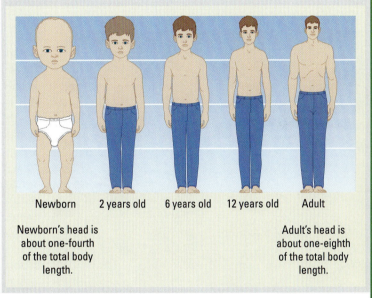

Newborn   2 years old   6 years old   12 years old   Adult

Newborn's head is about one-fourth of the total body length.

Adult's head is about one-eighth of the total body length.

Figure 4.5 • Changing Head/Body Proportions
The newborn's head is relatively large in proportion to the rest of the body. The cephalocaudal pattern of development is apparent here: the head and brain grow early, and the lower body grows more rapidly later. This gives the brain a head start in forming the complicated circuits that will govern movements, thoughts, and emotions.

This image from a scanning electron micrograph shows the web of connections that forms among neurons in the human brain. You can see the cell bodies (yellow) and the complex web of axons and dendrites that send messages throughout the web.

neurons
Specialized cells that process information and allow communication in the nervous system.

and occipital). The many convolutions (folds) in the cortex allow a greater amount of surface area to fit within the confines of the skull. The cortex is actually a thin layer of material, less than one eighth of an inch thick, so it is important that its surface area be maximized.

Many areas within the cortex have specialized functions. The motor area, in the middle of the cortex, controls voluntary muscle movements from raising the eyebrows to wiggling the toes. Just behind the motor area is the somatosensory area, which registers sensory input from all areas of the body. Wernicke's area processes speech input, and Broca's area organizes articulation for speech output. The visual area in the back of the brain receives messages from the eyes for visual processing. The large frontal lobe is involved in organizing, planning, and other executive functions that are important in higher-level thinking, problem solving, and creativity. Although researchers continue to discover specialized functions of various parts of the brain, it is also clear that most of our thoughts, perceptions, emotions, and memories are governed by complex communications occurring throughout the brain.

At the microscopic level, communication throughout the nervous system is controlled by specialized cells called **neurons.** The process involves neural impulses (electrical impulses) that travel through the neurons and neurotransmitters (chemical messengers) that transmit the impulses from one neuron to another. Neurons have three main parts, as shown in Figure 4.7. Dendrites are branchlike structures that receive input from other neurons. The cell body contains the nucleus and governs the function of the neuron. The axon, a relatively long fiber, carries electrical impulses that send messages to other cells. Mature axons are covered by a myelin sheath, a fatty substance that insulates the axon and speeds the axon's transmission of electrical

Figure 4.7 • Parts of a Neuron Each neuron in the brain and nervous system contains a cell body, dendrites, and an axon. Dendrites receive input from neighboring cells. Messages move down the length of the axon to the terminal buttons, and across the synapses to neighboring cells. (Adapted from Fabes & Martin, 2003.)

activity. The end of the axon branches out to form terminal buttons. Synapses are the open spaces between terminal buttons of one neuron and dendrites of the next neuron. When the electrical impulse reaches the end of the axon, it causes the release of chemical neurotransmitters from the terminal buttons. The neurotransmitters flow across the synapse to the dendrites, where they can stimulate or inhibit the response of the neighboring cells. This process of electrochemical stimulation allows neurons to communicate throughout the nervous system.

Forming the Brain and Nervous System

Now that you're familiar with the major parts of the nervous system, let's step back into prenatal development and take a look at how the brain forms and develops. At about 4 weeks after conception, the human embryo folds over to form a *neural tube*. The neural tube will later develop into the central nervous system (the brain and spinal cord). By 7 weeks after conception, neurons have begun to form at the neural tube. By 10 weeks, some of the neurons begin migrating to the top of the tube, where they form the first layer of the cerebral cortex. The cortex will eventually have six layers of neurons. The innermost layers form first. As more neurons grow, they migrate past the first layers to create the outer layers. New neurons form at an enormous pace. By 20 weeks of gestation, the cerebral cortex has approximately 80 billion neurons, and this is the approximate number that infants are born with (Kolb, 1999). To get to such a huge number, the brain needs to gain an

About four weeks after conception, the embryo folds over to form the neural tube. In another few weeks, neurons begin to form in the neural tube; later, they migrate to the top of the tube to form the beginnings of the brain.

your perspective

In your opinion, does brain growth allow children's thought processes to improve, or does exercising thought processes stimulate the brain to grow? What kinds of evidence would you need to have to address this question?

synaptogenesis
One form of neuron maturation in which dendrites and axons branch out to form an enormously large number of connections with neighboring neurons.

average of over half a million neurons per minute after neurons begin to form in week 7!

The focus of brain development now shifts from the creation of new neurons to the growth of connections among the neurons. By 20 weeks, axons and dendrites have begun growing (Huttenlocher, 1999). By 23 weeks, the first synapses have formed. The formation of new synapses is called **synaptogenesis.** Dendrites and axons grow longer and branch out to form an enormously large number of synapses with neighboring neurons. Thousands of synapses can form rather randomly as the axons of one neuron come into proximity with dendrites from another (Huttenlocher, 1999). Although the first synapses begin to form by the 23rd week of pregnancy, the process of synaptogenesis doesn't accelerate until late in pregnancy, and most synapses form after birth. By 31 weeks into pregnancy (only 7 to 9 weeks before a full-term birth), the cerebral cortex has grown enough that it begins to fold inside the skull, forming the convolutions that characterize this part of the brain. At birth, the newborn's brain has the same outward appearance as an adult's brain, although inside, much growth has yet to occur.

a social policy perspective

Can Mozart Stimulate Neural Connections in Infants?

In his 1999 budget, then Georgia Governor Zell Miller proposed that the state spend $105,000 to send a CD or cassette of classical music home with every baby born in the state. Miller commented that "[n]o one questions that listening to music at a very young age affects the spatial, temporal reasoning that underlies math and engineering and even chess" and that "[h]aving that infant listen to soothing music helps those trillions of brain connections to develop" (Sack, 1998).

Does research evidence support Miller's claims? Frances Rauscher and her colleagues published a series of intriguing studies suggesting that extensive music training significantly enhanced the spatial-temporal skills of preschool children. These researchers also found that listening to a Mozart sonata improved college students' spatial-reasoning IQ scores by eight to nine points (Rauscher, Shaw, & Ky, 1993, 1995; Rauscher et al., 1997). The spatial-reasoning scores involved were on tests of reasoning about proportions, ratios, and other concepts in mathematics. Improvements in these skills after exposure to classical music has been labeled the

"Mozart effect." Reports about the Mozart effect and about how early experience wires the developing brain led the proactive governor of Georgia to propose jump-starting infants' brain development with classical music.

But will it work? For the college students, the benefit of listening to classical music was temporary, lasting only 10 to 15 minutes (Rauscher et al., 1997), and several other researchers have been unable to replicate the Mozart effect (e.g., Nantais & Schellenberg, 1999; Steele, Bass, & Crook, 1999). Still, the excitement over the initial findings prompted the Florida legislature to pass a law requiring that toddlers in state-run schools hear classical music every day (Goode, 1999).

Q *On the basis of information in this chapter, how would you suggest that state and local governments, other agencies, schools, and parents enhance brain development in infants and toddlers? What information would you use to support new social policies in this area?*

Myelination is the growth of the myelin sheath around the axon. The myelin sheath insulates the axon, which more than triples the speed of transmission of the impulse and communication with other neurons (Bornstein & Arterberry, 1999). Although most axons are myelinated by birth, some areas of the brain are not completely myelinated for several years. For example, the motor and sensory areas in the cortex are still forming myelin until about 4 months after birth. It is not until after the motor areas are myelinated (after 4 months) that babies accomplish coordinated motor actions such as sitting, reaching, and standing. The frontal lobe is probably one of the last areas in the brain to be completely myelinated; some areas in the frontal lobe are still forming myelin all the way into our early 20s (National Research Council and Institute of Medicine, 2000).

Here is an interesting fact: Human beings lose half of their neurons before they are even born! Before birth, neurons proliferate at a tremendous rate and migrate to their final destinations, where they form the structures in the brain and the rest of the nervous system. But during migration and during periods of heavy synaptogenesis, about half of our neurons die. Researchers refer to this process as **programmed cell death** (Kandel, Schwartz, & Jessell, 2000). Neural activity determines which neurons will survive. The brain diverts its energy supplies toward the neurons that are more useful and active; the neurons that are less important or not very active begin to lose energy and die. Genetics provides an overabundance of neurons, and the brain manages to chisel away the excess until the final form is achieved.

Some years ago, a Georgia governor pushed for legislation aimed at enriching the environments of all newborn babies. To see how far his policy went, take a look at the Social Policy Perspective box called "Can Mozart Stimulate Neural Connections in Infants?"

myelination
A form of neuron maturation in which the fatty insulation (myelin sheath) grows around the axons.

programmed cell death
Process by which many neurons die during periods of migration and heavy synaptogenesis.

Think About Beverly...

What would you tell Beverly about the development of the brain and nervous system? How could this information be useful to her as she strives to enhance her baby's development?

■ Let's Review . . .

1. Children reach about half of their adult height by the time they are:
   - a. 1 year old.
   - b. 2 years old.
   - c. 5 years old.
   - d. 8 years old.

2. In the United States, how many mothers follow the recommendation of the American Academy of Pediatrics and breastfeed their babies until the babies are at least 12 months of age?
   - a. fewer than one quarter
   - b. about half
   - c. a little more than half
   - d. about two thirds

3. According to health experts, when should parents first introduce juices, soft foods, or other supplements to their breastfed babies?
   - a. after the first month
   - b. after 3 months
   - c. after 6 months
   - d. after 12 months

4. The first synapses form in the brain at around:
   - a. 10 weeks of gestation
   - b. 15 weeks of gestation
   - c. 23 weeks of gestation
   - d. 30 weeks of gestation

5. **True or False:** Compared to other babies, those who are breastfed are more likely to have a variety of infant diseases and illnesses.

6. **True or False:** Programmed cell death is nature's way of improving the efficiency of the brain as it develops.

Answers: 1. b, 2. a, 3. c, 4. c, 5. F, 6. T

Sensory Capabilities

When parents hold their newborn babies, they often wonder what their babies can see and hear and what their newborns can process with their other sensory modalities. In this section, we cover the basic sensory capabilities of newborn babies and track how some of these capabilities change during the infancy period. We return to this topic again in Chapter 5, where we describe how researchers study perceptual development and summarize what researchers have learned about how well infants and toddlers coordinate information across different sensory modalities.

As you study this section, ask yourself these questions:

- How clearly do infants see? How well do they see colors and depth?
- How well can infants hear? How early can they distinguish different sounds?
- When do infants begin to recognize smells and react to different odors? Can they distinguish different flavors?

Basic Components of Vision

How Clear Is Their Vision? One of the fundamental questions in perception concerns **visual acuity**—the ability to see fine detail. You are probably familiar with the standard eye chart used to measure visual acuity. According to this chart, a person with normal, 20/20 vision can read a certain row of letters on the chart from 20 feet away. A person with 20/40 vision would need to be 20 feet away to read what someone with normal vision could read from 40 feet away. But how can researchers test acuity in young infants who do not know the alphabet? To do this, researchers presented infants with the striped patterns shown in Figure 4.8. Each striped pattern was paired with a uniform gray square. If an infant doesn't have sufficient acuity to see the stripes, then the striped pattern blends to gray. As you can see in Figure 4.8, it is harder to see the most closely spaced stripes. (Back up several feet from your textbook, and the stripes will fade even more.) When infants can see the stripes, however, they tend to prefer to look at the stripes over the gray square. At a distance of 10 inches, 6-month-olds can see stripes as thin as 1/64 inch (and they prefer to look at those over the plain gray square), but 1-month-olds need the stripes to be at least 1/8 inch thick before they see them and prefer to look at them. Researchers estimate that visual acuity in newborns is somewhere between 20/150 and 20/600. Infants reach 20/20 vision by 6 to 12 months (Cohen, DeLoache, & Strauss, 1979). Even though acuity is poor in the first months, Hainline (1998) reminds us that when "development proceeds normally, infant vision seems perfectly adequate for the things that infants need to do" (p. 42), such as locate a caregiver, see a food source, or lock in on a smiling face.

visual acuity
The ability to see fine detail.

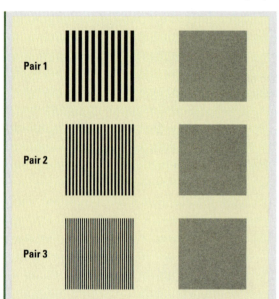

Figure 4.8 • Patterns Used to Test Visual Acuity in Infants Researchers determine which set of stripes infants differentiate from the plain gray square (Fantz, 1961).

Can They See Different Colors? It is unclear how well newborn infants are able to distinguish among various colors. Studies have found that newborns prefer to look at green, yellow, or red over gray (Adams, Maurer, & Davis, 1986). However, other evidence indicates that newborns can distinguish red from white but not blue, green, or yellow from white (Adams, Courage, & Mercer, 1994). Most of the evidence collected in the last few decades suggests that the photopigments in the eye that are necessary for normal color vision are present by at least 3 months, and it is safe to say that color vision is relatively mature by 6 months (Kellman & Arterberry, 2006; Suttle, Banks, & Graf, 2002).

How Deep Is That Drop? Early Depth Perception. When do infants first begin to perceive depth? Do they need to learn the dangers of deep drops, such as a set of stairs, through trial-and-error learning? The classic research on depth perception was Eleanor Gibson and Richard Walk's (1960) visual cliff experiment. Similar to the photo in Figure 4.9, a heavy sheet of glass extended across a solid surface and a deep drop-off. Infants from 6 to 14 months of age were tested. The researchers placed each infant in the middle; then the baby's mother called, first from one side and then the other. All of the 6-month-olds crawled out onto the solid side to reach their mothers, but they refused to crawl onto the deep side. Many cried, but still they didn't venture over the visual cliff. Gibson and Walk concluded that depth perception is available by the time infants learn to crawl. A decade later, other researchers demonstrated that infants just under 2 months of age could see the difference between the deep and solid sides (Campos et al., 1970). They placed infants face-down on each side of the visual cliff and measured their heart rates. Infants showed significantly more slowing of their heart rates on the deep side. In infants, heart rate deceleration indicates engrossed attention. Although it was clear that these young infants could perceive depth, it seems that they were more intrigued by than afraid of the "cliff."

What visual cues can infants use to perceive depth in the visual cliff experiments? Infants are first sensitive to cues involving the motion of objects, such as motion parallax: As the head and eyes move, the elements on the solid side of the visual cliff move more rapidly across the field of vision. Other studies find that infants as young as 1 month old show avoidance (e.g., blinking their eyes) in the face of approaching objects (Náñez & Yonas, 1994). A little later, by 3 to 4 months of age, infants can judge depth using *binocular disparity*—the difference between the images projected on the two eyes (Fox et al., 1980). Finally, there are *pictorial cues*—the relative size and density of the pattern elements shown beneath the glass. Neurological development and experience both play important roles in facilitating depth perception. As Bornstein and Arterberry (1999) put it, "no matter how early in life depth perception can be demonstrated, the ability still rests on some experience, and no matter how late its emergence, it can never be proved that only experience has mattered" (p. 238).

Figure 4.9 • Visual Cliff
A "visual cliff" like this was used in the classic study of depth perception by Gibson and Walk (1960). How can you tell whether the infant can see the deep drop under the glass?

How Well Do Infants Hear?

Research on young infants' auditory capabilities lets us draw several conclusions (Aslin, 1987). First, the auditory system is functional several weeks before birth; researchers have found that auditory stimuli such as loud sounds produce changes in fetal heart rate and brain-wave activity. Second, by 6 months of age, infants are capable of responding to a broad range of sounds. Even the youngest infants easily distinguish among rattles, voices, songs, and many other environmental noises. Infants seem to prefer more complex sounds (Richard et al., 2004). However, infants cannot yet detect very faint sounds, such as the softest of whispers, and they need changes in loudness and frequency (pitch) to be greater before they can detect these changes. For example, infants 6 to 9 months of age can barely detect a frequency change of 2 percent, but adults can detect a 0.5 percent change.

If you listen to adults speaking to infants, you will notice that adults take these developmental differences into account in a special style of speech: child-directed speech. In **child-directed speech** adults move close to the infant, speaking slowly, clearly, and with exaggerated changes in intonation. The "singsong" quality of child-directed speech provides greater changes in loudness and frequency, inducing infants to be more attentive.

A third characteristic of early auditory perception is that infants and young children might in fact be more sensitive than adults to higher frequencies of sound (e.g., 20,000 Hz). Sensitivity to higher frequencies begins to decline around the age of 6 years. Fourth, infants are able to locate sounds in the environment by turning their head or eyes in the direction of the sound source. Interestingly, this ability declines from birth to 2 months of age; then it improves again around 4 months of age. This trend might be due to the loss of the orienting reflex, which is controlled by lower brain centers. Then, as the higher cortex develops, the lower brain centers are overridden; this results in greater voluntary search behaviors (Aslin, 1987).

Researchers have devoted extensive study to infant reactions to the human voice. Newborns prefer the voices of their own mothers to the voices of unfamiliar females (DeCasper & Fifer, 1980). By 2 months, infants show a preference for speech with the rising and falling inflections typical of child-directed speech (Sullivan & Horowitz, 1983). At 4 months, infants prefer to listen to human voices over silence or white noise (Colombo & Bundy, 1981). By 5 months of age, infants can recognize their own names being spoken amid other names but only if their name is spoken more loudly than the other words (Newman, 2005).

A particularly intriguing experiment was conducted by DeCasper and Spence (1986). These researchers asked pregnant women to read aloud a particular children's story (e.g., *The Cat in the Hat*) twice each day during the last six weeks of pregnancy. Two to three days after birth, the experimenters tested the newborns for their recognition of the story. They connected a pacifier to an electronic switch that could activate one of two sound tracks. One sound track was a recording of the newborn's mother reading the familiar story (*The Cat in the Hat*). The other track was a recording of the mother reading a new story (e.g., *The King, the Mice, and the Cheese*). Newborns could choose which story to activate by adjusting their rate of sucking on the pacifier.

child-directed speech
The special singsong way in which adults and older children talk to infants, speaking slowly, clearly, and with exaggerated intonation.

This infant is participating in an experiment on auditory perception. By adjusting how fast he sucks on the pacifier, he can activate one of two tape recordings played into the headphones. If he adjusts his sucking rate, that is evidence that he hears the difference and is working to listen to one sound over the other.

For some, slower sucking would activate the familiar story; for others, this required faster sucking. In both cases, newborns adjusted their rate of sucking as required to activate the familiar story. Because both sound tracks were recordings of the mother's voice, the infants must have been choosing on the basis of certain qualities (e.g., pace) they heard in the stories. Further, these infants still preferred the familiar story when the stories were recorded by unfamiliar female voices. These results indicate that auditory perception before birth was adequate to process and retain the acoustic qualities of the story and that the newborns' perception and memory were sufficient to differentiate the two sound tracks and recognize which one was familiar. Quite a task for a baby only 2 to 3 days old!

Smell and Taste

Immediately after birth, their facial expressions show that that newborn babies react to certain odors in a manner similar to adults. Newborns show positive facial expressions in response to the aromas of bananas and butter, positive or indifferent responses to vanilla, some rejection to fishy odors, and complete disgust to rotten eggs (Bornstein & Arterberry, 1999; Steiner, 1979). In other experiments, Richard Porter and his colleagues studied newborns' recognition of their parents' smells. For example, parents in one study wore gauze pads under their arms for several hours; then researchers used the pads in a smelling test with the parents' newborn babies (Cernoch & Porter, 1985). At the age of 2 weeks, breastfed babies turned their heads toward the smell of their mothers more than to the smell of unfamiliar females (mothers of other babies). The newborns did not show recognition of the smell of their fathers, however. Also, bottle-fed newborns did not show a preference for the smell of their mothers. These results demonstrate that infants are capable of discerning small differences in complicated odors, at least when they have close and repeated contact with the odor—as breastfed infants would have with the smell of their mothers. But the perception of smell might become functional even before this time. Infants as young as 3 to 4 days of age prefer the smell of breast milk to that of formula milk, regardless of whether they are breastfed or bottle-fed (Marlier & Schall, 2005). There is also intriguing evidence that, just as for audition, the fetal system is well enough developed sometime near the end of gestation to sense and store information about odors encountered before birth. For example, newborns prefer the smell of their own amniotic fluid over that of other infants (Schall, Marlier, & Soussignan, 1998).

It is obvious that this child does not care for the taste of this lemon. Reactions to basic categories of smell and taste are controlled in the lower brain centers of babies.

Infants show taste preferences immediately after birth, even before their first feedings (Steiner, 1979). When given a sweet solution, newborns smile and make sucking movements. Infants will suck longer to obtain a solution that is sweeter as opposed to one that is less sweet (Crook, 1987). With a sour taste, they purse their lips and wrinkle their noses. A bitter taste causes newborns to spit and make a face that indicates disgust and rejection. These early taste preferences seem to be governed by areas in the lower brain, because they appear even in infants who are born without a cerebral cortex (Steiner, 1979). Reaction to salty flavors develops later, usually by 4 months of age (Beauchamp et al., 1994).

Motor Development

When babies are born, they can turn their heads in the direction of interesting sounds, and they move their eyes to track the movements of some objects. Even in the first weeks, they are beginning to gain control over muscles in the head and neck area, but it will still be a while before they can coordinate muscles in the rest of their bodies. With some trial and error, newborns may be able to get their hands to their mouths to suck their fingers or thumbs, but they still can't control their arm and hand muscles well enough to reach out and grasp an object. They are months away from being able to stand up, walk, and run.

In this section, we trace the typical patterns of motor development—gains that infants and children make in the ability to control their muscle movements. We begin with the muscle reflexes that infants show in the early months. Next we move to the ability of infants to coordinate voluntary muscle movements involved in actions such as sitting, standing, and walking. We look at the role of early experience and other factors that govern these patterns of development. We end the section with a discussion of toilet training.

As you study this section, ask yourself these questions:

■ What kinds of reflexes do infants have soon after birth, and what functions do these reflexes serve?

■ What patterns are seen as infants and toddlers learn to control their movements? What factors govern this phase of motor development?

■ Can motor development be accelerated with early experience, or is the rate of development limited by the growth and maturation of the brain?

■ When are toddlers ready for toilet training? What is the best approach for parents to use in toilet training?

Reflexes: The Infant's First Coordinated Movements

Human infants are equipped at birth with several interesting reflexes. **Reflexes** are involuntary movements that are elicited by environmental stimuli such as sound, light, touch, and body position. If you touch a newborn's cheek, the infant's head will turn in the direction of the touch. This is called the *rooting reflex*. If anything touches an infant's lips, the infant automatically begins to suck—the *sucking reflex*. As you read earlier in this chapter, the cerebral cortex (the upper part of the brain), which governs voluntary muscle movements, is not well developed at birth. So at first, it is the lower brain centers (spinal cord, brain stem, and midbrain) that control infants' involuntary reflexes. What purposes do these reflexes serve? Some help the infant to find nourishment, some help the infant to exercise muscles, and still others may be protective mechanisms. Let's consider three classes of reflexes: *primitive, postural,* and *locomotor* (Gabbard, 1992).

Primitive reflexes include rooting and sucking. As we have described, both of these reflexes help infants to find nourishment. When the breast or bottle touches their cheek, infants turn their head to the source of nutrition. When the nipple touches their mouth, they begin to suck. Other primitive reflexes are most likely remnants from earlier evolutionary forms in which the reflexes might have served protective functions. The Moro reflex (or startle reflex), for example, occurs when an infant is startled by a loud noise or begins to fall. A sharp bang on the crib will cause infants to extend their arms and legs outward, spread their fingers and toes, then bring their limbs back to their bodies. You will see the same response if you hold an infant in your arms, face upward, and then drop your arms suddenly a few inches. (Be sure to catch the baby!) The grasping reflex occurs when an object touches an infant's palm; the baby's fingers will automatically wrap around the object and grip strongly. These reflexes might have helped our ancestors grab onto their mothers or catch hold of support when falling. Most primitive reflexes are functional in the later months of prenatal development; for example, fetuses suck their thumbs by the fourth prenatal month. These reflexes tend to disappear by about four months after birth as the higher cortical centers in the brain begin to take over voluntary control of muscle movements.

Several **postural reflexes** help infants to keep their heads upright, maintain their postural balance, and roll their heads in the direction of their body motion. One interesting example is the parachute reflex. If infants are held upright and then quickly tilted face down, they will reflexively extend their arms outward as if to balance and brace against the movement. Postural reflexes emerge by the age of 2 to 4 months and then disappear by 12 months.

During the first few months of life, infants will show crawling motions if they are lying on their stomachs and their feet are stroked. If they are upright with their feet touching a surface such as a tabletop or the floor, they take small steps. If held horizontal in water with their heads up, infants make swimming motions with their arms and legs. These crawling, stepping, and swimming reflexes are examples of **locomotor reflexes.** The locomotor reflexes tend to emerge during the first month or so after birth and then disappear again by 4 months of age.

There has been much debate about the functional significance of infant reflexes. Some theorists have argued that with practice, early reflexes will evolve into coordinated voluntary movements. Infants who are given regular practice with the stepping reflex, for example, tend to maintain the reflex longer and tend to show voluntary walking about a month earlier than infants who are not given extra practice (Zelazo, 1983; Zelazo, Zelazo, & Kolb, 1972). Reflexes may provide valuable exercise that strengthens the muscles and helps the nervous system to make connections between the brain and the muscle groups. Other researchers contend that the lag between the disappearance of most reflexes and the onset of similar voluntary movements shows that these two phases of motor development are independent. Some even claim that the early reflexes must be suppressed so that the brain can take voluntary control of the muscles (Pontius, 1973).

reflexes
Involuntary movements that are elicited by environmental stimuli.

primitive reflexes
Reflexes that help the infant to find nourishment or might have served protective functions during earlier periods of evolution.

postural reflexes
Reflexes that help infants to keep their heads upright, maintain balance, and roll their heads in the direction of their body motion.

locomotor reflexes
Infant reflexes that mimic locomotor movements such as crawling, stepping, and swimming.

your perspective
Which reflexes have you observed in infants you have known? What purposes are served by these reflexes?

This newborn is demonstrating the Moro reflex. When startled, she extends her arms and legs and spreads her fingers. Why do infants have this reflex?

Either way, pediatricians have long used the existence and disappearance of reflexes as early indicators of nervous system function. Remember from Chapter 3 that the Apgar test includes a measure of "reflex irritability" as part of the assessment of early functioning in newborns. The Brazelton Neonatal Behavioral Assessment Scale, designed to assess the health of infants, measures some 20 different reflexes. A lack of reflexive response, or a delay in the emergence or disappearance of certain reflexes, can signal a problem with neurological development.

Voluntary Movements: The Motor Milestones

When our children were newborn babies, we loved the way they wiggled and squirmed when we held and played with them. Many of their movements were jerky and somewhat erratic, but it was a joy to watch them stretch and exercise their tiny muscles. Newborns can typically move their eyes and turn their heads to find one's face or track the sound of one's voice. Put your finger in the palm of a newborn's hand, and the strength of the infant's grip (from the grasping reflex) will surprise you. When newborn babies are awake, their arms and legs seem to be constantly stretching and flexing, their fingers gripping and extending. These early arm and leg movements are spontaneous and involuntary, not directed at reaching at or holding particular objects. It will be several months before the infant can coordinate voluntary and purposeful behaviors like reaching for a toy or dumping out a box of blocks. Over the next months, babies' reflexes, spontaneous movements, and later voluntary movements gradually strengthen the babies' muscles and stimulate neurological development in their brains and nervous systems.

Figure 4.10 illustrates the major milestones in gross motor development across the first year of life. **Gross motor development** refers to the process of coordinating

gross motor development
Process of coordinating movements with the large muscles in the body.

Figure 4.10 • Gross Motor Milestones You can see the cephalocaudal (head-to-tail) pattern of development by looking at the average ages at which infants achieve each of these gross motor milestones. Notice that they gain control over the neck and head before the trunk, and the trunk before the legs.

movements with the large muscles in the body. These muscles control the larger parts of the body such as the head, neck, torso, arms, and legs. Later, we will discuss **fine motor development,** the development of the smaller muscles that control our more intricate movements (e.g., finger movements).

Gross motor development follows the cephalocaudal pattern that we discussed before (Frankenburg et al., 1992). By 1 month of age, the muscles in infants' necks are strong enough to allow the infants to hold their heads upright. Next, the muscles in the trunk become more coordinated. Infants can roll over by 3 months and sit upright without support by 6 months. Around 7 months the legs are strong enough to allow infants to crawl—pushing with their legs and dragging their bodies along the floor. At 7 months, babies also can stand by holding onto a table or other form of support.

For many parents, the most significant of the early motor milestones is the baby's first step. Most infants take their first unaided steps sometime around their first birthday. But it is important to know that these ages are averages, and the rates of development for individual babies vary considerably. For example, 25 percent of infants are walking well at 11 months; another 25 percent begin walking well at 13 months; and 10 percent do not walk proficiently until 15 months (Frankenburg et al., 1992). Individual genetics, different rates of neurological development, and opportunities to practice muscle movements all contribute to this variability. Pediatricians will, however, see serious delays in motor development as a potential indication of neurological or muscular deficits. To learn more about how to identify and treat developmental delays in motor development, read the Professional Perspective box on page 144 called "Career Focus: Meet a Physical Therapist."

A proximodistal, or nearer-to-farther (from the body's midline), pattern can be seen in the progress infants make in reaching and grasping. At first, they reach with their arms; next come the fine motor skills of grasping with the hands and fingers (Gabbard, 1992). In Figure 4.11, you can see that voluntary control over the upper arm is shown by 4 to 5 months. The infant has voluntary control over the upper arm

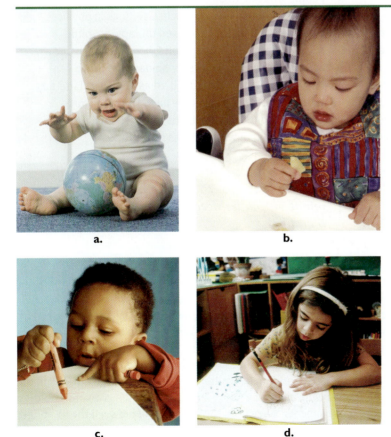

a.

b.

c.

d.

Figure 4.11 • Gross to Fine Motor Skills Gross-to fine-motor skills. The proximodistal (from nearer to farther from the body's center) pattern of development can be seen in the progress children make in reaching and grasping. (a.) Infants begin by reaching with both arms and using the palm to grasp objects. (b.) After gaining more fine motor control over the muscles in the hands and fingers, they can use the more effective pincer grasp. Later, they can (c.) hold smaller objects and (d.) produce intricate movements needed to write legibly.

Career Focus: Meet a Physical Therapist

Deanna Walsh
Madison, Wisconsin
Physical therapist at Meriter Hospital

What ages of children and what types of conditions do you work with? Are families involved in the children's therapy?

The youngest children I treat are premature infants, and the oldest may be up to 16 or 17 years old. I see children who are having a variety of movement problems. I see babies and children with torticollis (a tight muscle in their neck that restricts their movement), cerebral palsy, autism with associated movement difficulties, delays in their gross motor development (difficulty learning to crawl, walk, jump, etc.), spina bifida, muscular dystrophy, Down syndrome, other genetic syndromes that impact movement, and after surgery or fractures. The children I see may have problems with their balance or coordination, muscle weakness, muscle tightness, difficulty with mobility, or difficulty with specific movements. Some children require special equipment to make movement easier. This might include special braces or inserts in their shoes, crutches, walkers, adapted bicycles, or wheelchairs.

Typically, I see a child for one or two treatments per week, depending on the child's and family's needs. A great deal of my job is teaching families what they can do to help their child, since they are the people who are with the child most of the time. By involving families in their child's treatment, greater improvements are seen. Instead of working on an activity for one hour per week, the child will be incorporating it into their day, every day.

How do you determine whether a child is exhibiting delayed motor development?

I routinely use many different standardized tests when assessing a child's motor skills. Most tests address certain age groups and look at certain types of skills (e.g., balance, locomotor, coordination, and ball skills). I also observe the quality of a child's movements to determine whether she or he is having difficulty with mobility skills.

What education and training are needed to become a physical therapist?

Most physical therapy programs are now master's degree programs, and many are moving toward the doctorate level. Most include extensive clinical experience as part of the training, and this is typically where most students gain some hands-on experience working with children. Physical therapy is an excellent career for people who like to be involved with patients and their families. There are many practice settings in physical therapy—such as school-based therapy, hospital-based therapy, outpatient clinics, home health agencies, academics, research, nursing homes, and rehab centers. The great thing about all areas of physical therapy is that you get to help people meet their individual goals. Working with great kids and their families is an added benefit of working with pediatrics.

Q *What are some initial signs that parents can look for to determine whether their infant or toddler needs to see a physical therapist?*

and can reach out and pull an object in with both arms. At this age, infants wrap all four fingers and the thumb around the object in what is referred to as the palmar grasp. By 10 months, infants show the more advanced pincer grasp, using the thumb and the opposite forefinger. At 15 months, they can hold a writing implement (although they begin again with the palmar grasp) and make scribbles by using the large muscles in the upper arm. Later, children begin using the more precise "tripod" grasp for holding pencils and other writing implements: They hold the writing tool between the forefinger and thumb, and they steady the bottom of their hand on the writing surface. As you can see, control over the fine motor movements of the hands and fingers comes much later than control over the gross motor movements of the elbows, arms, and shoulders.

The cephalocaudal and proximodistal patterns in motor development mirror the progressive maturation of centers in the brain. Cells and connections in the part of the brain that controls muscle movements in the head and upper body tend to mature first. Neurological development then spreads, allowing control and coordination of muscles to proceed both downward and outward through the body. Of course, there are exceptions to every rule, and we point one out here. When young infants first start reaching for toys and other objects, they actually tend to reach with their feet first and do not try to reach with their hands until they are several weeks older (Galloway & Thelen, 2004). In general, however, motor development does tend to follow the head-to-tail and midline-out patterns of development.

Brain maturation also influences the appearance and disappearance of infant reflexes. The reflexes that are seen in early infancy are controlled mainly by pathways in the spinal cord, and the actions of these nerve pathways become inhibited once the higher cortical centers develop. The stepping reflex, for example, disappears as the motor area of the cortex matures enough to allow coordinated and voluntary movements of the legs. But is brain maturation the only factor driving motor development? Obviously not. For example, the disappearance of the stepping reflex is also related to weight gain during infancy. Infants who gain weight more rapidly tend to lose the stepping reflex earlier.

One group of researchers demonstrated this effect with 1-month-old infants. When they fitted these infants with leg weights that mimicked the amount of weight the infants would gain in the next few weeks, the stepping reflex diminished (Thelen, Fisher, & Ridley-Johnson, 1984). And when the researchers held other infants in water, the infants showed a more vigorous stepping reflex. The fatty leg tissue was more buoyant under water, so the reflex revived when the muscles were relieved of the extra weight load. Esther Thelen hypothesized that the normal disappearance of the stepping reflex is affected by the biomechanical load placed on the limbs and not caused entirely by maturation of the higher brain centers.

As we mentioned earlier, Philip Zelazo and his colleagues demonstrated that daily practice could strengthen the stepping reflex (Zelazo, Zelazo, & Kolb, 1972). Zelazo has even suggested that motor development may be subservient to cognitive development (Zelazo, 1983). Independent walking, for example, may occur only after infants develop certain information-processing and memory skills. According to this view, babies need to associate balance with stepping and to remember how to coordinate different body movements to walk successfully. So when it comes to motor development, cognitive practice may be as important as physical exercise and the strengthening of muscles.

Esther Thelen and her colleagues have proposed a dynamic systems theory (see Chapter 1) to describe the myriad interactive processes that are involved in motor development (Gershkoff-Stowe & Thelen, 2004; Thelen, 1989; Thelen & Smith, 2006). In this theory, coordinated movements such as reaching, crawling, walking, and throwing are dynamic actions that emerge from the complex interplay of individual muscles, nerve pathways, physical growth, learning, and motivation:

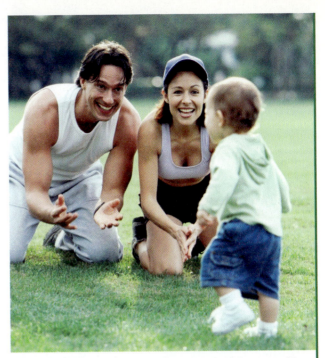

About half of all infants are taking their first steps alone at about 13 months of age. There is a good deal of variability, however, with some infants walking a few months earlier and some a few months later.

your perspective

Have you known an infant who began walking several months earlier or later than the average age of 13 months? What do you think caused this infant's timetable of development to be faster or slower than average?

- *Neurological development* gives infants the ability to exert voluntary control over their muscles.

- *Parental encouragement* and interesting objects in the environment motivate infants to raise their heads, turn their bodies, crawl, and take their first steps.

- *Opportunities to exercise* give babies the muscle strength they need to lift and control their growing limbs.

- *Maturation of cognitive systems* helps babies to remember where interesting objects are located and figure out how to coordinate their movements to get them.

Think About Beverly...

After her baby arrives, what could Beverly do to stimulate her baby's motor development?

The brain, the body, and the environment all work in concert to propel the child toward increased strength and coordination. Without the brain, the muscles won't move. Without muscular exercise, the brain won't develop. Without motivation, the child won't exercise. The important question is not which part of the system develops first, but rather how the various components work together to move the infant and child toward higher levels of development.

Cultural Differences in Early Experience

Because parenting practices differ across cultures, babies in some cultures receive more vigorous physical stimulation than do babies in other cultures. In Mali, for example, mothers often suspend babies by their arms or legs (which stretches the babies' muscles) and encourage babies to sit and stand at an early age (Bril & Sabatier, 1986). Researchers have also noted that some African cultures emphasize physical stimulation, and babies who are raised in these cultures are typically ahead of North American babies in the major motor milestones (Ainsworth, 1967; Rabain-Jamin & Wornham, 1993; Super, 1976).

Hopi Indians traditionally carried their infants on cradle boards like this one. What was the effect of this practice on their infants' ability to learn to walk?

In contrast, in some South American cultures, mothers are more protective of young infants and tend to limit their babies' opportunities to explore and exercise their motor skills. In Brazil, for example, researchers find that mothers carry their babies or hold the babies in their laps for a large part of the day. Many Brazilian mothers reportedly believe that sitting and standing positions can cause damage to the legs and spines of young infants, so they rarely allow their babies to sit or play on the floor by themselves (Santos, et al., 2001). During the first six months of infancy, these Brazilian babies lag behind their North American age-mates in motor skills such as sitting up and reaching for objects. By 8 months of age, however, they gain more physical exercise and catch up with babies raised in other cultures. Studies have found similar trends in babies in Chile (Andraca et al., 1998).

Infants among the Hopi tribe in Arizona and the Tewa of New Mexico take their first steps at about 14 months of age, or one to two months later than most other infants in North America (Dennis & Dennis, 1939/1991). For their classic study on cultural differences in motor development, Wayne and Marsena Dennis spent two summers living among the Hopi. In some villages, they found that Hopi mothers used the traditional practice of strapping their infants to cradle boards that the mothers then carried on their backs. For the first nine months of life, these infants spent most of their days restrained tightly on these boards, and they remained on the cradle boards even when they were nursing and when sleeping at night. Other Hopi villages were more "Americanized," and mothers in these villages had given up use of the cradle boards. Did the infants in these villages walk at an earlier age than the cradle board babies? Interestingly, the answer was no, not really: Use of the cradle board delayed the onset of walking by only two days on average (Dennis & Dennis, 1939/1991). Whether confined to the board or allowed to play and exercise more freely, all the Hopi infants took their first steps at about 14 months of age. As you can see, studies that investigate different cultures do not agree completely about the roles of physical practice and exercise in motor development.

Think About Beverly…
What advice would you give Beverly about providing exercise for her baby during the first year? Can exercise accelerate motor development significantly?

Toilet Training

Watching infants and toddlers move through the motor milestones is thrilling. Parents celebrate the first time their infants sit up, crawl, and stand on their own. And who can forget the excitement of those first few wobbly steps the toddler takes? For practical reasons, parents also celebrate a much less glamorous milestone: when their toddlers become toilet trained. As with crawling, walking, and other developmental milestones, toilet training develops from an interaction of physical maturity, cognitive understanding, cues and feedback from the environment, and motivation. Toilet training isn't solely a matter of motor development. This is a lesson that can be learned from the dynamic systems theory discussed earlier in the chapter.

Most toddlers gain voluntary control and coordination over the muscles that control their bladder and bowel movements by the time they are 18 to 24 months old. By this time, the toddlers are also walking well enough that they can get through the house and to the potty as the need arises. Once these physical developments have occurred, parents next need to assess their child's emotional and cognitive readiness. Can the child approach toilet training in a way that is positive and fairly relaxed? This is not the time to engage in a major power struggle with a testy 2-year-old, and children are not ready if they show fear of the potty or fear of bodily functions. Cognitive readiness is indicated when the child shows awareness of having soiled diapers, requests to be changed, asks to wear underwear, or shows a positive interest in the bathroom and toilet. It helps if the child is able to follow simple instructions and can stay dry for at least two or three hours during the day.

When the child seems ready for training, it's time to introduce the child to his or her own special potty (usually a child-sized potty chair), demonstrate or teach the basic skill, and be ready with lots of praise and rewards for a job well done. Most experts recommend a child-oriented approach to training, allowing the child to set the pace according to his or her own schedule of readiness (Brazelton, 1962; Stadtler, Gorski, & Brazelton, 1999).

Researchers studying a group of toddlers in the Milwaukee area found that at least half of girls showed an interest in using the toilet by 24 months of age and stayed dry during the day and night by 34 months (Schum et al., 2002). Boys achieved these milestones about two months later than girls. It is possible, however, for children to be trained at an even earlier age. In their review of other studies on this topic, the researchers conducting the Milwaukee study noted that the average age of daytime dryness was about 24 months during the 1950s (when parents tended to push children harder and use stricter methods). They also noted that children in some other countries

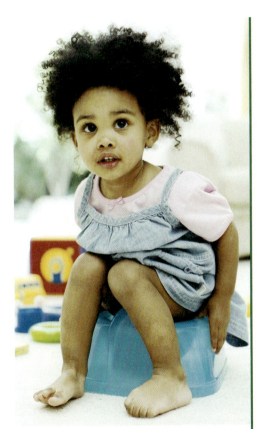

What do experts suggest about the best way to toilet train children?

your perspective

Do you think parents should push their toddlers to toilet train earlier, or do you think parents should follow the pace of the child? Why?

are trained earlier than most U.S. children and that many of the African American toddlers in their Milwaukee sample began training before 15 months of age. Although children can be pushed to train at an earlier age, most experts believe that there are psychological and emotional benefits to using a more child-oriented approach with most toddlers, even though it might delay training success by several months.

■ Let's Review . . .

1. What should you conclude about a 1-month-old infant who does not show the Moro reflex?
   a. This reflex normally does not emerge until 4 months, so the infant is developing normally.
   b. This reflex disappears by 3 weeks of age, so the infant is developing normally.
   c. Most infants do not show the Moro reflex, so there is no reason to be concerned.
   d. The infant may have a neurological problem or immaturity.

2. Which is the correct sequence of motor development for most infants?
   a. roll over, sit up, hold head up, walk
   b. hold head up, sit up, roll over, walk
   c. hold head up, roll over, sit up, walk
   d. hold head up, roll over, walk, sit up

3. Which of the following statements provides the best summary of the dynamic systems theory of motor development?
   a. Motor skills emerge from the combination of physical growth, learning, and motivation.
   b. Motor development is governed primarily by neurological development as maturation in the brain allows more coordinated motor movements.
   c. Motor development is governed primarily by experience as physical exercise stimulates the formation of neural circuits in the brain.
   d. Cognitive development precedes motor development; infants must first understand how to coordinate individual movements before they can execute complex motor skills.

4. **True or False:** Like most infants, Kelli learned to sit upright on her own before she learned to walk. This is an example of the proximodistal pattern of motor development.

5. **True or False:** Overall, children are being toilet trained at an earlier age today than they were 50 years ago.

Answers: 1. d, 2. c, 3. a, 4. F, 5. F

Thinking Back to Beverly . . .

Like most expectant parents, Beverly is concerned about how to stimulate her baby's development. With all the excitement generated by popular press reports about research on brain development, parents are eager to learn how experience helps to shape the communication pathways in the brain. During pregnancy, neurons will grow in the baby's brain, and synapses will begin to form to connect the neurons. The brain grows an overabundance of neurons, and half of the baby's neurons will die off in programmed cell death. Which neurons survive and which will die is determined partly by experience and the relative activity of the neurons, but this neuron loss is normal. Babies' brains use the variety of sights, sounds, and other sensations stimulated by the environment to govern brain growth and development, but Beverly should understand that stimulation is important throughout childhood, not just during the first year or two.

What about playing classical music during infancy? There is some slight evidence that classical music can stimulate spatial-reasoning and mathematics skills in preschool children and college students, but there is no evidence yet that this "Mozart effect" lasts over the long term or has the same impact on infants. At this point, we can say only that it probably won't hurt. The same goes for yoga and other exercise for infants. For example, practicing reflexes speeds the emergence of motor skills only slightly, so such classes probably do more for the social interaction between parent and baby than for the motor skills. The infant's nervous system and motor skills will develop well if the typical sources of stimulation are on hand: objects to manipulate, friendly voices and faces, hugs, things to climb on, and encouragement to explore a varied environment.

Unless there are conditions that prevent Beverly from breastfeeding, the expert advice is that Beverly should breastfeed her baby for at least the first year. Breast milk is all that her baby will need for the first six months, and then other foods and supplements can be introduced gradually. Experts also recommend that parents such as Beverly follow their children's pace when it comes to toilet training; toddlers learn this task relatively easily once they are physically and cognitively ready for the chore. These are some of the concepts and research findings that you might share with Beverly. Studying the chapter more closely, you can find even more helpful information.

■ Chapter Review . . .

How is prematurity defined, and what are the major risk factors associated with prematurity?

Premature infants can be defined as preterm (born before 37 weeks' gestation), low birth weight (weighing less than $5\frac{1}{2}$ pounds), very low birth weight (weighing less than $3\frac{1}{2}$ pounds), or small for gestational age (born below the tenth percentile for weight for their gestational age). SGA babies are especially at risk because something has prevented them from growing as well as would be expected, given the amount of time they spent in the uterus. A number of risk factors for preterm and low-birth-weight births have been identified. Several, such as lack of prenatal care, malnutrition, smoking, alcohol and drug use, and young maternal age, are controllable.

What is infant mortality, and how can it be reduced? How would prenatal care help?

Infant mortality refers to the number of babies who die before reaching 1 year of age. The rate is relatively high in the United States. Increasing access to and use of good prenatal care would reduce the rates of preterm and low-birth-weight births and would help to reduce infant mortality. With prenatal care, at-risk pregnancies can be identified early and parents learn how to reduce their risks by avoiding teratogens and engaging in healthy behaviors.

What are the main trends in physical growth during the infant and toddler years? What do experts recommend regarding breastfeeding versus bottle-feeding?

At birth, newborns average $7\frac{1}{2}$ pounds in weight and 20 inches in length. Weight doubles by 5 months of age, and children reach almost half of their adult height by 2 years of age. Health experts agree that human breast milk provides optimal nutrition and additional health benefits for infants and toddlers. Unless other conditions prevent healthy breastfeeding, infants should receive breast milk alone until 6 months; then juices and soft foods can gradually be introduced.

What are the major patterns that are seen in the formation of the brain and nervous system?

Development begins with the neural tube, which later forms the brain and spinal cord. Neurons form and migrate to the top of the neural tube to form the cerebral cortex. By 20 weeks of gestation, the cortex has nearly 80 billion neurons. Neurons will continue to proliferate, but many will later be lost through programmed cell death. Synaptogenesis (formation of synapses between neurons) begins after 23 weeks of gestation. Myelination of axons improves the neurons' capability to transmit information.

What is known about visual acuity, color vision, and depth perception in infants?

Newborn acuity is somewhat limited, with estimates ranging from 20/150 to 20/600. Normal 20/20 vision is achieved by 6 to 12 months of age. It is not clear how well newborns are able to distinguish various colors. Evidence suggests that color vision is adultlike by 3 to 6 months. Experiments with the visual cliff indicate that 2-month-olds can see the difference between the deep and shallow sides, and babies avoid the deep side by the time they can crawl (around 6 months). By 3 to 4 months, infants use binocular disparity to judge depth, and 1-month-olds show avoidance of approaching objects, indicating some sensitivity to depth and distance information.

What are the main conclusions about auditory capabilities of infants?

The auditory system is functional before birth, but young infants still need sounds to be louder; and to detect these changes, they need changes in intensity and frequency to be greater in comparison to the needs of adults. Infants might be more sensitive than adults to higher frequencies. Newborns prefer the voices of their own mothers, and they can recognize sounds that they heard while in the womb.

Can newborns differentiate between major odors and flavors?

Yes. For example, newborns react positively to the aromas of bananas and butter, but they reject the odors of fish and rotten eggs. Newborns prefer sweeter solutions but reject sour and bitter flavors.

What reflexes do infants have, and what is their significance?

Newborns show primitive reflexes (rooting, sucking, Moro, grasping, and Babinski) that normally disappear by 4 months of age. Rooting and sucking help newborns to obtain nourishment, but the other primitive reflexes are probably remnants from times earlier in evolution. Postural reflexes that help the baby to maintain balance and head direction emerge by 2 to 4 months of age and disappear by 12 months. Locomotor reflexes (crawling, stepping, swimming) emerge after birth and disappear by 4 months. These and other reflexes may provide exercise that helps to form connections between the muscles and brain; these connections will later support voluntary movements. When reflexes do not appear or disappear according to the usual timetable, neurological problems might be present.

What are the main patterns in the development of voluntary movements? What factors influence progress through the motor milestones?

Motor development generally proceeds according to cephalocaudal (head-to-tail) and proximodistal (near-to-far) patterns. Infants hold their heads up before they can sit alone, and they sit before they walk. They coordinate large muscles in the arms before gaining dexterity in the hands and fingers. Neurological development and opportunities to exercise muscle both contribute. According to dynamic systems theory, motor skills emerge from complex interactions among neurological development, physical growth, learning, and motivation. Cultural differences in exercise and stimulation can lead to small differences in attainment of motor milestones. Toilet training usually begins around age 2 years, and most toddlers can stay dry during the day by the time they are 3 years of age.

■ Key Terms

child-directed speech (138)
colostrum (128)
fine motor development (143)
gross motor development (142)
infant mortality (124)
locomotor reflexes (141)
low birth weight (123)
myelination (135)
neurons (132)

postural reflexes (141)
preterm birth (123)
primitive reflexes (141)
programmed cell death (135)
reflexes (141)
small for gestational age (SGA) (123)
synaptogenesis (134)
very low birth weight (123)
visual acuity (136)

mydevelopmentlab
Where human development comes to life!

If you are using MyDevelopmentLab, you have access to an ebook version of this textbook, along with dozens of valuable resources per chapter—including video and audio clips, simulations and activities, self-assessments, practice tests, and other study materials. Here is a sampling of the resources available for this chapter.

Explore
The Synapse
The Limbic System
Dendritic Spreading: Forming Interconnections in the Brain
Infant's Perceptual and Cognitive Milestones

Simulate
The Visual Cliff
Physiological Bases of Behavioral Problems

Watch
Brain Development and Nutrition
Breastfeeding

If you did not receive an access code to MyDevelopmentLab with this text and wish to purchase access online, please visit www.mydevelopmentlab.com.

chapter 5

Cognitive Development in Infants and Toddlers

Last week, Diana took her 10-month-old daughter Jamie to play in the neighborhood park. As the birds chirped, Jamie's eyes seemed to search everywhere for the source of the sound. As some children ran by, calling loudly to one another, Jamie looked and smiled at them, reaching out to touch them as they waved and said hello to her. Like most babies, Jamie seems eager to touch things, experiment, and experience the world. A friend told Diana that babies of this age don't even realize that something continues to exist if they can't see or touch it. Just as her friend predicted, it worked when Diana distracted Jamie from playing with the pinecones scattered on the ground at the park by hiding them under their blanket. But in other ways, Jamie seems very skilled. Even though she hasn't said any "real" words yet, Diana has no trouble understanding what Jamie needs, when she's happy, and when she wants another bite of her cereal.

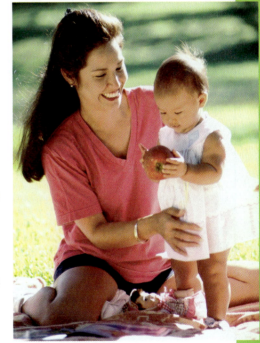

Diana wonders what babies this age understand about their world. Do infants connect the sounds they hear with what they see? Do toys that move and make sounds encourage development, or does all the clamor just confuse the young baby? How do babies come to realize that objects exist whether one can see them or not? And why does it seem so easy for babies to communicate, even before they are able to produce any words? Most important, Diana wonders what she can do to support her daughter's cognitive development.

As you read this chapter, look for the "Think About Diana . . ." questions that ask you to consider what you're learning from Diana's perspective.

Like Diana, you might have wondered what infants really understand about the world. How do babies put together the information from their senses and think about the things they experience? And how do they communicate their needs and thoughts to others? As you will learn in this chapter, even young infants have surprisingly well-developed capabilities in some areas (such as perceptual skills), and they are able to quickly and easily develop other complex skills (such as understanding the permanence of objects and using language). As you might recall from Chapter 1, *cognitive* refers to mental processes such as perceiving, thinking, remembering, solving problems, and communicating with language. While *sensation* is the physical process of detecting information about a stimulus in the environment through the five senses and transmitting that information to the brain, **perception** is the cognitive process of organizing, coordinating, and interpreting that information. Perception is an important part of cognition; it enables people to use sensory input to think, solve problems, and function in their environments. In this chapter, we will describe the perceptual, cognitive, and language abilities of infants and toddlers, and we will introduce you to some of the major theories that explain these areas of development.

perception
The cognitive process of organizing, coordinating, and interpreting sensory information.

Figure 5.1 • Looking Chamber Early researchers used the looking chamber to investigate visual preferences in young infants. The infant looked up from the bottom toward stimulus patterns illuminated within the chamber. A researcher monitored the infant's eyes, recording the amount of time the infant's gaze fixated on each stimulus pattern. (Based on Fantz, 1961.)

Perceptual Development

As you saw in Chapter 4, the human nervous system is relatively immature at the time of birth. Most of the synapses in the brain have not yet formed, and many of the neurons have not yet acquired the myelin sheath that insulates the axons and speeds transmission of neural impulses. Newborns can move their eyes to locate and track objects in their surroundings, but until they gain better control of the intricate muscles in and around their eyes, infants have trouble focusing on a target and coordinating the images coming from each eye. It is no wonder that John Locke and other early philosophers claimed that the newborn's mind was a "blank slate." According to this view, infants need to learn by trial and error to use their senses to form meaningful perceptions. One of the founders of psychology, William James (1890/1950), claimed that the mental experience of the infant was "one great blooming, buzzing confusion" (p. 488).

Do infants really begin life this helpless? Clearly, they do not. As we mentioned in Chapter 4, newborns come equipped with an array of sensory capabilities. In the 1950s, the emergence of reliable nonverbal techniques for testing infants opened the floodgates for research. Since then, scientists have learned an impressive amount about the perceptual capabilities of infants. It is apparent that, far from experiencing a "blooming, buzzing confusion," even young infants have a tremendous ability to organize and use sensory information in a meaningful way.

As you study this section, ask yourself these questions:

■ How do researchers know what infants can see and hear?

■ What kinds of information do infants prefer?

■ Do infants take a long time to learn to coordinate information from different senses, or do they show this capability soon after birth?

Robert Fantz and the Early Work in Testing Visual Preferences

As early as 1951, Robert Fantz was conducting experiments with newly hatched chickens and infant chimpanzees to determine whether perception of different forms (e.g., distinguishing squares from circles) was innate or learned (see Fantz, 1956, 1961). To study human infants, Fantz and his associates used a *looking chamber* (Figure 5.1). The researchers placed infants on the sliding tray at the bottom. A researcher, standing over the chamber, could slide patterns on cards through slots in the top of the chamber. Peering through a hole, the researcher could also observe the infants' eyes and use electronic devices to record the time infants spent fixating on (i.e., looking at) each pattern. "If an infant consistently turns its gaze toward some forms more often than toward others, it must be able to perceive form" (Fantz, 1961, p. 67). This became the logic of the **preferential-looking technique,** a simple but powerful procedure that many researchers have since used to investigate infant perception.

preferential-looking technique Technique used to test infant visual perception. If infants consistently look longer at some patterns than at others, researchers infer that the infants can see a difference between the patterns.

Figure 5.2 shows the results from one of Fantz's early experiments. Newborns who were only 2 to 5 days old looked more at a drawing of a face than at a bull's-eye or newsprint, but they preferred any of these detailed patterns over plain colored disks (Fantz, 1963). Infants spent approximately equal time looking at the colored disks, especially the yellow and white disks, so the experiment didn't show whether the infants could distinguish between these colors. Using this preferential-looking technique, Fantz collected some of the first scientific data that demonstrated conclusively that human infants are able to perceive form and pattern. Hundreds of researchers, in laboratories all around the world, have followed with their own studies investigating the kinds of visual information human infants can detect and process. Researchers have adapted Fantz's logic and procedures to assess perception in other senses as well.

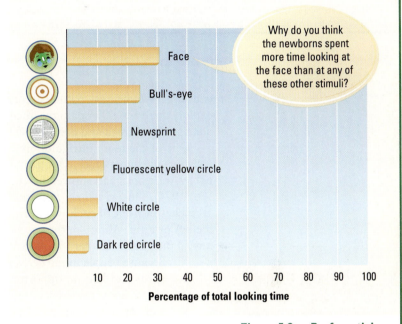

Percentage of total looking time

Figure 5.2 • Preferential Looking Results This graph shows results from an early preferential-looking study. Stimuli were presented one at a time in random order to newborns who were only 2 to 5 days old. What types of features caught the newborns' eyes? (Based on Fantz, 1963.)

Using Fantz's preferential-looking technique and similar techniques, researchers have discovered that newborn babies prefer the following types of visual information (see Bjorklund, 1989, for a review):

- Moving stimuli
- Outer contours or edges
- Sharp color contrasts (e.g., where black meets white or where red meets white)
- Patterns with some complexity or detail (but not too complex)
- Symmetrical patterns
- Curved patterns
- Patterns that resemble the human face

Some of these preferences are evident in Figure 5.2. Notice that infants preferred the bull's-eye over the plain disks, and they preferred the face most of all. Parents can use these preferences in shaping their babies' environments. To capture the infant's attention, crib mobiles, baby books, blocks, and other infant toys should feature sharp color

Figure 5.3 • Face Stimuli Researchers showed these patterns one at a time to newborns who were only a few minutes old. Although they had yet to see their first real face, the newborns preferred to look at the pattern that most resembled the arrangement of the human face. Why do you think this was so? (Goren, Sarty, & Wu, 1975.)

contrasts, symmetrical patterns, curves, and even human face patterns. As infants explore these and other patterns, their sensory systems get the input they need to stimulate further growth and development.

One of the more intriguing findings is that infants tend to prefer patterns that resemble the human face. One group of researchers entered the delivery room when babies were born and showed newborns the patterns in Figure 5.3 (Goren, Sarty, & Wu, 1975). One at a time, in a random series, they placed the patterns about 6 to 10 inches in front of each newborn's nose, then moved the patterns slowly toward the left or right. Although the newborns were only a few minutes old, they reliably turned their heads farther to follow the pattern that most resembled the human face.

Because people in the delivery room were wearing surgical masks, the newborns had had no opportunity to see a real human face before the testing began. Some researchers speculate that at birth, babies are already equipped with an innate *schema*, or mental framework, for the structure of the human face. However, other researchers remind us that these newborns might not recognize the patterns as "faces" per se. Instead, they might be responding to particular features that happen to be contained in faces—left-right symmetry and more details in the top than bottom half, for example. It might not be until 3 to 5 months of age that infants begin recognizing perceptual cues specific to faces (such as the location of the eyes and the space between them) (Bhatt et al., 2005; Turati et al., 2002; Turati et al., 2005).

The "specialness" of the human face has received much attention in the research literature (Cohen & Cashon, 2006; Kellman & Arterberry, 2006). Even newborns are able to recognize individual faces, and one study found that 3-month-old girls looked longer at photographs of their own mothers' faces than at photos of other adult females (Barrera & Maurer, 1981a; Turati et al., 2006). Interestingly, 3-month-old boys did not show the same pattern.

Beyond recognizing their mothers' faces, when do you think infants begin to judge the physical attractiveness of faces? Would you believe that they do this by 2 months of age? In an intriguing study, Judith Langlois and her colleagues asked college students to rate the attractiveness of photos of female adults. Then they slide-projected the photos in pairs on a large screen in front of infants (Langlois et al., 1987). When an "attractive" photo was paired with an "unattractive" photo, 2-month-olds looked longer at the attractive

Think About Diana…

On the basis of the preferential-looking research reviewed so far, what could you advise Diana regarding her baby's perceptual abilities? Do you have any suggestions about the types of patterns or decorations her baby might be able to see or prefer?

your perspective

Why do you believe 2-month-olds preferred looking at "attractive" faces? How did they learn or know which faces were more attractive?

photo. Langlois and her colleagues (1987) concluded that "the tendency to detect and prefer certain faces over others is present very early in life, long before any significant exposure to contemporary standards, definitions, and stereotypes" (p. 367). If beauty is in the eye of the beholder, it's there at a surprisingly early age!

Infant scanning of faces changes significantly from 1 to 2 months of age (Maurer & Salapatek, 1976). As Figure 5.4 shows, 1-month-olds tend to fixate more on the external features of faces (the chin and hairline), whereas 2-month-olds tend to focus on the internal features (especially the eyes and mouth). This change might help to explain why it is in the 2- to 3-month period that infants begin to show recognition of familiar faces (e.g., their mothers) and a preference for attractive faces: It's the internal features that help us to recognize people the most.

One-month-old's gaze

Fixations are primarily to the chin and outer hairline.

Two-month-old's gaze

Fixations are primarily between the eyes and mouth.

Figure 5.4 • Infant Visual Fixation on Facial Patterns
Tracking their eye movements, you can see that 1-month-old infants spend most of their time looking at the external features of the face—mostly the chin and outer hairline. By 2 months, infants are now looking more at the internal features, especially the eyes. (Based on Maurer & Salapatek, 1976.)

Habituation–Dishabituation Research

Recall from Figure 5.2 that young infants preferred to look at the face over the newsprint and any kind of detail over plain colors but did not show a preference among the plain colored disks. Can infants see the differences among these colors? On the basis of this test alone, it's not possible to know whether infants can visually discriminate between the colors. This is an important limitation of the preferential-looking technique: To show visual discrimination, infants not only must be able to *see* the difference between the stimuli, but also must have some reason to *prefer* one over the other. What if infants can see the difference but find both stimuli to be equally interesting?

To solve this problem, a more stringent test of visual discrimination involves the **habituation–dishabituation technique.** This technique capitalizes on infants' tendency to look longer at novel (new) stimuli than at familiar (old) stimuli. As an example, consider the experiment conducted by Cohen, Gelber, and Lazar (1971). Imagine that you show a red circle to a 4-month-old infant for several seconds, and you record the amount of time the infant spent looking at the circle. Then you remove the circle, and then you show it again. Repeat this procedure, each time recording how long the infant looks at the circle. Plotting the looking times, you might notice a trend, as shown in Figure 5.5. That is, the infant's interest in the stimulus has likely decreased across trials. The infant has shown **habituation**—the tendency to reduce a response to a stimulus that is presented repeatedly. Habituation indicates that the infant processed the stimulus and recognized it on its repeated appearances. Now look at what happens during the *dishabituation trials* in Figure 5.5. Here, the same infant sees a series of stimuli with familiar or novel forms and colors. Fixation time for the same familiar red circle remains low, continuing the trend shown in habituation trials. The infant continued to show habituation to the familiar color and form. But a change in color (to a green circle) or a change in form (to a red triangle) produces an *increase* in fixation time. Changing both color and form (to a green triangle) produces an even greater increase. These increases reflect **dishabituation**—the recovery or increase in response when a new stimulus replaces a familiar stimulus. Dishabituation indicates that the infant can see the difference between the novel and familiar stimuli. In this case, the infant can obviously see the difference between colors (red versus green) and forms (circle versus triangle).

Notice that at the outset of the experiment, there was no reason for the infants to prefer green over red or triangle over circle but that habituating infants to "red" and "circle" induced such preferences. The habituation–dishabituation technique thus avoids one of the problems with the preferential-looking technique because it can

habituation–dishabituation technique
Technique used to test infant perception. Infants are shown a stimulus repeatedly until they respond less (habituate) to it. Then a new stimulus is presented.

habituation
The tendency of infants to reduce their response to stimuli that are presented repeatedly.

dishabituation
The recovery or increase in infant's response when a familiar stimulus is replaced by one that is novel.

Figure 5.5 • Habituation–Dishabituation Example
This graph shows hypothetical data from a 4-month-old infant using the habituation–dishabituation technique. The infant shows habituation by looking less and less at a red circle that is presented repeatedly, but looking time increases (dishabituation) when novel forms or colors are presented. (Based on Cohen, Gelber, & Lazar, 1971.)

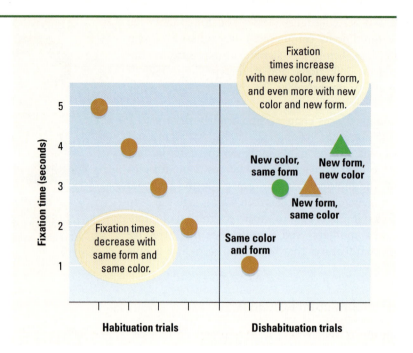

Fixation times increase with new color, new form, and even more with new color and new form.

Fixation times decrease with same form and same color.

New color, same form

New form, new color

New form, same color

Same color and form

Fixation time (seconds)

Habituation trials   **Dishabituation trials**

Think About Diana . . .

Would you expect Jamie to habituate to the decorations, toys, and other stimuli in her environment? Knowing about the habituation–dishabituation tendency, what would you advise Diana to do to enhance the stimulation value of her baby's surroundings?

intermodal perception
The process of combining or integrating information across sensory modalities.

demonstrate visual discrimination even when there is no chance that infants might have an already established preference for one stimulus over another.

An important practical application of these methods of studying infant perception is their use to predict later cognitive skills, even IQ (Fagan, 2000; Kavšek, 2004). To read more about issues surrounding the use of these techniques to predict cognitive skills, read the Social Policy Perspective box called "Assessing Infant Intelligence: A Good Idea?"

Intermodal Perception: Putting It All Together

Although we have treated the different sensory systems separately so far, in reality, most experiences involve multiple senses. For example, as you walk down the sidewalk, you feel the breeze on your face, see the colors of the sky, hear the voices of people walking around you, and smell the food in restaurants you walk by. In short, you experience the world through combined or integrated sensory inputs, or what researchers refer to as **intermodal perception.**

Do human beings need to learn to combine sensory information into unified impressions? According to the *constructivist* view, they do. Jean Piaget (1952b), for example, believed that young infants are not aware that what they see is related to what they hear. He hypothesized that infants need to learn, through experience, to coordinate their sensory systems. (We will discuss Piaget's constructivist theory of cognitive development in the next section.) At the other end of the spectrum, T. G. R. Bower (1974) speculated that infants have to learn to *separate* their sensory impressions. In the beginning, infants confuse their sensory impressions—they do not know whether they are seeing or hearing, tasting or smelling. Bower concluded that "the initial primitive unity [of the sensory systems] must go, leaving differentiated sensory systems in place of a unitary perceptual world" (p. 151). In a more moderate view, Eleanor Gibson pointed out that important features in the environment (she called them *invariants*) can be detected by multiple sensory systems (Gibson & Walker, 1984; Rose & Ruff, 1987). For example, you can see that a sidewalk is a solid surface (because its texture continues into the distance), and you can also feel its solidity beneath your feet. Similarly, infants can both smell and taste the sweetness of breast milk or formula and can both see and hear the movement of the rattle. Can infants

Assessing Infant Intelligence: A Good Idea?

For decades, researchers, educators, and policymakers have tried to find reliable ways to predict intelligence from early childhood, with limited success. Although intelligence test scores change over time, they are reasonably stable starting at about age 5 years of age. But correlations of scores for younger children and infants have typically shown low relationships to later IQ scores.

The habituation–dishabituation procedures that are used to study infant perception have shown promise in predicting cognitive skills later in childhood (Fagan, 2000; Kavšek, 2004; Neisser et al., 1996). Summary studies have found average correlations of about 0.45 between young infants' degrees of dishabituation and the same children's intelligence test scores at 1 to 8 years of age (McCall & Carriger, 1993). This correlation means that infants who show more dishabituation tend to score higher on IQ tests. The memory, discrimination, and recognition skills involved in habituation–dishabituation are related to the kinds of cognitive skills measured in typical intelligence tests. The habituation–dishabituation technique therefore can help researchers to assess cognitive functioning in early infancy and perhaps identify infants who are at risk for developmental delays. Infants who were exposed prenatally to cocaine, for example, show depressed habituation and dishabituation (Mayes et al., 1993). In one study, half of the 3-month-olds who were cocaine-exposed failed to achieve habituation at all (Mayes & Bornstein, 1995). Recent modifications of the procedure have even found that the rate of habituation *even before birth* is related to being at higher risk of cognitive problems at 6 months of age (Gaultney & Gingras, 2005).

Critics point out, however, that researchers do not completely understand what the infant assessments are measuring and how they relate to later cognitive skills. Habituation scores may reflect differences in cognitive speed of processing, but it is also possible that they are measuring differences in temperament or inhibition instead (Neisser et al., 1996). Some studies find that the aspect of the test that correlates with later cognitive skills (i.e., time to habituate versus degree of dishabituation) might be different for different types of infants (Kavšek, 2004). And while the infant assessments do predict later scores reasonably well, some studies have found that they do not show good test-retest reliabilities—that is, an individual baby's score changes if more than a few weeks go by before a second test (Andersson, 1996; Slater, 1997; Tasbihsazan, Nettelbeck, & Kirby, 2003). These apparent inconsistencies make it difficult to interpret correlations with later IQ scores. Some critics argue that the best predictor is already known: the home environment. Assessment of early processing abilities might help in understanding specific difficulties, but effective prevention and intervention programs must address multiple factors, including home environments (Meisels & Atkins-Burnett, 2000). Finally, although the researchers who develop these assessments have the best of intentions, the possibility of unfair discrimination against those who are found to be most at risk for later cognitive problems cannot be ignored.

Q *Do you think policymakers should pursue the development of predictive infant assessments? How could this information be useful in developing effective early interventions for children who are at risk? What guidelines would you suggest for the use of these interventions?*

make connections across these avenues of sensation? Research on intermodal (or intersensory), or cross-modal (or crosssensory), perception indicates that they can (Bahrick, 2000).

One of the classic demonstrations was an experiment conducted by Meltzoff and Borton (1979). These researchers placed a smooth or a "nubby" pacifier in the mouths of 1-month-old infants. They then removed the pacifier and showed both types of pacifiers simultaneously to the infants. The 1-month-olds looked significantly longer at the shape that had been in their mouths—they matched the shape they saw with the one they had felt. Also, Elizabeth Spelke and her colleagues found that infants can match the dynamic features of moving objects across senses. In one study, infants saw two films side by side (Spelke, 1979). One showed a kangaroo (or donkey) puppet bouncing quickly up and down. In the other film, the puppet bounced more slowly. At the same time the researchers played a slow or fast "thump" or "gong" sound that was synchronized with the bouncing in one of the films. Four-month-old infants looked significantly longer at the film that matched the pace of the sound. Of course, kangaroos do not normally make "thump" or "gong" noises when they jump, and it can be assumed that the infants had no prior experience with kangaroo activities. Still, these young infants matched the pace of the sound with the pace of the bouncing, showing that infants are quite capable of detecting features shared across the different senses.

your perspective

How do you think infants learn to match information across different sensory modalities? Is this ability available at birth? What real-life examples of intermodal perception have you observed in infants you have known?

In related research, 5-month-old infants matched the sound of an engine increasing or decreasing in volume with a video of an automobile coming toward or moving away from them (Walker-Andrews & Lennon, 1985). Five-and-a-half-month-old infants can use information about the hardness or softness of a ball that they touched but did not see to correctly judge which would fit through a tunnel opening that they saw but did not touch (Schweinle & Wilcox, 2004). Infants 6 to 8 months old matched the number they heard with the number they saw (Starkey, Spelke, & Gelman, 1983). For example, when they heard two drumbeats, they looked longer at a photo of two household objects; when they heard three drumbeats, they preferred to look at three objects. Again, these findings demonstrate intermodal perception of a variety of complicated events. Intermodal perception is sufficiently evident during infancy that its strength can serve as a reliable indicator of later cognitive functioning. For infants born preterm, scores on intermodal matching at 12 months of age predict cognitive abilities all the way through 6 years of age (Rose & Wallace, 1985). It takes a healthy nervous system to integrate the information flowing to the infant from multiple perceptual modalities.

As you can see, researchers have learned a lot about the perceptual capabilities of human infants. At birth, newborns can locate and track objects, and they can per-

ceive a variety of forms, colors, sounds, tastes, and smells. As their brains and nervous systems continue to develop, their perceptual abilities will become even more refined. With rapidly developing nervous systems and enhanced perceptual capabilities, young children are ready to absorb information and learn amazing amounts about their world. In the next section, we will look at one prominent theory that describes how infants and toddlers conceptualize information and learn to think about all of the wonders they encounter.

Does it take a significant amount of trial-and-error learning for infants to connect the voices they hear with the visual images of faces? Evidently not. Using a variety of interesting stimuli, research on intermodal (or intersensory) perception indicates that infants make such connections even when they have had very little experience with the events they are matching.

■ Let's Review . . .

1. With the preferential-looking technique, when an infant spends more time looking at a checkerboard pattern than at a plain colored square, it can be inferred that:
   a. the infant can see the difference between the checkerboard and the plain square.
   b. the infant is probably color-blind.
   c. the infant's visual acuity is very poor.
   d. the infant has habituated to the checkerboard pattern.

2. On the basis of research described in this section, it seems that infants recognize the configuration of the human face:
   a. by 3 months of age.   b. by 6 months of age.
   c. by 1 year of age.   d. immediately after birth.

3. Jamil shows his infant son a teddy bear several times. Each time Jamil shows the teddy bear, his son looks less at it. The decreased interest shown by Jamil's son shows an example of:
   a. habituation.   b. dishabituation.
   c. preferential looking.   d. cross-modal perception.

4. Which of the following is an example of intermodal (or intersensory) perception?
   a. Infants prefer to look at faces over most any other stimulus.
   b. Infants habituate before they show dishabituation.
   c. Infants prefer to look at attractive and happy-looking faces.
   d. Infants can match the sound of a happy voice with the film of a happy face.

5. **True or False:** Infants are more likely to show that they can discriminate red from blue when they are tested by using the habituation–dishabituation technique than when they are tested with the preferential-looking technique.

6. **True or False:** Jean Piaget believed that infants need to learn to separate sources of information coming from their different perceptual systems.

Answers: 1. a, 2. d, 3. a, 4. d, 5. T, 6. F

Explaining Cognitive Development: Piaget's Constructivist View

Vast changes in thinking are evident in every aspect of life as children grow from infants into toddlers, ranging from what they will pay attention to to the kinds of questions they ask and the explanations they can understand or offer. These changes in thinking, in which children's thought gradually becomes more organized and complex, are called *cognitive development*. The most influential theorist in the study of cognitive development was Jean Piaget (1896–1980). His prolific career in psychology spanned an astonishing seven decades and had an immense impact on the field (Beilin, 1994).

As you study this section, ask yourself these questions:

■ What influence did Piaget's background in biology have on his theory and research? What are some specific examples of this biological influence?

■ What is constructivism, and why is Piaget considered a constructivist?

■ According to Piaget, what processes guide children's interaction with the environment? How do these processes affect cognitive development?

- What are the main limitations in cognitive processing at the sensorimotor stage?

- What new cognitive structures or other cognitive advances emerge during this stage?

Piaget as a Child Prodigy

Jean Piaget was no ordinary child. From a very early age, he showed tremendous intellectual talent. Born in Neuchâtel, Switzerland, a small university town, Piaget showed an early interest in nature, particularly in observing wildlife in its natural setting. His observations led to the first of his many scientific publications. He was only 10 years old when he published his first article, a one-page report on an albino sparrow he observed in a park. At the Museum of Natural History in Neuchâtel, Piaget began working with a zoologist who specialized in mollusks (clams, oysters, snails, etc.). Piaget "catalogued and studied adaptation" (Bringuier, 1980, p. 8), detailing how mollusks' shells changed in relation to the movement of the water in which they lived. As you will see, the idea of adaptation came to play a central role in Piaget's later theory of human cognitive development.

Jean Piaget was a pioneer in child development research. His theory revolutionized how children's thinking is viewed.

After earning a Ph.D. degree at age 21, Piaget became interested in psychology. He worked for a time at a psychiatric clinic in Zurich, where he learned about Freudian psychoanalysis and how to conduct a clinical interview. Later, he moved to Paris to work with Theophile Simon in the Binet Laboratory. Theophile Simon and Alfred Binet were known for their work on intelligence testing, and Piaget's job in the laboratory was to help develop a standardized French version of some reasoning tasks. These years were important in several ways for Piaget and the development of his theory and methods. First, he realized that children were *active* in their thinking, not passive. He found that even very young children made admirable attempts to understand and answer questions, although their reasoning was far from what an adult would see as logical. Drawing on his biological background, Piaget interpreted these attempts as children's efforts to adapt cognitively to the situations they were in, to understand and succeed in their situations. Second, Piaget began to see that children's thinking showed a striking regularity and consistency, even though the thinking was often incorrect. Piaget noticed that children of the same age tended to give the same wrong answers, whereas children of a different age tended to give different wrong answers. There seemed to be age-related patterns in the children's thinking. These might not seem to be groundbreaking insights today, but at that time, most experts believed that children were passive recipients of information (simply memorizing information without interpreting or modifying it) and did not have coherent or regular ways of thinking. Piaget challenged these well-established views. Finally, Piaget realized that a *clinical method*, in which children are asked to explain the reasons for their answers rather than simply to give an answer, could be an invaluable tool in his efforts to understand children's thinking.

Constructivism and Interaction with the Environment

constructivist view
The view that people construct their own knowledge and understanding of the world by using what they already know and understand to interpret new experiences.

Piaget combined his background in biology with his interest in understanding how logic and knowledge develop and spent the rest of his career observing children and articulating his theory of cognitive development. He applied several concepts from biology and used them to explain how knowledge develops.

Piaget's theory is often described as a **constructivist view.** According to *constructivists*, people interpret their environments and experiences in light of the knowledge and experiences they already have. People do not simply take in an external reality and develop an unchanged, exact mental copy of objects or events. Instead, they build (or "construct") their own individual understandings and knowledge. For Piaget, the essential building block for cognition is the *scheme*. A **scheme** is an organized pattern of action or thought. It is a broad concept and can refer to organized patterns of physical action (such as an infant reaching to grasp an object) or mental action (such as a high school student thinking about how to solve an algebra problem).

As children interact with the environment, individual schemes become modified, combined, and reorganized to form more complex cognitive structures. Think of cognitive structures as the organizing framework of all a child's knowledge and cognitive skills. According to Piaget, structures are essential for understanding new knowledge, but structures are also changed by the new knowledge. As children mature, these structures allow more complex and sophisticated ways of thinking. These, in turn, allow children to interact in qualitatively different ways with their environment. For example, a little girl develops a scheme for noticing similarities between objects (we'll call this a "compare" scheme) and a separate one for noticing differences (a "contrast" scheme). Gradually, she coordinates and combines the two into a single cognitive structure that allows her to compare and contrast objects at the same time. When she encounters a new object, she uses this coordinated cognitive structure to develop a fuller understanding of the object. The first time she encounters an avocado, for example, she can compare and contrast it to other foods. This process will help her to determine what kind of food it is and will increase her understanding of the overall category (similar in size to an orange but different in shape, similar in color to a lime, different in texture from an apple).

Cognitive structures not only organize existing knowledge, but also serve as filters for all new experiences. That is, people interpret new experiences in light of their already existing cognitive structures. Because no two people ever have exactly the same experiences, no two cognitive structures ever are exactly the same, and no two people ever interpret events in exactly the same way. The way you interpret and understand the information you're learning about Piaget is different, at least slightly, from the way your classmates understand it, because each of you filters and interprets the information through a different cognitive structure.

Piaget believed that extensive interaction with the environment is absolutely essential for each person's cognitive development. Though Piaget acknowledged that biological maturation sets the general limits within which cognitive development occurs, he placed much more emphasis on the role of the environment. Children who have severely limited interactions with their environments simply will not have the opportunities to develop and reorganize their cognitive structures so as to achieve mature ways of thinking. The way people interact with the environment is not random, however. Three common processes guide their interactions: *organization, adaptation*, and *reflective abstraction*. If you have studied biology, you will recognize the influence of Piaget's biology background in the first two of these processes. Both concepts originate in the physical sciences, and Piaget used them in his theory of psychological development.

Organization is the tendency of all species to integrate separate elements into increasingly complex higher-order structures. For example, consider the human body. Cells themselves are organized systems of subcellular material. And cells organize into tissues, tissues into organs, organs into organ systems, and organ systems into the body. Piaget believed that the tendency to organize also occurs on the

scheme
An organized pattern of physical or mental action.

How is this child constructing her own understanding of science concepts?

organization
The tendency to integrate separate elements into increasingly complex higher-order structures.

adaptation
In cognitive development, the process of changing a cognitive structure or the environment (or both) in order to understand the environment.

assimilation
The process of bringing new objects or information into a scheme that already exists.

psychological level—that people try to organize their knowledge into coherent systems. In fact, Piaget believed that the tendency to organize is so basic that people cannot keep from trying to organize their knowledge. This explains why you might find yourself thinking about something that didn't make sense to you when you encountered it, even when you don't intend or want to spend time thinking about it. The advantage of this organizational tendency is that it gives people a way to understand and interpret events and objects they encounter; in short, it helps us to function more successfully in our psychological environments. The disadvantage is, of course, that the particular way in which you organize your knowledge might be completely wrong. If enough mistakes and misinterpretations occur, however, you might reexamine your cognitive organization and perhaps make adjustments. Piaget called this later process *adaptation*.

In biology, the term **adaptation** refers to every species' tendency to make modifications in order to survive and succeed in the environment. (Remember how the mollusks' shells adapted to the water currents?) Applied to cognitive development, *adaptation* means changing one's cognitive structure or one's environment (or both to some degree) in order to better understand the environment. Figure 5.6 diagrams the steps involved in adaptation: A child moves from assimilation through cognitive disequilibrium, accommodation, and cognitive equilibrium, then back to a new assimilation.

Let's explore this process using the example of Lily, a 2-year-old who is learning to name animals (see Figure 5.6). Lily has a dog at home, and according to her "dog scheme," "doggies" are animals that have four feet and fur and that bark and fetch balls. One day, riding in the car with her mother, Lily points to a field with several cows and exclaims, "Look, Mommy, doggies!" She is excited to see so many "doggies," especially ones that are so large! Lily is trying to understand these new animals by thinking about them as something she already understands: "doggies." This is an example of **assimilation**, the process of bringing new objects or information into a scheme that already exists.

Thinking of these new animals as "doggies," Lily fully expects that they will also bark and fetch balls. Such misunderstandings are common when a person tries to force new objects into an ill-fitting scheme. Lily's mother, however, comments, "No,

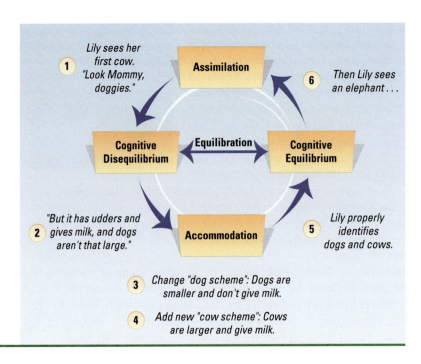

Figure 5.6 • Adaptation and Equilibration In the cycle of adaptation and equilibration, a new experience is first assimilated into an existing scheme. If it does not fit properly, cognitive disequilibrium results. Accommodating (adjusting) the scheme brings the child to cognitive equilibrium until a new assimilation challenges the scheme again.

1. Lily sees her first cow. "Look Mommy, doggies."
2. "But it has udders and gives milk, and dogs aren't that large."
3. Change "dog scheme": Dogs are smaller and don't give milk.
4. Add new "cow scheme": Cows are larger and give milk.
5. Lily properly identifies dogs and cows.
6. Then Lily sees an elephant . . .

Assimilation
Cognitive Disequilibrium
Equilibration
Cognitive Equilibrium
Accommodation

those are cows. They are bigger than dogs. And see the udders underneath? Cows give us milk." These comments place Lily into cognitive disequilibrium—she is confused. Lily realizes that she has never seen udders under dogs and also has never seen dogs that large. To resolve her cognitive conflict, Lily adjusts her understanding of animals. She adds new information about dogs (they are smaller and don't give us milk), and she learns a new animal (cows are like dogs but larger, and they give us milk). These adjustments are examples of **accommodation,** the process of modifying old schemes or creating new ones to fit better with assimilated information. Now Lily can properly identify dogs and cows, and her new success in naming the animals moves her into cognitive equilibrium. Lily remains in cognitive equilibrium until she visits the zoo and encounters a new animal: an elephant. How will she assimilate this animal?

Piaget claimed that people try to understand new experiences by assimilating these experiences into the schemes or cognitive structures that they already have. If the assimilation does not work completely, there is an imbalance between the new experience and the old scheme. Piaget described this imbalance as a state of *cognitive disequilibrium*. To resolve the disequilibrium, people accommodate, or adjust, their schemes to provide a better fit for the new experience. If this process is successful, they achieve *cognitive equilibrium*. **Equilibration** therefore is the dynamic process of moving between states of cognitive disequilibrium and equilibrium as new experiences are assimilated and schemes are accommodated.

Because of the process of organization, human beings are never satisfied with equilibrium. They stretch and extend their cognitive structures by assimilating new and challenging information. According to Piaget, the tendency to seek equilibrium is always present—people are constantly seeking to understand—but equilibration is a dynamic process and is never fully achieved. In other words, although there are certainly periods when a person understands and deals effectively with the environment, no one ever attains perfect, complete, and permanent understanding of everything. Piaget believed that "the normal state of mind is one of disequilibrium—or rather a state of 'moving equilibrium'" (Beilin, 1994, p. 263). There are always new things to learn.

A final process that guides thinking is reflective abstraction. In **reflective abstraction,** a person notices something in the environment (e.g., some specific property of an object or action), then reflects on it (Ginsburg & Opper, 1988; Piaget, 1971). That is, the person tries to relate it to his or her current cognitive structures. As a result of reflection, people modify their current cognitive structures. For example, a boy playing on the beach might notice that the number of rocks he has is the same regardless of whether he arranges them in a line or a circle or piles them on top of one another. Reflective abstraction in this case involves the child's *noticing* that he has the same number of rocks, then *thinking about the implication* of this fact—that number is not affected by how they are arranged. According to Piaget, people must engage in reflective abstraction to learn from their interactions with the environment. The process enables them to isolate and think about specific properties, compare and contrast them, and think about how they understand them. In this way, reflective abstraction *leads to* the accommodation of cognitive structures. A child can notice something in the environment, but if he does not think about its meaning or its relation to what he already knows, no cognitive reorganization will occur. In our earlier example, Lily would not have accommodated her understanding of "doggies" if she had not (1) *noticed* that the cows were much larger than dogs (and had udders) and (2) reflected or *thought about* what this meant.

The processes of organization, adaptation, and reflective abstraction play important roles in children's development. First, children are naturally curious. They are constantly probing and exploring their environments, looking for ways to challenge their existing schemes, and reflecting on whether the things they encounter make sense to them. But without opportunities for exploration

accommodation
The process of modifying old schemes or creating new ones to better fit assimilated information.

equilibration
The dynamic process of moving between states of cognitive disequilibrium and equilibrium.

reflective abstraction
The process of noticing and thinking about the implications of information and experiences.

Think About Diana...

What kinds of experiences could Diana provide to encourage Jamie to engage in adaptation, organization, and reflective abstraction? How can caregivers for infants use constructivist concepts to facilitate cognitive development?

and stimulating experiences, there would be nothing new to assimilate. Second, cognitive disequilibrium is a precursor to learning. When children are confused and perplexed, they are ready to make adjustments—they are ready to make accommodations in their schemes. Although it might be tempting to think of confusion as a sign of failure or as something to avoid, in Piaget's system it is a necessary step toward success. Finally, the concept of constructivism is embedded in the cycle. Faced with disequilibrium, children will accommodate their own schemes, engage in reflective abstraction, and improve and reorganize their cognitive structures. In short, children do not passively absorb structures from the adults and other people around them. They actively create their own accommodations and so construct their own understandings.

Piaget's Stage 1: Sensorimotor Thought (Birth to 2 Years)

We have seen that children adapt individual schemes (such as "doggie" and "cow") through equilibration. According to Piaget, our continual organization and adaptation lead to periodic major reorganizations of cognitive structures, which result in four broad stages of cognitive development. After a major reorganization, new and more powerful ways of thinking become possible. Each stage has certain skills and limitations, as summarized in Table 5.1. In this chapter, we will focus on stage 1, sensorimotor thought, which involves developments in infants and toddlers. We will discuss Stages 2, 3, and 4 in later chapters.

sensorimotor thought
Thought that is based only on sensory input and physical (motor) actions.

According to Piaget, infants can engage only in **sensorimotor thought**. That is, they know the world only in terms of their own sensory input (what they can see, smell, taste, touch, and hear) and their physical or motor actions on it (e.g., sucking, reaching, and grasping). They do not have internal mental representations of the objects and events that exist outside their own body. For example, consider what

TABLE 5.1 Piaget's Four Stages of Cognitive Development

COGNITIVE STAGE	LIMITATIONS	ACHIEVEMENTS
Sensorimotor Thought: Birth to 2 years	• No representational thought; infants cannot form internal symbols early in this stage. • Object permanence is lacking early in this stage.	• Representational, symbolic thought gradually emerges as the stage progresses. • Object permanence develops as the stage progresses.
Preoperational Thought: 2–7 years	• Intuitive logic leads to egocentrism, animism, artificialism, and an inability to use more objective forms of logic. • Schemes are not reversible, not operational. • Children fail conservation tasks because of centration, focus on static endpoints, and lack of reversibility.	• Flourishing mental representations and symbols are seen in language, art, and play.
Concrete Operational Thought: 7–12 years	• Logic is limited to concrete, tangible materials and experiences.	• Logical thought is more objective, allows skills such as class inclusion and transitivity. • Schemes can be reversible, operational. • Children pass conservation problems due to decentration, focus on dynamic transformations, reversibility.
Formal Operational Thought: 12 years and up	• Adolescent egocentrism is seen in the imaginary audience and personal fable.	• Hypothetico-deductive reasoning emerges. • Abstract thought emerges.

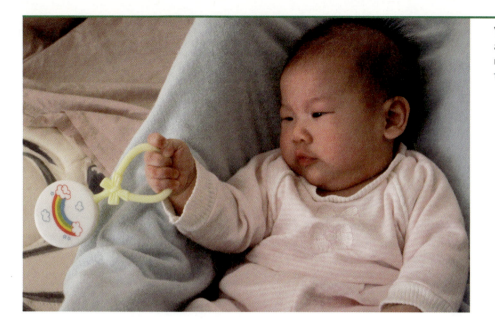

What does this infant understand about her rattle? If she drops the rattle out of sight, will she know that it still exists?

happens when you give 3-month-old Hyeree a plastic rattle. Hyeree grasps the rattle tightly in her hand, shakes it back and forth, and rubs it against her cheek. Then she brings the rattle to her mouth to explore it in detail by sucking and biting on it. Finally, she flings the rattle to the floor and stares brightly back at you. Now, what does Hyeree "know" about the rattle?

According to Piaget, Hyeree doesn't know anything about the rattle unless she is having direct sensory or motor contact with it. At the time when she is grasping and shaking the rattle, she knows how it feels in her hand and how it moves and sounds when she shakes it. She can feel its smooth surface against her cheek. She knows more about the detailed bumps, curves, and textures when she has it in her mouth. After she flings it to the floor, however, she has no way of maintaining an internalized mental representation of the rattle. She therefore can't "think" about the rattle, and she doesn't know or remember anything about it.

Most adults take mental representation for granted. When adults study an object, they form a mental code or image that represents what they know, and they can access this image later when the object is no longer physically available. They are capable of **symbolic (representational) thought**—the ability to form symbols in their minds that represent (or stand for) objects or events in the world. Piaget claimed that young infants cannot form symbols and are therefore stuck in the here-and-now world of their immediate sensory and motor actions. He believed that representational thought gradually emerges as babies develop the ability to form mental symbols. This represents an important achievement, because the emergence of representational thought frees children from the here and now. With representational thought, children can think about past events and anticipate future interactions. Mental representation also allows children to communicate with others, using language. By definition, language of any type requires that arbitrary symbols (words) represent actual things. Without mental representation, it is impossible to learn words and understand what they stand for.

Piaget proposed six substages of sensorimotor thought that describe how representational thought emerges during infancy. These substages are summarized in Table 5.2. If you look carefully across the substages, you will notice a general trend in babies' thinking. Infants begin in the early stages as simply *reflexive*—that is, reacting to environmental stimuli via inborn reflexes. They have no voluntary control over objects or events in their environment but can only react to whatever takes place. Gradually, however, infants begin to take more control. These first attempts occur because infants accidentally notice the effects of certain random actions. They

symbolic (representational) thought
The ability to form symbols (or mental representations) that stand for objects or events in the world.

TABLE 5.2   Piaget's Six Substages of Sensorimotor Thought

SENSORIMOTOR SUBSTAGE	AGE	CHARACTERISTIC	EXAMPLES
1. Basic Reflexes	Birth to 1 month	The first schemes are inborn reflexes.	Rooting, sucking, grasping reflexes.
2. Primary Circular Reactions	1–4 months	Infants discover actions involving their own bodies by accident, then learn by trial and error to repeat the actions until they become habits (schemes).	At first thumb comes to mouth by accident. Through trial and error, infants learn to reproduce the event until a thumb-sucking scheme becomes established.
3. Secondary Circular Reactions	4–10 months	Infants discover actions involving objects in the environment by accident, then learn by trial and error to repeat them until they become habits (schemes).	Holding a rattle, an infant might accidentally shake the rattle and enjoy the noise. Through trial and error, the infant learns to reproduce the event until a shaking scheme becomes established.
4. Coordination of Secondary Schemes	10–12 months	Infants intentionally put two schemes together to solve a problem or reach a goal. Intentionality is a new feature—these new behaviors are no longer discovered by accident.	An infant sees a toy behind a box, pushes the box aside, then reaches for the toy. The infant intentionally combined pushing and reaching schemes to reach the goal (the toy).
5. Tertiary Circular Reactions	12–18 months	Babies are curious about objects in the world and explore them in a trial-and-error fashion, trying to produce novel reactions.	A baby drops a ball from shoulder height and watches what happens. The baby then explores the dropping scheme by dropping the ball from hip height, then head height, then knee height, observing each new result.
6. Transition to Symbolic Thought	18–24 months	Toddlers begin to form symbolic representations of events, showing the beginnings of mental thought. Representations still tend to be physical (rather than purely mental), as when toddlers use their own body movements to represent movements of objects in the world.	A 1½-year-old girl would like to open the lid of a box; to think about this, she opens and closes her hand repeatedly. Rather than working directly on the box, she first uses her hand motion as a way to "think" about how to open it. She is thinking about the box using a symbolic representation (her hand).

begin trying to understand events by using *trial and error*, taking actions and simply observing what happens, then slightly modifying the actions, observing, and so on. Initially, these trial-and-error interactions are observations of effects with no anticipation of what the outcomes might be. Eventually, however, babies show evidence of *intentionality*. That is, they begin to take actions that they expect to have specific outcomes. Intentionality represents an effort to exert control over the environment because it involves taking actions that are intended to produce specific results.

How can parents tell when an infant has achieved representational thought? One line of evidence is the use of language, starting at about 1 year of age—because to use language, the child must have mental representations to attach labels to. A second indicator is *deferred imitation*, when a young child observes a behavior and imitates it later, after a period of several hours or days. If the child did not have a mental representation of the behavior, there would be no memory of the event, and imitation would not be possible. Finally, a third line of evidence for representational thought can be seen in babies' grasp of the concept Piaget called *object permanence*.

Piaget made the provocative claim that young infants do not understand **object permanence**—the fact that objects, events, or even people continue to exist when they are not in the infant's direct line of sensory or motor action. Recall Hyeree and her rattle. Once Hyeree flung the rattle to the floor, Piaget would say that she had no way to think or know about the rattle. Because she couldn't form a mental representation of it, she couldn't consider its continued existence. She couldn't want it or wonder about it. For Hyeree, "out of sight" was literally "out of mind."

Piaget traced understanding of object permanence through the substages of sensorimotor thought, from nonexistence at birth to its full achievement at about age 2 years (Ginsburg & Opper, 1988; Piaget, 1952a, 1954). In the earliest substages, infants simply do not look for an object once it is out of their immediate experience. They make no attempt to get the object back, though they might continue looking at the place where they last saw the object. Later, they might actively try to retrieve an object, but only if part of it is still visible (e.g., reaching for a toy that is partially hidden under a blanket). By about 1 year, babies will attempt to retrieve an object that is completely hidden. Interestingly, however, if babies watch the object being hidden in one location, then watch as a researcher moves the object to a different location (this is called a visible displacement problem), they will look in the first location rather than the second even though they witnessed the whole sequence. By about 18 months, babies are able to solve these *visible displacement* problems, but they still cannot find the object when the displacements are invisible. That is, they watch as the object is hidden in one location but when the researcher secretly moves the object to a different location, the babies look only in the first spot. They don't check other possible places nearby. Finally, by 2 years of age, the child is able to solve *invisible displacement* problems. Piaget described this ability as evidence of full mental representation. The Personal Perspective Box entitled "Where Did It Go?" describes three families as their infants solve a visible displacement problem.

In summary, there are two major developmental trends as an infant moves through the sensorimotor stage. First, the infant progresses from interacting reflexively with the environment through a trial-and-error phase to deliberate and intentional actions on the environment. Second, the child develops the ability to mentally represent objects, events, and people. Infants' early thought processes involve reflexes and immediate sensations and motor actions, but toddlers leave the sensorimotor stage with the ability to internalize their thought processes into a purely "mental" form. Internal and intentional thought provides the building blocks for the next stage of cognitive development.

Of course, not everyone agrees with Piaget's explanation of infant cognition. In particular, researchers from the information-processing approach (which you read about in Chapter 1 and will learn more about in Chapter 8) have found that Piaget underestimated the cognitive skills of infants and toddlers in many areas (Cohen & Cashon, 2006). We will discuss criticisms of Piaget's theory and alternative approaches in later chapters.

object permanence
The fact that objects, events, and people continue to exist even when they are out of a child's direct line of sensory input or motor action.

Think About Diana …

Does Jamie show evidence of object permanence yet? In a few months, how is she likely to react when Diana hides the pinecones under a blanket?

This infant is looking under the blanket for a hidden toy. What does this search behavior tell us about the mental representations formed by infants?

Where Did It Go?

Each of these parents was asked to play a game with their child, similar to the game that researchers sometimes use when studying object permanence. The parents showed their child a toy; then, making sure the child watched, they hid the toy under a blanket (Trial 1). They did the same thing a second time, except that they made sure the baby watched as they moved the toy and hid it in a different place (Trial 2). This is the *visible displacement* task that Piaget used. Here's how these children responded and what their parents' thought.

Hanah Shapiro, mother of Asher, 6 months old (Hollywood, Florida)

Trial 1:
Asher grasped for the rattle when I showed it to him. He watched me hide it but cried when he couldn't see it anymore—he didn't even try to look!

Trial 2:
Again, Asher cried when he could not see the rattle.

Parent's thoughts:
I was surprised Asher didn't even try to look for the rattle. He is normally very inquisitive, looking around a room and reaching for things. As Asher has grown, he explores objects more thoroughly—*everything* goes into his mouth! He particularly likes toys that play music and respond to him. Asher recently taught himself how to turn on the aquarium in his crib. He is, however, content to play with whatever is given to him rather than seeking out a favorite toy.

Paul Lewis, father of Paul David, 11 months old (Riverside, California)

Trial 1:
Paul David found the toy very quickly—after about ten seconds.

Trial 2:
He went looking for the toy under the first location. He searched there for about 15 seconds before losing interest. He never looked under the final destination of the toy!

Parents' thoughts:
Paul David is very interactive and inquisitive. On Trial 1, he went after the ball immediately and was eager to find it. We were very surprised that he did not find the ball the second time. He understood the game and found the ball in Trial 1 but had a hard time making a connection to the ball and its new location. Paul David is very hands-on; he likes most of his toys in his mouth. At this age, it's easy to distract him. If we hide "off-limits" items, he will immediately look for them, but he gives up and loses interest if we move them to a new location.

Nola Akala, mother of Akindele, 25 months old (Deerfield, Illinois)

Trial 1:
Akindele went directly to retrieve the train underneath the sofa cushion.

Trial 2:
He followed me to both locations and retrieved the toys. He looked for the toy in the new location within seconds. I was not surprised. My son is a determined little fellow!

Parent's thoughts:
Akindele knows where to go to get what he wants. This makes my life easier because I can say "Where is ABCD?" (his dog that sings the alphabet song) or "Where is Thomas the train?," and he goes to find them with no problems. When he was younger, Akindele played more by exploring with his mouth; he is more physical with his toys now, turning things over and around. Now he likes toys with a "cause and effect," ones that make a sound when you open a door or that speak when you press a button or slide a bar on the toy.

Q *Were you surprised at the 6- and 11-month-olds' reactions? What reaction do you think these three children would have to an invisible displacement problem? Try these games with some babies you know (with a parent's permission). What do their responses indicate about their cognitive development?*

■ Let's Review . . .

1. Adaptation is an important concept in Piaget's theory of cognitive development, and this concept can be traced back to Piaget's early work in:
   - a. psychology.
   - b. biology.
   - c. philosophy.
   - d. physics.

2. Two-year-old David points to a pickup truck and says, "Look, Mommy, a red car!" Calling the truck a car is an example of what Piaget would call:
   - a. equilibration.
   - b. accommodation.
   - c. abstraction.
   - d. assimilation.

3. When you consider Piaget's cycle of adaptation, what condition comes immediately before accommodation?
   - a. assimilation.
   - b. cognitive equilibrium.
   - c. cognitive disequilibrium.
   - d. organization.

4. According to Piaget, infants in the sensorimotor stage CANNOT:
   - a. use sensory impressions to understand the world.
   - b. use motor actions to understand the world.
   - c. form symbolic representations to understand the world.
   - d. display reflexes during the first month after birth.

5. **True or False:** Piaget is referred to as a "constructivist" because he believed that children learn primarily by copying the cognitive structures that have been constructed by the adults and other more mature people around them.

6. **True or False:** In Piaget's theory, cognitive equilibrium is achieved when children accommodate their schemes so that the schemes provide a better fit with new experiences.

Answers: 1. b, 2. d, 3. c, 4. c, 5. F, 6. T

Learning to Communicate

Language has long been a fascinating subject for psychologists. As you have just learned, it is seen as an indicator of mental representation, and it also seems to be one skill that sets humans apart from other species. Other species have many different ways to communicate with one another, that is, to send and receive information or messages. In this section, we will discuss what sets human language apart. Then we will describe theories of language development and how language develops in infants and toddlers.

As you study this section, ask yourself these questions:

- What are the defining characteristics of language?

- Is language learned or genetically programmed in humans? What role does the language acquisition device (LAD) play?

- How do social interactions and general cognitive level affect language development?

- What is the evidence for and against each of the three views of language development?

- How do infants' prelinguistic skills help to prepare them for language?

- What are the major developments in vocalizations, semantics, and grammar during infancy?

What Is Language?

Three key features distinguish human language (Brown, 1973; Gleason, 1997). First, language has *semanticity,* which means that it represents thoughts, objects, and events through specific and abstract symbols. For example, the word *baby* does not look or sound like a real baby. This word is an abstract symbol. Second, language is *productive,* which means that there is no limit to the number or types of utterances that humans can create. And as long as people follow the rules that their particular language has for how to put sounds together, their novel communications are completely understandable by others. Third, language has the quality of *displacement,* which means that people can communicate about things that are distant in time or space or even about things that are physically or logically impossible or nonexistent. Displacement allows humans to communicate about a vast range of things instead of being limited to the immediate circumstances.

So **language** is an arbitrary system of symbols (words) that is rule-governed and allows communication about things that are distant in time or space. In studying language, it is important to keep in mind the distinction between language *comprehension* and language *production.* Often, young children are able to understand and respond appropriately to spoken language well before they can produce grammatical speech. One point that most researchers agree on is that humans seem to have a very strong instinctive drive to acquire language. Although an impoverished language environment (i.e., one that provides and encourages less language) will affect a child's rate of language acquisition and the quality of the language the child achieves, it is quite difficult to keep humans from developing *any* language (Flavell, 1985; Hulit & Howard, 2007).

How do children grasp the complex rules of language? More intriguing, how are they able to master these rules so quickly? Three basic theories attempt to explain language development. The *learning* theory emphasizes the role of the environment, whereas *nativist* theory emphasizes the role of biology. *Interactionist* perspectives, as you might expect, focus on how various aspects of the environment interact with biological characteristics.

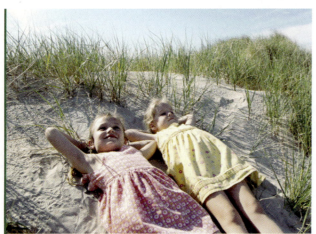

Language uses abstract symbols and allows communication about an infinite number of topics. What fantasies do you think these children could express with their language?

language
An arbitrary system of symbols (words) that is rule-governed and allows communication about things that are distant in time or space.

Learning Theory: Language as a Learned Skill

The **learning theory** of language development is based on behaviorist theories of learning, particularly B. F. Skinner's principles of operant conditioning and Albert Bandura's concept of learning through imitation (Bandura & Walters, 1963; Skinner, 1957). Sometimes referred to as the *environmental view,* this approach views language as a behavior that people learn just like any other skill (Watson, 1924). Learning theorists believe that specific language training governs language development and that biological predispositions do not play an important role.

According to the learning theory, *operant conditioning* principles, particularly the procedure of *shaping* (selectively reinforcing certain behaviors while ignoring or punishing others), explain how children come to produce speech. For example, as a child begins to make sounds, the people around the child tend to reinforce the ones that resemble real words (e.g., "dada") but ignore those that do not (e.g., "gaga"). As a result, the child tends to repeat the reinforced wordlike sounds, and the nonword-like sounds gradually die out. Caregivers also reinforce simple phrases such as "Me want juice" when they give the child what was requested. The more clearly the child says the phrase, the more likely an adult is to understand and comply with the request. As the child progresses, parents shift from shaping individual words to shaping longer phrases and sentences (Skinner, 1957).

learning theory
Theory that sees language as a skilled behavior that children learn through operant conditioning, imitation, and modeling.

Imitation and *modeling* are also important. At the same time that parents and others are selectively reinforcing closer approximations to real words and phrases, they also provide models of more advanced language. One way in which they do this is by repeating the word they think the child means to say. For example, if a young child says "Mmmm" while looking at his mother, the mother might respond by saying "Mommy, that's right, I'm your mommy." When the child tries to imitate the *mmmaaa* sound in the word "mommy," the mother reinforces the attempt. Adults also extend words or phrases, elaborating a bit on what the child said. For example, if the child says "Go" as she walks out the door, her father might say, "That's right, we're going bye-bye." Such interactions reinforce the child's language attempts, and they also provide a model of how to produce more mature words and phrases (Moerk, 1992, 2000).

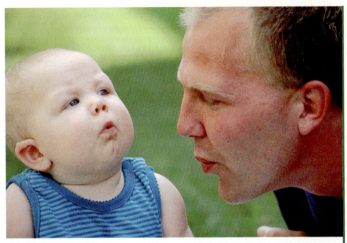

Behaviorists believe that parents use imitation, modeling, and shaping to teach language.

Word meanings can be learned through these conditioning processes. For example, therapists have successfully used shaping techniques to improve the language skills of children with mental retardation or autistic disorder. Simply providing models of language and grammar does not appear to affect these children's language skills, but if the children are actively encouraged to imitate the model, their language often improves (Bohannon & Bonvillian, 1997).

However, there are several criticisms of the learning theory of language development. First, it is not clear how consistent parents are in shaping their children's language. Some studies show that shaping is inconsistent and that parents tend to reinforce or punish the accuracy of the content of children's utterances rather than the grammatical correctness. Also, parents do not appear to explicitly teach their children language rules. In fact, most adults have a great deal of difficulty identifying and describing these complex rules for themselves, much less explicitly teaching them to children. Second, critics argue that much of the language children hear in their everyday lives is incomplete, ill formed, and full of errors—far from being a good model from which to learn. Third, learning principles can't really account for the degree of novelty of children's language utterances, or what linguists call *productivity*. From an early age, children regularly say things that they have never heard before, such as *I goed to the store*. They also express things they have heard in new and innovative ways. Critics argue that it would be impossible for all of children's utterances to result from imitation and shaping. Fourth, critics say that children learn language at a very fast pace—too fast to be explained by reinforcement, shaping, and imitation. Finally, critics question the learning theorists' idea that language is "simply another behavior." Research evidence that we will discuss in the next section suggests that humans are biologically predisposed to detect language and process it differently from other types of information (Brown & Hanlon, 1970; Eisenberg, 1976; Morgan, Bonamo, & Travis, 1995; Pinker, 1994).

Nativist Theory: Born to Talk

The famed linguist Noam Chomsky was one of the first to argue that learning theories could not adequately explain how children are able to master so quickly the complex systems of language. Chomsky proposed a **nativist theory**, the idea that language is an innate human capability. He suggested that humans are born with a **language acquisition device (LAD)**, a brain mechanism that is specialized for detecting and learning the rules of language (Chomsky, 1957, 1981; Lenneberg, 1967). Just as humans are born with specialized organs—a heart and lungs—to carry out the complex tasks of circulation and respiration, they are born with a specialized "language organ" in the brain

your perspective

Have you ever used, or seen someone using, language shaping, modeling, or imitation with young children? What did the adult do, and how did the child respond?

Think About Diana …

How could Diana use the learning theory view of language development to improve Jamie's language skills?

nativist theory
Theory that sees language as an innate human capability that develops when language input triggers a *language acquisition device* in the brain.

language acquisition device (LAD)
A brain mechanism in humans that is specialized for acquiring and processing language.

to carry out the complex task of acquiring language (Siegler, 1998, p. 140). Children must hear some amount of language to activate the LAD, but extensive language input is not necessary. Nor is it essential that the language that is heard be completely grammatically correct. Because the LAD is innate, language acquisition does not require great cognitive skill or cognitive effort. This explains why young children, as well as children with mental retardation and other cognitive delays, all develop at least some language ability quickly and easily. Another strength of the nativist view is that it explains both language acquisition patterns that are similar across different languages and patterns that differ. The LAD is innate but does not preprogram a child to learn a specific language.

Chomsky proposed that the LAD contains an innate knowledge of *universal grammar,* or the aspects of language rule systems that are common across all languages. When a child hears language, the LAD analyzes the language to determine its general type of grammatical construction system. Once the basic grammar of the language is recognized, the child can easily abstract important linguistic information and quickly acquire language. Other nativist theories suggest that the LAD contains more general *operating principles*—assumptions and biases that cause children to treat the language environment in special ways (Slobin, 1982, 1985b). In other words, children are predisposed to pay special attention to certain aspects of the language they hear, such as the ends of words, word order, and differences in intonation. Because of innate operating principles, children notice the subtle patterns their language uses to express things like plurality, possession, or relationships. Children become progressively more sensitive to the features that are most useful in their language (and less sensitive to less useful features). For example, a child learning Russian will gradually focus more closely on word endings to determine relationships between words. In contrast, a child learning English will focus more on the order of words. Regardless of the particular kinds of information contained in the LAD, all nativist theorists agree that a physiologically based LAD exists and that the role of the environment is to trigger its maturation. The environment does not shape or train verbal behavior (Bohannon & Bonvillian, 1997; Saffran et al., 2006).

Is Language Innate? If language acquisition is biologically programmed, then it should show developmental patterns similar to those of other biologically based systems, such as physical maturation. All humans should develop language, and they should develop it in a fairly consistent way. Language should be easy for humans to develop and hard to prevent, but nonhumans should not develop language. Also, there should be physical structures that specialize in language processing. Finally, language development should show *sensitive periods* (times during which a child is particularly sensitive to some aspect of the environment), as happens with many aspects of physical development. Language development shows several of these characteristics.

Do All Humans Develop Language? There is strong evidence from cross-cultural comparisons that all physically intact humans develop language easily and quickly and that the order and pace of achieving linguistic milestones are remarkably consistent across different languages (Caselli et al., 1995; Slobin, 1982, 1985a). Only extremely impoverished linguistic environments seem to keep children from developing some kind of language skill. Presumably, these environments simply don't provide enough language experience to trigger the LAD. Even children with significant cognitive delays develop near-average levels of language usage and syntactic knowledge (Bellugi & St. George, 2001; Fowler, 1998; Tager-Flusberg et al., 1999).

Can Nonhumans Develop Language? Whether nonhumans develop language has been an issue of some debate. Through sign language, by manipulating colored plastic tokens, or even by using specially designed computer keyboards, apes can learn to use words to describe things in their environment, ask and answer questions, and make requests. However, apes do not show knowledge of grammar, rarely include new information in their utterances, and show little understanding of language pragmatics

your perspective

Which language features seem most useful in your native language? Have you ever tried to learn a foreign language? If so, were the important features different from or similar to those of your native language?

such as taking turns in a conversation (Gleason, 1997; Terrace et al., 1980). Recent studies with a bonobo chimpanzee named Kanzi show that he became very good at understanding the meaning and grammar of verbal instructions (Goodall, 1986; Savage-Rumbaugh, Shanker, & Taylor, 1998). Although Kanzi's performance was impressive, nativists argue that it is unclear whether he could *produce* grammatically correct phrases, and they point out that it took eight years of intensive training to teach Kanzi his skills. Human children, by contrast, quickly and easily master the rules of grammar, meaning, and the social use of language. What explains the difference? Nativists argue that other species lack the specialized brain mechanism common to all humans: the LAD.

Can primates develop true language?

Are There Physical Structures That Are Specialized for Language? Although you might not have thought of them this way, the structures of the human mouth and throat are specially suited for producing the complex sounds of spoken language. Other species are not able to produce these sounds (Lenneberg, 1967). In addition, specific areas within the human brain specialize in processing linguistic information. Figure 5.7 shows some of these areas. In most people, the left hemisphere of the brain is chiefly responsible for processing language information. *Wernicke's area,* located in the left temporal lobe for most people, enables human beings to understand spoken words and produce coherent written and spoken language. *Broca's area,* located in the left frontal lobe, directs the patterns of muscle movements necessary for producing speech. Other brain areas that are specialized for language include the *arcuate fasciculus,* a band of fibers that connects Wernicke's area to Broca's area, and the *angular gyrus,* which is involved in processing written language (Gleason, 1997; Maratsos & Matheney, 1994).

So there is evidence of physical structures that are specialized for language processing. However, there does not appear to be a *single area* that is the LAD proposed

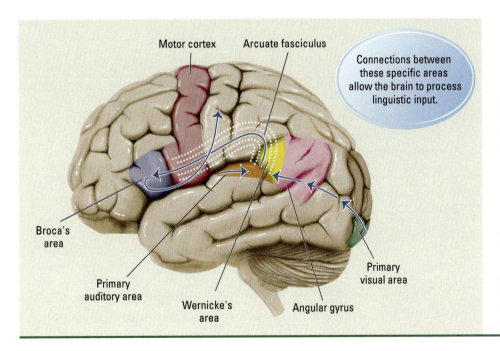

Figure 5.7 • Brain Structures Involved in Language Processing
Wernicke's area is important in comprehending spoken words and producing coherent written and spoken language. Nerves connect Wernicke's area to the *primary auditory cortex. Broca's area* directs the patterns of muscle movements necessary to produce speech sounds. The *arcuate fasciculus* connects Wernicke's area to Broca's area. The *angular gyrus* processes written language. (Based on Fabes & Martin, 2003.)

by Chomsky. Instead, the LAD may be more correctly thought of as several interconnected brain areas (Cornell et al., 1993; Krishner, 1995). As of now, there is still no agreement as to what kinds of innately hardwired information might exist within those structures.

Are There Sensitive Periods for Language Development? According to Lenneberg (1967), human beings acquire language almost exclusively during childhood, before the brain's organization becomes specialized and fixed. Areas of the brain are predisposed to respond to linguistic input, but children must experience language to activate these mechanisms. If a child does not receive enough linguistic input, the period of heightened sensitivity goes by. The key brain areas become specialized for other types of processing, and the opportunity for quick and easy language acquisition is lost. If Lenneberg is correct about sensitive periods, then several things should follow:

- Children who have been deprived of language should show poorer language skills, since the brain areas will not be activated.

- Older children and adults should have greater difficulty learning new languages than young children do.

- Older children and adults should recover less fully from damage to language areas of the brain, because the brain is already specialized.

There is evidence to support each of these predictions (Locke, 1993). First, case reports indicate that people who were deprived of linguistic input during childhood do not develop average linguistic skills; they have particular problems with grammar (Curtiss, 1977). Second, learning a new language seems to be more difficult for older children and adults than for younger children. For example, Johnson and Newport (1989) examined the English language skills of Chinese and Korean immigrants, focusing on the ages at which immigrants arrived in the United States. Figure 5.8 shows that English proficiency clearly relates to the immigrants' age on arrival. Proficiency was not related to the number of years the immigrants had spoken English or to the amount of formal English instruction they had received (Johnson & Newport, 1989). Other research found the same result for deaf children learning American Sign Language: Proficiency in ASL reflected the age at which children first encountered ASL but not how long they had used ASL (Newport, 1990). Finally, recovery of language functions after damage to the left hemisphere of the brain is much faster and more complete for younger children (Stiles & Thal, 1993; Witelson, 1987). In fact, if the left hemisphere is damaged

Figure 5.8 • Support for a Sensitive Period for Language Development
Johnson and Newport found that Chinese and Korean immigrants' proficiency in English was related to the age at which the immigrants arrived in the United States but not to the number of years they had spoken English or the amount of formal English instruction the immigrants had received. (Based on Johnson & Newport, 1989.)

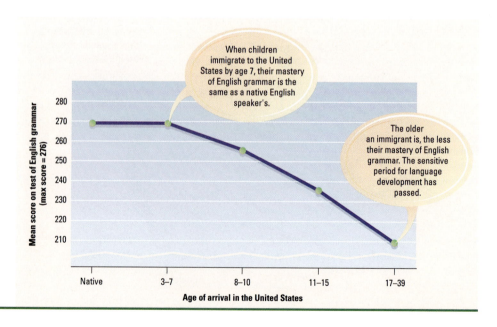

before the age of one year, the language functions can shift into the right hemisphere and "crowd out" the perceptual-spatial skills that usually localize there. The result is that language survives but perceptual-spatial skills suffer. So it seems that language development is biologically very important (Maratsos & Matheny, 1994; Siegler, 1998).

Criticisms of Nativist Theory. One of the major criticisms of nativist theory concerns the kind and amount of linguistic input and feedback that children actually receive. Pinker (1994), a nativist, suggested that language acquisition according to the learning model could occur only if children received explicit corrections of their language errors. Nativists claim that adults do not give this kind of feedback, so language must be innately driven (Morgan et al., 1995; Pinker, 1994). However, some studies show that adults do provide a great deal of corrective feedback (Bohannon & Bonvillian, 1997; Bohannon & Padgett, 1996; Farrar, 1992; Saxton, 1997). In addition, nativist theory predicts that any kind of exposure to language should activate the LAD and lead to average levels of language, regardless of the level of complexity, abstraction, or grammatical correctness of the linguistic input. But research has found that if language exposure comes only from television, children do not develop typical language skills (Sachs et al., 1981). Other critics point out that nativists have not identified a single universal grammar that applies to all known languages—a critical element in any theory that proposes a biologically programmed universal grammar (Tomasello, 1995). Finally, there is ongoing disagreement about whether other species can develop language.

Interaction Theories: Cognitive and Social Interactionist Approaches

Although both Skinner and Chomsky were right about some aspects of language development, many researchers came to believe that these two opposing theorists were too extreme. Dissatisfaction with both purely learning and purely nativist views led researchers to consider how multiple factors might interact to produce language development. Some interaction approaches emphasize the role of cognitive factors; others emphasize how social interactions contribute to language acquisition.

Cognitive Approach: Language Depends on Cognition. Not surprisingly, Jean Piaget, the famous cognitive development theorist you read about earlier in this chapter, stressed the role of the general cognitive abilities of the child in language acquisition. **Piaget's cognitive developmental theory** views language as only one of several different abilities that depend on overall cognitive maturation. Proper cognitive development is a necessary prerequisite for normal language development (Piaget, 1954). For example, you might remember that one of the major cognitive achievements by the end of Piaget's first stage of cognitive development—the sensorimotor stage—is object permanence, or the understanding that objects and people continue to exist even when the infant cannot directly experience them. If words are symbols that represent objects, then babies in the sensorimotor stage do not need them. Either babies directly experience objects (and so need no symbols) or objects are out of babies' immediate experience and no longer exist (requiring no symbols). Only when children develop cognitively to the point at which they need symbols to represent things do they have a reason to use words and develop language. Cognitive skills then interact with environmental demands and language experience to produce increasingly mature language skills.

Some correlational evidence is consistent with Piaget's cognitive developmental view. For example, children first begin using words that indicate something disappeared (e.g., "all gone") at about the same time they develop object permanence. Words that indicate evaluation of effort (e.g., "uh-oh," or "got it") appear at around the same time children start using intentional, goal-directed problem-solving strategies (Gopnik, 1984; Gopnik & Meltzoff, 1984). Some research indicates that children do not use grammatical markers for things like past tense or possession in their spontaneous speech until they have some understanding that there is such a thing as the past and that objects

Piaget's cognitive developmental theory
Theory that sees language as one of several abilities that depend on overall cognitive development. Proper cognitive development is a necessary prerequisite for normal language development.

can be owned (Slobin, 1982). However, these correlations do not prove that the cognitive skills *caused* the language skills to develop. Interestingly, many children with significant cognitive deficits still show normal language development; this should not occur if Piaget's theory is correct. Other work suggests that some specific aspects of language might result from general cognitive development, but others might not (Bellugi & St. George, 2001; Curtiss, 1981; Fowler, 1998; Levy et al., 2000). (We will describe another cognitive view of language development, which is based on current information-processing theory, in Chapter 11.)

social interactionist theory
Theory proposing that language development results from the interaction of biological and social factors and that social interaction is required.

Social Interactionist Theory. **Social interactionist theory** says that language development is the result of a complex interaction between the child's biological predispositions and social interactions. Most social interactionists agree with nativists that humans are biologically prepared to develop language, but they believe that simply hearing language is not enough. Instead, interacting with others is critical: To develop language, children must have conversations with other people. This theory also assumes that children have a strong drive to communicate effectively with others. Because humans are social by nature, children themselves play a significant role by seeking social interactions and trying to communicate with those around them (Akhtar & Tomasello, 2000).

What role do social interactions play for language development? As we noted earlier, it seems that parents provide much more feedback about language performance than some theorists used to think (Hart & Risley, 1995). Children often initiate language interaction by attempting some kind of sound, word, or phrase. If the utterance is grammatically correct, parents might imitate it—repeat or echo it—exactly. But parents also provide implicit feedback. For example, *recasts* are restatements of what the child said but with corrected grammar. If a child says, "I saw two deers in the yard," her mother might recast this and reply, "You saw two *deer*; that's great!" Parents also use *expansions*, repeating but also correcting and elaborating on the child's utterance. For example, a mother might expand the statement about *deers* by saying, "You saw two deer? Remember when we saw the deer at the forest preserve? Did those deer look like the ones in the yard?" Children respond to feedback by correcting their errors (Bohannon & Bonvillian, 1997; Farrar, 1992; Saxton, 1997, 2000).

Everyday activities and games serve as social structures that support language development. What language skills is this baby learning?

Caregivers also present language to children quite carefully and in a structured fashion through social interactions (Bruner, 1983). Examples are joint activities such as songs that have specific gestures, games such as peekaboo, and common daily activities such as baths and meals. These interactions have predictable structures, and all are very common across cultures (Fernald & O'Neill, 1993).

Adults and older children also change their linguistic style when they talk to young children—they use *child-directed speech,* sometimes called *motherese* (Sachs & Devine, 1976; Snow, 1972). As we described in Chapter 4, child-directed speech is slower and higher pitched, has more frequent and more extreme ups and downs in pitch, and includes more questions than does speech directed to adults. Child-directed speech also exaggerates key words and phrases for emphasis and often repeats such words several times. The sentences are short and simple, and they often focus on objects and activities to which the child is actively attending. Child-directed speech occurs in many different cultures and languages (Fernald, 1992; Kuhl et al., 1997). Even deaf mothers use child-directed sign language with their infants, signing more slowly, employing more repetition, and making exaggerated gestures (Masataka, 1996). Infants pay more attention to child-directed speech, and they are more successful in discriminating words both from nonwords and from other words with subtle differences in sound

Think About Diana ...

Develop some examples of how Diana might use recasts, expansions, imitation, joint social activities, and child-directed speech to help Jamie.

when they hear the words in child-directed speech (Cooper & Aslin, 1994; Masataka, 1998; Moore et al., 1997; Thiessen et al., 2005). However, the phenomenon of child-directed speech is not yet fully understood. Although it seems quite useful, it does not have the same features in all cultures. It is not yet known which particular features are most important or whether the central features are different for younger and older children (Bohannon & Bonvillian, 1997; Fee & Shaw, 1998).

your perspective

Have you ever used child-directed speech? What is different about it? What prompted you to use it, and what effect did it have on the child?

Early Communication: How Language Starts

We have explored some of the theories that explain how language develops, but what kinds of changes take place and when do they occur? During the first year of life, important changes relevant to language take place in three areas. First, perceptual skills improve, enabling infants to perceive and discriminate different speech sounds. Second, infants and their caregivers establish a social environment; this encourages babies to turn random sounds into words that communicate specific meanings. Third, having begun life with sounds that are reflexive and unintentional, by 1 year of age, babies begin to use real words.

Perceptual Skills. It does not take babies long to start recognizing differences between speech sounds. One classic study used a variation of the habituation procedure you learned about earlier in this chapter (Eimas et al., 1971). The researchers gave infants as young as 1 month of age a pacifier that activated a predetermined sound (e.g., "ba"). Babies gradually habituated to the sound, slowing their rate and intensity of sucking. When the sound was changed (e.g., to "pa"), the babies increased their rate of sucking. As you might recall, this pattern indicates that the babies remembered the first sound and could tell that the second was different. Other studies have shown the same result with a variety of different speech sounds (Aslin et al., 1998; Saffran et al., 2006). By 6 months, infants are able to discriminate among different sequences of sounds—an important skill, because words are made up of sometimes subtly different sound sequences (Goodsitt et al., 1984). Interestingly, it does not matter whether or not the speech sounds come from the infant's "native" language for 6- to 8-month-olds, but older babies have increasing difficulty with sounds from nonnative languages (Trehub, 1976; Werker & Tees, 1984). It seems that experience with language increases the ability to discriminate among speech sounds in one's own language, but people gradually lose the ability to make discriminations that are not required on a regular basis. Perception of the basic sounds of one's language is a good predictor of later language performance, including important skills such as word comprehension and production (Kuhl et al., 2005; Tsao et al., 2004).

Social Interactions. During the first year, babies are also beginning to understand that they can use sounds to communicate their needs and even to control other people's behavior. Successful communication requires a joint focus of attention; that is, it requires that both people focus their attention on the same object or event at the same time. You can imagine what odd "conversations" would take place if each conversational partner were talking about different objects, events, or topics! Joint focus of attention develops gradually over the first year of life (Carpenter et al., 1998; Hulit & Howard, 2006). Social interactions during infancy are also essential for developing an understanding of the social rules for language. For example, the games and routines you read about earlier (e.g., peekaboo) help to emphasize when and how the infant is expected to contribute to the conversation or interaction. These interactions help infants learn when it is their turn to talk and what kinds of contributions they should make (Bruner, 1983).

Think About Diana . . .
Would you expect Jamie to understand anything about taking turns in conversations yet? How can Diana help her to learn this skill?

From Crying to Words: Speech Production in Infancy. Table 5.3 summarizes the developmental progression in speech production during the first year. Examine this progression, and you will notice that the sounds become

TABLE 5.3 The Development of Speech Sounds in Infancy

AGE	TYPE OF SPEECH SOUND
Birth	• Vegetative and undifferentiated sounds: Reflexive, nonintentional sounds such as crying, burps, sneezing, coughing
2 months	• Greater variation in cries • Cooing to indicate comfort and pleasure
4 months	• Distinctive cries to signal specific states • Cooing and laughing
5 months	• Transitional babbling: Single syllables with one consonant and one vowel sound ("ma")
6 months	• True babbling: Repeated vowel-consonant pair ("mamama")
8 to 12 months	• Echolalia: Immediate imitation of words
9 to 18 months	• Variegated babbling: Multiple, differing syllables ("bapadaga") • Jargon babbling: Babbling that includes native language intonation patterns, rhythms, and stresses • Protowords: Consistent sound patterns used to refer to specific objects and events
One year	• First true words, usually accompanied by gestures, babbling, and/or protowords

(Adapted from Hulit & Howard, 1997.)

increasingly *differentiated*, which means that specific sounds are produced under specific conditions. The sounds also become increasingly *intentional*, which means that the baby produces them for a specific goal, such as showing a caregiver a toy or getting a caregiver to provide something. Both differentiation and intentionality help to lay the groundwork for the first real words around the age of one year.

An infant's first sounds are reflexive, nonintentional sounds such as crying, burping, sneezing, and coughing. Sometimes called *vegetative sounds,* these natural sounds come from many living creatures but are passive and do not convey an intentional meaning (Hulit & Howard, 2006). Also, a baby's first cries are undifferentiated; the cry that is produced because the baby is hungry sounds just like the one that is produced because the baby is wet, tired, angry, or in pain. By 2 months, the baby's cries show much more variation; and by 4 months, the baby is producing distinctive cries to signal such things as discomfort and request. *Cooing,* the production of vowellike sounds such as "o-o-o-o-u-u-u," is present by 2 months. Cooing communicates an infant's pleasure and comfort; infants often coo during social interactions, such as when their caregivers talk to or smile at them. By 4 months, babies both coo and laugh.

At about 6 months infants show *true babbling,* or repeated consonant–vowel syllables such as "mamama." True babbling occurs most often when infants are exploring their surroundings and when an infant is alone (Stark et al., 1993). It includes many different sounds, even sounds that are not part of the infant's native language. Gradually, the babbling comes to resemble more closely the speech sounds of the family's language. This means that all infants have the potential to develop any language. It is the language they experience during the first year or so of life that determines which speech sounds they will continue to produce and which will fade away. True babbling depends heavily on infants' being able to hear themselves clearly. As a result, it is at this point in development that babies with hearing impairments start to show delays, falling behind infants with normal hearing in the amount and variety of speech produced (Oller & Eilers, 1988; Stoel-Gammon & Otomo, 1986).

Between 8 and 12 months, infants start to show *echolalia*, the immediate imitation of others' sounds or words. Echolalia can be very accurate and might lead adults to believe that an infant has learned words, but infants do not understand the sounds they are producing. From 9 to 18 months, infants start to show *variegated babbling*, which includes syllables that differ from one another (e.g., "badagapa"), and jargon babbling, which includes the rhythms and stress patterns of the native language. Jargon babbling sounds just like a conversation but without using real words. It indicates that babies are attending to and beginning to master the rhythmic and intonation characteristics of the language they are hearing but haven't put these aspects together with real words yet.

Finally, around 9 to 10 months, infants begin to use *protowords* (also called *vocables*): consistent patterns of sounds that refer to specific people, objects, or events. For example, one of our sons used the protoword "nee-nee" to refer to his brother Andy, and many children use the protoword "baba" to refer to a baby bottle. Protowords mark an important transition from the random and nonmeaningful vocalizations of babbling to vocalizations that are intentional, consistent, and have specific meaning. Once a child begins using pro-towords, it is usually not long until the child begins using true words.

Think About Diana...
Does Jamie's language development during infancy seem to be progressing at an appropriate pace? What skills does she seem to be showing, and what can Diana expect to develop within the next year?

Semantics: Words and Their Meanings. Around the age of 1 year, children say their first true adult word. The transition from protowords to real words is gradual, and children continue to use gestures, babbling, and protowords along with real words for several months (Goldin-Meadow; 2006; Vihman & Miller, 1988). The average child can produce about 50 words by 18 months of age. Table 5.4 shows the kinds of words typically produced first. As you can see, children's earliest words are usually nouns. They are usually labels for familiar and important objects or people in the environment, such as family members, favorite toys, pets, or favorite foods (Childers & Tomasello, 2002; Nelson et al., 1993; Waxman & Lidz, 2006).

How Are Early Words Acquired? Toddlers learn the meanings of new words at an astonishing pace. One way is through their parents' modeling and labeling of objects and events. It is not surprising that the first words children acquire are the ones that are used most often by their parents. In addition, the more parents talk to their children, the faster the children's vocabulary grows. But children also use a process called *fast mapping*, in which they acquire at least a partial understanding of a word after only a single exposure (Carey, 1977; Woodward et al., 1994). Toddlers as young as 18 months show fast mapping if both the child and his or her conversational partner are attending to the object that is being labeled (Baldwin et al., 1996). Despite these impressive abilities, however, children's early words often include errors. Children frequently show *overextensions*, in which they expand a word's meaning to include more objects than it should (Naigles & Gelman, 1995). For example, a young child who is learning the word *parrot* might overextend this label and use it to refer to any feathered creature that flies with wings (what adults would call *birds*) rather than only to a certain type

TABLE 5.4 The Nature of Early Words

TYPE OF WORD	EXAMPLES	PERCENTAGE OF VOCABULARY WORDS
Names for *general examples* of a category	Mother, father, grandparent, doggy, kitty, toy	51
Names for *specific* members of a category	Mommy, Daddy, Grandma, Spot, Fluffy, Teddy	14
Words for *actions*	Go, up, swing, bounce, run, throw, cry	13
Words that *describe* objects or events	Big, little, mine, yummy, cold	9
Words that express *feelings or relationships*	No, sad, please	8
Words that serve *grammatical functions*	What, where, for, is	4

(Adapted from Nelson, 1973.)

holophrases
Single words used to express an entire idea or sentence.

of bird. Children also show *underextensions,* in which they use a word too narrowly. For example, a child might learn that the family's pet is a parrot and believe that this word applies only to this particular parrot, not to parrots in a zoo, on television, or in other places.

What Is the Function of Early Words? As you have read, young children's early words are often labels for familiar objects or people. Their early attempts at communication consist of single words, but these words often convey an entire idea or sentence. Words used in this way are called **holophrases.** For example, a toddler might say the word *hot* when he sees his father opening the oven door. Depending on the context and accompanying nonverbal cues, this single word might stand for several different and more complex ideas. The child could be saying, "Watch out, Dad! The oven is hot!" or "I need to stay away from that hot oven because it can burn me" or even "Is the oven hot?" Holophrases cannot communicate the wide range of meanings that children will be able to express once they start combining words, but holophrases do serve several communication functions, including demands, requests, desires, and questions. To understand holophrases, the listener needs to pay attention to intonational cues (i.e., which parts of a word or phrase are emphasized), gestures, and the specific context (Tomasello, 2006).

Toddler Grammar: Rules for Putting Words Together. Between 18 and 24 months of age, toddlers start to produce two- and three-word sentences. Many children's earliest sentences are of the form "familiar word + _____," though the particular familiar word differs from child to child (Bloom et al., 1975; Maratsos, 1983). For example, a child's early sentences might all consist of the phrase "No + ____," to produce "No *milk,*" "No *Mommy,*" "No *nap,*" "No *kitty,*" and so forth. The specific functions served by early sentences (e.g., to make demands, ask questions, or claim possession) are very similar across several different languages (Slobin, 1979).

As toddlers expand their language production to sentences, they often use telegraphic speech. Like telegrams, **telegraphic speech** includes words that are essential to get the meaning across but leaves out nonessential words. Instead of saying, "I'm going to watch my brother Will play baseball," a 2-year-old is likely to say, "I watch Will." Interestingly, even such limited utterances follow certain grammatical rules. Young children do not randomly combine words; they choose certain combinations of words and word orders (de Villiers & de Villiers, 1999; Mandel et al., 1996). For example, toddlers usually place nouns before verbs, as in "Daddy play" rather than "play Daddy"; and they place possessives before nouns, as in "my kitty" instead of "kitty my." Such combinations indicate a beginning understanding that the ordering of words, not just the words themselves, conveys important information.

telegraphic speech
Speech that includes only words that are essential to get the meaning across, leaving out unessential words.

This young child is likely using telegraphic speech to communicate. What words do you think he is saying, and what do you think his full meaning is?

The infant and toddler period is one of amazing change in language abilities. It is also a time when many parents might begin to notice the vast individual differences between their child and others in the pace of language development and to worry if their child is not saying words or putting together sentences as quickly as other children of the same age. When should parents worry about their child's pace of language development? What are some common language delays, and what kinds of therapy are available? The field of *speech-language pathology* helps to provide answers to these kinds of questions. To find out more about this field, read the Professional Perspective box called "Career Focus: Meet a Speech-Language Pathologist."

Career Focus: Meet a Speech-Language Pathologist

Deena Bernstein, Ph.D.
Bronx, New York
*Certified Speech-Language Pathologist,
Lehman College/City University of New York;
coauthor with Ellenmorris Tiegerman-Farber
of Language and Communication Disorders in
Children (2002), published by Allyn and Bacon*

What are the early signs of problems in language development?

Parents are often the first to suspect that a child might be delayed in acquiring language. They might notice that their infant does not do much babbling ("abbababa") or stops producing these playful sounds.

The child might not interact or make eye contact when parents try to talk and play with the child. Some young children will have problems learning to produce the sounds of speech. They will be difficult to understand, even beyond the preschool years. Others might be slow to learn new words, word endings (such as "-ing" or "-ed"), or small functional words (such as "is," "am," "was") or to string words together to make sentences.

Some might struggle with how to use language to communicate, not knowing how to ask for objects or actions they want. If parents notice these types of problems, they should seek help. Speech-language pathologists will conduct a speech-language evaluation and work with other professionals to help determine whether a language delay exists, the possible cause(s) for a delay, the skills the child has and/or needs to learn, and intervention strategies that would help the child. It is important that a child receive speech-language therapy as soon as he or she is diagnosed as having a language delay, no matter the cause. The earlier a child receives services, the greater are his or her chances for success.

What are other common problems that you see in your practice?

Some parents get concerned when they hear their 3-year-old say things like "I, I, I, I, I want the red car," but this is very common. Three- to three-and-a-half-year-olds often repeat not only whole words ("my, my, my, crayon")

but also phrases ("Mommy, I want, Mommy I want, Mommy I want a drink,") or even parts of words ("play, play, playschool"). However, if a child repeats the sounds of a word ("p, p, p, pot"), shows signs of struggle behaviors (such as tics, facial tension, or grimaces), or frequently produces a repetition or prolongation ("sssssssit," in more than one out of ten words), then this could indicate a stuttering condition.

Children who have language problems in the first five years of life are at risk for reading and writing problems later. When learning to read and write, children must actively think about all the components of the language system, and this can be difficult for children who have had a difficult time learning the oral language system. Parents should monitor and encourage their child's literacy skills and work with their child's teachers to provide any special help the child might need.

What causes problems in language development?

Often, the reason is not known. Some children have conditions that lead to language problems, such as hearing loss, mental retardation, autism, or attention deficit hyperactivity disorder. For some children, there is a genetic component. Researchers now believe that the "wiring" in the child's brain that is used to learn language is not operating at its optimum capacity, but they don't know why some individuals' "wiring" is less efficient than that of others.

What training is needed to work as a speech-language pathologist?

One needs a master's degree in speech-language pathology or communication disorders. Different states have different requirements, but some kind of certification and/or licensing is needed.

Q *Do any speech or language problems run in your family? On the basis of what you have learned about language development from this chapter, what techniques do you think might help people with speech and/or language problems?*

In this chapter, we have discussed some of the surprising capabilities of young infants and toddlers and have described how they integrate their perceptual experiences to support their cognitive and language development. Clearly, infants and toddlers need many more years and support from those around them to become sophisticated thinkers and conversationalists, but they are far from helpless even during infancy.

■ Let's Review . . .

1. The LAD refers to:
   a. a specific structure in the brain's left hemisphere that governs language development.
   b. the process of learning language.
   c. the specific structured parent–child interactions that help to teach language rules.
   d. several brain areas that together enable humans to detect and learn language rules.

2. The term *operating principles* refers to:
   a. an innate knowledge of universal grammar.
   b. innate predispositions to notice certain elements of language.
   c. the strategies that parents use to shape their children's use of grammar.
   d. rules that govern how connections between units change in response to external feedback.

3. Child-directed speech fosters language development in all of the following ways *except* by:
   a. providing feedback about grammar.
   b. drawing an infant's attention to the topic of conversation.
   c. explaining the operating principles for the native language.
   d. emphasizing important features of speech.

4. Which of the following provides the best support for the hypothesis that there are sensitive periods in language development?
   a. The existence of physical organs that are specialized for language processing.
   b. The fact that adults and children are both able to learn second languages.
   c. The fact that children are especially sensitive to child-directed speech.
   d. The greater degree of language recovery shown by children than by adults after damage to the brain's left hemisphere.

5. **True or False:** Human newborns are able to discriminate between speech sounds of their native language but not between sounds of other languages.

6. **True or False:** The use of protowords marks the first use of adult language.

Answers: 1. d, 2. b, 3. c, 4. d, 5. F, 6. F

Thinking Back to Diana...

Now that you have studied this chapter, you should be able to explain how Diana can use concepts about perceptual, cognitive, and language development to understand and support her baby's development. You should be able to list at least a dozen specific concepts and explain how each would relate to Diana and Jamie.

Like most parents of infants, Diana is interested in what her baby understands and how she can help to support her baby's learning. She might be interested to know about the perceptual skills that Jamie is developing, including the kinds of visual and auditory preferences she might show.

Diana might be especially interested in the fact that newborns really do prefer to look at human faces. This preference and the supportive behavior it elicits from adults might help to keep Diana and Jamie looking and "talking" to one another for extended periods, which helps to support Jamie's developing cognitive and language skills. It would be useful to tell Diana about infants' abilities to integrate their sensory experiences through intermodal perception. This skill also helps to support Jamie's cognitive development: According to Piaget, a critical part of cognitive development is combining and coordinating experiences to construct understanding. Piaget would encourage Diana to provide Jamie with as much sensory and motor experience as she can, since infant thought is based on these experiences and they lay the foundation for later stages. As Jamie encounters new things in her environment, her natural tendencies to adapt will lead her to construct new understandings of her world. Finally, Diana might be interested to know that even though human infants seem biologically prepared to develop language, the social and language interactions she helps to provide for Jamie are essential to support this important human skill.

■ Chapter Review...

How is the preferential-looking technique used to test infant perception?

Infants are shown two or more stimuli, and the amount of time spent looking at each one is recorded. When infants spend more time fixating on some stimuli than on others, it can be inferred that the infants are visually processing and discriminating the stimuli (i.e., they can see the differences among the stimuli). Using this technique, Robert Fantz and other researchers have demonstrated that young infants prefer to look at moving stimuli, outer contours and edges, areas of high contrast, detailed or complex patterns, symmetrical patterns, curves, and human face patterns.

How is the habituation–dishabituation technique used to test infant perception or avenues of sensation?

Infants are presented with the same stimulus repeatedly until they habituate (show decreased response). When a new stimulus is presented, dishabituation (renewed interest and response) indicates that the infant has processed the difference between the old and new stimuli.

Can infants coordinate information across different sensory modalities or avenues of sensation?

Yes. Research on intermodal perception indicates that young infants can match what they see with what they hear or feel. For example, one-month-olds look longer at the shape of a pacifier they previously held in their mouths, and older infants can match the sounds of objects with their filmed movements.

How is Piaget's background in biology reflected in his theory of cognitive development?

Piaget was a young scholar in biology, producing his first scientific publication at the age of 10. As a teen, he studied how sea mollusks adapt their shells to changes in water currents, and this image of adaptation formed the core of his theory of cognitive development. Piaget theorized that children create and adapt their own cognitive structures in response to their changing experiences with the world.

Why is Piaget's theory considered a constructivist view? What are the main concepts in Piaget's theory about how children develop cognitive structures?

Piaget's is considered a constructivist view because he emphasized that children learn primarily by interpreting their own environment and experiences in light of the knowledge and experiences they already have, thus constructing their own schemes and cognitive structures. Schemes are the cognitive structures that are constructed by the child, and they are modified through adaptation. New experiences are assimilated into existing schemes, and if the experiences do not fit adequately, cognitive disequilibrium results. Children can accommodate, or modify, their schemes to provide a better fit with the environment, returning the child to cognitive equilibrium. Organization is the tendency to integrate cognitive structures into larger coherent systems, and reflective abstraction is used to notice patterns and connections among related schemes.

What is Piaget's first stage of cognitive development, and what are the basic changes that occur as children progress through this stage?

In the stage of sensorimotor thought (birth to 2 years), infants begin by understanding the world through inborn reflexes and through their own direct sensory and motor actions. The ability to represent knowledge internally, in symbolic, mental form, develops gradually during this stage.

What are the defining characteristics of language?

Human language has *semanticity* and displacement and is productive. It is made up of arbitrary and abstract symbols and is governed by specific rules for how to communicate.

How do learning theorists explain language development?

Learning theorists say that language is learned through shaping of behavior, imitation, and modeling. Research indicates that language can be affected by differential reinforcement.

What evidence supports the idea that language is innate?

Nativist theory proposes that humans are endowed with an innate language acquisition device that contains either knowledge of universal grammar or operating principles that guide the processing of language information. Across many languages, children develop language quickly and easily, with marked consistency in the achievement of language milestones. There is disagreement as to whether nonhumans develop language, but the pace of animal language achievements is slower and the effort required is much greater than for humans. There are brain structures that are specialized for language processing, though there does not seem to be a single LAD brain organ. There is some evidence for the existence of sensitive periods in language development.

Describe the interaction theories of language development.

Cognitive approaches view language as dependent on other, more general cognitive skills. For Piaget, the broader ability to represent objects leads to the need for language. Social interaction theory emphasizes the importance of social interactions for acquiring language.

What abilities do infants have or develop that prepare them for language?

Infants have at birth or rapidly develop abilities to discriminate speech sounds and sequences of sounds, localize sound direction, and recognize a voice. Their recognition of speech sounds from their native language rapidly improves, but they lose the ability to discriminate sounds of other languages. Social interaction during the first year of life helps infants to learn that sounds can be used to communicate and fosters early pragmatic skills such as turn-taking. Child-directed speech and a developing joint focus of attention between infants and caregivers foster prelinguistic skills. Infants begin life making nonspeech sounds with no consistent meaning, then progress through cooing, babbling, echolalia, and protowords during the first year of life. Toddlers expand their vocabularies and learn grammatical rules for combining words into phrases and sentences.

■ Key Terms

accommodation (165)
adaptation (164)
assimilation (164)
constructivist view (162)
dishabituation (157)
equilibration (165)
habituation (157)
habituation–dishabituation technique
   (157)
holophrases (182)
intermodal perception (158)
language (172)
language acquisition device (LAD) (173)
learning theory (172)

nativist theory (173)
object permanence (169)
organization (163)
perception (154)
Piaget's cognitive developmental theory
   (177)
preferential-looking technique (155)
reflective abstraction (165)
scheme (163)
sensorimotor thought (166)
social interactionist theory (178)
symbolic (representational) thought
   (167)
telegraphic speech (182)

mydevelopmentlab Where human development comes to life!

If you are using MyDevelopmentLab, you have access to an ebook version of this textbook, along with dozens of valuable resources per chapter—including video and audio clips, simulations and activities, self-assessments, practice tests, and other study materials. Here is a sampling of the resources available for this chapter.

Explore
The Shaping Process

Watch
Noise and the Brain
B.F. Skinner Speaks
Language Learning
The Sensorimotor Stage

If you did not receive an access code to MyDevelopmentLab with this text and wish to purchase access online, please visit www.mydevelopmentlab.com.

chapter 6
Socioemotional Development in Infants and Toddlers

Erin remembers the first time she left her 1-year-old son Patrick at a day care center. Until then, Erin's mother had been taking care of Patrick during the day, but now it was time for him to spend some time in day care while Erin was at work. Erin had heard about Heartland Children's Daycare through friends and had taken Patrick for a visit during one of the center's open houses. Patrick was shy at first; he seemed overwhelmed by all of the new faces and things to do. Gradually, however, he warmed up and began playing with some of the toys and books. This was a good sign that Patrick might do well in day care.

On the drive over to the center on Patrick's first day, Erin tried to be as cheerful as she could. She mentioned all of the new things Patrick could do at day care: painting, listening to stories, playing outside, and meeting new friends. Patrick was quiet.

At the center, Patrick clung tightly to his mother and peered around. The center was busy, with lots of children running and playing. One of the teachers came over to greet Patrick. She bent down to talk to him, but Patrick shied away. Erin again reminded him of all of the fun he would have, but she was barely holding back her own tears. It was hard for her to leave Patrick in this new setting. Finally, Erin kissed Patrick on the cheek. After saying good-bye, she left Patrick with the teacher. When she got back to her car, Erin just sat and worried. Was she doing the right thing? Would Patrick be sad all day? Would he ever adjust to day care?

After studying this chapter, you should be able to use at least a dozen concepts to help Erin understand Patrick's reaction to his new setting. You will be able to explain what researchers know about infant–parent attachment and about when and why young children fear strangers and new settings. Does Patrick seem to have a secure attachment to his mother? What clues can you find in the scenario that you just read? How does Patrick's temperament factor into his reaction? What can Erin do to help Patrick cope with the emotions he feels? Finally, what should Erin expect regarding Patrick's adjustment to the new center and the kinds of friendships he might make there? Did Erin handle Patrick's first day well?

> As you read this chapter, look for the "Think About Erin . . ." questions that ask you to consider what you're learning from Erin's perspective.

Most parents remember the first time they left their child in a day care center or with a baby-sitter. That first time is usually not easy. Some children get very upset; others react more calmly. In this chapter, we explore some of the reasons behind these differences. We begin by looking at how researchers study human attachment and how they classify the various types of attachments that infants form with their parents. We also look at temperament and at the types of temperament that have been identified, and we discuss emotional development in infants and toddlers. We conclude the chapter by exploring the types of social interactions infants and toddlers develop and how they play with friends and peers. As you would imagine, children's attachment styles, temperaments, emotions, and social expectations and skills all contribute to their varied responses to situations like Patrick's first morning in day care.

Attachment

attachment
An emotional tie to a specific other person or people that endures across time and space.

In this first section, we look at the emotional bond that develops between an infant and his or her primary caregivers. Although most of us would call it "love," researchers refer to this bond by its more technical name: *attachment*. **Attachment** is an emotional tie to a specific person or people that endures across time and space (Ainsworth, 1973). Infants don't bond with everyone. They reserve this special emotional attachment for the select few who provide their primary care. From its beginnings in the 1950s, most research in this area has focused primarily on the attachments that infants form with their mothers. Of course, today, many infants receive a substantial amount of care from fathers, older siblings, grandparents, other close relatives, and day care providers, and they can form attachments with whoever provides consistent and loving care. In our discussion, we will sometimes refer to "caregivers," though this term sounds too technical for the special emotions and relationships that we will discuss. We'll use the term *mother* when describing research that primarily investigated mother attachments, but we hope that fathers and other caregivers will recognize that their relationships follow a similar path.

As you study this section, ask yourself these questions:

- What are the historical roots that gave rise to modern research on attachment? How do these roots affect our thinking about attachment today?

- How do researchers use the "Strange Situation" to measure infant attachment? What kinds of attachments have investigators identified?

- What primary factors influence healthy attachments? What primary factors influence less healthy attachments?

- How do the emotional bonds that are established early in life influence development throughout childhood?

The Story of Attachment Research

Modern research on human attachment has two important roots: the ethological theory of John Bowlby and the classic primate experiments conducted by Harry Harlow.

John Bowlby's Ethological Theory. In John Bowlby's (1958, 1988) ethological theory, attachment emerges from a system of traits and behaviors that have evolved over time to increase the infant's chances of survival. Human infants are dependent on their caregivers for a relatively long period of time. The deep emotional bond of attachment increases the amount of attention and the quality of care that an infant receives. Bowlby (1958) commented, "It is fortunate for their survival that babies are so designed by Nature that they beguile and enslave mothers" (p. 367). Smiling, crying, and calling are behaviors that infants use to bring adults closer. Newborns follow adults with their eyes. Later, as they learn to reach, crawl, and then walk, children are able to physically find, follow, and cling to their caregivers. Bowlby emphasized the infant's smile as a powerful social releaser of nurturing behavior in adults. Adults have evolved to respond positively to these social cues and to see the infant's round face, bright eyes, and chubby appearance as cute and cuddly.

Evolution, then, has provided an interactive system that links nurturing adults to infants who depend on the adults' loving care. Bowlby believed that attachment is especially evident when an infant seeks nearness or proximity to a protective adult in moments of distress or fear (Thompson, 1998). The attachment figure provides a secure base of emotional comfort for the infant.

Bowlby (1969) proposed that infants develop attachments in the following four stages:

1. *Orientation without discrimination* (first two to three months after birth). Infants signal and respond to any available and caring adult. In this initial stage, an attachment to a specific caregiver has not yet formed.

2. *Orientation with discrimination* (2 to 6 months of age). Infants begin to show a decided preference for their primary caregivers, signaling and responding more to the people who take care of them than to other people.

3. *Safe-base attachment* (6 months to 3 years of age). Infants and toddlers actively seek to be near their favored caregivers. They follow and cling to them, and they use them as a safe base to explore the environment. Infants and, later, toddlers often become visibly distressed when separated from their attachment figures, indicating that the emotional bond endures across both time and space. Fear of strangers also emerges.

4. *Goal-corrected partnerships* (3 years of age and up). Children begin to understand the feelings and motives of their caregivers. The relationship goes both ways now: Children can adjust or "correct" their behaviors to the changing needs and desires of their attachment figures, just as attachment figures adapt to children's changing needs. For example, children learn that sometimes their attachment figures are busy or have other demands that conflict with caregiving. There is now a more integrated emotional relationship between child and caregiver.

Since the 1950s, Bowlby's ethological theory has provided the dominant framework for study of the special bonds between infants and adults.

Harry Harlow's Research with Rhesus Monkeys. Also during the 1950s, psychologist Harry Harlow conducted one of the most famous series of experiments in child development research. Harlow raised infant rhesus monkeys with the two types of surrogate (substitute) "mothers" shown in Figure 6.1 (Harlow & Zimmermann, 1959). One surrogate was made of bare wire mesh; the other had a soft cloth covering. Would infant monkeys form an attachment to either of these objects? Would the presence of a surrogate provide any emotional support for the infant? The cloth-covered surrogate did. With his experiments Harlow provided a convincing demonstration that the critical ingredient in attachment formation is **contact comfort**—the comfortable feeling that infants gain by clinging to a soft attachment figure.

Who could resist this smile? Chubby cheeks, soft skin, and big smiles are just some of the features that induce adults to want to cuddle and take care of babies.

Think About Erin...

Which one of Bowlby's four stages best describes the attachment behaviors that Patrick showed on his first day in day care?

your perspective

What do you think were the qualities in your parents or other caregivers that made you become attached to them? Although you cannot remember back into your infancy, perhaps you can reflect back and think about the things they did for you that made you feel comfortable and attached to them.

contact comfort
The comfortable feeling that infants gain by clinging to a soft attachment figure.

Figure 6.1 • Surrogate Mothers from Harlow's Experiment Rhesus monkeys became emotionally attached to the cloth mother that provided contact comfort but not to the wire mother that provided food.

Harlow's finding contradicted the psychoanalytic and behavioral theories that were predominant at this time. These theories predicted that infants would form attachments with the caregiver who provided food. In psychoanalytic theory, oral gratification during feeding establishes the initial bond between infant and mother (recall Freud's oral stage, discussed in Chapter 1). In behavioral theory, food serves as a powerful reinforcer for behaviors related to attachment. Feeding was not what determined attachment for Harlow's monkeys, however. Even when the infants received milk from the wire mesh mother, they spent the great majority of their time clinging to the cloth mother. Harlow theorized that the cloth mother provided the infants with the kind of emotional security John Bowlby had described. When placed in an open room or an unfamiliar setting, infant monkeys without their cloth mothers showed extreme anxiety. They typically huddled in the corner, rocking and hugging themselves. But when their cloth mothers were in the room, these same infant monkeys showed a very different reaction. They would hug and cling to the mothers, and then, finding security in the mothers' presence, they would explore the room and play freely. When confronted with a fear stimulus (e.g., a clanging robot or a model of a giant insect), the infant monkeys first sought the comfort of their cloth mothers and then turned bravely to face their fears. The mother surrogates that provided contact comfort obviously served as the secure base that these infant monkeys needed. Mere feeding provided no such benefit.

Taken together, Bowlby and Harlow's findings provided the lens through which subsequent researchers have examined infant–parent attachments. Infants have formed an emotional bond to a specific person when they seek closeness to that person as a secure base. When separated from this person, the infant shows distress. When reunited with this person, the infant clings to the attachment figure and becomes emotionally comfortable again.

Think About Erin…

What similarities do you see between the reactions of Harlow's monkeys to strangers and separation and Patrick's behavior on his first day in day care? How were Harlow's experiments similar to situations faced by human children?

Where do infant monkeys turn when they are frightened? What does this response tell us about the attachment that they have formed with their caregivers?

Mary Ainsworth and the Strange Situation

Now let's look at how researchers built on Bowlby and Harlow's work to investigate human attachment relationships.

Secure Attachment in the Strange Situation. To investigate attachment in human infants, Mary Ainsworth developed the *Strange Situation* test (Ainsworth, 1973; Ainsworth et al., 1978; Ainsworth & Wittig, 1969). Following Bowlby and Harlow, Ainsworth based her procedure on the idea that infants will seek to be near their attachment figure when they are distressed by an unfamiliar setting or an unfamiliar person. The **Strange Situation** consists of eight episodes that are strictly scripted to allow researchers to observe attachment behaviors in human infants, as described in Table 6.1. The purpose is to place the infant in a "strange" or unfamiliar setting with the primary caregiver (in Ainsworth's time, this was almost exclusively the mother). Does the infant use the mother as a secure base for exploring the new setting? Does the infant become distressed when the mother leaves and seek her proximity when she returns? Does the infant prefer the mother over an unfamiliar adult?

Mary Ainsworth developed the Strange Situation, a method of testing attachment security that has been used by many researchers in the United States and in other countries.

Strange Situation
A structured laboratory procedure that is used to observe attachment behavior in human infants.

TABLE 6.1 Mary Ainsworth's Strange Situation Procedure

EPISODE	BEHAVIOR OF INFANT SHOWING SECURE ATTACHMENT
1. Introduction: Assistant introduces mother and baby to the room. This episode lasts 30 seconds; the other episodes last approximately 3 minutes each.	Baby is held by mother.
2. Unfamiliar room: Mother places baby on floor with toys and sits in chair. Mother is told not to direct baby's actions but otherwise to respond normally.	Baby might be wary of room at first but uses mother as a *safe base* of security. Plays with toys while mother is present. Usually maintains visual contact with mother during play.
3. Stranger enters: Unfamiliar female adult knocks on door, then enters. Stranger speaks with mother, then approaches baby to play.	Baby might show *stranger anxiety* and clearly prefers mother over stranger. While mother is present, baby might allow stranger to approach and play.
4. Mother leaves: Mother quietly leaves the room, leaving baby with the stranger. Stranger returns to sit in her chair.	Baby shows *separation anxiety* and renewed *stranger anxiety*. Baby might be somewhat comforted by stranger but clearly wants mother.
5. Reunion; stranger leaves: Mother returns, and stranger leaves. Mother comforts baby if baby wishes and returns baby to play with the toys.	Baby *seeks contact* with mother for joyful reunion. Seeks proximity, clings. Baby might continue playing while mother is present.
6. Mother leaves again: Mother says "bye-bye" and leaves infant alone in the room.	Baby shows *separation anxiety*, distress.
7. Stranger enters again: While baby is still alone, the same stranger enters again. Stranger sits in chair, then calls or approaches baby to play.	Baby might show *stranger anxiety* and clearly prefers that mother return.
8. Reunion; stranger leaves: Mother returns and stranger leaves. Mother picks up baby for a reunion that ends the procedure.	Joy on reunion. Baby *seeks proximity and contact* with mother.

stranger anxiety
Wariness or fear of unfamiliar adults.

separation anxiety
Distress infants experience when separated from their primary caregivers.

secure attachment
In Ainsworth's classification system, the healthy type of attachment between an infant and a caregiver. It is indicated when the infant seeks contact with the caregiver, clings, and is soothed by the caregiver and when the infant uses the caregiver as a safe base for exploring unfamiliar environments. Other indicators include *separation anxiety* and *stranger anxiety*.

The procedure begins when the mother brings her infant into a laboratory setting, almost always on a university campus. Infants are normally observed at about one year of age. The setting is an average-sized room with a few chairs and interesting toys strewn around. An observation mirror on one wall usually permits observers to videotape the sessions for later analysis. After a 30-second introductory period, the mother places the baby on the floor in the center of the room and sits in one of the chairs. Most infants are wary of the unfamiliar setting and usually situate themselves so that they can maintain visual contact with their mothers.

After 3 minutes, an unfamiliar female adult comes in. In a friendly manner, she speaks to the mother and then approaches the infant to play. Most infants show signs of **stranger anxiety**, a wariness or fear of unfamiliar adults. Infants might allow the stranger to approach and play, although most remain wary. Next, the mother calmly leaves the room. Losing their secure base, most infants show renewed stranger anxiety. They are no longer willing to play with the stranger and instead move to the door (or to the mother's chair), where they whine, cry, or show other visible signs of distress that indicate **separation anxiety**. For the next episode, the mother returns and the stranger leaves. Infants joyfully hug and cling tightly to their mothers. Feeling secure once more, infants resume their play. As the episodes continue, the mother exits again, leaving the infant alone; then the stranger reenters. These episodes allow additional opportunities to observe separation anxiety and stranger anxiety, respectively. The infant is reunited with the mother in the final episode.

Although anxieties are not normally considered positive, you can see from this description that *separation anxiety* and *stranger anxiety* both signify that the infant has formed a special emotional attachment to a specific other person. It is the mother, not the stranger, who provides the security the infant needs to feel comfortable in the new setting. The loss of this security is evident when the mother leaves. Wariness of the stranger and preference for the mother both indicate what Ainsworth termed **secure attachment**. The most reliable indicator of secure attachment, however, is the way in which the infant responds when the mother returns to the room: Securely attached infants seek contact with the mother, cling tightly, and allow the mother to soothe and comfort them. Of the thousands of infants and parents observed by Ainsworth and other U.S. researchers in the Strange Situation procedure, approximately 62 percent show secure attachment (Thompson, 2006). But what about the other 38 percent?

Think About Erin...

How were Patrick's behaviors similar to the ones Ainsworth observed with infants in her Strange Situation test? Does Patrick seem to have a secure attachment with his mother? How would you help Erin to understand that Patrick's crying and other behaviors indicate a healthy attachment with her?

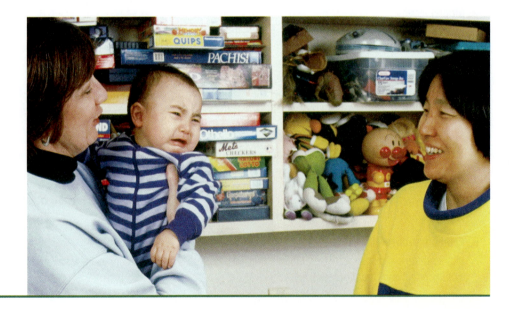

Like this baby, most infants go through a period of time when they are afraid of strangers. What does this behavior tell us about the attachment that has formed between the infant and mother?

Insecure Attachments. Ainsworth identified two patterns of *insecure attachment*. With **insecure–avoidant attachment,** seen in approximately 15 percent of infants studied in the United States, infants do not seem to use the mother as a secure base. When the stranger enters, these infants do not show a special preference for their mother; they might go directly to the stranger or play with the stranger without first needing to cling to the mother. When the mother leaves, these infants seem undisturbed. They might continue playing rather than going to the door and fussing. When the mother reenters, these infants turn away, ignore her, or avoid her. There is debate about how to interpret this pattern of behavior (Thompson, 1998). Are the infants actively avoiding contact with a parent who has rebuffed them in the past, or are they merely uninterested because they have not developed a special bond?

Insecure–resistant attachment is seen in about 8 percent of infants (Thompson, 2006). These infants usually seek the proximity of their mother, but they do not seem to gain comfort from the contact. Some show exaggerated stranger and separation anxiety or a strong need to stay close to the parent. But when the mother picks the baby up, some of these infants fight off her efforts to provide comfort, often showing signs of anger or heightened distress. Others seem passive when their mothers try to console them. Some researchers label this category *insecure–ambivalent attachment,* because the infant seeks proximity but then shows ambivalence about contact with the caregiver.

More recently, researchers have added another category called **insecure–disorganized (or disoriented) attachment,** seen in nearly 15 percent of infants who have been tested (Main & Solomon, 1986, 1990; Thompson, 2006). These infants seem confused or dazed, or they might show contradictory behaviors. They might be calm one moment and angry the next. They might remain motionless or might show apprehension as their parent approaches. Their behaviors are not consistently avoidant or resistant, so they do not fall neatly into either of those classifications of insecure attachment. Table 6.2 summarizes the types of attachment that Mary Ainsworth and other researchers have identified.

Other researchers have questioned whether infant–parent attachments should be classified into separate categories at all (Fraley & Spieker, 2003). They note that infants vary so much within these four attachment categories that it might be more informative to rate them all on two continuous scales: degree of avoidance of the

insecure–avoidant attachment
In Ainsworth's classification, an unhealthy type of attachment that is indicated when infants do not use their caregivers as a safe base for exploring unfamiliar environments, do not prefer the caregiver over unfamiliar adults, and are not visibly distressed by separation. Such infants ignore or avoid their caregivers when reunited after separation.

insecure–resistant attachment
In Ainsworth's classification, an unhealthy type of attachment that is indicated when infants seek the proximity of their caregiver but do not seem to gain comfort from the contact.

insecure–disorganized (or disoriented) attachment
An unhealthy type of attachment that is indicated when infants seem confused or dazed or show contradictory behaviors in the Strange Situation. Infants may be calm and then become angry, or they may be motionless or apprehensive.

TABLE 6.2 Different Types of Attachment Identified in the Strange Situation

TYPE OF ATTACHMENT	BEHAVIORS
Secure	• Baby uses mother as safe base for exploring unfamiliar room. • Baby prefers mother over stranger. • Baby might show distress when separated from mother. • Baby seeks proximity and contact with mother on reunion.
Insecure–avoidant	• Baby does not prefer mother over stranger. • Baby avoids contact with mother by turning or looking away.
Insecure–resistant	• Baby shows ambivalent approach–resist behavior: seeks proximity with mother but then resists contact. • Baby does not avoid mother. • Some infants show anger; others are passive.
Insecure–disorganized/disoriented	• Babies seem confused or dazed or may show contradictory behaviors. • Babies may be calm, then angry. • Babies may be motionless or show apprehension. • Behaviors are not consistently avoidant or resistant as in other categories.

parent and degree of hostility or resistance. In the future, research will show whether this strategy, or some other, provides a better description of the different types or degrees of attachment shown by infants and parents.

Parent, Infant, and Cultural Factors in Attachment

What causes these different types of attachments to develop? Parent, infant, and cultural factors are all involved.

Parent Factors. According to Ainsworth, it's the quality of the parenting during the first year of life that determines the type of attachment that is formed. Through extensive observation of mother–infant behaviors in the home environment, Ainsworth and others found that secure attachment relationships tend to be associated with mothers who respond positively, consistently, and warmly to their infants (Ainsworth, 1973; Ainsworth et al., 1978; Thompson, 2006). They hold their babies frequently, tenderly, and for long enough that the infants seem satisfied when they are put back down. When Ainsworth (1973) observed families in their homes, she found that securely attached infants showed very little distress when their mothers left the room briefly. They seemed conscious of their mothers' whereabouts and confident that the mothers would soon return. This was in contrast to the babies' behavior in the Strange Situation: These same infants showed separation distress when their mothers left them in the unfamiliar laboratory setting. During reunion episodes, securely attached infants gain considerable comfort by being held by their mothers. This response is consistent with Bowlby's view that maternal sensitivity would be most important when an infant was distressed, afraid, or anxious. Cross-culturally, maternal sensitivity was related to infant security in a study of families in the United States and in Bogota, Colombia (Posada et al., 2002; Posada et al., 2004).

A particularly important characteristic of secure attachments is the mother's sensitivity to the calls and signals of her baby. These mothers respond quickly when their infants cry or call out. They are not worried that their attention will "spoil" the baby. But it is more than just responding quickly and positively. These mothers show **sensitive responsiveness**—they see things from the baby's point of view and adjust their responses to meet the infant's needs. Consider a 1-year-old who opens a book, points to a balloon, and says "dat." The caregiver responds by smiling and saying, "Yes, that's a balloon, and here's another one." The caregiver has noticed the infant's signal and has responded to it by allowing the infant to initiate a game of pointing and naming. Contrast this to the caregiver who takes the book from the baby, turns to the beginning, and proceeds to read the book the "right" way. Which caregiver has shown sensitive responsiveness? Healthy attachments are facilitated when caregivers go along with the games, interactions, and other activities that their infants initiate. They adjust their babies' feeding and sleep schedules according to the signals and rhythms of the baby, and they otherwise show sensitivity toward the baby's perspective. With secure attachments, the relationship is mutual rather than being completely dominated by the caregiver.

On the basis of her home observations, Ainsworth (1973) believed that indifferent parenting led to insecure–avoidant attachments and that inconsistent parenting led to insecure–resistant (or ambivalent) relationships. Other researchers, however, have produced evidence that avoidant attachments arise more from parenting that is intrusive, overstimulating, or even hostile and that resistant attachments develop when care is unresponsive (Egeland & Farber, 1984; Isabella, 1995; Isabella & Belsky, 1991; Isabella et al., 1989; Lyons-Ruth et al., 1987). These researchers describe mothers of insecure–avoidant infants as being tense and irritable, showing little interest in their infants, handling them in a mechanical fashion, failing to adjust

sensitive responsiveness
A quality of infant care in which caregivers respond quickly and warmly to the baby's signals and adjust their responses to allow the infant to direct some of the interactions.

feedings to the baby's pace, being less responsive to infants' cries and calls, and otherwise reacting to motherhood in a resentful or negative way. Whether avoidant or resistant, insecurely attached infants learn that their caregivers will not respond sensitively to their needs. Thus, in times of stress, they might reject their parents' attempts to comfort them by looking away or by showing anger and frustration.

Insecure–disorganized (or disoriented) attachments have been associated with parenting that is abusive and/or with parents who themselves have suffered childhood traumas, have unresolved difficulties with their own parents, or are still mourning the death of their attachment figure (Main & Hesse, 1990; Main & Solomon, 1990). Infants who have been frightened by their parents might be confused about how to respond when they are in a stressful situation. They might also be fearful of how their parents will respond under stress. Can they use their parent as a safe base of security, or will their parent be dangerous? You can understand how an infant might respond in contradictory ways, such as approaching the parent but also cowering. Or an infant might freeze, immobilized by the dilemma. In less severe cases, disorganized/disoriented attachment behavior can occur when parents display anxiety or send conflicting signals to their infants.

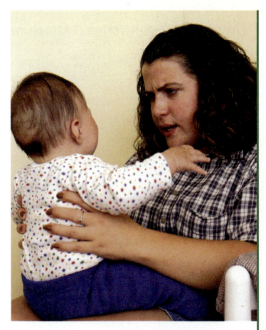

How is the attachment relationship affected when parents are frequently hostile or irritable? What if they are abusive?

Infant Factors. Attachment is a two-way relationship, and factors associated with infants themselves also can contribute to their security and insecurity. Infants who become securely attached tend to cry less frequently, greet their mothers more positively, and initiate more bodily contact with their mothers (Ainsworth et al., 1978). Conversely, infants with insecure attachments tend to cry more, often show anger, and show disruptions in bodily contact. Are these differences due to the infant or due to the parenting? Do securely attached infants cry less because their mothers respond more sensitively to them, or do the mothers respond more sensitively because their babies are more pleasant and congenial? It is difficult to determine the cause–effect relationships among these correlational associations. It has been found that insecure–disorganized attachments occur at a higher rate among infants with special needs, such as those with high-risk prematurity, Down syndrome, autism, and physical disabilities (Thompson, 1998; van IJzendoorn et al., 1992). There is also evidence that insecure–resistant infants, in particular, are less alert and active from birth and are more likely to show mental and motor delays throughout infancy (Egeland & Farber, 1984). Infants who are highly irritable are more likely to develop insecure attachments, but only when their mothers receive low levels of social support (Belsky & Isabella, 1988; Egeland & Farber, 1984). Other research suggests that shy infants are at a slightly higher risk for insecure–resistant attachments, while infants who are more active are more likely to show avoidant attachments (Shamir-Essakow et al., 2004). Otherwise, the basic personality or temperament of the infant is not a strong predictor of attachment outcome (Goldsmith & Alansky, 1987; Thompson, 1998). We will return to the issue of temperament later in this chapter.

Cultural Factors. Beyond the infant and parent, the values of the larger culture influence parental expectations and behaviors. Table 6.3 shows attachment classifications from the United States and seven other nations. Researchers observed infants in the Strange Situation, in most cases between 11 and 22 months of age. The newer category of insecure–disorganized/disoriented attachment does not appear in the table because most of the studies cited did not include it. You can see that Great Britain and Sweden registered the highest percentages of secure attachments. Chile and Germany showed the lowest national percentages, although the majority of infants observed in both countries were still securely attached. More variability is seen with insecure attachments. In the European countries (Great Britain, Sweden,

TABLE 6.3 Cross-National Attachment Data on Infants Observed in the Strange Situation

COUNTRY OR GROUP	NUMBER OF INFANTS SAMPLED	SECURE ATTACHMENT (PERCENTAGE)	INSECURE–AVOIDANT ATTACHMENT (PERCENTAGE)	INSECURE–RESISTANT ATTACHMENT (PERCENTAGE)
Great Britain	72	75	22	3
Sweden	51	74	22	4
Netherlands	115	68	26	6
Germany	136	57	35	8
Japan	96	68	5	27
Israel	166	64	5	31
Chile	38	53	24	24
U.S.: General population	1,584	67	21	12
U.S.: Chinese Americans	36	50	25	25
U.S.: Low-income Hispanics in South Bronx	50	50	30	20

(Data for U.S. general population taken from a review by van IJzendoorn, Goldberg, Kroonenberg, & Frankel, 1992. All other data taken from Thompson, 1998.)

the Netherlands, and Germany), nearly all of the insecure infants were classified as avoidant, and very few were classified as resistant. The reverse pattern occurred in Japan and Israel. Insecure infants in Chile were evenly divided between the avoidant and resistant categories.

What cultural factors might underlie these international differences? Japanese culture encourages close physical contact and intimacy between infants and mothers, and Japanese parents rarely leave their infants alone, especially when strangers are present (Takahashi, 1986). Similarly, Israeli infants, particularly those who live in communal kibbutz arrangements, are accustomed to close-knit relations and less experience with strangers and separation. When Japanese or Israeli infants encounter the Strange Situation, many show high levels of distress—sometimes to the point at which the researchers need to curtail the separation episodes. In the Strange Situation procedure, infants with high levels of distress level are classified with insecure–resistant attachment. In contrast, German culture stresses early independence in young children (Grossmann et al., 1981; Thompson, 1998). German infants learn that their mothers expect independence, so these infants might be less likely to seek proximity to their mothers in stressful situations. Remember that if infants ignore or avoid contact with their parents in the Strange Situation, they are typically classified as insecure–avoidant.

Within the United States, attachment patterns show socioeconomic and ethnic variability. Caucasian mothers tend to value independence and competence in infants and react more negatively to the clingy, dependent behavior that is typical of insecure–resistant infants (Harwood, 1992; Thompson, 1998). Other ethnic groups have somewhat different values. Puerto Rican mothers, for example, value familial love and respect and look most negatively on the independence shown by insecure–avoidant infants (Harwood, 1992). Many African Americans are raised in extended-family arrangements, in which caregiving is often shared among the mother, grandmother, aunts, sisters, and other relatives. Might these infants show less fear when their mothers leave? Parent–infant interactions also

your perspective

What cultural differences have you observed in how parents interact with their children?

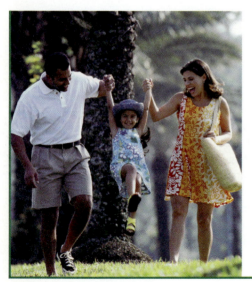

How do our cultural values influence the way we parent? How might the expression of attachment differ across cultures?

change in response to the environment in which the family lives. In urban communities where violence is pervasive, for example, some parents might be more restrictive with their children, allowing the children less independence and freedom to roam. In these situations, young children might be more afraid when their parents leave them and might display this fearfulness in the Strange Situation.

From this discussion, we hope you can see that environmental and cultural differences in parent–infant interactions influence behavior in the Strange Situation. Ainsworth originally developed her procedure with predominantly middle-class white American infants. Clearly, it is not always appropriate to use the typical behaviors of this group as a normative reference for categorizing infants who are being raised in other circumstances or cultures. Because of cultural differences, the behaviors children show in the strange situation may signify different types of attachments across different countries. Being "clingy," for example, may mean something different in Japan than it does in Germany.

Some infants spend a considerable amount of time with grandparents or other extended family members. How might these experiences relate to stranger anxiety and separation anxiety and how infants would respond when they are in Ainsworth's Strange Situation test with their mothers?

Fathers, Day Care, and Attachment

Attachments with Fathers. Until now, we have focused mostly on infant–mother attachments. What about fathers? Summing up the data from 11 studies of attachments with both mothers and fathers, Fox, Kimmerly, and Schafer (1991) concluded that infants were just as likely to form secure attachments with fathers as with mothers. In fact, among the 710 infants studied, the percentages of secure versus insecure attachments were 65 percent versus 35 percent for fathers and 65 percent versus 35 percent for mothers. Furthermore, the type of infant attachment tended to be consistent from one parent to the other. That is, infants with secure attachments with their mothers tended also to have secure attachments with their fathers; infants with avoidant attachments with their mothers tended also to have avoidant attachments to their fathers; and so on. It is unclear whether this consistency is due to characteristics in the infant that produce a similar attachment with each parent or whether both parents respond in similar ways to the infant.

Recent evidence from a twin study suggests that similarities in father-infant attachment are determined more by the way the twins were fathered than by any genetic predispositions the twins may have shared (Bakersman-Kranenburg et al., 2004). It is clear that the fathering relationship is very important and that infants do reach beyond their relationships with their mothers. When fathers, older siblings, and other important people provide sensitive care for infants, infants begin to rely on them as a secure base for emotional support.

Day Care and Attachment. Many parents worry that their attachment relationships will suffer if they are not with their infants full-time during the early months. Some research conducted during the 1980s suggested that infants who spend more than 20 hours per week in day care centers, family day care homes, or other baby-sitting arrangements are slightly more likely to be insecurely attached to their mothers than are infants who receive more maternal care or are cared for full-time at home (e.g., Belsky & Rovine, 1988). In these studies, although the majority of infants in day care (even those who are in day care more than 20 hours a week) were still securely attached to their mothers, the percentages were significantly lower than for infants with mothers at home. More recently, a large-scale nationwide study found that time spent in day care added to the risk of insecure attachment only when it was combined with mothering that was less sensitive and responsive (NICHD Early Child Care Research Network, 1997, 2001). According to this research, day care in itself does not

Children form attachments with their fathers and other close caregivers when they spend significant time together.

Parental Leave Policies in the United States and Other Nations

Many families in the United States face a troublesome dilemma when a new baby is born. Does the mother leave her job to stay at home with the baby? If so, how does the family survive her loss of income? What if she also loses her family's health insurance and other benefits? Will she be able to return to her job later, without penalty or loss of advancement? Or does the father leave his job, with all the same issues to consider? As you can imagine, this dilemma is especially acute for single mothers and in two-parent households in which neither parent makes a high wage. How do the parents do what is right for their new child without jeopardizing the family's economic security?

When parents who work outside the home look for day care for their infants, they encounter additional trouble. There are very few licensed care arrangements for infants (and toddlers under 2 years of age) in this country. When a family can find care, it often costs a substantial portion of one parent's wages. Many parents wonder whether it's worth staying at work. But again, can they afford to quit or take substantial time off?

Almost all other industrialized nations have recognized their important role in supporting healthy families. No one benefits when infants are left in substandard care or when families must live in poverty to care for their own children. On average, nations in the European Union provide 36 weeks of *paid leave* to families with new babies (Kamerman, 2000). Most provide similar benefits for adoption. Typically, mothers receive 14 to 16 weeks of maternity leave, paid at a full or substantial rate. An additional 20 or so weeks' leave for the mother (and sometimes for the father or for both parents) is available at a reduced rate of pay. Additional nonpaid time is usually available to one or both parents

if they choose. While on leave, parents maintain their job security and full benefits.

Table 6.4 summarizes the family leave policies of several industrialized nations. Out of 29 of the world's most developed nations, only the United States, Australia, and New Zealand have no paid leave benefits (Kamerman, 2000). In the United States, the *Family and Medical Leave Act (FMLA)* was signed into law in 1993. The FMLA requires employers that have 50 or more employees to provide up to 12 weeks of *unpaid leave* for the birth or adoption of a child or to care for other family members with serious medical conditions. Leaves are job protected. Employers may require, however, that accumulated sick leave or vacation time be used to cover some or all of the leave. Only about 55 percent of the U.S. workforce is covered by the FMLA (Kamerman, 2000). And although this statute pales in comparison to the provisions that are made in other nations, passage of the law still met considerable resistance. The impetus for the FMLA began in the 1970s but was not introduced in Congress until 1985. The law passed in Congress twice, in 1990 and 1991, but was vetoed both times by the president (Kamerman, 2000). Many employers were concerned that paid leaves would cripple their companies.

Q *Should the care of young infants be left up to the operation of a free-market economy? Or if paid leave were to be provided, how should it be financed? Should all taxpayers contribute equally, or should employers shoulder most of the burden? What do you think is the best policy?*

necessarily jeopardize attachment. The combination of parenting problems and full-time day care can have an impact, however. We will have much more to say about the effects of day care and the issue of quality of care in Chapter 9.

Many parents wish they could spend more time at home during the months after their babies are born, but often the parents must return to work sooner than they would like to avoid losing their jobs and the paychecks they need to pay the bills. In some countries, generous paid parental leave laws let parents spend more time at home with their new babies. To see how the United States compares, see the Social Policy Perspective box called "Parental Leave Policies in the United States and Other Nations."

TABLE 6.4 Family Leave Policies in Selected Countries

COUNTRY	DURATION OF LEAVE	WAGE REPLACED
Sweden	1 year parental leave	80%
	3 months' additional leave	Flat rate
	3 more months	Unpaid
Norway	42 weeks' parental leave	100%
	Parental leave until child is 2 years old	Unpaid
Portugal	6 months' maternity leave	100%
	24 months' additional parental leave	Unpaid
Poland	16–18 weeks' maternity leave	100%
	24 months' additional leave	Flat rate
Spain	16 weeks' maternity leave	100%
	Parental leave until child is 3 years old	Unpaid
Netherlands	16 weeks' maternity leave	100%
	6 months' additional leave per parent	Unpaid
Luxembourg	16 weeks' maternity leave	100%
Mexico	12 weeks' maternity leave	100%
Turkey	12 weeks' maternity leave	Two thirds
Great Britain	6 weeks' maternity leave	90%
	12 weeks' additional maternity leave	Flat rate
	13 weeks' parental leave	Unpaid
New Zealand	52 weeks' parental leave	Unpaid
United States	12 weeks' parental leave	Unpaid

(Adapted from Kamerman, 2000.)

Early Attachment and Long-Term Outcomes

So far, we have seen that there is a link between the quality of infant attachment and the quality of care an infant receives during the first year of life. Although interesting, this research would be less important if the effects applied only to the first year. They do not. Alan Sroufe, a psychologist and researcher at the University of Minnesota, and his colleagues continue to report on a longitudinal study of a large group of families who were originally recruited in Minneapolis in the early 1970s (e.g., Elicker et al., 1992; Sroufe, 1990, 1996; Sroufe et al., 1993; Sroufe & Egeland, 1991; see also a review in Thompson, 1998). Researchers observed these families' infants with their mothers in the Strange Situation when the infants were 12 and 18 months of age. During the preschool years, teachers and observers rated children who had been securely attached as infants as happier and more socially skilled, competent, compliant, and empathetic than were children who were insecurely attached as infants. Preschoolers with secure attachments also were more popular with their peers, had higher self-esteem, and were less dependent and negative. By age 10 years, children in the securely attached classification were still less dependent and received higher ratings on self-esteem, self-confidence, social skills, and emotional health. They made more friends than did children who had been insecurely attached as infants, and they spent more time with their friends. Adolescents who had been insecurely attached were somewhat more likely to experience psychological problems (Thompson, 1998).

This preschool child is being a good friend. How is this type of behavior related to the attachments that children form with their caregivers in the first year of life?

How do these long-term attachment effects work? According to Sroufe, human beings internalize the significant relationships that they have early in life and use those early experiences as interpretive filters when they develop later relationships. People come to expect others to interact with them in a way that mirrors their early attachment relationships. Securely attached infants, therefore, grow up to seek and expect others to be supportive and positive, and they behave in ways that elicit these qualities in people around them. Insecurely attached infants, however, might later expect and provoke hostility, ambivalence, or rejection in their relationships.

Michael Lamb, a child development researcher at the National Institute of Child Health and Development, provides a slightly different explanation (Lamb, 1987; Lamb et al., 1985). Lamb emphasizes the role of continuities in parenting. In other words, parents who foster secure attachments with their infants often remain sensitive, positive, and supportive through their children's preschool, middle-childhood, and even adolescent years. Warm parenting during childhood might be more important than first-year attachment in helping children to maintain positive behavioral, social, and personality characteristics in later years. Support for Lamb's position comes from research showing that early attachment categories do not necessarily correlate with later outcomes if characteristics of the family interactions change. Divorce, illness, and other negative circumstances can disrupt relationships even when children were securely attached as infants. Conversely, insecurely attached infants can benefit from later improvements in the quality of their care. Although the quality of the initial attachment is important in getting the infant off to a good start, it is clear that the quality and consistency of parental care after infancy also play an important role (Thompson, 2006).

Other Measures of Attachment

Ainsworth's Strange Situation procedure is a valuable tool for assessing attachment relationships in infants, and modified versions have been developed to measure attachments with toddlers and young children (Main & Cassidy, 1988; Moss et al., 2004; Moss et al., 2004). However, the most frequently used alternative to measuring attachment is the **Attachment Q-Sort (AQS)** method (Waters & Deane, 1985). The AQS can be used with children ages 12 months to 5 years. Parents, teachers, or other adults who have had a chance to observe the child are asked to sort through a stack of 90 cards. On each card is a short behavioral description, such as "acts to maintain social interaction." The adult places each card on one of nine piles ranked according to how well the descriptions fit the child—from most accurately to least accurately. Each card then gets a score based on the pile to which it was assigned.

Score patterns, when compared to established profiles, provide measures of security, dependency, sociability, and social desirability in the child. Descriptions related to high scores in security include "greets adult spontaneously" and "actively solicits comforting from adult when distressed." Low scores in security go with descriptions such as "expects adults will be unresponsive" and "does not solicit or enjoy affectionate physical contact with adult." One drawback of the AQS is that it does not involve the direct observation of the child by an unbiased and objective observer but rather relies on the observations and judgments of adults who know the child. When adults are well trained in using the AQS, scores show a reasonable, though not perfect, convergence with security as measured in Ainsworth's Strange Situation (Thompson, 1998; van Ijzendoorn et al., 2004; Vaughn & Waters, 1990).

Beginning with Bowlby and Harlow, attachment research has helped us understand the important link between caregiver behavior and child development. In the next section, we look at infant *temperament,* another characteristic that has received considerable attention from researchers who study parent–child interactions.

Attachment Q-Sort (AQS)
A method for classifying attachments in children between 12 months and 5 years of age. Parents or other adults who have observed the child sort through cards with behavioral descriptions and score the selected cards.

Let's Review...

1. What is the main point of John Bowlby's ethological theory of attachment?
   a. Infants are attached to the contact comfort they receive from their parents.
   b. Parents have to learn to love and nurture infants.
   c. Attachment behaviors have evolved over time to increase the chances of infant survival.
   d. Evolution has provided a system that causes parents to be attached to infants, but infants must learn to engage in behaviors that support the parents' nurturing tendency.

2. In Ainsworth's Strange Situation, infants who show stranger anxiety and separation anxiety are most likely to be classified as having:
   a. a secure attachment.
   b. an insecure–avoidant attachment.
   c. an insecure–disorganized/disoriented attachment.
   d. no attachment at all.

3. In which of the following cultures are infants expected to show the most independence from parents?
   a. Japanese   b. Israeli   c. German   d. Puerto Rican

4. **True or False:** Compared to other infants, infants with secure attachments with their parents tend to grow up to be preschool children who are happier, more competent, and popular with their peers.

5. **True or False:** The Attachment Q-Sort (AQS) uses direct observation of infant behaviors to sort infants into secure, avoidant, and resistant categories.

Answers: 1. c, 2. a, 3. c, 4. T, 5. F

Temperament

When our nonidentical twin girls were about 6 months old, our good friends Steve and Sue volunteered to baby-sit one evening to give us a much-needed break. After about 2 hours of quiet dinner and conversation, we returned home to an interesting sight. One of the twins, Lily, was playing on the couch with Steve and Sue. She was bouncing on their laps, giggling, and generally enjoying the attention that was being heaped on her by two loving adults. The other twin, Rachel, was gently rocking back and forth in an infant swing, but the swing was facing the wall.

Although our friends had visited several times before, Rachel was still not comfortable interacting with them without her parents around. She had become upset and cried for quite some time after we left. Our friends are very knowledgeable and experienced with parenting and children. After trying all the standard techniques to comfort Rachel, they came up with a resourceful and effective solution. They settled her in the swing (a familiar and comforting place), turned the swing so that Rachel couldn't see these less-familiar adults, and coached our 7-year-old son (Rachel's familiar and comforting older brother) in playing with her. It worked. By the time we got home, Rachel wasn't crying—though she seemed quite glad to see us when we walked in.

How can the extremely different reactions shown by our twin girls be explained? As recently as the 1970s, many child development theorists thought that infants entered the world as "blank slates" and that most of their behaviors and reactions were the result of parenting and other experiences (Foreman, 1995). Had we really

temperament
The infant or child's behavioral style or primary pattern of reacting to the environment.

treated our daughters so differently in their first few months? That is unlikely. Anyone who has spent considerable time with infants or toddlers recognizes that babies come into the world with their own behavioral styles or dispositions. Some are more sociable and outgoing and smile frequently. Others are more shy, afraid, or reluctant to engage in new situations. Today, researchers refer to the infant and child's behavioral style, or primary pattern of reacting to the environment, as **temperament.** In this section, we describe the most widely accepted classifications of temperament and discuss the practical reasons to understand this important characteristic.

As you study this section, ask yourself these questions:

- What are the behavioral dimensions that indicate a person's temperament?
- What main temperamental styles have researchers identified?
- How do different temperaments form? To what extent do nature and nurture influence temperament?

Types of Temperaments

The most widely accepted method of classifying temperaments is the system developed by two psychiatrists, Alexander Thomas and Stella Chess (Chess & Thomas, 1995; Thomas & Chess, 1977). In 1956, Thomas and Chess began an extensive longitudinal study with 141 children from 85 New York families. Later, they added several hundred children of working-class Puerto Rican parents, and they also added children who had been born prematurely or with physical, neurological, or intellectual disabilities. The study has followed most of these children well into adulthood. On the basis of detailed interviews with the parents, Thomas and Chess identified nine temperament dimensions that seemed to capture the diverse behavior patterns exhibited among the infants, as shown in Table 6.5. A child can receive a high, medium, or low score on each dimension. Together, the scores create a profile of the child's primary pattern of reacting to the environment.

TABLE 6.5 Nine Temperament Dimensions

TEMPERAMENT DIMENSION	DEFINITION
1. Activity Level	Degree of motor activity during daily activities such as bathing, eating, playing, and dressing: How *active* is the infant?
2. Rhythmicity	Degree of predictability/unpredictability in sleep, feeding, elimination, and other schedules: How *predictable and regular* are the infant's schedules?
3. Approach or Withdrawal	Degree of positive or negative response to a new stimulus: When the infant is presented with a new person, situation, or toy, how *positive or negative* is the infant's first response?
4. Adaptability	Ease with which infant modifies his or her responses in a desirable way when confronted with new or changing situations: How well does the infant *adapt to change*?
5. Threshold of Responsiveness	Intensity level of stimulation that is needed to cause a response: How strong does the new situation need to be to *cause a change* in the infant's behavior?
6. Intensity of Reaction	Energy level of the response: How *intense* is the infant's response?
7. Quality of Mood	Amount of pleasant or unpleasant response: How *joyful or friendly* is the infant's response?
8. Distractibility	Degree to which environmental stimuli interfere with ongoing behavior: How *distracted* is the infant?
9. Attention Span and Persistence	Degree to which the infant pursues and continues an activity, even in the face of obstacles: How long does the infant *continue activities*; how well does the infant *overcome obstacles* in continuing activities?

(Thomas & Chess, 1977.)

As all parents quickly learn, some infants are more easygoing and peaceful, while others are easily frustrated and difficult. Researchers believe that infants are born with a basic temperament—a style of reacting to new situations and stimuli.

Using the nine dimensions, Thomas and Chess (1977) identified three constellations of temperament that are particularly significant:

- The **easy temperament** is displayed when the child is primarily positive, smiles easily, has a positive and flexible approach to new situations, adapts to change, and quickly develops regular patterns of eating and sleeping.

- The **difficult temperament** exists when a child is frequently negative and easily frustrated, withdraws from new situations, is slow to adapt to change, and shows irregular patterns of eating and sleeping.

- The **slow-to-warm-up temperament** is shown when a child has mildly negative responses to new stimuli and situations but with repeated exposure gradually develops a quiet and positive interest. Compared to children with a difficult temperament, these children have less intense emotional reactions and more regular eating and sleeping schedules.

In Thomas and Chess's original longitudinal sample, 40 percent of the children were "easy," 10 percent were "difficult," and 15 percent were "slow to warm up." The remaining 35 percent did not fall neatly into any of these three categories, instead showing their own constellations of temperament dimensions. In some cases, a particular dimension—such as an extremely high activity level, high distractibility, or poor attention span—dominated a child's temperament.

How Do Different Temperaments Form? What shapes temperament? Thomas and Chess (1977) proposed an interactionist model that emphasizes the complementary forces of nature and nurture. As we saw in Chapter 2, behavior geneticists have come up with moderately high heritability estimates for temperament and personality. For example, heritability estimates range from about 0.44 to 0.70 for traits such as anxiety, sociability, activity level, emotionality, task orientation, and control (see Table 2.4 in Chapter 2). This means that 44 to 70 percent of the variation in these traits across the population is related to genetics—a substantial contribution. So infants are born with innate tendencies that can be reinforced, channeled, or frustrated by parents, the family, and the larger environment. For example, one family might see a child with a high activity level as "trouble," whereas another family might label such a child "vigorous." With warm and supportive parenting, an active child might learn self-control; harsh and punitive parenting, however, might lead such a child toward aggression (Rubin et al., 2003). This adaptation goes both ways: Parents adapt to the activity level of the child, and the child adapts to the parents' expectations and constraints. Also recall from Chapter 2 that the philosophical orientation of a whole society could have a relationship to the predominant temperament expressed in that particular gene pool (Kagan et al., 1993; Kagan et al., 1994). The emphasis on

easy temperament
Temperament in which a child is primarily positive, smiles easily, is adaptive and flexible, and has regular patterns of eating and sleeping.

difficult temperament
Temperament in which a child is frequently negative, is easily frustrated, withdraws from new situations, is slow to adapt to change, and shows irregular patterns of eating and sleeping.

slow-to-warm-up temperament
Temperament in which a child shows mildly negative responses to new stimuli and situations but with repeated exposure gradually develops a quiet and positive interest.

your perspective

Looking at these three types of temperaments and at the dimensions listed in Table 6.5, how would you rate your temperament?

serenity and harmony in Asian cultures, for example, might be an expression of a predominant temperament that in turn influences how parents and society treat children. Nature and nurture interact to facilitate some characteristics of temperament and suppress others. "It is a constantly evolving dynamic, as the child and family and society change over time" (Thomas & Chess, 1977, p. 68).

Goodness of Fit. As children mature, the key factor in their developmental outcomes will be what Thomas and Chess call the **goodness of fit** between their temperaments and their environments (Chess & Thomas, 1995). Healthy development occurs when a child and his or her environment are compatible. Highly active children, for example, will fare better when their parents are on the outgoing side and value physical activity. Conversely, a poor fit can impair development. Parents who are more reserved might not respond well to highly active children, and slow-to-warm-up children might not adapt well with parents who tend to rush them into new situations. When incompatibilities are severe, behavior disorders can emerge in the child (Chess & Thomas, 1995). Characteristics of the child and parent don't necessarily need to match to provide a good fit, however. Sometimes, good fits are complementary, as when a highly reactive child benefits from the calming influence of parents who are reflective, flexible, and patient. Good fits are important outside the family as well. Compatibility with peers, teachers, coworkers, and spouses becomes important as the child grows into adolescence and adulthood. Further, one culture might approve of active and assertive children, whereas another might view such children as rude and disrespectful.

To see how one parent provided a good fit for her difficult child, read the Personal Perspective box entitled "Meet the Parent of a Difficult Child."

Consistency over Time. Measures of temperament are not highly consistent over time. As with most other personality variables, numerous factors can influence temperament (or the behaviors that indicate temperament). With children in their longitudinal study, Thomas and Chess repeatedly collected measures on each of the nine temperament dimensions listed in Table 6.5. When comparing measures taken one year apart, the researchers found reliable correlations for six out of the nine dimensions. But only one dimension (threshold of responsiveness) showed a reliable correlation when measures were taken four years apart (Chess & Thomas, 1995). One reason for this variability is that the ways in which children express temperament can change over time. As children mature, they develop insight into their own temperaments and can use this self-awareness to adapt to their environments. One child might realize, "I'm shy, but I'm not a pushover." She therefore might assert herself more in social situations. Another might recognize that "I'm excitable, but I know the warning signs" and therefore might show more self-control. In both cases, the children's behavioral output might not reflect their true internal temperament. In some ways, individuals' temperaments change as they adapt to their environments, but in other ways, people learn to control how they express their temperaments. Both processes cause the outward measures of temperament to change across time.

Other Approaches to Temperament

Adding to Thomas and Chess's classification system, in this section, we describe two other methods for measuring and thinking about temperament.

Rothbart's Temperament Dimensions for Infants and Children. Mary Rothbart (1981) developed an instrument called the *Infant Behavior Questionnaire,* which asks parents to report the frequency of specific behaviors shown by their infants, ages 3 to 12 months. An advantage of this method of assessing temperament is that it

goodness of fit
The degree to which the child's temperament and environment are compatible or complementary, leading to better developmental outcomes.

Think About Erin...

How can Erin find a day care setting that would provide a good fit for Patrick's temperament? What factors should she and other parents consider?

your perspective

In what ways has your temperament changed over the years? In what ways is it still the same as it was when you were very young? How have you shaped the way you express your temperament to adapt to your environment?

Meet the Parent of a Difficult Child

Mary Jane
Portland, Maine
*Mother of Maria (15 years old), Rocco (13), John (9),
and Maggie (3)*

Describe your child's basic temperament (mood, behavior, outlook on life).

My concern is John. John has been challenging since he was 6 or 7 years old. He is quite moody, and mostly my concern is with his anger and lack of self-esteem. It seems to me that he has never quite felt that he is talented or good at anything. Most concerning to me was John's recent comment that there was nothing on this earth for him; it was boring and he hated it here.

Can you describe recent examples of John's behavior that concern you?

An example is playing family card games. When John loses, he becomes enraged, hitting and kicking everyone else involved. He also has a hard time with sudden changes in schedule. If we announce we are going for ice cream, John will be angry and refuse to go, or if he went, he wouldn't have any ice cream because no one asked whether that was what he wanted to do.

John loves to play computer games, but when we ask him to leave the game, he almost always ends up yelling loudly, stomping around, and being sent to his room.

How have you helped John? Can you give specific examples?

We did a little counseling to deal with the anger, and it was beneficial. The only way to get John to talk is to wait and go in with a positive attitude. I sit and talk to him (for over an hour sometimes) and validate that I understand that he feels badly. During this time, I make sure we have complete privacy (no other children barging in), and it usually ends nicely with him telling me how glad he is that we talked and could we please do it again. I try to plan something special just with him monthly—a hike or going out to a café for cocoa and cookies, et cetera. I really think time with a parent or grandparent once a week can be great therapy. I try to support him by showing him how much he is loved and cared for.

Q *What other advice would you have for parents who have children with difficult temperaments?*

---

yields useful information quickly; it does not require extensive interviews. The questionnaire includes 96 items. One example is: "During the past week, when being undressed, how often did your baby smile or laugh?" Parents respond along a six-point scale that ranges from *never* to *always*. The original questionnaire scored six dimensions of temperament: *activity level, smiling and laughter, fear, frustration, soothability,* and *duration of orienting*. The revised version now scores 14 dimensions (Rothbart, 2001). If you compare these dimensions to the ones in Table 6.5, you'll see that there is some overlap with the Thomas and Chess system. Among Rothbart's dimensions, *activity level* and *smiling and laughter* show the greatest stability across the first year of life. The other dimensions show only minimal consistency over time. Rothbart developed other questionnaires to measure temperament in children from 18 months to 15 years of age and in adults (Rothbart, 2001; Rothbart et al., 1994).

Kagan's Work with Shy Children. An aspect of temperament that has received considerable research attention is shyness. Longitudinal research conducted by Harvard University psychologist Jerome Kagan (1994, 1997) provides interesting insights about children who are extremely shy. In one study, Kagan presented 16-week-old infants with unfamiliar stimuli such as strong odors, unfamiliar voices, or brightly colored toys waved in front of their faces. About 20 percent of the infants reacted strongly, flailing their arms and legs or crying. By 1 to 2 years of age, one third of these reactive infants were very fearful in other laboratory situations, and by 4 years

This child is very shy. How might shyness be related to thresholds for arousal in the brain? How did shy children react to unfamiliar stimuli when they were infants?

of age, they were very shy and inhibited. Furthermore, as adolescents, they were at increased risk for developing *social phobia*—an intense and irrational fear of social situations.

Kagan surmises that these children had a genetic predisposition to shyness. He points to the amygdala and the hypothalamus, two structures in the brain that process environmental changes and help to produce our emotional reactions to new stimulation. Children with low thresholds for arousal in these systems tend to react more strongly to unfamiliar stimuli (Kagan & Fox, 2006). It doesn't take much stimulation to arouse fear states in these children. In the face of unfamiliar situations, their heart rates accelerate more than other children's do. Even when they are asleep, these children still show higher heart rates than other children do (Kagan, Reznick, & Snidman, 1988). As they grow into childhood, shy children learn to back away from social situations and other events that are highly stimulating for them.

What about the other extreme? In Kagan's study, about 40 percent of infants reacted calmly to unfamiliar odors, voices, and colored toys. They remained relatively still and were not distressed. Presumably, the new stimuli were not strong enough to arouse fear reactions in these infants—the infants had higher arousal thresholds. At 1 to 2 years of age, these children were not afraid of new laboratory situations, and as 4-year-olds, they tended to be sociable and talkative and smiled frequently. Kagan did warn, however, that children with extremely high arousal thresholds might seek intense or dangerous activities. In a small percentage of cases, this inclination might lead to problem behaviors, delinquency, or even violence (Kagan, 1997). Proper socialization and positive role models can help to steer such children away from thrill seeking with risk-prone peers or in dangerous circumstances.

Think About Erin...

If Patrick is very shy, what adjustments can Erin and his day care providers make to help Patrick cope with his new situation?

Let's Review...

1. The most widely accepted system for classifying infant temperaments is the one developed by:
    a. Mary Rothbart.
    b. Jerome Kagan.
    c. John Bowlby.
    d. Alexander Thomas and Stella Chess.

2. Healthy development occurs when there is compatibility between the child's temperament and the surrounding environment. This statement summarizes the concept of:
    a. goodness of fit.
    b. genetic–environmental interaction.
    c. longitudinal consistency.
    d. the reaction range of temperament.

3. Jerome Kagan believes that extreme shyness in children can be traced to:
    a. fear and anxiety shown by parents in social situations.
    b. the punishments children receive from peers and parents.
    c. low thresholds for arousal in the limbic system and hypothalamus.
    d. a dysfunction in the pituitary gland that causes a lack of energy and enthusiasm.

4. **True or False:** Compared to children with difficult temperaments, children who are slow to warm up have less intense emotional reactions and more regular eating and sleeping schedules.

5. **True or False:** Surgency, negative affectivity, and duration of orienting are three of the dimensions that Thomas and Chess use to identify infant temperaments.

Answers: 1. d, 2. a, 3. c, 4. T, 5. F

Emotion

We began this chapter with a discussion of attachment—the first emotional relationship that infants form with their caregivers. In this section, we explore a few of the other topics researchers investigate in the realm of *emotion*, or feelings. How do infants and toddlers develop their ability to understand and express emotions? When do they begin to tell emotions apart? For example, when are infants first able to see that happy faces look different from sad ones? We also explore what infants understand about the emotional expressions they see in people around them. As toddlers develop further, they become more aware of what other people expect of them, and they begin to compare themselves to these expectations; as a result, feelings of guilt, embarrassment, shame, and pride begin to emerge. We end this section by looking at how these more complex emotions emerge in toddlers.

As you study this section, ask yourself these questions:

- What are some of the first emotional reactions of newborn infants?

- When are infants able to tell different emotional expressions apart? How do adults know what kinds of information infants get from others' emotional expressions?

- When are children first able to feel guilt, embarrassment, shame, and pride?

Infant Responses to Emotions

Immediately after birth, newborn infants are responsive to certain emotional cues displayed by people around them. Visit any hospital nursery, and you will notice that when one newborn starts crying, they all start crying. This phenomenon is referred to as **emotion contagion**—the tendency of the emotional cues displayed by one individual to generate similar cues or emotional states in others. For newborns, some types of cries are more contagious than others. Newborns are more likely to cry when they hear other newborns cry than when they hear recordings of their own crying, of older infants' cries, or of artificially produced crying sounds (Martin & Clark, 1982; Sagi & Hoffman, 1976; Simner, 1971).

Newborns also can produce facial expressions that mimic the expressions of adults who are displaying various emotions. In the photos in Figure 6.2, the young infant imitates the adult's happy, sad, and surprised expressions remarkably well (Field et al., 1982). In one study, researchers asked mothers to make facial expressions and speak in ways that showed joy, sadness, and anger (Haviland & Lelwica, 1987). The mothers' 10-week-old infants responded differently to each of these emotions. The infants showed more joy and interest when their mothers were joyful. They made "mouthing" movements when their mothers were sad. They showed less interest and less movement when their mothers showed anger. Other researchers have found that 2-month-olds respond differently to happy faces than to faces that show no emotion at all (Nelson & Horowitz, 1983) and that 5-month-olds can tell the differences among anger, sadness, and fear (Schwartz et al., 1985). Infants can discriminate among facial expressions at a young age; however, they seem to rely more on vocal expressions for determining emotions (Saarni et al., 1998).

Even if infants can tell different emotional expressions apart, do they understand what the different expressions mean? Evidence suggests that they do: Infants as young as 4 months of age can understand the basic emotions behind facial expressions, including joy, anger, surprise, and sadness (Montague & Walker-Andrews, 2001). By 12 months of age, the evidence is even clearer. Consider a clever study that used the visual cliff that we described in Chapter 4. The researchers placed 12-month-old infants on the shallow side of the cliff and put

emotion contagion
The tendency of the emotional cues displayed by one person to generate similar cues or emotional states in other people.

an attractive toy at the other end of the deep side (Sorce et al., 1985). As infants approached the deep side, they looked up at their mothers, who had been instructed to show a joyful, interested, sad, angry, or fearful face. As Figure 6.3 shows, none of the infants crossed the deep side when the mothers showed fear. A few crossed when their mothers looked angry or sad, but many more crossed when the mothers appeared interested or joyful. These infants were doing more than just discriminating among various facial expressions: They were using the expressions to get information to guide their behavior. Trusting their mothers, they crossed the deep side when their mothers showed positive emotions, but they were reluctant or refused to cross when the mothers showed negative emotions. Still, keep in mind how difficult it is to know exactly what infants are understanding about emotional expressions. Are they really responding to the meaning in the expression (e.g., the joy or fear intended by the mother), or are they responding more to other aspects of the communication, such as the loudness of the mothers' voices (Saarni et al., 2006)?

Emotions communicate important information about the environment, and infants learn at an early age to use their parents' emotions as a guide in uncertain situations. Researchers refer to this as **social referencing**—the tendency of infants and children to look for emotional cues from parents and other caregivers to get information in uncertain situations (Thompson, 2006). When strangers approach, for example, infants often look to their parents for a cue. If the parent speaks to the stranger in a friendly manner, the infant reacts more positively to the stranger (Boccia & Campos, 1989; Feinman & Lewis, 1983). If the parent looks worried, the infant reacts more negatively. Similar interactions occur when infants are exposed to unfamiliar places and

social referencing
The tendency of infants and children to look for emotional cues from parents and other caregivers to get information in uncertain situations.

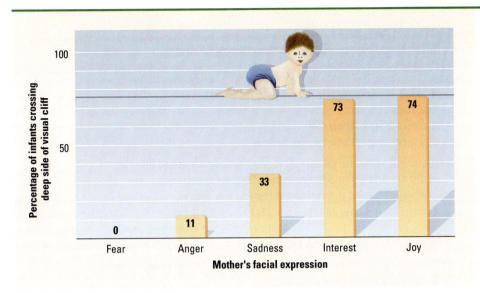

Figure 6.3 • Infants' Readings of Facial Expressions When 12-month-old infants were deciding whether to cross the deep side of the visual cliff, they relied on the their mothers' facial expressions. Infants did not cross when their mothers looked afraid, and infants were reluctant when mothers looked angry or sad. Most of the infants did cross when mothers looked interested or joyful. (Based on Sorce et al., 1985.)

toys (Crockenberg & Leerkes, 2004). One study showed that 12-month-old infants can even read the negative reactions of people they see on television (Mumme & Fernald, 2003). Researchers created a videotape of an actress viewing two objects (e.g., a bumpy ball and a garden hose connector). The actress showed a negative reaction to one of the objects—turning her head away, gasping, and showing a fearful facial expression. What did the infants do? They showed negative facial expressions when the actress did, and when given both objects to play with, infants avoided the one that the actress seemed to dislike. These and other studies demonstrate that by the time they reach their first birthdays, infants are capable of reading and understanding something about the emotions expressed by other people. So even before they understand a spoken language, infants are already receiving messages through the language of emotion.

self-conscious emotions
Emotions that relate to people's self-images or what people think about themselves; include shame, embarrassment, guilt, and pride.

Toddler Self-Conscious Emotions

By 15 months of age, **self-conscious emotions** begin to emerge (Lewis, 1993; Saarni et al., 2006). These are emotions related to people's thoughts about themselves—about how their thoughts and behaviors relate to their images of who they are and who they should be. A toddler who spilled his juice looks down and away, feeling *guilty* about the mess he made. If his siblings or other children are watching, he might feel *embarrassed* by his mistake. If he makes frequent mistakes, he might feel *shame*, believing that he is a "bad boy." If he pours his juice successfully, however, he might feel *pride* in his new accomplishment. By 15 months, he is comparing his own behavior to how he thinks he should behave, and his emotional reaction reflects this self-conscious comparison. For self-conscious emotions to emerge, the toddler must first have a sense of his own identity (who he is) and a sense of what others expect of him. As you will see in a later chapter, the self-conscious emotions become more complex as children's sense of self and others continues to develop during the preschool and following years.

"Oops. I made a mess!" Shame is a self-conscious emotion. Children begin to reflect on who they are and who they should be.

■ Let's Review . . .

1. Newborn babies are most likely to start crying when they hear:
   a. another newborn baby cry.
   b. an older child cry.
   c. a recording of their own crying.
   d. a recording of their mother crying.

2. Researchers using the visual cliff found that 12-month-old infants:
   a. did not understand their mothers' facial expressions.
   b. always crossed the cliff to get the toy.
   c. were more likely to cross the cliff when their mothers displayed expressions of joy or interest.
   d. were more likely to cross the cliff when their mothers displayed expressions of fear.

3. Self-conscious emotions (such as guilt and pride) emerge when toddlers:
   a. have a sense of their own identity.
   b. have a sense of what other people expect of them.
   c. have a sense of their own identity AND what other people expect of them.
   d. Research shows that self-conscious emotions do not develop until later childhood.

4. **True or False:** Infants cannot imitate the facial expressions that they see in other people until they are approximately 6 months of age.

5. **True or False:** When infants are in unfamiliar or uncertain situations, they sometimes use their parents' emotions as a guide for their own reactions.

Answers: 1. a, 2. c, 3. c, 4. F, 5. T

Social Relations and Play

If you are like most students, your earliest memory of a friend probably dates back to when you were about 5 or 6 years old. The first foundations of friendship began much earlier, however—when you were a small baby. To finish this chapter, we explore the social interactions and forms of play for infants and toddlers.

As you study this section, ask yourself these questions:

■ What are the first interactions that infants typically have with each other, and how do infants play?

■ What are friendships based on during the toddler period? What should parents and other caregivers do to help toddlers with their interpersonal conflicts?

■ What are the main themes in the play of toddlers?

Infant Social Interactions

mutual gaze
Intent eye contact between two people, as when young infants stare at each other.

By the age of only 2 months, infants show a special interest in other people their own size. When placed near each other, young infants show **mutual gaze**—they look intently at each other as if they are taking in all the information they can about this intriguing new peer (Eckerman, 1979; Fogel, 1979). They often express their excitement by flailing their arms and legs. By 6 months, infants interact with each other by babbling, smiling, and touching (Vandell et al., 1980). These are often the infants' first social interactions that involve mutual activity with people other than their family members.

Not surprisingly, infants vary greatly in social responsiveness. Some infants initiate interactions with peers frequently; others do so only rarely. Differences in temperament, in parent–infant relationships, and in opportunities to practice social skills all contribute to this variability. When infants have more exposure to other infants their age, they show more frequency and skill in their social interactions than infants with less exposure to peers (Vandell & Wilson, 1982). By the end of the first year, infants play by imitating each other's actions and by sharing and playing together with toys (Mueller & Silverman, 1989; Rubin et al., 1998).

Mutual gaze is one of the early social interactions in infancy. What do you think these infants think of each other?

Infant Sensorimotor Play

During the first year of life, play evolves mostly around the practice of sensory activity and the development of new motor actions. Researchers refer to this period of play as **sensorimotor play**, based on the sensorimotor stage in Piaget's theory (refer back to Chapter 5). For the first few months, infants spend most of their awake time lying on their backs and looking around at the world. They seem to be soaking up their new environments by staring at objects and colors and listening intently to the various sounds around them. The first noticeable signs of play involve activities infants discover with their own bodies. After accidentally bringing his fist to his mouth, for example, an infant might work to repeat this action. When he succeeds, the repetitive motion becomes a game that he repeats for several minutes, smiling and squirming with glee at his new discovery. Spitting bubbles and kicking their feet are similar games that infants discover and playfully repeat.

By 3 months of age, infants can reach out and grasp small objects. Now the world of play expands from actions involving infants' own bodies to interactions with objects in the world. Rattles, balls, pieces of cloth, and other small objects can now be grasped, mouthed, banged, and dropped. Infants repeat these playful actions as they develop new motor actions and explore new objects in their environments.

An interesting development occurs between the ages of 6 and 9 months. At 6 months infants usually treat all objects that are about the same size in the same way. Give a 6-month-old a spoon, for example, and the baby will bang the spoon on the table. If you then give the baby a ball, she will bang it, too, and will do the same with a rattle or a small doll (Hughes, 1999). At 6 months, babies incorporate every object into the action pattern they prefer at the moment (e.g., banging). At 9 months, however, infants pay more attention to the specific features of objects and begin treating objects differently (Hughes, 1999; Ruff, 1984). They bring the spoon to their mouth, throw the ball, shake the rattle, and hug the doll. Rather than forcing all objects into a fixed action pattern, 9-month-olds can adjust their play to fit the unique features of each object.

Infants appreciate having a variety of playthings with different shapes, sounds, textures, and actions. Toys that respond to babies' actions are especially interesting. When babies realize that pushing a particular button produces an exciting sound or a flash of light, a smile of recognition spreads across their faces. They recognize that they are having an influence on their environment and that the environment is now responding to them. It is exciting for parents to watch their infants form these early connections, and the infants derive self-confidence and a general sense of self from the realization that they can influence the environment (Hughes, 1999). To read more about how toy manufacturers use their knowledge of infant and child development to design interesting and educational toys, see the Professional Perspective box entitled "Career Focus: Meet a Toy Company Executive."

sensorimotor play
Play that evolves mostly around the practice of sensory activity and the development of new motor actions.

your perspective

Describe the kinds of sensorimotor play that you have observed in infants. Where do these kinds of play fit within the developmental trends that we presented?

Career Focus: Meet a Toy Company Executive

Susan Tice, B.A.
Parsippany, New Jersey
*Public Relations Director and Product
Manager for International Playthings,
Inc. (http://www.intplay.com).*

**What does International Playthings,
Inc. (IPI) do, and what is your role at
the company?**
IPI is one of the largest suppliers of
specialty toys in North America. We
make a wide variety of games, infant
toys, preschool toys, dolls, educational
toys, activity toys, and other playthings. I am the
director of public relations and a product manager.
I determine what products to submit to various toy
testing programs to obtain product recognition and
consumer awareness. I also make new product
suggestions. I work closely with manufacturers and
their factories to bring new product ideas to life.

**How do toy manufacturers decide what kinds of toys
to produce?**
Multiple factors are involved, and it depends on the age
of the child. We consider the child's developmental
skills, the educational benefits, age appropriateness,
and how unique or different our toy can be from similar
products that are already in the marketplace.

**What do you think infants and toddlers look for
in toys?**
Infants respond to toys that can stimulate one or more
of their senses. Contrasting colors provide visual
stimulation as well as a focal point for developing
eyesight. Different materials provide tactile stimulation. Jingles, rattles, crinkle, and music provide auditory
stimulation and so on. The product should not over-
stimulate the senses but should be able to provide
multiple experiences. For example, an infant will focus
on the toy and then touch it and then mouth it as she
learns all she can about it using her senses.

I think toddlers look for toys that "do" more—
products with a cause-and-effect reaction that lets
them be in control. For instance, if a toy plays music,
toddlers want to be the ones who do whatever is necessary to get the music to play. They are more mobile,
so they enjoy toys that can go with them, such as a
walker, ride-on toy, push toy, and
so forth. A great toy at this age is a
basic toy that allows the child's play
pattern to imitate life that he sees
every day, opening his imagination.
This can be done with something as
basic as a plush animal or a basic
plastic car. Here again, the product
needs to appeal to the child's initial
senses.

**How do you use child development
research when designing new toys?**
When we begin the design phase, we want to make
sure the toy is appropriate for a child of a certain age.
As a result, we need to keep in mind how children
develop—what basic skills they possess, what skills
they are in the process of developing, and how our toy
can encourage these developing skills. It's also
extremely important to be aware of a child's environment and exposure to society at that age so that our
products can be themed appropriately.

**What education or training does it take to work in
your area?**
You need a minimum of a four-year college degree. It's
excellent if you have taken marketing classes and have
an understanding of childhood development (perhaps
taking some child psychology classes could help here).
If you are looking to go more into the PR aspect, writing
classes are a tremendous asset. As for design of the
toy, you will work closely with an art department
and/or designers who can turn your ideas into graphics
that can be easily understood by factories. For this,
studying graphic design is definitely the way to go.
Finally, being familiar with how retail works is very
important, so your summer job at a retail store can
actually become something extremely useful for your
career.

Q *As you read through this interview, did
you recognize how this toy executive
used child development information in her role
at the company? If you had a job like hers,
what else would you like to know about child
development?*

Toddler Friends

After 1 year of age, emerging language and motor skills allow toddlers to interact in increasingly complex ways. They can seek each other out, follow each other around, and add verbal dialogue to their play. At the age of 2 years, **coordinated imitation** becomes much more frequent. Toddler playmates take turns imitating each other and—a new feature—become aware that they are being imitated (Eckerman, 1993; Rubin et al., 1998). Consider Josh and Jalen, two toddlers playing in a sandbox. Josh pours sand on his legs, and Jalen does the same. Josh throws sand at a toy, and Jalen copies again. Then Jalen throws sand straight up in the air, and Josh does too, both giggling and chuckling all the while. The fun in this toddler game is that each child knows that he is being imitated. Each act becomes an invitation for the other child to copy. This level of coordination rarely appears in children younger than 2 years of age (Eckerman, 1993).

Toddler interactions often evolve around games that children either repeat from prior experiences or create on the spot. Characteristically, these early games include taking turns, playing roles, and engaging in numerous repetitions of the game sequences (Ross, 1982). Common games are stacking and toppling blocks; throwing and catching; putting toys in a pail and pouring; requesting, receiving, and returning items; running and chasing; and climbing and jumping. These early interactions help children to acquire important social skills such as learning to play as equals, maintaining fun and interest for both players, and adapting to the characteristics of different playmates.

Toddlers choose playmates based largely on convenience—on who is available for play and who has interesting toys or materials to play with. By 2 years of age, however, pairs of children begin to select each other as mutually preferred playmates (Vandell & Mueller, 1980). That is, although other familiar peers are available for play, these friends pair off and voluntarily choose to play more with each other than with other children. For most children, this is the first time that a relationship contains all of the qualities of a true friendship: It is voluntary, mutual, and close, and it persists over time.

In a longitudinal study, Howes (1988) followed toddlers for up to 3 years as they maintained friends, lost friends, and made new friends. Her observations suggest that children who are more successful at maintaining friendships tend to enter into peer play more easily and to be more cooperative in social pretend play. For example, they are more likely to join in when asked, "You be the baby and I'll be the mommy, okay?" Children who were less successful in maintaining friendships showed less social skill and were more likely to be rebuffed by peers.

Toddler Conflicts

Anyone who has spent much time with toddlers knows that conflict is all too common. In one study, researchers paired up 2-year-old children who had never met before and allowed them to play together in several sessions that lasted 15 minutes each (Hay & Ross, 1982). After carefully analyzing videotapes of the play sessions, the researchers found that playmates averaged just over two instances of conflict for every 15-minute session. Most of the conflicts (84 percent) were struggles over toys. A few pairs of playmates had no conflicts, but one pair displayed 14 instances of protest, resistance, or retaliation in their 15 minutes of play. Other research suggests that children who are more socially outgoing tend to initiate more conflicts (Brown & Brownell, 1990).

Parents, child care workers, and others who work frequently with young children often need to help toddlers resolve their disputes. Lecturing and moralizing are usually ineffective, because toddlers have difficulty understanding abstract reasoning. The question "How do you think she feels?" is largely nonsensical for the average 2-year-old, who is motivated more by the concrete benefit of getting his or

coordinated imitation
Interaction in which toddler playmates take turns imitating each other and are aware that they are being imitated.

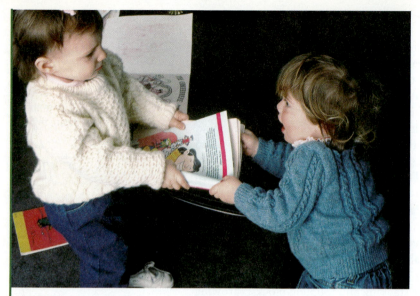

Conflict is common among toddlers. What is the best way to help children of this age handle conflict?

symbolic play
Play in which children use make-believe and pretend to embellish objects and actions.

her hands on a colored marker or a piece of candy. (In Chapter 8, we will describe the egocentric forms of thought that are typical for young children.) Distracting the toddlers with another attractive activity is a more practical way to resolve the dispute. Parents and caregivers can then gradually introduce moral reasoning and conflict resolution skills according to the cognitive and emotional maturity of the individual child.

Toddler Symbolic Play

As you saw in Chapter 5, a major change during the toddler period is the emergence of symbolic thinking—the ability to form mental representations of objects or events in the world. Symbolic thinking allows **symbolic play**, where children use make-believe and pretend to embellish the objects and actions in their play. Early symbols begin to emerge between 12 and 14 months as toddlers pretend to act out common activities. They might lie on the floor with a small blanket and pretend to go to sleep or use toy dishes to pretend to eat. By 2 to 3 years of age, toddlers pretend that an object is something else: A wooden block is a car, a spoon is an airplane, or the family cat is their baby. Still later, children integrate multiple objects and actions into dramatic play activities. Their bed becomes a castle, their pillow is a magic shield, and they engage in mythical duels with the Evil Knight of Doom (really a chair or their sister). Their play takes on all of the imagination allowed by their ever-expanding cognitive abilities.

■ Let's Review . . .

1. Which appears earliest in development?
   a. Mutual gaze.
   b. Symbolic play.
   c. Reaching for toys.
   d. Coordinated imitation.

2. An interesting change occurs by 9 months of age in how infants play with toys. What is it?
   a. Infants begin to babble at their toys.
   b. Infants begin to treat all toys alike.
   c. Infants begin to treat different toys differently.
   d. Infants temporarily lose interest in toys and prefer to play with other people.

3. At 18 months of age, Lauren is pretending to cook on a toy stove. This type of pretend represents the beginning of:
   a. social play.
   b. mutual play.
   c. symbolic play.
   d. coordinated imitation.

4. **True or False:** During the first three months of sensorimotor play, infants prefer activities that involve their own bodies such as kicking, waving their arms, or spitting bubbles.

5. **True or False:** Convenient availability is an important factor in determining which toddlers will play together and be friends.

Answers: 1. a, 2. c, 3. c, 4. T, 5. T

Thinking Back to Erin …

Now that you have studied this chapter, you should be able to help Erin understand Patrick's behavior on his first morning at day care. You should begin by explaining how Patrick's reactions reveal his attachment to his mother. By clinging to his mother in his new environment and by showing both stranger and separation anxiety, Patrick is demonstrating that he is securely attached to a specific other person: his mother. This is a positive attribute and will have benefits for Patrick as he continues to grow. Erin can help by letting Patrick see her interact in a friendly manner with the staff, signaling to Patrick that they are safe.

You should also discuss with Erin the research on day care and attachment. Many parents worry that day care will disrupt their child's attachment to them. Some research suggests that full-time day care can reduce attachment, but only if it is combined with parenting that is not sensitive or responsive. The majority of infants in day care still show secure attachments to their mothers, and Patrick's attachment to Erin is even more likely to be secure if Erin is sensitive and responsive when she is caring for Patrick.

Erin should also consider Patrick's temperament. On the basis of the few details that were provided in the opening vignette, it does not appear that Patrick is a difficult child. He might be slow to warm up; recall that he did eventually begin to play with toys and books when he visited the day care center's open house. If Patrick is very shy, the day care staff should introduce him gradually to the busy schedule and activities of the day care center, doing what they can to reduce his level of arousal. Erin should also work to find a day care center that provides a good fit for Patrick's temperament.

Erin did several things to try to help Patrick cope with the emotion of his first day. She took Patrick to the open house so that he could familiarize himself with the new setting, she spoke cheerfully about day care, and she comforted him as they entered the center. Although she herself was upset, she modeled good emotional control for Patrick. At Patrick's age, convenience plays an important role in making friends—children tend to play with whomever is available on a regular basis. After a few days at the center, Patrick will likely find one or more children who will enjoy playing with him.

■ Chapter Review...

How do researchers define attachment? What are the two main roots of modern attachment research?

Attachment is an emotional tie to a specific person or people that endures across time and space. Modern attachment research is rooted in John Bowlby's ethological theory and Harry Harlow's research with rhesus monkeys. Bowlby theorized that attachment behaviors evolved to increase survivability in infants. He emphasized how smiles and other infant behaviors trigger a nurturing response in adults. He also proposed four stages of attachment: orientation without discrimination, orientation with discrimination, safe-base attachment, and goal-corrected partnerships. Harlow demonstrated that contact comfort, not feeding as psychoanalytic and behavioral theorists had proposed, was the critical ingredient in attachment formation. Harlow showed how infant monkeys use their attachment figures as a secure base when they are frightened.

How do researchers use Mary Ainsworth's Strange Situation procedure to measure attachment relationships? What kinds of attachments does her procedure reveal?

In Ainsworth's Strange Situation test, eight episodes systematically expose the infant to unfamiliar situations involving a stranger and separation from the caregiver. The episodes reveal secure attachments when infants prefer the caregiver over the stranger, show separation anxiety when the caregiver leaves, and show joy on reunion when the caregiver returns. Other patterns of behavior can reveal insecure–avoidant, insecure–resistant, and insecure–disorganized/disoriented attachments.

Describe the parent, infant, and cultural factors associated with differences in attachment.

Ainsworth believed that the key to an infant's attachment style was the quality of the infant's interaction with his or her caregiver in the first year of life. When parents are consistently positive and warm in their response and when they are sensitively responsive to the calls and signals of the baby, secure attachments tend to develop. Indifferent, unresponsive, inconsistent, and abusive parenting often correlates with insecure attachments. Insecure attachments also are more likely when infants have special needs, are highly irritable, cry more, or are less alert and active. The prevalence of the different types of insecure attachments varies considerably across nations. Researchers believe that these cross-cultural variations are due to differences in the treatment and expectations of infants.

What are the long-term correlates of secure and insecure attachments in infancy?

Infants who are securely attached tend to become preschoolers who are more well liked, happy, competent, compliant, and empathetic. Later in childhood, they tend to have higher self-esteem and self-confidence, and they are more sociable and more emotionally healthy. Adolescents who were insecurely attached during infancy tend to have more psychological problems. Early attachment relationships can become internalized models that people use to guide their social relationships throughout life. Continuities in parenting might also contribute to the correlations between early attachment and later development.

What other measures of attachment have researchers developed?

Modified versions of the Strange Situation have been developed to use with toddlers and young children. Also, the Attachment Q-Sort was developed to use with children aged 12 months to 5 years, but it is a more indirect method, relying on the observations and judgments of people who know the child.

How do researchers define temperament? What is the most popular system for classifying infant temperaments?

Temperament is an infant's or child's behavioral style or primary pattern of reacting to the environment. The most popular method of classifying temperaments is the system developed by Thomas and Chess, who identified three main temperaments (easy, difficult, and slow to warm up) based on nine dimensions of behavior. Thomas and Chess believed that different temperaments result from interactions between genetics, parenting, and culture. They also emphasized the importance of an environment that is a good fit for the temperament of the individual child.

What are some other prominent systems for classifying or understanding temperament?

Mary Rothbart's revised Infant Behavior Questionnaire assesses infant temperament along 14 behavioral dimensions rated by parents. The original version scored 6 dimensions. Jerome Kagan observed infants who reacted strongly to unfamiliar stimuli. Later, these infants became children who were afraid in other laboratory situations and were very shy and inhibited. Kagan emphasized genetic and biological components involving the limbic system and hypothalamus, brain structures that process changes and new stimulation. Low thresholds of arousal in these systems cause shyness, and high thresholds are related to thrill seeking.

Describe several aspects of emotional development during infancy.

Emotion contagion and imitation of facial expressions are examples of emotional expressivity in newborns. Newborns tend to cry when they hear other newborns cry (contagion), and they can mimic facial expressions posed by adults (imitation). By 2 months of age, infants can discriminate among various facial expressions and respond differently to them. One-year-olds can use their mothers' facial expressions to gain information about how to respond in ambiguous situations.

What are self-conscious emotions, and when do they emerge?

Self-conscious emotions include guilt, embarrassment, shame, and pride. They begin to appear by 15 months of age as toddlers start to understand who they are and what other people expect of them.

What are the main trends in infant social interactions and play?

By 2 months of age, infants show mutual gaze—looking intently at other babies their size. By 6 months, they enjoy interacting with other babies by babbling, smiling, and touching. Infants engage in sensorimotor play—using their sensory systems and motor actions to interact with toys and other objects. During the first 3 months, infants try to repeat actions that involve their own bodies (e.g., kicking or spitting bubbles). By 3 months, they begin reaching out to grab and play with toys and other objects. By 9 months, they begin to play differently with different types of toys (e.g., shaking a rattle, squeezing a ball).

How do toddlers interact with friends, and how do they like to play?

By age 2 years, toddlers show coordinated imitation when they imitate each others' actions. They enjoy activities and games that involve taking turns. They make friends mostly by convenience, playing mainly with whoever is readily available. By age 2, they also begin pairing up in mutual friendships. Conflicts are common among toddlers, and these are often best handled by distracting the children off into different activities. Toddlers enjoy the beginnings of symbolic play—using make-believe and pretending to embellish objects and activities.

■ Key Terms

attachment (190)
Attachment Q-Sort (AQS) (202)
contact comfort (191)
coordinated imitation (215)
difficult temperament (205)
easy temperament (205)
emotion contagion (209)
goodness of fit (206)
insecure–avoidant attachment (195)
insecure–disorganized (or disoriented)
    attachment (195)
insecure–resistant attachment (195)

mutual gaze (212)
secure attachment (194)
self-conscious emotions (211)
sensitive responsiveness (196)
sensorimotor play (213)
separation anxiety (194)
slow-to-warm-up temperament (205)
social referencing (210)
Strange Situation (193)
stranger anxiety (194)
symbolic play (216)
temperament (204)

If you are using MyDevelopmentLab, you have access to an ebook version of this textbook, along with dozens of valuable resources per chapter—including video and audio clips, simulations and activities, self-assessments, practice tests, and other study materials. Here is a sampling of the resources available for this chapter.

Explore
Physiological, Evolutionary, and Cognitive Theories of Emotion

Simulate
Attachment Classifications in the Strange Situation

Watch
Contact Comfort
Attachment in Infants
Redefining Fatherhood

If you did not receive an access code to MyDevelopmentLab with this text and wish to purchase access online, please visit www.mydevelopmentlab.com.

Infants and Toddlers: The First Years

Physical Development

With proper prenatal care, babies have the best chance at being born full-term and healthy. Infants are at risk for a variety of developmental problems when they are born preterm, low in birth weight, or small for their gestational age. Experts recommend that infants receive breast milk for at least the first 12 months although that isn't always possible. They grow at an incredible rate, and children have already reached half of their adult height by the time they are 2 years old. Their brains are also developing rapidly as they form connections within the intricate network of neurons, as brain fibers become myelinated, and as they form the complex web of synapses that proliferate in the brain. Right from birth, infants have an impressive ability to see and hear and to distinguish basic odors and flavors. Over the first year, infant reflexes have been replaced by voluntary muscle movements as infants have learned to sit up, crawl, and take their first steps. These forms of physical development pave the way for the cognitive and socioemotional advances we see during these first years.

Cognitive Development

Even young infants have surprisingly well-developed abilities to remember and integrate sensory information. They can recognize sounds they've heard—even if they heard them before birth! Even as newborns, infants prefer to look at the human face over many other kinds of objects. By 6 months of age they can match information across different senses. Infants build on these experiences and gradually become able to mentally represent things and people in their environment—a significant achievement because it allows toddlers to think about things in the past and future. Their actions on the world become more intentional as well, and by the age of 2 toddlers are doing things on purpose to achieve specific goals. The average infant begins using sounds to communicate during the first year, and speaks the first real words around 1 year. From then on, toddlers' language proceeds at a phenomenal pace. It seems that humans are biologically predisposed to learn language, but the social interactions infants and toddlers have with those around them also help them as they learn words, grammar, and the social rules for using language.

Socioemotional Development

Over the first year, infants form a special emotional attachment to their parents and primary caregivers. They feel secure and comfortable when they are with their caregivers, and they show fear when they are separated from them or when strangers approach. Infant temperaments vary, and parents will find that some babies are easy to interact with while others are fussy and difficult or slow to warm up to new situations. Infants respond to other people's emotions at an early age. They gaze intently at other infants even before they have the physical coordination to crawl over and play. As children exit the toddler years, they are already playing creatively, forming new friendships, displaying their unique temperaments, and showing continued effects of the attachments they have formed with their parents and other important caregivers. With their physical, cognitive, and socioemotional developments, these toddlers are ready to explore the wider world. They are ready to enter the phase of *Early Childhood: The Playful Years.*

Some Developmental Landmarks

3 years
- Stands on one foot
- Holds pencil between thumb and forefinger
- Speaks in sentences
- Uses correct gender labels: boy, girl, mommy, daddy
- Prefers to play with same-sex friends
- Play is full of fantasy and pretend

4 years
- Mature walking gait
- Walks on balance beam, alternating feet as they step
- Puts on pants and shirts
- Speaks aloud to self in private speech
- Uses rewards and punishments to make judgments about right and wrong
- Coordinates roles in play with other children

5 years
- Hops several times on one foot
- Can work smaller buttons, zippers, and tools such as scissors
- Rides a two-wheel bicycle
- Can start kindergarten
- Holds four items in short-term memory
- Male versus female stereotypes are firmly formed

6 years
- Now 70 percent of adult height and 33 percent of adult weight
- Independent in many self-help skills such as dressing
- Vocabulary of 10,000 words
- Uses complex sentences, with accuracy
- Still has firm preference to play with same-sex friends

part three

Early Childhood: The Playful Years

The Playful Years, from ages 3 through 6, are some of the most enjoyable years to be around children! Their play is highly imaginative and full of fantasy and pretend. Children in this age group can one minute imagine they are superheroes and another imagine they are riding on a magic carpet over the world. In play, children practice their abilities to form mental symbols and to manipulate objects in their minds. They are also very energetic, gaining most of their exercise and learning new motor skills during play. They make friends with children who are similar to them and who are available for play. Boys prefer to play with other boys, and girls with girls, as both genders learn what to expect from each other.

Children's vocabularies soar after age 3. They internalize the speech they hear around them and use this to not only learn language but also to acquire the important concepts needed to understand the world. They actively explore and create their own understanding of things. Their logic is fanciful and personal at first, but after they begin kinder-garten and formal schooling, they will learn to think in ways that are more accurate and realistic. From ages 3 through 6, children progress rapidly in their physical, cognitive, and socioemotional development, as you will discover in the next three chapters.

Physical Development in Early Childhood

Tammi is concerned about the children who live next door. Her neighbors have two boys, ages 3 and 6, and they just had a new baby girl. The parents don't watch the children properly, in Tammi's opinion. The boys wander off through the neighborhood unsupervised. They are both dirty and wear the same clothes day after day. Most of the neighborhood children gather at the playground down the street for fun and games, but Tammi hasn't seen her neighbors' boys at the playground at all. They don't seem to fit in with the other children on her block. The older boy is in kindergarten, but Tammi has several times seen him playing in the yard alone at home on school days. Tammi has heard the parents yelling at the kids. She hasn't seen them hit the children, but she wonders what else might be happening inside the house. Are the children even getting enough to eat? Tammi wonders if she should call someone to report the situation before the children get hurt. Who should she call? She wants to do what is right for the children, but she'd also feel badly if the children were taken away.

What should people like Tammi do if they suspect that children are not receiving proper care and attention? Are neighbors obligated to report incidents like this to the authorities? What effects might this type of treatment have on the children's physical and psychological development? What advice would you give to Tammi and to families like the one that lives next door to her? After studying this chapter, you should be able to relate at least a dozen concepts and research findings to situations like the one Tammi observed. You should have concrete ideas about how situations like that at her neighbors' house can affect the development of young children.

As you read this chapter, look for the "Think About Tammi . . ." questions that ask you to consider what you're learning from Tammi's perspective.

The first section of this chapter describes the physical growth of children between the ages of 3 and 6 years, and it describes the nutritional needs they have during this early childhood period. It also covers the main events in brain growth and development and how experience with the environment influences brain development. The second section describes the development of muscle coordination and movement in early childhood, and the types of exercises and activities children need to foster their motor development. We also explore cerebral palsy—an example of a physical disability that afflicts many children. We end the chapter with a section on health and safety issues. What are the main causes of death in early childhood, and how can we prevent them? What are the categories of child abuse, and what are their effects?

Information in this chapter is important for anyone who is in charge of the physical care and well-being of children and for all of us who care about how children grow and develop. As you will see in the next chapters, early childhood is a wonderful period of play, imagination, and intellectual discovery. But to enjoy the magic of these early years, children first need to have their basic needs met. They need proper nutrition and exercise, basic health care, and the love and attention of parents and other caregivers who will keep the children safe and secure. All of these issues are discussed in this chapter, along with information about more unfortunate situations like the one Tammi observed.

Growth of the Body and Brain

Young children grow at a rapid rate. As parents, we always marveled at how fast our children outgrew their pants and shoes, and even when we were gone on business trips for just a few days we could notice how much they grew while we were away. In this section we describe the rapid changes that occur in height and weight during early childhood, and we discuss the importance of proper nutrition to support this growth. We also cover the growth and development of the child's brain—a type of growth that is less obvious from the outside but clearly important in understanding the many ways that children change, learn, and mature.

As you study this section, ask yourself these questions:

- How much do children grow during early childhood? When is their growth the fastest?

- What are the important elements of proper nutrition, and what do we know about the effects of poor nutrition?

- In what important ways does the brain grow and change during early childhood? How do experience and interaction with the environment shape these changes?

Physical Growth

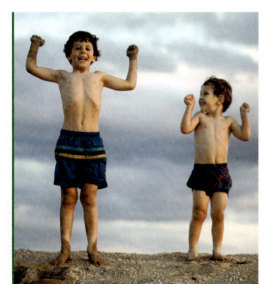

You can see how much taller this 6-year-old is than the 3-year-old. Young children grow so quickly!

During early childhood, children grow 2 or 3 inches per year, on average, and gain about $5\frac{1}{2}$ pounds per year (National Center for Health Statistics, 2004). Figure 7.1 plots these averages along with the variation in growth we expect for the middle 80 percent of children. Keep in mind that 10 percent of children will be smaller than the 10th percentile, while another 10 percent will be larger than the 90th percentile. The remaining 80 percent of children will fall somewhere between these two boundaries. By the time children are 6 years old, they have already gained about 70 percent of their adult height but only about one-third of their adult weight.

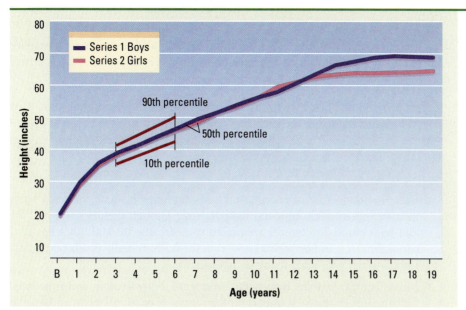

Figure 7.1 • Growth in Height (top graph) and Weight (bottom graph) from Birth through Adolescence The bracketed areas show the area between the 90th percentiles (largest 10% of children) and the 10th percentiles (smallest 10% of children). The 50th percentiles show where the middle (or average) heights and weights are for each age. (National Center for Health Statistics, 2004.)

Although growth at this age is rapid, children are not growing as fast as they did during infancy. From birth to one year of age, infants grow a full 10 inches, but after the age of 2 it takes young children nearly 4 years to add another 10 inches. Infants more than triple their weight in the first year, but after that it will take them 8 years to triple their weight again. As you can see in Figure 7.1, the rate of growth slows as children enter early childhood (around age 2 and 3), and it does not accelerate again until the adolescent growth spurt begins.

Children's body proportions also change. The head size becomes smaller relative to the rest of the body, and the chest and legs grow longer. The tummy is now flatter and the body becomes more trim. By the time children enter first grade their body proportions look like those seen in older children (Gallahue & Ozmun, 1995). On the inside, children's bones are getting thicker and children are gaining more muscle mass. Gender differences in growth are minimal. Boys have slightly more muscle mass and thicker bones than girls; otherwise boys and girls are remarkably similar in size and shape at this age.

Nutrition

Children need proper nutrition to fuel the rapid growth and the increasing activity levels we see in early childhood. At any age, a healthy diet includes adequate calories and the proper balance of these key nutrients (Gabbard, 1992):

- Proteins provide our bodies with amino acids, the essential building blocks of growth. Proteins from diet are necessary to support new growth in the body.

- Carbohydrates are an important source of fuel for the body, providing energy for muscle activity, the generation of body heat, and the enormous energy demands of the brain and nervous system.

- Fats provide a store of energy, and body fat helps insulate the body from fluctuations in environmental temperature. Though dietary saturated fat and high blood cholesterol are linked to heart disease and other harmful conditions, it is important to know that the body actually produces cholesterol and requires it for many bodily functions.

- Minerals and vitamins help maintain normal body growth and functions. Calcium, for example, is important for forming bones and teeth, and for the maintenance of healthy bones as we age.

your perspective

What were your favorite foods when you were young? Were you a picky eater? What do you or your parents remember?

---

a professional perspective

Career Focus: Meet a Family Nutrition Counselor

Kathryn Tromblay, RN, BSN
Naperville, Illinois

What eating patterns do you deal with most with children ages 3 to 6?
I work in a pediatrician's office in a suburb of Chicago, and I mostly see children who are constantly snacking. I talk with the parents and discuss using a schedule with three meals plus a morning and afternoon snack. I also stress that they decrease juice and switch to water in the children's sippy cups or drink cups.

How can parents get children to eat a more balanced and healthy meal?
Offer fun-looking meals that have all the food groups in them. Parent and family magazines always offer cute ideas for snacks and lunches such as mini pizzas made with whole wheat muffins and decorated with "faces" made of small pieces of vegetables. I always emphasize that parents should continue to offer all the food groups even if their children turn their noses up at the offering. Also, the parents must set good examples by eating healthy!

How should they handle a picky eater who wants to eat the same thing every day?
Offer new foods along with small amounts of a food that you know the child will eat. Parents must be consistent and not give in to a child's every request. Include something of what they like but always add the other food group or groups. If new foods are never offered, a child will never eat them! Never make the dinner table a place to argue—be calm, be consistent, and have the child leave the table if he/she becomes upset.

What education and experience does it take to work in your field?
I have a bachelor's degree in nursing and a Bachelor of Science degree in psychology. I feel this has been a good mix in working with the children and families. I can be successful only if the parents are willing to change. Eating habits are formed by parents! I tell my families we are not counting calories—we are talking about the food pyramid, how to use it at meals, and also how to change our activity levels in our day-to-day lives.

Q *What other nutrition issues do you think counselors deal with? What do you think the biggest nutrition problems are in the United States?*

Most young children tend to have a few foods they prefer to eat, and they don't usually like trying new foods. It's always a challenge to get young children to eat a balanced diet. What can parents do to encourage healthy eating in young children? Check out the advice given by a professional nutritionist in the Professional Perspective box called "Career Focus: Meet a Family Nutrition Counselor." Perhaps a career in nutrition is for you?

Malnutrition occurs when children do not consume adequate calories, protein, vitamins, and minerals. Although starvation is rare in the United States, malnutrition still plagues too many infants and children. A national survey taken between 1988 and 1994 indicated that as many as 12 million Americans lived in families that "sometimes" or "often" did not have food or money to buy food (Alaimo et al., 1998). Of these, nearly 70 percent went one or more days per month without food, and 4 percent went without food for 14 or more days per month. An estimated 3 to 4 million were children or adolescents under the age of 17. The survey found food insufficiency in 15 percent of Hispanic families, 8 percent of African American families, and 3 percent of non-Hispanic Caucasian families. This is an alarming record, given the great economic prosperity that the United States enjoys.

What are the short- and long-term effects of malnutrition? Children who lack adequate nutrition tend to show stunted growth. Inadequate calories or lack of a balanced diet can cause lowered intelligence. Malnourished children perform less well in school. As adults, children who were malnourished can continue to suffer physical and intellectual deficits that often limit their ability to earn an adequate income.

In developing countries the rate of malnutrition is even more alarming. According to the World Health Organization (WHO), in the developing countries 230 million children under the age of 5 are seriously malnourished (WHO, 2005; de Onis et al., 2002). These children are significantly underweight and show stunted growth. Approximately 80 percent live in Asia, 15 percent in Africa, and 5 percent in Latin America. As Table 7.1 shows, in various regions of the world, large segments of the population are not able to meet their basic nutritional requirements.

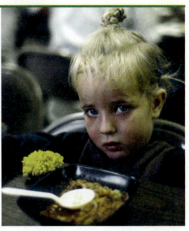

Millions of Americans are too poor to provide enough food for their families every day. Many rely on government programs and community food partners for help.

malnutrition
Nutritional deficiency caused by an inadequate intake of calories, protein, vitamins, and minerals.

Think About Tammi . . .
What might happen if the children who live next to Tammi are malnourished? What do these children need for proper nutrition?

TABLE 7.1 Children Under Age 5 in Developing Countries Who Are Significantly Malnourished and Underweight

REGION	EXAMPLE COUNTRIES	NUMBER OF CHILDREN (UNDER AGE 5)	PERCENTAGE OF CHILDREN (UNDER AGE 5)
South Asia	includes Bangladesh, India, Pakistan	101 million	60
East Asia	includes China, Mongolia	26 million	21
South-East Asia	includes Indonesia, Laos, Vietnam, Philippines	22 million	38
West Africa	includes Ghana, Namibia, Nigeria	12 million	33
East Africa	includes Ethiopia, Rwanda, Uganda	11 million	31
South America	includes Bolivia, Brazil, Colombia	3 million	8
Central America	includes Mexico, Guatemala, Honduras	3 million	18
North Africa	includes Algeria, Egypt	2 million	11
Caribbean	includes Dominican Republic, Haiti, Jamaica	0.6 million	19
United States (for comparison)			Less than 3

Note: "Underweight" is defined as being 2 standard deviations below the median weight for that age (equal to the lower 2.27 percent of a normal curve for children's weights).

(World Health Organization, 2005 and their report written by de Onis et al., 2002.)

your perspective

What do you think we need to do to combat the problem of world hunger? What can you and your friends do?

Figure 7.2 • This child has *kwashiorkor*, a terrible disease caused by a chronic lack of protein in the diet.

kwashiorkor
Disease caused by a lack of protein in the diet. Children are severly malnourished, with a swollen belly.

glial cells
Specialized cells in the nervous system that support neurons in several ways.

synaptic pruning
Process in which unused synapses are lost (pruned).

Maybe you have seen photos of children like the one shown in Figure 7.2. This child has **kwashiorkor,** a terrible disease caused by a chronic lack of protein in the diet. Children with kwashiorkor are seriously underweight but have swollen bellies. Their growth is retarded and they often have sores on their bodies and suffer from diarrhea. Untreated, the disease leads to coma and death. This level of malnutrition occurs mostly in developing nations that have suffered severe droughts or political unrest, and people are not able to get the food and nutrition they need. Writing about worldwide problems with nutrition, de Onis and colleagues commented that malnutrition "not only perpetuates the vicious cycle of poverty but also leads to an enormous waste of human potential" (2002, p. 10).

Another growing nutrition-related problem children face is obesity. Obesity problems have risen to epidemic proportions in the United States and elsewhere. We cover this important topic in detail in Chapter 10.

Growth and Development of the Brain

The brain grows in spurts (Epstein, 1978; Kolb, 1999; Kolb & Fantie, 1989). The first growth spurt is the greatest—during the infancy period between 3 and 18 months, the weight of the brain increases 30 percent. Brain weight then increases up to another 10 percent during each period from the years 2 to 4, 6 to 8, 10 to 12, and 14 to 16. These age periods correspond roughly with the stages of cognitive development Jean Piaget proposed several decades ago. Look back to Chapter 5 for an outline of Piaget's stages and the ages associated with each one.

Remember from Chapter 4 that most neurons are formed midway during pregnancy (by the 20th week of gestation). The rapid brain growth that occurs during postnatal growth spurts is therefore due mostly to an increase in blood vessels to feed the growing brain, the growth of the myelin sheath around axons (in the process of *myelination*), and the proliferation of *glial cells*. **Glial cells** are specialized cells in the nervous system that support neurons in several ways. First, they provide structural support, holding neurons together. The name *glial* refers to this property of "gluing" neurons together. In addition, glial cells provide nourishment, remove waste products, occupy injured sites in the nervous system, and form the myelin sheaths that insulate axons. There are more than 100 billion glial cells in a mature brain, outnumbering neurons (Kolb, 1999).

Although the brain is gaining size and weight, it is actually *shrinking* in another way. In Chapter 4 we mentioned that *synapses* (connections between neurons) form at a very rapid rate during the later weeks of pregnancy and into the infancy period. Synaptogenesis, governed largely by genetics, leads to a tremendous overabundance of synapses by the time the child reaches the age of 2. But from early childhood into adolescence, heavy **synaptic pruning** means that many more synapses are lost than gained. Synapses that are activated by environmental input and brain activity are maintained, but synapses that are not used are lost or "pruned." Figure 7.3 shows the developmental phases of heavy synaptogenesis followed by synaptic pruning. During childhood, as many as 100,000 synapses can be lost every second! About 40 percent of the synapses that existed at 2 years of age are lost by adulthood (Kolb, 1999). In the next section we explain how complex neural circuits in the brain are shaped by experience.

The Role of Experience in Brain Development

Researchers describe two types of brain development: *experience-expectant* and *experience-dependent* (Black & Greenough, 1986; Greenough & Black, 1999). With

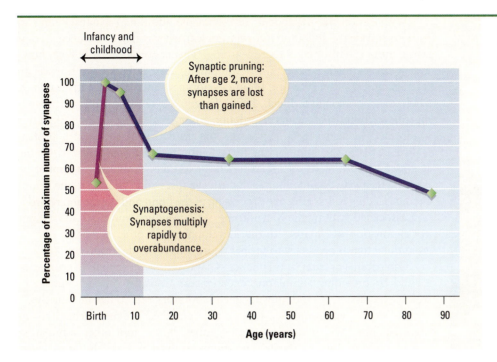

Figure 7.3 • Synaptogenesis and Synaptic Pruning New synapses form at an incredible rate during the first 2 years of life. During childhood, synaptic pruning reduces the total number of synapses. Synaptic density then remains relatively stable until the later years of life. (Adapted from Huttenlocher & Dabholkar, 1997.)

experience-expectant development, the brain has evolved to "expect" certain basic experiences or activities that all humans share—such as attachment to caregivers, recognition of human faces, hand–eye coordination, and communication by language (Nelson, 2001). The foundations for these types of experiences tend to be hardwired in the brain. Their development follows the pattern we've already described: Excess synapses form early in development ("expecting" the experience) and then are pruned throughout childhood (based on the actual experience). Genetics governs the rapid multiplication of synapses, and then experience determines which synapses survive. Scientists speculate that cycles of synapse overproduction and pruning are staggered across the various skills, yielding a schedule of critical or sensitive periods of development (Greenough & Black, 1999). Synapses related to hand–eye coordination, for example, may be produced and pruned earlier than synapses for language. With experience-expectant development, every human can develop the same set of basic skills, yet each person can develop his or her own twist on the universal theme.

    Experience-dependent development, on the other hand, has to do with experiences that are not universal. Examples include the vocabulary of a particular language (e.g., Portuguese), culture-specific behaviors (e.g., a handshake), and specific motor skills (e.g., skateboarding). The brain cannot "expect" these particular behaviors, so new synapses must form, stimulated by the experiences themselves, to encode them. As we learn to ride a skateboard, for example, new synapses form to code the motor movements required for this activity. Later some of these synapses may be pruned as we refine our skills. In addition to forming new synapses, researchers are now discovering that some new neurons do form and grow throughout life (especially in the hippocampus region of the brain) as a way to help us code new learning and memories (Schmidt-Hieberet et al., 2004). Experience-dependent development occurs throughout the life span, giving us the potential for lifelong learning and the retention of individualized skills, facts, and knowledge. This type of development contributes to the distinctive character coded into every individual's brain and sets each of us apart from all others.

experience-expectant development
Development of universal skills (such as hand–eye coordination) in which excess synapses form and are pruned according to experience.

Think About Tammi . . .

Where are Tammi's neighbors' children in the phases of synaptogenesis and synaptic pruning? Given their ages, are they mostly gaining synapses, or are they mostly losing synapses?

experience-dependent development
Development of specific skills (such as riding a skateboard) in which new synapses form to code the experience.

your perspective

Give an example of something you learned by experience-expectant development. What have you learned recently by experience-dependent development?

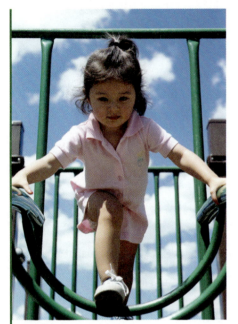

Safe places to climb, run, and play are part of the "enriched" environment all children need for optimal brain development.

Think About Tammi . . .

With this information on brain development, what concerns should Tammi have about the children next door? Are they getting the experiences needed to properly develop their brain circuits? Why or why not?

With experience-dependent development, additional synapses tend to form to encode the skills and information learned through experience. In that sense, more synapses code more learning. This is not necessarily true, however, with experience-expectant development. Researchers have learned an interesting lesson by studying brain development in children with fragile X syndrome (Greenough & Black, 1999). Fragile X syndrome is one of the leading inherited causes of mental retardation among males (see Chapter 2). In this syndrome a defective gene suppresses the normal production of a protein (called FMRP) that is important for synaptic pruning. Without FMRP, the synapses overproduced during experience-expectant development cannot be pruned effectively. Maintaining inefficient synapses adds "noise" to the neural circuits, leading to less effective processing in the brain and the mental retardation associated with fragile X syndrome. As Greenough and Black (1999) put it, "elimination of synapses during development, in other words, is often a good thing that is necessary to proper neurobehavioral development" (p. 35).

Can parents or caregivers enhance synaptogenesis and synaptic pruning in a child by providing stimulating experiences? Consider one experiment in which experimenters randomly assigned laboratory rats to live in "enriched" versus "sterile" environments. Rats in the "enriched" environments lived in cages equipped with numerous ramps, tubes, boxes, and other stimulating toys to explore. Rats in "sterile" environments lived in drab laboratory cages that lacked added stimulation. What effect did the added stimulation have on the development of the rats' brains? It depended on the age of the rats (Kolb et al., 1999). With rats in early adulthood, the enriched environment caused neurons to grow longer dendrites and increased the number of synapses per neuron. With young newly weaned rats, however, the enriched environment led to a decrease in synapses. That is, for the young rats, the enriched experience facilitated synaptic pruning during experience-expectant development, but for the older rats, the experience added synapses in experience-dependent development. The effect that experience has on the brain therefore depends on the age of the individual.

Clearly, exposure to stimulating environments is important for forming sophisticated neural networks in the young brain. Children deprived of adequate stimulation lose the positive benefits of synaptic pruning during experience-expectant development, and they lose the opportunity to gain new synapses during experience-dependent development. In both ways, they fail to reach their full cognitive potentials. But how far do we need to go to stimulate the developing brain? What does it take to create appropriately "enriched" environments? For children on a healthy developmental path the answer can be found in the everyday environment around them: colorful and varied visual patterns in their toys and books; voices speaking, reading, and singing to them; hugs, cuddles, and tickles; and the stimulation of running, jumping, and climbing. Opportunities to interact in rich and meaningful ways with the environment flood the developing brain with input and stimulate its development. Children deprived of these forms of stimulation, however, will be at greater risk for retarded or immature brain growth.

Larger Developmental Patterns in the Brain

So far, we have described microscopic development in the brain, focusing on individual neurons and synapses. Researchers also track the development of larger areas in the brain, correlating their development with corresponding advances in behavior and thought. The *visual area,* located in the occipital lobe in the back of the brain, develops early. This area reaches its peak in synapse density within 4 months after birth, and synapse density decreases to adult levels by approximately 10 years of age (Huttenlocher, 1990). As the visual area and the whole occipital lobe develop during early childhood, children become better able to process, recognize, and remember visual patterns that are more complex. The abilities to recognize specific faces and the emotional expressions from faces, for example, improve dramatically by the age of 6 to 8 years (Elias & Saucier, 2006; Kolb et al., 1992). At the same time, plasticity in the visual area is decreasing. For example, a doctor can correct *amblyopia* (one "lazy" eye) in a child under 4 by using a patch to block input to the healthy eye, pushing the other eye to process more input. After the age of 4, this intervention is not very effective.

Growth and myelination in the frontal lobes help children learn to pay attention, inhibit temptations, and cooperate in group situations.

As the *temporal lobes* develop, children make significant progress in learning language. Vocabulary increases sharply after age 3, and young children also absorb the structure and grammar of the language they hear around them. Improved communication between Wernicke's area (in the temporal lobe) and Broca's area (in the frontal lobe) helps children transform the language they hear into a language that they can speak and produce themselves. Language, hand–eye coordination, and the coordination of many other functions in the brain all improve as development continues in the *parietal lobes*. The parietal lobes begin to absorb more energy and become more active after children reach 2 to 3 years of age (Chugani, 1998; Elias & Saucier, 2006; Teeter & Semrud-Clikeman, 1997).

Heavy growth in the *frontal lobes* occurs between the ages of 3 and 6 years (Thompson et al., 2000). The frontal lobes are responsible for organizing and planning behavior, so by 3 to 6 years this brain growth helps children to participate more fully in group settings like preschool and kindergarten. As the frontal lobes develop, children become better able to control their emotions, inhibit their first reactions, and coordinate strategies to solve increasingly complex problems.

Areas elsewhere in the brain are also developing during early childhood. The hippocampus, for example, is an area deeper in the brain that is responsible for storing and processing memories. Most people cannot remember anything that happened to them before they were about 3 to 4 years old. **Infantile amnesia** is the term used to describe this type of memory failure, and it is believed to be related to immaturities in the hippocampus and other structures involved in memory (Elias & Saucier, 2006). As the hippocampus matures, our memories become more lasting and easier to retrieve.

These are just a few examples of how development of larger structures in the brain correlate with the improved skills and processes we see during early childhood.

infantile amnesia
Inability to remember things and events occurring before the age of 3 or 4.

your perspective
What is your earliest memory? Why do you think we don't remember more about our early years?

■ Let's Review . . .

1. When is the rate of physical growth the fastest?
   a. from birth to one year of age
   b. from 1 to 3 years of age
   c. from 3 to 6 years of age
   d. at the beginning of adolescence

2. Most of the children who are seriously malnourished live in _____.
    a. Africa
    b. Asia
    c. Latin America
    d. the urban sections of the United States

3. Which of the following is happening in the brains of typical 3-year-old children?
    a. They gain more neurons as they learn.
    b. Their axons are losing their myelin sheaths.
    c. Neurons are beginning to outnumber glial cells.
    d. They lose many more synapses than they gain.

4. Josh gets better grades in spelling and his twin brother gets better grades in reading. These differences in school performance are most likely due to differences in their _____.
    a. experience-expectant form of development.
    b. experience-dependent form of development.
    c. patterns of myelination in the occipital lobes.
    d. growth of glial cells before age 2.

5. **True or False:** *Kwashiorkor* is a disease caused by a chronic lack of protein in the diet.

6. **True or False:** Growth and development in the temporal lobes are primary reasons that children become better able to recognize faces and the emotions expressed by faces.

Answers: 1. a, 2. b, 3. d, 4. b, 5. T, 6. F

Motor Development and Physical Activity

As toddlers mature into the early childhood period, they are no longer trapped in their uncoordinated and unstable bodies. From birth to age two their mobility was very limited, and they stayed mostly in cribs, laps, playpens, and other spaces that were usually confined and safe. By the age of 3, however, most children are much more coordinated in their walking; they can walk up and down stairs, run, and even pedal a tricycle. Their world has opened into wide, new horizons!

Young children are very active and energetic. Most would rather run than walk. Have you noticed that many parents, childcare workers, and teachers often call after active children to slow down? By age 6, children are not only more mobile but they are also much more independent with activites such as eating and dressing themselves. They may still need help, however, opening lids and packages, cutting meats and tough foods, fastening buttons, and working tight zippers.

In this section we explore the major changes that occur in motor development and physical activity from the ages of 3 to 6 years. We begin with the gross-motor movements of children's large muscles, then we discuss the more intricate and delicate fine-motor movements of the hands and fingers. We also look at physical activity and exercise in early childhood. We conclude this section with a discussion of cerebral palsy—an example of a disability that profoundly affects the motor activities of many children and adults.

As you study this section, ask yourself these questions:

■ What improvements do young children make in the control and coordination of the larger muscles in their arms, legs, and torsos?

■ What improvements do we see in their ability to use smaller muscles to coordinate fine-motor skills?

- How physically active are most young children? How much do children differ in their levels of activity?

- What is cerebral palsy, and what do we know about the causes and consequences of this disability?

Gross-Motor Development

With advances in gross-motor development, children learn to use the large muscles in their legs, trunk, and upper arms to maintain their balance (Gallahue & Ozmun, 1995). At age 3, children can barely stand on one foot, but most 5-year-olds can hold their balance on one foot for several seconds. By age 4, children can walk a short distance on a low balance beam, alternating their feet as they walk. By age 4 they can also perform a basic forward roll, but it will be another few years before their forward and backward rolls look smooth and coordinated. At age 3, children use their leg muscles to pedal a tricycle, but they need to gain much more control of all of their large muscles to manage the balance necessary to ride a two-wheel bicycle. These are just a few examples of the improvements in balance that children make during these early childhood years.

As children improve their balance, they also improve their **locomotor skills,** or the skills used to move around, such as walking, running, and climbing. When toddlers walk, they take short, wobbly steps and their legs and arms are rather rigid. By age 4 we see a more mature walk with longer strides, relaxed movements, and a more rhythmic swinging of the arms to improve balance (Gallahue & Ozmun, 1995). By 5 years, children can run more efficiently, jump about 1 foot high, hop 8 to 10 times on one foot, and skip with both feet. In the gross-motor area, children also improve their ability to manipulate large objects with actions such as throwing, catching, and kicking. These skills improve as children gain balance, improve their hand–eye coordination, and learn to move one arm or leg independently from the other.

It is important to remember that children vary in their rates of progress in motor development. Some children improve their balance, strength, and coordination very quickly while others progress more slowly. The pace of physical development and coordination is controlled in part by genetics. It is also influenced by instruction and encouragement from adults and other children and by the opportunities that children have to practice particular motor skills. Even within a particular child, it is common to see uneven development across tasks. For example, one child may jump and skip with ease but be uncoordinated in throwing and catching. Another child may show the reverse pattern. The kinds of play activities children choose can be a major influence. Children who like to skip

locomotor skills
Skills used to move around, such as walking, running, and climbing.

your perspective
Did you learn some motor skills faster than others? Which forms of motor development were slowest to develop for you? Why?

By age 3, children have enough leg strength to pedal a tricycle, but it will be another few years before they typically have the balance and coordination to master a two-wheel bicycle.

Think About Tammi . . .

From what Tammi has observed, do you believe that the children next door are getting proper opportunities to develop their gross-motor skills? Why or why not?

rope will develop different motor skills than children who prefer to shoot basketballs. You can see this same pattern in the transition that "[c]hildren's play is the primary mode by which they learn about their bodies and movement capabilities" (Gallahue & Ozmun, 1995, p. 205). Keeping this in mind, parents, teachers, and childcare providers should offer children a variety of large motor activities. Play spaces, toys, and activities should encourage children to run, jump, climb, lift, catch, throw, balance, and otherwise help them strengthen and coordinate the larger muscles of their bodies.

Fine-Motor Development

Control over the delicate movements of the hands and fingers is required for fine-motor activities such as drawing, writing, typing, sewing, and stringing small beads. Young children are usually clumsy with these small movements. Their fine-motor development lags behind gross-motor development during this early childhood period.

Remember the proximodistal (midline-out) pattern of development we discussed in Chapters 3 and 4? You can see this pattern here in the transition children make from gross- to fine-motor development: Children learn to coordinate the larger muscles in their trunks, shoulders, and upper arms before they learn fine control over the smaller muscles further out in the hands and fingers. Coordination is spreading from the middle of their bodies outward into the extremities in a proximodistal pattern. We also see a cephalocaudal (head-to-tail) pattern in both gross- and fine-motor development as children learn to control their upper bodies (arms and hands) before their lower bodies (legs and feet). Most children, for example, can roll and catch a ball with their hands before they are very coordinated in kicking a ball with their feet.

Tying shoes is an example of a skill that requires considerable control over the fine-motor movements in the fingers and hands.

By age 3, children can put their shoes on, work easy buttons, wash their hands and face, and pour a drink from a pitcher (Gallahue & Ozmun, 1995). They can use a spoon to feed themselves, though they often spill and get as much food on their faces as in their mouths. By age 4, they can put on pants and shirts without help, brush their teeth, and lace their shoes. By 5 and 6 years of age, most children have gained remarkable control in fine-motor development: they can pour beverages and feed themselves without spilling; they can tie their shoes and work smaller buttons and zippers; and they can use pencils, scissors, and other tools with some precision.

Development of these skills often shows the patterns we just discussed. When 3-year-olds pour a beverage from a pitcher, for example, they often do it by standing up and turning their torsos and shoulders to pour the pitcher (Keogh & Sugden, 1985; Rosenbloom & Horton, 1975). Later, they will learn to keep their torsos and shoulders still, and they will pour by turning their arms and wrists instead. The transfer of control is moving in the proximodistal direction from the large muscles in and near the torso to the smaller muscles in the extremities. As they gain strength and dexterity in their fingers, they move from being able to use their hands to put their shoes on to using the fine-motor movements in their fingers to lace and tie their shoes.

As they enter school, it is important that children learn to use writing implements such as crayons, markers, and pencils. Figure 7.4 shows four phases children move through when developing a mature grip with pencils and other writing tools (Keogh & Sugden, 1985). At age 2, they usually use a **palmar grasp** by holding the pencil in the palm and moving the whole arm to draw on the paper. Many children then learn to hold the pencil through the fingers, still using large arm movements for drawing. By age 3 they learn to hold the pencil more delicately between the thumb and forefinger, but they are still using larger movements in the wrist to move the pencil. Finally, by around age 4, children show the **mature tripod grasp**—they place the base of their hands on the writing surface for support, they hold the pencil with the index finger and thumb, and move the wrist along with finer movements in the

palmar grasp
An immature grasp, holding the pencil in the palm and moving the whole arm to draw.

mature tripod grasp
Placing the base of the hand on the writing surface for support, holding the pencil with the index finger and thumb, and moving the wrist along with finer movements in the fingers to guide the pencil more precisely.

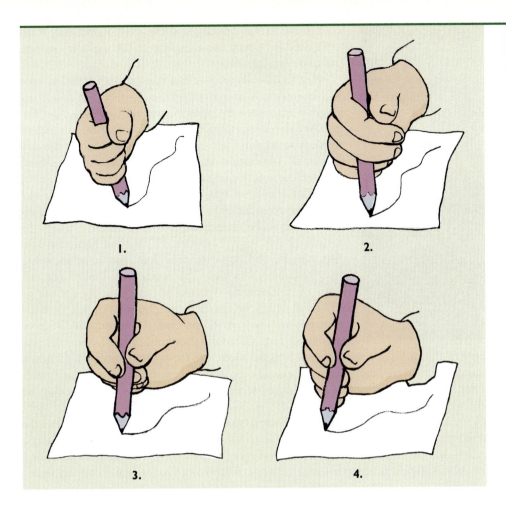

fingers to more precisely guide the pencil. They have gradually transferred the control of writing and drawing from the larger muscles in the upper arm to the smaller muscles in the hand and fingers. Similar progress can be seen in their coordination with scissors and other school tools.

As with gross-motor development, opportunity to practice is important. Children need to be encouraged to draw, color, cut, string beads, tie strings, work zippers and buttons, and practice a variety of other activities that involve fine-motor movements. With practice, they can learn to strengthen and control the smaller muscles that are so important in the many tasks we engage in every day.

And don't forget about the experience-expectant and experience-dependent patterns of brain development (discussed earlier in this chapter). Motor practice is important in helping the brain prune out ineffective synapses. If synapses in the motor areas remain too cluttered, motor movements will be clumsy. Practice also helps children grow new synapses to code the increasingly complex movements and skills that they are learning. Without practice, neither pattern of development can proceed normally.

Physical Activity and Exercise

Have you ever tried to keep up with young children? One minute they might be playing quietly with toys, but the next minute they are running in circles, racing up and down, or climbing over furniture. As we described above, physical activity is important in helping children strengthen their large muscles and coordinate their balance and fine-motor skills. Physical activity also provides the exercise children need to strengthen their cardiovascular systems (lungs and heart). Like everyone else, young children need

Young children get most of their physical exercise during games and playtime.

to be active to stay healthy, and the active habits they learn while they are young can remain with them as they mature and grow into adulthood.

Health officials recommend that children spend at least 60 minutes each day in physical activities that are structured or organized by parents, teachers, or other people, and they should accumulate at least another 60 minutes of physical activity in their free play sometime during the day (National Association for Sport and Physical Education, 2002). How many young children get this much exercise? In one study, children ages 3 to 5 wore a small watch-like device that recorded their heart rates every minute throughout the day (Benham-Deal, 2005). Children wore the devices all day on a Thursday, Friday, and Saturday, and their parents and day-care providers completed logs that described their activities. The researchers looked for evidence of moderate to vigorous physical activity, defined as activity in which the children's heart rates were 130 or more beats per minute (over 65 percent of a young child's maximum heart rate). What did they find? Overall, about 20 percent of the children's activities fell into the moderate to vigorous category. Children varied. Some were highly active almost all day, while others did not register any moderate or vigorous activity at all. Children were more active on the weekdays than on the weekend. Nearly three-quarters of the children accumulated 60 minutes or more of moderate to vigorous activity on Thursdays and Fridays, but just under half of the children met this level on Saturdays. The children played outside more on weekdays, when their parents and day-care workers reported that they played more at parks and on swings, slides, jungle gyms, and in games that involved running and chasing. Overall, children spent 65 percent to 87 percent of their time indoors where they mostly watched television, played with toys, and worked on arts and crafts. They evidently spent more time indoors on Saturdays. Another important finding was that almost all of the children's moderate to vigorous activities occurred in short bursts, lasting less than 10 minutes at a time. Young children do not pace themselves very well. Anyone working with young children needs to keep in mind that they tend to expend their energy very quickly, and then need frequent breaks to rest.

Children get most of their physical activity when they play. Running, climbing, chasing, and throwing are all common elements in young children's play. Parents and others can encourage children's activity by providing jungle gyms and play structures that allow swinging, climbing, and sliding. Push toys and riding toys are popular with young children. Three-year-olds love to pull things around in wagons and ride tricycles, and by the time they are 5 or 6 they are usually riding bicycles, scooters, and skateboards. Sand toys, pails and shovels, balls, and sporting equipment all give children opportunities to strengthen large and small muscles, improve hand–eye coordination, and otherwise enjoy their play and physical activity.

As children enter preschool and kindergarten, they have group activities and instruction that teach individual skills and also introduce turn-taking. At this age, most of their instruction in physical activity is incorporated into games, sports, and other fun activities. Music is a good motivator at this age, and one study showed that adding music and rhythmic movement exercises to young children's physical education classes helped them make more progress in their jumping and balance skills (Zachopoulou et al., 2004). A similar study showed that 5-year-old boys and girls did not differ in their gross-motor skills or music abilities, but girls did show an advantage over boys in rhythmic movement (Pollatou et al., 2005). As they

your perspective

What were your favorite physical activities between the ages of 3 and 6? Did you participate in organized sports or other programs for physical exercise at that age?

Think About Tammi . . .

Think about the 6-year-old boy who lives next to Tammi. What is he missing when he isn't in school or if his parents don't enroll him in community sports and exercise programs? What effect might this have on his physical development?

get older, children have gym classes in school and some children participate in dance or exercise programs sponsored by their local parks and recreation organizations. Many choose to join organized sports such as baseball, basketball, and swimming. We will have much more to say about organized sports participation in Chapter 10.

Cerebral Palsy

So far we have described the typical progress of motor development, but a large number of children have developmental delays or disorders in motor function, and they do not follow the typical pattern of development. **Cerebral palsy** (or CP) is one of the most serious disorders of motor development. It is caused by damage to one or more areas of the brain that control muscle movement and coordination (United Cerebral Palsy, 2005). "Cerebral" refers to the brain, and "palsy" refers to the muscle weakness and loss of muscle control that comes with the disorder. Cerebral palsy is actually a group of disorders, and the symptoms of CP vary depending on the specific areas of the brain that are damaged. Symptoms can include uncontrolled movements of the arms, legs, or other parts of the body. They may also include weak muscles, poor coordination, spastic (or jerky) movements, tight muscles, perceptual problems, and seizures. Children with CP usually have difficulty walking and engaging in many other physical activities (Østensjø et al., 2003, 2004). They may need help with common tasks such as dressing and going to the bathroom. They often have difficulty speaking, eating, and sometimes even breathing and swallowing. Children with CP often show mental retardation or learning disabilities. Read firsthand about a family living with cerebral palsy in our Personal Perspective box called "Living with Cerebral Palsy" on page 240.

Cerebral palsy is a serious disorder, but it is important to remember that it is not a disease. It is not curable, but with training and physical therapy children can learn to improve their muscle control and function. At United Cerebral Palsy (www.ucp.org) you can find a lot of other information about this disorder, including these facts:

- CP was first described by an English surgeon in the 1860s.

- In the U.S., approximately 10,000 new cases of CP are diagnosed in infants and young children each year.

- In about 70 percent of cases, the brain damage occurs during prenatal development (motor areas of the brain did not form properly); the symptoms may not be noticed for several months after the baby is born.

- In about 20 percent of cases, the brain is damaged during the process of birth, usually due to a lack of oxygen or severe pressure on the baby's head.

- About 10 percent of children have CP because of brain damage that occurred in the first months or years after birth, usually due to brain infections or other illnesses that affect the brain, head injuries in car accidents or falls, or damage inflicted from child abuse.

Today, many children with CP attend public schools, and some go on to college. The **Individuals with Disabilities Education Act** (IDEA) is a federal law (last amended in 2004) that requires that services be provided to assist all children with disabilities. When infants and toddlers are diagnosed with disabilities, states are required to work with families to coordinate services to help the children. When the children enter school, services are provided to help them work successfully in the school setting.

cerebral palsy (CP)
A serious disorder caused by damage to one or more areas of the brain that control muscle movement and coordination.

This child has cerebral palsy. The Individuals with Disabilities Education Act (IDEA) requires that all children be given the support they need to be successful in the school setting.

Individuals with Disabilities Education Act (IDEA)
Federal law requiring that services be provided to assist all children with disabilities.

Living with Cerebral Palsy

Betsy Carroll
South Berwick, ME
Parent of Jennifer, who has cerebral palsy

When and how did you first find out that your child had CP?

Jen was born 12 weeks early, weighing 2 pounds 10 ounces. Because she was born prematurely, we knew she would be delayed but didn't know how much. At six months of age they said she had increased tone but it wasn't until she had a 12-month check up with the developmental pediatrician that they said she would need physical therapy. I think it was about six months after that when a social worker handed me a book entitled *Handling the Cerebral Palsied Child at Home* so that I could take it home and read it. It was thick and purple and orange. I hate that book to this day!! I cried all the way home.

What was your reaction?

Probably shock. The delivery, hospitalization, caring for a sick child, coping with a child who didn't develop like others—it was all very overwhelming. The typical stress accompanying being a first time parent was magnified by all the questions I had of how to do the best for my child. The thrill and happiness of the birth of a child were coupled with fear and grief. The day she was born, Jennifer was taken by ambulance to another hospital 2½ hours away from home, where she stayed for 2 months. We lived far away from the NICU, it was winter, and I could only visit 3 times a week. I lived for those visits.

What treatments and supports has she needed?

From the time she was 12 months old, she has needed physical therapy and occupational therapy. She has had hip surgery and was in a body cast for 6 weeks. She has used a walker, a wheelchair, and crutches at various times. She had vision therapy and had "infant stimulation" when she was young. Jennifer has had an Individualized Educational Plan throughout her school years so that modifications and therapies could be provided. I struggled through many meetings at school, determined to get appropriate services for her. I learned about the laws and resources available for people with disabilities.

What advice do you have for other parents who might have a child with CP?

Enjoy them as children! You have many hats as a parent of a child with a disability. Don't let your jobs as occupational therapist, physical therapist, and social skills coach take over your job as a parent. The balance is not an easy one. Learn about your child's disability. Learn about special education and then be your child's greatest advocate. Connect with other parents whose children have a similar disability. They are some of the most wonderful, caring, and patient people you'll ever meet, and the support and resources shared by talking with other parents is incomparable. There will be many professionals in your life but as a parent, you know your child the best and don't forget that!

Q *How is the pattern of motor development different for children who have disabilities such as cerebral palsy? What accommodations can be made at home and school to help children with these types of disabilities?*

Before they graduate from high school, plans are developed to help the teens make the transition to life after high school. When it comes to helping children with cerebral palsy, all of this requires a great deal of work and coordination between parents, teachers, aides, pediatricians, physical therapists, social workers, and other helping professionals.

Health and Safety Issues

Young children are vulnerable and need our protection. They depend on us to keep them safe and to help them stay healthy. We've already discussed what parents and others can do to provide children with proper nutrition and the types of exercise and experiences they need for their growing bodies and brains. This section outlines the most frequent causes of death in early childhood, and we suggest things parents can do to help protect children from illnesses, accidents, and other health and safety problems. Unfortunately, many children are not properly cared for and protected, and we devote a large portion of this section to the issues of child abuse and neglect.

As you study this section, ask yourself these questions:

■ What are the most common causes of death during early childhood? How can they be prevented?

■ How many children in the U.S. suffer from child abuse or neglect?

- What is child maltreatment, and what are the different types?
- What are the effects of child abuse and neglect on young children?

Childhood Deaths and Safety Issues

Each year, more than 70,000 young people die in the United States (Kochanek et al., 2004). Table 7.2 shows the numbers of deaths that occurred in 2002 from various causes from infancy into early adulthood. As you can see in the table, the rate of death was highest for infants who were less than one year of age. The vast majority of infant deaths were due to genetic abnormalities, prenatal problems, complications that arise during the birth process, and diseases and illnesses contracted during the first year. Most of these infants were never healthy, and they were not able to survive their first years. After one year of age, the death rates dropped significantly, and then they rose again during the middle teenage and early adult years. As you can see in the table, automobile accidents were the leading cause of death among 15- to 24-year-olds, claiming more than one-third of all of the lives that were lost in 2002 in that age group. Deaths from other types of accidents and from homicides and suicides also rose sharply after age 14. Compared to these numbers, death rates were relatively low during early and middle childhood. Notice that across the 14 years from age 1 to age 14, the total number of deaths was still less than half of the number who died during their first year alone. And it was just over one-third of the number who died during the 10-year span from age 15 to 24.

From ages 1 to 4, more than 40 percent of all deaths were due to diseases and illnesses. Cancer, heart disease, and pneumonia were the most frequent killers among the major diseases and illnesses. Another 35 percent of deaths were due to accidents, and the top 3 killers in this category were automobile accidents, drowning, and fires. Although early childhood is a relatively safe

Cancer and other diseases are the most frequent causes of death among young children.

TABLE 7.2 Number of Deaths in the United States during 2002

CAUSE	UNDER 1 YEAR OF AGE	AGES 1 TO 4	AGES 5 TO 14	AGES 15 TO 24
Disease, illness, or medical condition	6,955	2,142	3,296	7,314
Prenatal or birthing problem, including genetic and chromosomal defects	19,729	595	448	513
Motor vehicle accidents	123	610	1,614	11,459
Other accidents, including falls, drowning, guns, poisons	924	1,088	1,172	4,531
Homicide	303	423	356	5,219
Suicide	–	–	264	4,010
Total from all causes	28,034	4,858	7,150	33,046
Rates per year	28,034	1,619	715	3,305

(Kochanek, Murphy, Anderson, & Scott, 2004.)

period of life, there are several things parents can do to protect young children:

Automobile accidents are a leading cause of death and injury in young children. Securing children safely in booster seats is an important precaution.

- Protect children against diseases by making sure they have proper immunizations. Make sure they get a thorough checkup from their pediatrician at least once each year, and have them checked any time they have a high fever or show other symptoms of serious illness.

- When traveling, always make sure children are secured properly in car seats or booster seats appropriate for their ages and sizes. Rear seats are safest. For your safety and theirs, never drink and drive.

- Never leave children unattended around water. It only takes a few inches of water in a bathtub or toddler swimming pool for a young child to drown. As children become more active and play more outdoors, make sure they do not stray into neighbors' pools or nearby ponds or streams.

- Secure all matches and lighters in your home. Always watch children carefully around candles, space heaters, kitchen stoves, and ovens. Keep a working smoke alarm in or near children's bedrooms, and have a family plan for getting everyone out of the house in case of fire.

- Avoid other accidents by keeping all guns, poisons, household cleaners, medications, and other dangerous materials safely locked and secured from children's reach. Cover electric outlets. Keep children safe around stairs, and make sure that the windows and screens on upper levels of the home or apartment are locked securely so children cannot climb or fall out.

- Although homicides and abductions by strangers don't happen often, it's still a good time to talk with young children about "stranger dangers." They need to learn who to trust and what to do when strangers approach them.

Think About Tammi . . .

If you were Tammi, what major risk factors would you worry about with the children next door? What major dangers or health problems would you worry about most for these children?

Child Maltreatment: Abuse and Neglect

Children depend on their parents and other caregivers for the physical, psychological, and emotional support they need for healthy development. Young children in particular are completely dependent on their parents—they can't make it on their own. Unfortunately, there are some parents and caregivers who don't (or can't) live up to their responsibilities, and there are others who exploit the vulnerable and powerless position of children. Child abuse is a tragedy that is very real and all too frequent in the lives of children. Before they grow up, about 1 in every 5 girls and 1 in every 9 boys in the United States will experience some form of sexual abuse (Finkelhor, 1994; Mash & Wolfe, 2005). In a national survey, 28 percent of parents reported that they use objects to hit or spank their children, and 13 percent said they physically shake their toddlers (Straus & Stewart, 1999). Who knows how many children suffer from other emotional and psychological abuses that remain hidden in family privacy?

Child maltreatment is a general category that includes all situations in which parents or other persons in charge of a child's well-being harm the child or otherwise neglect the child's needs. There are four standard categories of maltreatment.

- **Physical abuse** includes beating, slapping, hitting, kicking, burning, shaking, and otherwise causing physical harm to a child. Most cases are not intentional but result from discipline or physical punishment that got out of hand (Mash & Wolfe, 2005).

child maltreatment
A general category including all situations in which parents or other persons in charge of a child's well-being harm the child or otherwise neglect the child's needs.

physical abuse
Abuse that causes physical harm to a child.

neglect
Failure to provide for a child's basic physical, educational, or psychological needs.

sexual abuse
Abuse that includes fondling a child's genitals or breasts, committing intercourse or other sexual acts with a child, exposing the child to indecent acts, or involving the child in pornography.

psychological abuse
Abuse that includes verbal put-downs and other behavior that terrorizes, threatens, rejects, or isolates children.

■ **Neglect** is failure to provide for a child's basic physical, educational, or psychological needs. Neglect includes child abandonment, inadequate supervision, failing to provide proper nutrition or timely medical attention, failing to enroll a child in school, allowing truancy, failing to provide adequate affection, exposing the child to spousal conflict, and permitting drug or alcohol abuse (Mash & Wolfe, 2005).

■ **Sexual abuse** includes fondling a child's genitals or breasts, committing intercourse or other sexual acts with a child, exposing the child to indecent acts, or involving the child in pornography.

■ **Psychological abuse** includes verbal put-downs and other behavior that terrorizes, threatens, rejects, or isolates children or damages their self-esteem, thought processing, or ability to manage social interactions. This is also referred to as *emotional abuse.*

When cases of abuse exist, there is typically considerable overlap among these categories. For example, some degree of psychological abuse is present with every case of neglect or physical or sexual abuse.

In the United States, laws require anyone who comes in contact with children in the course of work or volunteer activities to report any suspected case of child maltreatment to child protection authorities or police (Mash & Wolfe, 1999). This requirement applies to teachers, bus drivers, camp counselors, childcare workers, babysitters, physicians, nurses, and anyone else who works with children. They all must report any credible suspicion they have regarding the abuse or neglect of a child. It is then up to child protection authorities to look into each report, investigate the case if it has merit, and take appropriate actions to protect the child.

To get a feel for the dimensions of the abuse problem in this country, consider that in the year 2003 authorities received nearly 3 million reports of suspected abuse or neglect (U.S. Department of Health and Human Services, 2005). Out of these, child protection agents investigated nearly 2 million cases and verified approximately 906,000 instances of child maltreatment. And this was for one year alone! At that rate, more than 16 million cases of maltreatment would occur in the 18 years that it takes for one child to grow up. Keep in mind that these statistics represent only the cases that were actually reported and then verified by child protection agents. How many more cases go unreported in a given year?

As you can see in Table 7.3, neglect is by far the most frequently reported type of maltreatment. The rates of child maltreatment increased significantly during the 1980s, but they started to decline slightly after 1993 (U.S. Department of Health and Human Services, 2005; Wekerle & Wolfe,

your perspective

Have you ever witnessed an incident of child maltreatment that you thought should be reported? Did you report it? Would you know whom to contact?

Think About Tammi . . .

Which categories of maltreatment would you suspect exist with the family next door to Tammi? Is she required by law to report her concerns? Why or why not? Should she report her concerns to someone?

TABLE 7.3 **Child Maltreatment Cases in the United States Verified by Child Protection Agencies in One Year (2003)**

906,000	verified cases of child maltreatment, approximately
551,754	due to neglect
171,234	due to physical abuse
86,694	due to sexual abuse
218,346	due to other types (or combinations) of abuse

Note: the numbers for neglect, physical abuse, sexual abuse, and other types total more than 906,000 because some cases involved multiple forms of abuse or repeated abuses during the year. In the United States., 1.2 percent of all children suffered verified cases of maltreatment.
(U.S. Department of Health and Human Services, Administration on Children, Youth, and Families, 2005. Data collected through the National Child Abuse and Neglect Data System, NCANDS.)

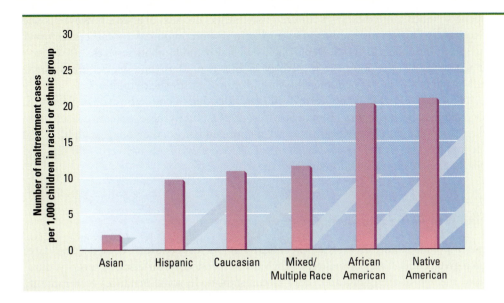

Figure 7.5 • U.S. Rates of Child Maltreatment by Race and Ethnicity, 2003 Rates of child maltreatment vary across racial and ethnic groups. This graph shows patterns of maltreatment reported to authorities during 2003. (U.S. Department of Health and Human Services, 2005.)

2003). We suspect that a large portion of the increase was due to wider implementation of the mandatory reporting laws through the 1980s, and that the decrease came as helpful services began to reach more at-risk families. Also remember that psychological abuse co-occurs with every other type of abuse. Psychological abuse does not have its own reporting category in Table 7.3, and we don't know how many cases go unreported; however, psychological abuse is the most frequent type of child maltreatment (Mash & Wolfe, 2005).

Which children are most likely to be abused? You may find it shocking to learn that overall maltreatment rates are highest for infants under the age of 1 (U.S. Department of Health and Human Services, 2005). Rates tend to decline as children grow older. When it comes to physical abuse, boys are most likely to be abused between the ages of 4 and 11, whereas girls most often suffer abuse between the ages of 12 and 15. Girls are four times more likely than boys to be sexually abused (U.S. Department of Health and Human Services, 2001; Wekerle & Wolfe, 2003). The maltreatment rates are also highest among Native Americans and African Americans, as Figure 7.5 shows.

Who is most likely to commit abuse? When we think of abuse, we may picture a mean father or stepfather yelling, hitting, or giving harsh punishment to children. It may surprise you to know, however, that mothers commit many more acts of physical abuse and neglect than do fathers (see Table 7.4). This is probably because mothers

Think About Tammi . . .

According to these statistics, which child in the family next door to Tammi is most likely to be abused? Who is most likely to be the abuser?

TABLE 7.4 Percentages of U.S. Child Maltreatment Cases for Each Type of Perpetrator: 2003

PERPETRATOR	PERCENTAGE OF CASES
Mother only	41%
Father only	19%
Both parents	17%
Mother and other	6%
Father and other	1%
Other and unknown	16%

Note: "Mother," "Father," and "Parent" includes biological, adoptive, and stepparents.
(U.S. Department of Health and Human Services, Administration on Children, Youth, and Families, 2005. Data collected through the National Child Abuse and Neglect Data System, NCANDS.)

spend so much more time with children than fathers do. Sexual abuse, however, is one exception: This type of abuse is more likely to be committed by fathers or other people in the child's life (U.S. Department of Health and Human Services, 2001). Isn't it alarming to know that over 80 percent of all acts of abuse and neglect are committed by parents—the very people who should care most for their children?

During 2003 alone there were 1,500 fatalities due to child abuse or neglect (U.S. Department of Health and Human Services, 2005). Out of these, parents caused more than three-quarters of the deaths. As we mentioned before, the youngest children are most vulnerable. A full 43 percent of the deaths were of infants not yet 1 year old, and nearly 80 percent were children under age 4.

Effects of Abuse and Neglect

It is impossible to determine the exact effect that any form of abuse or neglect will have on a given child. Cases of maltreatment vary tremendously, differing in severity, duration, the age of the child, and other circumstances. In some instances well-meaning parents try to "overprotect" their children but use discipline that is too harsh. In other cases violent parents strike their children in anger. Whenever abuse happens, it breaks the trust that should exist between child and caregiver. Although many abused children still claim love and affection for parents who have harmed them, the abuse often shatters their sense of security and well-being. When abuse occurs early, it threatens the formation of secure bonds of attachment between infants and their parents (recall Chapter 6). According to various studies, between 70 percent and 100 percent of abused infants show insecure attachments with their caregivers (Barnett et al., 1999; Cicchetti et al., 1988; Wekerle & Wolfe, 2003). When abuse occurs later, it still can cause physical pain, fear, and anxiety; it can lead to feelings of guilt, shame, and embarrassment in children; and it can disrupt children's social interactions as they try to hide their family secrets from their peers. Childhood abuse may also have a permanent effect on the brain's structure. The limbic system, important for regulating emotion and memory, seems to be especially affected. "Early stress [is] a toxic agent" that disrupts normal brain development (Teicher, 2002, p. 75).

As we mentioned before, the different types of maltreatment usually overlap. This adds to the difficulty of determining effects. For example, when a child experiences both physical abuse and neglect, any negative effects could result from the physical abuse alone, the neglect alone, the unique combination of both types of maltreatment, or other factors (such as parenting style) that correlate with them. Individual children also have their own individual reactions to the different types of abuse.

Although we can't specify the exact effects for any particular child, we can summarize what researchers have generally concluded about the effects of each type of maltreatment. In this section we will outline the main research findings regarding physical abuse and neglect, and we will discuss some of the effects of sexual abuse. (This topic will be discussed further in Chapter 10.) The effects of psychological abuse blend in with those of the other three categories, because this form of maltreatment tends to co-occur with all of the other types of abuse. As we describe these outcomes, bear in mind that the abuse is always an act perpetrated by the adult or other caregiver. It is never the fault of the child (Wekerle & Wolfe, 2003).

Effects of Physical Abuse. Aside from the deaths and physical injuries that can result from physical abuse, this type of abuse disrupts children's development in many ways. Children who have suffered physical abuse commonly have problems with aggression and hostility themselves (Nelson & Crick, 2002). From their abusive parents they learn to use violence as a way to confront conflict, and they also may learn to be unsympathetic about other people's feelings. One study showed how abused preschoolers reacted when their classmates were crying or in distress (Main & George, 1985). Rather than comforting their peers, the abused children responded with anger, fear, or hostility, sometimes even physically attacking children who were already in distress. Recent research indicates that abused children have a heightened sensitivity to situations in which other people express anger (Pollak et al., 2005). Other studies show that adolescents and adults who were abused as children are twice as likely to commit violent crimes and other criminal offenses as people who were not (McCord, 1983; Wekerle & Wolfe, 2003). Abused children are at greater risk for low self-esteem, depression, self-destructive behaviors, and suicide (Kim & Cicchetti, 2006; Wekerle & Wolfe, 1996).

Children who are physically abused sometimes develop compulsive compliance—they try to avoid severe punishment by complying with their parents' every demand.

A study conducted in China showed an interesting difference in how boys and girls respond to negative parenting (Nelson et al., 2006). Chinese parents who used more spanking, slapping, and physical punishment with their children tended to have sons who were more *physically aggressive*—their sons pushed, grabbed, and fought with other children more than did other boys their age. Chinese parents who used psychological strategies to make their children feel guilty, embarrassed, or not as good as other children tended to have daughters who were more *relationally aggressive*—they used emotional strategies to divide other children and make other children feel badly. The parenting these children received may not have risen to the level of full abuse, but the findings do show that different forms of negative parenting can have different effects on the aggressiveness of sons and daughters.

Contrary to popular belief, most abused children do not grow up to be abusers themselves. It is estimated that only about 30 percent of physically abused or neglected children grow up to abuse or neglect their own children. The remaining 70 percent develop more positive parenting skills (Kaufman & Zigler, 1989).

An interesting behavior pattern seen among some physically abused children is **compulsive compliance**—ready and quick responses aimed at pleasing adults by complying with their demands and wishes (Crittenden & DiLalla, 1988; Wekerle & Wolfe, 2003). Children who experience physical abuse sometimes become especially watchful of their own behavior, trying hard to avoid doing things that will make their abusive parents angry. Researchers report that this pattern is most noticeable in 1- to 3-year-olds. Most nonabused children this age are testing limits, saying no, and developing their own sense of autonomy (you've heard of the "terrible twos"?). Abused children, in contrast, are working to suppress these behaviors. The long-term effects of compulsive compliance are not yet known, but you can imagine the impact on children's sense of well-being, confidence, and self-esteem.

compulsive compliance
A behavior pattern seen among some physically abused children, marked by ready and quick responses aimed at pleasing adults by complying with their demands and wishes.

Language delays and poor academic performance also go hand in hand with physical abuse. Language disorders occur more frequently in abused children. Various studies have shown that physically abused children score an average of 20 points lower than their peers do on IQ tests. They also score about 2 years below their grade levels on standardized tests of verbal and math skills, and about one-third fail school subjects or must attend special education classes (Hoffman-Plotkin & Twentyman, 1984; Salzinger et al., 1984; Wekerle & Wolfe, 2003).

Effects of Neglect. The cognitive and academic achievement of neglected children is even worse than that of physically abused children (Wekerle & Wolfe, 2003). Parents who neglect their children don't provide as much stimulation for them when they are infants, don't read to them as much when they are preschoolers, and don't become involved or supportive in their schoolwork and other activities. Their children spend a lot of time unsupervised. Language delays, intelligence deficits, and lower academic performance are common. Neglected children often show poor impulse control and become highly dependent on their teachers. Some become extremely passive in school. Neglected children tend to be even more socially withdrawn than physically or sexually abused children, often shying away from playing with classmates. One of the difficult decisions child protection authorities often must make is how severe the neglect needs to be before they remove children from their homes. To learn more about this heart-wrenching issue, read the Social Policy Perspective box called "Protecting Children from Neglect."

As we mentioned before, the outcomes of child maltreatment are as varied as the individual children who suffer the abuse and the adults who perpetrate it. Also confusing the issue is the fact that it is virtually impossible to distinguish the effects of the abuse as such from the impacts of all the other factors surrounding these children and families. Abusing families tend to isolate themselves from friends and community, keeping the abuse private. They may move frequently, changing the children's schools and networks of friends. Family conflict and family dysfunction are common, so children may witness other acts of violence or abuse in addition to the maltreatment directed at them. Their homes may be overcrowded, and life may be chaotic and unpredictable. Although most abusers do not have officially diagnosed mental disorders, some do. Often, too, the families live in poverty. By interacting with all of these factors, child abuse and neglect can exact a considerable price.

Think About Tammi . . .

Given what Tammi has observed, what consequences should we be most concerned about regarding the children next door? What are the most likely effects of the way they are treated?

Abused children are usually trapped and powerless to change their environments. As one researcher put it, "She must find a way to preserve a sense of trust in people who are untrustworthy, safety in a situation that is unsafe, control in a situation that is terrifyingly unpredictable, power in a situation of helplessness" (Herman, 1992). Using cognitive and emotional skills that are not yet mature, abused children must struggle to understand their situations and the complex feelings evoked by them. When it comes to pointing fingers for the blame of child maltreatment, we need to focus on parents' lack of understanding of their children's needs, on the undue stressors many parents face, and on the failure of the society to offer families enough support.

How can we prevent child maltreatment? Solutions are not easy and must address multiple factors. One program that has been successful in significantly reducing the rate of child maltreatment is the Title I Child–Parent Center program begun in the Chicago public schools in 1967. This program offers preschool education for low-income children as well as a variety of services to support entire families. For example, training is offered in parenting skills and job-related skills, and the program actively encourages family involvement in children's schooling. The services are continued until the child weathers the transition to school (until second or third grade). Compared to other children, those who have participated in this program do better in school, have higher rates of graduation, and have lower arrest rates. Their parents are more involved in the children's schooling and have higher expectations for their children's academic achievement. And, most important for this discussion, the rate of child maltreatment is significantly lower in these families—about 50 percent lower than in similar families not in the program (Reynolds, 2000; Reynolds & Robertson, 2003; Reynolds et al., 2001).

Protecting Children from Neglect

Ana Diaz-DeJesus is a child protection caseworker in Bridgeport, Connecticut. She has a daunting caseload of more than 30 families, including nearly 150 children. Today she is visiting Maria R., a young mother of 3 children who lives in a filthy apartment with no heat and no food. Maria, a high school dropout and drug user, is raising her children alone on welfare. Moving from one cramped apartment to another, she barely stays ahead of eviction. Landlords, neighbors, and even relatives have called authorities to report that she is using drugs, not caring properly for her children, and living with a man who has a record of molesting children. One of the children had to be hospitalized in a coma after falling while unsupervised. At times the family has lived by candlelight because the electricity was turned off. Over many months Ana has often delivered groceries to the apartment and has arranged numerous services for Maria, including drug counseling, domestic violence counseling, and therapy for the children. Maria has never followed through. As she leaves the apartment this time, Ana prays, "God protect this family" (Gross, 1998, p. 1).

Not far from Bridgeport, in New York City, Sabrina Green was found dead several years ago, having suffered untreated burns, gangrene, and blows to the head. Sabrina was only 9 years old. She was living with her half-sister and 10 other children in a small apartment. The half-sister and her boyfriend claimed that Sabrina lit a fire and tried to put it out, resulting in the burns. Police, however, arrested the half-sister and boyfriend and charged them with manslaughter (Sexton & Swarns, 1997). A few years later in the Bronx, Ahsianea Carzan died of apparent malnutrition. Blind and disabled, she was not able to fend for herself. When she was found, her tiny body weighed only 17 pounds. Ahsianea was 5 years old (Bernstein & Chivers, 2000).

Abuse and neglect are a leading cause of death of children under the age of 4. The former secretary of Health and Human Services, Donna Shalala, reported that "children are being hurt more often and more seriously" (Pear, 1996, p. 1). Both Sabrina Green's and Ahsianea Carzan's families had numerous encounters with child protection agencies, but in neither case did the agencies put the child in foster care. Should the authorities have been more aggressive in protecting these children? Some people think so, and cases like these have prompted many child protection agencies to become more willing to remove children from their homes. Agencies once tried to keep families intact as long as possible, but they no longer feel they can allow families so many chances.

Other critics, however, believe that child protection agencies remove children too often. In a scathing opinion, one federal judge wrote that agencies are too quick in removing children from homes in which mothers suffer domestic violence, and one group of parents in New York City filed a class-action lawsuit claiming that child protection workers routinely violate the law by removing children from families when they are not in real danger (Glaberson, 2002; Swarns, 1999).

Meanwhile, in Bridgeport, Ana Diaz-DeJesus continues to do her best to provide support and services to families, taking heart in the glimmers of improvement she sometimes sees. The problems families face are complex, and the answers are never easy. Speaking about caseworkers like Ana, the deputy director of the Child Welfare League of America commented that "what they do is not rocket science—it's way harder than rocket science" (Gross, 1998, p. 1).

Q *Where do you think child protection authorities should draw the line between supporting families and removing children? What more can be done to ensure children's safety and well-being in cases where children are left in homes where there are substantiated instances of maltreatment?*

■ Let's Review . . .

1. Between 1 and 4 years of age, the most common cause of death is _____.
   a. homicide
   b. some type of accident
   c. a genetic or prenatal problem
   d. an illness, disease, or other type of medical condition

2. What are teachers, nurses, physicians, childcare workers, and other professionals required to do if they suspect that a child has been abused or neglected?
   a. Ignore it; it's a private family matter.
   b. Interview the child to find out what happened.
   c. Contact the parents to find out what happened.
   d. Report it to police or child protection authorities.

3. Who is most likely to physically abuse or neglect a child?
   a. fathers
   b. mothers
   c. childcare workers
   d. other relatives who care for children

4. School achievement and social withdrawal tend to be the worst for children who suffer _____.
   a. neglect
   b. physical abuse
   c. sexual abuse
   d. psychological abuse

5. **True or False:** Physical abuse increases the chances that children will use violence to solve their own problems.

6. **True or False:** Children who are neglected tend to become more dependent on their teachers.

Answers: 1. d, 2. d, 3. b, 4. a, 5. T, 6. T

Thinking Back to Tammi and Her Neighbors . . .

Now that you have studied this chapter, you should be able to apply at least a dozen concepts and research findings to the situation Tammi observed next door. The main concern here is that the children seem to be neglected. The parents do not seem to be providing proper care: The children wander off unsupervised, they wear dirty clothes, the older child doesn't always go to school, and Tammi wonders if they are even getting proper nutrition. The different categories of child maltreatment tend to co-occur, and Tammi suspects that the children may suffer physical abuse. Psychological abuse nearly always exists in cases of neglect and physical abuse. Ethically, Tammi should report her concerns to authorities if she believes the children's welfare is in jeopardy. Legally, however, she is not required to report her concerns because she doesn't interact with the children in any capacity of her job or volunteer work.

If the children are malnourished, we would have concerns about their growth and physical development. If they are neglected, they may miss physical activities in school and not join sports teams or other exercise programs. They already are not making use of the playground facilities on their block. Unless they find other ways to practice motor skills, their gross-motor development may be delayed. We should be more concerned, however, with other health and safety issues. Are they getting proper immunizations and health care? Are their illnesses being checked and treated? If they are not supervised, will they get into household poisons, find firearms in the house, or have other accidents in the house or around the neighborhood?

Early childhood is an important time for brain development. Synapses are being pruned at a rapid rate as the brain's circuits become shaped by the child's experiences. Axons are myelinating, and glial cells are proliferating in the brain. Without proper care, nutrition, and stimulation, will these processes be compromised for these children? What can be done to keep their brain development on the right track?

These are just a few of the concerns Tammi should have about her neighbors' children. The concepts you studied in this chapter can help you think about situations in which young children may not be receiving proper care. We can all use these concepts to better understand how children grow and develop and to help all children have an early childhood that is strong, safe, and healthy.

■ Chapter Review . . .

What do we know about growth and nutrition during early childhood?

Each year between the ages of 3 and 6, children grow about 2 or 3 inches in height and gain just over 5 pounds, on average. Growth during this period is not as rapid as it was during infancy or as rapid as it will be during the adolescent growth spurt yet to come. To support healthy growth, children need adequate calories and a balance of proteins, carbohydrates, fats, minerals, and vitamins. Malnutrition can result if the diet lacks enough calories or nutrients for proper growth. Starvation is rare in the U.S., but many families do not have enough food to eat. In developing countries, many millions of children are malnourished. *Kwashiorkor* is a disease caused by a chronic lack of protein in the diet.

What are the main trends in brain development during early childhood?

Brain weight increases about 10 percent between the ages of 2 and 4 and again between the ages of 6 and 8. Glial cells are proliferating, and these specialized cells provide structure, hold neurons together, provide nourishment, form myelin, and perform other important functions in the brain. During early childhood, children lose more synapses than they gain in a process called *synaptic pruning*. Basic human capacities develop via experience-expectant development in which the brain overproduces synapses and then prunes them back using experience and feedback from the environment. The unique skills and knowledge that set each of us apart develop more through experience-dependent development in which new synapses are created to code our experiences. Lobes of the cerebral cortex continue to develop as more axons become myelinated. Various skills and abilities emerge and improve as brain development proceeds.

What patterns do we see in gross- and fine-motor development?

Motor development tends to proceed in a cephalocaudal (head-to-tail) and a proximodistal (inside-out) direction. Children coordinate their arms before their legs, and they learn to control the larger muscles in the arms before the smaller muscles in the hands and fingers. Experience, exercise, and opportunities to practice are all important in facilitating motor development. As an example of fine-motor development, young children move from a palmar grasp to a mature tripod grasp when holding pencils and other writing tools.

What do we know about physical activity patterns in early childhood? What is cerebral palsy, and how is it caused?

Young children get most of their physical exercise when they play. Children tend to burn their energy in quick bursts of activity, and they need frequent breaks to rest. Officials recommend that children get at least 60 minutes of physical activity each day in structured activities and another 60 minutes in free play. Children vary. Most meet these recommendations, although they tend to be more active on weekdays than on weekends. Cerebral palsy is a serious disorder of motor development caused by damage to the brain during prenatal development or during birth, or by head trauma or brain illnesses that occur during childhood.

What are the main safety issues and causes of death in early childhood?

After one year of age, the death rates drop significantly and don't rise again until the teenage years. Relatively speaking, death rates are low during early childhood. Among children ages 1 to 4, diseases and illness account for 40 percent of deaths and accidents cause another 35 percent. Auto accidents, drowning, and fires are the top 3 causes of accidental deaths. Parents and others are responsible for seeing that young children get proper health care and that they are protected as much as possible from accidental injury and death.

What are the different types of child maltreatment, and what are their main effects?

Physical abuse, sexual abuse, psychological abuse, and neglect are the major categories of child maltreatment. Psychological abuse probably occurs with every case of child maltreatment. In 2003 there were nearly 3 million reports of child maltreatment, and about 906,000 cases were substantiated. Other than psychological abuse, neglect is the most frequent type. Infants suffer the highest rates of maltreatment. It is impossible to predict or determine the effects for any particular child. For physical abuse, common problems include aggression, hostility, conduct problems, depression, compulsive compliance, language and cognitive delays, and poor school performance. With neglect, delays in language, intelligence, and academic performance are common.

■ Key Terms

cerebral palsy (CP) (239)
child maltreatment (243)
compulsive compliance (247)
experience-dependent
    development (231)
experience-expectant
    development (231)
glial cells (230)
Individuals with Disabilities
    Education Act (IDEA) (239)
infantile amnesia (233)

kwashiorkor (230)
locomotor skills (235)
malnutrition (229)
mature tripod grasp (236)
neglect (244)
palmar grasp (236)
physical abuse (243)
psychological abuse (244)
sexual abuse (244)
synaptic pruning (230)

If you are using MyDevelopmentLab, you have access to an ebook version of this textbook, along with dozens of valuable resources per chapter—including video and audio clips, simulations and activities, self-assessments, practice tests, and other study materials. Here is a sampling of the resources available for this chapter.

Watch
Clotheslines for Violence

If you did not receive an access code to MyDevelopmentLab with this text and wish to purchase access online, please visit www.mydevelopmentlab.com.

Cognitive Development in Early Childhood

Maria is the mother of two boys, ages 4½ and 6. She and her children recently moved into a new community that has a school-choice program, allowing families to place their children in any school in the district. Maria wants to pick the best school for her sons, so she plans to observe and interview teachers and school officials at several schools. She's heard a lot about the importance of starting children in school early, but her younger son will have just turned 5 when the school year begins. Maria is concerned that he may not really be ready for formal schooling. She is also concerned because her boys are learning both Spanish and English at home.

She wants both boys to continue to learn Spanish (Maria's first language) but she doesn't want it to interfere with their work in school and with their mastering of the English language.

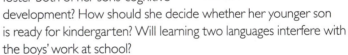

What should Maria look for when visiting schools and teachers? What kinds of classroom activities and teaching methods would best foster both of her sons' cognitive development? How should she decide whether her younger son is ready for kindergarten? Will learning two languages interfere with the boys' work at school?

After studying this chapter, you should be able to identify several important factors that Maria should consider. You will know the kinds of educational philosophy and practices that support and stimulate the cognitive growth of Maria's children. You will also learn the important aspects of language development that occur in early childhood, including the effects of learning two languages. As you work through this chapter, create a list of at least 12 concepts that might relate to Maria's situation. Explain how Maria could use each concept to identify the best educational environment for her sons.

As you read this chapter, look for the "Think About Maria . . ." questions that ask you to consider what you're learning from Maria's perspective.

The situation Maria faces is not uncommon. All of us who work with children need to understand cognitive development so that we can advocate for children, recognize their strengths and limitations, and provide stimulating academic and intellectual environments. As you learned in Chapters 4 and 7, children experience tremendous physical changes from birth through early childhood. Less visible but just as important are the enormous changes in children's thinking during these years. In this chapter, we revisit the theory of Jean Piaget to see how he described cognitive development during the early childhood period. We also introduce you to one of his contemporaries—the Soviet psychologist, Lev Vygotsky—who offered a different view of how young children build their knowledge and understanding of the world. Then we cover the more modern perspective offered by the information-processing approach. We end the chapter by exploring language development in early childhood and discussing the issues of early childhood education and kindergarten readiness.

Piaget's Stage 2: Preoperational Thought

preoperational thought
Thought characterized by the use of mental representations (symbols) and intuitive thought.

As you saw in Chapter 5, the Swiss psychologist, Jean Piaget, was very influential in shaping how we think about children's thinking. As toddlers emerge from Piaget's first stage (sensorimotor thought), they are beginning to use their minds to create mental representations that symbolize the objects and events they see in the world. During the early childhood years (roughly ages 3 through 6), children fall into Piaget's second stage: **preoperational thought**. In Stage 2, children can use mental representations to think about objects and events, even when the objects and events are not physically available to see, hear, and touch. According to Piaget, 3-month-old infants, for example, can't think about a toy unless they grab, shake, or mouth the toy. Grabbing, shaking, and mouthing are ways of thinking to a sensorimotor infant. By 3 years of age, however, children can internalize their understanding of the toy and think about it even when it is not physically available. They can remember what the toy looked like yesterday, they can imagine playing with it in a way they have never tried before, and they can even imagine what it tastes like without needing to put it in their mouths. Children's use of mental representations flourishes during this stage of preoperational thought, and Piaget claimed that children also begin to use intuitive logic in their thinking. We describe both of these trends in the next section.

operations
Logical processes that can be reversed.

As you will see shortly, children in Stage 2 are still not using full logic in their thinking. In Piaget's theory, **operations** are logical processes that can be reversed. If you pour liquid into a different container, for example, it is logical that you can reverse the process and pour it back into the original container. This logic seems obvious to you as an adult, but Piaget believed that children don't learn this type of logic until they reach middle childhood and Stage 3. During Stage 2, children do not think with *operations*, so Piaget called this level of thought *preoperational*.

As you study this section, ask yourself these questions:

■ What evidence of Stage 2 thinking do we see in children's language, art, and play?

■ What do Piaget's conservation problems tell us about children's thinking?

■ How has Piaget's theory influenced how teachers and others think about children's learning?

Flourishing Mental Representations

During the preoperational stage children will practice, and even playfully exaggerate, their new mental representation abilities. Let's look at the representations, or symbols, they use in language, art, and play.

Symbols in Language. Talk to a child who is just turning 2, and the conversation will be pretty simple and limited to objects and events currently present. Talk to a 4-year-old, however, and you'll find yourself engaged in a real conversation! As we discuss later in this chapter, there is an explosive increase in children's language ability after the age of 2. While the average vocabulary of a 2-year-old is 200 words, most 6-year-olds speak nearly 10,000 words (Anglin, 1993; Ganger & Brent, 2004). What makes this rapid escalation of linguistic skill possible? According to Piaget, language development is based on children's mental representational ability—their ability to let a symbol (e.g., a word) stand for an object in the environment. This ability gives children a way to communicate about the objects in the environment, even when the objects are not actually present. Since children are actively constructing their own langauge (look back to Chapter 5 for our discussion of constructivism), they often create their own inventive words and phrases. A young child may call a blanket a "winkie," describe a person with short hair as having "little hair," or say that a criminal is "under arrested."

Symbols in Art. Preoperational children's increasing ability to use mental representation is also seen clearly in the art they produce. When one of our daughters was 3 years old, she drew a heavy black horizontal line above a bright red horizontal line. "Look, Mom, I made a picture of you!" she said. "See, there's your head, and your hair on top, and that's your favorite red shirt!" What parent has not admired evidence of mental representation in his or her own child? To produce such artwork, the child must have mental representations—not only of the mother's face and hair, for example, but also of her favorite red shirt. Though the initial scribbles of 3-year-olds may not resemble any real object to an adult, they are evidence that the child has developed mental representation. Figure 8.1 exhibits drawings made by children of various ages; you can easily trace the development of more accurate and more complex mental representations in these drawings.

Symbols in Play. Watch children engaged in play and you will soon see clear evidence of symbol use. In *symbolic play,* children use one object to stand for another, such as when they pretend that a blanket is a magic carpet or a banana is a telephone. Children of 18 months seldom show such symbolic play; for example, they'll pretend to talk on

The ability to form mental representations allows these children to use fantasy and symbolism in their play. Using mental symbols, children can escape the reality of the here and now and pretend to be superheroes on exciting adventures in far-off places.

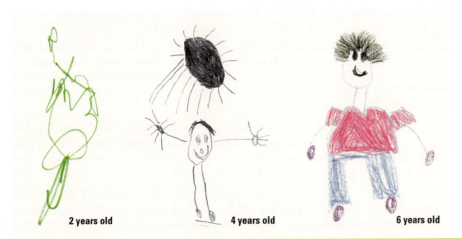

2 years old   4 years old   6 years old

Figure 8.1 • Artwork Showing the Development of Mental Representations The 2-year-old's drawing of a person is just a scribble. At age 4 the child draws the person as a happy head with arms and legs. By age 6, the body is represented more fully, including the neck and torso. What do these drawings tell us about the developing mental representation of what a person is?

Think About Maria . . .

For Maria's 4½-year-old son, how would language, art, and play activities be important in his cognitive development? Would art and play be important in his preschool and kindergarten classrooms? Explain.

intuitive thought
Thought and logic that is based on a child's personal experience rather than on a formal system of rules.

egocentrism
The child's inability to take another person's perspective.

animism
The idea that inanimate objects have conscious life and feelings.

artificialism
The notion that natural events or objects are under the control of people or of superhuman agents.

a telephone only when they have in hand a quite realistic-looking toy telephone. By the age of 2, children will use objects far less similar to the real item, such as using a banana for a telephone. Finally, by 5 years of age children are capable of using practically anything as a pretend "telephone." Their ability to mentally represent objects has progressed to the point that the symbol no longer has to bear any resemblance to the real thing (Corrigan, 1987; O'Reilly, 1995). Preoperational children use a lot of make-believe and fantasy in their play; we have a lot more to say about children's play in Chapter 9.

Emergence of Intuitive Thought: "It *Seems* Like . . ."

Another important development during the preoperational stage is the emergence of **intuitive thought,** or reasoning based on personal experience or on intuitive logic rather than on any formal logical system. Children reason according to what things "seem like," that is according to their personal experience with the objects and events involved. For example, on the way to preschool one foggy morning, our son, who was about 3½ years old, said, "Better turn your lights on—it's really *froggy* out." When asked what he meant, he explained that he had noticed a lot of this cloudy stuff in the air whenever we drove by ponds. "I know that frogs live in water, so when all the frogs breathe out, they make the air froggy." An admirable attempt, to be sure, but our son's intuitive explanation would not pass the objective tests of true logic. Evidence of intuitive thought can be seen in several characteristics of thinking that are common during the preoperational period, including egocentrism, animism, and artificialism.

Piaget used the term **egocentrism** to refer to a young child's inability to take another person's perspective. To young children it does seem that they are the center of the universe, and it seems that everyone must think about things just the way they do. Preoperational children are not able to understand that other people's perspectives might be different from their own. The classic demonstration of egocentrism is the three-mountain task. As pictured in Figure 8.2, experimenters show children a model of three mountains that have landmarks placed among them. A child sits at one location in relation to the mountains, and a doll sits at another location. The experimenter then asks the child to describe what the doll would see from its location. Preschool children typically describe the scene as they view it from their own location. Further, when given photographs depicting the views from each location around the table, children select the photos showing the view from their own locations, not the doll's (Piaget & Inhelder, 1948/1956). In other words, children select views based on their own personal and intuitive experience with the scene. They don't yet take into account the logical necessity that someone viewing the scene from a different place will have a different perspective. In other examples of egocentrism, children often think that the people they talk to on the telephone can see them, and they believe that their parents know what they are thinking and even know what they dream at night ("I saw my dream, why can't you?!").

Animism—the idea that inanimate objects have conscious life and feelings— is typical of the preoperational stage (Piaget, 1929, 1930, 1951). For example, children may say that the sun is shining brightly because "it's happy," or they may put their pencil down because "it's tired." **Artificialism** is the notion that natural events or objects (e.g., the sun, moon, rain, hurricanes) are under the control of people or of superhuman agents. A child might say that the sun went down because someone switched it off, or that the moon isn't shining because someone blew it out. As children's cognitive structures encounter more and more instances

Figure 8.2 • The Three-Mountains Task What would the doll see? Can children describe the perspective that would be seen from a different location? (Bee & Boyd, 2002).

in which animism and artificialism do not satisfactorily explain events, they begin to move away from these modes of intuitive thought and gradually move toward explanations based on physical facts and on a more objective logic.

Conservation Problems

The most famous examples of preoperational thought come from children's answers to Piaget's *conservation problems*. Piaget used the term **conservation** to refer to the concept that certain basic properties of an object (e.g., volume, mass, and weight) remain the same even if its physical appearance changes (Ginsburg & Opper, 1988; Piaget, 1952b, 1969, 1970; Piaget & Inhelder, 1974).

For example, look at the liquid conservation problem shown in Figure 8.3. An experimenter fills two identical beakers with liquid to the same level, as shown on the left. The experimenter asks the child, "Do these two have the same amount of liquid, or does one have more?" The child says that they have the same amount. Then, with the child watching, the experimenter pours the contents of one beaker into a taller and skinnier beaker. When asked if the two beakers "have the same amount, or does one have more?," younger children typically claim that the taller beaker has more liquid than the shorter beaker. When asked why, they usually point to the height of the liquid surface: "See, this one is taller, so it has more." Children using preoperational thought don't seem to understand that the volume of liquid is conserved (remains the same) even though the shape of the container changes. Children give similar responses for problems involving number and mass (see Figure 8.3).

Looking at Figure 8.3, you can see why preoperational children's tendency to use intuitive thought would lead them astray. At a quick glance, it does "seem like" the taller beaker has more. Piaget, however, analyzed children's responses further and was able to pinpoint other important limitations of preoperational thought.

- First, young children show *centration* in their thinking. Centration is the tendency to focus on only one aspect of a situation at a time instead of taking several aspects into consideration. In the liquid problem, for example, children tend to focus on the height of the liquid instead of considering that the greater width of one beaker compensates for the taller height of the other.

- Second, young children focus on the *static endpoints* of the transformation (how things look before and after) rather than considering what happened in the transformation itself. Children look at the beginning state (both levels are equal on the left side of Figure 8.3), then at the ending state (one level is higher on the right side), and they conclude that the higher level must have more. They fail to consider the transformation itself—it is actually the act of pouring that shows that the amount of liquid did not change.

- And finally, children at this stage lack a grasp of *reversibility*. That is, they do not imagine what would happen if they reversed the transformation; they don't visualize pouring the liquid back into its original container to demonstrate that the amount would still be the same. Remember, their thought is *preoperational* at this stage—they don't visualize the reversible operation of pouring the liquid back.

your perspective

Identify examples of egocentrism, animism, or artificialism from your own past, or from your experiences with children you know. What prompted changes in that thinking?

conservation
The understanding that some basic properties of objects remain the same even when a transformation changes the physical appearance.

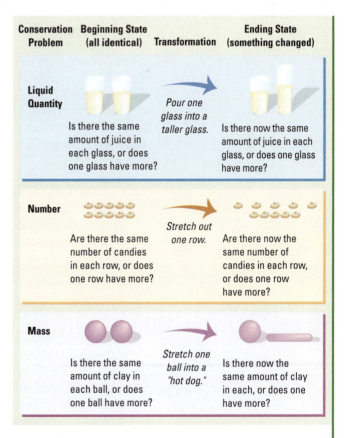

Figure 8.3 • Conservation Problems Three well-known conservation problems involve liquid quantity (top), number (middle), and mass (bottom).

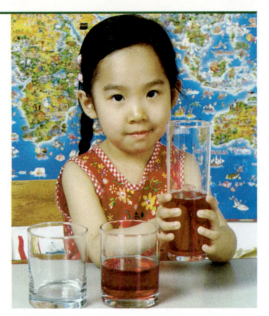

This child thinks the taller container has more liquid in it. What can her answer tell us about the thinking processes of young children?

When children focus on the height of the liquid, pay attention only to the static endpoints of the problem, and don't imagine pouring the liquid back, you can see why they usually reach such an intuitive answer as "this one is taller, so it has more."

Piaget saw the lack of mental reversibility as an important hallmark of preoperational thought. To be fully logical, our cognitive structures need to be reversible. Think about the logic of math, for example. If we have 4 and take 2 away, we need to understand that we can return to 4 by adding 2 back. Piaget believed that these dynamic mental operations were necessary for true logical thought. After continued experience with the environment, children realize that their intuitive thought does not adequately explain the events around them. As they realize the reversibility of many transformations and their thought structures become operational (reversible), we have the beginnings of the next stage of cognitive development. We describe Stage 3 in Chapter 11.

Piaget's Legacy

Before moving away from this topic, we want to make a few observations about the legacy left behind by Piaget's theory. *Piaget changed psychology's view of young children*. Before Piaget, theorists saw children as passive organisms capable mostly of reacting to events. After Piaget, they realized that children seek to understand their environments and actively explore and manipulate events simply to see how things work. Piaget's theory also *influenced the field of education* in several important ways.

- First, the notion of the child as an active and curious organism led to the design of interactive and hands-on curricula in schools and early childhood settings. These teaching materials encourage children to make use of their natural curiosity to explore concepts in science, mathematics, and other domains.

- Second, Piaget believed that children cannot skip stages but must move from one to another as their nervous systems biologically mature and they become cognitively ready. His stage ideas have shaped many guidelines for when to introduce different topics in schools.

- Third, educators have learned to make use of Piaget's ideas about schemes, assimilation, accommodation, disequilibrium, reflective abstraction, and similar topics (look back to Chapter 5). They do this by deliberately presenting children with puzzles, debates, and conflicting opinions to intentionally challenge children's existing cognitive structures and to encourage children to grow in understanding. Educators encourage students to think about the implications, usefulness, and limitations of their existing cognitive structures.

To learn more about how teachers use Piaget's theory to help children learn, read the Professional Perspective box called "Career Focus: Meet a Constructivist Teacher."

Career Focus: Meet a Constructivist Teacher

Stacie Anderson
Donnelsville, Ohio
First grade teacher at Donnelsville Elementary School

How do you use Piagetian concepts in your teaching?

It is critical to have an idea of the pre-existing schemes that students already have on a topic or skill area—it sets the stage for how I introduce a lesson. Next, I observe children's thought processes as a new concept, or a new layer of the concept, is introduced. How is it fitting (assimilating) into what they already know? I check to see how the new information is fitting by asking questions and having children evaluate their own thinking and each other's responses.

What specific activities do you use to help children construct knowledge?

Hands-on activities are critical in first grade, and all grades in my estimation. When teaching geometric shapes, I have children sort out squares, circles, and triangles and list what they know about each shape (the square has four sides, four corners, etc.). Then I show a rectangle and ask, "How many sides and angles does it have?" "Is it a square?" Some children will say "Yes." As we take a closer look, they recognize that the sides are different lengths. Now they understand that squares have four equal sides, but rectangles have two side lengths. Then we introduce a parallelogram, rhombus, trapezoid. . . . With counting, students build towers with Unifix cubes to represent each numeral (1 to 10). They observe that "It looks like stairs!" and "Every tower is one taller." They can visually see that each tower is one greater than the other, and this smoothly leads into the concept of adding one.

How do you use Piaget's stages as guidelines for your curriculum or classroom activities?

At the district level, we created benchmarks and indicators of success in critical skill areas. However, based on my experience, it is important to know that a child can exhibit various behaviors that are indicative of several of these stages. Still, first graders do think more concretely and have difficulty thinking beyond their home, family, and friends. It would be unrealistic to tackle national abstract issues with 6-year-olds!

What education and training is required to work in your area?

To be a licensed teacher, you need to have a degree or courses in education, and you need to be supervised as a student teacher for one year. The requirements differ in each state. Many states require teachers to get a master's degree to have a permanent teaching license, and others require an advanced degree to teach above the third grade. A *praxis* exam is required in most states.

Q *Which concepts from Piaget's theory do you see Stacie using? Explain why her approach is considered to be a constructivist approach.*

■ Let's Review . . .

1. According to Piaget, when children move from Stage 1 to Stage 2 in cognitive development, they begin to rely more on _____ in their thinking.
    a. sensorimotor impressions
    b. mental representations
    c. abstract thought
    d. true logic

Vygotsky's Sociocultural View of Cognitive Development

Of course, not everyone was satisfied with Piaget's account of cognitive development. Some theorists and practitioners have long felt that Piaget's account does not adequately consider one very important influence on cognition: the child's social environment. Lev Vygotsky is one theorist who gave the role of social interaction and culture a central place in his account of cognitive development.

As you study this section, ask yourself these questions:

■ What influence did Vygotsky's own cultural background have on his theory? What historical events were taking place during his lifetime and how did they affect his theory?

■ Why is Vygotsky's theory called a "sociocultural" view? According to this theory, what roles do culture and social interaction play in cognitive development?

■ What role does language play in cognitive development? How can adults facilitate children's development?

Vygotsky's Background: The Sociocultural Context for a New Theory

Vygotsky was born in 1896, the same year as Piaget but in Belorussia (later part of the Soviet Union). Vygotsky's family was Jewish, and they shared a rich cultural background with most of their fellow townspeople. Being Jewish, they also experienced prejudice, discrimination, and strict governmental restrictions. Vygotsky received his early education from a private tutor who taught by means of Socratic dialogue. In this method, the tutor poses questions and helps the student reason through and figure out answers rather than simply giving the student facts and information. At the University of Moscow, Vygotsky studied law, history, and philosophy. He graduated in 1917, the year of the Russian Revolution in which the centuries-old tsarist government fell and Vladimir Lenin came to power at the head of a Marxist government. Vygotsky was a committed Marxist. The new Soviet government seemed to promise an end to ethnic and religious discrimination, stating that everyone would be considered an equal Soviet citizen. Vygotsky also was a firm believer in Marx's emphasis on the importance of social history as an influence on people's behavior and development (Kozulin, 1990; Wertsch, 1985).

In 1924 Vygotsky took a position at Moscow's prestigious Psychological Institute to help restructure the institute and develop a Marxist psychology. Over the next decade this so-called "Mozart of psychology" (Toulmin, 1978) attracted many top Soviet scholars as students and colleagues to assist in developing and testing his theoretical ideas. Unfortunately, in 1934 Vygotsky died from tuberculosis. Although he was only 38, he had already written several important books and other articles, and his brilliance was recognized by all of those who worked around him (Kozulin, 1990; Wertsch, 1985).

It might seem that such a popular figure as Vygotsky would have had an immediate impact on psychology worldwide. He did not. Much of his writing was not published, even in the Soviet Union, until decades after his death. In part this was because the research to support Vygotsky's ideas had to be completed by his students after his death. Also, even as his followers completed the work, the Soviet regime banned much of it. Vygotsky often referenced foreign scientists, philosophers, and literary works, but officials in the Soviet government saw the influence of foreigners as undesirable. For two decades, therefore, few Soviet psychologists had access to Vygotsky's work. In addition, the cold war meant that there was little hope for dissemination to Western European and American psychologists. Josef Stalin (the successor to Lenin as the Soviet leader) died in 1953 and Vygotsky's work began to be published again. After the cold war ended, Vygotsky's influence on psychology steadily increased in the United States and around the world (Kozulin, 1990; Wertsch, 1985).

Soviet psychologist Lev Vygotsky proposed a sociocultural theory of cognitive development that continues to gain prominence. Can you see the influence of Vygotsky's own cultural background in his theory?

The Role of Speech and Language

The central theme in Vygotsky's theory is that children acquire cognitive structures from their culture and from their social interactions, primarily by listening to the language they hear around them. **Social speech** is the speech that we hear as people talk around us or to us. According to Vygotsky, children adopt important parts of social speech and make it their own **private speech**—the speech children say aloud to themselves. It is the language (speech) that carries the concepts and cognitive structures to the child, and these concepts become the "psychological tools" that the child will use (Vygotsky, 1962).

Consider the simple example of a little girl learning to draw a circle. At first the child has no concept of *circle*, so the adult uses social speech to talk her through the process. "Start your mark going around, like this [demonstrating an arc], then bring it all the way around until the marks meet each other." As the child tries to draw her own circle, she repeats the instructions aloud to herself, "I make the mark go 'round, like this, then I bring it 'round 'til it meets." The concept of *circle* was carried from the social speech (of the adult directing the child) to the private speech of the child.

Almost all children use private speech. When children are learning new concepts or difficult tasks, they often rely on the support of private speech, and the children who use private speech the most tend to be the ones who perform best in difficult tasks (Al-Namlah et al., 2006). "I'll bring the mark around. Oops! I went too far up. Now back down, and around this way. Not too far.

social speech
Speech that we hear as people talk around us or to us.

private speech
Speech that children say aloud to themselves; later internalized to form inner speech and mental activity.

Think About Maria . . .

According to Vygotsky's theory, why would it be important for Maria to spend time in the schools and classrooms listening to the verbal messages being conveyed? What kinds of messages, or cognitive structures, would she want to hear?

your perspective

Try to remember the last time that you mumbled or talked aloud to yourself when you were trying to do something difficult or challenging. How did your private speech help?

internalization
The process of taking external speech and making it internal and mental.

mediation
The process adults and more skilled peers use to introduce concepts and cognitive structures to less skilled children.

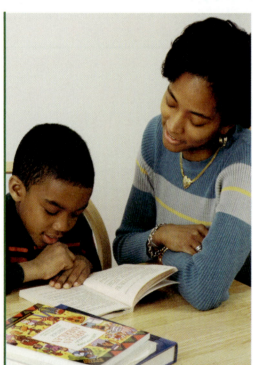

How do adults provide mediation for children's learning?

zone of proximal development (ZPD)
The distance between the current maximum independent performance level of the child and the tasks the child can perform if guided by adults or more capable peers.

Now the marks don't meet. I'll draw it over. There, a circle!" **Internalization** is the process by which external activity and speech become internal and come to be executed mentally. As children master a concept, they need private speech less and less. Eventually they internalize it completely as silent, inner speech. Private speech does not simply disappear forever, however. Have you ever found yourself mumbling or talking out loud when you are working on something that is complex or difficult? Private speech seems to help all of us focus our attention, regulate our strategies, and plan our problem-solving efforts (Behrend et al., 1992; Berk, 1992; Berk & Spuhl, 1995; Emerson & Miyake, 2003; Schneider, 2002).

Mediation: With a Little Help from Your Friends

In Vygotsky's theory interpersonal interactions with adults or more-skilled peers teach, or *mediate,* the cognitive structures created in the larger culture. **Mediation** is the process of introducing concepts, knowledge, skills, and strategies to the child (Karpov & Haywood, 1998; Vygotsky, 1981). For the mediating adult, mediation involves choosing which structures to introduce to the child, deciding when and how to teach them, and helping the child understand their usefulness. For example, think about helping a young child put together a jigsaw puzzle. Many adults encourage specific puzzle-making strategies such as starting with the corners, doing the borders first, or looking for clues (e.g., matching colors, matching shapes). In addition, adults often help children think about more general skills, such as being careful when matching shapes and colors or being systematic when trying a piece in different locations. However, most adults do not try to introduce all of these things at the same time. They mediate by selecting specific strategies and highlighting them; they help the child learn a few skills, then move on to others as the child gains expertise. Gradually the child internalizes all of the strategies, along with the verbal labels for them. In the end the child can use this information as a structure and tackle jigsaw puzzles independently.

Mediation can take place in structured settings (such as during formal schooling) or in informal day-to-day activities (such as when a parent talks about ecology while putting out the trash and recyclables). The key to making mediation effective is to tailor it to an appropriate level for the individual child. The structures being explained should be neither so easy that the child has already internalized them nor so difficult that the child cannot understand them. This optimal level of difficulty lies within what Vygotsky called the child's *zone of proximal development.*

The Zone of Proximal Development

Vygotsky defined the **zone of proximal development (ZPD)** as the distance between a child's "actual developmental level as determined by independent problem solving" and the child's level of "potential development as determined through problem solving under adult guidance or in collaboration with more capable peers" (Vygotsky, 1978, p. 86). The ZPD refers to the range of problems a child can solve if given some assistance. As shown in Figure 8.4, the bottom boundary of the ZPD consists of the most challenging problems a child can already solve independently. The top boundary of the ZPD consists of problems that the child cannot solve, no matter how much support others may offer. These tasks require higher mental functions that the child has not yet begun to internalize, so even very explicit assistance does not help. The ZPD is the zone between these two boundaries. The tasks within this zone require

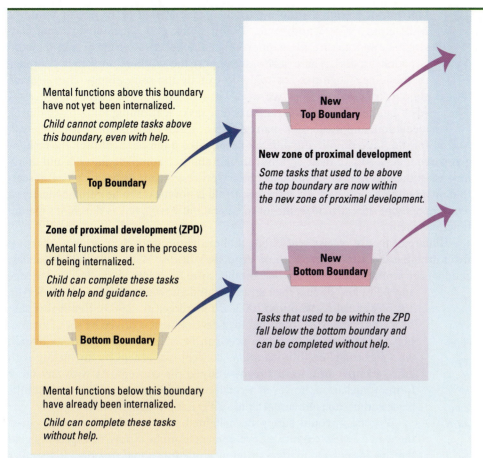

Figure 8.4 • The Zone of Proximal Development The range of tasks a child is capable of completing with help and guidance defines the zone of proximal development. The bottom boundary is defined by tasks the child already can complete independently. The top is defined by tasks the child cannot complete even with help. The zone changes with development, and both boundaries move up as more mental functions are internalized. As a result, tasks that used to be above the top boundary are within the child's zone; tasks that used to be within the zone become too easy and fall below the bottom boundary.

Labels within figure:

Mental functions above this boundary have not yet been internalized.

Child cannot complete tasks above this boundary, even with help.

Top Boundary

Zone of proximal development (ZPD)

Mental functions are in the process of being internalized.

Child can complete these tasks with help and guidance.

Bottom Boundary

Mental functions below this boundary have already been internalized.

Child can complete these tasks without help.

New Top Boundary

New zone of proximal development

Some tasks that used to be above the top boundary are now within the new zone of proximal development.

New Bottom Boundary

Tasks that used to be within the ZPD fall below the bottom boundary and can be completed without help.

mental functions that the child is in the process of internalizing but has not yet completely internalized.

An important point to remember about the ZPD is that it is dynamic—the top and bottom boundaries change as the child internalizes more and more mental functions (see Figure 8.4). The boundaries move up as the natural result of effective mediation within the ZPD. An adult interacts with a child, presenting problems that challenge the child. The adult helps the child work through the problem, sometimes needing to offer a great deal of assistance at first. The child gradually learns how to solve these challenging problems. Now some of the problems that used to be within the child's ZPD are below it.

There is an important implication here for instruction—can you see what it is? According to Vygotsky, the most effective instruction involves giving children *challenging material*, along with *help in mastering it*. Although children may need extensive help at first, Vygotsky said that challenging tasks promote cognitive development, as long as a given task is not beyond the top boundary of a given child's ZPD. And there is a related implication for assessment, or testing. That is, the most informative assessments are not tests of independent performance but tests of assisted performance. Such tests "take stock not only of . . . the processes of maturation that are completed" but also of "processes that are now in the state of coming into being, that are only ripening, or only developing" (Vygotsky, 1956, p. 448).

Scaffolding and Collaborative Learning

If mediation within the ZPD is so important, how do adults and other helpers do it? Scaffolding, a concept that has grown from Vygotsky's theory, helps answer this question. **Scaffolding** is providing supportive help when a child is developing a mental

> **Think About Maria . . .**
> *What could Maria look for that would indicate that her sons would be appropriately challenged within their own zones of proximal development? What kinds of mediation might teachers provide?*

scaffolding
Support given to a child as he or she develops a new mental function or learns to perform a particular task.

collaborative learning
Process where children work together to help one another solve problems, share their knowledge and skills, and discuss their strategies and knowledge.

Think About Maria . . .

If Maria observes children working together in groups, with teachers guiding and advising the groups, would this be a sign that the learning environment is conducive to cognitive development? Explain.

function or learning to do a particular task (Wood et al., 1976; Wood & Middleton, 1975; Wood et al., 1978). Think about a building being constructed, and picture the supports that the builders set up during the construction process. These scaffolds support the workers until they complete the building. Cognitive scaffolds do exactly the same thing—they provide support for children (the "workers") as they develop the cognitive processes (the "building") needed for a particular task. Scaffolding takes place during mediation, and it can take many different forms such as doing part of a task for the child, simplifying difficult parts, talking the child through the task, or giving reminders. Any of these actions can help children complete the task and therefore assist them as they develop the necessary processes. Just as with a physical scaffold on a building, however, a cognitive scaffold is not meant to be permanent. It is a *temporary supportive structure*, meant to be gradually removed as the child's mental functions mature.

Children can also receive scaffolding and mediation from their peers. Collaborative learning is a natural outgrowth of Vygotsky's theory. With **collaborative learning,** children can work together to help one another solve problems, share their knowledge and skills, and discuss their strategies and knowledge (Gillies, 2003; Slavin, 1995; Wentzel & Watkins, 2002; Zimbardo et al., 2003). Remember that Vygotsky emphasized that cognitive development is driven by social interaction and that a more capable peer can be an effective mediator. Children who are struggling to learn a new concept can benefit by interacting with other children who have already grasped the concept. As with any other form of mediation, however, a collaborative learning experience must take place within each individual child's ZPD if it is to be effective.

Vygotsky would surely be delighted that his ideas have influenced the way we view cognitive development. And he would be especially glad that his ideas have made a difference in educational practice. Remember that he lived in a tumultuous time, experiencing extraordinary social and intellectual upheavals. He saw firsthand how cultures and societies change over time, and he believed that such changes have a powerful influence on cognitive development. We can see that influence when we compare Vygotsky to Piaget. Piaget grew up in Switzerland, a country that prides itself on autonomy and independence; he theorized that children construct their own cognitive structures as they learn to adapt to the environment. For Piaget the child's own experiences are primary. For Vygotsky, however, the words of the community are primary. Vygotsky believed in the collectivist philosophy of the communist Soviet Union; he proposed that children learn by adopting the cognitive structures offered by the important people—and the larger community—around the child.

Can you see Vygotsky's sociocultural theory at work in this collaborative learning group? Use the concepts of social speech, mediation, zone of proximal development (ZPD), and scaffolding to explain why peer collaboration can be an effective way for children to learn.

■ Let's Review . . .

1. According to Vygotsky, children's thought structures develop from:
   a. the language they hear around them.
   b. their attempts to modify their own internal schemes.
   c. their own experimentation with characteristics in the environment.
   d. the biological maturation of their nervous systems.

Information Processing

Jean Piaget's theory was the dominant view of cognitive development for several decades. Researchers in the 1960s and 1970s, however, began to question some of Piaget's main assumptions, especially the idea that cognitive development proceeded through broad stages. At the same time, developments in computer and information technology offered developmental psychologists an alternative model—the idea that humans process information in much the same way that a computer does. This information-processing view has shaped the majority of the research in cognitive development since the early 1970s.

As you study this section, ask yourself these questions:

- What is the information-processing approach?

- How do processing capacity, processing efficiency, and attention change with development?

- What is metacognition, and how does it relate to children's theory of mind?

What Is the Information-Processing Approach?

Information processing is a term that comes from computer science; it refers to the way computers code information into computer symbols and how they sort, store, retrieve, and use these symbols. Information-processing psychologists have often used the computer as a metaphor for understanding how humans think and how they remember information (Munakata, 2006).

Figure 8.5 on page 268 compares information processing in computers and humans. Information enters the computer system using various input devices and is

Figure 8.5 • Information Processing in Computers and Humans Many information-processing psychologists use the computer as a metaphor for human thinking. This figure shows information flow in a prototypical computer (in the middle drawing). The bottom drawing depicts an information-processing model of human memory. Can you see the similarities between the computer's processing and that of humans?

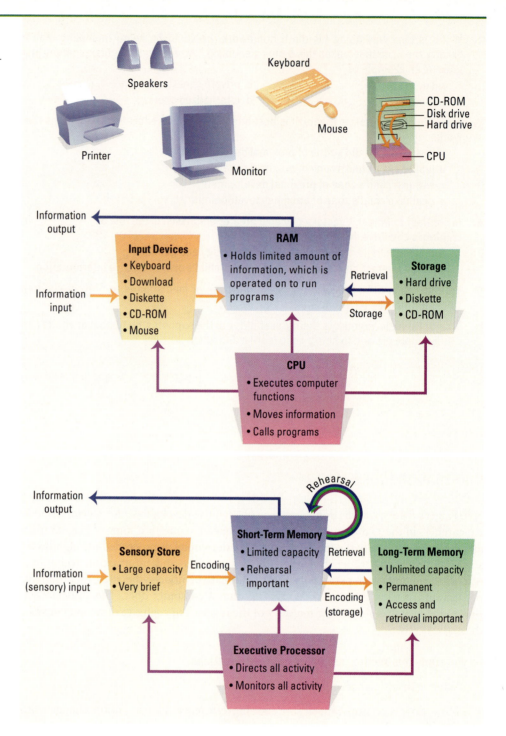

coded so it can be understood by the computer's central processing unit (CPU). The computer's working memory (RAM) holds the information and can transform it in various ways, depending on the software programs being used. Stored information can be accessed, retrieved, and used. The particular software that will work on the machine, how fast it can operate, and how much information can be processed at one time depend on the speed of the computer's CPU, the computer's operating system, and the size of its memory. The amount of information that can be stored and then retrieved depends on the size of the machine's internal hard drive and the capacity of any external storage devices (e.g., disks or external drives). Processed information is then output in various ways—on the monitor, printed on paper, delivered over the Internet, or stored for future use.

Similarly, information enters the human system and is encoded into a format that can be understood by the human CPU: the brain. Information can be held in short-term memory and transformed in various ways depending on the "software" (i.e., strategies) the person uses. Also, the person can access and retrieve information from long-term memory as needed. The speed and efficiency of processing, how much information can be processed at once, and the particular strategies that will be successful depend on various aspects of the person's brain and memory. The executive processor coordinates all activities. Processed information can then be output and presented in various ways, or it can be stored in memory.

Of course, information-processing psychologists would never claim that human thought is as mechanized, systematic, logical, and accurate as a computer's—we know that it is not. Nor do computers possess the full richness of human thinking. Clearly computers do not have emotional reactions to the information they are processing. Nor do they have internal motives or desires—not yet, anyway! Regardless of how explicitly we use the computer as a metaphor, however, the information-processing approach helps us think about how humans think and has extended our understanding of cognition and its development (Klahr, 1992; Kuhn, 1992).

One of the important assumptions of the information-processing view is that *humans are limited in their capacity to process information.* In other words, you can do only so much at once. The specific limit varies tremendously from one person to another, but everybody has one. Once we reach our personal limit, we begin to make errors or forget things. Much of cognitive development consists of developing strategies for making the most of our limited capacity. We develop strategies for learning, remembering, and using information as efficiently as possible so we can free up capacity to consider new information and new problems.

Think About Maria . . .

What can Maria look for in the schools that will tell her how well the teachers are helping students work with their limited capacities? What clues can she look for to determine whether teachers are overloading children's capacities?

The Development of Basic Cognitive Processes

A basic fact of cognitive development is that older children are able to process more information, process it faster, and control their attention better than younger children. Let's take a closer look at how developmental changes in these basic cognitive processes lead to superior cognitive performance as children grow older.

processing capacity
The amount of information a person can remember or think about at one time.

Changes in Processing Capacity. **Processing capacity** is the amount of information a person can remember or think about at one time. Researchers often measure it by presenting a series of pieces of information very quickly and counting how many items a person can remember in exact order. As you can see in Figure 8.6 on page 270, measures of processing capacity show consistent and regular increases throughout childhood and into early adulthood (Case, 1985; Dempster, 1981; Gathercole et al., 2004).

Changes in processing capacity help explain age differences in performance on many kinds of cognitive tasks. For example, do you remember the Piagetian conservation problem we described earlier in this chapter? When liquid is poured from a short beaker into a taller and skinnier one, young children often think that the taller one has more liquid. Piaget claimed that younger children center their thinking on only one aspect of the problem (the height of the liquid) but fail to consider the other element (the width of the beakers). Piaget believed that this was part of the child's inability to understand the logical structure of conservation. However, it is also possible that younger children's processing capacity may be too limited to allow them to work with both height and width at the same time. Perhaps younger children can switch their attention back and forth from one dimension to another, but cannot consider both of

Though some people have more processing capacity than others, everyone has a limit; once that limit is reached, people begin to make errors or forget things.

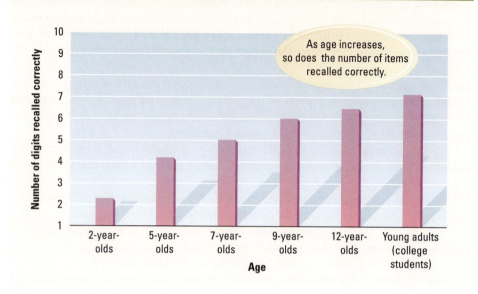

Figure 8.6 • Age-Related Changes in Memory Span
Adults remember about three times as much as 2-year-olds when asked to recall numbers in a specific order. Similar patterns are found in memory for words and for letters. (Adapted from Dempster, 1981, p. 66.)

the dimensions at once. As children mature and their capacity grows, they gain the ability to consider several sources of information at the same time, and their cognitive processing therefore becomes more flexible and powerful.

Changes in Processing Efficiency. Does processing capacity actually increase with development, or do older children simply learn to use the capacity they have more effectively? Some theorists focus on changes in **processing efficiency**—the speed and accuracy with which children can process information (Case, 1985; Case et al., 1982; Demetriou et al., 2002). Remember the key assumption of the information-processing view: There is a limited amount of capacity available at any given time. Part of this capacity is believed to be devoted to *operating space,* where the actual manipulation of information takes place. The rest is *storage space,* a place for storing and remembering the information we are manipulating. As shown in Figure 8.7, children use less of their limited operating space as they become faster at processing information. This frees up some of the operating space for other things, like storage of more information. The result is that the older child can remember more information. A child can also use the leftover operating space to do different kinds of processing, such as considering several aspects of a problem simultaneously, relating the current information to other information, and the like.

The *automaticity* of cognitive skills is important for increasing processing efficiency (Hasher & Zachs, 1979). **Automaticity** is the ability to perform a skill with little or no conscious effort. This frees up more cognitive capacity for other tasks. For example, think about young children who are learning to read. At first, the process is very laborious: Children recognize individual letters and attempt to combine their sounds to decode words. With practice, their recognition of letters, sounds, and common letter combinations becomes very fast and requires little conscious effort—it has become automatic. Cognitive capacity is now available for other tasks, such as reading with appropriate expression, monitoring comprehension, or wondering what will happen next. Eventually some of these higher-level processes also become more automatic. This allows children to consider additional dimensions as they read, such as comparing and contrasting the current text with

processing efficiency
The speed and accuracy with which a person can process information.

automaticity
The ability to carry out a process with little or no conscious effort, leaving more cognitive capacity to carry out other tasks.

As skills become more automatic, they require less processing capacity. This enables people to do multiple things at the same time.

Figure 8.7 • Storage Space and Operating Space in Working Memory What is 2 + 4 + 3? Younger children have difficulty with such questions because they need to use most of their processing capacity to figure out how to add the first two numbers; the capacity left available for storing and remembering other information is minimal. Adding is easy for older children, so more of their capacity is available for storage and other processes. (Based on Bjorklund, 1995.)

others they have read. In this way, automaticity of cognitive skills enables children to move to more sophisticated and complex ways of thinking—it is one of the mechanisms that fosters cognitive development.

Changes in Attention. **Attention** is the ability to focus on a particular stimulus (piece of information) without becoming distracted by other stimuli. As children get older they are better at maintaining their focus for longer periods of time and they also improve their ability to ignore information that can be distracting. Younger children often need help in knowing what to focus on and what to ignore. Good kindergarten teachers, for example, are skilled at directing children's attention to the topic of study (e.g., the alphabet on the blackboard) and away from other interesting sources of information (e.g., the frog in the aquarium or the noise coming in from the playground). Children gradually learn strategies that help them monitor and direct their own attentional focus, and this in turn helps them process information more deeply and accurately.

attention
The ability to focus on a particular stimulus without becoming distracted by other stimuli.

Metacognition and the Child's Developing Theory of Mind

Do you ever think about your own thinking? Do you ever wonder how in the world you will be able to remember a complicated set of information (like this whole chapter!), or even the name or phone number of someone you just met? If so, you have engaged in what psychologists call *metacognition*. **Metacognition** is the understanding or knowledge that people have about their own thought processes and memory. Several different types of metacognition develop during childhood. These include knowledge about cognitive *tasks* (such as knowing that a long list of words will be more difficult to remember than a short list), knowledge about cognitive *strategies* (such as knowing that simply repeating a telephone number will help you remember it for a short time), and knowledge about *people* (such as knowing that there are limits to what a person can remember).

Metacognitive skills tend to be pretty poor during early childhood, but they improve rapidly after the age of 5. Younger children are notoriously optimistic about their own memory abilities: They consistently overestimate how much they will be able to remember. However, they are more accurate when estimating how much

metacognition
The understanding or knowledge that people have about their own thought processes.

Teachers, parents, and the overall culture have a big impact on the metacognitive skills children develop and the beliefs children hold about their efforts.

Think About Maria . . .

How can teachers help young children learn metacognitive skills? What clues can Maria look for to indicate that the schools are doing a good job in this area?

theory of mind
An integrated understanding of what the mind is, how it works, and why it works that way.

someone else will remember on the same task (Flavell et al., 1970; Kreutzer et al., 1975). For example, ask 4-year-old Rachel how many words she thinks she could remember from a list of 20, and she's likely to say, "I could remember them all; I'm a good rememberer!" But ask her how many her twin sister will remember, and the answer is more likely to be, "Oh, maybe 5. It's hard to remember all that." This wishful thinking on the part of young children may actually be useful because it probably motivates children to keep trying. If young children accurately predicted their own poor memory performance, they might become frustrated and give up. This would reduce their chances to discover and practice memory strategies and gain metacognitive knowledge.

Theory of Mind. In recent decades work on metacognition has focused on how children develop their own *theory of mind*. A **theory of mind** is a coherent and integrated framework of concepts about the mind, how it works, and why it works that way (Wellman, 1990; Wellman et al., 2001; Wellman & Liu, 2004). Research on children's theory of mind has looked at what children know about thinking in general and at how well they understand the thoughts of other people.

Even young children have some understanding of thinking as a mental activity and know it is different from physical objects and behavior. For example, children as young as 3 years old know that mental objects are different from real objects. For example, they know that an imaginary ice cream cone is different from the real thing. They also know that it is possible to carry out mental activities that could not happen in the real world, such as flying to the moon in a cardboard box (Wellman & Estes, 1986). Three-year-olds can also understand that dreams are not real life, although many young children do believe that different people have the same dreams (Woolley & Wellman, 1992).

However, children's understanding of mental activities undergoes substantial development. For example, young children often do not understand the difference between how a real object *appears* to be and how it actually is. This is called the *appearance–reality distinction,* and it is a good indicator of theory of mind. If children are not able to tell the difference between appearance and reality, it means that they are not distinguishing between their beliefs about an object (which are based on how it appears) and how it really exists. For example, in one classic study researchers introduced children to a cat named Maynard (DeVries, 1969). The researchers then put a dog mask on Maynard's face. Even though Maynard's body and tail were unchanged and remained visible while the mask was put on, 3-year-olds said that Maynard was now a dog. To them the change in appearance changed the underlying reality. In contrast, 5- and 6-year-olds had no problem understanding that Maynard was still a cat despite his change in appearance. Other work using fake rocks (pieces of sponge painted to look like rocks) and "red milk" (white milk poured into a red cup) also showed that 3-year-olds did not distinguish appearance from reality. This result was consistent even when the tasks were simplified and even after children received explicit training in distinguishing between appearance and reality (Flavell et al., 1986; Flavell et al., 1987; Taylor & Hort, 1990). In other words, for young children, if it looks like a rock, it is a rock.

Do children understand the beliefs and desires of other people? To be able to do this, children must first understand that other people's thoughts are different from their own. If they can't make this distinction, then they can't understand that other people have their own unique beliefs and desires, and there is no reason even to try to figure out what others are thinking. It's not clear whether young children understand the difference between what they know themselves and what another person knows. Several studies have found that 3-year-olds have difficulty making this distinction, and cross-cultural studies have confirmed this result (Avis & Harris, 1991; Perner, 1991; Sullivan & Wimmer, 1993; Wellman & Bartsch, 1988).

Differentiating their own beliefs from other people's beliefs is an important part of developing an accurate theory of mind, but children must go beyond that to understand that *all* people differ in their thought processes. Five-year-olds, for example, believe that two people looking at the same picture will have the same thoughts about that picture (Eisbach, 2004). Over the next few years they learn that different people can have different mental reactions even when they see the same thing.

Recent studies indicate that language plays an important role in the development of a theory of mind. Talking to children beginning at a very early age about mental states such as desires, emotions, thinking, knowing, memory, understanding, and the like seems to help them develop a theory of mind (Meins et al., 2002; Ruffman et al., 2002). And children's performance on several different theory of mind tasks seems to be related to their experience in using language to communicate with those around them (Cheung et al., 2004; Deák et al., 2003; Lohmann & Tomasello, 2003; Nelson et al., 2003). Still, we have much yet to learn about what children understand about other people's thoughts and desires.

Young children have trouble understanding the distinction between appearance and reality. If this cat wears a mask of a dog's face, 3-year-olds are likely to believe that it has turned into a dog!

your perspective

How good are you at reading other people's thoughts? Do you think about what other people know and want as you work or socialize with them? How is your theory of mind different from those of any children you know?

■ Let's Review . . .

1. The term *processing capacity* refers to:
   a. the child's ability to understand math concepts.
   b. the amount of space a child has for storing information from the past.
   c. the amount of information a child can remember or think about at one time.
   d. the number of items that a child forgets in a given problem.

2. What does the term *metacognition* refer to?
   a. how people store and retrieve memories
   b. thought processes that are unconscious
   c. knowledge of one's own thought and memory processes
   d. the type of cognition used by younger children before they learn more mature forms of thinking

3. Renaldo pretends to play with a magic sword. He knows that the "magic" is really just pretend in his own head and that his toy sword is not really magic. Renaldo's understanding of the difference between pretend and reality is an example of his _____.
   a. cognitive strategies
   b. task knowledge
   c. attentional skill
   d. theory of mind

4. **True or False:** Processing capacity increases with age, but processing efficiency remains the same.

5. **True or False:** Three-year-old children are good at distinguishing appearance from reality.

Answers: 1. c, 2. c, 3. d, 4. F, 5. F

Language Development

Several years ago, some friends came to our house for dinner, bringing their 4-year-old daughter Kelly. When Kelly asked for a second helping of pasta, she remarked, "This is the bestest, most deliciousest dinner I have *ever* eated!" Kelly's interesting grammatical construction amused us all, but we had no difficulty understanding what she meant.

Like Kelly, most children learn very quickly to express their thoughts, desires, and emotions through language. They learn new words at an incredible rate of speed. And while most of us are still struggling with the intricate rules of grammar well into adulthood, young children make impressive progress in learning the complex rules of language. In this section we discuss how young children learn new words, learn rules of grammar, and learn to use language to communicate more effectively with other people. We also discuss children who are bilingual—learning more than one language at the same time.

As you study this section, ask yourself these questions:

- How much growth in vocabulary do we see during early childhood?

- How do young children learn grammar and the other complex rules that are part of any language?

- What are the advantages and disadvantages to learning two languages at the same time? Are bilingual children at a disadvantage?

An Expanding Vocabulary

Do you enjoy learning new vocabulary words? How many new words do you usually learn in a typical week? Consider this astounding statistic: While the average 2-year-old speaks about 200 different words, the typical 6-year-old produces approximately 10,000 (Anglin, 1993; Ganger & Brent, 2004; Nelson, 1973). That's an average gain of about 47 words per week or nearly seven new words every day! When you consider that children typically comprehend far more words than they produce, you can appreciate the phenomenal development that takes place during these early childhood years.

How do children learn new words so quickly? As you saw in Chapter 5, children use *fast-mapping* to learn new words after only one or two exposures. They also imitate words they hear around them, and their parents shape and reinforce new word utterances. Imitation and reinforcement are not enough, however. Children also analyze language and think about the patterns they notice. They use what they know about the grammatical structure of sentences (such as word order and word endings) to figure out the meanings of new words. This process of using syntax as a cue for determining word meaning is called *syntactical bootstrapping* (Gleitman, 1990). For example, if you encountered the sentence "Will is *pidding* his cereal," the placement of the new word along with its *-ing* ending would lead you to infer that *pidding* is an action, not an object. In contrast, the placement and word structure in the sentence "Will threw his *pid*" would lead you to infer that *pid* is an object, not an action (Naigles & Hoff-Ginsburg, 1995).

Learning Grammar

One of the most difficult challenges in learning any language is to learn all of the rules for properly combining words and forming sentences. Children learn these rules gradually. For example, they begin to produce *wh-* questions (asking *who, what, where, when,* or *why*) by first simply placing the *wh-* word before a noun, as in "Where kitty?" Later they include a helping verb but not in the correct order, producing such questions as "Where kitty is?" Finally, they produce the correct format: "Where is the kitty?"

A similar progression takes place as children learn to produce negative sentences. Young children start by simply putting *no* at the beginning of a word or statement, as in "No peas." Next, they add improperly ordered helping words, as in "I no peas" before arriving at the proper grammatical form: "I don't want peas." By 3 years of age, children's grammatical knowledge has already developed to the point that they are able to produce complex sentences. For example, they use conjunctions (e.g., *and*) to join simple sentences, they use clauses that modify preceding nouns (e.g., "The boy who lost his dog is outside."), and they produce embedded sentences (i.e., sentences within sentences). By age 6, children are quite good at producing complex and grammatically correct sentences (de Villiers & de Villiers, 1999).

Sometime by the age of 3, most children begin adding word endings such as *-s, -ing,* or *-ed* (Brown, 1973). As children learn these rules they sometimes apply them incorrectly and produce incorrect forms of irregular words. This is called **overregularization,** and it often leads children to make mistakes with words they were able to form correctly before they learned the rules. For example, a 3-year-old may be quite capable of saying, "I saw fish in the pond," but at 4 the same child might say, "I seed fishes." These errors occur when children are unable to recall the correct irregular form and so try to express their intent by applying a newly learned rule. Instances of overregularization sometimes cause parents to be concerned that their child is having language problems. However, these errors are nothing to worry about. Although they occur in many different languages, they are really relatively infrequent, occurring in less than 8 percent of the instances when children use irregular words (Marcus et al., 1992; Pinker, 1994). In fact, overregularizations actually indicate children's progress in grammatical knowledge and represent their attempts to use this knowledge to communicate. Table 8.1 on page 276 gives several suggestions parents can use to help their children learn language.

overregularization
Incorrect application of the linguistic rules for producing past tenses and plurals, resulting in incorrect forms of irregular words such as *goed* or *deers.*

your perspective
Have you ever heard examples of overregularization? What grammatical rules did the child or children seem to be trying to apply?

Learning the Social Rules of Discourse

Social rules of discourse are conventions that the speakers of a language follow when they are in a conversation with other people. The earliest social rule children acquire is *turn taking*—the idea that first one conversational partner makes a contribution to the exchange, then the other, going back and forth until the conversation ends. Parents

social rules of discourse
Conventions that speakers of a language follow when having a conversation.

TABLE 8.1 Facilitating Language Development: Suggestions for Parents

Be an active listener and participate in the conversation the child wants to have.
• Follow your child's lead.
• Ask open-ended questions ("Tell me more").
• Encourage your child to elaborate on topics that are important to him or her.

Provide good models.
• If your child is "misarticulating" sounds, make the sound correctly yourself.
• Don't ask your child to repeat the words or the sound he or she is having "trouble" with.
• Correct your child by saying things like, "Oh! You want soup?" instead of, "Say *soup*, not *thoup*."

Talk, talk, talk about events in your child's life.
• Talk about these events in a meaningful way.
• Don't talk too fast!

Provide a supportive atmosphere.
• Make sure your child feels free to communicate with you.
• Provide lots of good models of speech and language.
• Be encouraging and supportive.

Read, read, read to your child.
• Read to your child during infancy, toddlerhood, preschool years, and beyond.
• Point to the words, talk about the pictures.
• Talk about words that rhyme, different letters and the sounds they make.

Have the tools of written communication available.
• Have plenty of crayons, marking pencils, and paper available for your child.
• Encourage your child to use these tools to communicate.

Play sound and word games.
• "How many words are there in the sentence *I like to go to the store?*"
• "How many syllables are there in the word, *Baby?* Let's clap it out—*Ba* (clap) *by* (clap)."
• "Let's play a word game. I'm thinking of *glasses*—kinds that we wear and kinds that we drink from. Can you think of another word that can mean two different things?"

If your child shows *dysfluencies* (difficulties),
• Let your child finish each communication; don't finish sentences for him or her.
• Model easy, slower, less complex, speech.
• Be patient!

(Bernstein, personal communication, 2003.)

your perspective

Think of someone you know who is skilled in social rules of discourse and referential communication. Now think of someone with less skill. What do the two individuals do differently?

model this rule in child-directed speech and during countless daily activities, beginning when their children are infants. Children develop this knowledge further during early childhood and soon begin to apply it to conversations with other children as well as with adults. Other social rules of discourse, however, are not learned until later in childhood. For example, it is only around the age of 5 that children acquire the *answer-obviousness rule*. This rule says that if the answer to a question is obvious given the context and the speaker, then the listener should interpret the question as a request (or even a demand) rather than a true question. For example, suppose a mother finds her 6-year-old son jumping up and down on his bed and says, "Do you have to jump on your bed?" The child, who has acquired the answer-obviousness rule, understands that his mother is not really interested in whether or not he feels a need to jump on the bed. Instead, the mother's inquiry is an indirect way of commanding him to stop it. Other social rules of discourse involve even more sophisticated knowledge and are usually not acquired until the early school years. These include rules about saying something relevant to the topic being discussed, saying something related to what was just said in the conversation, and not repeating something that has already been said in the conversation.

What would this parent really mean if she said, "Do you *have* to jump on the bed?"

It is important to remember that there can be substantial cultural differences in rules for social discourse. For example, what constitutes an "obvious" answer depends on the particular culture. African Americans, for example, do not use question-demands as frequently as white Americans, so African American children might interpret the question about jumping on the bed as a true request for information rather than a demand. Rules for turn taking differ as well. Many African American children learn at home that they must take their turn and keep their audience's attention, rather than waiting until someone else finishes and they are given a turn (Delpit, 1995; Saville-Troike, 1986).

Think About Maria . . .

Looking back at this section on language, what language skills can Maria look for in her younger son to see if his skills are on par with other children of kindergarten age? What kinds of language mistakes or weaknesses are expected at this age?

Bilingual Children: Learning Two Languages

Do you speak more than one language? More than six million children in the United States are **bilingual,** or fluent in two languages. In *additive bilingualism*, a person learns a second language while maintaining a first language. In *subtractive bilingualism*, a person loses fluency in the first language as a result of acquiring a second language (Bialystok & Hakuta, 1994). Different social and cultural conditions usually accompany these two types of bilingualism. When the family and larger community see acquisition of a second language as a positive asset and highly value both languages, children are more likely to show additive bilingualism. On the contrary, if people see the second language as superior and the first as inferior in some way, children will be more likely to "subtract" their first language (Hamers & Blanc, 2000). Children can get a negative message about their first language when they don't see it used in their schools or in the media, or if their peers and other social contacts do not understand it. And it is not just children immigrating to the United States who experience conditions that encourage subtractive bilingualism. For example, U.S.-born Hispanic children who learn Spanish as their first language are often at a significant disadvantage when they enter a predominantly English-speaking school system. And in past decades Native American children were not allowed to speak their own languages in school (Harjo, 1999).

Children can become bilingual simultaneously or sequentially. *Simultaneous bilingualism* develops when a child learns two languages at the same time, starting from infancy. This situation often occurs when the child has parents who speak two languages. In *sequential bilingualism* a child learns one language first, then begins learning the second. Children who begin learning a second language by about the age of 3 usually become just as fluent in the second language as in the first. If second-language learning begins later in childhood or in adulthood, the person can use the second language effectively for

bilingual
Fluent in two languages.

Think About Maria . . .

What can Maria look for in the schools that will help her determine if they will properly support her bilingual sons? What clues would indicate that the schools foster additive bilingualism? What clues would suggest that they may promote subtractive bilingualism?

Will learning two languages be a positive or a negative experience for these bilingual children?

communication but usually will not attain such complete fluency. The accent of the second language is particularly problematic, and most older learners never acquire a native-sounding accent. Although they usually don't achieve a natural-sounding accent or a high level of fluency, older learners actually do learn vocabulary and grammar rules faster than younger children do (Krashen et al., 1982; Snow, 1987). Some theorists argue that young children are more successful at acquiring second languages not because of a special language-learning ability but because of the younger child's greater opportunity, longer time period in which to master the second language, and less interference from a first language because it is not already automatized (Ekstrand, 1981; MacWhinney, 1992). According to this view, younger children do not have any greater ability to acquire language than older children, but they do have "a less complex task for which [they have] more time" (Hamers & Blanc, 2000, p. 75). The skills learned in the first language may also apply to learning a second language, making the second language easier to learn (Snow & Kang, 2006).

In the early stages of learning two languages, children may occasionally mix words and grammar from both languages. It is not clear why this mixing, or *code switching,* occurs. It may happen because a child doesn't yet understand that the two languages are separate systems, or it may happen simply because the child has acquired words to express a specific thought in one language but not yet in the other language. Parent modeling also seems to play a role. Code switching occurs more often in children whose parents also code switch. The frequency of code switching decreases as children gain more vocabulary and a stronger grasp of grammar in each language, although even adult bilingual speakers sometimes code switch intentionally.

When they are learning two languages simultaneously, research shows that children learn the vocabulary and grammar of each language separately (Conboy & Thal, 2006). By the early preschool years, they show clear awareness that the two languages are independent systems. At first they may restrict their use of each language to certain contexts—for example, speaking only Spanish at home but speaking only English when outside the home. By the early school years, however, the bilingual child is able to switch automatically and appropriately from one language to another in either context (Cummins, 1991; Hamers & Blanc, 2000; Lanza, 1992; Volterra & Taeschner, 1978). To learn about one family's experience with bilingualism, read the Personal Perspective box called "Meet a Bilingual Family."

Learning two languages is not necessarily a difficult task for children. The rate of language acquisition is slightly slower for bilingual children, but the fact that they are learning two complex and abstract systems may actually provide some cognitive advantages. Studies have found that bilingual children sometimes score higher on measures of such things as concept formation, cognitive flexibility, language awareness, ability to correct ungrammatical sentences, verbal and nonverbal creativity, and logical thinking (Bialystok et al., 2003; Diaz & Kinger, 1991; Hamers, 1996; Hamers & Blanc, 2000). Bilingual children even have the edge on certain types of appearance–reality problems, like those we discussed earlier in this chapter (Bialystok & Senman, 2004). Because bilingual children must constantly examine and think about the particular language system they are using and the contexts for which each system is appropriate, they may develop an early awareness of the symbolic nature of language systems. This realization may encourage bilingual children to become more reflective about language and about how it can be used both for communication and as a tool for thinking (Mohanty & Perregaux, 1997).

Meet a Bilingual Family

Patrick, David, and Lori Glenn
El Paso, Texas
5-year-old bilingual child and his parents

We understand that Patrick's first language is English. When did he begin learning his second language (Spanish), and how is he progressing?
Patrick was exposed to both English and Spanish from birth. Both grandmothers spoke to Patrick strictly in Spanish. His mother, Lori, read and spoke to him in Spanish most of the time; his favorite book was *Lo que le encanta a Conejito.* His grandmothers sang and recited nursery rhymes to him in Spanish, and they also watched Spanish-language television in his presence.

His paternal grandfather and I [David] always spoke to him in English. Grampa repeated "Grampa" to him whenever he was with him, and Patrick's first word, at four months, was "Grampa!" Lori stopped speaking to him in Spanish when he went to day care (at 2 years, 9 months of age) so that he would better understand English. However, his maternal grandmother, *Abuela,* spent every afternoon with him. So he continued to be exposed to Spanish, while his day care providers and his parents stressed English. Patrick has progressed well in English, but unfortunately, his Spanish language skills are lacking.

What steps have you taken to help him learn either or both languages?
We speak and read to him in both languages. We have family living in Chihuahua, Mexico, and when we are together, they speak Spanish in his presence, and bring him into conversations. If he does not understand, they will speak to him in English. Funny thing is that we encourage his cousins to speak with him in Spanish, and his cousins' parents encourage them to practice their English around Patrick! It was suggested that we place him in a local magnet school with a bilingual curriculum. We have discussed the possibility of sending Patrick to school in Chihuahua for a semester.

How does your son seem to feel about speaking two languages?
Patrick understands Spanish fairly well, but speaks only a few words. He has his own imaginary Spanish that is mostly gibberish and sounds like the words being spoken in a conversation. He attempts to join a conversation in Spanish by using his phonetically similar made-up language; so we know he wants to converse, but just does not have the vocabulary. We attribute this to the time spent in school where English is the primary form of communication.

His 11-year-old cousin, Gerardo, is like a brother to Patrick. Gerardo is very articulate, and the Spanish language is melodious, so Patrick loves trying to imitate him. Plus, if Gerardo speaks Spanish, it's got to be cool! Or as Gerardo would say, *"Es bien padre!"*

Q *What do you think is the best way to help children learn more than one language? What would you advise is the best approach for schools to take regarding bilingual children?*

■ Let's Review . . .

1. Fast-mapping and syntactical bootstrapping are two ways that children learn _____.
   a. new grammar rules
   b. new vocabulary words
   c. new rules of social discourse
   d. subtractive bilingualism

2. A child says, "Mommy goed to the store." The child's incorrect use of the *-ed* suffix in the word *goed* is an example of _____.
   a. overregularization
   b. overextension
   c. fast-mapping
   d. syntactical bootstrapping

Early Childhood Education and Kindergarten Readiness

Most children start kindergarten at the age of 5, but many children are enrolled in some type of school-related program even before this age. Many children are enrolled in a preschool or nursery school program that includes an academic component where children are learning colors, shapes, the alphabet, counting, and rules for cooperating and getting along with teachers and other children in a school setting. Some programs are church-related and involve religious education, some are focused on ethnic education, and many others are run by community or public organizations. Parents enroll children to help them get an early start on academic learning, to give their children religious training, to involve their children in activities related to their ethnic backgrounds, or as a form of supervised child care while the parents work.

Other programs are designed to help children who are at special risk for falling behind after they start school. Children living in poor and disadvantaged areas, especially children in ethnic minority groups, are at a higher-than-average risk for performing poorly in school and dropping out before they graduate high school. These children can benefit from early school experiences that provide strong academic and emotional support (Hamre & Pianta, 2005). In the United States, most states now fund some type of educational program for children 4 years of age or younger, and the early indications are that these programs can help all children improve their learning and performance in school (Gormley et al., 2005).

In this last section of the chapter we focus on early childhood education programs that have been specifically designed to help disadvantaged children. We also explore issues related to preparation for kindergarten.

As you study this section, ask yourself these questions:

- What effects can Head Start and other early intervention programs have with children who are at risk for developmental problems? How do we know if they are effective?

- How do we know when children are ready to start kindergarten? Should they be held back if they don't seem ready to start school?

Early Childhood Education

A key theme of this book is that children's early experiences provide a critical foundation for positive development. Unfortunately, some children's early environments do not provide strong foundations, and these children are at risk for numerous academic and social problems. Many are already behind when they enter kindergarten or first grade. Early childhood education programs have been created to improve children's readiness to benefit from formal schooling, increase their success in school, and improve the quality of their lives.

Begun in 1965 as part of President Lyndon Johnson's War on Poverty, **Project Head Start** is a federally funded, comprehensive program designed to improve academic achievement and opportunity for children from ages 3 through 5. These children receive health and social services as well as educational support, and their parents are included as an integral part of the program (Washington & Oyemade, 1987; Zigler & Styfco, 1993). Interestingly, Urie Bronfenbrenner (refer back to Chapter 1 to review his ecological systems theory) was a member of the committee that designed the program. As you can imagine, he was a strong supporter of this comprehensive approach! Head Start has changed over the years, going from a part-time-only program to full-time in some places. The age range for services also expanded: In 1994 Congress authorized the *Early Head Start Program,* which assists even younger children, ages newborn through 3 years.

Before Project Head Start expanded to meet the needs of more children, there was the **Abecedarian Project.** Designed to assess the impact of full-time, high-quality intervention beginning in infancy, the Abecedarian Project served primarily African American children living in poverty (Ramey et al., 1998). Infants at high risk for problems in cognitive development entered the program at 4½ months, on average, and continued until at least 5 years of age. Another well-known early intervention program was the **High/Scope Perry Preschool Program** in Ypsilanti, Michigan. This program offered high quality, part-day (2½ hours per day) intervention during the school year (October to May) for poor African American children ages 3 to 5 (Schweinhart et al., 1993; Schweinhart & Weikart, 1998). The program focused on children's active involvement in directing their own learning. It also included weekly home visits to teach parents how to support their children's educational progress.

Project Head Start
Federally funded, comprehensive program designed to improve academic achievement and opportunity for young children.

Abecedarian Project
Project designed to assess the impact of full-time, high-quality intervention beginning in infancy; served primarily African American children living in poverty.

High/Scope Perry Preschool Program
Program offering high-quality partial-day intervention during the school year for young African American children living in poverty.

Effects of Early Education Programs. What effects have early childhood education programs had on children's development? Research has shown the following (Barnett, 1998; McKey et al., 1985; Reynolds et al., 2004; Schweinhart et al., 1993; Zigler et al., 1993):

The Abecedarian Project was created to give a head start to young African American children who were living in poverty and were at risk for doing poorly in school.

- Children in early intervention show an immediate gain of about 8 IQ points when compared with children who are not in such programs, but in many cases the difference "fades away" during the elementary school years. The Abecedarian Project is an exception, showing IQ differences up to 21 years of age (the oldest age tested so far), as you can see in Figure 8.8 on page 282 (Campbell et al., 2001).

- The children score higher on reading and mathematics achievement tests. Studies of Head Start programs find that these differences fade, but other programs show achievement differences up to adolescence or young adulthood (see Figure 8.8).

- The children show better academic progress on other measures such as fewer students placed in special education classes and higher rates of graduation from high school, as shown in Figure 8.9 on page 283.

- The children show other social and health benefits. For example, when surveyed as adults, participants in the High/Scope Perry Preschool Program were less likely to have been arrested or to have received welfare payments, and they were more likely to have a better-paying job (for the men), be employed (for the women), and own their own homes (see Figure 8.9 on page 283) (Schweinhart et al., 1993). As a group, children in Head Start have better overall health, immunization rates, and nutrition than nonprogram children.

Figure 8.8 • IQ, Reading, and Math Scores for Children in the Abecedarian Project
Children who participated in the Abecedarian Project continued to show higher scores for years after the program ended. (Data from Campbell et al., 2001.)

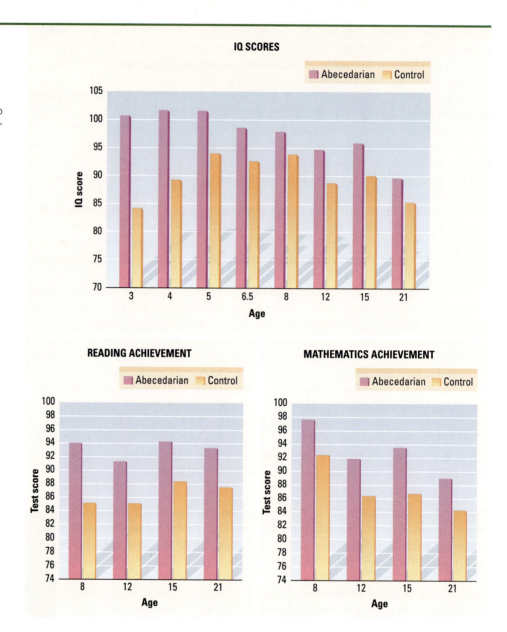

In general, programs such as the High/Scope Perry Preschool and Abecedarian projects show greater and longer-lasting benefits than Head Start. Why? Several factors probably play a role. Among these may be the quality of the instructional programs, the length of the programs, teacher training and pay, the numbers of at-risk children served, the seriousness of their challenges, and funding differences. However, the first large-scale evaluations of the Early Head Start Program offer encouraging results. Compared to disadvantaged children who were not enrolled in Early Head Start, the 3-year-old children in the program showed better cognitive and language skills, they were more able to maintain attention, and they were less aggressive. There were also positive effects on *parents'* skills and behaviors—parents were more emotionally supportive, read more to their children, provided more stimulation for learning, and spanked their children less (Love et al., 2002, 2005).

Controversy about the most effective ways to implement early intervention programs is intense. There is no better example of this than the debate that still surrounds Project Head Start even four decades after its beginning. To find out more about this program, read the Social Policy Perspective box on page 284 called "Project Head Start: What Lies Ahead?"

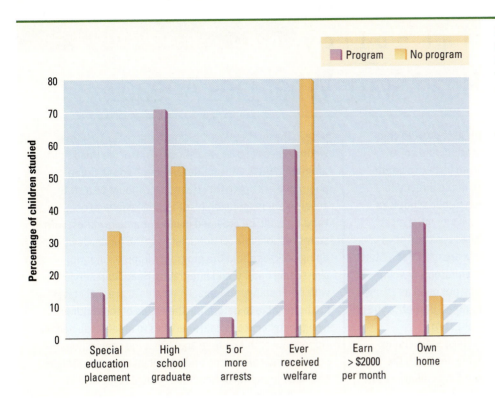

Figure 8.9 • Results from the High/Scope Perry Preschool Project Children in the High/Scope Perry Preschool Project showed long-lasting benefits on measures of academic progress and of social welfare. (Adapted from Schweinhart et al., 1993.)

Chart legend: ■ Program ■ No program

Y-axis: Percentage of children studied (0 to 80)

X-axis categories: Special education placement, High school graduate, 5 or more arrests, Ever received welfare, Earn > $2000 per month, Own home

Kindergarten Readiness

Although educators have long been interested in fostering children's readiness for schooling, defining readiness is not as easy as you might think. Schools often use chronological age to determine eligibility for entry, but several studies have shown that age is not a good predictor of academic success or learning (Carlton & Winsler, 1999; Morrison et al., 1997). National surveys have asked parents and kindergarten teachers to identify important readiness indicators. Both parents and teachers emphasize children's overall physical health, verbal communication skills, and enthusiasm. Teachers also emphasize social skills and ability to follow classroom rules and procedures. And parents—but not most teachers—see academic knowledge, such as familiarity with the alphabet or counting skills, as an important prerequisite (Lewit & Baker, 1995). Other educators believe that self-control over behavior and emotions, the ability to keep attention focused, and impulse control are major factors that underlie readiness (Blair, 2002; NICHD Early Child Care Research Network, 2003a). Many school districts use standardized assessments to assess readiness, but these tests show only low to moderate levels of predictive validity. In other words, the tests incorrectly identify many children as not ready for school (Carlton & Winsler, 1999).

How ready are our nation's children? On national surveys, kindergarten teachers rated approximately 65 percent of their students as ready for kindergarten on all five of the readiness characteristics the surveys assessed: rested, able to verbally communicate clearly, enthusiastic and interested, able to take turns and share, and able to sit still (Lewit & Baker, 1995). The overall health of children entering school, including immunization rates, has improved (National Education Goals Panel, 1999). One study assessed a nationally representative sample of 22,000 children. The majority of children had basic letter and number knowledge, showed good prosocial skills, persisted at tasks, were eager to learn, and could pay attention (Denton & Germino-Hausken, 2000). However, almost all the measures varied according to factors such as age (older kindergartners score higher); family type (children from single-parent homes tend to score lower); mothers' education (the higher the mothers' level of education,

Project Head Start: What Lies Ahead?

Project Head Start and Early Head Start provide comprehensive health, nutrition, education, and social services to low-income children from birth to school age. Federal Head Start grants are made directly to agencies that apply for them (often public schools or community agencies). Each program site must meet specific program standards, but sites typically have some freedom in how requirements are met. Head Start programs have positive effects on children's development, but the effects have generally not been as strong or long-lasting as some other programs (Barnett, 1998; McKey et al., 1985; Fenichel & Mann, 2001).

There is continuing debate over Head Start. Some have questioned whether the benefits are worth the immense cost of the program (about $6.5 billion in 2002). Few argue against providing services to needy preschoolers, but many contend that including infants substantially increases the overall program cost while having limited effects. Serious questions have also been raised about whether it is ethical to limit the early educational choices of disadvantaged preschoolers. As an alternative to spending billions on a governmentally controlled program, low-income parents could be given vouchers and allowed to select from any early-education or child-care arrangements, including Head Start centers. According to psychologist Sandra Scarr, "Head Start is a dinosaur, a remnant of the government-knows-best philosophy of an earlier era" and "should have to compete in the marketplace" (Scarr, 1999, p. 144). There is vigorous debate over who should control the Head Start program ("Bush Calls for Revamping," 2003). Some policy makers argue that Head Start should be a state government responsibility rather than a federal one. Funding could be provided in block grants to states, with states responsible for administering the funds, developing policies about the program's implementation, overseeing quality, and integrating Head Start services with other state programs. Advocates argue that states are better able to determine the needs of the children living there and coordinate services to meet those needs. Opponents of this change argue that the comprehensive services and community and parent involvement that are hallmark strengths of Head Start would likely be lost. Critics also assert that many states are unprepared to take on the responsibilities that would be involved if this change were made. While some states do an admirable job of providing early childhood intervention to low-income families, programs in other states are poor or nonexistent (Ramey, 1999; Ripple et al., 1999).

Q *Is early intervention worth its cost? How early should intervention begin, and which children should be targeted? Would a voucher system be more fair and effective? Who should control and pay for Head Start? What social policy recommendations would you make?*

the higher the children's scores); race/ethnicity (non-Hispanic white and Asian children score higher than African American and Hispanic children, especially on teacher ratings of behavior); and/or socioeconomic status (children from higher-income families score higher) (Stipek & Ryan, 1997). So although the majority of children seem reasonably ready for school and there have been important advancements, there is still much room for improvement.

Children old enough for school but identified as not ready present a dilemma for educators. Is it best to *redshirt*, or hold back, these children and keep them in their homes or in preschool for an additional year, place them in a transition class (either before kindergarten or between kindergarten and first grade), or retain them for an additional year of kindergarten? None of these options has been very successful in helping children catch up to peers who were not kept back. In fact, several studies have found that children who were recommended for delay, transition classes, or retention but were promoted anyway (perhaps at their parents' insistence) scored just as well on achievement tests as their classmates (Carlton & Winsler, 1999).

Some educators believe we need to rethink the idea of school readiness. They argue that it is the schools that must be ready, rather than placing the burden of readiness on the children (Carlton & Winsler, 1999; Dockett & Perry, 2003). These educators, drawing on Vygotsky's theory of cognitive development, say that holding back children who are not ready deprives them of the "very culture and learning situations [they] need" (Carlton & Winsler, 1999, p. 346). Also, postponing school entry keeps these children in the environments that created and maintained the lack of readiness in the first place. This view challenges schools to work with children's existing abilities, scaffolding their learning experiences to help them acquire the cognitive skills our culture sees as important for learning and academic achievement. Delaying children will only produce further academic problems and may well damage both motivation and self-esteem (Rose et al., 1983).

Think About Maria . . .
What concerns should Maria have regarding her younger son's readiness for kindergarten? Should she hold him back another year?

■ Let's Review . . .

1. Which of the following is true about early childhood education programs such as Head Start, High/Scope Perry Preschool, and the Abecedarian Project?
   a. These programs are not cost effective.
   b. These programs regularly produce permanent gains in IQ scores.
   c. These programs produce improved academic progress and graduation rates.
   d. These programs have little effect on social measures such as arrest records or employment.

2. According to a national survey of kindergarten teachers, what percentage of their students were fully ready for kindergarten?
   a. 65 percent
   b. 75 percent
   c. 85 percent
   d. 95 percent

3. When it comes to gauging a child's readiness for kindergarten, which characteristic is emphasized more by parents than by teachers?
   a. enthusiasm
   b. social skills
   c. physical health
   d. academic knowledge

4. **True or False:** Research shows that the Early Head Start Program that enrolls infants and toddlers is less effective than the regular Head Start Program.

5. **True or False:** Research suggests that it is best to "redshirt" children who do not seem to be socially and cognitively ready for kindergarten.

Answers: 1. c, 2. a, 3. d, 4. F, 5. F

Thinking Back to Maria . . .

Now that you have studied this chapter, you should be able to explain how Maria can use cognitive development concepts to identify schools and teachers that would facilitate her sons' learning and development. You should be able to list at least a dozen specific concepts and explain how each would relate to Maria's situation.

Using Piaget's theory, Maria would want to find classroom environments that promote active learning and look for teachers who use hands-on activities. Her sons are in the preoperational stage, so they are learning to use their representational abilities more effectively. Art and play are important activities for exploring symbolic and representational thought. Maria should look for signs that the teachers are sensitive to the intuitive logic commonly used by young children.

Using Vygotsky's sociocultural theory, Maria should understand that children also learn by adopting the cognitive structures embedded in the language and culture of the classroom and the school. She should spend time observing and listening for the messages contained in the school culture. Are the messages predominantly positive—as in "All students can learn" and "Celebrate diversity"? Social speech becomes private speech. Would Maria be proud to see her sons internalize the messages heard in the schools and classrooms she visits? What kinds of mediation and scaffolding do teachers provide? Do teachers properly challenge students within their own zones of proximal development?

From the information-processing perspective, Maria can watch for signs that the schools and teachers understand the processing limits of young children. What do they do to help children pay attention, think about, and remember information? Do they help children understand and overcome their own processing limits by teaching them metacognitive skills?

And how do the schools foster language development? Do they support bilingual children like Maria's? Regarding the younger son's school readiness, research does not suggest that it is helpful to hold younger children back a year before starting kindergarten. Are these schools ready for her younger son? By considering questions like these, Maria can more effectively evaluate the schools to determine which one will provide the best education for her sons.

■ Chapter Review . . .

What was Jean Piaget's description of preoperational thought during early childhood?
In the preoperational thought stage (2 through 7 years), children can form internal mental representations, and they practice using symbols in their language, art, and play. Thought in this stage is intuitive, based more on personal experience than on objective logic. Egocentrism, animism, and artificialism are prominent features. Children fail conservation problems because they center their thoughts on only one part of the problem, they focus on the static endpoints of the problem, and their cognitive schemes are not reversible (not yet *operational*).

What are the main ideas in Vygotsky's sociocultural view of cognitive development?
Vygotsky proposed that children learn primarily by adopting the cognitive structures embedded in the language and the larger culture around them. As adults and others speak, children adopt their social speech and transform it into their own private speech. Children then internalize their private speech to form internal thought structures. Adults and others mediate cognitive structures for children, often

providing scaffolds or supports as children attempt more difficult tasks. The zone of proximal development represents those tasks that the child can perform with mediation or support from more skilled mentors.

What is the information-processing approach, and what are its distinctive elements?
The information-processing approach views thinking as the processing of information and often uses the computer as a way to explain how humans think. From this approach, it is assumed that processing capacity is limited. Processing capacity, processing efficiency, and control of attention are all studied as ways that cognitive development advances in early childhood. Children also show improvements in metacognition and in their understanding of the theory of mind.

What are the major language accomplishments that take place during early childhood?
Vocabulary increases dramatically. Children learn grammar rules gradually. They learn rules for forming plurals and past tenses that are sometimes overregularized. Children

begin to learn social rules of discourse that help them communicate effectively with other people.

What is bilingualism, and how does it affect language development?

Bilingualism is fluency in two languages. Children may develop additive or subtractive bilingualism, and may develop it successively or sequentially. Code switching often appears in the early stages of learning two languages, but its frequency decreases by the early preschool years. Bilingualism may slow the rate of language acquisition, but it may have cognitive benefits by encouraging greater reflectiveness about language.

What do we know about the effectiveness of early education programs? Does it help to hold younger children back a year before starting them in kindergarten?

Programs such as Project Head Start, Early Head Start, the Abecedarian Project, and the High/Scope Perry Preschool Program were all created to help disadvantaged children succeed in school. Results vary, but the effects generally indicate improved rates of academic success, fewer school dropouts, and improved life conditions indicated by other measures. It does not seem to be helpful to hold younger children back before starting them in kindergarten; focus should be placed on preparing schools to educate all children.

■ Key Terms

Abecedarian Project (281)
animism (258)
artificialism (258)
attention (271)
automaticity (270)
bilingual (277)
collaborative learning (266)
conservation (259)
egocentrism (258)
High/Scope Perry Preschool
    Program (281)
internalization (264)
intuitive thought (258)
mediation (264)

metacognition (271)
operations (256)
overregularization (275)
preoperational thought (256)
private speech (263)
processing capacity (269)
processing efficiency (270)
Project Head Start (281)
scaffolding (265)
social rules of discourse (275)
social speech (263)
theory of mind (272)
zone of proximal
    development (ZPD) (264)

 mydevelopmentlab
Where human development comes to life!

If you are using MyDevelopmentLab, you have access to an ebook version of this textbook, along with dozens of valuable resources per chapter—including video and audio clips, simulations and activities, self-assessments, practice tests, and other study materials. Here is a sampling of the resources available for this chapter.

Explore
Piaget's Stages of Cognitive Development
Encoding, Storage, and Retrieval in Memory

Watch
Conservation of Liquids
Kindergarten: Ready for Success?

If you did not receive an access code to MyDevelopmentLab with this text and wish to purchase access online, please visit www.mydevelopmentlab.com.

chapter 9
Socioemotional Development in Early Childhood

Cassandra has two boys, ages 5 and 3, and she is having trouble handling them. The boys misbehave, they don't listen well, and Cassandra is concerned that she is yelling at them and being more harsh than she means to be. She is raising the boys by herself, and her low-paying job barely pays the bills. Jeremy, her older son, seems anxious about socializing with other children, and he mostly prefers to play alone. Nathan, who just turned 3, seems very aggressive. At day care, the teachers complain that he bites other children, takes their toys, and refuses to share. Cassandra is concerned that Nathan doesn't seem to understand the difference between "right" and "wrong." She wonders if his aggressiveness is coming more from the day care center or from how she treats the boys at home.

Cassandra knows she needs to do more to help the boys, but what should she do? What can she do at home to help the boys learn to behave? Should Cassandra be concerned that Jeremy isn't making more friends? How can she help Nathan learn "right" from "wrong" and help him learn to respect other children? How can she decide if the day care center she uses is appropriate for Nathan? After studying this chapter you should be able to apply at least a dozen concepts and research findings to help Cassandra sort through these issues with her sons. What helpful advice can you suggest?

As you read this chapter, look for the "Think About Cassandra . . ." questions that ask you to think about what you're learning from Cassandra's perspective.

Many parents have concerns and questions like Cassandra's. One of the great struggles for most parents is learning how to correct their children's behavior and help them learn right from wrong. During the early childhood period children are learning who they are, how to get along with other children, and how to operate in the wider world. Like Cassandra, most parents want to give their children all the help they can, and they would like to be helpful and supportive rather than overly negative and punitive. And like Cassandra, many parents worry about the effects of day care and whether their young children are learning right from wrong and how to make friends.

In this chapter we highlight many of the important topics related to the social and emotional development of young children. We begin by looking at how children learn self-concepts—understanding who they are. Emotions, gender concepts, and morality are all important components of this self discovery. We discuss parenting styles and some of the dos and don'ts of family discipline, how young children make friends and play, and how different cultures influence play in early childhood. We end the chapter by looking at day care and the factors that relate to the quality of care children receive in day care.

The Social and Emotional Self

You have obviously known yourself all of your life, but have you ever wondered when you first recognized who you were? When did you first look at a photograph and say, "Hey, that's me!"? Young children have the interesting task of discovering who they are and also learning to relate properly to the other people in their lives. As children begin to play with friends and interact with other people, they need to learn self-control, how to handle their emotions, and how to behave in ways that are moral, ethical, and fair. We look at these issues of self-discovery in the first section of this chapter.

As you study this section, ask yourself these questions:

- When do children develop a sense of "self," and how does their self identity help them control and regulate their behavior?

- What do young children think about their own emotions?

- When do children understand the differences and similarities between boys and girls?

- How do young children think about moral issues? How do they know what are the "right" and "wrong" things to do?

The Self

Based on the pioneering work of William James (1890/1950), psychologists distinguish between two basic aspects of the **self,** or the characteristics, emotions, and beliefs people have about themselves. The first aspect is the **I-self**—the conscious awareness that you exist as a separate, unique person. The I-self involves understanding that you have your own individual thoughts, perceptions, emotions, experiences, and actions, and that you continue to exist across time and contexts. Also part of the I-self is a sense of *personal agency,* the understanding that your actions and emotions can affect the environment, including the behavior and emotions of other people. The second aspect of the self is the **me-self,** or what you know about yourself. The me-self includes things like the categories by which people define themselves (e.g., gender, age) as well as people's

self
The characteristics, emotions, and beliefs people have about themselves, including an understanding that people are unique individuals.

I-self
The conscious awareness that you exist as a separate and unique person and that you can affect others.

me-self
What you know about yourself and how you describe yourself.

your perspective

For a moment, think about your "self." What are the main features in your self-description?

objective knowledge of their own personalities and physical and cognitive characteristics (Harter, 1999; James, 1890/1950; Thompson, 1999).

Most psychologists do not believe that a sense of self is present at birth. Instead, most believe that the I-self and the me-self are cognitive constructions that children create as their cognitive skills develop. Young children construct *working models of the self,* or increasingly complex cognitive representations of who they are. These working models change as children have more experiences and interact with more people. Their developing cognitive abilities enable children to recognize and integrate their personal characteristics, compare themselves to others, and deal with contradictory information. For example, a boy may think of himself as a nice person but also may realize that sometimes he does not want to do nice things like share his toys. His developing cognitive skills help him understand that there are situations in which it is okay not to share or that there are different ways to be nice other than sharing. He can still think of himself as "nice" even though he is not behaving nicely all the time.

What does this young child know about himself? Has he developed a me-self yet?

The me-self actually emerges by about 2 years of age. At first, the child's understanding of self is very concrete: "I have brown hair," and "I live in the yellow house." Younger children often give actual demonstrations of the things they mention, such as reciting their ABCs or running fast; their concepts are still closely tied to concrete behavior. Also, younger children's descriptions tend to be very disjointed, indicating that their self-representations are not integrated into an overall sense of self. Over the early childhood years, however, their self-descriptions become *increasingly abstract,* referring more and more to intangible qualities such as responsibility or conscientiousness. They also show *increasing differentiation* of aspects of the self and they are also more *realistic* in their assessments of their abilities. A 5-year-old, for example, may understand that he is very good at riding a bicycle but not very talented in math or spelling (Harter, 1999).

Think About Cassandra . . .
Given Nathan's age, do you think he recognizes himself? What do you think he understands about "self" at this age?

Self-Regulation

One of the most important skills that children develop is the ability to control aspects of the self. **Self-regulation** is the ability to control your own behavior, emotions, or thoughts, altering them in accordance with the demands of the situation. It includes the abilities to *inhibit* first responses, to *resist interference* from irrelevant stimulation, and to *persist* on relevant tasks even when we don't enjoy them. For example, when our son Will was young, he liked to play Monopoly Junior with his sisters. Will had developed reasonable self-regulation skills for his age, so he usually did not give in to the temptation to take money from his sisters' piles when they weren't looking (inhibiting first responses). Most of the time, he was able to ignore their incessant singing of "Jingle Bells" as he pondered whether to buy a property (resisting interference) or distract himself by focusing on the game when he started to feel irritated by the singing (emotional regulation). Though he might not do so on his own, Will did help clean up the game and put it away when we asked, even though he didn't really want to (persisting on less enjoyable tasks). Can you envision what this scene would be like if Will and his sisters had few or no self-regulation skills? We prefer to not think about it!

Mature self-regulation requires several sophisticated cognitive skills. These include awareness of the demands of any given situation; consistent monitoring of your own behavior, thoughts, and strategies; consideration of how successfully you are meeting the demands of the situation; and the ability to change aspects of your current functioning as needed to fit the situation or to accomplish a goal. Aspects of self-regulation correlate with various positive outcomes for children and adolescents—

self-regulation
The ability to control our own behavior, emotions, or thoughts and change them to meet the demands of the situation.

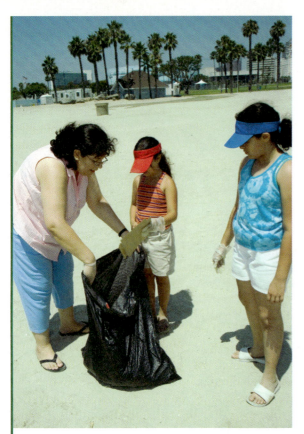

One way that children learn self-regulation is by watching adults. Children internalize and imitate the behaviors and self-regulation strategies that they see in the important people around them.

including better academic performance, problem-solving skills, and reading comprehension; more satisfying interactions with peers; higher levels of intrinsic motivation, self-worth, perceived competence, self-efficacy, moral cognition, and moral conduct; fewer behavior problems; and lower levels of psychopathology (e.g., depression) (Brown et al., 1983; Eisenberg et al., 2001; Grolnick et al., 1999; Howse et al., 2003; Kochanska et al., 1997; Ryan et al., 1992).

How do children develop self-regulation skills? From 3 through 7 years of age children grow steadily in their abilities to inhibit first responses. In one study, for example, older children were better than younger children were at not peeking while an experimenter wrapped a gift (Gerstadt et al., 1994; Kochanska et al., 1996; Kopp, 1982; Raffaelli et al., 2005). Several factors influence the development of self-regulation. Researchers have linked aspects of temperament (see Chapter 6) such as behavioral inhibition, effortful control, and fearfulness to several self-regulatory behaviors, including emotional regulation, cheating, compliance with adults' requests, and following rules (Kochanska et al., 2000; Kochanska et al., 2001; Rothbart & Bates, 1998). Maturation of certain areas of the brain, especially the frontal lobes, enables children to resist interference and inhibit responses. The frontal lobes undergo two periods of rapid growth, one during infancy and another between the ages of 4 and 7—and these periods are consistent with the developmental trends in self-regulation we've described (Hudspeth & Pribram, 1990; Luria, 1973).

But these biological links do not mean that self-regulation is completely innate. Aspects of the child's environment have a strong influence. In fact, most psychologists believe that self-regulation, though influenced by biological factors, begins with external control by others and gradually becomes internalized. For example, children learn specific strategies for regulating behavior and emotions by *modeling*—the process of imitating, practicing, and internalizing others' behavior (Schunk & Zimmerman, 1997). And children often use *private speech,* or speech they direct toward themselves (see the discussion of Vygotsky's theory in Chapter 8), to guide their problem-solving efforts and to regulate behavior, cognitive strategies, or emotions.

It also appears that the *way* adults try to direct children's behavior and emotions affects how quickly and how well self-regulatory skills develop. For example, children are more likely to change their behavior if they agree with a given request. When children comply because they agree with the request, there is a greater chance that they will view the request as being "self-generated and not interfering with" their attempts to be independent (Kochanska et al., 2001, p. 1108). In other words, they may think of the request as being their own idea, or at least regard it as sensible. Compliance under these conditions may ultimately lead to more effective self-regulation (Kochanska et al., 2001). When a child disagrees but is forced to comply anyway, there is less internalization of the parents' standards, and parents tend to resort to more power-based (rather than reason-based) control tactics.

Think for a moment about the implications of this. There will always be times when a child disagrees with parental requests, rules, or decisions. But forcing obedience through the use of power and control may delay the very thing that parents are trying to teach! Strategies that encourage internalization of social standards (e.g., explaining the rationale for a rule, involving children in establishing goals and rules, and so on) require more time and effort from caregivers but are probably more likely to produce voluntary self-regulation. Later in this chapter we explore parenting styles, including use of parental power, and their effects on children's cognitive, social, and emotional development.

your perspective

How well do you regulate your behavior and emotions? How could you do this more effectively?

Think About Cassandra . . .

How can Cassandra use these concepts to help Nathan learn self-regulation? What advice would you give?

The Self and Emotions

Infants don't fully understand that they are separate from other people and do not yet reflect on themselves as separate individuals. Consequently, their emotions often echo the emotional states of their caregivers and other people (Saarni et al., 1998); cry contagion (crying simply because they hear another infant's cry) and imitation of facial expressions are examples. Later, as children develop the capacity for self-reflection, they begin to appreciate that their emotions are their own personal responses to the situations and events around them. For example, they understand that they can enjoy a toy or TV show even if their friends don't, or that they may be more afraid of thunderstorms than their siblings or friends.

By age 2, children are spontaneously talking about their feelings and the feelings of other people (Saarni et al., 1998). They are also becoming aware that their emotional reactions may differ from those of other people. A child's emerging *theory of mind* (see Chapter 8) helps the child understand individual differences in emotions. By 2 to 3 years of age, children understand that emotions are connected to their mental appraisals of what they want, like, don't want, and don't like (Wellman et al., 1995). By the age of 5, children's understandings are more dynamic—they understand that events that confirm or disconfirm their beliefs or expectations can trigger emotions. If they think they "should" get a treat, they expect that they will be pleased, happy, or satisfied when they receive one. If they get an unexpected treat, they understand that surprise can result. Anger and sadness, however, can follow when expectations are not met. And because our beliefs, expectations, likes, dislikes, and other mental appraisals differ, we each have our own emotional reactions to events. By middle childhood, children understand these individual responses.

This child is happy because he anticipates that he will enjoy what is inside the present. By age 5, children's emotions can be triggered by what they expect or believe will happen.

As children begin to understand the individualized nature of emotions, they tend to see and report their own positive emotions more than their negative emotions—they show a **positive emotion bias** (Saarni et al., 1998). For example, if you describe a hypothetical scenario, 6-year-olds predict a more positive emotional reaction for themselves than for other children (Karniol & Koren, 1987). And 5-year-olds are less likely than 7-year-olds to report being sad (Glasberg & Aboud, 1982). Maybe adults seem to value happiness in children so much that younger children bow to the social pressure, exaggerating their positive emotions and denying or minimizing sadness and other negative emotions. Boys in particular seem to get a message to hide sadness, and they become more skilled at veiling this emotion as they mature (Chaplin et al., 2005). In one study boys and girls expressed sadness about equally at age 6 (Fuchs & Thelen, 1988). In middle childhood, however, gender differences emerged, and by age 11 boys were only half as likely as girls to express sad feelings. Further, boys reported that they would be less likely to communicate their sadness to their fathers than to their mothers. Boys seem to learn that sadness is not socially accepted for males, and it appears that they are getting this message during early childhood. Another aspect of the positive emotion bias is that children are more accurate in recognizing other people's positive emotions and less accurate in recognizing negative emotions (Fabes et al., 1991; Gross & Ballif, 1991).

positive emotion bias
Tendency of children to report positive more than negative emotions.

Developing Ideas about Gender

A major component of understanding the self is understanding what it means to be a boy or a girl. Table 9.1 on page 294 summarizes some of what we have learned about the developmental progression of the gender concept, gender roles, and sex-typed behavior. As you can see, some aspects of gender knowledge appear quite early in childhood. By about 2½ years, children are able to apply gender labels correctly (e.g., *boy, girl, mommy, daddy*). However, young children tend to use surface features such as hairstyles and clothing to determine if someone is female or male. For example,

TABLE 9.1 Trends in Gender Development

APPROXIMATE AGE/GRADE	TRENDS
2 through 3 years	• By 2 years of age, children show knowledge of gender differences in adult possessions, roles, physical appearance, and abstract characteristics (e.g., soft, cruel). • Children understand the category labels "boy" and "girl." They apply gender labels to adults before using them for children. By 3 years, most children understand gender identity (i.e., they can consistently label their own sex), but they rely on hairstyles and clothing cues. • Children show knowledge of gender stereotypes regarding objects, activities, and children's toys. Children increase play with same-sex toys. • Both boys and girls have increasing positive contact with same-sex peers and begin to show same-sex peer preferences.
Preschool (3 through 5 years)	• Children show increasing gender differences in toy preferences and play activities. • By 3 years, most children understand gender stability (i.e., that one's gender does not change over time). • Children show increasing stereotypes regarding children's toys, activities, colors, traits, and play preferences. Stereotypes increase rapidly and are well-established by 5 years; they are stronger for boys than for girls. • By 2 to 4 years, there is some evidence of children distinguishing between male and female traits, behavior, and emotions, especially along power/fearfulness dimension (e.g., boys are strong, fast, and they hit; girls cry, need help, and are fearful) and negative/positive evaluation (males as negative; females as positive). • Preference for same-sex peers and sex-segregation in play groups increases. This preference is found across cultures and even in nonhuman primates. • Stereotyped differences in personality-social characteristics begin to develop, especially in aggressive and helping behaviors. • The late preschool years are a period of high rigidity in gender beliefs and behavior.
Early elementary school (6 through 7 years)	• Rigidity in gender-stereotyped beliefs regarding activities, occupations, traits, sports, and school tasks is very high during kindergarten. • Segregation into same-sex play groups remains high and continues until early adolescence. • Gender-stereotyped preferences remain high or increase, though preferences are higher for some areas than others. When stereotyped preferences show declines, they are seen mostly in girls. • Stable or increasing gender differences are seen in such things as television show preferences (boys view more cartoons and action-adventure shows), sports participation, chores, hobbies, and outdoor/indoor play. • There is a strong negative reaction to cross-gender behavior, especially when it involves cross-gender appearance.

when asked whether she was a girl or a boy and how she knew, 5-year-old Rachel pointed to her shoulder-length hair and replied without hesitation, "I'm a girl, because my hair is long and sometimes I wear dresses." When asked, "What if you had short hair? Would you still be a girl?" Rachel replied with exasperation, "I wouldn't *have* short hair—I'm a girl!" It is not until about the age of 8 years that most children use genital cues to determine gender and understand that surface features can vary across boys and girls (Intons-Peterson, 1988; McConaghy, 1979).

Children begin to show *gender-stereotyped preferences* even before they have a full understanding of their own gender. For example, by age 2 they begin to prefer sex-typed toys (e.g., dolls if they are female, cars if they are male). Boys show a tendency to avoid playing with "girls' toys" as early as 2 to 3 years of age (Fagot et al., 1986; Powlishta et al., 1993). These experiences are also reflected in their vocabulary development—by 2 years of age, more boys are using male-oriented words such as *fire truck* and more girls are using female-oriented words such as *dress* (Stennes et al., 2005). By the time children are 3 years old, they are already beginning to show **gender segregation** in their peer preferences—the tendency to play and associate with peers of their own sex. This trend increases significantly, and gender segregation remains quite marked until adolescence. We have much more to say about gender segregation later in this chapter. By the time children are 5 years old, their gender stereotypes of activities, toys, behavior, and even personality traits are quite well developed.

Gender stereotypes during the late preschool and kindergarten years are also fairly rigid. For example, kindergartners react quite negatively to cross-gender behavior in peers, especially if it involves cross-gender appearance (e.g., a boy wearing a dress) (Signorella et al., 1993; Stoddart & Turiel, 1985). There is some evidence that boys' gender stereotypes develop earlier and are more rigid than girls'. In addition, both boys and girls tend to object to cross-gender behavior and appearance in boys; this may mean that the stereotype for "maleness" is more rigid than the one for "femaleness," at least in American culture (Ruble & Martin, 1998). After about 8 years of age, gender stereotypes will start to become more flexible as children begin to understand that most gender norms for behavior, activities, occupations, and the like are culturally determined rather than absolute.

Children sometimes receive explicit reinforcement for sex-typed behavior, but reinforcement can also be unspoken and subtle.

Remember Jean Piaget's cognitive developmental theory described in Chapters 5 and 8? Lawrence Kohlberg applied Piaget's theory and proposed that knowledge of gender and gender-related behavior constitutes a cognitive category and develops in the same way as knowledge of any other cognitive category: through interaction with the world that is filtered through existing cognitive structures. According to Kohlberg, children will not have a mature understanding of gender until they achieve the Piagetian stage of concrete operations, which happens by approximately age 7 (Kohlberg, 1966). The key concept children must grasp in order to understand gender is that of **gender constancy,** or the understanding that an individual's gender remains the same despite changes in outward appearance or behavior (e.g., in hairstyle, clothing, or mannerisms). As you may notice, this idea is simply another form of the Piagetian concept of *conservation* that we described in Chapters 8.

Researchers have used Kohlberg's theory to identify three stages of gender understanding (Slaby & Frey, 1975):

- *Gender identity* (by 2½ years): Children's ability to categorize themselves and others correctly as boys or girls.

- *Gender stability* (by 4 to 5 years): The understanding that gender is a stable characteristic over time—that boys continue to be boys, and girls continue to be girls.

- *Gender constancy* (also called *gender consistency;* by 6 to 7 years): The understanding that gender is consistent across changes in outward appearance such as hairstyles or clothing.

Kohlberg proposed that all children progress through these stages in the same order, and studies in several different cultures have supported this sequence of development (Munroe et al., 1984).

Moral Development

As children learn self-regulation and learn to understand their own emotions, they also begin to form a **conscience**—ideas children have about right and wrong. By 3 to 4 years of age, children have internalized many rules and have begun to feel guilt

morality
Knowing the difference between what is right and wrong and acting on that knowledge.

moral reasoning
The ways in which people think about right and wrong.

perspective taking
The ability to understand the psychological perspectives, motives, and needs of others.

convention
A rule or practice that members of a social group agree to abide by in their behaviors, choices, and decisions.

preconventional level
Level of moral reasoning where children do not yet understand that rules are social conventions; children accept the rules of powerful others.

your perspective

For each of Kohlberg's stages, try to think of someone who reasons about moral issues at that stage. What has helped some of these people move to higher stages? At what stage would you place yourself?

about their bad behavior and empathy for other children or people who have been wronged (Aksan & Kochanska, 2005). These feelings reflect the child's developing conscience and sense of *morality*. **Morality** involves knowing the difference between what is right and wrong and acting on that knowledge. **Moral reasoning** refers to the many ways people think about right and wrong. We mentioned that Lawrence Kohlberg applied Piaget's theory in order to understand gender development in children; Kohlberg also applied Piaget's theory to understand morality. To study morality, Kohlberg presented children with stories that contained moral dilemmas (Kohlberg, 1969; Kohlberg et al., 1984). How did the children reason through the dilemmas?

Pretend for a moment that someone dear to you is very sick and will soon die if they do not receive treatment. There is a new drug available that might help, but the pharmacist who developed it is asking a very high price, much more than it cost him to develop the drug. You cannot afford the price, and the druggist will not agree to sell it more cheaply or to let you pay for it later. You are becoming desperate and are considering stealing the drug. Should you? Why, or why not?

Moral dilemmas like this create a conflict between two values (e.g., saving a person's life versus obeying the law). Kohlberg believed that moral development depends on a person's level of cognitive development. You cannot think about moral issues in a sophisticated way if you do not have a fairly high level of overall cognitive development. **Perspective taking**—the ability to understand the psychological perspectives, motives, and needs of others—also is essential. To understand a person's intentions and reasons for acting, you have to be able to put yourself in the other person's place and view the situation as the other person might (Selman, 1980).

But cognitive development and perspective-taking ability alone are not enough. That is, they are *necessary but not sufficient* for moral development. Children also must directly experience and think about moral issues and dilemmas in order to understand that their current level of moral reasoning is not adequate. As you may recall, Piaget called this kind of imbalance between experiences and current understanding *cognitive disequilibrium*. Like Piaget, Kohlberg believed that moral development requires us to feel a certain degree of disequilibrium, or discomfort with our current way of thinking, to spur our cognitive construction of more complex and sophisticated reasoning about moral questions.

Kohlberg theorized that children progress through three broad levels of moral reasoning, with each level divided into two specific stages, as shown in Table 9.2. He believed that these stages were universal and constant—that all children move through the same stages in the same order. However, the pace of development and the final endpoint will differ depending on the specific moral experiences encountered, cognitive maturity, and perspective-taking ability.

Think about the meaning of the word *convention* and you'll understand why Kohlberg's levels are labeled as they are (Table 9.2). A **convention** is a rule or practice that members of a social group agree to abide by in their behavior, choices, and decisions. At Kohlberg's first level, children have not yet developed the understanding that rules are social conventions, so this is called the **preconventional level**. At this level children accept the rules of powerful others without thinking about where those rules come from, whether they are fixed or flexible, or whether some circumstances could allow changes in the rules. In Stage 1 children determine what is "moral" on the basis of rewards or punishments, regardless of whether the intention was good or not. Is it "wrong" to take a cookie (or steal some medicine)? Well, if you get caught and punished, then it is wrong; if you are not caught and punished, then it is not wrong! In Stage 2 children are beginning to understand that others have different perspectives, but they are not able to see a situation from another's perspective. Their moral reasoning at this stage is based on meeting their own egocentric needs—what is "good" is what serves their interests. During early childhood, most children use Stage 1 reasoning to think about moral

TABLE 9.2 Kohlberg's Levels and Stages of Moral Reasoning

Level I: Preconventional Moral Reasoning	*Stage 1: Punishment and obedience orientation* Children decide what is right based on whether the action will be punished or rewarded, but do not consider the interests of others. They obey because adults have greater power. *Stage 2: Individualism, instrumental purpose, and exchange* Children follow rules when it serves their own needs or interests. They are aware that others have interests, and that they may conflict with their own.
Level II: Conventional Moral Reasoning	*Stage 3: Mutual interpersonal expectations, relationships, and interpersonal conformity* Children are concerned with living up to others' expectations. "Being good" is important, and it means having good intentions, being concerned about others, being loyal and trustworthy. *Stage 4: Social system and conscience* Children define what is right according to what fulfills duties they have agreed to carry out. They abide by laws except in extreme cases. Moral actions are those that the larger society has determined are right.
Level III: Postconventional Moral Reasoning	*Stage 5: Social contract or utility and individual rights* Values and rules are seen as relative to a particular group and can be changed. Rules should be followed for the welfare and protection of all people's rights, and what is moral is what is best for the largest number of people. Some values, such as life and liberty, are recognized as nonrelative and must be upheld regardless of socially agreed upon laws. *Stage 6: Universal ethical principles* People develop and follow their own self-chosen ethical principles, which are part of an integrated and carefully thought-out system of values. If social laws violate these principles, the person's actions will be consistent with their ethical principles.

(Adapted from Kohlberg, 1984.)

issues, and a few may use Stage 2. The remaining stages are used by older children and adolescents, so we will discuss those stages in later chapters.

As you can see, the early childhood years are a period of self-discovery. Young children are learning who they are and what they are like. Although there is much progress yet to be made, they are learning how to handle their emotional reactions and how to think about what is right and wrong. This area of development is greatly affected by the style of parenting children receive and the types of discipline procedures used by their parents. Children's self-discovery continues as they play in social groups and learn to form close friendships with other children. We explore these topics in the next sections.

Think About Cassandra . . .

How can Cassandra use Kohlberg's stages to evaluate where Nathan is in his moral development? How can Cassandra help him understand the moral and ethical issues related to misbehaviors such as biting and taking toys from other children?

■ Let's Review . . .

1. The I–self is our _____.
   a. objective knowledge of our own characteristics
   b. understanding that we exist as a separate person
   c. ability to understand events from another person's perspective
   d. accumulation of feelings about our selves

2. Which of the following is the clearest example of self-regulation?
   a. Sarah knows what she likes and what she does not like.
   b. Mark cries when his mother leaves him all alone.
   c. Robbie would like to take his brother's toy, but he resists the temptation.
   d. Debbie is shy and does not like loud social situations.

3. Steven, a 3-year-old boy, once said that he might play with dolls someday when he grows up to be a girl. Steven's comment shows that he has not yet developed the concept of _____.
   a. gender stability
   b. gender constancy
   c. gender segregation
   d. gender identity

4. Lawrence Kohlberg gave children stories that contained ethical dilemmas, and he asked the children to decide what they would do in the story and why. In this study, Kohlberg was studying children's _____.
   a. gender concepts
   b. individualized emotions
   c. self-regulation
   d. moral reasoning

5. **True or False:** The "me-self" usually begins to emerge at about 3 years of age.

6. **True or False:** During early childhood, most children use what they know about rewards and punishments to determine which acts are "good" and which are "bad."

Answers: 1. b, 2. c, 3. a, 4. d, 5. F, 6. T

Parenting

Years ago, before we had children, we visited a friend who had two young children. As David served a quick post-swimming–pre-baseball-game summer dinner of hot dogs and canned green beans, he commented, "You got kids, you gotta serve a vegetable." Then he added thoughtfully, "You know, having kids is great, but it's the hardest thing I have ever done in my whole life."

We don't know any parent who would disagree with David's assessment. In this section, however, we hope to shed some light on parenting practices that can support the development of happy and well-adjusted children. Although parenting is never an easy task, this information should be helpful for parents or anyone else who works with children. We also point out that good parenting is important for children of all ages. We cover the topic in this chapter on early childhood to emphasize that family patterns and habits tend to become established early on. During infancy, parents provide for every need; as children move into the early childhood stages, a major task in parenting is to figure out how to set limits, enforce rules, and communicate care and respect for children while at the same time teaching them to be responsible.

As you study this section, ask yourself these questions:

■ How do parental warmth and parental control affect children's outcomes?

■ What are the four parenting styles described by Baumrind and other researchers? What outcomes are associated with each style?

■ What is the difference between *discipline* and *punishment*? Why is spanking an ineffective method of discipline? How can parents use discipline effectively?

Dimensions of Parenting

parental warmth
The degree to which parents are accepting, responsive, and compassionate with their children.

In studying characteristics of parenting, researchers have identified two dimensions that are especially important: *warmth* and *control*. **Parental warmth** is the degree to which parents are accepting, responsive, and compassionate with their children. Parents who are high in warmth are very supportive, nurturing, and caring. They pay close attention to their children's needs, and their parenting behaviors tend to be child centered (focused on the needs of the child rather than on the convenience or demands of the parents). Researchers see parental warmth as existing on a broad continuum—from parents who show a high degree of warmth to those who show little or no warmth. At the lower end of the continuum are parents who are rejecting, unresponsive to their children, and more parent centered than child centered. This *cold* type of parenting is obviously detrimental to the child's development. Numerous studies have shown that children who experience cold parenting are more aggressive, are less popular, and perform more poorly in school. Conversely, when parenting is high in warmth, children show better social and academic skills, and they show more love and respect for their parents and other people (see Maccoby & Martin [1983] and Parke & Buriel [1998] for reviews).

Parents high in warmth are supportive, nurturing, and caring, and pay close attention to their children's needs.

Parental control is the degree to which parents set limits, enforce rules, and maintain discipline with children. Parents who are high in control set firm limits on their children's behavior, and they consistently enforce rules. They are involved in their children's lives and use discipline to provide structure for their children's behaviors. Parents low in control, however, are lax, permissive, or uninvolved with their children. Like parental warmth, control is on a continuum: Some parents show a high degree of control, some only a moderate degree, and others very little control or involvement with their children.

When we look at parental warmth and parental control, it is important to consider their combined effects. When warm parents use firm control, for example, discipline tends to be child centered, age appropriate, and positive. When cold and rejecting parents use firm control, however, discipline can be very harsh, punitive, and even abusive. By itself, neither warmth nor control is sufficient for explaining the effects of parenting on children's developmental outcomes.

Researchers also draw a distinction between *physical control* and *psychological control*. Physical control involves the use of physical means to control children, such as hitting, spanking, pushing, and physically forcing children to do things. Psychological control uses guilt, humiliation, love withdrawal, or emotional manipulation to control children. Both forms of control can be harmful, especially when used by parents who are cold or rejecting with their children. One study of Chinese families, for example, showed that fathers who used more physical control had sons who were more physically aggressive with their peers. In this same study, psychological control by mothers was related to increases in physical and emotional aggressiveness in their daughters (Nelson et al., 2006). Therefore, the effects of physical and psychological control may depend on the parent inflicting the control and on the gender of the child who is being controlled.

parental control
The degree to which parents set limits, enforce rules, and maintain discipline with children.

Parenting Styles: Best Practices for Raising Children

In the mid-1960s Diana Baumrind began a longitudinal study investigating the effects of different styles of parenting. Her follow-up studies, and the many similar studies conducted by other researchers, have strongly influenced how parents and professionals think about parenting. The research has identified four distinct styles of parenting that represent the different combinations of high and low parental warmth combined with high and low parental control (Baumrind, 1973, 1991; Maccoby & Martin, 1983). Figure 9.1 on page 300 shows these four parenting styles in a 2 × 2 matrix of warmth and control. Let's look more closely at these styles. As we describe each style, consider what might happen if a 4-year-old child is caught hitting his sister. Ask yourself—what would you (or your parents) do in a situation like this?

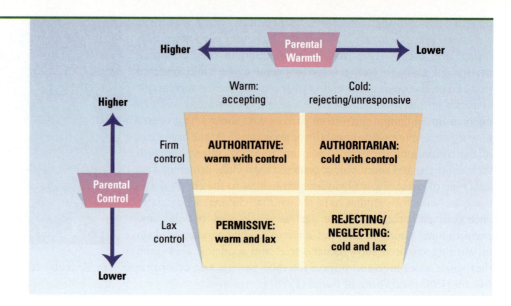

Figure 9.1 • Parental Warmth and Control Matrix Two dimensions of parenting (parental warmth and parental control) produce four styles of parenting: authoritative, authoritarian, permissive, and rejecting/neglecting. Research has associated the four styles with different outcomes for children.

authoritative parents
Parents who are warm and exert firm control.

Authoritative parents are warm and exert firm control. They monitor their children closely and have clear standards and high expectations for their behavior. They tend to use disciplinary methods that are supportive rather than punitive. There is clear communication between parent and child, and the lines of communication go both ways. Authoritative parents listen carefully to their children, and they allow give-and-take on disciplinary matters in a way that is age appropriate for the child. If their 4-year-old hits another child, their first response is likely to sit with the child and have a calm discussion about the incident. "Why did you hit her?" Authoritative parents are understanding and supportive ("We know you were frustrated and angry"), but they will set boundaries for their children and institute appropriate consequences if the child does not behave ("You know the family rule is 'no hitting,' so now you will lose your TV time"). The important point is that authoritative parents are rational, consistent, and child centered in their approaches to discipline.

Over time, authoritative parents expect their children to develop the ability to regulate their own behavior. Compared to other children, children raised by authoritative parents perform better in school, are less hostile and more popular among friends, have greater self-esteem, show more purpose and independence in their activities, and as adolescents they are more accurate in understanding their parents' values (Baumrind, 1973, 1991; Knafo & Schwartz, 2003; Parke & Buriel, 1998).

authoritarian parents
Parents who exert firm control but are rejecting or unresponsive to their children.

Authoritarian parents also exert firm control, but they do it in a way that is rejecting or unresponsive to the child. "No hitting!" they might yell. "What were you thinking!? Now you get over here right now!" Authoritarian parents set firm limits and expect that their children will behave. Their disciplinary methods tend to be harsh and punitive. Rather than having a rational discussion of an incident, they are more inclined to lower the boom immediately without regard for the child's perspective. Children raised in an authoritarian environment may feel trapped and angry but afraid to confront their parents (Parke & Buriel, 1998). They perform less well in school, are more hostile and aggressive, are less popular with their peers, and are less independent than children reared by authoritative parents (Baumrind, 1973).

permissive parents
Parents who are warm but have little control over their children.

Permissive parents are warm but have little control. They fail to set or enforce appropriate limits for their children. Permissive parents avoid confrontation with their children. Being too lenient they do not require that their children behave in a mature and responsible manner. Sometimes permissive parents justify their style by saying they'd rather be a friend than a parent to their children. A permissive parent might dismiss misbehavior lightly ("Now you know we don't hit, so don't let me see you do that again"). At the extreme, permissive parents can become *indulgent*—beyond merely allowing their children to misbehave, they may actually encourage or foster their misbehavior: "Well, if he hit you, then you just hit him back!" As their children and teens grow older, permissive–indulgent parents may encourage or condone inappropriate behaviors such as skipping school, vandalism, alcohol or drug abuse, or sexual promiscuity. Compared to authoritatively raised children, children from permissive homes are more impulsive, perform less well in school, and are less self-assured, independent, and confident in their activities (Parke & Buriel, 1998).

Rejecting/neglecting parents don't set limits and are unresponsive to their children's needs. This category of parenting has two substyles: *Rejecting parents* are harsh and actively reject their children, whereas *neglecting parents* ignore their children and fail to fulfill their responsibilities as parents. These parents don't monitor their children properly and may not notice misbehaviors. Rejecting/neglecting parents may be under too much stress to parent appropriately; they may not be committed to the task of raising children; or they may be depressed or otherwise psychologically or emotionally unavailable to their children. Children raised by rejecting/neglecting parents fare the worst of all. Compared to other children, rejected/neglected children grow up to show higher rates of delinquency, alcohol and drug use, and early sexual activity. They perform more poorly in school and show other disruptions in peer relations and cognitive development (Parke & Buriel, 1998).

rejecting/neglecting parents
Parents who don't set limits and are unresponsive to their children's needs.

a.

b.

c.

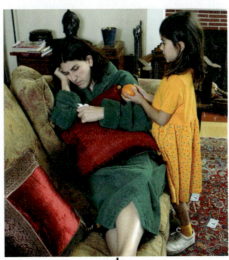

d.

(a.) Authoritative parents set limits and have appropriate control over children's behavior; they are warm, supportive, and respectful. (b.) Authoritarian parents exert firm control, but demonstrate little warmth and respect for the child's point of view. They tend to use harsh and punitive disciplinary methods. (c.) Permissive parents do not set or enforce limits, avoid confrontation with their children, and do not require their children to behave maturely or responsibly. (d.) Rejecting/neglecting parents ignore or actively reject their children. They do not discipline their children, or do so harshly and inconsistently.

In her later work Baumrind expanded the number of parenting styles to seven: *authoritative, democratic, nondirective, authoritarian–directive, nonauthoritarian–directive, unengaged,* and *good enough.* She also added two dimensions in addition to parental warmth and parental control. *Maturity demands* are parents' expectations that the child will show age-appropriate behavior, self-reliance, and self-control. *Democratic communication* is the degree to which parents ask for and consider the child's feelings and opinions. As you might expect, higher levels of each are indicative of more effective parenting. Research in this area also highlights the problem of *intrusiveness,* or control that parents maintain by psychologically manipulating and inhibiting children. Studies have linked higher levels of intrusiveness with poorer outcomes for children and adolescents. Researchers have confirmed this finding in several different cultures, although children of "unengaged" parents still seem to fare worst of all (Barber, 2002; Baumrind, 1991).

Quality parenting is an issue of great interest and concern to all who work with children, but there is little agreement on how to improve it. One proposal involves requiring people to get a license before they can become parents. To read more about the pros and cons of this intriguing idea, read the Social Policy Perspective box called "Should Parents Have to Be Licensed?"

Discipline: Spare the Rod and Spare the Child?

discipline
Techniques used to teach children appropriate behavior.

punishment
Techniques used to eliminate or reduce undesirable behavior.

The most important issue most parents face is how to provide appropriate discipline for their children. Psychologists use the word **discipline** to refer to the techniques parents and caregivers use to teach children appropriate behavior. Unfortunately, when most people think of *discipline,* they think immediately about **punishment,** or techniques used to eliminate or reduce undesirable behavior. Unless people have had special training in parenting or child development, they often overemphasize punishment when disciplining children. Too often, parents end up spanking, hitting, or yelling at children. Most parents don't want to be harsh with their children, but over time parents may lose their patience. Researchers who have observed parents interacting with young children have reported that, on average, parent–child conflicts occur three to 15 times per hour. Parents interrupt their children, on average, every seven minutes to get them to change their behavior (Baumrind, 1996; Lee & Bates, 1985; Minton et al., 1971). With young children, 65 percent of parent–child interactions involve the parent telling the child *not* to do something, as in "Don't touch that!" "Get down!" or "Don't do that!" (Baumrind, 1996; Hoffman, 1975).

What is a parent to do? One thing parents should *not* do is spank, hit, grab, or yell harshly at children. Although parents in this country generally treat children more humanely today than they did 50 or 100 years ago, spanking and other physical forms of punishment are still common. In surveys, 84 percent of American adults agree that "it is sometimes necessary to discipline a child with a good hard spanking" (Lehman, 1989; Straus, 1994). Also, 65 percent of parents report that they slap, hit, or spank their infants; 90 percent spank 3-year-olds; and 35 percent are still hitting or spanking their adolescents at age 16 (Straus, 1994). According to data from the National Longitudinal Study of Youth, two-thirds of mothers reported hitting or spanking their 6-year-old children (Straus, 1994). One out of every four parents uses a belt, wooden paddle, or other object to spank children (Straus & Stewart, 1999).

Sociologist Murray Straus (1991, 2001) has studied family violence for more than 20 years. His studies indicate that hitting and spanking is most widespread among parents who are relatively young; parents who themselves were hit or spanked as children or adolescents; and mothers whose husbands, boyfriends, or partners hit them. Straus also reports that a greater percentage of middle-income parents use spanking, but that the lower-income parents who do use spanking do so with more frequency.

Should Parents Have to Be Licensed?

We know a lot about different parenting styles and the child outcomes associated with them. As you can imagine, however, it isn't always easy to identify the "best" style. Different families' backgrounds, cultures, contexts, and temperaments may require different kinds of parenting behaviors. But have you ever seen a particularly troubling parent behavior and thought, "You ought to need a license to be a parent"?

Some are taking this idea very seriously (Lykken, 2000, 2001; Westman, 1994). They argue that parenting is a privilege and a responsibility, not a right. Requiring parents to obtain a license would communicate that parenting is just as important as all the other activities that we license, such as getting married, driving, or voting. Proponents of licensing also argue that people who wish to become foster or adoptive parents already must obtain official authorization; only parents raising their biological children need not be licensed. According to advocates of this idea, licensing would:

- Provide a way to determine parental competence "*before* rather than *after* damage to a child" (Westman, 1997, p. 201).
- Save millions of children the pain of neglect and abuse.
- Save society tremendous amounts of pain, suffering, and money. Advocates argue that incompetent parenting is a major cause of crime and violence, because it allows children to grow up unsocialized.
- Establish minimum parenting requirements, such as two parents "committed enough to be married to each other, who are mature and self-supporting, neither criminal nor incapacitated by mental illness" (Lykken, 2000, p. 599).
- Require that others who wish to raise a child (such as never-married women, divorced individuals, or gay and lesbian couples) obtain permission from a judge in family court.

As you might expect, this proposal is quite controversial. No one argues with the claim that it is better to have good parents than to have neglectful or abusive ones, but there are serious constitutionality questions about parental license requirements (Redding, 2002). In addition, licensing proponents clearly favor two-parent families, claiming that *both* biological parents should be present and committed to child rearing. Although a higher percentage of troubled youth come from single-parent rather than two-parent homes, opponents argue that the percentage is not nearly high enough to justify denying licenses to single parents (Scarr, 2000). Others point out that factors other than parenting, such as characteristics of a child's neighborhood culture, family income, and discrimination, also have important effects on children's outcomes. Opponents also maintain that it is only parents at the extremes who cause better or worse outcomes. "[P]retty good parents do not produce better children than average parents or pretty bad parents" (Harris, 2000, p. 630), and "very, very bad parents" are already addressed via (admittedly imperfect) social and child protective services. Perhaps most troubling to critics is the licensing scheme's distinct scent of social engineering. Would low-income parents be denied licenses? If so, ethnic minorities would be disproportionately affected, because they are more likely to be poor. Might not such a program limit the reproductive rights of certain groups to a greater degree than those of other segments of the population (Grigg, 1995)?

Q *What do you think of parent licensing? Would it be a good way to reduce child neglect, child abuse, and violent crime? How could it be structured so as not to discriminate unfairly against lower-income and minority individuals, single adults or gay and lesbian couples, or those with less education? Who would implement it? How would policies be enforced? If parents lost their licenses, would the authorities remove their children from the home? Perhaps the idea of parent licensing is more complicated than it first appears.*

In the short run, spanking does seem to work. For example, if a child runs into the street or is jumping up and down on the sofa, a quick swat usually terminates the misbehavior. After the spanking the child usually sits and cries, and refrains from immediately repeating the offending behavior. In the long run, however, spanking is not

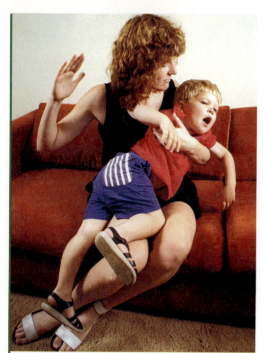

Spanking is not an effective form of discipline in the long term, and it can have a variety of negative side effects.

effective (Holden, 2002). When children are spanked, they eventually return to the misbehavior or replace it with other inappropriate behaviors. Why else would parents "need" to spank so often? Hitting and spanking can cause children to fear their parents. If children try to run, or if they strike back or talk back to their parents, the hitting usually becomes more severe. Although most spanking is not legally considered physically abusive, it is true that most physical abuse begins as physical punishment—punishment that then gets out of control (Straus, 1994).

Another thing to consider is the message that spanking sends to children. Do we want them to learn that "might makes right" or that it's appropriate for larger people to use physical force to get smaller people to obey? Ironically, "hitting other children" is the misbehavior that parents most often identify as calling for a spanking (Lehman, 1989; Straus, 1994). What message does the child get when the parent slaps them on the hand (or swats them on the behind) and says, "Don't hit other people!"?

Studies show that children who are spanked more often are more physically violent and aggressive; are twice as likely to attack their siblings; have lower moral standards and lower self-esteem; and as they grow up they are more likely to steal property, commit assaults, and commit other delinquent acts (Kerr et al., 2004; Straus, 1994; Straus et al., 1997). These studies also show that adolescents who are hit by their parents are more likely to be depressed and have suicidal thoughts, and that these problems worsen the more often they are hit. Adults who were spanked or hit during adolescence are three times more likely to hit their spouses; they are more likely to physically abuse their children; and they are more likely to link pain and violence with sexual activity.

Analyzing the results of 88 different studies, Gershoff (2002) found consistent correlations between physical punishment and increases in child aggression, delinquency, and antisocial behavior; increased rates of child abuse by parents; and poorer relationships between children and parents. Children whose parents physically punished them were less likely to internalize moral values, and later in life they were more likely to suffer from mental health problems such as low self-esteem, depression, and alcoholism. As adults they were more likely to be aggressive, commit crimes, and abuse their own children and spouses. And a recent study from New Zealand showed that mothers were less supportive with their children when they were treated harshly by their own parents, so the cycle of ineffective parenting continues across generations (Belsky et al., 2005). Researchers who studied families in Thailand, China, the Philippines, Italy, India, and Kenya found that physical punishment was related to higher levels of child aggression and anxiety in all of the countries. Interestingly, when physical punishment occurred, the negative effects were stronger in those countries where parents and children reported less overall use of physical punishment (Lansford et al., 2005).

Of course, all of these findings on physical punishment are correlational. It could be that children and adolescents who are more violent and engage in more misbehavior simply are spanked and hit more often. One study found a mild genetic link where children who had behavioral styles that were more aggressive and defiant received more spanking from their parents, but the same researchers reported that differences in the frequencies of spanking seemed to be related more to issues related to parents than to genetics in the children (Jaffee et al., 2004). To find out whether spanking actually causes negative outcomes for children, we would need to conduct an experiment: We'd need to randomly assign some children to a group that received spankings for misbehavior and other children to a group that did not. (Refer back to Chapter 1 to see how experiments determine cause and effect.) Obviously, we cannot ethically conduct this type of experiment, so we must rely on the suggestive evidence provided by correlational studies.

To be fair, too, we want to point out that other research suggests that the negative effects associated with spanking may be due to the style of parenting rather than to the spanking itself (Baumrind et al., 2002). As you can imagine, parents who rely heavily on spanking and hitting also tend to be less warm and affectionate, less involved, and less consistent in their parenting than parents who use more positive forms of discipline. When researchers control for differences in warmth and involvement, the correlations between spanking and aggression or delinquency sometimes disappear (Simons et al., 1994). In other studies, children showed increases in misbehavior when they were spanked by mothers who were rated as less warm and supportive toward their children or when parents were irritable and inconsistent in how they disciplined their children (McLoyd & Smith, 2002; Snyder et al., 2005). Spankings by more warm and supportive mothers didn't seem to increase misbehavior, although they didn't decrease it either. These results were similar across African American, non-Hispanic white, and Hispanic families. And one recent review suggests that mild spankings may not be harmful and that the negative effects are limited to situations where spanking is severe or is the main method of discipline used in the family (Larzelere & Kuhn, 2005).

Even when used by warm and loving parents, spanking obviously doesn't work as well as most American parents would like to believe. We can think of no misbehavior that would justify these forms of punishment. Austria, Croatia, Cyprus, Denmark, Finland, Germany, Israel, Italy, Latvia, Norway, and Sweden have all banned parents from using physical punishment with their children (Bitensky, 1998; Palmérus & Jutengren, 2004). Sweden was the first country to pass such a bill (in 1979). The Swedish statute states:

> Children are entitled to care, security, and a good upbringing. Children are to be treated with respect for their person and individuality and may not be subjected to physical punishment or other injurious or humiliating treatment. (Durrant, 1999, p. 436)

Under the Swedish law spanking or hitting children carries a civil penalty, but the law also provides considerable educational and social service support to help families learn more appropriate methods of discipline.

Positive Discipline

So, once again, what should parents do for discipline? There are many good books on the subject, and local community colleges and social service agencies usually offer excellent parent-education programs on effective discipline. We present here a basic positive program of discipline that is consistent with guidelines endorsed by the American Academy of Pediatrics (1998) and most parenting experts. First, remember that the term *discipline* refers to techniques used to *teach* children appropriate behavior. The emphasis is on *teaching* rather than on *punishing*. Also recognize that there is no technique that works all of the time and right away. With patience and a calm and positive approach to discipline, parents can set firm limits and help children learn to control their behavior in a way that is appropriate for their age. The AAP recommends that parents try the following steps.

1. *Manage the situation.* Parents should be aware of the situations their children are in and should try to manage each situation to reduce the temptations for misbehavior. Begin by childproofing the home. If there are items you don't want

Think About Cassandra . . .

From this research evidence, what advice would you give Cassandra about spanking and discipline for her boys?

your perspective

Were you spanked as a child? What is your opinion of the research findings regarding spanking? For every type of misbehavior for which you believe a child "deserves a good spanking," try to think of two specific alternatives for handling (or preventing) the misbehavior.

Preventing misbehavior through situation management is one of the most effective ways to teach children appropriate behavior.

your child to touch or break, put them out of reach. Notice other infractions that occur at home, and try to rearrange things so the misbehaviors are less tempting. Make sure there are plenty of positive things for children to do and appropriate objects to explore. Too often, parents set up situations in which the most interesting thing to do is misbehave. Is this really the child's fault?

2. *Set clear rules and limits.* Parents need to communicate clearly to children the dos and don'ts that are most important. Don't have too many rules, or it will be difficult for you and your child to keep up with them all. Pick the issues that are most important for the child's age. With younger children you might focus on safety rules like "Stay in the yard" and "Don't touch the stove." For older children there can be clear rules about homework, expectations for household chores, and safety issues like wearing a helmet while biking or skateboarding. Try to state rules positively so children know what they *should* do (instead of "Don't run" say "Please walk").

3. *Praise good behavior.* Have you heard the slogan "Catch them being good"? It's important to let children know when they are behaving appropriately. Work on strengthening the positive behaviors in your children. "I notice you shared with your brother today—great job!" Behaviors tend to be repeated when they are reinforced or rewarded. When children are busy behaving, they have less time to misbehave. Rewarding good behavior also helps parents keep a positive focus in their discipline.

Parents can use a timeout to remove a child from a situation when he is misbehaving. A safe, quiet place gives the child a chance to settle down and think about the rules.

4. *Use explanation and reasoning.* When misbehavior occurs, parents need to explain the rules and provide good reasons for compliance. A calm and reasoned discussion gives parents an opportunity to express warmth and compassion to the child and an opportunity to demonstrate positive ways to handle conflict.

5. *If you must punish, try removing privileges or using timeouts.* If you have followed all of the preceding steps and an unwanted behavior still persists, you might consider imposing an appropriate punishment. Remember, *punishment* is a technique that reduces the frequency of an undesirable behavior, but it doesn't mean that you have to resort to hitting or yelling. It's best to tie the punishment to the infraction as much as possible. If children are fighting over video games, for example, they could lose the privilege of playing the games for the rest of the day. Any such disciplinary action should begin with the mildest form and should take the child's age into account. For a toddler, losing a favorite toy for a few minutes may make a big impact, whereas a 7-year-old may need to lose a privilege for several hours or a day to get the point. As an alternative, try a mild timeout. Remove the child from the situation and from anything that is encouraging the misbehavior to continue, and place him in a safe, quiet environment. A short timeout (about one minute per year of the child's age) gives children a few minutes to collect themselves and reflect on what they have done. It also gives you time to gather your thoughts—and reduces the likelihood that you will lash out in anger and say or do something you will regret. After the brief timeout, try offering an explanation and reasoning again. Always be sure to praise children when their behavior improves.

You may feel that the steps we have outlined are not enough; you may believe that children need to "pay a price" for misbehavior. Keep in mind, however, that the focus should be on teaching good behavior. Research shows, for example, that children misbehave less when parents spend time teaching positive skills, provide children with engaging toys and learning materials, and take children on interesting trips (Bradley & Corwyn, 2005). Of course misbehavior can be very aggravating for parents, especially when they are dealing with difficult children and trying to balance

Think About Cassandra . . .

Describe a program of positive discipline that Cassandra could use with her boys. How should she handle Nathan's aggressive behaviors (biting, taking toys, and not sharing)?

Carrots or Sticks?
Family Discipline at Different Ages

What methods of discipline do you use regularly? Are they effective? Are there any methods that you have tried, but found they did not work?

Iris and Manuel Matos: Hispanic family
We like to talk to our children about what they did wrong. It lets them know how we feel and how the situation reflects on who they are as a person. Yelling did not work at all. They could handle 5 minutes of yelling, and that was that. Spanking also did not work. When a child thinks about their mom and dad, it should be wonderful thoughts about being safe, comfort, trust, and guidance. With spanking, our children would not have the bond with us we have today because we would have instilled fear in them. To us, the most effective way is communicating with our children.

Kristin and Marc Petraluzzi: French family (two boys, ages 2½ and 4½) We use timeouts. This has not been really effective, because they have quite a few timeouts daily (the older child). When we had nowhere else to go, we tried a spanking, but that did not seem to help either. I think we just have strong characters that we are dealing with!

Sharon Buenaventura: Asian family (three boys, ages 12, 9, and 20 months) My discipline methods are based on their personalities. My eldest son, Michael, fits the mold of the "first born." On the rare occasion that I've had to discipline him, it was really more of a discussion pointing out various reasons why I did not want him to repeat his actions. Michael is quite open to our discussions and will correct his behavior willingly once the reasons are spelled out to him. My second son, Nicky, responds to timeouts and the taking away of privileges

(e.g., soccer practice). Discussions do not work for Nicky. He tends to be more free-spirited and not as concerned about following the rules. Christian is still quite young, and I haven't figured out what method of discipline will work best for him. At this time, he may want to touch something that he shouldn't, and simply telling him to "look, not touch" will suffice.

One method I have discovered over the years is that "screaming" or "yelling" is definitely the least effective method for any of my boys. I find that they tend to shut me out and not really listen to anything I may be saying.

Kim Miller: African American family (two girls, ages 11 and 14) The 14-year-old got a poor grade on a history test because she spent more time instant-messaging her friends than studying for the test. I restricted her access to instant messaging and other unsupervised uses of the computer until she had another test and got a better grade. The key is not ever wavering from the imposed punishment—which in this case meant over 3 weeks of no instant messaging. To encourage getting in bed on time, I instituted a policy that for every minute they are late for bed, they are charged $1. The money goes in a top dresser drawer and can be earned back each night the appropriate behavior is achieved (i.e., five consecutive nights of going to bed on time will recoup $5).

Q *What discipline techniques do you think are most effective? How do the strategies used in these families compare with the recommendations for positive parenting presented in this textbook?*

multiple stresses at work and at home. Most parents want to have positive relationships with their children; but it takes time, effort, and considerable emotional control to maintain a warm and caring attitude when children are continually misbehaving. It's just plain easier to lash out, yell, or strike the child. If you find yourself in this situation, we hope that you will take some time to reflect on your own behavior and the potentially negative impact that it may have.

To read more about how some parents deal with everyday situations with children of various ages, read the Personal Perspective box called "Carrots or Sticks? Family Discipline at Different Ages."

■ Let's Review . . .

1. Which of the following parent comments would best illustrate an *authoritative* parenting style?
   a. You said you'd clean your room! You never follow through—you're grounded for 3 weeks!
   b. You didn't clean your room? Well, it's not that dirty. You can do it some other time.
   c. Go ahead and live in a pigsty—it's your room.
   d. No movies tonight. We agreed you would clean your room by Friday or you wouldn't go to the movies.

2. Children tend to fare worst of all when their parents use the _____.
   a. authoritative style of parenting
   b. authoritarian style of parenting
   c. permissive style of parenting
   d. neglecting/rejecting style of parenting

3. Compared to other children, children who are frequently spanked tend to be _____.
   a. more aggressive, more depressed, and lower in self-esteem than other children
   b. better behaved than other children
   c. less likely to use physical means to get what they want
   d. less likely to use physical punishment with their own children

4. In the context of positive parenting, the word *discipline* means _____.
   a. punish
   b. time out
   c. reward
   d. teach

5. **True or False:** Authoritarian parenting is high in control and high in warmth.

6. **True or False:** One of the best techniques for child discipline is the use of situation management to prevent misbehavior in the first place.

Answers: 1. d, 2. d, 3. a, 4. d, 5. F, 6. T

Friends and Play

As we mentioned in Chapter 6, toddlers form friendships based mostly on convenience—they play with whomever is available the most. During early childhood the main ingredients in forming friendships are opportunity and similarity. To become friends, children need to be available to each other for play and other activities. Children become good friends when they spend a lot of time playing together, sharing toys, and enjoying the same games and activities. Children who are neighbors, relatives, or schoolmates spend more time with each other and therefore have more opportunities to form friendships. Further, children's social contacts increase dramatically when they enter school. In school children encounter a much larger group of peers and tend to have less direct adult supervision when they are together. From the toddler period to the school-aged years, time spent with peers triples (Higgins & Parsons, 1983). Also, like adults, children are drawn to others who are like them. Friendships are more likely to form when children are similar in characteristics such as age, gender, race, attitudes, beliefs, and even play styles (Epstein, 1989; Hartup, 1989; Rubin et al., 1994).

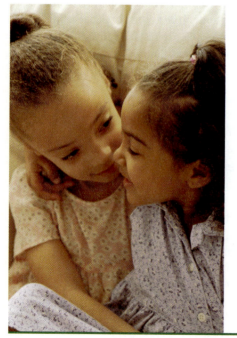

What do you think drew these 5-year-olds to each other as best friends? How do children of this age form close friendships?

In this section, we look at three topics that involve children's friends and play: the tendency of children to segregate into same-sex friendships, the basic types of play in early childhood, and the influence of culture on play.

As you study this section, ask yourself these questions:

- ■ Why do children play mostly with same-sex friends? Why don't they usually like to associate with children of the other sex?

- ■ How do researchers define "play," and what types of play have they studied?

- ■ How do different cultures influence how children play? What are some of the cultural differences that researchers have studied?

Gender Segregation

A prominent feature of children's friendships is *gender segregation*—the tendency of children to associate with others of their same sex. Consider the situation we observed while testing 4-year-old children in a preschool. As the children returned from their outside play period, a new boy in class took a seat in a circle of chairs. Several other boys ran immediately to him, yelling, "Get up, that's where the girls sit!" Hearing this, the new boy leaped up and began to furiously dust off the back of his pants! What did he think was on the chair? Cooties?

There is no doubt that gender segregation exists. In fact, it is nearly universal, occurring in every cultural setting where children have choice in selecting social groups (Fabes et al., 2003; Whiting & Edwards, 1988). But how does it begin, and why? There are no clear answers to these questions, but we can learn more by looking at how gender segregation evolves across childhood.

By 2 to 3 years of age, children are beginning to show a clear preference for playing with other children of their own sex (Serbin et al., 1994). At this age children are more interactive and sociable when playing with same-sex friends. When they are with the opposite sex, they tend to watch or play alongside the other child rather than interact directly. Gender segregation is very prominent after the age of 3. As you can see in Figure 9.2, preschool children spend very little time playing one-on-one with

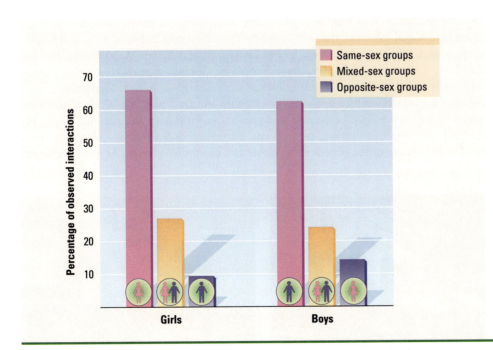

Figure 9.2 • Gender Interactions among Preschoolers In free play preschoolers (ages 3 to 6 years) choose to play with same-sex peers most often. When they do cross gender lines, they spend twice as much time playing in mixed-sex groups as with the opposite sex one-on-one. (Data from Fabes, 1994.)

the opposite sex. They spend some time in mixed-sex groups but spend most of their time, by far, playing with same-sex peers. By 6 years, segregation is so firm that if you watch 6-year-olds on the playground, you should expect to see only one girl–boy group for every 11 boy–boy or girl–girl groups (Maccoby & Jacklin, 1987).

Why does gender segregation exist? Let's consider the most prominent theories.

Play Compatibility. Some researchers believe that gender segregation occurs because children seek partners whose play styles match or complement their own (Serbin et al., 1994). Among the youngest children, the first to segregate tend to be the most active and disruptive boys and the most socially sensitive girls (Fabes, 1994; Serbin et al., 1994). Both types of children prefer to play with others like them.

Cognitive Schemas. According to the cognitive schemas view, children develop concepts or ideas (*schemas*) about what boys and girls are typically like. These concepts include stereotyped, and often exaggerated, notions about gender differences. Examples: "Boys are rough and like to fight and play with trucks" and "Girls are nice and like to talk and play with dolls." Children use these cognitive schemas as filters when they judge themselves and observe other children (Martin, 1994). As children learn gender schemas, their play and playmate preferences become more segregated.

your perspective

When you were a child, how did your peers respond when they saw you playing with someone of the opposite sex? Did their reactions have an encouraging or a discouraging effect on your choice of opposite-sex playmates?

Operant Conditioning. Reward and punishment also contribute to gender segregation. Boys in particular tend to incur harsh criticism when they cross gender lines to play with girls (Fagot, 1977, 1994; Fagot & Patterson, 1969). For most boys, being called a "sissy" is a major insult. Although some girls revel in being "tomboys," others can feel conflicted about being associated with stereotypically masculine activities. Whether consciously or only inadvertently, parents, teachers, peers, the media, and others contribute to gender segregation by reinforcing, or rewarding, sex-typed behaviors in boys and girls.

Psychoanalytic Theory. One of the oldest views on gender segregation was the theory formulated by Sigmund Freud (see Chapter 1). Although Freud's view of gender development isn't given much credence today, he offered the explanation that gender segregation occurs as children repress their sexual feelings during the "latency" stage of development. That is, children avoid interactions with the opposite sex so as to avoid the guilty feelings they associate with sexuality.

gender cultures
Different spheres of influence based on the differences that exist between male and female playgroups and affiliations.

Effects of Gender Segregation. Regardless of why gender segregation occurs, one of its consequences is that boys and girls grow up in different **gender cultures**—different spheres of social influence that are based on the differences between male and female groups and affiliations (Leaper, 1994; Leman et al., 2005; Maccoby & Jacklin, 1987). Rough-and-tumble play, chase, keep-away games, superhero warrior games, and competitive sports are more common among boys. Physical aggression, independence, and dominance are common themes in boys' play. Girls' play, however, tends to emphasize social closeness and sensitivity. Doll play and playing house, for example, involve role playing, turn taking, nurturing, and affection. Also, boys tend to play in larger groups; girls develop closer ties in smaller groups. As a consequence,

As you can see in these photos, boys and girls grow up in different gender cultures. Boys tend to engage in more rough and physical play while girls spend more time practicing interpersonal sensitivity. How do these experiences influence boys and girls differently?

girls may learn to share thoughts and feelings and practice being good listeners in intimate friendships. Boys, however, may see intimate sharing as a sign of weakness that would make them more vulnerable within their dominance hierarchies (Leaper, 1994). These different gender cultures may cause conflicts when girls and boys do begin to associate more together as they date and interact in adolescence and adulthood. Because they don't share the same gender culture, girls and boys may have difficulty understanding each others' perspectives.

What can adults do to reduce any negative effects of childhood gender segregation? Leaper (1994) provided several practical suggestions. For example, parents can model egalitarian roles at home, arrange more situations in which children can play and cooperate across genders, and reinforce and support children when they do cross stereotypical gender lines in their play. Teachers can arrange cooperative activities among boys and girls, and they can avoid grouping children by gender when they arrange seating and form lines. Teachers also should avoid using gender as a way to address students; for example, they shouldn't shout "Boys, sit down and be quiet!" unless all of the boys were indeed being loud. Of course, it would not be prudent or practical to try to eliminate all gender differences. Nevertheless, helping children develop more flexible expectations and skills in interacting with the opposite sex could be helpful. Read the Professional Perspective box on page 312 called "Career Focus: Meet the Director of a Child Care Center" for one expert's observations and advice regarding play preferences and gender segregation.

Play

Developmental psychologists define **play** as a pleasurable activity that is actively engaged in on a voluntary basis, is intrinsically motivated, and often contains some nonliteral element (Hughes, 1999). In plain words, play is something children (and older people) choose to do, on their own, for fun. They do it for the enjoyment of the play itself, not for outside rewards or in response to outside pressures. When children are truly "playing" baseball, for example, they are doing it because they enjoy the game. If they are doing it only to win a trophy or only because their parents made them do it, then it doesn't qualify as play. Finally, most play involves a nonliteral component—some element of make-believe, pretend, or symbolism. When children are playing, they pretend that dolls can talk, toy cars can zoom around imaginary racetracks, and a stick can become a powerful sword or a magic wand.

Play allows children to explore beyond the boundaries of reality. With imagination, fantasy, and creativity, children transform the objects and people in the real world to suit their own playful purposes. Through play children have opportunities to develop muscle coordination, social interaction skills, logical reasoning and problem-solving skills, and the ability to think about the world as it really is and as it could be.

The Social Levels of Play: Parten's Classic Study

In one of the classic studies of play, Mildred Parten (1932) made extensive observations of 42 children, ranging in age from 1 to 5, as they engaged in free play at their preschool. Parten observed them repeatedly over a period of nearly 8 months. She was particularly interested in the social nature of children's play. She identified six levels of play that ranged from completely nonsocial to highly integrated social play.

1. *Unoccupied behavior.* The child is not playing and not watching anyone or anything in particular. He may momentarily play with his own body, stand around, follow a teacher, or just sit alone. Example: Joey is sitting alone by the swings, apparently not playing with or watching anyone else.

2. *Onlooking.* The child spends most of his time watching other children play. He talks to the children he is watching and asks questions, but he does not engage in

play
A pleasurable activity that is actively engaged in on a voluntary basis, is intrinsically motivated, and contains some nonliteral element.

Career Focus: Meet the Director of a Child Care Center

Deborah Koshansky, Ph.D.
Bright Horizons Children's Center
in Washington, D.C.

Describe the children who attend your center. How many caregivers work there?
The Bright Horizons Children's Center in Washington, D.C., where I serve as Director is a work-site child care program managed by Bright Horizons Family Solutions for an international financial organization. We have 91 children enrolled ages 3 months through 5 years. We have 28 child care providers. Our family population is international in that most of the families are from countries other than the United States.

At your center, do you often see differences in the play preferences of boys and girls?
In our center we do see some differences in play preferences between the boys and girls. Usually this occurs initially in the 3-year-old group. It is most pronounced in the Pre-Kindergarten group and less so in the younger groups. As with any group, there is a continuum of behavior. We have some girls who enjoy rough and tumble play, construction play, and gross motor activities as much as some of the boys. Also, there are some boys who enjoy the dramatic play, art, and writing activities that usually attract the girls with greater frequency. We observe a great deal of tolerance and acceptance among the children if a child of the opposite gender joins them in play.

Why do you think children this age prefer to play with others of their same gender and not with the other gender?
As much as we would like to think that the genders are the same and if provided with similar encouragement and experiences we would not see gender differences, I think there are some inherent attractions for certain activities for boys and girls. My experience is that boys typically seek out more physically active activities such as super-heroes, block play, or gross motor activities, while girls prefer dramatic play, art, writing, and fine motor activities. Consequently, they self-select into those activities with other children of the same gender. We don't observe too much exclusionary behavior in our center such as "no girls allowed" or "boys don't wear dress-up clothes." I think that exclusionary behavior is more learned than innate and may reflect attitudes of adults that are transmitted to the children.

Do you encourage children to play across gender lines? Would this be helpful?
We don't make a practice of encouraging children to play across gender lines but we do monitor the play for exclusion. If we find that one group is excluding a child of either gender, we explore that with the children: "How can Susie participate in the dinosaur hunt?" "What role can Hank play in your family?" This is not always gender-related. It is sometimes just personalities. If we did see a pattern of gender segregation, I think it would be appropriate and useful to encourage play across genders. I would like to find subtle ways of encouraging it instead of making an overt issue of it. This could be accomplished by dividing the children into mixed gender small groups for specific activities. This would result in some mixed groups available for free choice play at the same time. I suspect they would play together at that time with greater regularity because of the need for a certain number of children to engage in associative and cooperative play successfully. As they gain experience with each other, they would be more likely to join each other in play at other times.

What education or training do child care providers and directors need to work in your field?
Our center is accredited by the National Association for the Education of Young Children. Consequently, we meet the NAEYC standards for teacher qualifications. Currently, all of our teachers hold at least a Child Development Associate credential (CDA). In order to meet the new, higher accreditation standards, they are working toward earning their associate degrees in Early Childhood Education.

Q *Is it appropriate and important to encourage boys and girls to play together? Why or why not? In what ways would you encourage this?*

the play himself. He focuses on the play of a particular child or group of children, and he stays near them so he can hear and observe. Example: Joey follows Sam around the sandbox as Sam plays; Joey asks questions and talks to Sam, but he does not play directly with Sam.

3. *Solitary play.* The child plays alone, and he makes no apparent connection between his play and the play of other children around him. Although he may play close to other children, he makes no attempt to make a connection with them. Example: Joey is playing in the sandbox; Sam is playing nearby, but Joey is not talking or sharing with him, and he is not watching Sam.

4. *Parallel play.* The child plays alone but with toys that are like those used by other children around him. His play may be similar to the play of nearby children, but he plays *beside* the other children, not *with* them. Example: Joey is pouring sand into his bucket and dumping it; Joey is sitting near Sam, who is also pouring and dumping sand, but they are not playing together.

5. *Associative play.* The child plays among other children, but his play is not well coordinated with their play. He may talk with the other children and share toys and materials, but his play is still relatively independent of others. The primary interest is in associating with other children but not in coordinating their play activity. Example: Joey and Sam are playing in the sandbox together; they talk, exchange buckets, and give sand to each other, but they are still pouring and dumping their own sand.

6. *Cooperative play.* The child plays with other children, and his play is integrated or coordinated with theirs. Play of this type often involves a group of children who are creating a common product, striving for a competitive goal, acting out adult situations, or playing formal games. There is a division of labor: Children play different roles, and their individual efforts contribute to a larger whole. Example: Several children are building a sand castle together. Joey is shoveling the sand into buckets while Sam dumps the sand to form spires and Sarah carefully pats and smoothes the spires. Together they build a large and beautiful castle.

Parten found a connection between children's ages and their types of play. The 1- and 2-year-olds spent most of their time in the first three levels of play: unoccupied behavior, onlooking, and solitary play. The 3- to 5-year-olds split their playtime about evenly among the upper three levels: parallel, associative, and cooperative play. Similar trends emerged in a study of young children in Taiwan (Pan, 1994).

Parten's observations highlighted the social nature of play. When children are young and lack social skills, they tend to play alone or beside other children—they rarely coordinate their play with peers or in a larger group. As children gain social skills, they tend to move toward more integrated play—they play with other children, and eventually they learn to coordinate their play roles to accomplish a larger group goal. When children do not make progress in learning to play socially, they are at risk for being rejected or excluded by their peers. Children who are anxious and fearful, for example, may play alone in solitary play and miss opportunities to learn to interact in more socially mature ways with other children. A cycle can erupt in which these children become even more fearful of social play, become more rejected, and become even more isolated in their solitary play (Coplan et al., 2004; Spinrad et al., 2004). It is important that parents, preschool teachers, and other adults help children make healthy social connections with other children.

> ## Think About Cassandra . . .
> *Looking at Parten's classification of play, what concerns do you have about Jeremy's play? What can Cassandra do to help Jeremy with social skills?*

Sociodramatic Play

Another type of play that becomes common by 3 years of age is **sociodramatic play**—acting out different social roles and characters. Sociodramatic play may be realistic ("I'll be the daddy and you be the baby.") or may involve a high degree of fantasy

sociodramatic play
Play that involves acting out different social roles or characters.

("I'm queen of the empire; behold my castle!"). Sociodramatic play can serve any of the following functions for young children (Hughes, 1999).

■ *Imitation of adults.* Children can act out adult roles they have observed, such as the role of a parent, teacher, cook, waiter, doctor, dentist, or veterinarian. Exploring these roles in play lets young children explore the activities of people in the larger world.

■ *Reenactment of family relationships.* Children often reenact events from their family lives. Most often, sociodramatic play involves simple, everyday activities: "Say good-bye to Mommy; she's going to work now." Sometimes, however, children use sociodramatic play to process larger and more traumatic events: "Daddy and Mommy don't love each other anymore; now we have to move to another house."

■ *Expression of needs.* Sociodramatic play gives children a chance to express unmet needs. For example, an only child may pretend to have a brother, or a child who misses his or her father may pretend to be playing ball with him.

■ *Outlet for forbidden impulses.* Sociodramatic play gives children a safer outlet for exploring roles and activities that would not be appropriate for them in real life. Children can pretend to be highly aggressive ("Beware, I'm going to smash down your whole house!"), and they can playact love, marriage, and aspects of sexuality.

■ *Reversal of roles.* Finally, in sociodramatic play children who usually feel helpless can act out more powerful roles, like those of parent, teacher, and superhero. They can turn the tables by disciplining their dolls or playmates ("Bad behavior—now you go to timeout!"), or they can be the ones giving the commands at preschool ("Now it's nap time, children."). This type of play helps children experience the more powerful perspective, and it can help them confront their anxieties about being the smaller and less powerful people in real life.

Of course, children often engage in sociodramatic play for the pure fun of acting out roles with playmates. Sometimes "You be the Mommy and I'll be the baby" is simply fun, and there doesn't have to be any deeper meaning to the play.

The early childhood years are an especially imaginative period of pretend play. The creativity that children show in their sociodramatic play reflects the new symbolic thinking skills they are developing, as we discussed in Chapter 8. As children exercise and explore the limits of symbolic thought, their play becomes ever more imaginative. This imaginativeness, however, will yield to an increasing realism as children move into the next stage of cognitive development.

Cultural Differences in Play

The culture in which children live has a tremendous influence on how much they play, where they play, and the main themes in their play. As an example, consider how different cultures value work and play. Children in the United States and Britain spend most of their after-school time in play, but children in Japan and Korea are more likely to spend time studying for school (Takeuchi, 1994). Japanese and Korean cultures place a high value on hard work, sacrifice, and educational achievement. In Japan, for example, students study hard in hopes of getting into the best universities and professional schools. Among the Hazda people

Young children enjoy pretending to be superheroes and other powerful characters. What are the potential benefits of this type of sociodramatic play?

of Tanzania, children are expected to forage for their own food by age 3; by age 10 they are expected to be productive hunters and gatherers (Lancy, 2002). Hazda children learn to work at a young age, and their parents have very little tolerance for play. In the West African nation of Senegal, children tend to live in communal "compounds" containing numerous households, all related to the eldest male in the compound (Bloch & Adler, 1994). Children play outdoors, roaming the compound in larger groups consisting mostly of siblings and cousins. As in most cultures, gender typing is clear in these children's sociodramatic play. Senegalese girls tend to playact family roles, nurturing younger children and doing domestic chores like cooking and carrying water. Senegalese boys playact farming, herding animals, fishing, and working with machines and automobiles (Bloch & Adler, 1994). Through their play these children learn the skills that are important in their culture.

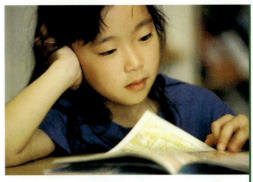

Cultural values regarding work and play have an enormous influence on how children develop. Japanese children, for example, spend much more time studying than do their U.S. counterparts.

Other effects of culture are apparent in the social themes and interactions in children's play. In one cross-cultural study, researchers gave 4-year-olds toy figurines to play with and asked the children to talk aloud and tell a story as they played with the figurines (Farver & Welles-Nystrom, 1997). Children in the United States incorporated significantly more aggressive words, unfriendly characters, and physical aggression in their play than did German, Swedish, or Indonesian children. U.S. children tended to solve the problems in their stories with force and violence. In contrast, Indonesian children's story characters were the most friendly, tended to be the most helpful, and solved problems in peaceful ways. In all four cultures, the children who showed the most aggression in their play were also the most aggressive with their peers in school and were rated by teachers as performing less well in school.

Are these trends reflected in the larger society? Consider the fact that the rate of serious crime (homicide, sex offenses, assault, theft, breaking and entering, and fraud) in the United States is higher than in most other industrialized nations (Farver & Welles-Nystrom, 1997). Children's play in this country reflects our society's attitudes toward aggression. Of course, U.S. society is itself diverse, and attitudes about aggression differ among subcultures. Korean American children, for example, show more cooperation, harmony, and social sensitivity in their play; European American children are more aggressive and antagonistic (Farver, 2000; Farver & Shin, 1997). These cultural values pass from one generation to the next in children's activities as they play.

■ Let's Review . . .

1. During early childhood, the main ingredients that promote friendships are similarity and _____.
   a. intimacy
   b. loyalty
   c. opportunity
   d. generosity

2. Karen and Tasha are both riding tricycles. Although they sometimes ride close together and talk to each other, they are not engaged with each other in any coordinated way. According to Parten's classification of play, Karen and Tasha are engaged in _____.
   a. onlooking
   b. solitary play
   c. associative play
   d. cooperative play

3. Imitating adults, reenacting family relationships, and expressing forbidden impulses are all functions that can be served by _____.
   a. solitary play
   b. gender segregation
   c. gender schemas
   d. sociodramatic play

4. Compared to children in Germany, Sweden, and Indonesia, children in the United States show more _____ in their play.
   a. aggression   b. cooperation
   c. group harmony   d. symbolic pretend

5. **True or False:** According to Freud's psychoanalytic theory, girls and boys avoid playing with each other because their styles of play do not match.

6. **True or False:** According to researchers, play is an activity that is pleasurable, voluntary, and intrinsically motivated.

Answers: 1. c, 2. c, 3. d, 4. a, 5. F, 6. T

Nonparental Child Care

nonparental child care
Care provided for a child by someone other than the child's parents.

Parents, friends, and playmates are obviously important figures in the lives of young children. Today, a great many young children also spend considerable time in **nonparental child care**—care provided by someone other than the child's parents. We close this chapter by looking at different types of child care arrangements, summarizing the research on the effects of nonparental child care, and discussing the issue of quality of care.

As you study this section, ask yourself these questions:

- What effect does nonparental child care have on children's social interactions and cognitive skills?

- What are the components of quality child care?

- What effect does quality of care have on children's developmental outcomes?

Nonparental Care and Its Effects

Figure 9.3 shows changes in child care arrangements for preschool children over the decades. As you can see, the percentage of children in family day care settings (where one provider cares for several children in her home) and in day care centers (facilities caring for larger numbers of children) increased dramatically; meanwhile, the percentage in the care of a parent or other relative decreased. The percentage in day care centers was more than four times higher in 1995 than in 1965. Given that so many children receive nonparental care, what are the effects of this kind of care on children's development?

Getting Along with Others. Simply experiencing nonparental care does not in itself help or harm children's social interaction skills and behavior. An important mediating factor is the quality of the care received. Research has found that higher-quality care is associated with such positive outcomes as greater cooperativeness with other children, more social participation, greater independence, less anxiety, and higher ratings of overall social competence (Andersson, 1992; Clarke-Stewart et al., 1994; Lamb, 1998; NICHD Early Child Care Research Network, 1998, 2002; Peisner-Feinberg et al., 2001; Vandell & Powers, 1983).

Effects on Cognitive Competence. Children who participate from a young age in child care programs specifically designed to improve school readiness, such as Head Start, have consistently shown positive effects on measures of cognitive development and school performance. These children achieve better results than children enrolled in community child care centers or those who are cared for mostly by parents at home

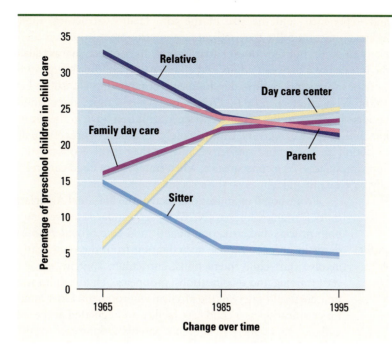

Figure 9.3 • Changes in Child Care Arrangements Since 1965 Arrangements for child care changed significantly over the decades. Since 1965, the number of children in family day care settings increased 1.5 times and the number in day care centers increased more than 400%. (Hofferth, 1996; Smith, 2000.)

(Campbell et al., 2001; Campell et al., 2002; Lamb, 1998). Furthermore, the effects are most pronounced for those children whose mothers are least educated and for children whose parents are more involved in the project. Children from disadvantaged families show cognitive benefits when they receive care from child care centers; children in family day care homes are less likely to show benefits (Loeb, Fuller, et al., 2004).

As with the other outcomes we have considered, the quality of the child care is an important mediating factor (Maccoby & Lewis, 2003; Votruba-Drzal et al., 2004). In Sweden, known for its high-quality child care, children who entered day care early showed higher scores on cognitive measures at ages 8 and 13 than those who entered day care later. Children who spent more time in center-based care and received higher-quality care also had better scores (Broberg et al., 1997; Hwang & Broberg, 1992). In the United States, recent analyses of data from the NICHD Early Child Care study found that the quality of care, especially the degree of language stimulation, had a moderate but consistent effect on children's cognitive and language development scores at 2 and 3 years, even after researchers took into account several family background variables (NICHD Early Child Care Research Network, 2000, 2002, 2003b; Peisner-Feinberg et al., 2001). In general, then, high-quality nonparental care can have positive effects on several aspects of children's cognitive competence, and children who come from more disadvantaged backgrounds show the greatest improvements. Lower-quality care, however, can have negative effects, especially if children would have received high-quality care at home and if children are moved from one provider to another (Lamb, 1998; Tran & Weinraub, 2006).

Child Care Quality

As you noticed throughout this discussion, the *quality* of care affects many of the outcomes of nonparental child care. This effect has become clear in studies from several countries, and quality seems to be especially important when children come from disadvantaged backgrounds (Lamb, 1998). But what is quality in child care? Two components have been identified: *structural quality* and *process quality*. **Structural quality** concerns objective aspects of the child care environment, such as the child–adult ratio (i.e., the number of children cared for by one caregiver), caregivers' formal education

> **Think About Cassandra . . .**
> *Considering the research on child care, what positive and negative effects would we expect to see with Nathan? Given Cassandra's situation, what would you advise?*

structural quality
The quality of objective aspects of the child care environment.

process quality
The quality of the actual experiences children have in child care.

and experience, and the size of the care facility. Structural quality measures are indirect—theoretically, they indicate an environment in which higher-quality care is likely to occur, but they do not guarantee it. In contrast, **process quality** has to do with the interactions between adults and children and children's exposure to materials and activities that support their development (Burchinal et al., 2002; Helburn & Howes, 1996; Wishard et al., 2003). Process quality is a more direct indication of quality, because it relates to the actual experiences children have in the setting, including their interactions with caregivers. Unfortunately, measures of process quality are also harder to obtain and are more subjective, in that they involve observations and ratings of appropriateness. As a consequence, when states adopt child care regulations, they usually base quality guidelines on the structural component.

Professional organizations such as the National Association for the Education of Young Children (NAEYC) set standards addressing many elements of both process and structural quality, and care providers must meet these standards in order to receive accreditation from the organization. The standards involve staff–child interactions, curriculum content, involvement of parents, staff training and qualifications, group size, child–adult ratios, and the appropriateness and safety of the physical environment. Governmental requirements for certification as a child care facility are regulated at the state level, however, and they vary widely. In addition, parents seeking care for their children do not always know which elements experts consider to be important. Or they may

Think About Cassandra . . .

List several specific things Cassandra should look at to determine if her child care center is of good quality. What are the key factors that she should consider in evaluating the quality of Nathan's child care?

TABLE 9.3   Questions to Ask When Seeking Quality Child Care

1. In general, are the children in this setting comfortable, relaxed, and happy? Are they happily involved in play and appropriate activities? Are they enjoying themselves?

2. Do the adults have specialized training in child development and early education?

3. What is the child-to-adult ratio? How many adults are there in all? How many children are there in all?

    NAEYC recommends that all groups have at least two teachers and that group sizes not exceed six to eight for infants, 10 to 14 for 2- to 3-year-olds, and 16 to 20 children for 4- to 5-year-olds."

4. Are the toys, materials, and teachers' expectations different for and appropriate for different ages? Do the caregivers recognize and respect individual differences in the children's abilities, interests, and preferences?

5. Do caregivers address all areas of children's development (e.g., cognitive skills, language skills, social interactions, fine and gross motor skills, emotional expression, self-management of positive and negative emotions, behavior self-management)?

6. Does the staff meet on a regular basis to plan and evaluate the program?

7. Do the activities offer a balance between quiet indoor and more vigorous outdoor play; between individual and small group play; between child-initiated and teacher-directed activities?

8. Is the caregiver flexible? Is she/he willing to adjust the daily activities to meet children's individual needs and interests?

9. Are parents welcome to observe, discuss policies or problems, make suggestions, and participate? Is there open and honest communication between the caregiver/staff and parents?

10. Does the caregiver show respect for all families' cultures, backgrounds, and traditions? Does the caregiver offer information about the child's daily activities?

(Adapted from National Association for the Education of Young Children, 2003.)

Figure 9.4 • Quality of Center-Based Child Care
Ratings of the quality of child care show that, on average, the care provided in centers and family day care homes is most often mediocre. (Helburn & Howes, 1996; Kontos et al., 1995.)

disagree with the experts; or other concerns such as cost, accessibility, and reliability of care may take precedence over quality (Scarr, 1998). If high-quality child care is important to you or someone you know, Table 9.3 presents some questions to keep in mind. Unfortunately, as Figure 9.4 illustrates, the majority of child care arrangements do not appear to be of high quality—or even of good quality.

■ Let's Review . . .

1. Since 1965, which type of nonparental care has shown the largest increase in use?
   a. baby sitters
   b. care by relatives
   c. family day cares
   d. day care centers

2. Research suggests that high-quality nonparental care _____.
   a. can have positive effects on children's social skills
   b. can have positive effects on children's cognitive skills
   c. can have positive effects on children's social and cognitive skills
   d. has no real effect on children's development when other characteristics of the family are factored out

3. Process quality in child care has to do with which of the following items?
   a. objective aspects of the child care setting
   b. the experiences and interactions a child has in the child care setting
   c. those aspects of the child care setting that are regulated by the government
   d. the degree of formal training in child development the caregiver has received

4. **True or False:** Children placed in higher-quality child care arrangements are more co-operative, more independent, and less anxious than other children.

5. **True or False:** An example of structural quality in a day care center is a low child–adult ratio.

Answers: 1. d, 2. c, 3. b, 4. T, 5. T

Thinking Back to Cassandra . . .

Now that you have studied this chapter, you should be able to apply at least a dozen concepts and research findings to Cassandra's situation. Her sons are both learning who they are and how to act in their larger social worlds. Her 3-year-old in particular is developing a me-self, learning what it means to be a boy, and just beginning to learn how to regulate his own behavior around other children. Children at his level of moral development are typically concerned about rewards and punishments, while Cassandra is focusing more on the ethics and fairness of his behavior with other children. Cassandra can learn positive techniques of discipline so she can help both boys learn positive behaviors. Using positive techniques, she will not need to rely so much on yelling and other negative forms of discipline.

At age 5, Jeremy is still playing mostly alone while most children his age are playing in social groups that are more integrated. Opportunity and similarity are important features in forming friendships at this age, so Cassandra might help by making sure Jeremy has opportunities to play and interact with children who are like him. Cassandra might consider Head Start or a similar program for Nathan, or at least evaluate the quality of the day care center she now uses for Nathan. With a high-quality center, Nathan may show benefits in his social and cognitive development.

Using these and other concepts from this chapter, you should be able to offer practical advice for Cassandra as she raises her two young boys. You should also be able to adjust the advice to fit families in other circumstances or other families you know.

■ Chapter Review . . .

What is the "self," and how does it develop in early childhood?

The "self" refers to characteristics, emotions, and beliefs people have about themselves; it includes the I-self and the me-self. Children recognize themselves by the age of 2, and with development their sense of self becomes more abstract, domain-specific, and differentitated, but also more integrated. As a sense of self develops, children become more skilled at self-regulation—controlling and changing their behaviors, thoughts, and emotions to meet the demands of different situations.

What do young children understand about gender—similarities and differences between boys and girls?

Children show gender-stereotyped preferences even before they fully understand their own gender. They prefer sex-typed toys and show high levels of gender segregation in their play by the time they are 3 years old. Gender stereotypes become increasingly rigid until early elementary school. Kohlberg proposed that gender concepts develop from gender identity, to gender stability, and then to gender constancy. Children's gender concepts greatly affect how they think about boys, girls, toys, friends, play, and other aspects of childhood.

What do young children think about moral issues?

Kohlberg proposed six stages of development of moral reasoning. Children's movement through the stages depends on their cognitive development, perspective-taking ability, and experience with moral issues. During early childhood, children's reasoning focuses on the roles of rewards and punishments (Stage 1) and on their own needs or interests (Stage 2).

What are Baumrind's four parenting styles? What outcomes are associated with each?

Parental warmth and control combine to create four parenting styles. *Authoritative* parents are warm and consistent, exert firm control, listen to their children, and use supportive methods of discipline. Their children show the most positive psychological, emotional, and academic outcomes. *Authoritarian* parents exert firm control but show little warmth or respect and use harsh and punitive disciplinary methods. Their children are more aggressive and hostile and do worse in school. *Permissive* parents do not set or enforce limits; they avoid confrontation with their children and do not require their children to behave maturely or responsibly. Their children are impulsive, less self-confident, and do less well in school. *Rejecting/neglecting* parents ignore or actively reject their children; they do not discipline their children, or do so harshly and inconsistently. Their children show the worst psychological, emotional, and academic outcomes.

What are the effects of using spanking for discipline? List some more appropriate discipline methods.

Spanking does not improve children's behavior over the long term, nor does it teach children appropriate behavior. Children who are spanked more often are more physically violent and aggressive, more depressed, and more likely to hit others. Alternative methods of discipline include managing the situation, setting clear rules and limits, praising good behavior, using explanation and reasoning, removing privileges, and using timeouts.

What are the important ingredients in forming friendships in early childhood, and why are young children so reluctant to play with opposite-sex peers?

Opportunity and similarity are important bases for friendships in childhood. The prominent theories for explaining gender segregation involve play compatibility, cognitive schemas, operant conditioning, and psychoanalytic theory. There is concern that boys and girls grow up in different gender cultures, making it more difficult for them to learn to communicate effectively across genders.

How do researchers define "play"? Describe the levels of social play that Parten identified.

Play is defined as a pleasurable activity that is actively engaged in by the child on a voluntary basis, is motivated intrinsically, and contains some nonliteral element. In her classic study Parten (1932) identified six levels of social play: unoccupied behavior; onlooking; and solitary, parallel, associative, and cooperative play.

Describe some of the cultural differences in the play of children around the world.

The opportunity to play and the central themes and styles of play differ across cultures. Some examples: Compared to U.S. and British children, Japanese and Korean children spend more time studying for school and less time playing. Children in Senegal play outside in large compounds where they are watched by any member of their large extended family. Indonesians and Korean Americans tend to be cooperative and socially sensitive in their play, whereas European American children often are more aggressive.

How does nonparental child care affect children's development?

Nonparental child care by itself does not seem to affect children's attachment, behavior, social interactions, or cognitive development. Effects depend on several factors, including the quality of the nonparental care and parent characteristics. High-quality nonparental care can have positive effects on cognitive skills, especially for children from disadvantaged backgrounds.

What is "quality" child care?

Structural quality has to do with objective environmental conditions in which higher-quality care is more likely to occur. Process quality, a more direct measure, relates to the interactions and experiences children have in the care setting. The average quality of child care in the United States is mediocre at best.

■ Key Terms

authoritarian parents (300)
authoritative parents (300)
conscience (295)
convention (296)
discipline (302)
gender constancy (295)
gender cultures (310)
gender segregation (295)
I-self (290)
me-self (290)
moral reasoning (296)
morality (296)
nonparental child care (316)
parental control (299)

parental warmth (298)
permissive parents (300)
perspective taking (296)
play (311)
positive emotion bias (293)
preconventional level (296)
process quality (318)
punishment (302)
rejecting/neglecting parents (301)
self (290)
self-regulation (291)
sociodramatic play (313)
structural quality (317)

mydevelopmentlab
Where human development comes to life!

If you are using MyDevelopmentLab, you have access to an ebook version of this textbook, along with dozens of valuable resources per chapter—including video and audio clips, simulations and activities, self-assessments, practice tests, and other study materials. Here is a sampling of the resources available for this chapter.

Explore
Ages and Stages of Cognitive and Moral Development
Different Gender Stereotypes

Simulate
Kohlberg's Stages of Moral Reasoning
Baumrind's Parenting Styles

Watch
Kohlberg and the Heinz Dilemma
Parenting Styles
Gender vs. Sex

If you did not receive an access code to MyDevelopmentLab with this text and wish to purchase access online, please visit www.mydevelopmentlab.com.

Early Childhood: The Playful Years

Physical Development

During early childhood, children grow 2 to 3 inches and gain about 5 pounds each year. Children need a well-balanced diet to support their growth and can be picky eaters at this age, often preferring a few favorite foods, even as parents encourage healthy eating habits. Malnutrition can have serious effects. By age 3, the brain is losing more synapses than it gains, but it is still growing in other ways. As larger brain areas mature, children's abilities to control emotions, inhibit behaviors, coordinate strategies, and learn language all improve. Children show great strides in muscle strength and coordination as they learn to walk with a mature gait, run, climb, peddle bicycles, and gain fine-motor control of their hands and fingers. Parents and other caregivers can provide them places and opportunities to play and encourage children to exercise and improve their motor skills. Health and safety are major concerns as children in this age group require regular medical care and safe environments in which to live and play.

Cognitive Development

Between the ages of 3 and 6, children's cognitive development equips them with the ability to imagine. This is a playful time when children's imaginations truly develop and their thinking becomes more internalized and fanciful. A scribble can be an ancient dinosaur, the moon can follow them home at night, and they believe the world sees everything from their perspective. Their logic is intuitive and personal, but not yet accurate. Children at this point in their development begin to pick up concepts in the social speech they hear from other people, and these concepts are internalized as they learn to mimic the speech inside their own minds. Children's capacities to process information are improving as they learn to handle more information more efficiently. Basic tasks become more automatic, freeing the mind to take in additional and more complex information. Tremendous gains are made in language development, and, by age 6, most children have a 10,000-word vocabulary and can speak using complex sentences. Some children even learn two or more languages simultaneously at this age. As the end of early childhood nears, children can begin kindergarten and formal schooling. Some children may benefit from Head Start or other early childhood education programs to help prepare them for the school years to come.

Socioemotional Development

During this time period, children begin the task of finding out who they are. They begin to learn "right" from "wrong" and how to regulate their own behaviors. Gender plays an important role in their lives as children learn what it means to be a boy or a girl, and which they prefer to play with—their own! Children benefit most from parenting that is warm but firm. Spanking, hitting, and yelling have negative effects while positive forms of discipline that focus on teaching rather than punishing are more effective. Early childhood is a time when children form friendships with children who are similar to them and with whom they have opportunities to play. Play is an essential activity in early childhood as it allows children to exercise their muscles, exercise their minds, expand their language, and learn to cooperate with other children. After age 6, fantasy and pretend give way to logic and reality. Children are now ready to enter the phase of *Middle Childhood: The School Years*.

Some Developmental Landmarks

7 years
- Average 4 feet tall and 55 pounds
- Logical thinking skills improve
- When reading, recognizes words faster
- Forms an overall opinion of self
- Will help others if it benefits the self
- Friendships are based on common activities

8 years
- Participates in organized sports
- Memory improves
- Better at controlling emotions
- Shows concern for others
- Video games popular

9 years
- Control and coordination of motor skills increases
- Effectively uses organizational strategies to improve memory
- Can identify and correct ambiguities in speech
- Shows increasing interest in riddles and verbal humor
- Increasing concern with gaining approval from others
- Influence of media increases

10 years
- Synaptic pruning results in shrinkage of some brain areas
- Flexibility in boys decreases
- Knowledge increases and becomes more organized
- 40,000-word vocabulary
- Self-evaluations more realistic
- Internet increasingly used

11 years
- Average 5 feet tall and 90 pounds
- Girls are 1½ inches taller and 8 pounds heavier than boys
- Rough play in boys decreases
- Understands social rules
- Reading to learn
- Deep friendships form

part four

Middle Childhood: The School Years

*T**he School Years,*** from ages 7 through 11, bring an amazing array of changes for children. While physical changes are not as obvious as they were during the first 6 years, children's bodies are becoming stronger, more coordinated, and more controlled. Their brains continue to be shaped by the experiences they have, and their thinking becomes more complex and sophisticated. Children in the middle childhood years go from beginning readers to being skilled and fluent; from counting on their fingers to solve math problems to solving complicated word problems; and from being unable to think about abstract concepts to being intrigued by subtle differences and abstract possibilities. These years are often busy ones as children try a variety of new sports, clubs, and musical activities.

Increasing cognitive skills have an important impact on children's emotions and social lives. Children become increasingly interested in how they compare to their peers, and their friendships become more mature, based on internal qualities like loyalty and shared interests instead of who happens to live next door. Children develop more realistic views of themselves and their own capabilities, and they learn many different strategies for learning, managing their behavior and emotions, and for coping with problems. Children make important strides in their physical, cognitive, and socioemotional development, as you will discover in the next three chapters.

chapter 10

Physical Development in Middle Childhood

Clayton just started working at the Parks and Recreation department in a small town near his college. He wants to be a physical education teacher when he finishes school, and this job will give him valuable experience. This morning, Clayton was the referee for a fourth grade soccer game, and he couldn't help comparing them to the first graders he coached last week. The difference between the groups in kicking, throwing, and dribbling the ball was amazing! The 12-year-olds practicing on the field next to him looked even better. But Clayton sees a lot of variation in skills and interest from one child to another, and a couple kids seem like they have trouble focusing and listening to his instructions. His supervisor has talked to him about working with one child who has a developmental delay, but Clayton isn't sure what the developmental delay is and has never worked with a child with exceptional needs before. He worries about the best ways to work with this child, and how he'll accommodate the wide range of skills he's sure to see when he's a PE teacher. He also wonders how he'll deal with some of the parents—some of them seem to be taking the soccer games *way* too seriously! One of Clayton's main goals is to help all the children he works with find some kind of physical activity they like and will stick with as they get older, but he wonders how much to teach and how much to just let the kids have fun running around the field.

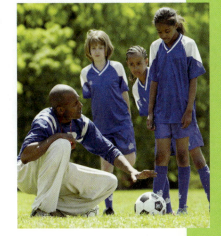

What advice would you give to Clayton as he works with these children over the summer? What can he expect from children in terms of their physical skills and development during the middle childhood years, and what should he do to ensure that they have a good experience? After studying this chapter, you should be able to relate at least a dozen concepts and research findings to Clayton's situation.

As you read this chapter, look for the "Think About Clayton . . ." questions that ask you to consider what you're learning from Clayton's perspective.

During the middle childhood years of ages 7 through 11, the pace of physical growth is not as obvious as during early childhood, but children are making big strides in many ways. The brain continues to change in important ways, and children's physical skills become increasingly controlled and coordinated. Children of these ages are generally quite healthy, but there are some significant threats to their health and safety, and some children begin experiencing more difficulty with disabilities due to the increasing demands of school. Like Clayton, many adults want to help children of this age develop good physical activity habits and protect them from potential problems and abuse. In this chapter, we will discuss typical patterns of body and brain growth during middle childhood, along with typical development of motor skills, the advantages and potential problems with organized sports, and the impact of some of the hazards and challenges children may face.

Growth of the Body and Brain

Children's bodies grow more slowly during the early part of middle childhood, but important changes are taking place. Unfortunately, increasing numbers of children experience problems with being overweight, which can cause immediate and long-term health problems. What are the typical patterns of body and brain growth during middle childhood, and what can be done to foster healthy growth during middle childhood? This section will address these issues.

As you study this section, ask yourself these questions:

- How do the average growth patterns for boys and girls differ during middle childhood?

- Why are more children in the United States becoming overweight? What is the impact of this trend, and what can adults do to help reverse this it?

- What influences brain growth during middle childhood?

Physical Growth

The average 7-year-old child stands about 4 feet tall (49 inches, to be more exact) and weighs about 55 pounds. By the time children reach the age of 11, they will grow another 9 inches and gain 35 pounds. You can look back to Figure 7.1 (in Chapter 7) to see how the average heights and weights change across childhood.

At the age of 9, the average girl is essentially the same size as the average boy. After age 10, however, a sex difference begins to emerge in rates of physical growth. Girls begin their adolescent growth spurt a little earlier than boys. By age 11, girls are 1½ inches taller than boys and about 8 pounds heavier. Boys then begin to grow at a faster rate, and they will be taller and heavier than girls by the age of 14. Of course, we are referring to averages here, and you should keep in mind that about half of all girls begin their growth spurt earlier than average and about half of boys begin later than average. What results is that awkward period of time, between ages 10 and 13, where some of the girls are substantially taller and larger than many of the boys. After that, boys grow faster, and by the end of the adolescent period they will be about 4 inches taller and over 20 pounds heavier than girls, on average. We will have much more to say about puberty and the psychological and emotional effects of early versus late maturation on young adolescents in Chapter 13.

Between the ages of 7 and 11 years, children on average will grow 9 inches in height and gain 35 pounds. What other trends in physical development are typical for this age range?

your perspective

Do you recall a time during childhood when girls were taller and heavier than boys were? What effect did this have on how you felt or behaved? When did this change?

Overweight Children

In Chapter 7 we gave the basic nutritional requirements for children, and we also covered the topic of child malnutrition. In this chapter we will devote our discussion to the opposite nutritional problem—children who are overweight.

In the United States, in contrast to developing nations, the most frequent nutritional problem is being **overweight** (called *obesity* in adults), defined as a body mass index at or above the 95th percentile for the child's age and sex. **Body mass index (BMI)** is an indicator of body fat based on weight and height, so a child with a BMI at or higher than 95 percent of all other children in the United States of the same age and sex is considered overweight. Children with a BMI between the 85th and 95th percentiles are considered at **risk of overweight** (Centers for Disease Control, 2006a). As you can see in Figure 10.1, from the 1960s to 2002 the percentage of U.S. children who were overweight quadrupled from 4 percent to 16 percent. The problem is even worse among adults: A full 65 percent of adults over the age of 20 were overweight during the 1999–2002 test period (National Center for Health Statistics, 2005). During childhood, the problem is especially serious among certain ethnic minorities. For example, in the 6- to 11-year-old age group, 26 percent of Mexican American boys and 23 percent of African American girls are overweight (National Center for Health Statistics, 2005).

Families rely more and more on fast foods and processed foods, and these foods boost children's intake of calories and saturated fat. In addition, children are becoming less physically active. Compared to a few decades ago, children today get less physical activity in school, they are less likely to walk to school, and their favorite hobbies and entertainment are more sedentary activities such as watching television, playing video games, and playing on computers (American Academy of Pediatrics, 2003). Over the years, the lives of both children and adults have become less strenuous. We all seem to be spending more time with electronics and passive forms of leisure entertainment and much less time with physical work and outdoor play than we did in past years. One national survey showed that 26 percent of U.S. children watch four or more hours of television per day, and these children were significantly heavier on average than children

overweight
Having a body mass index at or above the 95th percentile for the child's age and gender.

body mass index (BMI)
An indicator of body fat based on weight and height.

risk of overweight
Having a body mass index from the 85th to the 95th percentile for the child's age and gender.

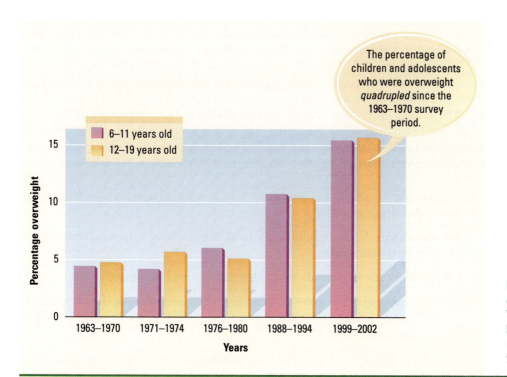

The percentage of children and adolescents who were overweight *quadrupled* since the 1963–1970 survey period.

Figure 10.1 • Percentage of Children and Adolescents Who Were Overweight between 1963 and 2002 (National Center for Health Statistics, 2005.)

An increasing number of children in the United States are overweight. Why is this an increasing trend?

who watched less television (Anderson et al., 1998). About 40 percent of children in lower-income families have TV sets in their bedrooms, and these children watch significantly more TV than other children and more of them are overweight (Dennison et al., 2002). The American Academy of Pediatrics has proclaimed that "we are in the midst of a youth fitness crisis" (1992, p. 1002). And of course, almost two-thirds of adults in the United States are now overweight, so children today have fewer positive role models for health and fitness than in earlier decades.

In childhood, as in adulthood, being overweight is a risk factor for a litany of health problems, including heart disease, diabetes, asthma, sleep apnea, depression, and low self-esteem. The surgeon general has even commented that obesity causes more health problems and preventable deaths than cigarette smoking does (American Academy of Pediatrics, 2003). It is important to help children learn to control their weight at an early age. Forty percent of overweight 4-year-olds will also be obese as adults, and 80 percent of overweight adolescents continue their obesity into adulthood.

A mix of genetic and environmental factors contribute to being overweight. Children are more likely to be overweight when they have a high birth weight, when their mother has diabetes, or when they have other family members who are overweight. When one parent is overweight, the child's risk of being overweight increases three times. When both parents are overweight, the child's risk increases 10 times (American Academy of Pediatrics, 2003). Children living below the poverty line are approximately 25 percent more likely to be overweight compared to other children (National Center for Health Statistics, 2005). Children in poor families tend to eat fewer fruits and vegetables and more foods with higher fat content, and they have fewer safe places to play outdoors and get physical activity (American Academy of Pediatrics, 2003). There is also some concern that parents who are overweight themselves may not worry about their children being overweight. They may see their children as "thick," "solid," or "big-boned" rather than focus on the potential health effects of their children being overweight. They may also think that the child's size is controlled mostly by genetics and an inherited metabolism rather than by diet, exercise, and other factors that they can control (Jain et al., 2001). By examining all of these factors you can see that a child's weight is influenced by a variety of factors including genetics, neighborhood safety, and even parental attitudes.

The number of children who are overweight has increased dramatically in recent years, and being overweight is a serious risk factor for both children and adults. To combat the problem, the American Academy of Pediatrics (2003) has made a number of recommendations for parents and caregivers that include the following:

- Offer nutritious meals and snacks such as fruits and vegetables, low-fat dairy foods, and whole grains.

- Set appropriate limits on children's food choices, and help children learn to monitor their own choices.

- Limit television and other video time to two hours per day.

- Encourage more physical activity in children's play—in their free time at home, in school-based activities, and in sports and fitness programs in the community.

- Be a good role model for healthy eating and exercise (many adults need to lose weight too!).

your perspective

How many of the factors that contribute to being overweight did you experience during childhood? How did you deal with them, and how could the adults in your life have helped?

Think About Clayton . . .

What are some ways in which Clayton could use these suggestions to help his current and future students?

Growth and Maturation of the Brain

By the age of 6, the child's brain is already 90 percent of its adult size (Giedd, 2003). The brain is obviously critical for most all of our functions, and we like to point out that it gets an early "head start" in development! In Chapters 4 and 7, we explained how the brain moves through two phases of growth and maturation: first it overproduces neurons and synapses (*synaptogenesis*), then it prunes back the circuits that are less useful in favor of the ones that are working more efficiently (*synaptic pruning*). The child's experiences will activate some circuits more than others, so experience plays an important role in this survival-of-the-fittest phase of brain development that occurs when the less useful circuits are pruned. We see this growth and shrinkage continue throughout middle childhood and into the adolescent years.

Until approximately age 10, most areas of the cerebral cortex are still growing and gaining mass. Most of this gain is due to growth in the blood vessels that spread through the brain, a gain in the number of glial cells that proliferate throughout the brain and support the function of neurons, and continued myelination of the axons that make up the brain's circuits. Recall from Chapters 4 and 7 that myelination involves the growth of fatty tissues (myelin) that cover the axons that carry nerve impulses from one neuron to other neurons. After myelin grows around an axon, it insulates the nerve impulse and speeds its action down the axon by as much as 100 times (Giedd, 2003). Brain circuits become much more efficient after they become myelinated.

After age 10, we begin to see the brain actually shrink in certain areas. Although it is still gaining glial cells and myelin, the rate of these gains begins to slow, and it is overtaken by a new wave of synaptic pruning. Pruning the less efficient circuits reduces the "noise" in the system, so this shrinkage is actually an important part of the maturation of the brain. As the shrinkage occurs, we see improvements in the child's functions controlled by those areas of the brain. The first areas to prune and mature in this way are the ones that control our basic sensory and motor functions (Gogtay et al., 2004). The occipital lobe on the back of the brain, for example, processes our visual signals, and it is one of the first areas to prune and mature. The motor cortex and sensory cortex also mature early, as does the area in the frontal cortex that controls smell and taste. The next areas to mature are the association areas in the parietal and temporal lobes. These areas integrate information, control language, and begin to perform our more advanced thought processes. Between the ages of 7 and 11, pruning results in a 50 percent loss in the circuits in the brain that control our fine-motor movements. Children at this age are beginning to master specific motor skills, for example by playing particular sports or by practicing musical instruments. It is no coincidence that "[c]oaches and music teachers readily agree that world-class athletes or musicians almost always have been practicing their skill during this developmental stage" (Giedd, 2003, p. 138). The prefrontal cortex is one of the last areas to mature. It is located deep inside the frontal lobes, and it is responsible for abstract reasoning and complex problem solving. This last area doesn't finish its prune-and-mature process until the end of adolescence (Gogtay et al., 2004).

As you consider these developmental phases, keep in mind that brain maturity helps us perform our important mental processes and functions, but mental and physical exercise provide the stimulation needed to prune the less efficient circuits. It's a reciprocal process. Stimulation, education, exercise, and challenge all help the brain mature. In turn, the improved efficiency helps us think, remember, coordinate information, and move with greater skill.

Trauma and other negative experiences can also have an effect on how the brain matures, and researchers are now beginning to find specific examples of how this works (Stien & Kendall, 2004; Teicher, 2002). Adults who have a history of early abuse have abnormal brain-wave patterns in the frontal and temporal lobes of their left cerebral hemispheres. These areas are important for processing language, emotion,

Think About Clayton . . .

How could knowing about brain development help Clayton be a more effective coach and teacher?

and higher cognitive functions. Abnormal brain-wave patterns in the left temporal lobe are often seen in people who are at high risk for suicidal and self-destructive behaviors. Some studies have linked abuse with slow growth in the left hippocampus (an area important for forming new memories), but other studies have shown no link. And some researchers have found that areas in the corpus collosum are smaller in children who have been abused. The corpus collosum is a bundle of fibers that connects the left and right cerebral hemispheres and helps the brain coordinate and integrate information from different areas of the brain. Although we still have a lot to learn about how the brain reacts to physical, sexual, and psychological forms of abuse, we are already getting a picture of how abuse can stunt the growth of important areas in the brain and disrupt the formation of healthy neural circuits. As the research continues, we may discover how disruptions in brain growth contribute to aggression, depression, suicidal behaviors, anxiety, memory losses and distortions, and many of the other unfortunate consequences of childhood abuse. We discussed some forms of abuse in Chapter 7, and we will have much more to say about child sexual abuse later in this chapter.

■ Let's Review . . .

1. Amanda and Samuel are neighbors who have always been similar in height and weight. If their rates of physical growth are typical, which of the following is likely to be true as they move through middle childhood?
    a. Samuel will get taller and heavier than Amanda and remain bigger.
    b. Amanda will get taller and heavier than Samuel and remain bigger until early adulthood.
    c. Amanda will get taller and heavier than Samuel, but Samuel will catch up; they will be equal in size after their mid-teens.
    d. Amanda will get taller and heavier than Samuel, but Samuel will catch up and be bigger by their late teens.

2. Which of the following children is most likely to be overweight?
    a. Amanda, who walks to school and to her friend's house to play every day.
    b. Aaron, who plays video games every day and eats fast food several times a week.
    c. Marnie, whose parents take a 30-minute walk with their children every night after dinner.
    d. Matt, whose parents make sure he eats several servings of fruits and vegetables every day.

3. Which of the following is TRUE regarding the effect of the environment on brain development?
    a. Abusive environments affect a child emotionally, but do not affect the structure of the brain.
    b. The environment helps shape the form and functioning of the brain.
    c. Environmental stimulation is important for forming new neural circuits, but not in pruning circuits.
    d. The specific environment a child is in has little effect on brain development.

4. **True or False:** Children in poor families are more likely to be overweight than children in non-poor families.

5. **True or False:** Brain maturity improves physical and mental skills, but the environment does not affect brain development.

Answers: 1. d, 2. b, 3. b, 4. T, 5. F

Motor Development and Physical Activity

Chapters 4 and 7 introduced you to the many physical changes of the first 6 years of life. The middle childhood years do not show the dramatic degrees of motor development that are found in the early years, but important changes are taking place nonetheless. Children of these ages become increasingly capable of a variety of complex and integrated physical feats. Many children during these years participate in organized sports as one way to be active and have fun while at the same time practicing a variety of physical skills. However, there is increasing concern over the level of children's physical activity. What skills do children develop during middle childhood, and how active are most children? In this section, we will talk about children's motor development, exercise, and participation in organized sports.

As you study this section, ask yourself these questions:

- In what ways do children's motor skills become more controlled and coordinated during middle childhood?

- How much physical activity do children at these ages get? What are some of the reasons they don't get more exercise?

- How can adults help children get more physical activity?

- What are the benefits and concerns of children's participation in organized sports?

Motor Development

Both gross-motor and fine-motor skills across the middle childhood years become more controlled and coordinated. For example, 6-year-old children can catch a ball—if it is relatively large, is not thrown too hard, and is thrown pretty accurately. By the time they are 12, however, most children can catch many different types of balls, easily and effectively adjusting their grasp to accommodate the different sizes. They can control their movements and run toward a pop-up fly ball during a baseball game, judge with reasonably good accuracy where the ball is going to land, coordinate their hands to catch and cover the ball—and at the same time think about which bases have runners and where and how hard they need to throw the ball in

These children have developed the motor control and coordination to do more detailed needlework. What other things will their fine- and gross-motor development enable them to do that they couldn't do when they were younger?

order to get the runners out! You may think of motor skills as being relevant mostly for sports and other physical activities, but they are important in many other areas as well. For example, the vast improvements in writing, artwork, playing musical instruments, and even playing video games are affected by the development of motor skills.

Overall strength improves during middle childhood—children can run faster, jump higher and farther, and throw harder than they used to. Boys tend to have greater strength than girls. Boys also continue to gain strength throughout middle childhood and adolescence, while girls' strength tends to increase until early adolescence and then stabilize. Both boys and girls show improvements in balance, with few consistent differences between genders. Children in this age range are more flexible than older children (i.e., they have a fuller range of motion when moving their arms and legs). Boys' flexibility starts to decrease at about 10 years of age, while girls' begins to decline around age 12. At all ages of middle childhood, girls show greater flexibility than boys (Gallahue & Ozmun, 1995; Keogh & Sugden, 1985).

Children also gradually gain much greater control over their movements during middle childhood. For example, they get better at adjusting their grasp when throwing and catching, and they are more precise when kicking, able to control where the ball will go and how hard they kick it. Increased control is evident in fine-motor skills as well. As students move through elementary school, handwriting improves as their fingers are able to grasp a pencil more delicately and they use their fingers and wrists more effectively, rather than moving the whole arm when they write. Look back at Figure 8.1 and you will notice striking changes in the level of detail and precision in artwork. Greater control over pens, pencils, and paintbrushes allows much better precision as children fill in color and details. And increasing fine-motor control is evident in many of the hobbies that children at these ages enjoy, such as accurately pressing the small buttons on hand-held electronic games, controlling knitting needles and crochet hooks, and producing small, even, neat stitches in needlework.

Finally, one of the most striking developments in both gross- and fine-motor skills during middle childhood is increasing coordination of skills. Spend some time watching 7-year-olds playing baseball, then watch 12-year-olds as they play. The older children are not only better at coordinating their arms and legs as they swing a bat, they are better at anticipating when the ball will arrive and integrating this information with their swings—so that they actually hit the ball much more often! Swimmers learning new strokes are able to coordinate their arm and leg movements to produce a fluid, effective movement through the water. Some of the increased coordination is due to the brain development you read about earlier in this chapter. Increased myelination allows faster transmission of neural impulses, decreased reaction times, and increased likelihood of integrating information. With continued practice, the neurons involved in physical skills are repeatedly activated together. Eventually, these neural pathways grow more synapses and/or the sensitivity of receptors increases, and they begin to fire more efficiently together—another example of the experience-dependent learning that you read about in Chapter 7 (Shonkoff & Phillips, 2000).

Physical Activity and Exercise

As you read in Chapter 7, health officials recommend that children get much more physical activity each day than most currently do (National Association for Sport and Physical Education, 2002). One nationally representative survey of 9- to 13-year-olds found that more than 60 percent of these children had not participated in any organized physical activity (i.e., one with a coach, teacher, or leader) in the week before the survey. While most of these students (77 percent) reported engaging in some sort of physical activity in their free time, the survey does not indicate how much time was spent in the activity (Centers for Disease Control, 2003). Girls reported significantly less free-time physical activity than boys. There were no ethnic group differences in free-time activity, but African American and Hispanic children reported less organized physical activity

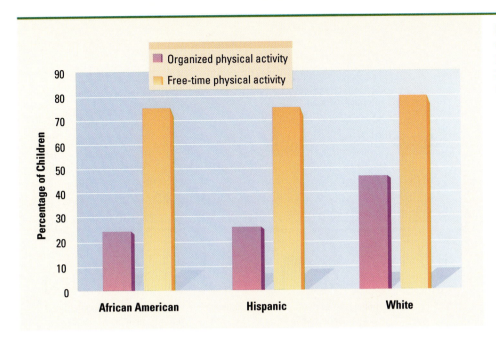

Figure 10.2 • Percentage of Children Participating in Physical Activity, by Ethnicity, 2002 (Centers for Disease Control, 2003.)

than white children, as shown in Figure 10.2. The benefits of regular exercise include physical effects such as weight control, healthy lung function, and cardiovascular health. There are emotional benefits as well; children who get regular exercise tend to feel better about themselves, have higher levels of self-esteem, and report having fewer negative moods (Annesi, 2005; Siegel, 2006; Parfitt & Eston, 2005).

Although most children report getting at least some physical activity, experts are still concerned. Children tend to get progressively less exercise as they move through adolescence, and some surveys indicate that only about 55 percent of 12th graders get regular vigorous exercise. For those children who are already less active, this may signal potentially serious health problems in adolescence and young adulthood. Unfortunately, only 28 percent of schools require daily physical education classes, and fewer than 10 percent of elementary schools provide for daily physical activity at the levels experts recommend (National Association for Sport and Physical Education & American Heart Association, 2006). Rates of physical activity during school recess vary widely, but boys are typically more physically active than girls during recess. Some have suggested that recess times be more structured to ensure that more children are active; others disagree, arguing that children already have too little free choice in their school day (Brinkman et al., 2005; Oliver et al., 2006).

Why don't children get more exercise? Part of the answer involves the increasing amount of time spent in sedentary activities such as watching television and playing video games, but there are other challenges as well. As shown in Figure 10.3 on page 336 the cost of participating in physical activities as well as transportation difficulties are obstacles for many families, particularly for ethnic minority families and those in lower income areas. Lack of opportunities and unsafe neighborhoods also make it more difficult for some children to be physically active (Centers for Disease Control, 2003). Incorporating more physical activity into

Most children report getting some daily physical activity, but experts are still worried. Why?

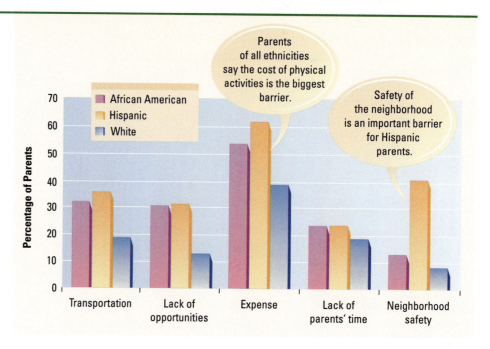

Parents of all ethnicities say the cost of physical activities is the biggest barrier.

Safety of the neighborhood is an important barrier for Hispanic parents.

Think About Clayton . . .

What are some specific things that Clayton could do to help the children he works with become more physically active and stay active?

rough-and-tumble play
Very physical, aggressive but friendly play common among boys during middle childhood.

your perspective

What gender differences in physical activity preferences have you experienced? What do you think caused them?

organized sports
Sporting activities organized, coached, or somehow supervised by adults.

daily activities can also be challenging. For example, many children now live too far away to walk to school, and concerns about traffic keep some of those who live close enough to walk from doing so (Centers for Disease Control, 2005). Not surprisingly, one thing that seems to help children get and stay more active is parental support of physical activity, whether in the form of being active with the child, supporting involvement in organized sports, or ensuring that the child has time to be physically active (Gustafson & Rhodes, 2006).

One consistent finding in the research on physical activity is the existence of gender differences, particularly in the physical activities they prefer. Girls are more likely to choose games that involve fine-motor skills and small groups and that do not emphasize competition. Boys, on the other hand, are more likely to prefer larger groups, competition, and games that require risk taking (Maccoby, 2002). For boys in particular, the amount of **rough-and-tumble play** increases during middle childhood. This type of play is very physical and often involves wrestling, chasing, shoving, and other aggressive behaviors, but it is done in a friendly and nonthreatening way. It likely improves gross-motor skills and may also provide a safe context in which boys can test their strength against peers. Rough-and-tumble play becomes less and less frequent once boys reach adolescence. Physical differences in strength, hormones, and skills account for some of the gender differences in activity preferences, but social and cultural differences are also a major factor. Until recent decades, girls were not encouraged to engage in sports and strenuous physical activities; in many cases, they were actively discouraged. Adults may expect more from boys in physical activities and be more supportive of their interests and skills. We know that being physically active is an important part of a healthy lifestyle, and it is important that *both* girls and boys be encouraged to find and regularly participate in physical activities they enjoy.

Organized Sports

There is no question that more children are participating in **organized sports**—sporting activities organized, coached, or somehow supervised by adults. Millions of children participate yearly in soccer, baseball, softball, basketball, tennis, swimming, golf, karate, dance, football, fencing, hockey—the choices include an almost mind-boggling variety. About 30 million youth participate in some sport each year, and some sources estimate that up to 55 percent of children from age 10 to 18 participate in some sort of organized sports activity outside of school. Although boys still outnumber girls in organized sports, the number of girls has increased significantly (Brady, 2004; Hofferth & Curtin, 2003). This increase in participation rate is good news, particularly in light of the facts we have discussed about rising rates of being overweight and declines in physical activity among children and adolescents. What are the benefits of participating in organized sports, and what are some of the potential problems?

Participation in organized youth sports has a number of potential physical, social, and emotional benefits. Muscle strength, endurance, lung and heart functioning, speed, flexibility, balance, and coordination can all be improved. Eye–hand coordination, visual and auditory perception skills, and body awareness (an awareness of where the body is in space, how it feels to coordinate left and right sides to accomplish a physical task) can also be improved. Of course, not all sports will affect every one of these physical skills, but participation in varied activities increases the likelihood of overall physical impact. Sports participation also offers the opportunity to learn valuable social skills and values, such as teamwork and cooperation, taking turns, coping with failure, understanding the importance of following rules, and good sportsmanship. There can also be emotional and cognitive benefits. For example, sports can offer children a socially acceptable way to handle feelings of frustration or aggression, an appropriate outlet for a child's naturally high energy level, and a way to help children feel good about themselves as they see their skills improve. Studies have found that participation in organized sports is associated with higher achievement test scores and greater success in school, lower rates of delinquency, and decreased likelihood of using tobacco and other drugs. For girls, participation in organized sports is associated with higher levels of self-esteem, lower levels of depression, a more positive body image, and a higher level of psychological well-being. Some of the studies are based on correlations, which makes it difficult to determine whether it is sports participation itself that accounts for the positive relationship. But others have used experimental designs and found that sports activity produces positive outcomes. And helping children establish a habit of regular physical activity encourages more sports activity in early adulthood, so it can help prevent serious future health problems such as obesity, diabetes, and heart disease (DeBate & Thompson, 2005; Fletcher et al., 2003; Hausenblas & Fallon, 2006; Hofferth & Curtin, 2003; Hofferth & Sandberg, 2001; Humphrey, 2003; National Alliance for Youth Sports, 2003; Perkins et al., 2004).

Increasing numbers of children participate in organized sports. What are some of the benefits of playing sports? How is this coach ensuring that her team members have a good experience?

Given the potential benefits, why wouldn't all parents get their children involved in organized sports? We have already mentioned money, time, transportation, and neighborhood safety considerations. Another concern about organized sports is the potential for injury. There are about 3 million sports-related injuries per year, but the rate of injury is higher for youths playing unorganized sports (e.g., a neighborhood pick-up basketball or baseball game) than organized sports. In organized youth sports, football has the highest rate and the most serious injuries. Fortunately, most injuries in organized sports are minor and the rate has decreased in recent years, thanks in part to changes in rules that restrict more aggressive play or risky moves, better safety equipment, and better training of coaches and referees. Many sports injuries are the result of contact with equipment or other players, but others are due to heat-related illness. Getting plenty of fluids is essential for

Experts are concerned about the behavior and attitudes of some adults involved in youth sports. What impact might these parents' behavior have on the children's experience with sports?

athletes of any age, especially during sports practices and events in warmer weather (Committee on Sports Medicine & Fitness, 2000; Hergenroeder, 1998; Radelet et al., 2002).

Another increasing concern about organized sports is the behavior and attitudes of the adults involved. As sports activities become more popular, some parents and coaches put increasing pressure on children to play sports they are not developmentally ready for, play too much, practice too hard, play with an injury, or simply put too much emphasis on the competitive aspects of the sport and winning. Given that 70 percent of the sports programs that children participate in are organized, coached, and run by adults, the impact of these inappropriate behaviors and attitudes can be strong. Seventy-four percent of the 3,000 children surveyed in one study reported that they had seen out-of-control adults at their sports games; 36 percent of these youngsters said that parents who couldn't control themselves appropriately should be banned from the games (National Alliance for Youth Sports, 2003)! Instead of developing their physical skills, feeling better about themselves, and having fun, children exposed to too much pressure and an overemphasis on winning can end up feeling anxious, inept, and disliking the sport altogether. Several national sports organizations now offer guidelines that emphasize positive and safe development of physical, social, and emotional skills rather than competition and winning to organizers, coaches, and parents (National Alliance for Youth Sports, 2001).

Think About Clayton . . .

How can Clayton help minimize the risks and maximize the benefits of organized sports for the children he's working with?

■ Let's Review . . .

1. Which of the following children is MOST typical of motor development by the end of middle childhood?
   a. Josh, who can catch a beach ball thrown directly at him but not a baseball.
   b. Emma, who can easily hit a softball most of the time.
   c. Michael, whose handwriting is made up of large and ill-formed letters.
   d. Jasmin, who is not able to control the direction of the soccer ball when she kicks it.

2. Which statement best summarizes motor development during middle childhood?
   a. Children become more flexible.
   b. Children are faster but cannot effectively control their movements.
   c. Children more effectively control and coordinate their bodies.
   d. Boys and girls show similar improvements in strength, balance, and flexibility.

3. Which of the following is NOT a likely explanation for why children fail to get adequate exercise?
   a. Most children do not like to play organized sports.
   b. Their parents lack time or money to support more physical activity.
   c. Children would rather watch TV and play video games.
   d. Their parents are concerned about neighborhood safety.

Health and Safety Issues

Look back to Table 7.2 in Chapter 7 and you will see that middle childhood is a relatively safe period of time. The vast majority of fatal accidents and illnesses occur during the first year of life and after age 14. Still, a large number of accidents, serious illnesses, and deaths do occur during the intervening years, and many are preventable. Unfortunately, one of the most devastating threats to child health and safety begins to increase during the middle childhood years: sexual abuse. In this section we explore the most serious health and safety issues that children and families face during middle childhood, and we offer concrete suggestions for protecting the health and safety of children of this age.

As you study this section, ask yourself these questions:

- What are the most common threats to health and safety during middle childhood? Why are these threats more common at these ages than at others?

- What are several things that adults can do to help protect children from the most common health and safety problems?

- Who is most at risk for child sexual abuse? Why are they more vulnerable?

- What immediate and long-term effects does sexual abuse have on children?

Childhood Injuries and Safety Issues

In the United States approximately 12 million children under age 12 are treated each year in hospital emergency rooms for injuries (Hunter et al., 2005). The most common causes of injuries treated in emergency rooms include falls, cuts, bicycle accidents, automobile accidents, dog bites, other bites and stings, and overexertion (Centers for Disease Control, 2006b). The most common causes of accidental death during middle childhood are automobile accidents, pedestrian accidents, drowning, fire, burns, and bicycle accidents (National SAFE KIDS Campaign, 2004). During middle childhood, children begin moving beyond the direct supervision of parents and other adults. They spend more time at home unsupervised, and they sometimes fix their own meals or work with household appliances. They ride bicycles, they walk or ride to friends' houses, and many

your perspective

What health and safety risks did you experience in middle childhood? What might have helped reduce these risks for you?

children walk to and from school. As they gain independence, children may still lack the developmental skills they need to stay safe. When crossing a street, for example, children often misjudge the speed and distance of oncoming traffic. They may have trouble seeing over taller bushes and parked cars, just as oncoming drivers may have trouble seeing them. They may not have the cognitive maturity to understand the full extent of many dangers or how to plan ahead to avoid danger. Children can be very active, curious, and even daring at this age, but their immaturity may still lead them to undersestimate the risks involved in many situations.

Adults and other caregivers need to remind children how to stay safe, and they need to minimize the hazards that exist in and around the places where children live and play. Here are several helpful tips:

- **Home Safety.** For U.S. children it is estimated that 40 percent of their accidental deaths and 50 percent of their accident-related injuries occur in or around their homes (National SAFE KIDS Campaign, 2004). There are many things parents and caregivers can do to improve safety at home. Remove or secure dangerous items such as firearms, matches, medicines, and household poisons. Prepare the house for children who will spend more time alone and will explore all through the house looking for interesting things to do. Equip the home with smoke and carbon monoxide detectors, and rehearse a family plan for fire safety. When children are alone at home, make sure that all doors and windows are locked and secure. Teach children about home safety, first aid, and how to keep strangers out of the home.

- **Automobile Safety.** Automobile accidents are the leading cause of accidental death in this age group. Remember that the majority of people who die in traffic accidents are not wearing seat belts. Every time you travel, make sure all children are secured in booster seats or seat belts that are appropriate for their size. Experts recommend that children use a booster seat until they are at least 4 feet and 10 inches tall and weigh at least 80 pounds (Centers for Disease Control, 2002a). Look back to the growth charts in Chapter 7 (Figure 7.1), and you'll see that the average child is not this large until the age of 11. Statistics show, however, that only about 6 percent of children aged 4 to 8 years actually ride in booster seats (Centers for Disease Control, 2002a). We obviously have a lot of room here to improve children's safety. When children transition out of booster seats, the seat belts should fit properly across the child's waist and the shoulder belt should be adjusted so it does not cross the neck. Children should never ride in front seats that have air bags; the rear seat is the safest location in most vehicle crashes. Drive defensively. Never drink and drive: 38 percent of all traffic deaths involve alcohol, and two-thirds of the children who die in alcohol-related crashes were riding with the driver who was drinking (Centers for Disease Control, 2002a).

- **Pedestrian Safety.** Most children under the age of 10 do not understand traffic safety and do not understand traffic signs and signals. Adults need to supervise children when crossing streets until they are sure the children have the skills and the maturity in judgment they need to stay safe. Teach children to stay on sidewalks, cross only at intersections, and watch for cars backing out of driveways. Remind children to never run into the street to chase a ball or for any other reason. When you are driving, always check carefully before backing up, and slow down in neighborhoods and other places where children play (Center for Disease Control, 2002b; National SAFE KIDS Campaign, 2006b).

- **Bicycle Safety.** In the United States, approximately 250,000 children are treated in emergency rooms each year for bicycle injuries (Centers for Disease Control, 2006b). More than 95 percent of all bicyclists killed each year were not wearing helmets (Centers for Disease Control, 2002c). Wearing a helmet can reduce the risks of serious head and brain injuries by as much as 85 percent, but only about one-quarter of children wear helmets. The percentage of teens who wear helmets is nearly zero. Children complain that it is not "cool" to wear helmets, their friends don't wear them, they are too hot and uncomfortable, and they don't believe they will be injured on their bicycles (Centers for Disease Control, 2002c). Parents and other adults can help by being good role models of helmet use and by teaching children the rules of the road for safe bicycling. When you are driving, always share the road with bicycles, and slow down around children. Children do not watch traffic carefully and they can turn or dart into traffic very suddenly. Many also do not have the coordination and skill to control their bicycles and to make sudden stops when danger approaches. Children should never ride in the dark, and they should be encouraged to take advantage of any bicycle safety programs offered in their communities.

Bicycle riding is an excellent way to be physically active. What steps are these children taking to make sure they stay safe?

■ **Water Safety.** Drowning is one of the leading causes of accidental death among children. During middle childhood, children still need to be supervised closely around water. All children should learn proper swimming techniques. But even when they have good swimming skills, remember that children this age may still lack the cognitive maturity to make sound judgments about how far they are from shore, the effect of currents, and the effects of fatigue. Children should always wear proper flotation devices when in boats or playing water sports. Out of all of the people who drown each year, nearly 90 percent were not wearing life jackets or flotation devices (Centers for Disease Control, 2002d). Diving accidents also cause serious injuries. Teach children to never dive head first into shallow water or water that was not first approved as safe for diving.

Many parenting books offer good advice on childhood safety. Table 10.1 shows some of the most common safety tips found in one review of best-selling parenting books.

Pediatricians are doctors who specialize in the treatment of children and adolescents. These doctors are often the major source of information that families have about health and safety issues. Read the Professional Perspective box on page 342 called "Career Focus: Meet a Pediatrician" to learn about one pediatrician's advice regarding health and safety for middle childhood.

Think About Clayton . . .

In your opinion, what are the two most effective things Clayton could do to reduce the risk of accidents and injury to his team members and future students?

TABLE 10.1   The Most Common Safety Tips Offered in Best-Selling Parenting Books*

- Have a working smoke alarm in the home.
- Keep the temperature of the hot water heater to 120°F or lower.
- Never leave a child alone near water; never let children swim alone.
- Keep household products (cleaners, medicines, etc.) out of sight and reach.
- Keep matches and lighters out of sight and reach.
- Do not keep guns in the home. If you do, keep them unloaded and locked.
- Children should always wear helmets when biking and wear reflective gear when biking at night.
- Children should wear protective gear when playing sports.

*Does not include tips for infant safety.
(Hunter et al., 2005.)

Career Focus: Meet a Pediatrician

Harlan R. Gephart, MD, FAAP
Woodinville, WA

What do you see as the biggest health and safety issues for children between the ages of 7 through 11?
One way to answer this question is to look at mortality statistics. The five leading causes of death for 5- to 9-year-olds (in descending order) are unintentional injury, malignant neoplasms (cancerous overgrowth of body cells), congenital anomalies (problems present at birth), homicide, and heart disease. In the 10- to 14-year range, suicide is third, followed by homicide and congenital anomalies. Homicide is sadly a recent newcomer to these lists! Chronic illness in childhood is also a concern. About 15 percent to 18 percent of children have ongoing health conditions that affect their functioning. The most frequent include asthma, recurrent middle ear infections, adolescent depression, ADHD, and developmental disabilities. All these conditions can persist into adulthood and impair the person's ability to be a functional and contributing citizen. Obviously, some conditions also shorten the person's life.

Who is at greatest risk for health and safety problems, and why? What might reduce the risk?
Poorer health status is directly related to general factors such as socioeconomic status and race/ethnicity. Increasing divorce rates and single-parent homes frequently result in lower SES, triggering a cascade of increased infections, inadequate housing, poorer nutrition, more exposure to environmental toxins, less physician contact, and reduced preventive care. There are also more specific situations that increase risk. For example, teenage pregnancies are often associated with lack of prenatal care, birth problems, prematurity, and child abuse and neglect. And there are the risks of each specific medical condition. For example, ADHD is associated with increased school and social failure, substance abuse, and driving accidents if it is not diagnosed and treated early.

These issues are very difficult to address, and experts do not always agree as to the best approaches in each situation. Yet there seems to be universal agreement, supported by data, that *early recognition and intervention* helps improve outcomes. The American Academy of Pediatrics Guidelines for treatment of ADHD, autism, hearing, vision, and many other pediatric issues emphasize this concept and provide screening and intervention tools for pediatricians.

What education and training is needed to become a pediatrician?
The minimal training for certification as a "qualified" pediatrician by the American Board of Pediatrics is a four-year college degree (heavily loaded with science), four years of medical school, then finally three years of specialty training in an approved pediatric residency training program. About 25 percent of pediatricians also obtain three additional years of training in a pediatric subspecialty such as cardiology, neonatology, allergy, etc. A thorough knowledge of child and adolescent development is crucial to a pediatrician—children are not "little adults." Because of the child's growth and development, any medical condition can have a profoundly different effect on a child than on an adult. Students who want a career in pediatrics should prepare for many arduous years of study and preparation, have a sincere love of children, and be motivated by even the small differences the practitioner can make in the daily life of children and families. Having a sense of humor is a real asset, as is an intellectual curiosity that drives one to self-examine one's practice and ask, "how do I know that what I am doing makes any difference" or "how could I do what I'm doing even better." After 42 years of practice I can look back and say it was the best vocation I could have ever chosen!

Q *What can you do to reduce these health and safety risks for the children you interact with? Are there other children's health issues you think are important? If so, what can be done to address them?*

Child Sexual Abuse

As we discussed in Chapter 7, far too many children suffer some form of maltreatment. An estimated 872,000 children were victims of neglect and abuse in 2004, with almost 10 percent of these victims suffering some form of sexual abuse (U.S. Dept. of Health & Human Services, 2006). **Child sexual abuse** involves fondling a child's genitals or breasts, committing intercourse or other sexual acts with a child, exposing the child to indecent acts, or involving the child in pornography. The rate of confirmed cases of child sexual abuse has declined dramatically since the early 1990s, but it isn't clear how much of this drop is due to a decrease in the actual number of sexual abuse cases and how much is due to other factors such as changes in reporting and investigation procedures. Nevertheless, before they grow up, about one in every five girls and one in every nine boys in the United States will experience some form of sexual abuse. Unfortunately, the majority of child sexual abuse victims never report their abuse (Berliner & Elliot, 2002; Finkelhor & Jones, 2004; Mash & Wolfe, 2005).

Who's at Risk? Child sexual abuse occurs in all ethnic, geographic, and economic groups. Sadly, children who are sexually abused are likely to experience other forms of maltreatment as well. Unlike most other forms of child maltreatment, child sexual abuse is more common in middle childhood and adolescence than in infancy and early childhood. This type of abuse is more likely to be committed by someone that the child knows, often a person with whom they have an ongoing relationship. Many people believe that only men commit child sexual abuse, but this is not true. In one study of adults who had suffered child sexual abuse, nearly 40 percent of the male and 6 percent of the female victims reported that their abuser was female (Dube et al., 2005). On average, sexual abuse continues for four years, and girls are four times more likely than boys to be sexually abused. Adolescents are the perpetrators in half the cases (Flinn, 1995; U.S. Department of Health and Human Services, 2001, 2006; Wekerle & Wolfe, 2003). Other risk factors include:

- *A poor family environment.* The risk for child sexual abuse is higher when the relationships between family members are not appropriate or supportive, there is no healthy emotional attachment between family members, parents are absent or otherwise not available, there is a higher rate of conflict or domestic violence, and/or the child does not live with either biological parent.

- *Marital disruptions.* Child sexual abuse is more likely in separated or divorced families and/or when there is a stepparent in the home.

- *Individual factors.* Children with few friends who are socially isolated are at higher risk for sexual abuse, as well as children who are physically attractive or who have gone through puberty earlier than peers. Gay and lesbian teens are also more likely to be victims of sexual abuse (Berliner & Elliot, 2002; Mullen & Fleming, 1998; Richardson et al., 1993; Savin-Williams, 1994).

Children who are sexually abused vary in the symptoms they exhibit, but some common signs of sexual abuse are shown in Table 10.2 on page 344.

Abusing families tend to isolate themselves from friends and community, keeping the abuse private. They may move frequently, changing the children's schools and networks of friends. Family conflict and family dysfunction are common, so children may witness other acts of violence or abuse in addition to the maltreatment directed at them. Their homes may be overcrowded, and life may be chaotic and unpredictable. Although most abusers do not have officially diagnosed mental disorders, some do. Often, too, the families live in poverty. By interacting with all of these factors, child abuse and neglect can exact a considerable price.

What Are the Effects of Child Sexual Abuse? As with other forms of abuse, the effects of sexual abuse depend on the frequency of the abuse and the length of time over which it

child sexual abuse
Abuse that includes fondling a child's genitals or breasts, committing intercourse or other sexual acts with a child, exposing the child to indecent acts, or involving the child in pornography.

TABLE 10.2   Signs That May Indicate Child Sexual Abuse

The child:

- has difficulty walking or sitting
- suddenly refuses to change for gym
- suddenly refuses to participate in physical activities
- reports nightmares or bedwetting
- shows symptoms that may indicate anxiety like chronic headaches or stomach pain
- shows a sudden change in appetite
- shows bizarre, seductive, sophisticated, or unusual sexual knowledge or behavior
- shows concern that there is something wrong with their genitals
- has redness, rashes, complains of swelling of the genital areas; contracts urinary tract infections
- begins showing behavioral problems, anger, rebellion, or aggressiveness
- becomes pregnant or contracts an STD, especially at an age younger than 14
- runs away
- reports abuse by a parent or other caregiver
- becomes depressed, withdrawn, and/or distrustful of adults; shows suicidal behavior
- shows behavior that is "too perfect"

Please note that some children show no clear signs at all!

The parent or caregiver:

- is overly protective of the child
- severely limits the child's contact with other children, especially those of the opposite sex
- is secretive and isolated
- is jealous or controlling with family members

(Adapted from National Clearinghouse on Child Abuse and Neglect, 2006; American Academy of Child & Adolescent Psychiatry, 2004; Darkness to Light, 2006.)

cortisol
A hormone released in response to stress.

This child has experienced sexual abuse, which can affect her physical, social, and emotional development. What signs might adults look for as indications of abuse?

occurs. In one study of randomly selected cases, more than half of female victims reported more than 50 incidents of abuse. The average number of incidents for the whole sample was 143, and the average age for the first abuse incident was 7 years old (Nash et al., 1993). With child sexual abuse, the outcomes are more negative when the abuse begins at an earlier age, the episodes are frequent, physical force is involved, sexual penetration occurs, and the abuser is a close relative such as a father or stepfather (Nash et al., 1993; Stien & Kendall, 2004; Wekerle & Wolfe, 1996). Outcomes are less severe when there is a relatively stable two-parent household and the abused child has a warm and supportive relationship with the mother. When mothers show anger, jealousy, or indifference, these responses compound the negative outcomes.

Some researchers have looked at the impact of trauma such as sexual abuse on brain functioning and structure (Shonkoff & Phillips, 2000; Stien & Kendall, 2004). Continued abuse wreaks havoc on the body in many ways and creates a state of chronic stress that results in abnormally high levels of stress hormones such as **cortisol**. Through a complex chain of reactions, chronic high levels of cortisol "eat away at the neural networks in the brain," damaging parts of the brain involved in memory processing and storage such as the hippocampus (Stien & Kendall, 2004, pg. 105). Cortisol may also damage the prefrontal cortex and cerebellum, both of which are important in behavioral and emotion regulation. It also stimulates **sensitization** in the areas of the brain involved in processing fear stimuli. This means that a tendency develops to overreact—strongly and quickly—to fearful situations even when they are relatively mild. Maltreatment is associated with a smaller corpus callosum, the part of the brain that connects the two hemispheres and aids in higher-order thinking and processing of emotions. Finally, sexual abuse has been linked to poorer functioning of the immune system. It isn't possible to conduct experimental studies with humans to study the effects of sexual abuse on the brain, but at least some of these effects are correlated with the severity and duration of abuse (Shonkoff & Phillips, 2000).

sensitization
The development of a tendency to overreact strongly and quickly to fearful situations even when they are relatively mild.

Depression is the symptom most often reported in children and adolescents following sexual abuse. In some studies, two-thirds of female victims showed depression and 42 percent showed evidence of suicidal thoughts in the aftermath of their abuse (Kendler et al., 2004; Koverola et al., 1993; Wozencraft et al., 1991). Another troubling symptom often seen in abused children is an increase in sexual behavior. A study of sexually abused preschoolers found that they engaged in more sexual kissing and used sexual words more often than their peers (Friedrich, 1993). And child sexual abuse correlates with increased sexual activity during adolescence as well as with teenage pregnancy and prostitution (Wekerle & Wolfe, 1996). Drug and alcohol abuse is more likely, with female victims about three times more likely to abuse drugs than non-victims (Kendler et al., 2000). About half of abused children show signs of post-traumatic stress disorder, and victims are at increased risk for a number of other problems such as feelings of guilt and shame, anxiety, low self-esteem, eating disorders, and running away from home. As adults, these individuals face an increased risk of continuing problems with intimate relationships and sexuality, particularly if the abuse involved penetration (Dube et al., 2005; Mullen & Fleming, 1998). Some studies have also found a relationship between child sexual abuse and lower levels of income during adulthood, perhaps because of continued problems in self-esteem and social interactions (Mullen & Fleming, 1998). However, compared to children who have been neglected or physically abused, sexually abused children show better school performance.

your perspective
Does it surprise you to learn about the effects of trauma and abuse on the brain? How does this information affect how you think about the behavior of those who have been abused?

Despite these negative effects of sexual abuse, children and adolescents who have suffered this type of abuse can survive and learn to cope. Removal from the abusive situation is a critical first step, because all the negative outcomes are worse the longer the abuse continues. Establishing a positive and healthy relationship with caring, trusted, and appropriate adults is important, as is receiving therapy as soon as possible from a professional who is skilled in working with victims of child sexual abuse. The Personal Perspective box on page 346 called "Surviving Child Sexual Abuse: One Survivor's Story" gives a moving firsthand account of child sexual abuse and one person's ongoing efforts to cope. We warn you that this is not an easy story to read; it was even more difficult for the person to tell. The survivor in our interview wanted others to know that there is help for those who have been sexually abused, and that courses like the one you're taking now helped her learn about appropriate parenting and positive family relationships; things she never had while growing up. With knowledge and therapy, victims can become survivors—good parents and partners who can break the cycle of abuse. Those of you who have had experiences similar to those described in the interview may find that reading this account makes you feel uncomfortable and unsettled. If so, we urge you to talk to your college or university counseling center, your instructor, or a local social services agency for help. You can also contact a national sexual abuse hotline such as *Darkness to Light* (1-800-FOR LIGHT; www.darkness2light.org), or the *National Child Abuse Hotline* (1-800-4ACHILD) for help and information.

Think About Clayton . . .
What should Clayton watch for that may indicate sexual abuse of his team members or students? What should he do if he notices these things, and how can he decide if he should do something?

Surviving Child Sexual Abuse:
One Survivor's Story

Dawn

A small town in the Midwest

Dawn is a survivor. She endured years of horrific treatment at the hands of people who should have protected her. But her main message is one of hope. She wants those who have been abused to know that help is available to stop the abuse and cope with the physical and emotional scars that remain. It is ongoing and difficult work, but it is possible. Here is her story.

My earliest memories of abuse are of my alcoholic father beating my mother and me. I even remember him beating my infant brother because he was crying—I was about 4 years old. My parents divorced, and my stepfather began immediately grooming our family for many, many years of severe sexual abuse. He would play seemingly innocent games with me, always physical, which happened mostly when my mother was at work. The games quickly led to rape a few times every week. My stepfather was violent and beat us, so I took seriously his threats to hurt us if I told. In third grade I stayed with my aunt in another state for a while. My teenage cousin, who had many behavior problems, babysat every day while my aunt worked. He soon began raping me, causing great pain and kidney infections. I wet the bed almost every night, which my aunt and uncle regularly embarrassed me about. Finally when I was 13, I told my mother about the abuse. She cursed at me and told me to leave, even after my stepfather admitted his guilt. From then on, I stayed with friends or slept outside. I married soon after I turned 18.

Why didn't anyone help? My mother could be quite violent when she was angry, so maybe she saw my stepfather's violence as acceptable. We lived in a very small town where it was just not acceptable to make waves, and the issue of abuse was only beginning to become public. I once told my best friend's mother and she became irate, accusing me of horrific lies—so I never mentioned it again. And my stepfather was respected in the community. He was from the largest family in town, taught Sunday school, and was a Boy Scout leader.

The effects of sexual abuse are pervasive. A person does not just "get over it," as has been suggested to me many times. It seeps into every part of a person's soul, mutating every cell and thought until there is nothing resembling normalcy, but this may not be evident from the outside. As an adult, I've been diagnosed with Major Depressive Disorder, Obsessive/Compulsive Disorder, Post-Traumatic Stress Disorder, and Generalized Anxiety Disorder. These are all linked to the abuse in my past, as are my lifelong eating disorders and weight-related problems. I have many issues when it comes to relationships, especially with trusting others. But the most precious thing that was ripped away from me was my true identity. I don't know the things I liked or disliked as a child, what my favorite colors were, or if I had favorite cartoon characters. I am 37 years old today and still attempting, on a daily basis, to learn who I am. Abuse strips away your identity and leaves only feelings of worthlessness, self-doubt, guilt, and shame.

In order to move on in life, it is important to seek professional help. I have been going to therapy for many, many years. I know I will need therapy on-and-off for life. I also use meditation, as well as reading just about everything I can about abuse. The biggest gift I have given myself, though, is continuing to learn who I am.

Adults need to know that if they were abused as children, there is no need to continue this terrible cycle. There are thousands of great books on parenting available, and classes are offered in almost every community. The cycle of abuse will not stop by itself; it takes conscious effort and much hard work, but it can be done. I feel it is important to speak out loudly about what happened to me as a child with the hope that more victims will do the same, so that people will become more aware of the extent of the effects of the abuse many children suffer. It is through awareness that we can work together to help stop the victimization of more innocent children.

Q *What could teachers, relatives, neighbors, and other adults in Dawn's life have done to prevent her suffering? What signs of abuse could they have looked for?*

■ Let's Review...

1. Aman is a 10-year-old boy who is being treated for an accident. Given his age, which of the following is most likely the cause of his accident?
   - a. accidental shooting
   - b. accidental poisoning
   - c. lawnmower accident
   - d. car accident

2. Which of the following is MOST important in keeping children safe when riding a bicycle?
   - a. Making sure children ride only on specially constructed bike paths.
   - b. Making sure children always wear a properly fitted bicycle helmet.
   - c. Making sure that children's bikes have nighttime lights that work properly.
   - d. Making sure that children never ride their bikes alone.

3. Which of the following children is at highest risk for child sexual abuse?
   - a. Nash, a boy whose family gets along well but is poor and moves a lot
   - b. Tony, a boy whose parents are divorced and who lives with his mother
   - c. Amanda, a girl who lives in foster care and has no real friends
   - d. Julie, a girl who fights with her mom a lot and spends a lot of time instant messaging with her friends

4. Which symptom is most frequently reported among children and adolescents who have suffered sexual abuse?
   - a. depression
   - b. anxiety disorders
   - c. conduct problems
   - d. sexual promiscuity

5. **True or False:** The most common cause of death during middle childhood is bicycle accidents.

6. **True or False:** Child sexual abuse can have an effect on the physical structure and functioning of the brain.

Answers: 1. d, 2. b, 3. c, 4. a, 5. F, 6. T

Children with Exceptional Needs

One out of every five children suffers from a mental illness or other serious developmental, emotional, or behavioral problem (Mash & Wolfe, 2005). **Children with exceptional needs** require extra help beyond what is needed by peers. Exceptional needs may be due to medical, physical, emotional, or developmental difficulties. Sometimes the needs interfere with learning because of cognitive difficulties, but other times the difficulties are caused by behavioral problems, physical disabilities, or absences from school because of medical conditions or the need for medical treatment. Because children with exceptional needs are included in regular classrooms, it is important that teachers understand a wide variety of problems and know how to effectively work with each child. And given the nature of their work, social workers, physicians, and nurses will encounter an even greater percentage of children who have serious problems. In this section, we will discuss the general approach that experts today use in thinking about problems or conditions that arise during childhood. Though there are many difficulties that children may experience, we will cover only a few in this chapter, including attention deficit/hyperactivity disorder, communication and learning disorders, and autism spectrum disorders. Others (such as conduct disorder, oppositional defiant disorder, depression, and eating disorders) will be discussed in Chapters 12 and 13.

children with exceptional needs
Children who require help beyond what is needed by peers.

As you study this section, ask yourself these questions:

■ What is the *developmental psychopathology perspective*? How does it help us better understand disorders of childhood and adolescence?

■ What is attention deficit/hyperactivity disorder (ADHD), and what are the subtypes of this disorder? What do researchers know about the causes of ADHD? Are drugs such as Ritalin effective in treating ADHD?

■ What are the different types of communication and learning disorders? What roles do abnormalities in brain functions play in these disorders?

■ What do researchers understand about autism spectrum disorders, and what treatment approaches exist for these conditions?

■ What is IDEA, and how has it affected the education of children with exceptional needs?

What Is Developmental Psychopathology?

Before we discuss specific conditions, it is important to understand that we rarely can identify the exact cause of any disorder in a particular child. In almost every case multiple causes or multiple conditions contribute to the problem. Today, most experts look at childhood problems from the **developmental psychopathology perspective** (Rutter & Sroufe, 2000). This view emphasizes the wide variety of factors that influence both typical and atypical paths of development. Among these factors are genetics, the interactions children have with their parents and family, the quality of their education, their peers, and many other elements in their social and cultural environments. The developmental outcome of any particular child is determined by the *transactions* that occur among all of these factors. A child with a genetic predisposition for depression, for example, could develop major depression, have minor symptoms, or possibly experience no symptoms at all, depending on interactions with his or her environment. Children with no genetic predispositions can still develop major depression if they suffer severe trauma or abuse. And some children who have the odds stacked against them still manage to escape without serious problems. The point is that for any particular child we cannot determine one single cause of mental illness or other problems. Still, we can report the general tendencies that researchers have discovered—the factors that may contribute to each type of problem or disorder, and the effects or developmental outcomes that typically result.

It's also important to understand that measuring how often a condition occurs can be difficult at times. **Prevalence rates** refer to the percentages or numbers of children who show the various problems or conditions. For each condition we discuss, we give the experts' best estimates. There are no hard numbers on prevalence rates, however, because a great many children with serious problems are not diagnosed or treated. Adults often think that a child will "outgrow" a problem, or they simply fail to recognize the child's problem because many children can't communicate their feelings effectively. Often, a child's problems can go unrecognized until the child begins to fail or have problems with peers in school.

Another important point is that you can't just add up the various prevalence rates to determine how many children are affected by the total of all of these problems. A high percentage of children with disorders have more than one disorder at once—a situation referred to as **comorbidity.** For example, about 40 percent of those with attention deficit/hyperactivity disorder also have another disorder; about 30 percent have both ADHD and a learning disability (Barkley, 2003; Faraone et al., 2001). And as you learned earlier in this chapter and in Chapter 7, children who suffer from mental illnesses are also more likely to experience abuse or neglect. The

---

developmental psychopathology perspective
The view that a wide variety of factors influences both normal and abnormal paths of development.

prevalence rates
Refers to the percentages or numbers of individuals who show particular problems or conditions.

comorbidity
Situation in which an individual has more than one psychological disorder or problem at the same time.

Think About Clayton . . .
How might an understanding of developmental psychopathology and comorbidity help Clayton be a more effective coach and teacher?

sad fact is that childhood problems and disorders tend to cluster or co-occur in individual children.

Attention Deficit/Hyperactivity Disorder

As a preschooler Tim was always on the go. Whether he was climbing and jumping on the furniture, rocking in his chair, running through the house, banging his toys, or talking constantly and loudly, it seemed that his motor was always running at high speed. When he started kindergarten, he was always interrupting other children, had a hard time waiting in line, and was too restless to sit for very long. Although his parents and teachers marveled at his energy and enthusiasm, they were exhausted trying to help him sit still, pay attention, and wait for his turn at home and school.

Most children prefer to be on the go, and they would rather learn by moving and doing than by sitting and listening quietly. But when their restlessness and high level of activity far exceed the norm for their age, then they are showing signs of **attention deficit/hyperactivity disorder (ADHD)**. Children with ADHD are unable to sustain attention, excessively active, and deficient in impulse control to a degree that is unusual for their developmental levels (Barkley, 2003). The signs of ADHD emerge early, usually before the age of 7, and they persist throughout childhood and often into adolescence and adulthood. Most children with ADHD show two phases with the disorder (Barkley, 2003).

> ■ First, parents and caregivers notice signs of hyperactivity, usually by the time the child is 3 or 4 years of age. Tim, for example, was showing the classic signs of hyperactivity.

> ■ Second, between the ages of 5 and 7, children with ADHD begin showing signs of inattentiveness. This side of the disorder usually becomes apparent when children begin formal schooling. They have a hard time finishing assignments, staying on task, and following rules and instructions. They can't concentrate; they seem to daydream; and they are disorganized, forgetful, and easily distracted.

As you can imagine, this combination of inattentiveness and hyperactivity can be challenging. As children grow into middle childhood, the hyperactive symptoms tend to decrease, but the attention problems remain. And adolescents who show more extreme levels of ADHD symptoms report having more negative moods and feeling less alert than those with lower levels of symptoms. They are also more likely to use tobacco and alcohol (Whalen et al., 2002). Currently, clinicians recognize four types of ADHD.

1. *ADHD—predominantly inattentive*
2. *ADHD—predominantly hyperactive–impulsive*
3. *ADHD—combined*
4. *ADHD—not otherwise specified* (American Psychiatric Association, 2000).

Although parents and teachers describe as many as one-half of all children as "hyperactive," only 4 percent to 6 percent of children actually meet the clinical criteria for some type of ADHD. Further, ADHD rates are three times higher among boys than girls. About 85 percent of children with ADHD show either type 2 or type 3: primarily hyperactive–impulsive or hyperactivity combined with inattentiveness (Barkley, 2003; Biederman et al., 2002).

The causes of ADHD are not known, but most of the research points to a genetic component and problems with areas in the frontal lobes of the brain that are responsible for attention, organization, and the inhibition and control of behavior. Researchers estimate that the heritability of ADHD is as high as .80 (Barkley, 2003; Levy et al., 2006). Identical twins share more ADHD symptoms than nonidentical twins, and children and their biological parents share more symptoms than adoptive families. Although genetics

attention deficit/hyperactivity disorder (ADHD)
A condition involving inablity to sustain attention, excessive activity, and deficiencies in impulse control that are unusual for the child's developmental level.

Stimulant medications are the most effective treatment for most cases of ADHD. Only 4 percent to 6 percent of children meet the clinical criteria for ADHD, and there are fears that many children are misdiagnosed and treated unnecessarily.

seems to play the larger role, research indicates that ADHD rates are slightly higher among children exposed to lead and among those exposed to alcohol and tobacco smoke during prenatal development. ADHD is somewhat more common in lower socioeconomic groups, but it exists at every socioeconomic level and in every country researchers have studied (Barkley, 2003; Linnet et al., 2003).

Family conflict is common when a child has ADHD. Children with ADHD are more talkative, defiant, and demanding than children without the disorder, and their parents (especially mothers) tend to be more negative and less rewarding (Barkley, 2003). Fathers seem to have less trouble with their ADHD children, perhaps because they spend less time with the children or because they tend to play in a rough-and-tumble style more suitable for highly active children. Parents with ADHD children tend to have more marital conflict; their separation and divorce rates are higher; they tend to consume more alcohol; and mothers are more likely to be depressed (Barkley, 2003). It is not clear whether these family problems are more a cause of ADHD or the result of the stress of dealing with difficult children with ADHD, but the evidence seems to suggest more of the latter.

In addition to family problems, children with ADHD have great difficulty in school. By the time they are adolescents, about 40 percent of children with ADHD have received some form of special education. One-quarter of students with ADHD get expelled from school, 35 percent are retained at least one grade level, and up to 30 percent drop out of school (Barkley, 1996). The majority do not go on to college (Barkley, 1998). Although there is little research on ADHD in adulthood, clinicians believe that nearly half of all children with ADHD carry the symptoms into their adult years—and experience significant problems in their work and social relations as a result.

There is no cure for ADHD, but there are effective treatments. Ironically, the most frequently used and effective treatment seems to consist of stimulant medications. The stimulants Ritalin, Dexedrine, and Cylert activate areas in the brain that relate to the inhibition and self-regulation of behavior. Although one-quarter of children with ADHD do not respond to stimulant medication, the remaining three-quarters often show significant improvements in concentration, motor control, cooperation, and the ability to stay on task (Barkley, 1998; Bedard et al., 2003; Rubia et al., 2003). A new stimulant called Adderall also shows promise in treating ADHD. In some cases antidepressant medications also have been effective. There are risks associated with some of these medications, however, including increased suicidal thoughts or actions, cardiac problems, slowed growth, liver problems, and addiction (Food and Drug Administration, 2005a, 2005b).

Behavior management programs can be helpful to children with ADHD. These programs train parents and teachers to reward children when they cooperate and stay on task and to remove privileges or give timeouts for disruptive behaviors. Behavior management programs work best when parents and teachers apply them consistently in both home and school settings and combine them with medications such as stimulants (Barkley, 1998; Owens et al., 2003).

Communication and Learning Disorders

Pretend that you are a child in a second-grade classroom. You have an above-average IQ, and you are motivated to learn. When you try to read printed text, however, you can't make sense out of the words and sentences. The print says, "Pam saw the dog play," but you invert the *m* in "Pam" into a *w*, you reverse the letters in "saw" to read "was," and you leave out the *l* in "play." To you, the sentence reads, "Paw was the dog pay." What sense does that make? After struggling day after day, you begin to give up. While other children are reading their books, you just sit and look around. And because so much of the information and instruction given in school involves reading, you are falling behind in most of your subjects. The teacher thinks you have an attention deficit, your classmates call you "names," and your parents wonder if you are just not trying. Inside, you know they are all wrong, but you can't figure out why you are having so much trouble. Actually, you are showing signs of a reading disorder—but it may be a long time before you get an official diagnosis and any real help with your difficulties in school.

Unless you have experienced a communication or learning disorder yourself, it is hard to imagine the frustrations that children with these problems feel every day in school. They are just as smart as other children are and can learn just as fast as other children, but in some specific area they have significant difficulty with language or learning. They fall behind in school, they may feel rejected by their classmates, and their self-esteem plummets. Many withdraw, show signs of depression or anxiety, or act out in school. Among adolescents with learning disorders, the high school dropout rate is about 40 percent (American Psychiatric Association, 2000).

Table 10.3 on page 352 describes the main communication and learning disorders. In **communication disorders** children have significant difficulty producing speech sounds, using spoken language to communicate, or understanding what other people say (Mash & Wolfe, 2005). **Learning disorders** (often referred to as *learning disabilities*) involve difficulties with specific skills such as reading, mathematics, or writing. With both types of disorders, children tend to have average to above-average intelligence. They should be capable of learning quickly in school, but their disorder slows them down and disrupts their performance. Communication and learning disorders are also highly connected.

Communication and learning disorders are sometimes thought of as "hidden" problems of childhood—they too often go undiagnosed and untreated. About 5 percent of U.S. students receive official diagnoses of learning disorders, but educators estimate that at least 20 percent of children suffer from reading disorders alone (Mash & Wolfe, 2005; Shaywitz et al., 1992). Children with communication and learning disorders already receive half of all of the special education services provided in schools, and even more children could obviously benefit from these programs.

Communication and learning disorders are strongly genetic and related to abnormalities in how the brain functions. When a parent has a communication disorder, about half of that person's children also have communication disorders. Children with phonological disorder (see Table 10.3) show less than normal activation in the left temporal region of their brains, a region

communication disorders
Conditions in which children have significant difficulty producing speech sounds, using spoken language to communicate, or understanding what other people say.

learning disorders
Conditions involving difficulties with specific skills such as reading, mathematics, or writing.

Think About Clayton . . .

How can teachers like Clayton tell the difference between a child with a learning or communication disorder, ASDs, or ADHD? What adjustments should teachers make for these different types of problems?

  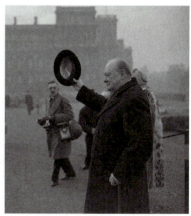

Well-known people such as Albert Einstein, Thomas Edison, and Winston Churchill managed high levels of success even though they were known to have or were suspected of having learning disorders (Mash & Wolfe, 1999).

TABLE 10.3 Communication and Learning Disorders

CATEGORIES OF DISORDERS	SYMPTOMS AND BEHAVIORS
Communication Disorders	
Phonological Disorder	Problems with the articulation or production of language sounds. Most frequent problems involve the *l, r, s, z,* and *th* sounds (e.g., saying "cwy" instead of "cry"). Problems persist beyond what is developmentally normal and interfere with school and social activities. About 10% of preschoolers show mild phonological problems. By age 7 years, 2% to 3% have a phonological disorder.
Expressive Language Disorder	Problems using words to communicate thoughts, desires, and feelings. Expression lags significantly behind the child's ability to understand language (receptive language). Speech usually begins late and progresses slowly. Limited vocabulary, short sentences, and simple grammatical structures characterize speech. Affects 2% to 3% of children.
Mixed Receptive-Expressive Language Disorder	Problems in expressive language combined with difficulty understanding language. Trouble making sense out of sounds, words, and sentences. Found in fewer than 3% of children.
Stuttering	Repeating or prolonging speech sounds (e.g., "g-g-g-g-g-go" or "Mo-ah-ah-ah-ah-mmy"). Child struggles to finish or continue sounds and words; may develop ways to avoid or compensate for problem sounds. Stuttering usually has a gradual onset between ages 2 and 7. Affects 1% of children; three times as many males as females. Usually self-correcting; 80% of children who stutter at age 5 no longer stutter by first grade.
Learning Disorders	
Reading Disorder	Reading ability substantially below the level expected given the child's age, intelligence, and education. Trouble recognizing basic words; common errors include letter reversals (b/d; p/q), transpositions (top/pot), letter inversions (m/w; u/n), and omissions (reading *place* instead of *palace*). Trouble decoding (separating the sounds in words). Difficulties with reading comprehension, spelling, and writing. Up to 20% of schoolchildren have significant reading problems.
Mathematics Disorder	Math ability is substantially below the level expected given the child's age, intelligence, and education. Trouble recognizing numbers and symbols, memorizing basic math facts (e.g., multiplication tables), aligning numbers, and understanding abstract concepts (e.g., place value and fractions). Child may also have problems with visual–spatial abilities. Disorder usually noticed when formal math instruction begins in grade 2 or 3. About 1% of children receive official diagnoses, but 6% score low enough on standardized math tests to be considered as having the disorder.
Writing Disorder	Writing ability is substantially below the level expected given the child's age, intelligence, and education. Problems with writing, drawing, copying figures, and other fine-motor skills involving hand–eye coordination. Large-motor skills (e.g., running, throwing, and climbing) are normal. Written work is low in interest and poorly organized; sentences are short; work contains many errors in spelling, punctuation, and grammar. Disorder affects up to 10% of children.

(Mash & Wolfe, 2005.)

strongly related to language function (Woo et al., 1991). Research has linked expressive language disorder to recurrent ear infections (Lonigan et al., 1992); such infections may lead to hearing loss that reduces input to the developing brain. And children with stuttering, reading, and writing disorders show more than normal activity in the right half of their brains (Mash & Wolfe, 1999). It seems that disruptions in prenatal brain development cause many of these disorders. Even minor defects can change how the brain sorts, organizes, and brings information together from specific brain areas; and these changes in turn hamper the child's ability to interpret and make sense out of the information.

In many of these cases, the disorders correct themselves or the children learn ways to compensate for their difficulties. Stuttering and expressive language disorders, for example, often correct themselves by the age of 6 or 7 (Mash & Wolfe, 2005). Or children who stutter can learn to slow down and breathe deeply before continuing. Speech therapists can train children with phonological disorder in articulation and help them learn to produce correct speech sounds. Children with reading, math, and writing disorders typically receive educational supports in school. They benefit from direct instruction, drill and practice, and learning strategies for breaking problems and assignments into smaller units. Counseling and therapy also can help children improve their self-esteem, deal with peer rejection, and learn how to monitor and control their own learning and thought processes. And with help, families can learn to provide more effective supports for children with communication and learning disorders. On the bright side, most people with these disorders find ways to compensate and go on to live normal lives.

Autism Spectrum Disorders

At the age of 9, Daniel still didn't speak, read, or write. Although he seemed to understand most of what other people said, he communicated mostly by pointing, grunting, and making nonsense sounds. For his birthday his uncle gave him a tape recorder, which Daniel began using to record short pieces of conversation he heard around him. At night he would lie in bed and replay the snippets he had recorded that day dozens of times. Using these recordings, Daniel began to teach himself to speak. As he learned two-way communication, he became fascinated with birth dates. When meeting you for the first time, he would immediately ask for your birth date and for the names and birth dates of all your pets. If you didn't have a pet, you had to make one up. Daniel insisted. In a split second, Daniel would then tell you *exactly* how old your pet was, down to the very day! Eventually Daniel's skill with birth dates grew into mastery of calendars (give him any date and he could figure out which day of the week it was) and an amazing ability to multiply and divide numbers in his head. Still, Daniel avoided eye contact, didn't respond properly to human emotions, showed little attachment to his family members, and had no reciprocal friendships. He did not attend school, living instead in a group home. This was where one of us (GC) met Daniel and worked with him, along with three other autistic children who lived in the same home.

Autism spectrum disorders (ASDs) are a group of serious developmental disorders characterized by impairments in social interaction and communication. Table 10.4 on page 354 lists some of the more common indicators. Formerly called *autism*, ASD is a *spectrum disorder*, which means it can take forms that range from milder (such as Asperger syndrome) to more severe (such as autistic disorder) (NICHD, 2005). In addition to the problems we've seen in the case of Daniel, children with ASDs often show repetitive body motions or self-stimulation activities such as rocking their bodies or waving their fingers in front of their eyes. They are inflexible about their daily routines and become upset by changes such as a different bedtime, a new arrangement of furniture, or an attempt to take them shopping at a new store. Children with ASDs tend to score low on IQ tests (in the range of mental retardation), but a small percentage show exceptional *splinter skills* like Daniel's gift for calculating dates and numbers. Other such skills include exceptional memory for music and speed in building puzzles. Language skills tend to be severely delayed in children with ASDs. Many of these children simply repeat back words and phrases they hear (a pattern called *echolalia*) without seeming to understand what is said.

ASDs affect approximately one to six out of every 1,000 children in the United States (Centers for Disease Control, 2006c; NICHD,

autism spectrum disorders (ASDs) A group of serious developmental disorders characterized by impairments in social interaction and communication.

Autistic children suffer from severe deficits in social interaction and communication. This child shows a kind of self-stimulation behavior that is typical for autistic children.

TABLE 10.4 Indicators of Autism Spectrum Disorders

Speech and Language	• Slow language and speech development:
	   • No meaningful gestures, no babbling by 1 year
	   • No words by 16 months
	   • No use of two-word combinations by 2 years
	• Language skills seemed normal, but has regressed in use of words and other communication
	• Does not respond to name
	• Does not follow directions
	• Is frequently not able to explain what is wanted
	• At times seems to not hear well; other times hearing seems normal

Social Interactions	• Shows poor eye contact when interacting with others • Does not smile in return when smiled at • Does not wave good-bye • Has violent or otherwise intense tantrums • Prefers to play alone; not interested in interacting with other children • Often seems to be absorbed in his/her own world • Used to show normal social interactions, but loses social skills
Behaviors	• Shows unusual attachment to a particular toy or object • Shows unusual need for a certain order of activities (e. g., becomes upset if asked to put on gloves before hat when she/he typically puts on hat first) • Unusual amounts of time spent lining things up in a certain order • Often repeats the same behaviors over and over; can't seem to move on to something else • Seems unusually active; is uncooperative or resistant to requests or demands • Frequently walks on his/her toes • Is ahead of peers in many behaviors and seems very independent

(NICHD, 2005.)

2005). It is four times more common among boys than girls. In recent years the number of children identified with ASDs has increased, perhaps due in part to changes in how ASDs are diagnosed. ASDs have a strong genetic component, being shared much more often between identical twins than between nonidentical twins (Bailey et al., 1995). Environmental contributors to ASDs are not well understood. Studies investigating a possible link between childhood vaccinations containing the preservative thimersol (which contains a form of mercury) have not supported the hypothesis that these vaccinations are linked to ASDs, but research continues on this question (as of 2001, thimersol is no longer used as a preservative in childhood vaccines in the United States, with the exception of some influenza vaccines) (DeStefano et al., 2004; NICHD, 2005; Parker et al., 2004). Researchers are just beginning to understand the brain mechanisms associated with ASDs. Early evidence indicates immaturity in the limbic system and in the frontal and midbrain areas of the brain (Kabotet al., 2003; Newsom, 1998). These areas regulate attention, emotion perception, and the control of planning and thought processes. Interestingly, ASDs are associated with increased neuron density in the hippocampal system (an area related to memory function) and with higher than normal brain weight.

With ASDs, the effectiveness of treatment varies depending on the severity of the disorder in individual children (Newsom, 1998). With severe levels of autism, therapy focuses on teaching self-care skills and helping the child learn to live as independently as possible. Lifelong care and supervision will probably still be essential. With more moderate to mild levels, treatment can be more effective if it starts early and involves intensive one-to-one training and therapy, preferably 20 to 40 hours per week. The work focuses on improving language, teaching social skills, and helping the child learn the skills and behaviors necessary for preschool and early elementary school (Autism Society of America, 2002; Newsom, 1998; Whalen & Schreibman, 2003). Parent education and training are also important parts of effective therapy (Kabot et al., 2003; Whitaker, 2002). With this kind of training and therapy, children with ASDs can show impressive gains, although most will still not function like their more typical peers.

Educating Children with Exceptional Needs

Like all children, students with exceptional needs are legally entitled to a free and appropriate public school education as outlined in United States Public Law 94-142. Enacted in 1975, this law also requires that each child identified as needing special education services have an **individualized education plan (IEP)** that describes the services needed and specific goals for instruction. Students must also be educated in the **least restrictive environment** that is appropriate. This means that students with disabilities should be educated in the classroom with their nondisabled peers whenever possible and appropriate. Table 10.5 shows the percentages of public school students who received federal funds to support their educations due to a disability during the

individualized education plan (IEP)
A written plan that describes the services needed and instructional goals for children identified as needing special education services.

least restrictive environment
Educational placement of students receiving special education services in the classroom with nondisabled peers whenever possible and appropriate.

TABLE 10.5 Percentage of Children Enrolled in Public Schools Who Received Federally Funded Services, 2001–2002

CATEGORY OF DISABILITY	PERCENT OF TOTAL STUDENT POPULATION RECEIVING FEDERAL SERVICES*
All disabilities	13.4
Specific learning disabilities	6.0
Speech or language impairments	2.3
Mental retardation	1.2
Emotional disturbance	1.0
Hearing impairments	0.1
Orthopedic impairments	0.2
Visual impairments	0.1
Other health impairments	0.7
Multiple disabilities	0.3
Autism spectrum disorders and traumatic brain injury	0.2
Developmental delay	0.1
Preschool disabled**	1.3

*Reported as percentage of all children ages 3 to 21 enrolled in U.S. public schools.
**Preschool disabled refers to preschool children ages 3 to 5 years who received services under Chapter 1 and IDEA, Part B (laws enacted to provide early childhood education services to disabled preschoolers).

(National Center for Education Statistics, 2005.)

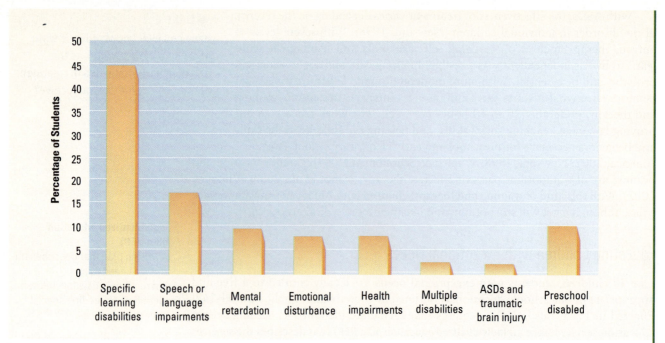

Figure 10.4 • Percentage of Students Receiving Federal Funds by Type of Disability*

*Percentages are the percent of all students receiving federal funding for a disability. Total number of students receiving federal education funds due to a disability during the 2001–2002 school year was 6.4 million.

Note: *Health impairments* include hearing, orthopedic, visual, and all other health impairments. *Preschool disabled* refers to preschool children ages 3 to 5 years who received services under Chapter 1 and IDEA, Part B (laws enacted to provide early childhood education services to disabled preschoolers). (National Center for Education Statistics, 2005.)

2001–2002 school year, and Figure 10.4 shows the types of disabilities these students received services for. Thirteen percent of all students enrolled received some sort of support due to a disability. Of these students, most (44 percent) received services for a specific learning disability such as reading or mathematics, 17 percent for speech and language impairments, and 9 percent due to mental retardation. PL 94-142 has made a significant impact in the lives of these students, but challenges remain. To learn more about ensuring that students with disabilities receive the education they are entitled to, read the Social Policy Perspective box called "Educating Children with Exceptional Needs."

In this chapter, we have reviewed typical patterns of growth during middle childhood, including overall physical growth, changes in the brain, and the development of motor skills. Most children are physically healthy during middle childhood, but threats to current and future physical and emotional health do exist. Parents and other caring adults can do a lot to protect children's safety—ensuring good eating habits, making sure that children take proper precautions when biking and playing sports, watching for signs of abuse, and advocating for fair and appropriate education of children with disabilities. Such efforts will help make the middle childhood years a more secure and happy time for all children.

Think About Clayton . . .

When he's a teacher, how can Clayton make sure he's meeting the needs of all his students and that he's not unnecessarily restricting their education?

Educating Children with Exceptional Needs

Karen Singer's son was diagnosed with autism spectrum disorder (ASD) at the age of 2 when he could not speak, he did not make eye contact with other people, and he had trouble with simple demands such as sitting still in his chair (Gross, 2005). After three years of a 40-hour-a-week home program with a behavioral therapist, her son learned the communication and academic skills he needed to enter a regular kindergarten class in school. With the advances being made in behavioral therapy, an increasing number of children with ASDs, communication problems, physical or sensory disabilities, cognitive deficits, and many other types of disabilities are now attending regular school classrooms.

Today, all children are entitled by law to a free and appropriate public education. In the 1970s, the U.S. congress passed the Individuals with Disabilities Education Act (IDEA). This law was last amended in 1997 and states that "Each State must establish procedures to assure that, to the maximum extent appropriate, children with disabilities . . . are educated with children who are not disabled, and that special education, separate schooling, or other removal of children with disabilities from the regular educational environment occurs only when the nature or severity of the disability is such that education in regular classes with the use of supplementary aids and services cannot be achieved satisfactorily" (as quoted by the Renaissance Group, 1999). The IDEA has done wonders to integrate children with all types of disabilities into mainstream society. Rather than attending separate schools or being pulled out for all-day special education classes, children with disabilities work alongside other children. All children can benefit. The children with disabilities have opportunities to make friends and learn from nondisabled children, and they have the challenge and stimulation offered in regular classes. Nondisabled children benefit too as they learn about diversity and see how they can adapt and have meaningful relationships with children who are different from themselves.

Unfortunately, full inclusion in regular education settings is not realistic for all children. Public schools emphasize academic skills, but they do little to help children learn the social skills they need to interact with diverse individuals. Karen Singer's son performed well in his school subjects, but by the time he entered middle school he did not feel comfortable in the regular school setting. He did not share the same teenage interests as his classmates, he was rigid about small matters such as what color ink to use on a school project, and he sometimes blurted out inappropriate remarks such as "You're stupid!" (Gross, 2005). As the years passed, he became more socially isolated, sometimes seeking the solace of the school bathroom to cry. In anguish, the Singers moved their son to a private school that specialized in disabilities, and so far their son seems more comfortable there.

Since passing the IDEA, public schools have made great strides in adapting their classrooms to accommodate students with all types of exceptional needs. We still have a long way to go, however, before all students feel equally challenged and supported in the academic realm while at the same time feeling equally accepted and comfortable in the social realm.

Q *What else do you think schools should do to help all children feel comfortable? What are the other pros and cons of full inclusion in regular education settings?*

1. Which component of ADHD usually emerges *first* in a child's development?
    a. inattention
    b. hyperactivity
    c. memory loss
    d. aggression

2. Which of the following contributes *most* to communication and learning disorders?
    a. quality of early parenting
    b. quality of early education
    c. genetic and biological factors
    d. social and cultural factors

3. Robbie is 10 years old, but he hardly speaks. Sometimes he repeats back small bits of what you say to him, but otherwise he doesn't communicate. He has a low IQ and spends a lot of time rocking his body back and forth or waving his fingers in front of his eyes. From this description, Robbie most likely suffers from _____.
    a. an autism spectrum disorder
    b. a communication disorder
    c. profound mental retardation
    d. cultural–familial retardation

4. **True or False:** Most children with learning disorders have below-average levels of intelligence.

5. **True or False:** The IDEA law requires that a child with exceptional needs be educated in classrooms with nondisabled peers regardless of the nature or extent of the disability.

Answers: 1. b, 2. c, 3. a, 4. F, 5. F

Thinking Back to Clayton . . .

Now that you have studied this chapter, you should be able to explain how Clayton can use information about typical physical development, safety, and the exceptional needs of some children to guide his coaching and teaching. You should be able to list at least a dozen specific concepts and explain how each would relate to Clayton and the children he is working with.

It will be very helpful for Clayton to learn about the typical levels of skills he can expect in children of these ages. This will help as he coaches this summer, and also as a PE teacher when he talks to parents about what's reasonable to expect from their children. It will also help him notice children who may benefit from more practice on certain skills. Clayton could benefit from knowing about gender differences in growth during middle childhood, and that some of the girls may be bigger and taller than boys for a time. They can certainly play sports together, but Clayton should also understand that they may not want to. Clayton probably is already aware that practicing physical skills helps improve control and coordination, but he might be interested in knowing more about the effect that these experiences have on children's brain development—and vice versa. It would also be good for him to understand that it's not very realistic to expect a high level of physical control and coordination from the kindergarten and first-graders he works with. Pushing them too hard may frustrate them and turn them off to exercise. Clayton's goal of helping kids develop lifelong exercise habits is an important one, and learning more about childhood weight problems should make him even more determined to achieve it.

It's important for Clayton to become very familiar with the rules, safety equipment, and other injury-prevention procedures in his job to guard against children getting hurt. Even this summer, he can help keep the children he is working with safe by reminding them to wear bike helmets and buckle up when riding in a car. He should always be watchful for signs of abuse in the children he works with, now and in the future, to help protect children from the extreme harm these situations can cause. He can learn more about the guidelines developed by different sports and medical organizations, and share these with parents. It might even be a good idea to talk directly to parents about the goals of the summer program, emphasizing being active, giving all the children a chance to play, developing their skills, and having fun—not winning games. Clayton can use the information on disorders to find ways to modify his coaching. For example, it will help Clayton be a more patient and effective coach if he understands that children with ADHD may need clearer structure and help focusing on instructions, and that children with communication disorders may need to receive instructions visually as well as verbally. Learning about the different needs that children have will help him more effectively teach each child.

■ Chapter Review . . .

What are the typical patterns of physical growth during middle childhood?
On average, children gain 9 inches and 35 pounds from the ages of 7 through 11 years. For a time, girls will be taller and heavier on average than boys. The brain gains blood vessels, glial cells, and myelination. After the age of 10, synaptic pruning of less efficient brain circuits decreases the size of some brain areas and improves their efficiency. Brain maturity and environmental stimulation have a reciprocal effect on each other.

What is considered to be overweight in children, and how big a problem is it?
Childhood overweight is defined as having a body mass index at or above the 95th percentile for the child's age and gender. It is increasingly common, and is a risk factor for many health problems. It is caused by both genetic and environmental factors, such as children's decreased activity levels and increased consumption of fast and processed foods. Parents can work to improve children's healthy eating and exercise habits, and provide a good role model.

What types of motor development and physical activity are typical of middle childhood?
Both gross- and fine-motor skills become more controlled and coordinated during middle childhood. There are improvements in strength and balance, but flexibility decreases after the age of 10 to 12 years. There are gender differences in the development of most motor skills and in physical activity preferences such as rough-and-tumble play, due to biological and sociocultural factors. Most children report getting some sort of physical activity, but experts are concerned that some groups of children remain at risk of future health problems. Barriers to physical activity include children's increasing preferences for more sedentary activities, the cost of participating in sports, lack of opportunities, and unsafe neighborhoods.

What are the pros and cons of children's participation in organized sports?
Organized sports offer physical benefits such as muscle strength and endurance, cardiovascular health, improved eye–hand coordination, and increased body awareness; social skills improvements such as cooperation and good sportsmanship; and chances to develop positive emotional coping strategies and improvement of self-esteem. Participation in organized sports is associated with positive outcomes such as greater school success and lower levels of negative behaviors such as drug use. However, there is the potential for injury. Inappropriate behavior of adults, such as overemphasis on competition and winning, can also be detrimental.

How can parents help reduce common threats to safety during middle childhood?
The most common threats to safety during middle childhood are accidents; the leading cause of death is auto accidents. Children are increasingly free of adult supervision but are not yet physically, emotionally, or cognitively mature enough to stay safe. Parents can improve safety around their homes, insist that children are always secured in booster seats or by seat belts when riding in a car, abstain from drinking alcohol and driving, insist that children always wear a helmet when riding a bicycle,

teach children how to swim, insist that they wear proper flotation devices around water, and always supervise children when they are around water.

How can sexual abuse affect a child's development?
Child sexual abuse occurs in all ethnic, geographic, and economic groups. It is more common in middle childhood and adolescence than in earlier years, and in children who have suffered other forms of maltreatment. Other risk factors include poor family relationships, marital disruptions, and individual factors such as being socially isolated and being female. There are a number of signs of possible child sexual abuse; some children show several but others show few, if any. The effects of child sexual abuse depend on the frequency, severity, and duration of the abuse, but can include depression, abnormally sexualized behavior, drug and alcohol use, posttraumatic stress disorder, feelings of guilt and shame, and difficulties with intimate relationships. There can also be physiological effects on the brain's structure and functioning.

What is the developmental psychopathology perspective?
This view of development emphasizes the wide variety of factors that affect both typical and atypical paths of development. A particular developmental outcome is determined by the transactions that occur among all the factors, and it is often difficult to pinpoint the exact cause(s) of a specific disorder or problem.

What are the symptoms of ADHD, and how is it treated?
ADHD involves the inability to sustain attention, excessive activity levels, and deficient impulse control for a child's developmental level. ADHD is associated with greater behavioral and emotional problems as children get older. There is a genetic component involved in ADHD, but environmental factors may also be involved. Children with ADHD tend to have higher levels of family conflict and difficulty in school. Treatment often involves the use of stimulant medications and behavioral management programs.

What are communication and learning disorders, and how do they affect children?
Communication disorders involve difficulty producing speech, using spoken language to communicate, or understanding spoken language. Learning disorders refer to problems with a specific skill such as reading, mathematics, or writing. Both types of disorders disrupt performance and slow learning. They are strongly genetic and are related to specific abnormalities in brain function. Some disorders correct themselves or children learn compensation strategies; counseling and therapy can also be effective.

What are autism spectrum disorders (ASDs)?
ASDs are a group of developmental disorders characterized by impairments in social interaction and communication. Children with ASDs tend to be rigid about routines, show repetitive body movements or self-stimulation activities, and have severely delayed language skills. Most show low IQ scores, but a few show narrow areas of exceptional skill. ASDs have a strong genetic component, and they are associated with brain abnormalities in the limbic system, hippocampus, frontal, and midbrain areas. Therapy depends on the level of severity, but early intervention for children with mild to moderate ASDs can help improve language and social skills.

What guidelines exist for the education of children with exceptional needs?
United States Public Law 94-142 requires that children with exceptional needs be provided a free and appropriate public school education, including an individualized education plan (IEP) for all those identified as needing special education services and placement in the least restrictive environment that is possible and appropriate. Most students who receive special education services do so because of a specific learning disability. Progress in the education of children with exceptional needs has been made, but challenges remain.

■ Key Terms

attention deficit/hyperactivity disorder (ADHD) (349)
autism spectrum disorders (ASDs) (353)
body mass index (BMI) (329)
child sexual abuse (343)
children with exceptional needs (347)
communication disorders (351)
comorbidity (348)
cortisol (344)
developmental psychopathology perspective (348)

individualized education plan (IEP) (355)
learning disorders (351)
least restrictive environment (355)
organized sports (336)
overweight (329)
prevalence rates (348)
risk of overweight (329)
rough-and-tumble play (336)
sensitization (345)

![mydevelopmentlab — Where human development comes to life!]

If you are using MyDevelopmentLab, you have access to an ebook version of this textbook, along with dozens of valuable resources per chapter—including video and audio clips, simulations and activities, self-assessments, practice tests, and other study materials. Here is a sampling of the resources available for this chapter.

Listen
Mental retardation

Watch
Effects of Emotional Disability on Peer Interactions
Medicating Kids
Are Intelligence Tests Valid?
Attention-Deficit Hyperactivity Disorder

If you did not receive an access code to MyDevelopmentLab with this text and wish to purchase access online, please visit www.mydevelopmentlab.com.

chapter 11

Cognitive Development in Middle Childhood

Manny is helping Angelique, his 8-year-old daughter, with her math homework. Angelique is having trouble solving math story problems. Manny asks her to read each problem aloud so he can help her understand it better. Reading the problem takes several minutes because Angelique is not a skilled reader. And when she gets to the end of the problem, she seems to have little idea of what she should do next. She has difficulty understanding that certain words in the problems, like *altogether*, are often good indicators of a specific math operation. When Manny asks her simple questions, Angelique seems confused and cannot remember what the problem is asking her to do. Even when Manny sets up the problem for her, Angelique has difficulty doing the computations. After getting an answer, Angelique writes it down but often forgets what the number refers to in the problem. When Manny asks Angelique to explain the problem in her own words, or even to talk about how she's thinking about the problems, Angelique has trouble expressing her thinking. Manny knows that his daughter is intelligent, but both he and Angelique are becoming frustrated. Why is she having such trouble with problems that seem so simple?

After studying this chapter, you should be able to identify several potential explanations for Angelique's difficulties with math story problems and suggest several things that Manny can do to help. What helpful advice can you suggest?

> As you read this chapter, look for the "Think About Angelique . . ." questions that ask you to consider what you are learning from Angelique's perspective.

Angelique is struggling to memorize her math facts and to understand how to solve word problems, and her father is struggling to find better ways to help her learn. Nearly every day, we all find ourselves pushed to our cognitive limits. What cognitive limitations do children from the ages of 7 through 11 face? What strategies do they use to think through complicated problems? When overwhelmed with new information, how do they focus on the information that is most important? How can children at these ages improve their memory skills and avoid forgetting important information? Can their language skills help them as they try to think through problems? As a college student, you are no doubt learning new ways to process and remember the information presented in your classes and textbooks. And although you have had many years to practice learning, it can still be a struggle. Children in elementary school encounter new and complex things every day. Simple acts like reading, understanding basic facts about the world, and verbally describing their thoughts can be just as bewildering to them as physics or calculus might be to you. What kinds of thought processes, memory abilities, and language skills do children of this age have?

These are questions that we explore in this chapter. We will begin with Jean Piaget's explanation of cognitive development during middle childhood. We then elaborate on the information-processing perspective you read about in Chapters 1 and 8 and describe what this view has taught us about the development of memory, knowledge, and strategies. We will review the typical language skills of the middle childhood period and introduce you to a recent approach to understanding language development. Finally, we will talk about development within three important academic areas: mathematics, reading, and writing.

Piaget's Stage 3: Concrete Operational Thought (Ages 7 through 11)

In Chapter 8, you learned that children in the preoperational thought stage (roughly ages 2 to 7) can form internal mental representations and use symbols in their language, art, and play. As you learned, thinking in early childhood is intuitive (based on personal experience but not logical) and characterized by egocentrism, animism, and artificialism. Young children fail conservation problems because their cognitive schemes are not yet reversible (not "operational"), they center their thought on only one dimension of the problem, and they focus on the static endpoints of the problem. As children enter middle childhood, however, new developments take place. According to Piaget's theory, what skills and limitations are typical of children during the middle childhood years?

As you study this section, ask yourself these questions:

- Why does Piaget call this stage of thought *concrete operational thinking*?
- What major skills do children in this stage show?
- What limitations do children in the concrete operational stage still face?

What Is Concrete Operational Thinking?

According to Piaget, children experience cognitive disequilibrium and engage in reflective abstraction (see Chapter 5). As a result, they gradually adapt their cognitive structures and reconstruct their understandings of the world. Given adequate experiences with their environment, most children progress to Piaget's third stage around 7 years of age. To these children, the conservation problems shown in Figure 8.3 are trivial. With the liquid conservation problem, a typical 10-year-old would say, "Of course they both still have the same amount; all you did was pour it over here. If you pour the taller one back into the short beaker, you'll see that it's just the same." Or "Sure, the taller one looks like it has more, but it is also skinnier, so it's really just the same." Children in this third stage, **concrete operational thought,** show thinking that is very different from that of the younger child. Their thought is *decentered*—they consider multiple aspects of the problem (understanding the importance of both height and width). They focus on the *dynamic transformations* in the problem (realizing that the true answer lies in the pouring). And, most importantly, they show the *reversibility* of true mental *operations* (just pour it back, and it's the same). In this third stage children's cognitive structures are operational—hence the name, concrete *operational* thought. This development allows them to think about the world using objective rules of logic, freeing them from the misconceptions of intuitive thought.

concrete operational thought
Stage of cognitive development in which children are able to think about two or more dimensions of a problem (decentered thought), dynamic transformations, and reversible operations.

Class Inclusion, Seriation, and Transitive Inference Skills

Children in the concrete operational stage also show their logical abilities when they solve *class inclusion* problems. For example, show a child a set of five dolls and three teddy bears, then ask this question: "Are there more dolls or more toys?" Children in the preoperational stage will typically answer "more dolls," because they tend to focus on only one part of the problem (dolls versus bears) and ignore the fact that all of the objects belong to the general class of toys. Most children in the concrete operational stage, however, understand that both dolls and bears are also toys. To them this is a silly question—of course there are more toys than dolls! In other words, older children understand *class inclusion*—the fact that objects can be classified in different ways and at different levels. Younger children don't understand this. When he was about 4, our younger son heard his mother referred to as "Doctor." He immediately spoke up: "She's not a doctor, she's my mommy!" Our older son just rolled his eyes. To young children, grandmothers can't also be mothers, and firemen can't also be fathers.

your perspective
Think about the last time you had to mentally reverse your thinking, such as when you were looking for an item you lost. What made this retracing of your steps more or less difficult for you? Could an 8- or 10-year-old have done this?

During the concrete operational stage, children develop the ability to *seriate,* or arrange a set of items into a series according to a quantitative dimension such as size, weight, or length. Seriation allows children to show another hallmark of concrete operational thought—*transitive inference,* or the process of mentally drawing inferences by comparing relations among objects. Consider the following example. Sue is taller than Jean, and Jean is taller than Lexi. Who is taller, Sue or Lexi? We can draw the inference that Sue is taller than Lexi by comparing the relationships from Sue and Jean to Jean and Lexi. Children in the preoperational stage have trouble following these transitivity problems; they may comment that they can't tell who is taller (after all, they can't see them!) or may just take a guess. With true operational logic, however, children in the concrete operational stage can represent the logical relationships and arrive at the correct answer. Recent work on various kinds of inferences, including transitive inferences and class inclusion problems, is consistent with Piaget's view that younger children's reasoning about inferences is consistently simpler than the reasoning of older children (Halford, 2004).

Think About Angelique . . .
Would Piaget predict that Angelique would be able to solve class inclusion, seriation, and transitivity problems? How might these skills improve her success in solving math story problems?

By age 7 most children are capable of using logical thought structures that are increasingly objective and reversible, and they can solve problems that involve class inclusion and transitivity. However, there is still one major limitation in their thinking: Their use of mental operations is still closely tied to *concrete* materials, contexts, and situations. In other words, if children have not had direct experience with the context or situation, or if the material is not tangible, then they are not successful in using their mental operations. This is why the stage is called *concrete* operational thought.

Children in the concrete operational stage develop the ability to *seriate,* or put things into a series according to a quantitative dimension, such as height or weight. This child has no difficulty seriating these objects. How well do you think she would do if she didn't have the objects in front of her, or if she was asked to reason about the relations?

Information Processing: Memory Development

In Chapter 8, we described changes in some of the basic elements of information processing—processing capacity, processing efficiency, and attention. Memory is influenced by all these basic processes, and memory development is one of the most studied topics in the information-processing literature. No matter what your capacity is for processing new information, and no matter how efficiently you focus your attention, it will do you very little good if you can't store the information and then remember it later. In this section we review many of the important research studies regarding the development of memory.

As you study this section, ask yourself these questions:

■ What are the differences between the stores model and network models of memory?

■ What are the characteristics of working memory and long-term memory? What develops in each?

■ What are some of the issues in memory development, and why is each important for cognitive development?

Two Models of Memory: Stores and Networks

For decades, variations of the **stores model** of memory guided research on memory development (Atkinson & Shiffrin, 1968). The stores model is the one you saw in the

stores model (of memory)
A model of human memory that views information as moving through a series of storage locations, from the sensory stores to short-term store to long-term store.

bottom part of Figure 8.5. This model views information as moving through a series of storage locations. Information enters the cognitive system through the *sensory store*, where large amounts of information can be maintained in their original modalities (e.g., visual, verbal, acoustic) for very brief periods of time (approximately half a second). Some of the information in the sensory store is selected and passed along to the *short-term store* (STS). The STS contains the information that you are consciously aware of at the moment, and its capacity is very limited. It can hold only between five and nine "chunks" of information (Miller, 1956). **Chunking** is the process of recoding individual elements in memory into larger groups of information. Larger chunks mean that more information can be maintained in STS. The size of one chunk can vary tremendously, however. For a young child learning the ABCs, a chunk might consist of a single letter; for an experienced reader, a chunk could be a whole section of text. Information can be maintained in the STS for long periods of time if we actively attend to it, but it will fade and disappear within seconds if we do not. To be stored more permanently, information must be passed along to the *long-term store* (LTS). The LTS has an infinite storage capacity, and information remains there permanently even when we are not actively attending to it. To understand the difference between the STS and LTS, notice what happens when you answer this simple question: What is your last name? If you are thinking about your last name and saying it to yourself, then it is now in your STS. But before you saw the question, you probably were not thinking about your last name. Where was your name stored then? It was in your LTS, the place where we store information that we are not consciously thinking about right now but might want to use later. According to the stores model, an *executive processor* controls all three stores and the processes that pass information among them. This processor determines which information will be attended to, and it governs the management of the system's limited capacity from moment to moment.

In recent years, **network models** of memory have largely replaced the stores model. There are several variations of network models, but in general they view memory as an interconnected network of associated information rather than as a series of separate mental storage boxes. Network models consist of *concept nodes* connected by *links*. The links vary in strength, with more heavily weighted links indicating a greater degree of association between the nodes. Rather than thinking of information as moving from STS into LTS, network theorists emphasize that information can be *activated* to different degrees at any point in time. A higher level of activation means that the information is easier to remember. For example, your own name usually has a much higher level of activation than the names of acquaintances. If someone asks your name, you are able to remember and answer much more quickly than if someone asks the name of an acquaintance.

Our son Andy is a skateboarder. Figure 11.1 on page 368 shows his memory network for topics related to skateboarding. Anytime he thinks about skateboarding, he quickly remembers his local skatepark, all of his skateboarding friends, and the ramps at the park. Trace the nodes of his network to see how the links are connected.

Nodes can be activated from either external sources (e.g., seeing an object in the environment) or internal sources (e.g., thinking about an object). Once started, the activation spreads along the connecting links like ripples on the surface of a pond, increasing the degree of activation of the nodes. The farther the activation travels from the original source, the weaker it becomes, until eventually it dies away. As a child grows, much development takes place in the memory network. The numbers of concept nodes and links increase, and the strengths of links change over time.

Working Memory

In the network model, the term **working memory** (WM) refers to the information that is currently active in the memory system and available for use in any mental task. From this "pool" of activated pieces of knowledge (i.e., stored information), a person

chunking
The process of recoding individual elements in memory into larger groups of information.

network models (of memory)
Models of human memory that view memory as an interconnected network of concept nodes connected by links of varying strength.

your perspective
Try making a sketch of your cognitive nodes and links for *information processing*. What are the main concept nodes? How are they linked? How has your network changed as you've read this book?

working memory
The information currently active in your memory system and currently available for use in a mental task.

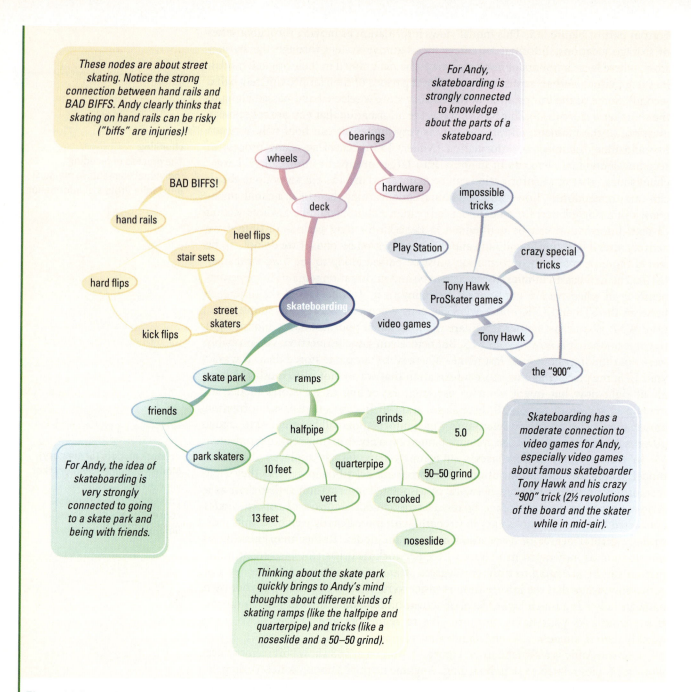

These nodes are about street skating. Notice the strong connection between hand rails and BAD BIFFS. Andy clearly thinks that skating on hand rails can be risky ("biffs" are injuries)!

For Andy, skateboarding is strongly connected to knowledge about the parts of a skateboard.

For Andy, the idea of skateboarding is very strongly connected to going to a skate park and being with friends.

Skateboarding has a moderate connection to video games for Andy, especially video games about famous skateboarder Tony Hawk and his crazy "900" trick (2½ revolutions of the board and the skater while in mid-air).

Thinking about the skate park quickly brings to Andy's mind thoughts about different kinds of skating ramps (like the halfpipe and quarterpipe) and tricks (like a noseslide and a 50–50 grind).

Figure 11.1 • A Partial Network for "Skateboarding" by Andy, Age 12 Network models of memory view memory as an interconnected network, with information stored as concept nodes connected by links. In this figure, thicker lines indicate knowledge that is strongly connected; thinner lines indicate weaker connections.

focuses on some pieces for more detailed processing, but all of the activated information is considered to be in working memory (Cowan, 1995, 1997). Working memory is similar to STS in the stores model—both consist of information that a person is consciously processing at any given time. But working memory differs from STS in that information is not thought of as being moved from one storage place to another. It is simply made available, as information in a book is made available when you open the book. Another difference between STS and WM is that WM has several distinct components. One component is centrally involved in processing verbal information, another in processing auditory information, and others in allocation and monitoring of cognitive resources such as attention as well as rehearsal and temporary storage of information (Baddeley, 1986; Bayliss et al., 2003; Hamilton et al.; Handley et al., 2002). The basic components of working memory are in place by the age of 6, but children learn to use each much more effectively across the school years (Gathercole et al., 2004).

Like STS, working memory has two important characteristics. It is *limited* in its capacity, and the information in working memory *decays over time*. In other words, only a certain amount of information can be activated at any given time. If activation is not maintained in some way, it decays and the information is no longer readily available for use in mental tasks. This information may be permanently lost, or it may simply take more effort to activate it again. As with STS, the amount of information that can be activated in working memory ranges from five to nine chunks of information. The length of time that information can remain activated is short, estimated at approximately 30 seconds, unless we do something to keep it active. For example, we can rehearse (i.e., repeat over and over) what we are trying to remember or relate it to other pieces of information that are active in working memory. Such strategies help keep information activated and therefore available in working memory for longer periods of time.

As you learned in our discussion of the basic processes of information processing in Chapter 8, it isn't clear whether the actual capacity of working memory increases with age or whether children simply learn to use their limited capacities more effectively. But you can probably see that the way a child allocates attention has an important effect on working memory. Consciously attending to information maintains activation and keeps the information readily available, which makes it more likely to be permanently stored in the network. In addition, keeping more pieces of information active increases a child's ability to consider several items at the same time. For example, think about a child learning to read. If a child keeps the letters of a word active in working memory (e.g., *c–a–t*), she can begin to chunk them into one word (*cat*). Because she is now processing these letters as one chunk, she can keep other letters and words active at the same time (*cat–in–the–hat*). As these chunk sizes increase, she can activate and process other information about these chunks: She can notice similarities in word structure; she can realize that *cat* and *hat* rhyme; and she can even use some of her working memory capacity to look for other words that might rhyme (Bayliss et al., 2005; Kuhn & Franklin, 2006).

As you might expect, working memory affects practically every cognitive task children undertake. If children could not keep information activated and accessible, they could not use the information to solve problems, answer test questions, or anything else. It is not surprising that scores on tests of short-term and working memory correlate with scores on many other cognitive abilities, including language, intelligence, reading ability, math performance, and comprehension ability. In all cases, the better a child's short-term or working memory performance, the higher the child's cognitive ability scores (Cantor et al.; Farmer & Klein, 1995; Geary et al., 2004; Gillam et al, 1995; Lee et al., 2004; Montgomery, 1995; Swanson & Beebe-Frankenberger, 2004).

Long-Term Memory

Long-term memory is just that—memory of information or events that endures over a relatively long time period. As you saw in Figure 8.5, the stores model of memory views long-term memory as a separate store (the LTS). In contrast, network models (Figure 11.1) view long-term memory as the nonactivated part of an integrated memory network. But regardless of how different theorists view the structure of long-term memory, they agree on several fundamental characteristics. First, long-term memory is *permanent*. Once information is stored in long-term memory, it never decays—it is never truly forgotten. Second, long-term memory is *unlimited* in its capacity. This means that theoretically you can store an infinite amount of information. This does not mean, however, that you can always remember the information you want, even when

long-term memory
Memory of knowledge or events that is permanent.

encoding
The process of forming a mental representation of information.

storage
Placing information in permanent, or long-term, memory.

accessing
The process of finding information in memory at the desired time.

retrieval
In the stores model, retrieval is the process of bringing information from the long-term store to the short-term store. In network models, retrieval is the process of activating information so that it becomes a part of the working memory and thus available for use.

you make concentrated efforts to do so. Trying to remember all of the definitions studied in yesterday's class is a prime example for most college students.

Although long-term memory does not suffer from difficulties with decay of information or lack of storage space as working memory does, there can be problems with the initial **encoding** of information (i.e., the process of forming a mental representation of the information), **storage** of information (i.e., putting it into the LTS or into the network), **accessing** stored information (i.e., finding the right information at the desired time), and **retrieval** of stored information (i.e., activating it so that it can become part of working memory or STS and thus available for use). For example, when walking down the sidewalk, do you ever see someone you know but find yourself unable to remember the person's name? The problem may be that you never encoded the person's name; this means you will never be able to remember it, because the name was never mentally represented. Maybe you encoded it but never stored it; since the name never entered your memory network, there is nothing there to remember. Or perhaps you encoded it incorrectly, so you might call the person *Helen* when her name is really *Ellen*. Maybe you encoded the name correctly but cannot access it at the moment. We often recognize a person's face (and "know" that we know the person) but fail to access or retrieve the person's name. Finally, you may be able to access the name, but the retrieval cues (things in the mind or environment that increase the likelihood you will be able to remember something) may not be adequate to actually allow you to retrieve it—or, in network model terms, fully activate it. As you might guess, it can be especially difficult to tell whether a memory problem is due to an access or a retrieval problem—access and retrieval tend to be associated, but they are not the

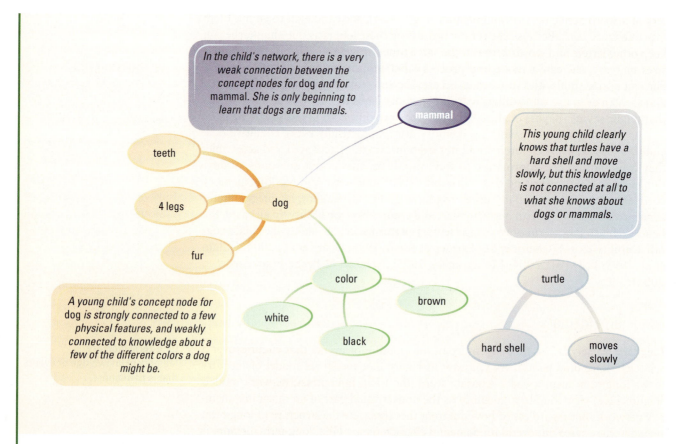

Figure 11.2 • Developmental Changes in a Long-Term Memory Network A young child's initial network for the concept of "dog" is shown above; a more elaborate network for "dog" (shown on the facing page) develops as the child learns and grows. Thicker lines indicate stronger connections; thinner lines indicate weaker connections.

same thing. If you've ever experienced the "tip-of-the-tongue" phenomenon, in which you know for sure that you know something but you just can't remember it at the moment, you've experienced access but an inability to retrieve.

This child is having a *tip-of-the-tongue* experience as he tries to remember his new teacher's name. What does this experience tell us about his access and retrieval of information in his memory?

What develops in long-term memory? Clearly, the amount of knowledge in long-term memory grows tremendously with age—older children simply have stored more information. In addition, the organization of the stored information changes with development. Information becomes more interconnected as children understand the relations between concepts. Older children have more connections between stored concepts, and they add different types of links between concepts. For example, Figure 11.2 shows how a child may initially connect an animal such as a dog with its network attributes, in effect representing the things a dog "has" (fur, four legs, a certain color, etc.). Eventually the child will add different kinds of links to this understanding of dogs, such as links that identify the different categories a dog belongs to and represent what a dog "is" (an animal, warm-blooded, etc.). The strengths of associations between concepts also change with development. Some connections become stronger—such as the link between "mammal" and "platypus" when a child learns that a platypus is a mammal. Others become weaker—such as the link between

your perspective

Have you ever had a "tip-of-the-tongue" experience? How did you finally remember the information? Think of other examples of encoding, access, or retrieval problems. How would the stores model and network models explain these problems?

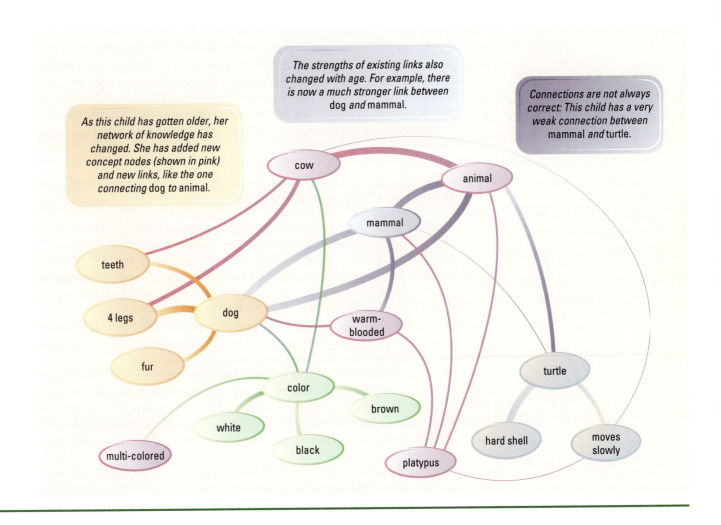

The strengths of existing links also changed with age. For example, there is now a much stronger link between dog *and* mammal.

Connections are not always correct: This child has a very weak connection between mammal *and* turtle.

As this child has gotten older, her network of knowledge has changed. She has added new concept nodes (shown in pink) and new links, like the one connecting dog *to* animal.

cow · animal · mammal · teeth · 4 legs · dog · warm-blooded · fur · color · brown · turtle · white · black · hard shell · moves slowly · multi-colored · platypus

Scripts are formed for events that are encountered repeatedly, like getting ready for bed.

scripts
Mental representations of the way things typically occur in certain settings or for certain events.

Think About Angelique . . .

How can Angelique's links between basic math facts and their correct answers be strengthened?

Think About Angelique . . .

How could Manny help Angelique develop scripts for the problems she's working with? How would this help her be more successful in solving these types of problems?

reconstructive memory
A characteristic of human memory. We store parts of events and knowledge; during recall we retrieve the stored pieces and draw inferences about the rest.

"mammal" and "turtle." Changes in the number, types, and strengths of interconnections of stored information are the things that create change in the organization of long-term memory.

For many years, much of the research on long-term memory concerned *semantic memory,* or knowledge of words and concepts. Children clearly develop semantic memory networks, but their earliest memories seem to be of a different type. *Episodic memory* is memory for events, or episodes, that one experiences in day-to-day life (Tulving, 1972). Some researchers have suggested that children's memories are primarily memories of events and that these episodic memories are organized into **scripts,** mental representations of the way things typically occur in certain settings or for certain events (Bauer, 2006; Nelson, 1986). For example, many children in this country have a script for going to a fast-food restaurant. They know that you go to a counter and tell a person what you want to eat, but that you can order only the foods listed on big signs behind the counter; that you pay for the food before you get it, not after you're done eating; that you take your food to a table and throw everything away when you are finished; and that sometimes there is a playground where you can have fun.

Scripts reflect real-world events, and they indicate what usually happens for a given type of event. They form most readily for events children encounter repeatedly, such as getting ready for bed, going to visit relatives, or eating out in restaurants. Children's first scripts contain only the most central events, and even children as young as one year of age show evidence of scripts (Bauer & Dow, 1994; Bauer & Mandler, 1992; Fivush et al., 1992). As children grow, they need fewer encounters with an event to form a script, and the scripts become more detailed (Farrar & Goodman, 1992; Hudson et al., 1992). For example, a 2-year-old's script for eating in a fast-food restaurant may include only the information that first you order your food, then you play on the playground. A 9-year-old's script will likely contain many more details, such as what kinds of food are available, how loud and rowdy you can be, whether the toys that come with the kids' meals are too babyish to play with, and the fact that food must be paid for before you eat. By organizing knowledge, scripts help children predict what will happen next and help them remember events that take place (Hudson & Nelson, 1983; Hudson et al., 1995).

Other Characteristics of Memory Development

Reconstructive Memory. On an episode of a popular reality television show, two former friends were appearing in small-claims court. One friend (we'll call her Kim) had purchased some expensive airline tickets for a beach vacation. She claimed that her friend "Samantha" had promised to reimburse her for one of the tickets. Kim's mother caught the girls and would not allow them to go (the girls were only 15!), but the tickets could not be returned for a refund. Samantha denied having promised to pay for her ticket, saying that she had stated only that she would help pay for the trip. Because the trip did not take place, Samantha felt she was under no obligation to pay for anything.

Do you think of memory as a mental copy of information and events? Many people do. The story of Kim and Samantha, however, clearly illustrates that memory is anything but a "mental copy." Instead, memory is *reconstructive.* This means that memory stores only some aspects of events and some pieces of information—and when you try to recall the information or event, you access and retrieve these pieces then infer the rest. In other words, in **reconstructive memory** you patch together what probably happened based on the bits and pieces you actually stored, along with other relevant information from memory and from external cues. Perhaps Samantha actually said something like "I'll help pay for the trip." But Kim's reconstruction, influenced by her past eagerness to get to the beach and her present need to recover some of her lost money, was more like "She said she'd pay for her ticket." Our memory of experiences and knowledge draws on previous knowledge, memories, and the current context—it is sometimes changed in subtle ways but sometimes altered substantially.

Numerous studies have confirmed that memory can be significantly affected by what people already know, as well as by the way they are asked to recall it. For example, people give very different answers to this question: "How fast was the car going when it crashed into the house?" as opposed to this one: "Can you estimate the car's speed at the time of the accident?" Also—and especially with children—prompted recall, which uses questions like either of the two above, produces more detailed *but more incorrect* recall than unprompted recall (e.g., responses to "Tell me all you can remember about the event") (Ceci & Bruck, 1998; Loftus & Ketcham, 1994).

Why does it matter whether memory is literal or reconstructed? Sometimes it doesn't. It doesn't matter whether you can remember the dialogue from a television show word for word or only the gist of the story. Other times, however, the difference is crucial. For example, read the Social Policy Perspective box on page 374 called "Children's Eyewitness Testimony: The Truth, the Whole Truth, and Nothing but the Truth?"

Autobiographical Memory. One of us (JLC) had a bicycle accident at about 8 years of age. Whenever I think about it, I can almost feel the pain in my knee, see the bright red of the blood, and remember the words I was thinking: "Just get home, just get home. Dad will help me." I remember remaining reasonably calm until I saw my father standing at the edge of the yard, and then bursting into tears. Do you have any such vivid memories?

Such long-lasting memories of personally experienced events are called **autobiographical memories.** Autobiographical memories are a special subgroup of episodic memories. They are memories of events that had a high level of personal significance. Such meaningful memories form the core experiences of a child's "life story." Not surprisingly, autobiographical memories are often quite vivid and detailed, sometimes even including emotions, sights, and sounds. Children begin to form autobiographical memories early in life and begin talking about such past events when they are as young as 2 years of age. Children's descriptions of past events become more organized and detailed between ages 3 and 6. During middle childhood, children add more background information and provide more of the contexts of the events—such as where they were, what they were thinking and feeling at the time, who was present, and the like. Children learn to describe their autobiographical memories as narratives or stories by interacting with adults; adults elaborate on the information the child provides, ask questions to clarify details or elicit more information, and teach children a cultural format to use in talking about their memories. For example, parents and children often have "remember when you . . ." conversations: "Remember when you had your big bike accident in second grade? Do you remember the bike trick you were trying to do when it happened?" Interactions like these teach children a form for describing memories, and they also help children fill in forgotten details. In other words, such conversations strengthen events that might have become inaccessible in memory so that the child is better able to remember them later (Bauer, 2006; Cleveland & Reese, 2005; Fivush, 1995; Fivush et al., 1995; Howe & Courage, 2004; Howe et al., 1995). Differences in the types of interactions, such as how mothers talk with their children about past events (by elaborating on details and evaluating them versus providing fewer elaborations and evaluations) or cultural tendencies (such as storytelling as entertainment versus to teach moral lessons), affect the age of earliest memories and how detailed they are (Nelson & Fivush, 2004).

your perspective
Have you and a friend or sibling ever experienced the same event, only to have very different memories of what happened? Explain how this is an example of reconstructive memory.

Reconstruction in memory is vitally important for understanding eyewitness testimony, especially when the witness is a child. The accuracy and detail of children's eyewitness testimony can be good if children are questioned soon after the event in a nonmisleading way and in a comfortable and relaxing atmosphere.

autobiographical memories Memories of events of great personal importance. They are episodic memories and are often vivid and detailed.

your perspective
Are your earliest memories about events? Are they autobiographical? Ask several friends about their earliest memories. Do you see a pattern?

Children's Eyewitness Testimony: The Truth, the Whole Truth, and Nothing but the Truth?

In the winter of 1989, a co-owner of the Little Rascals Day Care Center in North Carolina was accused of sexually abusing one of the children attending the school. Over the next several months and years, dozens of adults would be accused of sexually abusing 90 children. Few children made accusations early on, but after repeated questioning by parents and police and months of therapy, dozens of children did so, and seven adults were arrested. Two were found guilty at trial and two pleaded no contest to the charges, but the convictions were later reversed on appeal and the prosecution eventually dropped all charges (Ceci & Bruck, 1998).

Children are being called on in ever-increasing numbers to provide testimony in legal court cases. Often the cases involve serious crimes, such as child abuse or homicide, and the witnesses are sometimes as young as 4 years of age. Can children provide reliable and valid information under such circumstances? Are they able to tell the truth, the whole truth, and nothing but the truth? What effect does repeated questioning by therapists, police, or lawyers have on children's memories?

There is growing research literature looking at these questions. Even preschoolers are *capable* of accurately reporting information, though it is often not as detailed as the reports of older children and adults and they forget more as time passes. Repeated questioning does increase the amount recalled for both children and adults, but unfortunately the additional information is not necessarily accurate. Both children and adults become more confident in their memories if they receive feedback confirming their reports—even when their reports are incorrect (Neuschatz et al., 2005)! Preschool children also have more difficulty than adults remembering the sources of information and details, so they are more likely to mistakenly think that things they were told about or even imagined actually happened to them. And younger children's memories are more easily affected by the way questions are phrased, the status and attitude of the person asking the questions, and other details of the interview context. If questioning is misleading, younger children are more likely to change their answers to include the misleading information.

They may even expand on it, using the "suggestions in highly productive ways to reconstruct and at times distort reality" (Bruck et al., 1995; Ceci & Bruck, 1998, p. 738; Schneider & Bjorklund, 1998). The false information can be integrated into memory, becoming a stable part of it to be repeated as being true when asked about the events at a later time (Brainerd et al., 1995). In other words, the inaccurate information can essentially *become* the truth more easily for children than for adults. And just as important is that experts often cannot tell for certain whether a child is reporting events that actually happened or not (Leichtman & Ceci, 1995).

The news is not all bad, however. When questions are asked in a nonmisleading way, children are questioned in a nonfrightening and nondemanding atmosphere, and children are given permission to acknowledge when they do not know the answer, the accuracy and details of children's eyewitness reports can be good. Repeated questioning under these optimal conditions results in more complete and more accurate reporting of details and better memory for the events during later questioning (Ceci & Bruck, 1998; Pipe et al., 2004). Some evidence suggests that when misleading information is given long after the event and the event being recalled is highly memorable (for example, it concerns being injured and treated in an emergency room), recall is *more* accurate than if misleading details are not offered (Peterson, Parsons, & Dean, 2004). Using props during questioning (such as anatomically correct dolls) has had mixed results, but encouraging children to think more deeply by doing things such as drawing a picture about an event in addition to talking about it can increase how much is remembered (Bruck & Ceci, 1999; Butler et al., 1995; Steward & Steward, 1996).

Q *If you were a social worker, prosecutor, jury member, or judge in the Little Rascals case or one like it, how would you proceed? What safeguards would you put into place to ensure that children's testimony is as accurate as possible, and what details of the questioning and therapy processes would you want to know?*

Autobiographical memories are interesting because they seem so different from our memory for other kinds of information, such as facts and categories. These memories are also important in helping children develop a sense of their own identity, a topic we will discuss in Chapter 15. Given what you've learned about the reconstructive nature of memory, however, can you see a potential problem with autobiographical memories? It can be difficult for a person to figure out how much of an autobiographical memory, particularly one of a traumatic event such as a serious accident or abuse, might be influenced by other people's interpretations of the event or even by imagining an event (Mazzoni & Memon, 2003; Niedzwienska, 2003). To learn about how clinical psychologists deal with autobiographical memories their clients may have, read the Professional Perspective box on page 376 called "Career Focus: Meet a Child and Family Therapist."

Autobiographical memories are memories of events that are very important to the person. They are often very vivid, and can include the emotions, sights, and sounds that were present at the original event.

■ Let's Review . . .

1. Which model describes human memory as a set of concept nodes with links that vary in strength?
   - a. the stores model
   - b. the network model
   - c. the short-term model
   - d. the autobiographical model

2. According to some researchers, children organize their long-term memories of events into special mental structures called _____.
   - a. scripts
   - b. semantic networks
   - c. reconstructive stores
   - d. autobiographical networks

3. Two witnesses to a robbery offer very different reports of what happened. Which of the following BEST explains why the reports differ?
   - a. autobiographical memory
   - b. unintentional memory
   - c. reconstructive memory
   - d. episodic memory

4. **True or False:** As their processing speed increases, children tend to maintain less information in their working memories.

5. **True or False:** With development, the amount of information held in long-term memory increases, and the organization of the information changes.

Answers: 1. b, 2. a, 3. c, 4. F, 5. T

Information Processing: Knowledge, Strategies, and New Approaches

When our two sons were about 9 and 5 years old, they asked me (JLC) to play Pokémon cards with them. Each card had a picture of a different Pokémon character. Different characters had distinctive beginning strength levels and "tricks" they could use to defeat

Career Focus: Meet a Child and Family Therapist

Dr. Anne Updegrove, Licensed Clinical Psychologist and adjunct faculty at Loyola University
Chicago, Illinois

In therapy situations, how do you use research information about autobiographical and reconstructive memory?
Since therapists rely on children's reports, it is important to be familiar with research that explains what factors influence children's memory of their own experiences and events in their lives. Using research gives clinicians a sense of the "big picture" and helps us to not rely solely on our own unique experience, but to be more objective in our evaluation of children.

In your experience, do children seem more prone than adults to making errors when they reconstruct memories in therapy?
I don't think they make more errors. Instead, I think they remember differently and are differentially affected by how questions are asked. Children's memories tend to be less elaborate, more concrete, and often include details that may seem less relevant or more idiosyncratic. For example, a traumatized child may focus on a stuffed animal that was lost during the traumatic incident or the smell of an individual who has abused them. Also, children are more easily influenced by the way questions are asked if they sense that an adult, authority figure wants them to respond in a particular way. The younger the child, the more this seems to be true.

How do you help children accurately recall events, without leading them into inaccurate memories?
It's difficult. We want to help clients remember as much detail as possible but without influencing the nature of their memories. We do several things to enhance accurate recall. First, clients must trust the therapist and feel that he or she is supportive and nonjudgmental. Second, questions should be open-ended. Clients should be asked to "Tell me more about that" rather than given leading questions. Good training in assessment and interviewing helps clinicians learn how to ask questions the right way. For example, clinicians learn that using the client's own words when phrasing a question reduces the possibility that you are introducing your own biases into the interview. Third, it can be helpful to ask someone to tell the story in their *own* words. Memories that seem unusually rehearsed or include words that children do not typically know are suspect. Likewise, if a child describes an experience in some detail that is unusual for a child to know about (for example, a sexual act), this lends credibility to the accuracy of the memory.

What kinds of education and training are needed to work as a child or family therapist?
Most therapists have a Master's degree or a Ph.D. in clinical psychology, counseling, or clinical social work. Course work in child development, family dynamics, assessment, and therapy is needed, with supervised practice in a therapy situation. Most states require a licensing exam.

Q *What aspects of memory research seem important in clinical work as a therapist? How would you use what you have learned about memory, its processes, and its characteristics to ensure accurate memory in important situations like this?*

opponents. The object was to defeat the opposing Pokémon and win the card. My sons gave me a few cards to start with and we began our game. Within minutes, I had lost all of my cards. The boys had quickly determined which Pokémon to start with, which trick to use, how much damage they had suffered, and who won the game—all before I could even figure out which of my cards had the highest beginning strength!

What could explain my sons' clear superiority with Pokémon? It wasn't overall level of intelligence. I like to think my sons are intelligent, but so am I. It was not due to their having better memory in general—just ask them about homework or if they've brushed their teeth, and it is as if they have no memory at all! The answer has to do with **knowledge base** (the amount of information a person knows about a particular

knowledge base
The amount of information a person knows about a particular topic.

topic) and **strategies** (the conscious, intentional, and controllable plans we adopt to enhance our performance).

As you may have realized by now, information processors pay a great deal of attention to how people acquire and use knowledge. In this section we explore how children develop their knowledge base and how knowledge base affects other cognitive processes. We also look at how children develop strategies to improve their memories and cognitive processing. Finally, we will review some of the more recent explanations of cognitive development that have grown from the information-processing perspective and evaluate some of the pros and cons of this approach to cognitive development.

As you study this section, ask yourself these questions:

- What effect does knowledge base have on cognitive development?

- How do strategies develop? What factors affect strategy use, and how does increasing strategy use foster cognitive development?

- What are production systems and connectionist models? How do they help us understand cognitive development?

- What are fuzzy traces? How do they explain age differences in memory?

- What are the strengths and weaknesses of the information-processing approach to cognitive development?

Knowledge Base

Though we haven't seen any studies of Pokémon experts (yet), researchers have looked at the effects of knowledge base in many other areas of life. Not surprisingly, the more you know about a particular topic, the more you can remember about it—but that is not the only effect of knowledge base. For example, when you get new information about a topic you already know well, you are more likely to notice details and relationships than someone who has less prior knowledge. You are also better able to group the information in useful ways. So my sons were good at categorizing their Pokémon cards according to the types and overall amount of "powers" they had (a useful category for the card battles), whereas I began by sorting the cards according to color and size (which is not very helpful for the battles). In other words, your knowledge base enables you to encode new information differently. You can also store the new information more effectively. In essence, you are better able to integrate the new information with previous knowledge, which increases the likelihood that you will be able to access and retrieve the new information when you need it. Finally, you are able to carry out all these processes more quickly than someone who does not know much about the topic. And, as you'll recall from Chapter 8, the faster you can process information, the less processing capacity you use, and the more of your limited capacity is available for other mental processes. So not only will you be able to remember more of the new information, you will be able to think about it more quickly and at a higher level than someone with less knowledge. Given all this, I suppose it isn't surprising that my sons defeated me so quickly in our Pokémon game.

The influence of prior knowledge is very clear when you study *experts* versus *novices*—that is, when you contrast people who know a lot about a given area with people who know very little about it. Some of the earliest and best-known research on expert–novice differences focused on chess players (Chi, 1978). In one well-known study the chess experts were only 10 years old, whereas the novices were graduate students. The experimenters showed both groups chess pieces in chessboard arrangements that would be likely to occur during a real game. The participants saw the pieces for about one second. Then the researchers asked them to remember the positions and place the pieces on another chessboard in the same arrangements they had viewed. The results

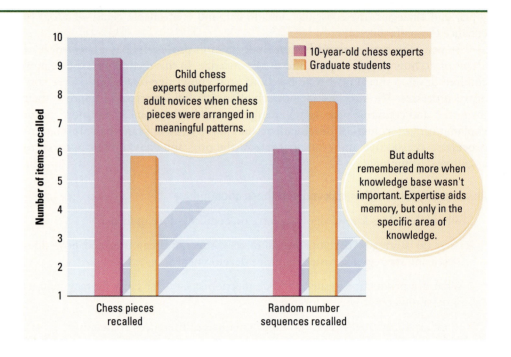

10-year-old chess experts
Graduate students

Child chess experts outperformed adult novices when chess pieces were arranged in meaningful patterns.

But adults remembered more when knowledge base wasn't important. Expertise aids memory, but only in the specific area of knowledge.

Number of items recalled

Chess pieces recalled

Random number sequences recalled

No matter what their age, experts have a greater knowledge base and organize their knowledge differently than novices.

are shown in Figure 11.3. Because of their greater knowledge of chess, the children clearly outperformed the adults. This did not happen because the children had better memories in general: When the task was to remember random sequences of numbers, the graduate students did better, as shown in Figure 11.3. In other words, greater prior knowledge of chess produced better memory, but only for chess. Expert–novice differences in memory and problem-solving performance are evident in many realms, including academic areas (e.g., mathematics, physics, information seeking, and evaluation), sports (e.g., soccer, baseball), and even hobbies and entertainment (e.g., dinosaurs, cartoon characters like Superman or Spider-Man, or *Star Wars* characters and plots) (Brand-Gruval et al., 2005; Chi et al., 1988; Chi & Koeske, 1983; Means & Voss, 1985; Schneider et al., 1993).

Perhaps the most interesting finding from all the work on expert–novice differences is that experts not only have more information but also mentally organize their knowledge about their topics differently than do novices. Instead of storing information about individual chess pieces as a novice would, chess experts mentally group entire board configurations (which are made up of many individual pieces). They store the entire thing as a single chunk in memory. They sometimes even store common *sequences* of moves as a single chunk! In other words, for a chess expert one chunk may contain dozens of individual pieces arranged in successive moves. In contrast, novices think about, store, and retrieve only a few pieces of information at a time. Experts also mentally categorize information based on general principles instead of according to surface-level characteristics. For example, physics novices mentally store physics information according to the kinds of objects they see in the problem situation (e.g., an inclined plane). In contrast, experts mentally organize their knowledge according to general principles of physics (e.g., the principle of inertia) (Chi et al., 1981). As a result, physics experts can quickly recognize the underlying principles involved, categorize the general type of problem they are dealing with, and access relevant information and possible solution strategies. Meanwhile, novices are stuck trying to figure out what, if anything, the existence of an inclined plane means. A novice is like a detective who may notice clues but doesn't think about how they fit together to solve a mystery.

Given that knowledge base affects memory and knowledge organization, how does it help explain cognitive development? Young children are, in essence, "universal novices" (Brown & DeLoache, 1978). They know about fewer topics than older children, and they know less about the topics they have encountered. Because young children have less knowledge, the information in their knowledge bases is less connected than that of older children. Also, it tends to be organized according to surface features rather than according to underlying principles. All these features lead to poorer memory and less efficient cognitive processing. Information-processing psychologists agree that age differences in knowledge base play an important role in explaining cognitive development. In fact, some claim that knowledge base is the *most* important factor in explaining why adults are better than children on most cognitive tasks (Carey, 1985). Notice how different this explanation of cognitive development is from the Piagetian view.

If a rich knowledge base has such important effects, what does it take for children to acquire one? The few longitudinal studies that have been done confirm what you are probably thinking—lots of practice is absolutely necessary. In studies of both chess experts and tennis experts, it seems that practice, along with motivational factors such as interest and dedication, were more important than general aptitude measures (Renniger et al., 1992; Schneider, 1993). How extensive a knowledge base is necessary? Not surprisingly, it appears that it takes a fairly high degree of knowledge to enhance children's performance and produce changes in the structure of their knowledge (DeMarie-Dreblow, 1991).

Think About Angelique . . .

What parts of Angelique's knowledge base must improve to help her solve story problems more effectively? How can Manny help with this?

Strategy Development

While reading a new book one day, 10-year-old Will encounters the word *facilitates*. He pauses and looks carefully at the picture on the page, but cannot figure out the word. He tries to sound out the individual letters but still doesn't understand the text. Finally, Will points to the word and asks his teacher for help. Will's attempts to understand the book are *strategies*—the conscious, intentional, and controllable plans that people use to improve performance at all stages of information processing (Schneider & Bjorklund, 1998). As you can see, Will tried three different strategies to encode the new word: using the context, sounding it out, and asking for help. He will probably use several other strategies to understand the story, store it in memory, and recall it later on. Information-processing psychologists have given enormous attention to children's development of cognitive strategies, because they believe that strategies have a strong impact on thinking, remembering, and solving problems.

Research has looked in depth at the development of several specific memory strategies. One strategy is *rehearsal,* or repeating information that you want to remember. Rehearsal can be a very effective memory strategy, because it increases the likelihood that information will be stored in memory. As you might expect, the amount of rehearsal is important—more rehearsal tends to produce better memory performance, but the style of rehearsal may be even more important. Older children tend to use a cumulative (or active) rehearsal style, in which they repeat several items together. In contrast, younger children use a more passive style—they repeat only the last item they are trying to remember. This passive style does not encourage further processing of other items, and it doesn't encourage the child to look for relationships among the items. Younger children can be trained to use cumulative rehearsal; doing so improves their memory performance, but they do not tend to continue using it after training (Naus et al., 1977).

Two other useful memory strategies are *organization,* in which we use relationships among items to improve our memory for the items, and *elaboration,* in which we create visual or verbal associations to link the items. In

your perspective

Think of a problem you had to solve recently. Did you use only one strategy or several? How (and why) have your "favorite" strategies changed over the years?

These children are likely using different strategies. How might they use rehearsal, elaboration, and organization to improve their memory of their spelling words?

general, all three strategies show similar changes across ages (Pressley & Hilden, 2006).

- Preschool children are less likely to use these strategies spontaneously than school-age children, but younger children can easily be taught to use the strategies. And when used correctly, the strategies can help their memory performance.

- Even after training, younger children usually do not use the strategies as effectively or as consistently as older children. Even when younger children are trained to the point that they spontaneously use a strategy on new information, their memory of the information does not always improve (Bjorklund & Coyle, 1995; Bjorklund et al., 1997).

- The three strategies typically appear at different ages. Simple forms of rehearsal are found in preschool children, but organization is not common until the elementary school years, and spontaneous use of elaboration does not occur until adolescence or even later (Hasselhorn, 1992; Pressley & Afflerbach, 1995).

- Children use strategies more often and more effectively with familiar materials and meaningful, interesting activities (Rogoff & Mistry, 1990).

It is also important to keep in mind that strategies do not function in isolation. Children do not use only one strategy at a time, and they do not move neatly from less sophisticated to more sophisticated strategies. Instead, they typically use a variety of different strategies from one problem to the next. Sometimes—as with 10-year-old Will and the word *facilitates*—children use combinations of multiple strategies on a single problem (Coyle & Bjorklund, 1997; Siegler, 1995). Children's strategy development can be thought of as a series of *overlapping waves* in which children use a variety of different strategies, some simpler and some more complex. The particular strategies used most often gradually shift from the simpler to the more complex (Geary et al., 2004; Kwong & Varnhagen, 2005; Siegler, 2006; Torbeyns et al., 2005). The shift occurs as the child becomes more efficient in using the more complex strategy, which reduces the "cost" in terms of cognitive capacity and provides greater "benefits" in terms of better performance.

Think About Angelique . . .

How could Angelique use rehearsal, organization, and elaboration to improve her math performance? Can you think of other reading or math strategies that might help her?

Newer Approaches to Understanding Cognitive Development

Research on information processing began in the mid-twentieth century when computers became available on most university campuses and research sites. Since those days computers have obviously become much more powerful and sophisticated. The primitive computers of the 1950s would have been hard pressed to perform the functions of one of today's cheap pocket calculators! And just as computers have grown and developed, so has our understanding of children's cognitive processing. The stores model you saw in Figure 8.5 was first proposed in the 1960s, and it is very simple compared to the models and theories of cognitive processing being developed today. In this last section we will introduce you to some of the ideas that information-processing theorists are exploring today.

Computational Models of Thought. Some information-processing researchers try to map the exact steps that people go through as they solve problems or perform other cognitive tasks. To test their conclusions, these researchers create computer programs that attempt to mimic the thought processes of humans. These theories of cognition that are programmed and tested on computers are known as **computational models**

computational models
Models of cognition that are programmed on computers: output of the programs is compared to human performance.

(Klahr & MacWhinney, 1998; Munakatu, 2006). Researchers have been developing and testing computational models of adult cognition since the early days of information processing, but we include this as a new approach because of these models' more recent use in work on children's cognitive development. There are two general types of computational models: *production systems* and *connectionist models*.

Production systems are sets of computerized *if–then statements*, or "productions," that state the specific actions that a person will take under certain conditions. For example, Table 11.1 shows hypothetical productions for solving a Piagetian liquid conservation problem like those you learned about in Chapter 8. Each production

production systems
Sets of computerized *if–then statements* that state the specific actions that will be taken under certain conditions.

TABLE 11.1 Examples of Possible Productions for a Piagetian Liquid Conservation Task

The task is to say whether the two containers still have the same amount of liquid, or if one has more. This hypothetical production system proposes four different ways that children can solve this problem. If these models were run on a computer, the researcher could compare the computer's output to that of real children to see how well the production system matches the children's performance.

Model I.
Considers only the height of liquid in each container.

P1: ((Same Height) → (Say "same"))
P2: ((Container C more Height) → (Say "C has more"))

Model II.
Considers both the height and the width of the liquid in each container, but only if the height and width information are consistent.

P1: ((Same Height) → (Say "same"))
P2: ((Container C more Height) → (Say "C has more"))
P3: ((Same Height) (Container C more Width) → (Say "C has more"))

Model III.
Considers both height and width, but not sure how to coordinate them.

P1: ((Same Height) → (Say "same"))
P2: ((Container C more Height) → (Say "C has more"))
P3: ((Same Height) (Container C more Width) → (Say "C has more"))
P4: ((Container C more Height) (Container C less Width) → muddle through)
P5: ((Container C more Height) (Container C more Width) → (Say "C has more"))

Model IV.
Considers both height and width of both containers, coordinating them by estimating volume.

P1: ((Same Height) → (Say "same"))
P2: ((Container C more Height) → (Say "C has more"))
P3: ((Same Height) (Container C more Width) → (Say "C has more"))
P4: ((Container C more Height) (Container C less Width) → (get Volume))
P5: ((Container C more Height) (Container C more Width) → (Say "C has more"))
P6: ((Same Volume) → (Say "same"))
P7: ((Container C more Volume) → (Say "C has more"))

P = An individual production, or *if-then statement*, e.g., IF both containers have the same height, THEN say "same."
C = The container holding the liquid.
Height = Height of the liquid in the container.
Width = Width of the liquid in the container.
(Adapted from Klahr & Siegler, 1978, p. 78.)

---

specifies a *condition* that must be met before the production will be implemented (this is the *if* part) and a specific *action* that will be taken (the *then* part). When you look closely at Table 11.1, it is easy to see how production systems quickly become complex. The system must specify the many different conditions a person might encounter and the specific actions to be taken under each condition. The system also must include *decision rules* for deciding which productions to implement when the conditions of more than one production are met, when none of the conditions for any existing production are met, or when other complicating situations exist (Klahr & Siegler, 1978; Munakatu, 2006).

Think About Angelique . . .

How would it help Angelique to notice the conditions *and* actions *in the problems she's trying to solve? How can Manny help her notice and remember these relations?*

Researchers use production systems to clarify and test hypotheses about development. They specify the exact conditions that must be met, the exact actions that will be taken, and the exact input information needed. They then compare the computer-produced output with the solutions real children produce for similar problems. This allows the researchers to identify parts of the model that are wrong or vague. Earlier production systems emphasized matching children's performance at different ages. More recently, researchers have focused on developing self-modifying production systems, or systems that "learn," in order to simulate the actual process of developmental change (Halford et al., 1995; Siegler & Shipley, 1995; Simon & Klahr, 1995). These models provide invaluable information about the precise processes that change as a child develops (e.g., exactly what happens when a child generalizes, discriminates, or chunks information) and about the conditions under which the changes occur.

connectionist models
"Neurally inspired" or neural network models of cognition that view knowledge as based on patterns of activation among interconnected sets of individual units rather than stored as entire concepts.

Like production systems, **connectionist models** are computational in that they are implemented in a computer simulation and focus on cognitive processes. However, they differ from most other cognitive theories in one important way: Connectionist models hypothesize that knowledge is not "stored" at all. Instead, all knowledge is believed to be reconstructed based on different patterns of activations among interconnected sets of numerous individual components. These models reflect what is known about the workings of neurons in the brain and so are said to be "neurally inspired." They are often referred to as *neural networks*. Figure 11.4 shows a simple connectionist model. The basic elements are its *units*—simple elements that combine to form different patterns. Each unit has a certain *level of activation*—the degree to which it is "turned on" at any given time. The individual units are connected by *links*. The links vary in how strongly they are weighted, with heavily weighted links capable of transmitting activation between two units more easily than lightly weighted links. As shown in the figure, the input layer represents the signals that initially enter the network, the output layer represents the decisions made by the network, and various layers hidden in between enable the network to make a variety of different connections between the input and output layers (Munakatu, 2006).

Researchers "train" these connectionist models; that is, they compare a program's output to people's performance, then adjust the program to produce a better match. The main point is to match humans' *developmental changes*—to get the computer model to show the same learning patterns that humans show, including patterns of generalization to new problems. "Learning" occurs through changes in the weights of the links between units. Many different learning rules can be incorporated into the computer program, and each one has different effects on the network. The different learning rules correspond to different hypotheses about how learning takes place, and the different patterns of connections represent different levels of knowledge. By identifying the learning rules and connection patterns that provide the best fit between computer and human learning patterns, we can begin to understand changes in human learning (Bates & Elman, 2002; Thomas & Karmiloff-Smith, 2003).

As you might expect, developing connectionist models is quite complex and time consuming, and each model must be specific to a single domain. Models have been developed and tested to investigate the learning processes in such diverse areas as learning second languages, acquiring vocabulary, learning word meanings, solving

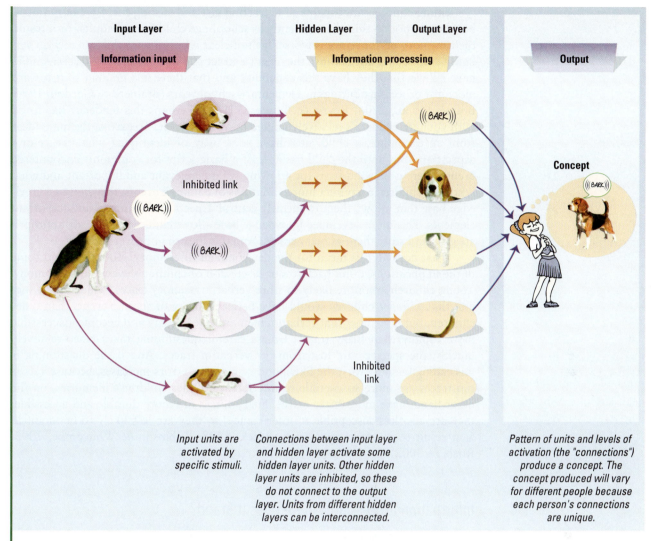

Information input

Information processing

Output

Inhibited link

(((BARK)))

Concept

(((BARK)))

Inhibited link

| Input units are activated by specific stimuli. | Connections between input layer and hidden layer activate some hidden layer units. Other hidden layer units are inhibited, so these do not connect to the output layer. Units from different hidden layers can be interconnected. | Pattern of units and levels of activation (the "connections") produce a concept. The concept produced will vary for different people because each person's connections are unique. |

Figure 11.4 • A Simple Connectionist Model The ovals are the individual units of this model. There are three different layers: an input layer, one hidden layer, and an output layer. The lines with arrows represent the links between individual units, and the different widths of lines represent degrees of strength between particular units. Notice that the input units can connect to all the output units, but not directly. Their connection is mediated by the hidden layers of units. (Based on Klahr & MacWhinney, 1998, p. 649.)

balance-beam problems, and even forming emotional attachments (Klahr & MacWhinney, 1998; Rodd et al., 2004; Zevin & Seidenberg, 2004).

Fuzzy Trace Theory. Think back to something you did yesterday. Now try to remember something interesting that happened several years ago. Do you remember the exact details of the events, or do you instead recall the general gist and then reconstruct the details? The main idea of **fuzzy trace theory** is that memory representations (or traces) vary on a continuum from very exact and literal traces to imprecise, general, and "fuzzy" traces based on the gist of the message (Brainerd, 2005; Brainerd & Reyna, 1993, 1995, 2004). This view says that people typically do not reason logically from precise, verbatim recollections. Instead, we have a strong tendency toward intuitive reasoning based on the main ideas. These fuzzy memory traces are less detailed and are better integrated with our prior knowledge than verbatim traces. Better integration means that there are multiple access and retrieval cues associated with fuzzy traces. As a result, they last longer and are easier to access, less effortful to use, and less susceptible to interference and forgetting than are verbatim traces.

fuzzy trace theory
The view that memory representations vary on a continuum from exact and literal to imprecise and general memory traces based on the gist of the information or event.

Young children are capable of extracting gist and storing fuzzy memory traces, but they do not do this as consistently as school-age children and adults. As a result, their memory performance is worse. It's not clear why younger children rely on verbatim traces. It is not because they can't extract gist and form fuzzy traces; studies have shown that they have this capability and that there is a gradual shift toward more gist processing during the elementary school years (Brainerd & Gordon, 1994; Brainerd et al., 2004; Reyna & Brainerd, 1995). Perhaps this tendency has to do with younger children's relatively limited knowledge base. To extract the main ideas from an encounter, a child must have some way of identifying what the central aspects are. But until the child has at least a basic script for commonly encountered events, there is no solid basis for knowing what is relevant and important and what is not. As children encounter more variations of common events, they build a knowledge base that allows them to identify central aspects and common and important elements. This more developed knowledge base allows children to identify appropriate gists and store them as fuzzy traces. And this in turn improves memory.

What does all this mean for the development of memory? To understand some of the implications, think back to our discussion of children's eyewitness testimony. Young children are more likely to store verbatim memory traces, which might suggest that younger children would have better memory of specific events than older children. But remember that verbatim memory traces decay and become inaccessible more rapidly than fuzzy traces. Unless careful questioning takes place relatively quickly, the specifics are lost from the verbatim traces. And if the questioning is misleading in some way, the likelihood of memory errors increases, because verbatim traces are more susceptible to interference. Older children's memories, on the other hand, have more fuzzy traces. Fuzzy traces are more durable and accessible; they are also less susceptible to interference, so they are less likely to be modified as a result of questioning (Ceci & Bruck, 1998; Robinson & Whitcombe, 2003; Roebers, 2002).

Information Processing: Where Does It Stand?

Since the early 1960s information processing has become the dominant model for understanding cognitive development. Through its emphasis on detailed analysis of specific cognitive processes, the computer metaphor of "thinking as the processing of information" has greatly increased our understanding of developmental change.

There are limits to this approach, however. The most obvious is that despite the detailed information it has provided, the information-processing approach does not offer a comprehensive, overarching structure for explaining cognitive development like that of Piaget's theory. We know a lot about many specific areas of development, and we have many "toy versions" of the real-life cognitive processes we wish to understand (Klahr & MacWhinney, 1998). Yet no comprehensive theory addresses the whole of cognitive development and how it might be related to other areas of development. Second, the information-processing approach has been described as "cold" cognition because of its emphasis on thoughts based on logical reasoning. Information-processing models rarely consider such factors as social interaction, emotional reactions, or motivation, even though these factors are quite important in real-life cognition. In the past, these models have also been slow to incorporate new information about the biological bases of cognitive development, though newer connectionist models are now attempting to do this. And finally, critics have long pointed out that most information-processing models depend on an "executive processor" (something that oversees all processes and determines the allocation of cognitive resources, strategy use, and the like)—but lack details on how the executive works or develops. Both fuzzy trace theory and connectionist models, which explain change without the need for an executive processor, address this criticism.

■ Let's Review . . .

1. Children who were chess experts were compared to adults who were chess novices. What differences were found in their memory for chess pieces?
   a. Child novices remembered as many chess pieces as adult novices.
   b. Child experts remembered fewer chess pieces than adult experts.
   c. Child experts remembered as many chess pieces as adult novices.
   d. Child experts remembered more chess pieces than adult novices.

2. As children's knowledge bases increase, they tend to do all of the following, except _____.
   a. use information-processing strategies more effectively
   b. organize information into smaller "chunks" or pieces of information
   c. notice details about and relationships among pieces of information
   d. encode, store, and retrieve information more quickly

3. Neural networks are an example of a _____.
   a. production system   b. fuzzy trace model
   c. stores model   d. connectionist model

4. Fuzzy traces tend to be:
   a. remembered longer than memories that are exact and precise.
   b. remembered for less time than memories that are exact and precise.
   c. remembered about as long as memories that are exact and precise.
   d. more effortful to use than memories that are exact and precise.

5. **True or False:** In connectionist models, learning is represented by changes in the weights of the links among units in the model.

6. **True or False:** The connectionist and fuzzy trace theories both say there is an executive processor that directs ongoing cognitive activity.

Answers: 1. d, 2. b, 3. d, 4. a, 5. T, 6. F

Learning to Communicate: Language in Middle Childhood

Language development during early childhood is quite impressive, but it is far from complete by the time a child enters school. The middle childhood years see development in several important areas of language.

As you study this section, ask yourself these questions:

■ What language skills do children develop between 7 and 11 years of age?

■ What is metalinguistic awareness and why is it important for language skill? Why does it not develop before the middle childhood years?

■ How do 7- to 11-year-olds differ from younger children in their use of language?

■ What are connectionist models of language development, and what evidence supports these approaches?

Experts in the Basics

Semantic knowledge, or what words mean, continues to increase dramatically over middle childhood. While a typical 2-year-old knows about 200 words and a 6-year-old about 10,000, the vocabulary of a typical 10-year-old contains about 40,000 words—and this grows to about 80,000 words by high school age (Anglin, 1993; McLaughlin, 2006). The kinds of words that older children acquire are more abstract words such as *irony* or *justice* because increases in cognitive development allow them to better understand these abstract concepts (Hulit & Howard, 2006; McGhee-Bidlack, 1991). *Phonemic* development (knowing about basic speech sounds) continues as well. As children enter elementary school, they begin to master more difficult phonemes such as *j* or *th*. During middle childhood, children continue to show increased understanding of how to use intonation (or tone of voice) to change the meaning of utterances. For example, a sentence such as "Rachel took a bracelet from Mom and she took one from Lily." can have two different meanings, depending on whether *and* or *she* is emphasized.

The school-age years also see increases in children's mastery of grammar and *syntax* (rules for combining words into sentences). For example, English-speaking preschool children rarely use the passive voice in their speech, and show only incomplete understanding when they hear it. Sentences such as "The dog was patted by the girl" or "Donald was liked by Goofy" are quite difficult for young children and are likely to be understood as "The dog patted the girl" and "Donald liked Goofy." At ages 8 or 9, however, children begin to produce full passive sentences, though some forms of the passive voice remain difficult throughout middle childhood (Bever, 1970; Horgan, 1978; Maratsos et al., 1979). However, this sequence of grammatical development is not universal. In languages where the passive voice is more important and frequent, such as the Southern African language Sesotho, it is understood and used correctly much earlier (by 2 to 4 years of age) (Demuth, 1990; Tomasello, 2006). By 9 to 11 years of age, children are also able to draw inferences from what they hear or read and recognize that the inferred information was not directly stated. The ability to draw inferences is essential for understanding and producing many of the more subtle uses of language, including sarcasm, humor, or metaphor (Casteel, 1993; Dews et al., 1996).

Children's *pragmatic* language skills (using language to effectively interact with others) continue to improve throughout middle childhood. Referential communication skills improve from early childhood such that older children are now able to spontaneously identify and correct ambiguities in their own and others' speech, and they are able to take effective steps to correct the ambiguities (Beal & Belgrad, 1990; Kemper & Vernoog, 1994). Children of this age are also becoming much more skilled in the social rules of discourse. Just listen to any 10-year-old child on the phone with her friends and it's clear that they know how to have successful conversations!

your perspective

Evaluate your own metalinguistic awareness. How does this awareness affect your ability to use language effectively? How might you increase your level of metalinguistic awareness?

metalinguistic awareness
A person's explicit knowledge about language itself and about his or her own use of it.

These children are using their language skills to tell jokes and understand humor. How does their metalinguistic awareness help them enjoy riddles and jokes?

Metalinguistic Awareness

One of the most notable features of language development during the middle childhood years is the increase in **metalinguistic awareness,** or the explicit knowledge about language itself and one's own use of it (McLaughlin, 2006). Metalinguistic awareness is the result of a great deal of experience with using language along with increases in cognitive abilities, and it contributes to a number of linguistic skills. For example, one aspect of metalinguistic awareness is the understanding that a single word can have multiple meanings. This enables children to use language more flexibly and even to create and appreciate humor based on different word meanings. Metalinguistic awareness also helps children self-monitor and self-correct the speech they produce and receive, which means they can communicate more effectively. Finally, explicit knowledge of the social rules of discourse helps children have more effective and socially acceptable conversations. Not surprisingly, a higher level of metalinguistic awareness at early ages is related to higher reading ability in the early elementary school years (McBride-Chang, 1996; Warren-Leubecker & Carter, 1988).

Changes in How Language Is Used

During middle childhood, children not only develop a more complete and explicit understanding of language, they also begin to use language in different ways. Preschool children play with language, creating nonsense words that rhyme or adding morphemes to create words that express strong feelings, such as "icky" or "gooey" (Ely & McCabe, 1994). School-age children continue to create words in this way, and they also begin to show a great interest in riddles and other forms of verbal humor. These kinds of language play require a more advanced understanding of language rules, especially the understanding that word meanings and syntax can be ambiguous (Ely, 1997; Ely & McCabe, 1994).

Finally, older children begin to use language to describe and understand important aspects of themselves. **Personal narratives** are stories about the storyteller's experiences. They involve the use of language to inform others about the self, as well as using language as a tool for increased self-understanding. While even 2-year-olds are able to give rudimentary narratives, it is during middle childhood that children become able to provide coherent narratives that fully describe and evaluate their personal experiences. For example, 4-year-olds' personal narratives tend to have a *leap-frog* structure in which they jump from one topic to another without giving a complete account of what happened and how they felt about it. Between 4 and 8 years of age, personal narratives often have more of a *chronological* structure in which the storyteller reports a sequence of events without adding details or evaluating the events. By the age of 8 or 9, children show a *classic narrative* structure in which the story leads up to a main event (called the high point), an evaluation of how the storyteller feels about the event is offered, and then the event is resolved. Narrative skills are strong predictors of later language and literacy skills, and educational television programs can help children learn the classic narrative structure. The evaluation aspect of personal narratives will continue to increase in complexity and variety throughout adolescence (Berman & Slobin, 1994; Engel, 1995; Peterson & McCabe, 1983; Uchikoshi, 2005).

However, the preferred style of a personal narrative varies depending upon the child's culture. In addition to helping children better understand themselves, personal narratives serve to help children come to know and understand their broader cultures (Gee, 1992). For example, Hispanic children's narratives have been found to focus more on family relationships, while Japanese children's narratives include events that are related to a central theme rather than by time, place, or family membership. The narratives of middle- and working-class white children in North America typically focus on a single topic, while working-class African-American children tell personal narratives that are longer and include several different characters and events linked by a general theme (Ely, 1997; Michaels, 1991; Minami & McCabe, 1990). The different narrative styles reflect the values and structure of their respective cultures, and thus are one way in which language helps children come to understand the central aspects of their cultures in a very personal way.

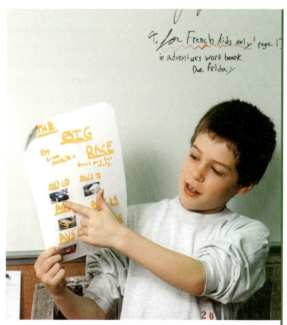

Children use personal narratives to discover and communicate things about themselves. What do you think this child is communicating in his personal narrative?

personal narratives
Stories about personal experiences that use language to inform others about the self and that provide increased self-understanding.

Think About Angelique . . .
What are some ways in which Angelique could use narratives to help her understand and solve math story problems more effectively?

Connectionist Models of Language Development

In Chapter 5, we talked about several main theories of language development—the learning theory (based primarily on Skinner's operant conditioning principles and proposing that language is a learned skill), the nativist view (based on Chomsky and others' theory that language is largely a biologically programmed skill in humans), and interaction theories (with some, like Piaget, emphasizing the role of cognitive factors and others emphasizing the role of social interactions for language acquisition).

A more recent and very intriguing cognitive approach to understanding language development is based on the *connectionist models* of cognition you read about in the last section. Recall that connectionist models are neural network models in which links of varying strengths connect simple elements called *units*. Applied to language development, connectionist models say that language acquisition results from changes in the strengths of connections between units based on how closely the language produced matches external criteria. For example, imagine that a boy sees an animal that looks a lot like the animal he associates with the word *dog*. Units corresponding to characteristics of the input (the dog) stimulate the pattern of connections the boy has developed for these input features in the past, so he says "Look at that dog." But his dad says, "Wow, look at that coyote—right in our yard!" Even though the father is not explicitly correcting his son's utterance, he is providing a model by using a specific word consistently for the new animal. As the boy continues to encounter the animal (by seeing it, seeing pictures of it, talking or thinking about it) and hear the same name, the links between the units that produce *dog* will decrease in strength, and those that lead to the production of the word *coyote* will increase. Eventually, he will come to call this animal a coyote.

The strongest support for connectionism comes from computer simulations. Researchers presented verbs to a computer with the same frequency that children typically encounter them in everyday language. Even though the computer never received and did not learn any explicit rules, it gradually learned to produce correct past tenses for both regular and irregular verbs, and it showed patterns of acquiring past tenses that were quite similar to those of children (Rumelhart & McClelland, 1986). Even more convincing are the findings that the simulation showed the same kinds of error patterns as children—and that the connectionist model successfully predicts which specific grammatical cues (such as word endings or word order) children will acquire first in specific languages (MacWhinney, 1987, 1999). However, critics argue that language development based on gradual changes in connection strengths would take far longer than it actually does for real children. A related criticism is that children often learn new words after a single exposure to them. Such *one-trial learning* can be difficult for these models to explain.

■ Let's Review . . .

1. Which of the following children is showing metalinguistic awareness?
   a. Andy, who knows that *hammer* can be both a thing and an action.
   b. Will, who knows how to use a *hammer*.
   c. Rachel, who knows that *hammer* means to hit something.
   d. Lily, who knows that both *hammers* and *mallets* can be used to pound things.

2. Personal narratives are important in language development primarily because they _____.
   a. indicate a child's level of semantic development
   b. force the child to use more complex grammatical structures
   c. allow the child to use language to inform others about the self
   d. provide a way for parents to offer explicit feedback about social rules of language use

3. **True or False:** Children do not understand correct use of the passive voice in grammar until well into the middle childhood years regardless of the language they speak.

4. **True or False:** Connectionist models of language development say that children must receive direct and explicit feedback in order to learn language.

Answers: 1. a, 2. c, 3. F, 4. F

Cognition in Context

The first sections of this chapter presented information about the development of children's cognitive skills during middle childhood. But an important part of children's lives during middle childhood involves learning in school. How do children use their cognitive abilities to deal with academic tasks? This section will discuss the development of mathematical, reading, and writing skills. Our descriptions begin with the foundations laid down during infancy and early childhood and continue past the middle childhood years, but we have included this broader range of ages in this chapter because of the importance of these academic skills in the middle childhood years.

As you study this section, ask yourself these questions:

- What are some of the major skills children develop in mathematics? What mathematical competencies and limitations do children of different ages typically show?

- What stages do children go through as they learn to read? What are some important factors that predict reading skill? How can families and schools encourage reading skill?

- What are the major accomplishments that children achieve as they learn to write?

Development of Mathematical Skills

Laying the Foundation for Mathematical Skills. Amazing but true: Researchers have found evidence that even *newborns* have rudimentary mathematical skills. Humans seem to be "born with a fundamental sense of quantity" (Geary, 1994, p. 1). For example, researchers showed newborn infants (less than one week old!) a card with two black dots (Antell & Keating, 1983). The newborns looked at the dots for a bit, then started looking away. Looking away signals boredom; in Chapter five we referred to this as *habituation*. When researchers then switched to a card that had three dots, the newborns regained interest in looking at the dots—they *dishabituated*. These patterns of habituation and dishabituation show that newborns can see the difference between two and three dots.

How are infants able to show such skills? They clearly cannot count objects. They have no experience with a number system, and they don't have the language skills they need to say the words that go with the numbers. Researchers propose that infants enumerate small sets by **subitizing,** a perceptual process that we all use to quickly and easily determine the basic quantity in a small set of objects. To see how subitizing works, try the following experiment. Have your friend toss three or four pennies onto a table while you have your eyes closed. Now open your eyes and, as quickly as you can, look to see how many pennies there are. Most people can "see" that there are three pennies, or four pennies, without needing to actually count each penny. There is something about the visual arrangement of the pennies that lets you know immediately how many there are.

During the preschool years, children *learn to count*. At about the age of 2, children begin to associate the counting words used in their language with the correct number of objects. By about 4 years of age, they begin to use counting as a tool to solve simple arithmetic problems rather than rely on subitizing. This represents an important advance in their mathematical skills—a child can use counting with sets of any size and in the absence of concrete objects, whereas subitizing works only with small sets and visible objects. Children quickly begin to use several different **counting strategies,** approaches to solving problems that involve counting of the quantities. For example: A child figures out that $2 + 2 = 4$ by first counting to 2 and then counting on (2 more

subitizing
A perceptual process where people quickly and easily determine how many objects are in a small set without actually counting them.

counting strategies
Approaches to solving math problems that involve counting of the quantities.

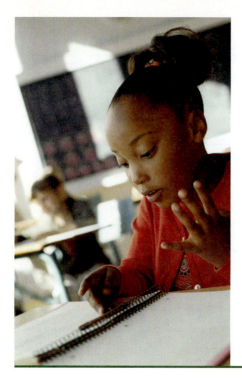

steps) to 3 and then 4. Preschoolers learn to solve simple problems whether the change in number is visible to them, screened from their view, or even described verbally in the absence of any concrete objects. Gradually, over the later preschool and elementary school years, children increase the complexity and sophistication of their counting strategies (Aunola et al.; Geary, 2006).

Mathematical Skills during the Elementary School Years. Over the course of the elementary school years, the counting strategies children use to solve addition and subtraction problems gradually become more efficient. Table 11.2 shows some of these strategies. Younger children tend to use strategies that require more counting. This is cumbersome and increases the opportunity for errors, but it reduces the burden on their working memory. As children gain experience, they tend to move to strategies that require more memory but can be executed more quickly. Children begin to store basic math facts and simply retrieve them from memory instead of relying on counting strategies. Once a child has memorized a fact, he or she has a tool for deriving the answers to other, nonmemorized problems. For example, given the problem $5 + 8$, a child who knows that $5 + 5 = 10$ may use this known fact, reason that 8 is 3 more than 5, and add 3 to 10 to obtain the answer 13 (Ashcraft, 1992; for reviews, see Geary, 1994, and Ginsburg et al., 1998).

When given addition and subtraction problems, should children be allowed to use back-up strategies such as counting on their fingers?

TABLE 11.2 Examples of Common Counting Strategies for Addition

STRATEGY	EXAMPLE PROBLEM	USE OF STRATEGY
Counting manipulatives	2 + 5	Child counts two manipulatives (e.g., blocks, coins, candies), then counts five more manipulatives, then counts all seven objects.
Counting fingers	2 + 5	Child raises two fingers on one hand, then five on the other hand. Child then counts all seven fingers one at a time, moving each one as it is counted.
Counting all (sum)	2 + 5	Child counts the first number aloud "1, 2." Child then continues counting on by the second number "3, 4, 5, 6, 7"—then states the answer as "7."
Counting on from first	2 + 5	Child states the first number "2"; counts on by the second number "3, 4, 5, 6, 7"; then states the answer as "7."
Counting on from larger (also called minimum strategy or min)	2 + 5	Child states the biggest number, regardless of whether it is first or second. Here, the child says "5," then counts on by the smaller number ("6, 7"), then states the answer as "7."
Decomposition (deriving a fact)	7 + 6	Child decomposes the 6 into "3 + 3", adds 7 + 3 and gets 10, adds the other 3 to 10, and gives the answer: 13. (The child could choose to decompose the other number, 7, into 4 + 3, add 4 + 6 to get 10, then add the remaining 3 to 10.)
Fact retrieval	2 + 5	Child retrieves the answer from long-term memory and states the answer as "7."
Regrouping	16 + 23	Child decomposes both numbers into tens and ones (16 = 10 + 6; 23 = 20 + 3), sums the tens and ones separately (10 + 20 = 30; 6 + 3 = 9), adds the subtotals (30 + 9 = 39), states answer: 39.

(Adapted from Geary, 1994.)

How do elementary school children memorize and retrieve math facts? One possibility is the **strategy choice model** (Siegler & Jenkins, 1989). According to this model, "Children tend to choose the fastest approach that they can execute accurately" (Siegler, 1998, p. 286). Using a fast strategy increases the likelihood that the problem and answer will both be present in working memory, and therefore increases their degree of association. Using the most accurate strategy helps ensure that the association will develop between the problem and its *correct* answer. The more often a correct answer (e.g., 7) is associated with a problem (e.g., 4 + 3), the stronger the association between them and the more likely that the child will retrieve this answer on future occasions. If the degree of association is not strong, the child will use a *backup strategy* such as counting, guessing, or deriving an answer based on known facts or rules. According to the strategy choice model, discouraging children from using backup strategies (like counting on their fingers) may actually *delay* their memorizing basic math facts (Siegler, 1998). Can you explain why?

Though children gradually move from less to more efficient strategies, they do not rely on a single strategy for solving arithmetic problems. Instead, they consistently use a variety of strategies. The strategy choice model helps explain why. The availability of multiple strategies increases the likelihood that a child can obtain a correct answer quickly. This helps the child succeed in solving problems and helps build strong associations between problems and their correct answers. Researchers have found evidence of multiple strategies for a variety of arithmetic operations and across a wide range of student ages, abilities, and nationalities (Fuson & Kwon, 1992; Geary, 1996; LeFevre & Bisanz, 1996; Lemaire & Siegler, 1995; Mabbott & Bisanz, 2003).

For better or worse, elementary school children spend many hours working on mathematical *word problems,* or verbal descriptions of mathematical situations. As you may recall from personal experience, word problems can cause even the best math students to groan with dread. Several factors contribute to the difficulty of a word problem—among them the number of words in the problem, the number of required arithmetic operations, and the number of mathematical terms. The context of the problem has an important effect as well. Sometimes problems are difficult because their content is simply not interesting to the child, their wording is confusing, or their context is unfamiliar. In one study, for example, Brazilian children experienced at selling products at street stands were quite good at solving word problems that had a "selling" context, even when the items named in the problems were not ones they had sold. Their performance was much worse when problems did not have the sales context, even though the required computations were identical to those in the other problems (Carraher et al., 1985). Unfamiliar details and situations may not provide effective cues to help children access and use relevant knowledge, or they may simply overload working memory. With familiar contexts, children have a greater chance of comprehending the situation being described, understanding what they are being asked to figure out, and being motivated to solve the problem (Mayer et al., 1992; Stern, 1993; Vlahovicetic et al., 2004).

Children continue to increase their knowledge of basic mathematical principles throughout their school years, although some principles take a long time to develop (Geary, 2006). Sometimes misunderstandings of fundamental math principles lead to *bugs,* or systematic errors in children's problem-solving procedures. Buggy procedures are common in all arithmetic operations, and they can persist well into the late elementary school years. During the later part of middle childhood, children begin to learn about more complex math topics such as fractions, geometry, and algebra.

strategy choice model
The idea that children solve math problems by choosing the fastest approach that they can execute accurately.

Think About Angelique . . .
How could Manny use the strategy choice model to better understand the problems Angelique has in remembering math facts? According to this model, what strategies might help Angelique improve?

your perspective
Are word problems difficult for you? How are your mathematical problem-solving efforts affected by problem context and the types of relations in the problem?

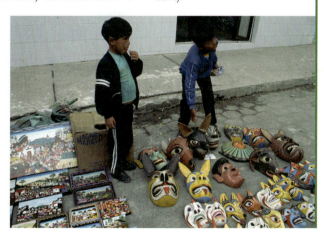

This Brazilian street vendor shows a great deal of math skill when he is calculating prices and making change for customers. With the traditional math problems that are used in classrooms, however, he will likely show much less skill. Context has a powerful effect on children's math problem-solving ability.

As they do so, they consistently attempt to build new understanding on what they already know. At times this leads to misunderstandings of new principles; but when students recognize their mistakes, they begin to debug their math knowledge and understand the accurate procedures. Instruction that builds on prior knowledge is typically more effective in helping students understand new mathematical concepts. In contrast, instruction that focuses on memorization of facts and rules gives students less opportunity to work out their buggy procedures. As a result, mistakes can take longer to correct (Clement, 1982).

Development of Reading Skills

Reading is perhaps the single most important academic skill we acquire. Western cultures tend to be reading- and writing-based, so we get much of our knowledge and information through books, magazines, newspapers, instruction manuals, the Internet and television, and other print media. An expert on reading development, Jeanne Chall, surmised that "the learning and uses of literacy are among the most advanced forms of intelligence, and, compared to other forms, depend more on instruction and practice" (1983, p. 2). Chall (1983) proposed six developmental stages that describe how children typically learn to read, as summarized in Table 11.3. Chall commented that many adults may never reach the most mature stage of reading, even after four years of college.

In fact, too many people have trouble reaching even Chall's fourth stage, "Reading for New Learning." Researchers estimate that in the United States 25 percent of people are poor readers and 36 percent of fourth graders score below the basic reading level for their grade (Adams et al., 1998; Donahue et al., 1999; Perie et al., 2005). To see how volunteers can help children and adults overcome illiteracy, read the Personal Perspective box on page 394 called "Meet a Literacy Volunteer."

Two of the factors that best predict success in early reading are *familiarity with letters of the alphabet* and *phonemic awareness* (Adams et al., 1998). Preschoolers who show early familiarity with letters tend to be more successful in reading through the primary grades. In contrast, preschoolers who are less familiar with letters tend to have more difficulty learning to read. Children whose primary language is not English tend to be less familiar with letters and have greater difficulty learning to read in English in school. Reading difficulty really emerges, however, when children cannot blend the printed letters together to form whole words.

Phonemic awareness is the understanding that words are made up of smaller units of sound, or *phonemes*. This understanding involves associating printed letters with the sounds that go with them. Phonemic awareness usually begins developing during the first year of formal schooling as children learn to make the speech sounds associated with each letter and with various letter combinations. Success with phonemic awareness is a strong predictor of later reading success—even stronger than the child's overall IQ (Adams et al., 1998; Eldredge, 2005; Spira et al., 2005; Strattman & Hodson, 2005; Vellutino & Scanlon, 1987). A major source of reading weakness is difficulty in decoding (or breaking down) printed words into their individual speech sounds. Instructional activities that emphasize phonemic awareness can facilitate reading growth. Even during the preschool years, play with letters and letter sounds is helpful. Popular TV programs like *Sesame Street* show young children how to link sounds to letters and to blend speech sounds (e.g., "Today's program is brought to you by the letter *T* as in *Toy, Tiger,* and *Teddy*").

Once children develop phonemic awareness, it is important that they pick up speed in recognizing whole words: They need to *automatize* their recognition of words (Eldredge, 2005). Strong readers quickly learn to recognize words, increasing their reading fluency. Reitsma (1983, 1989) studied second graders who were reading at and below

phonemic awareness
The understanding that words are made up of smaller units of sound; also, association of printed letters with the sounds that go with them.

As children become more accomplished readers, they become better at understanding the meaning of text and considering different interpretations. How has automaticity in reading enabled this child to enjoy reading to her class?

TABLE 11.3 Chall's Six Developmental Stages in Reading

STAGE & AGE RANGE	DESCRIPTION OF ACTIVITIES AND SKILLS
Prereading: Birth to kindergarten	Parents "read" to infants and toddlers by pointing to and naming objects and colors in books and reading simple stories. Many 3-year-olds pretend to read—flipping through pages, reciting memorized stories, and creating their own stories as they point to words and pictures. By the time children enter kindergarten many of them can recite the alphabet, recognize written letters, and print their own names. These are examples of prereading skills that lay the foundation for further development.
Reading/Decoding: Grades 1–2	Children learn to associate letters with their corresponding sounds. Using *phonics*, children sound out letters, decoding the word that is formed when they run the sounds together. With the *whole word method*, children recognize words based on context, pictures, and the shapes of the words. Readers at this stage often focus on individual words and phrases and miss the larger meaning of the story.
Fluency: Grades 2–3	Children become more fluent in recognizing or decoding words. Rereading familiar books and reading stories with familiar or stereotyped structures, children gain speed, fluency, and confidence in their reading ability. Chall (1983) commented that children are "learning to read" by associating printed words with stories they already know and understand.
Reading for New Learning: Grades 4–8	Fluency with words allows children to move to less familiar material. With the decoding load reduced, children can focus on meaning and messages, gaining a new way to learn new information. Fourth graders typically begin using books and printed materials to study subject areas such as science, history, and geography. In this stage children are "reading to learn," focusing on fact-based information.
Multiple Viewpoints: High school	Adolescents move beyond basic facts. They begin to appreciate layers of information representing different viewpoints or theories. *Examples:* History texts might describe events from differing perspectives; biology can be discussed at the cellular, organismic, and ecological levels. School assignments and free-reading of more mature fiction and nonfiction facilitate this development.
Construction and Reconstruction: College and adulthood	Mature readers can read multiple sources, opinions, and views and then construct their own understanding. They read to suit their purposes, whether it's to gain understanding, for entertainment, or to consider views of others. They decide how fast or to deeply to read and when to gloss, skim, or attend to detail. They know what *not* to read as well as what to read in order to suit their purposes.

grade level. After accomplished readers reread and decoded unfamiliar words a few times, they became significantly faster at recognizing those words. Less accomplished readers, however, showed little or no gain in recognition speed. When children fail to automatize word recognition, they must continue to decode words by sounding out the individual letters and speech sounds. The decoding process occupies a great deal of processing capacity, so struggling readers have less capacity available to attend to meaning and get less out of their reading. These kinds of decoding and automaticity difficulties are common in children with learning disabilities in reading.

In sum, when it comes to reading, "the rich get richer." Children with strong decoding skills and phonemic awareness are better able to sound out words. With repeated exposures, they automatize their word recognition. This makes it easier for them to read—and as a result they tend to read more.

Think About Angelique . . .

Do you think that Angelique's math difficulties are being affected by her reading skills? Would it be helpful for Manny to work with her on reading? How might this help?

Meet a Literacy Volunteer

Kim Davenport, Vice President of Education & Training at Jumpstart Literacy Programs
Boston, Massachusetts

What do you do to help others learn to read?
Jumpstart Corps members work one-on-one with preschool children to develop language, literacy, and social-emotional skills. Corps members are trained on how to read effectively with children using the Dialogic Reading Method, an interactive reading method that encourages children and adults to have conversations about a book.

Why did you decide to become involved with this program?
Literacy is a key component to school success for children. Research tells us that reading with young children builds vocabulary, promotes engagement with books, fosters lifelong reading habits, and develops strong literacy and language skills. Reading with children supports emergent literacy skills such as print awareness, letter knowledge, phonemic awareness, and builds vocabulary and comprehension skills. My work supports Jumpstart's key mission: to work toward the day that every child succeeds in school. I can think of no more globally pressing issue for children today. It is our responsibility as citizens to support and develop our children. They are our future.

What do you know about the need for programs of this type?
Each year more than 35 percent of children enter school unprepared to succeed. First grade children from low-income families have an average of 5,000-word vocabularies. In contrast, children from more affluent families enter school with vocabularies of 20,000 words. That difference is startling.
We understand how to solve the problem of literacy, now we need a way to reach each child.

How can others become involved with literacy programs?
College students can become involved with Jumpstart through their college campuses. This year, Jumpstart hosts programs in 33 communities around the country. You can find a list of cities and programs and ways you can help at www.jstart.org. Across the country there are numerous literacy programs. Check with your local library, child care resource and referral center, or schools for information about opportunities to read with young children.

Q *What aspects of information processing theory do you think would be useful in helping someone learn to read? How could you help someone develop phonemic awareness and automaticity?*

Increased reading further enhances their reading skills; it also exposes them to a broader array of knowledge and information, which, in turn, facilitates their cognitive development. When you consider all that we can learn through reading, you can see why it is critically important that children get off to a good start in the early reading stages (see Adams et al., 1998, for a review).

Development of Writing Skills

You probably know from experience that reading and writing skills are highly correlated (Spivey & King, 1989). Children who learn the alphabet early, become skilled decoders, and automatize word recognition will later have a strong foundation for spelling and some of the other mechanics of writing. Also, children who can read and synthesize text from multiple perspectives will likely write more effectively because they can keep the perspective of the audience in mind. And both reading and writing show similar developmental progressions. That is, children move from early mastery of the alphabet, to greater fluency and confidence with words and language, to greater sophistication in comprehension and the ability to use reading and writing to suit their purposes or fulfill their goals. In this section we outline some of the major accomplishments that children achieve in the writing process as they move from the early phases of inventive spelling to the more mature phase of successful revision.

Inventive Spelling. In the early phases of writing, children struggle to learn spelling. Before they memorize conventional word spellings, they frequently invent their own made-up versions, a process called **inventive spellings.** For example, a beginner might write *two* as *tu* or *sometimes* as *sumtyms*. We are all painfully aware of the myriad complexities, letter blends, and spelling exceptions that exist in English. Schools today generally accept and encourage inventive spelling, teaching beginners to focus more on their meaning and message than on writing mechanics. Research indicates that inventive spelling does not interfere with children's ability to learn to correctly spell words later on. Instead, as children construct their own spellings, they gain practice with letter sounds and blends, enhancing their phonemic awareness. The use of inventive spelling therefore correlates with later success in conventional spelling, word recognition, and reading fluency (Adams et al., 1998; Uhry & Shepard, 1993).

inventive spellings
Incorrect spellings that children create by sounding out words and writing the associated letters.

Mechanics and Intermediate Writing. During the elementary school years, children gradually learn conventional spellings and begin to form increasingly complex sentence structures. In the earlier grades children must devote most of their processing capacity to the technical requirements of writing: spelling, capitalization, punctuation, and the formation of complete sentences. Children tend to write from an egocentric perspective—they have a difficult time keeping the needs of the reader in mind. Organization also tends to be lacking. Beginning writers tend to engage in **knowledge telling,** a strategy in which children simply add ideas to their essays as they come to mind (Bereiter & Scardamalia, 1987). Even high school and college writers show this strategy, in fact. It seems that many assignments in formal education encourage students to "dump in" all they know about a topic. Few assignments require or encourage students to write creatively, so children often rely on rudimentary and stereotyped structures during this intermediate phase of their writing development.

knowledge telling
Adding or "dumping" in ideas as they come to mind; a failure to selectively organize ideas in writing.

Planning and Revising. Young writers have particular difficulty knowing when and what to revise. Once weaknesses are pointed out, however, they do seem capable of correcting most mistakes. As students move into more mature phases of writing, they spend increasing amounts of time on planning and revising. Before writing their first sentence, mature writers spend time gathering facts and sources and organizing their ideas; the first draft is not the last draft. They realize that good writing evolves through the dynamic process of *recursive revision*. That is, after planning and writing, they reevaluate their plan and rewrite several times. In early revisions accomplished writers attend above all to the meaning and message of their writing. They tend to defer the mechanics of spelling, grammar, and punctuation to later revisions (Adams et al., 1998). Strong writers become skilled at reviewing their own material from the reader's perspective—even reading it aloud—and continually revise their work to meet their writing goals.

These children are working together to plan and revise their stories in a writer's workshop. What writing skills are these children displaying?

In this chapter we have described the cognitive skills of children during the middle childhood years, from ages 7 to 11. We described the skills and limitations of these ages according to Piagetian theory. We discussed in detail the important developments in memory, knowledge base, strategies, and language skills, and we introduced recent views of cognition and language development. To offer a

your perspective

When writing, how much time do you spend on planning and revising your text? Looking at one of your most recent writing assignments, how could it be improved if you spent more time revising?

glimpse of how children put their cognitive skills to use in one important practical setting—school—we also described the development of three important academic skills. Hopefully, it is clear to you that children of this age have an amazing array of cognitive skills, and that these skills are built upon the cognitive foundation developed during the infancy, toddler, and early childhood periods. While they still face important limitations, anyone who works with children of these ages cannot help but be impressed with the level and range of skills most children show during the middle childhood years.

■ Let's Review . . .

1. Which of the following is TRUE regarding the effect of context familiarity on solving story problems?
   a. Children become bored with familiar contexts and so pay less attention to problem details.
   b. Familiar contexts provide more effective cues for children to use relevant knowledge.
   c. Unfamiliar contexts encourage more effective strategies and reduce working memory load.
   d. There is no difference in problem difficulty for unfamiliar versus familiar contexts.

2. This year Jeremy is able to learn new material by reading textbooks. Before, he could barely understand individual words and sentences. Now Jeremy can process the meaning of text passages and absorb new information. Jeremy's ability to learn by reading shows that he is in Jeanne Chall's stage of _____.
   a. reading/decoding
   b. fluency
   c. reading for new learning
   d. multiple viewpoints

3. One important part of learning to read is the understanding that words are made up of smaller units of sound. What is this concept called?
   a. word fluency
   b. phonemic awareness
   c. automatizing word recognition
   d. the prereading component

4. **True or False:** According to the strategy choice model, children who are discouraged from using counting strategies to solve mathematics problems may take longer to memorize and retrieve basic math facts.

5. **True or False:** The use of inventive spelling in the early elementary school years interferes with children's ability to learn to spell words correctly in the later school years.

Answers: 1. b, 2. c, 3. b, 4. T, 5. F

Thinking Back to Manny and Angelique . . .

Now that you have studied this chapter, you should be able to list at least a dozen specific concepts and explain how Manny could use each to help Angelique. According to Piaget, Angelique is likely in the early stages of concrete operational thinking. Manny may be able to help her use her ability to mentally reverse actions to understand mathematical operations and the dynamics being described in the story problems she must solve. Manny should keep in mind that although Angelique probably has basic class inclusion and transitive inference skills, she may need more experience with these kinds of problems before she can successfully apply them to story problems. You probably noticed the effects of Angelique's limited processing capacity and overloaded working memory. By the time she finishes the effortful task of reading the problem, she doesn't have enough capacity left over to remember what she is supposed to do in the problem! If Manny can help Angelique develop automaticity in reading and basic math facts, she can focus on other aspects of the problems. Manny can also help Angelique develop attentional skills by teaching her to identify and selectively attend to the most informative parts of the problem.

Manny can help Angelique's memory for math facts become better organized and easier to access by helping her see the relations among them. Organizing fact "families" that contain complementary addition, subtraction, and (later) multiplication and division facts will strengthen the associations in her memory network, making retrieval faster and more accurate. After more experiences with similar kinds of problems, Angelique will probably develop some scripts for common types of story problems, which will help her figure out the most likely questions and operations. It might be helpful to encourage Angelique to use her language skills to write a personal narrative, and to write about any "natural" story problems she encounters. This could help her understand the connection between the story problems she's trying to solve and real-life situations involving math. Manny might also help Angelique identify the strategies she is using and help her develop more effective ones.

Manny and Angelique's situation provides a good example of how research on cognitve development helps people solve real-life problems. Teachers and parents alike can benefit from understanding how factors such as mental reversibility, processing efficiency, knowledge base, and learning specific strategies contribute to memory and problem solving. The information-processing view in particular can offer specific ideas about what is causing problems for a child; it also offers specific ideas about how to help the child improve.

■ Chapter Review . . .

What changes occur in Piaget's third stage of cognitive development?
In the concrete operational stage (7 to 11 years of age), children can solve conservation problems: Schemes are reversible ("operational"), and children represent multiple dimensions of the problems and the dynamic transformations. Logic is more objective and allows the child to understand class inclusion and transitive inference. Logic still requires tangible or concrete material or experience, however.

What are the differences between a stores model of memory and network models?
The stores model proposes a series of storage locations (sensory store, short-term memory, long-term memory) into which information is placed. It focuses on characteristics of each store and how an executive processor directs the use of processing capacity within the stores. Network models view memory as an interconnected system of concept nodes connected by links. These models focus on how information is organized and on how activation spreads along the links.

What develops in working memory and in long-term memory?
Functional capacity of working memory changes with age, even if actual capacity does not. The size of chunks that can be kept active in working memory and the speed with which activation spreads within the memory network both increase with age. In long-term memory, the amount of

knowledge and its organization change with age. Children get better at encoding information, storing it in long-term memory, accessing and retrieving it.

What are some other important aspects of memory development?

Memory is reconstructive rather than based on mental copies. Younger children's reconstructions are affected more than older children's by several factors. Autobiographical memories, or memories of personally important events, help form the basis for a child's sense of self.

How do increases in knowledge base contribute to cognitive development?

Greater knowledge in a domain leads to more effective and efficient processing of new information in that domain. Experts organize their knowledge differently than novices, which allows them to quickly identify important aspects of a situation and focus on problem solutions.

How do strategies change with age?

Young children's strategy use is inconsistent and inflexible and does not always improve their performance. Younger children can be trained to use a strategy, but they often do not generalize it. Parental and cultural expectations and encouragement strongly influence strategy use. Children seem to have a variety of strategies available, and development consists of changes in which strategy is used most often.

What new approaches have grown out of the information-processing perspective?

New in the developmental sphere are computational models—theories of cognition that are programmed into and run on a computer. Researchers compare the programs' output with that of real children in order to better explain development. Production systems are sets of computerized *if–then* statements that specify the actions involved in a cognitive task. Connectionist models contain many simple units arranged into layers and connected by links of different weights. Fuzzy trace theory says that memory traces vary from verbatim to imprecise and general. Verbatim traces require more effort to store and use and are more likely to be forgotten or modified. Older children and adults tend to store and reason with fuzzy traces, while younger children tend to use verbatim traces.

What are limitations of the information-processing perspective?

The information-processing view emphasizes detailed analysis of specific processes and highlights the importance of cognitive efficiency and the knowledge base. However, it does not offer an overarching theory to explain all of cognitive development. Nor does it address social or emotional issues in cognitive development.

How does language continue to develop during middle childhood?

Vocabulary development continues, and more abstract words are learned. Children become skilled in the use of passive voice, making inferences, referential communication, and social rules of discourse. Metalinguistic awareness improves, which enables them to use language more flexibly and understand subtle humor. Children use language in different ways, becoming more skilled at language play such as riddles. They use language as a tool for informing others about themselves and to better understand themselves through personal narratives.

Describe the connectionist model of language development.

Cognitive connectionist models explain language development as progressive changes in the strength of connections among cognitive units.

What mathematical skills do children develop as they move from infancy to late childhood?

Even young infants can distinguish between small sets and recognize the effects of addition and subtraction through subitizing. Preschoolers develop several counting strategies, and strategy efficiency increases throughout elementary school. Children develop strong associations between problems and correct answers and become able to retrieve answers, though they continue to use multiple strategies to solve arithmetic problems. Word problems are difficult for many students; problems with unfamiliar contexts and involving static relations between sets are especially difficult. Buggy procedures in mathematics result from lack of understanding of math principles.

What are the main phases that children go through as they learn to read?

Chall identified six stages of reading development: pre-reading, reading/decoding, fluency, reading for new learning, multiple viewpoints, and construction/reconstruction. For young children, familiarity with the alphabet and phonemic awareness predict later reading success. After learning to decode or recognize whole words, children must automatize word recognition.

What are the main phases that children go through as they learn to write?

Reading and writing skills are correlated and follow similar developmental pathways. Early writers use inventive spellings. After automatizing proper spellings, children can focus on other technical requirements of writing. Early writers tend to be egocentric, have poor organization, and use unsophisticated "knowledge-telling" strategies. As writers mature, they engage in more planning and revising.

■ Key Terms

accessing (370)
autobiographical memories (373)
chunking (367)
computational models (380)
concrete operational thought (365)
connectionist models (382)
counting strategies (389)
encoding (370)
fuzzy trace theory (383)
inventive spelling (395)
knowledge base (376)
knowledge telling (395)
long-term memory (369)
metalinguistic awareness (386)

network models (of memory) (367)
personal narratives (387)
phonemic awareness (392)
production systems (381)
reconstructive memory (372)
retrieval (370)
scripts (372)
storage (370)
stores model (of memory) (366)
strategies (377)
strategy choice model (391)
subitizing (389)
working memory (367)

mydevelopmentlab
Where human development comes to life!

If you are using MyDevelopmentLab, you have access to an ebook version of this textbook, along with dozens of valuable resources per chapter—including video and audio clips, simulations and activities, self-assessments, practice tests, and other study materials. Here is a sampling of the resources available for this chapter.

Explore
Key Processes in Stages of Memory

Simulate
How Good is Your Memory for Stories?
The Mind's Organization of Conceptual Knowledge

Watch
Encouraging Literacy
Learning Language
Hands-On Learning in Elementary Math
Online and Grades

If you did not receive an access code to MyDevelopmentLab with this text and wish to purchase access online, please visit www.mydevelopmentlab.com.

The Transition toward Adulthood, ages 12 and beyond, brings adolescents from childhood to the brink of adulthood. Rapid physical changes are both exciting and bewildering, and increasingly mature cognitive skills allow adolescents to tackle complex academic subjects and ponder important social issues. Brain development helps them gradually become less impulsive and more reasoned decision makers, but at times their judgment is clouded by a sense of invulnerability to harm. Adolescents stretch their wings as they seek more independence from parents, but at the same time they learn to develop and maintain social relationships that are emotionally and sometimes physically intimate. Throughout these years, adolescents are striving to develop a sense of identity; who they are will impact important decisions about their future education, careers, and relationships.

Adolescents cope with many difficult issues and choices. Figuring out which of their peers to spend time with and how to be accepted by them, when to become sexually active, whether to experiment with drugs and alcohol, how to cope with peer pressure, how to handle academic demands, and how to gain more independence from parents are only a few of the many issues that confront them. While peers and media gain influence, families are still important sources of support during these years. From the age of 12 on, adolescents become increasingly mature in their physical, cognitive, and socioemotional development, as you will discover in the next three chapters.

Physical Development in Adolescence

Fifteen-year-old Marcus spends a lot of time thinking these days. His health teacher keeps talking about hormones and puberty, but Marcus still looks younger than most of the other freshmen guys. His parents talk about his "moodiness" a lot. They've even asked if he's depressed. They talk about how he'll have so much more responsibility when he (finally!) gets his driver's license. Between them and his teachers, it feels like he is constantly being told to think ahead, plan his time, and make good choices. It's as if they're afraid he's going to suddenly become a sex-crazed, drug-using, crazy-driving fiend!

But Marcus does spend a lot of time thinking about girls. He really likes one girl, Lavone, but he's not sure how to act around her. He's excited, anxious, and fearful all at once. Some of his friends talk like they've already had sex, but he's not sure if it's true. In sex education classes they make it sound like awful things will happen if you even *think* about doing it. His 16-year-old cousin got pregnant last year so Marcus knows he should use protection, but it seems like having condoms on hand is a little too planned.

Marcus is also trying to figure out how he feels about alcohol and marijuana. He knows that some of his friends are experimenting. He doesn't want to ruin his grades or his place on the track team, but it seems like a lot of people are trying it and having fun—could it be that bad?

Is Marcus unusual in the things he's thinking and worrying about? What kinds of physical issues do most adolescents face, and how can parents and teachers help? After studying this chapter, you should be able to identify at least a dozen research findings or concepts that will help Marcus as he thinks about these issues.

> As you read this chapter, look for the "Think About Marcus . . ." questions that ask you to consider what you're learning from Marcus's perspective.

Growth of the Body and Brain During Adolescence

Adolescence is the period of life that serves as a transition between childhood and adulthood. It is a time of tremendous physical, cognitive, and socioemotional development. Individuals enter this period looking like children, but in a few short years they blossom into young adults. Like Marcus, many teens worry about whether their physical development is keeping up with, or is too far ahead of, their peers. While many of the physical changes of adolescence are easily seen, some of the most important are hidden—important changes are taking place in the brain that will enable adolescents to get better and better at directing their behaviors, thoughts, and emotions. In this chapter, we'll discuss the normal physical changes of adolescence. We'll also talk about several important health and safety issues, including sexual activity, nutrition and exercise, sleep, substance use, depression and suicide, and teen driving.

As you study this section, ask yourself these questions:

- What is the typical sequence of events in puberty?
- What are the psychological effects of early and late maturation for boys and for girls?
- What major changes take place in the brain during adolescence? How are these changes related to adolescent behavior?

Puberty

puberty
The process of physical maturation that leads to the physical capability to reproduce.

One of the most recognized landmarks of adolescent development is **puberty,** the process of physical maturation that leads to the physical capability to reproduce. During puberty, there are rapid increases in height, weight, and strength as well as changes in the amount and distribution of body muscle and fat. The *primary sex characteristics* (the organs needed for reproduction) mature and begin producing eggs and sperm. *Secondary sex characteristics* (physical indicators of sexual maturation that do not involve the sex organs) develop, including enlargement of the breasts; body growth; appearance of pubic, underarm, facial, and body hair; increased output of oil- and sweat-producing glands; and changes in the voice. In males, the most noticeable changes tend to occur in this order: The penis and testicles increase in size, pubic hair appears, the voice begins to deepen, **spermarche** (the first ejaculation) occurs, hair grows in the armpits, and facial hair begins to grow. In females, changes usually occur as follows: Breasts begin to enlarge, pubic hair appears, hair grows in the armpits, hips enlarge, and the first menstruation occurs.

spermarche
The first ejaculation.

The primary factors governing the onset of puberty are genetics and two types of sex hormones: **androgens** (male hormones) and **estrogens** (female hormones). Puberty involves several different *glands* in the body's *endocrine system,* the system of organs that produce, secrete, and regulate levels of a variety of body *hormones* (chemicals secreted by the endocrine system that affect the functioning of other cells). The biological processes are diagrammed in Figure 13.1. Although scientists are not entirely sure, there is evidence that increasing levels of *leptin*—a protein produced by fat cells—could play an important role in initiating puberty. Rising levels of leptin signal that there is enough body fat to support menstruation and pregnancy in females (it is less clear how leptin relates to puberty initiation in boys) (Sussman & Rogol, 2004). Leptin affects the hypothalamus, part of the lower forebrain, and causes the hypothalamus to increase production of several *releasing factors,* hormones that signal other glands to increase production of specific hormones. These releasing factors signal the pituitary gland to produce more of certain hormones (e.g., luteinizing hormone, follicle-stimulating hormone), a process that occurs mostly during sleep during the early stages of puberty, then later during awake periods as well. Increasing levels

androgens
One type of sex hormone, released in greater concentration by males.

estrogens
One type of sex hormone, released in greater concentration by females.

of hormones from the pituitary signals the release of sex hormones from the gonads (ovaries in females and testes in males). The gonads in both males and females secrete both types of sex hormones, but at different concentrations. The male testes secrete higher levels of *testosterone* (an androgen), and the female ovaries secrete higher levels of *estradiol* (an estrogen). The sex hormones stimulate the growth and maturation of the reproductive systems as well as secondary sexual characteristics, and they provide feedback to the hypothalamus about current levels of sex hormones. This feedback loop from hypothalamus to pituitary gland to gonads and back to the hypothalamus is known as the *HPG axis,* and serves to regulate the levels of sex hormones. It is functional early in life, but the levels of hormones it maintains gradually change during late childhood and early adolescence based on genetic factors and input from other sources, such as leptin levels.

The HPG axis is what most people think of as puberty, but it is only one part of it, *gonadarche.* Through different hormones, the pituitary gland also stimulates the adrenal gland to release hormones that contribute to the development of secondary sex characteristics and increased sexual attraction. This process is called *adrenarche.* It occurs about two years earlier than gonadarche, which means that increased sexual attraction and subtle changes in secondary sex characteristics begin happening much earlier than most people think—around 7 years of age (Sussman & Rogol, 2004).

Sexual maturation tends to occur earlier in girls than in boys. Many girls show noticeable changes by age 10 or 11, but most boys enter puberty a year or two later. For most girls **menarche** (the first menstrual period) occurs at 12 or 13, though African American girls start to menstruate earlier than girls of other ethnicities (Chumlea et al., 2003). The average age at menarche, however, has been decreasing. In the United States, for example, the average age at menarche fell from 13.8 in 1920 to 12.8 around 1960 and is currently estimated at 12.43 (Chumlea et al., 2003; Marshall & Tanner, 1986; Tanner, 1991). Over the last 100 years, children have grown larger and matured faster than in previous generations. Improved nutrition and overall health have contributed greatly to this long-term pattern, called the *secular trend.* Weight gain is related to menarche; perhaps improved nutrition and health cause earlier weight gain, signaling the female body to begin the reproductive phase of life. Although the same secular trend has occurred in other industrialized nations, girls in the United States have always reached menarche a bit earlier than girls in other nations. The reasons for this are not known. The secular trend toward earlier puberty

Figure 13.1 • The Biological Processes of Puberty

Gonadarche, shown in the right side of the figure, involves the HPG axis and results in the development of the primary sex characteristics. *Adrenarche,* shown on the left side, results in the development of sexual attraction and contributes to secondary sex characteristics. Adrenarche begins around ages 7 to 10, about two years before the onset of gonadarche.

menarche
The first menstrual period for females, usually occurring around 12 to 13 years of age.

Do you recall the age period when the girls in your class were taller than the boys? After being about equal in height throughout childhood, girls enter their adolescent growth spurt at an earlier age than boys. By the end of adolescence, boys will stand 5 inches taller (on average) than girls.

adolescent growth spurt
The increase in growth associated with the onset of puberty.

appears to be slowing, but not for all groups (Sun et al., 2005). While the overall average age of menarche has not changed over the past few decades in the United States, there is evidence of earlier onset of puberty over the last few decades for non-Hispanic white boys and for Mexican American boys and girls (Chumlea et al., 2003; Herman-Giddens, 2006; Sun et al., 2005).

The **adolescent growth spurt** is an increase in growth that begins with the onset of puberty. As we've seen, sex hormones at puberty trigger the process of sexual maturation. This release of sex hormones also stimulates the release of additional growth hormones from the pituitary gland. As Figure 13.2 indicates, boys and girls grow at about the same rate until adolescence. Then comes the growth spurt, usually peaking around 12 years of age for girls. For boys the growth spurt peaks a few years later, usually around 14 years. This lag in growth spurt means that there is a short time period between the ages of 11 and 14, when females are taller than males, on average. The growth spurt lasts longer for boys, however. By the time he reaches 18 years of age, the average male is now about 5 inches taller than the average female. Both sexes have nearly reached their adult heights. In both sexes the long bones (e.g., in the arms and legs) may continue to grow slightly until age 25, and minor growth in the vertebral column can continue until age 30 (Tanner, 1978).

Early and Late Maturation

Of course, these are just the physical changes associated with puberty and sexual maturation—but what about the psychological effects? For many adolescents puberty is a confusing and awkward time. Their bodies are changing rapidly and in dramatic ways, and these changes affect their thoughts and emotions. And, as you'll learn in Chapters 14 and 15, adolescents' developing cognitive skills and changing social roles affect how they cope with their rapidly changing bodies. No longer children,

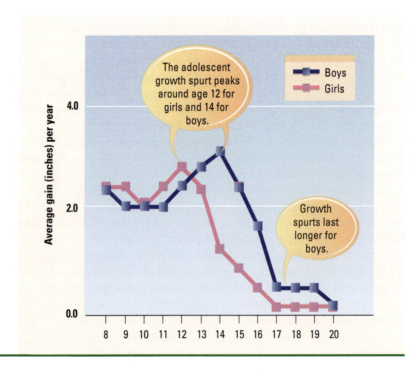

Figure 13.2 • Height Curves for Girls and Boys
These curves show the average height gained per year from late childhood through adolescence. (National Center for Health Statistics, 2000b.)

Part Five: Adolescence

teenagers may look toward late adolescence and adulthood with mixed feelings of excitement and apprehension. Researchers have devoted considerable attention to adolescents' changing **body image,** or the way a person thinks about his or her body and how it looks to others. During adolescent growth, boys tend to add muscle mass and height, and with these changes they tend to become more satisfied with their bodies (Duncan et al., 1985; Simmons & Blyth, 1987). In contrast, girls tend to add more fat tissue, and many become less satisfied with their bodies. This is particularly true among girls who reach menarche before age 12, because their build tends to be shorter and stockier by late adolescence. In **early maturation,** the physical changes of puberty occur in a child before these changes occur in

Adolescents go through puberty at very different times. What advantages and disadvantages do you think early maturing girls experience? What about later maturing girls?

the majority of other children of the same age. In **late maturation,** the physical changes do not occur until after the majority of one's peers. Early and late maturation can have an important psychological impact. A study of nearly 5,000 girls in Scotland, for example, showed that girls who matured earlier perceived their bodies as "too fat." More late-maturing girls saw themselves as "too thin" (Williams & Currie, 2000). Girls with both types of negative body image tended to have lower self-esteem. Early-maturing girls also tend to have older friends, engage in more delinquency, have more problems in school, begin dating at a younger age, and tend to have more problems with depression and substance abuse (Magnusson, 1988; Simmons & Blyth, 1987; Stice et al., 2001; Wiesner & Ittel, 2002). You can imagine how the social context can put added pressure on early-maturing girls—they receive more attention from boys and may feel somewhat alienated from slower-developing girls their own age. For more on this issue, read the Personal Perspective box on page 446 called "Meet a Young Adolescent."

Early maturation can enhance the self-image of boys, however (Nottelmann et al., 1987; Simmons & Blyth, 1987). Thanks to their size and strength, early-maturing boys have the advantage in sports. Also, peers may see their more developed musculature, facial hair, and deeper voices as being attractive. Late-maturing boys often feel uncomfortable about comparing themselves with their more developed peers. Remember entering the gym showers at this age? On the negative side, however, early-maturing boys tend to engage in more delinquent behavior than do boys who mature later (Duncan et al., 1985; Ge et al., 2002). Being larger and stronger than their age-mates, these boys often affiliate with older adolescents. They may get into situations they are not prepared to handle—and get into trouble as a result. One study indicated that early-maturing boys felt more hostile and distressed than other boys (Ge et al., 2001).

Brain Development

Until recently, most researchers believed that brain development was for the most part complete before adolescence. However, the adolescent brain appears to still be under construction in many ways. Some of the changes in the brain seem to come before puberty while others come after. Hormonal changes during puberty are probably involved in brain development during adolescence, but they do not appear to have a direct influence and their role isn't clear (Dahl & Spear, 2004).

As you might recall from Chapter 4, *myelination* is the process in which the fatty myelin sheath is deposited on the axons of neurons in the brain. The myelin sheath insulates the axon, and increased myelination leads to faster transmission of neural impulses, faster processing of information, and faster speed of responding. While most brain pathways are myelinated in infancy and early childhood, myelination of some

body image
The way a person thinks about his or her body and how it looks to others.

early maturation
When the physical changes of puberty occur earlier than they do in the majority of one's peers.

late maturation
When the physical changes of puberty do not occur until after they do in the majority of one's peers.

your perspective
Did you begin puberty earlier or later than other adolescents your age? How did your rate of maturation affect your feelings about yourself and how you compared with your classmates?

Think About Marcus . . .
What sorts of difficulties is Marcus likely to experience as a result of being a later maturing boy? What advantages might he have over early maturing boys?

Meet a Young Adolescent

Hannah Lee Vestal
Bristol, Tennessee
Age 15, discussing the impact of physical changes during adolescence

Which physical changes do you and your friends notice most? What differences do you notice between early and late "bloomers"?

I notice a lot of physical changes in myself and in others. I notice hair, clothing, body, nails, and much more. But, for some reason, I think I am always looking for faults; I always notice them so much. I think developed girls look at not-so-developed girls and wish they could be that way, and vice versa! I see some late "bloomers" who are very self-conscious and limit their clothing due to the fact that they are not fully developed. But I also see late bloomers who are very comfortable with themselves and their bodies, so they are more willing to wear the clothing of choice. Some early bloomers (like me) are a lot more inclined to cover themselves and hide the fact that they have bloomed. But again, I see some early bloomers who embrace the fact that they are developed. They sometimes wear low-cut shirts or strapless tops, which I guess is good in a way. They are so comfortable with themselves that they *can* wear those clothes.

What do you think are the most exciting, awkward, and stressful aspects of puberty?

Starting to date, friends, and drugs. Starting to date is very difficult because if you don't date, you start to feel like you are ugly and no one wants to date you. Dating makes you feel very critical of yourself. It makes you want to change things about yourself, mainly your looks. If you do date, you might feel pressured to do things you aren't ready for. Friends can also be very stressful. High school is like one big soap opera, one that you can't miss a single episode of. The drama of who's dating who and the "he said, she said" stuff is very aggravating and childish. But pressure from friends is not as bad as TV and politicians make it out to be, at least not at my school. Drugs are readily available, but I have never been asked if I would like to take drugs, smoke anything, or drink. I think to get involved in that stuff you have to go looking for it. Teens can't blame all their mess-ups on pressure, because it's not really there as much as adults think. Most of it is in the individual.

What advice would you give adults about an adolescent's perspective during puberty?

I think parents should be very honest with their children, especially at this age. If you tell your kids about the experiences you had, they'll learn more from that than they would from watching a movie on it or reading a book about it. If you tell your kids if or how your experiences changed your life, for good or bad, they will respect that. They'll tell you more and trust you. I know I can talk to my mom about almost anything. She won't yell at me, but will listen and tell me how she feels, and about her experiences and the effects they had on her.

Q *What have you learned so far in this book that could help adolescents cope successfully with the "soap opera" of adolescence?*

areas such as the prefrontal cortex continues throughout adolescence. This increased efficiency of neural transmission is one reason teens are able to process information faster and more efficiently than younger children. Increased myelination is sometimes referred to as increases in the white matter in the brain (Kail & Salthouse, 1994; Keating, 2004; National Research Council and Institute of Medicine, 2000).

A more recent discovery is that there are also important changes in the gray matter of the brain (the neurons themselves and the connections between them). Again, as you may recall from Chapter 4, the brain during early childhood shows *synaptogenesis*, a rapid increase in the number of neural connections (or synapses) followed by *synaptic pruning,* or a decrease as connections that are not used fade away. The same process happens just before and during the early part of adolescence. This indicates a second growth spurt in synaptic connections followed by a pruning away of unused connections. Synaptic pruning highlights the importance of experience in adolescence, since the connections that are pruned are those that are not used. Given that teens have far more control than infants over how they spend their time, teens may actually be able to control to some extent how their brains "grow" through their choices of activities during these critical years (Giedd et al., 1999).

Myelination, synaptogenesis, and synaptic pruning are especially evident in the **prefrontal cortex** of the adolescent's brain. This area (part of the frontal lobe, located behind the forehead) is especially important in planning, judgment and decision making, and inhibiting impulsive responding. There is also evidence that, contrary to what we used to think, some new neurons are formed throughout adolescence and into adulthood in certain areas such as the hippocampus, which is heavily involved in storing memory of facts and relations between places and events (Blakemore & Choudhury, 2006; Dahl & Spear, 2004; Eriksson et al., 1998; Keating, 2004).

The relative lateness in maturation of the prefrontal cortex has implications for many aspects of self-regulation. For example, adolescents are known for reacting quickly and emotionally to things. The traditional explanation is that hormones are to blame. However, differences in the relative functioning of brain structures may also be involved. One study compared adolescents and adults in their understanding of emotional cues in facial expressions (Baird et al., 1999). Compared to adults, teens were less accurate in identifying the emotions being portrayed and they showed significantly more activity in the *amygdala,* a part of the brain's temporal lobe that is important in processing emotional stimuli and distinguishing among different emotions. In contrast, adults showed more activity in the *frontal lobes,* the area of the brain associated with rational thinking, goal-directed behavior, and inhibiting impulsive responses. So adolescents' classic emotion-based responding may also have a basis in the relative immaturity of parts of their frontal lobes.

Finally, adolescents experience changes in the levels of several different neurotransmitters (e.g., glutamate, GABA, dopamine, and serotonin) in both the prefrontal cortex and the limbic system of the brain. The limbic system (which includes the amygdala mentioned above) is important for processing and responding to emotional and stressful stimuli. Dopamine levels in the brain are very sensitive to stress, and dopamine plays a role in assessing the motivational value of stimuli. During adolescence, changes in the prefrontal cortex and the limbic system combine with changes in the levels of dopamine to these brain areas to increase the degree of emotionality and reaction to stress. But these changes also make adolescents *less* responsive to rewards. As a result, adolescents may increase their risk-taking behaviors as a way to seek more novel and engaging stimuli (Spear, 2000).

As you'll learn later in this chapter, many of the major threats to adolescent health and well-being involve impulsive behavior, taking risks, and generally making poor decisions in areas such as sexual behavior, substance use, and driving. Adolescents can control their impulses and behavior, but immaturity of the prefrontal cortex and changing neurotransmitter levels may make this more difficult than adults realize. In addition, we are just beginning to understand the potential long-term impact of some of these impulsive behaviors on a brain that is still developing. For example, heavy alcohol consumption may have more negative effects on adolescents than on adults because of differences in brain structure and function (Brown et al., 2000; Dahl & Spear, 2004; Keating, 2004; Tapert et al., 2004/2005).

prefrontal cortex
A large part of the frontal lobe of the brain that is important for planning, judgment, decision making, and inhibiting impulsive responding.

During puberty, adolescents sometimes react impulsively and emotionally, partly because of immaturity in their prefrontal cortex. Could this teen be misunderstanding her parents' emotional cues?

Think About Marcus . . .

What effect might brain development be having on Marcus's emotions and his decisions about sex and drug use?

Sexual Activity During Adolescence

One of the hallmarks of physical development in adolescence is increased interest in sex. Many adolescents become sexually active, but there is great variation in when and why they become sexually active. The majority of the research literature on sexual activity in adolescence has focused on the negative consequences that can occur; there is little information to guide teens and parents as to what is a *good* age to become sexually active (Savin-Williams & Diamond, 2004). When do most teens become sexually active, and what reasons do they give for having or not having sex? The sexual landscape has changed tremendously over the last few decades due to social changes as well as diseases that have serious long-term effects. What do teens know about these issues, and how consistently do they use their knowledge for safer sexual practices?

As you study this section, ask yourself these questions:

■ What patterns of sexual activity are found during adolescence? How have these patterns changed over the last few decades?

■ Why do some teens become sexually active relatively early, while others wait?

■ What sexual risks do adolescents tend to take? Why do they take these risks?

■ What approaches to sex education are commonly used? How effective are these programs in delaying sexual activity or increasing safer sex practices among teens?

Patterns of Sexual Activity

The majority of adolescents in the United States have had sexual intercourse by the time they finish high school. Figure 13.3 shows the percentages of adolescents who reported ever having sexual intercourse. These data from a nationwide survey of high school students show that more than one-third of adolescents have had intercourse by the ninth grade, and nearly two-thirds by 12th grade. African Americans are much more likely than Hispanics or non-Hispanic whites to have engaged in sexual intercourse. In other data from the survey, 30 percent of African American males reported that they had sexual intercourse before the age of 13. In contrast, among all high school students (including male African Americans), 12 percent of males and 4 percent of females reported sexual intercourse before age 13 (Coles & Stokes, 1985). The overall rate of sexual intercourse among adolescents increased steadily beginning in the 1960s, but has recently declined. Until recently, there was a consistent trend toward intercourse at younger ages, especially among teen girls, though this trend too has declined. In 2002, for example, 13 percent of girls and 15 percent of boys between the ages of 15 and 19 reported having sex before the age of 15, compared with 19 percent and 21 percent in 1995 (Abma et al., 2004; Santelli et al., 2000a; Savin-Williams & Diamond, 2004). These differences could be a result of adolescents having a better understanding of the health risks of unprotected sex as well as an increased emphasis on abstinence in some sex education programs (Santelli et al., 2004a, 2006).

One difficulty with estimating sexual activity among teens is establishing a common definition for what "counts" as sex. While adults may consider any kind of sexual contact to be sexual activity (including vaginal, oral, and anal sex as well as masturbation), teens are more likely to only consider vaginal intercourse to be sex (Remez, 2000). Recently, researchers have begun investigating the frequency of oral sex among teens. There are few large-scale nationally representative studies available, so it is difficult to know how reliable the estimates are. The available studies indicate that between

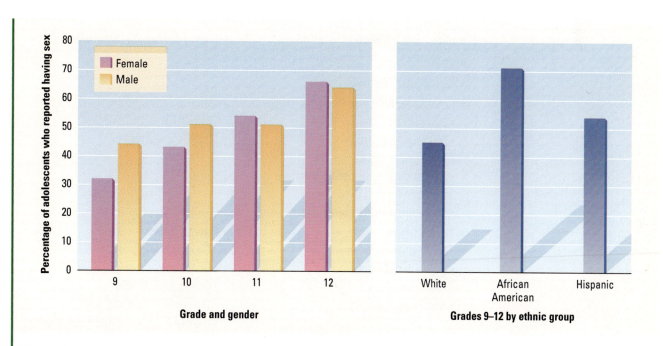

Figure 13.3 • Percentages of High School Students Who Have Ever Had Sexual Intercourse This graph shows the percentages of male and female high school students who reported in a nationwide survey that they have ever had sexual intercourse. The bars at the right show percentages by ethnic group. (National Center for Health Statistics, 2000a.)

20 percent and 30 percent of high school students and approximately 18 percent of younger teens between the ages of 12 and 15 had engaged in oral sex at least once. The rates for teens appear to have modestly increased since the early 1990s, but the rates within the adult population have also increased. What is perhaps most interesting about these studies are the beliefs that many teens hold about oral sex. A significant minority (13 percent) of adolescents in one study believed that the risk of pregnancy, of contracting **sexually transmitted diseases** (or STDs, diseases that are transmitted mostly through sexual contact), or of becoming infected with HIV is completely eliminated by engaging in oral rather than vaginal sex. While this is true for pregnancy, STDs like chlamydia, herpes, gonorrhea, and syphilis can be transmitted via unprotected oral sex. Teens also report that oral sex has fewer social and emotional risks than vaginal sex, that it is more socially acceptable and more appropriate for people of their own age in both dating and casual relationships, and is less of a threat to their personal values and morals (Halpern-Felsher et al., 2005; McKay, 2004).

Reasons for Becoming Sexually Active

Why do some adolescents become sexually active at an early age while others wait? The reasons vary, but several tendencies do exist and are summarized in Table 13.1. In general, adolescents who engage in earlier sexual activity are more likely to perform poorly in school, to achieve lower intelligence-test scores, to lack clear

TABLE 13.1   Factors Associated with Earlier and Later Sexual Activity Among Teens

EARLIER SEXUAL ACTIVITY	LATER SEXUAL ACTIVITY
■ Poverty	■ Higher income
■ History of sexual abuse	■ Higher adult expectations of them
■ Violence in home	
■ Peer pressure (perceived, actual)	
■ Individual factors	■ Individual factors
• Early puberty	• More religious affiliation
• Less religious affiliation	• Better impulse control
• Poor impulse control	
• Alcohol, drug use (especially binge drinking)	
• Thrill seeking, risk-taking personality	
■ Parental factors	■ Parental factors
• Poor relationship w/parents	• Good relationship w/parents
• Lack of parental support	• Good parental monitoring
• Poor parental monitoring	• Good parenting skills
• Single-parent household	• Dual-parent household
	• Parental disapproval of early sexual activity
■ Cognitive and educational factors	■ Cognitive and educational factors
• Lack of school, career goals	• Clear school, career goals
• Poor school performance	• Better school performance
• Lower IQ scores	

educational goals, to live in single-parent homes, to report poor parental communication and lack of parental support, to be more impulsive, and to use alcohol and other drugs and engage in binge drinking. The top reasons teens give for being sexually active are peer pressure, curiosity, and the idea that "everyone does it." Girls also cite pressure from boys as a top reason, and girls who mature earlier and look older are more likely to be sexually active than those who mature later (Dunn et al., 2003; Katchadourian, 1990; Savin-Williams & Diamond, 2004; Raffaelli & Crockett, 2003). Among teens who had abstained from sex, 65 percent told researchers they abstained because they feared sexually transmitted diseases, 62 percent feared pregnancy, 50 percent feared parents, and 29 percent feared they would lose their reputations among friends (Katchadourian, 1990).

Lack of parental supervision is an important risk factor for many teen behaviors, including early sexual activity and drug use. What can the families of these teens do to help reduce their risks?

Lack of parental supervision is also an important factor in teens' sexual activity. One study reported that higher levels of parental supervision were significantly linked to lower levels of sexual activity, fewer sexual partners, and lower incidence of STDs, especially for boys (Cohen et al., 2002). The majority of high school students said the most frequent place they had sex was in their own homes (74 percent of boys and 87 percent of girls) and more than half said they had sex at home after school—when their parents were not home. Supervision of adolescents is a difficult issue for parents, especially for those parents who work outside of the home. Unfortunately, there are fewer supervised after-school activities available to middle and high school youths than there are for younger kids. And at some point, parents do need to "loosen the reins" and allow teens more unsupervised time. The questions are how much, how soon, and under what conditions—difficult questions to answer.

The impact of peer pressure and the belief that "everyone is doing it" are more complicated than they may first appear. For example, Latino and African American girls report experiencing pressure to become sexually active, but also to conform to traditional norms to not be sexually permissive—and these pressures come from both girls and boys (O'Sullivan & Meyer-Bahlberg, 2003). One interesting study asked adolescents which of a range of sexual behaviors they believed were appropriate at a given stage of dating (Roche & Ramsbey, 1993). They were then asked if they had engaged in these behaviors and at what stage of dating, and finally they were asked to estimate how many of their peers they believed had engaged in these behaviors. The results are shown in Table 13.2. If you look closely, it's clear that a higher percentage of teens report engaging in behaviors than the percentage of teens who believed it was appropriate. Even more interesting, however, is that several behaviors seem to be influenced by *misperceptions* of how many peers are engaging in the behavior. For example, only 5 percent of females believed that heavy petting is appropriate in stage 2 of dating but 14 percent report doing so—and they believe that a full 40 percent of their peers are doing this. Similarly, 44 percent of males said that intercourse was appropriate when they are dating and in love (Stage 3), but 60 percent engage in this behavior—and they think that 72 percent of their peers are having sex in this situation. Overall, 72 percent of the "proper, self, other" cells fit the pattern that would be expected if teens are changing their behaviors in accordance with misperceptions (these cells are shaded in Table 13.2). While peer pressure to be sexually active clearly exists, these data indicate that sometimes teens *think* that more of their peers are engaging in sexual activities than really are; therefore they may be changing their behavior and doing things they don't feel are appropriate in order to conform to a "peer pressure" that isn't even real! In talking to teens about becoming sexually active, it seems important to help them realize when they may be overestimating the sexual activity of their peers and not let their behavior be influenced by these misperceptions.

Think About Marcus ...

What important information should Marcus have as he thinks about sexual activity? How could his parents improve the odds that he'll make thoughtful decisions regarding sex?

TABLE 13.2 Reported and Perceived Sexual Activity at Different Stages of Dating

	STAGE 1 (Dating, no affection)			STAGE 2 (Dating with affection, not love)			STAGE 3 (Dating and in love)			STAGE 4 (Dating only one person and in love)			STAGE 5 (Engaged)		
	Proper	Self	Other	Proper	Self	Other	Proper	Self	Other	Proper	Self	Other	Proper	Self	Other
Light Petting															
Males	7	37	38	41	58	61	69	74	91	87	91	94	93	100	97
Females	1	8	22	13	21	50	50	57	88	81	85	96	93	95	99
Heavy Petting															
Males	6	32	29	32	50	49	54	69	83	77	82	91	90	81	96
Females	0	6	15	5	14	40	31	38	76	69	76	92	83	90	98
Intercourse															
Males	3	23	10	17	33	29	44	60	72	69	80	83	76	69	96
Females	0	2	10	1	7	18	15	16	58	52	59	84	67	75	96
Oral sex (received)															
Males	1	37	40	36	59	69	56	66	91	86	85	97	89	87	99
Females	0	5	16	4	13	45	20	23	73	68	68	95	79	74	99
Oral sex (given)															
Males	1	21	39	29	49	66	50	62	89	84	85	99	84	87	99
Females	0	5	18	3	8	46	14	18	75	65	64	94	76	72	98

Do teens change their behavior according to *misperceptions* about peer pressure? Shaded cells are ones that fit the pattern of behavior change in accordance with misperceptions of how many peers are engaging in the behavior. Overall, 72% of the *Proper*, *Self*, and *Other* cells fit the pattern that would be expected.

Note: Proper is the percentage of teens who said the behavior would be appropriate at the given stage of dating; *Self* is the percentage of teens who reported they had engaged in the behavior at the given stage of dating; and *Other* is the percentage of their peers that teens estimate are engaging in the behavior at the given stage of dating.

(Data from Roche & Ramsbey, 1993.)

Contraceptive Use in Adolescence

Not surprisingly, many adults are concerned about adolescents' consistent and correct use of **contraception,** methods used to prevent pregnancy and sexually transmitted diseases. More adolescents report using contraception (particularly condoms and birth control pills) now than in past years. But teens are still notoriously inconsistent in this regard. For example, as you can see in Figure 13.4, 45 percent of adolescent girls under age 16 in a recent survey did not use any contraception at first intercourse. More teens who consider themselves to be sexually active report using contraception at last intercourse—83 percent of females and 91 percent of males used some method. However, it is difficult to tell from these surveys whether sexually active teens *always* use some form of contraception and whether they correctly use contraceptives; several studies indicate that they do not (Kourtis et al., 2006). The best predictor of consistent contraceptive use is age—though not perfect, older teens are more reliable than younger ones. Family factors are also important. Teens who have good relationships with their families are less likely to be sexually active, and they're more likely to consistently use contraceptives if they are sexually active (Abma et al., 2004; Breheny & Stephens, 2004; Mosher et al., 2004; Santelli et al., 2000b).

Why don't teens consistently use contraception? Many teens simply are not mature enough to admit to themselves that they are sexually active or that they plan to be. Consistent contraceptive use, especially hormonal methods like birth control pills, requires that adolescents recognize they are sexually active and plan for sex far in advance of the act itself—something that is incompatible with many teens' views of sexual activity as being spontaneous. Not surprisingly, teens who are able to talk with their partners about contraception and their intent to use it are more likely to do so; but as we just learned, many teens have trouble showing this level of maturity,

Many teens aren't mature enough to admit that they are sexually active and need to consistently use contraception. What factors do you think encouraged this teenage boy to be more responsible?

contraception
Methods such as condoms and birth control pills used to prevent pregnancy.

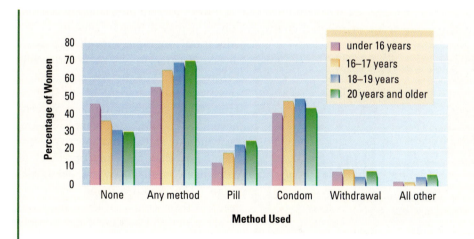

Figure 13.4 • Teens' Use of Contraceptives at First Intercourse This figure shows the percentage of women who did and did not report using contraception at first intercourse. Of those who reported using contraceptives, the percentages of women using different types of contraceptives are also shown. Younger teens are less likely to use any type of contraception. Condoms are the most often used type of protection of all ages surveyed. *Note: Any method* includes all methods reported by women in the survey such as surgical sterilization, hormonal methods, barrier and chemical methods, IUD, rhythm methods, withdrawal, and other. (Mosher et al., 2004.)

planning, and reasoned decision making about sex. Some teens do not use contraceptives because they're afraid their parents will discover that they are sexually active. Others say they do not know where to get contraceptives or that they aren't easily available. Surprisingly, despite the years of sex education that most teens have, some still have misunderstandings about sex and pregnancy or hold misconceptions about the need for contraceptives and how to use them. For example, some teens believe that if they do not have sex frequently, they do not need contraceptives, or that taking a single birth control pill shortly before or after having sex will protect them. And some teens simply don't believe that things like pregnancy or STDs will happen to them. The belief that one is special and invincible is called the *personal fable,* and is related to cognitive development during adolescence (see Chapter 14). Finally, for some adolescents, lack of contraceptive use is part of a broader pattern of risk-taking behaviors and impulsivity (Averett et al., 2002; Iuliano et al., 2006; Kaplan, 2004; Miller & Moore, 1990).

Sexual Knowledge and Sex Education

Almost all public school systems provide sex education programs. Churches and community organizations such as Planned Parenthood, the YMCA, Boy Scouts, and Girl Scouts also offer these programs. Most teens are often not willing to openly talk with their parents about sex, and they don't have independent access to health care or their own health insurance. Without school and community programs, where would they get reliable information? Almost everyone agrees that it is essential to provide sex education in schools, but there is heated debate about what to teach in sex-ed classes. Read about the debate between *abstinence-only* and *comprehensive* sex-ed programs in the Social Policy Perspective box called "The Sex Education Debate."

Given all these educational efforts, what do teens know about sex, sexuality, pregnancy, STDs, and contraception? Early reports were discouraging. For example, high school students in one early study had an average score of 42 percent on an assessment of sexual knowledge, despite the fact that many were already sexually active (Carver et al., 1990; Padilla & Baird, 1991; Trussell, 1988). Fortunately, recent studies find that teens have better knowledge of how to prevent pregnancy. In general, students' knowledge of sex and contraception is increased by participating in sex education programs, though they don't always participate in these programs before they become sexually active (Kirby, 2002; Lindberg et al., 2000). However, a surprising number of teens have little knowledge of what STDs are, how they are spread, and how to prevent them. For example, only one-third of teens in one study knew that chlamydia is an STD. Another found that many teens in their sample believed that condoms *cause* STDs. Knowledge is only one of the many factors that influence sexual behavior, but recent drops in the rate of teen pregnancy may indicate that students are putting their knowledge of contraception into practice. More efforts are needed regarding STDs (Downs et al., 2006; Garside et al., 2001; Halpern-Felsher et al., 2005; Hamilton et al., 2005; Lagerberg, 2004).

your perspective

Was the sex education program in your school system adequate and effective? How do you think it could be improved?

Most schools in the United States teach sex education in some form. What information should be included in these programs for them to be effective in reducing teen pregnancy and STDs?

The Sex Education Debate

In 2001 the surgeon general of the United States, David Satcher, released a report about sex education in U.S. schools. After reviewing hundreds of scientific studies of teenage pregnancy, teen rates of sexually transmitted disease, and adolescent sexual activity, Satcher recommended that sex education programs teach the importance of abstaining from sex but also teach teens who are already sexually active how to prevent STDs and unintended pregnancies (Alan Guttmacher Institute, 2002).

The issue of teaching teens how to use condoms and other methods of pregnancy and disease prevention has been hotly debated since the federal government began playing a role in sex education in the 1980s. In 1981 Congress passed the Adolescent Family Life Act (AFLA), creating a federally funded program to prevent teen pregnancy by teaching abstinence and self-discipline in the schools. Later, a welfare reform law passed in 1996 and a maternal and child health block grant passed in 2000 began providing additional federal funds to promote *abstinence-only* programs in schools. Abstinence-only programs condemn all sex outside of marriage (for people of any age), and they completely prohibit any positive discussion of contraception. Abstinence-only programs may discuss condoms and other contraceptive methods only in order to explain how often they fail in preventing pregnancy and disease in adolescents.

Since the 1980s U.S. schools overall have shifted toward the abstinence-only approach. They have moved away from giving teens detailed information about how to obtain and use condoms and other contraceptive methods. According to a nationwide survey published in 1999, out of the school districts with sex education programs, 35 percent mandated the abstinence-only approach; 51 percent required that abstinence be taught as the preferred method but allowed some discussion of contraception in preventing pregnancy and STDs; and only 14 percent offered the kind of comprehensive approach recommended by Satcher (Alan Guttmacher Institute, 2002).

Conservative lawmakers and some religious groups worry that teaching children and adolescents about condoms and contraception sends the wrong moral message—the message that premarital sex is acceptable. Satcher and others argue that the reality is that most teens *are* sexually active and need accurate and unbiased information about how to protect themselves. In a 1995 survey fewer than 60 percent of teenage males (ages 15 to 19) said they received information in school

about birth control and STDs before their first sexual intercourse (Lindberg et al., 2000). Less than half had instruction on how to say no to sex, and fewer than 40 percent were taught how to put on a condom. Only half said they spoke to their parents about these issues. Girls are more likely to get these messages, with about 70 percent reporting formal education about birth control, HIV/AIDS, STDs, and abstinence before their first intercourse. Other surveys indicate that 81 percent of parents want their children's schools to provide comprehensive sex education that includes abstinence as well as condom use, birth control, abortion, and disease prevention. About half of all teens say they want more information about these and other sex-related topics (Kaiser Family Foundation, 2002).

Satcher's report pointed out that there was no available research evidence that abstinence-only programs work in preventing or delaying teen sex. Comprehensive programs that teach abstinence and contraception, however, have been associated with slight delays in the onset of sexual activity, reductions in the numbers of sexual partners, and increased contraceptive use among sexually active teens. The teenage pregnancy rate did decline slightly during the 1990s, with most of the decline due to increased use of contraception (Alan Guttmacher Institute, 2002).

The debate still rages. Abstinence promotion was a prominent feature of George W. Bush's 2000 presidential campaign. During the early part of the Bush administration, information about condom use, ways to reduce sex among teenagers, and abortion were removed from government Web sites. On the other side, a federal judge in New Orleans ordered Louisiana to change its federally funded abstinence programs because some programs used the federal funds to advance religious beliefs (Clymer, 2002; Liptak, 2002; Santelli et al., 2006).

The battle over sex education in schools involves conflicting views on government control, religious morals, family and personal values, and the realities of teen sex. The stakes are high, given our nation's high rate of teen pregnancy and the devastating consequences of HIV infection and other STDs.

Q *What should schools do? What role should the federal government play? What kinds of information and values do you think should be taught in sex education classes?*

■ Let's Review . . .

1. Based on research of adolescents' knowledge of sex after participating in sex education programs, which of the following is *true?*
   a. Adolescents' knowledge about sex is improved, but many still do not have a good understanding of STDs and how to prevent them.
   b. Adolescents are very knowledgeable about sex, STDs, and contraception.
   c. Despite participation in sex education programs, adolescents know little about sex, STDs, and contraception.
   d. Adolescents' knowledge about sex is improved, but there is little evidence that they use this knowledge to prevent pregnancy and STDs.

2. Teens who are sexually active do not use contraception consistently because they _____.
   a. are less likely to become pregnant than older sexually active individuals
   b. do not have sex frequently enough to warrant the use of contraception
   c. believe that contraceptive methods are not effective in preventing pregnancy and infections
   d. believe that pregnancy and STDs won't happen to them

3. Regarding the reasons for becoming sexually active, which of the following is *false?*
   a. Girls report pressure from boys as the biggest factor for becoming sexually active.
   b. Teens' perceptions of their peers' sexual activity are accurate.
   c. Girls report pressure to be active as well as the conflicting pressure to not be sexually active.
   d. Both boys and girls who have less parental supervision are more likely to be sexually active.

4. Which of the following is a risk factor for early sexual activity?
   a. Later physical maturation compared to peers
   b. Fear of STD infection
   c. Lack of adequate parental supervision
   d. Lack of knowledge about sex

5. **True or False:** The majority of teens have had sexual intercourse by the age of 18.

6. **True or False:** Oral sex eliminates the risk of STD infection.

Answers: 1. a, 2. d, 3. b, 4. c, 5. T, 6. F

Special Concerns about Teenage Sexual Activity

Most adults recognize that an important part of adolescence involves understanding sexual needs and learning to meet these needs in a mature way. Three important issues that arise are preventing STDs, preventing teenage pregnancy, and keeping adolescents safe from sexual assault. Who is at risk? What are the outcomes and how can they be prevented?

As you study this section, ask yourself these questions:

■ Why are adolesescents at higher risk for STDs? How can they reduce their risk?

■ Who is at risk for teenage pregnancy? What are the effects of teen parenthood, and what elements characterize effective pregnancy prevention and teenage parent support programs?

■ Why are adolescents at higher risk of sexual assault than those of other ages? What can parents, schools, and communities do to reduce the risk?

Sexually Transmitted Diseases and Adolescents

Sexually transmitted diseases, or STDs, constitute a major concern for teenage sexual activity, and rightly so. Adolescents and young adults from the ages of 15 to 24 account for almost half of all new cases of STDs each year, even though they only make up 25 percent of the sexually active population. Figure 13.5 shows the rates of infection for chlamydia and gonorrhea, two STDs for which the highest rates of infection are among teens (CDC, 2005).

Chlamydia, caused by a bacteria, is one of the most commonly reported diseases in the United States. It is known as a "silent" disease because it often produces no symptoms. It is spread through vaginal, oral, or anal sexual contact, and is much more commonly diagnosed in women. Though not serious in the short-term, chlamydia can lead to difficulties becoming pregnant. Babies born to women with chlamydia are at risk for preterm birth, eye and respiratory tract infections, and pneumonia (CDC Fact Sheets on Sexually Transmitted Diseases, 2006).

Gonorrhea is also caused by a bacteria spread by vaginal, oral, or anal sex. Symptoms are often mild and mistaken for kidney or bladder infections, and include pain or burning during urination, a discharge, bleeding, or a sore throat (CDC Fact Sheets on Sexually Transmitted Diseases, 2006). Gonorrhea can lead to infertility in both men and women, and to serious blood or joint problems. An infected mother can pass the infection to her baby during birth, which can cause blindness, joint infection, or serious blood infection in the infant. Both chlamydia and gonorrhea can be easily cured with antibiotics, but treatment does not reverse any damage that is done before treatment begins.

Human papillomavirus (HPV) is a group of viruses with more than 100 different strains. Infection sometimes produces visible warts in the genital area, but there are often no symptoms. Infection with HPV is very common; at least 50 percent of sexually active men and women will be infected at some point. Persistent infection with some HPV strains, although rare, is the main risk factor for cervical cancer (CDC Fact Sheets on Sexually Transmitted Diseases, 2006). There is no cure for HPV, but a vaccine that appears to reduce the likelihood of becoming infected was recently approved by the U.S. Food and Drug Administration. Many doctors are now recommending that girls receive the vaccination before becoming sexually active—at 11 to 12 years of age (Koutsky et al., 2002; Lo, 2006; Poland et al., 2005). As you probably noticed,

Many teens do not have accurate knowledge about STDs, how they are transmitted, and how they are treated. How can parents and schools help teens become more aware of these infections and how to protect themselves?

chlamydia
A common STD caused by a bacteria that often produces no symptoms, but that can lead to infertility if untreated.

gonorrhea
A common STD caused by a bacteria with often mild symptoms, but that can lead to infertility, blood, or joint problems if untreated.

human papillomavirus (HPV)
A common STD caused by any of a group of viruses with more than 100 different strains. Persistent infection is the main risk factor for cervical cancer.

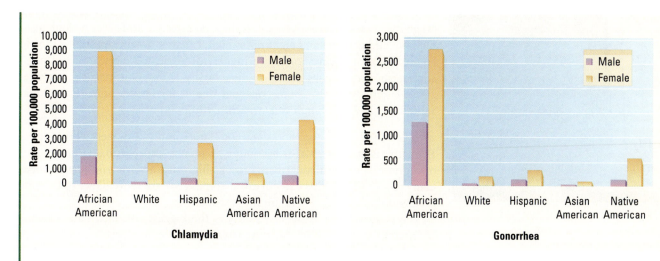

Figure 13.5 • Rate of Chlamydia and Gonorrhea Infection among Teens Age 15 to 19, by Ethnicity This figure shows the rate of reported infection among teens for chlamydia and gonorrhea, two of the most common STDs. These graphs show that females in general, and African American females in particular, are at high risk. (Data from CDC, 2005.)

your perspective

What did you and your peers know about STDs when you were 13, 14, and 15 years old? How did this knowledge (or lack of it) affect your choices about sexual activities?

all three of these infections can be difficult to recognize because they often have mild symptoms or none at all. This makes it even more important for sexually active individuals of any age to have regular screenings for these and other STDs. (Several other STDs that have serious consequences for fetuses were discussed in Chapter 3.)

As you can see in Figure 13.5, the rate of STD infection varies by ethnicity. Rates for most of these infections are higher among ethnic minorities. For example, in 2004, 70 percent of the reported cases of gonorrhea occurred in African Americans. It is important to remember that ethnic minority status is frequently confounded with other factors that are associated with higher rates of STDs such as poverty, lack of access to health care, and living in communities that have higher rates of STDs (CDC, 2005; Upchurch et al., 2004).

Adolescents are more likely to engage in casual sex and, as we learned in the last section, are less likely to use protection than adults. For both these reasons, sexually active teens are at high risk for STDs. In addition, adolescent females are at an increased risk for some STDs because the cervix is not fully mature (CDC, 2005). Many of these infections have vague symptoms or none at all so teens are often not aware that they carry them. Unfortunately, infection puts them at risk for a number of serious health risks. Having an STD makes people of any age more susceptible to other infections, including HIV. Someone who has an STD is also more likely to pass HIV on to someone else—the concentration of HIV in semen is up to 10 times higher in men who have both gonorrhea and HIV than in those who have only HIV (Wasserheit, 1992). Women with STDs are also at increased risk of pelvic inflammatory disease (PID), an infection of reproductive organs that can lead to infertility or ectopic (tubal) pregnancies. PID is frequently associated with the two STDs mentioned above that are commonly found in teens—chlamydia and gonorrhea. More teens are using condoms, but more effective efforts are needed to reduce STDs in adolescents.

Teenage Pregnancy

Each year approximately 850,000 U.S. teenage girls become pregnant. About 34 percent of U.S. teens will become pregnant *at least once* before they turn 20 years old. Adolescent girls account for about 14 percent of all pregnancies and 10 percent of all births each year (Hamilton et al., 2005; National Campaign to Prevent Teen Pregnancy, 2005; National Center for Health Statistics, 2000a; Ventura et al., 2003). Increased use of contraception and delaying having sex until later ages have contributed to a decline in teenage pregnancy rates in recent years, but the U.S. rates are still twice as high as in England and Canada and eight times higher than in Japan. As you can see in Figure 13.6, pregnancy rates are higher for African Americans, and most adolescent pregnancies result in live births (Alan Guttmacher Institute, 2004; Hamilton et al., 2005; National Center for Health Statistics, 2000a; Santelli et al., 2004; Singh & Darroch, 2000).

Who Is at Risk for Teenage Parenthood? Put simply, any teen who is sexually active is at some risk for becoming pregnant. Those who do not use contraception or use it inconsistently are at high risk and, as you just learned, many teens fall into this category. But some teens are more likely to become pregnant than others. What are the risk factors?

Most experts agree that living in poverty is the biggest risk factor for teenage pregnancy (Santelli et al., 2000b). As you probably realize, however, it's not lack of money per se that increases the risk. Poverty is associated with many factors related to teen pregnancy including poorer educational systems, lack of educational and job opportunities, family instability, less parental monitoring, and early age of first intercourse. Earlier age of first intercourse increases the risk of pregnancy in large part

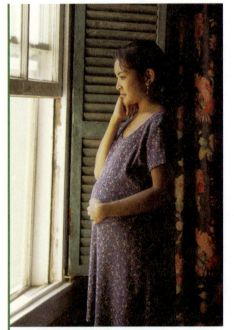

Teens who live in poverty, both external and internal, are at higher risk for teen pregnancy. What problems does this young woman face, and how can her family and community help her?

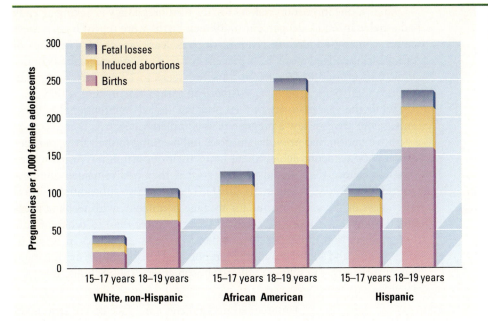

Figure 13.6 • Teenage Pregnancy Rates Pregnancy rates and pregnancy outcomes among 15- to 19-year-olds in the United States vary at different ages and among different ethnic groups. The data here come from a 1996 survey. (National Center for Health Statistics, 2000a.)

because younger teens are much less likely than older teens to use contraception reliably. Younger age of intercourse is also related to other family and personal problems, such as poorer parental monitoring and increased risk-taking. Regardless of socioeconomic status, lack of parental supervision increases the risk of a teen pregnancy. Growing up in a single parent home, poor academic performance, cognitive deficits, aggressiveness and social withdrawal during childhood, and alcohol and other drug use in early adolescence all increase the risk of teen pregnancy (Serbin et al., 1998; Stack et al., 2005).

Individual cognitive factors also play a role. One study assessed the locus of control and self-efficacy (both are related to feelings of control over outcomes and competence) along with educational and career expectations of almost 2000 8th grade girls from a large national data set. Four years later, teens who reported becoming pregnant by 12th grade were compared to nonpregnant teens of the same race and age. By 8th grade, those who would later become pregnant showed significantly lower self-efficacy, higher external locus of control, and lower expectations regarding their overall educational achievement. In essence, these teens seem to suffer from an "internal poverty," or the belief that they were less able to achieve their goals and that their lives were under others' control rather than their own (Young et al., 2001, p. 290; Young et al., 2004). Other studies report that expectations about life options play a role in teen pregnancy, with those who perceive fewer or more negative life options at a higher risk. For these teens, becoming pregnant may not represent a great loss of potential because, in their eyes, they did not have many positive options in the first place. Therefore, they see a pregnancy as causing less disruption to their lives, which may lead them to be less concerned about consistent use of contraception (Bickel et al., 1997; Bissel, 2000).

Less is known about risk factors for becoming a teenage father. Only about 7 percent of teen boys become fathers. Most are poor, do not do well in school (many have dropped out of high school), and are more likely to engage in drug use and delinquent activities than teens who are not fathers. Many come from single-parent and lower income homes, and from homes in which parents showed the poor discipline practices of *coercive homes* that we described in Chapter 12. Teen fathers show some of the same cognitive deficits as teen mothers, such as poor planning skills and childhood aggression. Substance use and involvement in deviant peer groups were also related to teen parenthood, all of which suggests a pattern of poor impulse control (Fagot et al., 1998; Miller-Johnson et al., 2004; Trad, 1995).

your perspective

Do you know anyone who became pregnant as a teenager? How has this person dealt with this challenge? What were the outcomes for this person?

Think About Marcus ...

Does Marcus have any of the risk factors for teen pregnancy? What can his family and community do to reduce the chances of his becoming a teen father?

Finally, one important risk factor for teen pregnancy is having already had a baby. In 2003, 20 percent of all teen births were repeat births; these young women had already given birth to at least one child. The rates of repeat births ranged from 15.5 percent for teens of Asian/Pacific Islander ethnic background to 16 percent for white teens to 19 percent for African American, Hispanic, and Native American teens (Martin et al., 2005).

While the vast majority of teen pregnancies are unintentional, adolescents do not always view a pregnancy as completely negative. Some see it as a positive option that provides purpose and meaning to their lives, particularly if poor academic achievement limits their opportunities. At least, they may not believe they would be better off if they had remained childless (SmithBathe, 2005; Young et al., 2001). There are also substantial cultural differences in the social norms for teenage pregnancy, with teenage pregnancy being much more accepted in some cultures than in others. Some teen mothers and fathers see a pregnancy as having benefits in terms of social status, and some teen mothers report that their children are the main reason they persist in school (Miller-Johnson et al., 2004; Schultz, 2001).

The Impact of Teen Parenthood. Unintended pregnancies can place severe strains on adolescents. These teens are often not physically or emotionally ready to bear and raise children. Teenage parenthood is associated with a number of negative outcomes; some of them are listed below (Coley & Chase-Lansdale, 1998; Furstenberg et al., 1989; Planned Parenthood, 2006; Stoiber & McIntyre, 2006).

- *Poorer educational achievement:* Both teen mothers and fathers finish fewer years of school than their peers (Hofferth et al., 2001).

- *Lower levels of financial success:* Nearly 80 percent of teen mothers receive welfare, most within the first five years of giving birth. Many do return to the work force after their children begin school; few receive financial help from the fathers of their children.

- *Disruptions in emotional development:* Identity development of teen mothers may suffer if parenthood limits their opportunity to explore different identities, and the development of autonomy may be curtailed if she is dependent on her parents for help. Some teenage mothers view their pregnancy[ies] and infant[s] as interfering with independence and options, and they may become resentful. Depending on the level of emotional maturity before the pregnancy, teen mothers may have difficulty putting their infants' needs first (Trad, 1999).

The children of teenage parents fare less well than those of older parents. As infants they are more likely to suffer from preterm birth, low birth weight, birthing complications, and infant mortality; second children of teen mothers have an even higher mortality rate (Cowden & Funkhouser, 2001). This may be due in part to the fact that younger mothers are less likely to receive consistent prenatal care, and they are less knowledgeable about and less inclined to engage in healthy behaviors during pregnancy and avoid unhealthy ones. The parenting skills of teen parents are often not well-developed, and their children are at increased risk for accidents, illnesses, child abuse, and neglect. Adolescent mothers are more likely to show an unresponsive parenting style and they tend to have unrealistic expectations of their children. Both teen mothers and fathers use discipline styles that are more negative, directive, and physical—much like the coercive parenting described in Chapter 12. These young parents are less empathetic toward their children, less patient, less verbal, and provide less stimulating environments for their babies. Problems for children of adolescent parents tend to worsen as they get older, especially for sons. They are at greater risk for educational, behavioral, emotional, and financial problems—including early parenthood themselves (Bunting & McAuley, 2004; Fagot et al., 1998; Pogarsky et al., 2006).

Clearly, teen parenthood is associated with a host of problems for mothers, fathers, and babies. What is less clear, however, is the extent to which these problems are the *result* of, rather than the *cause* of, teen parenthood. For example, the educational achievement differences between teen mothers and those who delay having a child are frequently in place long before early parenthood, though they do tend to worsen afterward. And a number of the behavioral problems shown by the children of young parents, such as early aggressiveness and poor impulse control, are very similar to the behaviors that put these parents at risk for early parenthood in the first place. Are these educational and behavioral problems due to early parenthood per se, to the poorer parenting skills of young parents, or to genetically related tendencies shared by these parents and children? The research has only begun to sort out these issues. Finally, the pervasive effects of poverty, both as a contributing factor to teen pregnancy and a result of young parenthood, may have a bigger impact on outcomes for teenage moms, dads, and their children than early parenthood itself (Bissell, 2000; Coley & Chase-Lansdale, 1998; Furstenberg et al., 1989; Levine et al., 2001).

Not all teen pregnancies have dire outcomes. If the young parents are able to continue their education, delay having a second child, and form supportive and positive relationships with family and friends, these young families can be more successful.

Recent research also indicates that there is a great deal of diversity in the outcomes for teen parents and their children (Furstenberg et al., 1989; Klein & the Committee on Adolescence, 2005; Schiefelbein et al., 2005). Many teen parents eventually achieve stability, especially if they are able to continue their education and delay having subsequent children. A stable marriage can contribute to better outcomes, but unstable relationships are associated with worse outcomes. While becoming a teenage parent is clearly not optimal, it does not necessarily doom the parents and children to negative outcomes. Prevention programs that foster self-esteem, feelings of self-competence, hopefulness, and plans for the future, and that help adolescents remain engaged in school help reduce the occurrence of teenage pregnancy (Bennett & Assefi, 2005; Klein & the Committee on Adolescence, 2005). Programs that help teen parents after a pregnancy has occurred can improve outcomes for parents and children, particularly when they:

- Emphasize correct and consistent use of contraceptives to delay a second pregnancy

- Support continued schooling and occupational training

- Encourage family support and provide help from community health/development experts

- Provide training in parenting skills and child development

- Help teen parents develop and maintain a strong sense of self-esteem and competence (American Academy of Pediatrics, 2001; Benson, 2004; Parra-Cardona, Sangalang et al., 2006; Wampler et al., 2006).

Forced Sexual Behavior

Unfortunately, many teens report that they were forced to have sex. Among sexually active girls, for example, 14 percent reported being victims of rape, and a quarter of these rapes occurred before the girl was even 10 years old (Coles & Stokes, 1985). According to a recent study, first intercourse was forced for 9 percent of females (Abma et al., 2004). In about half of the cases, the rapist was a boyfriend or casual friend. In other cases the rapists included relatives and family friends. **Rape** refers to sexual intercourse as a result of physical force or psychological coercion, while **sexual assault** refers to sexual contact due to physical force or psychological coercion that

rape
Sexual intercourse as a result of physical force or psychological coercion.

sexual assault
Sexual contact due to physical force or psychological coercion that may or may not involve penetration.

sexual harassment
Any unwanted behavior of a sexual nature that creates a hostile or offensive environment.

may or may not involve penetration. **Sexual harrassment** refers to any sort of unwanted behavior of a sexual nature and includes unwelcome sexual requests, demands, rumors, jokes, taunts, or other actions that create a hostile or offensive environment.

Adolescents are at higher risk for rape and other sexual assault than any other age group. Most victims are female, and most know the person who assaults them. Estimates of the prevalence of forced sex vary widely. Some studies report that about 10 percent of girls and 5 percent of boys will experience forced sex at some point; others estimate that as many as 68 percent of adolescents will suffer *acquaintance* or *date* rape (in which the victim knows, or is on a date with, the perpetrator). Twenty-six percent of college-aged men report having attempted acquaintance or date rape. The rate of sexual harrassment is even higher—in one study, 83 percent of adolescent girls and 79 percent of adolescent boys reported that they had experienced it, and 25 percent said they experienced it frequently (American Association of University Women, 2001; National Center for Victims of Crime, 2006; Rickert & Weimann, 1998).

Why are adolescents at higher risk of sexual assault? They usually have more freedom than younger children in terms of where they go and who they are with, they often want to experiment with new behaviors and therefore take more risks than older or younger individuals, they may not yet be skilled in "reading the signs" that indicate a potentially dangerous situation is developing, and they are in close contact with many other adolescents for a large part of the day during the school year (Howard & Wang, 2005; Rickert & Weimann, 1998).

Which adolescents are at highest risk for sexual assault? Unfortunately, one of the best predictors of being a victim of rape in adolescence is having been a victim of

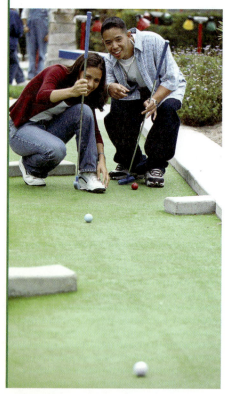

Date rape and other types of sexual assault are far too common. What can these teens do to reduce the likelihood of becoming victims of sexual assault?

rape during childhood (Clements et al., 2004; Rickert et al., 2004). As you learned in Chapter 10, the consequences of childhood sexual abuse are severe and far-reaching and, for many youth, the abuse does not stop. Other predictors of sexual assault during adolescence are early age for first date and early sexual activity, both of which place teens in situations where sexual coercion and rape are more likely. Drug use, particularly use of alcohol, is also associated with sexual assault for adolescents. For perpetrators of sexual violence, drug and alcohol use increases the chance of misinterpreting cues from the victim as sexual invitations. In addition, others may not hold perpetrators as responsible for their behavior if they were intoxicated; ironically, victims who are intoxicated may be viewed as more to blame (Johnson et al., 1997; Rickert & Weimann, 1998). For victims, alcohol and other drugs make it harder to cope with or escape the situation. One particular drug, flunitrazepam (Rohypnol), has received a lot of attention. This so-called *date rape drug* produces sleepiness, decreased anxiety and muscle control, and may cause amnesia. These effects put the victim at greater risk of not only being sexually assaulted but also unable to remember details that might be helpful in reporting and prosecuting an attack. Rape-tolerant attitudes also play an important role in the risk for rape. In some studies, date and acquaintence rape were not considered to be rape at all, or there was a stronger tendency in these situations to blame the victim. Both male and female high school students are more likely to assign blame to the victim if she dresses provocatively, though some studies find that more males assign this blame than females (White & Kurpius, 2002).

As you might expect, forced sexual activity has a number of negative consequences. Victims report feeling afraid, anxious, sad, and hopeless. Feelings of depression are common for both males and females, and they are worse when the victim knows the attacker. Victims may also experience problems with academic achievement, risky sexual behavior, increased drug and alcohol use, and increased risk of post-traumatic stress disorder. Not surprisingly, the more severe an assault and the longer the attacks continue before they are stopped, the more emotionally, psychologically, and physically difficult it is for the victims (Clements et al., 2004; Demaris & Kaukinen, 2005; National Center for Victims of Crime, 2006). Some prevention programs have been effective in changing both males' and females' attitudes and behaviors associated with sexual assault and in increasing knowledge of strategies for preventing rape. Awareness of sexual harassment and assault has been heightened, and guidelines have been published to help schools develop policies for preventing and reporting unwanted sexual activities. Given the statistics on adolescent sexual assault and harassment, however, there remains a need to improve and expand these programs (American Council on Education, 1992).

■ Let's Review . . .

1. Compared to white teens, teens who are ethnic minorities are at higher risk for STDs because a higher percentage of ethnic minority teens tend to _____.
   a. use drugs at a higher rate
   b. live in poverty
   c. avoid using health care even though it is easily available
   d. live in places where STDs are uncommon so they don't want to be screened for them

2. Why is poverty a risk factor for teen pregnancy?
   a. Poor teens are more likely to see a pregnancy as disrupting their future plans.
   b. Poor teens tend to become sexually active later and have less knowledge about contraception.
   c. Poor teens have fewer job and education opportunities.
   d. Poor teens are more aggressive and socially withdrawn during childhood.

3. Which of the following teen girls is at highest risk of a teenage pregnancy?
   a. Olivia, who loves school and enjoys working on school-related activities with her friends
   b. Julia, who believes that success in life is mostly about being lucky
   c. Bernadette, who plans to be a clinical psychologist
   d. Maya, whose parents check up on her regularly

4. Which of the following teens is at highest risk for becoming a victim of sexual assault?
   a. Brady, who binge drinks regularly
   b. Tevin, who is not yet sexually active at age 16
   c. Daniel, who helped organize his school's sexual assault prevention program
   d. Sam, who suffers from depression

5. **True or False:** The biggest risk factor for teenage pregnancy is aggressiveness during childhood.

6. **True or False:** Children of teen parents tend to have significant problems early in life, but their problems get better as they get older.

Answers: 1. b, 2. c, 3. b, 4. a, 5. F, 6. F

Adolescent Health Issues

In terms of physical illness and chronic health problems, adolescents are much healthier than the rest of the population. Leading causes of death among adults such as heart disease, cancer, and stroke are far less prevalent during adolescence (Miniño et al., 2002). However, experts have become increasingly concerned with adolescents' health. One reason is that adolescence is a time when long-lasting behavior patterns begin. If adolescents can be encouraged to develop positive health habits, they may avoid problems in adulthood. Experts also recognize that the major things that threaten adolescent health are *completely preventable*. For example, the leading cause of death by far among adolescents is unintentional injury, particularly motor vehicle accidents. And many adolescents each year compromise their health by misusing alcohol and other drugs; others suffer from depression and may even attempt suicide. Clearly, encouraging adolescents to develop positive health behaviors and avoid negative ones will reduce their risk for health problems and injury.

As you study this section, ask yourself these questions:

■ How good (or bad) are adolescents' eating and exercise habits? How can they be improved?

■ Who is at risk for eating disorders, and what factors contribute to their development?

■ Why don't adolescents get enough sleep? What are the effects of lack of sleep on behavior and emotions?

■ Which teens are at higher risk for substance abuse problems? What are *gateway drugs,* and why are adults concerned about teens' use of them?

■ What are the major causes of death in adolescence? How can these risks be reduced?

Nutrition and Exercise

You're probably well aware that the average teen today does not have very good eating habits. But just how good (or bad) is the state of adolescent nutrition? Recent surveys found that only 22 percent of high school students eat the recommended five servings of fruits and vegetables daily—unless you count french fries and potato chips. In fact, for any given category in the USDA's Food Pyramid (grains, vegetables, fruits, meat and beans, milk), fewer than half the teens surveyed ate the recommended number of servings. But their intake of fat and sugars was much higher than recommended. Two-thirds exceeded the guidelines for overall fat intake and almost 75 percent ate too much saturated fat—the kind that is associated with a host of health problems (Enns et al., 2003; Grunbaum et al., 2004). Adolescents are also more likely than other age groups to have inconsistent eating patterns. Skipping meals is quite common, with about 20 percent of teens not eating breakfast and 50 percent not eating lunch. Skipping meals often leads to adolescents eating more snacks, and snack choices are often as bad or worse than meal choices (Siega-Riz et al., 2001). All foods are much more available to teens than in past generations, but the availability of fast food in particular plays an important role in the teens' food choices. Increased portion sizes encourage many to overeat less healthy foods. Family eating habits are also important—more families eat away from home than in the past and parents often provide poorer models of food choices for children (Briefel & Johnson, 2004).

What about exercise? About two-thirds of adolescents engage in regular vigorous physical activity, though less than one-third do so in a physical education class at school. Teens are less physically active than younger children, however, and teen girls are significantly less likely to get regular physical exercise than teen boys. Teens who are more physically active see themselves as healthier, have a more positive body image, and have healthier overall lifestyles. Both teen boys and girls report that they are more likely to exercise regularly when they have a friend to exercise with, when they like the activity they engage in, and when they think of exercise as something that is typical among their friends (Godin et al., 2005; Tergerson & King, 2002). The level of physical activity among minority females is lower than among whites, but they have similar perceptions of

Teens eat out much more frequently than in years past and overeat fat and sugars. How can teens, parents, and communities improve the health habits of adolescents?

the benefits (e.g., staying in shape) and negative aspects of exercise (e.g., getting hurt, sweating, having to deal with aggressive players, and embarassment) (Grieser et al., 2006). Higher levels of support from parents and peers is related to higher levels of regular physical activity (DeBourdeaudhuij, Lefevre, & Deforche, 2005; Gustafson & Rhodes, 2006). One important factor that is sometimes overlooked in attempts to increase physical activity in children and teens is neighborhood safety. Teens who live in neighborhoods that are perceived as being less safe are less likely to engage in physical activity (Molnar et al., 2004).

Think About Marcus …
What steps can Marcus take as a teen to improve his lifelong health? What are some things his parents and his school could do to encourage Marcus to develop positive health habits?

Eating Disorders

As you may have experienced yourself, there is considerable pressure toward unhealthy thinness for children and teens, especially for girls and women. For example, consider the story of Sarah. At the age of 13 Sarah was already thinner than most girls her age, but she still believed that she was fat and unattractive. On a typical day Sarah ate a plain piece of toast in the morning and a cup of yogurt and fruit for dinner. She rarely snacked. She exercised vigorously every day, determined to lose another 5 to 10 pounds. By the time she was 15, Sarah weighed only 85 pounds (more than 25 percent less than the average weight for her age). Because of her severe weight loss, she stopped having menstrual periods, but she was still determined to lose more weight. Sarah was never satisfied with how she looked, and she felt that she was losing control of her weight. In despair, Sarah tried to end her life by taking an overdose of sleeping pills. Fortunately, her parents found her before it was too late, and they admitted her to the hospital. Before she was released from the hospital, she gained 14 pounds. Sarah and her parents now attend counseling sessions, and only time will tell if she will recover from her condition.

You have probably recognized that Sarah suffers from **anorexia nervosa**. This serious condition involves a distorted body image, an intense fear of gaining weight, and the refusal to maintain a minimally healthy body weight. People with anorexia, like Sarah, have an irrational view of their own bodies. By objective standards they are already thin, but they are still convinced that they are fat and unattractive. They show a relentless determination to be even more thin. People with anorexia have a very restricted diet, and they attempt to lose additional weight through vigorous exercise or by purging food through self-induced vomiting or the misuse of laxatives or enemas.

Bulimia nervosa, or bulimia, is a related condition that involves cycles of binge eating (consumption of huge amounts of food) followed by purging, fasting, or excessive exercise as a means to compensate for overeating. People with bulimia experience a loss of control during binge episodes: They know they are overeating, but they feel powerless to stop. Afterwards, they feel intense guilt. In contrast to some anorexics, who purge after eating only small amounts of food, bulimics purge after uncontrolled eating binges.

Both types of eating disorders are most common among female adolescents. Approximately one out of every 100 female adolescents is anorexic, two to three times as many are bulimic (Mash & Wolfe, 1999). In the past these disorders were rare in males, but body dissatisfaction and eating disorders may be increasing among male adolescents, along with use of anabolic steroids and other untested supplements to increase muscle mass (Labre, 2002; McCabe & Ricciardelli, 2004). Anorexia typically appears between the ages of 14 and 18, whereas bulimia usually emerges in later adolescence. There is a mild to moderate genetic link to eating disorders. These disorders tend to run in families, and compared to nonidentical twins, identical twins are three to five times more likely to share an eating disorder (Hsu et al., 1990). Researchers believe that adolescents can inherit emotional tendencies that make them vulnerable to eating disorders. Too often, these vulnerabilities can combine with

anorexia nervosa
A serious eating disorder involving distorted body image, intense fear of gaining weight, and refusal to maintain a healthy weight.

bulimia nervosa
A serious eating disorder with binge eating, followed by purging, fasting, or excessive exercise.

Some teens suffer from serious eating disorders. What does this young woman see when she looks in the mirror? What are some of the factors that might have led to her illness?

your perspective

Have you known anyone with an eating disorder? What impact did it have on his or her life? Did this person receive treatment? Was it effective?

low self-esteem, family pressures, and the strong societal message that "thin is beautiful" to lead to eating disorders (Davison & Birch, 2002; Stice & Whitenton, 2002). Unfortunately, eating disorders have a higher death rate than any other psychiatric disorder (Sullivan, 1995).

We all know that society places too much emphasis on being thin. The mass media are full of images of attractive women who are significantly thinner than the general population. In fact many models are so thin that they are unhealthy. Very few adolescent girls can "measure up" to these unreasonable standards. Most adolescent girls are not satisfied with their body image, and 80 percent diet to control their weight (Mash & Wolfe, 1999). For ethnic minority teens, the stress of trying to fit into the majority culture adds additional pressures (Perez et al., 2002). Striving to be thin, some adolescent girls spiral into a dangerous cycle of anorexia or bulimia. For many anorexics, food is the only thing they feel they can control. And for bulimics, binging and purging is another symptom of their lack of control over life events. Psychological therapy and medications have shown promise in treating adolescent eating disorders (DeAngelis, 2002). Some recent approaches combine a school-based prevention program that addresses issues of body image, cultural ideals, and self-esteem with a more intensive family-based program for students identified as being at high risk of developing eating disorders (Varnado-Sullivan & Zucker, 2004). Severe cases, like Sarah's, may require hospitalization to force weight gain or to treat other symptoms such as suicidal behavior or chronic depression. To read more about eating disorders, their impact on teens and their families, and how they are treated, read the Professional Perspective box called "Career Focus: Meet an Eating Disorders Counselor."

Adolescents Need More Sleep

It will probably come as no surprise to you that many adolescents don't get enough sleep. One large study found that only 20 percent of high school students averaged at least 8 hours of sleep on school nights and almost half slept 7 hours or less. Of these students, 87 percent said they did not get enough sleep (Wolfson & Carskadon, 1998). But adolescents and young adults *need* as much sleep as younger children to be alert and function well during the day—about 9.2 hours. Lack of sleep is associated with greater levels of depression and anxiety, poorer grades in school, lapses of attention, slower cognitive and motor reactions, mental errors, poorer task performance, decreased motivation, and increased risk of accidents. Difficulties with regulating emotions and attention may be due to the effect of sleep deprivation on the prefrontal cortex. As you learned earlier in this chapter, this area of the brain is still undergoing important developmental changes during adolescence and lack of sleep may affect this development in ways we do not yet understand (Dahl & Spear, 2004; Mitru et al., 2002). Remember, though, that the problems associated with lack of sleep are based on correlations so we can't be certain if less sleep is causing these difficulties, the difficulties are causing sleep problems, or if some other factor such as having a more anxiety-prone personality is causing both.

As you may have experienced, sleep deprivation can lead teenagers to nap during the day. Some have *microsleeps* in which they fall asleep from a few seconds up to a minute but aren't aware that they've been asleep— clearly a dangerous situation if they happen to be driving at the time! Many attempt to catch up on lost sleep on weekends, but it's not clear whether this is a good strategy. Some studies have found that inconsistency in weekday versus weekend bedtimes is associated with more sleep-related difficulties such as having a hard time falling asleep and needing more than one reminder to get up. The strategies that teens (indeed, that many of us) use to cope with daytime sleepiness often involve consuming some form of caffeine, which can create even more sleep problems (Millman, 2005; O'Brien & Mindell, 2005; Orbeta et al., 2006).

Most teens do not get enough sleep, which leads to problems with concentrating, staying alert, and performing tasks. What role might biological changes in circadian rhythms play in this student's difficulties staying awake?

Career Focus: Meet an Eating Disorders Counselor

Douglas Bunnell, Ph.D., FAED
Wilton, CT
Counselor specializing in treatment of eating disorders; Past president of the National Eating Disorders Association

What eating disorders are common in teens? What factors lead to an eating disorder?

Most teens with eating disorders have tried to diet by restricting their food intake. Some go on to develop full blown anorexia nervosa, but many are not able to sustain the food restriction. They develop symptoms such as binge eating. This often leads to guilt and anxiety about weight gain and can provoke overexercising, using laxatives, or inducing vomiting. Eating disorders are never caused by a single factor. There is no question that cultural messages about the importance of being thin help create tremendous body image distress in teens, boys and girls alike. This is a pervasive risk factor for developing eating disorders. Teens who have other risk factors, such as predisposing genetics, anxiety, or depression are most likely to develop a serious eating disorder.

What symptoms and effects do teens with eating disorders and their families experience?

Eating disorders are serious illnesses that have an enormous impact on both the individual and the people who know and love her or him. Teens with eating disorders often feel anxious and depressed. Many feel that nothing they accomplish can make them feel satisfied, so they push themselves to incredible lengths just to feel "good enough." They can develop dangerous cardiac problems, weakened bones, and serious dental problems. Their families also struggle.

What kinds of treatments are available? How can parents and teens prevent eating disorders?

Eating disorders are complicated illnesses. Treatment has to be equally complex, but it can be hard to find, expensive, and it can take a long time. Most patients have an individual or family therapist who helps them develop new ways to cope with their feelings. Family therapy is often the most effective treatment. Patients may work with a nutritionist for help with meal planning and eating disorder behaviors. Psychiatric medications can be very helpful—a medical doctor is an important part of every patient's treatment team. Many patients can be treated as outpatients, but a significant number will need a residential or hospital-based program. The structure and supervision of these programs often make it easier for patients to give up their symptoms.

Teaching children to decode cultural messages about body image may help them resist the pressure to be thin at any cost. Identifying early warning signs of an eating disorder like body image distress, attempts to diet when there is no need to lose weight, ritualized eating habits, or evidence of purging can help by starting treatment before more serious symptoms occur.

What advice do you have for students who are considering a career in this area?

Clinicians need to be fully aware of the mental, psychological, relational, and biological aspects of adolescence, because eating disorders are mostly teen disorders. Whether their specialty is medicine, psychology, nutrition, or social work, students need to be able to integrate information from a wide variety of perspectives. Patients with eating disorders may be reluctant to let themselves get help. Clinicians need to be empathic, informed, and creative to establish a connection with them. The best background is one that exposes you to a wide variety of literature, arts, science, and humanities. There are no simple answers with these disorders and clinicians need to be comfortable with complexity and ambiguity. They also need to be a bit stubborn while still being respectful and caring.

Q *What can families and communities do to help their children and adolescents cope with the pervasive cultural messages about being thin?*

Why do adolescents get less sleep than they need? Parents don't monitor bedtimes as closely as with younger children, and teens often have more demands on their time and tasks to complete before they go to bed such as homework, jobs, volunteer activities, sports practices, music lessons, clubs, and the like. Television, instant messaging, and other technological distractions also keep them up late. But there may also be a biological reason for their later bedtimes. As adolescents go through puberty, circadian rhythms that help regulate many of the body's systems (including the sleep/wake cycle) change to a **delayed phase preference**—so teens simply aren't sleepy until later at night (Carskadon et al., 1998; Carskadon et al., 1993; Millman, 2005).

Research on the biology of adolescent sleep patterns has led to attempts to change school start times. Between 35 percent and 50 percent of high schools in the United States begin by 7:30 a.m. (Millman, 2005). However, high school students perform better in afternoon classes than in morning classes, and they report being less alert in earlier classes. Early start times are also associated with higher levels of sleep deprivation and overall daytime sleepiness (Carskadon et al., 1998; Hansen et al., 2005). In 1997 the Minneapolis school district changed the start times for its schools so that older students started later, affecting 50,000 students at all grades. High schoolers reported feeling more alert, tardiness due to oversleeping decreased, and teachers reported fewer students sleeping in class. The effects on student behavior and grades were less clear. Only about one-third of teachers in one survey reported that behavior improved. Grades were higher than in comparison schools, but it's not clear whether this was because of later start times or other differences in grading practices (Kubow et al., 1999). Not all students seemed to benefit from the changes. Middle schoolers, whose school start time changed from 7:40 a.m. to 9:40 a.m., seemed tired and impatient by the end of the day and many had to miss late afternoon classes because of conflicts with sports and other after-school activities. Changing school start times also presents challenges with scheduling buses, sports practices, and other after-school activities, as well as conflicts with teens' after-school job schedules.

Substance Use and Abuse

A major threat to adolescent health is substance use and abuse. **Substance use** can be somewhat difficult to define, but in general it refers to ingesting any legal or illegal substance that alters psychological functioning on more than a few occasions. **Substance abuse** refers to the use of a substance (legal or illegal) to the extent that it creates difficulties in day-to-day life. How prevalent is substance use and abuse? A large nationwide survey of U.S. high school students indicated that the majority of ninth graders had tried both alcohol and tobacco, and more than one-third had tried marijuana (CDC, 2004). As Figure 13.7 shows, smaller percentages of ninth graders had tried cocaine and other drugs. Almost 20 percent of ninth graders also admitted that they still used marijuana or tobacco, and about 35 percent still used alcohol. Although the percentages were somewhat higher for 12th graders, the patterns of alcohol and drug use were already well established by the first year of high school. Use of inhalants (sniffing glue, paint, or aerosols) is a more recent phenomenon. More 9th graders than 12th graders had ever tried inhalants; about twice as many ninth graders still used inhalants. Use of ecstasy (also known as MDMA), is becoming more common, with 11 percent of teens nationwide reporting having used it at least once. Table 13.3 shows ethnic differences in substance use from the same nationwide survey. Use of alcohol, tobacco, cocaine, inhalants, ecstasy, and methamphetamines was lower among African Americans than among non-Hispanic whites or Hispanics. Hispanics reported the highest use of cocaine and ecstasy. Other large-scale surveys show that the rate of using many illegal drugs has declined in recent years, by about 10 percent among 12th graders. However, the use of inhalants, sedatives, and the addictive prescription drug OxyContin has increased (Cleveland & Wiebe, 2003; Dishion & Owen, 2002; Johnston et al., 2006).

delayed phase preference
Changes in natural circadian rhythms during puberty that cause teens to become sleepy later in the evening and awaken later in the morning.

Think About Marcus …

What can Marcus do to make sure he gets enough sleep? Why is it important that he do this?

substance use
Ingesting on more than a few occasions any substance that alters psychological functioning.

substance abuse
The use of a substance that alters psychological functioning to the extent that it creates difficulties in day-to-day life.

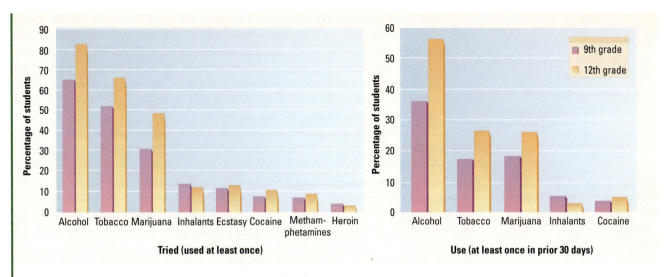

Figure 13.7 • Alcohol and Drug Use in 9th and 12th Grades The data graphed here come from a nationwide survey of high school students. Compare the percentages of students in the 9th and 12th grades who reported trying and using alcohol and other drugs. *Note: Tried* means used the substance at least once; *use* means used the substance at least once during the 30 days prior to the survey. *Cocaine* includes powder, "crack," and "freebase"; *inhalants* include sniffing glue or breathing aerosols, paints, or sprays; *heroin* includes "smack," "junk," and "China white." (Data from CDC, 2004.)

The rates of alcohol and tobacco (and increasingly, marijuana) use are concerning. As you saw above, a majority of teens have at least tried alcohol by the time they reach high school and many drink regularly. Most obtain alcohol from their own homes. **Binge drinking,** defined as consuming five or more drinks on a single occasion, is also becoming more common among high school students, with 20 percent of 9th graders and 37 percent of 12th graders saying they have binged at least once. Alcohol use by teens is related to many problem behaviors and outcomes, including traffic accidents and fatalities, early sexual activity, rape, poor school performance, and poorer mental health. It can be difficult to tease apart which factors lead to and which result from alcohol use, but alcohol use by teens is clearly linked to many problems. Tobacco use has declined significantly since the mid-1990s, but this trend is weakening for both cigarettes and smokeless tobacco (currently used by about 7 percent

binge drinking
Consuming five or more alcoholic drinks on a single occasion.

TABLE 13.3 High School Students' Alcohol and Drug Use by Ethnic Group

	NON-HISPANIC WHITE	AFRICAN AMERICAN	HISPANIC
Use alcohol	47	37	46
Use tobacco	25	15	18
Use marijuana	22	24	24
Use cocaine	4	2	6
Use inhalants	4	3	4
Tried ecstasy	11	6	13
Tried methamphetamines	8	3	8
Tried heroin	3	3	4

Note: Use means the students used the substance at least once during the 30 days prior to the survey.
Tried means the students ever used heroin in any form.
(CDC, 2004.)

your perspective

Were your parents concerned about you using gateway drugs? How did they communicate this to you, and did it make a difference?

gateway drugs
Drugs such as alcohol, tobacco, and marijuana that are typically used prior to the onset of using harder drugs such as cocaine and heroin.

of teens). Teens hold much more negative attitudes toward smoking and its health risks than in past years, there is less cigarette advertising that targets them, and they see much more antismoking advertising. The skyrocketing cost of cigarettes is probably also a factor in declining rates of tobacco use (Johnston et al., 2006). Finally, marijuana is by far the most frequently used drug that is illegal for both adolescents and adults. It equals tobacco in the percentage of teens who are regular users.

Substance use usually starts during adolescence, and it usually begins with legal-for-adults drugs such as alcohol and tobacco. If it progresses, marijuana is typically used next, then other illegal drugs. Alcohol, tobacco, and marijuana are often called **gateway drugs** because the vast majority of those who use harder drugs first used one of these three. Across several studies, 90 percent of those who used illegal drugs first used marijuana, and the risk of using marijuana is 65 times greater for those who have smoked cigarettes or used alcohol compared to those who have not. Earlier and more frequent use of the gateway drugs is also associated with a greater chance of using harder illegal drugs. The gateway theory does not say that progression to harder drugs is inevitable or even likely—in fact, most who use alcohol, tobacco, and marijuana do not go on to harder drug use. But monitoring the use of these substances is still important for parents because it is a signal for potential problems, particularly if their adolescent shows other risk factors for drug abuse (Fergusson, Boden, & Horwood, 2006; Kandel, 2002; Kandel et al., 1992).

Risk Factors for Drug Use. One risk factor for drug use is simply being an adolescent. Adolescents are far more likely to experiment with alcohol and drugs than younger or older individuals. But not all teens who experiment are at equal risk of developing problems or having negative long-term outcomes. Many who experiment or only use occasionally do not experience long-term effects—as long as they escape short-term negative outcomes such as accidents and sexual risk-taking. As you might expect, early onset of use (e.g., using alcohol before age 14 or illegal drugs before age 15) is associated with increasing use over time and greater risk for alcohol and drug disorders (Chassin et al., 2004). But what risk factors can adults watch for before substance use begins?

Characteristics of the individual are related to substance use. Those who develop substance problems are more likely to be sensation seeking, aggressive, impulsive, and have poor behavioral control—and many of these qualities are evident between 3 and 5 years of age. Problems with cognitive skills related to self-regulation such as planning, organizing, and selective attention are also related to increased risk of substance abuse. A history of antisocial behavior, including aggressiveness and conduct problems, is also a risk factor (Chassin et al., 2004).

Teens' beliefs, values, and experiences also play a role in whether they use alcohol and drugs. Those who believe that alcohol and drugs are a threat to their health or their future goals are less likely to use them, while those that think of drug use as less risky and more fun are at increased risk. Teens who describe themselves as more religious are less likely to try alcohol or drugs. And those who experience high levels of stress are at an increased risk. Having experienced physical or sexual abuse in childhood or witnessed family or neighborhood violence increases the risk. For these teens, substance use may be an attempt to cope with circumstances that are overwhelming to them (McIntosh et al., 2005; Merrill et al., 2001; Wallace et al., 2003).

Family factors are important in predicting substance problems. Those with a family history of substance abuse are at higher risk, probably for several reasons. Families may share a genetic susceptibility for drug use and dependence, and parents who abuse alcohol or drugs provide a model of substance use for their children. Prenatal exposure to alcohol or drugs may increase the sensitivity of receptors for the substances in the child's brain or may contribute to conduct and self-control problems in the child. Alcohol and drugs are also likely to be more available in homes with a family history of substance use.

Parenting practices are also important. Harsh, inconsistent, or permissive discipline is associated with higher levels of substance use. Not surprisingly, poor parental monitoring increases the risk as well because these parents have less knowledge of what their teens are doing and who they're with. More authoritative parenting (high in warmth and responsiveness, but with appropriate expectations and discipline) is associated with lower levels of substance use. A close relationship with parents reduces the likelihood of drug use, probably because these parents monitor their adolescents more closely and perhaps have more influence on their teens' friendships. Parents also communicate their beliefs and values about substance use by their behavior and through discussions with their children, and they can reinforce positive connections with peers, school, clubs, churches, and other organizations that affect the risk of substance use.

Like many adolescents, these teens are experimenting with alcohol and tobacco. Why do some teens choose not to drink and smoke? What are the effects of occasional substance use and of heavier substance use during adolescence?

Of all the factors that have been studied, having friends who use alcohol and other drugs is the strongest predictor of teen substance use. Friends who use provide a model of substance use, opportunity to engage in substance use, access to the substances, and reinforcement for using. Of course, it is difficult to know exactly how to interpret this relationship. Do teens who are more likely to use substances *select* friends who are also likely to do so? Or are teens who would otherwise be unlikely to use drugs being *influenced to use* by their friends? As you might expect, it can be difficult for research to sort out these possibilities but it seems that both selection and socialization influences are important. Regardless, it's a good idea for parents to monitor who their teens are spending time with and get to know their teen's friends.

As you can see, adolescents with more difficult temperaments, cognitive difficulties, and poor self-control of behavior and emotions are at higher risk for substance problems. These individual vulnerabilities may interact with more coercive or lax parenting practices, leading to problems with schooling and lack of acceptance into a positive peer group. These children and teens may then become increasingly involved with deviant peer groups that model, reinforce, and provide opportunities to engage in substance use—much the same way that these elements work together to produce conduct problems, aggression, and delinquent behavior (see Chapters 12 and 15).

Think About Marcus . . .

How great is the risk that Marcus will develop a substance abuse problem? Which risk factors does he show? What can he and his parents do to help him make good decisions about alcohol and drugs?

Depression

Teri's father died when she was 11. Since then, she has become increasingly withdrawn and moody. Now at the age of 15, she is disobedient, skips school, and refers to herself as "stupid." As she looks at her life, Teri wonders why she should go on. She tries every day to see the point of living, but there is none. On three occasions she cut her wrists, but the wounds were only superficial (adapted from Berman & Jobes, 1991, pp. 95–96).

Most of us use the word *depression* to refer to the kind of sadness and loss of energy that periodically occurs in our lives. **Clinical depression,** however, refers to a constellation of symptoms that can include sadness, loss of interest in activities, feelings of worthlessness, sleep problems, and changes in appetite (Kazdin & Marciano, 1998). The symptoms are prolonged, lasting longer than normal for periods of grief or loss. It is normal, for example, for someone to feel intense sadness for several months after losing a loved one. But when the symptoms continue for an unusually long time, as they did with Teri, then clinical depression is indicated. With depression, the symptoms also cause significant distress and impair the person's ability to perform at school, at work, and in social situations.

clinical depression
A condition that involves sadness, loss of interest in activities, feelings of worthlessness, sleep problems, and changes in appetite that persist for an unusually long time.

It is normal for children to feel intense sadness after experiencing a significant loss. It is considered to be a clinical depression when the symptoms continue after an unusually long time and when they impair the child's ability to perform at school and in social situations.

Adolescents who are depressed tend to have low self-esteem and they have negative thoughts about themselves and the events around them. They are less popular among their peers and are more likely to feel rejected and isolated. They tend to perform poorly in school, and are more likely to miss assignments, miss school, and fail a grade. When they become adults, they are at an increased risk for having marriage problems, being unemployed, abusing drugs, and engaging in criminal activity (Kazdin & Marciano, 1998).

Depression is relatively rare (less than 1 percent) among preschoolers, increases during the elementary school years (up to 2 percent), and increases again during adolescence (to around 2 percent to 8 percent). There is some evidence that, during childhood, depression is more common among boys than girls. By puberty, however, depression is five times more common among girls than boys (Kazdin & Marciano, 1998). When boys are angry, they tend to act out their feelings in physical and sometimes aggressive ways, but girls are socialized from an early age to hold these feelings inside. Researchers believe that many more children and adolescents suffer from serious symptoms of depression, even if they don't meet the full criteria for a clinical disorder. And the rates of depression seem to be significantly increasing. The most serious forms of clinical depression run in families. The heritability index for depression is as high as .60, with identical twins much more likely to share symptoms of depression than fraternal twins (Nurnberger & Gershon, 1992). The milder forms of depression, however, do not have a consistent genetic link. Depression is also thought to be related to faulty cognitive processes (pessimistic and negative thought patterns), learned behaviors, and stressful life events.

Children and adolescents who suffer from depression tend to show significant improvements after receiving psychotherapy. Therapy is especially effective when it focuses on decreasing negative and destructive thought processes, improving self-esteem, enhancing social skills, and techniques for relaxation and the management of anxiety (Kazdin & Marciano, 1998). Surprisingly, the antidepressant medications (such as *Prozac*) that seem to work for adults don't work as well with younger individuals. Controlled studies with children have failed to show that antidepressants work any better than placebo (sugar) pills, and there is concern about the possibility of serious side effects. By 1996, three-quarters of a million prescriptions were written to provide *Prozac* to children and adolescents (it even comes in peppermint flavor!), but there simply is not sufficient research evidence to indicate that these types of drugs are working for them (Kazdin & Marciano, 1998; Mash & Wolfe, 1999). Unfortunately, 70 percent to 80 percent of depressed adolescents do not receive treatment of any kind (Kazdin & Marciano, 1998). Because they are more withdrawn, and their symptoms are turned inward, depressed adolescents are often overlooked. Parents, teachers, and others often expect adolescents to be moody and dramatic, and the symptoms of depression are sometimes mistaken for a "phase that will pass."

Causes of Death

The leading cause of death among adolescents is unintentional injury, led by motor vehicle accidents. In fact, a recent national study found that the *only* groups of adolescents for whom unintentional injuries were not the leading cause of death were 15- to 19-year-old African American males (homicide was the leading cause of death in this group) and 10- to 14-year-old Asian American males (cancers were the leading cause for this group). Homicide and suicide are within the top 10 causes of adolescent death for all ethnic groups except 10- to 14-year-old African American females—for this group, accidents were the leading cause of death and homicide was third, but suicide was not in the top 10 causes (Anderson & Smith, 2002).

Part Five: Adolescence

Adolescent Drivers. The statistics are striking. For every mile they drive, 16-year-old drivers are seven times more likely to have an accident than 25- to 29-year-olds. Despite accounting for only about 5 percent of licensed drivers, teens are involved in 12 percent of fatal crashes. Accidents involving teens are especially likely during the first six months after obtaining a license, when driving at night (between 9 p.m and 6 a.m.), when carrying passengers, and when drinking alcohol. Teenagers are less likely than adults to wear seatbelts, which increases the likelihood of serious injury when they are in an accident. Teens' greater tendencies to take risks accounts for some of their increased accident rate, but simple inexperience with driving is also a major contributor (CDC Injury Fact Book, 2002; Sherman et al., 2004; Williams, 2003).

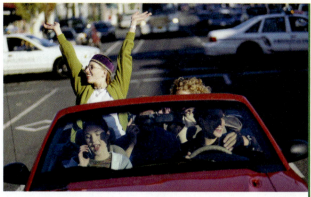

Teen drivers have more accidents than any other age group, especially in the first six months after getting their licenses. What should parents do to help their teens gain experience and avoid accidents?

Graduated driver licensing laws (GDL laws) have been enacted by many states to reduce the frequency of teen vehicle accidents. GDL laws typically have a 6-month period of supervised driving, then an intermediate period during which teens are allowed to drive unsupervised in lower risk conditions (e.g., daytime, with limited numbers of passengers), and finally full licensure. Since enacting GDL, states report reductions in teen accidents ranging from 5 percent to 60 percent, so it seems these laws can be effective (Sherman et al., 2004; Simons-Morton et al., 2005). States vary in how stringently they enforce GDL laws, and the accident rate for teens is still higher than for older drivers even in states where these laws are enforced. Experts point out that "parents remain the true enforcers of driving privileges among teenagers, because parents can control access to the car" (Simons-Morton et al., 2005, p. 447). Parents are encouraged to closely monitor their teens' driving skills, control how often and under what conditions their teen is allowed to drive, and establish and enforce restrictions in accordance with appropriate driving behaviors.

Think About Marcus . . .

How can Marcus and his parents reduce the likelihood that Marcus will have an accident when he gets his license? Will GDL laws be enough, or should his parents do more?

Suicide. It is estimated that between 3 percent and 11 percent of all adolescents have attempted suicide at some point (Lewinsohn et al., 1994). In one set of studies, researchers interviewed a large representative sample of adolescents in the state of Oregon (Andrews & Lewinsohn, 1992; Lewinsohn et al., 1993; Lewinsohn et al., 1994). When interviewed again one year later, 26 (out of 1,508) of the adolescents reported that they had attempted suicide since the first interview. That means that, in one year alone, 1.7 percent of the adolescents attempted suicide!

What distinguished these 26 adolescents from the ones who did not attempt suicide? Adolescents were more likely to attempt suicide when they were born to teenage mothers, suffered from depression or other psychological disorders, had suicidal thoughts or ideas during the first interview, had a friend who attempted suicide recently, or had low self-esteem. Similar evidence indicates that adolescents are more likely to attempt suicide when they live in single-parent homes, their parents have less education, they lack support from family and friends, and they show problems with appetite (Lewinsohn et al., 1994). Also, females are about three times more likely than males to attempt suicide, but males are more than four times more likely to die from their suicide attempts (Lewinsohn et al., 1994; Stillion & McDowell, 1996). Suicide rates are nearly twice as high among Latino American adolescents as among African American or white teens. Researchers speculate that in Latino families that recently immigrated to the United States, teens are especially stressed by the conflict between their Latino culture and mainstream America (Canino & Roberts, 2001). Researchers are still trying to assemble a list of risk factors that might indicate which adolescents are at especially high risk for trying to take their own lives, but as you can tell from the discussion above, a great many adolescents show one or more of the risks. It is therefore very difficult to identify (in advance) which ones will actually make suicide attempts.

Since 1960, the rate of suicide deaths has remained steady for the whole U.S. population, but it has steadily increased for younger individuals. For 15- to 24-year-olds, there were about five suicides per 100,000 individuals in 1960 and about 13 per 100,000 by 1990. It is rare for younger children to actually commit suicide, but as many as one in five say that they have seriously thought about killing themselves (Stillion & McDowell, 1996). These numbers should give us all reason to pause and consider how children's lives have changed in recent decades. Researchers have not yet identified the specific causes of the increase in suicide rates, but you can imagine that speculation centers on changes in family structure, the increased pace of life, and the loss of family support systems. One way to reduce the rate is to make sure that the symptoms of depression (and other psychological disturbances) are noticed and treated at an earlier age.

Although G. Stanley Hall (1904) and other theorists characterized adolescence as a time of "storm and stress," most manage to work their way through puberty and adolescent transitions in a relatively peaceful manner. In this chapter, we described the many physical changes that characterize the move toward adulthood, as well as some of the major challenges to adolescent health and safety. Good relationships with parents make these transitions easier, and affiliating with a positive peer group can influence teens to use positive and adaptive coping strategies. And as we saw at earlier ages, physical changes have an important influence on cognitive and socioemotional development, but adolescents' health and safety are also clearly influenced by cognitive and social development. We will talk more about these areas of development in the next two chapters.

■ Let's Review . . .

1. Which of the following is *true* about adolescents and sleep?
   a. On average, teens get about 9.2 hours of sleep per night.
   b. Teens' circadian rhythms lead them to become sleepy later at night than when they were younger.
   c. Changing to later school start times does not affect teens' school performance.
   d. Teens need less sleep than younger children.

2. For most drugs, the rate of use is lowest for which of the following ethnicities?
   a. African American
   b. Hispanic
   c. white
   d. Native American

3. Which of the following best defines the gateway drug effect theory?
   a. Teens who use harder drugs begin doing so before or at the same time as using alcohol.
   b. Teens who use harder drugs almost always started out with alcohol, tobacco, or marijuana.
   c. Teens who use alcohol, tobacco, or marijuana will likely progress to using harder drugs.
   d. Teens who use alcohol, tobacco, or marijuana are not at any higher risk for progressing to harder drugs.

4. GDL laws are intended to _____.
   a. keep teens from driving until they are older
   b. get parents more involved in teaching their teens to drive
   c. explicitly teach teens how to drive in high-risk situations
   d. reduce the number of motor vehicle accidents for teens

5. **True or False:** A majority of teens report that they get regular vigorous exercise.

6. **True or False:** Anorexia and bulimia are most likely caused by a combination of genetic, social, and psychological factors.

Answers: 1. b, 2. a, 3. b, 4. d, 5. T, 6. T

Thinking Back to Marcus . . .

Now that you have studied this chapter, you should be able to help Marcus better understand the things he's concerned about and make good choices. His concerns are not at all unusual—many teens worry about whether their physical development is normal. You might help reassure him that even though it seems that the early-maturing guys have all the advantages, they do face problems with getting into situations they aren't mature enough to handle.

Helping Marcus develop some nonphysical attributes like his intelligence and sense of humor might help him feel more competent until his physical development catches up. Marcus is probably focused on his physical size and appearance, but you might tell him about the important ways in which his brain is developing too—this might help him understand why parents and teachers worry about impulsive teenage behavior and rash decisions!

The fact that Marcus is thinking a lot about sex is also very normal for someone his age. Remind him to think about what the sex education classes are teaching him, but expand on the information a little to help him see how the sexual decisions he makes can have important consequences for his education and future goals. To help him make more informed decisions, talk with him about the emotional aspects of sexual activity as well as his goals for the future, and encourage him to talk with his parents about these things. Marcus seems to have learned from his cousin's pregnancy, but he may still need help understanding the importance of being sexually responsible—both to prevent pregnancy and to protect himself from STDs. If possible, have a frank discussion about the different sexual practices his friends might be boasting about, like oral sex. And Marcus is probably smart to doubt some of the things his friends are saying. It might be interesting for him to learn that many teens overestimate the sexual activity of their peers, so that he can make more informed decisions about sexual activity.

Marcus's thoughts about trying alcohol and marijuana are difficult issues for many teens. Hopefully he has a good relationship with his parents and can talk with them about this. While teens do like to experiment, it would help for Marcus to know where his parents stand regarding drinking and drugs, and why. It's important that Marcus understand that, while occasional users might not suffer long-term ill effects, the short-term risks like car accidents can be very large. It seems that Marcus is involved in school and athletics. It might be helpful to encourage him to think how he might begin making more health-enhancing choices (like getting proper nutrition, exercise, and sleep) and fewer health-compromising choices (like poor nutrition, using alcohol and drugs, and engaging in unsafe sex).

■ Chapter Review . . .

What are the main changes that occur with puberty, and how does early versus late maturation affect adolescents?
With the onset of puberty, sex hormones (androgens and estrogens) initiate increased growth and sexual maturation. These changes typically begin earlier for girls than for boys. Early maturation in girls is associated with a stockier and shorter build during later adolescence, less satisfaction with body image, lower self-esteem, a tendency to affiliate with older peers, increased delinquency and problems in school, and earlier dating behavior. Early maturation in boys may give them an advantage in sports and social situations, but also an increased risk of delinquency.

How does the brain develop during adolescence?
The neurons in the brain become increasingly myelinated during adolescence. Their brains show synaptogenesis just before and synaptic pruning during the early part of adolescence, particularly in the prefrontal cortex. Changing levels of several neurotransmitters in the prefrontal cortex and the limbic system may make adolescents less responsive to rewards, which explains in part why adolescents are more prone to taking risks.

How common is sexual activity among adolescents?
A majority of adolescents have had sexual intercourse by 12th grade, though age of first intercourse varies by ethnicity and gender. In recent years, adolescents are waiting until they are older to have intercourse, though rates of oral sex have increased. Many teens believe that oral sex is less physically and emotionally risky and are not aware of the risk of STDs for oral sex.

Do adolescents use contraception appropriately?
More adolescents use contraception than in past years, but many still do not use them consistently or correctly. Older teens are more consistent than younger ones, and teens who have good relationships with parents are more likely to consistently use contraceptives when they become sexually active. Some teens are not mature enough to admit they are having sex, have misunderstandings about how to effectively obtain and use contraception, or believe they are immune from negative consequences.

What do teens know about sex, and what factors predict becoming sexually active?
Teens have better knowledge than in past years regarding contraception, but many still do not understand STDs very well. Teens are at higher risk for STDs, and many STDs can have few symptoms initially but serious consequences later. Factors that predict earlier sexual activity include lack of parental support and supervision, impulsivity, alcohol use, and peer pressure. Teens' sexual activity may be affected by misperceptions of peers' sexual activity.

What are the risk factors for and outcomes of teen pregnancy?
Fewer teens become pregnant now than in the last few decades. Poverty is the biggest risk factor for teen pregnancy, and lack of parental supervision also increases the risk. Teen moms are also more likely to suffer from low self-efficacy and external locus of control. Both teen moms and dads tend to have histories of aggression, and alcohol and other drug use. Educational and financial outcomes for teen moms and dads are negative; their children have higher rates of physical, behavioral, and cognitive problems. Teens who continue their education, delay having a second child, and are supported by family and/or community programs fare better.

Which teens are at highest risk for suffering a sexual assault?
Adolescents who were victimized during childhood are at greatest risk. Other risk factors include early dating and early sexual activity, and drug use by either the teen or his or her parents. Teens who suffer a sexual assault may suffer from fear, anxiety, sadness, depression, academic difficulties, increased drug/alcohol use, and risky sexual behavior.

What is the state of adolescent nutrition and exercise today?
Few teens get the recommended daily servings for any category of the USDA food pyramid, but most overconsume fat and sugars. Most adolescents report getting regular vigorous exercise. A small percentage of teens develop eating disorders such as anorexia and bulimia—serious disorders of body image and control that can be fatal if not treated.

What other health-related issues do teens face?
Most adolescents need more sleep than they get, which can lead to academic, behavioral, and emotional problems as well as increased accidents. Social factors, increased responsibilities, decreased parental monitoring, early school start times, and biologically based changes in circadian rhythms all play a role. Many teens experiment with alcohol, tobacco, and marijuana. The strongest predictor of teen substance use is having friends who use alcohol and/or drugs, but impulsivity, parental substance use, and lack of parental monitoring are also important. The rate of depression increases during adolescence. The leading causes of adolescent death are accidents, homicide, and suicide. Teens are much more likely to have motor vehicle accidents during the first six months after obtaining a license. Suicide rates increase at adolescence, with girls more likely to attempt suicide but boys more likely to actually die from suicide.

■ Key Terms

adolescent growth spurt (444)
androgens (442)
anorexia nervosa (465)
binge drinking (469)
body image (445)
bulimia nervosa (465)
chlamydia (457)
clinical depression (471)
contraception (453)
delayed phase preference (468)
early maturation (445)
estrogens (442)
gateway drugs (470)
gonorrhea (457)

human papillomavirus
(HPV) (457)
late maturation (445)
menarche (443)
prefrontal cortex (447)
puberty (442)
rape (461)
sexual assault (461)
sexual harrassment (462)
sexually transmitted diseases
(STDs) (450)
spermarche (442)
substance abuse (468)
substance use (468)

mydevelopmentlab Where human development comes to life!

If you are using MyDevelopmentLab, you have access to an ebook version of this textbook, along with dozens of valuable resources per chapter—including video and audio clips, simulations and activities, self-assessments, practice tests, and other study materials. Here is a sampling of the resources available for this chapter.

Explore
The Endocrine System

Simulate
General Model of Drug Addiction

Watch
Brain Building
Sex and Mating Behavior
Male Body Image
AIDS Report
Smoking Damage
Stress and Sleep
Common Misconceptions About STDs
Marijuana and Performance
Eating Disorders

If you did not receive an access code to MyDevelopmentLab with this text and wish to purchase access online, please visit www.mydevelopmentlab.com.

Cognitive Development in Adolescence

Maya is a 17-year-old African American teen who is nearing the end of her junior year in high school. She is working hard to keep up in school. Though English continues to be fun and relatively easy for her, math and science were a lot more challenging this year. She has always done well by working in study groups with friends, but this is no longer helping. Maya is also distracted because she really wants to get a part-time job so she'll have spending money over the summer. She'd like to keep working during her senior year, but her parents worry that this will interfere with her schoolwork and soccer, something she's loved since elementary school. On top of these concerns, Maya has become increasingly worried about what she'll do after she finishes high school. She has always wanted to go to college, and her parents encourage this, but Maya's recent academic struggles make her wonder if she'll be able to make it in college. She always thought she was fairly smart, but now she won-

ders. She also has no idea of what kind of job or career she wants to work toward. She likes writing, especially poems and short stories, but doubts there's much of a job market for poets! Her friends seem to know just what they want to do and how to achieve it, and she's worried about her inability to decide.

Are Maya's cognitive skills and intelligence causes for worry? Should she have a more definite post-high school plan? Is working during her senior year a good idea? After studying this chapter, you should be able to identify several potential reasons for Maya's difficulties and be able to suggest several things that might help. What helpful advice can you suggest?

As you read this chapter, look for the "Think About Maya . . ." questions that ask you to consider what you're learning from Maya's perspective.

Maya is dealing with several important issues and feels a need to make some important decisions about her future. Like many teens her age, schoolwork seems to demand higher levels of thinking about abstract concepts, and she's beginning to doubt her intelligence. She wonders what kind of careers might inspire her to succeed. What cognitive skills are typical for teens of this age, and what does it mean to be intelligent? How do adolescents use their cognitive skills to make decisions, particularly about important issues like career paths? In this chapter we will describe Piaget's view of adolescents' cognitive skills and evaluate his tremendous contribution to our understanding of development. We will introduce you to several newer views of cognitive development that grew from the Vygotskyian theory you learned about in Chapter 8. We will consider different theories of intelligence, and describe some interesting features of how adolescents use language. Finally, we will talk about one important way that adolescents must learn to apply their cognitive skills—to make decisions.

Piaget's Stage 4: Formal Operational Thought (12 Years and Above)

In earlier chapters, you learned about Piaget's view of the cognitive skills and limitations of children from infancy through age 11, up to the end of the concrete operational stage. By the end of the middle childhood years, children have developed impressive reasoning abilities. They can use logical thought structures that are increasingly objective and reversible, and they can solve problems that involve class inclusion and transitivity. As they enter adolescence, their thinking finally becomes abstract—they no longer need to have direct experience with tangible materials to be able to reason logically. According to Piaget's theory, what are the characteristics of this highest level of cognitive development?

As you study this section, ask yourself these questions:

- What new forms of logical thought and cognitive advances emerge during the formal operational stage?

- What limitations in cognitive processing still exist at this stage?

- What is *adolescent egocentrism,* and why is it important for understanding adolescents' thinking and behavior?

- What is the practical usefulness of understanding Piaget's stages of cognitive development?

What Is Formal Operational Thought?

According to Piaget, it is during adolescence that cognitive development reaches its fullest potential—**formal operational thought.** Formal operational thought is characterized by five important higher-level cognitive abilities: hypothetico-deductive reasoning; reasoning logically about abstract concepts; separating reality from possibilities; considering all logical possible combinations; and thinking about one's own thinking (Inhelder & Piaget, 1958; Kaplan, 2004). However, they are still limited by adolescent egocentrism, especially during the early part of adolescence.

Hypothetico-Deductive Reasoning. For Piaget one of the most important achievements in cognitive development is the ability to use hypothetico-deductive reasoning. **Hypothetico-deductive reasoning** is the use of *deductive reasoning* (reasoning from general principles to particular conclusions) to systematically manipulate several variables, test

formal operational thought
Piaget's final stage of cognitive development, when an adolescent gradually learns to use hypothetico-deductive reasoning and to extend logical thinking to abstract concepts.

hypothetico-deductive reasoning
The ability to use deductive reasoning (reasoning from general to specific facts) to systematically manipulate several variables, test the effects in a systematic way, and reach correct conclusions in complex problems; scientific reasoning.

Length of string	Amount of weight	Height at which oscillation is started

Figure 14.1 • Piaget's Pendulum Problem The pendulum problem asks you to figure out what causes the rate of the swing to vary. Is it the length of the string, the amount of weight at the end, or the height from which the weight is dropped? What tests would you conduct to isolate the relevant factor?

hypotheses about their effects in a systematic way, and reach correct conclusions. Piaget tested adolescents' developing use of hypothetico-deductive reasoning by using several tasks, many of which involved physics or chemistry (Ginsburg & Opper, 1988; Inhelder & Piaget, 1958). In his famous pendulum problem, children and adolescents of different ages were given a set of weights and strings of different lengths. As you can see in Figure 14.1, the weights could be hung from the strings and swung like pendulums. The investigators asked the children and adolescents to determine what caused the pendulums to swing at different rates. Was it the length of the string, the amount of weight, or how high the weight was held before it was released? The answer can be found on page 486. Children in the concrete operational stage are not good at systematically testing all of the factors; they tend to report whatever answer seems to be correct after conducting only a few tests. Adolescents using formal operations, however, start by considering all of the variables and all of their possible combinations, reasoning that any single factor could be responsible for the pendulum's rate of swing. They then systematically test each factor one at a time, holding the other factors constant, until they arrive at the correct solution. The adolescent shows hypothetico-deductive reasoning, or formal scientific reasoning—the ability to plan systematic tests to explore multiple variables.

Abstract Thought. A second major development that takes place during the formal operational stage is the adolescent's growing ability to engage in abstract thought. **Abstract thought** is the ability to think about things that are not concrete or tangible, such as general concepts or ideas. During the stage of formal operations, the adolescent learns to think logically about such abstract concepts as truth, justice, fairness, and morality. "Whereas earlier the adolescent could love his mother or hate a peer, now he can love freedom or hate exploitation" (Ginsburg & Opper, 1979, p. 201). Such concepts are at the heart of many important social, political, and ethical issues faced the world over. Not only are adolescents beginning to comprehend these concepts, they also develop the ability to reason flexibly about them and understand their relativity. For example, adolescents gradually become able to understand that *justice* may mean very different things to different people, depending on the context and intent of an action. They learn that it can be difficult to assess the justness of any particular action without considering these complex factors. The black-and-white meanings of childhood have given way to the grays of adulthood.

Adolescents are fond of discussing deep thoughts and abstract ideas. What kinds of discussions do you remember having with your friends during adolescence?

abstract thought
Thought about things that are not real or things that are only possibilities.

Think About Maya . . .
Could Maya's problems with her math and science classes be related to her skills in hypothetico-deductive reasoning and abstract thought? How would Piaget suggest she improve these skills?

Adolescents' increasing ability to imagine how things *could* be may lead them to be idealistic—but they may also become discouraged when comparing their idealistic visions with reality.

combinational logic
The ability to generate and systematically consider all possible combinations of a set of elements.

adolescent egocentrism
A cognitive immaturity seen in adolescents—their inability to distinguish between one's own abstract reasoning and thoughts and the reasoning and thoughts of others.

imaginary audience
Adolescents' belief that other people are just as concerned with their behavior, feelings, thoughts, and appearance as they are themselves.

Separating Reality from Possibilities. Related to the developing skill of abstract thinking is the adolescent's increasing ability to separate what is real from what is possible. You saw an example of this in the pendulum problem. When solving the problem, adolescents took as their starting point *all possible solutions;* this allowed them to efficiently reach an accurate solution. Piaget argued that during the formal operational stage, the direction of thinking about reality and possibility actually reverses: Possibility is not thought of as an extension of an existing situation, but instead reality is thought of as only one of many possible outcomes (Inhelder & Piaget, 1958). As you can probably imagine, the ability to envision how things *could* be offers an exhilarating freedom—adolescents are no longer bound by reality but can imagine all kinds of different situations, from the swinging of a pendulum to the nature of justice to the career path they might choose. As a result, adolescents may become very idealistic about the possibilities for their own lives, the environment, or for those in difficult and unfair situations around the world. They sometimes become discouraged when they compare the reality they or others experience with these idealistic visions. And the ability to envision multitudes of possibilities can also lead adolescents to spend extraordinary amounts of time speculating on all the possible outcomes of seemingly simple actions—as when they spend 4 hours discussing whether to wear *this* dress or *that* dress to a school social event. Although these behaviors may drive parents crazy, they really are signs of increasing cognitive maturity!

Combinational Logic. The pendulum problem in Figure 14.1 also illustrates the use of **combinational logic,** or the adolescent's ability to generate and systematically consider all possible combinations of a set of elements. When asked to solve the pendulum problem, younger children may test the factors individually (the weight, the length of the string, or the height), and some may haphazardly combine them. But adolescents are much more likely to generate all the possible combinations of the three factors and conduct systematic tests. As you might imagine, the ability to use combinational logic along with hypothetico-deductive logic is essential for solving problems in chemistry, physics, and other academic areas. But it is also helpful in thinking about social and personal problems. For example, suppose an adolescent is thinking about what career path she might follow. She may realize that she has multiple interests, skills, and goals such as writing, traveling, helping others, creating new products, and spending time with friends and family. Using combinational thinking will help her think through different ways to combine these elements and, hopefully, achieve her goals.

Reflective Thinking. As a result of many of the developing abilities we have just described, adolescents are able to think about their own thinking, a skill that Piaget called *reflective thinking*. They are able to critically analyze their thoughts, opinions, and beliefs and construct their own theories about how their thoughts develop, change, and compare with others' thoughts. As you may recall from Chapter 8, information-processing psychologists call the ability to analyze one's own thoughts *metacognition* and, like Piaget, believe it plays an important role in mature thinking.

Adolescent Egocentrism

Although adolescents are developing impressive thinking skills, Piaget observed that they still show a level of immaturity. He defined **adolescent egocentrism** as a young person's inability to distinguish between his or her own abstract reasoning and thoughts and those of others (Inhelder & Piaget, 1958). Two particular forms of adolescent egocentrism have been described (Elkind, 1967). The first is the **imaginary audience,** or adolescents' belief that other people are just as concerned with their behavior, feelings, thoughts, and appearance as they are themselves. This leads to a sometimes excruciating degree of self-consciousness. Many adolescents feel "on stage," as if everyone else were noticing every embarrassing thing they do. The second facet of adolescent egocentrism involves the **personal fable,** or false beliefs that adolescents have about their own thoughts, influence, and risk (Aalsma et al., 2006; Elkind, 1967). Adolescents tend to believe that they and their newly abstract thoughts are unique (*personal uniqueness*)—they often believe that no one has ever thought about issues in the same way they do, and that no one else (especially parents!) could ever understand the way they feel. They also believe that they are a source of special information and influence over events (*omnipotence*), and that bad things will not happen to them because they are so unique (*invulnerability*). Unfortunately, feelings of invulnerability can lead adolescents to engage in very risky behavior, like unprotected sexual activity or drinking and driving—after all, their invulnerability assures them that they will not suffer the bad outcomes that happen to others.

personal fable
False beliefs that adolescents have about their own thoughts, influence, and risks.

Adolescent egocentrism is an indicator of increasing cognitive development, but it has usually been linked to negative behaviors such as risk-taking. Recent research indicates that this concept is more complex than first thought, and some aspects serve more positive functions. For example, omnipotence is correlated with *better* mental health and adjustment—believing that you have control in a situation may lead you to take steps to do something about it, rather than do nothing to try to cope. In contrast, personal uniqueness predicts depression and suicidal thoughts; after all, if your thoughts and emotions are so different from anyone else's, then how can anyone help you deal with them? Invulnerability predicts risk-taking, but this can be a difficult relationship to interpret. Researchers have tended to focus on the negative outcomes of adolescent risk-taking, but a moderate degree of risk-taking in many situations may not be a bad thing. For example, invulnerability also predicts positive adjustment, better coping, and feelings of self-worth. Perhaps believing that they won't be physically or emotionally harmed encourages teenagers to try new sports, relationships, hobbies, jobs, or even academic areas (Aalsma et al., 2006).

With the achievement of the cognitive skills described above and with the eventual decline of adolescent egocentrism, emerging adults gradually attain what Piaget considered mature cognition. They become able to reason about anything, real or imagined, and have the capability to use scientific reasoning to solve complex problems. But this does not mean that no further changes in cognition occur. On the contrary, Piaget claimed that we never reach a permanent state of equilibrium. He believed that we are forever adapting and reorganizing our cognitive structures and working "toward *better* equilibrium" (Piaget, 1985, p. 26). Piaget did not, however, envision further major reorganizations of cognitive structure or the development of qualitatively more advanced or different kinds of thought. Others disagree, arguing that older adolescents and adults show *postformal reasoning,* characterized by (Kaplan, 2004; Labouvie-Vief, 2006):

■ Increasing emphasis on what is *practical within a given context.* As you learned earlier, adolescents are able to separate reality from possibilities and come up with all the possible combinations. But it is not until they are a few years older that they begin to recognize that real-life problems are often best solved by balancing what is theoretically best and what is realistically practical (Labouvie-Vief, 1980).

■ Increasing ability to *accept contradiction in the world.* Adolescents become increasingly able to use hypothetico-deductive reasoning, but they may be troubled by the discovery that the world is full of events and behaviors that aren't consistent with their logical conclusions. For example, young adolescents may have great difficulty understanding that a person can be a good friend but also willing to shoplift.

■ *Relativistic reasoning,* the understanding that knowledge is subjective and depends on the experiences and perspective of the individual. As adolescents begin to understand that knowledge is subjective, they may overgeneralize this knowledge and begin to believe that everything is debatable and without a definite

your perspective
Do you ever recall having an imaginary audience? What examples of personal fable can you think of from your own adolescent experiences or from those of other adolescents you have known?

answer. This can lead to seemingly endless debates with parents (which often end in the dreaded "because I said so" reasoning that every parent swore they'd never resort to!). Fortunately, teenagers gradually come to understand that while knowledge may be based on subjective experience, one can still develop consistent views that are supported by evidence.

your perspective

In what ways do you think differently now, as an adult, than you did as an adolescent? Think of some examples of post-formal reasoning that you have shown.

Think About Maya . . .

In what way is Maya's thinking likely to change over the next few years? How will these changes help her deal with schoolwork and her decisions?

■ Judgments and decisions based on increasing *wisdom,* or knowledge and beliefs about what it means to live a "good life," including an understanding of how to balance one's own well-being with others' (Baltes & Kunzmann, 2004; Baltes & Staudinger, 2000). Humans never achieve a state of perfect wisdom, but recent research supports the idea of significant growth in wisdom-related knowledge and judgments across later adolescence and early adulthood. For example, adolescents (ages 13 through 20) and young adults (ages 20 through 37) were asked to reason about dilemmas involving issues such as peer pressure, academic achievement, relationships with parents, sexuality, suicide, or the meaning of life. Overall, the young adults were significantly more likely to consider several aspects of the person's life circumstances, the relative nature of values and life priorities, and uncertainties in life and decision-making. The rate of growth in these types of considerations, however, was much higher for those between the ages of 13 and 24 (Pasupathi et al., 2001). Contrary to Piaget's theory, important changes in thinking may occur throughout late adolescence and early adulthood.

Evaluating Piaget's Theory

An astounding amount of research has been done to evaluate Piaget's theory. We will not attempt to cover all of this work. Instead, we will discuss the general conclusions about Piaget's most important and well-known claims, and we'll give you an overview of Piaget's legacy today.

Many important aspects of Piaget's views on cognitive development have been supported by research. In general, children do seem to move from being more egocentric to less egocentric. They also move from being less systematic and less able to reason logically to being more able to think in these ways. Many studies over many years have also replicated Piaget's results on tasks such as object permanence and conservation, if the experimenters conduct the tasks in the same ways as Piaget conducted them. Finally, studies from different cultures indicate that children seem to pass through Piaget's four stages in the same order—although the age brackets of the stages show great variability. Also, whether children ever achieve the formal operational stage depends on several different factors such as educational level and the kinds of cognitive skills valued in a culture (Gelman & Baillargeon, 1983; Ginsburg & Opper, 1988; Harris, 1983; Opper, 1977).

Research studies have also, however, highlighted two important weaknesses in Piaget's theory. First, Piaget underestimated the abilities of children, especially during infancy (Gelman & Baillargeon, 1983; Haith & Benson, 1998; Wellman & Gelman, 1998). Under the proper conditions, infants as young as 3½ months demonstrate a grasp of object permanence (Baillargeon, 1993; Spelke, 1991). Also, research demonstrates that young infants do code information and store mental representations in the form of memories (Barr et al., 2003; DeCasper & Spence, 1986; Rovee-Collier & Gerhardstein, 1997). Other research shows that preschool children can handle conservation and other problems when the tasks are simple enough and the children have appropriate training (Au et al., 1993; Beilin, 1978; Donaldson, 1982; Gelman, 1972; McCabe & Siegel, 1987). At the same time, it turns out that Piaget may have *overestimated* the abilities of most adolescents and adults. Researchers now believe that only 50 percent to 60 percent of 18- to 20-year-olds in industrialized countries use formal operations and that the rates are even lower in nonindustrialized countries

(Commons et al., 1982; Keating, 1980). Recent research also questions how consistently adolescent egocentrism is found. Studies have suggested that it may indicate more about young adolescents' attempts to develop an identity and psychologically separate from their families than a general cognitive immaturity (Vartanian, 2000, 2001). And, as we noted earlier, many researchers are finding evidence of changes in the types of thought well beyond adolescence.

A second general criticism addresses the notion of developmental stages. Piaget's theory implies that as children reorganize their cognitive structures, they rise to a higher level of logical thought. Once achieved, these new structures and organizations presumably apply across all contexts. In real life, however, this is not what happens (Gelman, 2000; Gelman & Baillargeon, 1983; Harris, 1983; Larivée et al., 2000). Let's take conservation problems as an example. Research shows that most children pass tests on number conservation problems by age 6 or 7; they pass weight conservation problems by age 9 or 10; but they don't pass volume conservation problems until about age 11 or 12 (Ginsburg & Opper, 1988). If children understand the concept of conservation (showing decentered and reversible thought) in the number problem, why don't they transfer this understanding to the weight and volume problems until years later? And how do we mark the transition from preoperational to concrete operational thought? Does it occur when a child passes the number conservation problem, or do we wait until the child comprehends conservation in all its forms? Not only is it difficult to define these transitions, but children also frequently show evidence of being in two or more stages at once. For these and other reasons, most modern-day researchers reject the concept of broad cognitive developmental stages (Flavell et al., 1993).

What is least criticized is Piaget's constructivist view of development. Children do seem to be active participants in their own learning and development, assimilating new information into their existing cognitive structures, and modifying or reorganizing their structures when necessary to fit new information. The process of adaptation that Piaget observed in sea mollusks seems a fitting analogy for the adaptive processes children engage in as they achieve cognitive maturity.

Piaget's Legacy

Piaget's theory of cognitive development has left a legacy that no other theory in developmental psychology has even approached. His contributions can be summarized as follows.

- Piaget changed *psychology's view of young children*. Before, theorists saw children as passive organisms capable only of reacting to events. After Piaget, they realized that children actively seek to understand their environments and actively initiate events simply to see how things work.

- Piaget gave to future generations a *vast store of facts about children* and child development. This knowledge came both directly—from Piaget's own research, observations, and writings—and indirectly, from the research that others conducted attempting to either support or refute his theory.

- Piaget's theory has had important *applications in the field of education*. First, the notion of the child as an active and curious organism led to the design of interactive and hands-on curricula in schools. These teaching materials encourage children to make use of their natural curiosity to explore concepts in science, mathematics, and other domains. Second, Piaget's four stages and his concept of cognitive readiness (i.e., the idea that children cannot skip stages but must move from one to another as they are maturationally and cognitively ready) have shaped many guidelines for when to introduce different topics. Third, educators have learned to make use of the notion of cognitive disequilibrium. They do this by deliberately presenting students with puzzles, debates, and conflicting opinions to intentionally upset students' existing cognitive structures and encourage students to grow in understanding. Finally, educators explicitly urge reflective abstraction; they encourage students to think about the implications, usefulness, and limitations of their existing cognitive structures.

■ Piaget's work and writing stimulated *vast amounts of research* in a variety of areas of child development. In doing this work, researchers developed new methodologies, tested new ideas of how children think, and opened and pursued new areas of inquiry. There is an old saying in scientific circles that the clear sign of a good theory is not whether the theory is ultimately shown to be right or wrong, but how much research and knowledge it stimulates. Whether or not any aspects of Piaget's theory are ultimately shown to be true, the theory can be considered great by this standard alone.

■ Let's Review . . .

1. All of the following are abilities that develop during the formal operational period *except* _____.
   a. the ability to mentally reverse actions
   b. the ability to mentally separate what is real from what is possible
   c. the ability to critically analyze one's own thoughts
   d. the ability to think about general principles and arrive at specific conclusions

2. When asked to help figure out why the DVD player won't work, which of the following suggestions shows evidence of formal operational thought?
   a. Remembering that the problem last time was that the cord wasn't plugged in.
   b. Checking that both the power cord and the connections to the screen are tight.
   c. Thinking through the possible sources of the problem and systematically testing them one-by-one.
   d. Thinking through the possible sources of the problem and systematically testing them both alone and in all possible combinations.

3. According to Piaget, the imaginary audience and the personal fable are both parts of _____.
   a. intuitive thought   b. object thought
   c. conservation problems   d. adolescent egocentrism

4. **True or False:** Compared to young adults, adolescents show less evidence of wisdom in their reasoning.

5. **True or False:** One criticism of Piaget's theory is that he underestimated the cognitive abilities of adolescents.

Answers: 1. a, 2. d, 3. d, 4. T, 5. F

■ *Answer to the pendulum problem in Figure 14.1:* Length of the string is the factor that determines how fast the pendulum swings.

Recent Sociocultural Views of Cognitive Development

In Chapter 8, you learned about another approach to cognitive development, the sociocultural view of Lev Vygotsky. Vygotsky's theory served as the foundation for several more recent views of cognitive development. These views emphasize the important influence of social interaction and the larger cultural context on cognitive development, and they reveal how Vygotsky's theory has stimulated researchers to think about cognitive development in new ways.

As you study this section, ask yourself these questions:

- What influence did Vygotsky have on the development of the newer sociocultural views of cognitive development?

- According to these newer views, how do the social context, groups, and the larger culture influence cognitive development?

- What specific ideas can we take from these newer sociocultural views that could help us facilitate cognitive development?

Situated Cognition

"If you were selling candy, would you make more profit by selling one piece for 200 cruzeiros or by selling three pieces for 500 cruzeiros?" When Geoffrey Saxe (1988) asked Brazilian schoolchildren questions like this, he found that most were not able to answer correctly. But when he went into city streets in Brazil and asked children who were not attending school at all, he got accurate answers. Why the difference? Those he interviewed in the streets were vendors who sold things to support themselves and their families. Although they lacked formal education in mathematics, they had developed their own strategies for solving complicated problems. The street vendors probably would not have succeeded in school math tests, because these tests tend to use problems that are rather abstract and taken out of context. Within their familiar context, however, the vendors were quite adept. Similar results have been found in the cultures of other countries, such as Beirut (Jurdak & Shahin, 1999). These mathematical skills were situation-specific—an example of *situated cognition.*

The **situated cognition** view of cognitive development holds that thinking always takes place within a specific context, and always in relation to a particular problem, situation, or interaction. According to this view you cannot really understand thought or its quality or level without also examining the context in which the thought takes place. For example, suppose you ask a sixth grader, "Find the value of X in the expression $6X = 750$." She may have trouble finding the answer, perhaps saying she hasn't "had algebra yet." But tell her that she and her friends are getting $750 for band camp and it has to be divided equally among all six girls, and watch how quickly she figures out how much money each girl will get. Embedding questions in concrete and meaningful contexts enables people to solve problems that they cannot otherwise understand. The situated cognition view emphasizes that the particular kinds of thinking that occur in different cultures result from adaptations to the particular contexts in which the members of the cultures find themselves. The key factors are the kinds of problems people encounter frequently and the cognitive structures that they find to be effective. In sum, this view reminds us that to properly understand cognitive development, we need also to consider its social and cultural context (Sternberg & Grigorenko, 2006). In keeping with this view, many educators strive to teach cognitive skills within contexts—drawing on the types of situations most important within their students' cultures.

situated cognition
The idea that we cannot fully understand children's thinking and cognition without considering the context in which it occurs.

Guided Participation and Communities of Practice

Another recent sociocultural view emphasizes **guided participation** within a *community of practice.* A community of practice is a broad term that refers to the people, activities, and social interactions that take place as people work together to learn and accomplish goals. The central idea here is that development consists of a person's

guided participation
The idea that children are involved in sociocultural activities to the degree that their level of cognitive development allows.

This adolescent boy is a *legitimate peripheral participant* in auto mechanics, contributing to the extent he can right now. With guidance and support from those who know more about this area, his participation will increase.

your perspective

Identify an activity in which you have moved from being a legitimate peripheral participant to being a more central participant. What skills and knowledge did you learn as a legitimate peripheral participant, and how did they help you become more of a central participant?

socially shared cognition
The idea that thought is a shared group activity and that the thoughts held by an individual are derived at least in part from dynamic interactions occurring between people and in groups.

Think About Maya . . .
What aspects of these sociocultural views could be used to help make Maya's study groups more effective in helping her learn?

gradually increasing participation in sociocultural activity—with gradually decreasing guidance and support from those around them (Cox, 2005; Fuller et al., 2005; Lave & Wenger, 1991; Rogoff, 2003; Rogoff et al., 1993; Wenger, 1998). For example, think about a high school student (a participant) learning about auto mechanics (a community of practice). Initially, he does not understand concepts of engine timing, compression, and torque, so his participation is marginal. But he is a *legitimate peripheral participant* (Lave & Wenger, 1991, 1996), which means that he is involved in the activity to the degree that his current skill allows. He can clean tools, check air pressure in tires, and help change the oil. As he learns more, his degree of participation increases and its nature changes. He can now perform a basic engine tune-up, change spark plugs, drain a radiator, and even replace an exhaust system—but he is still not able to diagnose more than simple problems without help, and he needs guidance on more complicated repairs. His participation continues to change as he gradually becomes more of a *central participant,* able to do a great deal of the work himself and even teach the basics to other, less central participants.

The guided participation view is similar to Vygotsky's in that more central participants initially guide the activity, and the learner gradually takes on increasing responsibility. But whereas Vygotsky emphasized how learners internalize the psychological tools represented in their cultures, the guided participation view instead emphasizes how a person's social roles or shared interactions with other people change as the person develops. Also, whereas Vygotsky tended to focus on the internalization of such things as a culture's language or number system, the guided participation view emphasizes participation in more routine, day-to-day activities.

Thinking as Socially Shared Cognition: Two Heads Are Better Than One

Vygotsky claimed that even after children internalize cognitive structures, thought is still a social phenomenon because its roots are in social interaction.

Recent work emphasizes this point, describing cognition as a socially shared activity rather than an individual activity (Resnick et al., 1991; Wertsch et al., 1993). In this view, cognition does not involve an individual's activities alone, or even an individual's contributions to a social interaction. This view holds that thinking extends "beyond the skin" of the individual and includes the "thinking" of pairs and groups of people (Wertsch et al., 1993, p. 337). It does not make sense to ask, "Whose idea is that?" because thought takes place across the members of a group—it is **socially shared cognition.** This theory does not deny that an individual can think independently. But it argues that even "independent" thought is the culmination of many others' input. Thinking resides in the dynamic interactions between individuals within the group, not solely inside the head of any individual.

The three views we have summarized here all draw on different aspects of Vygotsky's theory. These modern sociocultural views of cognition are still in the formative stages. But the key point is that today's sociocultural cognition theorists no longer see thought as something that takes place inside one individual's head and consists of abstract skills applied across many different problems and contexts. Instead, they view cognition as much more complex. They suggest that cognition makes use of specific features and contexts and involves individuals collaborating to create ideas and think in ways that no individual could accomplish alone. In short, they see cognition as a very dynamic, social, and interactive process.

1. Children show more advanced cognitive processing when they are tested within contexts that are familiar and well practiced. This is one of the main points of the:
   a. socially shared cognition view.
   b. guided participation view.
   c. social speech view.
   d. situated cognition view.

2. Which of the following would be an example of development in the guided participation view?
   a. John moves from watching children play basketball to playing in the game himself.
   b. Sue and Lisa work together to solve a problem that neither could solve alone.
   c. Henri can read his favorite books at home but has trouble reading the practice sheets in school.
   d. Tonya needs social scaffolds to help her understand algebra problems.

3. **True or False:** The sociocultural theories are a reaction against Vygotsky's view of cognitive development.

4. **True or False:** According to the sociocultural view, cognition is the product of social interaction more than the private construction of individual thinkers.

Answers: 1. d, 2. a, 3. F, 4. T

Intelligence

Piaget's theory of cognitive development, Vygotsky's sociocultural theory, information processing, sociocultural views—each of these theories attempts to explain the development of cognitive skills. In many important ways, each theory can be thought of as explaining the development of intelligence. But intelligence can be defined in many different ways. Most of the psychological research on intelligence comes from the Western, industrialized perspective of Europe and the United States. Theorists within this perspective generally define **intelligence** as the ability to learn, think logically about abstract concepts, and adapt to the environment—very similar to Piaget's views of formal operational thought. Even within this Western perspective, however, there has been great disagreement about how to define and understand human intelligence, and even greater disagreement about how to fairly measure intelligence. In this section we will introduce you to three different approaches to intelligence: the psychometric approach, Sternberg's triarchic theory, and Gardner's multiple-intelligences approach. We will also discuss some frequently used intelligence tests, as well as the issue of cultural bias in using these assessments.

intelligence
As generally defined in Western cultures, the ability to learn, think logically about abstract concepts, and adapt to the environment.

As you study this section, ask yourself these questions:

■ Is intelligence a general and broad ability, or is it a constellation of many separate skills?

■ What are the major similarities and differences among the different theories of intelligence?

■ How is intelligence assessed?

■ How is *mental retardation* defined, and how do genetic and environmental factors contribute to its development? What characteristics are typical of gifted and talented individuals?

■ Do today's intelligence tests take into account cultural differences among groups of people? How might the fairness of intelligence tests be improved?

Theories of Intelligence

psychometric approach
The attempt to quantify people's psychological skills and abilities, usually by means of paper-and-pencil tests and/or physical measurements.

general intelligence (g)
A broad thinking ability or mental power that underlies all intellectual tasks and functions.

specific intelligence (s)
Abilities people have in particular areas, such as reading, verbal, and spatial skills.

fluid ability
A biological-based ability to think and perceive relations among elements.

crystallized ability
The body of specific knowledge and skills acquired in a particular culture.

Psychometric Approaches. With the **psychometric approach** to studying intelligence, researchers use paper-and-pencil tests and/or physical measurements in an attempt to quantify people's psychological skills and abilities. One of the most influential psychometric theorists was Charles Spearman (1863–1945), who gathered information on school children in a village in England. Spearman studied children's physical and perceptual attributes as well as children's cleverness, common sense, and exam scores in various subject areas. Spearman found strong positive correlations among all his measures and proposed a *two-factor theory of intelligence* to explain his results (Spearman, 1904, 1927). The first factor he called **general intelligence (g).** General intelligence is a broad ability that applies to some extent to all intellectual tasks—essentially, the ability to see how things relate and fit together. Spearman thought that *g* was neurologically based, and he saw *g* as providing the driving force behind most intellectual accomplishments (Spearman, 1923, p. 5). Spearman called his second factor **specific intelligence (s),** referring to the abilities people have in particular areas, such as reading, verbal, and spatial skills.

The biggest area of disagreement among different psychometric theories is the question of how many abilities fall under the heading of "intelligence." For example, Louis Thurstone identified seven mental abilities that he saw as separate and distinct from general intelligence (Thurstone, 1938; Thurstone & Thurstone, 1941). J. P. Guilford identified at least 150 abilities as important in defining intelligence (Guilford, 1967, 1982). John Horn and Raymond B. Cattell proposed two broad factors, **fluid ability** and **crystallized ability,** along with several other more specific factors (Horn & Cattell, 1966). Fluid ability, much like Spearman's *g*, is a biologically based ability to think. It essentially involves the ability to perceive relations among elements, and it peaks by around age 18. In contrast, crystallized ability consists of the knowledge and skills people acquire in a particular culture. Crystallized ability includes such things as number ability, mechanical skills, and vocabulary, and it can increase throughout adulthood.

The important point to remember about these later psychometric theories of intelligence is this: They began to challenge the idea that a *g*-factor theory like Spearman's could adequately explain differences among individuals' intellectual performance. The controversy reminds us that there has always been disagreement about whether each person has a level of "general" intelligence underlying performance across all tasks. Modern cognitive psychologists have argued that psychometric theories place too much emphasis on static indicators of intelligence (such as facts and vocabulary) and disregard the cognitive *processes* involved in intelligent thought. These criticisms have led to new theories of intelligence that take more contemporary cognitive and neuropsychological views into account (Garlick, 2002).

Think About Maya . . .

How is Maya's view of intelligence related to Spearman's concepts of g and s?

your perspective
Do you agree with the idea of a *g* factor in intelligence that underlies all intellectual accomplishments? Explain why or why not.

triarchic theory of intelligence
Theory of intelligence emphasizing how mental processes, experience, and situational contexts relate to intellectual thought. Includes componential, experiential, and contextual subtheories.

Sternberg's Triarchic Theory. Starting in the early 1980s, Yale University psychologist Robert Sternberg developed a **triarchic theory of intelligence.** Sternberg's theory embraces the information-processing concept you read about in earlier chapters. It describes the mental processes involved in thinking as well as the aspects of experience and the environmental context for intelligence. The theory is called "triarchic" because it consists of three interrelated subtheories, as shown in Figure 14.2.

Figure 14.2 • Sternberg's Triarchic Theory of Intelligence In Sternberg's theory, analytic intelligence, experience, and real-life contexts combine to yield intelligent thought and behavior.

The **componential subtheory** describes how mental processes work together to give us intellectual thought (Sternberg, 1985, 1999). In this subtheory a "component" is a mental process (such as planning, reading, or remembering) that gathers or works with information. Sternberg described three types of components (he is famous for doing things in threes!). *Knowledge-acquisition components* selectively encode, combine, and compare information, allowing us to acquire new knowledge. *Performance components* perform tasks such as sorting, classifying, remembering, and otherwise processing information. *Metacomponents* "supervise" and evaluate the functioning of the other two types of components.

As an example, Sternberg described how these three components work together when we write a paper (Sternberg, 1988). We use metacomponents to define a topic, decide on an organization, monitor the writing progress, and evaluate the finished product. Thanks to *performance components* we can do such things as retrieve appropriate words from memory, remember how to use the word-processing system on our computer, or remember the rules of grammar. Knowledge-acquisition components help us during the research phase, allowing us to sift through vast amounts of information and decide what to include in the paper. Because these mental components enable us to analyze information, they are sometimes called *analytical intelligence*. Analytical intelligence is the type of intelligence that is usually measured in typical paper-and-pencils tests.

The **experiential subtheory** addresses the role of novelty and experience in intelligence. According to this subtheory, we become more intelligent as we master new tasks and learn how to perform them more automatically. For example, think of adolescents learning to drive. At first processes such as steering, braking, and accelerating are new, so new drivers have to think hard about each one. With more experience they begin to carry out more and more of the processes automatically. Eventually the processes flow smoothly and together, so the drivers are able to control a car's speed and direction easily. Now adolescents can begin to deal with other aspects of driving—looking ahead at intersections, noticing other drivers' behavior, and noticing the effects of different weather conditions. Like driving, most complex tasks are difficult to perform at first, but with experience become more automatic. This frees up more mental capacity for other aspects of the task. As you can see, this part of Sternberg's theory uses the concept of *automaticity,* which we discussed in Chapter 8. The experiential subtheory ties in with what we typically call *creative*

componential subtheory Describes how mental processes work together to give us intellectual thought ("analytical intelligence").

experiential subtheory Describes how we become more intelligent as we master new tasks and learn how to perform them more automatically ("creative intelligence").

Robert Sternberg's triarchic theory describes how mental processes, experience, and the environmental context all interact to produce intelligent thought and behavior.

intelligence. That is, some people are quick at figuring out new tasks—they see new patterns easily and find creative new ways to solve problems.

The **contextual subtheory** describes individuals' abilities to show intelligent behavior in real-life contexts. That is an aspect of intelligent behavior that Sternberg thought was missing in most other theories of intelligence (Sternberg, 1985). It involves adapting to, selecting, and shaping real-life situations. (Yes, *another* set of three.) When placed in a new situation, people usually try first to *adapt to* their environment: They try to achieve a good fit between themselves and the environment without changing either in any significant way. Sometimes, however, they must do something to improve the fit. One possibility is to *select* a different environment; another is to attempt to *shape* the existing environment. Sternberg (1985) used the example of marriage to illustrate these three processes. If a marriage is not satisfying in some way, a person will try first to adapt by ignoring the negatives and focusing on the marriage's positive aspects. If that does not work, then the person may select a different environment by leaving the marriage—or may try to shape the existing environment by changing its unsatisfactory aspects. Some people are especially good at dealing with their environments. Contextual intelligence is related to what most people call *common sense, street smarts,* or *practical intelligence.*

Sternberg's theory is an ambitious attempt to account for the varied facets of intelligent behavior. His comprehensive explanation is a strength of this theory. Another strength is that empirical research studies have investigated each of the subtheories and have provided at least modest support for many of the ideas (Sternberg, 1985). However, critics charge that although the theory is comprehensive, it is not clear how the three subtheories relate to one another. Nor is it clear why some elements are included but other possible elements are not. Finally, Sternberg does not link his components and processes to the biology of intelligence or to what is known about how the brain functions (Gardner et al., 1996).

contextual subtheory
Describes how intelligent behavior is related to real-life situations as people adapt to, select, and/or shape their environments ("practical intelligence").

Think About Maya . . .

How might Sternberg's theory help Maya deal with her concerns about her intelligence and her fears about succeeding in college?

theory of multiple intelligences
Theory of intelligence emphasizing that we all have multiple intelligences that operate relatively independently of one another; the theory includes eight intelligences.

Gardner's Theory of Multiple Intelligences. In 1983 Harvard psychologist Howard Gardner proposed a **theory of multiple intelligences.** This theory defines *an intelligence* as a "biopsychological potential to process information that can be activated in a cultural setting to solve problems or create products that are of value in a culture" (Gardner, 1999, p. 34). Notice several important aspects of this definition. First, Gardner is not defining *intelligence;* rather, he is defining *an intelligence.* This is the heart of his theory. Gardner proposes that intelligence is neither a unitary *g* factor, nor a broad factor made up of subcomponents or specific abilities. Instead, he argues that there are several different types of intelligence, each relatively independent of the others. A person's overall level of functioning is determined by his profile of strengths and weaknesses among these different intelligences in interaction with a particular cultural setting. A second important point is that an intelligence is a *biopsychological potential;* this means that there is an underlying biological, and most likely genetic, component. Being genetic, however, does not mean that this potential is unaffected by the environment. A particular biopsychological potential *may or may not be fully realized,* depending on environmental factors. Cultural values, opportunities, and individual choices all affect the developing intelligence. For example, think of a girl born with strong logical–mathematical potential. If she grows up in a culture that does not permit females to be educated, such as under the former Taliban government in Afghanistan, it is very unlikely that the girl will fulfill this particular potential. In other countries girls may go to school, but the culture may steer them toward more "domestic" topics and away from advanced mathematics. Finally, even if the culture is encouraging, the girl herself may decide not to pursue math; again, her mathematics potential is not going to be fully realized.

Gardner identifies eight intelligences, shown in Table 14.1 (Gardner, 1983, 1999). Clearly, he is not the first to identify several of these areas—all the theorists we have discussed recognize at least two, and sometimes many more, factors. Gardner differs from other approaches, though, in that he does not base his analysis solely on statistical analysis of a battery of paper-and-pencil tests. Instead, he identified a set of specific criteria to determine whether a given skill qualifies as an intelligence. These criteria

Howard Gardner believes there is more than one type of intelligence. His theory of multiple intelligences includes eight different types.

TABLE 14.1 Eight Types of Intelligences Proposed by Gardner, with Examples of Occupations Involving Each Type

TYPE OF INTELLIGENCE	DESCRIPTION AND EXAMPLES
Linguistic intelligence	• Acute sensitivity to spoken and written language; includes abilities to learn languages, use language effectively to achieve specific goals • *Examples:* Lawyers, speakers, writers, and poets
Logical–mathematical intelligence	• Recognizing and using abstract relations to logically analyze problems, carry out mathematical operations, and investigate issues scientifically • Gardner believes that Piaget's theory of cognitive development is mostly a description of the development of this intelligence • *Examples:* Mathematicians, computer programmers, accountants, engineers, and scientists
Musical intelligence	• Sensitivity to aspects of sound (such as tone, pitch, and rhythm) and skill in creating and communicating with sounds and musical patterns • *Examples:* Composers, conductors, audio engineers, and acousticians
Bodily–kinesthetic intelligence	• The ability to use the whole body, or parts of it, to solve problems or make products; involves a high degree of control over fine- and gross-motor skills • *Examples:* Dancers, athletes, surgeons, craftspeople, actors, and mechanics
Spatial intelligence	• The abilities to perceive, transform, and re-create spatial information for large-scale or small-scale projects • *Examples:* Sailors, pilots, engineers, surgeons, sculptors, and painters
Interpersonal intelligence	• The capacity to understand and work effectively with other people, including understanding other people's motivations, intentions, and desires • *Examples:* Successful salespeople, politicians, teachers, clinicians, and religious leaders
Intrapersonal intelligence	• The ability to understand and regulate your own emotions; involves sensitivity to and understanding of own desires, fears, intentions, and capacities • Gardner believes intrapersonal intelligence allows people to build accurate "mental models" of themselves and to use these models to make good personal decisions. • *Examples:* Writers, therapists, and communities' "wise elders"
Naturalist intelligence	• Skill in recognizing and classifying plants and animals, including an ability to distinguish among species and chart relations among species • *Examples:* Biologists, environmentalists, hunters, fishermen, farmers, gardeners, and cooks

What will happen with this girl's biopsychological potential if she has a genetic strength for math and science but grows up in a culture that forbids her from pursuing these topics in school? How has your culture affected your intellectual potential?

include not only psychometric findings but also such things as the potential for isolation by brain damage (which indicates a biological basis for the skill), an evolutionary history (to explain why the intelligence would have evolved), identifiable core operation(s) (to specify the skills involved in the intelligence), and the existence of exceptional people (both those with strength and those with weakness in the particular intelligence). Thus, Gardner's analysis depends on support from more than just psychometric test scores.

Gardner emphasizes that all eight intelligences exist to some degree in every individual, because the intelligences are part of being human. However, each person has a different *profile of intelligences*—a different combination of strengths and weaknesses (Chen & Gardner, 2005). According to Gardner, it is important that parents and educators recognize each child's individual strengths and weaknesses and provide adequate opportunities for each child to activate his or her own areas of strength. When looking at a school curriculum, for example, we need to recognize that one size doesn't fit all. In addition to covering areas such as reading, math, and science, we need to offer opportunities in art, music, sports, and technical training. Exploring these options lets students activate their unique potentials or strengthen their individual intellectual profiles.

Gardner's theory has broadened our view of what constitutes intelligence. He is not without critics, however (Kincheloe, 2004). One complaint critics have is that his roster of intelligences really does not further our understanding of the concept of intelligence. They argue that the theory blurs the distinction between intelligence and other, nonintellectual, human characteristics (Herrnstein & Murray, 1994). Critics also have pointed out that Gardner's measures of the intelligences often correlate with one another, perhaps weakening the argument that they are independent. Gardner responds that this intercorrelation occurs because of the types of tests that have traditionally been available. If more appropriate measures existed for each of the intelligences, he suggests, we could test their independence more fairly (Gardner et al., 1996; Scarr, 1985). Finally, it is not clear what coordinates the intelligences when they work together on a given task. Gardner says that the intrapersonal intelligence may play this role; but critics claim that such coordination necessarily implies a *g* factor—the very concept that Gardner was reacting against.

your perspective

For each intelligence proposed by Gardner, identify a person you know who is strong in this intelligence. What would your profile look like across these types of intelligences?

Think About Maya . . .

How would you describe Maya's intelligences profile? How could she use her strengths to improve her weaknesses? How could her parents and teachers help with this?

Howard Gardner proposes that there are several different types of intelligence. What types of intelligences are shown by the people in these photos?

Assessing Intelligence

As you have just learned, experts have never agreed on how to define intelligence. Even so, there have been many attempts to try to assess intelligence for practical purposes such as selecting those who might do well in various types of training programs or identifying those who may need extra help in learning. The first practical intelligence scale came out in France in 1905. Alfred Binet and Theodore Simon devised the scale to help French schools predict which children would perform well in regular education settings and which would benefit from special education. The scale posed a series of increasingly difficult questions, such as pointing to an object in a picture, defining a common word, and explaining the difference between "boredom" and "weariness" (Gregory, 1996). Then each child's progress through the tests was compared to the average pattern shown by other children of the same age (called *age norms*). Through these comparisons, Binet and Simon stated, they could determine "how much above or below average" a child was (Simon & Binet, 1905, as quoted in Thorndike & Lohman, 1990, p. 13).

In 1916 Lewis Terman, an American psychologist at Stanford University, published his own modified version of the Binet–Simon scale (Gregory, 1996). Terman's test popularized the term *intelligence quotient* (IQ), a concept that was originally developed in Germany by William Stern in 1912. Stern suggested that each child's mental level be adjusted by their chronological age to yield a ratio showing their mental standing. IQ was defined as mental age (MA) divided by chronological age (CA). Later it became popular to multiply the result by 100 to eliminate decimals, giving the formula $(MA \div CA) \times 100$. With this formula, a child who shows a mental age of 12 on the test, but who is actually 15 years old, would score an IQ of 80 $[(12 \div 15) \times 100 = 80]$. A child who shows a mental age of 15 on the test, but actually has a chronological age of only 12, would score an IQ of 125 $[(15 \div 12) \times 100 = 125]$. A 12-year-old who shows a mental age of 12 on the test would have an IQ of 100 $[(12 \div 12) \times 100 = 100]$. With this scoring system, 100 is the average IQ for children of a given age. Scores below 100 show performance that is below what is typical for that age, and scores above 100 show above-average performance.

Intelligence Testing Today. Today, psychologists and other mental health professionals often use intelligence tests to help diagnose and treat numerous problems in children and adolescents. Measures of intelligence help professionals identify those who have cognitive deficits; learning disabilities; attention deficits; or problems with specific processes such as reading, spatial reasoning, or memory. Test results can also help practitioners determine if a child has an emotional disturbance, brain disorder, or serious mental illness. Taken alone, intelligence scores do not provide enough information to enable a practitioner to make any of these diagnoses. In combination with clinical interviews (of the child, parents, and teachers), physical examinations, and results from other psychological tests and observations, however, the scores can add an important piece to the larger puzzle. Educators also use intelligence tests to screen children for entry into special education programs. In addition, the tests can measure children's progress as they receive special programs or other forms of therapy or counseling. Still, we always need to heed the lessons from the past: Any professional who uses intelligence tests (or any other assessment tool) needs to be aware of the tests' potential for cultural bias, misinterpretation, and misuse. We'll discuss this issue more thoroughly later in the chapter.

A variety of tests exist for assessing intelligence across different ages and for different purposes. The most widely used are the Stanford–Binet scale and the tests developed by David Wechsler. But before we describe these tests, we need to explain the two essential ingredients that any assessment device needs: *reliability* and *validity*.

The term **reliability** refers to the consistency of scores when a test is repeated under the same or similar conditions. If the same person takes an intelligence test twice, the results should be about the same both times (assuming there has been no

reliability
The consistency of scores when a test is repeated under the same or similar conditions.

intervention aimed at improving intelligence between test sessions). Otherwise, how could we trust that either score was accurate? Researchers measure the reliability of intelligence tests by having the same groups of people retake the test and then computing correlations to determine how similar the scores are across the test and retest sessions. Another way to check reliability is to split a test into two equivalent halves, then see if scores across the two halves are similar. Correlations above .80 usually indicate a high degree of reliability (Sattler, 2001).

A test's **validity** is its ability to measure what it intends to measure—in this case, intelligence. In contrast to the situation with reliability, there are no direct measures of a test's validity. As a result, validity has to be assessed more indirectly. We deem intelligence tests to be valid when the scores accurately predict which children will perform better or worse in school; or when they predict success in other areas of life, such as job performance. That is, we assume that higher intelligence will be related to greater success in school and on the job—so when test scores predict success in these areas, we conclude that the test does indeed measure intelligence. We also have evidence of a test's validity when the scores correlate highly with scores on other tests that are presumed to measure intelligence.

The Stanford–Binet Intelligence Scale. Terman's Stanford–Binet scale has undergone several revisions since its introduction in 1916. A complete restructuring in 1986 and further revisions led to what is now known as the *Stanford–Binet Intelligence Scale,* Fifth Edition (or SB5) (Roid, 2003). Figure 14.3 shows items like those in the SB5. Whereas the earlier Stanford–Binet tests yielded only a single intelligence score, the SB5 provides an overall intelligence score along with scores in five subareas (fluid reasoning, knowledge, quantitative reasoning, visual–spatial processing, and working verbal memory), and it yields both a verbal and a nonverbal IQ score. Test items were reviewed for several sources of possible bias (gender, ethnic, cultural, religious, regional, and socioeconomic status); the standardization process used a sample of almost 5,000 individuals ranging in age from 2 to 85 years and closely matched the 2000 census in terms of socioeconomic and ethnic groups in the United States. The SB5 is very reliable, with reliability correlations typically above .90 (Roid, 2003). The test also shows moderately high correlations with other measures of intelligence, demonstrating a reasonable degree of validity.

The Wechsler Scales. In the 1930s David Wechsler constructed an intelligence test to use with the diverse patients he treated in the psychiatric unit of Bellevue Hospital in New York. He began his work with adults, but gradually developed a family of intelligence scales designed for people of different ages: the *Wechsler Preschool and Primary Scale of Intelligence, Third Edition* (WPPSI–III) for children aged 2½ through 7, the *Wechsler Intelligence Scale for Children, Fourth Edition* (WISC–IV) for children 6 through 16, and the *Wechsler Adult Intelligence Scale, Third Edition* (WAIS–III) for people 16 and up. Each of these scales provides an overall or composite intelligence score and two general subscale scores—verbal and performance. The verbal subscale includes subtests in basic information, vocabulary, arithmetic, comprehension, and similarities. The performance subscale includes picture completion, block design, and object assembly. Additional verbal and performance subtests are available but vary across the tests. A few sample items like those from the WISC–IV appear in Figure 14.3.

As with the SB5, standardization of the Wechsler scales used large samples representing all income and ethnic segments of the U.S. population. The tests have reliability correlations around .90 or higher. They also have demonstrated adequate validity (Sattler, 2001; Zhu & Weiss, 2005). That is, Wechsler scores predict later school success moderately well, with correlations ranging around .50 to .65 in most studies (Kamphaus, 2001). In general, children who score higher on these intelligence tests tend to receive higher grades in school, are more likely to go to college, and tend to receive more favorable job performance ratings.

validity
The ability of a test to measure what it intends to measure (e.g., intelligence).

Figure 14.3 • Sample
Intelligence Test Items
The *Stanford–Binet Intelligence
Scale*, Fifth Edition (top) and the
*Wechsler Intelligence Scale for
Children*, Fourth Edition (bottom)
include items such as the questions
shown here. (Sattler, 2001.)

Verbal	Name pictures. Define *train, dime, taut, cryptography.*
Quantitative	What is the smallest whole number evenly divisible by 1, 2, and 3?
Short-term memory	Recall series of digits (e.g., 4, 6, 9, 0, 3, 2, 5). Recall similar series backwards.
Abstract/visual	Select the picture that shows how a folded and cut piece of paper would look unfolded.

Verbal

Basic information	Who discovered the North Pole? What is the capital of France?
Vocabulary	Define *summer, poet, obstreperous.*
Arithmetic	If a suit sells for one-half of the regular price, what is the cost of a $120 suit?
Comprehension	Why are we tried by a jury of our peers?
Similarities	In what way are *inch* and *mile* alike?

Performance

Picture completion	**Block design**	**Object assembly**
What is missing from this picture?	Reproduce the design below using four or nine blocks.	Arrange the pieces into a meaningful object.

For some examples of uses of intelligence tests in a professional setting, see the Professional Perspective box on page 498 called "Career Focus: Meet a School Psychologist."

Extremes of Intelligence: Mental Retardation and Giftedness

Most current tools for assessing intelligence come from the psychometric approaches we described earlier in this chapter. These tests compare people's scores to averages of others of the same chronological age, so most people by definition show average intelligence scores. But what about those whose IQ scores are significantly below or above average? What outcomes are common for these individuals?

Mental Retardation. Children with mental retardation learn more slowly than other children, have more difficulty solving problems, and show language and communication

Career Focus: Meet a School Psychologist

Sandy Roland, Ph.D., Licensed Specialist in School Psychology
Richardson Independent School District in Dallas and Richardson, Texas

In what circumstances are intelligence tests useful in your practice?

Intelligence tests are used to acquire a general level of functioning of the child when considering what strategies may help the child progress in learning. Mainly, we use intelligence tests when determining if a child has mental retardation or a learning disability. Intelligence scores are also sometimes helpful when a child is being screened or evaluated for ADHD.

How do you decide what tests to use?

The child's age, developmental level, special needs, and background are important to consider when choosing an intelligence test. First, the test must have norms for the age of the child. Second, it is important to consider the child's developmental level and if he/she has any special needs such as a physical disability or speech/language impairment. Finally, the background of the child, including cultural differences and socioeconomic challenges need to be considered. We have a wide range of tests to choose from including developmental screenings, neuropsychological batteries, nonverbal tests, and the typical Wechsler-like tests.

What do scores on intelligence tests tell you about a child?

Scores usually tell us a lot about a child, but there are times when the scores are not as useful as the information gained from observation during the testing session. Most tests yield at least one composite score, usually, a score to describe the overall cognitive ability of a child. Many tests have subtest scores that give additional information that can be used when looking at a profile of strengths and weaknesses for the child. Cognitive processing and problem solving can also be gauged. During the test, observing the frustration level of the child is also a very important result of the testing situation.

What precautions do you take when interpreting and using scores?

It is important to make sure that the most appropriate test is given to the child and if the most appropriate is unavailable, then the next appropriate test can be used with some precautions. If the child's frustration level is too high and he/she "shuts-down" during the testing session, it should be noted. If the child's attention has to be constantly redirected to the task at hand, if speech/language issues make the testing session difficult, or if there are language or cultural differences to consider, then caution should be used in interpreting those scores.

Describe the education and training required to become a school psychologist.

In Texas we need the LSSP (Licensed Specialist in School Psychology) certification. This is a master's level certification. Practicum and internship are required, as well as a year of post-internship supervision before working independently. Many school psychologists also have a doctorate degree.

Q *Do you think educators should use intelligence tests to determine which students qualify for services or to gauge students' progress? Why or why not? How should eligibility and progress be determined?*

---

mental retardation (MR)
A condition characterized by below-normal intellectual functioning, deficits in adaptive behavior, and an onset early in life (before age 18).

deficits. As a result, they perform less well in school and have more difficulty making friends and engaging in social activities. With special services and support, children with mild to moderate levels of retardation can adjust to many of the normal challenges in life. They can attend regular classrooms, learn to care for themselves, and develop friendships with peers. With more severe levels of retardation, a child may need extensive support merely to negotiate everyday activities such as brushing teeth and getting dressed. Approximately 2 percent to 3 percent of the U.S. population has mental retardation. There are three components to the formal definition of **mental retardation (MR)**.

1. *Below-normal intellectual functioning* (usually indicated by an IQ of less than 70 or 75)

2. *Deficits in adaptive behavior,* the daily activities required for personal and social independence (e.g., communicating needs to others, eating, dressing, grooming, toileting, following rules, and working and playing with others)

3. *An onset early in life* (before age 18) (Hodapp & Dykens, 2003)

This teenager needs help with many of the self-care activities that most of us take for granted. Deficits in adaptive behavior, low IQ, and early onset (before age 18) are all elements of mental retardation.

Literally thousands of biological and environmental factors can cause mental retardation. The most severe forms of MR tend to result from genetic disorders. Down syndrome and fragile-X syndrome (see Chapter 2) are the two most common types of genetic disorders that cause mental retardation. Together these two disorders alone affect one in every 500 children born, and more than 700 other genetic diseases also can contribute to MR (Hodapp & Dykens, 2003). Mental retardation can also result from prenatal damage to the brain and nervous system by toxins such as alcohol and drugs. As you read in Chapter 3, prenatal alcohol exposure is the leading *known* cause of mental retardation in the United States (Abel & Sokol, 1987; Institute of Medicine, 1996). And MR can occur when infants suffer oxygen deprivation or other traumas during birth, and when they are born prematurely.

After children are born, numerous factors in the environment can retard mental development. The best-known environmental factors related to MR include exposure to lead and other toxins, poor nutrition, lack of stimulation, and parents who are illiterate or mentally retarded themselves. Rates of mental retardation are higher among children living in poverty, minority children, and males (Hodapp & Dykens, 2003). Mental health researchers often refer to retardation caused by lack of educational opportunity and stimulation as *cultural–familial retardation.* Mental retardation also can have multiple causes. For example, children may inherit low intelligence from their parents; on top of this, they may suffer poor nutrition, and their parents may fail to provide a stimulating learning environment. When both parents have mental retardation, the odds are more than 40 percent that their children also will have MR. The odds drop to 20 percent when only one parent has MR and to less than 10 percent when neither parent has MR (Mash & Wolfe, 1999).

Clinicians typically divide mental retardation into the four levels shown in Table 14.2. Approximately 85 percent of people with mental retardation are in the mild category (Mash & Wolfe, 2005). Toddlers and preschoolers with mild MR usually show only small delays. When they reach early elementary school, however, they fall behind in academic subjects. With some special education and support, these children can learn up to the sixth- or seventh-grade level. They may have only minor problems with peers and other social relationships, and after finishing school they can live and work independently or with a modest amount of supervision. At the other end of the

TABLE 14.2 Four Levels of Mental Retardation

LEVEL OF MENTAL RETARDATION	APPROXIMATE IQ*
Mild	50 to 70 or 75
Moderate	35 to 50
Severe	20 to 40
Profound	Below 20 or 25

Note: An IQ score of 100 indicates an "average" level of intelligence.
(Mash & Wolfe, 2005.)

scale, 1 percent to 2 percent of all people with mental retardation are in the profound category. As infants, they show serious delays in sensory and motor functions, and by the age of 4 they are still responding like typical 1-year-olds (Mash & Wolfe, 2005). These children need considerable training to learn to perform self-care activities such as eating, dressing, and toileting. They will need lifelong care. At present, most people with profound MR in the United States eventually go to live in group homes or residential facilities. Almost all cases of profound MR have a genetic or biological cause.

There are several things family members and other people can do to help children with mental retardation improve the quality of their lives (Mash & Wolfe, 2005; Ramey & Ramey, 1992). They can encourage children with MR to explore the environment so they can learn and gather information, and work with them on basic learning skills such as labeling, sorting, and comparing objects. Children with MR need consistent care from a responsible adult—someone they can trust and depend on. Caregivers can also help by celebrating the achievements and developmental milestones of children with MR, and protecting them from harmful teasing, punishment, and criticism. None of these steps can erase the retardation, but they can go a long way in helping the child live a more happy and satisfying life.

gifted (or talented) children
Children who show extraordinary achievement in one or more areas.

Gifted and Talented Children. **Gifted (or talented) children** show achievement that is well above average in one or more areas—usually in language, math, music, art, or athletics. Some children are *globally gifted:* They show exceptional talent in all areas. Other children are *unevenly gifted:* They are exceptional in one or two areas but are at (or below) average levels in others. While a high IQ score may be an indicator of giftedness, it is not the only indicator, and some talent areas are not included on intelligence tests. Winner (1996) describes three characteristics that are typical of gifted (or talented) children.

1. Gifted children are *precocious*. They begin learning early and progress faster than others.

2. Gifted children *march to their own drummer*. They don't need much assistance to master information in their favorite subjects. They often teach themselves, have their own way of learning and unique ways of organizing and sorting information, and they don't always conform to the conventional learning methods of schools.

3. Gifted children have a *rage to master*—an intense craving for information and an obsessive need to make sense out of their favorite topics. They devour information, spend endless hours on their chosen subjects, and rarely engage in any other pursuits. Parents don't push them to achieve; instead, gifted children push their parents for more materials and stimulation.

One of the most ambitious longitudinal studies in history was begun by Lewis Terman in 1921 to study the development of highly gifted individuals. Contrary to common stereotypes, Terman found that gifted and talented individuals were not neurotic, frail, eccentric, or emotionally sensitive individuals. Instead, they were larger, healthier, and generally more well adjusted than most other children. Overall, they tended to live longer, enjoyed better health, had a lower divorce rate, and were happier than most people (Shurkin, 1992; Terman, 1925). More recent research has found that gifted and talented adolescents are more focused in school, spend much of their free time working in their talent areas, and spend more time alone than their "average" peers. Their parents tend to have more education, and their families have higher incomes, as well as more supportive and positive family environments. For example, most talented teenagers rate their family interactions as more affectionate, cohesive, flexible, and happy than other students (Csikszentmihalyi et al., 1997; Shurkin, 1992; Terman, 1925). If others had these benefits, how many more would show exceptional talent?

your perspective
Have you ever had a "rage to master" a particular topic? What was the experience like, and what do you think motivated you? If you haven't experienced this intense level of motivation, what subject comes closest to motivating you to learn at a higher level?

Ethnic Differences and Questions about Cultural Bias

Imagine the challenges that faced many immigrants arriving in the United States in the early 1900s. Often malnourished, exhausted, and in poor health after a long journey in a crowded ship, they stepped out on Ellis Island. Anxious to find relatives and explore their new country, they learned that first they must take several tests. One was an intelligence test—perhaps the Stanford–Binet, which was a French test translated into English. If the immigrants didn't speak English, then they would take a version retranslated into their native languages. The test administrators would then compare their scores to the norms established by U.S.-born citizens who were tested under far more comfortable conditions. Is it surprising that the immigrants' scores were lower? Further, could the questions in the French and American tests adequately measure the general intelligence of people raised in Hungary, Russia, Italy, African nations, or other parts of the world? Did the questions even make sense to people from other cultures? In other words, were the tests culturally fair?

your perspective

What would it take to develop an intelligence test that is truly culturally fair?

Numerous studies conducted since the 1960s have documented differences in intelligence scores among various U.S. ethnic groups (see Gregory, 1996 and Sattler, 2001 for reviews). Typically, composite scores for non-Hispanic whites are about 100. Asians score slightly higher, African Americans score about 15 points lower, and Hispanics score between whites and African Americans. You must keep in mind that these are group differences; scores vary much more *within* these groups than *among* them. It is impossible to predict any one person's score based on the person's ethnic group identity. Still, these group differences have generated a fierce debate about the cultural fairness of intelligence tests. To read more about the social implications of ethnic differences in IQ scores, see the Social Policy Perspective box on page 502 called "Ethnicity and IQ."

Because of intelligence tests' potential for cultural bias, some critics have argued that these tests should not be used with students from ethnic minority groups. Below are some of the most common arguments *against* testing (Onwuegbuzie & Daley, 2001; Sattler, 2001).

- *Intelligence tests are culturally biased.* The developers of most tests are middle-class whites who bring their own experiences to test construction. If they lack knowledge of other cultures, they may inadvertently create biased instruments. Some test items require knowledge that is specific to middle-class white culture. Cultural bias disadvantages test takers from minority cultures.

- *Minorities have less test-taking skill and experience.* Ethnic minority groups tend to focus more on oral skills, so paper-and-pencil tests may not be a good fit with their learning styles. Children from these groups also may have had less practice with standardized tests. Because the tests reflect the values and norms of the dominant majority, these children may be less motivated to perform at their highest levels or may not appreciate the importance and implications of doing well on the test.

- *Most test examiners are white.* Communication and rapport between white examiners and minority children may be less than optimal, and this may depress scores.

- *Test results lead to inadequate and inferior educational placements.* Because of their lower test scores, schools often disproportionately place minority children in special education classes, where curriculum and support may fall short of what other children receive. Special education placements also create negative expectancies in teachers and other school officials—and even in the minds of minority children themselves. In this negative cycle, called *stereotype threat*, the child begins to accept the negative views and expectations; this can lead to poorer intellectual performance (Steele & Aronson, 1995).

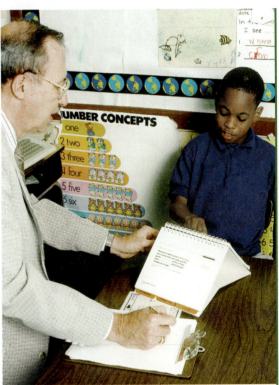

Does racial uneasiness between examiner and child affect children's performance on IQ tests? What other potential problems must we consider when comparing IQ scores across different ethnic groups?

Ethnicity and IQ

How important is intelligence for doing well in school, getting a good job, and for explaining social problems like poverty, unemployment, crime, and poor parenting? Why are there persistent differences in the average IQ scores of different ethnic groups? These questions have been addressed for decades, with heated debate about the answers and their implications for social policies.

The most recent controversy has centered on *The Bell Curve,* a book that presents intelligence as a general trait, significantly influenced by genetics and successfully estimated by IQ tests (Herrnstein & Murray, 1994). The authors argue that differences in intelligence play a central role in many of the vexing problems faced by society such as poverty, unemployment, crime, education, and poor home environment, and that "large proportions of the people who exhibit the behaviors and problems that dominate the nation's social policy agenda have limited cognitive ability" (Herrnstein & Murray, 1994, p. 386).

The biggest controversy centers on the discussion of ethnic differences in IQ scores. While most experts agree that there are consistent differences in the average IQ scores of different ethnic groups, there is heated disagreement as to why. Herrnstein and Murray argue that the differences are not due to poverty, education, or test bias, but to real differences in cognitive abilities. They acknowledge that the environment undoubtedly plays a role in the development of intelligence, but argue that increasing intelligence has proven to be difficult. And finally, they urge consideration of social policies that recognize the central role of intelligence. For example, they urge a return to emphasizing quality education for gifted students because these students will benefit more from good education than less intelligent students. They also advocate a re-examination of affirmative action policies in education and employment to give preference to disadvantaged individuals only when their qualifications are very similar to those of nondisadvantaged peers.

Reaction to *The Bell Curve* was swift, furious, and often negative. Critics claim the book does not describe problems in the data they use to support their arguments, the theories and data on which it is based have been replaced by newer views of intelligence and cognitive processing, and that the social policy recommendations are "exotic, neither following from the analyses nor justified on their own terms" (Gardner, 1995, p. 23; Fraser, 1995). Others believe that the authors dismiss the impact of such things as poverty, discrimination, and testing bias far too quickly, and overemphasize a narrowly defined view of intelligence to explain complex social problems (Fish, 2002; Miele, 1995; Neisser, 1998; Neisser et al., 1996).

Q *What role do you think intelligence plays in the important social issues we currently face? What are the social policy implications of thinking of intelligence as a strongly genetically influenced general factor that is difficult to change? If you were developing social policies to address such things as poverty, crime, and fairness in educational and job opportunities, what role would group differences in intelligence play in your thinking?*

In view of these arguments, examiners administering psychological tests need to be sensitive to cultural differences. They should always interpret test results with caution, and they should never base special education placements or other diagnoses solely on the results of a single test. However, it's also important to evaluate criticisms of cultural bias in the light of objective research data. For example, it might seem that the verbal subscales of intelligence tests, which involve vocabulary, factual knowledge, and text comprehension (e.g., define the word *obfuscate*), would reflect more cultural bias than nonverbal subscales involving picture completion, object assembly, and block design (e.g., use blocks to copy a design). However, Taylor and Richards (1991) researched this question and found that African American children actually scored *higher* on the verbal subscales of the WISC–R (an earlier version of the WISC–IV) than they did on the nonverbal subscales. Further, when people have identified test items as culturally biased, test statistics often showed the same ethnic group differences on those items as on the whole test. Sometimes, in fact, results on these "biased" items favor ethnic minorities (Sattler, 2001).

One factor with a clear link to IQ scores is socioeconomic status, or SES. When SES and other living conditions are the same, IQ differences between non-Hispanic whites and African Americans are far smaller—less than five points in some studies (Sattler, 1992). After all, ethnic minority groups make up a disproportionately high percentage of families living in poverty in the United States. And children living in poverty have worse schools and fewer educational opportunities, both leading to lower IQ scores.

Jerome Sattler (1992, 2001), a researcher and expert in childhood assessment, summarized arguments that *favor* using intelligence tests with minority students.

Think About Maya . . .
How might Maya's ethnicity impact her performance on intelligence tests? What steps can she, her parents, and test administrators take to make assessments more fair for her?

- *Tests are useful in evaluating present functioning.* The subscales of intelligence tests can help educators identify students' cognitive strengths and weaknesses. Some subscale profiles may suggest brain damage or psychological difficulties; more specific tests can then follow up on these potential problems. A significant drop in IQ score can signal the need for follow-up.

- *Tests help students get access to special programs.* When used properly, test scores can be an important part of the justification for providing special education programming and other services that some minority children need—services to which they are legally entitled.

- *Tests help families, educators, and communities evaluate programs.* By helping to document gains and losses, IQ scores can help hold schools and programs accountable for benefiting all children. When test scores reveal significant differences among ethnic groups, these findings can stimulate special interventions to address inequalities. Rather than seeing the tests as marred by bias, we can see them as tools for identifying bias in existing systems.

- *Finally, tests are useful in indicating future functioning.* Binet originally designed his scales to predict future school performance, and this is still one of the most important uses of intelligence tests today. IQ scores do correlate with academic success and performance.

Biases that exist in intelligence tests reflect the values and assumptions that operate in the dominant culture. The reality is that educational opportunities, and the likelihood of success in school and work, also reflect the dominant culture. Childhood IQ scores provide early evidence of this effect. They demonstrate the importance of achieving a truly multiethnic and pluralistic society where students of all cultures have an equal chance of success, achievement, and happiness.

■ Let's Review . . .

1. Most experts agree that intelligence involves _____.
   a. the ability to learn
   b. the ability to think logically about abstract concepts
   c. the ability to adapt to the environment
   d. all of the above

2. Now in fifth grade, Lisa has practiced her division math facts so thoroughly that she can fly through her flash cards at an impressive speed. Which subtheory in Sternberg's triarchic theory of intelligence would relate most closely to Lisa's speed with division facts?
   a. the componential subtheory b. the experiential subtheory
   c. the contextual subtheory d. the metacomponent subtheory

Learning to Communicate: Language in Adolescence

As you learned in Chapters 5, 8, and 11, language development during childhood is quite impressive, but it is far from complete by the time a child enters adolescence. The teenage years see development in several important aspects of language. Some of these developments seem almost intentionally designed to keep parents and other adults from knowing what adolescents are talking about! Others aspects arise from the social and cultural contexts in which a teen develops.

As you study this section, ask yourself these questions:

■ What is the adolescent register and what role does it play in adolescent development?

■ How does the speech of girls and boys differ?

■ What are dialects and how do they develop? What advantages and disadvantages do dialects present?

The Adolescent Register

adolescent register
Special form of speech adolescents use to identify themselves as belonging to a particular social, cultural, or generational group.

During adolescence children begin to use language as a tool for identifying peer groups and for excluding those outside their peer group. The **adolescent register** is a special form of speech that adolescents use to identify themselves as belonging to a particular social, cultural, or generational group (Romaine, 1984). If you have ever overheard a group of adolescents talking with one another, you will recognize that their patterns of language include several distinctive features, including phonemes and syntax that are markedly different from those used by younger and older speakers of the same language. In particular, the adolescent register has an interesting vocabulary that includes many novel slang terms. Think back to movies from or about prior decades—can you recall any of the odd-sounding words and phrases that adolescents used? What was *groovy* in the 1960s, *cool* in the 1970s, and *awesome* in the 1990s became *phat* in the early 2000s; yesterday's *nerds* are today's *posers*. Although adolescent registers exist across social, regional, and ethnic groups, the specific terms, syntax, and phonemes vary widely. Also, because the purpose of an adolescent register is to identify an adolescent as belonging to

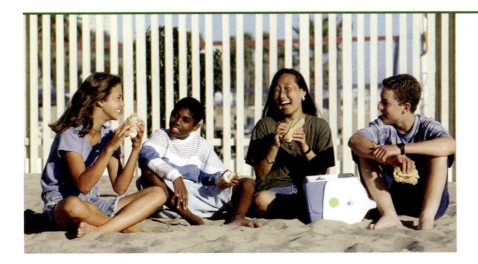

What features of their adolescent registers do you think these teenagers are using?

a particular generation, place, and group, registers change quickly. As adolescents grow to adulthood, the patterns and terms that marked their groups either fade away or, in some cases, become part of the overall culture. (Pretty cool, huh?)

Genderlects

Genderlects, different ways of talking for males and females, begin in early child-hood, probably as a result of differential treatment by adults and peers as well as parent modeling (Gleason et al., 1994; Kramer, 1974; Perlmann & Gleason, 1994; Sadker & Sadker, 1994). Evidence of developing genderlects has been found in tod-dlers as young as 2 (Sachs, 1987), but these differences become more pronounced during middle childhood and adolescence. For example, the language of boys play-ing with other boys includes more verbal conflict, coercive terms, slang terms, and profanity than girls' language (Cheshire, 1982; Jay, 1992; Sheldon, 1990). In contrast, girls' interactions with other girls include more questions, collaborative suggestions, attempts to verbally manage and control interactions, and communications about emotions and feelings (Blair, 2000; Goodwin & Goodwin, 1987; Lloyd & Goodwin, 1993; Warren & McCloskey, 1997). Some theorists argue that genderlects develop because of differences in the goals boys and girls are pursuing when using language. The idea is that boys focus more on gaining power and autonomy, whereas girls focus more on affiliation or relationship building (Gilligan, 1982). However, genderlect differences seem to be somewhat situ-ation- and culture-specific. More pronounced differences are found in same-sex than in mixed-sex interactions, and some studies have not found female genderlect features among African American adolescent girls (Goodwin, 1990; McCloskey & Coleman, 1992).

your perspective
What was your adolescent register? How was it different from those of your parents or of members of other social and ethnic groups? Do you notice genderlects in your language or that of your friends?

Social and Cultural Dialects

Even though people in different geographic regions and cultural groups within a country may all speak the same language, there are often differences in vocabulary, grammar/syntax, pragmatics, and style of language interactions. A **dialect** is a consistent and sys-tematic variety of a single language that is shared by a certain subgroup of speakers (McLaughlin, 2006; Oetting, 2003a). In contrast, an *accent* consists of audible speech characteristics or differences in how words are pronounced and is one component of a dialect. A given language usually has several dialects, some of which are associated with specific geographic regions (e.g., Boston English, Southern English) and others with ethnic and cultural groups (e.g., African American English). A dialect may get its name from a particular ethnic group, but not all members of that ethnic group will

dialect
A consistent and systematic variety of a single language that is shared by a certain subgroup of speakers.

African American English (AAE), spoken by many African Americans, includes elements of several western African languages, Portuguese, Dutch, and French. Like other cultural dialects, AAE is a consistent system with its own linguistic rules and vocabulary, not an incorrect form of Standard American English.

necessarily speak the dialect—nor will members of the ethnic group be the only people who can speak it. Dialects develop in response to social and cultural conditions, not according to race, although these factors often go together (Hulit & Howard, 2006).

The most studied social dialect of Standard American English is *African American English* (AAE), also known as *Black English* or *Ebonics* (Green, 2002; Wolfram & Thomas, 2002). AAE is a distinct dialect of English, complete with its own linguistic rules and vocabulary, not a simplistic or incorrect form of Standard American English. *Hispanic English* and *Asian English* are other common dialects. As with AAE, not all Hispanic American or Asian American children use these dialects. Also, Hispanic and Asian populations in the United States come from a variety of different Spanish and Asian language backgrounds, so these dialects can vary a great deal. All these dialects show consistent differences from Standard American English in vocabulary, phonology, and grammar rules (Cheng, 1987; Hulit & Howard, 2006; McLaughlin, 2006; Taylor, 1986).

Different dialects are simply different from one another; no one dialect is inherently better or worse than any other. And even though dialects differ in systematic ways, they also share many similarities (Oetting, 2003a; Oetting & McDonald, 2001). However, the reality is that people often make negative judgments about those who speak a dialect other than their own. People may rate dialect speakers as lower in competence, professionalism, intelligence, ambition, education, success, and wealth—even when the raters are themselves speakers of the dialects (Atkins, 1993; Luhman, 1990). Often such judgments affect the treatment of people who speak different dialects in schools or workplaces. There is a tendency to treat such individuals as less competent and less intelligent, and speaking a dialect in educational and work settings often brings reprimands or even punishments (Romaine, 1995). Perhaps wider understanding that social dialects have their own complex rule systems and develop as a result of cultural and social circumstances might decrease these negative and unfair judgments (Oetting, 2003b).

Think About Maya . . .

Is it likely that Maya speaks a dialect of English? If so, how might this affect how she is treated by others who do not speak the same dialect?

your perspective

Do you speak a dialect of English? What are some examples of its vocabulary and grammar? Do you think your dialect has affected the judgments others who speak different dialects make of you? If so, in what ways?

■ Let's Review . . .

1. The adolescent register helps adolescents identify themselves as _____.
   a. being members of adult society
   b. being popular among peers
   c. belonging to a particular generation
   d. being aware of the abstract nature of language

Cognition in Context: Adolescents Making Decisions

As adolescents develop, they are increasingly called upon to use their intelligence in a variety of different ways. They have more freedom to make decisions about day-to-day matters as well as serious and far-reaching issues. Deciding what courses to take, how much effort to put into studying, whether to continue with further schooling past high school, which extracurricular activities to participate in, when they are ready for sexual activity, and whether to try drugs and alcohol are only a few of the choices most adolescents face. How well do adolescents make decisions? In this section we will briefly review research on adolescent decision making in general, then talk in more detail about adolescents' choices of jobs and careers.

As you study this section, ask yourself these questions:

- What skills are involved in making decisions? How well-developed are these skills in adolescents compared to children and adults?

- What factors are involved in making career decisions? What difficulties do adolescents have in thinking about possible jobs and the paths to achieve their occupational goals?

- What is the *forgotten third*, and what can be done to help improve their economic prospects?

How Well Do Adolescents Make Decisions?

Decision making is a complex process. It involves the coordination of a number of cognitive skills, including recognizing that there is a decision to be made; generating alternatives and identifying possible problems or biases with each; objectively evaluating the likelihood that an alternative will produce the results you want, and the likely consequences whether it does or does not; and taking into consideration the social, personal, and emotional contexts at each step in the process. And it all happens with at least some degree of uncertainty, because we can never be sure if a decision is the "right" one or not until it has already been made (Halpern, 2003).

Think back to our discussions of formal operations, and to the information-processing research in earlier chapters, and it is easy to understand why we might expect adolescents to be better than children at making sound decisions. For example, generating alternatives requires the ability to think about abstract possibilities and use combinational logic, and evaluating possibilities is aided by systematic logical thinking. Determining likely consequences is based in part on reasoning about logical conclusions and abstract concepts as well as reflective thinking. As information-processing psychologists point out, adolescents also have a great deal more knowledge and a greater repertoire of strategies to bring to bear when making decisions. Their cognitive processing is faster and more efficient—this enables them to keep several perspectives in mind at once and allows them to compare and contrast possible courses of action.

The research in this area supports the conclusion that adolescents are better than children at making "good" decisions, or ones that reflect reasonably careful consideration of different options. By 14 years of age, adolescents are able to evaluate options and defend their decisions. And as you might expect, older adolescents (over age 14) show better performance than younger ones in a variety of decision-making skills. Younger teens tend to use less of the information that is available to them, are not as good at identifying possible negative consequences, and are not as good at determining whether the source of information is credible or not (Kaplan, 2004; Keating, 1990). Younger adolescents may also be more susceptible to peer pressure in their decision making, and may give more weight to what adults think of as less important factors (such as appearance or being viewed positively by their friends). However, it is also clear that decision-making skills continue to improve throughout adolescence and into adulthood. For example, one study asked adolescents ranging in age from 11 to 17 and 23-year-old young adults to help a teen think through a decision (such as whether to have cosmetic surgery or whether to live with their mother or their father following a divorce). Compared to the adolescents, young adults were more likely to consider the risks and benefits of the decisions and to suggest that the teen seek help from an impartial expert (Halpern-Felsher & Cauffman, 2001; Lewis, 1981). It's also important to keep in mind that most of the studies comparing adolescent and adult decision-making processes involve hypothetical dilemmas in laboratory settings. It's been suggested that the differences in decision making may be greater than we realize when the choices involve personally relevant issues in emotional, real-world contexts (Steinberg & Scott, 2003). Finally, the level of thinking in both adolescence and adulthood varies a great deal and depends to a great extent on a person's particular experiences (Moshman, 2005).

The issue of adolescent decision making can have critical real-world implications, particularly when considering issues such as legal rights and responsibilities and risky behavior. At what age should one be legally allowed to seek health care without parental permission? At what age should teens be prosecuted as adults for criminal activities? And, if adolescents approach adults in their abilities to make sound decisions, why do they have the reputation of engaging in risky behaviors with potentially devastating consequences? Is this behavior due to immature decision-making skills, immature brain development, the adolescent egocentric feeling of invulnerability, or a different system of perceived costs and benefits (Beckman, 2004; Goldberg, Halpern-Felsher, & Millstein, 2002; Gruber, 2001; Steinberg & Scott, 2003)? The research on decision making, and adolescent cognitive development in general, will be important to consider as society makes these decisions and tries to understand these adolescent behaviors.

your perspective

Think about a difficult decision you had to make during your adolescence. How did you think through the issue—what factors did you consider? How would you think about it differently now?

Making Vocational Choices

One of the biggest decisions that adolescents must grapple with is what occupation to work toward. It may surprise you to learn that the foundations for making choices about vocations begin well before adolescence, as even young children begin recognizing and developing their talents, attitudes, and needs (Hartung et al., 2005). Occupational development is a developmental process, with individuals first observing and thinking about the occupations they see around them and becoming progressively more specific and realistic about their choices (Super, 1957). During early and middle adolescence, increasing cognitive skills enable adolescents to think more realistically about their own skills and interests as well as to consider what is required in different occupations.

What factors influence the specific vocational decisions that an individual makes? Several factors are involved, including one's interests, values regarding the rewards one wants from working, and several aspects of the social context such as socioeconomic status, parents, peers, the job market, gender, and ethnicity. One well-known theory of career choice was developed by John Holland (1997) and focuses on the role of personality, particularly a person's interests. According to Holland, successful career choice involves making a good match between one's interests and the demands of their occupational environment. Holland argued that interests can be organized into six general occupational categories, as shown in Figure 14.4, and that different occupational environments are more suited to some categories than others. For example, someone whose personality characteristics are more investigative would likely be better suited to and more satisfied with a career in a scientific or technical field rather than in a clerical or sales position. According to Holland, a good fit will increase the likelihood of career satisfaction, achievement, and stability as well as greater overall well-being. In general, these relationships are supported by research, though some studies find stronger relations than others (Luzzo & MacGregor, 2001; Mullis & Mullis, 1997). In addition, predicting occupational success may be more complicated than finding a good match between personality and occupational demands, particularly for members of minority groups. These individuals may have the interests, desire, and talents to succeed in a specific career but have to contend with discrimination or other barriers in educational or job opportunities (Brown, 1995; Greenlee et al., 1988).

Other researchers emphasize the role of *work values,* or the types of rewards a person wishes to get from work, rather than interests per se when explaining career choice (Johnson, 2002). For example, some people are very motivated by money when making job choices while others seek job stability, opportunities to be creative, power over others, helping others, or having time for recreation. Adolescents may be unrealistic in this regard. For example, teens rate many different types of rewards as being very important, and say they are very confident they will find a job that meets them all (Schneider & Stevenson, 1999). As they gain more experience in the

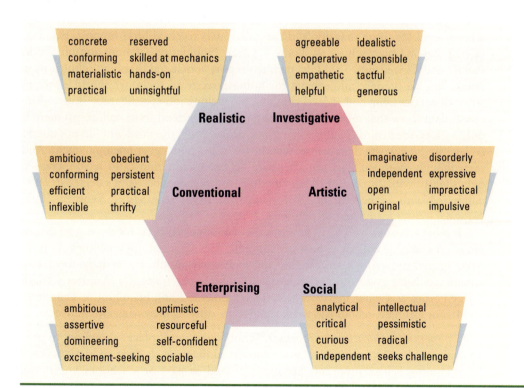

Figure 14.4 • Holland's Six Occupational Categories In Holland's theory, an individual's pattern of interests can be categorized into the six occupational categories shown here. The better the match between these interest categories and the demands of the occupation, the more satisfied and successful the person will be. (Based on Holland, 1997.)

work world, work values change. Emphasis on making a lot of money, helping others, and enjoying relationships with co-workers decreases while job stability and opportunities to be creative continue to be important (Johnson, 2002).

This research is an important reminder of one of the main difficulties of relying on interest-based or work value-based models when talking with adolescents about career decisions: These things can change. While some 18-year-olds are quite sure of their identities, interests, and values, others are not. By this age they may have a general sense of their interests and talents but are still in the process of exploring alternatives and trying different possibilities (Tracey et al., 2005). Adolescents and young adults are making vocational choices at later ages now than in past decades, and work environments themselves can have an important influence on the development of interests and values. As with many aspects of development, the factors involved have bidirectional effects.

It is also important to remember that vocational decisions are not based solely on the individual's characteristics. Instead, they are made within and significantly affected by the social context. For example, overall socioeconomic status affects many job-relevant factors, including the occupational models the adolescent sees, job opportunities, types of schooling and training available, work values, degree and types of career exploration available and encouraged, and family connections to list only a few (Mullis et al., 1998; Steinberg, 2005). Adolescents are also affected by expectations of their families and their culture. For example, stereotypes of appropriate careers for women and cultural expectations to balance family and work affect young women's thinking about careers. And cultural values regarding group connectedness and community responsibility require that adolescents and young adults from some ethnic minority backgrounds balance these values with occupational environments that may be quite different (Kaplan, 2004). Given the complexities of vocational decision making, it is not surprising that it takes many years to make career decisions.

The Forgotten Third: Improving the Transition from School to Work

When considering vocational decision making, the majority of attention is focused on adolescents who will attend college. In the late 1980s, a report drew nationwide attention to the fact that almost half of adolescents do not go to college after high school—and for those that don't, these individuals received little support, training, or help beyond high school (William T. Grant Foundation Commission on Work, Family and Citizenship, 1988). In fact, the report concluded that high schools were doing little to prepare adolescents for going directly to the work world either in terms of encouraging higher-level thinking or teaching job-specific trade skills. More recent data show that more students are going on to attend some college (so there is only a "forgotten third") but the economic prospects of the third who do not attend college are even worse than before, with lower wages and higher unemployment. And even though more students are attending college, graduation rates have increased only slightly, with 28 percent of young adults completing a bachelor's degree in 2004 compared with 22 percent in 1971 (Halperin, 1998; Jennings & Rentner, 2005; National Center for Education Statistics, 2005).

It is in everyone's interest to improve the economic prospects for those who do not attend or complete college. A host of economic, social, and health outcomes are positively related to having a more stable and higher-paying job. Fortunately, increasing attention is being given to improving the *school-to-work transition* (American Youth Policy Forum & Center for Workforce Development, 2000; Hamilton & Hamilton, 2004). For example, school and work settings are offering increasing alternatives.

■ *Cooperative educational programs.* Schools and work places cooperate to provide paid work experience with specific skill goals as part of the student's schooling. These programs are often offered as part of a school's vocational educational curriculum.

- *Internships*. Interns are placed in a work setting either during the school year or summer. Work hours, responsibilities, and compensation are negotiated among the student, work supervisor, and academic supervisor.

- *Youth apprenticeships*. These are formal, structured, systematic programs with the explicit goal of teaching the skills of a specific trade to a certain standard.

- *Service-learning experiences*. These experiences combine the opportunity to learn skills with performing a service for others. They are unpaid and short-term activities, but may be required as part of a school's community service expectations.

For school-to-work experiences to be beneficial and successful, the quality of *mentoring* the students receive must be considered. **Mentoring** refers to adults in the work and/or school setting taking responsibility for teaching and advising the student to make sure that the work being done contributes to students' learning. Good mentoring in school-to-work programs helps adolescents achieve competence in the academic skills and knowledge required by the job, responsibility in their personal job-related actions, the skills and willingness to behave and communicate according to the norms of the professions, and the skills and willingness to learn effectively and perform well in school in general (Hamilton & Hamilton, 2004). Good mentoring can also help students build important social networks, which will help them find full-time employment after they graduate. When done well, school-to-work mentoring programs have positive effects on a variety of social, academic, and occupational outcomes though the size of the effects are relatively modest (DuBois et al., 2002). To learn more about the experiences of one of the Forgotten Third, read the Personal Perspective box on page 512 called "I Graduated—Now What?"

Finally, what about the effects of simply working for pay during adolescence— not as part of a structured school-to-work program? Most teenagers have part-time jobs, usually in retail or service jobs as cashiers, cooks, stock handlers/baggers, or fast-food servers. Working more than 20 hours per week during the school year is associated with poorer grades and increased negative behaviors. Some of this negative effect may be due to selection factors (i.e., students who work longer hours may also be less interested and less successful in school to begin with). In general, however, adolescents who balance work, school, and extracurricular activities (spending less than 20 hours per week working for pay) are most successful in high school and beyond (Mortimer, 2003; Staff et al., 2004). As you might expect, number of hours worked is not the only important factor in thinking about the effects of teen employment. Working conditions that encourage school–work connections and provide opportunities to learn new career-related skills reduce the chances of school problems, drug and alcohol use, and criminal activity. These working conditions, which school-to-work transition programs try to encourage, also have the positive effects of helping teens become more independent, confident, and responsible as well as helping them develop work values and beliefs that will help them succeed in the adult workplace (Staff et al., 2004).

In this chapter, we have described important cognitive changes that occur during adolescence as well as several ways to think about and assess intelligence. We also described how adolescents use these skills to make decisions about daily aspects of their lives and their future occupations. As we look back over the course of cognitive development, it is clear that adolescents have made tremendous strides in their abilities to reason, and have become very capable at making important decisions. Their cognitive skills will continue to grow in important ways over the rest of their lives, but adolescents' reasoning is quite impressive indeed!

The school-to-work transition for adolescents who do not further their schooling after high school graduation can be difficult. How can schools and potential employers help ease this transition?

mentoring
The process of taking responsibility for teaching and advising students in a work or school setting to ensure student learning.

Think About Maya . . .
How could a part-time job help Maya as she thinks about her future? What type of job might help her most, and what should she be cautious about?

I Graduated—Now What?

Donna Rowland
Pittsburgh, PA

Why did you decide to not continue your schooling after high school?
It was more of an assumption than a decision. I grew up in a very blue-collar environment. Going off to college was not something that was discussed or even thought about in my immediate family. I did have friends that went on to college, and I would look at them with such amazement and curiosity. Why were they going off to college and leaving me behind to jump-start a future with really no knowledge? I am not bitter about my decision, but I do daydream about what I might have been and what my life would be like now had I gone to college.

What was the school-to-work transition like for you?
I was looking for that glamorous secretarial position, not realizing that you have to start out as the lowly file clerk. You could always find employment as a sales clerk or cashier but that was not something I wanted to do. My first job was processing payment checks in the credit office of a major department store. It doesn't sound like much fun or excitement, but this was my entrance into the business world. What I do remember are the great friends I made and what fun we had planning what we were going to do on the weekend.

What could the school system have done to make the transition easier?
I was in the academic program in high school, so in some ways I was not as efficient as those who concentrated on their typing and shorthand skills—Yes, I did say shorthand! It would have been beneficial if my school had an intern program. This would have prepared the people not going on to college for what the real world had to offer. That in itself may have convinced more of us to try to further their education.

Looking back, would you change anything about your decision-making process, your choices, or your preparation for life after high school?
This is a very hard question to answer. I am very pleased with my life but there are times when I think about what I would have done differently. I love art and spend a lot of my free time painting. This talent might have been channeled into a profession such as an art teacher. I love children and if someone had shown me how these two could have come together, I might have pursued a career as an elementary art teacher.

> **Q** *What school-to-work programs would you design to ease the school-to-work transition and help students become more aware of their options as well as the real world of work? What elements seem most important, and why?*

■ Let's Review . . .

1. Adolescents are better decision makers than younger children because of adolescents'_____.
   a. less detailed knowledge base
   b. more mature cognitive skills
   c. slower cognitive processing
   d. greater emphasis on peer opinion

2. According to Holland's theory of career decision making, which of the following factors would be *most* important for a high school guidance counselor to know in order to help a teen make occupational plans?
   a. what the teen's parents do for an occupation
   b. the teen's ethnic background
   c. the teen's work values
   d. the teen's interests

3. Compared to adults, adolescents' work values _____.
   a. are more idealistic
   b. focus more on having free time for recreation
   c. are less realistic
   d. are very similar and do not change much with age

4. **True or False:** By age 14, most adolescents are just as good as adults at making decisions.

5. **True or False:** The economic conditions for teens who do not continue their schooling after high school graduation are better now than they were two decades ago.

Answers: 1. b, 2. d, 3. c, 4. F, 5. F

Thinking Back to Maya . . .

Now that you have studied this chapter, you should be able to help Maya understand more about her cognitive strengths and weaknesses, as well as how she might use her skills to make important decisions in her life. You can explain some of the higher level thinking skills that Piaget's theory predicts will develop during adolescence. This theory may help Maya see how skills like hypothetico-deductive reasoning, abstract thought, and combinational thinking are needed more in her coursework than before. Understanding adolescent egocentrism might help her better understand her own and her friends' behaviors, and prompt her to think more carefully about important choices and taking risks. Knowledge of situated and socially shared cognition may give her some ideas of how to better use her study groups and aspects of both her in-school and out-of-school contexts to understand the concepts she is learning. Understanding more about her developing ability to separate reality from possibilities may also help Maya as she thinks through the pros and cons of working and possible options for her future. She may be comforted to know that things will not always seem so confusing—her skills will become more mature and she will probably develop aspects of postformal reasoning.

It is concerning that Maya is starting to doubt her intelligence, especially since there is so little agreement as to how to define this concept! It would be helpful to tell Maya about some of the ways of conceptualizing intelligence. Perhaps if she thinks about the different factors, components, or types of intelligence, she might see her own profile of skills more realistically. You could work with her to identify her areas of strength (like verbal skills) and help her find ways to use those to improve her skills and performance in weaker areas. She and her parents should also be made aware of the potential bias of the standardized tests she may have taken (and will surely take, if she decides to apply for college admissions) and take whatever steps they can to ensure that these assessments are fair and used appropriately.

Working while still in high school offers some benefits, but Maya should be careful to balance her work, school, and other activities. Maya's parents might try to find people within her general areas of interest to provide mentoring for her; perhaps her school or local businesses offer structured school-to-work programs. Participating in these might help Maya understand the usefulness of what she is learning in school, connect her schoolwork to the real world, develop more mature work values, and think of herself as a legitimate peripheral participant in a field that interests her. Maya and her parents should definitely work with one another and the school system to help prepare her for her transition after high school, whether she attends college or not.

■ Chapter Review . . .

What basic changes occur during Piaget's stage of formal operational thought?

Adolescents develop the abilities to use hypothetico-deductive reasoning, abstract thought, combinational logic, reflective thought, and separate reality from possibilties. They can systematically work through all possible solutions to complex problems and are able to envision how things *could* be in contrast to how they really exist. Adolescents maintain a form of adolescent egocentrism, reflected in the imaginary audience and the personal fable.

What are the main criticisms and contributions of Piaget's theory?

Piaget underestimated children's abilities, and there does not seem to be evidence for the unified stages he proposed. Still, Piaget left a tremendous legacy for child development. He emphasized the active, constructive nature of children's learning, and many of the cognitive developmental trends he observed have been verified by research.

What are the more recent sociocultural views stimulated by Vygotsky's theory?

The situated cognition view emphasizes adaptation to the cultural context, and that development cannot be understood or measured without considering the situation. The guided participation view stresses how other social agents guide children from being peripheral participants to central participants in important cognitive activities. With socially shared cognition, two heads are better than one: Working together, children can construct more advanced cognitive products than when working alone.

What are the main approaches to defining intelligence?

Most experts agree that intelligence involves the ability to learn, think logically about abstract concepts, and adapt to the environment. The psychometric approach relies on numerous paper-and-pencil tests and physical measures; the data are analyzed to identify a smaller set of factors that underlie intelligence. Sternberg proposed three subtheories: componential, experiential, and contextual that explain how one acquires skills, processes information, and copes with the environment. Gardner proposed eight independent types of intelligence. People inherit biopsychological potentials to be stronger or weaker in each intelligence but environmental factors and individual choices are important for developing these potentials.

What tests are used to assess intelligence?

Binet and Simon developed the first practical intelligence test to determine which French schoolchildren would benefit from special education. Frequently used intelligence tests today are the most recent edition of the Stanford–Binet scale (SB5) and the series of assessments developed by David Wechsler. All provide an overall IQ score as well as subtest scores.

What characterizes those with below-normal and above-normal levels of intelligence?

Mental retardation refers to below-normal intellectual functioning, deficits in adaptive behavior, and an onset before age 18. Thousands of biological and environmental factors can cause mental retardation. Gifted children are precocious, march to their own drummers, and have a "rage to master." Most gifted children are healthy, well adjusted, and well liked by peers; most come from families with the financial and emotional resources to support giftedness.

What ethnic group differences in average IQ scores are typically found?

African Americans tend to score about 15 points lower than non-Hispanic whites on IQs tests; Asian Americans have scored slightly higher than non-Hispanic whites, and Hispanics have scored between non-Hispanic whites and African Americans. There is much more variability within these groups than between, and ethnic group differences are smaller when SES levels are equal. Critics have concerns about possible bias in test items, testing situations, and use of test results. Provided they are used and interpreted properly, tests can be useful in evaluating individuals and programs, qualifying children for needed services, and predicting future school functioning.

How does language continue to develop during adolescence?

Adolescents develop an adolescent register, and gender-lect differences become more pronounced. Social dialects are common. People who speak social dialects are often subject to negative judgments.

How do adolescents and adults differ in their decision-making skills? How do adolescents make occupational decisions?

Adolescents are better than younger children in many decision-making skills, but they are less likely than adults to weigh risks and benefits of decisions. The level of adolescent skills has important implications for real-world decisions concerning high-risk behavior and legal responsibility for decisions. Holland's theory of career choice emphasizes a good match between an individual's interests and occupation, while others emphasize the role of work values. Other factors are also involved, such as SES and cultural values.

What do we know about the transition from school-to-work for teens?

This transition is especially difficult for those who do not continue their schooling after high school graduation, and their economic prospects are difficult. Several transition programs can ease the transition, and the role of quality mentoring by an adult is key. Working for pay during high school offers several benefits as long as adolescents are careful to balance work with school demands and extracurricular activities.

■ Key Terms

abstract thought (481)
adolescent egocentrism (482)
adolescent register (504)
combinational logic (482)
componential subtheory (491)
contextual subtheory (492)
crystallized ability (490)
dialect (505)
experiential subtheory (491)
fluid ability (490)

formal operational thought (480)
general intelligence *(g)* (490)
gifted (or talented) children (500)
guided participation (487)
hypothetico-deductive reasoning (480)
imaginary audience (482)
intelligence (489)
mental retardation (498)
mentoring (511)

personal fable (483)
psychometric approach (490)
reliability (495)
situated cognition (487)
socially shared cognition (488)
specific intelligence *(s)* (490)
theory of multiple intelligences (492)
triarchic theory of intelligence (490)
validity (496)

mydevelopmentlab

If you are using MyDevelopmentLab, you have access to an ebook version of this textbook, along with dozens of valuable resources per chapter—including video and audio clips, simulations and activities, self-assessments, practice tests, and other study materials. Here is a sampling of the resources available for this chapter.

Explore
Gardner's Multiple Intelligences
Sternberg's Triarchic Theory of Intelligence
How to Be a Critical Thinker

Simulate
Gardner's Theory of Intelligence

Watch
Adolescent Egocentrism
Cultural Influences
Giftedness
Demographics and Intelligence Testing
Multiple Roles of Women

If you did not receive an access code to MyDevelopmentLab with this text and wish to purchase access online, please visit www.mydevelopmentlab.com.

chapter 15

Socioemotional Development in Adolescence

Luis is almost 16. He has always been fairly easygoing, but lately it seems like he and his parents are arguing about all kinds of little things. He feels like his parents stay on him all the time about his grades and "contributing" more around the house. They even asked him if anyone he knows has tried smoking marijuana. Although his grades aren't stellar, he's passing all his classes. Luis will be taking his driver's license test soon. He's really looking forward to the freedom he hopes having a driver's license will give him, but he hasn't yet figured out how he'll get a car like he wants. His parents don't have much money, and Luis doesn't have a job.

Although he doesn't talk much about it, Luis is thinking quite a bit about his future. He always thought that he would go to college, but he feels clueless about what he wants to study, and he feels like he should stay close to home to help his family financially. He doesn't feel like he has really connected with any of his teachers or subjects in a long time. His interests change from week to week, and he feels torn between wanting to make lots of money and wanting to do something that's more helpful to people. Luis likes hanging out with the friends he's had since middle school, but they seem to be gradually growing apart. Luis also recently broke up with his girlfriend because he didn't want to be tied to one person. But now he sees her going out with a senior and wonders if he made the right decision.

Are the concerns and feelings Luis is having about his future, family, friends, and romantic relationships normal for this age? After studying this chapter, you should be able to identify several potential reasons for his concerns and suggest several things that might help.

As you read this chapter, look for the "Think About Luis . . ." questions that ask you to consider what you're learning from Luis' perspective.

Like Luis, many adolescents feel excitement, anxiety, eagerness to experience adult activities, and fear of not being able to handle adult responsibilties—sometimes all within a matter of minutes! Adolescents face three central developmental tasks in their socioemotional development: identity, autonomy, and intimacy. This is a time when individuals begin to develop a clearer sense of their skills, interests, personal and occupational goals. They usually develop close friendships during these years as well as experience the first feelings of romance and sexual attraction. The family still exerts a strong influence on attitudes and behavior, but the impact of peers increases substantially as adolescents gradually become more independent. With their increased freedom and more mature thinking skills, some adolescents encounter conflicts between their developing moral guidelines and what they experience; many begin to think about ethical dilemmas in more mature ways. As with younger children, adolescents' development is affected by the different social contexts in which they live, such as the schools they attend as well as their overall cultural context. The concepts and research findings presented in this chapter should help you understand the many aspects of adolescent social and emotional development. It is also important to remember that, although these developmental tasks are typically discussed as socio-emotional tasks, all three are directly affected by the physical and cognitive developments you learned about in Chapters 13 and 14.

Who Am I? Adolescents' Understanding of Themselves

As you might recall from Chapter 1, Erik Erikson believed that one of the central developmental tasks for adolescent social-emotional development is to develop a clear sense of their own identities. **Identity** refers to a person's self-definition, including a knowledge and understanding of the combination of skills, interests, and characteristics that make her a unique person. In this section, we will describe the development of several different aspects of identity: identity status and ethnic identity, sexual orientation, and morality.

identity
A person's self-definition, including a knowledge and understanding of the combination of skills, interests, and characteristics that make her a unique person.

As you study this section, ask yourself these questions:

- What are the four identity statuses described by Marcia?
- How are ethnic majority and minority adolescents similar and different in the process they go through to develop a sense of identity?
- What factors contribute to the development of sexual orientation?
- What evidence supports Kohlberg's theory of moral development? What are some of the criticisms of this theory?

Identity

Adolescents' developing self-representation becomes an important issue as young people strive to develop their own identities. You may recall Erik Erikson's famous theory of psychosocial development (see Table 1.2 on page 15 in Chapter 1) (Erikson, 1968). Erikson believed that adolescents grapple with the stage of *identity versus role confusion*. Their increasing cognitive abilities enable them to think about abstract qualities of the self, to compare their "real selves" to their "ideal selves," and to think about other "possible selves." During adolescence, too, social demands increase rapidly: Teenagers take on different roles and responsibilities in areas such as work, religion, politics, and sexual relationships. Erikson proposed that adolescents must come to a resolution of who they are and what they believe. In other words, they must integrate in some way the many aspects of their self-representation and develop a sense of identity. If adolescents do not resolve the crisis of identity, their unclear sense of self will make it more difficult to deal with the crises that will arise during the adulthood years (i.e., intimacy, generativity, and integrity).

Think About Luis . . .
Which identity status do you think Luis is in? Does it seem that his changing interests and confusion are typical for his age, or do they indicate a problem? Why or why not?

Identity Status. James Marcia put forth a well-known elaboration of Erikson's theory, as shown in Figure 15.1 (Marcia, 1966). Marcia proposed two components of adolescent identity development. The first component is a *crisis* (sometimes referred to as *exploration*). In this crisis we question and think about what we know about ourself, how it all fits together, and how it compares to the ideal vision we have of ourself. Second, after some period of questioning and thought, we may make a *commitment* to an identity, reaching some conclusion or decision about ourself. As shown in Figure 15.1, Marcia described four possible identity statuses during adolescence.

1. **Identity achievement** is the status in which an adolescent has experienced and worked through the crisis and has made a commitment.

2. **Identity foreclosure** is the status in which an adolescent has experienced very little crisis but has made a commitment based on what others have said he is and should be. The adolescent has taken on an identity without much self-examination or questioning.

3. **Identity diffusion** is the status in which an adolescent may or may not have experienced a crisis, but is not currently in a state of crisis. The adolescent in identity diffusion either has stopped trying to reach a commitment or for some reason is still unable to do so—there is a clear *lack* of commitment.

4. **Identity moratorium** is the status of an adolescent who is still in the process of working through the crisis. The experience of the crisis is relatively high, but commitment is low.

As you might expect, adolescents who experience the period of crisis before making a commitment show greater complexity in their self-concepts than those in the foreclosed identity status, who have not experienced a period of exploration (Low, 1999).

identity achievement
A state of identity development in which a person has experienced and worked through the crisis and has made a commitment.

identity foreclosure
A state of identity development in which a person has experienced very little crisis but has made a commitment based on what others have said he is and should be.

identity diffusion
A state of identity development in which a person is not currently in a state of crisis, but there is a lack of commitment. The person either has stopped trying or is unable to reach a commitment.

identity moratorium
A state of identity development in which a person is still in the process of working through the crisis.

Figure 15.1 • The Four Identity Statuses of James Marcia Each of Marcia's identity statuses reflects the degree of *crisis* experienced and the degree of *commitment* reached. (Based on Marcia, 1966.)

ethnic identity
A person's understanding of his or her ethnic background and a feeling of belonging to a minority group.

The Development of Ethnic Identity. Adolescents who are members of an ethnic minority must also develop an **ethnic** or racial **identity**—an understanding of their ethnic backgrounds and a feeling of belonging within their minority groups. The groundwork for this development occurs during middle childhood, when minority children first begin to identify themselves as members of specific minority groups. Children as young as 5 understand the differences between themselves and majority-group children and typically prefer children of their own ethnicity (Aboud & Doyle, 1995; Wright, 1998). According to Phinney (1990), the development of ethnic identity takes place in three stages during adolescence, as shown in Table 15.1.

If you examine Phinney's stages, you will notice parallels to Marcia's identity statuses. Minority teens may begin with an *unexamined ethnic identity*. In this stage, as in the foreclosed identity status, adolescents have not gone through a period of exploration or questioning but they have clear feelings about their ethnicity based on outside sources. These sources may convey a positive image, such as an image held by parents; or they may convey a more negative identity, such as stereotypes from the majority culture (Spencer & Dornbusch, 1990). Alternatively, the unexamined stage may be more of an identity diffusion status in which adolescents have not really explored identity issues and have no clear sense of ethnicity. The second stage, *ethnic identity search*, is a period of identity moratorium during which teenagers reexamine their ethnic identities and search for what makes sense to them personally. This questioning process occurs when teens apply their growing cognitive abilities to social experiences—typically, experiences that in some way highlight their ethnicities, such as encounters with people of other ethnicities or personal experiences of prejudice. The *resolution of conflict* stage is comparable to Marcia's achieved identity status. In this stage adolescents come to a resolution regarding their ethnicities

TABLE 15.1   Phinney's Three-Stage Model of Ethnic Identity Development

STAGE	DESCRIPTION
Unexamined Ethnic Identity	■ Child holds an identity based on outside sources, or has no clear sense of identity ■ A foreclosed or diffused identity status ■ May be based on positive image (e.g., from parents) ■ May be based on negative image (e.g., stereotypes)
Ethnic Identity Search	■ Increasing cognitive abilities and social experiences combine to prompt reexamination and questioning of ethnic identity ■ A period of moratorium

Achieved Ethnic Identity	■ Adolescent settles on an ethnic identity
	■ Achieved identity status
	■ Can resolve the crisis by:
	  • *Distancing* themselves from his or her ethnic culture;
	  • Adopting a *blended bicultural identity,* in which aspects of both the majority and ethnic culture are adopted;
	  • Adopting an *alternating bicultural identity,* in which two different identities are created and the individual switches between them depending on the social context;
	  • Making a *complete commitment* to their ethnicity, even if it means loss of acceptance and access to the majority culture.

(Phinney, 1990.)

that is comfortable and makes sense to them. Developing an ethnic identity is often a long and difficult process, however. It is made more difficult because ethnic minority adolescents often must deal with stress and conflict created by racial discrimination at the same time (Fisher et al., 2000; Verkuyten, 2003).

Teens may go about resolving ethnic identity conflicts in a variety of ways, as Table 15.1 indicates. *Acculturation strategies*—the particular strategies a family uses to deal with differences between the customs and beliefs of their ethnic background and the majority culture—affect the development of ethnic identity (Berry, 1993; Phinney, 2003; Saito, 2003). For example,

Adolescents from ethnic minority groups progress through several stages as they develop an ethnic identity.

some families emphasize and celebrate their ethnicities as a proud cultural heritage. Such families are likely to encourage their children to learn more about and be proud of their backgrounds. And in some cultures, identity development is less a process of individual discovery and more of coming to understand one's role within the family. The further minority adolescents progress through the three stages, the better their levels of psychological adjustment and self-esteem (Phinney et al., 1997). To learn more about how one family has accomplished the task of developing an ethnic identity, read the Personal Perspective box on page 522 called "Developing an Ethnic Identity."

Remember that identity is multifaceted; an adolescent may reach commitment in some facets well before others. Culture plays an important role in identity development by suggesting such things as how long it is acceptable to remain in moratorium and what kinds of identities are acceptable to consider (we will discuss culture's influence on identity in more detail later in this chapter). Relationships with parents also affect how adolescents deal with issues of identity. Both younger children and adolescents benefit from parenting that is supportive and accepting, that lets youngsters express themselves, but that also provides reasonable expectations and limits for behavior (Harter, 2006). Contrary to what many people believe, parents continue to be just as important in their children's lives during adolescence as they were during childhood, even as the influence of friends increases (Lamborn & Steinberg, 1993).

Sexual Orientation

One aspect of self-understanding that becomes prominent during adolescence is sexual orientation. Most children begin experiencing feelings of sexual attraction during late childhood or early adolescence. The object of their attraction is usually a member of the opposite sex, but some are attracted to people of the same sex. **Sexual orientation** is the tendency to be attracted to people of the same sex (homosexual orientation), of the opposite sex (heterosexual orientation), or of both sexes (bisexual orientation). Why an individual develops a specific sexual orientation is a matter of great debate, as you are probably well aware. The basic issue is the one we have discussed throughout this book: What are the relative influences of nature (genetics and biology) and nurture (the environment in which a child develops), and how do these two factors interact?

When studying sexual behavior, we need to distinguish between *homosexual orientation* and *homosexual experiences*. **Homosexual orientation** is a sexual identity in which the person is sexually attracted primarily to people of the same sex. Homosexuals include *gay males* and *lesbian females*. *Bisexuals* have an attraction to both sexes. A **homosexual experience,** however, is simply a sexual encounter with someone

sexual orientation
Tendency to be attracted to people of the same sex (homosexual orientation), of the opposite sex (heterosexual orientation), or to both sexes (bisexual orientation).

homosexual orientation
The sexual identity where the person's sexual attraction is primarily to someone of the same sex.

homosexual experience
A sexual encounter with someone of the same sex.

Developing an Ethnic Identity

Angela Watkins
Atlanta, Georgia
*African American professor, author,
and parent*

How did your ethnic identity develop?

I was born during a most promising time for African Americans—the Civil Rights Movement was in full motion, and it was a time of massive social change. My agents of socialization were African Americans in positions of authority, power, and influence. My family members were key players in the Civil Rights Movement. I grew up in Ebenezer Baptist Church in Atlanta, Georgia, the church of world-renowned Civil Rights leader, Reverend Dr. Martin Luther King, Jr. The administrators, teachers, and babysitters that I interacted with in preschool and elementary school were African Americans. Each had a clear sense of ethnicity and an unspoken responsibility to continue the struggle for justice and equality. I remember learning words like "slavery," "Jim Crow," "Ku Klux Klan," "segregation," and "discrimination" early in life. I also remember messages of empowerment that counteracted such evil. Throughout my childhood I observed African American pride and dignity firsthand. Although I was keenly aware of racial differences and the evils of racism, I was also aware of the possibilities of active protest.

My teenage years were more challenging, consumed by a personal struggle for ethnic identity congruence. Others' perceptions of me were critically important. I looked for confirmation of my intelligence, my worth, and my potential for success. I remember many positive and affirming experiences, which buffered me for the more difficult ones of prejudice that I often faced. It was clear that society viewed whites as cleaner, better, and smarter and African Americans as less clean, less intelligent, and of lesser value. Fortunately, the buffers I had, coupled with the excellent models in my immediate and extended family, church, and school, saved me from a life of delusion, depression, and defeat.

Now I am married, with a 6-year-old daughter and a flourishing career. Although I am still reminded of the prestige of whites and the subordination of Blacks every morning when I turn on the television, now I am more confident, secure, and proud. I have learned to appreciate the history of our resilience, despite slavery and oppression, and I recognize our brilliance and significant inventions. I reject demeaning messages and seek out inspiration and truth. I share these truths in my courses,

my writings, and in daily interactions with family and friends. I actively advocate positive social change and participate in acts of protest. Now my own story of survival empowers me. An added benefit is that as I have learned to embrace my own ethnicity, I have a greater appreciation for other cultures of the world.

How have you approached teaching your children about their ethnic heritage?

The task of instilling a healthy sense of ethnic pride in my daughter is a challenging one. At times I wish that I could free her from the evil and the pain. I see her confusion as she notices particular inequalities and tries to understand them. She wants to know why she sees so many white people in magazines, on television, in books, in stores, and in hotels. She ponders the meaning behind her observation of a little white girl who bought a Black "Bratz" doll. She has noticed that her skin is light, compared to mine, and wonders if it's okay. I want to give her both the truth of the harsh realities and the richness of our culture. I surround her with symbols of African American culture, Black art in our home, a host of books with African American characters and names, Black dolls, educational software infused with our cultural flair, Black music (spirituals, blues, gospel, and jazz), and greeting cards with African American faces and expressions. I also expose her to lessons of African American history. We watch documentaries that give accurate portrayals of our people. We participate in the Kwanza celebration (a traditional 7-day emphasis on Africentric value systems that occurs around the Christmas holiday season). We attend plays and concerts that highlight the beauty and uniqueness of our culture. We talk a lot. She asks lots of questions and I try to answer them all. I want her to be as equipped as I am to navigate the dominant society and to appreciate the many cultures of the world. I realize that until she develops a love of her own ethnicity, she will not be able to accept and appreciate those who are different. She must learn to be multicultural and to respect diversity. In fact, that is a lesson for us all!

Q *What can parents and community do to help a child develop a positive ethnic identity? What challenges do you think children from ethnic backgrounds face in their development of identity?*

of the same sex. When experimenting with sexuality, adolescents may have some type of *homosexual experience*. These same-sex experiences may be exploratory and not lead to a *homosexual orientation* in adulthood. For example, in a large national survey, 22 percent of men and 17 percent of women reported having some type of homosexual experience at some point in their lives (Janus & Janus, 1993). But only 9 percent of these men and 5 percent of the women reported they were currently actively engaged in same-sex relationships. As you can see, most of those who had homosexual experiences were not gay or lesbian, or at least did not report being in a homosexual relationship at the time.

Development of a Homosexual Identity. Researchers estimate that 5 percent to 10 percent of adults in the United States identify themselves as gay, lesbian, or bisexual (Patterson, 1995). One study of young homosexual and bisexual men reported that the men experienced feelings of same-sex attraction by the age of 10 and had their first homosexual experiences at around 14 (Savin-Williams, 1995). Some differences between homosexual and heterosexual individuals are apparent during childhood. For example, homosexual men and women report having had cross-gender interests during childhood more often than heterosexuals. Though the process differs in some respects for men versus women, homosexual identity is usually described as developing through several stages (Rub et al., 2006; Troiden, 1988).

■ *Stage 1: Sensitization.* In this stage, which usually occurs before puberty, a child has a general feeling of being different from his or her same-sex peers.

■ *Stage 2: Identity confusion.* Usually first experienced during adolescence, this stage involves a conflict between a teenager's prior self-image and his or her current feelings of same-sex arousal (or lack of heterosexual arousal). Men tend to report same-sex attraction at younger ages than women.

■ *Stage 3: Identity assumption.* This stage often begins during the early 20s. The person defines and accepts himself or herself as homosexual and associates regularly with homosexual peer groups.

■ *Stage 4: Commitment.* This stage begins when the person enters a same-sex love relationship. Women may be less likely to say they are in love with a same-sex partner, despite engaging in lesbian sexual activity (Diamond, 2003; Ruble et al., 2006). The person adopts homosexuality "as a way of life," views a homosexual identity as a valid and satisfying self-identity, and may "come out" to others (Troiden, 1988, p. 110).

One of the myths about homosexuality is what researchers call the *heterosexual assumption*—the idea that all adolescents are heterosexual at first and "discover" their homosexuality only after having several failed relationships with members of the opposite sex (Hunter & Mallon, 2000). For most gay people this assumption couldn't be further from the truth. After extensive interviews with gay and bisexual men aged 17 to 23, for example, Savin-Williams (1995) reported that most of the men experienced homosexual sex first. If they tried heterosexual relations at all, they did so later and with much less frequency. On average these gay and bisexual men had their first homosexual experiences at age 14 and their first heterosexual experiences later. Most did not try heterosexual sex until after they graduated from high school. Across their sexual histories the men reported having sex with an average of eight male partners and only one female partner. Most of the men noticed at an early age that they were attracted to the same sex. Some reported having same-sex attractions from their earliest memories; the average was at 8 years old, although a few had their first male attraction as late as age 16. Individuals obviously differ, but it is clear that in most of these men their attraction to other males emerged at an early age and before any attraction they may have had to the opposite sex.

Causes of Sexual Orientation. Descriptions of different childhood characteristics of heterosexual and homosexual individuals are interesting and indicate that orientations may begin to develop early in life—but they do not explain *why* children have these characteristics. There may be a genetic influence: Twin studies have found higher concordance in homosexuality in identical than in nonidentical twins (Bailey & Pillard, 1991). Prenatal hormone levels may play a role as well. For example, there is a relationship between abnormal prenatal hormone levels and later behavior, personality characteristics, and sexual orientation. Girls exposed to higher than normal prenatal levels of *androgens* (male hormones) tend to show traits and preferences more typical of males, and males exposed to lower than normal levels of androgens show more female-typical patterns and choices (Berenbaum & Snyder, 1995; Meyer-Bahlburg et al., 1995; Ruble et al., 2006). And autopsy studies have found that some areas of the brains of homosexual men are more similar to those of heterosexual women than of heterosexual men; remember, however, that differences in brain structure could result from biological factors or from differences in experience (Byrnes, 2001b; LeVay, 1993; Swaab et al., 1995). And reinforcement, punishment, and observational learning—all aspects of the environment—also play a role.

One interesting theory tries to integrate the findings on biological and environmental influences (Bem, 1996, 2000). According to this "exotic becomes erotic" theory, adolescents begin to see "exotic," or very different, attributes and behaviors as erotic, or sexually attractive. In this process biology exerts an indirect influence through temperamental characteristics such as activity level and aggressiveness. First, in the preschool and elementary school years, children who are by nature active and aggressive enjoy more active, rough, and energetic activities and peers—

The development of sexual attraction is complex. One theory describes the process as moving from a dislike of those we see as different from ourselves (*exotic*) to thinking of them as sexually attractive (*erotic*).

that is, more typically male interests and activities. Children with less active and less aggressive tendencies gravitate toward a more female-typical pattern. The key factor, according to this theory, is not a child's overall activity level and degree of aggressiveness but how different the child feels from his or her own or opposite-sex peers during childhood. During childhood each group will tend to view the other as different ("exotic") and undesirable, and these perceptions will cause arousal. Children interpret this arousal as dislike, discomfort, or sometimes even anger or fear. Puberty then changes things—a lot! At this point youngsters cognitively reinterpret the arousal and gradually come to experience it as attraction. As a result, most adolescents develop sexual attraction toward members of the group they have not identified themselves as belonging to. Notice that this theory tries to explain both heterosexual and homosexual development. The groups that form during early and middle childhood are based not on gender but on traits like activity level and aggressiveness. More active and aggressive girls are more likely to identify with boys early on; less active and less aggressive boys are more likely to identify with girls. Some evidence supports the "exotic becomes erotic" idea. Gender segregation during early and middle childhood is very strong, and young children often describe the opposite sex as undesirable and different ("yucky," to use one 6-year-old's word). And homosexual men and women report higher levels of childhood cross-gender play and preferences, as well as feelings of being different from others of their gender (Bailey & Zucker, 1995; Ruble et al., 2006). However, others have suggested that the process may work in the opposite way. That is, rather than behavioral differences leading to feelings of being different from others of the same sex, it may be that feelings of being different lead to progressively more atypical gender behavior and a homosexual self-concept (Carver et al., 2004; Hammack, 2005; Nicolosi & Byrd, 2002; Ruble et al., 2006). Clearly, the development of sexual identity is complex and more research is needed.

The Experience of Being Gay. Although homosexuality is becoming more widely accepted in today's culture, gay men and lesbians still experience tremendous discrimination and harsh treatment from peers and family. Most homosexuals are keenly aware that heterosexuals view their same-sex attraction as "different" or "deviant." When they reveal their feelings, gay males and lesbians typically suffer intense social isolation (Hunter & Mallon, 2000). The vast majority of lesbian and gay adolescents report that they feel separated and emotionally isolated from their peers (Savin-Williams, 1994). Many are victims of violent physical attacks, and you may be surprised to learn that most of these attacks actually come from members of the teenagers' own families (Hunter, 1990; Savin-Williams, 1994). The verbal and physical abuse that many homosexual students receive from peers, parents, and others is harmful to their sense of self-worth and mental health. Compared to their heterosexual peers, homosexual youths are at a much higher risk of failing a grade in school, skipping school, dropping out of school, running away from home, being kicked out of their own homes, and/or engaging in substance abuse and prostitution. In a review of the research in this area, Savin-Williams (1994) reported that "suicide is the leading cause of death among lesbian, gay male, and bisexual youths, primarily because of the debilitating effects of growing up in a homophobic society" (p. 266). The suicide rate is two to three times higher among homosexual than among heterosexual youths. And when gay and lesbian adolescents try to take their own lives, family conflict is the reason cited most often.

Among gay and lesbian youths who do show positive development, self-acceptance is the best predictor of positive growth (Hershberger & D'Augelli, 1995). A general sense of personal worth and a positive view of their sexual orientation are critical for these adolescents' healthy development. Strong family support is also important: It can provide a buffer against the harsh treatment the adolescent receives at school and elsewhere (Hershberger & D'Augelli, 1995). And many homosexuals report that they find great comfort in having good friends who understand and appreciate their sexual orientations (Hunter & Mallon, 2000).

your perspective

Do you know anyone who has a homosexual orientation? What stage of homosexual identity development is he/she likely in? What family and friendship supports or challenges has this person experienced, and what effect have these experiences had?

Morality

Another aspect of self-understanding that adolescents often struggle with is figuring out a set of personal values and morals to guide their behavior. As you might recall from Chapter 9, Lawrence Kohlberg described three levels of moral reasoning (look back at Table 9.2 to review Kohlberg's levels). While many adolescents continue to think about moral issues at Kohlberg's earlier levels (preconventional and conventional), some will progress to the third level.

postconventional level
The level of moral reasoning at which people base moral reasoning on an understanding of social contract and utility and universal ethical principles.

Kohlberg's Level III.   The highest level of Kohlberg's theory is the **postconventional level,** at which people move beyond social conventions as the basis for moral reasoning. They no longer obey societal rules without at least questioning them. They understand that others can have opinions that are different from their own, and that different opinions can be equally "right." In Stage 5 they obey rules and laws because this helps protect the rights of individuals. Laws (conventions) can be interpreted and changed for greater fairness, however. In Stage 6 individuals reason about moral issues on the basis of self-chosen, abstract ethical principles that they apply to all humans and social systems. People at this stage may choose to disobey laws they believe are immoral rather than violating their ethical principles. They accept the legal or social consequences of breaking the rules. Adolescents certainly grapple with moral issues and some may achieve the postconventional level, but people usually do not attain this level until adulthood, if ever. Kohlberg emphasized that it is the way a person *reasons* about the issue that determines the level of moral reasoning, not the specific choice the person makes.

At Stage 6, the highest level of Lawrence Kohlberg's theory of moral reasoning, a person's thinking about moral issues is based on self-chosen abstract ethical principles that apply to all humans. While Mother Teresa clearly achieved Stage 6, few people appear to function consistently at this level.

your perspective

Think of someone who reasons about moral issues at Kohlberg's Stage 6 or the possible Stage 7. What has helped them develop to these levels? At what level would you place yourself?

Think About Luis . . .

Does Luis' ambivalence about a career reflect a higher level of moral reasoning and concern with abstract ethical issues?

Later Work and Research on Kohlberg's Theory. Kohlberg revised his theory several times. In later work, he said that some aspects of moral development (the levels of reasoning) are universal, whereas others (the particular moral values developed and choices made) depend on the specific social conditions in which a child develops. Kohlberg also acknowledged that Stage 6 is rare in real life; it may be more of a theoretical endpoint than a stage many people actually achieve. However, he also speculated that there may be a seventh stage that goes past the postconventional level. The seventh stage would represent an "ethical orientation arising from . . . existential or religious experience and thinking rather than from moral experience alone" (Kohlberg & Power, 1981, p. 354).

Research has supported several aspects of Kohlberg's theory. For example, Figure 15.2 shows some of the results of a well-known 20-year longitudinal study of Kohlberg's original sample. Participants showed the expected sequence of stages from Stage 1 up to Stage 5, with no evidence of skipping stages or of falling back to lower stages once they had reached a higher level. The correlation between age and stage of moral development was .78, indicating a strong positive relationship. Other studies have verified the predicted sequences across several different cultures (Colby et al., 1983; Snarey et al., 1985; Tietjen & Walker, 1985; Walker, 1989). There is also good support for Kohlberg's ideas about the relationship among cognitive development, perspective-taking skill, and moral development (Krebs & Gillmore, 1982; Selman, 1976; Walker & Hennig, 1997).

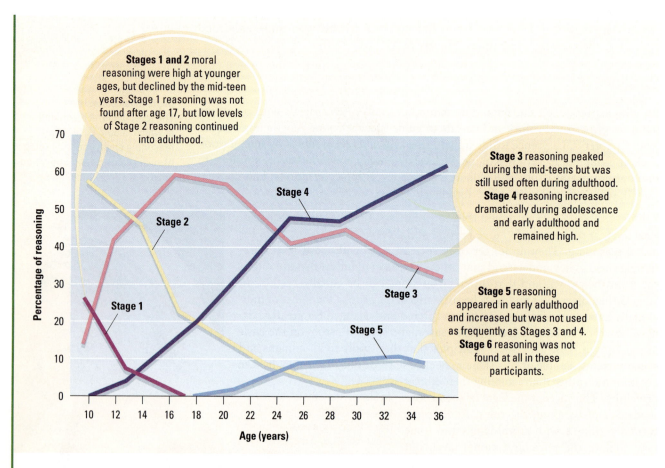

Figure 15.2 • Follow-up Research on Kohlberg's Theory of Moral Development A 20-year follow-up of Lawrence Kohlberg's original sample supported the sequence of stages proposed in his developmental theory of moral reasoning. Ages and stages of moral reasoning showed strong correlations. (Adapted from Colby et al., 1983.)

Other Moral Orientations and Moral Domains. Nevertheless, critics have raised important questions about Kohlberg's model. Cross-cultural studies support his sequence of stages, but they have also found that people in less technologically advanced and more rural cultures move through the stages more slowly and achieve a lower end stage than those in more advanced and urban cultures (Snarey, 1995). These findings are not necessarily a problem for Kohlberg's theory; to the degree that different cultures provide different kinds of experience with moral issues, the theory would expect differences (Kohlberg, 1969; Snarey et al., 1985). However, these results could be due to a bigger issue: a fundamental difference between the moral orientation of these cultures and the orientation Kohlberg's theory reflects. Critics argue that Kohlberg's stages are based on a *justice orientation* of morality. That is, in Kohlberg's theory morality involves justice, individual responsibility, and preservation of individual rights. In some cultures, however, justice is not the factor people emphasize when making moral judgments. For example, some cultures emphasize a morality based on *community,* in which social order, status, and duty to others are key. Others emphasize *divinity,* which involves restraint from sinful acts, duty to a God, and the sanctity of people, objects, or places. Others, like Kohlberg's, emphasize *autonomy* and focus on justice, preservation of individual rights, and fairness (Shweder et al., 1997; Turiel, 2006). Kohlberg's theory (and the dilemmas used to test it) reflect an orientation that may not be relevant in other cultures.

Cultures differ in their moral orientations. Some emphasize community, others divinity, and others autonomy. Kohlberg's stages of moral reasoning may pertain more to some cultures than others.

Therefore, the theory may apply to only a small or unimportant part of moral development in these cultures. If so, then conclusions about the people's levels of moral reasoning or the universality of moral development will be incomplete or even invalid.

A similar criticism has arisen regarding the validity of Kohlberg's model for women. In 1982 Carol Gilligan proposed that women's moral reasoning derives from a *care ethic,* which emphasizes concern for the welfare of others, preservation of interpersonal relationships, and an obligation to take care of others (Gilligan, 1982). Gilligan said that Kohlberg's emphasis on autonomy, justice, and impartial fairness is more consistent with a traditionally male perspective. She argued that Kohlberg's theory does not fully consider the elements that are central to women's moral reasoning. Are her criticisms supported by research? No and yes. There is little evidence of systematic gender differences in studies using Kohlberg's materials and stages. That is, when participants offer reasons involving care for others, the materials do not systematically score these reasons as being at a lower level (Jadack et al., 1995; Jaffee & Hyde, 2000; Walker, 1995). However, a care orientation does exist and females are somewhat more likely to use it, especially when reasoning about personal and real-life issues (Garmon et al., 1996; Wark & Krebs, 1996). But it is not the case that males do not use a care orientation. Instead, it appears that both men and women can and do use both care and justice orientations. It's just that the typical moral issues encountered by each gender may lead men to use a justice orientation more often and women to use a care orientation more often (Clopton & Sorell, 1993; Gilligan & Attanucci, 1988).

Other studies have questioned the degree to which moral reasoning is consistent across contexts. For example, when reasoning about real-life moral dilemmas instead of hypothetical ones, people use a lower level of moral reasoning, report having strong emotions as they think about the dilemma, and often suggest several different strategies for addressing the dilemma (Walker & Hennig, 1997; Walker et al., 1995). Moral reasoning also seems to be different for different types of moral issues such as protection of human rights versus matters of individual choice; in other words, moral reasoning is more domain-specific than Kohlberg believed. And finally, Kohlberg's theory does not consider how emotions such as guilt, fear, shame, sympathy, or empathy affect moral reasoning (Nucci, 1996; Turiel, 2006).

In sum, as with Piaget's theory of cognitive development, it appears that levels of moral reasoning can be influenced significantly by features of the context and are more domain-specific than Kohlberg believed. In addition, as you might have gathered from the discussion so far in this chapter and from Chapters 9 and 12, moral development is multifaceted and includes many aspects of reasoning, emotion, context, and behavior—*reasoning* about what is morally right in a given situation by no means guarantees moral *behavior.*

■ Let's Review . . .

1. Andrew has tried three different majors in college. After carefully considering his interests and skills, he believes he has finally found the best major for him. Andrew is probably in which of Marcia's identity statuses?
    a. foreclosure
    b. moratorium
    c. achieved
    d. diffusion

2. Which of the following best exemplifies the *resolution of conflict* stage of ethnic identity development?
   a. Sage is proud to be a Chippewa tribal member, but she's never really thought much about what it means.
   b. At times, Choong-youl is unhappy about his culture's emphasis on family, especially when his friends want him to do something that his family disapproves of.
   c. Marta is trying to learn more about her ethnic background.
   d. LaToya struggled for a while, but she found ways to blend her cultural values and her professional training as a doctor.

3. Which of the following quotes from a 10-year-old boy is the best example of Daniel Bem's "exotic becomes erotic" theory of the development of sexual orientation?
   a. "Girls really stink."
   b. "Boys really stink."
   c. "Everybody stinks and they always did."
   d. "Girls used to really stink, but they don't seem to stink so much anymore."

4. Research on Kohlberg's stages of moral reasoning has found that _____.
   a. the sequence of stages is consistent across many cultures
   b. the sequence of stages is not valid for cultures that emphasize autonomy and justice.
   c. the sequence of stages applies only to Western cultures
   d. the sequence of stages is evident in men but not in women

5. **True or False:** The care ethic proposed by Gilligan is used by women but not by men.

Answers: 1. c, 2. d, 3. d, 4. a, 5. F

Social Relationships: Family

A second major developmental task that adolescents face is to develop emotional and behavioral **autonomy,** or the ability to be independent in thought and action. Autonomy also involves being able to control impulses and accept responsibility for your own behavior. Developing autonomy can become a source of conflict between teens and parents, especially during early and middle adolescence. As you learned in earlier chapters, parenting style and family structure can have an impact on children's outcomes. In this section, we will discuss the nature and function of conflict during adolescence, as well as research on the characteristics of three family structures we have not yet considered: adoptive, gay or lesbian, and ethnic families.

autonomy
The ability to be independent in thought and action, control impulses, and accept responsibility for one's behavior.

As you study this section, ask yourself these questions:

■ How much conflict is normal for adolescents and their parents to experience? Why do they argue, and how can families cope positively with this conflict?

■ What developmental outcomes are typical for adopted children? What developmental challenges do they face?

■ What academic, social, and emotional outcomes are found for children raised by gay or lesbian parents?

■ What family practices and parenting styles are helpful in promoting strength and resilience in ethnic families? Why are these practices beneficial?

Teens Developing Autonomy: Conflict with Parents

Conflict between Teens and Parents. G. Stanley Hall, often considered the "father" of the study of adolescent development, strongly believed that adolescence was a time of *storm and stress*, during which frequent and intense levels of teen–parent conflict were to be expected. In fact, the prevailing view for many years was that if there was *not* conflict, then something was wrong. Conflict was seen as an indication that the adolescent was developing a unique identity and becoming emotionally and behaviorally independent. Little conflict meant the adolescent was not trying to separate or parents were not allowing separation to happen. And in early research, indeed it seemed that adolescent–parent relationships were characterized by frequent and rather intense conflict (Laursen & Collins, 1994; Steinberg, 2001).

your perspective

How frequent and how intense was the conflict you and your parents experienced? How did your family cope with it, and how might you have dealt with it more positively?

On closer examination, however, the story seems more complicated—and fortunately more positive. Recent research indicates that stormy and stressful encounters between parents and teens are not the norm. Much of the early research was based on families seeking mental health services. When *nonclinical* samples were studied, 75 percent of teens reported positive relationships with parents; most who reported poorer relationships had experienced family difficulties well before adolescence (Rutter et al., 1976). One study interviewed teens about conflicts with their parents on three different randomly selected days. On average, these teens reported conflicts with their parents only about once every three days (Montemayor, 1982). Girls report more conflicts than boys, and both report more conflicts with moms than with dads; they also report spending more time with moms than with dads. As teens get older, the rate of conflict with moms decreases more than the rate with dads (Collins & Laursen, 2004).

However, it would be inaccurate to say that there is *no* conflict during this period of development. Adolescents and their parents do disagree, but they typically argue about everyday issues rather than major issues such as educational importance, religious values, sexual activity, or drug use (Gecas & Seff, 1990; Montemayor, 1982). Teens and parents most often argue about things like clothes and music, keeping the teen's bedroom clean enough and doing household chores, curfew and bedtimes, appropriate age for dating, and choice of leisure activities. Whether teens will argue about parents' rules depends on how the teen views the issue involved. For example, teens are more likely to resist their parents' rules when they see the issue as one of a personal choice (such as what clothes to wear or how clean to keep their rooms) than when they believe the issue involves something parents have a right to regulate, as when a moral or safety issue is involved (such as knowing when the teen is expected to be home or whether to drink alcohol). When the expectations of either the teen or the parents are violated, conflict is more likely to occur (Steinberg, 2001).

Overall, the rate of conflict declines as adolescents move from early through middle and later adolescence, perhaps in part because parents and teens spend progressively less time together. The emotional intensity of the conflicts, however, increases from early to middle adolescence; teens at these ages are encountering new social situations as well as many physical changes, but at the same time are striving to become more autonomous and often show heightened emotional responses (Laursen et al., 1998). There are cultural differences in adolescent–parent conflict. For example, conflict is reported more frequently in North American and European families than in families from Asian countries. As you might expect, immigration to a different culture also impacts teen–parent conflict, with increases in conflict between parents attempting to maintain their original cultural values while their teens adopt the values of the new country (Collins & Laursen, 2004).

Much of the focus in this area of research has been on what the adolescent experiences. But some authors note that "the popular image of the individual sulking in the wake of a family argument may be a more accurate portrayal of the emotional state of the *parent,* rather than the teenager" (Steinberg, 2001, p. 5). Many teens seem to recover rather quickly from quarrels while parents, especially mothers, see the conflicts as much more meaningful and involving more important issues—so moms tend to be more concerned about disagreements. In addition, many parents of teens are entering middle age and are coping with physical and emotional issues that often arise during this period of life. Finally, parents may have difficulty coping with the fact that their teens no longer view them as positively as they did when the teens were younger. In teens' eyes, parents become astoundingly less capable and less intelligent—and teens are not very skilled at hiding their change of opinion from their parents (Steinberg, 2001).

Many teens recover quickly from arguments with parents but parents see the conflicts as much more meaningful and involving more important issues.

Dealing Effectively with Adolescent–Parent Conflict. So if some conflict is inevitable, how should parents deal with it? The first thing to remember is that even though conflict is not a pleasant thing, it can have some positive effects such as improved reasoning and conflict resolution skills, increased understanding of others' perspectives, and enhanced identity development. In fact, adolescents who experience moderate levels of conflict with their parents perform better in school and have fewer overall adjustment difficulties than *either* those who report higher levels of conflict or no conflict at all (Adams & Laursen, 2001; Collins & Laursen, 2004; Kaplan, 2004). Second, just because teenagers argue with their parents from time to time does not mean they do not have a close relationship overall. Indeed, in families with healthy and secure attachment between parents and teens, conflict serves the positive function of helping the family talk about issues that need attention, revise expectations, and renegotiate rules to allow increasing autonomy to the teen within appropriately changing boundaries. This type of interaction can have the effect of actually improving the overall relationship (Collins & Laursen, 2004).

A key in effectively handling conflict and achieving positive and productive outcomes is something you read about in Chapter 9—*authoritative parenting.* As you might recall, this parenting style involves developmentally appropriate expectations and firm, consistent limits within the context of warmth, involvement, and supportiveness. During adolescence, a third dimension also seems to become important: **psychological autonomy granting,** or encouraging adolescents to develop their own individual opinions and beliefs (Steinberg, 2001). This style of parenting is associated with a number of positive social, cognitive, and behavioral outcomes as well as positive identity development. The effects have been found for both males and females and across a number of ethnic groups (Collins & Laursen, 2004; Steinberg, 2001). Unfortunately, most parent–teen conflicts are resolved by submission (one party giving in) or disengagement (the topic is dropped and one party leaves the conflict) instead of through compromise (Laursen & Collins, 1994). Developing a more authoritative parenting style might help families deal more constructively with conflict as their teens strive for autonomy.

> **Think About Luis . . .**
> *Does the conflict between Luis and his parents seem atypical in any way? How can they deal with it constructively?*

psychological autonomy granting
A dimension of parenting that involves encouraging adolescents to develop their own individual opinions and beliefs.

Family Structures

Adopted Adolescents. Millions of adolescents grow up in adoptive families, whether adopted by relatives, stepparents, nonrelated adults, or adults of a different country or ethnicity. Adopted individuals do much better on many psychological, educational, social, and emotional measures than those in residential institutions, long-term foster care, or returned from foster care to parents who are unable or unwilling to parent effectively (Morgan, 1998; Triseliotis & Hill, 1990). Greater financial resources and stability, higher-quality parenting, highly motivated parents, significant parental emotional involvement and support, and a clear long-term parental commitment help adopted adolescents develop a stronger sense of identity and enable them to take advantage of available financial and community resources. Children in transracial adoptions, in which parents of one racial group adopt a child of a different race, are the same as children adopted by same-race parents in terms of racial self-identity, general adjustment, or self-esteem (Baden, 2002; Feigelman, 2000; Silverman & Feigelman, 1990; Vroegh, 1997).

Most adopted individuals adjust well and function normally. However, they do face special challenges and are at greater risk for negative outcomes than biological offspring, particularly when the problems become more severe (Miller et al., 2000). Adopted children and adolescents are more likely than others to be referred for psychological treatment and more likely to show aggressive and delinquent behavior, learning disabilities, drug use, and school adjustment problems. In general, adopted children have greater difficulty when they are older (e.g., over 5 years of age) at the time of adoption, perhaps more because of negative early experiences than because of adoption. Adopted boys seem to have more difficulty than adopted girls. Sometimes problems do not emerge during infancy or early childhood but seem to emerge as children move through middle childhood and adolescence. However, adopted children show better scores on measures such as participation in academic clubs, prosocial behavior, self-reports of social problems, and self-reported withdrawal. The majority of adopted individuals report being satisfied with their adoptive status and report feeling emotionally attached to their adoptive parents (Brodzinsky, 1990, 1993; Howe, 1998; Kirschner, 1995; Miller et al., 2000; Morgan, 1998; Sharma et al., 1996, 1998; Stams et al., 2000; Triseliotis, 2000).

Families with Lesbian or Gay Parents. Researchers estimate that as many as 14 million children and adolescents in the United States have lesbian or gay parents (Patterson, 1992). The majority were born while their biological parents were in heterosexual marriages. An increasing number of lesbians, however, are using donor insemination to conceive biological children or are adopting or providing foster care for children. More gay men are also adopting children, providing foster care, or fathering their own biological children. Does exposure to a gay or lesbian lifestyle disrupt the adolescent's developing sense of identity or cause any other negative developmental outcomes? Charlotte Patterson (1992) conducted a thorough review of the research and concluded that "not a single study has found children of gay or lesbian parents to be disadvantaged in any significant respect relative to children of heterosexual parents" (p. 1036). Recent work has also found that those with lesbian parents are well adjusted and show positive relationships with their parents (Bos et al., 2005; Golombok et al., 2003; MacCallum & Golombok, 2004). They are no different from children raised by heterosexual parents in activity preferences, interests, popularity, social skills, occupational goals, sociability, hyperactivity, emotional difficulty, behavior problems, moral maturity, or measures of intelligence.

In her review, Patterson found that children and adolescents raised by lesbian or gay parents showed no disturbances in gender identity. Compared to those raised by heterosexual parents, they were just as happy with the gender to which they belonged and had no wish to be the opposite sex. Sexual orientation also did not differ. Children raised by gay or lesbian parents were not more likely to become homosexuals themselves. This finding is particularly interesting in view of the fact that these adolescents received significant portions of their genes from gay or lesbian parents and grew up in environments created in part by those same parents.

Finally, although courts often award child custody on the condition that the homosexual parent *not* live with his or her romantic partner, the research evidence actually shows advantages for children whose gay or lesbian parents live with committed partners (Patterson, 1992). One study documented higher self-esteem in daughters of lesbian mothers living with partners than in girls whose lesbian mothers lived alone (Huggins, 1989). Mothers in lesbian partnerships are more likely to arrange male role models for their children. Lesbian couples who conceived children

TABLE 15.2 Growth in U.S. Ethnic Diversity 1990–2000 (Figures in Millions)

RACE OR LATINO ORIGIN	1990	2000	PERCENT INCREASE FROM 1990	GROWTH RATE VS. WHITE GROWTH RATE
Whites (non-Latino)*	188.9	194.6	3	—
Latinos (of any race)*	22.4	35.3	58	19.3 times faster
African Americans	30.0	34.7	16	5.3 times faster
Asian Americans and Pacific Islanders	7.3	10.6	45	15 times faster
Native Americans and Alaskans	2.0	2.5	25	8.3 times faster
Other races	9.8	15.4	57	19 times faster
More than one race	NA	6.8	—	—

*The total U.S. population in the year 2000 was 281.4 million. The U.S. Census considers race separately from Latino origin. In the 2000 Census, 48 percent of Latinos identified themselves as white. In this table we present the number of whites who did not identify themselves as Latino (estimated by subtracting 48 percent of the Latinos totals from the 1990 and 2000 census total for whites). The 2000 Census was the first to allow respondents to identify themselves as belonging to more than one race (e.g., white *and* Asian).
(U.S. Census Bureau, 2001.)

by donor insemination showed as much awareness of parenting skills as heterosexual mothers and more awareness than heterosexual fathers, and both lesbian partners were equally involved in the child's activities (Flaks et al., 1995; MacCallum & Golombok, 2004; Vanfraussen et al., 2003). In short, it is evident that lesbian and gay parents can and do provide healthy living environments for children.

Ethnically Diverse Families. Ethnic minority families are the fastest growing segment of the U.S. population, as shown in Table 15.2. In earlier decades most of the research on family ethnicity focused on negative factors and outcomes. As you are no doubt aware, the rates of poverty, crime, homicide, incarceration, and other such problems are higher among minority groups than among white European Americans. Researchers compared ethnically diverse families to white families and emphasized things that were "going wrong" in minority-group families. This **cultural deficit perspective** assumed negative outcomes were due to ways in which minority families were not "measuring up" to the majority population. Recently, however, researchers have learned that many of the negative outcomes associated with minority families are due more to poverty and difficulties in the neighborhoods that many minority families live in than to ethnic culture itself (Caspi et al., 2000; Leventhal & Brooks-Gunn, 2000; McLoyd, 1998; Pinderhughes et al., Zelli, 2000). A more positive approach to looking at minority families, the **strength and resilience perspective,** has emerged (Parke & Buriel, 2006). Researchers are now exploring ways in which minority families have survived in spite of historical patterns of racism, bigotry, and inequality.

What characteristics of ethnic families have contributed to their strength and resilience? Table 15.3 on page 534 summarizes some of the characteristics of several ethnic groups identified by researchers. One important factor seems to be the central role that the family often plays, particularly the extended family. For example, Latino parents teach children that their personal identity is inseparable from the larger identity of the family (*la familia*). In many ethnic groups, people value family and group cooperation over competition and personal achievement. Researchers have noted that African American families tend to show a strong sense of family and family obligation, fluid household boundaries (and great willingness to have relatives move into and out of the household), frequent interaction with relatives, frequent extended-family

cultural deficit perspective
Research perspective that assumed the problems associated with minority group families were due to the ways these families were not "measuring up" to the standards of majority white families.

strength and resilience perspective
Research perspective that explores ways that minority families have survived in spite of historical patterns of racism, bigotry, and inequality.

your perspective
Think about a family you know who fosters strength and resilience in their teens. What parenting practices do they use? How do these practices help their children become more resilient?

TABLE 15.3 Sources of Ethnic Groups' Strength and Resilience

ETHNIC GROUP	REFERS TO	FAMILY FACTORS	CULTURAL TRADITIONS
Latino	Primarily immigrants from Mexico, Central and South America, Puerto Rico, Cuba, and descendents of Spanish explorers	Personal identity connected to family identity Emphasis on extended-family systems First few years following immigration often spent living with extended-family members	Cooperation Group harmony Respect Obedience and respect for elders Traditional gender roles
African American	Primarily descendents of slaves originally from West African tribes	Emphasis on extended-family systems Strong sense of family and family obligation Frequent interactions with relatives Grandmothers play important role in moral and religious focus, provide sense of family solidarity Emphasis on strict discipline, especially among working-class and poor families	West African traditions of spirituality, harmony, and communalism Emphasis on ethnic pride
Asian American	Immigrants from 28 countries or ethnic groups from Far East and Southeast Asia, including India, China, Philippines, Vietnam, Cambodia, Laos, Japan, Korea, Pakistan, Thailand, Hmong	Father dominant but emotionally distant Emphasis on *chiao shun* and *guan* styles of strict discipline among some groups	Religious traditions of respect for elders and family harmony Obedience and loyalty to parents Family needs placed above individual needs Traditional gender roles
Native American and Alaskan	Numerous peoples including 450 different tribal units with more than 100 different languages, among them Cherokee, Navajo, Chippewa, Sioux, Pueblos, Aleuts, Eskimos	Emphasis on extended-family systems, communal village structure Grandparents play important official and symbolic role Prior government policies disrupted family structure, producing lack of cultural and family role models	Cooperation Partnership Respect for elders Increasing emphasis on ethnic pride

(Boykin & Toms, 1985; Chao, 1994; Parke & Buriel, 2006; Reed, 1982; Trimble & Medicine, 1993.)

gatherings for holidays and special occasions, and a strong system of mutual aid and support among family members (Hatchett & Jackson, 1999; Parke & Buriel, 2006). Asian American families teach their children to be obedient and loyal to their parents and to place the family above individual needs. Extended-family systems have also been crucial in helping Native Americans cope with the discrimination and many forms of adversity they have faced. Even when living in urban areas, Native Americans often organize around several households of relatives that operate like a communal village (Parke & Buriel, 2006).

An emphasis on strict discipline is also characteristic of many ethnic groups. Both working-class African American parents and Latino families tend to rely on physical punishment, power assertion, and obedience in their efforts to control their children (Parke & Buriel, 2006). However, this approach to discipline correlates more with poverty and dangerous neighborhoods than with ethnicity—lower-income whites also tend to use strict authoritarian discipline, while middle-class African American parents tend to use a more authoritative approach. Lower-income parents may use physical discipline to try to protect their children in dangerous communities and as a way to emphasize the importance of performing well in school (Kelley et al., 1993; Parke & Buriel, 2006).

Mothers in China are more restrictive and controlling than Euro-American mothers (Chiu, 1987). As Chinese Americans adapt to life in the United States, they tend to take on parenting styles that lie between these two extremes. In her cross-cultural studies, Chao (1994, 2001) has pointed out that the strict control used by Chinese parents is not the same as the harsh and punitive style used by authoritarian parents in the United States. Chinese parents practice the concepts of *chiao shun* (meaning "training" or "teaching") and *guan* ("to govern" or "to care for or love"). They model appropriate behaviors for their children, and they govern their children firmly but with great care and love. Whereas harsh and punitive parenting (the authoritarian style) correlates with poor school performance in Euro-American students, children raised in the strict *chiao shun* and *guan* style used by many Asian American parents show superior school performance (Chao, 1994; Dornbusch et al., 1987). This type of cross-cultural research reminds us that we cannot always view other cultures through the same lenses that we develop using Euro-American research samples.

A sense of ethnic pride can help buffer some of the hardships that ethnic children often face. Many African American families foster ethnic pride in their children as a way to help them confront the discrimination they will face in U.S. society (Parke & Buriel, 2006). In a national study of African American families, the children who were eventually more successful and upwardly mobile were the ones whose parents had emphasized ethnic pride, the importance of self-development, and an awareness of the racial barriers that they would face (Bowman & Howard, 1985). Similarly, Native Americans are increasingly working to build ethnic pride in their children, both to reconnect with the traditions of their cultures and to support their children's development. We all benefit by recognizing the unique strengths demonstrated by cultures and ethnic groups other than our own.

Asian American parents tend to be strict, but they are generally caring and loving rather than harsh and punitive. Their *chiao shun* and *guan* styles are linked to superior school performance in their children.

Think About Luis ...

What parenting practices might Luis' parents try to help their son develop resilience? How might these practices differ if this family were of a different ethnic background?

■ Let's Review ...

1. It is normal for adolescent–parent conflict to _____.
    a. be frequent and intense
    b. decline in frequency and emotional intensity from early to middle to later adolescence
    c. be more upsetting for moms than for adolescents
    d. occur more often over moral and safety issues than over issues of personal choice

2. Which of the following is *not* true of adopted children?
    a. Most adopted children adjust well and are emotionally attached to their adoptive parents.
    b. Adopted children are at greater risk than nonadopted children for many negative outcomes.
    c. Children who were older when adopted are at greater risk for poorer outcomes than those adopted at a younger age.
    d. Transracial adoptees have more difficulty with identity development than adoptees with same-race parents.

Social Relationships: Peers

intimacy
An emotional attachment to another person that involves sharing important personal information and trusting others to hold confidences and be supportive.

A third important developmental task for adolescents is to develop **intimacy,** both within the context of friendships and in romantic relationships. Intimacy is an emotional attachment to another person and involves sharing important personal information and trusting one another to hold confidences and be supportive. Earlier, we described the development of sexual orientation, but how do adolescents learn the skills needed to make and maintain intimate relationships? What impact do peers have on teens' behavior? And when are adolescents ready to move from nonromantic friendship groups to dating in couples? In this section, we will discuss the nature of friendships and dating during the teenage years.

As you study this section, ask yourself these questions:

- Why are friendships important during adolescence? How do adolescents develop the skills needed for intimate romantic and nonromantic relationships?

- What are cliques and crowds, and how do they affect adolescents' development?

- What influence does peer pressure have on adolescent behavior?

- How do adolescents spend their leisure time?

Friends and Peers in Adolescence

Intimate friends share their most personal thoughts and feelings. They trust each other to keep personal secrets, and they use each other as a safe base for exploring issues and problems that they may not discuss with anyone else, including parents, teachers, and close siblings. During adolescence, intimacy and self-disclosure distinguish best friends from other friends. Intimacy emerges in early adolescence for girls but only in later adolescence for most boys (Berndt, 1986). Adolescents spend twice as much time with their friends (outside of the classroom) as with their parents, siblings, and other adults (Csikszentmihalyi & Larson, 1984). As Savin-Williams and Berndt (1990) put it:

> Adolescents typically report that they enjoy their activities with friends more than any other. With friends, they feel that they are understood and can fully be themselves. Friends spend much time together simply talking about themselves, other adolescents, or events in the wider world. They relax, joke, watch television or videos, and participate in sports. These moments of enjoyment and companionship contribute to a generational sense of belonging with others who are respected and liked. (p. 279)

In their review of the research literature on adolescent friendships and peer relations, Savin-Williams and Berndt (1990) found that adolescents who have close and supportive friendships tend to have higher self-esteem, to understand other people's feelings better, and to be more generally popular among their peers. In school they are better behaved, receive higher grades, and score higher on tests of intelligence. Adolescents who do not have close friendships don't fare as well (Rubin, Bukowski, & Parker, 2006). Keep in mind, however, that these findings are correlational. In other words, we don't know the direction of the causal link between friendships and adolescent development. Do close and supportive friendships facilitate social and academic growth, or do adolescents who are more socially and academically skilled attract more close friends?

Beginning in adolescence, our closest friends are the people we can trust and with whom we share our personal thoughts and feelings. A shared sense of intimacy bonds best friends together.

How do teens develop the skills needed to start and maintain intimate friendships and, later, romantic relationships? One view is based on the attachment research that you read about in Chapter 6. According to Alan Sroufe and his colleagues, children internalize the significant relationships they have early in life and use those early experiences as a basis for understanding what it means to have an intimate relationship (Hazan & Shaver, 1987; Roisman et al., 2005; Sroufe et al., 2005). A different view emphasizes the role of peers more strongly. Harry Stack Sullivan (1953) says that youngsters develop *chumships*, or close nonromantic relationships, over the course of late childhood and early adolescence. It is within these chumships that teens learn the skills needed to have successful intimacy such as loyalty, trustworthiness, honesty, and supportiveness. After these skills are developed to some degree, teens begin to shift the focus of their intimacy to romantic relationships. The chumships allow young teens to "practice" intimacy without the added element of romantic attraction. Perhaps attachment relations in early childhood set the stage for the development of intimacy and serve as a foundation for early nonromantic relationships, and chumships both modify teens' understanding of intimacy and help them develop specific relationship skills.

> ### Think About Luis . . .
> *In what ways have Luis' family and friends helped him develop the skills he needs to develop intimate friendships?*

When it comes to forming friendships, similarity is still the rule in adolescence. Adolescents who become close friends tend to share similar attitudes; educational aspirations; religious and political orientations; and patterns of drinking, drug use, and delinquency (Rubin et al., 2006; Savin-Williams & Berndt, 1990). As we mentioned earlier, shared intimacy is an important feature of adolescent friendships. Strong bonds form when intimate friends share personal stories and help one other cope with problems. Although it can be difficult to maintain friendships as adolescents move through the transitions from middle school to high school and later into college or work, many lifelong friends trace their relationships back to their adolescent years.

Cliques and Crowds

Another aspect of adolescent peer relations is the emergence of *cliques* and *crowds*. **Cliques** are small groups, usually including three to nine friends, who hang out together on a voluntary basis (Rubin et al., 2006). Friends in cliques are almost always of the same sex and race. By the age of 11, most children report being a member of a clique, and this social group forms the context for most of their peer interactions (Crockett et al., 1984). Most cliques are closed circles—members often put down or exclude people outside their clique, although they understand that excluding peers is sometimes wrong and harmful (Horn, 2003). Between ages 11 and 18, however, bonds within individual cliques loosen and adolescents begin associating simultaneously with several loosely defined cliques (Rubin et al., 2006).

Crowds are larger groups made up of individuals who have similar reputations or share primary attitudes or activities (B. Brown, 2004). When asked to describe the different groups of students that make up their schools, teenagers typically identify crowds such as *jocks, brains, nerds, druggies, goths, populars, normals, nobodies,*

cliques
Small groups, of usually three to nine friends, who spend time together on a voluntary basis.

crowds
Groups of adolescent peers who have similar reputations or share primary attitudes or activities.

your perspective

Describe the different "crowds" that you recall from your high school. Which crowd did you fit best with? What effect did your crowd have on your identity?

and *loners*. Specific names for crowds vary across geographic locations and schools, but they tend to fall into these general categories.

Individual students usually can't pick their favorite crowd to join. Instead, they acquire crowd "membership" based on stereotyped perceptions held across the school population. Your crowd designation has to do mostly with what other people think about you and who they think you are like. In one study researchers asked students to guess which crowd their peers had assigned them to. Although 75 percent of the "jocks" and "druggies" correctly guessed their crowd assignment, only 15 percent of the "nobodies" and "loners" were accurate (Brown et al., 1987). In many schools students see members of ethnic minority groups as separate crowds—the Hispanic crowd, the African American crowd, and so on (Brown & Klute, 2003). Perhaps because of the prejudice and discrimination they experience, ethnic minority students may feel more comfortable associating with other members of their racial or ethnic group. In other cases, perhaps ethnic groups are segregated because of cultural differences in behavior, dress, religion, or other characteristics.

Research has shown a link between self-esteem and membership in particular crowds. In one midwestern community, students in junior and senior high schools rank-ordered five crowds that they identified in their schools (Brown & Lohr, 1987). Most admired were the *jocks*, followed (in order) by *populars*, *normals*, *druggies/ toughs*, and *nobodies*. Not surprisingly, self-esteem scores were highest among students who were jocks and populars, moderate among normals and druggies/toughs, and lowest for nobodies. For outsiders (students who were not associated with any of the crowds), self-esteem depended on how much they cared about being in a crowd. Self-esteem was relatively high among outsiders who gave little importance to crowd membership, but it was low among students who wanted to—but didn't— belong to a crowd.

Just as clique memberships loosen by mid-adolescence, crowd affiliations begin to soften by the end of high school. Researchers have commented on the cohesiveness that often develops among high school seniors (Rubin et al., 2006). Differences and animosities seem to fade a bit as members of the different crowds reflect back on their years together and look ahead to what awaits them after they leave school.

Peer Pressure, Delinquent Behavior, and Aggression

Conformity to peer pressure is highest during early adolescence, peaking around age 14. Parents often worry that peers will influence their teens to do things they shouldn't, like drink alcohol or use drugs. After all, as you learned in Chapter 13, the best predictor of drug and alcohol use is having friends who do these things. Another concern is that some adolescent crowds can put pressure on peers to engage in violence or aggression (Espelage et al., 2003). A recent report from the U.S. surgeon general indicated that having antisocial or delinquent peers was one of the strongest risk factors for adolescent violence (U.S. Department of Health and Human Services, 2001). But is peer pressure to blame for delinquent behavior? Involvement in delinquent activity is relatively common during adolescence (especially for boys), and most delinquent acts such as stealing or trespassing are committed by middle adolescent boys in groups. Further, boys who are more autonomous compared to their peers are less likely to engage in delinquent acts—so it seems that peer pressure does play a role.

your perspective

What are examples of both positive and negative peer pressure you experienced during adolescence?

Fortunately, most adolescents who begin delinquent behavior during adolescence do not continue it. Some, however, show a **life-course persistent pattern** in which they engage in antisocial and delinquent behavior from childhood and continuing into adulthood (Moffitt, 1993). Peer pressure is not the main factor for these adolescents' behavior. They have several things working against them from an early age, including a difficult temperament, subtle cognitive deficits, poor impulse control, poor parenting, high-conflict home environments (such as the coercive homes you read about in Chapter 12), and dangerous neighborhoods. This combination leads to academic and behavior problems.

life-course persistent pattern
A pattern of antisocial and delinquent behavior that begins in childhood and continues into adulthood.

At greatest risk are adolescents who are aggressive and also unpopular. These teens tend to be rejected by nonaggressive peers, so they often seek the company of other aggressive and rejected adolescents, and sometimes form groups that further encourage violence and aggression. Most studies of delinquent and aggressive behavior focus on boys; the few that examine girls' delinquent behavior find similar factors to be involved (Carroll et al., 2006; Dodge et al., 2006; Farrington, 2004; Moffitt et al., 1996). Juvenile delinquency is a difficult problem with no easy answers. The number of juveniles, particularly girls, entering the justice system has increased significantly over the past decade. To learn more about how the justice system helps youths, see the Professional Perspective box called "Career Focus: Meet a Juvenile Probation Officer."

The good news about peer pressure is that, for most adolescents, the strongest pressures actually tend to be positive. Adolescents claim that the greatest peer pressures they experience are to get along with others, get good grades, graduate from high school, and attend college (B. Brown, 1990). While some students do commit delinquent acts

a professional perspective

Career Focus: Meet a Juvenile Probation Officer

Nancy Magowan
Philadelphia, Pennsylvania
Juvenile probation officer in the Family Division of the Common Pleas Court, Special Offender Unit

What are the most common offenses that youths supervised by the Special Offender Unit commit?
The Special Offender Unit supervises juveniles who are placed in a residential treatment facility for mental therapy and treatment. The offenses include assault, theft, robbery, auto theft, burglary, controlled substance offenses, criminal conspiracy, and sexual offenses such as rape, indecent assault, indecent exposure, and involuntary deviate sexual intercourse.

What do juvenile probation officers do to help youths avoid future offenses?
Once the juvenile completes treatment and is recommended for discharge from the facility, we develop a Probation Supervision Plan. The plan holds the youth accountable for his/her actions, offers some restoration to the victim, protects the community, and develops the youth's competencies. I monitor the youth's progress and success. I often connect the youth with community-based support programs that provide educational or vocational schooling, substance abuse treatment, individual or family therapy, and employment services. We customize the plans to meet the needs of each youth.

What do you think is the most important thing that can be done to prevent behavior problems, violence, and crime among youths?
Preventing youth from entering the juvenile justice system is an ongoing and difficult task. The breakdown of the family seems to affect so many. Family support, guidance, and encouragement are key in a youth's ability to develop positive and appropriate social skills and self-esteem to adjust to the challenges of adolescence and life. Communication among parents, schools, and support programs is essential to maintain continuity and encouragement for the young people in our society in their efforts to succeed. Empowering youth with education and emphasizing their strengths will help reduce the juvenile crime rate.

What education and training is needed to work in your occupation?
After I got my bachelor's degree in Administration of Justice from Penn State University and did an internship at the court where I work now, most of my training was on the job. Additional training and education (40-plus hours) is provided and required by the courts on a yearly basis. My only regret regarding education is not being bilingual.

Q *What delinquent behavior should families watch for that might indicate the beginnings of delinquent behaviors? What can parents and communities do to prevent delinquent behaviors and encourage adolescents to focus on positive activities.*

and behave aggressively, many do not. And adolescents are just as concerned by aggressiveness in their peers as adults are—after all, they are the most frequent victims of delinquent and aggressive behavior (Dodge et al., 2006). Since the tragic school shootings at Columbine High School in Colorado and other places across the country, communities and schools have struggled to confront the issue of aggression and school safety. All agree that something must be done, but there is no consensus on what steps to take. For more information about this issue, read the Social Policy Perspective box called "How Should We Deal with Aggressive Students?"

From Gender Segregation to Dating

Although most cliques form among same-sex peers in early adolescence, many relationships do form across the sexes by middle adolescence. The classic study of the transition from gender segregation to dating is a naturalistic field study that Dexter Dunphy (1963) performed in Sydney, Australia. Dunphy observed that young adolescents (around age 13) congregated in same-sex cliques containing between three and nine close friends. Then group-to-group interactions began to occur between male and

In early adolescence, members of the same larger crowd begin pairing off and dating. Cross-sex intimacy (the ability to share personal thoughts and feelings with a member of the opposite sex) typically develops faster in girls than in boys.

female cliques. As you probably recall from your own adolescence, these interactions often begin as teasing and chasing. Eventually, however, they evolve into relationships that are more cooperative. In Dunphy's study the cross-sex interactions occurred almost exclusively between cliques in the same larger crowd (between male jocks and female jocks, for example), so the cross-sex relationships were among adolescents who had similar attitudes, values, and economic status. When asked to choose partners in social situations, adolescents picked members of their own clique most often. They chose other members of their crowd (not in their clique) less frequently. Only rarely (6 percent of the time) did they select partners outside their crowds. In the next phase, the higher-status members of each clique began heterosexual dating. Gradually, the boundaries between cliques dissolved as more members began dating. Now the most recognizable social unit was the crowd, in which some members were dating and some were not. By late adolescence (ages 18 to 21), Dunphy reported, crowd boundaries also began to dissolve as more couples paired off for dating. This pattern echoes the trends we described earlier, with clique boundaries softening earlier in adolescence and crowds blending by high school graduation.

The trends Dunphy (1963) found in Australia seem to apply worldwide. For example, researchers asked Israeli students to rate the degree of intimacy (sharing of personal thoughts and feelings) they perceived in their closest same- and opposite-sex friendships (Sharabany et al., 1981). Intimacy among same-sex friends remained constant across adolescence, but intimacy among opposite-sex friends increased substantially over adolescence. Overall, girls reported more intimacy than boys, and the intimacy girls reported in their opposite-sex relationships increased faster than the opposite-sex intimacy reported by boys. By late adolescence the intimacy of cross-sex couples was comparable to the intimacy shared between same-sex friends. As you can see from these studies, children share their personal thoughts and feelings first with the friends who are most like them—their closest same-sex friends. Later, adolescents gradually begin sharing intimacy with opposite-sex friends, first within the safe confines of common cliques and crowds, and later in individualistic dating patterns.

Leisure Time in Adolescence

Adolescence brings a shift from the concrete and realistic thought of the grade school child to the more hypothetical and idealistic thought characteristic of the formal operational stage. In some sense this represents a return to the fantasy of earlier years, but this time adolescents use their imaginations to speculate about how the world could be or should be (Hughes, 1999). Movies, TV, music, video games, and surfing the Internet (particularly instant messaging programs) are popular; they give

How Should We Deal with Aggressive Students?

BURLINGTON, WISCONSIN (November 1998). Five teens were arrested and expelled after their plans to kill school staff and 12 children were reported to police. The boys confessed; three received probation and two were ordered to undergo psychiatric treatment (Kertscher, 1999; Kertscher et al., 1998). A similar incident, thwarted by a friend who contacted police, recently occurred in Green Bay, Wisconsin (Phelps, 2006).

LITTLETON, COLORADO (April 1999). Eric Harris and Dylan Klebold entered Columbine High School carrying two shotguns, a rifle, a pistol, and numerous bombs. They killed 12 students and one teacher, and seriously wounded about 23 others before killing themselves (Luzadder & Vaughan, 1999).

Casenovia, Wisconsin (September 2006). Weston Schools principal John Klang was shot and killed by Eric Hainstock, a 15-year-old ninth grader at the school. Hainstock was reportedly upset over being teased by classmates, as well as for being reprimanded for behavior problems and having tobacco in school (Principal Killed . . .", 2006).

BEDFORD, TEXAS (March 2002). A high school junior was expelled from school after a guard found a 10-inch bread knife in the bed of his truck. The student says the knife fell from a box of his grandmother's belongings that he was taking to a thrift shop ("High School Expels Junior," 2002).

Reports like these have become all too common over the last decade; violence in schools seems to have reached epidemic levels. But how frequent are violent behavior and crime among children and youth? In reality, the rate of many of the most violent school crimes actually decreased across the 1990s. By 2000 fewer students reported carrying a weapon to school, and students reported feeling more secure at school. Children are far more likely to be victims of crime when they are *not* at school (Kaufman et al., 2001, 2000). However, the rate of threats and injuries with weapons on school property remained constant across the 1990s, as did the number of physical fights not involving weapons. And although horrifying incidents like the Columbine massacre are rare, even one such tragedy is too many.

How should communities and schools deal with aggressive students? The majority of public schools in the United States have adopted some form of *zero tolerance policy* toward firearms, violence, alcohol, and drugs. These policies mandate a specific punishment (often expulsion) for specific offenses. Unfortunately, critics argue, in practice these well-intentioned policies often use suspension and expulsion to punish both serious and trivial incidents. The policies are used inconsistently across schools and disproportionately affect minority students; compared to white students, black students are two to three times more likely to be suspended, and black students receive harsher punishments for less serious offenses (Skiba & Knesting, 2001). Above all, critics say, there is little evidence that zero tolerance policies are effective in reducing student aggression—and they may actually increase students' risk of dropping out of school and engaging in juvenile delinquency (Browne et al., 2001; Skiba & Knesting, 2001). Other approaches advocate prevention; they focus on early identification and treatment of such things as truancy, bullying (treating both the bullies and the victims), anger, and aggression through school-based group therapy run by trained psychologists or counselors (Larson & Lochman, 2002). School and districtwide policies and staff training emphasizing conflict resolution skills, effective discipline strategies, and social skills training have helped produce more prosocial environments in some schools (Gagnon & Leone, 2001). Many experts point out that aggression and school violence have multiple causes; schools, parents, and the overall community must coordinate their efforts and resources to deal with these problems effectively.

Q *What policies seem to work best with aggressive students and school violence? How can schools balance the needs and rights of students against the urgency of identifying and dealing with potential problems so as to prevent violence? What social policy suggestions would you make?*

Think About Luis …

How could Luis use leisure activities to make new friends who share more of his current interests? Describe two or three activities he might try as a way to meet and socialize with a different crowd.

adolescents opportunities to escape the realities of life, explore more exciting possibilities, and connect with one another. Activities that enable adolescents to be around one another, sharing their ideas and interests, often lead to dating and other intimate contacts. Even when alone, adolescents use music, TV, and similar activities as ways to explore their own interests, examine how they fit with peers, and reflect on where they are going in their lives. Self-understanding, sexual attraction, and intimate communication are important aspects of leisure-time activities in adolescence (Hughes, 1999).

As Figure 15.3 shows, adolescents devote more time to TV than to homework, and their hours spent watching TV outnumber hours spent reading books and magazines by more than 3 to 1. One recent study looked at time spent on computer activities and found that adolescents from 11 to 18 years of age report an average of 29 minutes a day in non-school-related computer activities—but almost 3 hours watching television (Roberts et al., 2004). Adolescents don't spend all of their time watching TV, of course. They put a considerable amount of time into paid employment and some time into household chores. Adults often complain that adolescents waste too much time watching TV, but research data suggest that their criticism may be misdirected. According to one British study, for example, 12- to 15-year-olds and 16- to 24-year-olds spent approximately 2.7 hours per day watching TV, but adults (25 to 54 years old) spent 3.5 hours glued to the tube (Gunter & McAleer, 1997). Older adults (ages 55 and up) watched nearly 5 hours per day! Estimates of media usage by teens are complicated by the fact that many teenagers do several things at once, *multitasking* at every possible opportunity. For example, 15- to 18-year-olds average 2.75 hours per day listening to CDs, radio, and other media—but they are usually listening while they are doing something else (like homework) (Roberts et al., 2004). Many adolescents also engage in more active pursuits of course, such as organized sports, skateboarding, or dancing. At this age, however, they tend to focus selectively on the one or two activities in which they excel (Hughes, 1999). Even in adolescence, these activities still qualify as play: They are pleasurable, and the adolescent engages in them actively, voluntarily, and for intrinsic motivations.

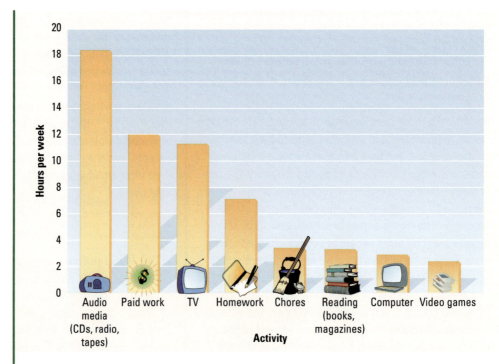

Figure 15.3 • Common Activities in Adolescence Shown here are average hours per week that U.S. adolescents spend in various activities, based on reports from students mostly 15 to 18 years old. (Data from Anderson et al., 2001; Roberts et al., 2004.)

1. Which statement best summarizes the type of friendships children have during adolescence?
    a. "He's my friend because we have known each other forever."
    b. "She's my friend because she is my neighbor and we play soccer together a lot."
    c. "She's my friend because we are in the same class in school."
    d. "He's my friend because we can talk about things that upset me and he'll keep it secret."

2. According to Harry Stack Sullivan, which of the following is *most* important for the development of successful intimate relationships in adolescence?
    a. having close nonromantic relationships during late childhood
    b. having a secure attachment to caregivers during infancy
    c. having a lot of loyal and honest friends
    d. having friends who are similar to yourself in important ways

3. Research on adolescent crowds indicates that self-esteem is highest among _____.
    a. *druggies/toughs*   b. *nobodies*   c. *normals*   d. *jocks*

4. **True or False:** Most adolescents experience stronger peer pressure to engage in positive behaviors than in negative behaviors.

5. **True or False:** In general, adolescents who do *not* have close friendships have just as good outcomes as those who do have close friendships.

Answers: 1. d, 2. a, 3. d, 4. T, 5. F

Contexts of Development

Adolescents do not face the developmental tasks of forming their identity, developing intimate relationships, and achieving autonomy in a vacuum. Their attempts are strongly affected by aspects of their social context. Two contexts that are particularly important are the schools they attend and the overall cultural context in which they develop. In this section, we will examine the impact of these contexts on adolescent development.

As you study this section, ask yourself these questions:

■ What is *stage–environment fit* and how does it affect adolescent development?

■ How do U.S. students compare to those in other countries in academic achievement? Which U.S. students are especially at risk for achievement problems, and why?

■ What are *individualism* and *collectivism*? In what ways are they different?

■ How does poverty affect development?

■ What is *acculturation,* and how are children and adolescents affected by it?

Adolescents in School

School Climate and Structure. Just as classroom climate can encourage certain goals, activities, beliefs, emotions, and behavior, overall school climate influences students and teachers alike (Roeser et al., 1996). Schoolwide practices such as honor roll assemblies,

Think About Luis . . .

*How good do you think Luis'
stage–environment fit has been in
the past few years? What could the
schools or his parents have done or
still do to improve the fit?*

stage–environment fit
The degree to which the
environment is successful in
meeting the cognitive, social, and
emotional needs of a child in a
particular stage of development.

Middle school practices such as
publicly posting honor rolls emphasize competition and ability rather
than cooperation and effort at a
time when students need greater
support and chances to maintain
friendships. This is an example of a
poor *stage–environment fit*, and it
can produce long-lasting negative
effects—especially for young adolescents who are at academic risk
or psychologically vulnerable.

public posting of honor rolls, and class ranking on student report cards and permanent records encourage a schoolwide emphasis on ability, competition, and social comparison. In contrast, recognition of effort and improvement, coupled with instruction that encourages mastery, produces a schoolwide learning orientation (Eccles & Roeser, 1999; Roeser & Eccles, 1998).

School structure has important effects as students transition to middle school or junior high. At this point schools typically increase the emphasis on competition, grades, teacher control, and social comparison. At the same time, schools decrease individual attention and support from teachers and provide fewer opportunities for students to maintain close networks of friendships. Long-lasting declines in students' self-esteem, motivation, and achievement can occur—particularly for students who are at academic risk or are more psychologically vulnerable (Eccles et al., 1997). This mismatch between school structure and adolescents' developmental needs is an example of a poor **stage–environment fit:** a poor match between the environment and the cognitive, social, and emotional needs of a particular stage of development (Eccles, 2004; Eccles & Roeser, 1999). School structures can be modified to be more appropriate for middle school students by encouraging learning-oriented goals (rather than performance-oriented goals); using cooperative learning techniques; focusing honors and awards on initiative, effort, and improvement; allowing students more control in classroom and school decision making; and scheduling regular advisory sessions so teachers get to know individual students and identify potential problems early (Anderman & Maehr, 1994; Eccles, 2004; Seidman & French, 1997).

Differences in Academic Performance

How do students in the United States compare to those in other countries in academic achievement? In the latest international assessment of mathematics and science achievement, U.S. eighth-graders ranked 15th in math and ninth in science out of 45 countries assessed—significantly above the international average and much improved from previous years, but still below the scores of the top-ranked countries (Lemke & Gonzales, 2006). Twelfth graders have fared even worse, ranking 19th in math and 16th in science out of 21 countries assessed in past years (Mullis et al., 1998). Findings like these are disappointing, particularly because of the heavy emphasis on educational improvement over the past few decades.

Researchers have examined educational practices in the United States, Japan, China, and Taiwan and found interesting differences between practices in Asian cultures (which often lead the world in math and science scores) and in the United States. Differences have been especially apparent in such areas as beliefs about effort and ability, active engagement in learning activities, parent expectations and involvement, and how time on academics is spent by students and teachers (Lee, 1998; Shen, 2001; Stevenson & Lee, 1990). It would be unrealistic to propose that the same educational practices that work in Asian cultures be implemented wholesale in the United States as there are quite different cultural systems operating (Shen, 2001). But some school systems have attempted changes inspired by Asian educational practices. For example, one study found that extending the school year by 30 days produced higher achievement scores in several areas (Frazier & Morrison, 1998). It's interesting to note that many of the practices long advocated by educational researchers and developmental psychologists are common in Asian cultures. Examples include active learning by students, emphasis on effort rather than ability, and focus on problem solving and conceptual knowledge. As you're probably well aware, many U.S. schools have made changes to try to improve education, but it will likely take several years before we can see the effects of these changes.

What about ethnic group differences among U.S. students? As Figure 15.4 shows, the 2005 National Assessment of Educational Progress found large ethnic group differences in math achievement. Similar differences were found in all the subjects tested, and the gaps have narrowed little or none since 1990 (Braswell et al., 2001; Grigg et al., 2006; Perie et al., 2005). And although the rate of dropping out of school declined for all ethnicities during the 1970s and 1980s, ethnic differences persist. For example, the dropout rate among Hispanic students (41 percent) is almost four times the rate for non-Hispanic white students (11 percent); African American students' dropout rate (21 percent) is almost twice that of white students (U.S. Census Bureau, 2004).

Why do substantial ethnic differences remain in spite of years of attention and concern? Poverty and its effects are a crucial factor. Ethnic minority students are far more likely to live in poverty than are white students. And poverty affects the quality of schools available, money available for materials and enrichment activities, parents' abilities and opportunities to help, and students' overall health, to name but a few factors (Byrnes, 2003; Skiba et al., 2002). Cultural differences also are important, particularly the extent to which schools are compatible with students' home cultures and the degree to which children's cultures value the kinds of skills taught in schools (Byrnes, 2001a). One important result of cultural incompatibility is that students are less likely to care about their performance, put in extra effort, or seek help. Schools that are sensitive to the cultures of their students and try to involve parents can have a positive impact on children's academic achievement (Fan & Chen, 2001; Parker et al., 1999).

Is it true that boys are better than girls in mathematics, as so many people seem to believe? It depends on students' ages as well as on the particular area of mathematics being assessed. The only consistent differences found in elementary school favor girls, both for computation and for grades in math (Halpern, 2000). Girls continue to earn higher math grades, but their superior performance in computation disappears after about age 15. Gender differences favoring boys appear at adolescence and increase during high school, but only in areas involving mathematics problem

Asian cultures place a strong emphasis on hard work. In these societies, there are high expectations for students' achievement and active involvement in learning. Teachers have more preparation time than in the United States; children have ample recess time; and parents are very involved in their children's schoolwork.

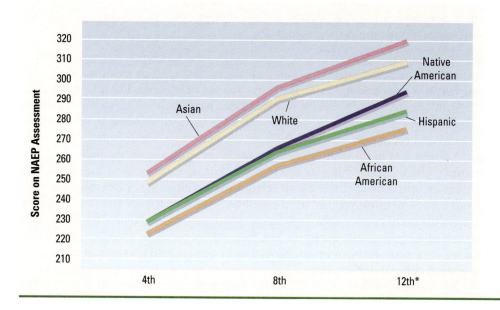

Figure 15.4 • Ethnic Group Differences in Achievement This figure shows the ethnic group differences in math. Ethnic group differences in achievement are large in all subject areas tested. *Note:* Data for 12th grade students are from the year 2000. Year 2005 data not available. (Braswell et al., 2001; Perie et al., 2005.)

solving. Since the late 1970s boys have consistently scored about 10 percent higher than girls on the math portion of the Scholastic Aptitude Test (the SAT). However, on national assessments of fourth, eighth, and twelfth graders, math gender differences have decreased since the early 1980s, and the most recent national assessment shows no significant differences at any of these grade levels (Byrnes, 2001a; Campbell et al., 2000). Some studies find that girls hold less positive attitudes toward math, show less interest in math, and receive less encouragement for engaging in math-related activities (Eccles et al., 1998; Maccoby, 1998). Schools have struggled with these issues for many years, but stereotypes still exist.

In more general cognitive skills the largest and most consistent gender differences are in verbal, language, and certain spatial skills (Halpern, 2000; Hyde & Linn, 1988). The biggest differences in verbal skills during school-age years—all favoring girls—are in spelling, overall language measures, and writing. Some of these differences get smaller during adolescence, whereas others (e.g., writing) remain. Boys score higher in some spatial skills such as mental rotation (the ability to visualize how an object would look if you viewed it from a different angle). Differences in these areas emerge at around 9 to 13 years and widen throughout adolescence (Masters & Sanders, 1993; Voyer et al., 1995).

How Can We Prevent Problems in Schooling? What can we do to prevent difficulties in schooling? You may soon be in a position to help, perhaps by working in health and social services, early childhood education, schools, or government or private agencies. You may also have children of your own. Table 15.4 presents suggestions for all of us who work with children, from preschool through high school. It is vital that each student begin school ready to learn, experience early success to gain a solid foundation for learning, and learn that effort and persistence make a difference. Each child must feel that school is relevant and important in his or her life, and each must feel individually known and valued by teachers and schools. These are challenging goals that require active involvement of all who care about students' academic success and overall quality of life.

Cultural Contexts for Development

Throughout this book we have often mentioned the influence of culture when explaining why children behave, think, or feel in certain ways. In every chapter we have pointed out differences among cultures. But what is *culture,* and how does it affect development? In this section we will discuss types of cultures and consider their impact on children's development.

Cultural Orientations: Individualism and Collectivism. A **culture** is a system of shared customs and meanings that allows individuals to participate as members of a group and that is transmitted from one generation to the next (Cole, 1999; Goodenough, 1994). A culture includes clearly specified rules (such as laws) as well as attitudes, beliefs, goals, values, and traditions. Cultures can be vastly different in their specific customs and meanings, but one important dimension on which people often compare cultures has to do with their emphasis on the group or on the individual. For example, think about how you describe yourself. Do you tend to use terms that emphasize your individuality or your relationships with others? Now think honestly about how responsible you feel for the well-being of your friends and family: Would you readily sacrifice your own desires, independence, and happiness for their sake? Psychologists have posed questions like these to people from a variety of different places. Their responses can be categorized as having an individualistic or collectivistic general cultural orientation.

Individualism involves the general belief that people are independent of each other. Individualistic cultures focus on an individual's "rights above duties, a concern for

culture
A system of shared customs and meanings that allow individuals to participate as a member of a group and that are transmitted from one generation to the next.

individualism
A cultural orientation based on the belief that people are independent of each other; emphasizes individual rights, self-fulfillment, and personal accomplishments.

TABLE 15.4 Preventing Problems with Schooling

STRATEGIES	PARENTS CAN . . .	SCHOOLS CAN . . .
Promote school readiness to help children get off to a good start academically	Immunize children, encourage good eating and exercise habits, and make sure children get enough sleep. Use quality preschool programs that teach basic skills and encourage positive attitudes toward learning and schooling. Read to children *daily* and encourage them to use descriptive words. Encourage curiosity and questions. Encourage children's efforts, not just their results. Let your child know you believe he can learn through effort and persistence.	Offer specific suggestions to parents for increasing school readiness. Thoroughly screen all preschoolers to identify those at highest need of early intervention. Establish an environment that values and encourages curiosity, questioning, and enthusiasm for learning. Develop policies that emphasize effort, persistence, and a mastery orientation. Hold positive expectations for students.
Help create a positive school environment to help children feel comfortable, confident, and happy to be in school	Be involved in your child's school. Volunteer, and attend school events. Meet with your child's teacher(s) periodically, even if your child is not having any problems. Request teachers who emphasize effort, persistence, and mastery, and who have positive expectations for children. Consider the climate of your child's class—is it warm and supportive or chilly and uninviting?	Encourage meaningful and regular parent involvement. Take steps to eliminate negative classroom environments. Hold regular in-service training on strategies that foster positive classroom climates and mastery learning orientations. Make strong efforts to keep class sizes below 20 students, especially at early grade levels.
Think about the consequences of school structure and policies to provide a good stage–environment fit	Ask questions about school policies that emphasize grades or competition. Ask how learning orientations, effort, and persistence are encouraged. Support programs in middle/junior high schools that make it a friendlier place for students, like block schedules or homeroom "advisory" programs. Watch for signs that your child is having difficulty transitioning to a new school.	Think about whether school policies focus too much on ability. Try to emphasize effort, persistence, and learning orientations more often. Consider having "advisory" programs and/or block-type schedules so teachers and students can get to know one another better. Watch for signs that individual students are having adjustment difficulties. Establish routines that are student-friendly and teach self-management and self-control strategies. Maintain contact with parents to ensure that children's needs are being met.
Understand different cultures to make school more relevant and interesting for students	Get to know your child's teachers. Help them understand differences between their culture and yours. Help organize a multicultural event in your child's class or school. Try to understand *why* the school curriculum contains the things it does. Try to find reasons that make sense to your child. Point out to your child examples of the content and skills he or she is learning, especially for topics your child thinks are irrelevant.	Plan events that encourage parents and teachers to get to know one another. Offer in-service training to help teachers understand the cultures, expectations, and customs of their students. Encourage teachers to incorporate information about their students' cultural backgrounds into instruction. Ask community members about school topics that seem irrelevant to them or their children. Get suggestions to improve the relevance of the curriculum.
Do more than just teach content so students' non-academic needs are not an obstacle to learning	Help children develop positive, supportive friendships. Encourage children to talk about school—about what they're learning, what they like or don't like, and why. Encourage your child to develop positive relationships with other trusted adults such as teachers.	Talk with students about attitudes toward learning, strategies for self-control, and how to deal with strong or negative emotions. Provide counseling services or referrals for students having academic, social, or emotional difficulties. Serve as an information resource for academic as well as nonacademic services and issues.

(Anderman & Maehr, 1994; Deci & Ryan, 1985; Dweck, 2001; Eccles, 2004; Fan & Chen, 2001; Ford & Harris, 2000; Good & Brophy, 2003; Keith et al., 1998; Parker et al., 1999; Seidman & French, 1997.)

collectivism
A cultural orientation based on the belief people are interdependent members of a social group; emphasizes duty to others and group goals, values, and well-being.

oneself and immediate family, an emphasis on personal autonomy and self-fulfillment," and an identity based on personal accomplishments (Oyserman et al., 2002, p. 4). In contrast, **collectivism** is the view that individuals are interdependent members of a social group and that the greatest concern is with the group's goals, values, and well-being. In collectivism the emphasis is on fulfilling duties to others, even if it means sacrificing your own desires and happiness; identity has to do with group beliefs, accomplishments, and characteristics rather than individual ones. Group membership in such a culture may be based on kinship, religion, ethnicity, or something else. Researchers often talk about whole countries as having an individualistic or collectivistic cultural orientation, but any specific individual within the country may not have the same orientation. Within a given country there can be large differences in how strictly individuals adhere to the overall cultural orientation or to any of the culture's specific customs or meanings (Chirkov et al., 2003; Triandis, 1995).

Studies have found differences related to individualism and collectivism in many cultural beliefs and behaviors relevant for development, including parenting practices, emotional attachment type, attitudes toward academic effort and ability, school discipline strategies, cooperation and competition, conflict resolution, helping behaviors, and preferences for working alone versus in groups (Greenfield et al., 2006; Oyserman et al., 2002; Rothbaum et al., 2000). For example, many European Americans (not to mention developmental researchers) view authoritative parenting as effective because it encourages outcomes such as self-reliance, self-regulation, and exploration—outcomes that an individualistic cultural orientation finds desirable. But as you learned earlier in this chapter, this parenting style is not the norm and these outcomes are not the goal in other, less individualistic cultures such as those of East Asian and African countries (Greenfield et al., 2006).

your perspective

Do you consider your cultural orientation to be individualistic or collectivistic? If you've known anyone with a different cultural orientation, describe any differences you have noticed.

Think About Luis . . .

Do you see indications of a collectivist or individualistic cultural orientation in Luis and his family? How might their cultural orientations affect their beliefs, behavior, and expectations?

As you have probably guessed, researchers often describe Western cultures like that of the United States as individualistic. Within U.S. culture, they typically see European Americans as the most individualistic. East Asian cultures such as those of China and Japan are often thought of as more collectivistic. However, recent research is challenging some of the established beliefs about individualistic and collectivistic cultures. It appears that some theories and measures may be biased toward one orientation or the other; also, some studies question the traditional beliefs about which cultures show strong tendencies toward one orientation or the other (Oyserman et al., 2002; Rothbaum et al., 2000).

What's the Neighborhood Like? Urban and Rural Poverty. In recent years, developmental researchers have focused a great deal of attention on characteristics of the neighborhoods in which children live. Neighborhoods often consist of people who are similar in important ways; for example, in attitudes, beliefs, ethnicity, language, and/or behavior. The resources a community supports, the private and public behavior it encourages, the parenting practices it encourages, and the social activities it organizes and allows can all affect children for better or for worse, directly and indirectly (Furstenberg & Hughes, 1997). One factor that stands out is the impact of living in a poor neighborhood. Living in poverty has pervasive negative effects on children's development.

Poverty: A Culture of Economics. As of 2004, the overall poverty rate for U.S. families was 12.7 percent. This is among the lowest in two decades, but the rate has risen every year since 2000. Look carefully at Figure 15.5. What does this figure show about the poverty status of *children and adolescents* as a group relative to the overall population? Although the situation is improving, the poverty rate of children up to age 18 is still almost 1.5 times higher than the rate for all ages. In other words, children, particularly young children, are more likely to live in poverty than any other age group. This is especially true for African American and Hispanic children; three out of 10 children in these ethnic groups live in poverty. Even more striking is the fact that

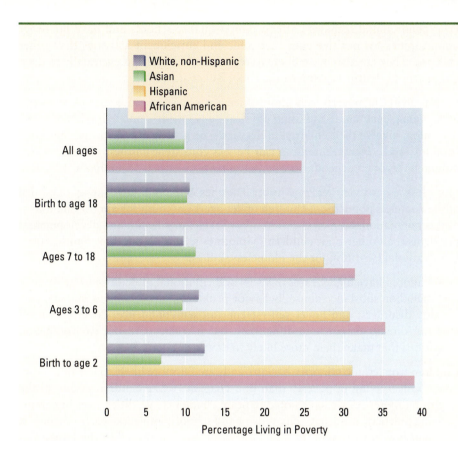

Figure 15.5 • Percentages of U.S. Age Groups Living in Poverty, 2004 People living in poverty in the United States include more children than any other age group—especially children under the age of 2. African American and Hispanic children are especially at risk. (*Current Population Survey*, 2005.)

over half (54 percent) of families living in poverty include at least one person who works *full-time* and *year-round* (*Current Population Survey*, 2005; National Center for Children in Poverty, 2006). In 2002, the U.S. Census Bureau defined the poverty level as a total annual income of not more than $13,078 for a household of two people ($19,806 for four). What difficulties do you think a family of four would have on this income?

In general, children and adolescents living in poverty face seriously limited options and many difficulties in their day-to-day lives. Lack of resources, continuous hassles, and relatively frequent negative life events create high levels of stress for all family members, and the stress never seems to abate. The younger a child is and the longer the child lives in poverty, the larger the impact tends to be. And the more poverty risk factors an individual experiences (such as poor health, inadequate parenting, and low social support), the worse the effect. Living in poverty affects well-being in numerous ways, including the following (Bradley & Corwyn, 2002; Brooks-Gunn et al., 1995; Duncan & Brooks-Gunn, 1997; Linver et al., 2002; McLoyd et al., 2006).

■ Poor children are more likely than children who are not poor to suffer physical health problems, including higher rates of preterm birth, low birth weight, illnesses, injuries, poisoning, parental neglect, exposure to toxic substances, and abuse (Pelton, 1989). They have less access to adequate health care and lower rates of immunizations, so illnesses and injuries often progress to more serious levels before they receive treatment.

■ Poverty correlates significantly with lower IQ scores, lower academic achievement, and lower scores on a variety of cognitive measures (Bradley et al., 1996). Poor children are less ready for school in terms of knowledge, cognitive skills, social skills, and self-regulation.

your perspective

Think about the things you've done in the last week or so. How might these activities have been different or more difficult (or easy) if you were poor or if you were wealthy?

- Poor children and teenagers attend poorer-quality schools and have far fewer opportunities for positive extracurricular and enrichment activities than other children. They are also more likely to repeat grade levels and eventually to drop out of school (Battin-Pearson et al., 2000; Zill et al., 1995).

- Parents living in poverty rely more often on power-assertive discipline tactics (e.g., issuing commands and using physical punishment) and are less likely to use reasoning, involve their children in decisions, or give praise for proper behavior (Bradley et al., 2001). Parenting can be less consistent and less child centered, although this often depends on whether other problems arise (Halpern, 1993).

- Homelessness is a very real possibility. Families with children make up one-third of the homeless population; children under age 18 account for almost one-fourth of this population. Homeless children have even more health and developmental problems than other poor children (Molnar et al., 1990; Smith & Smith, 2001; U.S. National Coalition for the Homeless, 2001).

- Poor children have higher rates of social and emotional difficulties from an early age, including substance abuse, behavior problems, mental illness, suicide, personality disorders, and lower self-esteem and self-confidence. Poverty in itself may not directly cause these difficulties, but it creates stressful environmental conditions that make them more likely to develop.

Children from ethnic minority backgrounds are far more likely to live in poverty and spend longer living in poverty than non-Hispanic white children. Many of the ethnic-group differences we have noted in other chapters (e.g., differences in parenting practices, academic achievement and school completion, early pregnancy, and low birth weight, to name a few) at least partly reflect the impacts of poverty. For many outcomes, in fact, differences between ethnic groups fade or disappear when analysts take the effects of poverty into account. Moving from a poor neighborhood to one with little poverty has many positive effects, including decreased emotional distress, less reliance on harsh parenting practices, and less violent behavior (DeAngelis, 2001).

Think About Luis . . .

What effect might the lack of money in Luis' family have on him? How can he and his family deal with these effects?

The Inner City. Inner-city poverty is an especially difficult context for children and adolescents. Almost one-quarter of all children in U.S. inner cities are poor. All of the effects of poverty we've already discussed weigh especially heavily on those living in inner-city poverty, and the vast majority of these children are members of ethnic minorities (Brooks-Gunn et al., 1997). There are additional problems as well. Crime, particularly violent crime, is much more frequent in the inner city. Housing is often substandard, crowded, and inconsistent. Positive options are less available, and negative options like gangs and drug use are more common. Children and parents alike focus more on the present than on the future; "simply surviving in the inner city is viewed by these families as evidence" of success (Brookins et al., 1997, p. 54; Burton et al., 1996). Parents lack financial and emotional resources, often facing chronic unemployment or inconsistent employment as well as insufficient support and help from the community. Often there is a sense of social isolation from other parts of the city, and families may keep to themselves because of fear for children's safety. Inner-city

In addition to the obstacles poor children face, inner-city adolescents living in poverty must deal with higher levels of violent crime, bad housing, lack of positive options, less support from parents, temptation from gangs and drugs, and a sense of isolation from the larger community.

children have far less academic success, with a 50 percent high school dropout rate in some areas. These outcomes limit options for these children even further and serve to perpetuate the cycle of poverty for the next generation.

How can families living in poor neighborhoods find a way out? Numerous social programs try to help create economic opportunities and improve the educational success of inner-city youth, with varying degrees of success (Brown & Richman, 1997; Lehman & Smeeding, 1997). Although there is no doubt that neighborhood factors are important, a child's family can overcome the influence of a poor neighborhood. For example, researchers have identified several family behaviors that help inner-city African American adolescents be more successful (Jarrett, 1995). These behaviors characterize *community-bridging families*, which can help children find and take advantage of opportunities within and outside the immediate neighborhood. For example, community-bridging families:

Community-bridging families help children find and take advantage of opportunities by closely monitoring their activities and friendships, maintaining social support networks, encouraging their involvement in positive activities, and expecting them to help with family responsibilities.

- Establish and maintain networks among family members (immediate and extended) that provide support and resources

- Restrict children's interaction with people whose lifestyles are inconsistent with the family's goals and values; this reduces children's exposure to negative influences

- Carefully and consistently monitor their children's activities and friendships

- Encourage involvement in positive activities—activities that increase contact with like-minded families and friends and help children develop their skills and talents

- Expect children to contribute to the family's well-being through chores, responsibilities, part-time jobs, and the like, all of which help increase children's self-esteem and family cohesion

Rural Poverty. The fact that the poverty rate in rural areas is almost as high as in inner cities is often overlooked. In the year 2000, for example, 24 percent of children in inner cities and 19 percent of children in rural areas were poor, compared to 10.8 percent of children in suburbs (Children's Defense Fund, 2001a). Like all poor children, children living in rural poverty face more difficulties and stress than nonpoor children. They experience many of the effects we have reviewed, with one possible, but important, exception. One extensive study of rural Iowa farm children found that family ties are often strong

and serve to connect several generations, and that strong social networks connect these farm communities (Elder & Conger, 2000). Strong family loyalty also is frequent in Appalachian poor families. At least for these rural families, poverty does not seem to disrupt social supports as much as it does in the inner city (Crockett et al., 2000; Wilson & Peterson, 2000).

The poverty rate in rural areas is almost as high as in inner cities, and children in rural poverty suffer many of the same effects as the inner-city poor. The rural poor are from a wide range of ethnic backgrounds, cultures, and geographic regions.

Think About Luis . . .

What aspects of community-bridging families *might be helpful to Luis and his family? How could they use these ideas to help Luis as he moves through adolescence?*

your perspective

Do you know any "community-bridging" families? Think about what kinds of things they do differently than other families and how this affects their children's development.

acculturation
The process of learning the language, values, customs, and social skills of a new culture.

Coming to America: Immigration and Acculturation. Throughout the history of the United States, immigrants have coped with the stresses of settling in a new country, usually arriving with few resources and little knowledge of the language and customs. **Acculturation** is the process of learning the language, values, customs, and social skills of a new culture (Chun et al., 2003; Parke & Buriel, 2006). It is a lengthy process, often spanning several generations, and it can create conflict and stress for families, particularly during adolescence. For example, when adolescents speak different languages than their parents (i.e., the parents talk to their children in the native language, but the children usually respond in English), the teenagers report less communication and closeness with their parents than do teenagers who use the same language as their parents (Tseng & Fuligni, 2000). In addition, U.S.-born adolescents in immigrant families tend to change their values and beliefs more rapidly than their parents, creating a bigger difference in values between parents and adolescents in these families than in other immigrant or nonimmigrant families. Because many immigrants come from cultures that emphasize respect for and obedience to adults, this difference can create much family stress and disruption. The more differences there are in the acculturation of parents and children, the more family conflict there tends to be (Farver et al., 2002; Phinney et al., 2000).

Regardless of their countries of origin, immigrants must develop strategies in order to adapt successfully. For example, studies find that Mexican immigrants emphasize and strengthen family ties; this strategy provides additional sources of economic, emotional, and social support. They also cultivate **biculturalism,** or adoption of two cultural orientations at the same time. Biculturalism allows families to maintain the cultural values they brought from their homeland but also understand and function successfully in the new culture. The adolescents (and sometimes even younger children) of immigrants often find themselves serving as **child cultural brokers**—as interpreters not only of the language but also of the culture of the new country for their parents and other family members (Parke & Buriel, 2006). This can be a difficult position for children. They must try to represent the family to members of the majority culture and to cope with important adult responsibilities like legal matters, tax forms, and insurance claims. Child cultural brokers are supposed to teach their parents about these matters and other subtleties of the new culture, but they must do it in a way that allows their parents to maintain their status and respect within the family and community. Being a child cultural broker can have some positive effects, too; these children can develop a greater knowledge of U.S. culture, greater sensitivity to the challenges facing their parents, and stronger bonds with their parents.

biculturalism
Adopting two cultural orientations at the same time.

child cultural brokers
Children of immigrants who serve as interpreters of the language and culture of the new country for their family members.

Immigrants to the United States gradually acculturate to the mainstream culture, but it's important to remember that mainstream U.S. culture also changes. Latinos and Asian Americans are the fastest-growing ethnic minority groups in the United States, and each of these groups represents a varied collection of home cultures and languages. As the population of the United States becomes more diverse, the mainstream culture will evolve to incorporate new customs and reflect this rich diversity.

Adolescence can be a stressful time for immigrant families. This adolescent is likely to have adopted American customs faster than her parents, which can lead to conflict. Her grandparent is likely to maintain an identity of her country of origin, while the girl and her parents are likely to have an Asian American ethnic identity.

Explaining Culture's Influence. In essence, culture provides a "set of lenses for seeing the world" (Triandis, 1994, p. 13). Back in Chapter 1 we described an experience one of the authors had in East Germany in 1989, months after the fall of the Communist government. The citizens there often said, "It's not possible" when they encountered an impediment, which sounded odd to an American. A lifetime in the United States led us to believe that problems can be overcome given enough effort, time, and resources. Being steeped in communist culture led East Germans to the very different belief that trying to remove obstructions was futile and perhaps even dangerous.

Think back to the layers of Bronfenbrenner's ecological systems theory, shown in Figure 1.3, and look at the many different systems that affect development directly or indirectly. All of these systems exist within and are affected by a specific cultural setting. At the broadest levels (the macrosystem and the exosystem), culture affects the options that are available to children and families, the resources they have to draw on, the governmental policies and laws that help or hurt them, the types of neighborhoods they live in, and the types of lifestyles they have and wish for. On more individual levels (the microsystem and the mesosystem), culture affects how and with whom social interactions take place; what kinds of parenting are considered appropriate; what people see as important or problematic, possible or impossible; what constitutes acceptable versus inappropriate behavior; and what children expect of themselves and others. In short, culture permeates all these levels to affect children's thoughts, emotions, beliefs, and behaviors. Yet so often we aren't even aware of the pervasive effects of our own culture—that is, until we encounter someone else's culture! Because cultural beliefs and customs are so thoroughly ingrained, it's not surprising that we sometimes misconstrue cultural differences as deficits. We are so accustomed to doing and thinking about things in the ways our own culture considers correct that we forget there are often other, equally correct, ways to go about things. "Like the air one breathes, under ordinary conditions, these values frameworks do not rise to conscious awareness" (Greenfield & Suzuki, 1998, p. 1060).

In this chapter we described three central developmental tasks adolescents face in their socioemotional development—identity, autonomy, and intimacy—along with several factors that influence their efforts to accomplish these tasks. Families, peers, and social context have a substantial impact. We discussed each influence as a separate topic, but it is important to remember that these and other factors all interact to influence the adolescent's development.

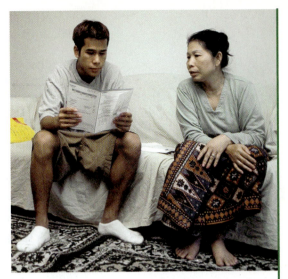

Children of immigrants may find themselves serving as cultural brokers. This son is expected to teach his parents about the majority culture and represent his family to others, but he must also make sure his parents retain status and respect both inside and outside the family.

■ Let's Review . . .

1. Which of the following does *not* explain the negative effect of the transition to junior high after sixth grade?
   a. Junior high schools usually decrease individual attention but increase competition.
   b. Students are given too much control too quickly over school-related decisions.
   c. Teachers rely too heavily on competitive learning techniques and performance-oriented goals.
   d. Class structure in junior high schools makes it harder to maintain friendship networks.

2. Andre has been offered a well-paying job that requires moving far away from his parents and extended family. His family does not want him to leave their town, so Andre does not take the job because he doesn't want to go against his family's wishes. Andre is most likely _____.
   a. individualistic in his cultural orientation
   b. collectivistic in his cultural orientation
   c. neutral in his cultural orientation
   d. European American

3. Which of the following is *true* about the effects of poverty on child development?

    a. Poor children have more physical health problems than other children.

    b. Poor children perform just as well in school as other children.

    c. Poor children's parents are just as consistent and child centered as other parents.

    d. Poor children are more likely to attend preschool than other children.

4. Twelve-year-old Miguel helps his parents with paperwork for their medical forms, translates for them when they must deal with their landlord, and helps them understand which kinds of stores are likely to negotiate prices and which are not. Miguel is a _____.

    a. individualist   b. collectivist

    c. child cultural broker   d. community bridger

5. **True or False:** Ethnic differences in academic achievement scores are large and stable.

6. **True or False:** Community bridging families protect their children by severely restricting the children's interactions with all community members.

Answers: 1. b, 2. b, 3. a, 4. c, 5. T, 6. F

Thinking Back to Luis . . .

Now that you have studied this chapter, you should be able to apply at least a dozen concepts and research findings to Luis' situation. The description of Luis clearly shows that he is dealing with all three of the socioemotional developmental tasks of adolescence: identity, autonomy, and intimacy. His concerns about what he wants to do in the future and his frequent changes of mind about his interests are a normal part of the identity exploration process. While it's frustrating for Luis, it's important for him to think about a variety of different possibilities. This will increase the likelihood that he'll find an area that is a good fit for his interests and talents. The fact that he isn't "connecting" with school anymore is troublesome because this may lead him to be less interested in exploring different subject areas and continued education. Hopefully his parents are monitoring his interest in school as well as his overall grades. Perhaps they can work with his teachers and a guidance counselor as Luis moves toward his junior and senior years of high school to help him as he searches for areas of strength and interest.

Luis is also working to develop autonomy, evidenced by the conflicts he's having with his parents. The amount and degree of conflict do not seem excessive, and it may serve the positive purpose of helping Luis learn to deal with conflict and increased responsibility; the conflict may help his parents learn to allow Luis more autonomy as he is ready for it. It will be important for his parents to maintain appropriate expectations and offer positive support, but also recognize Luis' need to become more independent. The conflicts Luis and his parents are having may actually help them learn to communicate more clearly and build a stronger relationship, factors that may help buffer Luis from any of the ill effects of coming from a poorer neighborhood.

Finally, Luis is also continuing to develop the skills he'll need for forming successful and positive intimate relationships. He is learning the difficult lesson that friendships sometimes change as people mature and their interests change. The friendship skills he has developed, along with the model of relationships he has experienced in his family, will be important as he moves to intimate romantic relationships.

■ Chapter Review . . .

What major changes take place in the development of identity during adolescence?
Adolescents compare their real with ideal selves and think about many possible selves. Two components of identity development have been proposed (crisis, commitment) resulting in four identity statuses (moratorium, foreclosed, achieved, and diffused). Adolescents from ethnic minority groups work to develop an ethnic identity, possibly moving through several stages.

How and why does a homosexual orientation develop?
The development of a homosexual orientation begins in childhood and progresses through stages. The reasons for developing a particular sexual orienation are not completely understood but genetic factors, prenatal hormones, and the environment may all play a role. Teens with a homosexual orientation face increased risk of emotional, behavioral, and physical difficulties.

How do adolescents reason about moral issues?
Kohlberg's postconventional level of moral reasoning begins in adolescence, but few people reason consistently at this level. The justice orientation of Kohlberg's theory is less central in some cultures. Men and women use both care and justice orientations when thinking about moral issues. Moral reasoning is not as consistent across tasks as Kohlberg's theory suggests.

How much conflict is normal between teens and parents?
Some conflict over day-to-day issues is common and helps families address issues and learn to resolve conflict, and it indicates the adolescent is working toward autonomy. Parents, rather than teens, seem to be most bothered by conflict. Authoritative parenting, with the additional factor of psychological autonomy granting, helps adolescents constructively deal with conflict.

What are the effects of growing up in alternative family structures?
Most adopted children and teenagers are well-adjusted, but they do face challenges that non-adopted individuals do not. There is increased risk of psychological, behavioral, and academic problems, and some problems emerge in late childhood and adolescence. Being raised by gay or lesbian parents is not associated with negative developmental outcomes. Ethnic minority families and immigrant families often face challenges that majority group children do not, such as an increased risk of poverty and discrimination. Research has identified a number of characteristics of families that foster these teens' strength and resilience. A strict discipline style is common in many ethnic groups, but may be a protective response to dangerous neighborhoods.

How do adolescents develop friendships and romantic relationships?
The skills to form intimate relationships may be based in part on the attachment relations the child has with parents early in life, but childhood friendships also teach relationship skills. Adolescents form closely knit cliques and socialize in larger crowds. Crowd membership can affect behavior, identity, relationships, and emotions in both positive and negative ways. Most, but not all, peer pressure is toward positive behaviors. Some adolescents face challenges from early childhood that increase their likelihood of ongoing delinquent behavior.

What impact does the school context have on adolescent development?
School structure is not always supportive of the emotional, social, physical, and cognitive changes that young adolescents face. Cross-national assessments of achievement indicate that U.S. students fare worse than expected. Comparisons of American and Asian educational systems and beliefs have found interesting differences. There are substantial and consistent ethnic group differences in academic performance despite years of attempts to address the differences. Gender differences in cognitive skills are most consistent in verbal, language, and some spatial skills, but similarities in academic achievement between boys and girls far outweigh the differences.

What aspects of culture are important for understanding adolescent development?
A culture's overall orientation impacts a number of factors that are important for development including parenting practices, attitudes toward academic effort and achievement, and responsibility to family. One's culture affects every system of development.

How does poverty affect adolescent development?
Poverty affects all aspects of development directly and/or indirectly through lack of opportunity, lack of having basic needs met, increased difficulty of accomplishing day-to-day tasks, increased likelihood of poor parenting practices, and increased risk of social and emotional problems.

Inner-city poverty is especially difficult because of the added burdens of crime, violence, poor housing, lack of positive options, and social isolation. Community bridging families create strong family networks and connections to protect and support children and adolescents. Rural poverty presents similar risks and challenges, but strong family loyalty and connections across generations within a family are a source of support.

What is it like to be an adolescent in a family that has immigrated to another country?
Children and adolescents in immigrant families must cope with the process of *acculturation,* which can span several generations and create conflict during the adolescent years. Children and teens in immigrant families frequently become the cultural brokers for their parents, interpreting language as well as important adult responsibilities.

■ Key Terms

acculturation (552)
autonomy (529)
biculturalism (552)
child cultural brokers (552)
cliques (537)
collectivism (548)
crowds (537)
cultural deficit perspective (533)
culture (546)
ethnic identity (520)
homosexual experience (521)
homosexual orientation (521)
identity (518)

identity achievement (519)
identity diffusion (519)
identity foreclosure (519)
identity moratorium (519)
individualism (546)
intimacy (536)
life-course persistent pattern (538)
postconventional level (525)
psychological autonomy granting (531)
sexual orientation (521)
stage–environment fit (544)
strength and resilience
    perspective (533)

mydevelopmentlab

If you are using MyDevelopmentLab, you have access to an ebook version of this textbook, along with dozens of valuable resources per chapter—including video and audio clips, simulations and activities, self-assessments, practice tests, and other study materials. Here is a sampling of the resources available for this chapter.

Simulate
Identity Status

Watch
Peer Groups in Adolescence
Mentoring At-Risk Children
Men, Women, and Attraction
Adolescent Shyness
Social Influence
Sexual Orientation and Gender

If you did not receive an access code to MyDevelopmentLab with this text and wish to purchase access online, please visit www.mydevelopmentlab.com.

part five

Adolescence: The Transition toward Adulthood

Physical Development

Puberty produces drastic changes in appearance—adolescents enter this period looking like children and leave it looking like physically mature adults. The timing of puberty varies across adolescents, and those who mature significantly earlier or later than peers may experience different social and emotional effects. Continued brain development enables better reasoning and planning skills but also makes adolescents less responsive to rewards, which contributes to risk-taking behaviors. Two-thirds of adolescents are sexually active by 12th grade. Many are inconsistent in their use of contraceptives, which puts them at high risk for STDs and unintended pregnancies. Teen parenthood is associated with many problems for both parents and children, but outcomes are better if the teens stay in school, delay having another child, and receive support. Overall, adolescence is one of the healthiest periods of life, despite the fact that many teens do not eat well-balanced diets, get less vigorous exercise than recommended, and get too little sleep. Major threats to health and safety are most often the result of auto accidents and risk-taking behaviors such as drug and alcohol use and unprotected sexual activity. The risks of depression, suicide, and eating disorders also increase.

Cognitive Development

Adolescents gradually develop the abilities to think logically and systematically about abstract, hypothetical problems and possibilities. In later adolescence, thinking may progress even further to the understanding that knowledge is relative rather than absolute and that practical aspects of a situation often must take precedence over ideals when solving a problem. Teens gradually become more central participants in academic, social, and sports activities as their skills increase. Intellectual skills are defined differently depending on the theory of intelligence, and they continue to develop throughout adolescence. Adolescents often intentionally use slang words and phrases to set them apart from other generations. During adolescence, decision-making skills improve, gradually including a more thorough consideration of risks and benefits. Teens are called upon to begin making important decisions about schooling and careers as well as behavioral choices such as sexual activity and experimentation with drugs and alcohol.

Socioemotional Development

Adolescents face three main developmental tasks in their socioemotional development: identity, autonomy, and intimacy. They explore different possible selves and are influenced by the cliques and crowds they associate with. Crowd membership is less important to older adolescents, who are more secure in their identities and relationships. Most families experience some conflict between teens and parents, especially during early adolescence. Conflict can help teens become independent as long as the conflict is dealt with constructively and is not too intense or frequent. Adolescents build on skills learned in relationships with parents and childhood friends to create intimate friendships and romantic relationships. Important contexts that affect socioemotional development include adolescents' school settings, background culture, and poverty status.

By the end of adolescence, most teenagers have developed a deeper understanding of their individual preferences, skills, and limitations. Most have become relatively autonomous, no longer dependent on parents for making decisions and regulating behavior and emotions. Most have learned how to have good social relationships. Clearly, development does not end with adolescence—there are many important physical, cognitive, and socioemotional changes that happen during adulthood as well. Looking back over the chapters in this book, however, it's clear that adolescents have made tremendous accomplishments on their path to maturity.

A Few Final Thoughts

Throughout this book, we have emphasized many of the different factors that influence children's development. We'd like to leave you with a few general points to keep in mind.

Children's Development Is Complex

Children develop physically, emotionally, socially, and cognitively—and all these aspects interact with one another as well as with children's overall family and cultural context. As you have seen over and over, it is usually difficult to give one specific answer to the question of *why*: Why do children do, think, or feel what they do? Why do some children thrive even in the worst of living conditions? Why do others seem to have such difficulty even when they have many advantages? While this complexity may be frustrating at times, it is important to understand that usually there are no quick and easy solutions to the issues that children and their families face.

Think about Children's Development from Several Different Perspectives

Throughout this book we have emphasized different perspectives—from the different explanations that theorists offer for a developmental phenomenon, to the different professions that deal with children, to the different ways to understand and interpret the data from a single experiment. People (and even entire professions) see things differently, focus on different aspects of a situation, and consider different types of solutions. By trying to look at an issue through another person's eyes we can better understand it. For example, while taking a walk one day with our then 8-year-old skateboarder son, we commented on the remodeling that our neighbors had done to their house. We noticed the inviting front porch and beautifully restored brickwork along the front of the home. Our son had a very different perspective. He exclaimed, "Wow, those steps would be awesome to ollie [meaning, jump over on a skateboard]!" We hadn't even noticed the steps, but our son analyzed them in detail and saw that they offered exciting possibilities. Different people think in different ways; this has a profound impact on what they notice, what they see as a problem, and what they see as possible solutions.

Be Active in Your Thinking about and Analysis of Child Development Information

As we've pointed out numerous times, sometimes research data can be interpreted in different ways, and often things are more complex than they seem on the surface. Cultivate the habit of asking why a result makes sense and thinking about how the information might be useful to you in your professional and personal life. The more deeply you think about the information you've encountered, the more likely you are to remember it, to use it in the future, and to understand the vast amount of new information you'll encounter in the years to come.

Most Importantly, Be an Active Advocate for Children

This textbook has given you a foundation for your knowledge of development. You're not expected to be an expert on children and adolescents—no one could be after only one course! But you have gained valuable information that many people you work with, live with, or meet in your life may not have. Build on what you've learned, and use your knowledge to help make children's lives more healthy, positive, and supported. Children depend on caring and supportive adults to help them learn and develop in positive ways. Take the responsibility seriously and help provide the best environment you can for all the children you interact with!

Glossary

Abecedarian Project Project designed to assess the impact of full-time, high-quality intervention beginning in infancy; served primarily African American children living in poverty. (p. 281)

ability grouping Placing children in instructional groups based on their ability levels. (p. 427)

abstract thought Thought about things that are not real or things that are only possibilities. (p. 481)

accessing The process of finding information in memory at the desired time. (p. 370)

accommodation The process of modifying old schemes or creating new ones to better fit assimilated information. (p. 165)

acculturation The process of learning the language, values, customs, and social skills of a new culture. (p. 552)

achievement motivation The degree to which a person chooses to engage in and keep trying to accomplish challenging tasks. (p. 425)

adaptation In cognitive development, the process of changing a cognitive structure or the environment (or both) in order to understand the environment. (p. 164)

adolescent egocentrism A cognitive immaturity seen in adolescents—their inability to distinguish between one's own abstract reasoning and thoughts and the reasoning and thoughts of others. (p. 482)

adolescent growth spurt The increase in growth associated with the onset of puberty. (p. 444)

adolescent register Special form of speech adolescents use to identify themselves as belonging to a particular social, cultural, or generational group. (p. 504)

adoption studies Comparisons between measurements of children and their adoptive and biological parents used to estimate the genetic contribution to traits and characteristics. (p. 72)

afterbirth The third and last stage of birth, in which the placenta and other membranes are delivered through the birth canal. (p. 101)

allele An alternative version of a gene; alleles operate in pairs across matched chromosomes. (p. 48)

amniocentesis Procedure used to detect chromosomal and genetic abnormalities in the fetus. A needle is inserted through the mother's abdomen and uterus and into the amniotic sac, and fetal cells are withdrawn from the amniotic fluid. (p. 62)

androgens One type of sex hormone, released in greater concentration by males. (p. 442)

animism The idea that inanimate objects have conscious life and feelings. (p. 258)

anorexia nervosa A serious eating disorder involving distorted body image, intense fear of gaining weight, and refusal to maintain a healthy weight. (p. 465)

Apgar test A brief assessment of the newborn conducted at 1 and 5 minutes after birth; used to identify newborns who are at risk and need medical attention. (p. 104)

artificialism The notion that natural events or objects are under the control of people or of superhuman agents. (p. 258)

assimilation The process of bringing new objects or information into a scheme that already exists. (p. 164)

Attachment Q-Sort (AQS) A method for classifying attachments in children between 12 months and 5 years of age. Parents or other adults who have observed the child sort through cards with behavioral descriptions and score the selected cards. (p. 202)

attachment An emotional tie to a specific other person or people that endures across time and space. (p. 190)

attention deficit/hyperactivity disorder (ADHD) A condition involving inablity to sustain attention, excessive activity, and deficiencies in impulse control that are unusual for the child's developmental level. (p. 349)

attention The ability to focus on a particular stimulus without becoming distracted by other stimuli. (p. 271)

attributions Individuals' beliefs about why they or others succeed or fail. (p. 426)

authoritarian parents Parents who exert firm control but are rejecting or unresponsive to their children. (p. 300)

authoritative parents Parents who are warm and exert firm control. (p. 300)

autism spectrum disorders (ASDs) A group of serious developmental disorders characterized by impairments in social interaction and communication. (p. 353)

autobiographical memories Memories of events of great personal importance. They are episodic memories and are often vivid and detailed. (p. 373)

automaticity The ability to carry out a process with little or no conscious effort, leaving more cognitive capacity to carry out other tasks. (p. 270)

autonomy The ability to be independent in thought and action, control impulses, and accept responsibility for one's behavior. (p. 529)

average children Children who receive moderate numbers of both "like best" and "like least" nominations. (p. 422)

behavior genetics Field of study that compares the influence of genetics (nature) to the influence of learning and the environment (nurture), and examines how these forces interact to influence development. (p. 8)

behaviorism An American movement to develop a psychology that was objective and scientific, focusing on the principles of classical conditioning and operant conditioning. (p. 14)

biculturalism Adopting two cultural orientations at the same time. (p. 552)

bilingual Fluent in two languages. (p. 277)

binge drinking Consuming five or more alcoholic drinks on a single occasion. (p. 469)

body image The way a person thinks about his or her body and how it looks to others. (p. 445)

body mass index (BMI) An indicator of body fat based on weight and height. (p. 329)

bulimia nervosa A serious eating disorder with binge eating, followed by purging, fasting, or excessive exercise. (p. 465)

canalization Genetic limits on the effects of the environment. In experiential canalization, in contrast, it is the environment that limits the expression of genes. (p. 66)

cephalocaudal pattern Pattern of growth where areas in the head and upper body tend to form and grow before the areas in the lower body grow. (p. 88)

cerebral palsy (CP) A serious disorder caused by damage to one or more areas of the brain that control muscle movement and coordination. (p. 239)

cesarean section (C-section) births Surgical procedure in which the baby is removed through an incision made through the mother's abdomen and into the uterus. (p. 96)

child cultural brokers Children of immigrants who serve as interpreters of the language and culture of the new country for their family members. (p. 552)

child development Field of study in which researchers from many disciplines work to describe and understand the important changes that take place as children grow through childhood. (p. 6)

child maltreatment A general category including all situations in which parents or other persons in charge of a child's well-being harm the child or otherwise neglect the child's needs. (p. 243)

child sexual abuse Abuse that includes fondling a child's genitals or breasts, committing intercourse or other sexual acts with a child, exposing the child to indecent acts, or involving the child in pornography. (p. 343)

child-directed speech The special singsong way in which adults and older children talk to infants, speaking slowly, clearly, and with exaggerated intonation. (p. 138)

children with exceptional needs Children who require help beyond what is needed by peers. (p. 347)

chlamydia A common STD caused by a bacteria that often produces no symptoms, but that can lead to infertility if untreated. (p. 457)

chorionic villus sampling (CVS) Procedure used to detect chromosomal and genetic abnormalities in the fetus. A catheter (tube) is inserted into the uterus and cells are taken from the chorionic layer of the placenta around the fetus. Chromosomes are removed to conduct genetic tests. (p. 63)

chromosomes Strands of deoxyribonucleic acid (DNA) molecules that contain the genetic codes. (p. 44)

chunking The process of recoding individual elements in memory into larger groups of information. (p. 367)

classical conditioning Process where neutral stimuli are paired with unconditioned stimuli until they come to evoke conditioned responses. (p. 15)

classroom climate The social and emotional environment within a classroom; the way the classroom feels to those in it. (p. 427)

clinical depression A condition that involves sadness, loss of interest in activities, feelings of worthlessness, sleep problems, and changes in appetite that persist for an unusually long time. (p. 471)

cliques Small groups, of usually three to nine friends, who spend time together on a voluntary basis. (p. 537)

cognitive development Component of development related to changes in how children think, remember, and communicate. (p. 7)

cognitive developmental theory A theory that focuses on how children adjust their own understanding as they explore and learn about the world. (p. 17)

collaborative learning Process where children work together to help one another solve problems, share their knowledge and skills, and discuss their strategies and knowledge. (p. 266)

collectivism A cultural orientation based on the belief people are interdependent members of a social group; emphasizes duty to others and group goals, values, and well-being. (p. 548)

colostrum A thick, yellowish substance in breast milk containing important antibodies. (p. 128)

combinational logic The ability to generate and systematically consider all possible combinations of a set of elements. (p. 482)

communication disorders Conditions in which children have significant difficulty producing speech sounds, using spoken language to communicate, or understanding what other people say. (p. 351)

comorbidity Situation in which an individual has more than one psychological disorder or problem at the same time. (p. 348)

componential subtheory Describes how mental processes work together to give us intellectual thought ("analytical intelligence"). (p. 491)

compulsive compliance A behavior pattern seen among some physically abused children, marked by ready and quick responses aimed at pleasing adults by complying with their demands and wishes. (p. 247)

computational models Models of cognition that are programmed on computers: output of the programs is compared to human performance. (p. 380)

concrete operational thought Stage of cognitive development in which children are able to think about two or more dimensions of a problem (decentered thought), dynamic transformations, and reversible operations. (p. 365)

conduct disorder (CD) A conduct problem involving consistent violations of other people's basic rights or the breaking of major societal rules. (p. 409)

conduct problems A general category of rule-breaking behaviors. (p. 409)

connectionist models "Neurally inspired" or neural network models of cognition that view knowledge as based on patterns of activation among interconnected sets of individual units rather than stored as entire concepts. (p. 382)

conscience Ideas children have about right and wrong. (p. 295)

conservation The understanding that some basic properties of objects remain the same even when a transformation changes the physical appearance. (p. 259)

constructivist view The view that people construct their own knowledge and understanding of the world by using what they already know and understand to interpret new experiences. (p. 162)

contact comfort The comfortable feeling that infants gain by clinging to a soft attachment figure. (p. 191)

contextual subtheory Describes how intelligent behavior is related to real-life situations as people adapt to, select, and/or shape their environments ("practical intelligence"). (p. 492)

contraception Methods such as condoms and birth control pills used to prevent pregnancy. (p. 453)

controversial children Children who receive large numbers of both "like best" and "like least" nominations. (p. 422)

convention A rule or practice that members of a social group agree to abide by in their behaviors, choices, and decisions. (p. 296)

coordinated imitation Interaction in which toddler playmates take turns imitating each other and are aware that they are being imitated. (p. 215)

correlational method Research method that measures the degree to which two or more variables are related or associated. (p. 26)

cortisol A hormone released in response to stress. (p. 344)

counting strategies Approaches to solving math problems that involve counting of the quantities. (p. 389)

critical periods Segments of time when structures are first forming and are most vulnerable to damage. (p. 88)

cross-sectional method A type of research design that studies development by comparing groups of children of different ages against one another at the same point in time. (p. 30)

crowds Groups of adolescent peers who have similar reputations or share primary attitudes or activities. (p. 538)

crystallized ability The body of specific knowledge and skills acquired in a particular culture. (p. 490)

cultural deficit perspective Research perspective that assumed the problems associated with minority group families were due to the ways these families were not "measuring up" to the standards of majority white families. (p. 533)

culture A system of shared customs and meanings that allow individuals to participate as a member of a group and that are transmitted from one generation to the next. (p. 548)

delayed phase preference Changes in natural circadian rhythms during puberty that cause teens to become sleepy later in the evening and awaken later in the morning. (p. 468)

descriptive methods Research methods that describe a behavior of interest, such as how often it occurs and under what conditions. (p. 25)

developmental psychopathology perspective The view that a wide variety of factors influences both normal and abnormal paths of development. (p. 348)

dialect A consistent and systematic variety of a single language that is shared by a certain subgroup of speakers. (p. 505)

differentiation Process that occurs during cell division in which each new cell, as it divides, is committed to becoming a particular structure and serving a particular function. (p. 85)

difficult temperament Temperament in which a child is frequently negative, is easily frustrated, withdraws from new situations, is slow to adapt to change, and shows irregular patterns of eating and sleeping. (p. 205)

dilation The gradual opening of the cervix caused by labor contractions during the first stage of birth. (p. 101)

discipline Techniques used to teach children appropriate behavior. (p. 302)

dishabituation The recovery or increase in an infant's response when a familiar stimulus is replaced by one that is novel. (p. 157)

divorce-stress-adjustment perspective A model used to understand divorce outcomes; emphasizes that a complex interaction of stressors, specific vulnerabilities, and protective factors determine an individual child's adjustment to divorce. (p. 411)

dizygotic (DZ) twins Nonidentical twins. These twins form when two eggs are fertilized by two different sperm cells. (p. 53)

DNA Two strands of molecules that twist around each other like a spiral staircase. Connected by a series of nucleotide bases (adenine, thymine, guanine, and cytosine). (p. 44)

dominant–recessive relationship Relationship between genes where the dominant allele will govern a particular trait, and the recessive allele will be repressed. To express a recessive trait, the individual needs to inherit two recessive alleles—one on each chromosome. (p. 56)

Down syndrome Trisomy 21, a genetic disorder that occurs when there is an extra 21st chromosome. Lower IQ, facial defects, heart problems, and shortened life span are characteristic problems. (p. 60)

dynamic systems theories Theories that use models from mathematics and physics to understand complex systems of development. (p. 22)

early maturation When the physical changes of puberty occur earlier than they do in the majority of one's peers. (p. 445)

easy temperament Temperament in which a child is primarily positive, smiles easily, is adaptive and flexible, and has regular patterns of eating and sleeping. (p. 205)

ecological systems theory Theory focusing on the complex set of systems and interacting social layers that can affect a child's development. (p. 20)

egocentrism The child's inability to take another person's perspective. (p. 258)

embryonic stage The second stage of prenatal development, weeks 3 through 8. The embryo forms tissue representing every system and major part of the body. (p. 87)

emotion contagion The tendency of the emotional cues displayed by one person to generate similar cues or emotional states in other people. (p. 209)

encoding The process of forming a mental representation of information. (p. 370)

equilibration The dynamic process of moving between states of cognitive disequilibrium and equilibrium. (p. 165)

estrogens One type of sex hormone, released in greater concentration by females. (p. 442)

ethnic identity A person's understanding of his or her ethnic background and a feeling of belonging to a minority group. (p. 520)

ethology Area of study focusing on the adaptive significance or survival value of behaviors. (p. 19)

experience-dependent development Development of specific skills (such as riding a skateboard) in which new synapses form to code the experience. (p. 231)

experience-expectant development Development of universal skills (such as hand–eye coordination) in which excess synapses form and are pruned according to experience. (p. 231)

experiential subtheory Describes how we become more intelligent as we master new tasks and learn how to perform them more automatically ("creative intelligence"). (p. 491)

experiment Method where researchers systematically manipulate an independent variable to determine if it causes a difference in a dependent variable. (p. 29)

fertilization The union of the father's sperm cell with the mother's egg, yielding one fertilized cell with a unique combination of genes along 46 chromosomes—23 from the father and 23 from the mother. (p. 52)

fetal alcohol effects (FAE) Individual or multiple birth defects caused by prenatal exposure to alcohol. Lowered IQ, hyperactivity, growth deficiencies, and physical malformations can exist alone or in combinations but not in a way that indicates FAS. (p. 94)

fetal alcohol syndrome (FAS) A syndrome of birth defects caused by prenatal exposure to alcohol. Includes growth deficiencies, head and facial malformations, and central nervous system dysfunction. (p. 94)

fetal distress A condition that indicates that the fetus is at risk; usually includes a sudden lack of oxygen (anoxia), a change in fetal heart rate, and/or a change in fetal respiration. (p. 103)

fetal stage The third and final stage of prenatal development, lasting from 8 weeks after conception until birth. (p. 89)

fine motor development Process of coordinating intricate movements with smaller muscles. (p. 143)

fluid ability A biological-based ability to think and perceive relations among elements. (p. 490)

formal operational thought Piaget's final stage of cognitive development, when an adolescent gradually learns to use hypothetico-deductive reasoning and to extend logical thinking to abstract concepts. (p. 480)

fuzzy trace theory   The view that memory representations vary on a continuum from exact and literal to imprecise and general memory traces based on the gist of the information or event. (p. 383)

G x E interaction   The interacting effects of genetics and the environment on the development of traits and characteristics. (p. 65)

gateway drugs   Drugs such as alcohol, tobacco, and marijuana that are typically used prior to the onset of using harder drugs such as cocaine and heroin. (p. 470)

gender constancy   The understanding that gender remains the same despite superficial changes in appearance or behavior. (p. 295)

gender cultures   Different spheres of influence based on the differences that exist between male and female playgroups and affiliations. (p. 310)

gender segregation   The tendency of children to associate with others of their same sex. (p. 295)

gene   A segment of DNA that provides an instruction for a particular structure, function, or trait. (p. 45)

general intelligence *(g)*   A broad thinking ability or mental power that underlies all intellectual tasks and functions. (p. 490)

genotype   The genetic code a person inherits. (p. 66)

germinal stage   The first stage of prenatal development, from conception to 2 weeks. (p. 86)

gifted (or talented) children   Children who show extraordinary achievement in one or more areas. (p. 500)

glial cells   Specialized cells in the nervous system that support neurons in several ways. (p. 230)

gonorrhea   A common STD caused by a bacteria with often mild symptoms, but that can lead to infertility, blood, or joint problems if untreated. (p. 457)

goodness of fit   The degree to which the child's temperament and environment are compatible or complementary, leading to better developmental outcomes. (p. 206)

gross motor development   Process of coordinating movements with the large muscles in the body. (p. 142)

guided participation   The idea that children are involved in sociocultural activities to the degree that their level of cognitive development allows. (p. 487)

habituation   The tendency of infants to reduce their response to stimuli that are presented repeatedly. (p. 157)

habituation–dishabituation technique   Technique used to test infant perception. Infants are shown a stimulus repeatedly until they respond less (habituate) to it. Then a new stimulus is presented. (p. 157)

helpless orientation   The tendency to attribute success to external and uncontrollable factors such as luck, and to attribute failure to internal and stable factors such as lack of ability. (p. 426)

heritability   A mathematical estimate of the degree of genetic influence for a given trait or behavior. (p. 71)

High/Scope Perry Preschool Program   Program offering high-quality partial-day intervention during the school year for young African American children living in poverty. (p. 281)

holophrases   Single words used to express an entire idea or sentence. (p. 182)

homosexual experience   A sexual encounter with someone of the same sex. (p. 523)

homosexual orientation   The sexual identity where the person's sexual attraction is primarily to someone of the same sex. (p. 523)

Human Genome Project   A multinational effort by governments and scientists to map the 3 billion pairs of nucleotide bases and the genes contained in human chromosomes. (p. 46)

human papillomavirus (HPV)   A common STD caused by any of a group of viruses with more than 100 different strains. Persistent infection is the main risk factor for cervical cancer. (p. 457)

hypotheses   Specific inferences drawn from theories; researchers test hypotheses by collecting scientific observations. (p. 10)

hypothetico-deductive reasoning   The ability to use deductive reasoning (reasoning from general to specific facts) to systematically manipulate several variables, test the effects in a systematic way, and reach correct conclusions in complex problems; scientific reasoning. (p. 480)

identity   A person's self-definition, including a knowledge and understanding of the combination of skills, interests, and characteristics that make her a unique person. (p. 518)

identity achievement   A state of identity development in which a person has experienced and worked through the crisis and has made a commitment. (p. 519)

identity diffusion   A state of identity development in which a person is not currently in a state of crisis, but there is a lack of commitment. The person either has stopped trying or is unable to reach a commitment. (p. 519)

identity foreclosure   A state of identity development in which a person has experienced very little crisis but has made a commitment based on what others have said he is and should be. (p. 519)

identity moratorium   A state of identity development in which a person is still in the process of working through the crisis. (p. 519)

imaginary audience   Adolescents' belief that other people are just as concerned with their behavior, feelings, thoughts, and appearance as they are themselves. (p. 482)

implantation   Process where the zygote embeds itself into the inner lining of the mother's uterus. (p. 87)

individualism   A cultural orientation based on the belief that people are independent of each other; emphasizes individual rights, self-fulfillment, and personal accomplishments. (p. 548)

individualized education plan (IEP)   A written plan that describes the services needed and instructional goals for children identified as needing special education services. (p. 355)

Individuals with Disabilities Education Act (IDEA)   Federal law requiring that services be provided to assist all children with disabilities. (p. 239)

infant mortality   Deaths that occur between birth and 1 year of age. (p. 124)

infantile amnesia   Inability to remember things and events occurring before the age of 3 or 4. (p. 233)

information-processing approach   A theoretical approach focusing on how children perceive, store, and retrieve information, and on the strategies they use to solve problems. (p. 18)

insecure–avoidant attachment   In Ainsworth's classification, an unhealthy type of attachment that is indicated when infants do not use their caregivers as a safe base for exploring unfamiliar environments, do not prefer the caregiver over unfamiliar adults, and are not visibly distressed by separation. Such infants ignore or avoid their caregivers when reunited after separation. (p. 195)

insecure–disorganized (or disoriented) attachment   An unhealthy type of attachment that is indicated when infants seem confused or dazed or show contradictory behaviors in the Strange Situation. Infants may be calm and then become angry; or they may be motionless or apprehensive. (p. 195)

insecure–resistant attachment   In Ainsworth's classification, an unhealthy type of attachment that is indicated when infants seek the proximity of their caregiver but do not seem to gain comfort from the contact. (p. 195)

intelligence   As generally defined in Western cultures, the ability to learn, think logically about abstract concepts, and adapt to the environment. (p. 489)

intermodal perception   The process of combining or integrating information across sensory modalities. (p. 158)

internalization   The process of taking external speech and making it internal and mental. (p. 264)

intimacy   An emotional attachment to another person that involves sharing important personal information and trusting others to hold confidences and be supportive. (p. 536)

intuitive thought   Thought and logic that is based on a child's personal experience rather than on a formal system of rules. (p. 258)

inventive spelling   Incorrect spellings that children create by sounding out words and writing the associated letters. (p. 395)

I-self   The conscious awareness that you exist as a separate and unique person and that you can affect others. (p. 290)

knowledge base   The amount of information a person knows about a particular topic. (p. 376)

knowledge telling   Adding or "dumping" in ideas as they come to mind; a failure to selectively organize ideas in writing. (p. 395)

kwashiorkor   Disease caused by a lack of protein in the diet. Children are severly malnourished, with a swollen belly. (p. 230)

language   An arbitrary system of symbols (words) that is rule-governed and allows communication about things that are distant in time or space. (p. 172)

language acquisition device (LAD)   A brain mechanism in humans that is specialized for acquiring and processing language. (p. 173)

late maturation   When the physical changes of puberty do not occur until after they do in the majority of one's peers. (p. 445)

learning disorders   Conditions involving difficulties with specific skills such as reading, mathematics, or writing. (p. 351)

learning theory   Theory that sees language as a skilled behavior that children learn through operant conditioning, imitation, and modeling. (p. 172)

least restrictive environment   Educational placement of students receiving special education services in the classroom with non-disabled peers whenever possible and appropriate. (p. 355)

life-course persistent pattern   A pattern of antisocial and delinquent behavior that begins in childhood and continues into adulthood. (p. 539)

locomotor reflexes   Infant reflexes that mimic locomotor movements such as crawling, stepping, and swimming. (p. 141)

locomotor skills   Skills used to move around, such as walking, running, and climbing. (p. 235)

longitudinal method   A type of research design that studies development by measuring or observing the same children across time as they grow and mature. (p. 31)

long-term memory   Memory of knowledge or events that is permanent. (p. 369)

low birth weight   Weight less than 5½ pounds at birth (2 pounds lighter than average); indicates potential for health risks. (pp. 92, 123)

malnutrition   Nutritional deficiency caused by an inadequate intake of calories, protein, vitamins, and minerals. (p. 229)

malpresentation   Improper positioning of the fetus in the mother's uterus. (p. 103)

mastery orientation   The tendency to attribute success to internal and controllable factors such as hard work and ability, and to attribute failure to controllable or changeable factors such as effort, strategy, or task difficulty. (p. 426)

mature tripod grasp   Placing the base of the hand on the writing surface for support, holding the pencil with the index finger and thumb, and moving the wrist along with finer movements in the fingers to guide the pencil more precisely. (p. 236)

mediation   The process adults and more skilled peers use to introduce concepts and cognitive structures to less skilled children. (p. 264)

meiosis   "Reduction division," the type of cell division that occurs during the formation of gametes (sperm and eggs). (p. 51)

menarche   The first menstrual period for females, usually occurring around 12 to 13 years of age. (p. 443)

mental retardation (MR)   A condition characterized by below-normal intellectual functioning, deficits in adaptive behavior, and an onset early in life (before age 18). (p. 498)

mentoring   The process of taking responsibility for teaching and advising students in a work or school setting to ensure student learning. (p. 511)

me-self   What you know about yourself and how you describe yourself. (p. 290)

metacognition   The understanding or knowledge that people have about their own thought processes. (p. 271)

metalinguistic awareness   A person's explicit knowledge about language itself and about his or her own use of it. (p. 386)

miscarriage   Naturally occurring termination of a pregnancy before the baby is born alive. Also referred to as *spontaneous abortion*. (p. 87)

mitosis   "Copy division," the type of cell division that occurs when chromosomes are copied into each new cell. (p. 51)

monozygotic (MZ) twins   Identical twins. These twins form when one zygote divides to make two zygotes. (p. 53)

moral reasoning   The ways in which people think about right and wrong. (p. 296)

morality   Knowing the difference between what is right and wrong and acting on that knowledge. (p. 296)

mutual gaze   Intent eye contact between two people, as when young infants stare at each other. (p. 212)

myelination   A form of neuron maturation in which the fatty insulation (myelin sheath) grows around the axons. (p. 135)

nativist theory   Theory that sees language as an innate human capability that develops when language input triggers a *language acquisition device* in the brain. (p. 173)

nature   The biological forces (e.g., genetics) that govern development. (p. 8)

neglect   Failure to provide for a child's basic physical, educational, or psychological needs. (p. 244)

neglected children   Children who have very few peers who like them best or least. (p. 422)

network models (of memory)   Models of human memory that view memory as an interconnected network of concept nodes connected by links of varying strength. (p. 367)

neurons   Specialized cells that process information and allow communication in the nervous system. (p. 132)

neuropsychology   An area of study that focuses on the brain and nervous system; researchers often observe brain function using technology such as CT scans, PET, and *f*MRI. (p. 19)

niche-picking   The tendency to pick activities and environments that fit with our genetic predispositions. (p. 68)

nonparental child care   Care provided for a child by someone other than the child's parents. (p. 316)

nonshared environment   Experiences and aspects of the environment that differ across people. (p. 71)

nurture   The environmental conditions and supports that impact development. (p. 8)

object permanence   The fact that objects, events, and people continue to exist even when they are out of a child's direct line of sensory input or motor action. (p. 169)

operant conditioning Process where reinforcing or punishing consequences of actions affect behaviors. (p. 16)

operations Logical processes that can be reversed. (p. 256)

oppositional defiant disorder (ODD) A conduct problem involving a repetitive pattern of defiance, disobedience, and hostility toward authority figures. (p. 409)

organization The tendency to integrate separate elements into increasingly complex higher-order structures. (p. 163)

organized sports Sporting activities organized, coached, or somehow supervised by adults. (p. 336)

organogenesis Organ formation: Process where each major organ and system in the body differentiates within the embryo. (p. 88)

overregularization Incorrect application of the linguistic rules for producing past tenses and plurals, resulting in incorrect forms of irregular words such as *goed* or *deers*. (p. 275)

overweight Having a body mass index at or above the 95th percentile for the child's age and gender. (p. 329)

ovulation Release of an egg (ovum) from the female ovary. (p. 84)

palmar grasp An immature grasp, holding the pencil in the palm and moving the whole arm to draw. (p. 236)

parental control The degree to which parents set limits, enforce rules, and maintain discipline with children. (p. 299)

parental warmth The degree to which parents are accepting, responsive, and compassionate with their children. (p. 298)

parentification Role reversal in which a child assumes responsibilities usually taken care of by parents. (p. 413)

peer nomination technique A polling technique used to identify categories of popular and unpopular children. (p. 420)

perception The cognitive process of organizing, coordinating, and interpreting sensory information. (p. 154)

permissive parents Parents who are warm but have little control over their children. (p. 300)

personal fable False beliefs that adolescents have about their own thoughts, influence, and risks. (p. 483)

personal narratives Stories about personal experiences that use language to inform others about the self and that provide increased self-understanding. (p. 387)

perspective taking The ability to understand the psychological perspectives, motives, and needs of others. (p. 296)

phenotype The observable trait a person shows, resulting in part from the genotype they inherit. (p. 66)

phonemic awareness The understanding that words are made up of smaller units of sound; also, association of printed letters with the sounds that go with them. (p. 392)

physical abuse Abuse that causes physical harm to a child. (p. 243)

physical development Component of development related to growth in size, strength, and muscle coordination. (p. 7)

Piaget's cognitive developmental theory Theory that sees language as one of several abilities that depend on overall cognitive development. Proper cognitive development is a necessary prerequisite for normal language development. (p. 177)

play A pleasurable activity that is actively engaged in on a voluntary basis, is intrinsically motivated, and contains some nonliteral element. (p. 311)

popular children Children whom a large number of peers have chosen as classmates they "like best." (p. 120)

positive emotion bias Tendency of children to report positive more than negative emotions. (p. 293)

postconventional level The level of moral reasoning at which people base moral reasoning on an understanding of social contract and utility and universal ethical principles. (pp. 296, 525)

postural reflexes Reflexes that help infants to keep their heads upright, maintain balance, and roll their heads in the direction of their body motion. (p. 141)

preconventional level Level of moral reasoning where children do not yet understand that rules are social conventions; children accept the rules of powerful others. (p. 296)

preferential-looking technique Technique used to test infant visual perception. If infants consistently look longer at some patterns than at others, researchers infer that the infants can see a difference between the patterns. (p. 155)

prefrontal cortex A large part of the frontal lobe of the brain that is important for planning, judgment, decision making, and inhibiting impulsive responding. (p. 447)

premature (or prematurity) Refers to babies who are born earlier or smaller than average. (p. 90)

prenatal development Development of the organism that occurs before (*pre*) its birth (*natal*). (p. 84)

preoperational thought Thought characterized by the use of mental representations (symbols) and intuitive thought. (p. 256)

prepared childbirth Use of birthing techniques designed to reduce muscle tension, promote relaxation, and reduce pain during labor and delivery. (p. 107)

preterm birth Birth that occurs before 37 weeks of gestation, or about 3 weeks earlier than the normal due date. (p. 92, 123)

prevalence rates Refers to the percentages or numbers of individuals who show particular problems or conditions. (p. 348)

primitive reflexes Reflexes that help the infant to find nourishment or might have served protective functions during earlier periods of evolution. (p. 141)

private speech Speech that children say aloud to themselves; later internalized to form inner speech and mental activity. (p. 263)

probabilistic epigenesis The likelihood that specific environmental conditions will activate specific genes that lead to particular traits or behavioral outcomes. (p. 69)

process quality The quality of the actual experiences children have in child care. (p. 318)

processing capacity The amount of information a person can remember or think about at one time. (p. 269)

processing efficiency The speed and accuracy with which a person can process information. (p. 270)

production systems Sets of computerized *if–then* statements that state the specific actions that will be taken under certain conditions. (p. 381)

programmed cell death Process by which many neurons die during periods of migration and heavy synaptogenesis. (p. 135)

Project Head Start Federally funded, comprehensive program designed to improve academic achievement and opportunity for young children. (p. 281)

prosocial reasoning How children think about helping others, including their reasons for deciding whether to help another person. (p. 407)

proximodistal pattern Pattern of growth where areas closer to the center of the body tend to form and grow before the areas toward the extremities grow. (p. 88)

psychoanalytic theories Theories that focus on the structure of personality and how the conscious and unconscious portions of the self influence behavior and development. (p. 11)

psychological abuse Abuse that includes verbal put-downs and other behavior that terrorizes, threatens, rejects, or isolates children. (p. 244)

psychological autonomy granting A dimension of parenting that involves encouraging adolescents to develop their own individual opinions and beliefs. (p. 531)

psychometric approach The attempt to quantify people's psychological skills and abilities, usually by means of paper-and-pencil tests and/or physical measurements. (p. 490)

puberty The process of physical maturation that leads to the physical capability to reproduce. (p. 442)

punishment Techniques used to eliminate or reduce undesirable behavior. (p. 302)

range of reaction The range of possible phenotypes that exist for a particular genotype. (p. 66)

rape Sexual intercourse as a result of physical force or psychological coercion. (p. 461)

reconstructive memory A characteristic of human memory. We store parts of events and knowledge; during recall we retrieve the stored pieces and draw inferences about the rest. (p. 372)

reflective abstraction The process of noticing and thinking about the implications of information and experiences. (p. 165)

reflexes Involuntary movements that are elicited by environmental stimuli. (p. 141)

rejected children Children who are actively disliked; a large number of peers have chosen them as classmates they "like least." (p. 422)

rejecting/neglecting parents Parents who don't set limits and are unresponsive to their children's needs. (p. 301)

relational aggression Withdrawing friendship or otherwise disrupting or threatening social relationships as a way to hurt other people. (p. 406)

reliability The consistency of scores when a test is repeated under the same or similar conditions. (p. 495)

resilient children Children who succeed, achieve, or otherwise have positive developmental outcomes despite growing up under negative conditions. (p. 410)

retrieval In the stores model, retrieval is the process of bringing information from the long-term store to the short-term store. In network models, retrieval is the process of activating information so that it becomes a part of the working memory and thus available for use. (p. 370)

risk of overweight Having a body mass index from the 85th to the 95th percentile for the child's age and gender. (p. 329)

rough-and-tumble play Very physical, aggressive but friendly play common among boys during middle childhood. (p. 336)

scaffolding Support given to a child as he or she develops a new mental function or learns to perform a particular task. (p. 265)

scheme An organized pattern of physical or mental action. (p. 163)

scientific method Process where researchers test hypotheses by making systematic observations. (p. 24)

scripts Mental representations of the way things typically occur in certain settings or for certain events. (p. 372)

secure attachment In Ainsworth's classification system, the healthy type of attachment between an infant and a caregiver. It is indicated when the infant seeks contact with the caregiver, clings, and is soothed by the caregiver and when the infant uses the caregiver as a safe base for exploring unfamiliar environments. Other indicators include *separation anxiety* and *stranger anxiety*. (p. 194)

selection model A model used to understand divorce outcomes; emphasizes that certain characteristics of parents (e.g., abusiveness) rather than the divorce itself cause children's negative outcomes. (p. 412)

self The characteristics, emotions, and beliefs people have about themselves, including an understanding that people are unique individuals. (p. 290)

self-conscious emotions Emotions that relate to people's self-images or what people think about themselves; include shame, embarrassment, guilt, and pride. (p. 211)

self-esteem The emotions people feel about themselves. (p. 402)

self-evaluations The judgments people make about themselves. (p. 402)

self-fulfilling prophecy A prediction that comes true because people believe the prediction and behave in ways that produce the expected outcome. (p. 427)

self-regulation The ability to control our own behavior, emotions, or thoughts and change them to meet the demands of the situation. (p. 291)

self-representations The ways people describe themselves; also called *self-concepts*. (p. 402)

sensitive responsiveness A quality of infant care in which caregivers respond quickly and warmly to the baby's signals and adjust their responses to allow the infant to direct some of the interactions. (p. 196)

sensitization The development of a tendency to overreact strongly and quickly to fearful situations even when they are relatively mild. (p. 345)

sensorimotor play Play that evolves mostly around the practice of sensory activity and the development of new motor actions. (p. 213)

sensorimotor thought Thought that is based only on sensory input and physical (motor) actions. (p. 166)

separation anxiety Distress infants experience when separated from their primary caregivers. (p. 194)

sex chromosomes The 23rd pair of chromosomes (in humans), specialized to determine the sex of the child and other characteristics. Males are XY and females are XX. (p. 54)

sexual abuse Abuse that includes fondling a child's genitals or breasts, committing intercourse or other sexual acts with a child, exposing the child to indecent acts, or involving the child in pornography. (p. 244)

sexual assault Sexual contact due to physical force or psychological coercion that may or may not involve penetration. (p. 461)

sexual harassment Any unwanted behavior of a sexual nature that creates a hostile or offensive environment. (p. 462)

sexual orientation Tendency to be attracted to people of the same sex (homosexual orientation), of the opposite sex (heterosexual orientation), or to both sexes (bisexual orientation). (p. 521)

sexually transmitted diseases (STDs) A disease transmitted primarily through sexual contact. (p. 450)

shared environment Experiences and aspects of the environment that are common across all individuals who are living together. (p. 71)

situated cognition The idea that we cannot fully understand children's thinking and cognition without considering the context in which it occurs. (p. 487)

sleeper effect Subtle effects of divorce that may not become apparent until children reach adolescence or young adulthood and have difficulty forming intimate and stable relationships. (p. 413)

slow-to-warm-up temperament Temperament in which a child shows mildly negative responses to new stimuli and situations but with repeated exposure gradually develops a quiet and positive interest. (p. 205)

small for gestational age (SGA) Born below the tenth percentile of birth weight for gestational age; indicates serious health risks. (p. 123)

social cognition model A model that explains how different children perceive, interpret, and respond to information in social settings. (p. 423)

social comparison The process where children compare their own qualities and performances to those of their peers. (p. 402)

social interactionist theory Theory proposing that language development results from the interaction of biological and social factors and that social interaction is required. (p. 178)

social learning Process where children learn by observing and imitating the behaviors of other people. (p. 16)

social policy Attempts to improve the lives of children and families by using child development research to affect laws, regulations, and programs. (p. 36)

social referencing The tendency of infants and children to look for emotional cues from parents and other caregivers to get information in uncertain situations. (p. 210)

social rules of discourse Conventions that speakers of a language follow when having a conversation. (p. 275)

social speech Speech that we hear as people talk around us or to us. (p. 263)

socially shared cognition The idea that thought is a shared group activity and that the thoughts held by an individual are derived at least in part from dynamic interactions occurring between people and in groups. (p. 488)

sociocultural theory A theory that focuses on how language and culture influence the growth of thought in children. (p. 17)

sociodramatic play Play that involves acting out different social roles or characters. (p. 313)

socioemotional development Component of development related to changes in how children interact with other people (e.g., family members, peers, and playmates) and manage their emotions. (p. 7)

specific intelligence *(s)* Abilities people have in particular areas, such as reading, verbal, and spatial skills. (p. 490)

spermarche The first ejaculation. (p. 442)

stage–environment fit The degree to which the environment is successful in meeting the cognitive, social, and emotional needs of a child in a particular stage of development. (p. 544)

storage Placing information in permanent, or long-term, memory. (p. 370)

stores model (of memory) A model of human memory that views information as moving through a series of storage locations, from the sensory stores to short-term store to long-term store. (p. 366)

Strange Situation A structured laboratory procedure that is used to observe attachment behavior in human infants. (p. 193)

stranger anxiety Wariness or fear of unfamiliar adults. (p. 194)

strategies Conscious, intentional, and controllable plans used to improve performance. (p. 377)

strategy choice model The idea that children solve math problems by choosing the fastest approach that they can execute accurately. (p. 391)

strength and resilience perspective Research perspective that explores ways that minority families have survived in spite of historical patterns of racism, bigotry, and inequality. (p. 533)

structural quality The quality of objective aspects of the child care environment. (p. 317)

subitizing A perceptual process where people quickly and easily determine how many objects are in a small set without actually counting them. (p. 389)

substance abuse The use of a substance that alters psychological functioning to the extent that it creates difficulties in day to day life. (p. 468)

substance use Ingesting on more than a few occasions any substance that alters psychological functioning. (p. 468)

symbolic play Play in which children use make-believe and pretend to embellish objects and actions. (p. 216)

symbolic (representational) thought The ability to form symbols (or mental representations) that stand for objects or events in the world. (p. 167)

synaptic pruning Process in which unused synapses are lost (pruned). (p. 230)

synaptogenesis One form of neuron maturation in which dendrites and axons branch out to form an enormously large number of connections with neighboring neurons. (p. 134)

telegraphic speech Speech that includes only words that are essential to get the meaning across, leaving out unessential words. (p. 182)

temperament The infant or child's behavioral style or primary pattern of reacting to the environment. (p. 204)

teratogen Any substance or condition that might disrupt prenatal development and cause birth defects. (p. 90)

theory An explanation of how facts fit together, allowing us to understand and predict behavior. (p. 10)

theory of mind An integrated understanding of what the mind is, how it works, and why it works that way. (p. 272)

theory of multiple intelligences Theory of intelligence emphasizing that we all have multiple intelligences that operate relatively independently of one another; the theory includes 8 intelligences. (p. 492)

triarchic theory of intelligence Theory of intelligence emphasizing how mental processes, experience, and situational contexts relate to intellectual thought. Includes componential, experiential, and contextual subtheories. (p. 490)

twin studies Comparisons between measurements of identical and nonidentical twins, used to estimate the genetic contribution to traits and characteristics. (p. 72)

ultrasonography (ultrasound) Images of the fetus inside the mother's womb produced by sound waves. Ultrasound can be used to help physicians monitor fetal growth and detect physical defects. (p. 62)

validity The ability of a test to measure what it intends to measure (e.g., intelligence). (p. 496)

very low birth weight Weight less than $3\frac{1}{2}$ pounds at birth (4 pounds lighter than average); indicates serious health risks. (p. 123)

visual acuity The ability to see fine detail. (p. 136)

working memory The information currently active in your memory system and currently available for use in a mental task. (p. 367)

X-linked (sex-linked) traits Traits that differ in rate of occurrence between males and females, caused by dominant and recessive alleles on the X and Y chromosomes. (p. 59)

zone of proximal development (ZPD) The distance between the current maximum independent performance level of the child and the tasks the child can perform if guided by adults or more capable peers. (p. 264)

zygote Term used to refer to the human organism after the fertilized egg cell begins to divide. (p. 50)

References

Aalsma, M. C., Lapsley, D. K., & Flannery, D. J. (2006). Personal fables, narcissism, and adolescent adjustment. *Psychology in the Schools, 43,* 481–491.

ABC News. (2001). An evil smile: Witnesses say suspect looked like he was "getting even." Retrieved March 6, 2001, from http://abcnews.go.com/sections/us/dailynews/shooting_calif010306.html.

Abel, E. L. (1992). Paternal exposure to alcohol. In T. B. Sonderegger (Ed.), *Perinatal Substance Abuse: Research Findings and Clinical Implications* (pp. 132–160). Baltimore: The Johns Hopkins University Press.

Abel, E. L. (1993). Paternal alcohol exposure and hyperactivity in rat offspring: Effects of amphetamine. *Neurotoxicology and Teratology, 15,* 445–449.

Abel, E. L. (2004). Paternal contribution to fetal alcohol syndrome. *Addiction Biology, 9,* 127–133.

Abel, E. L., & Sokol, R. J. (1987). Incidence of fetal alcohol syndrome and economic impact of FAS–related anomalies. *Drug and Alcohol Dependence, 19,* 51–70.

Abma, J. C., Martinez, G. M., Mosher, W. D., & Dawson, B. S. (2004). *Teenagers in the United States: Sexual activity, contraceptive use, and childbearing, 2002.* National Center for Health Statistics. Vital Health Statistics Series 23 (24). Retrieved May 27, 2006, from http://www.cdc.gov/nchs/data/series/sr_23/sr23_024.pdf.

Aboud, F. E., & Doyle, A. B. (1995). The development of in-group pride in black Canadians. *Journal of Cross-Cultural Psychology, 26,* 243–254.

Ackermann–Liebrich, U., Voegeli, T., Gÿanter–Witt, K., Kunz, I., Zÿallig, M., Schindler, C., & Maurer, M. (1996). Home versus hospital deliveries: Follow up study of matched pairs for procedures and outcome. *British Journal of Medicine, 313,* 1313–1318.

Adams, M. J., Treiman, R., & Pressley, M. (1998). Reading, writing, and literacy. In Damon (Ed.), *Handbook of Child Psychology* (Vol. 4). New York: John Wiley & Sons, Inc.

Adams, R. J., Courage, M. L., & Mercer, M. E. (1994). Systematic measurement of human neonatal color vision. *Vision Research, 34,* 1691–1701.

Adams, R. J., Maurer, D., & Davis, M. (1986). Newborns' discrimination of chromatic from achromatic stimuli. *Journal of Experimental Child Psychology, 41,* 267–281.

Adams, R., & Laursen, B. (2001). The organization and dynamics of adolescent conflict with parents and friends. *Journal of Marriage and the Family, 63,* 97–110.

Ainsworth, M. D. S. (1973). The development of infant-mother attachment. In B. M. Caldwell & H. N. Ricciuti (Eds.), *Review of Child Development Research* (Vol. 3, pp. 1–94). Chicago: University of Chicago Press.

Ainsworth, M. D. S., & Wittig, B. A. (1969). Attachment and exploratory behavior of one-year-olds in a Strange Situation. In B. M. Foss (Ed.), *Determinants of Infant Behavior* (Vol. 4, pp. 111–136). London: Methuen.

Ainsworth, M. D. S., Blehar, M. C., Waters, E., & Wall, S. (1978). *Patterns of attachment: A psychological study of the strange situation.* Hillsdale, NJ: Lawrence Erlbaum Associates.

Ainsworth, M. S. (1967). *Infancy in Uganda.* Baltimore: The Johns Hopkins University Press.

Akhtar, N., & Tomasello, M. (2000). The social nature of words and word learning. In R. M. Golinkoff, K. Hirsh-Pasek, L. Bloom, L. B. Smith, A. L. Woodward, N. Akhtar, M. Tomasello, & G. Hollich (Eds.), *Becoming a Word Learner: A Debate on Lexical Acquisition* (pp. 115–135). Oxford, England: Oxford University Press.

Aksan, N., & Kochanska, G. (2005). Conscience in childhood: Old questions, new answers. *Developmental Psychology, 41,* 506–516.

Alaimo, K., Briefel, R. R., Frongillo, E. A., & Olson, C. M. (1998). Food insufficiency exists in the United States: Results from the Third National Health and Nutrition Examination Survey (NHANES III). *American Journal of Public Health, 88,* 419–426.

Alan Guttmacher Institute (1994). *Sex and America's Teenagers.* New York: Alan Guttmacher Institute.

Alan Guttmacher Institute (2002). State-level policies on sexuality, STD education. Retrieved January 6, 2003, from www.guttmacher.org/pubs/ib_5-01.html.

Alan Guttmacher Institute (2004). U.S. teenage pregnancy statistics: Overall trends, trends by race and ethnicity and state-by-state information. Retrieved May 24, 2006, from http://www.guttmacher.org/.

Alarcón, M., Plomin, R., Fulker, D. W., Corley, R., & DeFries, J. C. (1998). Multivariate path analysis of specific cognitive abilities data at 12 years of age in the Colorado adoption project. *Behavior Genetics, 28*(4), 255–264.

Alderman, M. K. (1999). *Motivation for achievement: Possibilities for teaching and learning.* Mahwah, NJ: Erlbaum.

Al-Namlah, A. S., Fernyhough, C., & Meins, E. (2006). Sociocultural influences on the development of verbal mediation: Private speech and phonological recoding in Saudi Arabian and British samples. *Developmental Psychology, 42,* 117–131.

Altman, L. K. (2000, June 27). Reading the book of life: The doctor's world; genomic chief has high hopes, and great fears, for genetic testing. *The New York Times.* Retrieved February 15, 2002, from http://www.nytimes.com.

Amato, P. R. (1994). The implications of research findings on children in stepfamilies. In A. Booth & J. Dunn (Eds.), *Stepfamilies: Who Benefits? Who does Not?* (pp. 81–87). Hillsdale, NJ: Erlbaum.

Amato, P. R. (1999). Children of divorced parents as young adults. In E. M. Hetherington (Ed.), *Coping with Divorce, Single Parenting, and Remarriage: A Risk and Resiliency Perspective* (pp. 147–163). Mahwah, NJ: Erlbaum.

Amato, P. R. (2000). The consequences of divorce for adults and children. *Journal of Marriage and the Family, 62,* 1269–1287.

Amato, P. R. (2001). Children of divorce in the 1990s: An update of the Amato and Keith (1991) meta-analysis. *Journal of Family Psychology, 15,* 355–370.

Amato, P. R., & Booth, A. (1997). *A generation at risk: Growing up in an era of family upheaval.* Cambridge, MA: Harvard University Press.

Amato, P. R., & Keith, B. (1991). Parental divorce and the well-being of children: A meta-analysis. *Psychological Bulletin, 110,* 26–46.

American Academy of Child & Adolescent Psychiatry (2004). *Child sexual abuse.* Retrieved June 22, 2006, from http://www.aacap.org/publications/factsfam/sexabuse.htm.

American Academy of Pediatrics. (1992). Fitness, activity, and sports participation in the preschool child. *Pediatrics, 90,* 1002–1004.

American Academy of Pediatrics. (1998). Guidance for effective discipline. *Pediatrics, 101,* 723–728.

American Academy of Pediatrics (2001). Care of adolescent parents and their children. *Pediatrics, 107,* 429–434.

American Academy of Pediatrics (2003). Prevention of Pediatric Overweight and Obesity. *Pediatrics, 112*(2), 424–430.

American Academy of Pediatrics. (2005). Breastfeeding and the use of human milk. *Pediatrics, 115*(2), 496–506.

American Association of University Women (2001). *Hostile hallways: Bullying, teasing, and sexual harassment in school.* Washington, DC: AAUW.

American Council on Education, (1992). *Sexual harassment on campus: A policy and program of deterrence.* Washington, DC: American Council on Education.

American Psychiatric Association (2000). *Diagnostic and statistical manual of mental disorders*-TR (4th ed.). Washington, DC: Author.

American Psychological Association. www.apa.org/ethics.

American Youth Policy Forum & Center for Workforce Development (June, 2000). *Looking forward: School-to-work principles and strategies for sustainability.* Washington, DC. Retrieved July 14, 2005, from www.aypf.org.

Ames, C. (1992). Classrooms: Goals, structures, and student motivation. *Journal of Educational Psychology, 84,* 261–271.

Anderman, E. M., & Maehr, M. L. (1994). Motivation and schooling in the middle grades. *Review of Educational Research, 64,* 287–309.

Anderson, C. A., & Bushman, B. J. (2001). Effects of violent video games on aggressive behavior, aggressive cognition, aggressive affect, physiological arousal, and prosocial behavior: A meta-analytic review of the scientific literature. *Psychological Science, 12,* 353–359.

Anderson, D. K., Rhees, R. W., & Fleming, D. E. (1985). Effects of prenatal stress on differentiation of the sexually dimorphic nucleus of the preoptic area (SDN–POA) of the rat brain. *Brain Research, 332,* 113–118.

Anderson, D. R., Huston, A. C., Schmitt, K. L., Linebarger, D. L., & Wright, J. C. (2001). Early childhood television viewing and adolescent behavior. *Monographs of the Society for Research in Child Development, 66*(Serial No. 264), 1–156.

Anderson, R. E., Crespo, C. J., Bartlett, S. J., Cheskin, L. J., & Pratt, M. (1998). Relationship of physical activity and television watching with body weight and level of fatness among children. *Journal of the American Medical Association, 279*(12), 938–942.

Anderson, R. N., & Smith, B. L. (2005). Deaths: Leading causes for 2002. National Vital Statistics Reports, 23(17). Hyattsville, MD: National Center for Health Statistics. Retrieved July 22, 2006, from http://www.cdc.gov/nchs/data/nvsr/nvsr53/nvsr53_17.pdf.

Andersson, B. E. (1992). Effects of day care on cognitive and socioemotional competence of thirteen-year-old Swedish school children. *Child Development, 63,* 20–36.

Andersson, H. W. (1996). The Fagan Test of Infant Intelligence: Predictive validity in a random sample. *Psychological Reports, 78,* 1015–1026.

Andraca, I., Pino, P., LaParra, A., & Castillo, F. R. (1998). Risk factors for psychomotor development among infants born under optimal biological conditions. *Revista de Saude Publica, 32,* 138–147. (As cited in Santos et al. 2001.)

Andrews, J. A., & Lewinsohn, P. M. (1992). Suicidal attempts among older adolescents: Prevalence and co-occurrence with psychiatric disorders. *Journal of the American Academy of Child and Adolescent Psychiatry, 31,* 655–662.

Anglin, J. M. (1993). Vocabulary development: A morphological analysis. *Monographs of the Society for Research in Child Development, 58*(10, Serial No. 238).

Annesi, J. J. (2005). Improvements in self-concept associated with reductions in negative mood in preadolescents enrolled in an after-school physical activity program. *Psychological Reports, 97,* 400–404.

Antell, S., & Keating, D. (1983). Perception of numerical invariance in neonates. *Child Development, 54,* 695–701.

Apgar, V. (1953). A proposal for a new method of evaluation in the newborn infant. *Current Research in Anesthesia and Analgesia, 32,* 260.

Arditti, J. A. (1999). Rethinking relationships between divorced mothers and their children: Capitalizing on family strengths. *Family Relations, 48,* 109–119.

Arendt, R. E., Short, E. J., & Singer, L. T. (2004). Children prenatally exposed to cocaine: Developmental outcomes and environmental risks at seven years of age. *Journal of Developmental and Behavioral Pediatrics, 25,* 83–90.

Ashcraft, M. H. (1992). Cognitive arithmetic: A review of data and theory. *Cognition, 44,* 75–106.

Asher, S. R., Parker, J. G., & Walker, D. L. (1996). Distinguishing friendship from acceptance: Implications for intervention and assessment. In W. M. Bukowski, A. F. Newcomb, & W. W. Hartup (Eds.), *The Company They Keep: Friendship in Childhood and Adolescence* (pp. 366–405). New York: Cambridge University Press.

Aslin, R. N. (1987). Visual and auditory development in infancy. In J. D. Osofsky (Ed.), *Handbook of Infant Development* (2nd ed., pp. 5–97). New York: Wiley.

Aslin, R. N., Jusczyk, P. W., & Pisoni, D. B. (1998). Speech and auditory processing during infancy. In D. Kuhn & R. S. Siegler (Eds.), *Cognitive, Language, and Perceptual Develoment* (Vol. 2, pp. 147–198), in W. Damon (Gen. Ed.), *Handbook of Child Psychology.* New York: Wiley.

Associated Press (1999, January 15). Mom wins parole after drug rehab. *The State* (Columbia, South Carolina Newspaper), p. B1.

Atkins, C. P. (1993). Do employment recruiters discriminate on the basis of nonstandard dialect? *Journal of Employment Counseling, 30,* 108–118.

Atkinson, R. C., & Shiffrin, R. M. (1968). Human memory: A proposed system and its control processes. In K. W. Spence & J. T. Spence (Eds.), *The Psychology of Learning and Motivation: Advances in Research and Theory* (Vol. 2, pp. 89–195). New York: Academic Press.

Attinasi, J. J. (1998). English only for California children and the aftermath of proposition 227. *Education, 119,* 263–284.

Atwater, E. (1992). *Adolescence* (2nd ed.). Englewood Cliffs, NJ: Prentice Hall.

Au, T. K., Sidle, A. L., & Rollins, K. B. (1993). Developing an intuitive understanding of conservation and contamination: Invisible particles as a plausible mechanism. *Developmental Psychology, 29,* 286–299.

Aunola, K., Leskinen, E., Lerkkanen, M-K., & Nurmi, J-E. (2004). Developmental dynamics of math performance from preschool to grade 2. *Journal of Educational Psychology, 96,* 699–713.

Autism Society of America (2002). What is autism? Retrieved June 28, 2002, from www.autism-society.org.

Averett, S. L., Rees, D. I., & Argus, L. M. (2002). The impact of government policies and neighborhood characteristics on teenage sexual activity and contraceptive use. *American Journal of Public Health, 92,* 1773–1778.

Avis, J., & Harris, P. L. (1991). Belief-desire reasoning among Baka children: Evidence for a universal conception of mind. *Child Development, 62,* 460–467.

Babrick, L. E. (2000). Increasing specificity in the development of intermodal perception. In D. Muir & A. Slater (Eds.), *Infant development: The Essential Readings* (pp. 119–136). Malden, MA: Blackwell.

Baddeley, A. D. (1986). *Working memory.* New York: Oxford University Press.

Baden, A. L. (2002). The psychological adjustment of transracial adoptees: An application of the cultural-racial identity model. *Journal of Social Distress and the Homeless, 11,* 167–191.

Bailey, J. M., LeCouteur, A., Gottesman, I., Bolton, P., Simonoff, E., Yuzda, E., et al. (1995). Autism as a strongly genetic disorder: Evidence from a British twin study. *Psychological Medicine, 25,* 63–77.

Bailey, J. M., & Pillard, R. C. (1991). A genetic study of male sexual orientation. *Archives of General Psychiatry, 48,* 1089–1096.

Bailey, J. M., & Zucker, K. J. (1995). Childhood sex-typed behavior and sexual orientation: A conceptual analysis and quantitative review. *Developmental Psychology, 31,* 43–55.

Baillargeon, R. (1993). The object concept revisited: New directions in the investigation of infants' physical knowledge. In C. E. Granrud (Ed.), *Visual Perception and Cognition in Infancy* (pp. 265–315). Hillsdale, NJ: Erlbaum.

Baird, A. A., Burber, S. A., Rein, D. A., Maas, L. C., Steingard, R. J., Renshaw, P. F., et al. (1999). Functional magnetic resonance imaging of facial affect recognition in children and adolescents. *Journal of the American Academy of Child and Adolescent Psychiatry, 38,* 195–199.

Baker, K. (1998). Structured English immersion: Breakthrough in teaching limited-English-proficient students. *Phi Delta Kappan,*

Bakermans-Kranenburg, M. J., van IJzendoorn, M. H., Bokhorst, C. L., & Schuengel, C. (2004). The importance of shared environment in infant-father attachment: A behavioral genetic study of the Attachment Q-Sort. *Journal of Family Psychology, 18,* 545–549.

Baldwin, D. A., Markman, E. M., Bill, B., Desjardins, R. N., Irwin, R. N., & Tidball, G. (1996). Infants' reliance on social criterion for establishing word-object relations. *Child Development, 67,* 3135–3153.

Baltes, P. B., & Kunzmann, U. (2004). The two faces of wisdom: Wisdom as a general theory of knowledge and judgment about excellence in mind and virtue vs. wisdom as everyday realization in people and products. *Human Development, 47,* 290–299.

Baltes, P. B., & Staudinger, U. M. (2000). Wisdom: A metaheuristic (pragmatic) to orchestrate mind and virtue toward excellence. *American Psychologist, 55,* 122–136.

Bandura, A. (1997). *Self-efficacy: The exercise of control.* New York: W. H. Freeman.

Bandura, A., & Walters, R. (1963). *Social learning and personality development.* New York: Holt, Rinehart, & Winston.

Barber, B. K. (2002). *Intrusive parenting: How psychological control affects children and adolescents.* Washington, DC: American Psychological Association.

Barkley, R. A. (1996). Attention Deficit/Hyperactivity Disorder. In E. J. Mash & R. A. Barkley (Eds.), *Child Psychopathology* (pp. 63–112). New York: Guilford Press.

Barkley, R. A. (1998). Attention Deficit/Hyperactivity Disorder. In E. J. Mash & R. A. Barkley (Eds.), *Treatment of Childhood Disorders* (pp. 55–110). New York: Guilford Press.

Barkley, R. A. (2003). Attention Deficit/Hyperactivity Disorder. In E. J. Mash & R. A. Barkley (Eds.), *Child Psychopathology* (2nd ed., pp. 63–112). New York: Guilford Press.

Barlow, S. M., Knight, A. F., & Sullivan, F. M. (1979). Prevention by diazepam of adverse effects of maternal restraint stress on postnatal development and learning in the rat. *Teratology, 19,* 105–110.

Barnett, D., Ganiban, J., & Cicchetti, D. (1999). Maltreatment, negative expressivity, and the development of Type D attachments from 12 to 24 months of age. *Monographs of the Society for Research in Child Development, 64*(3), 97–118.

Barnett, W. S. (1998). Long-term effects on cognitive development and school success. In W. S. Barnett & S. S. Boocock (Eds.), *Early Care and Education for Children in Poverty: Promises, Programs, and Long-term Results* (pp. 11–44). Albany, NY: State University of New York Press.

Barr, R., Marott, H., & Rovee-Collier, C. K. (2003). The role of sensory preconditioning in memory retrieval by preverbal infants. *Learning & Behavior, 31,* 11–123.

Barrera, M. E., & Maurer, D. (1981a). Recognition of mother's photographed face by the three-month-old infant. *Child Development, 52,* 714–716.

Bates, E. A., & Elman, J. L. (2002). Connectionism and the study of change. In M. H. Johnson, Y. Munakata, & R. O. Gilmore (Eds.), *Brain Development and Cognition: A Reader* (2nd ed., pp. 420–440). Malden, MA: Blackwell Publishers.

Battin-Pearson, S., Newcomb, M. D., Abbott, R. D., Hill, K. G., Catalano, R. F., & Hawkins, J. D. (2000). Predictors of early high school drop-out: A test of five theories. *Journal of Educational Psychology, 92,* 568–582.

Bauer, P. J. (2006). Event memory. In D. Kuhn & R. S. Siegler (Eds.), *Cognitive, Language, and Perceptual Development* (Vol. 2, pp. 373–425), in W. Damon (Gen. Ed.), *Handbook of Child Psychology.* New York: Wiley.

Bauer, P. J., & Dow, G. A. (1994). Episodic memory in 16- and 20-month-old children: Specifics are generalized but not forgotten. *Developmental Psychology, 30,* 403–417.

Bauer, P. J., & Mandler, J. M. (1992). Putting the horse before the cart: The use of temporal order in recall of events by one-year-old children. *Developmental Psychology, 28,* 441–452.

Baumrind, D. (1973). The development of instrumental competence through socialization. In A. D. Pick (Ed.), *Minnesota Symposia on Child Psychology* (Vol. 7, pp. 3–46). Minneapolis: University of Minnesota Press.

Baumrind, D. (1991). Effective parenting during the early adolescent transition. In P. A. Cowan & M. Heatherington (Eds.), *Family Transitions* (pp. 111–164). Hillsdale, NJ: Erlbaum.

Baumrind, D. (1996). The discipline controversy revisited. *Family Relations, 45,* 405–414.

Baumrind, D., Larzelere, R. E., & Cowan, P. A. (2002). Ordinary physical punishment: Is it harmful? Comment on Gershoff (2002). *Psychological Bulletin, 128,* 580–589.

Baydar, N., & Greek, A. (1997). A longitudinal study of the effects of the birth of a sibling during the first six years of life. *Journal of Marriage and the Family, 59*(4), 939–957.

Baydar, N., & Hyle, P. (1997). A longitudinal study of the effects of the birth of a sibling during preschool and early grade school years. *Journal of Marriage and the Family, 59*(4), 957–966.

Bayliss, D. M., Jarrold, C., Baddeley, A. D., Gunn, D. M., & Leigh E. (2005). Mapping the developmental constraints on working memory span performance. *Developmental Psychology, 41,* 579–597.

Bayliss, D. M., Jarrold, C., Gunn, D. M., & Baddeley, A. D. (2003). The complexities of complex span: Explaining individual differences in working memory in children and adults. *Journal of Experimental Psychology: General, 132,* 71–92.

Beal, C., & Belgrad, S. (1990). The development of message evaluation skills in young children. *Child Development, 61,* 705–712.

Beauchamp, G. K., Cowart, B. J., Mennella, J. A., & Marsh, R. R. (1994). Infant salt taste: Developmental, methodological, and contextual factors. *Developmental Psychobiology, 27,* 353–365.

Beckman, M. (2004). Crime, culpability, and the adolescent brain. *Science, 305,* 596–599.

Bedard, A., Ickowicz, A., Logan, G. D., Hogg-Johnson, S., Schachar, R., & Tannock, R. (2003). Selective inhibition in children with attention deficit hyperactivity disorder off and on stimulant medication. *Journal of Abnormal Child Psychology, 31,* 315–327.

Behrend, D. A., Rosengren, K. S., & Perlmutter, M. (1992). The relation between private speech and parental interactive style. In R. M. Diaz & L. E. Berk (Eds.), *Private Speech: From Social Interaction to Self-regulation* (pp. 85–100). Hillsdale, NJ: Erlbaum.

Beilin, H. (1978). Inducing conservation through training. In G. Steiner (Ed.), *Psychology of the Twentieth Century* (Vol. 7, pp. 260–289). Munich: Kindler.

Beilin, H. (1994). Jean Piaget's enduring contribution to developmental psychology. In R. D. Parke, P. A. Ornstein, J. J. Rieser, & C. Zahn-Waxler (Eds.), *A Century of Developmental Psychology* (pp. 257–290). Washington, DC: American Psychological Association.

Beller, E. K., & Pohl, A. (1986, April). *The strange situation revisited.* Paper presented at the biennial meeting of the International Conference on Infant Studies, Beverly Hills, CA.

Bellugi, U., & St. George, M. (Eds.). (2001). *Journal from cognition to brain to gene: Perspectives from Williams syndrome.* Cambridge, MA: MIT Press.

Belsky, J., & Isabella, R. (1985). Marital and parent–child relationships in family of origin and marital change following the birth of a baby: A retrospective analysis. *Child Development, 56,* 342–349.

Belsky, J., & Isabella, R. (1988). Maternal, infant, and social-contextual determinants of attachment security. In J. Belsky & T. Nezworski (Eds.), *Clinical Applications of Attachment* (pp. 41–94). Hillsdale, NJ: Lawrence Erlbaum Associates.

Belsky, J., & Rovine, M. J. (1988). Nonmaternal care in the first year of life and the security of infant-parent attachment. *Child Development, 59,* 157–167.

Belsky, J., Jaffee, S. R., Sligo, J., Woodward, L., & Silva, P. A. (2005). Intergenerational transmission of warm-sensitive-stimulating parenting: A prospective study of mothers and fathers of 3-year-olds. *Child Development, 76,* 384–396.

Belsky, J., Lerner, R. M., & Spanier, G. B. (1984). *The child in the family.* New York: Random House.

Bem, D. J. (1996). Exotic becomes erotic: A developmental theory of sexual orientation. *Psychological Review, 103,* 320–335.

Bem, D. J. (2000). Exotic becomes erotic: Interpreting the biological correlates of sexual orientation. *Archives of Sexual Behavior, 29,* 531–548.

Ben-Ari, R., & Eliassy, L. (2003). The differential effects of the learning environment on student achievement motivation: A comparison between frontal and complex instruction strategies. *Social Behavior and Personality, 31,* 143–166.

Benham-Deal, T. (2005). Preschool children's accumulated and sustained physical activity. *Perceptual and Motor Skills, 100,* 443–450.

Bennett, S. E., & Assefi, N. P. (2005). School-based teenage pregnancy prevention programs: A systematic review of randomized controlled trials. *Journal of Adolescent Health, 36,* 72–81.

Benson, M. J. (2004). After the adolescent pregnancy: Parents, teens, and families. *Child and Adolescent Social Work, 21,* 435–455.

Bentur, Y. (1994). Ionizing and nonionizing radiation in pregnancy. In G. Koren (Ed.), *Maternal–Fetal Toxicology: A Clinician's Guide* (pp. 515–572). New York: Marcel Dekker, Inc.

Bentur, Y., & Koren, G. (1994). The common occupational exposures encountered by pregnant women. In G. Koren (Ed.), *Maternal–Fetal Toxicology: A Clinician's Guide* (pp. 425–445). New York: Marcel Dekker, Inc.

Bereiter, C., & Scardamalia, M. (1987). *The psychology of written composition.* Hillsdale, NJ: Erlbaum.

Berenbaum, S. A., & Snyder, E. (1995). Early hormonal influences on childhood sex-typed activity and playmate preferences: Implications for the development of sexual orientation. *Developmental Psychology, 31,* 31–42.

Berk, L. E. (1992). Children's private speech: An overview of theory and the status of research. In R. M. Diaz & L. E. Berk (Eds.), *Private Speech: From Social Interaction to Self-regulation* (pp. 17–53). Hillsdale, NJ: Erlbaum.

Berk, L. E., & Spuhl, S. T. (1995). Maternal interaction, private speech, and task performance in preschool children. *Early Childhood Research Quarterly, 10,* 145–169.

Berkowitz, G. S., & Kasl, S. V. (1983). The role of psychosocial factors in spontaneous preterm delivery. *Journal of Psychosomatic Research, 27,* 283–290.

Berkowitz, G. S., Skovron, M. L., Lapinski, R. H., & Berkowitz, R. L. (1990). Delayed childbearing and the outcome of pregnancy. *The New England Journal of Medicine, 322,* 659–664.

Berliner, L., & Elliot, D. M. (2002). Sexual abuse of children. In J. E. B. Myers, L. Berliner, J. Briere, C. T. Hendrix, T. A. Reid, & C. A. Jenny (Eds.), *The APSAC Handbook on Child Maltreatment* (2nd ed., pp. 55–78). Thousand Oaks, CA: Sage Publications.

Berman, A. L., & Jobes, D. A. (1991). *Adolescent suicide: Assessment and intervention.* Washington, DC: American Psychological Association.

Berman, R. A., & Slobin, D. I. (1994). *Relating events in narrative: A crosslinguistic developmental study.* Hillsdale, NJ: Erlbaum.

Berndt, T. J. (1986). Children's comments about their friendships. In M. Perlmutter (Ed.), *Cognitive Perspectives on Children's Social and Behavioral Development* (pp. 189–212). Hillsdale, NJ: Lawrence Erlbaum Associates.

Bernstein, N., & Chivers, C. J. (2000, May 19). Disabled girl is found dead, amid signs of malnutrition. *New York Times.* Retrieved August 2, 2002, from www.nytimes.com.

Berry, J. W. (1993). Ethnic identity in plural societies. In M. E. Bernal & G. P. Knight (Eds.), *Ethnic Identity: Formation and Transmission Among Hispanic and Other Minorities* (pp. 271–296). Albany, NY: SUNY Press.

Bettencourt, B. A., & Miller, N. (1996). Gender differences in aggression as a function of provocation: A meta-analysis. *Psychological Bulletin, 119,* 422–447.

Bever, T. G. (1970). The cognitive basis for linguistic structure. In J. R. Hayes (Ed.), *Cognition and the Development of Language* (pp. 279–362). New York: Wiley.

Bhatt, R. S., Bertin, E., Hayden, A., & Reed, A. (2005). Face processing in infancy: Developmental changes in the use of different kinds of relational information. *Child Development, 76,* 169–181.

Bialystok, E., & Hakuta, K. (1994). *In other words: The science and psychology of second-language acquisition.* New York: Basic Books.

Bialystok, E., & Senman, L. (2004). Executive processes in appearance-reality tasks: The role of inhibition of attention and symbolic representation. *Child Development, 75,* 562–579.

Bialystok, E., Majumder, S., & Martin, M. M. (2003). Developing phonological awareness: Is there a bilingual advantage? *Applied Psycholinguistics, 24,* 27–44.

Bickel, R., Weaver, S., Williams, T., & Lange, L. (1997). Opportunity, community, and teen pregnancy in an Appalachian state. *Journal of Educational Research, 90,* 175–181.

Biederman, J., Mick, E., Faraone, S. V., Braaten, E., Doyle, A., Spencer, T., Wilens, T. E., et al. (2002). Influence of gender on attention deficit hyperactivity disorder in children referred to a psychiatric clinic. *American Journal of Psychiatry, 159*(1), 36–42.

Bigelow, B. J. (1977). Children's friendship expectations: A cognitive developmental study. *Child Development, 48,* 246–253.

Bishop, E. G., Cherny, S. S., Corley, R., Plomin, R., DeFries, J. C., & Hewitt, J. K. (2003). Development genetic analysis of general cognitive ability from 1 to 12 years in a sample of adoptees, biological siblings, and twins. *Intelligence, 31,* 31–50.

Bissel, M. (2000). Socio-economic outcomes of teen pregnancy and parenthood: A review of the literature. *The Canadian Journal of Human Sexuality, 9,* 191–204.

Bitensky, S. H. (1998). Spare the rod, embrace our humanity: Toward a new legal regime prohibiting corporal punishment of children. *University of Michigan Journal of Law Reform, 31,* 353–474. As cited in Gershoff (2002).

Bjorklund, D. F. (1995). *Children's thinking: Developmental functions and individual differences* (2nd ed.). Pacific Grove, CA: Brooks/Cole Publishing Company.

Bjorklund, D. F., & Coyle, T. R. (1995). Utilization deficiencies in the development of memory strategies. In F. E. Weinert & W. Schneider (Eds.), *Memory Performance and Competencies: Issues in Growth and development* (pp. 161–180). Hillsdale, NJ: Erlbaum.

Bjorklund, D. F., Miller, P. H., Coyle, T. R., & Slawinski, J. L. (1997). Instructing children to use memory strategies: Evidence of utilization deficiencies in memory training studies. *Developmental Review, 17,* 411–422.

Black, J. E., & Greenough, W. T. (1986). Induction of pattern in neural structure by experience: Implications for cognitive development. In M. E. Lamb, A. L. Brown, & B. Rogoff (Eds.), *Advances in Developmental Psychology* (Vol. 4, pp. 1–50). Hillsdale, NJ: Erlbaum.

Blair, C. (2002). School readiness: Integrating cognition and emotion in a neurobiological conceptualization of children's functioning at school entry. *American Psychologist, 57,* 111–127.

Blair, H. A. (2000). Genderlects: Girl talk and boy talk in a middle-years classroom. *Language Arts, 77,* 315–323.

Blakemore, S., & Choudhury, S. (2006). Development of the adolescent brain: Implications for executive function and social cognition. *Journal of Child Psychology and Psychiatry, 47,* 296–312.

Bloch, M. N., & Adler, S. M. (1994). African children's play and the emergence of the sexual division of labor. In J. L. Roopnarine, J. E. Johnson, & F. H. Hooper (Eds.), *Children's Play in Diverse Cultures* (pp. 148–178). Albany, NY: State University of New York Press.

Bloom, L., Lightbrown, P., & Hood, L. (1975). Structure and variation in child language. *Monographs of the Society for Research in Child Development, 40*(Serial No. 160).

Boccia, M., & Campos, J. J. (1989). Maternal emotional signals, social referencing, and infants' reactions to strangers. In N. Eisenberg (Ed.), *New Directions for Child Development* (Vol. 44, pp. 25–49). San Francisco: Jossey-Bass.

Bogatz, G. A., & Ball, S. (1977). *The second year of "Sesame Street": A continuing evaluation.* Princeton, NJ: Educational Testing Service.

Bohannon, J. N., & Bonvillian, J. D. (1997). Theoretical approaches to language acquisition. In J. B. Gleason (Ed.), *The Development of Language* (pp. 259–316). Needham Heights, MA: Allyn and Bacon.

Bohannon, J. N., & Padgett, R. (1996). Useful evidence on negative evidence. *Developmental Psychology, 32,* 551–555.

Bojanowski, J. (2005). Sickle cell disease. *The Gale Encyclopedia of Genetic Disorders* (2nd ed.), Vol. 1, 1181–1188. Detroit, MI: Thomson Gale.

Bondas-Salonen, T. (1998). How women experience the presence of their partners at the births of their babies. *Qualitative Health Research, 8,* 784–800.

Boomsma, D. I. (1993). Current status and future prospects in twin studies of the development of cognitive abilities: Infancy to old age. In T. J. Bouchard, Jr. & P. Propping (Eds.), *Twins as a Tool of Behavioral Genetics* (pp. 67–82). West Sussex, England: Wiley.

Booth, A., & Amato, P. R. (2001). Parental predivorce relations and offspring postdivorce well-being. *Journal of Marriage and the Family, 63,* 197–212.

Bornstein, M. H., & Arterberry, M. E. (1999). Perceptual development. In M. H. Bornstein & M. E. Lamb (Eds.), *Developmental Psychology: An Advanced Textbook* (4th ed., pp. 231–274). Mahwah, NJ: Lawrence Erlbaum Associates.

Bos, H. M. W., van Balen, F., & van den Boom, D. C. (2005). Lesbian families and family functioning: An overview. *Patient Education and Counseling, 59,* 263–275.

Bouchard, T. J., & McGue, M. (1981). Familial studies of intelligence: A review. *Science, 212,* 1055–1059.

Bouchard, T. J., Jr. (1994). Genes, environment, and personality. *Science, 264,* 1700–1701.

Bouchard, T. J., Jr. (1997). Experience producing drive theory: How genes drive experience and shape personality. *Acta Paediatr Supplement, 422,* 60–64.

Bower, T. G. R. (1974). The evolution of sensory systems. In R. B. MacLeod & H. L. Pick, Jr. (Eds.), *Perception: Essays in Honor of James J. Gibson* (pp. 141–165). Ithaca, NY: Cornell University Press.

Bowlby, J. (1958). The nature of the child's tie to his mother. *International Journal of Psycho-Analysis, 39,* 350–373.

Bowlby, J. (1969). *Attachment and loss: Attachment* (Vol. 1). New York: Basic Books.

Bowlby, J. (1988). *A secure base: Parent-child attachment and healthy human development.* New York: Basic Books.

Bowman, P. J., & Howard, C. S. (1985). Race-related socialization, motivation and academic achievement: A study of Black youth in three-generation families. *Journal of the American Academy of Child Psychiatry, 24,* 134–141.

Boykin, A. W., & Toms, F. D. (1985). Black child socialization: A conceptual framework. In H. P. McAdoo & J. L. McAdoo (Eds.), *Black Children: Social, Educational, and Parental Environments* (pp. 33–51). Newbury Park, CA: Sage.

Brackbill, Y., McManus, K., & Woodward, L. (1985). *Medication in maternity: Infant exposure and maternal information.* Ann Arbor, MI: The University of Michigan Press.

Bradley, R. H., & Corwyn, R. F. (2002). Socioeconomic status and child development. *Annual Review of Psychology, 53,* 371–399.

Bradley, R. H., & Corwyn, R. F. (2005). Productive activity and the prevention of behavior problems. *Developmental Psychology, 41,* 89–98.

Bradley, R. H., Corwyn, R. F., & Whiteside-Mansell, L. (1996). Life at home: Same time, different places. *Early Development Parental, 5,* 251–269.

Bradley, R. H., Corwyn, R. F., McAdoo, H. P., & Coll, C. G. (2001). The home environments of children in the United States. Part I: Variations by age, ethnicity, and poverty status. *Child Development, 72,* 1844–1867.

Brady, F. (2004). Children's organized sports: A developmental perspective. *JOPERD: The Journal of Physical Education, Recreation and Dance, 75,* 35–53.

Brainerd, C. J. (2005). Fuzzy-trace theory: Memory. In C. Izawa & N. Ohta (Eds.), *Human Learning and Memory: Advances in Theory and Application: The 4th Tsukuba International Conference on Memory* (pp. 219–238). Mahwah, NJ: Erlbaum.

Brainerd, C. J., & Gordon, L. L. (1994). Development of verbatim and gist memory for numbers. *Developmental Psychology, 30,* 163–177.

Brainerd, C. J., & Reyna, V. F. (1993). Memory independence and memory interference in cognitive development. *Psychological Review, 100,* 42–67.

Brainerd, C. J., & Reyna, V. F. (1995). Learning rate, learning opportunities, and the development of forgetting. *Developmental Psychology, 31,* 251–262.

Brainerd, C. J., & Reyna, V. F. (2004). Fuzzy-trace theory and memory development. *Developmental Review, 24,* 396–439.

Brainerd, C. J., Holliday, R. E., & Reyna, V. F. (2004). Behavioral measurement of remembering phenomenologies: So simple a child can do it. *Child Development, 75,* 505–522.

Brainerd, C. J., Reyna, V., & Brandes, E. (1995). Are children's false memories more persistent than their true memories? *Psychological Science, 4,* 141–148.

Brand-Gruwel, S., Wopereis, I., & Vermetten, Y. (2005). Information problem solving by experts and novices: Analysis of a complex cognitive skill. *Computers in Human Behavior, 21,* 487–508.

Braswell, J. S., Lutkus, A. D., Grigg, W. S., Santapau, S. L., Tay-Lim, B. S.-H., & Johnson, M. S. (2001). *The Nation's Report Card: Mathematics 2000* (NCES 2001–517). U.S. Department of Education, National Center for Education Statistics. Washington, DC: U.S. Government Printing Office.

Braungart, J. M., Plomin, R., DeFries, J. C., & Fulker, D. W. (1992). Genetic influence on tester-rated infant temperament as assessed by Bayley's Infant Behavior Record: Nonadoptive and adoptive siblings and twins. *Developmental Psychology, 28,* 40–47.

Bray, J. H. (1999). From marriage to remarriage and beyond: Findings from the developmental issues in stepfamilies research project. In E. M. Hetherington (Ed.), *Coping with Divorce, Single Parenting, and Remarriage: A Risk and Resiliency Perspective* (pp. 253–271). Mahwah, NJ: Erlbaum.

Brazelton, T. B. (1962). A child-oriented approach to toilet training. *Pediatrics, 29*(1), 121–128.

Breheny, M., & Stephens, C. (2004). Barriers to effective contraception and strategies for overcoming them among adolescent mothers. *Public Health Nursing, 21,* 220–227.

Briefel, R. R., & Johnson, C. L. (2004). Secular trends in dietary intake in the United States. *Annual Review of Nutrition, 24,* 401–431.

Bril, B., & Sabatier, C. (1986). The cultural context of motor development: Postural manipulations in the daily life of Bambara babies (Mali). *International Journal of Behavioral Development, 9,* 439–453.

Bringuier, J. (1980). *Conversations with Jean Piaget.* Chicago: University of Chicago Press.

Brinkman, B., Cook, K. L., Kahan, D., Elliott, G., Myrick, S., Greene, B., et al. (2005). Should recess be more structured and supervised in order to increase students' physical activity? *JOPERD: The Journal of Physical Education, Recreation and Dance, 76,* 9–49.

Broberg, A. G., Wessels, H., Lamb, M. E., & Hwang, C. P. (1997). Effects of day care on the development of cognitive abilities in 8-year-olds: A longitudinal study. *Developmental Psychology, 33,* 62–69.

Brodzinsky, D. M. (1990). A stress and coping model of adoption adjustment. In D. M. Brodzinsky & M. D. Schechter (Eds.), *The Psychology of Adoption* (pp. 3–24). New York: Oxford University Press.

Brodzinsky, D. M. (1993). Long-term outcomes in adoption. In R. E. Behrman (Ed.), *The Future of Children: Adoption* (pp. 153–166). Los Altos, CA: Center for the Future of Children, the Davis and Lucile Packard Foundation.

Bronfenbrenner, U. (1989). Ecological systems theory. In R. Vasta (Ed.), *Annals of Child Development* (Vol. 6, pp. 187–251). Greenwich, CT: JAI Press.

Bronfenbrenner, U. (1995). The bioecological model from a life course perspective: Reflections of a participant observer. In P. Moen, G. H. Elder, Jr., & K. Lüscher (Eds.), *Examining Lives in Context* (pp. 599–618). Washington, DC: American Psychological Association.

Bronfenbrenner, U. (Ed.). (2005). *Making human beings human: Bioecological perspectives on human development.* Thousand Oaks, CA: SAGE Publications.

Brookins, G. K., Petersen, A. C., & Brooks, L. M. (1997). Youth and families in the inner city: Influencing positive outcomes. In H. J. Walberg, O. Reyes, & R. P. Weissberg (Eds.), *Children and Youth: Interdisciplinary Perspectives* (pp. 45–66). Thousand Oaks, CA: SAGE Publications.

Brooks-Gunn, J., Duncan, G. J., & Aber, J. L. (Eds.). (1997). *Neighborhood Poverty: Vol. I. Context and Consequences for Children.* New York: Russell Sage Foundation.

Broome, M. E., & Koehler, C. (1986). Childbirth education: A review of effects on the woman and her family. *Family and Community Health, 9,* 33–44.

Brown, A. L., & DeLoache, J. S. (1978). Skills, plans, and self-regulation. In R. S. Siegler (Ed.), *Children's Thinking: What Develops?* (pp. 3–35). Hillsdale, NJ: Erlbaum.

Brown, A. L., Bransford, J. D., Ferrara, R., & Campione, J. (1983). Learning, understanding and remembering. In J. H. Flavell & E. Markman (Eds.), *Handbook of Child Psychology: Cognitive development* (4th ed., Vol. 1). New York: Wiley.

Brown, B. B. (1990). Peer groups and peer cultures. In S. S. Feldman & G. R. Elliott (Eds.), *At the Threshold: The Developing Adolescent* (pp. 171–196). Cambridge, MA: Harvard University Press.

Brown, B. B. (2004). Adolescents' relationships with peers. In R. M. Lerner & L. Steinberg (Eds.), *Handbook of Adolescent Psychology* (2nd ed., pp. 363–394). Hoboken, NJ: John Wiley & Sons, Inc.,

Brown, B. B., & Klute, C. (2003). Friendships, cliques, and crowds. In G. R. Adams & M. D. Berzonsky (Eds.), *Blackwell Handbook of Adolescence* (pp. 330–348). Malden, MA: Blackwell Publishing, Ltd.

Brown, B. B., & Lohr, M. J. (1987). Peer-group affiliation and adolescent self-esteem: An integration of ego-identity and symbolic-interaction theories. *Journal of Personality and Social Psychology, 52,* 47–55.

Brown, B. B., Clasen, D. R., & Niess, J. D. (1987, April). *Smoke in the looking glass: Adolescents' perceptions of their peer group status.* Paper presented at the biennial meeting of the Society for Research in Child Development, Baltimore. (As cited in B. Brown, 1989).

Brown, E., & Brownell, C. (1990). Individual differences in toddlers' interaction styles. Paper presented at the International Conference on Infant Studies, Montreal, Canada. (As cited in Rubin et al., 1998).

Brown, M. T. (1995). The career development of African Americans: Theoretical and empirical issues. In F. T. L. Leong (Ed.), *Career Development and Vocational Behavior of Racial and Ethnic Minorities* (pp. 7–36). Mahwah, NJ: Erlbaum.

Brown, P., & Richman, H. A. (1997). Neighborhood effects and state and local policy. In J. Brooks-Gunn, G. J. Duncan, & J. L. Aber (Eds.), *Neighborhood Poverty: Vol. II. Policy Implications in Studying Neighborhoods* (pp. 164–181). New York: Russell Sage Foundation.

Brown, R. (1973). *A first language: The early stages.* Cambridge, MA: Harvard University Press.

Brown, R., & Hanlon, C. (1970). Derivational complexity and the order of acquisition in child speech. In J. R. Hayes (Ed.), *Cognition and the Development of Language* (pp. 11–53). New York: Wiley.

Brown, S. A., Tapert, S. F., Granholm, E., & Delis, D. C. (2000). Neurocognitive functioning of adolescents: Effects of protracted alcohol use. *Alcoholism: Clinical and Experimental Research, 24,* 164–171.

Browne, J. A., Losen, D. J., & Wald, J. (2001). Zero tolerance: Unfair, with little recourse. In R. J. Skiba & G. G. Noam (Eds.), *Zero Tolerance: Can Suspension and Expulsion Keep Schools Safe?* (pp. 73–100). San Francisco: Jossey-Bass.

Bruck, M., & Ceci, S. J. (1999). The suggestibility of children's memory. *Annual Review of Psychology, 50,* 419–439.

Bruck, M., Ceci, S. J., Francouer, E., & Barr, R. J. (1995). "I hardly cried when I got my shot!": Influencing children's reports about a visit to their pediatrician. *Child Development, 66,* 193–208.

Bruner, J. S. (1983). *Child's talk: Learning to use language.* New York: Norton.

Buchanan, C. M., Maccoby, E. E., & Dornbusch, S. M. (1996). *Adolescents after divorce.* Cambridge, MA: Harvard University Press.

Bumpass, L., (1984). Children and marital disruption: A replication and update. *Demography, 21,* 71–82.

Bunting, L., & McAuley, C. (2004). Research review: Teenage pregnancy and parenthood: The role of fathers. *Child and Family Social Work, 9,* 295–303.

Burchinal, M. R., Howes, C., & Kontos, S. (2002). Structural predictors of child care quality in child care homes. *Early Childhood Research Quarterly, 17,* 87–105.

Burstein, I., Kinch, R. A., & Stern, L. (1974). Anxiety, pregnancy, labor, and the neonate. *American Journal of Obstetrics and Gynecology, 118,* 195–199.

Burton, L. M., Obeidallah, D. A., & Allison, K. (1996). Ethnographic insights on social context and adolescent development among inner-city African American teens. In R. Jessor, A. Colby, & R. Schweder (Eds.), *Ethnography and Human Development: Context and Meaning in Social Inquiry* (pp. 395–418). Chicago: University of Chicago Press.

Bushman, B. J., & Huesmann, L. R. (2001). Effects of televised violence on aggression. In D. G. Singer & J. L. Singer (Eds.), *Handbook of Children and the Media* (pp. 223–254). Thousand Oaks, CA: Sage.

Butler, S., Gross, J., & Hayne, H. (1995). The effect of drawing on memory performance in young children. *Developmental Psychology, 31,* 597–608.

Byrnes, J. P. (2001a). *Cognitive development and learning in instructional contexts* (2nd ed.). Boston: Allyn and Bacon.

Byrnes, J. P. (2001b). *Minds, brains, and education: Understanding the psychological and educational relevance of neuroscientific research.* New York: Guilford.

Byrnes, J. P. (2003). Factors predictive of mathematics achievement in White, Black, and Hispanic 12th graders. *Journal of Educational Psychology, 95,* 316–326.

Campbell, F. A., Pungello, E. P., Miller-Johnson, S., Burchinal, M., & Ramey, C. T. (2001). The development of cognitive and academic abilities: Growth curves from an early childhood educational experiment. *Developmental Psychology, 37,* 231–242.

Campbell, F. A., Ramey, C. T., Pungello, E., Sparling, J., & Miller-Johnson, S. (2002). Early childhood education: Young adult outcomes from the Abecedarian Project. *Applied Developmental Science, 6,* 42–57.

Campos, J. J., Langer, A., & Krowitz, A. (1970). Cardiac responses on the visual cliff in prelocomotor human infants. *Science, 170,* 196–197.

Canino, G., & Roberts, R. E. (2001). Suicidal behavior among Latino youth. *Suicide and Life-Threatening Behavior, 31,* 122–131.

Cantor, J. R., Engle, W., & Hamilton, G. (1991). Short-term memory, working memory, and verbal abilities: How do they relate? *Intelligence, 15,* 229–246.

Carey, G., & DiLalla, D. L. (1994). Personality and psychopathology: Genetic perspectives. *Journal of Abnormal Psychology, 103*(1), 32–43.

Carey, S. (1977). The child as a word learner. In M. Halle, J. Bresnan, & G. A. Miller (Eds.), *Linguistic Theory and Psychological Reality* (pp. 264–293). Cambridge, MA: MIT Press.

Carey, S. (1985). Are children fundamentally different kinds of thinkers and learners than adults? In S. F. Chipman, J. W. Segal, & R. Glaser (Eds.), *Thinking and Learning Skills* (Vol. 2, pp. 485–517). Hillsdale, NJ: Erlbaum.

Carlton, M. P., & Winsler, A. (1999). School readiness: The need for a paradigm shift. *School Psychology Review, 28,* 338–352.

Carpenter, M., Nagell, K., & Tomasello, M. (1998). Social cognition, joint attention, and communicative competence from 9 to 15 months of age. *Monographs of the Society for Research in Child Development, 63*(4, Serial No. 255).

Carraher, T. N., Carraher, D. W., & Schliemann, A. D. (1985). Mathematics in the streets and in the schools. *British Journal of Developmental Psychology, 3,* 21–29.

Carroll, A., Hemingway, F., Bower, J., Ashman, A., Houghton, S., & Durkin, K. (2006). Impulsivity in juvenile delinquency: Differences among early-onset, late-onset, and non-offenders. *Journal of Youth and Adolescence, 35,* 519–529.

Carskadon, M. A., Vieira, C., & Acebo, C. (1993). Association between puberty and delayed phase preference. *Sleep, 16,* 258–262.

Carskadon, M. A., Wolfson, A. R., Acebo, C., Tzischinsky, O., & Seifer, R. (1998). Adolescent sleep patterns, circadian timing, and sleepiness at a transition to early school days. *Sleep, 21,* 871–881.

Carver, P. R., Egan, S. K., & Perry, D. G. (2004). Children who question their heterosexuality. *Developmental Psychology, 40,* 43–53.

Carver, V. C., Kittleson, M. J., & Lacey, E. P. (1990). Adolescent pregnancy: A reason to examine gender differences in sexual knowledge, attitudes and behavior. *Heath Values: Health, Behavior, Education and Promotion, 14,* 24–29.

Case, R. (1985). *Intellectual development: Birth to adulthood.* New York: Academic Press.

Case, R., Kurland, M., & Goldberg, J. (1982). Operational efficiency and the growth of short-term memory span. *Journal of Experimental Child Psychology, 33,* 386–404.

Caselli, M. C., Bates, E., Casadio, P., Fenson, J., Fenson, L., Sanderl, L., & Weir, J. (1995). A cross-linguistic study of early lexical development. *Cognitive Development, 10,* 159–199.

Caspi, A., Moffitt, T. E., Morgan, J., Rutter, M., Taylor, A., Arseneault, L., et al. (2004). Maternal expressed emotion predicts children's antisocial behavior problems: Using monozygotic-twin differences to identify environmental effects on behavioral development. *Developmental Psychology, 40,* 149–161.

Caspi, A., Taylor, A., Moffitt, T. E., & Plomin, R. (2000). Neighborhood deprivation affects children's mental health: Environmental risks identified in a genetic design. *Psychological Science, 11,* 338–342.

Cassidy, J., Parke, R. D., Butkovsky, L., & Braungart, J. M. (1992). Family–peer connections: The roles of emotional expressiveness within the family and children's understanding of emotions. *Child Development, 63,* 603–618.

Casteel, M. A. (1993). Effects of inference necessity and reading goal on children's inferential generation. *Developmental Psychology, 29,* 346–357.

CDC (May, 2004). *Surveillance Summaries,* May 21, 2004. *Morbidity and Mortality Weekly Report 2004, 53*(SS-2), 1–95. Retrieved May 31, 2006, from http://www.cdc.gov/mmwr/PDF/SS/SS5302.pdf.

CDC (September, 2005). *Sexually transmitted disease surveillance, 2004.* Atlanta, GA: U.S. Department of Health and Human Services. Retrieved May 29, 2005, from http://www.cdc.gov/std/stats/04pdf/2004SurveillanceAll.pdf.

CDC Fact Sheets on Sexually Transmitted Diseases (2006). Retrieved May 29, 2005, from http://www.cdc.gov/std/HealthComm/fact_sheets.htm.

CDC Injury Fact Book (2002). *Teens Behind the Wheel.* Retrieved May 30, 2006, from http://www.cdc.gov/ncipc/fact_book/27_Teens_Behind_Wheel.htm.

Ceci, S. J., & Bruck, M. (1998). Children's testimony: Applied and basic issues. In W. Damon, I. E. Sigel, & K. A. Renninger (Eds.), *Handbook of Child Psychology* (5th ed.), *Vol. 4: Child Psychology in Practice* (pp. 713–774).

Centers for Disease Control (2001a). Congenital syphilis—United States, 2000. *Morbidity and Mortality Weekly Report, 50* (No. 27, pp. 573–577). Retrieved March 1, 2002, from http://www.cdc.gov/mmwr/preview/mmwrhtml/mm5027a1.htm.

Centers for Disease Control (2001b). CDC report regarding selected public health topics affecting women's health. *Morbidity and Mortality Weekly Report, 50* (No. RR–6, pp. 15–28). Retrieved March 1, 2002, from http://www.cdc.gov/mmwr/ indrr_2001.html.

Centers for Disease Control (2002a). Child passenger safety. Retrieved December 6, 2005, from http://www.cdc.gov/ncipc/fact_book/13_child_passenger_safetyt.htm.

Centers for Disease Control (2002b). Pedestrian injuries. Retrieved December 6, 2005, from http://www.cdc.gov/ncipc/fact_book/19_pedestrian.htm.

Centers for Disease Control (2002c). Bicycle-related injuries. Retrieved December 6, 2005, from http://www.cdc.gov/ncipc/fact_book/11_bicycle_related_injuries.htm.

Centers for Disease Control (2002d). Water-related injuries. Retrieved December 6, 2005, from http://www.cdc.gov/ncipc/fact_book/30_waterrelated_injuries.htm.

Centers for Disease Control (2003). Physical activity levels among children aged 9–13 years—United States, 2002. *Morbidity and Mortality Weekly Report, 52,* 785–788. Retrieved June 20, 2006 from http://www.cdc.gov/mmwr/PDF/wk/mm5233.pdf.

Centers for Disease Control (2004). Alcohol consumption among women who are pregnant or who might become pregnant—United States, 2002. *Morbidity and Mortality Weekly Report, 53* (50, pp. 1178–1181). Retrieved June 9, 2006 from http://www.cdc.gov/mmwr/preview/mmwrhtml/mm5350a4.htm#tab1.

Centers for Disease Control (2005). Barriers to children walking to or from school—United States, 2004. *Morbidity and Mortality Weekly Report, 54,* 949–952. Retrieved June 20, 2006, from http://www.cdc.gov/mmwr/PDF/wk/mm5438.pdf.

Centers for Disease Control (2005). Fetal Alcohol Syndrome. From the National Center on Birth Defects and Developmental Disabilities. Retrieved June 9, 2006. from http://www.cdc.gov/ncbddd/fas/faqs.htm.

Centers for Disease Control (2006a). BMI—Body Mass Index: About BMI for Children and Teens. Retrieved June 24, 2006, from http://www.cdc.gov/nccdphp/dnpa/bmi/childrens_BMI/about_childrens_BMI.htm.

Centers for Disease Control (2006b). National estimates of the 10 leading causes of nonfatal injuries treated in hospital emergency departments, United States, 2003. Retrieved January 26, 2006, from http://ftp.cdc.gov/pub/ncipc/10LC-2003/PDF/10lc-2003-nonfatal.pdf.

Centers for Disease Control (2006c). Autism. Retrieved September 12, 2006, from http://www.cdc.gov/ncbddd/autism/index.htm.

Cernoch, J. M., & Porter, R. H. (1985). Recognition of maternal axillary odors by infants. *Child Development, 56,* 1593–1598.

Chall, J. S. (1983). *Stages of Reading Development.* New York: McGraw-Hill Book Company.

Chang, L. (2003). Variable effects of children's aggression, social withdrawal, and prosocial leadership as functions of teacher beliefs and behaviors. *Child Development, 74,* 535–548.

Chao, R. K. (1994). Beyond parental control and authoritarian parenting style: Understanding Chinese parenting through the cultural notion of training. *Child Development, 65,* 1111–1119.

Chao, R. K. (2001). Extending research on the consequences of parenting styles for Chinese Americans and European Americans. *Child Development, 72,* 1832–1843.

Chaplin, T. M., Cole, P. M., & Zahn-Waxler, C. (2005). Parental socialization of emotion expression: Gender differences and relations to child adjustment. *Emotion, 5,* 80–88.

Chassin, L., Hussong, A., Barrera, M., Molina, B. S. G., Trim, R., & Ritter, J. (2004). Adolescent substance use. In R. M. Lerner & L. Steinberg (Eds.), *Handbook of Adolescent Psychology* (pp. 665–696). Hoboken, NJ: John Wiley & Sons, Inc.

Chen, J., & Gardner, H. (2005). Assessment based on multiple-intelligences theory. In D. P. Flanagan & P. L. Harrison (Eds.), *Contemporary Intellectual Assessment: Theories, Tests, and Issues* (pp. 77–102). New York: Guilford Press.

Cheng, L. L. (1987). Cross-cultural and linguistic considerations in working with Asian populations. *ASHA, 29,* 33–38.

Cherny, S. S., Fulker, D. W., Emde, R. N., Robinson, J., Corley, R. P., Reznick, J. S., et al. (1994). A developmental-genetic analysis of continuity and change in the Bayley mental development index from 14 to 24 months: The MacArthur Longitudinal Twin Study. *Psychological Science, 5,* 354–360.

Cheshire, J. (1982). *Variations in an English dialect.* Cambridge, England: Cambridge University Press.

Chess, S., & Thomas, A. (1995). *Temperament in clinical practice.* New York: Guilford Press.

Cheung, H., Hsuan-Chih, C., Creed, N., Ng, L., Wang, S. P., & Mo, L. (2004). Relative roles of general and complementation language in theory-of-mind development: Evidence from Cantonese and English. *Child Development, 75,* 1155–1170.

Chi, M. T. H. (1978). Knowledge structure and memory development. In R. Siegler (Ed.), *Children's Thinking: What Develops?* (pp. 73–96) Hillsdale, NJ: Erlbaum.

Chi, M. T. H., & Koeske, R. D. (1983). Network representation of a child's dinosaur knowledge. *Developmental Psychology, 19,* 29–39.

Chi, M. T. H., Feltovich, P. J., & Glaser, R. (1981). Categorization and representation of physics problems by experts and novices. *Cognitive Science, 5,* 121–152.

Chi, M. T. H., Glaser, R., & Farr, M. (Eds.). (1988). *The Nature of Expertise.* Hillsdale, NJ: Erlbaum.

Childers, J. B., & Tomasello, M. (2002). Two-year-olds learn novel nouns, verbs, and conventional actions from massed or distributed exposures. *Developmental Psychology, 38,* 967–978.

Children's Defense Fund (2001). Overall child poverty rate dropped in 2000 but poverty rose for children in full-time working families. Retrieved July 19, 2002, from http://www.childrensdefense.org.

Children's Defense Fund (2001). *The state of America's children yearbook 2001.* Washington, DC: CDF Publications.

Children's Defense Fund (2006). *Each day in America; Child Health; and Census 2000 Supplementary Survey: Poverty Status During Previous 12 Months, by age.* Three reports retrieved March 17, 2006 from www.childrensdefense.org.

Ching, J., & Newton, N. (1982). A prospective study of psychological and social factors in pregnancy related to preterm and low-birth-weight deliveries. In H. J. Prill & M. Stauber (Eds.), *Advances in Psychosomatic Obstetrics and Gynecology* (pp. 384–385). New York: Springer–Verlag.

Chirkov, V., Ryan, R. M., Kim, Y., & Kaplan, U. (2003). Differentiating autonomy from individualism and independence: A self-determination theory perspective on internalization of cultural orientations and well-being. *Journal of Personality and Social Psychology, 84,* 97–101.

Chiu, L. H. (1987). Child-rearing attitudes of Chinese, Chinese-American, and Anglo-American mothers. *International Journal of Psychology, 22,* 409–419.

Chomsky, N. S. (1957). *Syntactic structures.* The Hague: Mouton.

Chomsky, N. S. (1981). *Lectures on government and binding.* New York: Foris.

Chugani, H. T. (1998). A critical period of brain development: Studies of cerebral glucose utilization with PET. *Preventive Medicine, 27*(2), 184–188.

Chumlea, W. C., Schubert, C. M., Roche, A. F., Kulin, H. E., Lee, P. A., Himes, J. H., et al. (2003). Age at menarche and racial comparisons in U.S. girls. *Pediatrics, 111,* 110–113.

Chun, K. M., Organista, P. B., & Marin, G. (Eds.). (2003). *Acculturation: Advances in theory, measurement, and applied research.* Washington, DC: American Psychological Association.

Cicchetti, D., Toth, S., & Bush, M. (1988). Developmental psychopathology and incompetence in childhood: Suggestions for intervention. In B. B. Lahey & A. E. Kazdin (Eds.), *Advances in Clinical Child Psychology* (Vol. 11, pp. 1–77). New York: Plenum.

Clarke-Stewart, K. A., Gruber, C. P., & Fitzgerald, L. M. (1994). *Children at home and in day-care*. Hillsdale, NJ: Erlbaum.

Clarke-Stewart, K. A., Vandell, D. L., McCartney, K., Owen, M. T., & Booth, C. (2000). Effects of parental separation and divorce on very young children. *Journal of Family Psychology, 14*, 304–326.

Clement, J. (1982). Algebra word problem solutions: Thought processes underlying a common misconception. *Journal for Research in Mathematics Education, 13*, 16–30.

Clements, P. T., Speck, P. M., Crane, P. A., & Faulkner, M. J. (2004). Issues and dynamics of sexually assaulted adolescents and their families. *International Journal of Mental Health Nursing, 13*, 267–274.

Cleveland, E. S., & Reese, E. (2005). Maternal structure and autonomy support in conversations about the past: Contributions to children's autobiographical memory. *Developmental Psychology, 41*, 376–388.

Cleveland, H. H., & Wiebe, R. P. (2003). The moderation of adolescent-to-peer similarity in tobacco and alcohol use by school levels of substance use. *Child Development, 74*, 279–291.

Cloninger, C. R., Adolfsson, R., & Svrakic, N. M. (1996). Mapping genes for human personality. *Nature Geneetics, 12*, 3–4.

Clopton, N. A., & Sorell, G. T. (1993). Gender differences in moral reasoning: Stable or situational? *Psychology of Women Quarterly, 17*, 85–101.

Clymer, A. (2002, November 26). Critics say government deleted sexual material from Web sites to push abstinence. *New York Times*. Retrieved January 6, 2003, from www.nytimes.com.

Cnattingius, S. (2004). The epidemiology of smoking during pregnancy: Smoking prevalence, maternal characteristics, and pregnancy outcomes. *Nicotine and Tobacco Research, 6 (Suppl. 2)*, S125–S140.

Cnattingius, S., Forman, M. R., Berendes, H. W., & Isotalo, L. (1992). Delayed childbearing and risk of adverse perinatal outcome. *Journal of the American Medical Association, 19*, 886–890.

Coalson, D. W., & Glosten, B. (1991). Alternatives to epidural analgesia. *Seminars in Perinatology, 15*, 375–385.

Cohen, D. A., Farley, T. A., Taylor, S. N., Martin, D. H., & Schuster, M. A. (2002). When and where do youths have sex? The potential role of adult supervision. *Pediatrics, 110*, e66. Retrieved May 28, 2006, from http://www.pediatrics.org/cgi/content/full/110/6/e66.

Cohen, L. B., & Cashon, C. H. (2006). Infant cognition. In D. Kuhn & R. S. Siegler (Eds.), *Cognition, Perception, and Language* (Vol. 2, pp. 214–251), in W. Damon & R. M. Lerner (Gen. Eds.), *Handbook of Child Psychology* (6th ed.). New York: Wiley.

Cohen, L. B., DeLoache, J. S., & Strauss, M. S. (1979). Infant visual perception. In J. D. Osofsky (Ed.), *Handbook of Infant Development* (pp. 393–438). New York: Wiley.

Cohen, L. B., Gelber, E. R., & Lazar, M. A. (1971). Infant habituation and generalization to differing degrees of stimulus novelty. *Journal of Experimental Child Psychology, 11*, 379–389.

Cohen, R. (1981). Factors influencing maternal choice of childbirth alternatives. *Journal of the American Academy of Child Psychiatry, 20*, 1–15.

Coie, J. D., & Dodge, K. A. (1988). Multiple sources of data on social behavior and social status. *Child Development, 59*, 815–829.

Coie, J. D., & Dodge, K. A. (1998). Aggression and antisocial behavior. In W. Damon & N. Eisenberg (Eds.), *Handbook of Child Psychology: Vol. 3. Social, Emotional, and Personality Development* (pp. 779–862). New York: Wiley.

Colby, A., Kohlberg, L., Gibbs, J. C., & Lieberman, M. (1983). A longitudinal study of moral judgment. *Monographs of the Society for Research in Child Development, 48* (1–2, Serial No. 200).

Cole, M. (1999). Culture in development. In M. H. Bornstein & M. E. Lamb (Eds.), *Developmental Psychology: An Advanced Textbook* (pp. 73–123). Mahwah, NJ: Erlbaum.

Coles, R., & Stokes, G. (1985). *Sex and the American teenager*. New York: Harper & Row.

Coley, R. L., & Chase-Lansdale, P. L. (1998). Adolescent pregnancy and parenthood: Recent evidence and future direction. *American Psychologist, 53*, 152–166.

Collins, M., & Nowicki, S. (2001). African American children's ability to identify emotion in facial expressions and tones of voice of European Americans. *Journal of Genetic Psychology, 162*, 334–346.

Collins, W. A., & Laursen, B. (2004). Parent-adolescent relationships and influences. In R. M. Lerner & L. Steinberg (Eds.), *Handbook of Adolescent Psychology* (2nd ed., pp. 331–361). Hoboken, NJ: John Wiley & Sons, Inc.

Colombo, J., & Bundy, R. S. (1981). A method for the measurement of infant auditory selectivity. *Infant Behavior and Development, 4*, 219–233.

Committee on Sports Medicine & Fitness (2000). Injuries in youth soccer: A subject review. *Pediatrics, 105*, 659–661.

Commons, M. L., Miller, P. M., & Kuhn, D. (1982). The relation between formal operational reasoning and academic course selection and performance among college freshmen and sophomores. *Journal of Applied Developmental Psychology, 3*, 1–10.

Comstock, G. A., & Paik, H. (1991). *Television and the American child*. New York: Academic Press.

Comstock, G., & Scharrer, E. (2006). Media and popular culture. In K. A. Renninger & I. E. Sigel (Vol. Ed.) and W. Damon & R. M. Lerner (editors-in-chief), *Handbook of Child Psychology*, (6th ed., Vol. 4, pp. 817–863).

Conboy, B. T., & Thal, D. J. (2006). Ties between the lexicon and grammar: Cross-sectional and longitudinal studies of bilingual toddlers. *Child Development, 77*, 712–735.

Cooper, R. P., & Aslin, R. N. (1994). Developmental differences in infant attention to the spectral properties of infant-directed speech. *Child Development, 65*, 1663–1677.

Coplan, R. J., Prakash, K., O'Neil, K., & Armer, M. (2004). Do you "want" to play? Distinguishing between conflicted shyness and social disinterest in early childhood. *Developmental Psychology, 40*, 244–258.

Copper, R. L., Goldenberg, R. L., Creasy, R. K., DuBard, M. B., Davis, R. O., Entman, S. S., Iams, J. D., & Cliver, S. P. (1993). A multicenter study of preterm birth weight and gestational age-specific neonatal mortality. *American Journal of Obstetrics and Gynecology, 168*, 78–84.

Cornelius, M. D., Goldschmidt, L., Day, N. L., & Larkby, C. (2002). Alcohol, tobacco and marijuana use among pregnant teenagers: Six-year follow-up of offspring growth effects. *Neurotoxicology and Teratology, 24(6)*, 703–710.

Cornell, T. L., Fromkin, V. A., & Mauner, G. (1993). A linguistic approach to language processing in Broca's aphasia: A paradox resolved. *Current Directions in Psychological Science*, (Vol. 2, pp. 47–52).

Corrigan, R. (1987). A developmental sequence of actor-object pretend play in young children. *Merrill-Palmer Quarterly, 33*, 87–106.

Cowan, N. (1995). *Attention and memory: An integrated framework*. New York: Oxford University Press.

Cowan, N. (1997). The development of working memory. In N. Cowan & C. Hulme (Eds.), *The Development of Memory in Childhood* (pp. 163–200). Hove East Sussex, UK: Psychology Press.

Cowan, N., Nugent, L. D., Elliot, E. M., Ponomarev, I., & Saults, J. S. (1999). The role of attention in the development of short-term memory: Age differences in the verbal span of apprehension. *Child Development, 70*, 1082–1097.

Cowden, A. J., & Funkhouser, E. (2001). Adolescent pregnancy, infant mortality, and source of payment for birth: Alabama residential live births, 1991–1994. *Journal of Adolescent Health, 29*, 37–45.

Cox, A. (2005). What are communities of practice? A comparative review of four seminal works. *Journal of Information Science, 31*, 527–540.

Coyle, T. R., & Bjorklund, D. F. (1997). Age differences in, and consequences of, multiple- and variable-strategy use on a multitrial sort-recall task. *Developmental Psychology, 33*, 372–380.

Crawford, J. (1997). *Best evidence: Research foundations of the Bilingual Education Act*. Washington, DC: National Clearinghouse for Bilingual Education. Retrieved June 24, 2002, from http://www.ncela.gwu.edu/ncbepugs/reports/bestevidence/.

Crick, N. R., & Dodge, K. A. (1994). A review and reformulation of social information-processing mechanisms in children's social adjustment. *Psychological Bulletin, 115*, 74–101.

Crick, N. R., & Grotpeter, J. K. (1995). Relational aggression, gender, and social–psychological adjustment. *Child Development, 66*, 710–722.

Crittenden, P. M., & DiLalla, D. L. (1988). Compulsive compliance: The development of an inhibitory coping strategy in infancy. *Journal of Abnormal Child Psychology, 16*, 585–599.

Crockenberg, S. C., & Leerkes, E. M. (2004). Infant and maternal behaviors regulate infant reactivity to novelty at 6 months. *Developmental Psychology, 40*, 1123–1132.

Crockett, L., Losoff, M., & Petersen, A. C. (1984). Perceptions of the peer group and friendship in early adolescence. *Journal of Early Adolescence, 4*, 155–181.

Crockett, L. J., Shanahan, M. J., & Jackson-Newsom, J. (2000). Rural youth: Ecological and life course perspectives. In R. Montemayor, G. R. Adams, & T. P. Gullotta (Eds.), *Adolescent Diversity in Ethnic, Economic, and Cultural Contexts* (pp. 43–74). Thousand Oaks, CA: SAGE Publications.

Cronenwett, L. R., & Newmark, L. L. (1974). Fathers' responses to childbirth. *Nursing Research, 23*, 210–217.

Crook, C. K. (1987). Taste and olfaction. In P. Salapatek & L. B. Cohen (Eds.), *Handbook of Infant Perception* (Vol. 1, pp. 237–264). New York: Academic Press.

Crosnoe, R., & Elder, G. H., Jr. (2002). Adolescent twins and emotional distress: The interrelated influence of nonshared environment and social structure. *Child Development, 73*, 1761–1774.

Csikszentmihalyi, M., & Larson, R. (1984). *Being adolescent: Conflict and growth in the teenage years.* New York: Basic Books.

Csikszentmihalyi, M., Rathunde, K., & Whalen, S. (1997). *Talented teenagers: The roots of success and failure.* Cambridge, England: Cambridge University Press.

Cummins, J. (1991). Interdependence of first- and second-language proficiency in bilingual children. In E. Bialystok (Ed.), *Language Processing in Bilingual Children* (pp. 70–89). Cambridge: Cambridge University Press.

Curran, M. J. A. (1991). Options for labor analgesia: Techniques of epidural and spinal analgesia. *Seminars in Perinatology, 15*, 348–357.

Current Population Survey (2005). Annual demographic survey, March supplement. Retrieved August 2, 2006. http://pubdb3.census.gov/macro/032005/pov/new34_100.htm.

Curtiss, S. (1977). *Genie: A psycholinguistic study of a modern-day "wild child."* New York: Academic Press.

Curtiss, S. (1981). Dissociations between language and cognition: Cases and implications. *Journal of Autism and Developmental Disorders, 11*, 15–30.

D'Alessandro, M. P. (2002). Rickets, vitamin-D resistant. Retrieved March 1, 2002, from http://www.vh.org.

Dahl, R. E., & Spear, L. P. (2004). *Adolescent brain development: Vulnerabilities and opportunities.* New York: New York Academy of Sciences.

Dalterio, S. L., & Fried, P. A. (1992). The effects of marijuana use on offspring. In T. B. Sonderegger (Ed.), *Perinatal Substance Abuse: Research Findings and Clinical Applications* (pp. 161–183). Baltimore: The Johns Hopkins University Press.

Davenport–Slack, B., & Boylan, C. H. (1974). Psychological correlates of childbirth pain. *Psychosomatic Medicine, 36*, 215–223.

Davison, K. K., & Birch, L. L. (2002). Processes linking weight status and self-concept among girls ages 5 to 7 years. *Developmental Psychology, 38*, 735–748.

de Onis, M., Monteiro, C., Akré, J., & Clugston, G. (2002). *The worldwide magnitude of protein–energy malnutrition: An overview from the WHO Global Database on Child Growth.* Retrieved March 22, 2002, from www.who.int/whosis/cgrowth/bulletin.htm.

de Villiers, J. G., & de Villiers, P. A. (1999). Language development. In M. H. Bornstein & M. E. Lamb (Eds.), *Developmental Psychology: An Advanced Textbook* (4th ed., pp. 313–373). Hillsdale, NJ: Lawrence Erlbaum Associates.

de Waal, F. B. M. (1999). The end of nature versus nurture. *Scientific American, 281*(6), 94–99.

Deák, G. O., Ray, S. D., & Brenneman, K. (2003). Children's perseverative appearance-reality errors are related to emerging language skills. *Child Development, 74*, 944–964.

DeAngelis, T. (2001). Movin' on up? *Monitor on Psychology,* July/August, 2001, 70–73.

DeAngelis, T. (2002). Promising treatments for anorexia and bulimia. *Monitor on Psychology, 33*, 38–41.

DeBate, R. D., & Thompson, S. H. (2005). Girls on the run: Improvements in self-esteem, body size satisfaction and eating attitudes/behavior. *Eating and Weight Disorders, 10*, 25–32.

DeBourdeaudhuij, I., Lefevre, J., & Deforche, B. (2005). Physical activity and psychosocial correlates in normal weight and overweight 11 to 19 year olds. *Obesity Research, 13*, 1097–1105.

DeCasper, A. J., & Fifer, W. P. (1980). Of human bonding: Newborns prefer their mothers' voices. *Science, 208*, 1174–1176.

DeCasper, A. J., & Spence, M. J. (1986). Prenatal maternal speech influences newborns' perception of speech sounds. *Infant Behavior and Development, 9*, 133–150.

Deci, E. L., & Ryan, R. M. (1985). *Intrinsic motivation and self-determination in human behavior.* New York: Plenum.

DeFries, J. C., Gervais, M. C., & Thomas, E. A. (1978). Response to 30 generations of selection for open-field activity in laboratory mice. *Behavior Genetics, 8*, 3–13.

DeGarmo, D. S., Forgatch, M. S., & Martinez, C. R. (1999). Parenting of divorced mothers as a link between social status and boys' academic outcomes: Unpacking the effects of socioeconomic status. *Child Development, 70*, 1231–1245.

Delaney-Black, V., Covington, C., Nordstrom, B., Ager, J., Janisse, J., Hannigan, J. H., et al. (2004). Prenatal cocaine: Quantity of exposure and gender moderation. *Journal of Developmental and Behavioral Pediatrics, 25*, 254–263.

Delpit, L. (1995). *Other people's children: Cultural conflict in the classroom.* New York: New Press/W. W. Norton.

DeMarie-Dreblow, D. (1991). Relation between knowledge and memory: A reminder that correlation does not imply causality. *Child Development, 62*, 484–498.

Demaris, A., & Kaukinen, C. (2005). Violent victimization and women's mental and physical health: Evidence from a national sample. *Journal of Research in Crime and Delinquency, 42*, 384–411.

Demetriou, A., Christou, C., Spanoudis, G., & Platsidou, M. (2002). The development of mental processing: Efficiency, working memory, and thinking. *Monographs of the Society for Research in Child Development, 67*(1); Serial No. 268.

Dempster, F. N. (1981). Memory span: Sources of individual and developmental differences. *Psychological Bulletin, 89*, 63–100.

Demuth, K. (1990). Subject, topic and Sesotho passive. *Journal of Child Language, 17*, 67–84.

Denham, S. A., Blair, K. A., DeMulder, E., Levitas, J., Sawyer, K., Auerbach-Major, S., & Queenan, P. (2003). Preschool emotional competence: Pathway to social competence? *Child Development, 74*, 238–256.

Denham, S. A., McKinley, M., Couchoud, E. A., & Holt, R. (1990). Emotional and behavioral predictors of preschool peer ratings. *Child Development, 61*, 1145–1152.

Dennis, W., & Dennis, M. G. (1939/1991). The effect of cradling practices upon the onset of walking in Hopi children. *Journal of Genetic Psychology, 152*, 563–573.

Dennison, B. A., Erb, T. A., & Jenkins, P. L. (2002). Television viewing and television in bedroom associated with overweight risk among low-income preschool children. *Pediatrics, 109*(6), 1028–1035.

Denton, K., & Germino-Hausken, E. (2000). *America's Kindergartners.* Washington, DC: U.S. Department of Education, National Center for Education Statistics.

DeStefano, F., Bhasin, T. K., Thompson, W. W., Yeargin-Allsopp, M., & Boyle, C. (2004). Age at first measles-mumps-rubella vaccination in children with autism and school-matched control subjects: A population-based study in metropolitan Atlanta. *Pediatrics, 113*, 259–266.

Devlin, B., Daniels, M., & Roeder, K. (1997). Heritability of IQ. *Nature, 388*, 468–471.

DeVries, R. (1969). Constancy of generic identity in the years three to six. *Monographs of the Society for Research in Child Development, 34*(Serial No. 127).

Dews, S., Winner, E., Kaplan, J., Rosenblatt, E., Hunt, M., Lim, K. M., et al. (1996). Children's understanding of the meaning and functions of verbal irony. *Child Development, 67*, 3071–3085.

Diamond, D., Heinicke, C., & Mintz, J. (1996). Separation—individuation as a family transactional process in the transition to parenthood. *Infant Mental Health Journal, 17*(1), 24–42.

Diamond, L. M. (2003). What does sexual orientation orient? A biobehavioral model distinguishing romantic love and sexual desire. *Psychological Review, 110,* 173–192.

Diaz, R. M., & Kinger, C. (1991). Towards an explanatory model of the interaction between bilingualism and cognitive development. In E. Bialystok (Ed.), *Language Processing in Bilingual Children* (pp. 167–192). Cambridge: Cambridge University Press.

Dick–Read, G. (1933/1972). *Childbirth without fear: The original approach to natural childbirth.* (Originally published 1933). (Rev. ed.). H. Wessel & H. Ellis (Eds.). New York: Harper & Row.

DiPietro, J. A., Novak, M. F. S. X., Costigan, K. A., Atella, L. D., & Reusing, S. P. (2006). Maternal psychological distress during pregnancy in relation to child development at age two. *Child Development, 77,* 573–587.

Dishion, T. J., & Owen, L. D. (2002). A longitudinal analysis of friendships and substance use: Bidirectional influence from adolescence to adulthood. *Developmental Psychology, 38*(4), 480–491.

Dockett, S., & Perry, B. (2003). The transition to school: What's important? *Educational Leadership, 60*(7), 30–33.

Dodge, K. A. (1986). A social information processing model of social competence in children. In M. Perlmutter (Ed.), *Minnesota Symposium on Child Psychology* (Vol. 18, pp. 77–125). Hillsdale, NJ: Erlbaum.

Dodge, K. A., Doie, J. D., & Lynam, D. (2006). Aggression and antisocial behavior in youth. In W. Damon & R. Lerner (Series Ed.) and N. Eisenberg (Vol. Ed.), *Handbook of Child Psychology: Vol. 3. Social, Emotional, and Personality Development* (6th ed., pp. 719–788). New York: Wiley.

Dodge, K. A., Lansford, J. E., Burks, V. S., Bates, J. E., Pettit, G. S., Fontaine, R., et al. (2003). Peer rejection and social information-processing factors in the development of aggressive behavior problems in children. *Child Development, 74*(2), 374–393.

Dodge, K. A., Pettit, G. S., & Bates, J. E. (1994). Socialization mediators of the relation between socioeconomic status and child conduct problems. *Child Development, 65,* 649–665.

Dodge, K. A., Pettit, G. S., McClaskey, C. L., & Brown, M. W. (1986). Social competence in children. *Monographs of the Society for Research in Child Development, 51*(2), 1–80.

Donahue, P. L., Voelkl, K. E., Campbell, J. R., & Mazzeo, J. (1999). *NAEP 1998 reading report card for the nation and the states.* Washington, DC: U.S. Department of Education, Office of Educational Research and Improvement.

Donaldson, M. (1982). Conservation: What is the question? *British Journal of Psychology, 73,* 199–207.

Dornbusch, S. M., Ritter, P. L., Leiderman, P. H., Roberts, D. F., & Fraleigh, M. J. (1987). The relation of parenting style to adolescent school performance. *Child Development, 58,* 1244–1257.

Downey, D. B., Ainsworth-Darnell, J. W., & Dufur, M. J. (1998). Sex of parent and children's well-being in single-parent households. *Journal of Marriage and the Family, 60,* 878–893.

Downs, J. S., deBruin, W. B., Murray, P. J., & Fischhoff, B. (2006). Specific STI knowledge may be acquired too late. *Journal of Adolescent Health, 38,* 65–67.

Dragonas, T. G. (1992). Greek fathers' participation in labour and care of the infant. *Scandinavian Journal of Caring Sciences, 6,* 151–159.

Dube, S. R., Whitfield, C. L., Brown, D. W., Felitti, V. J., Dong, M., & Giles, W. H. (2005). Long-term consequences of childhood sexual abuse by gender of victim. *American Journal of Preventative Medicine, 28,* 430–438.

DuBois, D. L., Holloway, B. E., Valentine, J. C., & Cooper, H. (2002). Effectiveness of mentoring programs for youth: A meta-analytic review. *American Journal of Community Psychology, 30,* 157–197.

Duncan, G. J., & Brooks-Gunn, J. (Eds.). (1997). *Consequences of growing up poor.* New York: Russell Sage Foundation.

Duncan, P. D., Ritter, P. L., Dornbusch, S. M., Gross, R. T., & Carlsmith, J. M. (1985). The effects of pubertal timing on body image, school behavior, and deviance. *Journal of Youth and Adolescence, 14,* 227–235.

Duncan, S. W., & Markham, H. J. (1988). Intervention programs for the transition to parenthood: Current status from a preventive perspective. In G. Y. Michaels & W. A. Goldberg (Eds.), *The Transition to Parenthood: Current Theory and Research* (pp. 227–310). Cambridge, England: Cambridge University Press.

Dunn, M. S., Bartee, R. T., & Perko, M. A. (2003). Self-reported alcohol use and sexual behaviors of adolescents. *Psychological Reports, 92,* 339–348.

Dunphy, D. (1963). The social structure of urban adolescent peer groups. *Sociometry, 26,* 230–246.

Durrant, J. E. (1999). Evaluating the success of Sweden's corporal punishment ban. *Child Abuse and Neglect, 23,* 435–448.

Durrett, M. E., Otaki, M., & Richards, P. (1984). Attachment and the mother's perception of support from the father. *International Journal of Behavioral Development, 7,* 167–176.

Dweck, C. S. (2001). The development of ability conceptions. In A. Wigfield & J. S. Eccles (Eds.), *Development of Achievement Motivation* (pp. 57–88). San Diego, CA: Academic Press.

Dweck, C. S., & Leggett, E. L. (1988). A social-cognitive approach to motivation and personality. *Psychological Review, 95,* 256–273.

East, P. L., & Jacobson, L. J. (2001). The younger siblings of teenage mothers: A follow-up of their pregnancy risk. *Developmental Psychology, 37,* 254–264.

Eaton, W. O., & Enns, L. R. (1986). Sex differences in human motor activity level. *Psychological Bulletin, 100,* 19–28.

Eccles, J. S. (2004). Schools, academic motivation, and stage-environment fit. In R. M. Lerner & L. Steinberg (Eds.), *Handbook of Adolescent Psychology* (2nd ed., pp. 125–153). Hoboken, NJ: John Wiley & Sons, Inc.

Eccles, J. S., & Roeser, R. W. (1999). School and community influences on human development. In M. H. Bornstein & M. E. Lamb (Eds.), *Developmental Psychology: An Advanced Textbook* (pp. 503–554). Mahwah, NJ: Erlbaum.

Eccles, J. S., Lord, S. E., Roeser, R. W., Barber, B. L., & Jozefowicz, D. M. H. (1997). The association of school transitions in early adolescence with developmental trajectories through high school. In J. Schulenberg, J. Maggs, & K. Hurrelmann (Eds.), *Health Risks and Developmental Transitions During Adolescence* (pp. 283–320). New York: Cambridge University Press.

Eccles, J. S., Wigfield, A., & Schiefele, U. (1998). Motivation to succeed. In W. Damon & N. Eisenberg (Eds.), *Handbook of Child Psychology: Vol. 3. Social, Emotional, and Personality Development* (pp. 1018–1095). New York: John Wiley & Sons, Inc.

Eckerman, C. O. (1979). The human infant in social interaction. In R. Cairns (Ed.), *The Analysis of Social Interactions: Methods, Issues, and Illustrations* (pp. 163–178). Hillsdale, NJ: Lawrence Erlbaum Associates.

Eckerman, C. O. (1993). Imitation and toddlers' achievement of co-ordinated action with others. In J. Nadel & L. Camaioni (Eds.), *New Perspectives in Early Communicative Development* (pp. 116–138). London: Routledge.

Egeland, B., & Farber, E. A. (1984). Infant-mother attachment: Factors related to its development and changes over time. *Child Development, 55,* 753–771.

Eimas, P. D., Siqueland, E. R., Jusczyk, P., & Vigorito, J. (1971). Speech perception in infants. *Science, 71,* 303–306.

Eisbach, A. O. (2004). Children's developing awareness of diversity in people's trains of thought. *Child Development, 75,* 1694–1707.

Eisenberg, N. (1986). *Altruistic emotion, cognition, and behavior.* Hillsdale, NJ: Erlbaum.

Eisenberg, N., & Fabes, R. A. (1998). Prosocial development. In W. Damon & N. Eisenberg (Eds.), *Handbook of Child Psychology: Vol. 3. Social, Emotional, and Personality Development* (pp. 701–778). New York: Wiley.

Eisenberg, N., & Shell, R. (1986). The relation of prosocial moral judgment and behavior in children: The mediating role of cost. *Personality and Social Psychology Bulletin, 12,* 426–433.

Eisenberg, N., Carlo, G., Murphy, B., & Van Court, P. (1995). Prosocial development in late adolescence: A longitudinal study. *Child Development, 66,* 1179–1197.

Eisenberg, N., Cumberland, A., Spinrad, T. L., Fabes, R. A., Shepard, S. A., Reiser, M., et al. (2001). The relations of regulation and emotionality to children's externalizing and internalizing problem behavior. *Child Development, 72,* 1112–1134.

Eisenberg, N., Guthrie, I. K., Murphy, B. C., Shepard, S. A., Cumberland, A., & Carlo, G. (1999). Consistency and development of prosocial dispositions: A longitudinal study. *Child Development, 70,* 1360–1372.

Eisenberg, N., Lennon, R., & Roth, K. (1983). Prosocial development: A longitudinal study. *Developmental Psychology, 19,* 846–855.

Eisenberg, N., Sadovsky, A., Spinrad, T. L., Fabes, R. A., Losoya, S. H., Valiente, C., et al. (2005). The relations of problem behavior status to children's negative emotionality, effortful control, and impulsivity: Concurrent relations and prediction of change. *Developmental Psychology, 41,* 193–211.

Eisenberg, R. (1976). *Auditory competence in early life: The roots of communicative-behavior.* Baltimore: University Park Press.

Ekstrand, L. H. (1981). Theories and facts about early bilingualism in native and migrant children. (As cited in J. F. Hamers & M. H. A. Blanc, 2000). *Bilinguality and Bilingualism* (2nd ed.). Cambridge: Cambridge University Press.

Elashoff, J. D., & Snow, R. E. (1971). *Pygmalion reconsidered.* Worthington, OH: Charles A. Jones.

Elder, G. H., Jr., & Conger, R. D. (2000). *Children of the land: Adversity and success in rural America.* Chicago: University of Chicago Press.

Eldredge, J. L. (2005). Foundations of fluency: An exploration. *Reading Psychology, 26,* 161–182.

Elias, L. J., & Saucier, D. M. (2006). *Neuropsychology: Clinical and Experimental Foundations.* Boston: Pearson Education.

Elicker, J., Englund, M., & Sroufe, L. A. (1992). Predicting peer competence and peer relationships in childhood from early parent-child relationships. In R. D. Parke & G. W. Ladd (Eds.), *Family-peer Relationships: Modes of Linkage* (pp. 77–106). Hillsdale, NJ: Lawrence Erlbaum Associates.

Elkind, D. (1967). Egocentrism in adolescence. *Child Development, 38,* 1025–1034.

Elliott, E. S., & Dweck, C. S. (1988). Goals: An approach to motivation and achievement. *Journal of Personality and Social Psychology, 54,* 5–12.

Elliott, S. N., Kratochwill, T. R., Cook, J. L., & Travers, J. F. (2000). *Educational psychology: Effective teaching, effective learning* (3rd ed.). Boston: McGraw-Hill.

El-Sheikh, M., & Harger, J. (2001). Appraisals of marital conflict and children's adjustment, health, and physiological reactivity. *Developmental Psychology, 37,* 875–885.

Ely, R. (1997). Language and literacy in the school years. In J. B. Gleason (Ed.), *The Development of Language* (pp. 398–439). Boston: Allyn and Bacon.

Ely, R., & McCabe, A. (1994). The language play of kindergarten children. *First Language, 14,* 19–35.

Embury, S., Hebbel, R., Mohandas, N., & Steinberg, M. (Eds.) (1994). *Sickle cell disease: Basic principles and clinical practice.* New York: Raven Press.

Emde, R. M., Plomin, R., Robinson, J., Corley, R., DeFries, J., Fulker, D. W., et al. (1992). Temperament, emotion, and cognition at fourteen months: The MacArthur Longitudinal Twin Study. *Child Development, 63,* 1437–1455.

Emerson, M. J., & Miyake, A. (2003). The role of inner speech in task switching: A dual-task investigation. *Journal of Memory and Language, 48,* 148–168.

Emery, R. E. (1982). Interparental conflict and the children of discord and divorce. *Psychological Bulletin, 92,* 310–330.

Emery, R. E. (1999a). *Marriage, divorce, and children's adjustment* (2nd ed.). Thousand Oaks, CA: Sage.

Emery, R. E. (1999b). Postdivorce family life for children: An overview of research and some implications for policy. In R. A. Thompson & P. R. Amato (Eds.), *The Postdivorce Family: Children, Parenting, and Society* (pp. 3–27). Thousand Oaks, CA: Sage.

Emery, R. E., Kitzman, K. M., & Waldron, M. (1999). Psychological interventions for separated and divorced families. In E. M. Hetherington (Ed.), *Coping with Divorce, Single Parenting, and Remarriage: A Risk and Resiliency Perspective* (pp. 323–344). Mahwah, NJ: Erlbaum.

Engel, S. (1995). *The stories children tell: Making sense of the narratives of children.* New York: W. H. Freeman.

Enns, C. W., Mickle, S. J., & Goldman, J. D. (2003). Trends in food and nutrient intakes by adolescents in the United States. *Family Economics and Nutrition Review, 15,* 15–27.

Epstein, H. T. (1978). Growth spurts during brain development: Implications for educational policy and practice. In J. S. Chall & A. F. Mirsky (Eds.), *Education and the Brain: The Seventy-seventh Yearbook of the National Society for the Study of Education* (pp. 343–370). Chicago: University of Chicago Press.

Epstein, J. L. (1986). Friendship selection: Developmental and environmental influences. In E. Mueller & C. Cooper (Eds.), *Process and Outcome in Peer Relationships.* New York: Academic Press.

Epstein, J. L. (1989). The selection of friends: Changes across the grades and in different school environments. In T. J. Berndt & G. W. Ladd (Eds.), *Peer Relationships in Child Development* (pp. 158–187). New York: Wiley.

Erikson, E. H. (1968). *Identity: Youth and crisis.* New York: Norton. As cited in Thomas, R. M. (1992), *Comparing Theories of Child Development.* Belmont, CA: Wadsworth, pp. 163–164.

Eriksson, P. S., Perfilieva, E., Bjork-Eriksson, T., Alborn, A. M., Nordborg, C., Peterson, D. A., et al. (1998). Neurogenesis in the adult human hippocampus. *Nature Medicine, 4,* 1313–1317.

Eron, L. D., Huesmann, L. R., Lefkowitz, M. M., & Walder, L. O. (1972). Does television violence cause aggression? *American Psychologist, 27,* 253–263.

Espelage, D. L., Holt, M. K., & Henkel, R. R. (2003). Examination of peer-group contextual effects on aggression during early adolescence. *Child Development, 74*(1), 205–220.

Fabes, R. A. (1994). Physiological, emotional, and behavioral correlates of gender segregation. In W. Damon (Ed.), *New Directions for Child Development* (No. 65, pp. 19–34). San Francisco: Jossey-Bass.

Fabes, R. A., Eisenberg, N., Nyman, M., & Michealieu, Q. (1991). Young children's appraisals of others' spontaneous emotional reactions. *Developmental Psychology, 27,* 858–866.

Fabes, R. A., Martin, C. L., & Hanish, L. D. (2003). Young children's play qualities in same-, other-, and mixed-sex peer groups. *Child Development, 74*(3), 921–932.

Fabes, R., & Martin, C. L. (2003). *Exploring child development* (2nd ed.). Boston: Allyn and Bacon.

Fagan, J. F. (2000). A theory of intelligence as processing: Implications for society. *Psychology, Public Policy, and Law, 6,* 168–179.

Fagot, B. I. (1977). Consequences of moderate cross-gender behavior in preschool children. *Child Development, 48,* 902–907.

Fagot, B. I. (1994). Peer relations and the development of competence in boys and girls. In W. Damon (Ed.), *New Directions for Child Development* (No. 65, pp. 53–65). San Francisco: Jossey-Bass.

Fagot, B. I., & Patterson, G. R. (1969). An in vivo analysis of reinforcing contingencies for sex-role behaviors in the preschool child. *Developmental Psychology, 1,* 563–568.

Fagot, B. I., Leinbach, M. D., & Hagan, R. (1986). Gender labeling and the adoption of sex-typed behaviors. *Developmental Psychology, 22,* 440–443.

Fagot, B. I., Pears, K. C., Capaldi, D. M., Crosby, L., & Leve, C. S. (1998). Becoming an adolescent father: Precursors and parenting. *Developmental Psychology, 34,* 1209–1219.

Falorni, M. L., Fornasarig, A., & Stefanile, C. (1979). Research about anxiety effects on the pregnant woman and her newborn child. In L. Carenza & L. Zichella (Eds.), *Emotion and Reproduction. Proceedings of the Serono Symposium* (Vol. 20B, pp. 1147–1153). London: Academic Press.

Fan, X., & Chen, M. (2001). Parental involvement and students' academic achievement: A meta-analysis. *Educational Psychology Review, 13,* 1–22.

Fantz, R. L. (1956). A method for studying early visual development. *Perceptual Motor Skills, 6,* 13–15.

Fantz, R. L. (1961). The origin of form perception. *Scientific American, 204,* 66–72.

Fantz, R. L. (1963). Pattern vision in newborn infants. *Science, 140,* 296–297.

Faraone, S. V., Biederman, J., Monuteaux, M. C., Doyle, A. E., & Seidman, L. J. (2001). A psychometric measure of learning disability predicts educational failure four years later in boys with attention deficit/hyperactivity disorder. *Journal of Attention Disorders, 4,* 220–230.

Farmer, M. E., & Klein, R. M. (1995). The evidence for a temporal processing deficit linked to dyslexia: A review. *Psychonomic Bulletin and Review, 2,* 460–493.

Farrar, J. (1992). Negative evidence and grammatical morpheme acquisition. *Developmental Psychology, 28,* 90–98.

Farrar, M. J., & Goodman, G. S. (1992). Developmental changes in event memory. *Child Development, 63,* 173–187.

Farrington, D. P. (2004). Conduct disorder, aggression, and delinquency. In R. M. Lerner & L. Steinberg (Eds.), *Handbook of Adolescent Psychology* (2nd ed., pp. 627–664). Hoboken, NJ: John Wiley & Sons, Inc.

Farver, J. A. M., Narang, S. K., & Bhadha, B. R. (2002). East meets West: Ethnic identity, acculturation, and conflict in Asian Indian families. *Journal of Family Psychology, 16,* 338–350.

Farver, J. M. (2000). Within cultural differences. *Journal of Cross-Cultural Psychology, 31,* 583–602.

Farver, J. M., & Shin, Y. L. (1997). Social pretend play in Korean- and Anglo-American preschoolers. *Child Development, 68,* 544–556.

Farver, J. M., & Welles-Nystrom, B. (1997). Toy stories. *Journal of Cross-Cultural Psychology, 28,* 393–420.

Fee, E. J., & Shaw, K. (1998). Pitch modifications in Mi'kmaq child-directed speech. In E. V. Clark (Ed.), *The Proceedings of the Twenty-ninth Annual Child Language Research Forum* (pp. 47–54). Chicago: Center for the Study of Language and Information.

Feigelman, W. (2000). Adjustments of transracially and inracially adopted young adults. *Child and Adolescent Social Work Journal, 17,* 165–183.

Feingold, A. (1994). Gender differences in personality: A meta-analysis. *Psychological Bulletin, 116,* 429–456.

Feinman, S., & Lewis, M. (1983). Social referencing at ten months: A second-order effect on infants' responses to strangers. *Child Development, 54,* 878–887.

Fergusson, D. M., Boden, J. M., & Horwood, L. J. (2006). Cannabis use and other illicit drug use: Testing the cannabis gateway hypothesis. *Addiction, 101,* 556–569.

Fernald, A. (1992). Human maternal vocalizations to infants as biologically relevant signals: An evolutionary perspective. In J. H. Barkow, L. Cosmides, & J. Tooby (Eds.), *The Adaptive Mind: Evolutionary Psychology and the Generation of Culture* (pp. 391–428). New York: Oxford University Press.

Fernald, A., & O'Neill, D. K. (1993). Peek-a-boo across cultures: How mothers and infants play with voices, faces and expectations. In K. Macdonald (Ed.), *Parent-child Play* (pp. 259–285). Albany: State University of New York Press.

Field, T. M., Woodson, R., Greenberg, R., & Cohen, D. (1982). Discrimination and imitation of facial expressions by neonates. *Science, 218,* 179–181.

Finkelhor, D. (1994). The international epidemiology of child sexual abuse. *Child Abuse and Neglect, 18,* 409–417.

Finkelhor, D., & Jones, L. M. (2004). Explanations for the decline in child sexual abuse cases. *Juvenile Justice Bulletin, January 2004.* U.S. Department of Justice, Office of Justice Programs, Office of Juvenile Justice and Delinquency Prevention. Retrieved June 22, 2006, from http://www.ncjrs.gov/pdffiles1/ojjdp/199298.pdf.

Fischer, K. W., & Bidell, T. R. (1998). Dynamic development of psychological structures in action and thought. In W. Damon (Series Ed.) and R. M. Lerner (Vol. Ed.), *Handbook of Child Psychology: Vol. 1. Theoretical Models of Human Development* (5th ed., pp. 467–561). New York: Wiley.

Fish, J. M. (2002). *Race and intelligence: Separating science from myth.* Mahwah, NJ: Erlbaum.

Fisher, C. B., Wallace, S. A., & Fenton, R. E. (2000). Discrimination distress during adolescence. *Journal of Youth and Adolescence, 29,* 679–695.

Fisher, P. A., Leve, L. D., O'Leary, C. C., & Leve, C. (2003). Parental monitoring of children's behavior: Variation across stepmother, stepfather, and two-parent biological families. *Family Relations, 52,* 45–52.

Fivush, R. (1995). Language, narrative, and autobiography. *Consciousness and Cognition, 4,* 100–103.

Fivush, R., Haden, C., & Adam, S. (1995). Structure and coherence of preschoolers' personal narratives over time: Implications for childhood amnesia. *Journal of Experimental Child Psychology, 60,* 32–56.

Fivush, R., Kuebli, J., & Clubb, P. A. (1992). The structure of events and event representations: A developmental analysis. *Child Development, 63,* 188–201.

Flaks, D. K., Ficher, I., Masterpasqua, F., & Joseph, G. (1995). Lesbians choosing motherhood: A comparative study of lesbian and heterosexual parents and their children. *Developmental Psychology, 31,* 105–114.

Flavell, J. H., Friedrichs, A. G., & Hoyt, J. D. (1970). Developmental changes in memorization processes. *Cognitive Psychology, 1,* 324–340.

Flavell, J. H., Green, F. L., & Flavell, E. R. (1986). Development of knowledge about the appearance-reality distinction. *Monographs of the Society for Research in Child Development, 51,* (Serial No. 212).

Flavell, J. H., Green, F. R., Wahl, K. E., & Flavell, E. R. (1987). The effects of question clarification and memory aids on young children's performance on appearance-reality tasks. *Cognitive Development, 2,* 127–144.

Flavell, J. H., Miller, P. H., & Miller, S. A. (1993). *Cognitive development* (3rd ed.). Englewood Cliffs, NJ: Prentice Hall.

Flavell, J. R. (1985). *Cognitive development* (2nd ed.). Englewood Cliffs, NJ: Prentice Hall.

Fletcher, A. C., Nickerson, P., & Wright, K. L. (2003). Structured leisure activities in middle childhood: Links to well-being. *Journal of Community Psychology, 31,* 641–659.

Flinn, S. K. (1995). *Child sexual abuse I: An overview.* Advocates for Youth. Retrieved June 22, 2006, from http://www.advocates-foryouth.org/publications/factsheet/fsabuse1.htm.

Flook, L., Repetti, R. L., & Ullman, J. B. (2005). Classroom social experiences as predictors of academic performance. *Developmental Psychology, 41,* 319–327.

Fogel, A. (1979). Peer- vs. mother-directed behavior in 1- to 3-month-old infants. In T. J. Berndt & G. W. Ladd (Eds.), *Peer Relationships in Child Development* (pp. 46–70). New York: Wiley.

Fogel, A. (1997). *Infancy: Infant, Family, and Society* (3rd ed.). Minneapolis/St. Paul: West Publishing Company.

Fogelman, K. (1980). Smoking in pregnancy and subsequent development of the child. *Child Care Health and Development, 6,* 233–249.

Food and Drug Administration (2005a, September). Public health advisory: Suicidal thinking in children and adolescents being treated with Strattera (Atomoxetine). Author. Retrieved September 11, 2006 from http://www.fda.gov/cder/drug/advisory/atomoxetine .htm.

Food and Drug Administration (2005b, September). Public health advisory for Adderall and Adderall XR. Author. Retrieved September 11, 2006 from http://www.fda.gov/cder/drug/advisory/adderall.htm.

Ford, D. Y., & Harris, J. J. (2000). A framework for infusing multicultural curriculum into gifted education. *Roeper Review, 23,* 4–10.

Foreman, M. A. (1995). Foreword. In S. Chess & A. Thomas, *Temperament in Clinical Practice* (pp. v–viii). New York: Guilford Press.

Fowler, A. E. (1998). Language in mental retardation: Associations with and dissociations from general cognition. In J. A. Burack, R. M. Hodapp, & E. Zigler (Eds.), *Handbook of Mental Retardation and Development* (pp. 290–333). New York: Cambridge University Press.

Fox, N. A., Kimmerly, N. L., & Schafer, W. D. (1991). Attachment to mother/attachment to father: A meta-analysis. *Child Development, 62,* 210–225.

Fox, R., Aslin, R. N., Shea, S. L., & Dumais, S. T. (1980). Stereopsis in human infants. *Science, 207,* 323–324.

Fracasso, M. P., Busch-Rossnagel, N. A., & Fisher, C. B. (1993). The relationship of maternal behavior and acculturation to the quality of attachment in Hispanic infants living in New York City. *Hispanic Journal of Behavioral Sciences, 16,* 143–154.

Fraley, R. C., & Spieker, S. J. (2003). Are infant attachment patterns continuously or categorically distributed?: A taxonomic analysis of strange situation behavior. *Developmental Psychology, 39,* 387–404.

Frankenburg, W. K., Dodds, J., Archer, P., Bresnick, B., Maschka, P., Edelman, N., & Shapiro, H. (1992). *Denver II: Training manual.* Denver, CO: Denver Developmental Materials, Inc.

Fraser, S. (1995). *The bell curve wars: Race, intelligence, and the future of America.* New York: Basic Books.

Frazier, J. A., & Morrison, F. J. (1998). The influence of extended-year schooling on growth of achievement and perceived competence in early elementary school. *Child Development, 69,* 495–517.

French, D. C. (1988). Heterogeneity of peer rejected boys: Aggressive and nonaggressive subtypes. *Child Development, 59,* 976–985.

Fretts, R. C., Schmittdiel, J., McLean, F. H., Usher, R. H., & Goldman, M. B. (1995). Increased maternal age and the risk of fetal death. *The New England Journal of Medicine, 333,* 953–957.

Frey, K. S., Hirschstein, M. K., Snell, J. L., Edstrom, L. V., MacKenzie, E. P., & Broderick, C. J. (2005). Reducing playground bullying and supporting beliefs: An experimental trial of the *Steps to Respect* program. *Developmental Psychology, 41,* 479–491.

Friedrich, W. N. (1993). Sexual behavior in sexually abused children. *Violence Update, 3,* 1–7.

Frosch, C. A., Mangelsdorf, S. C., & McHale, J. L. (1998). Correlates of marital behavior at six months postpartum. *Developmental Psychology, 34,* 1438–1449.

Fuchs, D., & Thelen, M. H. (1988). Children's expected interpersonal consequences of communicating their affective state and reported likelihood of expression. *Child Development, 59,* 1314–1322.

Fuller, A., Hodkinson, H., Hodkinson, P., & Unwin, L. (2005). Learning as peripheral participation in communities of practice: A reassessment of key concepts in workplace learning. *British Educational Research Journal, 31,* 49–68.

Furstenberg, F. F., & Hughes, M. E. (1997). The influence of neighborhoods on children's development: A theoretical perspective and a research agenda. In J. Brooks-Gunn, G. J. Duncan, & J. L. Aber (Eds.), *Neighborhood Poverty: Vol. II. Policy Implications in Studying Neighborhoods* (pp. 23–47). New York: Russell Sage Foundation.

Furstenberg, F. F., Brooks-Gunn, J., & Chase-Lansdale, L. (1989) Teenaged pregnancy and childbearing. *American Psychologist, 44,* 313–320.

Fuson, K. C., & Kwon, Y. (1992). Korean children's single-digit addition and subtraction: Numbers structured by ten. *Journal for Research in Mathematics Education, 23,* 148–165.

Gabbard, C. P. (1992). *Lifelong motor development* (2nd ed.). Madison, WI: Brown & Benchmark.

Gagnon, J. C., & Leone, P. E. (2001). Alternative strategies for school violence prevention. In R. J. Skiba & G. G. Noam (Eds.), *Zero Tolerance: Can Suspension and Expulsion Keep Schools Safe?* (pp. 101–126). San Francisco: Jossey-Bass.

Gale Encyclopedia of Genetic Disorders, Vol. 2. (2005). Detroit: Thomson Gale.

Gallahue, D. L., & Ozmun, J. C. (1995). *Understanding motor development: Infants, children, adolescents, adults.* Madison, WI: Wm. C. Brown Communications, Inc.

Gallahue, D. L., & Ozmun, J. C. (1995). *Understanding motor development: Infants, children, adolescents, adults* (3rd ed.). Madison, WI: Brown & Benchmark.

Galloway, J. C., & Thelen, E. (2004). Feet first: Object exploration in young infants. *Infant Behavior and Development, 27,* 107–112.

Ganger, J., & Brent, M. R. (2004). Reexamining the vocabulary spurt. *Developmental Psychology, 40,* 621–632.

Gardner, H. (1983). *Frames of mind: The theory of multiple intelligences.* New York: Basic Books.

Gardner, H. (1995). Cracking open the IQ box. In S. Fraser (Ed.), *The Bell Curve Wars: Race, Intelligence, and the Future of America* (pp. 23–35). New York: Basic Books.

Gardner, H. (1999). *Intelligence reframed: Multiple intelligences for the 21st century.* New York: Basic Books.

Gardner, H., Kornhaber, M. L., & Wake, W. K. (1996). *Intelligence: Multiple perspectives.* Fort Worth, TX: Harcourt Brace College.

Gardner, R. M., Friedman, B. N., & Jackson, N. A. (1999). Body size estimations, body dissatisfaction, and ideal size preferences in children six through thirteen. *Journal of Youth and Adolescence, 28,* 603–618.

Garlick, D. (2002). Understanding the nature of the general factor of intelligence: The role of individual differences in neural plasticity as an explanatory mechanism. *Psychological Review, 109,* 116–136.

Garmezy, N. (1985). Stress-resistant children: The search for protective factors. In J. E. Stevenson (Ed.), *Recent Research in Developmental Psychopathology* (pp. 213–233). Oxford: Pergamon Press.

Garmon, A., Nystrand, M., Berends, M., & LePore, P. C. (1995). An organizational analysis of the effects of ability grouping. *American Education Research Journal, 32,* 687–715.

Garmon, L. C., Basinger, K. S., Gregg, V. R., & Gibbs, J. C. (1996). Gender differences in stage and expression of moral judgment. *Merrill-Palmer Quarterly, 42,* 418–437.

Garside, R., Ayres, R., & Owen, M. (2001). 'They never tell you about the consequences': Young people's awareness of sexually transmitted infections. *International Journal of STD and AIDS, 12,* 582–588.

Gathercole, S. E., Pickering, S. J., Ambridge, B., & Wearing, H. (2004). The structure of working memory from 4 to 15 years of age. *Developmental Psychology, 40,* 177–190.

Gaultney, J. F., & Gingras, J. L. (2005). Fetal rate of behavioral inhibition and preference for novelty during infancy. *Early Human Development, 81,* 379–386.

Ge, X., Brody, G. H., Conger, R. D., Simons, R. L., & Murry, V. M. (2002). Contextual amplification of pubertal transition effects on deviant peer affiliation and externalizing behavior among African American children. *Developmental Psychology, 38,* 42–54.

Ge, X., Conger, R. D., & Elder, G. H. (2001). The relation between puberty and psychological distress in adolescent boys. *Journal of Research on Adolescence, 11,* 49–70.

Geary, D. (1994). *Children's mathematical development: Research and practical applications.* Washington, DC: American Psychological Association.

Geary, D. C. (1996). International differences in mathematical achievement: Their nature, courses, and consequences. *Current Directions in Psychological Science, 5,* 133–137.

Geary, D. C. (2006). Development of mathematical understanding. In D. Kuhn & R. S. Siegler (Eds.), *Cognitive, Language, and Perceptual Development* (Vol. 2, pp. 777–810), in W. Damon (Gen. Ed.), *Handbook of Child Psychology.* New York: Wiley.

Geary, D. C., Hoard, M. K., Byrd-Craven, J., & DeSoto, M. C. (2004). Strategy choices in simple and complex addition: Contributions of working memory and counting knowledge for children with mathematical disability. *Journal of Experimental Child Psychology, 88,* 121–151.

Gecas, V., & Seff, M. (1990). Families and adolescents: A review of the 1980s. *Journal of Marriage and the Family, 52,* 941–958.

Gee, J. P. (1992). *The social mind: Language, ideology and social practice.* New York: Bergin & Garvey.

Gelman, R. (1972). Logical capacity of very young children: Number invariance rules. *Child Development, 43,* 75–90.

Gelman, R. (2000). Domain specificity and variability in cognitive development. *Child Development, 71,* 854–856.

Gelman, R., & Baillargeon, R. (1983). A review of some Piagetian concepts. In P. H. Mussen (Series Ed.) and J. H. Flavell & E. M. Markman (Vol. Eds.), *Handbook of Child Psychology: Vol. 3. Cognitive Development* (pp. 163–230). New York: Wiley.

Gershkoff-Stowe, L., & Thelen, E. (2004). U-shaped changes in behavior: A dynamic systems perspective. *Journal of Cognition and Development, 5,* 11–36.

Gershoff, E. T. (2002). Corporal punishment by parents and associated child behaviors and experiences: A meta-analytic and theoretical review. *Psychological Bulletin, 128,* 539–579.

Gerstadt, C. L., Hong, Y. J., & Diamond, A. (1994). The relationship between cognition and action: Performance of children 3.5–7 years old on a Stroop-like day-night test. *Cognition, 53,* 129–153.

Gibbs, C. P., Krischer, J., Peckham, B. M., Sharp, H., & Kirschbaum, T. H. (1986). Obstetric anesthesia: A national survey. *Anesthesiology, 65,* 298–306.

Gibson, E. J., & Walk, R. D. (1960). The "visual cliff." *Scientific American, 202,* 64–71.

Gibson, E. J., & Walker, A. S. (1984). Development of knowledge of visual-tactual affordances of substance. *Child Development, 55,* 453–460.

Giedd, J. N. (2003). The anatomy of mentalization: A view from developmental neuroimaging. *Bulletin of the Menninger Clinic, 67*(2), 132–142.

Giedd, J. N., Blumenthal, J., Jeffries, N.O., Castellanos, F. X., Liu, H., Zijdenbos, A., et al. (1999). Brain development during childhood and adolescence: A longitudinal MRI study. *Nature Neuroscience, 2,* 861–863.

Giles, J. W., & Heyman, G. D. (2005). Young children's beliefs about the relationship between gender and aggressive behavior. *Child Development, 76,* 107–121.

Gillam, R. B., Cowan, N., & Day, L. S. (1995). Sequential memory in children with and without language impairment. *Journal of Speech and Hearing Research, 38,* 393–402.

Gillies, R. M. (2003). The behaviors, interactions, and perceptions of junior high school students during small-group learning. *Journal of Educational Psychology, 95,* 137–147.

Gilligan, C. (1982). *In a different voice: Psychological theory and women's development.* Cambridge, MA: Harvard University Press.

Gilligan, C., & Attanucci, J. (1988). Two moral orientations: Gender differences and similarities. *Merrill-Palmer Quarterly, 34,* 223–237.

Ginsburg, H. P., & Opper, S. (1988). *Piaget's theory of intellectual development* (3rd ed.). Englewood Cliffs, NJ: Prentice Hall.

Ginsburg, H. P., Klein, A., & Starkey, P. (1998). Development of children's mathematical thinking: Connecting research with practice. In W. Damon, I. E. Sigel, & K. A. Renninger (Eds.), *Handbook of Child Psychology (Vol. 4): Child psychology in Practice.* New York: John Wiley & Sons, Inc.

Ginsburg, H., & Opper, S. (1979). *Piaget's theory of intellectual development* (2nd ed.). Englewood Cliffs, NJ: Prentice-Hall.

Glaberson, W. (2002, March 5). Judge rebukes city officials for removing children from homes of battered women. *New York Times.* Retrieved August 2, 2002, from www.nytimes.com.

Glasberg, R., & Aboud, F. (1982). Keeping one's distance from sadness: Children's self-reports of emotional experience. *Developmental Psychology, 18,* 287–293.

Gleason, J. B. (1997). *The development of language.* Boston, MA: Allyn and Bacon.

Gleason, J. B., Perlmann, R. Y., Ely, D., & Evans, D. (1994). The babytalk register: Parents' use of diminutives. In J. L. Sokolov & C. E. Snow (Eds.), *Handbook of Research in Language Development using CHILDES* (pp. 50–76). Hillsdale, NJ: Erlbaum.

Gleitman, L. (1990). The structural sources of verb meanings. *Language Acquisition, 1,* 3–55.

Godin, G., Anderson, D., & Lambert, L. D. (2005). Identifying factors associated with regular physical activity in leisure time among Canadian adolescents. *American Journal of Health Promotion, 20,* 20–27.

Gogtay, N., Giedd, J. N., Lusk, L., Hayashi, K. M., Greenstein, D., Vaituzis, A. C., et al. (2004). Dynamic mapping of human cortical development during childhood through early adolescence. *Proceedings of the National Academy of Science, 101*(21), 8174–8179.

Goldberg, J. H., Halpern-Felsher, B. L., & Millstein, S. G. (2002). Beyond invulnerability: The importance of benefits in adolescents' decision to drink alcohol. *Health Psychology, 21,* 477–484.

Goldin-Meadow, S. (2006). Nonverbal communication: The hand's role in talking and thinking. In D. Kuhn & R. S. Siegler (Eds.), *Cognition, Perception, and Language* (Vol. 2, pp. 336–369), in W. Damon & R. M. Lerner (Gen. Eds.), *Handbook of Child Psychology* (6th ed.). New York: Wiley.

Goldsmith, H. H., & Alansky, J. A. (1987). Maternal and infant temperamental predictors of attachment: A meta-analytic review. *Journal of Consulting and Clinical Psychology, 55,* 805–816.

Golombok, G., Perry, B., Burson, A., Murray, C., Mooney-Somers, J., Stevens, M., & Golding, J. (2003). Children with lesbian parents: A community study. *Developmental Psychology, 39,* 20–33.

Golombok, S., Lycett, E., MacCallum, F., Jadva, V., Murray, C., Rust, J., et al. (2004a). Parenting infants conceived by gamete donation. *Journal of Family Psychology, 18,* 443–452.

Golombok, S., MacCallum, F., & Goodman, E. (2001). The "test-tube" generation: Parent–child relationships and the psychological well-being of in vitro fertilization children at adolescence. *Child Development, 72,* 599–608.

Golombok, S., MacCallum, F., Goodman, E., & Rutter, M. (2002). Families with children conceived by donor insemination: A follow-up at age twelve. *Child Development, 73,* 952–968.

Golombok, S., Murray, C., Jadva, V., MacCallum, F., & Lycett, E. (2004b). Families created through surrogacy arrangements: Parent-child relationships in the 1st year of life. *Developmental Psychology, 40,* 400–411.

Goodall, J. (1986). *The chimpanzees of Bombe: Patterns of behavior.* Cambridge, MA: Harvard University Press.

Good, T. L., & Brophy, J. E. (2003). *Lokking in classrooms* (9th ed.). Boston: Allyn & Bacon.

Goode, E. (1999, August 3). Mozart for baby? Some say, maybe not. *New York Times.* Retrieved September 14, 2000, from www.nytimes.com.

Goodenough, W. H. (1994). Toward a working theory of culture. In R. Borotsky (Ed.), *Assessing Cultural Anthropology* (pp. 262–273). New York: McGraw-Hill.

Goodsitt, J., Morse, P., VerHoeve, J., & Cowan, N. (1984). Infant speech recognition in multisyllabic contexts. *Child Development, 55,* 903–910.

Goodwin, M. H. (1990). *He-said-she-said: Talk as a social organization among black children.* Bloomington, IN: Indiana University Press.

Goodwin, M. H., & Goodwin, C. (1987). Children's arguing. In S. U. Philips, S. Steele, & C. Tanz (Eds.), *Language, Gender, and Sex in Comparative Perspective* (pp. 200–247). New York: Cambridge University Press.

Goossens, F. A., & van IJzendoorn, M. H. (1990). Quality of infants' attachments to professional caregivers: Relation to infant–parent attachment and day care characteristics. *Child Development, 61,* 832–837.

Gopnik, A. (1984). The acquisition of "gone" and the development of the object concept. *Journal of Child Language, 11,* 273–292.

Gopnik, A., & Meltzoff, A. (1984). Semantic and cognitive development in 15- to 21-month old children. *Journal of Child Language, 11,* 495–513.

Goren, C. C., Sarty, M., & Wu, P. Y. K. (1975). Visual following and pattern discrimination of face-like stimuli by newborn infants. *Pediatrics, 56,* 544–549.

Gormley, W. T. Jr., Gayer, T., Phillips, D., & Dawson, B. (2005). The effects of universal pre-K on cognitive development. *Developmental Psychology, 41,* 872–884.

Gorn, G. I., Goldberg, M. E., & Kanningo, R. N. (1976). The role of educational television in changing intergroup attitudes to children. *Child Development, 47,* 277–280.

Gosselin, P., & Larocque, C. (2000). Facial morphology and children's categorization of facial expressions of emotions: A comparison between Asian and Caucasian faces. *Journal of Genetic Psychology, 161,* 346–358.

Gostin, L. O. (2001). The rights of pregnant women: The Supreme Court and drug testing. *Hastings Center Report, 31*(5), 8–9.

Gottesman, I. I. (1963). Genetic aspects of intelligent behavior. In N. Ellis (Ed.), *Handbook of Mental Deficiency.* New York: McGraw-Hill.

Gottesman, I. I. (1991). *Schizophrenia genetics: The origins of madness.* New York: Freeman.

Gottleib, G. (1997). *Synthesizing nature–nurture: Prenatal roots of instinctive behavior.* Mahwah: NJ: Erlbaum.

Gottlieb, G. (2003). On making behavioral genetics truly developmental. *Human Development, 46,* 337–355.

Graham, S., Hudley, C., & Williams, E. (1992). Attributional and emotional determinants of aggression among African-American and Latino young adolescents. *Developmental Psychology, 28,* 731–740.

Green, L. J. (2002). *African American English: A linguistic introduction.* New York: Cambridge University Press.

Greenfield, P. M., & Suzuki, L. K. (1998). Culture and human development: Implications for parenting, education, pediatrics, and mental health. In W. Damon, I. E. Sigel, & K. A. Renninger (Eds.), *Handbook of Child Psychology, Vol. 4: Child Psychology in Practice* (pp. 1059–1109). New York: John Wiley & Sons.

Greenfield, P. M., Suzuki, L. K., & Rothstein-Fisch, C. (2006). Cultural pathways through human development. In W. Damon & R. M. Lerner (Series Eds.) and K. A. Renninger & I. E. Sigel (Vol. Eds.), *Handbook of Child Psychology, Vol. 4: Child Psychology in Practice* (pp. 665–699). New York: John Wiley & Sons.

Greenlee, S. P., Damarin, F. L., & Walsh, W. G. (1988). Congruence and differentiation among Black and White males in two non-college-degreed occupations. *Journal of Vocational Behavior, 32,* 298–306.

Greenough, W. T., & Black, J. E. (1999). Experience, neural plasticity, and psychological development. In N. A. Fox, L. A. Leavitt, & J. G. Warhol (Eds.), *The Role of Early Experience in Infant Development* (pp. 29–40). New York: Johnson & Johnson Pediatric Institute.

Gregory, R. (1996). *Psychological testing: History, principles, and applications* (2nd ed.). Boston: Allyn and Bacon.

Grieser, M., Vu, M. B., & Bedimo-Rung, A. L. (2006). Physical activity attitudes, preferences, and practices in African American, Hispanic, and Caucasian girls. *Health Education and Behavior, 33,* 40–51.

Griffiths, M. D., & Hunt, N. (1995). Computer game playing in adolescence: Prevalence and demographic indicators. *Journal of Community and Applied Social Psychology, 5,* 189–193.

Grigg, W. N. (1995). Are you fit to be a parent? *The New American, 11*(2). Retrieved January 9, 2003, from www.thenewamerican.com.

Grigg, W., Lauko, M., & Brockway, D. (2006). *The Nation's Report Card: Science 2005* (NCES 2006-466). U.S. Department of Education, National Center for Education Statistics. Washington, DC: U.S. Government Printing Office.

Grolnick, W. S., Kurowski, C. O., & Gurland, S. T. (1999). Family processes and the development of children's self-regulation. *Educational Psychologist, 34,* 3–14.

Gross, A. L., & Ballif, B. (1991). Children's understanding of emotion from facial expressions and situations: A review. *Developmental Review, 11,* 368–398.

Gross, J. (1998, January 18). On the case: A special report. Child welfare foot soldier treads fine line. *New York Times.* Retrieved August 2, 2002, from www.nytimes.com.

Gross, J. (2005, February 26). As autistic children grow, so does social gap. *The New York Times.* Retrieved February 13, 2006, from www.nytimes.com.

Grossmann, K. E., Grossmann, K., Huber, F., & Wartner, U. (1981). German children's behavior towards their mothers at 12 months and their fathers at 18 months in Ainsworth's Strange Situation. *International Journal of Behavioral Development, 4,* 157–181.

Gruber, J. (2001). *Risky behavior among youths: An economic analysis.* Chicago: University of Chicago Press.

Grunbaum, J. A., Kann, L., Kinchen, S., Ross, J., Hawkins, J., Lowry, R., et al. (2004). Youth risk behavior surveillance—United States, 2003. *Morbidity and Mortality Weekly Report 2004, 53*(SS-2), 1–95. Retrieved May 31, 2006, from http://www.cdc.gov/mmwr/PDF/SS/SS5302.pdf.

Guilford, J. P. (1967). *The nature of human intelligence.* New York: McGraw-Hill.

Guilford, J. P. (1982). Cognitive psychology's ambiguities: Some suggested remedies. *Psychological Review, 89,* 48–59.

Gulli, L. (2005). Huntington disease. *The Gale Encyclopedia of Genetic Disorders* (2nd ed., Vol. 1, pp. 646–649). Detroit, MI: Thomson Gale.

Gunter, B., & McAleer, J. (1997). *Children and television.* London: Routledge.

Gustafson, S. L., & Rhodes, R. E. (2006). Parental correlates of physical activity in chlidren and early adolescents. *Sports Medicine, 36,* 79–97.

Hainline, L. (1998). The development of basic visual abilities. In A. Slater (Ed.), *Perceptual Development: Visual, Auditory, and Speech Perception in Infancy* (pp. 5–50). East Sussex, UK: Psychology Press.

Haith, M. M., & Benson, J. B. (1998). Infant cognition, In W. Damon (Series Ed.) and D. Kuhn & R. S. Siegler (Vol. Eds.), *Handbook of Child Psychology: Vol. 2. Cognition, Perception, and Language* (5th ed., pp. 199–254). New York: Wiley.

Halford, G. S. (2004). The development of deductive reasoning: How important is complexity? *Thinking and Reasoning, 10,* 123–145.

Halford, G. S., Smith, S. B., Dickson, J. C., Mayberry, M. T., Kelly, M. E., Bain, J. D., et al. (1995). Modeling the development of reasoning strategies: The roles of analogy, knowledge, and capacity. In T. Simon & G. Halford (Eds.), *Developing Cognitive Competence: New Approaches to Process Modeling* (pp. 77–156). Hillsdale, NJ: Erlbaum.

Hall, G. S. (1904). *Adolescence: Its psychology and its relations to physiology, anthropology, sociology, sex, crime, religion, and education* (Vols. 1 and 2). New York: Appleton.

Halperin, S. (ed.) (1998). *The forgotten half revisited: American youth and young families, 1988–2008.* Washington, DC: American Youth Policy Forum.

Halpern, D. F. (2000). *Sex differences in cognitive abilities* (3rd ed.). Hillsdale, NJ: Erlbaum.

Halpern, D. F. (2003). *Thought and knowledge: An introduction to critical thinking* (4th ed.). Mahwah, NJ: Erlbaum.

Halpern, R. (1993). Poverty and infant development. In C. H. Zeanah, Jr. (Ed.), *Handbook of Infant Mental Health* (pp. 73–86). New York: The Guilford Press.

Halpern-Felsher, B. L., & Cauffman, E. (2001). Costs and benefits of a decision: Decision-making competence in adolescents and adults. *Journal of Applied Developmental Psychology, 22,* 257–273.

Halpern-Felsher, B. L., Cornell, J. L., Kropp, R. Y., & Tschann, J. M. (2005). Oral versus vaginal sex among adolescents: Perceptions, attitudes, and behavior. *Pediatrics, 115,* 845–851.

Hamers, J. F. (1996). Cognitive and language development of bilingual children. In I. Parasnis (Ed.), *Cultural and Language Diversity and the Deaf Experience* (pp. 51–75). Cambridge: Cambridge University Press.

Hamers, J. F., & Blanc, M.H.A. (2000). *Bilinguality and bilingualism* (2nd ed.). Cambridge: Cambridge University Press.

Hamilton, B. E., Ventura, S. J., Martin, J. A., & Sutton, P. D. (2005). Preliminary births for 2004. Health E-stats. Hyattsville, MD: National Center for Health Statistics. Released October 28, 2005. Retrieved May 24, 2006, from http://www.cdc.gov.

Hamilton, C. J., Coates, R. O., & Heffernan, T. (2003). What develops in visuo-spatial working memory development? *European Journal of Cognitive Psychology, 15,* 43–70.

Hamilton, S. F., & Hamilton, M. A. (2004). Contexts for mentoring: Adolescent-adult relationships in workplaces and communities (pp. 395–428). In R. M. Lerner & L. Steinberg (Eds.), *Handbook of Adolescent Psychology* (2nd ed.). Hoboken, NJ: John Wiley & Sons.

Hammack, P. L. (2005). The life course development of human sexual orientation: An integrative paradigm. *Human Development, 48,* 267–290.

Hamre, B. K., & Pianta, R. C. (2005). Can instructional and emotional support in the first-grade classroom make a difference for children at risk of school failure? *Child Development, 76,* 949–967.

Handley, S. J., Capon, A., Copp, C., & Harper, C. (2002). Conditional reasoning and the Tower of Hanoi: The role of spatial and verbal working memory. *British Journal of Psychology, 93,* 501–518.

Hansen, M., Janssen, I., Schiff, A., Zee, P. C., & Dubocovich, M. L. (2005). The impact of school daily schedule on adolescent sleep. *Pediatrics, 115,* 1555–1561.

Hanson, T. L. (1999). Does parental conflict explain why divorce is negatively associated with child welfare? *Social Forces, 77,* 1283–1316.

Harjo, S. S. (1999). The American Indian Experience. In H. P. McAdoo (Ed.), *Family Ethnicity: Strength in Diversity* (pp. 63–71). Thousand Oaks, CA: Sage Publications, Inc.

Harlow, H. F., & Zimmermann, R. R. (1959). Affectional responses in the infant monkey. *Science, 130,* 421–432.

Harris, J. R. (1998). *The nurture assumption: Why children turn out the way they do.* New York: Free Press.

Harris, J. R. (2000). The outcome of parenting: What do we really know? *Journal of Personality, 68,* 625–637.

Harris, P. L. (1983). Infant cognition. In P. H. Mussen (Series Ed.) and M. M. Haith & J. J. Campos (Vol. Eds.), *Handbook of Child Psychology: Vol. 2. Infancy and Developmental Psychobiology* (pp. 689–782). New York: Wiley.

Hart, B., & Risley, T. R. (1995). *Meaningful differences in the everyday experience of young American children.* Baltimore: Paul H. Brookes.

Hart, C. H., Olsen, S. F., Robinson, C. C., & Mandleco, B. L. (1997). The relation of childhood personality types to adolescent behavior and development: A longitudinal study of Icelandic children. *Developmental Psychology, 33,* 195–205.

Harter, S. (1993). Causes and consequences of low self-esteem in children and adolescents. In R. F. Baumeister (Ed.), *Self-esteem: The Puzzle of Low Self-regard* (pp. 87–116). New York: Plenum.

Harter, S. (1998). The development of self-representations. In W. Damon & N. Eisenberg (Eds.), *Handbook of Child Psychology: Vol. 3. Social, Emotional, and Personality Development* (pp. 553–617). New York: Wiley.

Harter, S. (1999). *The construction of the self: A developmental perspective.* New York: The Guilford Press.

Harter, S. (2006). The self. In W. Damon & R. M. Lerner (Series Eds.) and N. Eisenberg (Vol. Ed.), *Handbook of Child Psychology, Vol. 3: Social, Emotional, and Personality Development* (6th ed., pp. 505–570). New York: John Wiley & Sons.

Hartung, P. J., Porfeli, E. J., & Vondracek, F. W. (2005). Child vocational development: A review and reconsideration. *Journal of Vocational Behavior, 66,* 385–419.

Hartup, W. W. (1989). Behavioral manifestations of children's friendships. In T. J. Berndt & G. W. Ladd (Eds.), *Peer Relationships in Child Development* (pp. 46–70). New York: Wiley.

Harwood, R. L. (1992). The influence of culturally derived values on Anglo and Puerto Rican mothers' perceptions of attachment behavior. *Child Development, 63,* 822–839.

Hasher, L., & Zachs, R. T. (1979). Automatic and effortful processes in memory. *Journal of Experimental Psychology: General, 108,* 356–388.

Hasselhorn, M. (1992). Task dependency and the role of category typicality and metamemory in the development of an organizational strategy. *Child Development, 63,* 202–214.

Hatch, M. C., Shu, X. O., McLean, D. E., Levin, B., Begg, M., Reuss, L., et al. (1993). Maternal exercise during pregnancy, physical fitness, and fetal growth. *American Journal of Epidemiology, 137*(10), 1105–1114.

Hatchett, S. J., & Jackson, J. S. (1999). African American extended kin systems: An empirical assessment in the National Survey of Black Americans. In H. P. McAdoo (Ed.), *Family Ethnicity: Strength in diversity* (2nd ed., pp. 171–190). Thousand Oaks, CA: Sage.

Hausenblas, H. A., & Fallon, E. A. (2006). Exercise and body image: A meta-analysis. *Psychology and Health, 21,* 33–47.

Haviland, J. M., & Lelwica, M. (1987). The induced affect response: 10-week-old infants' responses to three emotion expressions. *Developmental Psychology, 23,* 97–104.

Hay, D. F., & Ross, H. S. (1982). The social nature of early conflict. *Child Development, 53,* 105–113.

Hazan, C., & Shaver, P. (1987). Romantic love conceptualized as an attachment process. *Journal of Personality and Social Psychology, 52*(3), 511–524.

Hazell, L. (1975). A study of 300 elective home births. *Birth and the Family Journal, 2,* 11–18.

Hearold, S. (1986). A synthesis of 1,043 effects of television on social behavior. In G. Comstock (Ed.), *Public Communication and Behavior* (Vol. 1, pp. 65–133). New York: Academic Press.

Heinicke, C. M., & Guthrie, D. (1996). Prebirth marital interactions and postbirth marital development. *Infant Mental Health Journal, 17*(2), 140–151.

Helburn, S. W., & Howes, C. (1996). Child care cost and quality. *The Future of Children, 6,* 62–82.

Hergenroeder, A. C. (1998). Prevention of sports injuries. *Pediatrics, 101,* 1057–1063.

Herman, J. L. (1992). *Trauma and recovery: The aftermath of violence—from domestic abuse to political terror.* New York: Basic Books. As cited in Werkerle & Wolfe (1996), p. 508.

Herman-Giddens, M. E. (2006). Recent data on pubertal milestones in United States children: The secular trend toward earlier development. *International Journal of Andrology, 29,* 241–246.

Herpes.com (2002). "Good" virus/"Bad" virus: The truth about HSV-1 and HSV-2; Herpes and Pregnancy; and Transmission. All articles retrieved March 1, 2002, from www.herpes.com.

Herrnstein, R. J., & Murray, C. (1994). *The bell curve: Intelligence and class structure in American life.* New York: Free Press.

Hershberger, S. L., & D'Augelli, A. R. (1995). The impact of victimization on the mental health and suicidality of lesbian, gay, and bisexual youths. *Developmental Psychology, 31,* 65–74.

Hetherington, E. M. (1999). Should we stay together for the sake of the children? In E. M. Hetherington (Ed.), *Coping with Divorce, Single Parenting, and Remarriage: A Risk and Resiliency Perspective* (pp. 93–116). Mahwah, NJ: Erlbaum.

Hetherington, E. M., & Clingempeel, W. G. (1992). Coping with marital transitions. *Monographs of the Society for Research in Child Development, 57* (No. 2–3). Chicago: University of Chicago Press.

Hetherington, E. M., & Jodl, K. M. (1994). Stepfamilies as settings for child development. In A. Booth & J. Dunn (Eds.), *Stepfamilies: Who Benefits? Who does Not?* (pp. 55–79). Hillsdale, NJ: Erlbaum.

Hetherington, E. M., & Kelly, J. (2002). *For better or for worse: Divorce reconsidered.* New York: W. W. Norton.

Hetherington, E. M., & Stanley-Hagan, M. M. (1995). Parenting in divorced and remarried families. In M. H. Bornstein (Ed.), *Handbook of Parenting: Vol. 3. Status and Social Conditions of Parenting* (pp. 233–254). Mahwah, NJ: Erlbaum.

Hetherington, E. M., Bridges, M., & Insabella, G. M. (1998). What matters? What does not? *American Psychologist, 53,* 167–184.

Hetherington, E. M., Cox, M., & Cox. R. (1982). Effects of divorce on parents and children. In M. E. Lamb (Ed.), *Nontraditional Families: Parenting and Child Development* (pp. 233–288). Hillsdale, NJ: Erlbaum.

Hetherington, E. M., Reiss, D., & Plomin, R. (Eds.). (1994). *Separate social worlds of siblings: The impact of nonshared environment on development.* Hillsdale, NJ: Erlbaum.

Higgins, E. T., & Parsons, J. E. (1983). Social cognition and the social life of the child: Stages as subcultures. In E. T. Higgins, D. N. Ruble, & W. W. Hartup (Eds.), *Social Cognition and Social Development* (pp. 15–62). Cambridge, England: Cambridge University Press.

High school expels junior after guard finds knife in truck. (2002, March 21). *New York Times.* Retrieved August 7, 2002, from www.nytimes.com.

Hilton, J. M. (2002). Children's behavior problems in single-parent and married-parent families: Development of a predictive model. *Journal of Divorce and Remarriage, 37,* 13–36.

Ho, M.-W. (1984). Environment and heredity in development and evolution. In M.-W. Ho & P. T. Saunders (Eds.), *Beyond Neo-Darwinism: An Introduction to the New Evolutionary Paradigm* (pp. 267–289). London: Academic Press.

Hodapp, R. M., & Dykens, E. M. (2003). Mental retardation (Intellectual Disabilities). In E. J. Mash & R. A. Barkley (Eds.), *Child Psychopathology* (2nd ed., pp. 486–519). New York: Guilford Press.

Hodnett, E. D., & Osborn, R. W. (1989). Effects of continuous intrapartum professional support on childbirth outcomes. *Research in Nursing and Health, 12,* 289–297.

Hofferth, S. L. (1996). Child care in the United States today. *The Future of Children, 6,* 41–61.

Hofferth, S. L., & Curtin, S. C. (2003). *Leisure time activities in middle childhood.* Paper presented at the Positive Outcomes Conference, Washington, DC, March 12-13, 2003. Retrieved June 21, 2006, from http://www.childtrends.org/Files/Hofferth CurtinPaper.pdf.

Hofferth, S. L., & Sandberg, J. F. (2001). How American children use their time. *Journal of Marriage and the Family, 63,* 295–308.

Hofferth, S. L., Reid, L., & Mott, F. L. (2001). The effects of early childbearing on schooling over time. *Family Planning Perspectives, 33,* 259–267.

Hoffman, M. L. (1975). Moral internalization, parental power, and the nature of parent–child interaction. *Developmental Psychology, 11,* 228–239.

Hoffman-Plotkin, D., & Twentyman, C. T. (1984). A multimodal assessment of behavioral and cognitive deficits in abused and neglected preschoolers. *Child Development, 55,* 794–802.

Hogben, M. (1998). Factors moderating the effect of televised aggression on viewer behavior. *Communication Research, 25,* 220–247.

Hoglund, W. L., & Leadbeater, B. J. (2004). The effects of family, school, and classroom ecologies on changes in children's social competence and emotional behavioral problems in first grade. *Developmental Psychology, 40,* 533–544.

Holden, C. (1995). More on genes and homosexuality. *Science, 268,* 1571.

Holden, G. W. (2002). Perspectives on the effects of corporal punishment: Comment on Gershoff (2002). *Psychological Bulletin, 128,* 590–595.

Holland, J. L. (1997). *Making vocational choices* (3rd ed.). Lutz, FL: Psychological Assessment Resources.

Horgan, D. (1978). The development of the full passive. *Journal of Child Language, 5,* 65–80.

Horn, J., & Cattell, R. B. (1966). Refinement and test of the theory of fluid and crystallized general intelligences. *Journal of Educational Psychology, 57*(5), 253–270.

Horn, S. S. (2003). Adolescents' reasoning about exclusion from social groups. *Developmental Psychology, 39*(1), 71–84.

Howard, D. E., & Wang, M. Q. (2005). Psychosocial correlates of U.S. adolescents who report a history of forced sexual intercourse. *Journal of Adolescent Health, 36,* 372–379.

Howe, D. (1998). *Patterns of adoption: Nature, nurture, and psychosocial development*. Oxford: Blackwell Science, Ltd.

Howe, M. L., & Courage, M. L. (2004). Demystifying the beginnings of memory. *Developmental Review, 24*, 1–5.

Howe, M. L., Courage, M. L., & Bryant-Brown, L. (1995). Reinstating preschoolers' memories. *Developmental Psychology, 29*, 854–869.

Howes, C. (1988). Peer interaction of young children. *Monographs of the Society for Research in Child Development, 53* (Serial No. 217), pp. 1–78.

Howse, R. B., Lange, G., Farran, D. C., & Boyles, C. D. (2003). Motivation and self-regulation as predictors of achievement in economically disadvantaged young children. *Journal of Experimental Education, 71*, 151–174.

Hsu, L. K. G., Chesler, B. E., & Santhouse, R. (1990). Bulimia nervosa in eleven sets of twins: A clinical report. *International Journal of Eating Disorders, 9*, 275–282.

Hudson, J. A., & Nelson, K. (1983). Effects of script structure on children's story recall. *Developmental Psychology, 19*, 625–635.

Hudson, J. A., Fivush, R., & Kuebli, J. (1992). Scripts and episodes: The development of event memory. *Applied Cognitive Psychology, 6*, 483–505.

Hudson, J. A., Shapiro, L. R., & Sosa, B. B. (1995). Planning in the real world: Preschool children's scripts for familiar events. *Child Development, 66*, 984–998.

Hudspeth, W. J., & Pribram, K. H. (1990). Stages of brain and cognitive maturation. *Journal of Educational Psychology, 82*, 881–884.

Huesmann, L. R., & Miller, L. S. (1994). Long-term effects of repeated exposure to media violence in childhood. In L. R. Huesmann (Ed.), *Aggressive Behavior: Current Perspectives* (pp. 153–186). New York: Plenum.

Huesmann, L. R., Eron, L. D., Lefkowitz, M. M., & Walder, L. O. (1984). Stability of aggression over time and generations. *Developmental Psychology, 20*, 1120–1134.

Huesmann, L. R., Moise-Titus, J., Podolski, C., & Eron, L. D. (2003). Longitudinal relations between children's exposure to TV violence and their aggressive and violent behavior in young adulthood: 1977–1992. *Developmental Psychology, 38*, 201–221.

Huggins, S. L. (1989). A comparative study of self-esteem of adolescent children of divorced lesbian mothers and divorced heterosexual mothers. *Journal of Homosexuality, 18*, 123–135.

Hughes, F. P. (1999). *Children, play, and development*. Boston: Allyn and Bacon.

Hulit, L. M., & Howard, M. R. (1997). *Born to talk: An introduction to speech and language development*. Boston, MA: Allyn and Bacon.

Hulit, L. M., & Howard, M. R. (2006). *Born to talk: An introduction to speech and language development* (4th ed.). Boston: Allyn and Bacon.

Human Genome Program, U.S. Department of Energy (1992). Primer on Molecular Genetics, Washington, DC, www.ornl.gov/hgmis/publicat/primer/intro.html.

Human Genome Program, U.S. Department of Energy (2000). Human Genome Project milestones celebrated at White House. Human Genome News, 11, No. 1–2. Retrieved January 18, 2002, from http://www.ornl.gov/hgmis/publicat/hgn/v11n1/04draft.html.

Human Genome Program, U.S. Department of Energy (2001). Human Genome Project information. Retrieved January 18, 2002, from http://www.ornl.gov/hgmis/.

Human Genome Program, U.S. Department of Energy (2006). How many genes are in the human genome? Washington, DC. Retrieved August 24, 2006 from www.ornl.gov/sci/techresources/Human_Genome/faq/genenumber.shtml.

Humphrey, J. H. (2003). *Child development through sports*. New York: The Haworth Press.

Hunter, J. (1990). Violence against lesbian and gay male youths. *Journal of Interpersonal Violence, 5*, 295–300.

Hunter, J., & Mallon, G. P. (2000). Lesbian, gay, and bisexual adolescent development: Dancing with your feet tied together. In B. Greene & G. L. Croom (Eds.), *Education, Research, and Practice in Lesbian, Gay, Bisexual, and Transgendered Psychology: A Resource Manual* (pp. 226–243). Thousand Oaks, CA: Sage.

Hunter, W. M., Helou, S., Saluja, G., Runyan, C. W., & Coyne-Beasley, T. (2005). Injury prevention advice in top-selling parenting books. *Pediatrics, 116*(5), 1080–1088.

Huston, A. C., & Wright, J. C. (1998). Mass media and children's development. In W. Damon, I. E. Sigel, & K. A. Renninger (Eds.), *Handbook of Child Psychology: Vol. 4. Child Psychology in Practice* (pp. 999–1058). New York: Wiley.

Huston, A. C., Donnerstein, E., Fairchild, H., Feshbach, N. D., Katz, P. A., Murray, J. P., et al. (1992). *Big world, small screen: The role of television in American society*. Lincoln: University of Nebraska Press.

Huttenlocher, P. R. (1990). Morphometric study of human cerebral cortex development. *Neuropsychologia, 28*, 517–527.

Huttenlocher, P. R. (1999). Synaptogenesis in human cerebral cortex and the concept of critical periods. In N. A. Fox, L. A. Leavitt, & J. G. Warhol (Eds.), *The Role of Early Experience in Infant Development* (pp. 15–28). New Brunswick, NJ: Johnson & Johnson Pediatric Institute.

Huttenlocher, P. R., & Dabholkar, A. S. (1997). Regional differences in synaptogenesis in human cerebral cortex. *Journal of Comparative Neurology, 387*, 167–178.

Hwang, C. P., & Broberg, A. G. (1992). The historical and social context of child care in Sweden. In M. E. Lamb, K. J. Sternberg, C. P. Hwang & A. G. Broberg (Eds.), *Child Care in Context: Cross-cultural Perspectives* (pp. 27–54). Hillsdale, NJ: Erlbaum.

Hyde, J. S., & Linn, M. C. (1988). Gender differences in verbal ability: A meta-analysis. *Psychological Bulletin, 104*, 53–69.

Hymel, S., Rubin, K. H., Rowden, L., & LeMare, L. (1990). Children's peer relationships: Longitudinal predictions of internalizing and externalizing problems from middle to late childhood. *Child Development, 61*, 2004–2021.

Inhelder, B., & Piaget, J. (1958). *The growth of logical thinking from childhood to adolescence: An essay on the construction of formal operational structures*. New York: Basic Books.

Institute of Medicine, Committee to Study Fetal Alcohol Syndrome (1996). In K. Stratton, C. Howe, & F. Battaglia (Eds.), *Fetal Alcohol Syndrome: Diagnosis, Epidemiology, Prevention, and Treatment*. Washington, DC: National Academy Press.

Intons-Peterson, M. J. (1988). *Children's concepts of gender*. Norwood, NJ: ABLEX.

Isabella, R. A. (1995). The origins of infant-mother attachment: Maternal behavior and infant development. *Annals of Child Development, 10*, 57–81.

Isabella, R. A., & Belsky, J. (1991). Interactional synchrony and the origins of infant-mother attachment: A replication study. *Child Development, 62*, 373–384.

Isabella, R. A., Belsky, J., & von Eye, A. (1989). Origins of infant-mother attachment: An examination of interactional synchrony during the infant's first year. *Developmental Psychology, 25*, 12–21.

Istvan, J. (1986). Stress, anxiety, and birth outcomes: A critical review of the evidence. *Psychological Bulletin, 100*, 331–348.

Iuliano, A. D., Speizer, I. S., Santelli, J., & Kendall, C. (2006). Reasons for contraceptive nonuse at first sex and unintended pregnancy. *American Journal of Health Behavior, 30*, 92–102.

Jacobson, J. L., & Jacobson, S. W. (1996). Intellectual impairment in children exposed to polychlorinated biphenyls in utero. *New England Journal of Medicine, 335*, 783–789.

Jacobson, J. L., & Jacobson, S. W. (2002). Effects of prenatal alcohol exposure on child development. *Alcohol Research and Health, 26*, 282–286.

Jacobson, J. L., Jacobson, S. W., & Humphrey, H. E. B. (1990). Effects of in utero exposure to polychlorinated biphenyls (PCBs) and related contaminants on cognitive functioning in young children. *Journal of Pediatrics, 116*, 38–45.

Jadack, R. A., Hyde, J. S., Moore, C. F., & Keller, M. L. (1995). Moral reasoning about sexually transmitted diseases. *Child Development, 66*, 167–177.

Jaffee, S. R., Caspi, A., Moffitt, T. E., Polo-Tomas, M., Price, T. S., & Taylor, A. (2004). The limits of child effects: Evidence for genetically mediated child effects on corporal punishment but not on physical maltreatment. *Developmental Psychology, 40*, 1047–1058.

Jaffee, S. R., Moffitt, T. E., Caspi, A., & Taylor, A. (2003). Life with (or without) father: The benefits of living with two biological parents depend on the father's antisocial behavior. *Child Development, 74,* 109–126.

Jaffee, S., & Hyde, J. S. (2000). Gender differences in moral orientation: A meta-analysis. *Psychological Bulletin, 126,* 703–726.

Jain, A., Sherman, S. N., Chamberlin, L. A., Carter, Y., Powers, S. W., & Whitaker, R. C. (2001). Why don't low-income mothers worry about their preschoolers being overweight? *Pediatrics, 107*(5), 1138–1146.

James, K. A., Phelps, L., & Bross, A. L. (2001). Body dissatisfaction, drive for thinness, and self-esteem in African American college females. *Psychology in the Schools, 38,* 491–495.

James, W. (1890/1950). *The principles of psychology.* New York: Dover. (Originally published in 1890.)

Janssens, J. M. A. M., & Dekovic, M. (1997). Child rearing, prosocial moral reasoning, and prosocial behavior. *International Journal of Behavioral Development, 20,* 509–527.

Janus, S. S., & Janus, C. L. (1993). *The Janus report on sexual behavior.* New York: Wiley.

Jarrett, R. L. (1995). Growing up poor: The family experiences of socially mobile youth in low-income African American neighborhoods. *Journal of Adolescent Research, 10,* 111–135.

Jay, T. (1992). *Cursing in America.* Philadelphia: J. Benjamins.

Jekielek, S. M. (1998). Parental conflict, marital disruption and children's emotional well-being. *Social Forces, 76,* 905–935.

Jenkins, J., Dunn, J., O'Connor, T. G., Rasbash, J., & Simpson, A. (2005). Mutual influence of marital conflict and children's behavior problems: Shared and nonshared family risks. *Child Development, 76,* 24–39.

Jennings, J., & Rentner, D. S. (2005). Youth and school reform: From the forgotten half to the forgotten third. Washington, DC: Center on Education Policy. Retrieved July 13, 2005, from http://www.ctredpol.org/policy_papers/.

Johnson, B. E., Kuck, D. L., & Schander, P. R. (1997). Rape myth acceptance and sociodemographic characteristics: A multidimensional analysis. *Sex Roles, 36,* 693–708.

Johnson, J. S., & Newport, E. L. (1989). Critical period effects in second language learning: The influence of maturational state on the acquisition of English as a second language. *Cognitive Psychology, 21,* 60–99.

Johnson, M. K. (2002). Social origins, adolescent experiences, and work value trajectories during the transition to adulthood. *Social Forces, 80,* 1307–1341.

Johnston, J. (1990). Role diffusion and role reversal: Structural variations in divorced families and children's functioning. *Family Relations, 39,* 405–413.

Johnston, L. D., O'Malley, P. M., Bachman, J. G., & Schulenberg, J. E. (2006). Monitoring the future: National results on adolescent drug use, Overview of key findings, 2005. (NIH Publication No. 06-5882). Bethesda, MD: National Institute on Drug Abuse. Retrieved May 30, 2006, from http://monitoringthefuture.org/.

Jurdak, M., & Shahin, I. (1999). An ethnographic study of the computational strategies of a group of young street vendors in Beirut. *Educational Studies in Mathematics, 40,* 155–172.

Kabot, S., Masi, W., & Segal, M. (2003). Advances in the diagnosis and treatment of autism spectrum disorders. *Professional Psychology: Research and Practice, 34,* 26–33.

Kagan, J. (1994). *Galen's prophecy.* New York: Basic.

Kagan, J. (1997). Temperament and the reactions to unfamiliarity. *Child Development, 68,* 139–143.

Kagan, J., & Fox, N. A. (2006). Biology, culture, and temperamental biases. In N. Eisenberg (Vol. Ed.), and W. Damon & R. M. Lerner (Eds.), *Handbook of Child Psychology* (6th ed., Vol. 3, pp. 167–225). New York: John Wiley & Sons.

Kagan, J., Arcus, D., & Snidman, N. (1993). The idea of temperament: Where do we go from here? In R. Plomin & G. E. McClearn (Eds.), *Nature, Nurture, and Psychology* (pp. 197–210). Washington, DC: American Psychological Association.

Kagan, J., Arcus, D., Snidman, N., Feng, W. Y., Hendler, J., & Greene, S. (1994). Reactivity in infants: A cross-national comparison. *Developmental Psychology, 30,* 342–345.

Kagan, J., Reznick, J. S., & Snidman, N. (1988). Biological bases of childhood shyness. *Science, 240,* 167–171.

Kail, R., & Salthouse, T. A. (1994). Processing speed as a mental capacity. *Acta Psychologica, 86,* 199–225.

Kaiser Family Foundation. (2002, March). Sex education in the U.S.: Policy and politics. Retrieved January 7, 2003, from www.kff.org/content/2002/3224.

Kaltenbach, K., & Finnegan, L. (1992). Methadone maintenance during pregnancy: Implications for perinatal and developmental outcome. In T. B. Sonderegger (Ed.), *Perinatal Substance Abuse: Research Findings and Clinical Applications* (pp. 239–253). Baltimore: The Johns Hopkins University Press.

Kamerman, S. B. (2000). Parental leave policies: An essential ingredient in early childhood education and care policies. *Social Policy Report* (Vol. 14, Pt. 2). Ann Arbor, MI: The Society for Research in Child Development.

Kamphaus, R. W. (2001). *Clinical assessment of child and adolescent intelligence* (2nd ed.). Boston: Allyn and Bacon.

Kandel, D. B. (2002). *Stages and pathways of drug involvement: Examining the gateway hypothesis.* New York: Cambridge University Press.

Kandel, D. B., Yamaguchi, K., & Chen, K. (1992). Stages of progression in drug involvement from adolescence to adulthood: Further evidence for the gateway theory. *Journal of Studies on Alcohol, 53,* 447–457.

Kandel, E. R., Schwartz, J. H., & Jessell, T. M. (2000). *Principles of neural science* (4th ed.). New York: McGraw-Hill.

Kann, R. T., & Hanna, F. J. (2000). Disruptive behavior disorders in children and adolescents: How do girls differ from boys? *Journal of Counseling and Development, 78,* 267–274.

Kaplan, P. S. (2004). *Adolescence.* Boston: Houghton Mifflin Company.

Karniol, R., & Koren, L. (1987). How would you feel? Children's inferences regarding their own and others' affective reactions. *Cognitive Development, 2,* 271–278.

Karpov, Y. V., & Haywood, H. C. (1998). Two ways to elaborate Vygotsky's concept of mediation. *American Psychologist, 53,* 27–36.

Kaslow, N. J., Collins, M. H., Rashid, F. L., Baskin, M. L., Grifith, J. R., Hollins, L., et al. (2000). The efficacy of a pilot family psychoeducational intervention for pediatric sickle cell disease (SCD). *Families, Systems, and Health, 18,* 381–404.

Katchadourian, H. (1990). Sexuality. In S. S. Feldman & G. R. Elliott (Eds.), *At the threshold: The developing adolescent* (pp. 330–351). Cambridge, MA: Harvard University Press.

Katz, L. F., & Woodin, E. M. (2002). Hostility, hostile detachment, and conflict engagement in marriages: Effects on child and family functioning. *Child Development, 73,* 636–652.

Kaufman, J., & Zigler, E. (1989). The intergenerational transmission of child abuse and the prospect of predicting future abusers. In D. Cicchetti & V. Carlson (Eds.), *Child Maltreatment: Research and Theory on the Causes and Consequences of Child Abuse and Neglect* (pp. 129–150). New York: Cambridge University Press.

Kaufman, P., Chen, X., Choy, S. P., Peter, K., Ruddy, S. A., Miller, A. K., et al. (2001). *Indicators of school crime and safety, 2001.* Washington, DC: U.S. Departments of Education and Justice. NCES 2002-113/NCJ-190075. Retrieved August 8, 2002, from http://nces.ed.gov.

Kaufman, P., Chen, X., Choy, S. P., Ruddy, S. A., Miller, A. K., Fleury, J. K., et al. (2000). *Indicators of school crime and safety, 2000.* Washington, DC: U.S. Departments of Education and Justice. NCES 2001-017/NCJ-184176. Retrieved August 8, 2002, from http://nces.ed.gov.

Kavšek, M. (2004). Predicting later IQ from infant visual habituation and dishabituation: A meta-analysis. *Journal of Applied Developmental Psychology, 25,* 369–393.

Kazdin, A. E., & Marciano, P. L. (1998). Childhood and adolescent depression. In E. J. Mash & R. A. Barkley (Eds.), *Treatment of Childhood Disorders* (pp. 211–248). New York: Guilford Press.

Keating, D. P. (1980). Thinking processes in adolescence. In J. Adelson (Ed.), *Handbook of Adolescent Psychology* (pp. 211–246). New York: Wiley.

Keating, D. P. (1990). Adolescent thinking. In S. S. Feldman & G. R. Elliott (Eds.), *At the Threshold: The Developing Adolescent* (pp. 54–89). Cambridge, MA: Harvard University Press.

Keating, D. P. (2004). Cognitive and brain development. In R. M. Lerner & L. Steinberg (Eds.), *Handbook of Adolescent Psychology* (2nd ed., pp. 45–84). Hoboken, NJ: John Wiley & Sons, Inc.

Keith, T. Z., Keith, P. B., Quirk, K. J., Sperduto, J., Santillo, S., & Killings, S. (1998). Longitudinal effects of parent involvement on high school grades: Similarities and differences across gender and ethnic groups. *Journal of School Psychology, 36,* 335–363.

Kelley, M. L., Sanchez-Hucles, J., & Walker, R. (1993). Correlates of disciplinary practices in working- to middle-class African-American mothers. *Merrill-Palmer Quarterly, 39,* 252–264.

Kellman, P. J., & Arterberry, M. E. (2006). Infant visual perception. In D. Kuhn & R. S. Siegler (Eds.), *Cognition, Perception, and Language* (Vol. 2, pp. 109–160), in W. Damon & R. M. Lerner (Gen. Eds.), *Handbook of Child Psychology* (6th ed.). New York: Wiley.

Kemper, R. L., & Vernoog, A. R. (1994). Metalinguistic awareness in first graders: A qualitative perspective. *Journal of Psycholinguistic Research, 22,* 41–57.

Kendler, K. S., Bulik, C. M., Silberg, J., Hettema, J. M., Myers, J., & Prescott, C. A. (2000). Childhood sexual abuse and adult psychiatric and substance use disorders in women: An epidemiological and co-twin control analysis. *Archives of General Psychiatry, 57,* 953–959.

Kendler, K. S., Kuhn, J. W., & Prescott, C. A. (2004). Childhood sexual abuse, stressful life events and risk for major depression in women. *Psychological Medicine, 34,* 1475–1482.

Kendler, K. S., Neale, M. C., Kessler, R. C., Heath, A. C., & Eaves, L. J. (1993). A test of the equal-environment assumption in twin studies of psychiatric illness. *Behavior Genetics, 23*(1), 21–27.

Keogh, J., & Sugden, D. (1985). *Movement skill development.* New York: Macmillan Publishing Co.

Kerr, D. C. R., Lopez, N. L., Olson, S. L., & Sameroff, A. J. (2004). Parental discipline and externalizing behavior problems in early childhood: The roles of moral regulation and child gender. *Journal of Abnormal Child Psychology, 32,* 369–383.

Kertscher, T. (1999, April 6). Burlington teenager gets probation. *Milwaukee Journal Sentinel.* Retrieved July 19, 2002, from http://proquest.umi.com.

Kertscher, T., Spice, L., Johnson, M., Krantz, C., & Ortiz, V. (1998, November 19). Pewaukee High student arrested after threat. In separate case, three Burlington teens charged with planning killings. *Milwaukee Journal Sentinel.* Retrieved July 19, 2003, from http://proquest.umi.com.

Khanna, N. (1998). Effects of exercise on pregnancy. *American Family Physician, 57*(8), 1764–1768.

Kim, J., & Cicchetti, D. (2006). Longitudinal trajectories of self-esteem processes and depressive symptoms among maltreated and nonmaltreated children. *Child Development, 77,* 624–639.

Kincheloe, J. L. (2004). *Multiple intelligences reconsidered.* New York: Peter Lang.

King, V. (2002). Parental divorce and interpersonal trust in adult offspring. *Journal of Marriage and Family, 64,* 642–656.

Kirby, D. (2002). Effective approaches to reducing adolescent unprotected sex, pregnancy, and childbearing. *The Journal of Sex Research, 39,* 51–57.

Kirschner, D. (1995). Adoption psychopathology and the "adopted child syndrome." In *The Hatherleigh Guide to Child and Adolescent Therapy* (pp. 103–123). New York: Hatherleigh Press.

Klahr, D. (1992). Information-processing approaches to cognitive development. In M. H. Bornstein & M. E. Lamb (Eds.), *Developmental Psychology: An Advanced Textbook* (3rd ed., pp. 273–335). Hillsdale, NJ: Erlbaum.

Klahr, D., & MacWhinney, B. (1998). Information processing. In W. Damon, D. Kuhn, & R. S. Siegler (Eds.), *Handbook of Child Psychology* (5th ed.), *Vol. 2: Cognition, Perception, and Language* (pp. 631–678). New York: John Wiley & Sons.

Klahr, D., & Siegler, R. S. (1978). The representation of children's knowledge. In H. W. Reese & L. P. Lipsitt (Eds.), *Advances in Child Development and Behavior* (Vol. 12, pp. 61–116). New York: Academic Press.

Klaus, M. H., & Kennell, J. H. (1976). *Maternal-infant bonding.* St. Louis: Mosby.

Klein, J. D., & the Committee on Adolescence (2005). Adolescent pregnancy: Current trends and issues. *Pediatrics, 116,* 281–286. Retrieved May 28, 2006, from http://pediatrics.aappublications .org/cgi/content/full/116/1/281.

Knafo, A., & Schwartz, S. H. (2003). Parenting and adolescents' accuracy in perceiving parental values. *Child Development, 74,* 595–611.

Kochanek, K. D., Murphy, S. L., Anderson, R. N., & Scott, C. (2004). Deaths: Final Data for 2002. Centers for Disease Control and Prevention, *National Vital Statistics Reports, 53*(5), 1–116. Retrieved October 29, 2005, from www.cdc.gov/nchs/data/nvsr/ nvsr53/nvsr53_05.pdf.

Kochanska, G., Coy, K. C., & Murray, K. T. (2001). The development of self-regulation in the first four years of life. *Child Development, 72,* 1091–1111.

Kochanska, G., Murray, K. T., & Harlan, E. T. (2000). Effortful control in early childhood: Continuity and change, antecedents, and implications for social development. *Developmental Psychology, 36,* 220–232.

Kochanska, G., Murray, K., & Coy, K. C. (1997). Inhibitory control as a contributor to conscience in childhood: From toddler to early school age. *Child Development, 68,* 263–277.

Kochanska, G., Murray, K., Jacques, T. Y., Koenig, A. L., & Vandegeest, K. A. (1996). Inhibitory control in young children and its role in emerging internalization. *Child Development, 67,* 490–507.

Koestner, R., Franz, C., & Weinberger, J. (1990). The family origins of empathetic concern: A 26-year longitudinal study. *Journal of Personality and Social Psychology, 58,* 709–717.

Kohlberg, L. A. (1966). A cognitive-developmental analysis of children's sex role concepts and attitudes. In E. E. Maccoby (Ed.), *The Development of Sex Differences* (pp. 82–173). Stanford, CA: Stanford University Press.

Kohlberg, L. A. (1969). Stage and sequence: The cognitive-developmental approach to socialization. In D. Goslin (Ed.), *Handbook of Socialization Theory and Research* (pp. 347–480). Chicago: Rand McNally.

Kohlberg, L. A. (1984). Moral stages and moralization: The cognitive-developmental approach. In L. Kohlberg, *Essays on Moral Development: Vol. II. The Psychology of Moral Development: The Nature and Validity of Moral Stages* (pp. 170–211). San Francisco: Harper & Row Publishers.

Kohlberg, L., & Power, C. (1981). Moral development, religious thinking, and the question of a seventh stage. In L. Kohlberg, *Essays on Moral Development: Vol. I. The Philosophy of Moral Development: Moral Stages and the Idea of Justice* (pp. 311–372). Cambridge: Harper & Row.

Kohlberg, L., Levine, C., & Hewer, A. (1984). The current formulation of the theory. In L. Kohlberg, *Essays on Moral Development: Vol. II. The Psychology of Moral Development: The Nature and Validity of Moral Stages* (pp. 212–319). San Francisco: Harper & Row.

Kolb, B. (1999). Neuroanatomy and development overview. In N. A. Fox, L. A. Leavitt, & J. G. Warhol (Eds.), *The Role of Early Experience in Infant Development* (pp. 5–14). New Brunswick, NJ: Johnson & Johnson Pediatric Institute.

Kolb, B., & Fantie, B. (1989). Development of the child's brain and behavior. In C. R. Reynolds & E. F. Janzen (Eds.), *Handbook of Clinical Child Neuropsychology* (pp. 17–40). New York: Plenum.

Kolb, B., Gibb, R., & Dallison, A. (1999). Early experience, behavior, and the changing brain. In N. A. Fox, L. A. Leavitt, & J. G. Warhol (Eds.), *The Role of Early Experience in Infant Development* (pp. 41–63). New York: Johnson & Johnson Pediatric Institute.

Kolb, B., Wilson, B., & Taylor, L. (1992). Developmental changes in the recognition and comprehension of facial expression: Implications for frontal lobe function. *Brain and Cognition, 20*(1), 74–84.

Kollar, E. J., & Fisher, C. (1980). Tooth induction in chick epithelium: Expression of quiescent genes for enamel synthesis. *Science, 207,* 993–995.

Kontos, S., Howes, C., Shinn, M., & Galinsky, E. (1995). *Quality in Family Child Care and Relative Care.* New York: Teachers College Press.

Kopp, C. B. (1982). Antecedents of self-regulation: A developmental perspective. *Developmental Psychology, 18,* 199–214.

Korkman, M., Kettunen, S., & Autti-Rämö, I. (2003). Neurocognitive impairment in early adolescence following prenatal alcohol exposure of varying duration. *Child Neuropsychology, 9,* 117–128.

Korkman, M., Liikanen, A., & Fellman, V. (1996). Neuropsychological consequences of very low birth weight and asphyxia at term: Follow-up until school-age. *Journal of Clinical and Experimental Neuropsychology, 18,* 220–233.

Kourtis, A. P., Kraft, J. M., Gavin, L., Kissin, D., McMichen-Wright, P., & Jamieson, D. J. (2006). Prevention of sexually transmitted human immunodeficiency virus (HIV) infection in adolescents. *Current HIV Research, 4,* 209–219.

Koutsky, L. A., Ault, K. A., Wheeler, C. M., Brown, D. R., Barr, E., Alvarez, F. B., et al. (2002). A controlled trial of a human papillomavirus type 16 vaccine. *New England Journal of Medicine, 347*(21), 1645–1651.

Koverola, C., Pound, J., Heger, A., & Lytle, C. (1993). Relationship of child sexual abuse to depression. *Child Abuse and Neglect, 17,* 393–400.

Kozulin, A. (1990). *Vygotsky's psychology: A biography of ideas.* Cambridge, MA: Harvard University Press.

Kramer, C. (1974). Women's speech: Separate but unequal? *Quarterly Journal of Speech, 60,* 14–24.

Krashen, S. (1999). What the research really says about structured English immersion. *Phi Delta Kappan, 80,* 705–706.

Krashen, S., Long, M., & Scarcella, R. (1982). Age, rate, and eventual attainment in second language acquisition. In S. Krashen, R. Scarcella, & M. Long (Eds.), *Child-adult Differences in Second Language Acquisition* (pp. 161–174). Rowley, MA: Newbury House.

Kraut, R., Scherlis, W., Mukhopadhyay, T., Manning, J., & Kiesler, S. (1996). The HomeNet field trial of residential Internet services. *Communications of the ACM, 39,* 55–63.

Krebs, D., & Gillmore, J. (1982). The relationship among the first stages of cognitive development, role-taking abilities, and moral development. *Child Development, 53,* 877–886.

Kreutzer, M. A., Leonard, C., & Flavell, J. H. (1975). An interview study of children's knowledge about memory. *Monographs of the Society for Research in Child Development, 40* (Serial No. 159.).

Krishner, H. S. (1995). *Classical aphasia syndromes.* New York: Marcel Dekker.

Kubow, P. K., Wahlstrom, K. L., & Bemis, A. E. (1999). Starting time and school life: Reflections from educators and students. *Phi Delta Kappan, 80,* 366–371.

Kuhl, P. K., Andruski, J. E., Christovich, I. A., Christovich, L. A., Kozhevnikova, E. V., Ryskina, V. L., Stolyarova, E. I., Sundberg, U., & Lacerda, F. (1997). Cross-language analsyis of phonetic units in language addressed to infants. *Science, 277*(1 August), 684–686.

Kuhl, P. K., Conboy, B. T., Padden, D., Nelson, T., & Pruitt, J. (2005). Early speech perception and later language development: Implications for the "critical period." *Language Learning and Development, 1,* 237–264.

Kuhn, D. (1992). Cognitive development. In M. H. Bornstein & M. E. Lamb (Eds.), *Developmental Psychology: An Advanced Textbook* (3rd ed., pp. 211–272). Hillsdale, NJ: Erlbaum.

Kuhn, D., & Franklin, S. (2006). The second decade: What develops (and how). In D. Kuhn & R. S. Siegler (Eds.), *Cognitive, Language, and Perceptual Development* (Vol. 2, pp. 953–993), in W. Damon (Gen. Ed.), *Handbook of Child Psychology.* New York: Wiley.

Kupersmidt, J. B., & Coie, J. D. (1990). Preadolescent peer status, aggression, and school adjustment as predictors of externalizing problems in adolescence. *Child Development, 61,* 1350–1362.

Kupersmidt, J. B., Briesler, P. C., DeRosier, M. E., Patterson, C. J., & Davis, P. W. (1995). Childhood aggression and peer relations in the context of family and neighborhood factors. *Child Development, 66,* 360–375.

Kwong, T. E., & Varnhagen, C. K. (2005). Strategy development and learning to spell new words: Generalization of a process. *Developmental Psychology, 41,* 148–159.

Labouvie-Vief, G. (1980). Beyond formal operations: Uses and limits of pure logic in life-span development. *Human Development, 23,* 141–161.

Labouvie-Vief, G. (2006). Emerging structures of adult thought. In J. J. Arnett & J. L. Tanner (Eds.), *Emerging Adults in America: Coming of Age in the 21st Century* (pp. 59–84). Washington, DC: American Psychological Association.

Labre, M. P. (2002). Adolescent boys and the muscular male body ideal. *Journal of Adolescent Health, 30* (4, supplement), 233–242.

Ladd, G. W., Birch, S. H., & Buhs, E. S. (1999). Children's social and scholastic lives in kindergarten: Related spheres of influence? *Child Development, 70,* 1373–1400.

Lagerberg, D. (2004). Sexual knowledge and behavior in South African students: A case for prevention with focus on behavior. *Acta Paediatrica, 93,* 159–161.

Lamaze, F. (1958). *Painless childbirth.* London: Burke.

Lamb, M. E. (1987). Predictive implications of individual differences in attachment. *Journal of Consulting and Clinical Psychology, 55,* 817–824.

Lamb, M. E. (1998). Nonparental child care: Context, quality, correlates, and consequences. In W. Damon, I. E. Sigel, & K. A. Renninger (Eds.), *Handbook of Child Psychology: Vol 4. Child Psychology in Practice* (pp. 73–133). New York: Wiley.

Lamb, M. E., Hwang, C. P., Frodi, A., & Frodi, M. (1982). Security of mother– and father–infant attachment and its relation to sociability with strangers in traditional and non-traditional Swedish families. *Infant Behavior and Development, 5,* 355–367.

Lamb, M. E., Thompson, R. A., Gardner, W., & Charnov, E. L. (1985). *Infant–mother attachment: The origins and developmental significance of individual differences in Strange Situation behavior.* Hillsdale, NJ: Lawrence Erlbaum Associates.

Lamborn, S. D., & Steinberg, L. (1993). Emotional autonomy redux: Revisiting Ryan and Lynch. *Child Development, 64,* 483–499.

Lancy, D. F. (2002). Cultural constraints on children's play. In J. L. Roopnarine (Ed.), *Conceptual, Social-cognitive, and Contextual Issues in the Fields of Play. Play and Culture Studies* (Vol. 4, pp. 53–60). Westport, CT: Ablex.

Langlois, J. H., Roggman, L. A., Casey, R. J., Ritter, J. M., Rieser-Danner, A., & Jenkins, V. Y. (1987). Infant preferences for attractive faces: Rudiments of a stereotype? *Developmental Psychology, 23,* 363–369.

Lansford, J. E., Chang, L., Dodge, K. A., Malone, P. S., Oburu, P., Palmérus, K., et al. (2005). Physical discipline and children's adjustment: Cultural normativeness as a moderator. *Child Development, 76,* 1234–1246.

Lanza, E. (1992). Can bilingual two-year-olds code-switch? *Journal of Child Language, 19,* 633–658.

Larivée, S., Normandeau, S., & Parent, S. (2000). The French connection: Some contributions of French-language research in the Post-Piagetian era. *Child Development, 71,* 823–839.

Larson, J., & Lochman, J. E. (2002). *Helping schoolchildren cope with anger.* New York: Guilford Press.

Larzelere, R. E., & Kuhn, B. R. (2005). Comparing child outcomes of physical punishment and alternative disciplinary tactics: A meta-analysis. *Clinical Child and Family Psychology Review, 8,* 1–37.

Laumann-Billings, L., & Emery, R. E. (2000). Distress among young adults from divorced families. *Journal of Family Psychology, 14,* 671–688.

Laursen, B., & Collins, W. A. (1994). Interpersonal conflict during adolescence. *Psychological Bulletin, 115,* 197–209.

Laursen, B., Coy, K. C., & Collins, W. A. (1998). Reconsidering changes in parent–child conflict across adolescence: A meta-analysis. *Child Development, 69,* 817–832.

Lave, J., & Wenger, E. (1991). *Situated learning: Legitimate peripheral participation.* Cambridge, England: Cambridge University Press.

Lave, J., & Wenger, E. (1996). Practice, person, social world. In H. Daniels (Ed.), *An Introduction to Vygotsky* (pp. 143–150). London: Routledge.

Leaper, C. (1994). Exploring the consequences of gender segregation on social relationships. In W. Damon (Ed.), *New Directions for Child Development* (No. 65, pp. 67–86). San Francisco: Jossey-Bass.

Leboyer, F. (1975). *Birth without violence.* New York: Knopf.

Lee, C. L., & Bates, J. E. (1985). Mother–child interactions at age two years and perceived difficult temperament. *Child Development, 56,* 1314–1325.

Lee, K., Swee-Fong, N., Ee-Lynn, N., Zee-Ying, L. (2004). Working memory and literacy as predictors of performance on algebraic word problems. *Journal of Experimental Child Psychology, 89,* 140–158.

Lee, S. (1998). Mathematics learning and teaching in the school context: Reflections from cross-cultural comparisons. In S. G. Paris & H. M. Wellman (Eds.), *Global Prospects for Education: Development, Culture, and Schooling* (pp. 45–77). Washington, DC: American Psychological Association.

LeFevre, J., & Bisanz, J. (1996). Multiple routes to solution of single-digit multiplication problems. *Journal of Experimental Psychology: General, 125,* 284–307.

Lehman, B. A. (1989, March 13). Spanking teaches the wrong lesson. *Boston Globe,* p. 27.

Lehman, J. S., & Smeeding, T. M. (1997). Neighborhood effects and federal policy. In J. Brooks-Gunn, G. J. Duncan, & J. L. Aber (Eds.), *Neighborhood Poverty: Vol. I. Context and Consequences for Children* (pp. 251–278). New York: Russell Sage Foundation.

Leichtman, M. D., & Ceci, S. J. (1995). The effect of stereotypes and suggestions on preschoolers' reports. *Developmental Psychology, 31,* 568–578.

Lemaire, P., & Siegler, R. S. (1995). Four aspects of strategic change: Contributions to children's learning of multiplication. *Journal of Experimental Psychology: General, 124,* 83–98.

Leman, P. J., Ahmed, S., & Ozarow, L. (2005). Gender, gender relations, and the social dynamics of children's conversations. *Developmental Psychology, 41,* 64–74.

Lemke, M., & Gonzales, P. (2006). *U.S. Student and Adult Performance on International Assessments of Educational Achievement: Findings from the Condition of Education 2006* (NCES 2006-073). U.S. Department of Education. Washington, DC: National Center for Education Statistics.

Lemoine, P., Harousseau, H., Borteyru, J. P., & Menuet, J. C. (1968). Les enfants de parents aicooliques: Anomalies observies. A proposos de 127 cas. [Children of alcoholic parents: Abnormalities observed in 127 cases.] *Ouest Medicine, 21,* 476–482. As cited in Mattson & Riley, 1998.

Lenneberg, E. H. (1967). *Biological foundations of language.* New York: Wiley.

Lerner, R. M. (2006). Developmental science, developmental systems, and contemporary theories of human development. In W. Damon & R. M. Lerner (Series Eds.) and R. M. Lerner (Vol. Ed.), *Handbook of Child Psychology: Vol. 1. Theoretical Models of Human Development* (6th ed., pp. 1–17). Hoboken, NJ: Wiley.

LeVay, S. (1993). *The sexual brain.* Cambridge: MIT Press.

Leventhal, T., & Brooks-Gunn, J. (2000). The neighborhoods they live in: The effects of neighborhood residence on child and adolescent outcomes. *Psychological Bulletin, 126,* 309–337.

Levine, J. A., Pollack, H., & Comfort, M. E. (2001). Academic and behavioral outcomes among the children of young mothers. *Journal of Marriage and Family, 63,* 355–369.

Levy, F., Hay, D. A., & Bennett, K. S. (2006). Genetics of attention deficit hyperactivity disorder: A current review and future prospects. *International Journal of Disability and Education, 53,* 5–20.

Levy, Y., Tennenbaum, A., & Ornoy, A. (2000). Spontaneous language of children with specific neurological syndromes. *Journal of Speech, Language, and Hearing Research, 43,* 351–365.

Lewinsohn, P. M., Rohde, P., & Seeley, J. R. (1993). Psychosocial characteristics of adolescents with a history of suicide attempt. *Journal of the American Academy of Child and Adolescent Psychiatry, 32,* 60–68.

Lewinsohn, P. M., Rohde, P., & Seeley, J. R. (1994). Psychosocial risk factors for future adolescent suicide attempts. *Journal of Consulting and Clinical Psychology, 62,* 297–305.

Lewis, B. A., Singer, L.T., & Short, E. J. (2004). Four-year language outcomes of children exposed to cocaine in utero. *Neurotoxicology and Teratology, 26,* 617–627.

Lewis, C. C. (1981). How adolescents approach decisions: Changes over grades seven to twelve and policy implications. *Child Development, 52,* 538–544.

Lewis, M. (1993). Self-conscious emotions: Embarrassment, pride, shame, and guilt. In M. Lewis & J. Haviland (Eds.), *The Handbook of Emotions* (pp. 563–573). New York: Guilford Press.

Lewis, M.W., Misra, S., Johnson, H. L., & Rosen, T. S. (2004). Neurological and developmental outcomes of prenatally cocaine-exposed offspring from 12 to 36 months. *American Journal of Drug and Alcohol Abuse, 30,* 299–321.

Lewit, E. M., & Baker, L. S. (1995). School readiness. *The Future of Children, 5,* 128–139.

Li, J. (2004). Learning as a task or a virtue: U.S. and Chinese preschoolers explain learning. *Developmental Psychology, 40,* 595–605.

Lindberg, L. D., Ku, L., & Sonenstein, F. (2000). Adolescents' reports of reproductive health education, 1988 and 1995. *Family Planning Perspectives, 32,* 220–226.

Lindsey, E. W., Mize, J., & Pettit, G. S. (1997). Differential play patterns of mothers and fathers of sons and daughters: Implications for children's gender role development. *Sex Roles, 17,* 643–661.

Linnet, K. M., Dalsgaard, S., Obel, C., Wisborg, K., Henriksen, T. B., Rodriguez, A., et al. (2003). Maternal lifestyle factors in pregnancy risk of attention deficit hyperactivity disorder and associated behaviors: Review of the current evidence. *American Journal of Psychiatry, 160,* 1028–1040.

Linver, M. R., Brooks-Gunn, J., & Kohen, D. E. (2002). Family processes as pathways from income to young childrens' development. *Developmental Psychology, 38,* 719–734.

Liptak, A. (2002, July 26). Judge orders abstinence program changed. *New York Times.* Retrieved January 6, 2003, from www.nytimes.com.

Li-Repac, D. C. (1982). *The impact of acculturation on the child-rearing attitudes and practices of Chinese-American families: Consequences for the attachment process.* Unpublished doctoral dissertation, University of California–Berkeley.

Lloyd, B., & Goodwin, R. (1993). Girls' and boys' use of directives in pretend play. *Social Development, 2,* 122–130.

Lo, B. (2006). HPV vaccine and adolescents' sexual activity. *British Medical Journal, 332,* 1106–1107.

Locke, J. L. (1993). *The child's path to spoken language.* Cambridge, MA: Harvard University Press.

Loeb, S., Fuller, B., Kagan, S. L., & Carrol, B. (2004). Child care in poor communities: Early learning effects of type, quality, and stability. *Child Development, 75,* 47–65.

Loehlin, J. C., & Nichols, R. C. (1976). *Heredity, environment, and personality.* Austin: University of Texas Press.

Loehlin, J. C., Horn, J. M., & Willerman, L. (1994). Differential inheritance of mental abilities in the Texas Adoption Project. *Intelligence, 19,* 325–336.

Loftus, E. F., & Ketcham, K. (1994). *The myth of repressed memory.* New York: St. Martin's Press.

Lohmann, H., & Tomasello, M. (2003). Language and social understanding: Commentary on Nelson et al. *Human Development, 46,* 47–50.

Lonigan, C. J., Fischel, J. E., Whitehurst, G. J., Arnold, D. S., & Valdez-Menchaca, M. C. (1992). The role of otitis media in the development of expressive language disorder. *Developmental Psychology, 28,* 430–440.

Lorenz, K. Z. (1973/1977). *Behind the mirror: A search for a natural history of human knowledge.* New York: Harcourt Brace Jovanovich.

Love, J. M., Kisker, E. E., Ross, C. M., Schochet, P. Z., Brooks-Gunn, J., Paulsell, D., et al. (2002). *Making a difference in the lives of infants and toddlers and their families: The impact of Early Head Start.* Department of Health and Human Services Document. Retrieved July 11, 2003, from www.headstartinfo.org/cgi-bin/pubcatstore.cfm.

Love, J. M., Kisker, E. E., Ross, C., Raikes, H., Constantine, J., Boller, K., et al. (2005). The effectiveness of Early Head Start for 3-year-old children and their parents: Lessons for policy and programs. *Developmental Psychology, 41,* 885–901.

Low, J. M. (1999). Differences in cognitive complexity of adolescents with foreclosed and achieved identity status. *Psychological Reports, 85,* 1093–1099.

Luhman, R. (1990). Appalachian English stereotypes: Language attitudes in Kentucky. *Language in Society, 19,* 331–348.

Luria, A. R. (1973). *The working brain: An introduction to neuropsychology.* New York: Basic.

Luthar, S. S., Cicchetti, D., & Becker, B. (2000). The construct of resilience: A critical evaluation and guidelines for future work. *Child Development, 71*, 543–562.

Luzadder, D., & Vaughan, K. (1999, December 12). Inside the Columbine investigation. Retrieved January 3, 2003, from http://denver.rockymountainnews.com.

Luzzo, D. A., & MacGregor, M. W. (2001). Practice and research in career counseling and development 2000. *Career Development Quarterly, 50*, 98–140.

Lykken, D. T. (2000). The causes and costs of crime and a controversial cure. *Journal of Personality, 68*, 559–605.

Lykken, D. T. (2001). Parental licensure. *American Psychologist, 56*, 885–894.

Lyons-Ruth, K., Connell, D. B., Zoll, D., & Stahl, J. (1987). Infants at social risk: Relations among infant maltreatment, maternal behavior, and infant attachment behavior. *Developmental Psychology, 23*, 223–232.

Mabbott, D. J., & Bisanz, J. (2003). Developmental change and individual differences in children's multiplication. *Child Development, 74*, 1091–1107.

MacAulay, D. J. (1990). Classroom environment: A literature review. *Educational Psychology, 10*, 239–253.

MacCallum, F., & Golombok, S. (2004). Children raised in fatherless families from infancy: A follow-up of children from lesbian and single heterosexual mothers at early adolescence. *Journal of Child Psychology and Psychiatry, 45*, 1407–1419.

Maccoby, E. E. (1998). *The two sexes: Growing up apart, coming together.* Boston: Harvard University Press.

Maccoby, E. E. (2002). Gender and group process: A developmental perspective. *Current Directions in Psychological Science, 11*, 54–58.

Maccoby, E. E., & Jacklin, C. N. (1974). *The psychology of sex differences.* Stanford, CA: Stanford University Press.

Maccoby, E. E., & Jacklin, C. N. (1987). Gender segregation in childhood. In E. H. Reese (Ed.), *Advances in Child Development and Behavior* (Vol. 20, pp. 239–287). New York: Academic Press.

Maccoby, E. E., & Lewis, C. C. (2003). Less day care or different day care? *Child Development, 74*, 1069–1075.

Maccoby, E. E., & Martin, J. A. (1983). Socialization in the context of the family: Parent–child interaction. In P. H. Mussen (Ed.), *Handbook of Child Psychology* (Vol. 4, pp. 1–101). New York: Wiley.

MacWhinney, B. (1987) (Ed.), *Mechanisms of language acquisition.* Hillsdale, NJ: Erlbaum.

MacWhinney, B. (1992). Transfer and competition in second language learning. In R. J. Harris (Eds.), *Cognitive Processing in Bilinguals.* Amsterdam, North Holland: Elsevier.

MacWhinney, B. (1999) (Ed.), *The emergence of language.* Hillsdale, NJ: Erlbaum

Maes, H. H. M., Neale, M. C., & Eaves, L. J. (1997). Genetic and environmental factors in relative body weight and human adiposity. *Behavior Genetics, 27*(4), 325–351.

Magnusson, D. (1988). *Individual development from an interactional perspective: A longitudinal study.* Hillsdale, NJ: Erlbaum.

Main, M., & Cassidy, J. (1988). Categories of response to reunion with the parent at age 6: Predicted from infant attachment classifications and stable over a 1-month period. *Developmental Psychology, 24*, 415–426.

Main, M., & George, C. (1985). Responses of abused and disadvantaged toddlers to distress in agemates: A study in the day care setting. *Developmental Psychology, 21*, 407–412.

Main, M., & Hesse, E. (1990). Parents' unresolved traumatic experiences are related to infant disorganized attachment status: Is frightened and/or frightening parental behavior the linking mechanism? In M. T. Greenberg, D. Cicchetti, & E. M. Cummings (Eds.), *Attachment in the Preschool Years: Theory, Research, and Intervention* (pp. 161–182). Chicago: University of Chicago Press.

Main, M., & Solomon, J. (1986). Discovery of an insecure-disorganized/disoriented attachment pattern. In T. B. Brazelton & M. W. Yogman (Eds.), *Affective Development in Infancy* (pp. 95–124). Norwood, NJ: Ablex.

Main, M., & Solomon, J. (1990). Procedures for identifying infants as disorganized/disoriented during the Ainsworth Strange Situation. In M. T. Greenberg, D. Cicchetti, & E. M. Cummings (Eds.), *Attachment in the Preschool Years: Theory, Research, and Intervention* (pp. 121–182). Chicago: University of Chicago Press.

Mandel, D., Kemler Nelson, D. G., & Jusczyk, P. W. (1996). Infants remember the order of words in a spoken sentence. *Cognitive Development, 11*, 181–196.

Maratsos, M. (1983). Some current issues in the study of the acquisition of grammar. In J. H. Flavell & E. M. Markman (Eds.), *Handbook of Child Psychology: Vol. 3. Cognitive Development* (pp. 707–786). New York: Wiley.

Maratsos, M., & Matheney, L. (1994). Language specificity and elasticity: Brain and clinical syndrome studies. *Annual Review of Psychology, 45*, 487–516.

Maratsos, M., Kuczaj, S. A., Fox, D. E. C., & Chalkley, M. A. (1979). Some empirical studies in the acquisition of transformational relations: Passives, negatives and the past tense. In W. A. Collins (Ed.), *Children's Language and Communication* (pp. 1–45). Hillsdale, NJ: Erlbaum.

Marble, M. (1995). Guidelines for pregnant women. *Women's Health Weekly, 1/4/95, N,* 10–12.

Marcia, J. E. (1966). Development and validation of ego identity status. *Journal of Personality and Social Psychology, 38*, 551–558.

Marcus, G. F., Pinker, S., Ullman, M., Hollander, M., Rosen, T. J., & Xu, F. (1992). Overrregularization in language acquisition. *Monographs of the Society for Research in Child Development, 57*(4, Serial No. 228).

Mares, M., & Woodard, E. H. (2001). Prosocial effects on children's social interactions. In D. G. Singer & J. L. Singer (Eds.), *Handbook of Children and the Media* (pp. 183–203). Thousand Oaks, CA: Sage.

Marlier, L., & Schall, B. (2005). Human newborns prefer human milk: Conspecific milk odor is attractive without postnatal exposure. *Child Development, 76*, 155–168.

Marshall, W. A., & Tanner, J. M. (1986). Puberty. In F. Falkner & J. M. Tanner (Eds.), *Human Growth* (2nd ed., Vol. 2, pp. 171–209). New York: Plenum Press.

Martin, C. L. (1994). Cognitive influences on the development and maintenance of gender segregation. In W. Damon (Ed.), *New Directions for Child Development* (No. 65, pp. 35–51). San Francisco: Jossey-Bass.

Martin, G. B., & Clark, R. D. (1982). Distress crying in neonates: Species and peer specificity. *Developmental Psychology, 18*, 3–9.

Martin, J. A., Hamilton, B. E., Sutton, P. D., Ventura, S. J., Menacker, F., & Munson, M. L. (2003, Dec. 17). Births: Final data for 2002. *National Vital Statistics Reports, 52*(10), 1–116. Retrieved March 20, 2005, from http://www.cdc.gov/nchs/data/nvsr/nvsr52/nvsr52_10.pdf.

Martin, J. A., Hamilton, B. E., Sutton, P. D., Ventura, S. J., Menacker, F., & Munson, M. L. (2005). Births: Final data for 2003. *National Vital Statistics Reports, 54*(2). Sept. 8, 2005. Retrieved May 24, 2006, from http://www.cdc.gov/nchs/products/pubs/pubd/nvsr/nvsr.htm.

Martin, J. C. (1992). The effects of maternal use of tobacco products or amphetamines on offspring. In T. B. Sonderegger (Ed.), *Perinatal Substance Abuse: Research Findings and Clinical Applications* (pp. 279–305). Baltimore: The Johns Hopkins University Press.

Martin, N. G., & Heath, A. C. (1993). The genetics of voting: An Australian twin-family study. *Behavior Genetics, 23*, 558.

Martin, N. G., Eaves, L. J., Heath, A. C., Jardine, R., Feingold, L. M., & Eysenck, H. J. (1986). Transmission of social attitudes. *Proceedings of the National Academy of Sciences, USA, 83*, 4364–4368.

Masataka, N. (1996). Perception of motherese in a signed language by 6-month-old deaf infants. *Developmental Psychology, 32*, 874–879.

Masataka, N. (1998). Perception of motherese in Japanese sign language by 6-month-old hearing infants. *Developmental Psychology, 34*, 241–246.

Mash, E. J., & Wolfe, D. A. (1999). *Abnormal child psychology.* Belmont, CA: Brooks/Cole.

Mash, E. J., & Wolfe, D. A. (2005). *Abnormal child psychology* (3rd ed.). Belmont, CA: Wadsworth.

Mason, C. A., Cauce, A. M., Gonzales, N., & Hiraga, Y. (1996). Neither too sweet nor too sour: Problem peers, maternal control, and problem behavior in African American adolescents. *Child Development, 67,* 2115–2130.

Masters, M. S., & Sanders, B. (1993). Is the gender difference in mental rotation disappearing? *Behavior Genetics, 23,* 337–341.

Matthews, T. J., Menacher, F., & MacDorman, M. F. (2002). Infant mortality statistics from the 2000 period linked birth/infant death data set. *National Vital Statistics Reports, 50*(12). Hyattsville, MD: National Center for Health Statistics.

Mattson, S. N., & Riley, E. P. (1998). A review of the neurobehavioral deficits in children with fetal alcohol syndrome or prenatal exposure to alcohol. *Alcoholism: Clinical and Experimental Research, 22,* 279–294.

Maurer, D., & Salapatek, P. (1976). Developmental changes in the scanning of faces by young infants. *Child Development, 47,* 523–527.

Mayer, R. E., Lewis, A., & Hegarty, M. (1992). Mathematical misunderstandings: Qualitative reasoning about quantitative problems. In J. I. D. Campbell (Ed.), *Advances in Psychology, Vol. 91: The Nature and Origins of Mathematical Skills* (pp. 137–153). Oxford, England: North-Holland.

Mayes, L. C., Granger, R. H., Frank, M. A., Schottenfeld, R., & Bornstein, M. (1993). Neurobehavioral profiles of infants exposed to cocaine prenatally. *Pediatrics, 91,* 778–783.

Mayes, L., & Bornstein, M. H. (1995). Information processing and developmental assessments in 3-month-old infants exposed prenatally to cocaine. *Pediatrics, 95,* 539–545.

Mayo Clinic (2003, March 17). HIV/AIDS. Retrieved March 21, 2003, from http://www.MayoClinic.com.

Mazzoni, G., & Memon, A. (2003). Imagination can create false autobiographical memories. *Psychological Science, 14,* 186–188.

McBride-Chang, C. (1996). Models of speech perception and phonological processing in reading. *Child Development, 67,* 1836–1856.

McCabe, A. E., & Siegel, L. S. (1987). The stability of training effects in young children's class inclusion reasoning. *Merrill-Palmer Quarterly, 33,* 187–194.

McCabe, M. P., & Ricciardelli, L. A. (2004). Body image dissatisfaction among males across the lifespan: A review of past literature. *Journal of Psychosomatic Research, 56,* 675–685.

McCall, R. B., & Carriger, M. S. (1993). A meta-analysis of infant habituation and recognition memory performance as predictors of later IQ. *Child Development, 64,* 57–79.

McCartney, K., Harris, M. J., & Bernieri, F. (1990). Growing up and growing apart: A developmental meta-analysis of twin studies. *Psychological Bulletin, 107,* 226–237.

McCloskey, L. A., & Coleman, L. (1992). Difference without dominance: Children's talk in mixed- and same-sex dyads. *Sex Roles, 27,* 241–257.

McConaghy, M. J. (1979). Gender permanence and the genital basis of gender: Stages in the development of constancy of gender identity. *Child Development, 50,* 1223–1226.

McCord, J. (1983). A forty-year perspective on effects of child abuse and neglect. *Child Abuse and Neglect, 7,* 265–270.

McCormick, M. C. (1985). The contribution of low birth weight to infant mortality and childhood morbidity. *The New England Journal of Medicine, 312,* 82–90.

McGhee-Bidlack, B. (1991). The development of noun definitions: A metalinguistic analysis. *Journal of Child Languages, 18,* 417–434.

McGue, M., Bacon, S., & Lykken, D. T. (1993). Personality stability and change in early adulthood: A behavioral genetic analysis. *Developmental Psychology, 29,* 96–109.

McHale, J. P., Kazali, C., & Rotman, T. (2004). The transition to coparenthood: Parents' prebirth expectations and early coparental adjustment at 3 months postpartum. *Development and Psychopathology, 16,* 711–733.

McIntosh, J., MacDonald, F., & McKeganey, N. (2005). The reasons why children in their pre and early teenage years do or do not use illegal drugs. *International Journal of Drug Policy, 16,* 254–261.

McKay, A. (2004). Oral sex among teenagers: Research, discourse, and education. *The Candian Journal of Human Sexuality, 13,* 201–203.

McKey, R., Condelli, L., Ganson, H., et al. (1985). *The impact of Head Start on children, families, and communities* (Final report of the Head Start Evaluation, Synthesis, and Utilization Project). Washington, DC: U.S. Department of Health and Human Services.

McKusick, V. A. (1998). *Mendelian inheritance in man: A catalog of human genes and genetic disorders* (12th ed., Vols. 1–3). Baltimore: The Johns Hopkins University Press.

McLanahan, S. S. (1999). Father absence and the welfare of children. In E. M. Hetherington (Ed.), *Coping with Divorce, Single Parenting, and Remarriage: A Risk and Resiliency Perspective* (pp. 117–145). Mahwah, NJ: Erlbaum.

McLaughlin, S. (2006). *Introduction to language development* (2nd ed). San Diego, CA: Singular Publishing Group, Inc. Cliffton Park, NY: Thomson Delmar Learning.

McLoyd, V. C. (1998). Socioeconomic disadvantage and child development. *American Psychologist, 53,* 185–204.

McLoyd, V. C., & Smith, J. (2002). Physical discipline and behavior problems in African American, European American, and Hispanic children: Emotional support as a moderator. *Journal of Marriage and the Family, 64,* 40–53.

McLoyd, V. C., Aikens, N. L., & Burton, L. M. (2006). Childhood poverty, policy, and practice. In W. Damon & R. M. Lerner (Series Eds.) and K. A. Renninger & I. E. Sigel (Vol. Eds.), *Handbook of Child Psychology: Vol. 4. Child Psychology in Practice* (pp. 700–775). New York: John Wiley & Sons.

McMahon, R. J., & Wells, K. C. (1998). Conduct problems. In E. J. Mash & R. A. Barkley (Eds.), *Treatment of Childhood Disorders* (pp. 111–207). New York: Guilford Press.

Means, M., & Voss, J. (1985). Star wars: A developmental study of expert and novice knowledge structures. *Memory and Language, 24,* 746–757.

Meins, E., Fernyhough, C., Wainwright, R., Gupta, M. D., Fradley, E., & Tuckey, M. (2002). Maternal mind-mindedness and attachment security as predictors of theory of mind understanding. *Child Development, 73,* 1715–1726.

Meisels, S. J., & Atkins-Burnett, S. (2000). The elements of early childhood assessment. In J. P. Shonkoff & S. J. Meisels (Eds.), *Handbook of Early Childhood Intervention* (2nd ed., pp. 231–257). New York: Cambridge University Press.

Meltzoff, A. N., & Borton, R. W. (1979). Intermodal matching by human neonates. *Nature, 282,* 403–404.

Merrill, R. M., Salazar, R. D., & Gardner, N. W. (2001). Relationship between family religiosity and drug use behavior among youth. *Social Behavior and Personality, 29,* 347–358.

Messinger, D. S., Bauer, C. R., Das, A., Seifer, R., Lester, B. M., Lagasse, L. L., et al. (2004). The maternal lifestyle study: Cognitive, motor, and behavioral outcomes of cocaine-exposed and opiate-exposed infants through three years of age. *Pediatrics, 113*(6), 1677–1686.

Meyer, D. R. (1999). Compliance with child support orders in paternity and divorce cases. In R. A. Thompson & P. R. Amato (Eds.), *The Postdivorce Family: Children, Parenting, and Society* (pp. 127–157). Thousand Oaks, CA: Sage.

Meyer-Bahlburg, H. F. L., Ehrhardt, A. A., Rosen, L. R., Gruen, R. S., Veridiano, N. P., Vann, F. H., et al. (1995). Prenatal estrogens and the development of homosexual orientation. *Developmental Psychology, 31,* 12–21.

Michaels, S. (1991). The dismantling of narrative. In A. McCabe & C. Peterson (Eds.), *Developing Narrative Structure* (pp. 303–351). Hillsdale, NJ: Erlbaum.

Mick, E., Biederman, J., Faraone, S. V., Sayer, J., & Kleinman, S. (2002). Case-control study of attention-deficit hyperactivity disorder and maternal smoking, alcohol use and drug use during pregnancy. *Journal of the American Academy of Child and Adolescent Psychiatry, 41*(4), 378–385.

Miele, F. (1995). *Skeptic Magazine* interview with Robert Sternberg on *The Bell Curve. Skeptic, 3,* 72–80.

Miller, B. C., Xitao, F., Christensen, M., Grotevant, H. D., & van Dulmen, M. (2000). Comparisons of adopted and nonadopted adolescents in a large, nationally representative sample. *Child Development, 71,* 1458–1473.

Miller, B., & Moore, K. (1990). Adolescent sexual behavior, pregnancy, and parenting: Research through the 1980s. *Journal of Marriage and the Family, 52,* 1025–1044.

Miller, G. A. (1956). The magical number seven, plus or minus two: Some limits on our capacity for processing information. *Psychological Review, 63*, 81–97.

Miller, P. A., Eisenberg, N., Fabes, R. A., & Shell, R. (1996). Relations of moral reasoning and vicarious emotion to young children's prosocial behavior toward peers and adults. *Developmental Psychology, 32*, 210–219.

Miller-Johnson, S., Winn, D. C., Coie, J. D., Malone, P. S., & Lochman, J. (2004). Risk factors for adolescent pregnancy reports among African American males. *Journal of Research on Adolescence, 14*, 471–495.

Millman, R. P. (2005). Excessive sleepiness in adolescents and young adults: Causes, consequences, and treatment strategies. *Pediatrics, 115*, 1774–1786.

Minami, M., & McCabe, A. (1990). Haiku as a discourse regulation device: A stanza analysis of Japanese children's personal narratives. *Language in Society, 20*, 577–599.

Miniño, A. M., Arias, E., Kochanek, K. D., Murphy, S. L., & Smith, B. L. (2002). Deaths: Final Data for 2000. *National Vital Statistics Reports, 50*(15). Hyattsville, Maryland: National Center for Health Statistics.

Minton, C., Kagan, J., & Levine, J. (1971). Maternal control and obedience in the two-year-old. *Child Development, 42*, 1873–1894.

Mitru, G., Millrood, D. L., & Mateika, J. H. (2002). The impact of sleep on learning and behavior in adolescents. *Teachers College Record, 104*, 704–726.

Moerk, E. L. (1992). *A first language taught and learned.* Baltimore: Paul H. Brooks.

Moerk, E. L. (2000). *The guided acquisition of first language skills.* Stamford, CT: Ablex.

Moffitt, T. E. (1993). Adolescence-limited and life-course-persistent antisocial behavior: A developmental taxonomy. *Psychological Review, 100*, 674–701.

Moffitt, T. E., Caspi, A., Dickson, N., Silva, P., & Stanton, W. (1996). Childhood-onset versus adolescent-onset antisocial conduct problems in males: Natural history from ages 3 to 18 years. *Development and Psychopathology, 8*, 399–424.

Mohanty, A. K., & Perregaux, C. (1997). Language acquisition and bilingualism. In J. W. Berry, P. R. Dasen, & T. S. Saraswathi (Eds.), *Handbook of Cross-Cultural Psychology. Vol. 2: Basic Processes and Human Development.* (2nd ed.). Boston: Allyn and Bacon.

Moir, D. D. (1986). *Pain relief in labour: A handbook for midwives* (5th ed.). Edinburgh: Churchill Livingstone.

Molnar, B. E., Gortmaker, S. L., & Bull, F. C. (2004). Unsafe to play? Neighborhood disorder and lack of safety predict reduced physical activity among urban children and adolescents. *American Journal of Health Promotion, 18*, 378–386.

Molnar, J., Roth, W., & Klein, T. (1990). Constantly compromised: The impact of homelessness on children. *Journal of Social Issues, 46*, 109–124.

Montague, D. P. F., & Walker-Andrews, A. S. (2001). Peekaboo: A new look at infants' perception of emotion expressions. *Developmental Psychology, 37*, 826–838.

Montemayor, R. (1982). The relationship between parent-adolescent conflict and the amount of time adolescents spend alone and with parents and peers. *Child Development, 53*, 1512–1519.

Montgomery, J. W. (1995). Sentence comprehension in children with specific language impairment: The role of phonological working memory. *Journal of Speech and Hearing Research, 38*, 187–199.

Moore, D. S., Spence, M. J., & Katz, G. S. (1997). Six-month-olds' categorization of natural infant-directed utterances. *Developmental Psychology, 33*, 980–989.

Moore, K. L., & Persaud, T. V. N. (1998). *The developing human: Clinically oriented embryology* (6th ed.). Philadelphia: W. B. Saunders Company.

Morgan, J., Bonamo, K. M., & Travis, L. L. (1995). Negative evidence on negative evidence. *Developmental Psychology, 31*, 180–197.

Morgan, P. (1998). *Adoption and the care of children.* London: IEA Health and Welfare Unit.

Morrison, F. J., Griffith, E. M., & Alberts, D. M. (1997). Nature–nurture in the classroom: Entrance age, school readiness, and learning in children. *Developmental Psychology, 33*, 254–262.

Morrow, C. E., Vogel, A. L., & Anthony, J. C. (2004). Expressive and receptive language functioning in preschool children with prenatal cocaine exposure. *Journal of Pediatric Psychology, 29*, 543–554.

Mortimer, J. T. (2003). *Working and growing up in America.* Cambridge, MA: Harvard University Press.

Mosher, W. D., Martinez, G. M., Chandra, A., Abma, J. C., & Willson, S. J. (2004). *Use of contraception and use of family planning services in the United States: 1982–2002. Advance data from vital and health statistics; No. 350.* Hyattsville, MD: National Center for Health Statistics. 2004. Retrieved May 29, 2005, from http://www.cdc.gov/nchs/data/ad/ad350.pdf.

Moshman, D. (2005). *Adolescent psychological development: Rationality, morality, and identity* (2nd ed.). Mahwah, NJ: Erlbaum.

Moss, E., Bureau, J. F., Cyr, C., Mongeau, C., & St-Laurent, D. (2004). Correlates of attachment at age 3: Construct validity of the preschool attachment classification system. *Developmental Psychology, 40*, 323–334.

Moss, E., Cyr, C., & Dubois-Comtois, K. (2004). Attachment at early school age and developmental risk: Examining family contexts and behavior problems of controlling-caregiving, controlling-punitive, and behaviorally disorganized children. *Developmental Psychology, 40*, 519–532.

Mueller, E., & Silverman, N. (1989). Peer relations in maltreated children. In D. Cicchetti & V. Carlson (Eds.), *Child Maltreatment: Theory and Research on the Causes and Consequences of Child Abuse and Neglect* (pp. 529–578). New York: Cambridge University Press.

Mullen, P. E., & Fleming, J. (1998). Long-term effects of child sexual abuse. *Issues in Child Abuse Prevention, 9.* National Child Protection Clearinghouse. Retrieved June 22, 2006, from http://www.aifs.gov.au/nch/issues9.html.

Mullis, A. K., & Mullis, R. L. (1997). Vocational interests of adolescents: Relationships between self-esteem and locus of control. *Psychological Reports, 81*, 1363–1371.

Mullis, I. V. S., Martin, M. O., Beaton, A. E., Gonzalez, E. J., Kelly, D. L., & Smith, T. A. (1998). *Mathematics and science achievement in the final year of secondary school: IEA's third international mathematics and science study (TIMSS).* Chestnut Hill, MA: Center for the Study of Testing, Evaluation, and Educational Policy, Boston College.

Mullis, R. L., Mullis, A. K., & Gerwels, D. (1998). Stability of vocational interests among high school students. *Adolescence, 33*, 699–707.

Mumme, D. L., & Fernald, A. (2003). The infant as onlooker: Learning from emotional reactions observed in a television scenario. *Child Development, 74*, 221–237.

Munakata, Y. (2006). Information processing approaches to development. In D. Kuhn & R. Siegler (Vol. Eds.) and W. Damon & R. M. Lerner (Eds.-in-chief), *Handbook of Child Psychology* (6th ed., Vol. 1, pp. 426–463). Hoboken, NJ: Wiley.

Munroe, R. H., Shimmin, H. S., & Munroe, R. L. (1984). Gender understanding and sex role preferences in four cultures. *Developmental Psychology, 20*, 673–682.

Naeye, R., & Peters, E. (1984). Mental development of children whose mothers smoked during pregnancy. *Obstetrics and Gynecology, 64*, 601–607.

Naigles, L., & Gelman, S. A. (1995). Overextensions in comprehension and production revisited: Preferential-looking in a study of *dog, cat,* and *cow. Journal of Child Language, 22*, 19–46.

Naigles, L.G., & Hoff-Ginsburg, E. (1995). Input to verb learning: Evidence for the plausibility of syntactic bootstrapping. *Developmental Psychology, 31*, 827–837.

Náñez, J. E., & Yonas, A. (1994). Effects of luminance and texture motion on infant defensive reactions to optical collision. *Infant Behavior and Development, 17*, 165–174.

Nantais, K. M., & Schellenberg, E. G. (1999). The Mozart effect: An artifact of preference. *Psychological Science, 10*, 370–373.

Nash, M. R., Zivney, O. A., & Hulsey, T. (1993). Characteristics of sexual abuse associated with greater psychological impairment among children. *Child Abuse and Neglect, 17*, 401–408.

Nathanielsz, P. W. (1992). *Life before birth: The challenges of fetal development.* New York: W. H. Freeman and Company.

National Alliance for Youth Sports (2001). *Standards.* Retrieved June 22, 2006, from http://www.nays.org/TimeOut/National%20Standards.pdf.

National Alliance for Youth Sports (2003). *Recommendations for Communities*. Retrieved June 22, 2006, from http://www.nays.org/nays_community_recommendations.pdf.

National Association for Education of Young Children (2003). Questions to ask when seeking quality child care. Retreived January 12, 2003 from www.naeyc.org/accreditation/naeyc_accred/info_general-fag3.asp.

National Association for Sport and Physical Education & American Heart Association (2006). 2006 Shape of the nation report: Status of physical education in the USA. Reston, VA: National Association for Sport and Physical Education. Retrieved June 20, 2006, from http://www.aahperd.org/naspe/ShapeOfTheNation/PDF/ShapeOfTheNation.pdf.

National Association for Sport and Physical Education (2002). *Active Start: A statement of physical activity guidelines for children birth to five years*. National Association for Sport and Physical Education: Reston, Virginia.

National Association for the Education of Young Children (2003). Retrieved January 12, 2003, from www.naeyc.org/accreditation/naeyc_accred/info_general-faq3.asp.

National Campaign to Prevent Teen Pregnancy (2005). *General Facts and Stats*. Retrieved May 26, 2006, from. http://www.teenpregnancy.org/resoursces/data/genlfact.asp.

National Center for Children in Poverty (2006). *Most low-income parents are employed*. Retrieved August 2, 2006, from http://www.nccp.org/media/pel06_text.pdf.

National Center for Chronic Disease Prevention and Health Promotion. (2004). Breastfeeding practices: Results from the 2003 National Immunization Survey. Retrieved September 10, 2004, from http://www.cdc.gov/breastfeeding/NIS_data/index.htm.

National Center for Health Statistics. (2005). Health, United States, 2005, with chartbook on trends in the health of Americans. Hyattsville, MD: U.S. Government Printing Office. Retrieved May 30, 2006, from http://www.cdc.gov/nchs/data/hus/hus05.pdf#highlights.

National Center for Education Statistics (2005). *Digest of Education Statistics Tables and Figures, 2005* (Table 11). Retrieved July 28, 2006, from http://nces.ed.gov/programs/digest/d05/tables/dt05_011.asp.

National Center for Education Statistics (2005a). *Digest of Education Statistics, 2004*. Retrieved June 19, 2006, from http://nces.ed.gov/pubsearch/pubsinfo.asp?pubid=2006005.

National Center for Health Statistics (2000a). *Adolescent health chartbook (DHHS publication No. 2000-1232-1)*, (pp. 63 and 110). Hyattsville, MD: U.S. Department of Health and Human Services.

National Center for Health Statistics (2000b). *National health and nutrition examinations survey: Clinical growth charts*. Retrieved October 21, 2002, from www.cdd.gov/nchs/about/major/nhanes/growthcharts/clinical_charts.htm#clin1.

National Center for Health Statistics (2004). *2000 CDC Growth charts: United States,* for the U.S. Department of Health and Human Services and the Centers for Disease Control and Prevention. Last accessed November 7, 2005, from http://www.cdc.gov/growthcharts/.

National Center for Health Statistics (2005). *Health, United States, 2005, with Chartbook on Trends in the Health of Americans* (pp. 42–43, 275–279). Hyattsville, MD: National Center for Health Statistics. Retrieved December 13, 2005, from http://www.cdc.gov/nchs/hus.htm.

National Center for Victims of Crime (2006). *Sexual assault fact sheet*. Accessed May 27, 2006, from. http://www.ncvc.org/ncvc/AGP.Net/Components/documentViewer/Download.aspxnz?DocumentID=39727.

National Clearinghouse on Child Abuse and Neglect (2006). *Recognizing child abuse and neglect: Signs and symptoms.* Retrieved June 22, 2006, from http://nccahch.acf.hhs.gov.

National Education Goals Panel. (1999). *The National Education Goals report: Building a nation of learners*. Washington, DC: U.S. Government Printing Office.

National Institute on Drug Abuse (2001). Pregnancy and drug use trends. *NIDA InfoFax*. Retrieved March 3, 2002, from www.nida.nih.gov/infofax/pregnancytrends.html.

National Research Council and Institute of Medicine. (2000). *From Neurons to Neighborhoods: The Science of Early Childhood Development*. In J. P. Shonkoff & D. A. Phillips, (Eds.), *Board on Children, Youth, and Families, Commission on Behavioral and Social Sciences and Education*. Washington, DC: National Academy Press.

National SAFE KIDS Campaign (2004). *Childhood injury fact sheet*. Washington, DC: NSKC. Retrieved December 6, 2005, from http://www.usa.safekids.org/tier3_printable.cfm?content_item_id=1030&folder_id=540.

National SAFE KIDS Campaign (2006). *Preventing injuries to child pedestrians*. Retrieved January 27, 2006, from http://www.usa.safekids.org/content_documents/ACF43B4.pdf.

Naus, M. J., Ornstein, P. A., & Aivano, S. (1977). Developmental changes in memory: The effects of processing time and rehearsal instructions. *Journal of Experimental Child Psychology, 23,* 237–251.

Neisser, U. (1998). *The rising curve: Long-term gains in IQ and related measures*. Washington, DC: American Psychological Association.

Neisser, U., Boodoo, G., Touchard, T. J., Boykin, A. W., Brody, N., Ceci, S. J., Halpern, D. F., Loehlin, J. C., Perloff, R., Sternberg, R. J., & Urbina, S. (1996). Intelligence: Knowns and unknowns. *American Psychologist, 51,* 77–101.

Nelson, C. A. (2001). The development and neural bases of face recognition. *Infant and Child Development, 10*(1–2), 3–18.

Nelson, C. A., & Horowitz, F. D. (1983). The perception of facial expressions and stimulus motion by two- and five-month-old infants using holographic stimuli. *Child Development, 54,* 868–877.

Nelson, D. A., & Crick, N. R. (2002). Parental psychological control: Implications for childhood physical and relational aggression. In B. K. Barber (Ed.), *Intrusive Parenting: How Psychological Control Affects Children and Adolescents* (pp. 168–189). Washington, DC: American Psychological Association.

Nelson, D. A., Hart, C. H., Yang, C., Olsen, J. A., & Jin, S. (2006). Aversive parenting in China: Associations with child physical and relational aggression. *Child Development, 77,* 554–572.

Nelson, K. (1973). Structure and strategy in learning to talk. *Monographs of the Society for Research in Child Development, 38* (Serial No. 149).

Nelson, K. (1986). *Event knowledge: Structure and function in development*. Hillsdale, NJ: Erlbaum.

Nelson, K., & Fivush, R. (2004). The emergence of autobiographical memory: A social cultural developmental theory. *Psychological Review, 111,* 486–511.

Nelson, K., Hampson, J., & Shaw, L. K. (1993). Nouns in early lexicons: Evidence, explanations and implications. *Journal of Child Language, 20,* 61–84.

Nelson, K., Skwerer, D. P., Goldman, S., Henseler, S., Presler, N., & Walkenfeld, F. F. (2003). Entering a community of minds: An experiential approach to "theory of mind." *Human Development, 46,* 24–46.

Nelson, N. M., Enkin, M. W., Saigel, S., Bennett, K. J., Milner, R., & Sackett, D. L. (1980). A randomized clinical trial of the Leboyer approach to childbirth. *New England Journal of Medicine, 299,* 655–660.

Nettlebladt, P., Fagerstrom, C., & Udderberg, N. (1976). The significance of reported childbirth pain. *Journal of Psychosomatic Research, 20,* 215–221.

Neuschatz, J. S., Preston, E. L., Burkett, A. D., Toglia, M. P., Lampinen, J. M., Neuschatz, Jo, S., et al. (2005). The effects of post-identification feedback and age on retrospective eyewitness memory. *Applied Cognitive Psychology, 19,* 435–453.

New York Times. (2001). Shooting at California school leaves 2 dead and 13 hurt. Retrieved March 6, 2001, from www.nytimes.com/2001/03/06/national/06SHOO.html.

Newburger, E. C. (2001). Home computers and Internet use in the United States: August 2000. *Current Population Reports*. Washington, DC: U.S. Census Bureau. Retrieved July 8, 2002, from www.census.gov.

Newman, D. L., Caspi, A., Moffitt, T. E., & Silva, P. A. (1997). Antecedents of adult interpersonal functioning: Effects of individual differences in age 3 temperament. *Developmental Psychology, 33,* 206–217.

Newman, R. S. (2005). The cocktail party effect in infants revisited: Listening to one's name in noise. *Developmental Psychology, 41,* 352–362.

Newport, E. L. (1990). Maturational constraints on language learning. *Cognitive Science, 14,* 11–28.

Newsom, C. (1998). Autistic disorder. In E. J. Mash & R. A. Barkley (Eds.), *Treatment of childhood disorders* (2nd ed., pp. 416–467). New York: Guilford Press.

Newton, R. W., & Hunt, L. P. (1984). Psychosocial stress in pregnancy and its relation to low birth weight. *British Medical Journal, 288,* 1191–1194.

NICHD (2005). Autism overview: What we know. Retrieved 9/12/06 from http://www.nichd.nih.gov/publications/pubs/autism_overview_2005.pdf.

NICHD Early Child Care Research Network (1997). The effects of infant child care on infant-mother attachment security: Results of the NICHD study of early child care. *Child Development, 68,* 860–879.

NICHD Early Child Care Research Network. (1998). Early child care and self-control, compliance, and problem behavior at twenty-four and thirty-six months. *Child Development, 69,* 1145–1170.

NICHD Early Child Care Research Network. (2000). The relation of child care to cognitive and language development. *Child Development, 71,* 960–980.

NICHD Early Child Care Research Network (2001). Child-care and family predictors of preschool attachment and stability from infancy. *Developmental Psychology, 37,* 847–862.

NICHD Early Child Care Research Network. (2002). Child-care structure → process → outcome: Direct and indirect effects of child-care quality on young children's development. *Psychological Science, 13,* 199–206.

NICHD Early Child Care Research Network. (2003a). Do children's attention processes mediate the link between family predictors and school readiness? *Developmental Psychology, 39,* 581–593.

NICHD Early Child Care Research Network. (2003b). Does quality of child care affect child outcomes at age 4½? *Developmental Psychology, 39,* 451–469.

NICHD Early Child Care Research Network. (2004). Does class size in first grade relate to children's academic and social performance or observed classroom processes? *Developmental Psychology, 40,* 651–664.

Nichols, R. C. (1978). Twin studies of ability, personality, and interests. *Homo, 29,* 158–173.

Nicolosi, J., & Byrd, A. D. (2002). A critique of Bem's "exotic becomes erotic" theory of sexual orientation development. *Psychological Reports, 90,* 931–946.

Niedzwienska, A. (2003). Distortion of autobiographical memories. *Applied Cognitive Psychology, 17,* 81–91.

Nottelmann, E. D., Susman, E. J., Blue, J. H., Inoff-Germain, G., Dorn, L. D., Loriaux, D. L., et al. (1987). Gonadal and adrenal hormone correlates of adjustment in early adolescence. In R. M. Lerner & T. T. Foch (Eds.), *Biological-Psychosocial Interactions in Early Adolescence.* Hillsdale, NJ: Erlbaum.

Nucci, L. P. (1996). Morality and the personal sphere of action. In E. Reed, E. Turiel, & T. Brown (Eds.), *Values and Knowledge* (pp. 41–60). Hillsdale, NJ: Erlbaum.

Nurnberger, J. I., & Gershon, E. S. (1992). Genetics. In E. S. Paykel (Ed.), *Handbook of Affective Disorders* (2nd ed., pp. 131–148). New York: Guilford Press.

O'Brien, E. M., & Mindell, J. A. (2005). Sleep and risk-taking behavior in adolescents. *Behavioral Sleep Medicine, 3,* 113–133.

O'Connor, T. G., & Croft, C. M. (2001). A twin study of attachment in preschool children. *Child Development, 72,* 1501–1511.

O'Reilly, A. W. (1995). Using representations: Comprehension and production of actions with imagined objects. *Child Development, 66,* 999–1010.

O'Sullivan, L. R., & Meyer-Bahlberg, H. F. L. (2003). African American and Latina inner-city girls' reports of romantic and sexual development. *Journal of Social and Personal Relationships, 20,* 221–238.

Oetting, J. B. (2003a). Dialect speakers. In R. Kent (Ed.), *MIT Encyclopedia of Communication Sciences and Disorders.* Cambridge, MA: MIT Press.

Oetting, J. B. (2003b). Dialect vs. disorder. In R. Kent (Ed.), *MIT Encyclopedia of Communication Sciences and Disorders.* Cambridge, MA: MIT Press.

Oetting, J. B., & McDonald, J. L. (2001). Nonmainstream dialect use and specific language impairment. *Journal of Speech, Language, and Hearing Research, 44,* 207–223.

Oliver, M., Schofield, G., & McEvoy, E. (2006). An integrated curriculum approach to increasing habitual physical activity in children: A feasibility study. *Journal of School Health, 76,* 74–79.

Ollendick, T. H., Weist, M. D., Borden, M. G., & Greene, R. W. (1992). Sociometric status and academic, behavioral, and psychological adjustment: A five-year longitudinal study. *Journal of Consulting and Clinical Psychology, 60,* 80–87.

Oller, D. K., & Eilers, R. E. (1988). The role of audition in infant babbling. *Child Development, 59,* 441–449.

Onwuegbuzie, A. J., & Daley, C. E. (2001). Racial differences in IQ revisited: A synthesis of nearly a century of research. *Journal of Black Psychology, 27,* 209–220.

Opper, S. (1977). Concept development in Thai urban and rural children. In P. R. Dasen (Ed.), *Piagetian Psychology: Cross-cultural Contributions* (pp. 89–122). New York: Gardner Press.

Orbeta, R. L., Overpeck, M. D., Ramcharran, D., Kogan, M. D., & Ledsky, R. (2006). High caffeine intake in adolescents: Associations with difficulty sleeping and feeling tired in the morning. *Journal of Adolescent Health, 38,* 451–453.

Orr, J. E., & Hakuta, K. (2000). Inadequate conclusions from an inadequate assessment: What can SAT-9 scores tell us about the impact of Proposition 227 in California? *Bilingual Research Journal, 24,* 141–155.

Osofsky, J. D. (1999). The impact of violence on children. *The Future of Children, 9,* 33–49.

Østensjø, S., Carlberg, E. B., & Vøllestad, N. K. (2003). Everyday functioning in young children with cerebral palsy: Functional skills, caregiver assistance, and modifications of the environment. *Developmental Medicine and Child Neurology, 45*(9), 603–612.

Østensjø, S., Carlberg, E. B., & Vøllestad, N. K. (2004). Motor impairments in young children with cerebral palsy: Relationship to gross-motor function and everyday activities. *Developmental Medicine and Child Neurology, 46*(9), 580–589.

Owens, E. B., Hinshaw, S. P., Arnold, L. E., Cantwell, D. P., Elliott, G., Hechtman, L., et al. (2003). Which treatment for whom for ADHD? Moderators of treatment response in the MTA. *Journal of Consulting and Clinical Psychology, 71,* 540–552.

Oyserman, D., Coon, H. M., & Kemmelmeier, M. (2002). Rethinking individualism and collectivism: Evaluation of theoretical assumptions and meta-analyses. *Psychological Bulletin, 128,* 3–72.

Padilla, A. M., & Baird, T. L. (1991). Mexican-American adolescent sexuality and sexual knowledge: An exploratory study. *Hispanic Journal of Behavioral Sciences, 13,* 95–104.

Paik, H., & Comstock, G. (1994). The effects of television violence on antisocial behavior: A meta-analysis. *Communication Research, 21,* 516–546.

Palmérus, K., & Jutengren, G. (2004). Swedish parents' self-reported use of discipline in response to continued misconduct by their pre-school children. *Infant and Child Development, 13,* 79–90.

Pam, A., Kemker, S. S., Ross, C. A., & Golden, R. (1996). The "equal environments assumption" in MZ–DZ twin comparisons: An untenable premise of psychiatric genetics? *Acta Geneticae Medicae et Gemellologiae: Twin Research, 45*(3), 349–360.

Pan, H. W. (1994). Children's play in Taiwan. In J. L. Roopnarine, J. E. Johnson, & F. H. Hooper (Eds.), *Children's Play in Diverse Cultures* (pp. 31–50). Albany, NY: State University of New York Press.

Parfitt, G., & Eston, R. G. (2005). The relationship between children's habitual activity level and psychological well-being. *Acta Paediatrica, 94,* 1791–1797.

Parke, R. D., & Buriel, R. (1998). Socialization in the family: Ethnic and ecological perspectives. In W. Damon & N. Eisenberg (Eds.), *Handbook of Child Psychology: Vol. 3. Social, Emotional, and Personality Development* (pp. 463–552). New York: Wiley.

Parke, R. D., & Buriel, R. (2006). Socialization in the family: Ethnic and ecological perspectives. In W. Damon & R. Lerner (Series Eds.) and N. Eisenberg (Vol. Ed.), *Handbook of Child Psychology: Vol. 3. Social, Emotional, and Personality Development* (6th ed., pp. 429–504). New York: Wiley.

Parker, F. L., Boak, A. Y., Griffin, K. W., Ripple, C., & Peay, L. (1999). Parent–child relationship, home learning environment, and school readiness. *School Psychology Review, 28,* 413–425.

Parker, S. K., Schwartz, B., Todd, J., & Pickering, L. K. (2004). Thimersol-containing vaccines and Autistic Spectrum Disorder:

A critical review of published original data. *Pediatrics, 114,* 793–804.

Parra-Cardona, J. R., Wampler, R. S., & Sharp, E. A. (2006). "Wanting to be a good father": Experiences of adolescent fathers of Mexican descent in a teen fathers program. *Journal of Marital and Family Therapy, 32,* 215–231.

Parten, M. B. (1932). Social participation among pre-school children. *Journal of Abnormal and Social Psychology, 27,* 243–269.

Pasupathi, M., Staudinger, U. M., & Baltes, P. B. (2001). Seeds of wisdom: Adolescents' knowledge and judgment about difficult life problems. *Developmental Psychology, 37,* 351–361.

Patterson, C. J. (1992). Children of lesbian and gay parents. *Child Development, 63,* 1025–1042.

Patterson, C. J. (1995). Sexual orientation and human development: An overview: *Developmental Psychology, 31,* 3–11.

Patterson, G. R. (1995). Coercion—a basis for early age of onset for arrest. In J. McCord (Ed.), *Coercion and Punishment in Long-term Perspective* (pp. 81–105). New York: Cambridge University Press.

Patterson, G. R. (1997). Performance models for parenting: A social interactional perspective. In J. E. Grusec & L. Kuczynski (Eds.), *Parenting and Children's Internalization of Values* (pp. 193–226). New York: Wiley.

Pear, R. (1996, March 17). Many states fail to fulfill child welfare. *New York Times.* Retrieved August 2, 2002, from www.nytimes.com.

Pedersen, N. L. (1993). Genetic and environmental continuity and change in personality. In T. J. Bouchard, Jr. & P. Propping (Eds.), *Twins as a Tool of Behavioral Genetics* (pp. 147–162). West Sussex, England: Wiley.

Pedro-Carroll, J. (2001). The promotion of wellness in children and families: Challenges and opportunities. *American Psychologist, 56,* 993–1004.

Peisner-Feinberg, E. S., Burchinal, M. R., Clifford, R. M., Culkin, M. L., Howes, C., Kagan, S. L., et al. (2001). The relation of preschool child-care quality to children's cognitive and social developmental trajectories through second grade. *Child Development, 72,* 1534–1553.

Pelton, L. (1989). *For reasons of poverty: A critical analysis of the public child welfare system in the United States.* New York: Praeger.

Pennington, B. F., Moon, J., Edgin, J., Stedron, J., & Nadel, L. (2003). The neuropsychology of Down Syndrome: Evidence for hippocampal dysfunction. *Child Development, 74,* 75–93.

Perez, M., Voelz, Z. R., Pettit, J. W., & Joiner, T. E., Jr. (2002). The role of acculturative stress and body dissatisfaction in predicting bulimic symptomology across ethnic groups. *International Journal of Eating Disorders, 31,* 442–454.

Perie, M., Grigg, W., & Dion, G. (2005). *The Nation's Report Card: Mathematics 2005* (NCES 2006-453). U.S. Department of Education, National Center for Education Statistics. Washington, DC: U.S. Government Printing Office.

Perie, M., Grigg, W., & Donahue, P. (2005). *The Nation's Report Card: Reading 2005* (NCES 2006-451). U.S. Department of Education, National Center for Education Statistics. Washington, DC: U.S. Government Printing Office. Retrieved June 11, 2006, from http://nces.ed.gov/nationsreportcard/pdf/main2005/2006451.pdf.

Perie, M., Grigg, W., & Donahue, P. (2005). *The Nation's Report Card: Reading 2005* (NCES 2006-451). U.S. Department of Education, National Center for Education Statistics. Washington, DC: U.S. Government Printing Office.

Perkins, D. F., Jacobs, J. E., Barber, B. L., & Eccles, J. S. (2004). Childhood and adolescent sports participation as predictors of participation in sports and physical fitness activities during young adulthood. *Youth and Society, 35,* 495–520.

Perlmann, R. Y., & Gleason, J. B. (1994). The neglected role of fathers in children's communicative development. *Seminars in Speech and Language, 14,* 314–324.

Perner, J. (1991). *Understanding the representational mind.* Cambridge, MA: MIT Press.

Peterson, C., & McCabe, A. (1983). *Developmental psycholinguistics: Three ways of looking at a child's narrative.* New York: Plenum.

Peterson, C., Parsons, T., & Dean, M. (2004). Providing misleading and reinstatement information a year after it happened: Effects on long-term memory. *Memory, 12,* 1–13.

Petrill, S. A., Lipton, P. A., Hewitt, J. K., Plomin, R., Cherny, S. S., Corley, R., et al. (2004). Genetic and environmental contributions to general cognitive ability through the first 16 years of life. *Developmental Psychology, 40,* 805–812.

Phelps, N. (2006). Teen says he had to stop school plot. Retrieved October 14, 2006 from http://www.thenorthwestern.com/apps/pbcs.dll/article?AID=/20060921/OSH/309210013/1128/OSHnews Principal killed at Wisconsin school; 9th-grader charged. (2006, September 30). *CNN.com.* Retrieved October 14, 2006, from CNN.com.

Phinney, J. S. (1990). Ethnic identity in adolescents and adults: Review of research. *Psychological Bulletin, 108,* 499–514.

Phinney, J. S. (2003). Ethnic identity and acculturation. In K. M. Chun, P. B. Organista, & G. Marín (Eds.), *Acculturation: Advances in Theory, Measurement, and Applied Research* (pp. 63–81). Washington, DC: American Psychological Association.

Phinney, J. S., Cantu, C. L., & Kurtz, D. A. (1997). Ethnic and American identity as predictors of self-esteem among African American, Latino, and White adolescents. *Journal of Youth and Adolescence, 26,* 165–185.

Phinney, J. S., Ong, A., & Madden, T. (2000). Cultural values and intergenerational value discrepancies in immigrant and non-immigrant families. *Child Development, 71,* 528–539.

Piaget, J. (1929). *The child's conception of the world.* New York: Harcourt, Brace & World.

Piaget, J. (1930). *The child's conception of physical causality.* New York: Harcourt, Brace & World. (Original work published in 1926).

Piaget, J. (1951). *Play, dreams, and imitation in childhood.* New York: Norton.

Piaget, J. (1952a). *The child's conception of number* (C. Gattegno & F. M. Hodgson, Trans.). London: Routledge & Paul.

Piaget, J. (1952b). *The origins of intelligence in children* (M. Cook, Trans.). New York: International Universities Press.

Piaget, J. (1954). *The construction of reality in the child* (M. Cook, Trans.). New York: Basic Books.

Piaget, J. (1954). *The origins of intelligence.* New York: Basic Books.

Piaget, J. (1969). *The child's conception of time.* London: Routledge & Kegan Paul.

Piaget, J. (1970). *The child's conception of movement and speed.* London: Routledge & Kegan Paul.

Piaget, J. (1971). *Biology and knowledge* (B. Walsh, Trans.). Chicago: University of Chicago Press.

Piaget, J. (1985). *The equilibration of cognitive structures.* Chicago: University of Chicago Press.

Piaget, J., & Inhelder, B. (1948/1956). *The child's conception of space.* London: Routledge & Kegan Paul. (Original work published in 1948).

Piaget, J., & Inhelder, B. (1974). *The child's construction of quantities: Conservation and atomism* (A. J. Pomerans, Trans.). London: Routledge & Kegan Paul.

Pinderhughes, E. E., Dodge, K. A., Bates, J. E., Pettit, G. S., & Zelli, A. (2000). Discipline responses: Influences of parents' socioeconomic status, ethnicity, beliefs about parenting, stress, and cognitive-emotional processes. *Journal of Family Psychology, 14,* 380–400.

Pinker, S. (1994). *The language instinct.* New York: William Morrow.

Pipe, M-E., Lamb, M. E., Orbach, Y., & Esplin, P. W. (2004). Recent research on children's testimony about experienced and witnessed events. *Developmental Review, 24,* 440–468.

Planned Parenthood (2006). *Pregnancy and childbearing among U.S. teens.* Retrieved May 26, 2005, from. http://www.plannedparenthood.org/.

Plomin, R. (1986). *Development, genetics, and psychology.* Hillsdale, NJ: Erlbaum.

Plomin, R. (1990). *Nature and nurture: An introduction to human behavioral genetics.* Pacific Grove, CA: Brooks/Cole Publishing Co.

Plomin, R. (1994). *Genetics and experience: the interplay between nature and nurture.* Thousand Oaks, CA: Sage.

Plomin, R., & DeFries, J. C. (1998). The genetics of cognitive abilities and disabilities. *Scientific American, 278,* 62–69.

Plomin, R., & McGuffin, P. (2003). Psychopathology in the postgenomic era. *Annual Review of Psychology, 54,* 205–228.

Plomin, R., & Spinath, F. M. (2004). Intelligence: Genetics, genes, and genomics. *Journal of Personality and Social Psychology, 86,* 112–129.

Plomin, R., Corley, R., DeFries, J. C., & Fulker, D. W. (1990). Individual differences in television viewing in early childhood: Nature as well as nurture. *Psychological Science, 1,* 371–377.

Plomin, R., DeFries, J. C., Craig, I. W., & McGuffin, P. (2003). *Behavioral genetics in the postgenomic era.* Washington, DC: APA.

Plomin, R., Emde, R. N., Braungart, J. M., Campos, J., Corley, R., et al. (1993). Genetic change and continuity from 14 to 20 months: The MacArthur longitudinal twin study. *Child Development, 64,* 1354–1376.

Plomin, R., Owen, M. J., & McGuffin, P. (1994). The genetic basis of complex human behaviors. *Science, 264,* 1733–1739.

Pogarsky, G., Thornberry, T. P., & Lizotte, A. J. (2006). Developmental outcomes for children of young mothers. *Journal of Marriage and Family, 68,* 332–344.

Poland, G., Jacobson, R. M., Koutsky, L. A., Tamms, G. M., Railkar, R., Smith, J. F., et al. (2005). Immunogenicity and reactogenicity of a novel vaccine for human papillomavirus 16: A 2-year randomized controlled clinical trial. *Mayo Clinic Proceedings, 80*(5), 601–610.

Pollak, S. D., Vardi, S., Putzer Bechner, A. M., & Curtin, J. J. (2005). Physically abused children's regulation of attention in response to hostility. *Child Development, 76,* 968–977.

Pollatou, E., Karadimou, K., & Gerodimos, V. (2005). Gender differences in musical aptitude, rhythmic ability and motor performance in preschool children. *Early Child Development and Care, 175*(4), 361–369.

Pontius, A. A. (1973). Neuro-ethics of "walking" in the newborn. *Perceptual and Motor Skills, 37,* 235–245.

Posada, G., Carbonell, O. A., Alzate, G., & Plata, S. J. (2004). Through Columbian lenses: Ethnographic and conventional analyses of maternal care and their associations with secure base behavior. *Developmental Psychology, 40,* 508–518.

Posada, G., Jacobs, A., Richmond, M. K., Carbonell, O. A., Alzate, G., Bustamante, M. R., & Quiceno, J. (2002). Maternal caregiving and infant security in two cultures. *Developmental Psychology, 38,* 67–78.

Powlishta, K. K., Serbin, L. A., & Moller, L. C. (1993). The stability of individual differences in gender typing: Implications for understanding gender segregation. *Sex Roles, 29,* 723–737.

Pressley, M. (1995). *Advanced educational psychology for educators, researchers, and policymakers.* New York: HarperCollins.

Pressley, M., & Afflerbach, P. (1995). *Verbal protocols of reading: The nature of constructively responsive reading.* Hillsdale, NJ: Erlbaum.

Pressley, M., & Hilden, K. (2006). Cognitive strategies. In D. Kuhn & R. S. Siegler (Eds.), *Cognitive, Language, and Perceptual Development* (Vol. 2, pp. 511–556), in W. Damon (Gen. Ed.), *Handbook of Child Psychology.* New York: Wiley.

Principal killed at Wisconsin school; 9th-grader charged. (2006, September 30). *CNN.com.* Retrieved October 14, 2006, from CNN.com.

Putallaz, M. (1983). Predicting children's sociometric status from their behavior. *Child Development, 54,* 1417–1426.

Quercia, N. (2005). Fragile X syndrome. *The Gale Encyclopedia of Genetic Disorders* (2nd ed., Vol. 1, pp. 472–475). Detroit, MI: Thomson Gale.

Rabain-Jamin, J., & Wornham, W. L. (1993). Practices and representations of child care and motor development among West Africans in Paris. *Early Development and Parenting, 2,* 107–119.

Radelet, M. A., Lephart, S. M., Rubinstein, E. N., & Myers, J. B. (2002). Survey of the injury rate for children in community sports. *Pediatrics, 110*(3), e28. Retrieved June 22, 2006, from http://www.pediatrics.org/cgi/content/full/110/3/e28.

Raffaelli, M., & Crockett, L. J. (2003). Sexual risk taking in adolescence: The role of self-regulation and attraction to risk. *Developmental Psychology, 39,* 1036–1046.

Raffaelli, M., Crockett, L. J., & Shen, Y. (2005). Developmental stability and change in self-regulation from childhood to adolescence. *The Journal of Genetic Psychology, 166,* 54–75.

Ramey, C. T., & Ramey, S. L. (1992). Effective early intervention. *Mental Retardation, 6,* 337–345.

Ramey, C. T., Campbell, F. A., & Blair, C. (1998). Enhancing the life course for high-risk children: Results from the Abecedarian Project. In J. Crane (Ed.), *Social Programs That Work* (pp. 163–183). New York: Russell Sage Foundation.

Rauscher, F. H., Shaw, G. L., & Ky, K. N. (1993). Music and spatial task performance. *Nature, 365,* 611.

Rauscher, F. H., Shaw, G. L., & Ky, K. N. (1995). Listening to Mozart enhances spatial-temporal reasoning: Towards a neurophysiological basis. *Neuroscience Letters, 185,* 44–47.

Rauscher, F. H., Shaw, G. L., Levine, L. J., Wright, E. L., Dennis, W. R., & Newcomb, R. L. (1997). Music training causes long-term enhancement of preschool children's spatial-temporal reasoning. *Neurological Research, 19,* 2–8.

Redding, R. E. (2002). The impossibility of parental licensure. *American Psychologist, 57,* 987–988.

Reed, J. (1982). Black Americans in the 1980s. *Population Bulletin, 37,* 1–37.

Reifman, A., Villa, L. C., Amans, J. A., Rethinam, V., & Telesca, T. Y. (2001). Children of divorce in the 1990s: A meta-analysis. *Journal of Divorce and Remarriage, 36,* 27–36.

Reitsma, P. (1983). Printed word learning in beginning readers. *Journal of Experimental Child Psychology, 36,* 321–339.

Reitsma, P. (1989). Orthographic memory and learning to read. In P. G. Aaron & R. M. Joshi (Eds.), *Reading and Writing Disorders in Different Orthographic Systems* (pp. 51–73). The Hague, The Netherlands: Kluwer Academic.

Rempel, L. A., & Rempel, J. K. (2004). Partner influence on health behavior decision-making: Increasing breastfeeding duration. *Journal of Social and Personal Relationships, 21,* 92–111.

Renaissance Group (1999). Legal requirements: Children that learn together, learn to live together. Retrieved February 13, 2006, from http://www.uni.edu/coe/inclusion/legal/index.html.

Renniger, A., Hidi, S., & Krapp, A. (Eds.). (1992). *The Role of Interest in Learning and Development.* Hillsdale, NJ: Erlbaum.

Renshaw, P. E., & Brown, P. J. (1993). Loneliness in middle childhood: Concurrent and longitudinal predictors. *Child Development, 64,* 1271–1284.

Resnick, L. B., Levine, J. M., & Teasley, S. D. (Eds.). (1991). *Perspectives on Socially Shared Cognition.* Washington, DC: American Psychological Association.

Reyna, V. F., & Brainerd, C. J. (1995). Fuzzy-trace theory: An interim synthesis. *Learning and Individual Differences, 7,* 1–75.

Reynolds, A. J. (2000). *Success in early intervention: The Chicago child–parent centers.* Lincoln: University of Nebraska Press.

Reynolds, A. J., & Robertson, D. L. (2003). School-based early intervention and later child maltreatment in the Chicago longitudinal study. *Child Development, 74,* 3–26.

Reynolds, A. J., Ou, S., & Topitzes, J. W. (2004). Paths of effects of early childhood intervention on educational attainment and delinquency: A confirmatory analysis of the Chicago child-parent centers. *Child Development, 75,* 1299–1328.

Reynolds, A. J., Temple, J. A., Robertson, D. L., & Mann, E. A. (2001). Long-term effects of an early childhood intervention on educational achievement and juvenile arrest: A 15-year follow-up of low-income children in public schools. *JAMA: Journal of the American Medical Association, 285,* 2339–2346.

Richard, J. F., Normandeau, J., Brun, V., & Maillet, M. (2004). Attracting and maintaining infant attention during habituation: Further evidence of the importance of stimulus complexity. *Infant and Child Development, 13*(4), 277–286.

Richardson, M. F., Meredith, W., & Abbot, D. A. (1993). Sex-typed role in male adolescent sexual abuse survivors. *Journal of Family Violence, 8,* 89–100.

Rickert, V. I., Wiemann, C. M., Vaughan, R. D., & White, J. W. (2004). Rates and risk factors for sexual violence among an ethnically diverse sample of adolescents. *Archives of Pediatrics and Adolescent Medicine, 158,* 1132–1139.

Rickert, V. J., & Weimann, C. M. (1998). Date rape among adolescents and young adults. *Journal of Pediatric Adolescent Gynecology, 11,* 167–175.

Roberts, D. F., & Foehr, U. G. (2004). *Kids and media in America.* New York: Cambridge University Press.

Roberts, D. F., Foehr, U. G., Rideout, V. J., & Brodie, M. (1999). *Kids and media at the new millennium.* Menlo Park, CA: Kaiser Family Foundation.

Roberts, D. F., Henriksen, L., & Foehr, U. G. (2004). Adolescents and media. In R. M. Lerner & L. Steinberg (Eds.), *Handbook of Adolescent Psychology* (2nd ed., pp. 487–521). Hoboken, NJ: John Wiley & Sons, Inc.

Robinson, E. J., & Whitcombe, E. L. (2003). Children's suggestibility in relation to their understanding about sources of knowledge. *Child Development, 74,* 48–62.

Robinson, J. L., Reznick, J. S., Kagan, J., & Corley, R. (1992). The heritability of inhibited and uninhibited behavior: A twin study. *Developmental Psychology, 28,* 1030–1037.

Robinson, L. L., Buckley, J. D., Daigle, A. E., Wells, R., Benjamin, D., & Hammond, G. D. (1989). Maternal drug use and risk of childhood nonlymphoblastic leukemia among offspring: An epidemiologic investigation implicating marijuana (a report from the Children's Cancer Study Group). *Cancer, 63,* 1904–1911.

Roche, J. P., & Ramsbey, T. W. (1993). Premarital sexuality: A five-year follow-up study of attitudes and behavior by dating stage. *Adolescence, 28,* 67–80.

Rodd, J. M., Gaskell, M. G., & Marslen-Wilson, W. D. (2004). Modeling the effects of semantic ambiguity in word recognition. *Cognitive Science, 28,* 89–104.

Roebers, C. M. (2002). Confidence judgments in children's and adults' event recall and suggestibility. *Developmental Psychology, 38,* 1052–1067.

Roeser, R. W., & Eccles, J. S. (1998). Adolescents' perceptions of middle school: Relation to longitudinal changes in academic and psychological adjustment. *Journal of Research on Adolescence, 88,* 123–158.

Roeser, R. W., Midgley, C. M., & Urdan, T. C. (1996). Perceptions of the school psychological environment and early adolescents' psychological and behavioral functioning in school: The mediating role of goals and belonging. *Journal of Educational Psychology, 88,* 408–422.

Rogoff, B. (2003). *The cultural nature of human development.* London: Oxford University Press.

Rogoff, B., & Mistry, J. (1990). The social and functional context of children's remembering. In R. Fivush & J. A. Hudson (Eds.), *Knowing and Remembering in Young Children* (pp. 197–222). Cambridge, England: Cambridge University Press.

Rogoff, B., Mistry, J., Göncü, A., & Mosier, C. (1993). Guided participation in cultural activity by toddlers and caregivers. *Monographs of the Society for Research in Child Development, 58*(8, Serial No. 236).

Roid, G. (2003). *Stanford-Binet Intelligence Scales* (5th ed.). Itasca, IL: Riverside.

Roisman, G. I., Collins, W. A., & Sroufe, L. A. (2005). Predictors of young adults' representations of and behavior in their current romantic relationship: Prospective tests of the prototype hypothesis. *Attachment and Human Development, 7*(2), 105–121.

Romaine, S. (1984). *The language of children and adolescents—the acquisition of communicative competence.* New York: Blackwell.

Romaine, S. (1995). *Bilingualism* (2nd ed.). Oxford, England: Blackwell.

Rose, J. S., Medway, F. J., Cantrell, V. L., & Marus, S. H. (1983). A fresh look at the retention–promotion controversy. *Journal of School Psychology, 21,* 201–211.

Rose, R. J. (1995). Genes and human behavior. In J. T. Spence, J. M. Darley, & D. J. Foss (Eds.), *Annual Review of Psychology* (Vol. 46, pp. 625–654). Palo Alto, CA: Annual Reviews Inc.

Rose, S. A., & Ruff, H. A. (1987). Cross-modal abilities in human infants. In J. D. Osofsky (Ed.), *Handbook of Infant Development* (2nd ed., pp. 318–362). New York: Wiley.

Rose, S. A., & Wallace, I. F. (1985). Cross-modal and intramodal transfer as predictors of mental development in fullterm and preterm infants. *Developmental Psychology, 21,* 949–962.

Rosenblith, J. R., & Sims–Knight, J. E. (1985). *In the beginning: Development in the first two years.* Belmont, CA: Brooks–Cole.

Rosenbloom, L., & Horton, M. E. (1975). Observing motor skill: A developmental approach. In K. S. Holt (Ed.), *Movement and Child Development, Clinics in Developmental Medicine* (Vol. 55, pp. 111–118). London: William Heinemann Medical Books.

Rosenthal, R., & Jacobson, L. (1968). *Pygmalion in the classroom: Teacher expectation and pupils' intellectual development.* New York: Holt, Rinehart & Winston.

Rosick, E. (2005). Cystic fibrosis. *The Gale Encyclopedia of Genetic Disorders* (2nd ed., Vol. 1, pp. 315–322). Detroit, MI: Thomson Gale.

Ross, H. S. (1982). Establishment of social games among toddlers. *Developmental Psychology, 18,* 509–518.

Rossell, C. H., & Baker, K. (1996). The educational effectiveness of bilingual education. *Research in the Teaching of English, 30,* 7–74.

Roth, R. (2000). *Making women pay: The hidden costs of fetal rights.* Ithaca, NY: Cornell University Press.

Rothbart, M. K. (1981). Measurement of temperament in infancy. *Child Development, 52,* 569–578.

Rothbart, M. K. (2001). *Mary Rothbart's temperament laboratory at the University of Oregon.* Accessed on November 17, 2004, at http://www.uoregon.edu/~maryroth/.

Rothbart, M. K., Ahadi, S. A., & Hershey, K. L. (1994). Temperament and social behavior in childhood. *Merrill-Palmer Quarterly, 40,* 21–39.

Rothbart, M. K., & Bates, J. E. (1998). *Temperament.* In W. Damon & N. Eisenberg (Eds.), *Handbook of Child Psychology (Vol. 3): Social, Emotional, and Personality Development* (pp. 105–176). New York: John Wiley & Sons, Inc.

Rothbaum, F., Weisz, J., Pott, M., Miyake, K., & Morelli, G. (2000). Attachment and culture: Security in the United States and Japan. *American Psychologist, 55,* 1093–1104.

Rovee-Collier, C. K., & Gerharstein, P. (1997). The development of infant memory. In N. Cowan & C. Hulme (Eds.), *The Development of Memory in Childhood* (pp. 5–40). Hove, East Sussex, England: Psychology Press.

Rubia, K., Noorloos, J., Smith, A., Gunning, B., & Sergeant, J. (2003). Motor timing deficits in community and clinical boys with hyperactive behavior: The effect of methylphenidate on motor timing. *Journal of Abnormal Child Psychology, 31,* 301–313.

Rubin, K. H., Bukowski, W., & Parker, J. G. (1998). Peer interactions, relationships, and groups. In W. Damon (Ed.), *Handbook of Child Psychology* (5th ed., Vol. 3, pp. 619–700). New York: Wiley.

Rubin, K. H., Bukowski, W., & Parker, J. G. (2006). Peer interactions, relationships, and groups. In W. Damon & R. Lerner (Series Eds.) and N. Eisenberg (Vol. Ed.), *Handbook of Child Psychology: Vol. 3. Social, Emotional, and Personality Developmenty* (6th ed., pp. 571–645). New York: Wiley.

Rubin, K. H., Burgess, K. B., Dwyer, K. M., & Hastings, P. D. (2003). Predicting preschoolers' externalizing behaviors from toddler temperament, conflict, and maternal negativity. *Developmental Psychology, 39,* 164–176.

Rubin, K. H., Chen, X., McDougall, P., Bowker, A., & McKinnon, J. (1995). The Waterloo Longitudinal Project: Predicting internalizing and externalizing problems in adolescence. *Development and Psychopathology, 7,* 751–764.

Rubin, K. H., Lynch, D., Coplan, R., Rose-Krasnor, L., & Booth, C. L. (1994). "Birds of a feather . . . ": Behavioral concordances and preferential personal attraction in children. *Child Development, 65,* 1778–1785.

Ruble, D. N., Martin, C. L., & Berenbaum, S. A. (2006). Gender development. In W. Damon & R. Lerner (Series Ed.) and N. Eisenberg (Vol. Ed.), *Handbook of Child Psychology: Vol. 3. Social, Emotional, and Personality Development* (6th ed., pp. 858–932). New York: Wiley.

Ruble, D. N., & Martin, C. L. (1998). Gender development. In W. Damon & N. Eisenberg (Eds.), *Handbook of Child Psychology (Vol. 3): Social, Emotional, and Personality Development* (pp. 933–1016). New York: John Wiley & Sons.

Ruff, H. A. (1984). Infants' manipulative exploration of objects: Basic cognitive processes and individual differences. In M. H. Bornstein & A. W. O'Reilly (Eds.), *The Role of Play in the Development of Thought* (pp. 5–15). San Francisco: Jossey-Bass.

Ruffman, T., Slade, L., & Crowe, E. (2002). The relation between children's and mothers' mental state language and theory-of-mind understanding. *Child Development, 73,* 734–751.

Rumelhart, D. E., & McClelland, J. L. (1986). On learning the past tenses of English verbs. In J. L. McClelland, D. E. Rumelhart, & PDP Research Group, *Parallel Distributed Processing: Explorations in the Microstructure of Cognition, Vol. 2: Psychological and Biological Models* (pp. 216–271). Cambridge, MA: The MIT Press.

Rutter, M. (1987). Psychosocial resilience and protective mechanisms. *American Journal of Orthopsychiatry, 57,* 316–331.

Rutter, M. (2002). Nature, nurture, and development: From evangelism through science toward policy and practice. *Child Development, 73,* 1–21.

Rutter, M., & Sroufe, L. A. (2000). Developmental psychopathology: Concepts and challenges. *Development and Psychopathology, 12,* 265–296.

Rutter, M., Graham, P., Chadwick, R., & Yule, W. (1976). Adolescent turmoil: Fact or fiction? *Journal of Child Psychology and Psychiatry, 17,* 35–56.

Ryan, R. M., Connell, J. P., & Grolnick, W.S. (1992). When achievement is not intrinsically motivated: A theory of self-regulation in school. In A. K. Boggiano & T. S. Pittman (Eds.), *Achievement and Motivation: A Social-developmental Perspective* (pp. 167–188). New York: Cambridge University Press.

Saarni, C., Campos, J. J., Camras, L. A., & Witherington, D. (2006). Emotional development: Action, communication, and understanding. In N. Eisenberg (Vol. Ed.) and W. Damon & R. M. Lerner (Eds.), *Handbook of Child Psychology* (6th ed., Vol. 3, pp. 226–299). New York: John Wiley & Sons.

Saarni, C., Mumme, D. L., & Campos, J. J. (1998). Emotional development: Action, communication, and understanding. In W. Damon (Ed.), *Handbook of Child Psychology* (Vol. 3, pp. 237–309). New York: John Wiley & Sons.

Sachs, J. (1987). Preschool boys' and girls' language use in pretend play. In S. U. Philips, S. Steele, & C. Tanz (Eds.), *Language, Gender, and Sex in Comparative Perspective* (pp. 178–188). New York: Cambridge University Press.

Sachs, J., & Devine, J. (1976). Young children's use of age-appropriate speech styles in social interaction and role-playing. *Journal of Child Language, 3,* 81–98.

Sachs, J., Bard, B., & Johnson, M. L. (1981). Language learning with restricted input: Case studies of two hearing children of deaf parents. *Applied Psycholinguistics, 2*(1), 33–54.

Sack, K. (1998, January 15). Georgia's governor seeks musical start for babies. *New York Times.* Retrieved September 17, 2000, from www.nytimes.com.

Sadker, M., & Sadker, D. (1994). *Failing at fairness: How America's schools cheat girls.* New York: Scribners.

Saffran, J. R., Werker, J. F., & Werner, L. A. (2006). The infant's auditory world: Hearing, speech, and the beginnings of language. In D. Kuhn & R. S. Siegler (Eds.), *Cognition, Perception, and Language* (Vol. 2, pp. 58–108), in W. Damon & R. M. Lerner (Gen. Eds.), *Handbook of Child Psychology* (6th ed). New York: Wiley.

Sagi, A., & Hoffman, M. L. (1976). Empathetic distress in the newborn. *Developmental Psychology, 12,* 175–176.

Sagi, A., & Lewkowicz, K. S. (1987). A cross-cultural evaluation of attachment research. In L. W. C. Tavecchio & M. H. van IJzendoorn (Eds.), *Attachment in Social Networks* (pp. 427–459). Amsterdam, Netherlands: Elsevier.

Sagi, A., Lamb, M. E., Lewkowicz, K. S., Shoham, R., Dvir, R., & Estes, D. (1985). Security of infant–mother–father, and *metapelet* attachments among kibbutz-reared Israeli children. In I. Bretherton & E. Waters (Eds.), Growing points of attachment theory and research. *Monographs of the Society for Research in Child Development, 50*(Serial No. 209), 257–275.

Sagi, A., van IJzendoorn, M. H., Aviezer, O., Donnell, F., & Mayseless, O. (1994). Sleeping out of home in a kibbutz communal arrangement: It makes a difference for infant–mother attachment. *Child Development, 65,* 992–1004.

Saito, L. T. (2003). *Ethnic identity and motivation: Socio-cultural factors in the educational achievement of Vietnamese American students.* Levittown, PA: LFB Scholarly.

Salzinger, S., Kaplan, S., Pelcovitz, D., Samit, C., & Krieger, R. (1984). Parent and teacher assessment of children's behavior in child maltreating families. *Journal of the American Academy of Child Psychiatry, 23,* 458–464.

Sandler, I. N., Tein, J., Mehta, P., Wolchik, S., & Ayers, T. (2000). Coping efficacy and psychological problems of children of divorce. *Child Development, 71,* 1099–1118.

Sangalang, B. B., Barth, R. P., & Painter, J. S. (2006). First-birth outcomes and timing of second births: A statewide case management program for adolescent mothers. *Health and Social Work, 31,* 54–63.

Santelli, J. S., Lingberg, L. D., Abma, J., McNeely, C. S., & Resnick, M. (2000a). Adolescent sexual behavior: Estimates and trends from four nationally representative surveys. *Family Planning Perspectives, 32,* 156–165; 194.

Santelli, J. S., Lowry, R., Brener, N. D., & Robin, L. (2000b). The association of sexual behaviors with socioeconomic status, family structure, and race/ethnicity among U.S. adolescents. *American Journal of Public Health, 90,* 1582–1588.

Santelli, J., Abma, J., Ventura, S., Lindberg, L., Morrow, B., Anderson, J. E., et al. (2004). Can changes in sexual behaviors among high school students explain the decline in teen pregnancy rates in the 1990s? *Journal of Adolescent Health, 35,* 80–90.

Santelli, J., Ott, M. A., Lyon, M., Rogers, J., & Summers, D. (2006). Abstinence-only education policies and programs: A position paper of the Society for Adolescent Medicine. *Journal of Adolescent Health, 38,* 83–87.

Santos, D. C. C., Gabbard, C., & Goncalves, V. M. G. (2001). Motor development during the first year: A comparative study. *Journal of Genetic Psychology, 162,* 143–154.

Sattler, J. (1992). *Assessment of children* (3rd ed.). San Diego, CA: Jerome M. Sattler.

Sattler, J. (2001). *Assessment of children* (4th ed.). San Diego, CA: Jerome M. Sattler.

Savage-Rumbaugh, S., Shanker, S. G., & Taylor, T. J. (1998). *Apes, language, and the human mind.* Oxford, England: Oxford University Press.

Saville-Troike, M. (1986). Anthropological considerations in the study of communication. In O. L. Taylor (Ed.), *Nature of Communication Disorders in Culturally and Linguistically Diverse Populations* (pp. 47–72). San Diego, CA: College-Hill Press.

Savin-Williams, R. (1994). Verbal and physical abuse as stressors in the lives of lesbian, gay male, and bisexual youths: Associations with school problems, running away, substance abuse, prostitution, and suicide. *Journal of Consulting and Clinical Psychology, 62,* 261–269.

Savin-Williams, R. C. (1995). An exploratory study of pubertal maturation timing and self-esteem among gay and bisexual male youths. *Developmental Psychology, 31,* 56–64.

Savin-Williams, R. C., & Berndt, T. J. (1990). Friendship and peer relations. In S. S. Feldman & G. R. Elliott (Eds.), *At the Threshold: The Developing Adolescent* (pp. 277–307). Cambridge, MA: Harvard University Press.

Savin-Williams, R. C., & Diamond, L. M. (2004). Sex. In R. M. Lerner & L. Steinberg (Eds.), *Handbook of Adolescent Psychology* (2nd ed., pp. 189–231). Hoboken, NJ: Wiley.

Saxe, G. B. (1988). The mathematics of child street vendors. *Child Development, 59,* 1415–1425.

Saxton, M. (1997). The contrast theory of negative input. *Journal of Child Language, 24,* 139–161.

Saxton, M. (2000). Negative evidence and negative feedback: Immediate effects on the grammaticality of child speech. *First Language, 20* (60, Pt. 3), 221–252.

Scarr, S. (1985). Constructing psychology: Making facts and fables for our times. *American Psychologist, 40,* 499–512.

Scarr, S. (1992). Developmental theories for the 1990s: Development and individual differences. *Child Development, 63,* 1–19.

Scarr, S. (1993). Biological and cultural diversity: The legacy of Darwin for development. *Child Development, 64,* 1333–1353.

Scarr, S. (1998). American child care today. *American Psychologist, 53,* 95–108.

Scarr, S. (2000). Toward voluntary parenthood. *Journal of Personality, 68,* 615–623.

Scarr, S., & McCartney, K. (1983). How people make their own environments: A theory of genotype-environment effects. *Child Development, 54,* 424–435.

Scarr, S., Weinberg, R. A., & Waldman, I. D. (1993). IQ correlations in transracial adoptive families. *Intelligence, 17,* 541–555.

Schall, B., Marlier, L., & Soussignan, R. (1998). Olfactory function in the human fetus: Evidence from selective neonatal responsiveness to the odor of amniotic fluid. *Behavioral Neuroscience, 112,* 1438–1449.

Schiefelbein, V. L., Susman, E. J., & Dorn, L. D. (2005). Self-competence mediates earlier and later anxiety in adolescent mothers: A 3-year longitudinal perspective. *Journal of Research on Adolescence, 15,* 625–655.

Schmidt-Hieber, C., Jonas, P., & Bischofberger, J. (2004). Enhanced synaptic plasticity in newly generated granule cells of the adult hippocampus. *Nature, 429 (May),* 184–187.

Schneider, B. L., & Stevenson, D. (1999). *The ambitious generation: America's teenagers, motivated but directionless.* New Haven: Yale University Press.

Schneider, J. F. (2002). Relations among self-talk, self-consciousness, and self-knowledge. *Psychological Reports, 91,* 807–812.

Schneider, W. (1993). Acquiring expertise: Determinants of exceptional performance. In K. A. Keller, F. J. Monks, & A. H. Passow (Eds.), *International Handbook of Research on and Development of Giftedness and Talent* (pp. 311–324). Oxford, UK: Pergamon Press.

Schneider, W., & Bjorklund, D. F. (1998). Memory. In W. Damon, D. Kuhn, & R. S. Siegler (Eds.), *Handbook of Child Psychology* (5th ed.), *Vol. 2: Cognition, Perception, and Language* (pp. 467–521). New York: John Wiley & Sons.

Schneider, W., Gruber, H., Gold, A., & Opwis, K. (1993). Chess expertise and memory for chess positions in children and adults. *Journal of Experimental Child Psychology, 56,* 328–349.

Schultz, K. (2001). Constructing failure, narrating success: Rethinking the "problem" of teen pregnancy. *Teachers College Record, 103*(4), 582–607.

Schum, T. R., Kolb, T. M., McAuliffe, T. L., Simms, M. D., Underhill, R. L., & Lewis, M. (2002). Sequential acquisition of toilet-training skills: A descriptive study of gender and age differences in normal children. *Pediatrics, 109*(3). Retrieved September 20, 2004, from http://www.pediatrics.org/cgi/content/full/109/3/e48.

Schunk, D. H., & Zimmerman, B. J. (1997). Social origins of self-regulatory competence. *Educational Psychologist, 32,* 195–208.

Schutzman, D. L., Frankenfield-Chernicoff, M., Clatterbaugh, H. E., & Singer, J. (1991). Incidence of intrauterine cocaine exposure in a suburban setting. *Pediatrics, 88,* 825–827.

Schwartz, G. M., Izard, C. E., & Ansul, S. E. (1985). The 5-month-old's ability to discriminate facial expressions of emotion. *Infant Behavior and Development, 8,* 65–77.

Schweinhart, L. J., & Weikart, D. P. (1998). High/Scope Perry Preschool program effects at age twenty-seven. In J. Crane (Ed.), *Social Programs that Work* (pp. 148–162). New York: Russell Sage Foundation.

Schweinhart, L. J., Barnes, H. V., & Weikart, D. P. (1993). *Significant benefits: The High/Scope Perry Preschool study through age 27* (Monographs of the High/Scope Educational Research Foundation, Number Ten). Ypsilanti, MI: The High/Scope Press.

Schweinle, A., & Wilcox, T. (2004). Intermodal perception and physical reasoning in young infants. *Infant Behavior and Development, 27*(2), 246–265.

Seidman, E., & French, S. E. (1997). Normative school transitions among urban adolescents: When, where, and how to intervene. In H. J. Walberg, O. Reyes, & R. P. Weissberg (Eds.), *Children and Youth: Interdisciplinary Perspectives* (pp. 166–189). Thousand Oaks, CA: Sage.

Selman, R. L. (1976). Social-cognitive understanding: A guide to educational and clinical practices. In T. Likona (Ed.), *Moral Development and Behavior: Theory, Research, and Social Issues* (pp. 299–316). New York: Holt, Rinehart, and Winston.

Selman, R. L. (1980). *The growth of interpersonal understanding.* New York: Academic Press.

Serbin, L. A., Cooperman, J. M., Peters, P. L., Lehoux, P. M., Stack, D. M., & Schwartzman, A. E. (1998). Intergenerational transfer of psychosocial risk in women with childhood histories of aggression, withdrawal, or aggression and withdrawal. *Developmental Psychology, 34,* 1246–1262.

Serbin, L. A., Moller, L. C., Gulko, J., Powlishta, K. K., & Colburne, K. A. (1994). The emergence of gender segregation in toddler playgroups. In W. Damon (Ed.), *New Directions for Child Development* (No. 65, pp. 7–17). San Francisco: Jossey-Bass.

Sexton, J., & Swarns, R. L. (1997, November 15). Pictures of Sabrina: A special report. A slide into peril, with no one to catch her. *New York Times.* Retrieved August 2, 2002, from www.nytimes.com.

Shamir-Essakow, G., Ungerer, J. A., Rapee, R. M., & Safier, R. (2004). Caregiving representations of mothers of behaviorally inhibited and uninhibited preschool children. *Developmental Psychology, 40,* 899–910.

Sharabany, R., Gershoni, R., & Hofman, J. E. (1981). Girlfriend, boyfriend: Age and sex differences in intimate friendship. *Developmental Psychology, 17,* 800–808.

Sharma, A. R., McGue, M. K., & Benson, P. L. (1996). The emotional and behavioral adjustment of United States adopted adolescents: I. A comparison study. *Children and Youth Services Review, 18,* 77–94.

Sharma, A. R., McGue, M. K., & Benson, P. L. (1998). The psychological adjustment of United States adopted adolescents and their nonadopted siblings. *Child Development, 69,* 791–802.

Shaywitz, S. E., Escobar, M. D., Shaywitz, B. A., Fletcher, J. M., & Makuch, R. (1992). Evidence that dyslexia may represent the lower tail of a normal distribution of reading ability. *The New England Journal of Medicine, 326*(3), 145–150.

Sheldon, A. (1990). Pickle fights: Genderlect talk in preschool disputes. *Discourse Processes, 13,* 5–31.

Shen, C. (2001). Social values associated with cross-national differences in mathematics and science achievement: A cross-national analysis. *Assessment in Education, 8,* 193–223.

Sherman, K., Lapidus, G., Gelven, E., & Banco, L. (2004). New teen drivers and their parents: What they know and what they expect. *American Journal of Health Behavior, 28,* 387–396.

Shonkoff, J. P., & Phillips, D. A. (2000). *From neurons to neighborhoods: The science of early childhood development.* Washington, DC: National Academy Press.

Shurkin, J. N. (1992). *Terman's kids: The groundbreaking study of how the gifted grow up.* Boston: Little, Brown and Company.

Shweder, R. A., Much, N. C., Mahapatra, M., & Park, L. (1997). The "Big Three" of morality (Autonomy, Community, and Divinity) and the "Big Three" explanations of suffering. In A. Brandt & P. Rozin (Eds.), *Morality and Health* (pp. 119–169). Stanford, CA: Stanford University Press.

Sickle cell anemia. Retrieved October 13, 2002, from http://www.mayoclinic.com.

Siega-Riz, A. M., Cavadini, C., & Popkin, B. M. (2001). U.S. teens and the nutrient contribution and differences of their selected meal patterns. *Family Economics and Nutrition Review, 13,* 15–26.

Siegel, D. (2006). The effects of physical activity on the health and well-being of youths. *JOPERD: The Journal of Physical Education, Recreation and Dance, 77,* 11–11.

Siegler, R. S. (1995). Children's thinking: How does change occur. In W. Schneider & F. E. Weinert (Eds.), *Memory Performance and Competencies: Issues in Growth and Development* (pp. 405–430). Hillsdale, NJ: Erlbaum.

Siegler, R. S. (1996). *Emerging minds: The process of change in children's thinking.* New York: Oxford University Press.

Siegler, R. S. (1998). *Children's thinking* (3rd ed.). Upper Saddle River, NJ: Prentice Hall.

Siegler, R. S. (2006). Microgenetic analyses of learning. In D. Kuhn & R. S. Siegler (Eds.), *Cognitive, Language, and Perceptual Development,* (Vol. 2, pp. 464–510), in W. Damon (Gen. Ed.), *Handbook of Child Psychology.* New York: Wiley.

Siegler, R. S., & Jenkins, E. (1989). *How children discover strategies.* Hillsdale, NJ: Erlbaum.

Siegler, R. S., & Shipley, C. (1995). Variation, selection, and cognitive change. In T. Simon & G. Halford (Eds.), *Developing Cognitive Competence: New Approaches to Process Modeling* (pp. 31–76). Hillsdale, NJ: Erlbaum.

Signorella, M. L., Bigler, R. S., & Liben, L. S. (1993). Developmental differences in children's gender schemata about others: A meta-analytic review. *Developmental Review, 13,* 147–183.

Signorielli, N. (2001). Television's gender role images and contribution to stereotyping: Past, present, and future. In D. G. Singer & J. L. Singer (Eds.), *Handbook of Children and the Media* (pp. 341–358). Thousand Oaks, CA: Sage.

Silverman, A. R., & Feigelman, W. (1990). Adjustment in interracial adoptees: An overview. In D. M. Brodzinsky & M. D. Schechter (Eds.), *The Psychology of Adoption* (pp. 187–200). New York: Oxford University Press.

Simmons, R. G., & Blyth, D. A. (1987). *Moving into adolescence: The impact of pubertal change and school context.* New York: Aldine De Gruyter.

Simner, M. L. (1971). Newborn's response to the cry of another infant. *Developmental Psychology, 5,* 136–150.

Simon, T., & Klahr, D. (1995). A theory of children's learning about number conservation. In T. Simon & G. Halford (Eds.), *Developing Cognitive Competence: New Approaches to Process Modeling* (pp. 315–354). Hillsdale, NJ: Erlbaum.

Simons, R. L., Johnson, C., & Conger, R. D. (1994). Harsh corporal punishment versus quality of parental involvement as an explanation of adolescent maladjustment. *Journal of Marriage and the Family, 56,* 591–607.

Simons-Morton, B. G., Hartos, J. L., Leaf, W. A., & Preusser, D. F. (2005). Persistence of effects of the checkpoints program on parental restrictions of teen driving privileges. *American Journal of Public Health, 95,* 447–452.

Singer, L. T., Arendt, R., Minnes, S., Farkas, K., Salvator, A., Kirchner, H. L., et al. (2002). Cognitive and motor outcomes of cocaine-exposed infants. *Journal of the American Medical Association, 287,* 1952–1959.

Singh, S., & Darroch, J. E. (2000). Adolescent pregnancy and childbearing: Levels and trends in developed countries. *Family Planning Perspectives, 32,* 14–23.

Skiba, R. J., & Knesting, K. (2001). Zero tolerance, zero evidence: An analysis of school disciplinary practice. In R. J. Skiba & G. G. Noam (Eds.), *Zero Tolerance: Can Suspension and Expulsion Keep Schools Safe?* (pp. 17–43). San Francisco: Jossey-Bass.

Skiba, R. J., Knesting, K., & Bush, L. D. (2002). Culturally competent assessment: More than unbiased tests. *Journal of Child and Family Studies, 11,* 61–78.

Skinner, B. F. (1957). *Verbal behavior.* Englewood Cliffs, NJ: Prentice-Hall.

Slaby, R. G., & Frey, K. S. (1975). Development of gender constancy and selective attention to same-sex models. *Child Development, 46,* 849–856.

Slater, A. (1997). Can measures of infant habituation predict later intellectual ability? *Archives of Disease in Childhood, 77,* 474–476. Retrieved June 12, 2006, from http://adc.bmjjournals .com/cgi/content/full/77/6/474.

Slavin, R. E. (1990). Achievement effects of ability grouping in secondary schools: A best-evidence synthesis. *Review of Education Research, 60,* 471–499.

Slavin, R. E. (1995). *Cooperative learning* (2nd ed.). Boston: Allyn and Bacon.

Slobin, D. I. (1979). *Psycholinguistics.* Glenview, IL: Scott, Foresman.

Slobin, D. I. (1982). Universal and particular in the acquisiton of language. In E. Wanner & L. Gleitman (Eds.), *Language Acquisition: The State of the Art* (pp. 128–170). Cambridge, England: Cambridge University Press.

Slobin, D. I. (1985a). *The crosslinguistic study of language acquisition: Vol. 1. The data.* Hillsdale, NJ: Lawrence Erlbaum Associates.

Slobin, D. I. (1985b). Crosslinguistic evidence for the language-making capacity. In D. I. Slobin (Ed.), *The Crosslinguistic Study of Language Acquisition: Vol. 2. Theoretical Issues.* (pp. 1157–1249). Hillsdale, NJ: Lawrence Erlbaum Associates.

Smith, A. C., & Smith, D. I. (2001). Emergency and transitional shelter population: 2000. U.S. Census Bureau, Census Special Reports, Series CENSR/01-2. Washington, DC: U.S. Government Printing Office.

Smith, J. C. (2001). Rett syndrome in boys. Accessed March 1, 2002, from http://www.rettsyndrome.org.

Smith, K. (2000). *Who's Minding the Kids? Child Care Arrangements: Fall 1995.* Current Population Reports, P70-70. Washington, DC: U.S. Census Bureau.

Smith, P. K., & Noble, R. (1987). Factors affecting the development of caregiver–infant relationships. In L. W. C. Tavecchio & M. H. van IJzendoorn (Eds.), *Attachment in Social Networks* (pp. 93–134). Amsterdam, Netherlands: Elsevier.

SmithBathe, L. (2005). Examining assumptions about teen mothers. *American Journal of Nursing, 105,* 13.

Smollar, J., & Youniss, J. (1982). Social development through friendship. In K. H. Rubin & H. S. Ross (Eds.), *Peer RelationShips and Social Skills in Childhood* (pp. 279–298). New York: Springer.

Snarey, J. R. (1995). In a communitarian voice: The sociobiological expansion of Kohlbergian theory, research, and practice. In W. M. Kurtines & J. L. Gewirtz (Eds.), *Moral Development: An Introduction* (pp. 109–134). Boston: Allyn and Bacon.

Snarey, J. R., Reimer, J., & Kohlberg, L. (1985). The development of social-moral reasoning among kibbutz adolescents: A longitudinal cross-cultural study. *Developmental Psychology, 20,* 3–17.

Snow, C. (1972). Mother's speech to children learning language. *Child Development, 43,* 549–565.

Snow, C. E. (1987). Relevance of the notion of a critical period to language acquisition. In M. Bornstein (Ed.), *Sensitive Periods in Development: An Interdisciplinary Perspective* (pp. 183–209). Hillsdale, NJ: Erlbaum.

Snow, C. E., & Kang, J. Y. (2006). Becoming bilingual, biliterate, and bicultural. In K. A. Renninger & I. E. Sigel (Vol. Eds.) and W. Damon & R. M. Lerner (Eds.-in-chief), *Handbook of Child Psychology* (6th ed., Vol. 1, pp. 75–102). Hoboken, NJ: Wiley.

Snow, R. E. (1995). Pygmalion and intelligence. *Current Directions in Psychological Science, 4,* 169–171.

Snyder, J., Cramer, A., Afrank, J., & Patterson, G. R. (2005). The contributions of ineffective discipline and parental hostile attributions of child misbehavior to the development of conduct problems at home and school. *Developmental Psychology, 41,* 30–41.

Society for Research in Child Development. www.srcd.org/about.

Sokol, R. J., Delaney-Black, V., Nordstrom, B. (2003). Fetal alcohol spectrum disorder. *Journal of the American Medical Association, 290,* 2996–2999.

Sorce, J. F., Emde, R. N., Campos, J., & Klinnert, M. D. (1985). Maternal emotional signaling: Its effect on the visual cliff behavior of 1-year-olds. *Developmental Psychology, 21,* 195–200.

Spear, L. P. (2000). The adolescent brain and age-related behavioral manifestations. *Neuroscience and Biobehavioral Reviews, 24,* 417–463.

Spearman, C. (1904). General intelligence, objectively determined and measured. *American Journal of Psychology, 15,* 201–293.

Spearman, C. (1923). *The nature of "intelligence" and the principles of cognition.* London: Macmillan.

Spearman, C. (1927). *The abilities of man.* New York: Macmillan.

Spelke, E. S. (1979). Perceiving bimodally specified events in infancy. *Developmental Psychology, 15,* 626–636.

Spelke, E. S. (1991). Physical knowledge in infancy: Reflections on Piaget's theory. In S. Carey & R. Gelman (Eds.), *The Epigenesis of Mind* (pp. 133–169). Hillsdale, NJ: Erlbaum.

Spencer, M. B., & Dornbusch, S. M. (1990). Challenges in studying minority youth. In S. S. Feldman & G. R. Elliott (Eds.), *At the Threshold: The Developing Adolescent* (pp. 123–146). Cambridge, MA: Harvard University Press.

Spinrad, T. L., Eisenberg, N., Harris, E., Hanish, L., Fabes, R. A., Kupanoff, K., et al. (2004). The relation of children's everyday nonsocial peer play behavior to their emotionality, regulation, and social functioning. *Developmental Psychology, 40,* 67–80.

Spira, E. G., Bracken, S. S., & Fischel, J. E. (2005). Predicting improvement after first-grade reading difficulties: The effects of oral language, emergent literacy, and behavior skills. *Developmental Psychology, 41,* 225–234.

Spivey, N. N., & King, J. R. (1989). Readers as writers composing from sources. *Reading Research Quarterly, 24,* 7–26.

Sroufe, L. A. (1990). An organizational perspective on the self. In D. Cicchetti & M. Beeghly (Eds.), *The Self in Transition: Infancy to Childhood* (pp. 281–307). Chicago: University of Chicago Press.

Sroufe, L. A. (1996). *Emotional development.* Cambridge, England: Cambridge University Press.

Sroufe, L. A., & Egeland, B. (1991). Illustrations of person-environment interaction from a longitudinal study. In T. D. Wachs & R. Plomin (Eds.), *Conceptualization and Measurement of Organism-environment Interaction* (pp. 68–84). Washington, DC: American Psychological Association.

Sroufe, L. A., Carlson, E., & Schulman, S. (1993). Individuals in relationships: Development from infancy through adolescence. In D. C. Funder, R. D. Parke, C. Tomlinson-Keasy, & K. Widaman (Eds.), *Studying Lives through Time: Personality and Development* (pp. 315–342). Washington, DC: American Psychological Association.

Sroufe, L. A., Egeland, B., & Carlson, E. (2005). Placing early attachment experiences in developmental context: The Minnesota Longitudinal Study. In K. E. Grossmann, K. Grossmann, & E. Waters (Eds.), *Attachment from Infancy to Adulthood: The Major Longitudinal Studies* (pp. 48–70). New York: Guilford Publications, Inc.

Stack, D. M., Serbin, L. A., Schwartzman, A. E., & Ledingham, J. (2005). Girls' aggression across the life course: Long-term outcomes and intergenerational risk. In D. J. Pepler, K. C. Madsen,

C. Webster, & K. S. Levene (Eds.), *The Development and Treatment of Girlhood Aggression* (pp. 253–283). Mahwah, NJ: Erlbaum.

Stadtler, A. C., Gorski, P. A., & Brazelton, T. B. (1999). Toilet training methods, clinical interventions, and recommendations. *Pediatrics, 103*(6), 1359–1361.

Staff, J., Mortimer, J. T., & Uggen, C. (2004). Work and leisure in adolescence (pp. 429–450). In R. M. Lerner & L. Steinberg (Eds.), *Handbook of Adolescent Psychology* (2nd ed.). Hoboken, NJ: John Wiley & Sons, Inc.

Stams, G. J. M., Juffer, F., Rispens, J., & Hoksbergen, R. A. C. (2000). The development and adjustment of 7-year-old children adopted in infancy. *Journal of Child Psychology and Psychiatry, 41*, 1025–1037.

Standley, K., Soule, B., & Copans, S. (1979). Dimensions of prenatal anxiety and their influence on pregnancy outcome. *American Journal of Obstetrics and Gynecology, 135*, 22–26.

Stark, R., Bernstein, L., & Demorest, M. (1993). Vocal communication in the first 18 months of life. *Journal of Speech and Hearing Research, 36*, 548–558.

Starkey, P., Spelke, E. S., & Gelman, R. (1983). Detection of intermodal numerical correspondences by human infants. *Science, 222*, 179–181.

Starr, C., & Taggart, R. (1998). *Biology: The unity and diversity of life.* Belmont, CA: Wadsworth.

Stechler, G., & Halton, A. (1982). Prenatal influences on human development. In B. B. Wolman (Ed.), *Handbook of Developmental Psychology* (pp. 175–189). Englewood Cliffs, NJ: Prentice-Hall.

Steele, C. M., & Aronson, J. (1995). Stereotype threat and the intellectual test performance of African Americans. *Journal of Personality and Social Psychology, 69*, 797–811.

Steele, K. M., Bass, K. E., & Crook, M. D. (1999). The mystery of the Mozart effect: Failure to replicate. *Psychological Science, 10*, 366–369.

Steinberg, L. (2001). We know some things: Parent-adolescent relationships in retrospect and prospect. *Journal of Research on Adolescence, 11*, 1–19.

Steinberg, L. (2005). *Adolescence* (7th ed.). Boston: McGraw Hill.

Steinberg, L., & Scott, E. S. (2003). Less guilty by reason of adolescence: Developmental immaturity, diminished responsibility, and the juvenile death penalty. *American Psychologist, 58*, 1009–1018.

Steiner, J. E. (1979). Human facial expressions in response to taste and smell stimulation. In H. Reese & L. Lipsitt (Eds.), *Advances in Child Development and Behavior* (Vol. 13, pp. 257–295). New York: Academic Press.

Stennes, L. M., Burch, M. M., Sen, M. G., & Bauer, P. J. (2005). A longitudinal study of gendered vocabulary and communicative action in young children. *Developmental Psychology, 41*, 75–88.

Stern, E. (1993). What makes certain arithmetic word problems involving comparison of sets so difficult for children? *Journal of Educational Psychology, 85*, 7–23.

Sternberg, R. J. (1985). *Beyond IQ: A triarchic theory of human intelligence.* Cambridge, England: Cambridge University Press.

Sternberg, R. J. (1988). *The triarchic mind: A new theory of human intelligence.* New York: Viking.

Sternberg, R. J. (1999). The theory of successful intelligence. *Review of General Psychology, 3*, 292–316.

Sternberg, R. J., & Grigorenko, E. L. (2006). Cultural intelligence and successful intelligence. *Group and Organizational Management, 31*, 27–39.

Stevenson, H. W., & Lee, S. (1990). Contexts of achievement: A study of American, Chinese, and Japanese children. *Monographs of the Society for Research in Child Development, 55*(1-2, Serial No. 221).

Stevenson, J. (1992). Evidence for genetic etiology in hyperactivity in children. *Behavior Genetics, 22*(3), 337–344.

Stevenson, L. (1997). Exercise in pregnancy. Part 1: Update on pathophysiology. *Canadian Family Physician, 43*(1), 97–104.

Steward, M. S., & Steward, D. S. (1996). Interviewing young children about body touch and handling. *Monographs of the Society for Research in Child Development, 61*(Serial No. 248).

Stewart, S. L., & Rubin, K. H. (1995). The social problem-solving skills of anxious–withdrawn children. *Development and Psychopathology, 7*, 323–336.

Stice, E., & Whitenton, K. (2002). Risk factors for body dissatisfaction in adolescent girls: A longitudinal investigation. *Developmental Psychology, 38*(5), 669–678.

Stice, E., Presnell, K., & Bearman, S. K. (2001). Relation of early menarche to depression, eating disorders, substance abuse, and comorbid psychopathology among adolescent girls. *Developmental Psychology, 37*(5), 608–619.

Stien, P. T., & Kendall, J. (2004). *Psychological trauma and the developing brain.* New York: The Haworth Press, Inc.

Stiles, J., & Thal, D. (1993). Linguistic and spatial cognitive development following early focal brain injury: Patterns of deficit and recovery. In M. Johnson (Ed.), *Brain Development and Cognition: A Reader* (pp. 643–664). Oxford: Blackwell.

Stillion, J. M., & McDowell, E. E. (1996). *Suicide across the life span* (2nd ed.). Washington, DC: Taylor & Francis.

Stipek, D. J., & Ryan, R. H. (1997). Economically disadvantaged preschoolers: Ready to learn but further to go. *Developmental Psychology, 33*, 711–723.

Stipek, D., Recchia, S., & McClintic, S. (1992). Self-evaluation in young children. *Monographs of the Society for Research in Child Development, 57*(1, Serial No. 226).

Stoddart, T., & Turiel, E. (1985). Children's concepts of cross-gender activities. *Child Development, 56*, 1241–1252.

Stoel-Gammon, C., & Otomo, K. (1986). Babbling development of hearing-impaired and normally hearing subjects. *Journal of Speech and Hearing Disorders, 51*, 33–41.

Stoiber, K. C., & McIntyre, H. (2006). Adolescent pregnancy and parenting. In G. G. Bear & K. M. Minke (Eds.), *Children's Needs III: Development, Prevention, and Intervention* (pp. 705–719). Washington, DC: National Association of School Psychologists.

Strattman, K., & Hodson, B. W. (2005). Variables that influence decoding and spelling in beginning readers. *Child Language Teaching and Therapy, 21*, 165–191.

Straus, M. A. (1991). Discipline and deviance: Physical punishment of children and violence and other crime in adulthood. *Social Problems, 38*, 133–154.

Straus, M. A. (2001). *Beating the devil out of them: Corporal punishment in American families and its effects on children.* New York: Lexington Books.

Straus, M. A., & Stewart, J. H. (1999). Corporal punishment by American parents: National data on prevalence, chronicity, severity, and duration, in relation to child and family characteristics. *Clinical Child and Family Psychology Review, 2*, 55–70.

Straus, M. A., Sugarman, D. B., & Giles-Sims, J. (1997). Spanking by parents and subsequent antisocial behavior of children. *Archives of Pediatric and Adolescent Medicine, 151*, 761–767.

Subrahmanyam, K., Kraut, R., Greenfield, P., & Gross, E. (2001). New forms of electronic media. In D. G. Singer & J. L. Singer (Eds.), *Handbook of Children and the Media* (pp. 73–99). Thousand Oaks, CA: Sage.

Sullivan, A. (2000, July 23). The way we live now: 7-23-00: Counter culture; promotion of the fittest. *The New York Times.* Retrieved February 15, 2002, from http://www.nytimes.com.

Sullivan, H. S. (1953). *The interpersonal theory of psychiatry.* New York: Norton.

Sullivan, J., & Horowitz, F. D. (1983). The effects of intonation on infant attention: The role of the rising intonation contour. *Journal of Child Language, 10*, 521–534.

Sullivan, K., & Wimmer, E. (1993). Three-year-olds' understanding of mental states: The influence of trickery. *Journal of Experimental Child Psychology, 56*, 135–148.

Sullivan, P. F. (1995). Mortality in anorexia nervosa. *American Journal of Psychiatry, 152*, 1073–1074.

Sun, S. S., Schubert, C. M., Liang, R., Roche, A. F., Kulin, H. E., Lee, P. A., et al. (2005). Is sexual maturity occurring earlier among U.S. children? *Journal of Adolescent Health, 37*, 345–355.

Sun, Y., & Li, Y. (2002). Children's well-being during parents' marital disruption process: A pooled time-series analysis. *Journal of Marriage and Family, 64*, 472–488.

Super, C. (1976). Environmental effects on motor development: The case of "African infant precocity." *Developmental Medicine and Child Neurology, 18*, 561–567.

Super, D. E. (1957). *The psychology of careers: An introduction to vocational development.* New York: Harper.

Sussman, E. J., & Rogol, A. (2004). Puberty and psychological development. In R. M. Lerner & L. S. Steinberg (Eds.), *Handbook of Adolescent Psychology* (2nd ed., pp. 15–44). Hoboken, NJ: John Wiley & Sons, Inc.

Suttle, C. M., Banks, M. S., & Graf, E. W. (2002). FPL and sweep VEP to tritan stimuli in young human infants. *Vision Research, 42*(26), 2879–2891.

Swaab, D. F., Gooren, L. J. G., & Hofman, M. A. (1995). Brain research, gender, and sexual orientation. *Journal of Homosexuality, 28*, 283–301.

Swanson, H. L., & Beebe-Frankenberger, M. (2004). The relationship between working memory and mathematical problem solving in children at risk and not at risk for serious math difficulties. *Journal of Educational Psychology, 96*, 471–491.

Swarns, R. L. (1999, January 30). Children go to foster care needlessly, suit charges. *New York Times*. Retrieved August 2, 2002, from www.nytimes.com.

Szeverenyi, P., Hetey, A., Kovacsne, Z. T., & Muennich, A. (1995). Does the father's presence at delivery have an influence on the parental judgment of the father–child relationship? *Magyar Pszichologiai Szemle, 51*, 83–95.

Tager-Flusberg, H., Boshart, J., & Baron-Cohen, S. (1999). Reading the windows to the soul: Evidence of domain-specific sparing in Williams syndrome. *Journal of Cognitive Neuroscience, 10*, 631–639.

Takahashi, K. (1986). Examining the Strange-Situation procedure with Japanese mothers and 12-month-old infants. *Developmental Psychology, 22*, 265–270.

Takahashi, K. (1990). Are the key assumptions of the "strange situation" procedure universal?: A view from Japanese research. *Human Development, 33*, 23–30.

Takeuchi, M. (1994). Children's play in Japan. In J. L. Roopnarine, J. E. Johnson, & F. H. Hooper (Eds.), *Children's Play in Diverse Cultures* (pp. 51–72). Albany: State University of New York Press.

Tanner, J. M. (1978). *Fetus into man: Physical growth from conception to maturity*. Cambridge, MA: Harvard University Press.

Tanner, J. M. (1991). Menarche, secular trend in age of. In R. M. Lerner, A. C. Petersen, & J. Brooks-Gunn (Eds.), *Encyclopedia of Adolescence* (Vol. 2, pp. 637–641). New York: Garland Publishing, Inc.

Tapert, S. F., Caldwell, L., & Burke, C. (2004/2005). Alcohol and the adolescent brain. *Alcohol Research and Health, 28*, 205–212.

Tasbihsazan, R., Nettelbeck, T., & Kirby, N. (2003). Predictive validity of the Fagan Test of Infant Intelligence. *British Journal of Developmental Psychology, 21*, 585–597.

Taylor, M., & Hort, B. (1990). Can children be trained in making the distinction between appearance and reality? *Child Development, 5*, 89–99.

Taylor, O. L. (1986). *Nature of communication disorders in culturally and linguistically diverse populations*. San Diego, CA: College-Hill Press.

Taylor, R., & Richards, S. (1991). Patterns of intellectual differences of black, Hispanic, and white children. *Psychology in the Schools, 28*, 5–9.

Teeter , P. A., & Semrud-Clikeman, M. (1997). *Child neuropsychology: Assessment and interventions for neurodevelopmental Disorders*. Boston: Allyn and Bacon.

Teicher, M. H. (2002). Scars that won't heal: The neurobiology of child abuse. *Scientific American, 286*(3), 68–75.

Tergerson, J. L., & King, K. A. (2002). Do perceived cues, benefits, and barriers to physical activity differ between male and female adolescents? *Journal of School Health, 72*, 374–380.

Terman, L. M. (1925). *Genetic studies of genius, Vol. 1: Mental and physical traits of a thousand gifted children*. Stanford, CA: Stanford University Press.

Terrace, H. S., Petitto, L. A., Sanders, R. J., & Bever, T. G. (1980). One the grammatical capacity of apes. In K. E. Nelson (Ed.), *Children's Language*. New York: Gardner Press.

Thapar, A., Fowler, T., & Rice, F. (2003). Maternal smoking during pregnancy and Attention Deficit Hyperactivity Disorder symptoms in offspring. *American Journal of Psychiatry, 160*, 1985–1989.

Thelen, E. (1989). The (re)discovery of motor development: Learning new things from an old field. *Developmental Psychology, 25*, 946–949.

Thelen, E., & Smith, L. B. (2006). Dynamic systems theories. In W. Damon & R. M. Lerner (Series Eds.) and R. M. Lerner (Vol. Ed.), *Handbook of Child Psychology: Vol. 1. Theoretical Models of Human Development* (6th ed., pp. 258–312). Hoboken, NJ: Wiley.

Thelen, E., Fisher, D. M., & Ridley-Johnson, R. (1984). The relationship between physical growth and a newborn reflex. *Infant Behavior and Development, 7*, 479–493.

Thiessen, E. D., Hill, E. A., & Saffran, J. R. (2005). Infant-directed speech facilitates word segmentation. *Infancy, 7*(1), 53–71.

Thomas, A., & Chess, S. (1977). *Temperament and development*. New York: Brunner/Mazel.

Thomas, M., & Karmiloff-Smith, A. (2003). Connectionist models of development, developmental disorders, and individual differences. In R. J. Sternberg, J. Lautrey, & T. Lubart, (Eds.), *Models of Intelligence: International Perspectives* (pp. 133–150). Washington, DC: American Psychological Association.

Thomas, R. M. (2000). *Comparing Theories of Child Development*. Belmont, CA: Wadsworth Publishing Company.

Thompson, M. W., McInnes, R. R., & Willard, H. F. (1991). *Thompson & Thompson genetics in medicine* (5th ed.). Philadelphia: W. B. Saunders Company.

Thompson, P. M., Giedd, J. N., Woods, R. P., MacDonald, D., Evans, A. C., & Toga, A. W. (2000). Growth patterns in the developing brain detected by using continuum mechanical tensor maps. *Nature, 404*, 190–193.

Thompson, R. A. (1998). Early sociopersonality development. In W. Damon (Ed.), *Handbook of Child Psychology* (Vol. 3, pp. 25–104). New York: John Wiley & Sons.

Thompson, R. A. (2006). The development of the person: Social understanding, relationships, conscience, self. In N. Eisenberg (Vol. Ed.) and W. Damon & R. M. Lerner (Eds.), *Handbook of Child Psychology* (6th ed., Vol. 3, pp. 24–98). New York: John Wiley & Sons.

Thompson, R. A. (1999). The individual child: Temperament, emotion, self, and personality. In M. H. Bornstein & M. S. Lamb (Eds.), *Developmental Psychology: An Advanced Textbook* (4th ed., pp. 377–409). Mahwah, NJ: Erlbaum.

Thorndike, R., & Lohman, D. (1990). *A century of ability testing*. Chicago: Riverside.

Thurstone, L. L. (1938). *Primary mental abilities*. Chicago: University of Chicago Press.

Thurstone, L. L., & Thurstone, T. G. (1941). *Factorial studies of intelligence*. Chicago: University of Chicago Press.

Tietjen, A., & Walker, L. (1985). Moral reasoning and leadership among men in a Papua, New Guinea village. *Developmental Psychology, 21*, 982–992.

Tomasello, M. (1995). Language is not an instinct. *Cognitive Development, 10*, 131–156.

Tomasello, M. (2006). Acquiring linguistic construction. In D. Kuhn & R. S. Siegler (Eds.), *Cognition, Perception, and Language* (Vol. 2, pp. 255–298), in W. Damon & R. M. Lerner (Gen. Eds.), *Handbook of Child Psychology* (6th ed.). New York: Wiley.

Tomkins, A. J., & Kepfield, S. S. (1992). Policy responses: When women use drugs during pregnancy: Using child abuse laws to combat substance abuse. In T. B. Sonderegger (Ed.), *Perinatal Substance Abuse: Research Findings and Clinical Applications* (pp. 306–345). Baltimore: The Johns Hopkins University Press.

Torbeyns, J., Verschaffel, L., & Ghesquiere, P. (2005). Simple addition strategies in a first-grade class with multiple strategy instruction. *Cognition and Instruction, 23*, 1–21.

Toulmin, S. (1978, September). The Mozart of psychology. *New York Review of Books*. (As cited in Wertsch, 1985).

Tracey, J. G., Robbins, S. B., & Hofsess, C. D. (2005). Stability and change in interests: A longitudinal study of adolescents from grades 8 through 12. *Journal of Vocational Behavior, 66*, 1–25.

Trad, P. V. (1995). Mental health of adolescent mothers. *Journal of the American Academy of Child and Adolescent Psychiatry, 34*, 130–142.

Trad, P. V. (1999). Assessing the patterns that prevent teenage pregnancy. *Adolescence, 34*, 221–240.

Tran, H., & Weinraub, M. (2006). Child care effects in context: Quality, stability, and multiplicity in nonmaternal child care arrangements during the first 15 months of life. *Developmental Psychology, 42,* 566–582.

Trehub, S. E. (1976). The discrimination of foreign speech contrasts by infants and adults. *Child Development, 47,* 466–472.

Triandis, H. C. (1994). *Culture and social behavior.* New York: McGraw-Hill.

Triandis, H. C. (1995). *Individualism and collectivism.* Boulder, CO: Westview Press.

Trimble, J. E., & Medicine, B. (1993). Diversification of American Indians: Forming an indigenous perspective. In U. Kim & J. W. Berry (Eds.), *Indigenous Psychologies* (pp. 133–151). Newbury Park, CA: Sage.

Triseliotis, J. (2000). Identity formation and the adopted person revisited. In A. Treacher & I. Katz (Eds.), *The Dynamics of Adoption* (pp. 81–97). London: Jessica Kingsley Publishers.

Triseliotis, J., & Hill, M. (1990). Contrasting adoption, foster care, and residential rearing. In D. M. Brodzinsky & M. D. Schechter (Eds.), *The Psychology of Adoption* (pp. 107–120). New York: Oxford University Press.

Troiden, R. R. (1988). Homosexual identity development. *Journal of Adolescent Health Care, 9,* 105–113.

Trussell, J. (1988). Teenage pregnancy in the United States. *Family Planning Perspectives, 20,* 262–272.

Tsao, R., Liu, H., & Kuhl, P. K. (2004). Speech perception in infancy predicts language development in the second year of life: A longitudinal study. *Child Development, 75,* 1067–1084.

Tschannen-Moran, M., Woolfolk Hoy, A., & Hoy, W. K. (1998). Teacher efficacy: Its meaning and measure. *Review of Educational Research, 68,* 202–248.

Tseng, V., & Fuligni, A. J. (2000). Parent-adolescent language use and relationships among immigrant families with East Asian, Filipino, and Latin American backgrounds. *Journal of Marriage and the Family, 62,* 465–476.

Tulving, E. (1972). Episodic and semantic memory. In E. Tulving & W. Donaldson (Eds.), *Organization of Memory* (pp. 382–403). New York: Academic Press.

Turati, C., Cassia, V. M., Simion, F., & Leo, I. (2006). Newborns' face recognition: Role of inner and outer facial features. *Child Development, 77,* 297–311.

Turati, C., Simion, F., Milani, I., & Umiltá, C. (2002). Newborns' preferences for faces: What is crucial? *Developmental Psychology, 38*(6), 875–882.

Turati, C., Valenza, E., Leo, I., & Simion, F. (2005). Three-month-olds' preference for faces and its underlying visual processing mechanisms. *Journal of Experimental Child Psychology, 90,* 255–273.

Turiel, E. (1998, 2006). The development of morality. In W. Damon & R. Lerner (Series Ed.) and N. Eisenberg (Vol. Ed.), *Handbook of Child Psychology: Vol. 3. Social, Emotional, and Personality Development* (6th ed., pp. 789–857). New York: Wiley. In W. Damon & N. Eisenberg (Eds.), *Handbook of Child Psychology: Vol. 3. Social, Emotional, and Personality Development* (pp. 863–932). New York: John Wiley & Sons, Inc.

U.S. Census Bureau. (2000). *Profile of general demographic characteristics for the United States: 2000* (Table DP-1). Washington, DC: Government Printing Office.

U.S. Census Bureau. (2001). *Overview of race and Hispanic origin: Census 2000 Brief.* Issued March, 2001, by the U.S. Department of Commerce. Also, census data retrieved June 1, 2001: 1990 data from http://homer.ssd.census.gov/cdrom/lookup/991424885 and 2000 data from www.census.gov/Press-Release/www/2001/cb01cn61.html.

U.S. Census Bureau (2004). *Current Population Survey (March 2005).* Retrieved August 2, 2006, from http://www.census.gov/population/www/socdemo/education/cps2004.html.

U.S. Census Bureau. (2006). *America's Children in Brief: Key National Indicators of Well-Being, 2006.* Last accessed July 28, 2006, from http://www.childstats.gov/amchildren06/tables.asp.

U.S. Department of Education. (2001). National Center for Education Statistics. *Internet Access in U.S. public schools and classrooms: 1994–2000* (NCES 2001-071), by A. Cattagni & E. F. Westat. Washington, DC: U.S. Government Printing Office.

U.S. Department of Health and Human Services, Administration on Children, Youth, and Families. (2001). *Child Maltreatment 1999.* Washington, DC: U.S. Government Printing Office.

U.S. Department of Health and Human Services. (2001). *Youth violence: A report of the Surgeon General.* Rockville, MD: U.S. Department of Health and Human Services, Centers for Disease Control and Prevention, National Center for Injury Prevention and Control; Substance Abuse and Mental Health Services Administration, Center for Mental Health Services; and National Institutes of Mental Health, National Institute of Mental Health.

U.S. Department of Health and Human Services (2005). *Child Maltreatment 2003.* Administration on Children, Youth and Families. Washington, DC: U.S. Government Printing Office.

U.S. Department of Health and Human Services (2006). *Child Maltreatment, 2004.* Washington, DC: U.S. Government Printing Office. Retrieved June 22, 2006, from http://www.acf.hhs.gov/programs/cb/pubs/cm04/cm04.pdf.

U.S. National Coalition for the Homeless (2001). Homeless families with children (NCH fact sheet #7). Retrieved July 19, 2002, from http://www.nationalhomeless.org/families.html.

U.S. Teens and Technology [online]. (1997). Retrieved July 11, 2002, from www.nsf.gov/lpa/nstw/teenov.htm.

Uchikoshi, Y. (2005). Narrative development in bilingual kindergartners: Can *Arthur* help? *Developmental Psychology, 41,* 464–478.

Uhlmann, W. R. (2000, February 29). When genes are decoded, who should see the results?: "Every one of us is at risk." *The New York Times.* Retrieved February 15, 2002, from http://www.nytimes.com.

Uhry, J. K., & Shepard, M. J. (1993). Segmentation/spelling instruction as part of a first-grade reading program: Effects on several measures of reading. *Reading Research Quarterly, 28,* 218–233.

United Cerebral Palsy. (2005). *United Cerebral Palsy.* Retrieved October 27, 2005, from www.ucp.org.

Upchurch, D. M., Mason, W. M., Kusunoki, Y., & Kriechbaum, M. J. (2004). Social and behavioral determinants of self-reported STD among adolescents. *Perspectives on Sexual and Reproductive Health, 36,* 276–287.

Valenzuela, M. (1990). Attachment in chronically underweight young children. *Child Development, 61,* 1984–1996.

Valian, V., Hoeffner, J., & Aubry, S. (1996). Young children's imitation of sentence subjects: Evidence of processing limitations. *Developmental Psychology, 32,* 153–164.

van Ijzendoorn, M. H., Goldberg, S., Kroonenberg, P. M., & Frenkel, O. J. (1992). The relative effects of maternal and child problems on the quality of attachment: A meta-analysis of attachment in clinical samples. *Child Development, 63,* 840–858.

Van Ijzendoorn, M. H., Goossens, F. A., Kroonenberg, P. M., & Tavecchio, L. W. C. (1985). Dependent attachment: B4-children in the strange situation. *Psychological Reports, 57,* 439–451.

van Ijzendoorn, M. H., Verijken, C. M. J. L., Bakermans-Kranenburg, M. J., & Riksen-Walraven, J. M. (2004). Assessing attachment security with the Attachment Q Sort: Meta-analytic evidence for the validity of the observer AQS. *Child Development, 75,* 1188–1213.

Vandell, D. L., & Mueller, E. C. (1980). Peer play and friendships during the first two years. In H. C. Foot, A. J. Chapman, & J. R. Smith (Eds.), *Friendship and Social Relations in Children* (pp. 181–208). New York: Wiley.

Vandell, D. L., & Powers, C. (1983). Day care quality and children's free play activities. *American Journal of Orthopsychiatry, 53,* 493–500.

Vandell, D. L., & Wilson, K. S. (1982). Social interaction in the first year: Infants' social skills with peers versus mother. In K. H. Rubin & H. S. Ross (Eds.), *Peer Relationships and Social Skills in Childhood* (pp. 187–208). New York: Springer-Verlag.

Vandell, D. L., Wilson, K. S., & Buchanan, N. R. (1980). Peer interaction in the first year of life: An examination of its structure, content, and sensitivity to toys. *Child Development, 51,* 481–488.

Vanfraussen, K., Ponjaert-Kristoffersen, I., & Brewaeys, A. (2003). Family functioning in lesbian families created by donor insemination. *American Journal of Orthopsychiatry, 73,* 78–90.

Varnado-Sullivan, P. J., & Zucker, N. (2004). The body logic program for adolescents. *Behavior Modification, 28,* 854–875.

Vartanian, L. R. (2000). Revisiting the imaginary audience and personal fable constructs of adolescent egocentrism: A conceptual review. *Adolescence, 35,* 639–661.

Vartanian, L. R. (2001). Adolescents' reactions to hypothetical peer group conversations: Evidence for an imaginary audience? *Adolescence, 36,* 347–380.

Vaughn, B. E., & Waters, E. (1990). Attachment behavior at home and in the laboratory: Q-sort observations and Strange Situation classifications of one-year-olds. *Child Development, 61,* 1965–1973.

Vellutino, F. R., & Scanlon, D. M. (1987). Phonological coding, phonological awareness, and reading ability: Evidence from a longitudinal and experimental study. *Merrill-Palmer Quarterly, 33,* 321–363.

Venter, J. C., Adams, M. D., Myers, E. W., Li, P. W., Mural, R. J., Sutton, G. G., et al. (2001). The sequence of the human genome. *Science, 291,* 1304–1351.

Ventura, S. J., Abma, J. C., Mosher, W. D., & Henshaw, S. (2003). Revised pregnancy rates, 1990–97, and new rates for 1998–99: United States. *National Vital Statistics Reports, 52*(7). Oct. 31, 2003. Retrieved May 24, 2005, from http://www.cdc.gov/nchs/products/pubs/pubd/nvsr/nvsr.htm.

Ventura, S. J., Mosher, W. D., Curtin, S. C., Abma, J. C., & Henshaw, S. (2001). Trends in pregnancy rates for the United States, 1976–97: An update. *National vital statistics reports, 49*(4). Retrieved March 27, 2003, from www.cdc.gov/nchs/data/nvsr/nvsr49/nvsr49_04. pdf.

Ventura, S. J., Peters, K. D., Martin, J. A., & Maurer, J. D. (1997). Births and deaths: United States, 1996. *Monthly Vital Statistics Report, 46*(1), supp. 2. Hyattsville, MD: National Center for Health Statistics.

Verkuyten, M. (2003). Postive and negative self-esteem among ethnic minority early adolescents: Social and cultural sources and threats. *Journal of Youth and Adolescence, 32,* 267–277.

Vihman, M., & Miller, R. (1988). Words and babble at the threshold of language acquisition. In M. Smith & J. Locke (Eds.), *The Emergent Lexicon: The Child's Development of a Linguistic Vocabulary* (pp. 151–184). New York: Academic Press.

Viken, R. J., Rose, R. J., Kaprio, J., & Koskenvuo, M. (1994). A developmental-genetic analysis of adult personality: Extraversion and neuroticism from 18 to 59. *Journal of Personality and Social Psychology, 66,* 722–730.

Vlahovic-Stetic, V., Rovan, D., & Mendek, Z. (2004). The role of students' age, problem type and situational context in solving mathematical word problems. *Review of Psychology, 11,* 25–33.

Volterra, V., & Taeschner, T. (1978). The acquisition and development of language by bilingual children. *Journal of Child Language, 5,* 311–326.

Votruba-Drzal, E., Coley, R. L., & Chase-Lansdale, P. L. (2004). Child care and low-income children's development: Direct and moderated effects. *Child Development, 75,* 296–312.

Voyer, D., Voyer, S., & Bryden, M. P. (1995). Magnitude of sex differences in spatial abilities: A meta-analysis and consideration of critical variables. *Psychological Bulletin, 117,* 250–270.

Vroegh, K. S. (1997). Transracial adoptees: Developmental status after 17 years. *American Journal of Orthopsychiatry, 67,* 568–575.

Vygotsky, L. S. (1956). *Izbrannye psikhologicheskie issledovaniya. [Selected psychological investigations].* Moscow: Izdatel'stvo Akademii Pedagogicheskikh Nauk. (As cited in Wertsch & Tulviste, 1992).

Vygotsky, L. S. (1962). *Thought and language.* New York: Wiley.

Vygotsky, L. S. (1978). *Mind in society: The development of higher psychological processes.* Cambridge, MA: Harvard University Press.

Vygotsky, L. S. (1981). The genesis of higher mental functions. In J. V. Wertsch (Ed.), *The Concept of Activity in Soviet Psychology* (pp. 144–188). Armonk, NJ: M. E. Sharpe.

Waddington, C. H. (1942). Canalization of development and the inheritance of acquired characters. *Nature, 150,* 563–564.

Waddington, C. H. (1957). *The strategy of the genes.* London: Allen and Unwin.

Walker, L. J. (1989). A longitudinal study of moral reasoning. *Child Development, 60,* 157–166.

Walker, L. J. (1995). Sexism in Kohlberg's moral psychology? In W. M. Kurtines & J. L. Gerwitz (Eds.), *Moral Development: An Introduction* (pp. 83–107). Boston: Allyn and Bacon.

Walker, L. J., & Hennig, K. H. (1997). Moral development in the broader context of personality. In S. Hala (Ed.), *The Development of Social Cognition* (pp. 297–327). Hove, UK: Psychology Press.

Walker, L. J., Pitts, R., Hennig, K., & Matsuba, M. K. (1995). Reasoning about morality and real-life moral problems. In M. Killen & D. Hart (Eds.), *Morality in Everyday Life: Developmental Perspectives* (pp. 371–407). New York: Cambridge University Press.

Walker, S. O., Petrill, S. A., Spinath, F. M., & Plomin, R. (2004). Nature, nurture and academic achievement: A twin study of teacher assessments of 7-year-olds. *British Journal of Educational Psychology, 74,* 323–342.

Walker-Andrews, A. S., & Lennon, E. M. (1985). Auditory-visual perception of changing distance by human infants. *Child Development, 56,* 544–548.

Wallace, J. M., Brown, T. N., & Bachman, J. G. (2003). The influence of race and religion on abstinence from alcohol, cigarettes, and marijuana among adolescents. *Journal of Studies on Alcohol, 64,* 843–848.

Wallerstein, J. S. (2001). The challenges of divorce for parents and children. In J. C. Westman (Ed.), *Parenthood in America: Undervalued, Underpaid, Under Siege* (pp. 127–139). Madison: University of Wisconsin Press.

Wallerstein, J. S., Lewis, J. M., & Blakeslee, S. (2000). *The unexpected legacy of divorce: A 25-year landmark study.* New York: Hyperion.

Ward, L. M. (2004). Wading through the stereotypes: Positive and negative associations between media use and black adolescents' conceptions of self. *Developmental Psychology, 40,* 284–294.

Wark, G. R., & Krebs, D. L. (1996). Gender and dilemma differences in real-life moral judgments. *Developmental Psychology, 32,* 220–230.

Warren, A. R., & McCloskey, L. A. (1997). Language in social contexts. In J. B. Gleason (Ed.), *The Development of Language* (4th ed., pp. 210–258). Boston: Allyn and Bacon.

Warren-Leubecker, A., & Carter, B. W. (1988). Reading and growth in metalinguistic awareness: Relations to socioeconomic status and reading readiness skills. *Child Development, 59,* 728–742.

Washington, V., & Oyemade, U. J. (1987). *Project Head Start: Past, present, and future trends in the context of family needs.* New York: Garland.

Wasserheit, J. N. (1992). Epidemiologic synergy: Interrelationships between human immunodeficiency virus infection and other sexually transmitted diseases. *Sexually Transmitted Diseases, 9,* 61–77.

Waters, E., & Deane, K. E. (1985). Defining and assessing individual differences in attachment relationships: Q-methodology and the organization of behavior in infancy and early childhood. In I. Bretherton & E. Waters (Eds.), Growing Points of Attachment Theory and Research. *Monographs of the Society for Research in Child Development, 50*(1/2, Serial No. 209), 41–65.

Watson, J. B. (1924). *Behaviorism.* Chicago: University of Chicago Press.

Watson, J. B. (1928). *Psychological care of infant and child.* New York: W. W. Norton & Company, Inc.

Watson, J. B. (1930). *Behaviorism.* Chicago: The University of Chicago Press. Original edition published in 1924.

Watson, J. B., & Rayner, R. (1920). Conditioned emotional reactions. *Journal of Experimental Psychology, 3,* 1–14.

Watson, J. D., & Crick, F. H. C. (1953). Molecular structure of nucleic acids: A structure for deoxyribose nucleic acid. *Nature, 171,* pp. 737–738.

Waxman, S. R., & Lidz, J. L. (2006). Early word learning. In D. Kuhn & R. S. Siegler (Eds.), *Cognition, Perception, and Language* (Vol. 2, pp. 299–335), in W. Damon & R. M. Lerner (Gen. Eds.), *Handbook of Child Psychology* (6th ed.). New York: Wiley.

Weiner, B. (1992). *Human motivation: Metaphors, theories, and research.* Newbury Park, CA: Sage.

Weiner, B. (2000). Intrapersonal and interpersonal theories of motivation from an attributional perspective. *Educational Psychology Review, 12,* 1–14.

Wekerle, C., & Wolfe, D. A. (1996). Child maltreatment. In E. J. Mash & R. A. Barkley (Eds.), *Child Psychopathology* (pp. 492–537). New York: Guilford Press.

Wekerle, C., & Wolfe, D. A. (2003). Child maltreatment. In E. J. Mash & R. A. Barkley (Eds.), *Child Psychopathology* (pp. 632–684). New York: Guilford Press.

Wellman, H. M. (1990). *The child's theory of mind*. Cambridge, MA: MIT Press.

Wellman, H. M., & Bartsch, K. (1988). Young children's reasoning about beliefs. *Cognition, 30,* 239–277.

Wellman, H. M., & Estes, D. (1986). Early understanding of mental entities: A reexamination of childhood realism. *Child Development, 57,* 910–923.

Wellman, H. M., & Gelman, S. A. (1998). Knowledge acquisition in foundational domains. In W. Damon (Series Ed.) and D. Kuhn & R. S. Siegler (Vol. Eds.), *Handbook of Child Psychology: Vol. 2. Cognition, Perception, and Language* (5th ed., pp. 523–573). New York: Wiley.

Wellman, H. M., & Liu, D. (2004). Scaling of theory-of-mind tasks. *Child Development, 75,* 523–541.

Wellman, H. M., Cross, D., & Watson, J. (2001). Meta-analysis of theory-of-mind development: The truth about false belief. *Child Development, 72,* 655–684.

Wellman, H., Harris, P. L., Banerjee, M., & Sinclair, A. (1995). Early understanding of emotion: Evidence from natural language. *Cognition and Emotion, 9,* 117–149.

Wenger, E. (1998). *Communities of practice: Learning, meaning, and identity*. Cambridge, England: Cambridge University Press.

Wentzel, K. R., & Watkins, D. E. (2002). Peer relationships and collaborative learning as contexts for academic enablers. *School Psychology Review, 31,* 366–377.

Werker, J. F., & Tees, R. C. (1984). Cross-language speech perception: Evidence for perceptual reorganization during the first year of life. *Infant Behavior and Development, 7,* 49–63.

Werker, J., & Tees, R. (1984). Cross-language speech perception: Evidence for perceptual reorganization during the first year of life. *Infant Behavior and Development, 7,* 49–64.

Werner, E. E. (1989). High-risk children in young adulthood: A longitudinal study from birth to 32 years. *American Journal of Orthopsychiatry, 59,* 72–81.

Werner, E. E. (2000). Protective factors and individual resilience. In J. P. Shonkoff & S. J. Meisels (Eds.), *Handbook of Early Childhood Intervention* (2nd ed., pp. 115–132). Cambridge, UK: Cambridge University Press.

Werner, E. E., & Smith, R. S. (2001). *Journeys from childhood to midlife: Risk, resilience, and recovery*. Ithaca, NJ: Cornell University Press.

Wertsch, J. V. (1985). *Vygotsky and the social formation of mind*. Cambridge, MA: Harvard University Press.

Wertsch, J. V., Tulviste, P., & Hagstrom, F. (1993). A sociocultural approach to agency. In E. A. Forman, N. Minick, & C. A. Stone (Eds.), *Contexts for Learning* (pp. 336–356). New York: Oxford University Press.

Westman, J. C. (1994). *Licensing parents: Can we prevent child abuse and neglect?* New York: Insight Books.

Whalen, C. K., & Schreibman, L. (2003). Joint attention training for children with autism using behavior modification procedures. *Journal of Child Psychology and Psychiatry and Allied Disciplines, 44,* 456–468.

Whalen, C. K., Jamner, L. D., Henker, B., Delfino, R. J., & Lozano, J. M. (2002). The ADHD spectrum and everyday life: Experience sampling of adolescent moods, activities, smoking, and drinking. *Child Development, 73,* 209–227.

Whitaker, P. (2002). Supporting families of preschool children with autism: What parents want and what helps. *Autism, 6,* 411–426.

White, B. H., & Kurpius, S. E. R. (2002). Effects of victim sex and sexual orientation on perceptions of rape. *Sex Roles, 46,* 191–200.

Whiting, B. B., & Edwards, C. P. (1988). *Children of different worlds*. Cambridge, MA: Harvard University Press.

Wiesner, M., & Ittel, A. (2002). Relations of pubertal timing and depressive symptoms to substance use in early adolescence. *Journal of Early Adolescence, 22(1),* 5–23.

Wigfield, A., & Eccles, J. S. (2001). Introduction. In A. Wigfield & J. S. Eccles (Eds.), *Development of Achievement Motivation* (pp. 1–11). San Diego, CA: Academic Press.

Wilcox, A. J., Baird, D. D., & Weinberg, C. R. (1999). Time of implantation of the conceptus and loss of pregnancy. *The New England Journal of Medicine, 340,* 1796–1799.

William T. Grant Foundation Commission on Work, Family and Citizenship (1988). *The forgotten half: Pathways to success for America's youth and young families: Final report*. Washington, DC: William T. Grant Foundation Commission on Work, Family, and Citizenship.

Williams, A. F. (2003). Teenage drivers: Patterns of risk. *Journal of Safety Research, 34,* 5–15.

Williams, J. M., & Currie, C. (2000). Self-esteem and physical development in early adolescence: Pubertal timing and body image. *Journal of Early Adolescence, 20,* 129–149.

Wilson, G. S. (1992). Heroin use during pregnancy: Clinical studies of long-term effects. In T. B. Sonderegger (Ed.), *Perinatal Substance Abuse: Research Findings and Clinical Applications* (pp. 224–238). Baltimore: The Johns Hopkins University Press.

Wilson, S. M., & Peterson, G. W. (2000). Growing up in Appalachia: Ecological influences on adolescent development. In R. Montemayor, G. R. Adams, & T. P. Gullotta (Eds.), *Adolescent Diversity in Ethnic, Economic, and Cultural Contexts* (pp. 75–109). Thousand Oaks, CA: SAGE Publications.

Winner, E. (1996). *Gifted children: Myths and realities*. New York: Basic Books.

Wishard, A. G., Shivers, E. M., Howes, C., & Ritchie, S. (2003). Child care program and teacher practices: Associations with quality and children's experiences. *Early Childhood Research Quarterly, 18,* 65–103.

Witelson, S. F. (1987). Neurobiological aspects of language in children. *Child Development, 58,* 653–688.

Wolfram, W., & Thomas, E. R. (2002). *The development of African American English*. Oxford, England: Blackwell Publishers.

Wolfson, A. R., & Carskadon, M. A. (1998). Sleep schedules and daytime functioning in adolescents. *Child Development, 69,* 875–887.

Wood, D., & Middleton, D. (1975). A study of assisted problem solving. *British Journal of Psychology, 66,* 181–191.

Wood, D., Bruner, J. S., & Ross, G. (1976). The role of tutoring in problem solving. *Journal of Child Psychology and Psychiatry, 17,* 89–100.

Wood, D., Wood, H., & Middleton, D. (1978). An experimental evaluation of four face-to-face teaching strategies. *International Journal of Behavioral Development, 2,* 131–147.

Wood, F., Felton, R., Flowers, L., & Naylor, C. (1991). Neurobehavioral definition of dyslexia. In D. D. Duane & D. B. Gray (Eds.), *The Reading Brain: The Biological Basis of Dyslexia* (pp. 1–25). Parkton, MD: York Press.

Woodward, A. L., Markman, E. M., & Fitzsimmons, C. M. (1994). Rapid word learning in 13- and 18-month-olds. *Developmental Psychology, 30,* 553–566.

Woolley, J. D., & Wellman, H. M. (1992). Children's conceptions of dreams. *Cognitive Development, 7,* 365–380.

World Health Organization (2005). Global Database on Child Growth and Malnutrition. Retrieved September 30, 2005, from http://www.who.int/nutgrowthdb/database/en/.

World Health Organization. (2003). Nutrition Data Banks: Global Data Bank on Breastfeeding. Retrieved September 13, 2004, from http://www.who.int/nut/db_bfd.htm.

Wozencraft, T., Wagner, W., & Pellegrin, A. (1991). Depression and suicidal ideation in sexually abused children. *Child Abuse and Neglect, 15,* 505–511.

Wright, M. A. (1998). *I'm chocolate, you're vanilla*. San Francisco: Jossey-Bass Publishers.

Yazigi, R. A., Odem, R. R., & Polakoski, K. L. (1991). Demonstration of specific binding of cocaine to human spermatozoa. *Journal of the American Medical Association, 266,* 1956–1959.

Young, T. M., Martin, S. S., Young, M. E., & Ting, L. (2001). Internal poverty and teen pregnancy. *Adolescence, 36,* 289–304.

Young, T., Turner, J., & Denny, G. (2004). Examining external and internal poverty as antecedents of teen pregnancy. *American Journal of Health Behavior, 28,* 361–373.

Zachopoulou, E., Tsapakidou, A., & Derri, V. (2004). The effects of a developmentally appropriate music and movement program on motor performance. *Early Childhood Research Quarterly, 19,* 631–642.

Zahn, G. L., Kagan, S., & Widaman, K. F. (1986). Cooperative learning and classroom climate. *Journal of School Psychology, 24,* 351–362.

Zahn-Waxler, C., & Robinson, J. (1995). Empathy and guilt: Early origins of feelings of responsibility. In J. Tangney & K. Fischer (Eds.), *Self-conscious Emotions* (pp. 143–173). New York: Guilford Press.

Zehr, M.A. (2002). Colorado extends *Bilingual Education*, but Massachusetts voters reject it. *Education Week, 22*(11), November 13, 2002.

Zelazo, P. R. (1983). The development of walking: New findings and old assumptions. *Journal of Motor Behavior, 15,* 99–137.

Zelazo, P. R., Zelazo, N. A., & Kolb, S. (1972). "Walking" in the newborn. *Science, 176,* 314–315.

Zevin, J. D., & Seidenberg, M. S. (2004). Age-of-acquisition effects in reading aloud: Tests of cumulative frequency and frequency trajectory. *Memory and Cognition, 32,* 31–38.

Zhu, J., & Weiss, L. (2005). The Wechsler scales. In D. P. Flanagan & P. L. Harrison (Eds.), *Contemporary Intellectual Assessment: Theories, Tests, and Issues* (pp. 297–324). New York: Guilford Press.

Zigler, E., & Styfco, S. J. (1993). *Head Start and beyond: A national plan for extended childhood intervention.* New Haven, CT: Yale University Press.

Zigler, E., Styfco, S. J., & Gilman, E. (1993). The national Head Start program for disadvantaged preschoolers. In E. Zigler & S. J. Styfco (Eds.), *Head Start and Beyond: A National Plan for Extended Childhood Intervention* (pp. 1–41). New Haven, CT: Yale University Press.

Zill, N., Moore, K. A., Smith, E. W., Stief, T., & Coiro, M. J. (1995). The life circumstances and development of children in welfare families: A profile based on national survey data. In P. L. Chase-Lansdale & J. Brooks-Gunn (Eds.), *Escape from Poverty: What Makes a Difference for Children?* (pp. 39–59). Cambridge, England: Cambridge University Press.

Zimbardo, P. G., Butler, L. D., & Wolfe, V. A. (2003). Cooperative college examinations: More gain, less pain when students share information and grades. *The Journal of Experimental Education, 71,* 101–125.

Name Index

Subject Index

Credits

Figure and Table Credits

Figure 1.6, G.W. Ladd, S.H. Birch, & E.S. Banks. (1989). "Children's social and scholastic lives in kindergarten: Related spheres of influence?" *Child Development, 70,* 1373–1400. Reprinted with permission.

Figure 2.12, From H. Bee & D. Boyd. (2004). *Lifespan Development,* 3/e. Published by Allyn & Bacon, Boston, MA. Copyright © 2004 by Pearson Education. By permission of the publisher.

Figure 2.14, Adapted from C.H. Waddington. (1974). "A catastrophe theory of evolution." *Annals of the New York Academy of Sciences, 231,* 32–42. Adapted with permission.

Figure 4.6, From Richard Fabes, Carol Lynn Martin, *Exploring Child Development,* 2/e. Published by Allyn & Bacon, Boston, MA. Copyright © 2004 by Pearson Education. By permission of the publisher.

Figure 4.7, From Richard Fabes, Carol Lynn Martin, *Exploring Child Development,* 2/e. Published by Allyn & Bacon, Boston, MA. Copyright © 2004 by Pearson Education. By permission of the publisher.

Figure 5.3, Reproduced with permission from *Pediatrics, 56,* 544–549. Copyright © 1975 by the AAP.

Figure 5.10, Reprinted from *Cognitive Psychology, 21,* J.S. Johnson & E.L. Newport, "Critical period effects in second language learning: The influence of maturational state on the acquisition of English as a second language," p. 79. Copyright © 1989, with permission from Elsevier.

Table 6.4, Adapted from S.B. Kamerman, (2000). "Parental leave policies: An essential ingredient in early childhood education and care policies." *Social Policy Report, 14*(2), pp. 5–6.

Figure 7.3, P.R. Huttenlocher & A.S. Dabholkar (1997), "Regional differences in synaptogenesis in human cerebral cortex." *Journal of Comparative Neurology 387,* 167–178. Copyright © 1997, John Wiley & Sons, Inc. Reprinted with permission of Wiley-Liss, Inc., a subsidiary of John Wiley & Sons, Inc.

Figure 7.4, From J. Keough & D. Sugden, *Movement Skill Development,* Macmillan. Copyright © by J. Keough and D. Sugden.

Figure 8.2, From H. Bee & D. Boyd. (2004). *Lifespan Development,* 3/e. Published by Allyn & Bacon, Boston, MA. Copyright © 2004 by Pearson Education. By permission of the publisher.

Figure 8.9, Adapted from L.J. Schweinert, H.V. Barnes, & D.P. Weikart. (1993). *Significant benefits: The High/Scope Perry Preschool study through age 27* (Monographs of the High/Scope Educational Research Foundation, Number 10), pp. xvi–xvii. Ypsilanti, MI: The High/Scope Press.

Table 9.3, Adapted from National Association for the Education of Young Children (2003).

Table 10.1, From Wanda M. Hunter, Samah Helou, Gitanjali Saluja, Carol W. Runyan, & Tamera Coyne-Beasley, "Injury Prevention Advice in Top-Selling Parenting Books." *Pediatrics 116*(5), pp. 1080–1088. Reproduced with permission from Pediatrics, 116,(5), 1080–1088, Table 5. Copyright © 2005 by the AAP.

Table 11.2, Adapted from Geary, D.C. (1994). *Children's mathematical development: Research and practical applications.* Washington DC: American Psychological Association.

Figure 12.1, From Huesmann, L.R., Eron, L.D., Lefkowitz, M.M., & Walder, L.O. (1984). "Stability of aggression over time and generations." *Developmental Psychology, 20*(6), p. 1125. Reprinted with permission.

Figure 12.2, Adapted with permission of National Council on Family Relations, from Paul R. Amato, "The consequences of divorce for adults and children." *Journal of Marriage and the Family, 62,* pp. 1269–1287. Copyright © 2000. Conveyed through Copyright Clearance Center, Inc.

Figure 12.4, Adapted from I.D. Eron (1987). "The development of aggressive behavior from the perspective of a developing behaviorism." *American Psychologist, 42*(5). Adapted with permission. Aggression score from Eron, Huesmann, Lefkowitz, & Walder (1972), p. 256.

Table 13.2, Data from J.P. Roche & T.W. Ramsbey (1993). "Premarital sexuality: A five-year follow-up study of attitudes and behavior by dating stage." *Adolescence, 28,* 67–80.

Figure 14.3, J. Sattler. (2001). *Assessment of Children,* 4th ed. San Diego, CA: Jerome M. Sattler. Reprinted with permission.

Figure 15.2, Adapted from A. Colby, L. Kohlberg, J. Gibbs, & M. Lieberman. (1983). "A longitudinal study of moral judgment." *Monograph of the Society for Research in Child Development, 40* (1–2, Serial No. 200), p. 48. Reprinted with permission of the Society for Research in Child Development.

Photo Credits

PART ONE
pp. 2–3, Jupiter Images

CHAPTER 1
p. 4, Stockbyte/Getty Images; p. 5, Jim Whitmer; p. 6, Photodisc Blue/Getty Images; p. 7 (top), Kathy McLaughlin/Image Works; p. 7 (bottom), Ellen Sinisi/The Image Works; p. 11, Image Works/Mary Evans Picture Library Ltd; p. 13 (far left), Marden Smith/Taxi/Getty Images; p. 13 (second left), Nancy Sheehan/PhotoEdit; p. 13 (center), Bob Daemmrich/PhotoEdit; p. 13 (second right): Tom Stewart/Corbis; p. 13 (far right), Michael Newman/PhotoEdit; p. 14 (top), Courtesy of the Library of Congress; p. 14 (bottom), Benjamin Harris, Ph.D; p. 16 (top), Nina Leen/Getty Images/Time Life Pictures; p. 16 (bottom), John Brenneis/Life Magazine/Time & Life Pictures/Getty Images; p. 17, Judith Behling Ford; p. 18 (top), Elizabeth Crews/The Image Works; p. 18 (bottom), Sovfoto/Eastfoto; p. 19 (top), Nena Leen/Getty Images/Time Life Pictures; p. 19 (bottom), Scott K. Holland, Ph.D.; p. 20, AP Images; p. 21, Dorling Kindersley

Media Library; p. 35, Courtesy of Carolyn and Bob Landers; p. 38, Courtesy of Pamela Talbot; p. 39, Jim Whitmer

CHAPTER 2
p. 42, Photofusion Picture Library/Alamy Images; p. 43, Rick Gomez/Corbis; p. 45, CNRI/SPL/Photo Researchers; p. 46, SSPL/The Image Works; p. 47, OnRequest Images/Index Stock Imagery; p. 49, Alix/ Photo Researchers; p. 50, Courtesy of Lea Adams; p. 51, CNRI/Phototake; p. 54 (top), Custom Medical Stock Photo; p. 54 (bottom left, Eric Dreyer/Stone Allstock/Getty Images; p. 54 (bottom right):, Tony Freeman/PhotoEdit; p. 60, Will Hart/PhotoEdit; p. 62, UHB Trust/Stone Allstock/Getty Images; p. 64, Courtesy of Robin L. Bennett; p. 68, Sean Murphy/Getty Images; p. 71, Photolibrary.com; p. 74, Bob Daemmrich/The Image Works; p. 77, Viviane Moos/Corbis; p. 78, Rick Gomez/Corbis

CHAPTER 3
p. 82, Ewasko/Getty Images; p. 83, Tom Prettyman/PhotoEdit; p. 84, Lennart Nilsson/Albert Bonniers Forlag AB; p. 85, Dr. Yorgos Nikas/Phototake; p. 87, ICAM/Mona Lisa/Eurelios; p. 88 (top), Lennart Nilsson/Albert Bonniers Forlag AB; p. 88 (bottom left), Lennart Nilsson/Albert Bonniers Forlag AB; p. 88 (bottom right), Albert Bonniers Forlag AB; p. 89, Albert Bonniers Forlag AB; p. 92, Fetal Alcohol & Drug Unit (FAS); p. 93, Stevie Grand/Photo Researchers; p. 94, Courtesy of Cheri and Allan Scott; p. 98, Nick Emm/Alamy; p. 100, Tim Kiusalaas/Masterfile; p. 104 (top), Vince Streano/Corbis; p. 104 (bottom), Laura Dwight Photography; p. 108, Courtesy of Abbi Beuby; p. 109 (top), Chip East/Reuters; p. 109 (bottom), Hattie Young/Photo Researchers; p. 110, Dumbarton Oaks Pre-Columbian Collection, Washington, DC; p. 111, Ruth Jenkinson/MIDIRS/Photo Researchers; p. 113, Tom Prettyman/PhotoEdit; p. 117, Jupiter Images

PART TWO
pp. 118–119, Veer

CHAPTER 4
p. 120, Ariel Skelley/Corbis; p. 121, Jose Luis Pelaez/Corbis; p. 122 (top), David Young-Wolff/PhotoEdit; p. 122 (bottom), Jonathan Nourok/PhotoEdit; p. 123, Superstock; p. 125, Courtesy of Kim Powell and Larry Sikkink; p. 126, Chad Ehlers/Alamy; p. 128 (left), Spencer Grant/PhotoEdit; p. 128 (right), Chuck Savage/Corbis; p. 129, Ariel Skelley/Corbis; p. 130, Per-Anders Pettersson/Getty Images; p. 132, CNRI/ Photo Researchers; p. 133, Anatomical Travelogue/Photo Researchers; p. 137, Mark Richards/PhotoEdit; p. 138, William P. Fifer; p. 139, Dion Ogust/Image Works; p. 142 (top), Jennie Woodcock/Reflections Photolibrary/Corbis; p. 142 (mid left), Elizabeth Crews Photography; p. 142 (mid center), Elizabeth Crews Photography; p. 142 (mid right), Laura Dwight Photography; p. 142 (bottom left), Elizabeth Crews Photography; p. 142 (bottom center), Laura Dwight/Corbis; p. 142 (bottom right):, Laura Dwight Photography; p. 143 (top left), Comstock; p. 143 (top right), Laura Dwight Photography; p. 143 (bottom left), Bill Miles/Corbis; p. 143 (bottom right):, Elizabeth Crews Photography; p. 144, Courtesy of Deanna Walsh; p. 145, Rick Gomez/Corbis; p. 146, Mike Greeniar/Image Works; p. 147, Bananastock/Alamy; p. 148, Jose Louis Palaez/Corbis

CHAPTER 5
p. 152, Jose Luis Pelaez/Corbis; p. 153, Sri Maiava Rusden/Pacific Stock; p. 160, Michael Newman/ PhotoEdit; p. 162, Corbis/Bettmann; p. 163, Geri Engberg/Image Works; p. 167, Laura Dwight/Corbis; p. 169, Laura Dwight Photography; p. 170 (top left) Courtesy of Hanah Shapiro; p. 170 (bottom left) Courtesy of Paul Lewis; p. 170 (right) Courtesy of Nola Akala; p. 172, John Henley/Corbis; p. 173, Cleo Photography/PhotoEdit; p. 175, Susan Kuklin/Photo Researchers; p. 178, Peter Southwick/Stock Boston; p. 182, Laura Dwight Photography; p. 183, Courtesy of Deena Bernstein; p. 185, Sri Maiava Rusden/ Pacific Stock

CHAPTER 6
p. 188, Raoul Minsart/Masterfile; p. 189, Natalie Fobes/Stone Allstock/Getty Images; p. 191, Laura Dwight Photography; p. 192 (top), Nina Leen/Time Life Pictures/Getty Images; p. 192 (bottom), Harlow Primate Laboratory/University of Wisconsin; p. 193, Daniel Grogan Photography; p. 194, Laura Dwight Photography; p. 197, Michael Newman/PhotoEdit; p. 198, Ariel Skelley/Corbis; p. 199 (top), Medioimages/ Getty Images; p. 199 (bottom), Dynamic Graphics Group/IT Stock Free/Alamy; p. 201, Ellen Senisi/Image Works; p. 205 (left), ANA/Image Works; p. 205 (right), Corbis Royalty Free; p. 208, Ellen Senisi/Image Works; p. 210, Tiffany M. Field, Ph.D.; p. 211, Elizabeth Crews Photography; p. 213, Norbert Shaefer/ Corbis; p. 214, Courtesy of Susan Tice; p. 216, Laura Dwight Photography; p. 217, Natalie Fobes/Stone Allstock/Getty Images; p. 221, Veer

PART THREE
pp. 222–223, Blend Images/Alamy

CHAPTER 7
p. 224, Zelick Nagel/Getty Images; p. 225, Alan Oddie/PhotoEdit; p. 226, Bob Daemmrich/Image Works; p. 228, Courtesy of Kathryn Tromblay; p. 229, Robin Nelson/PhotoEdit; p. 230, AP Images/Brennan Linsley; p. 232, Karl Weatherly/Getty Images; p. 233, AP Images/John Russell; p. 235 (left), Nancy Sheehan/ Index Stock; p. 235 (right), Peter Griffith/Masterfile; p. 236, Laura Dwight Photography; p. 238, Michelle D. Bridwell/PhotoEdit; p. 239, Richard Hutchings/PhotoEdit; p. 240, Courtesy of Betsy Carroll; p. 242, G. Tompkinson/Photo Researchers; p. 243, Rommel/Masterfile; p. 247, Roy Morsch/Corbis; p. 250, Alan Oddie/PhotoEdit

CHAPTER 8
p. 254, Michael Newman/PhotoEdit; p. 255, Robin Sachs/PhotoEdit; p. 257, Jonathan Skow/Stone Allstock/Getty Images; p. 260, Laura Dwight Photography; p. 261, Courtesy of Stacie Anderson; p. 263, Sovfoto/Eastfoto; p. 264, Laura Dwight/Corbis; p. 266, Katy McDonnell/Digital Vision/Getty Images; p. 269, Daniel Bosler/Stone Allstock/Getty Images; p. 270, Bob Elsdale/Getty Images; p. 272, Mug

Shots/Stock Market/Corbis; p. 273, Barbara Peacock/Stock Market/Corbis; p. 277, Corbis Royalty Free; p. 278, Jeff Greenberg/Index Stock Imagery; p. 279, Courtesy of David and Lori Glenn; p. 281, Robin Nelson/PhotoEdit; p. 285, Robin Sachs/PhotoEdit

CHAPTER 9
p. 288, Photodisc Blue.Getty Images; p. 289, Anderson Ross/Digital Vision/Getty Images; p. 291, Peter Hendrie/Getty Images; p. 292, David Young-Wolff/PhotoEdit; p. 293, Image Source/Alamy; p. 295, Blend Images/Alamy; p. 299, Myrleen Ferguson Cate/PhotoEdit; p. 301 (top left), Myrleen Ferguson Cate/PhotoEdit; p. 301 (top right), Michael Newman/PhotoEdit; p. 301 (bottom right), Steve Murez/Image Bank/Getty Images; p. 301 (bottom left), Tony Freeman/PhotoEdit; p. 304, Spencer Grant/PhotoEdit; p. 305, Nancy Sheehan/PhotoEdit; p. 306, Cindy Roesinger/Photo Researchers; p. 307, Courtesy of Iris and Manuel Matos; p. 308, Rob Lewine/Corbis; p. 310 (left), James Shaffer/PhotoEdit; p. 310 (right), Laura Dwight Photography; p. 312, Courtesy of Deborah Koshansky; p. 314, Dennis O'Clair/Image Bank/Getty Images; p. 315, INGRAM/Jupiter Images; p. 320, Anderson Ross/Digital Vision/Getty Images; p. 323, Blend Images/Alamy

PART FOUR
pp. 324–325, Pat O'Hara/Stone/Getty Images

CHAPTER 10
p. 326, Kathy Ferguson-Johnson/PhotoEdit; p. 327, Corbis Royalty Free; p. 328, Dann Tardif/Corbis; p. 330, Bob Daemmrich/Stock Boston; p. 333, Richard Hutchings/Corbis; p. 334, ImageState/Alamy; p. 335, Myrleen Ferguson Cate/PhotoEdit; p. 337, Brand X Pictures/Alamy; p. 338, Michael Cogliantry/Getty Images; p. 341, Myrleen Ferguson Cate/PhotoEdit; p. 342, Courtesy of Harlan R. Gephardt; p. 344, Rob Crandall/The Stock Connection; p. 350, Lezlie Sterling/Zuma Press; p. 351 (left), AP Images; p. 351 (center), Corbis/Bettmann; p. 351 (right), Hulton Archive/Getty Images; p. 353, Robin Sachs/PhotoEdit; p. 358, Corbis Royalty Free

CHAPTER 11
p. 362, Jim Wes/The Image Works; p. 363, Corbis Royalty Free; p. 365, Laura Dwight/Corbis; p. 371, Larry Williams/Corbis; p. 372, Lawrence Migdale/Stock Boston; p. 373, Jim Pickerell/The Image Works; p. 375, David J. Sams/Stock Boston; p. 376, Courtesy of Anne Updegrove; p. 378, David Young-Wolff/PhotoEdit; p. 380, Bob Daemmrich/Stone Allstock/Getty Images; p. 386, Elyse Lewin/Getty Images; p. 387, Laura Dwight Photography; p. 390, LWA- JDC/Corbis; p. 391, Carl & Ann Purcell/Corbis; p. 392, Image100/Alamy; p. 394, Courtesy of Kim Davenport; p. 395, Image Source/Alamy; p. 396, Corbis Royalty Free

CHAPTER 12
p. 400, Anne Ackermann/Getty Images; p. 401, Corbis Royalty Free; p. 402, Eric R. Bernd/Unicorn Stock Photos; p. 403, George Shelley/Corbis; p. 406 (top), Bob Daemmrich/The Image Works; p. 406 (bottom), Tony Freeman/PhotoEdit; p. 409, Richard Hutchings/PhotoEdit; p. 413, Lon C. Diehl/PhotoEdit; p. 415, Corbis Royalty Free; p. 420, Courtesy of Sophia Martin; p. 423, Catherine Ledner/Stone Allstock/Getty Images; p. 427, Jim Cummins/Corbis; p. 428, David Young-Wolff/PhotoEdit; p. 431, Albert Bandura; p. 432, Andrew Lichtenstein/The Image Works; p. 433, Courtesy of Jan Craige Singer; p. 434, Corbis Royalty Free; p. 437, Pat O'Hara/Stone/Getty Images

PART FOUR
pp. 438–439, Jeff Greenberg/Age Fotostock

CHAPTER 13
p. 440, Big Cheese Photo/SuperStock; p. 441, Donna Day/Age Fotostock; p. 444, Elena Rooraid/Photo Edit; p. 445, Jon Feingersh/Masterfile; p. 446, Courtesy of Hannah Lee Vestal; p. 447, Corbis Royalty Free; p. 451, PunchStock; p. 453, Peter D. Byron/PhotoEdit; p. 454, Time & Life Pictures/Getty Images Pictures; p. 457, Will Hart; p. 458, Michael Hart/Getty Images; p. 461, Bill Aron/PhotoEdit; p. 462, Brand X Pictures/Alamy; p. 464, Superstock; p. 465, Staffordshire Sentinel/SOLO/Zuma Press; p. 466, Corbis Royalty Free; p. 467, Courtesy of Douglas Bunnell; p. 471, Photodisc Green/Getty Images; p. 472, Alan Lewis/Corbis; p. 473, Photodisc Green/Getty Images; p. 475, Donna Day/Age Fotostock

CHAPTER 14
p. 478, Superstock; p. 479, Jeff Greenberg/PhotoEdit; p. 481, Esbin-Anderson/Image Works; p. 482, Bob Daemmrich/PhotoEdit; p. 488, Photodisc/Getty Images; p. 492, AP Images; p. 493, President and Fellows of Harvard College; p. 494 (top), AP Images; p. 494 (bottom left), Tom & Dee Ann McCarthy; p. 494 (bottom center), Bob Daemmrich/Stock Boston; p. 494 (bottom right), Ariel Skelley/Corbis; p. 498, Courtesy of Sandy Roland; p. 499, James Shaffer/PhotoEdit; p. 501, Laura Dwight Photography; p. 505, David Young-Wolff/PhotoEdit; p. 506, Yva Momatuik/Stock Boston; p. 511, Chuck Savage/Corbis; p. 513, Jeff Greenberg/PhotoEdit; p. 512, Courtesy of Donna Rowland

CHAPTER 15
p. 516, Photodisc/Getty Images; p. 517, Photodisc/Getty Images; p. 521, Jim Whitmer; p. 522, Courtesy of Angela Watkins; p. 524, Purestock/Alamy; p. 525, AP Images/Plinio Lepri; p. 527 (top left), Vicki Silbert/PhotoEdit; p. 527 (bottom left), Spencer Grant/PhotoEdit; p. 527 (right), Reuters/Corbis; p. 531, John Powell/Topham/Image Works; p. 535, Corbis Royalty Free; p. 537, Alan Veldenzer/Index Stock; p. 539, Courtesy of Nancy Magowan; p. 540, Tony Anderson/Image Bank/Getty Images; p. 544, HIRB/Index Stock; p. 545, Digital Vision/Getty Images; p. 550, Peter Byron/PhotoEdit; p. 551 (bottom), Peter Blakely/Corbis SABA; p. 551 (top), Ariel Skelley/Corbis; p. 552, Kindra Clineff/Index Stock; p. 553, Richard Lord/Image Works; p. 554, Photodisc/Getty Images; p. 557, Jeff Greenberg/Age Fotostock